Introduction to Probability
for
Data Science

Stanley H. Chan
Purdue University

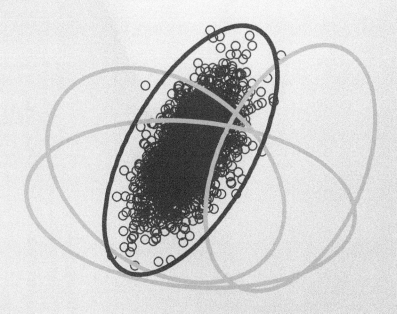

Published in the United States of America by
Michigan Publishing
Manufactured in the United States of America

ISBN 978-1-60785-746-4 (hardcover)
ISBN 978-1-60785-747-1 (electronic)

The Free ECE Textbook Initiative is sponsored by the ECE Department at the University of Michigan.

ELECTRICAL &
COMPUTER ENGINEERING
UNIVERSITY OF MICHIGAN

To Vivian, Joanna, and Cynthia Chan

And ye shall know the truth, and the truth shall make you free.

John 8:32

Preface

This book is an introductory textbook in undergraduate probability. It has a mission: to spell out the *motivation*, *intuition*, and *implication* of the probabilistic tools we use in science and engineering. From over half a decade of teaching the course, I have distilled what I believe to be the core of probabilistic methods. I put the book in the context of data science to emphasize the inseparability between data (computing) and probability (theory) in our time.

Probability is one of the most interesting subjects in electrical engineering and computer science. It bridges our favorite engineering principles to the practical reality, a world that is full of uncertainty. However, because probability is such a mature subject, the undergraduate textbooks alone might fill several rows of shelves in a library. When the literature is so rich, the challenge becomes how one can pierce through to the insight while diving into the details. For example, many of you have used a normal random variable before, but have you ever wondered where the "bell shape" comes from? Every probability class will teach you about flipping a coin, but how can "flipping a coin" ever be useful in machine learning today? Data scientists use the Poisson random variables to model the internet traffic, but where does the gorgeous Poisson equation come from? This book is designed to fill these gaps with knowledge that is essential to all data science students.

This leads to the three goals of the book. (i) Motivation: In the ocean of mathematical definitions, theorems, and equations, why should we spend our time on this particular topic but not another? (ii) Intuition: When going through the derivations, is there a geometric interpretation or physics beyond those equations? (iii) Implication: After we have learned a topic, what new problems can we solve?

The book's intended audience is undergraduate juniors/seniors and first-year graduate students majoring in electrical engineering and computer science. The prerequisites are standard undergraduate linear algebra and calculus, except for the section about characteristic functions, where Fourier transforms are needed. An undergraduate course in signals and systems would suffice, even taken concurrently while studying this book.

The length of the book is suitable for a two-semester course. Instructors are encouraged to use the set of chapters that best fits their classes. For example, a basic probability course can use Chapters 1-5 as its backbone. Chapter 6 on sample statistics is suitable for students who wish to gain theoretical insights into probabilistic convergence. Chapter 7 on regression and Chapter 8 on estimation best suit students who want to pursue machine learning and signal processing. Chapter 9 discusses confidence intervals and hypothesis testing, which are critical to modern data analysis. Chapter 10 introduces random processes. My approach for random processes is more tailored to information processing and communication systems, which are usually more relevant to electrical engineering students.

Additional teaching resources can be found on the book's website, where you can find lecture videos and homework videos. Throughout the book you will see many "practice exercises", which are easy problems with worked-out solutions. They can be skipped without loss to the flow of the book.

Acknowledgements: If I could thank only one person, it must be Professor Fawwaz Ulaby of the University of Michigan. Professor Ulaby has been the source of support in all aspects, from the book's layout to technical content, proofreading, and marketing. The book would not have been published without the help of Professor Ulaby. I am deeply moved by Professor Ulaby's vision that education should be made accessible to all students. With textbook prices rocketing up, the EECS free textbook initiative launched by Professor Ulaby is the most direct response to the publishers, teachers, parents, and students. Thank you, Fawwaz, for your unbounded support — technically, mentally, and financially. Thank you also for recommending Richard Carnes. The meticulous details Richard offered have significantly improved the fluency of the book. Thank you, Richard.

I thank my colleagues at Purdue who had shared many thoughts with me when I taught the course (in alphabetical order): Professors Mark Bell, Mary Comer, Saul Gelfand, Amy Reibman, and Chih-Chun Wang. My teaching assistant I-Fan Lin was instrumental in the early development of this book. To the graduate students of my lab (Yiheng Chi, Nick Chimitt, Kent Gauen, Abhiram Gnanasambandam, Guanzhe Hong, Chengxi Li, Zhiyuan Mao, Xiangyu Qu, and Yash Sanghvi): Thank you! It would have been impossible to finish the book without your participation. A few students I taught volunteered to help edit the book: Benjamin Gottfried, Harrison Hsueh, Dawoon Jung, Antonio Kincaid, Deepak Ravikumar, Krister Ulvog, Peace Umoru, Zhijing Yao. I would like to thank my Ph.D. advisor Professor Truong Nguyen for encouraging me to write the book.

Finally, I would like to thank my wife Vivian and my daughters, Joanna and Cynthia, for their love, patience, and support.

Stanley H. Chan, *West Lafayette, Indiana*

May, 2021

Companion website:

https://probability4datascience.com/

Contents

CONTENTS

CONTENTS

Chapter 1

Mathematical Background

"Data science" has different meanings to different people. If you ask a biologist, data science could mean analyzing DNA sequences. If you ask a banker, data science could mean predicting the stock market. If you ask a software engineer, data science could mean programs and data structures; if you ask a machine learning scientist, data science could mean models and algorithms. However, one thing that is common in all these disciplines is the concept of **uncertainty**. We choose to learn from data because we believe that the latent information is embedded in the data — unprocessed, contains noise, and could have missing entries. If there is no randomness, all data scientists can close their business because there is simply no problem to solve. However, the moment we see randomness, our business comes back. Therefore, data science is the subject of making decisions in uncertainty.

The mathematics of analyzing uncertainty is **probability**. It is *the* tool to help us model, analyze, and predict random events. Probability can be studied in as many ways as you can think of. You can take a rigorous course in probability theory, or a "probability for dummies" on the internet, or a typical undergraduate probability course offered by your school. This book is different from all these. Our goal is to tell you *how things work* in the context of data science. For example, why do we need those three axioms of probabilities and not others? Where does the "bell shape" Gaussian random variable come from? How many samples do we need to construct a reliable histogram? These questions are at the core of data science, and they deserve close attention rather than sweeping them under the rug.

To help you get used to the pace and style of this book, in this chapter, we review some of the very familiar topics in undergraduate algebra and calculus. These topics are meant to warm up your mathematics background so that you can follow the subsequent chapters. Specifically, in this chapter, we cover several topics. First, in Section 1.1 we discuss infinite series, something that will be used frequently when we evaluate the expectation and variance of random variables in Chapter 3. In Section 1.2 we review the Taylor approximation, which will be helpful when we discuss continuous random variables. Section 1.3 discusses integration and reviews several tricks we can use to make integration easy. Section 1.4 deals with linear algebra, aka matrices and vectors, which are fundamental to modern data analysis. Finally, Section 1.5 discusses permutation and combination, two basic techniques to count events.

1

1.1   Infinite Series

Imagine that you have a **fair coin**. If you get a tail, you flip it again. You do this repeatedly until you finally get a head. What is the probability that you need to flip the coin three times to get one head?

This is a warm-up exercise. Since the coin is fair, the probability of obtaining a head is $\frac{1}{2}$. The probability of getting a tail followed by a head is $\frac{1}{2} \times \frac{1}{2} = \frac{1}{4}$. Similarly, the probability of getting two tails and then a head is $\frac{1}{2} \times \frac{1}{2} \times \frac{1}{2} = \frac{1}{8}$. If you follow this logic, you can write down the probabilities for all other cases. For your convenience, we have drawn the first few in **Figure 1.1**. As you have probably noticed, the probabilities follow the pattern $\{\frac{1}{2}, \frac{1}{4}, \frac{1}{8}, \ldots\}$.

$$\frac{1}{2} \qquad\qquad \frac{1}{4} \qquad\qquad \frac{1}{8} \qquad\qquad\qquad \frac{1}{16}$$

Figure 1.1: Suppose you flip a coin until you see a head. This requires you to have $N - 1$ tails followed by a head. The probability of this sequence of events are $\frac{1}{2}, \frac{1}{4}, \frac{1}{8}, \ldots$, which forms an infinite sequence.

We can also summarize these probabilities using a familiar plot called the **histogram** as shown in **Figure 1.2**. The histogram for this problem has a special pattern, that every value is one order higher than the preceding one, and the sequence is infinitely long.

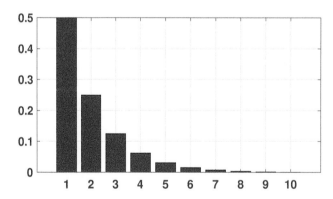

Figure 1.2: The histogram of flipping a coin until we see a head. The x-axis is the number of coin flips, and the y-axis is the probability.

Let us ask something harder: On average, if you want to be 90% sure that you will get a head, what is the minimum number of attempts you need to try? Five attempts? Ten attempts? Indeed, if you try ten attempts, you will very likely accomplish your goal. However, this would seem to be overkill. If you try five attempts, then it becomes unclear whether you will be 90% sure.

This problem can be answered by analyzing the sequence of probabilities. If we make two attempts, then the probability of getting a head is the sum of the probabilities for one attempt and that of two attempts:

$$\mathbb{P}[\text{success after 1 attempt}] = \frac{1}{2} = 0.5$$

$$\mathbb{P}[\text{success after 2 attempts}] = \frac{1}{2} + \frac{1}{4} = 0.75$$

Therefore, if you make 3 attempts or 4 attempts, you get the following probabilities:

$$\mathbb{P}[\text{success after 3 attempts}] = \frac{1}{2} + \frac{1}{4} + \frac{1}{8} = 0.875$$

$$\mathbb{P}[\text{success after 4 attempts}] = \frac{1}{2} + \frac{1}{4} + \frac{1}{8} + \frac{1}{16} = 0.9375.$$

So if we try four attempts, we will have a 93.75% probability of getting a head. Thus, four attempts is the answer.

The MATLAB / Python codes we used to generate **Figure 1.2** are shown below.

```matlab
% MATLAB code to generate a geometric sequence
p = 1/2;
n = 1:10;
X = p.^n;
bar(n,X,'FaceColor',[0.8, 0.2,0.2]);
```

```python
# Python code to generate a geometric sequence
import numpy as np
import matplotlib.pyplot as plt
p = 1/2
n = np.arange(1,10)
X = np.power(p,n)
plt.bar(n,X); plt.show()
```

This warm-up exercise has perhaps raised some of your interest in the subject. However, we will not tell you everything now. We will come back to the probability in Chapter 3 when we discuss geometric random variables. In the present section, we want to make sure you have the basic mathematical tools to calculate quantities, such as a sum of fractional numbers. For example, what if we want to calculate $\mathbb{P}[\text{success after 107 attempts}]$? Is there a systematic way of performing the calculation?

Remark. You should be aware that the 93.75% only says that the probability of achieving the goal is high. If you have a bad day, you may still need more than four attempts. Therefore, when we stated the question, we asked for 90% "on average". Sometimes you may need more attempts and sometimes fewer attempts, but on average, you have a 93.75% chance of succeeding.

1.1.1 Geometric Series

A geometric series is the sum of a finite or an infinite sequence of numbers with a constant ratio between successive terms. As we have seen in the previous example, a geometric series appears naturally in the context of discrete events. In Chapter 3 of this book, we will use geometric series when calculating the **expectation** and **moments** of a random variable.

Definition 1.1. *Let* $0 < r < 1$, *a* **finite geometric sequence** *of power n is a sequence of numbers*

$$\left\{1, r, r^2, \ldots, r^n\right\}.$$

An **infinite geometric sequence** *is a sequence of numbers*

$$\left\{1, r, r^2, r^3, \ldots\right\}.$$

Theorem 1.1. *The sum of a* **finite geometric series** *of power n is*

$$\sum_{k=0}^{n} r^k = 1 + r + r^2 + \cdots + r^n = \frac{1 - r^{n+1}}{1 - r}. \tag{1.1}$$

Proof. We multiply both sides by $1 - r$. The left hand side becomes

$$\left(\sum_{k=0}^{n} r^k\right)(1 - r) = \left(1 + r + r^2 + \cdots + r^n\right)(1 - r)$$

$$= \left(1 + r + r^2 + \cdots + r^n\right) - \left(r + r^2 + r^3 + \cdots + r^{n+1}\right)$$

$$\stackrel{(a)}{=} 1 - r^{n+1},$$

where (a) holds because terms are canceled due to subtractions.

$\square$

A corollary of Equation (1.1) is the sum of an infinite geometric sequence.

Corollary 1.1. *Let* $0 < r < 1$. *The sum of an* **infinite geometric series** *is*

$$\sum_{k=0}^{\infty} r^k = 1 + r + r^2 + \cdots = \frac{1}{1 - r}. \tag{1.2}$$

Proof. We take the limit in Equation (1.1). This yields

$$\sum_{k=0}^{\infty} r^k = \lim_{n \to \infty} \sum_{k=0}^{n} r^k = \lim_{n \to \infty} \frac{1 - r^{n+1}}{1 - r} = \frac{1}{1 - r}.$$

$\square$

Remark. Note that the condition $0 < r < 1$ is important. If $r > 1$, then the limit $\lim_{n \to \infty} r^{n+1}$ in Equation (1.2) will diverge. The constant r cannot equal to 1, for otherwise the fraction $(1 - r^{n+1})/(1 - r)$ is undefined. We are not interested in the case when $r = 0$, because the sum is trivially 1: $\sum_{k=0}^{\infty} 0^k = 1 + 0^1 + 0^2 + \cdots = 1$.

Practice Exercise 1.1. Compute the infinite series $\sum\limits_{k=2}^{\infty} \frac{1}{2^k}$.

Solution.

$$\sum_{k=2}^{\infty} \frac{1}{2^k} = \frac{1}{4} + \frac{1}{8} + \cdots +$$

$$= \frac{1}{4}\left(1 + \frac{1}{2} + \frac{1}{4} + \cdots\right)$$

$$= \frac{1}{4} \cdot \frac{1}{1 - \frac{1}{2}} = \frac{1}{2}.$$

Remark. You should not be confused about a geometric series and a **harmonic series**. A harmonic series concerns with the sum of $\{1, \frac{1}{2}, \frac{1}{3}, \frac{1}{4}, \ldots\}$. It turns out that[1]

$$\sum_{n=1}^{\infty} \frac{1}{n} = 1 + \frac{1}{2} + \frac{1}{3} + \frac{1}{4} + \cdots = \infty.$$

On the other hand, a squared harmonic series $\{1, \frac{1}{2^2}, \frac{1}{3^2}, \frac{1}{4^2}, \ldots\}$ converges:

$$\sum_{n=1}^{\infty} \frac{1}{n^2} = 1 + \frac{1}{2^2} + \frac{1}{3^2} + \frac{1}{4^2} + \cdots = \frac{\pi^2}{6}.$$

The latter result is known as the **Basel problem**.

We can extend the main theorem by considering more complicated series, for example the following one.

Corollary 1.2. *Let* $0 < r < 1$. *It holds that*

$$\sum_{k=1}^{\infty} k r^{k-1} = 1 + 2r + 3r^2 + \cdots = \frac{1}{(1-r)^2}. \tag{1.3}$$

Proof. Take the derivative on both sides of Equation (1.2). The left hand side becomes

$$\frac{d}{dr} \sum_{k=0}^{\infty} r^k = \frac{d}{dr}\left(1 + r + r^2 + \cdots\right)$$

$$= 1 + 2r + 3r^2 + \cdots = \sum_{k=1}^{\infty} k r^{k-1}$$

The right hand side becomes $\dfrac{d}{dr}\left(\dfrac{1}{1-r}\right) = \dfrac{1}{(1-r)^2}$.

$\square$

---

[1]This result can be found in Tom Apostol, *Mathematical Analysis*, 2nd Edition, Theorem 8.11.

Practice Exercise 1.2. Compute the infinite sum $\sum_{k=1}^{\infty} k \cdot \frac{1}{3^k}$.

Solution. We can use the derivative result:

$$\sum_{k=1}^{\infty} k \cdot \frac{1}{3^k} = 1 \cdot \frac{1}{3} + 2 \cdot \frac{1}{9} + 3 \cdot \frac{1}{27} + \cdots$$

$$= \frac{1}{3} \cdot \left(1 + 2 \cdot \frac{1}{3} + 3 \cdot \frac{1}{9} + \cdots\right) = \frac{1}{3} \cdot \frac{1}{(1-\frac{1}{3})^2} = \frac{1}{3} \cdot \frac{1}{\frac{4}{9}} = \frac{3}{4}.$$

1.1.2 Binomial Series

A geometric series is useful when handling situations such as $N-1$ failures followed by a success. However, we can easily twist the problem by asking: What is the probability of getting one head out of 3 independent coin tosses? In this case, the probability can be determined by enumerating all possible cases:

$$\mathbb{P}[1 \text{ head in 3 coins}] = \mathbb{P}[\text{H,T,T}] + \mathbb{P}[\text{T,H,T}] + \mathbb{P}[\text{T,T,H}]$$

$$= \left(\frac{1}{2} \times \frac{1}{2} \times \frac{1}{2}\right) + \left(\frac{1}{2} \times \frac{1}{2} \times \frac{1}{2}\right) + \left(\frac{1}{2} \times \frac{1}{2} \times \frac{1}{2}\right)$$

$$= \frac{3}{8}.$$

Figure 1.3 illustrates the situation.

Figure 1.3: When flipping three coins independently, the probability of getting exactly one head can come from three different possibilities.

What lessons have we learned in this example? Notice that you need to enumerate all possible combinations of one head and two tails to solve this problem. The number is 3 in our example. In general, the number of combinations can be systematically studied using **combinatorics**, which we will discuss later in the chapter. However, the number of combinations motivates us to discuss another background technique known as the binomial series. The binomial series is instrumental in algebra when handling polynomials such as $(a+b)^2$ or $(1+x)^3$. It provides a valuable formula when computing these powers.

Theorem 1.2 (Binomial theorem). *For any real numbers a and b, the binomial series of power n is*

$$(a+b)^n = \sum_{k=0}^{n} \binom{n}{k} a^{n-k} b^k, \tag{1.4}$$

where $\binom{n}{k} = \frac{n!}{k!(n-k)!}$.

The **binomial theorem** is valid for any real numbers a and b. The quantity $\binom{n}{k}$ reads as "n choose k". Its definition is

$$\binom{n}{k} \stackrel{\text{def}}{=} \frac{n!}{k!(n-k)!},$$

where $n! = n(n-1)(n-2)\cdots 3 \cdot 2 \cdot 1$. We shall discuss the physical meaning of $\binom{n}{k}$ in Section 1.5. But we can quickly plug in the "n choose k" into the coin flipping example by letting $n = 3$ and $k = 1$:

$$\text{Number of combinations for 1 head and 2 tails} = \binom{3}{1} = \frac{3!}{1!2!} = 3.$$

So you can see why we want you to spend your precious time learning about the binomial theorem. In MATLAB and Python, $\binom{n}{k}$ can be computed using the commands as follows.

```
% MATLAB code to compute (N choose K) and K!
n = 10;
k = 2;
nchoosek(n,k)
factorial(k)
```

```
# Python code to compute (N choose K) and K!
from scipy.special import comb, factorial
n = 10
k = 2
comb(n, k)
factorial(k)
```

The binomial theorem makes the most sense when we also learn about the **Pascal's identity**.

Theorem 1.3 (Pascal's identity). *Let n and k be positive integers such that $k \leq n$. Then,*

$$\binom{n}{k} + \binom{n}{k-1} = \binom{n+1}{k}. \tag{1.5}$$

Proof. We start by recalling the definition of $\binom{n}{k}$. This gives us

$$\binom{n}{k} + \binom{n}{k-1} = \frac{n!}{k!(n-k)!} + \frac{n!}{(k-1)!(n-(k-1))!}$$

$$= n! \left(\frac{1}{k!(n-k)!} + \frac{1}{(k-1)!(n-k+1)!} \right),$$

where we factor out $n!$ to obtain the second equation. Next, we observe that

$$\frac{1}{k!(n-k)!} \times \frac{(n-k+1)}{(n-k+1)} = \frac{n-k+1}{k!(n-k+1)!},$$

$$\frac{1}{(k-1)!(n-k+1)!} \times \frac{k}{k} = \frac{k}{k!(n-k+1)!}.$$

Substituting into the previous equation we obtain

$$\binom{n}{k} + \binom{n}{k-1} = n!\left(\frac{n-k+1}{k!(n-k+1)!} + \frac{k}{k!(n-k+1)!}\right)$$
$$= n!\left(\frac{n+1}{k!(n-k+1)!}\right)$$
$$= \frac{(n+1)!}{k!(n+1-k)!} = \binom{n+1}{k}.$$

□

The Pascal triangle is a visualization of the coefficients of $(a+b)^n$ as shown in **Figure 1.4**. For example, when $n = 5$, we know that $\binom{5}{3} = 10$. However, by Pascal's identity, we know that $\binom{5}{3} = \binom{4}{2} + \binom{4}{3}$. So the number 10 is actually obtained by summing the numbers 4 and 6 of the previous row.

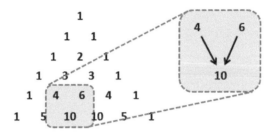

Figure 1.4: Pascal triangle for $n = 0, \ldots, 5$. Note that a number in one row is obtained by summing two numbers directly above it.

Practice Exercise 1.3. Find $(1+x)^3$.

Solution. Using the binomial theorem, we can show that

$$(1+x)^3 = \sum_{k=0}^{n} \binom{3}{k} 1^{3-k} x^k = 1 + 3x + 3x^2 + x^3.$$

Practice Exercise 1.4. Let $0 < p < 1$. Find

$$\sum_{k=0}^{n} \binom{n}{k} p^{n-k}(1-p)^k.$$

Solution. By using the binomial theorem, we have

$$\sum_{k=0}^{n} \binom{n}{k} p^{n-k}(1-p)^k = (p + (1-p))^n = 1.$$

This result will be helpful when evaluating binomial random variables in Chapter 3.

We now prove the binomial theorem. Please feel free to skip the proof if this is your first time reading the book.

Proof of the binomial theorem. We prove by induction. When $n = 1$,

$$(a + b)^1 = a + b = \sum_{k=0}^{1} a^{1-k} b^k.$$

Therefore, the base case is verified. Assume up to case n. We need to verify case $n + 1$.

$$(a + b)^{n+1} = (a + b)(a + b)^n = (a + b) \sum_{k=0}^{n} \binom{n}{k} a^{n-k} b^k$$

$$= \sum_{k=0}^{n} \binom{n}{k} a^{n-k+1} b^k + \sum_{k=0}^{n} \binom{n}{k} a^{n-k} b^{k+1}.$$

We want to apply the Pascal's identity to combine the two terms. In order to do so, we note that the second term in this sum can be rewritten as

$$\sum_{k=0}^{n} \binom{n}{k} a^{n-k} b^{k+1} = \sum_{k=0}^{n} \binom{n}{k} a^{n+1-k-1} b^{k+1}$$

$$= \sum_{\ell=1}^{n+1} \binom{n}{\ell-1} a^{n+1-\ell} b^\ell, \qquad \text{where} \quad \ell = k + 1$$

$$= \sum_{\ell=1}^{n} \binom{n}{\ell-1} a^{n+1-\ell} b^\ell + b^{n+1}.$$

The first term in the sum can be written as

$$\sum_{k=0}^{n} \binom{n}{k} a^{n-k+1} b^k = \sum_{\ell=1}^{n} \binom{n}{\ell} a^{n+1-\ell} b^\ell + a^{n+1}, \qquad \text{where} \quad \ell = k.$$

Therefore, the two terms can be combined using Pascal's identity to yield

$$(a + b)^{n+1} = \sum_{\ell=1}^{n} \left[\binom{n}{\ell} + \binom{n}{\ell-1} \right] a^{n+1-\ell} b^\ell + a^{n+1} + b^{n+1}$$

$$= \sum_{\ell=1}^{n} \binom{n+1}{\ell} a^{n+1-\ell} b^\ell + a^{n+1} + b^{n+1} = \sum_{\ell=0}^{n+1} \binom{n+1}{\ell} a^{n+1-\ell} b^\ell.$$

Hence, the $(n + 1)$th case is also verified. By the principle of mathematical induction, we have completed the proof. □

The end of the proof. Please join us again.

1.2   Approximation

Consider a function $f(x) = \log(1+x)$, for $x > 0$ as shown in **Figure 1.5**. This is a nonlinear function, and we all know that nonlinear functions are not fun to deal with. For example, if you want to integrate the function $\int_a^b x \log(1+x) \, dx$, then the logarithm will force you to do integration by parts. However, in many practical problems, you may not need the full range of $x > 0$. Suppose that you are only interested in values $x \ll 1$. Then the logarithm can be approximated, and thus the integral can also be approximated.

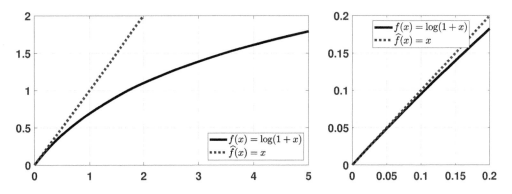

Figure 1.5: The function $f(x) = \log(1+x)$ and the approximation $\widehat{f}(x) = x$.

To see how this is even possible, we show in **Figure 1.5** the nonlinear function $f(x) = \log(1+x)$ and an approximation $\widehat{f}(x) = x$. The approximation is carefully chosen such that for $x \ll 1$, the approximation $\widehat{f}(x)$ is close to the true function $f(x)$. Therefore, we can argue that for $x \ll 1$,

$$\log(1+x) \approx x, \tag{1.6}$$

thereby simplifying the calculation. For example, if you want to integrate $x \log(1+x)$ for $0 < x < 0.1$, then the integral can be approximated by $\int_0^{0.1} x \log(1+x) \, dx \approx \int_0^{0.1} x^2 \, dx = \frac{x^3}{3} = 3.33 \times 10^{-4}$. (The actual integral is 3.21×10^{-4}.) In this section we will learn about the basic approximation techniques. We will use them when we discuss limit theorems in Chapter 6, as well as various distributions, such as from binomial to Poisson.

1.2.1   Taylor approximation

Given a function $f : \mathbb{R} \to \mathbb{R}$, it is often useful to analyze its behavior by approximating f using its local information. **Taylor approximation** (or Taylor series) is one of the tools for such a task. We will use the Taylor approximation on many occasions.

Definition 1.2 (Taylor Approximation). *Let $f : \mathbb{R} \to \mathbb{R}$ be a continuous function with infinite derivatives. Let $a \in \mathbb{R}$ be a fixed constant. The Taylor approximation of f at*

$x = a$ *is*

$$f(x) = f(a) + f'(a)(x-a) + \frac{f''(a)}{2!}(x-a)^2 + \cdots$$

$$= \sum_{n=0}^{\infty} \frac{f^{(n)}(a)}{n!}(x-a)^n, \qquad (1.7)$$

where $f^{(n)}$ denotes the nth-order derivative of f.

Taylor approximation is a geometry-based approximation. It approximates the function according to the offset, slope, curvature, and so on. According to Definition 1.2, the Taylor series has an infinite number of terms. If we use a finite number of terms, we obtain the nth-order Taylor approximation:

First-Order :
$$f(x) = \underbrace{f(a)}_{\text{offset}} + \underbrace{f'(a)(x-a)}_{\text{slope}} + \mathcal{O}((x-a)^2)$$

Second-Order :
$$f(x) = \underbrace{f(a)}_{\text{offset}} + \underbrace{f'(a)(x-a)}_{\text{slope}} + \underbrace{\frac{f''(a)}{2!}(x-a)^2}_{\text{curvature}} + \mathcal{O}((x-a)^3).$$

Here, the big-O notation $\mathcal{O}(\varepsilon^k)$ means any term that has an order at least power k. For small ε, i.e., $\varepsilon \ll 1$, a high-order term $\mathcal{O}(\varepsilon^k) \approx 0$ for large k.

Example 1.1. Let $f(x) = \sin x$. Then the Taylor approximation at $x = 0$ is

$$f(x) \approx f(0) + f'(0)(x-0) + \frac{f''(0)}{2!}(x-0)^2 + \frac{f'''(0)}{3!}(x-0)^3$$

$$= \sin(0) + (\cos 0)(x-0) - \frac{\sin(0)}{2!}(x-0)^2 - \frac{\cos(0)}{3!}(x-0)^3$$

$$= 0 + x - 0 - \frac{x^3}{6} = x - \frac{x^3}{6}.$$

We can expand further to higher orders, which yields

$$f(x) = x - \frac{x^3}{3!} + \frac{x^5}{5!} - \frac{x^7}{7!} + \cdots$$

We show the first few approximations in **Figure 1.6**.

One should be reminded that Taylor approximation approximates a function $f(x)$ at a particular point $x = a$. Therefore, the approximation of f near $x = 0$ and the approximation of f near $x = \pi/2$ are different. For example, the Taylor approximation at $x = \pi/2$ for $f(x) = \sin x$ is

$$f(x) = \sin\frac{\pi}{2} + \cos\frac{\pi}{2}\left(x - \frac{\pi}{2}\right) - \frac{\sin\frac{\pi}{2}}{2!}\left(x - \frac{\pi}{2}\right)^2 - \frac{\cos\frac{\pi}{2}}{3!}\left(x - \frac{\pi}{2}\right)^3$$

$$= 1 + 0 - \frac{1}{4}\left(x - \frac{\pi}{2}\right)^2 - 0 = 1 - \frac{1}{4}\left(x - \frac{\pi}{2}\right)^2.$$

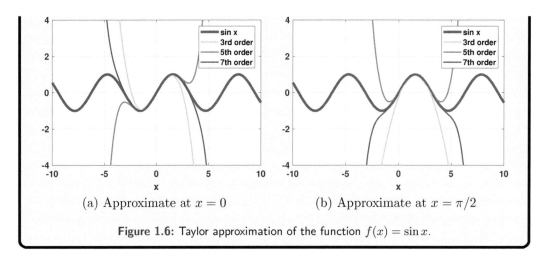

(a) Approximate at $x = 0$ (b) Approximate at $x = \pi/2$

Figure 1.6: Taylor approximation of the function $f(x) = \sin x$.

1.2.2 Exponential series

An immediate application of the Taylor approximation is to derive the **exponential series**.

Theorem 1.4. *Let x be any real number. Then,*

$$e^x = 1 + x + \frac{x^2}{2} + \frac{x^3}{3!} + \cdots = \sum_{k=0}^{\infty} \frac{x^k}{k!}. \tag{1.8}$$

Proof. Let $f(x) = e^x$ for any x. Then, the Taylor approximation around $x = 0$ is

$$f(x) = f(0) + f'(0)(x - 0) + \frac{f''(0)}{2!}(x - 0)^2 + \cdots$$

$$= e^0 + e^0(x - 0) + \frac{e^0}{2!}(x - 0)^2 + \cdots$$

$$= 1 + x + \frac{x^2}{2} + \cdots = \sum_{k=0}^{\infty} \frac{x^k}{k!}.$$

□

Practice Exercise 1.5. Evaluate $\sum_{k=0}^{\infty} \frac{\lambda^k e^{-\lambda}}{k!}$.

Solution.

$$\sum_{k=0}^{\infty} \frac{\lambda^k e^{-\lambda}}{k!} = e^{-\lambda} \sum_{k=0}^{\infty} \frac{\lambda^k}{k!} = e^{-\lambda} e^{\lambda} = 1.$$

This result will be useful for **Poisson random variables** in Chapter 3.

If we substitute $x = j\theta$ where $j = \sqrt{-1}$, then we can show that

$$\underbrace{e^{j\theta}}_{=\cos\theta + j\sin\theta} = 1 + j\theta + \frac{(j\theta)^2}{2!} + \cdots$$

$$= \underbrace{\left(1 - \frac{\theta^2}{2!} + \frac{\theta^4}{4!} + \cdots\right)}_{\text{real}} + j\underbrace{\left(\theta - \frac{\theta^3}{3!} + \cdots\right)}_{\text{imaginary}}$$

Matching the real and the imaginary terms, we can show that

$$\cos\theta = 1 - \frac{\theta^2}{2!} + \frac{\theta^4}{4!} + \cdots$$

$$\sin\theta = \theta - \frac{\theta^3}{3!} + \frac{\theta^5}{5!} + \cdots$$

This gives the infinite series representations of the two trigonometric functions.

1.2.3 Logarithmic approximation

Taylor approximation also allows us to find approximations to logarithmic functions. We start by presenting a lemma.

Lemma 1.1. *Let $0 < x < 1$ be a constant. Then,*

$$\log(1 + x) = x - \frac{x^2}{2} + \mathcal{O}(x^3). \tag{1.9}$$

Proof. Let $f(x) = \log(1 + x)$. Then, the derivatives of f are

$$f'(x) = \frac{1}{(1+x)}, \quad \text{and} \quad f''(x) = -\frac{1}{(1+x)^2}.$$

Taylor approximation at $x = 0$ gives

$$f(x) = f(0) + f'(0)(x - 0) + \frac{f''(0)}{2}(x - 0)^2 + \mathcal{O}(x^3)$$

$$= \log 1 + \left(\frac{1}{(1+0)}\right)x - \left(\frac{1}{(1+0)^2}\right)\frac{x^2}{2} + \mathcal{O}(x^3)$$

$$= x - \frac{x^2}{2} + \mathcal{O}(x^3).$$

$\square$

The difference between this result and the result we showed in the beginning of this section is the order of polynomials we used to approximate the logarithm:

- First-order: $\log(1 + x) = x$
- Second-order: $\log(1 + x) = x - x^2/2$.

What order of approximation is good? It depends on *where* you want the approximation to be good, and how *far* you want the approximation to go. The difference between first-order and second-order approximations is shown in **Figure 1.7**.

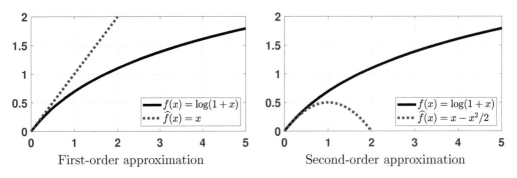

First-order approximation   Second-order approximation

Figure 1.7: The function $f(x) = \log(1+x)$, the first-order approximation $\widehat{f}(x) = x$, and the second-order approximation $\widehat{f}(x) = x - x^2/2$.

Example 1.2. When we prove the **Central Limit Theorem** in Chapter 6, we need to use the following result.

$$\lim_{N \to \infty} \left(1 + \frac{s^2}{2N}\right)^N = e^{s^2/2}.$$

The proof of this equation can be done using the Taylor approximation. Consider $N \log\left(1 + \frac{s^2}{2N}\right)$. By the logarithmic lemma, we can obtain the second-order approximation:

$$\log\left(1 + \frac{s^2}{2N}\right) = \frac{s^2}{2N} - \frac{s^4}{4N^2}.$$

Therefore, multiplying both sides by N yields

$$N \log\left(1 + \frac{s^2}{2N}\right) = \frac{s^2}{2} - \frac{s^4}{4N}.$$

Putting the limit $N \to \infty$ we can show that

$$\lim_{N \to \infty} \left\{ N \log\left(1 + \frac{s^2}{2N}\right) \right\} = \frac{s^2}{2}.$$

Taking exponential on both sides yields

$$\exp\left\{ \lim_{N \to \infty} N \log\left(1 + \frac{s^2}{2N}\right) \right\} = \exp\left\{ \frac{s^2}{2} \right\}.$$

Moving the limit outside the exponential yields the result. **Figure 1.8** provides a pictorial illustration.

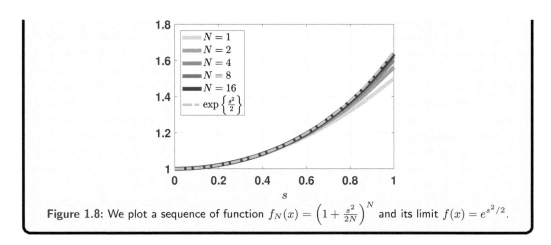

Figure 1.8: We plot a sequence of function $f_N(x) = \left(1 + \frac{s^2}{2N}\right)^N$ and its limit $f(x) = e^{s^2/2}$.

1.3 Integration

When you learned calculus, your teacher probably told you that there are two ways to compute an integral:

- **Substitution:**

$$\int f(ax)\, dx = \frac{1}{a}\int f(u)\, du.$$

- **By parts:**

$$\int u\, dv = u\, v - \int v\, du.$$

Besides these two, we want to teach you two more. The first technique is even and odd functions when integrating a function symmetrically about the y-axis. If a function is even, you just need to integrate half of the function. If a function is odd, you will get a zero. The second technique is to leverage the fact that a probability density function integrates to 1. We will discuss the first technique here and defer the second technique to Chapter 4.

Besides the two integration techniques, we will review the fundamental theorem of calculus. We will need it when we study cumulative distribution functions in Chapter 4.

1.3.1 Odd and even functions

Definition 1.3. *A function $f : \mathbb{R} \to \mathbb{R}$ is **even** if for any $x \in \mathbb{R}$,*

$$f(x) = f(-x), \tag{1.10}$$

*and f is **odd** if*

$$f(x) = -f(-x). \tag{1.11}$$

Essentially, an even function flips over about the y-axis, whereas an odd function flips over both the x- and y-axes.

Example 1.3. The function $f(x) = x^2 - 0.4x^4$ is even, because

$$f(-x) = (-x)^2 - 0.4(-x)^4 = x^2 - 0.4x^4 = f(x).$$

See **Figure 1.9**(a) for illustration. When integrating the function, we have

$$\int_{-1}^{1} f(x)\, dx = 2\int_{0}^{1} f(x)\, dx = 2\int_{0}^{1} x^2 - 0.4^4\, dx = 2\left[\frac{x^3}{3} - \frac{0.4}{5}x^5\right]_{x=0}^{x=1} = \frac{38}{75}.$$

Example 1.4. The function $f(x) = x\exp(-x^2/2)$ is odd, because

$$f(-x) = (-x)\exp\left\{-\frac{(-x)^2}{2}\right\} = -x\exp\left\{-\frac{x^2}{2}\right\} = -f(x).$$

See **Figure 1.9**(b) for illustration. When integrating the function, we can let $u = -x$. Then, the integral becomes

$$\int_{-1}^{1} f(x)\, dx = \int_{-1}^{0} f(x)\, dx + \int_{0}^{1} f(x)\, dx$$

$$= \int_{0}^{1} f(-u)\, du + \int_{0}^{1} f(x)\, dx$$

$$= -\int_{0}^{1} f(u)\, du + \int_{0}^{1} f(x)\, dx = 0.$$

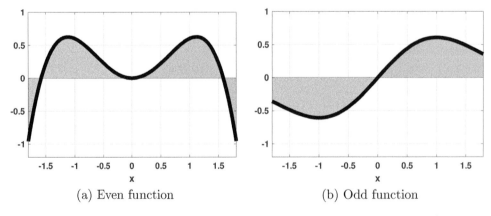

(a) Even function   (b) Odd function

Figure 1.9: An even function is symmetric about the y-axis, and so the integration $\int_{-a}^{a} f(x)\, dx = 2\int_{0}^{a} f(x)\, dx$. An odd function is anti-symmetric about the y-axis. Thus, $\int_{-a}^{a} f(x)\, dx = 0$.

1.3.2 Fundamental Theorem of Calculus

Our following result is the **Fundamental Theorem of Calculus**. It is a handy tool that links integration and differentiation.

Theorem 1.5 (Fundamental Theorem of Calculus). *Let $f : [a, b] \to \mathbb{R}$ be a continuous function defined on a closed interval $[a, b]$. Then, for any $x \in (a, b)$,*

$$f(x) = \frac{d}{dx} \int_a^x f(t)\, dt, \qquad (1.12)$$

Before we prove the result, let us understand the theorem if you have forgotten its meaning.

Example 1.5. Consider a function $f(t) = t^2$. If we integrate the function from 0 to x, we will obtain another function

$$F(x) \stackrel{\text{def}}{=} \int_0^x f(t)\, dt = \int_0^x t^2\, dt = \frac{x^3}{3}.$$

On the other hand, we can differentiate $F(x)$ to obtain $f(x)$:

$$f(x) = \frac{d}{dx} F(x) = \frac{d}{dx} \frac{x^3}{3} = x^2.$$

The fundamental theorem of calculus basically puts the two together:

$$f(x) = \frac{d}{dx} \int_0^x f(t)\, dt.$$

That's it. Nothing more and nothing less.

How can the fundamental theorem of calculus ever be useful when studying probability? Very soon you will learn two concepts: **probability density function** and **cumulative distribution function**. These two functions are related to each other by the fundamental theorem of calculus. To give you a concrete example, we write down the probability density function of an exponential random variable. (Please do not panic about the exponential random variable. Just think of it as a "rapidly decaying" function.)

$$f(x) = e^{-x}, \quad x \geq 0.$$

It turns out that the cumulative distribution function is

$$F(x) = \int_0^x f(t)\, dt = \int_0^x e^{-t}\, dt = 1 - e^{-x}.$$

You can also check that $f(x) = \frac{d}{dx} F(x)$. The fundamental theorem of calculus says that if you tell me $F(x) = \int_0^x e^{-t}\, dt$ (for whatever reason), I will be able to tell you that $f(x) = e^{-x}$ merely by visually inspecting the integrand without doing the differentiation.

Figure 1.10 illustrates the pair of functions $f(x) = e^{-x}$ and $F(x) = 1 - e^{-x}$. One thing you should notice is that the *height* of $F(x)$ is the area under the curve of $f(t)$ from $-\infty$ to x. For example, in **Figure 1.10** we show the area under the curve from 0 to 2. Correspondingly in $F(x)$, the height is $F(2)$.

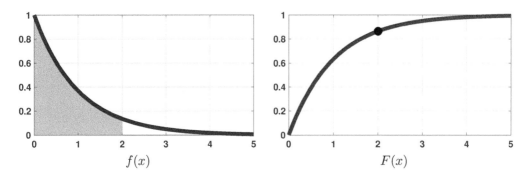

Figure 1.10: The pair of functions $f(x) = e^{-x}$ and $F(x) = 1 - e^{-x}$

The following proof of the Fundamental Theorem of Calculus can be skipped if it is your first time reading the book.

Proof. Our proof is based on Stewart (6th Edition), Section 5.3. Define the integral as a function F:

$$F(x) = \int_a^x f(t) \, dt.$$

The derivative of F with respect to x is

$$\begin{aligned}
\frac{d}{dx}F(x) &= \lim_{h \to 0} \frac{F(x+h) - F(x)}{h} \\
&= \lim_{h \to 0} \frac{1}{h} \left(\int_a^{x+h} f(t) \, dt - \int_a^x f(t) \, dt \right) \\
&= \lim_{h \to 0} \frac{1}{h} \int_x^{x+h} f(t) \, dt \\
&\overset{(a)}{\leq} \lim_{h \to 0} \frac{1}{h} \int_x^{x+h} \left\{ \max_{x \leq \tau \leq x+h} f(\tau) \right\} dt \\
&= \lim_{h \to 0} \left\{ \max_{x \leq \tau \leq x+h} f(\tau) \right\}.
\end{aligned}$$

Here, the inequality in (a) holds because

$$f(t) \leq \max_{x \leq \tau \leq x+h} f(\tau)$$

for all $x \leq t \leq x + h$. The maximum exists because f is continuous in a closed interval.

Using the parallel argument, we can show that

$$\frac{d}{dx}F(x) = \lim_{h \to 0} \frac{F(x+h) - F(x)}{h}$$

$$= \lim_{h \to 0} \frac{1}{h} \left(\int_a^{x+h} f(t)\,dt - \int_a^x f(t)\,dt \right)$$

$$= \lim_{h \to 0} \frac{1}{h} \int_x^{x+h} f(t)\,dt$$

$$\geq \lim_{h \to 0} \frac{1}{h} \int_x^{x+h} \left\{ \min_{x \leq \tau \leq x+h} f(\tau) \right\} dt$$

$$= \lim_{h \to 0} \left\{ \min_{x \leq \tau \leq x+h} f(\tau) \right\}.$$

Combining the two results, we have that

$$\lim_{h \to 0} \left\{ \min_{x \leq \tau \leq x+h} f(\tau) \right\} \leq \frac{d}{dx}F(x) \leq \lim_{h \to 0} \left\{ \max_{x \leq \tau \leq x+h} f(\tau) \right\}.$$

However, since the two limits are both converging to $f(x)$ as $h \to 0$, we conclude that $\frac{d}{dx}F(x) = f(x)$.

□

Remark. An alternative proof is to use Mean Value Theorem in terms of Riemann-Stieltjes integrals (see, e.g., Tom Apostol, *Mathematical Analysis*, 2nd edition, Theorem 7.34). To handle more general functions such as delta functions, one can use techniques in Lebesgue's integration. However, this is beyond the scope of this book.

> This is the end of the proof. Please join us again.

In many practical problems, the fundamental theorem of calculus needs to be used in conjunction with the **chain rule**.

> **Corollary 1.3.** *Let $f : [a, b] \to \mathbb{R}$ be a continuous function defined on a closed interval $[a, b]$. Let $g : \mathbb{R} \to [a, b]$ be a continuously differentiable function. Then, for any $x \in (a, b)$,*
>
> $$\frac{d}{dx} \int_a^{g(x)} f(t)\,dt = g'(x) \cdot f(g(x)). \tag{1.13}$$

Proof. We can prove this with the chain rule: Let $y = g(x)$. Then we have

$$\frac{d}{dx} \int_a^{g(x)} f(t)\,dt = \frac{dy}{dx} \cdot \frac{d}{dy} \int_a^y f(t)\,dt = g'(x)\,f(y),$$

which completes the proof.

□

Practice Exercise 1.6. Evaluate the integral

$$\frac{d}{dx}\int_0^{x-\mu}\frac{1}{\sqrt{2\pi\sigma^2}}\exp\left\{-\frac{t^2}{2\sigma^2}\right\}dt.$$

Solution. Let $y = x - \mu$. Then by using the fundamental theorem of calculus, we can show that

$$\frac{d}{dx}\int_0^{x-\mu}\frac{1}{\sqrt{2\pi\sigma^2}}\exp\left\{-\frac{t^2}{2\sigma^2}\right\}dt = \frac{dy}{dx}\cdot\frac{d}{dy}\int_0^{y}\frac{1}{\sqrt{2\pi\sigma^2}}\exp\left\{-\frac{t^2}{2\sigma^2}\right\}dt$$

$$= \frac{d(x-\mu)}{dx}\cdot\frac{1}{\sqrt{2\pi\sigma^2}}\exp\left\{-\frac{y^2}{2\sigma^2}\right\}$$

$$= \frac{1}{\sqrt{2\pi\sigma^2}}\exp\left\{-\frac{(x-\mu)^2}{2\sigma^2}\right\}.$$

This result will be useful when we do linear transformations of a Gaussian random variable in Chapter 4.

1.4 Linear Algebra

The two most important subjects for data science are *probability*, which is the subject of the book you are reading, and *linear algebra*, which concerns matrices and vectors. We cannot cover linear algebra in detail because this would require another book. However, we need to highlight some ideas that are important for doing data analysis.

1.4.1 Why do we need linear algebra in data science?

Consider a dataset of the crime rate of several cities as shown below, downloaded from https://web.stanford.edu/~hastie/StatLearnSparsity/data.html.

The table shows that the crime rate depends on several factors such as funding for the police department, the percentage of high school graduates, etc.

city	crime rate	funding	hs	no-hs	college	college4
1	478	40	74	11	31	20
2	494	32	72	11	43	18
3	643	57	71	18	16	16
4	341	31	71	11	25	19
⋮	⋮	⋮	⋮	⋮	⋮	⋮
50	940	66	67	26	18	16

What questions can we ask about this table? We can ask: What is the most influential cause of the crime rate? What are the leading contributions to the crime rate? To answer these questions, we need to describe these numbers. One way to do it is to put the numbers in matrices and vectors. For example,

$$\boldsymbol{y}_{\text{crime}} = \begin{bmatrix} 478 \\ 494 \\ \vdots \\ 940 \end{bmatrix}, \quad \boldsymbol{x}_{\text{fund}} = \begin{bmatrix} 40 \\ 32 \\ \vdots \\ 66 \end{bmatrix}, \quad \boldsymbol{x}_{\text{hs}} = \begin{bmatrix} 74 \\ 72 \\ \vdots \\ 67 \end{bmatrix}, \dots$$

With this vector expression of the data, the analysis questions can roughly be translated to finding β's in the following equation:

$$\boldsymbol{y}_{\text{crime}} = \beta_{\text{fund}}\boldsymbol{x}_{\text{fund}} + \beta_{\text{hs}}\boldsymbol{x}_{\text{hs}} + \cdots + \beta_{\text{college4}}\boldsymbol{x}_{\text{college4}}.$$

This equation offers a lot of useful insights. First, it is a **linear model** of $\boldsymbol{y}_{\text{crime}}$. We call it a linear model because the observable $\boldsymbol{y}_{\text{crime}}$ is written as a **linear combination** of the variables $\boldsymbol{x}_{\text{fund}}, \boldsymbol{x}_{\text{hs}}$, etc. The linear model assumes that the variables are scaled and added to generate the observed phenomena. This assumption is not always realistic, but it is often a fair assumption that greatly simplifies the problem. For example, if we can show that all β's are zero except β_{fund}, then we can conclude that the crime rate is solely dependent on the police funding. If two variables are correlated, e.g., high school graduate and college graduate, we would expect the β's to change simultaneously.

The linear model can further be simplified to a matrix-vector equation:

$$\begin{bmatrix} | \\ \boldsymbol{y}_{\text{crime}} \\ | \end{bmatrix} = \begin{bmatrix} | & | & & | \\ \boldsymbol{x}_{\text{fund}} & \boldsymbol{x}_{\text{hs}} & \cdots & \boldsymbol{x}_{\text{college4}} \\ | & | & & | \end{bmatrix} \begin{bmatrix} \beta_{\text{fund}} \\ \beta_{\text{hs}} \\ \vdots \\ \beta_{\text{college4}} \end{bmatrix}$$

Here, the lines "|" emphasize that the vectors are column vectors. If we denote the matrix in the middle as $\boldsymbol{A}$ and the vector as $\boldsymbol{\beta}$, then the equation is equivalent to $\boldsymbol{y} = \boldsymbol{A}\boldsymbol{\beta}$. So we can find $\boldsymbol{\beta}$ by appropriately inverting the matrix $\boldsymbol{A}$. If two columns of $\boldsymbol{A}$ are dependent, we will not be able to resolve the corresponding β's uniquely.

As you can see from the above data analysis problem, matrices and vectors offer a way to describe the data. We will discuss the calculations in Chapter 7. However, to understand how to interpret the results from the matrix-vector equations, we need to review some basic ideas about matrices and vectors.

1.4.2 Everything you need to know about linear algebra

Throughout this book, you will see different sets of notations. For linear algebra, we also have a set of notations. We denote $\boldsymbol{x} \in \mathbb{R}^d$ a d-dimensional vector taking real numbers as its entries. An M-by-N matrix is denoted as $\boldsymbol{X} \in \mathbb{R}^{M \times N}$. The transpose of a matrix is denoted as $\boldsymbol{X}^T$. A matrix $\boldsymbol{X}$ can be viewed according to its columns and its rows:

$$\boldsymbol{X} = \begin{bmatrix} | & | & & | \\ \boldsymbol{x}_1 & \boldsymbol{x}_2 & \cdots & \boldsymbol{x}_N \\ | & | & & | \end{bmatrix}, \quad \text{and} \quad \boldsymbol{X} = \begin{bmatrix} - & \boldsymbol{x}^1 & - \\ - & \boldsymbol{x}^2 & - \\ & \vdots & \\ - & \boldsymbol{x}^M & - \end{bmatrix}.$$

Here, $\boldsymbol{x}_j$ denotes the jth column of $\boldsymbol{X}$, and $\boldsymbol{x}^i$ denotes the ith row of $\boldsymbol{X}$. The (i,j)th element of $\boldsymbol{X}$ is denoted as x_{ij} or $[\boldsymbol{X}]_{ij}$. The identity matrix is denoted as $\boldsymbol{I}$. The ith column of $\boldsymbol{I}$ is denoted as $\boldsymbol{e}_i = [0, \ldots, 1, \ldots, 0]^T$, and is called the ith **standard basis vector**. An all-zero vector is denoted as $\boldsymbol{0} = [0, \ldots, 0]^T$.

What is the most important thing to know about linear algebra? From a data analysis point of view, **Figure 1.11** gives us the answer. The picture is straightforward, but it captures all the essence. In almost all the data analysis problems, ultimately, there are three things we care about: (i) The observable vector $\boldsymbol{y}$, (ii) the variable vectors $\boldsymbol{x}_n$, and (iii) the coefficients β_n. The set of variable vectors $\{\boldsymbol{x}_n\}_{n=1}^N$ **spans** a vector space in which all vectors are living. Some of these variable vectors are correlated, and some are not. However, for the sake of this discussion, let us assume they are independent of each other. Then for any observable vector $\boldsymbol{y}$, we can always project $\boldsymbol{y}$ in the directions determined by $\{\boldsymbol{x}_n\}_{n=1}^N$. The projection of $\boldsymbol{y}$ onto $\boldsymbol{x}_n$ is the coefficient β_n. A larger value of β_n means that the variable $\boldsymbol{x}_n$ has more contributions.

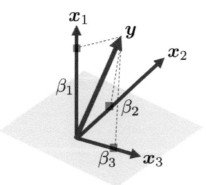

Figure 1.11: Representing an observable vector $\boldsymbol{y}$ by a linear combination of variable vectors $\boldsymbol{x}_1$, $\boldsymbol{x}_2$ and $\boldsymbol{x}_3$. The combination weights are $\beta_1, \beta_2, \beta_3$.

Why is this picture so important? Because most of the data analysis problems can be expressed, or approximately expressed, by the picture:

$$\boldsymbol{y} = \sum_{n=1}^N \beta_n \boldsymbol{x}_n.$$

If you recall the crime rate example, this equation is precisely the linear model we used to describe the crime rate. This equation can also describe many other problems.

Example 1.6. Polynomial fitting. Consider a dataset of pairs of numbers (t_m, y_m) for $m = 1, \ldots, M$, as shown in **Figure 1.12**. After a visual inspection of the dataset, we propose to use a line to fit the data. A line is specified by the equation

$$y_m = a t_m + b, \qquad m = 1, \ldots, M,$$

where $a \in \mathbb{R}$ is the slope and $b \in \mathbb{R}$ is the y-intercept. The goal of this problem is to find one line (which is fully characterized by (a, b)) such that it has the best fit to *all* the data pairs (t_m, y_m) for $m = 1, \ldots, M$. This problem can be described in matrices

---

and vectors by noting that

$$
\underbrace{\begin{bmatrix} y_1 \\ \vdots \\ y_M \end{bmatrix}}_{y} = \underbrace{a}_{\beta_1} \underbrace{\begin{bmatrix} t_1 \\ \vdots \\ t_M \end{bmatrix}}_{x_1} + \underbrace{b}_{\beta_2} \underbrace{\begin{bmatrix} 1 \\ \vdots \\ 1 \end{bmatrix}}_{x_2},
$$

or more compactly,

$$
y = \beta_1 x_1 + \beta_2 x_2.
$$

Here, $x_1 = [t_1, \ldots, t_M]^T$ contains all the variable values, and $x_2 = [1, \ldots, 1]^T$ contains a constant offset.

t_m	y_m
0.1622	2.1227
0.7943	3.3354
$\vdots$	$\vdots$
0.7379	3.4054
0.2691	2.5672
0.4228	2.3796
0.6020	3.2942

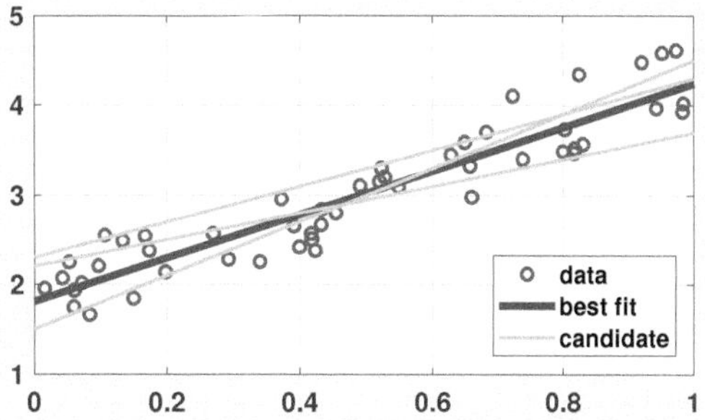

Figure 1.12: Example of fitting a set of data points. The problem can be described by $y = \beta_1 x_1 + \beta_2 x_2$.

Example 1.7. Image compression. The JPEG compression for images is based on the concept of **discrete cosine transform** (DCT). The DCT consists of a set of **basis vectors**, or $\{x_n\}_{n=1}^N$ using our notation. In the most standard setting, each basis vector x_n consists of 8×8 pixels, and there are $N = 64$ of these x_n's. Given an image, we can partition the image into M small blocks of 8×8 pixels. Let us call one of these blocks y. Then, DCT represents the observation y as a linear combination of the DCT basis vectors:

$$
y = \sum_{n=1}^N \beta_n x_n.
$$

The coefficients $\{\beta_n\}_{n=1}^N$ are called the DCT coefficients. They provide a **representation** of y, because once we know $\{\beta_n\}_{n=1}^N$, we can completely describe y because the basis vectors $\{x_n\}_{n=1}^N$ are known and fixed. The situation is depicted in **Figure 1.13**.

How can we compress images using DCT? In the 1970s, scientists found that most images have strong leading DCT coefficients but weak tail DCT coefficients. In other words, among the $N = 64$ β_n's, only the first few are important. If we truncate the number of DCT coefficients, we can effectively compress the number of bits required to represent the image.

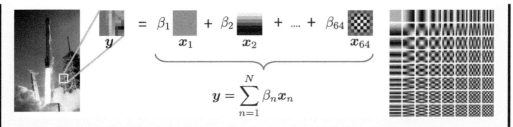

Figure 1.13: JPEG image compression is based on the concept of discrete cosine transform, which can be formulated as a matrix-vector problem.

We hope by now you are convinced of the importance of matrices and vectors in the context of data science. They are not "yet another" subject but an essential tool you must know how to use. So, what are the technical materials you must master? Here we go.

1.4.3 Inner products and norms

We assume that you know the basic operations such as matrix-vector multiplication, taking the transpose, etc. If you have forgotten these, please consult any undergraduate linear algebra textbook such as Gilbert Strang's *Linear Algebra and its Applications*. We will highlight a few of the most important operations for our purposes.

Definition 1.4 (Inner product). *Let $\boldsymbol{x} = [x_1, \ldots, x_N]^T$, and $\boldsymbol{y} = [y_1, \ldots, y_N]^T$. The inner product $\boldsymbol{x}^T \boldsymbol{y}$ is*

$$\boldsymbol{x}^T \boldsymbol{y} = \sum_{i=1}^{N} x_i y_i. \tag{1.14}$$

Practice Exercise 1.7. Let $\boldsymbol{x} = [1,\ 0,\ -1]^T$, and $\boldsymbol{y} = [3,\ 2,\ 0]^T$. Find $\boldsymbol{x}^T \boldsymbol{y}$.

Solution. The inner product is $\boldsymbol{x}^T \boldsymbol{y} = (1)(3) + (0)(2) + (-1)(0) = 3$.

Inner products are important because they tell us how two vectors are correlated. **Figure 1.14** depicts the geometric meaning of an inner product. If two vectors are correlated (i.e., nearly parallel), then the inner product will give us a large value. Conversely, if the two vectors are close to perpendicular, then the inner product will be small. Therefore, the inner product provides a measure of the closeness/similarity between two vectors.

Figure 1.14: Geometric interpretation of inner product: We project one vector onto the other vector. The projected distance is the inner product.

Creating vectors and computing the inner products are straightforward in MATLAB. We simply need to define the column vectors x and y by using the command [] with ; to denote the next row. The inner product is done using the transpose operation x' and vector multiplication *.

```
% MATLAB code to perform an inner product
x = [1 0 -1];
y = [3 2 0];
z = x'*y;
```

In Python, constructing a vector is done using the command `np.array`. Inside this command, one needs to enter the array. For a column vector, we write `[[1],[2],[3]]`, with an outer `[]`, and three inner `[]` for each entry. If the vector is a row vector, the one can omit the inner `[]`'s by just calling `np.array([1, 2, 3])`. Given two column vectors x and y, the inner product is computed via `np.dot(x.T,y)`, where `np.dot` is the command for inner product, and `x.T` returns the transpose of x. One can also call `np.transpose(x)`, which is the same as `x.T`.

```
# Python code to perform an inner product
import numpy as np
x = np.array([[1],[0],[-1]])
y = np.array([[3],[2],[0]])
z = np.dot(np.transpose(x),y)
print(z)
```

In data analytics, the inner product of two vectors can be useful. Consider the vectors in **Table 1.1**. Just from looking at the numbers, you probably will not see anything wrong. However, let's compute the inner products. It turns out that $x_1^T x_2 = -0.0031$, whereas $x_1^T x_3 = 2.0020$. There is almost no correlation between x_1 and x_2, but there is a substantial correlation between x_1 and x_3. What happened? The vectors x_1 and x_2 are random vectors constructed independently and uncorrelated to each other. The last vector x_3 was constructed by $x_3 = 2x_1 - \pi/1000$. Since x_3 is completely constructed from x_1, they have to be correlated.

x_1	x_2	x_3
0.0006	−0.0011	−0.0020
−0.0014	−0.0024	−0.0059
−0.0034	0.0073	−0.0099
⋮	⋮	⋮
0.0001	−0.0066	−0.0030
0.0074	0.0046	0.0116
0.0007	−0.0061	−0.0017

Table 1.1: Three example vectors.

One caveat for this example is that the naive inner product $x_i^T x_j$ is scale-dependent. For example, the vectors $x_3 = x_1$ and $x_3 = 1000x_1$ have the same amount of correlation, but the simple inner product will give a larger value for the latter case. To solve this problem we first define the **norm** of the vectors:

Definition 1.5 (Norm). *Let $x = [x_1, \ldots, x_N]^T$ be a vector. The ℓ_p-norm of x is*

$$\|x\|_p = \left(\sum_{i=1}^{N} |x_i|^p \right)^{1/p}, \qquad (1.15)$$

for any $p \geq 1$.

The norm essentially tells us the **length** of the vector. This is most obvious if we consider the ℓ_2-norm:

$$\|x\|_2 = \left(\sum_{i=1}^{N} x_i^2 \right)^{1/2}.$$

By taking the square on both sides, one can show that $\|x\|_2^2 = x^T x$. This is called the **squared ℓ_2-norm**, and is the sum of the squares.

On MATLAB, computing the norm is done using the command `norm`. Here, we can indicate the types of norms, e.g., `norm(x,1)` returns the ℓ_1-norm whereas `norm(x,2)` returns the ℓ_2-norm (which is also the default).

```
% MATLAB code to compute the norm
x = [1 0 -1];
x_norm = norm(x);
```

On Python, the norm command is listed in the `np.linalg`. To call the ℓ_1-norm, we use `np.linalg.norm(x,1)`, and by default the ℓ_2-norm is `np.linalg.norm(x)`.

```
# Python code to compute the norm
import numpy as np
x = np.array([[1],[0],[-1]])
x_norm = np.linalg.norm(x)
```

Using the norm, one can define an angle called the **cosine angle** between two vectors.

Definition 1.6. *The **cosine angle** between two vectors x and y is*

$$\cos \theta = \frac{x^T y}{\|x\|_2 \|y\|_2}. \qquad (1.16)$$

The difference between the cosine angle and the basic inner product is the **normalization** in the denominator, which is the product $\|x\|_2 \|y\|_2$. This normalization factor scales the vector x to $x/\|x\|_2$ and y to $y/\|y\|_2$. The scaling makes the length of the new vector equal to unity, but it does not change the vector's orientation. Therefore, the cosine angle is not affected by a very long vector or a very short vector. Only the angle matters. See **Figure 1.15**.

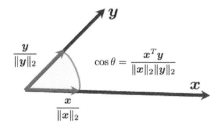

Figure 1.15: The cosine angle is the inner product divided by the norms of the vectors.

Going back to the previous example, after normalization we can show that the cosine angle between x_1 and x_2 is $\cos\theta_{1,2} = -0.0031$, whereas the cosine angle between x_1 and x_3 is $\cos\theta_{1,3} = 0.8958$. There is still a strong correlation between x_1 and x_3, but now using the cosine angle the value is between -1 and $+1$.

Remark 1: There are other norms one can use. The ℓ_1-norm is useful for **sparse** models where we want to have the fewest possible non-zeros. The ℓ_1-norm of x is

$$\|x\|_1 = \sum_{i=1}^{N} |x_i|,$$

which is the sum of absolute values. The ℓ_∞-norm picks the maximum of $\{x_1, \ldots, x_N\}$:

$$\|x\|_\infty = \lim_{p\to\infty} \left(\sum_{i=1}^{N} |x_i|^p \right)^{1/p}$$

$$= \max\{|x_1|, \ldots, |x_N|\},$$

because as $p \to \infty$, only the largest element will be amplified.

Remark 2: The standard ℓ_2-norm is a circle: Just consider $x = [x_1, x_2]^T$. The norm is $\|x\|_2 = \sqrt{x_1^2 + x_2^2}$. We can convert the circle to ellipses by considering a weighted norm.

Definition 1.7 (Weighted ℓ_2-norm square). *Let* $x = [x_1, \ldots, x_N]^T$ *and let* $W = diag(w_1, \ldots, w_N)$ *be a non-negative diagonal matrix. The weighted ℓ_2-norm square of* x *is*

$$\|x\|_W^2 = x^T W x$$

$$= \begin{bmatrix} x_1 & \cdots & x_N \end{bmatrix} \begin{bmatrix} w_1 & \cdots & 0 \\ \vdots & \ddots & \vdots \\ 0 & \cdots & w_N \end{bmatrix} \begin{bmatrix} x_1 \\ \vdots \\ x_N \end{bmatrix} = \sum_{i=1}^{N} w_i x_i^2. \quad (1.17)$$

The geometry of the weighted ℓ_2-norm is determined by the matrix W. For example, if $W = I$ (the identity operator), then $\|x\|_W^2 = \|x\|_2^2$, which defines a circle. If W is any "non-negative" matrix[2], then $\|x\|_W^2$ defines an ellipse.

---

[2]The technical term for these matrices is *positive semi-definite* matrices.

In MATLAB, the weighted inner product is just a sequence of two matrix-vector multiplications. This can be done using the command `x'*W*x` as shown below.

```
% MATLAB code to compute the weighted norm
W = [1 2 3; 4 5 6; 7 8 9];
x = [2; -1; 1];
z = x'*W*x
```

In Python, constructing the matrix $\boldsymbol{W}$ and the column vector $\boldsymbol{x}$ is done using `np.array`. The matrix-vector multiplication is done using two `np.dot` commands: one for `np.dot(W,x)` and the other one for `np.dot(x.T, np.dot(W,x))`.

```
# Python code to compute the weighted norm
import numpy as np
W = np.array([[1, 2, 3], [4, 5, 6], [7, 8, 9]])
x = np.array([[2],[-1],[1]])
z = np.dot(x.T, np.dot(W,x))
print(z)
```

1.4.4 Matrix calculus

The last linear algebra topic we need to review is matrix calculus. As its name indicates, matrix calculus is about the differentiation of matrices and vectors. Why do we need differentiation for matrices and vectors? Because we want to find the **minimum or maximum** of a scalar function with a vector input.

Let us go back to the crime rate problem we discussed earlier. Given the data, we want to find the model coefficients $\beta_1, \ldots, \beta_N$ such that the variables can best explain the observation. In other words, we want to minimize the deviation between $\boldsymbol{y}$ and the prediction offered by our model:

$$\underset{\beta_1, \ldots, \beta_N}{\text{minimize}} \left\| \boldsymbol{y} - \sum_{n=1}^{N} \beta_n \boldsymbol{x}_n \right\|^2.$$

This equation is self-explanatory. The norm $\|\clubsuit - \heartsuit\|^2$ measures the deviation. If $\boldsymbol{y}$ can be perfectly explained by $\{\boldsymbol{x}_n\}_{n=1}^{N}$, then the norm can eventually go to zero by finding a good set of $\{\beta_1, \ldots, \beta_N\}$. The symbol $\underset{\beta_1, \ldots, \beta_N}{\text{minimize}}$ means to minimize the function by finding $\{\beta_1, \ldots, \beta_N\}$. Note that the norm is taking a vector as the input and generating a scalar as the output. It can be expressed as

$$\varepsilon(\boldsymbol{\beta}) \overset{\text{def}}{=} \left\| \boldsymbol{y} - \sum_{n=1}^{N} \beta_n \boldsymbol{x}_n \right\|^2,$$

to emphasize this relationship. Here we define $\boldsymbol{\beta} = [\beta_1, \ldots, \beta_N]^T$ as the collection of all coefficients.

Given this setup, how would you determine $\boldsymbol{\beta}$ such that the deviation is minimized? Our calculus teachers told us that we could take the function's derivative and set it to zero for scalar problems. It is the same story for vectors. What we do is to take the derivative of the error and set it equal to zero:

$$\frac{d}{d\beta}\,\varepsilon(\beta) = 0.$$

Now the question arises, how do we take the derivatives of $\varepsilon(\beta)$ when it takes a vector as input? If we can answer this question, we will find the best β. The answer is straightforward. Since the function has one output and many inputs, take the derivative for each element independently. This is called the **scalar differentiation of vectors**.

Definition 1.8 (Scalar differentiation of vectors). *Let $f : \mathbb{R}^N \to \mathbb{R}$ be a differentiable scalar function, and let $y = f(x)$ for some input $x \in \mathbb{R}^N$. Then,*

$$\frac{dy}{dx} = \begin{bmatrix} dy/dx_1 \\ \vdots \\ dy/dx_N \end{bmatrix}.$$

As you can see from this definition, there is nothing conceptually challenging here. The only difficulty is that things can get tedious because there will be many terms. However, the good news is that mathematicians have already compiled a list of identities for common matrix differentiation. So instead of deriving every equation from scratch, we can enjoy the fruit of their hard work by referring to those formulae. The best place to find these equations is the *Matrix Cookbook* by Petersen and Pedersen.[3] Here, we will mention two of the most useful results.

Example 1.8. Let $y = x^T A x$ for any matrix $A \in \mathbb{R}^{N \times N}$. Find $\frac{dy}{dx}$.

Solution.

$$\frac{d}{dx}\left(x^T A x\right) = A x + A^T x.$$

Now, if A is symmetric, i.e., $A = A^T$, then

$$\frac{d}{dx}\left(x^T A x\right) = 2A x.$$

Example 1.9. Let $\varepsilon = \|Ax - y\|_2^2$, where $A \in \mathbb{R}^{N \times N}$ is symmetric. Find $\frac{d\varepsilon}{dx}$.

Solution. First, we note that

$$\varepsilon = \|Ax - y\|_2^2$$
$$= x^T A^T A x - 2y^T A x + y^T y.$$

---

[3]https://www.math.uwaterloo.ca/~hwolkowi/matrixcookbook.pdf

Taking the derivative with respect to $\boldsymbol{x}$ yields

$$\frac{d\varepsilon}{d\boldsymbol{x}} = 2\boldsymbol{A}^T\boldsymbol{A}\boldsymbol{x} - 2\boldsymbol{A}^T\boldsymbol{y}$$
$$= 2\boldsymbol{A}^T(\boldsymbol{A}\boldsymbol{x} - \boldsymbol{y}).$$

Going back to the crime rate problem, we can now show that

$$0 = \frac{d\varepsilon}{d\boldsymbol{\beta}}\|\boldsymbol{y} - \boldsymbol{X}\boldsymbol{\beta}\|^2 = 2\boldsymbol{X}^T(\boldsymbol{X}\boldsymbol{\beta} - \boldsymbol{y}).$$

Therefore, the solution is

$$\widehat{\boldsymbol{\beta}} = (\boldsymbol{X}^T\boldsymbol{X})^{-1}\boldsymbol{X}^T\boldsymbol{y}.$$

As you can see, if we do not have access to the matrix calculus, we will not be able to solve the minimization problem. (There are alternative paths that do not require matrix calculus, but they require an understanding of linear subspaces and properties of the projection operators. So in some sense, matrix calculus is the easiest way to solve the problem.) When we discuss the linear regression methods in Chapter 7, we will cover the interpretation of the inverses and related topics.

In MATLAB and Python, matrix inversion is done using the command `inv` in MAT-LAB and `np.linalg.inv` in Python. Below is an example in Python.

```
# Python code to compute a matrix inverse
import numpy as np
X      = np.array([[1, 3], [-2, 7], [0, 1]])
XtX    = np.dot(X.T, X)
XtXinv = np.linalg.inv(XtX)
print(XtXinv)
```

Sometimes, instead of computing the matrix inverse we are more interested in solving a linear equation $\boldsymbol{X}\boldsymbol{\beta} = \boldsymbol{y}$ (the solution of which is $\widehat{\boldsymbol{\beta}} = (\boldsymbol{X}^T\boldsymbol{X})^{-1}\boldsymbol{X}\boldsymbol{y}$). In both MATLAB and Python, there are built-in commands to do this. In MATLAB, the command is \ (backslash).

```
% MATLAB code to solve X beta = y
X      = [1 3; -2 7; 0 1];
y      = [2; 1; 0];
beta   = X\y;
```

In Python, the built-in command is `np.linalg.lstsq`.

```
# Python code to solve X beta = y
import numpy as np
X      = np.array([[1, 3], [-2, 7], [0, 1]])
y      = np.array([[2],[1],[0]])
beta   = np.linalg.lstsq(X, y, rcond=None)[0]
print(beta)
```

Closing remark: In this section, we have given a brief introduction to a few of the most relevant concepts in linear algebra. We will introduce further concepts in linear algebra in later chapters, such as eigenvalues, principal component analysis, linear transformations, and regularization, as they become useful for our discussion.

1.5 Basic Combinatorics

The last topic we review in this chapter is **combinatorics**. Combinatorics concerns the number of configurations that can be obtained from certain discrete experiments. It is useful because it provides a systematic way of enumerating cases. Combinatorics often becomes very challenging as the complexity of the event grows. However, you may rest assured that in this book, we will not tackle the more difficult problems of combinatorics; we will confine our discussion to two of the most basic principles: **permutation** and **combination**.

1.5.1 Birthday paradox

To motivate the discussion of combinatorics, let us start with the following problem. Suppose there are 50 people in a room. What is the probability that at least one pair of people have the same birthday (month and day)? (We exclude Feb. 29 in this problem.)

The first thing you might be thinking is that since there are 365 days, we need at least 366 people to ensure that one pair has the same birthday. Therefore, the chance that 2 of 50 people have the same birthday is low. This seems reasonable, but let's do a simulated experiment. In **Figure 1.16** we plot the probability as a function of the number of people. For a room containing 50 people, the probability is 97%. To get a 50% probability, we just need 23 people! How is this possible?

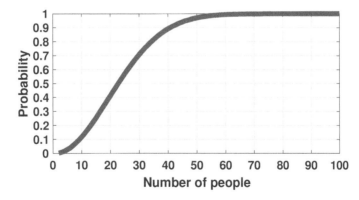

Figure 1.16: The probability for two people in a group to have the same birthday as a function of the number of people in the group.

If you think about this problem more deeply, you will probably realize that to solve the problem, we must carefully enumerate all the possible configurations. How can we do this?

Well, suppose you walk into the room and sequentially pick two people. The probability that they have *different* birthdays is

$$\mathbb{P}[\text{The first 2 people have different birthdays}] = \frac{365}{365} \times \frac{364}{365}.$$

When you ask the first person to tell you their birthday, he or she can occupy any of the 365 slots. This gives us $\frac{365}{365}$. The second person has one slot short because the first person has taken it, and so the probability that he or she has a different birthday from the first person is $\frac{364}{365}$. Note that this calculation is independent of how many people you have in the room because you are picking them sequentially.

If you now choose a third person, the probability that they have different birthdays is

$$\mathbb{P}[\text{The first 3 people have different birthdays}] = \frac{365}{365} \times \frac{364}{365} \times \frac{363}{365}.$$

This process can be visualized in **Figure 1.17**.

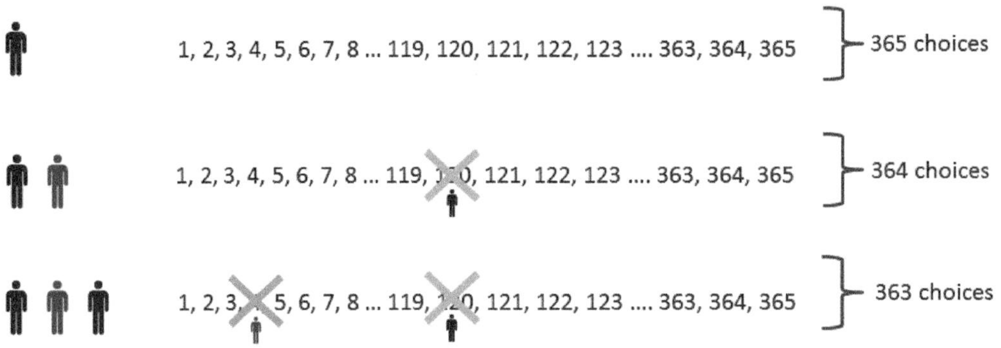

Figure 1.17: The probability for two people to have the same birthday as a function of the number of people in the group. When there is only one person, this person can land on any of the 365 days. When there are two people, the first person has already taken one day (out of 365 days), so the second person can only choose 364 days. When there are three people, the first two people have occupied two days, so there are only 363 days left. If we generalize this process, we see that the number of configurations is $365 \times 364 \times \cdots \times (365 - k + 1)$, where k is the number of people in the room.

So imagine that you keep going down the list to the 50th person. The probability that none of these 50 people will have the same birthday is

$$\mathbb{P}[\text{The first 50 people have different birthdays}]$$
$$= \frac{365}{365} \times \frac{364}{365} \times \frac{363}{365} \times \cdots \times \frac{316}{365} \approx 0.03.$$

That means that the probability for 50 people to have different birthdays, the probability is as little as 3%. If you take the complement, you can show that with 97% probability, there is at least one pair of people having the same birthday.

The general equation for this problem is now easy to see:

$$\mathbb{P}[\text{The first } k \text{ people have different birthdays}] = \frac{365 \times 364 \times \cdots \times (365 - k + 1)}{365 \times 365 \times \cdots \times 365}$$
$$= \frac{365!}{(365 - k)!} \times \frac{1}{365^k}.$$

The first term in our equation, $\frac{365!}{(365-k)!}$, is called the **permutation** of picking k days from 365 options. We shall discuss this operation shortly.

Why is the probability so high with only 50 people while it seems that we need 366 people to ensure two identical birthdays? The difference is the notion of **probabilistic** and **deterministic**. The 366-people argument is deterministic. If you have 366 people, you are certain that two people will have the same birthday. This has no conflict with the probabilistic argument because the probabilistic argument says that with 50 people, we have a 97% chance of getting two identical birthdays. With a 97% success rate, you still have a 3% chance of failing. It is unlikely to happen, but it can still happen. The more people you put into the room, the stronger guarantee you will have. However, even if you have 364 people and the probability is almost 100%, there is still no guarantee. So there is no conflict between the two arguments since they are answering two different questions.

Now, let's discuss the two combinatorics questions.

1.5.2 Permutation

Permutation concerns the following question:

Consider a set of n distinct balls. Suppose we want to pick k balls from the set without replacement. How many ordered configurations can we obtain?

Note that in the above question, the word "ordered" is crucial. For example, the set $A = \{a, b, c\}$ can lead to 6 different ordered configurations

$$(a, b, c), \ (a, c, b), \ (b, a, c), \ (b, c, a), \ (c, a, b), \ (c, b, a).$$

As a simple illustration of how to compute the permutation, we can consider a set of 5 colored balls as shown in **Figure 1.18**.

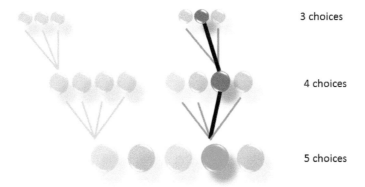

Figure 1.18: Permutation. The number of choices is reduced in every stage. Therefore, the total number is $n \times (n-1) \times \cdots \times (n-k+1)$ if there are k stages.

If you start with the base, which contains five balls, you will have five choices. At one level up, since one ball has already been taken, you have only four choices. You continue the process until you reached the number of balls you want to collect. The number of configurations you have generated is the permutation. Here is the formula:

Theorem 1.6. *The number of* **permutations** *of choosing k out of n is*

$$\frac{n!}{(n-k)!}$$

where $n! = n(n-1)(n-2)\cdots 3 \cdot 2 \cdot 1$.

Proof. Let's list all possible ways:

Which ball to pick	Number of choices	Why?
The 1st ball	n	No has been picked, so we have n choices
The 2nd ball	$n-1$	The first ball has been picked
The 3rd ball	$n-2$	The first two balls have been picked
$\vdots$	$\vdots$	$\vdots$
The kth ball	$n-k+1$	The first $k-1$ balls have been picked
Total:	$n(n-1)\cdots(n-k+1)$	

The total number of ordered configurations is $n(n-1)\cdots(n-k+1)$. This simplifies to

$$n(n-1)(n-2)\cdots(n-k+1)$$
$$= n(n-1)(n-2)\cdots(n-k+1) \cdot \frac{(n-k)(n-k-1)\cdots 3 \cdot 2 \cdot 1}{(n-k)(n-k-1)\cdots 3 \cdot 2 \cdot 1}$$
$$= \frac{n!}{(n-k)!}.$$

$\square$

Practice Exercise 1.8. Consider a set of 4 balls $\{1, 2, 3, 4\}$. We want to pick two balls at random without replacement. The ordering matters. How many permutations can we obtain?

Solution. The possible configurations are (1,2), (2,1), (1,3), (3,1), (1,4), (4,1), (2,3), (3,2), (2,4), (4,2), (3,4), (4,3). So totally there are 12 configurations. We can also verify this number by noting that there are 4 balls altogether and so the number of choices for picking the first ball is 4 and the number of choices for picking the second ball is $(4-1) = 3$. Thus, the total is $4 \cdot 3 = 12$. Referring to the formula, this result coincides with the theorem, which states that the number of permutations is $\frac{4!}{(4-2)!} = \frac{4 \cdot 3 \cdot 2 \cdot 1}{2 \cdot 1} = 12$.

1.5.3 Combination

Another operation in combinatorics is combination. Combination concerns the following question:

*Consider a set of n distinct balls. Suppose we want to pick k balls from the set without replacement. How many **unordered** configurations can we obtain?*

Unlike permutation, combination treats a subset of balls with whatever ordering as one single configuration. For example, the subset (a, b, c) is considered the same as (a, c, b) or (b, c, a), etc.

Let's go back to the 5-ball exercise. Suppose you have picked orange, green, and light blue. This is the same combination as if you have picked {green, orange, and light blue}, or {green, light blue, and orange}. **Figure 1.19** lists all the six possible configurations for these three balls. So what is combination? Combination needs to take these repeated cases into account.

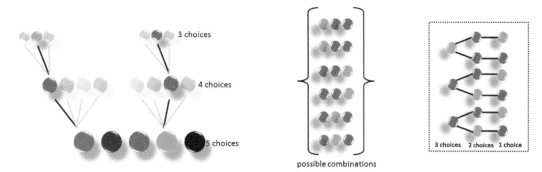

Figure 1.19: Combination. In this problem, we are interested in picking 3 colored balls out of 5. This will give us $5 \times 4 \times 3 = 60$ permutations. However, since we are not interested in the ordering, some of the permutations are repeated. For example, there are 6 combos of (green, light blue, orange), which is computed from $3 \times 2 \times 1$. Dividing 60 permutations by these 6 choices of the orderings will give us 10 distinct combinations of the colors.

Theorem 1.7. *The number of* **combinations** *of choosing k out of n is*

$$\frac{n!}{k!(n-k)!}$$

where $n! = n(n-1)(n-2)\cdots 3 \cdot 2 \cdot 1.$

Proof. We start with the permutation result, which gives us $\frac{n!}{(n-k)!}$ permutations. Note that every permutation has exactly k balls. However, while these k balls can be arranged in any order, in combination, we treat them as one single configuration. Therefore, the task is to count the number of possible orderings for these k balls.

To this end, we note that for a set of k balls, there are in total $k!$ possible ways of ordering them. The number $k!$ comes from the following table.

Which ball to pick	Number of choices
The 1st ball	k
The 2nd ball	$k-1$
$\vdots$	$\vdots$
The kth ball	1
Total:	$k(k-1)\cdots 3\cdot 2\cdot 1$

Therefore, the total number of orderings for a set of k balls is $k!$. Since permutation gives us $\frac{n!}{(n-k)!}$ and every permutation has $k!$ repetitions due to ordering, we divide the number by $k!$. Thus the number of combinations is

$$\frac{n!}{k!(n-k)!}.$$

$\square$

Practice Exercise 1.9. Consider a set of 4 balls $\{1,2,3,4\}$. We want to pick two balls at random without replacement. The ordering does not matter. How many combinations can we obtain?

Solution. The permutation result gives us 12 permutations. However, among all these 12 permutations, there are only 6 distinct pairs of numbers. We can confirm this by noting that since we picked 2 balls, there are exactly 2 possible orderings for these 2 balls. Therefore, we have $\frac{12}{2} = 6$ number of combinations. Using the formula of the theorem, we check that the number of combinations is

$$\frac{4!}{2!(4-2)!} = \frac{4\cdot 3\cdot 2\cdot 1}{(2\cdot 1)(2\cdot 1)} = 6.$$

Example 1.10. (Ross, 8th edition, Section 1.6) Consider the equation

$$x_1 + x_2 + \cdots + x_K = N,$$

where $\{x_k\}$ are positive integers. How many combinations of solutions of this equation are there?

Solution. We can determine the number of combinations by considering the figure below. The integer N can be modeled as N balls in an urn. The number of variables K is equivalent to the number of colors of these balls. Since all variables are positive, the problem can be translated to partitioning the N balls into K buckets. This, in turn, is the same as inserting $K-1$ dividers among $N-1$ holes. Therefore, the number of combinations is

$$\binom{N-1}{K-1} = \frac{(N-1)!}{(K-1)!(N-K)!}.$$

For example, if $N = 16$ and $K = 4$, then the number of solutions is

$$\binom{16-1}{4-1} = \frac{15!}{3!12!} = 455.$$

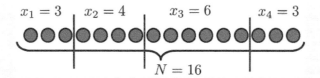

Figure 1.20: One possible solution for $N = 16$ and $K = 4$. In general, the problem is equivalent to inserting $K - 1$ dividers among $N - 1$ balls.

Closing remark. Permutations and combinations are two ways to enumerate all the possible cases. While the conclusions are probabilistic, as the birthday paradox shows, permutation and combination are deterministic. We do not need to worry about the distribution of the samples, and we are not taking averages of anything. Thus, modern data analysis seldom uses the concepts of permutation and combination. Accordingly, combinatorics does not play a large role in this book.

Does it mean that combinatorics is not useful? Not quite, because it still provides us with powerful tools for theoretical analysis. For example, in binomial random variables, we need the concept of combination to calculate the repeated cases. The Poisson random variable can be regarded as a limiting case of the binomial random variable, and so combination is also used. Therefore, while we do not use the concepts of permutation per se, we use them to define random variables.

1.6 Summary

In this chapter, we have reviewed several background mathematical concepts that will become useful later in the book. You will find that these concepts are important for understanding the rest of this book. When studying these materials, we recommend not just remembering the "recipes" of the steps but focusing on the **motivations** and **intuitions** behind the techniques.

We would like to highlight the significance of the birthday paradox. Many of us come from an engineering background in which we were told to ensure reliability and guarantee success. We want to ensure that the product we deliver to our customers can survive even in the worst-case scenario. We tend to apply deterministic arguments such as requiring 366 people to ensure complete coverage of the 365 days. In modern data analysis, the worst-case scenario may not always be relevant because of the complexity of the problem and the cost of such a warranty. The probabilistic argument, or the average argument, is more reasonable and cost-effective, as you can see from our analysis of the birthday problem. The heart of the problem is the trade-off between how much confidence you need versus how much effort you need to expend. Suppose an event is unlikely to happen, but if it happens, it will be a disaster. In that case, you might prefer to be very conservative to ensure that such a disaster event has a low chance of happening. Industries related to risk management such as insurance and investment banking are all operating under this principle.

1.7 References

Introductory materials

1-1 Erwin Kreyszig, *Advanced Engineering Mathematics*, Wiley, 10th Edition, 2011.

1-2 Henry Stark and John W. Woods, *Probability and Random Processes with Applications to Signal Processing*, Prentice Hall, 3rd Edition, 2002. Appendix.

1-3 Michael J. Evans and Jeffrey S. Rosenthal, *Probability and Statistics: The Science of Uncertainty*, W. H. Freeman, 2nd Edition, 2009. Appendix.

1-4 James Stewart, *Single Variable Calculus, Early Transcendentals*, Thomson Brooks/Cole, 6th Edition, 2008. Chapter 5.

Combinatorics

1-5 Dimitri P. Bertsekas and John N. Tsitsiklis, *Introduction to Probability*, Athena Scientific, 2nd Edition, 2008. Section 1.6.

1-6 Alberto Leon-Garcia, *Probability, Statistics, and Random Processes for Electrical Engineering*, Prentice Hall, 3rd Edition, 2008. Section 2.6.

1-7 Athanasios Papoulis and S. Unnikrishna Pillai, *Probability, Random Variables and Stochastic Processes*, McGraw-Hill, 4th Edition, 2001. Chapter 3.

Analysis

In some sections of this chapter, we use results from calculus and infinite series. Many formal proofs can be found in the standard undergraduate real analysis textbooks.

1-8 Tom M. Apostol, *Mathematical Analysis*, Pearson, 1974.

1-9 Walter Rudin, *Principles of Mathematical Analysis*, McGraw Hill, 1976.

1.8   Problems

Exercise 1. (VIDEO SOLUTION)

(a) Show that
$$\sum_{k=0}^{n} r^k = \frac{1 - r^{n+1}}{1 - r}.$$
for any $0 < r < 1$. Evaluate $\sum_{k=0}^{\infty} r^k$.

(b) Using the result of (a), evaluate
$$1 + 2r + 3r^2 + \cdots.$$

(c) Evaluate the sums
$$\sum_{k=0}^{\infty} k \left(\frac{1}{3}\right)^{k+1}, \quad \text{and} \quad \sum_{k=2}^{\infty} k \left(\frac{1}{4}\right)^{k-1}.$$

Exercise 2. (VIDEO SOLUTION)
Recall that
$$\sum_{k=0}^{\infty} \frac{\lambda^k}{k!} = e^\lambda.$$
Evaluate
$$\sum_{k=0}^{\infty} k \frac{\lambda^k e^{-\lambda}}{k!}, \quad \text{and} \quad \sum_{k=0}^{\infty} k^2 \frac{\lambda^k e^{-\lambda}}{k!}.$$

Exercise 3. (VIDEO SOLUTION)
Evaluate the integrals

(a)
$$\int_a^b \frac{1}{b-a} \left(x - \frac{a+b}{2}\right)^2 dx.$$

(b)
$$\int_0^\infty \lambda x e^{-\lambda x} \, dx.$$

(c)
$$\int_{-\infty}^\infty \frac{\lambda x}{2} e^{-\lambda |x|} \, dx.$$

Exercise 4.

(a) Compute the result of the following matrix vector multiplication using Numpy. Submit your result and codes.

$$\begin{bmatrix} 1 & 2 & 3 \\ 4 & 5 & 6 \\ 7 & 8 & 9 \end{bmatrix} \times \begin{bmatrix} 1 \\ 2 \\ 3 \end{bmatrix}.$$

(b) Plot a sine function on the interval $[-\pi, \pi]$ with 1000 data points.

(c) Generate 10,000 uniformly distributed random numbers on interval $[0, 1)$.

Use `matplotlib.pyplot.hist` to generate a histogram of all the random numbers.

Exercise 5.

Calculate

$$\sum_{k=0}^{\infty} k \left(\frac{2}{3} \right)^{k+1}.$$

Exercise 6.

Let

$$\mathbf{x} = \begin{bmatrix} x \\ y \end{bmatrix}, \quad \boldsymbol{\mu} = \begin{bmatrix} 1 \\ 0 \end{bmatrix}, \quad \boldsymbol{\Sigma} = \begin{bmatrix} 4 & 1 \\ 1 & 1 \end{bmatrix}.$$

(a) Find $\boldsymbol{\Sigma}^{-1}$, the inverse of $\boldsymbol{\Sigma}$.

(b) Find $|\boldsymbol{\Sigma}|$, the determinant of $\boldsymbol{\Sigma}$.

(c) Simplify the two-dimensional function

$$f(\mathbf{x}) = \frac{1}{2\pi|\boldsymbol{\Sigma}|^{1/2}} \exp\left\{ -\frac{1}{2}(\mathbf{x} - \boldsymbol{\mu})^T \boldsymbol{\Sigma}^{-1} (\mathbf{x} - \boldsymbol{\mu}) \right\}.$$

(d) Use `matplotlib.pyplot.contour`, plot the function $f(\mathbf{x})$ for the range $[-3, 3] \times [-3, 3]$.

Exercise 7.

Out of seven electrical engineering (EE) students and five mechanical engineering (ME) students, a committee consisting of three EEs and two MEs is to be formed. In how many ways can this be done if

(a) any of the EEs and any of the MEs can be included?

(b) one particular EE must be on the committee?

(c) two particular MEs cannot be on the committee?

Exercise 8.
Five blue balls, three red balls, and three white balls are placed in an urn. Three balls are drawn at random without regard to the order in which they are drawn. Using the counting approach to probability, find the probability that

(a) one blue ball, one red ball, and one white ball are drawn.

(b) all three balls drawn are red.

(c) exactly two of the balls drawn are blue.

Exercise 9.
A collection of 26 English letters, a-z, is mixed in a jar. Two letters are drawn at random, one after the other.

(a) What is the probability of drawing a vowel (a,e,i,o,u) and a consonant in either order?

(b) Write a MATLAB / Python program to verify your answer in part (a). Randomly draw two letters without replacement and check whether one is a vowel and the other is a consonant. Compute the probability by repeating the experiment 10000 times.

Exercise 10.
There are 50 students in a classroom.

(a) What is the probability that there is at least one pair of students having the same birthday? Show your steps.

(b) Write a MATLAB / Python program to simulate the event and verify your answer in (a). Hint: You probably need to repeat the simulation many times to obtain a probability. Submit your code and result.

You may assume that a year only has 365 days. You may also assume that all days have an equal likelihood of being taken.

Chapter 2

Probability

Data and probability are inseparable. Data is the **computational** side of the story, whereas probability is the **theoretical** side of the story. Any data science practice must be built on the foundation of probability, and probability needs to address practical problems. However, what exactly is "probability"? Mathematicians have been debating this for centuries. The **frequentists** argue that probability is the relative frequency of an outcome. For example, flipping a fair coin has a 1/2 probability of getting a head because if you flip the coin infinitely many times, you will have half of the time getting a head. The **Bayesians** argue that probability is a subjective belief. For example, the probability of getting an A in a class is subjective because no one would want to take a class infinitely many times to obtain the relative frequency. Both the frequentists and Bayesians have valid points. However, the differentiation is often non-essential because the context of your problem will force you to align with one or the other. For example, when you have a shortage of data, then the subjectivity of the Bayesians allows you to use prior knowledge, whereas the frequentists tell us how to compute the confidence interval of an estimate.

No matter whether you prefer the frequentist's view or the Bayesian's view, there is something more fundamental thanks to **Andrey Kolmogorov** (1903-1987). The development of this fundamental definition will take some effort on our part, but if we distill the essence, we can summarize it as follows:

> **Probability is a measure of the size of a set.**

This sentence is not a formal definition; instead, it summarizes what we believe to be the essence of probability. We need to clarify some puzzles later in this chapter, but if you can understand what this sentence means, you are halfway done with this book. To spell out the details, we will describe an elementary problem that everyone knows how to solve. As we discuss this problem, we will highlight a few key concepts that will give you some intuitive insights into our definition of probability, after which we will explain the sequence of topics to be covered in this chapter.

Prelude: Probability of throwing a die

Suppose that you have a fair die. It has 6 faces: $\{1, 2, 3, 4, 5, 6\}$. What is the probability that you get a number that is "less than 5" and is "an even number"? This is a straightforward problem. You probably have already found the answer, which is $\frac{2}{6}$ because "less than 5" and "an even number" means $\{2, 4\}$. However, let's go through the thinking process slowly by explicitly writing down the steps.

First of all, how do we know that the denominator in $\frac{2}{6}$ is 6? Well, because there are six faces. These six faces form a set called the **sample space**. A sample space is the set containing all possible outcomes, which in our case is $\Omega = \{1, 2, 3, 4, 5, 6\}$. The denominator 6 is the size of the sample space.

How do we know that the numerator is 2? Again, implicitly in our minds, we have constructed two **events**: $E_1 = $ "less than 5" $= \{1, 2, 3, 4\}$, and $E_2 = $ "an even number" $= \{2, 4, 6\}$. Then we take the intersection between these two events to conclude the event $E = \{2, 4\}$. The numerical value "2" is the size of this event E.

So, when we say that "the probability is $\frac{2}{6}$," we are saying that the size of the event E relative to the sample space Ω is the ratio $\frac{2}{6}$. This process involves **measuring** the size of E and Ω. In this particular example, the measure we use is a "counter" that counts the number of elements.

This example shows us all the necessary components of probability: (i) There is a **sample space**, which is the set that contains all the possible outcomes. (ii) There is an **event**, which is a subset inside the sample space. (iii) Two events E_1 and E_2 can be **combined** to construct another event E that is still a subset inside the sample space. (iv) Probability is a number assigned by certain **rules** such that it describes the **relative size** of the event E compared with the sample space Ω. So, when we say that **probability is a measure of the size of a set**, we create a mapping that takes in a set and outputs the size of that set.

Organization of this chapter

As you can see from this example, since probability is a measure of the size of a set, we need to understand the operations of sets to understand probability. Accordingly, in Section 2.1 we first define sets and discuss their operations. After learning these basic concepts, we move on to define the sample space and event space in Section 2.2. There, we discuss sample spaces that are not necessarily countable and how probabilities are assigned to events. Of course, assigning a probability value to an event cannot be arbitrary; otherwise, the probabilities may be inconsistent. Consequently, in Section 2.3 we introduce the probability axioms and formalize the notion of measure. Section 2.4 consists of a trio of topics that concern the relationship between events using conditioning. We discuss conditional probability in Section 2.4.1, independence in Section 2.4.2, and Bayes' theorem in Section 2.4.3.

2.1 Set Theory

2.1.1 Why study set theory?

In mathematics, we are often interested in describing a collection of numbers, for example, a positive interval $[a, b]$ on the real line or the ordered pairs of numbers that define a circle on a graph with two axes. These collections of numbers can be abstractly defined as **sets**. In a nutshell, a set is simply a collection of things. These things can be numbers, but they can also be alphabets, objects, or anything. Set theory is a mathematical tool that defines operations on sets. It provides the basic arithmetic for us to combine, separate, and decompose sets.

Why do we start the chapter by describing set theory? Because **probability is a measure of the size of a set**. Yes, probability is not just a number telling us the relative frequency of events; it is an operator that takes a set and tells us how large the set is. Using the example we showed in the prelude, the event "even number" of a die is a set containing numbers $\{2, 4, 6\}$. When we apply probability to this set, we obtain the number $\frac{3}{6}$, as shown in **Figure 2.1**. Thus sets are the foundation of the study of probability.

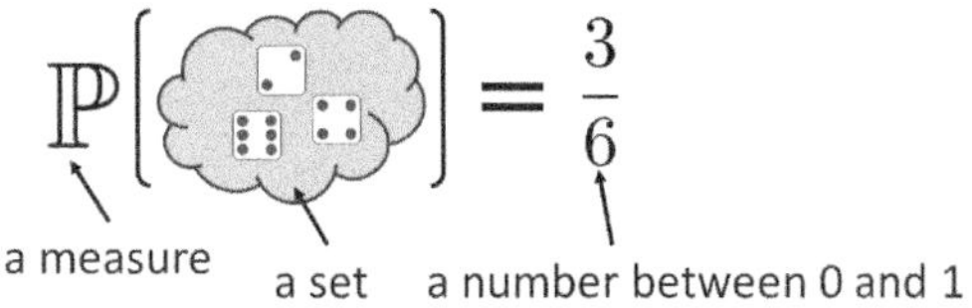

Figure 2.1: Probability is a measure of the size of a set. Whenever we talk about probability, it has to be the probability of a **set**.

2.1.2 Basic concepts of a set

Definition 2.1 (Set). *A **set** is a collection of elements. We denote*

$$A = \{\xi_1, \xi_2, \ldots, \xi_n\} \tag{2.1}$$

as a set, where ξ_i is the ith element in the set.

In this definition, A is called a set. It is nothing but a collection of elements $\xi_1, \ldots, \xi_n$. What are these ξ_i's? They can be anything. Let's see a few examples below.

Example 2.1(a). $A = \{\text{apple}, \text{orange}, \text{pear}\}$ is a finite set.

Example 2.1(b). $A = \{1, 2, 3, 4, 5, 6\}$ is a finite set.

Example 2.1(c). $A = \{2, 4, 6, 8, \ldots\}$ is a countable but infinite set.

Example 2.1(d). $A = \{x \mid 0 < x < 1\}$ is a uncountable set.

To say that an element ξ is drawn from A, we write $\xi \in A$. For example, the number 1 is an element in the set $\{1, 2, 3\}$. We write $1 \in \{1, 2, 3\}$. There are a few common sets that we will encounter. For example,

---

Example 2.2(a). $\mathbb{R}$ is the set of all real numbers including $\pm\infty$.

Example 2.2(b). $\mathbb{R}^2$ is the set of ordered pairs of real numbers.

Example 2.2(c). $[a, b] = \{x \mid a \le x \le b\}$ is a closed interval on $\mathbb{R}$.

Example 2.2(d). $(a, b) = \{x \mid a < x < b\}$ is an open interval on $\mathbb{R}$.

Example 2.2(e). $(a, b] = \{x \mid a < x \le b\}$ is a semi-closed interval on $\mathbb{R}$.

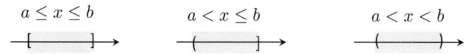

Figure 2.2: From left to right: a closed interval, a semi-closed (or semi-open) interval, and an open interval.

Sets are not limited to numbers. A set can be used to describe a collection of **functions**.

Example 2.3. $A = \{f : \mathbb{R} \to \mathbb{R} \mid f(x) = ax+b,\ a, b \in \mathbb{R}\}$. This is the set of all straight lines in 2D. The notation $f : \mathbb{R} \to \mathbb{R}$ means that the function f takes an argument from $\mathbb{R}$ and sends it to another real number in $\mathbb{R}$. The definition $f(x) = ax + b$ says that f is taking the specific form of $ax + b$. Since the constants a and b can be any real number, the equation $f(x) = ax + b$ enumerates all possible straight lines in 2D. See **Figure 2.3**(a).

Example 2.4. $A = \{f : \mathbb{R} \to [-1,1] \mid f(t) = \cos(\omega_0 t + \theta),\ \theta \in [0, 2\pi]\}$. This is the set of all cosine functions of a fixed carrier frequency ω_0. The phase θ, however, is changing. Therefore, the equation $f(t) = \cos(\omega_0 t + \theta)$ says that the set A is the collection of all possible cosines with different phases. See **Figure 2.3**(b).

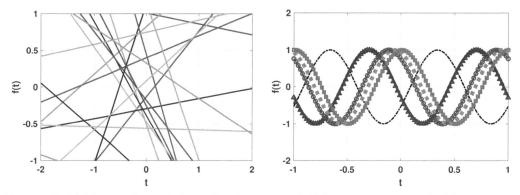

Figure 2.3: (a) The set of straight lines $A = \{f : \mathbb{R} \to \mathbb{R} \mid f(x) = ax + b,\ a, b \in \mathbb{R}\}$. (b) The set of phase-shifted cosines $A = \{f : \mathbb{R} \to [-1, 1] \mid f(t) = \cos(\omega_0 t + \theta),\ \theta \in [0, 2\pi]\}$.

A set can also be used to describe a collection of sets. Let A and B be two sets. Then $\mathcal{C} = \{A, B\}$ is a set of sets.

Example 2.5. Let $A = \{1, 2\}$ and $B = \{\text{apple}, \text{orange}\}$. Then

$$\mathcal{C} = \{A, B\} = \{\{1, 2\}, \{\text{apple}, \text{orange}\}\}$$

is a collection of sets. Note that here we are not saying $\mathcal{C}$ is the union of two sets. We are only saying that $\mathcal{C}$ is a collection of two sets. See the next example.

Example 2.6. Let $A = \{1, 2\}$ and $B = \{3\}$, then $\mathcal{C} = \{A, B\}$ means that

$$\mathcal{C} = \{\{1, 2\}, \{3\}\}.$$

Therefore $\mathcal{C}$ contains only two elements. One is the set $\{1, 2\}$ and the other is the set $\{3\}$. Note that $\{\{1, 2\}, \{3\}\} \neq \{1, 2, 3\}$. The former is a set of two sets. The latter is a set of three elements.

2.1.3 Subsets

Given a set, we often want to specify a portion of the set, which is called a **subset**.

Definition 2.2 (Subset). *B is a **subset** of A if for any $\xi \in B$, ξ is also in A. We write*

$$B \subseteq A \tag{2.2}$$

to denote that B is a subset of A.

B is called a **proper subset** of A if B is a subset of A and $B \neq A$. We denote a proper subset as $B \subset A$. Two sets A and B are equal if and only if $A \subseteq B$ and $B \subseteq A$.

Example 2.7.

- If $A = \{1, 2, 3, 4, 5, 6\}$, then $B = \{1, 3, 5\}$ is a proper subset of A.
- If $A = \{1, 2\}$, then $B = \{1, 2\}$ is an improper subset of A.
- If $A = \{t \mid t \geq 0\}$, then $B = \{t \mid t > 0\}$ is a proper subset of A.

Practice Exercise 2.1. Let $A = \{1, 2, 3\}$. List all the subsets of A.
Solution. The subsets of A are:

$$\mathcal{A} = \{\emptyset, \{1\}, \{2\}, \{3\}, \{1, 2\}, \{1, 3\}, \{2, 3\}, \{1, 2, 3\}\}.$$

Practice Exercise 2.2. Prove that two sets A and B are equal if and only if $A \subseteq B$ and $B \subseteq A$.

Solution. Suppose $A \subseteq B$ and $B \subseteq A$. Assume by contradiction that $A \neq B$. Then necessarily there must exist an x such that $x \in A$ but $x \notin B$ (or vice versa). But $A \subseteq B$ means that $x \in A$ will necessarily be in B. So it is impossible to have $x \notin B$. Conversely, suppose that $A = B$. Then any $x \in A$ will necessarily be in B. Therefore, we have $A \subseteq B$. Similarly, if $A = B$ then any $x \in B$ will be in A, and so $B \subseteq A$.

2.1.4 Empty set and universal set

> **Definition 2.3** (**Empty Set**). *A set is* **empty** *if it contains no element. We denote an empty set as*
> $$A = \emptyset. \tag{2.3}$$

A set containing an element 0 is not an empty set. It is a set of one element, $\{0\}$. The number of elements of the empty set is 0. The empty set is a subset of any set, i.e., $\emptyset \subseteq A$ for any A. We use $\subseteq$ because A could also be an empty set.

> **Example 2.8(a).** The set $A = \{x \mid \sin x > 1\}$ is empty because no $x \in \mathbb{R}$ can make $\sin x > 1$.
>
> **Example 2.8(b).** The set $A = \{x \mid x > 5 \text{ and } x < 1\}$ is empty because the two conditions $x > 5$ and $x < 1$ are contradictory.

> **Definition 2.4** (**Universal Set**). *The* **universal set** *is the set containing all elements under consideration. We denote a universal set as*
> $$A = \Omega. \tag{2.4}$$

The universal set Ω contains itself, i.e., $\Omega \subseteq \Omega$. The universal set is a relative concept. Usually, we first define a universal set Ω before referring to subsets of Ω. For example, we can define $\Omega = \mathbb{R}$ and refer to intervals in $\mathbb{R}$. We can also define $\Omega = [0, 1]$ and refer to subintervals inside $[0, 1]$.

2.1.5 Union

We now discuss basic set operations. By operations, we mean functions of two or more sets whose output value is a set. We use these operations to combine and separate sets. Let us first consdier the union of two sets. See **Figure 2.4** for a graphical depiction.

> **Definition 2.5** (**Finite Union**). *The* **union** *of two sets A and B contains all elements in A* **or** *in B. That is,*
> $$A \cup B = \{\xi \mid \xi \in A \text{ or } \xi \in B\}. \tag{2.5}$$

As the definition suggests, the union of two sets connects the sets using the logical operator "**or**". Therefore, the union of two sets is always larger than or equal to the individual sets.

> **Example 2.9(a).** If $A = \{1, 2\}$, $B = \{1, 5\}$, then $A \cup B = \{1, 2, 5\}$. The overlapping element 1 is absorbed. Also, note that $A \cup B \neq \{\{1, 2\}, \{1, 5\}\}$. The latter is a set of sets.
>
> **Example 2.9(b).** If $A = (3, 4]$, $B = (3.5, \infty)$, then $A \cup B = (3, \infty)$.
>
> **Example 2.9(c).** If $A = \{f : \mathbb{R} \to \mathbb{R} \mid f(x) = ax\}$ and $B = \{f : \mathbb{R} \to \mathbb{R} \mid f(x) = b\}$, then $A \cup B = $ a set of sloped lines with a slope a plus a set of constant lines with

height b. Note that $A \cup B \neq \{f : \mathbb{R} \to \mathbb{R} \mid f(x) = ax + b\}$ because the latter is a set of sloped lines with arbitrary y-intercept.

Example 2.9(d). If $A = \{1, 2\}$ and $B = \emptyset$, then $A \cup B = \{1, 2\}$.

Example. If $A = \{1, 2\}$ and $B = \Omega$, then $A \cup B = \Omega$.

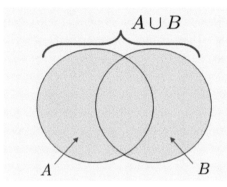

Figure 2.4: The union of two sets contains elements that are either in A or B or both.

The previous example can be generalized in the following exercise. What it says is that if A is a subset of another set B, then the union of A and B is just B. Intuitively, this should be straightforward because whatever you have in A is already in B, so the union will just be B. Below is a formal proof that illustrates how to state the arguments clearly. You may like to draw a picture to convince yourself that the proof is correct.

Practice Exercise 2.3: Prove that if $A \subseteq B$, then $A \cup B = B$.

Solution: We will show that $A \cup B \subseteq B$ and $B \subseteq A \cup B$. Let $\xi \in A \cup B$. Then ξ must be inside either A or B (or both). In any case, since we know that $A \subseteq B$, it holds that if $\xi \in A$ then ξ must also be in B. Therefore, for any $\xi \in A \cup B$ we have $\xi \in B$. This shows $A \cup B \subseteq B$. Conversely, if $\xi \in B$, then ξ must be inside $A \cup B$ because $A \cup B$ is a larger set than B. So if $\xi \in B$ then $\xi \in A \cup B$ and hence $B \subseteq A \cup B$. Since $A \cup B$ is a subset of B or equal to B, and B is a subset of $A \cup B$ or equal to $A \cup B$, it follows that $A \cup B = B$.

What should we do if we want to take the union of an infinite number of sets? First, we need to define the concept of an **infinite union**.

Definition 2.6 (Infinite Union). *For an infinite sequence of sets $A_1, A_2, \ldots$, the* **infinite union** *is defined as*

$$\bigcup_{n=1}^{\infty} A_n = \{\xi \mid \xi \in A_n \text{ for } \textbf{at least one } n \text{ that is finite.}\}. \tag{2.6}$$

An infinite union is a natural extension of a finite union. It is not difficult to see that

$$\xi \in A \text{ or } \xi \in B \iff \xi \text{ is in } \textbf{at least one of } A \text{ and } B.$$

Similarly, an infinite union means that

$$\xi \in A_1 \ \textbf{or} \ \xi \in A_2 \ \textbf{or} \ \xi \in A_3 \ldots \quad \Longleftrightarrow \quad \xi \text{ is in } \textbf{at least one of } A_1, A_2, A_3, \ldots.$$

The finite n requirement says that we only evaluate the sets for a finite number of n's. This n can be arbitrarily large, but it is finite. Why are we able to do this? Because the concept of an infinite union is to determine A_∞, which is the limit of a sequence. Like any sequence of real numbers, the limit of a sequence of sets has to be defined by evaluating the instances of all possible finite cases.

Consider a sequence of sets $A_n = \left[-1, 1 - \frac{1}{n}\right]$, for $n = 1, 2, \ldots$. For example, $A_1 = [-1, 0]$, $A_2 = \left[-1, \frac{1}{2}\right]$, $A_3 = \left[-1, \frac{2}{3}\right]$, $A_4 = \left[-1, \frac{3}{4}\right]$, etc.

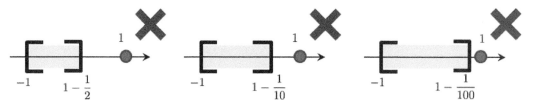

Figure 2.5: The infinite union of $\bigcup_{n=1}^{\infty}\left[-1, 1 - \frac{1}{n}\right]$. No matter how large n gets, the point 1 is never included. So the infinite union is $[-1, 1)$

To take the infinite union, we know that the set $[-1, 1)$ is always included, because the right-hand limit $1 - \frac{1}{n}$ approaches 1 as n approaches ∞. So the only question concerns the number 1. Should 1 be included? According to the definition above, we ask: Is 1 an element of **at least one** of the sets $A_1, A_2, \ldots, A_n$? Clearly it is not: $1 \notin A_1$, $1 \notin A_2$, $\ldots$. In fact, $1 \notin A_n$ for any finite n. Therefore 1 is not an element of the infinite union, and we conclude that

$$\bigcup_{n=1}^{\infty} A_n = \bigcup_{n=1}^{\infty} \left[-1, 1 - \frac{1}{n}\right] = [-1, 1).$$

Practice Exercise 2.4. Find the infinite union of the sequences where (a) $A_n = \left[-1, 1 - \frac{1}{n}\right)$, (b) $A_n = \left(-1, 1 - \frac{1}{n}\right]$.
Solution. (a) $\bigcup_{n=1}^{\infty} A_n = [-1, 1)$. (b) $\bigcup_{n=1}^{\infty} A_n = (-1, 1)$.

2.1.6 Intersection

The union of two sets is based on the logical operator **or**. If we use the logical operator **and**, then the result is the **intersection** of two sets.

Definition 2.7 (Finite Intersection). *The **intersection** of two sets A and B contains all elements in A **and** in B. That is,*

$$A \cap B = \{\xi \mid \xi \in A \text{ and } \xi \in B\}. \tag{2.7}$$

Figure 2.6 portrays intersection graphically. Intersection finds the common elements of the two sets. It is not difficult to show that $A \cap B \subseteq A$ and $A \cap B \subseteq B$.

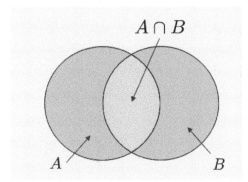

$A \cap B$

A B

Figure 2.6: The intersection of two sets contains elements in both A and B.

Example 2.10(a). If $A = \{1, 2, 3, 4\}$, $B = \{1, 5, 6\}$, then $A \cap B = \{1\}$.

Example 2.10(b). If $A = \{1, 2\}$, $B = \{5, 6\}$, then $A \cap B = \emptyset$.

Example 2.10(c). If $A = (3, 4]$, $B = [3.5, \infty)$, then $A \cap B = [3.5, 4]$.

Example 2.10(d). If $A = (3, 4]$, $B = \emptyset$, then $A \cap B = \emptyset$.

Example 2.10(e). If $A = (3, 4]$, $B = \Omega$, then $A \cap B = (3, 4]$.

Example 2.11. If $A = \{f : \mathbb{R} \to \mathbb{R} \mid f(x) = ax\}$ and $B = \{f : \mathbb{R} \to \mathbb{R} \mid f(x) = b\}$, then $A \cap B =$ the intersection of a set of sloped lines with a slope a and a set of constant lines with height b. The only line that can satisfy both sets is the line $f(x) = 0$. Therefore, $A \cap B = \{f \mid f(x) = 0\}$.

Example 2.12. If $A = \{\{1\}, \{2\}\}$ and $B = \{\{2, 3\}, \{4\}\}$, then $A \cap B = \emptyset$. This is because A is a set containing two sets, and B is a set containing two sets. The two sets $\{2\}$ and $\{2, 3\}$ are not the same. Thus, A and B have no elements in common, and so $A \cap B = \emptyset$.

Similarly to the infinite union, we can define the concept of **infinite intersection**.

Definition 2.8 (Infinite Intersection). *For an infinite sequence of sets $A_1, A_2, \ldots$, the* **infinite intersection** *is defined as*

$$\bigcap_{n=1}^{\infty} A_n = \{\xi \mid \xi \in A_n \text{ for every finite } n.\} \tag{2.8}$$

To understand this definition, we note that

$$\xi \in A \text{ and } \xi \in B \iff \xi \text{ is in every one of } A \text{ and } B.$$

As a result, it follows that

$$\xi \in A_1 \text{ and } \xi \in A_2 \text{ and } \xi \in A_3 \ldots \iff \xi \text{ is in every one of } A_1, A_2, A_3, \ldots.$$

Since the infinite intersection requires that ξ is in every one of A_1, A_2, ..., A_n, if there is a set A_i that does not contain ξ, the infinite intersection is an empty set.

Consider the problem of finding the infinite intersection of $\bigcap_{n=1}^{\infty} A_n$, where

$$A_n = \left[0, 1 + \frac{1}{n}\right).$$

We note that the sequence of sets is $[0, 2]$, $[0, 1.5]$, $[0, 1.33]$, ... As $n \to \infty$, we note that the limit is either $[0, 1)$ or $[0, 1]$. Should the right-hand limit 1 be included in the infinite intersection? According to the definition above, we know that $1 \in A_1$, $1 \in A_2$, ..., $1 \in A_n$ for any finite n. Therefore, 1 is included and so

$$\bigcap_{n=1}^{\infty} A_n = \bigcap_{n=1}^{\infty} \left[0, 1 + \frac{1}{n}\right) = [0, 1].$$

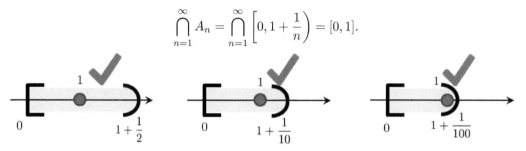

Figure 2.7: The infinite intersection of $\bigcap_{n=1}^{\infty} \left[0, 1 + \frac{1}{n}\right)$. No matter how large n gets, the point 1 is never included. So the infinite intersection is $[0, 1]$

Practice Exercise 2.5. Find the infinite intersection of the sequences where (a) $A_n = \left[0, 1 + \frac{1}{n}\right]$, (b) $A_n = \left(0, 1 + \frac{1}{n}\right)$, (c) $A_n = \left[0, 1 - \frac{1}{n}\right)$, (d) $A_n = \left[0, 1 - \frac{1}{n}\right]$.

Solution.

(a) $\bigcap_{n=1}^{\infty} A_n = [0, 1]$.

(b) $\bigcap_{n=1}^{\infty} A_n = (0, 1]$.

(c) $\bigcap_{n=1}^{\infty} A_n = [0, 0) = \emptyset$.

(d) $\bigcap_{n=1}^{\infty} A_n = [0, 0] = \{0\}$.

2.1.7 Complement and difference

Besides union and intersection, there is a third basic operation on sets known as the **complement**.

Definition 2.9 (Complement). *The **complement** of a set A is the set containing all elements that are in Ω but not in A. That is,*

$$A^c = \{\xi \mid \xi \in \Omega \text{ and } \xi \notin A\}. \tag{2.9}$$

Figure 2.8 graphically portrays the idea of a complement. The complement is a set that contains everything in the universal set that is not in A. Thus the complement of a set is always relative to a specified universal set.

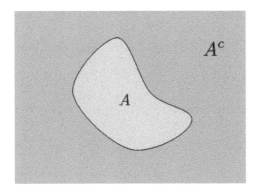
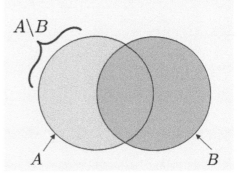

Figure 2.8: [Left] The complement of a set A contains all elements that are not in A. [Right] The difference $A \backslash B$ contains elements that are in A but not in B.

Example 2.13(a). Let $A = \{1,2,3\}$ and $\Omega = \{1,2,3,4,5,6\}$. Then $A^c = \{4,5,6\}$.

Example 2.13(b). Let $A = \{\text{even integers}\}$ and $\Omega = \{\text{integers}\}$. Then $A^c = \{\text{odd integers}\}$.

Example 2.13(c). Let $A = \{\text{integers}\}$ and $\Omega = \mathbb{R}$. Then $A^c = \{\text{any real number that is not an integer}\}$.

Example 2.13(d). Let $A = [0,5)$ and $\Omega = \mathbb{R}$. Then $A^c = (-\infty, 0) \cup [5, \infty)$.

Example 2.13(e). Let $A = \mathbb{R}$ and $\Omega = \mathbb{R}$. Then $A^c = \emptyset$.

The concept of the complement will help us understand the concept of **difference**.

Definition 2.10 (Difference). *The **difference** $A \backslash B$ is the set containing all elements in A but not in B.*

$$A \backslash B = \{\xi \mid \xi \in A \text{ and } \xi \notin B\}. \tag{2.10}$$

Figure 2.8 portrays the concept of difference graphically. Note that $A \backslash B \neq B \backslash A$. The former removes the elements in B whereas the latter removes the elements in A.

Example 2.14(a). Let $A = \{1,3,5,6\}$ and $B = \{2,3,4\}$. Then $A \backslash B = \{1,5,6\}$ and $B \backslash A = \{2,4\}$.

Example 2.14(b). Let $A = [0,1]$, $B = [2,3]$, then $A \backslash B = [0,1]$, and $B \backslash A = [2,3]$. This example shows that if the two sets do not overlap, there is nothing to subtract.

Example 2.14(c). Let $A = [0,1]$, $B = \mathbb{R}$, then $A \backslash B = \emptyset$, and $B \backslash A = (-\infty, 0) \cup (1, \infty)$. This example shows that if one of the sets is the universal set, then the difference will either return the empty set or the complement.

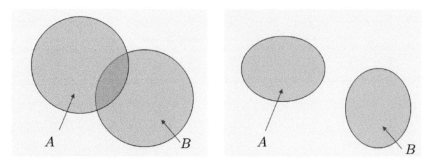

Figure 2.9: [Left] A and B are overlapping. [Right] A and B are disjoint.

Practice Exercise 2.6. Show that for any two sets A and B, the differences $A\backslash B$ and $B\backslash A$ never overlap, i.e., $(A\backslash B) \cap (B\backslash A) = \emptyset$.

Solution. Suppose, by contradiction, that the intersection is not empty so that there exists an $\xi \in (A\backslash B) \cap (B\backslash A)$. Then, by the definition of intersection, ξ is an element of $(A\backslash B)$ **and** $(B\backslash A)$. But if ξ is an element of $(A\backslash B)$, it cannot be an element of B. This implies that ξ cannot be an element of $(B\backslash A)$ since it is a subset of B. This is a contradiction because we just assumed that the ξ can live in both $(A\backslash B)$ and $(B\backslash A)$.

Difference can be defined in terms of intersection and complement:

Theorem 2.1. *Let A and B be two sets. Then*

$$A\backslash B = A \cap B^c \tag{2.11}$$

Proof. Let $x \in A\backslash B$. Then $x \in A$ and $x \notin B$. Since $x \notin B$, we have $x \in B^c$. Therefore, $x \in A$ and $x \in B^c$. By the definition of intersection, we have $x \in A \cap B^c$. This shows that $A\backslash B \subseteq A \cap B^c$. Conversely, let $x \in A \cap B^c$. Then, $x \in A$ and $x \in B^c$, which implies that $x \in A$ and $x \notin B$. By the definition of $A\backslash B$, we have that $x \in A\backslash B$. This shows that $A \cap B^c \subseteq A\backslash B$.

$\square$

2.1.8 Disjoint and partition

It is important to be able to quantify situations in which two sets are not overlapping. In this situation, we say that the sets are **disjoint**.

Definition 2.11 (Disjoint). *Two sets A and B are **disjoint** if*

$$A \cap B = \emptyset. \tag{2.12}$$

For a collection of sets $\{A_1, A_2, \ldots, A_n\}$, we say that the collection is disjoint if, for any pair $i \neq j$,

$$A_i \cap A_j = \emptyset. \tag{2.13}$$

A pictorial interpretation can be found in **Figure 2.9**.

Example 2.15(a). Let $A = \{x > 1\}$ and $B = \{x < 0\}$. Then A and B are disjoint.

Example 2.15(b). Let $A = \{1, 2, 3\}$ and $B = \emptyset$. Then A and B are disjoint.

Example 2.15(c). Let $A = (0, 1)$ and $B = [1, 2)$. Then A and B are disjoint.

With the definition of disjoint, we can now define the powerful concept of **partition**.

Definition 2.12 (Partition). *A collection of sets* $\{A_1, \ldots, A_n\}$ *is a* **partition** *of the universal set* Ω *if it satisfies the following conditions:*

- *(**non-overlap**)* $\{A_1, \ldots, A_n\}$ *is disjoint:*

$$A_i \cap A_j = \emptyset. \tag{2.14}$$

- *(**decompose**)* *Union of* $\{A_1, \ldots, A_n\}$ *gives the universal set:*

$$\bigcup_{i=1}^{n} A_i = \Omega. \tag{2.15}$$

In plain language, a partition is a collection of non-overlapping subsets whose union is the universal set. Partition is important because it is a **decomposition** of Ω into a smaller subset, and since these subsets do not overlap, they can be analyzed separately. Partition is a handy tool for studying probability because it allows us to decouple complex events by treating them as isolated sub-events.

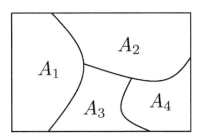

Figure 2.10: A partition of Ω contains disjoint subsets of which the union gives us Ω.

Example 2.16. Let $\Omega = \{1, 2, 3, 4, 5, 6\}$. The following sets form a partition:

$$A_1 = \{1, 2, 3\}, \quad A_2 = \{4, 5\}, \quad A_3 = \{6\}$$

Example 2.17. Let $\Omega = \{1, 2, 3, 4, 5, 6\}$. The collection

$$A_1 = \{1, 2, 3\}, \quad A_2 = \{4, 5\}, \quad A_3 = \{5, 6\}$$

does not form a partition, because $A_2 \cap A_3 = \{5\}$.

If $\{A_1, A_2, \ldots, A_n\}$ forms a partition of the universal set Ω, then for any $B \subseteq \Omega$, we can decompose B into n disjoint subsets: $B \cap A_1$, $B \cap A_2$, $\ldots B \cap A_n$. Two properties hold:

- $B \cap A_i$ and $B \cap A_j$ are disjoint if $i \neq j$.
- The union of $B \cap A_1$, $B \cap A_2$, $\ldots B \cap A_n$ is B.

Practice Exercise 2.7. Prove the above two statements.

Solution. To prove the first statement, we can pick $\xi \in (B \cap A_i)$. This means that $\xi \in B$ and $\xi \in A_i$. Since $\xi \in A_i$, it cannot be in A_j because A_i and A_j are disjoint. Therefore ξ cannot live in $B \cap A_j$. This completes the proof, because we just showed that any $\xi \in B \cap A_i$ cannot simultaneously live in $B \cap A_j$.

To prove the second statement, we pick $\xi \in \bigcup_{i=1}^{n}(B \cap A_i)$. Since ξ lives in the union, it has to live in at least one of the $(B \cap A_i)$ for some i. Now suppose $\xi \in B \cap A_i$. This means that ξ is in both B and A_i, so it must live in B. Therefore, $\bigcup_{i=1}^{n}(B \cap A_i) \subseteq B$. Now, suppose we pick $\xi \in B$. Then since it is an element in B, it must be an element in all of the $(B \cap A_i)$'s for any i. Therefore, $\xi \in \bigcup_{i=1}^{n}(B \cap A_i)$, and so we showed that $B \subseteq \bigcup_{i=1}^{n}(B \cap A_i)$. Combining the two directions, we conclude that $\bigcup_{i=1}^{n}(B \cap A_i) = B$.

Example 2.18. Let $\Omega = \{1, 2, 3, 4, 5, 6\}$ and let a partition of Ω be $A_1 = \{1, 2, 3\}$, $A_2 = \{4, 5\}$, $A_3 = \{6\}$. Let $B = \{1, 3, 4\}$. Then, by the result we just proved, B can be decomposed into three subsets:

$$B \cap A_1 = \{1, 3\}, \quad B \cap A_2 = \{4\}, \quad B \cap A_3 = \emptyset.$$

Thus we can see that $B \cap A_1$, $B \cap A_2$ and $B \cap A_3$ are disjoint. Furthermore, the union of these three sets gives B.

2.1.9 Set operations

When handling multiple sets, it would be useful to have some basic set operations. There are four basic theorems concerning set operations that you need to know for our purposes in this book:

Theorem 2.2 (Commutative). *(Order does not matter)*

$$A \cap B = B \cap A, \quad and \quad A \cup B = B \cup A. \tag{2.16}$$

Theorem 2.3 (Associative). *(How to do multiple union and intersection)*

$$A \cup (B \cup C) = (A \cup B) \cup C,$$
$$A \cap (B \cap C) = (A \cap B) \cap C. \tag{2.17}$$

Theorem 2.4 (Distributive). *(How to mix union and intersection)*

$$A \cap (B \cup C) = (A \cap B) \cup (A \cap C),$$
$$A \cup (B \cap C) = (A \cup B) \cap (A \cup C). \tag{2.18}$$

Theorem 2.5 (De Morgan's Law). *(How to complement over intersection and union)*

$$(A \cap B)^c = A^c \cup B^c,$$
$$(A \cup B)^c = A^c \cap B^c. \tag{2.19}$$

Example 2.19. Consider $[1,4] \cap ([0,2] \cup [3,5])$. By the distributive property we can simplify the set as

$$[1,4] \cap ([0,2] \cup [3,5]) = ([1,4] \cap [0,2]) \cup ([1,4] \cap [3,5])$$
$$= [1,2] \cup [3,4].$$

Example 2.20. Consider $([0,1] \cup [2,3])^c$. By De Morgan's Law we can rewrite the set as

$$([0,1] \cup [2,3])^c = [0,1]^c \cap [2,3]^c.$$

2.1.10 Closing remarks about set theory

It should be apparent why set theory is useful: it shows us how to combine, split, and remove sets. In **Figure 2.11** we depict the intersection of two sets $A = \{$even number$\}$ and $B = \{$less than or equal to 3$\}$. Set theory tells us how to define the intersection so that the probability can be applied to the resulting set.

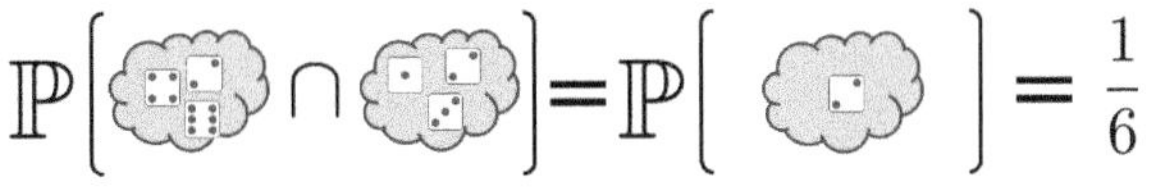

$$\mathbb{P}\left[\bigcirc \cap \bigcirc \right] = \mathbb{P}\left[\bigcirc \right] = \frac{1}{6}$$

Figure 2.11: When there are two events A and B, the probability of $A \cap B$ is determined by first taking the intersection of the two sets and then evaluating its probability.

Universal sets and empty sets are useful too. Universal sets cover all the possible outcomes of an experiment, so we should expect $\mathbb{P}[\Omega] = 1$. Empty sets contain nothing, and so we should expect $\mathbb{P}[\emptyset] = 0$. These two properties are essential to define a probability because no probability can be greater than 1, and no probability can be less than 0.

2.2   Probability Space

We now formally define probability. Our discussion will be based on the slogan **probability is a measure of the size of a set**. Three elements constitute a **probability space**:

- **Sample Space** Ω: The set of all possible outcomes from an experiment.
- **Event Space** $\mathcal{F}$: The collection of all possible events. An event E is a subset in Ω that defines an outcome or a combination of outcomes.
- **Probability Law** $\mathbb{P}$: A mapping from an event E to a number $\mathbb{P}[E]$ which, ideally, measures the size of the event.

Therefore, whenever you talk about "probability," you need to specify the triplet $(\Omega, \mathcal{F}, \mathbb{P})$ to define the probability space.

The necessity of the three elements is illustrated in **Figure 2.12**. The **sample space** is the interface with the **physical world**. It is the collection of all possible states that can result from an experiment. Some outcomes are more likely to happen, and some are less likely, but this does not matter because the sample space contains every possible outcome. The **probability law** is the interface with the **data analysis**. It is this law that defines the likelihood of each of the outcomes. However, since the probability law measures the size of a set, the probability law itself must be a function, a function whose argument is a set and whose value is a number. An outcome in the sample space is not a set. Instead, a subset in the sample space is a set. Therefore, the probability should input a subset and map it to a number. The collection of all possible subsets is the **event space**.

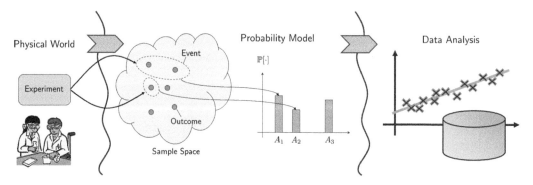

Figure 2.12: Given an experiment, we define the collection of all outcomes as the sample space. A subset in the sample space is called an event. The probability law is a mapping that maps an event to a number that denotes the size of the event.

A perceptive reader like you may be wondering why we want to complicate things to this degree when calculating probability is trivial, e.g., throwing a die gives us a probability $\frac{1}{6}$ per face. In a simple world where problems are that easy, you can surely ignore all these complications and proceed to the answer $\frac{1}{6}$. However, modern data analysis is not so easy. If we are given an image of size 64×64 pixels, how do we tell whether this image is of a cat or a dog? We need to construct a probability model that tells us the likelihood of having a particular 64×64 image. What should be included in this probability model? We need to know all the possible cases (**the sample space**), all the possible events (**the event space**), and the probability of each of the events (**the probability law**). If we know all these, then our decision will be theoretically optimal. Of course, for high-dimensional data like images, we need approximations to such a probability model. However, we first need to understand the theoretical foundation of the probability space to know what approximations would make sense.

2.2.1 Sample space Ω

We start by defining the sample space Ω. Given an experiment, the **sample space** Ω is the set containing all possible outcomes of the experiment.

Definition 2.13. *A sample space Ω is the set of all possible outcomes from an experiment. We denote ξ as an element in Ω.*

A sample space can contain discrete outcomes or continuous outcomes, as shown in the examples below and **Figure 2.13**.

Example 2.21: (Discrete Outcomes)

- Coin flip: $\Omega = \{H,\, T\}$.
- Throw a die: $\Omega = \{1, 2, 3, 4, 5, 6\}$.
- Paper / scissor / stone: $\Omega = \{\text{paper}, \text{scissor}, \text{stone}\}$.
- Draw an even integer: $\Omega = \{2, 4, 6, 8, \ldots\}$.

Example 2.22: (Continuous Outcomes)

- Waiting time for a bus in West Lafayette: $\Omega = \{t \mid 0 \leq t \leq 30 \text{ minutes}\}$.
- Phase angle of a voltage: $\Omega = \{\theta \mid 0 \leq \theta \leq 2\pi\}$.
- Frequency of a pitch: $\Omega = \{f \mid 0 \leq f \leq f_{\max}\}$.

Figure 2.13 also shows a **functional** example of the sample space. In this case, the sample space contains **functions**. For example,

- Set of all straight lines in 2D:

$$\Omega = \{f \mid f(x) = ax + b,\ a, b \in \mathbb{R}\}.$$

- Set of all cosine functions with a phase offset:

$$\Omega = \{f \mid f(t) = \cos(2\pi\omega_0 t + \Theta),\ 0 \leq \Theta \leq 2\pi\}.$$

As we see from the above examples, the sample space is nothing but a universal set. The elements inside the sample space are the outcomes of the experiment. If you change

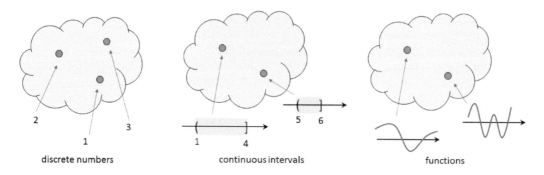

discrete numbers   continuous intervals   functions

Figure 2.13: The sample space can take various forms: it can contain discrete numbers, or continuous intervals, or even functions.

the experiment, the possible outcomes will be different so that the sample space will be different. For example, flipping a coin has different possible outcomes from throwing a die.

What if we want to describe a composite experiment where we flip a coin and throw a die? Here is the sample space:

Example 2.23: If the experiment contains flipping a coin and throwing a die, then the sample space is

$$\Big\{(H,1), (H,2), (H,3), (H,4), (H,5), (H,6),$$

$$(T,1), (T,2), (T,3), (T,4), (T,5), (T,6)\Big\}.$$

In this sample space, each element is a pair of outcomes.

Practice Exercise 2.8. There are 8 processors on a computer. A computer job scheduler chooses one processor randomly. What is the sample space? If the computer job scheduler can choose two processors at once, what is the sample space then?

Solution. The sample space of the first case is $\Omega = \{1, 2, 3, 4, 5, 6, 7, 8\}$. The sample space of the second case is $\Omega = \{(1, 2), (1, 3), (1, 4), \ldots, (7, 8)\}$.

Practice Exercise 2.9. A cell phone tower has a circular average coverage area of radius of 10 km. We observe the source locations of calls received by the tower. What is the sample space of all possible source locations?

Solution. Assume that the center of the tower is located at (x_0, y_0). The sample space is the set

$$\Omega = \{(x, y) \mid \sqrt{(x - x_0)^2 + (y - y_0)^2} \leq 10\}.$$

Not every set can be a sample space. A sample space must be **exhaustive** and **exclusive**. The term "exhaustive" means that the sample space has to cover **all** possible outcomes. If there is one possible outcome that is left out, then the set is no longer a sample space. The term "exclusive" means that the sample space contains unique elements so that there is no repetition of elements.

Example 2.24. (Counterexamples)

The following two examples are NOT sample spaces.

- Throw a die: $\Omega = \{1, 2, 3\}$ is not a sample space because it is not **exhaustive**.
- Throw a die: $\Omega = \{1, 1, 2, 3, 4, 5, 6\}$ is not a sample space because it is not **exclusive**.

Therefore, a valid sample space must contain all possible outcomes, and each element must be unique.

We summarize the concept of a sample space as follows.

What is a sample space Ω?

- A sample space Ω is the collection of all possible outcomes.
- The outcomes can be numbers, alphabets, vectors, or functions. The outcomes can also be images, videos, EEG signals, audio speeches, etc.
- Ω must be exhaustive and exclusive.

2.2.2 Event space $\mathcal{F}$

The sample space contains all the possible outcomes. However, in many practical situations, we are not interested in each of the individual outcomes; we are interested in the *combinations* of the outcomes. For example, when throwing a die, we may ask "What is the probability of rolling an odd number?" or "What is the probability of rolling a number that is less than 3?" Clearly, "odd number" is not an outcome of the experiment because the possible outcomes are $\{1, 2, 3, 4, 5, 6\}$. We call "odd number" an **event**. An event must be a subset in the sample space.

Definition 2.14. *An **event** E is a subset in the sample space Ω. The set of all possible events is denoted as $\mathcal{F}$.*

While this definition is extremely simple, we need to keep in mind a few facts about events. First, an outcome ξ is an element in Ω but an event E is a subset contained in Ω, i.e., $E \subseteq \Omega$. Thus, an event can contain one outcome but it can also contain many outcomes. The following example shows a few cases of events:

Example 2.25. Throw a die. Let $\Omega = \{1, 2, 3, 4, 5, 6\}$. The following are two possible events, as illustrated in **Figure 2.14**.

- $E_1 = \{\text{even numbers}\} = \{2, 4, 6\}$.

- $E_2 = \{\text{less than } 3\} = \{1, 2\}$.

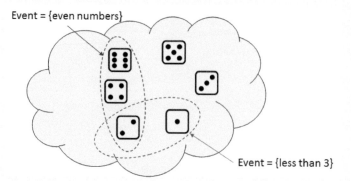

Event = {even numbers}

Event = {less than 3}

Figure 2.14: Two examples of events: The first event contains numbers $\{2, 4, 6\}$, and the second event contains numbers $\{1, 2\}$.

Practice Exercise 2.10. The "ping" command is used to measure round-trip times for Internet packets. What is the sample space of all possible round-trip times? What is the event that a round-trip time is between 10 ms and 20 ms?

Solution. The sample space is $\Omega = [0, \infty)$. The event is $E = [10, 20]$.

Practice Exercise 2.11. A cell phone tower has a circular average coverage area of radius 10 km. We observe the source locations of calls received by the tower. What is the event when the source location of a call is between 2 km and 5 km from the tower?

Solution. Assume that the center of the tower is located at (x_0, y_0). The event is $E = \{(x, y) \mid 2 \leq \sqrt{(x - x_0)^2 + (y - y_0)^2} \leq 5\}$.

The second point we should remember is the cardinality of Ω and that of $\mathcal{F}$. A sample space containing n elements has a cardinality n. However, the event space constructed from Ω will contain 2^n events. To see why this is so, let's consider the following example.

Example 2.26. Consider an experiment with 3 outcomes $\Omega = \{\clubsuit, \heartsuit, \maltese\}$. We can list out all the possible events: $\emptyset$, $\{\clubsuit\}$, $\{\heartsuit\}$, $\{\maltese\}$, $\{\clubsuit, \heartsuit\}$, $\{\clubsuit, \maltese\}$, $\{\heartsuit, \clubsuit\}$, $\{\clubsuit, \heartsuit, \maltese\}$. So in total there are $2^3 = 8$ possible events. **Figure 2.15** depicts the situation. What is the difference between $\clubsuit$ and $\{\clubsuit\}$? The former is an element, whereas the latter is a set. Thus, $\{\clubsuit\}$ is an event but $\clubsuit$ is not an event. Why is $\emptyset$ an event? Because we can ask "What is the probability that we get an odd number and an even number?" The probability is obviously zero, but the reason it is zero is that the event is an empty set.

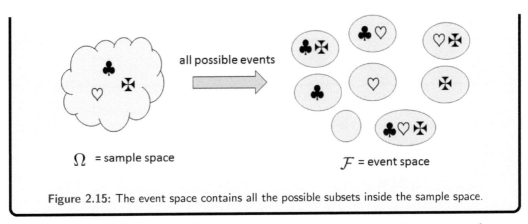

Figure 2.15: The event space contains all the possible subsets inside the sample space.

In general, if there are n elements in the sample space, then the number of events is 2^n. To see why this is true, we can assign to each element a binary value: either 0 or 1. For example, in Table 2.1 we consider throwing a die. For each of the six faces, we assign a binary code. This will give us a binary string for each event. For example, the event $\{1, 5\}$ is encoded as the binary string 100010 because only 1 and 5 are activated. We can count the total number of unique strings, which is the number of strings that can be constructed from n bits. It is easily seen that this number is 2^n.

Event	1	2	3	4	5	6	Binary Code
$\emptyset$	×	×	×	×	×	×	000000
$\{1, 5\}$	○	×	×	×	○	×	100010
$\{3, 4, 5\}$	×	×	○	○	○	×	001110
⋮		⋮		⋮			⋮
$\{2, 3, 4, 5, 6\}$	×	○	○	○	○	○	011111
$\{1, 2, 3, 4, 5, 6\}$	○	○	○	○	○	○	111111

Table 2.1: An event space contains 2^n events, where n is the number of elements in the sample space. To see this, we encode each outcome with a binary code. The resulting binary string then forms a unique index of the event. Counting the total number of events gives us the cardinality of the event space.

The box below summarizes what you need to know about event spaces.

What is an event space $\mathcal{F}$?

- An event space $\mathcal{F}$ is the set of all possible subsets. It is a set of sets.
- We need $\mathcal{F}$ because the probability law $\mathbb{P}$ is mapping a set to a number. $\mathbb{P}$ does not take an outcome from Ω but a subset inside Ω.

Event spaces: Some advanced topics

> The following discussions can be skipped if it is your first time reading the book.

What else do we need to take care of in order to ensure that an event is well defined? A few set operations seem to be necessary. For example, if $E_1 = \{1\}$ and $E_2 = \{2\}$ are events, it is necessary that $E = E_1 \cup E_2 = \{1, 2\}$ is an event too. Another example: if $E_1 = \{5, 6\}$ and $E_2 = \{1, 5\}$ are events, then it is necessary that $E = E_1 \cap E_2 = \{5\}$ is also an event. The third example: if $E_1 = \{3, 4, 5, 6\}$ is an event, then $E = E_1^c = \{1, 2\}$ should be an event. As you can see, there is nothing sophisticated in these examples. They are just some basic set operations. We want to ensure that the event space is **closed** under these set operations. That is, we do not want to be surprised by finding that a set constructed from two events is not an event. However, since all set operations can be constructed from union, intersection and complement, ensuring that the event space is closed under these three operations effectively ensures that it is closed to **all** set operations.

The formal way to guarantee these is the notion of a **field**. This term may seem to be abstract, but it is indeed quite useful:

Definition 2.15. *For an event space $\mathcal{F}$ to be valid, $\mathcal{F}$ must be a* **field** $\mathcal{F}$. *It is a field if it satisfies the following conditions*

- $\emptyset \in \mathcal{F}$ *and* $\Omega \in \mathcal{F}$.
- *(Closed under complement) If* $F \in \mathcal{F}$, *then also* $F^c \in \mathcal{F}$.
- *(Closed under union and intersection) If* $F_1 \in \mathcal{F}$ *and* $F_2 \in \mathcal{F}$, *then* $F_1 \cap F_2 \in \mathcal{F}$ *and* $F_1 \cup F_2 \in \mathcal{F}$.

For a finite set, i.e., a set that contains n elements, the collection of all possible subsets is indeed a field. This is not difficult to see if you consider rolling a die. For example, if $E = \{3, 4, 5, 6\}$ is inside $\mathcal{F}$, then $E^c = \{1, 2\}$ is also inside $\mathcal{F}$. This is because $\mathcal{F}$ consists of 2^n subsets each being encoded by a unique binary string. So if $E = 001111$, then $E^c = 110000$, which is also in $\mathcal{F}$. Similar reasoning applies to intersection and union.

At this point, you may ask:

- **Why bother constructing a field?** The answer is that probability is a measure of the size of a set, so we must input a set to a probability measure $\mathbb{P}$ to get a number. The set being input to $\mathbb{P}$ must be a subset inside the sample space; otherwise, it will be undefined. If we regard $\mathbb{P}$ as a mapping, we need to specify the collection of all its inputs, which is the set of all subsets, i.e., the event space. So if we do not define the field, there is no way to define the measure $\mathbb{P}$.

- **What if the event space is not a field?** If the event space is not a field, then we can easily construct pathological cases where we cannot assign a probability. For example, if the event space is not a field, then it would be possible that the complement of $E = \{3, 4, 5, 6\}$ (which is $E^c = \{1, 2\}$) is not an event. This just does not make sense.

The concept of a field is sufficient for finite sample spaces. However, there are two other types of sample spaces where the concept of a field is inadequate. The first type of sets consists of the **countably infinite** sets, and the second type consists of the sets defined on the **real line**. There are other types of sets, but these two have important practical applications. Therefore, we need to have a basic understanding of these two types.

Sigma-field

The difficulty of a countably infinite set is that there are infinitely many subsets in the field of a countably infinite set. Having a finite union and a finite intersection is insufficient to ensure the closedness of all intersections and unions. In particular, having $F_1 \cup F_2 \in \mathcal{F}$ does not automatically give us $\bigcup_{n=1}^{\infty} F_n \in \mathcal{F}$ because the latter is an infinite union. Therefore, for countably infinite sets, their requirements to be a field are more restrictive as we need to ensure infinite intersection and union. The resulting field is called the σ-field.

> **Definition 2.16.** *A sigma-field (σ-**field**) $\mathcal{F}$ is a field such that*
>
> - $\mathcal{F}$ *is a field, and*
> - *if $F_1, F_2, \ldots \in \mathcal{F}$, then the union $\bigcup_{i=1}^{\infty} F_i$ and the intersection $\bigcap_{i=1}^{\infty} F_i$ are both in $\mathcal{F}$.*

When do we need a σ-field? When the sample space is countable and has infinitely many elements. For example, if the sample space contains all integers, then the collection of all possible subsets is a σ-field. For another, if $E_1 = \{2\}$, $E_2 = \{4\}$, $E_3 = \{6\}$, ..., then $\bigcup_{n=1}^{\infty} E_n = \{2, 4, 6, 8, \ldots\} = \{$positive even numbers$\}$. Clearly, we want $\bigcup_{n=1}^{\infty} E_n$ to live in the sample space.

Borel sigma-field

While a sigma-field allows us to consider countable sets of events, it is still insufficient for considering events defined on the real line, e.g., time, as these events are not countable. So how do we define an event on the real line? It turns out that we need a different way to define the **smallest unit**. For finite sets and countable sets, the smallest units are the elements themselves because we can **count** them. For the real line, we cannot count the elements because any non-empty interval is uncountably infinite.

The smallest unit we use to construct a field for the real line is a semi-closed interval

$$(-\infty, b] \stackrel{\text{def}}{=} \{x \mid -\infty < x \le b\}.$$

The **Borel σ-field** is defined as the sigma-field generated by the semi-closed intervals.

> **Definition 2.17.** *The **Borel σ-field** $\mathcal{B}$ is a σ-field generated from semi-closed intervals:*
>
> $$(-\infty, b] \stackrel{\text{def}}{=} \{x \mid -\infty < x \le b\}.$$

The difference between the Borel σ-field $\mathcal{B}$ and a regular σ-field is how we measure the subsets. In a σ-field, we count the elements in the subsets, whereas, in a Borel σ-field, we use the semi-closed intervals to measure the subsets.

Being a field, the Borel σ-field is closed under complement, union, and intersection. In particular, subsets of the following forms are also in the Borel σ-field $\mathcal{B}$:

$$(a, b), \ [a, b], \ (a, b], \ [a, b), \ [a, \infty), \ (a, \infty), \ (-\infty, b], \ \{b\}.$$

For example, (a, ∞) can be constructed from $(-\infty, a]^c$, and $(a, b]$ can be constructed by taking the intersection of $(-\infty, b]$ and (a, ∞).

Example 2.27: Waiting for a bus. Let $\Omega = \{0 \le t \le 30\}$. The Borel σ-field contains all semi-closed intervals $(a, b]$, where $0 \le a \le b \le 30$. Here are two possible events:

- $F_1 = \{\text{less than 10 minutes}\} = \{0 \le t < 10\} = \{0\} \cup (\{0 < t \le 10\} \cap \{10\}^c)$.
- $F_2 = \{\text{more than 20 minutes}\} = \{20 < t \le 30\}$.

Further discussion of the Borel σ-field can be found in Leon-Garcia (3rd Edition,) Chapter 2.9.

This is the end of the discussion. Please join us again.

2.2.3   Probability law $\mathbb{P}$

The third component of a probability space is the probability law $\mathbb{P}$. Its job is to assign a number to an event.

Definition 2.18. *A **probability law** is a function $\mathbb{P} : \mathcal{F} \to [0, 1]$ of an event E to a real number in $[0, 1]$.*

The probability law is thus a **function**, and therefore we must specify the input and the output. The input to $\mathbb{P}$ is an event E, which is a subset in Ω and an element in $\mathcal{F}$. The output of $\mathbb{P}$ is a number between 0 and 1, which we call the **probability**.

The definition above does not specify how an event is being mapped to a number. However, since probability is a measure of the size of a set, a meaningful $\mathbb{P}$ should be **consistent** for all events in $\mathcal{F}$. This requires some rules, known as the **axioms of probability**, when we define the $\mathbb{P}$. Any probability law $\mathbb{P}$ must satisfy these axioms; otherwise, we will see contradictions. We will discuss the axioms in the next section. For now, let us look at two examples to make sure we understand the functional nature of $\mathbb{P}$.

Example 2.28. Consider flipping a coin. The event space is $\mathcal{F} = \{\emptyset, \{H\}, \{T\}, \Omega\}$. We can define the probability law as

$$\mathbb{P}[\emptyset] = 0, \ \ \mathbb{P}[\{H\}] = \frac{1}{2}, \ \ \mathbb{P}[\{T\}] = \frac{1}{2}, \ \ \mathbb{P}[\Omega] = 1,$$

as shown in **Figure 2.16**. This $\mathbb{P}$ is clearly consistent for all the events in $\mathcal{F}$.

Is it possible to construct an invalid $\mathbb{P}$? Certainly. Consider the following proba-

---

bility law:

$$\mathbb{P}[\emptyset] = 0, \quad \mathbb{P}[\{H\}] = \frac{1}{3}, \quad \mathbb{P}[\{T\}] = \frac{1}{3}, \quad \mathbb{P}[\Omega] = 1.$$

This law is invalid because the individual events are $\mathbb{P}[\{H\}] = \frac{1}{3}$ and $\mathbb{P}[\{T\}] = \frac{1}{3}$ but the union is $\mathbb{P}[\Omega] = 1$. To fix this problem, one possible solution is to define the probability law as

$$\mathbb{P}[\emptyset] = 0, \quad \mathbb{P}[\{H\}] = \frac{1}{3}, \quad \mathbb{P}[\{T\}] = \frac{2}{3}, \quad \mathbb{P}[\Omega] = 1.$$

Then, the probabilities for all the events are well defined and consistent.

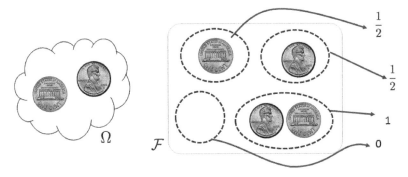

Figure 2.16: A probability law is a mapping from an event to a number. A probability law cannot be arbitrarily assigned; it must satisfy the axioms of probability.

Example 2.29. Consider a sample space containing three elements $\Omega = \{\clubsuit, \heartsuit, \maltese\}$. The event space is then $\mathcal{F} = \left\{ \emptyset, \{\clubsuit\}, \{\heartsuit\}, \{\maltese\}, \{\clubsuit, \heartsuit\}, \{\heartsuit, \maltese\}, \{\clubsuit, \maltese\}, \{\clubsuit, \heartsuit, \maltese\} \right\}$. One possible $\mathbb{P}$ we could define would be

$$\mathbb{P}[\emptyset] = 0, \quad \mathbb{P}[\{\clubsuit\}] = \mathbb{P}[\{\heartsuit\}] = \mathbb{P}[\{\maltese\}] = \frac{1}{3},$$

$$\mathbb{P}[\{\clubsuit, \heartsuit\}] = \mathbb{P}[\{\clubsuit, \maltese\}] = \mathbb{P}[\{\heartsuit, \maltese\}] = \frac{2}{3}, \quad \mathbb{P}[\{\clubsuit, \heartsuit, \maltese\}] = 1.$$

What is a probability law $\mathbb{P}$?

- A probability law $\mathbb{P}$ is a **function**.
- It takes a subset (an element in $\mathcal{F}$) and maps it to a number between 0 and 1.
- $\mathbb{P}$ is a **measure** of the size of a set.
- For $\mathbb{P}$ to be valid, it must satisfy the **axioms of probability**.

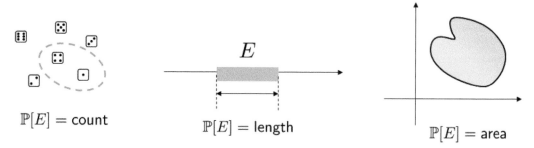

$\mathbb{P}[E] = \text{count}$ $\mathbb{P}[E] = \text{length}$ $\mathbb{P}[E] = \text{area}$

Figure 2.17: Probability is a measure of the size of a set. The probability can be a counter that counts the number of elements, a ruler that measures the length of an interval, or an integration that measures the area of a region.

A probability law $\mathbb{P}$ is a measure

Consider the word "measure" in our slogan: **probability is a measure of the size of a set**. Depending on the nature of the set, the measure can be a counter, ruler, scale, or even a stopwatch. So far, all the examples we have seen are based on sets with a finite number of elements. For these sets, the natural choice of the probability measure is a counter. However, if the sets are intervals on the real line or regions in a plane, we need a different probability law to measure their size. Let's look at the examples shown in **Figure 2.17**.

Example 2.30 (Finite Set). Consider throwing a die, so that

$$\Omega = \{1, 2, 3, 4, 5, 6\}.$$

Then the probability measure is a counter that reports the number of elements. If the die is fair, i.e., all the 6 faces have equal probability of happening, then an event $E = \{1, 3\}$ will have a probability $\mathbb{P}[E] = \frac{2}{6}$.

Example 2.31 (Intervals). Suppose that the sample space is a unit interval $\Omega = [0, 1]$. Let E be an event such that $E = [a, b]$ where a, b are numbers in $[0, 1]$. Then the probability measure is a ruler that measures the length of the intervals. If all the numbers on the real line have equal probability of appearing, then $\mathbb{P}[E] = b - a$.

Example 2.32 (Regions). Suppose that the sample space is the square $\Omega = [-1, 1] \times [-1, 1]$. Let E be a circle such that $E = \{(x, y) | x^2 + y^2 < r^2\}$, where $r < 1$. Then the probability measure is an area measure that returns us the area of E. If we assume that all coordinates in Ω are equally probable, then $\mathbb{P}[E] = \pi r^2$, for $r < 1$.

Because probability is a measure of the size of a set, two sets can be compared according to their probability measures. For example, if $\Omega = \{\clubsuit, \heartsuit, \maltese\}$, and if $E_1 = \{\clubsuit\}$ and $E_2 = \{\clubsuit, \heartsuit\}$, then one possible $\mathbb{P}$ is to assign $\mathbb{P}[E_1] = \mathbb{P}[\{\clubsuit\}] = \frac{1}{3}$ and $\mathbb{P}[E_2] = \mathbb{P}[\{\clubsuit, \heartsuit\}] = 2/3$.

In this particular case, we see that $E_1 \subseteq E_2$ and thus

$$\mathbb{P}[E_1] \leq \mathbb{P}[E_2].$$

Let's now consider the term "size." Notice that the concept of the size of a set is not limited to the number of elements. A better way to think about size is to imagine that it is the weight of the set. This might may seem fanciful at first, but it is quite natural. Consider the following example.

Example 2.33. (Discrete events with different weights) Suppose we have a sample space $\Omega = \{\clubsuit, \heartsuit, \maltese\}$. Let us assign a different probability to each outcome:

$$\mathbb{P}[\{\clubsuit\}] = \frac{2}{6}, \quad \mathbb{P}[\{\heartsuit\}] = \frac{1}{6}, \quad \mathbb{P}[\{\maltese\}] = \frac{3}{6}.$$

As illustrated in **Figure 2.18**, since each outcome has a different weight, when determining the probability of a set of outcomes we can add these weights (instead of counting the number of outcomes). For example, when reporting $\mathbb{P}[\{\clubsuit\}]$ we find its weight $\mathbb{P}[\{\clubsuit\}] = \frac{2}{6}$, whereas when reporting $\mathbb{P}[\{\heartsuit, \maltese\}]$ we find the sum of their weights $\mathbb{P}[\{\heartsuit, \maltese\}] = \frac{1}{6} + \frac{3}{6} = \frac{4}{6}$. Therefore, the notion of size does not refer to the number of elements but to the total weight of these elements.

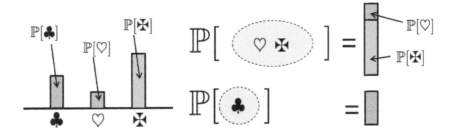

Figure 2.18: This example shows the "weights" of three elements in a set. The weights are numbers between 0 and 1 such that the sum is 1. When applying a probability measure to this set, we sum the weights for the elements in the events being considered. For example, $\mathbb{P}[\heartsuit, \maltese]$ = yellow + green, and $\mathbb{P}[\clubsuit]$ = purple.

Example 2.34. (Continuous events with different weights) Suppose that the sample space is an interval, say $\Omega = [-1, 1]$. On this interval we define a weighting function $f(x)$ where $f(x_0)$ specifies the weight for x_0. Because Ω is an interval, events defined on this Ω must also be intervals. For example, we can consider two events $E_1 = [a, b]$ and $E_2 = [c, d]$. The probabilities of these events are $\mathbb{P}[E_1] = \int_a^b f(x)\, dx$ and $\mathbb{P}[E_2] = \int_c^d f(x)\, dx$, as shown in **Figure 2.19**.

Viewing probability as a measure is not just a game for mathematicians; rather, it has fundamental significance for several reasons. First, it eliminates any dependency on probability as relative frequency from the frequentist point of view. Relative frequency is a

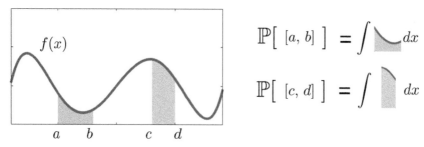

Figure 2.19: If the sample space is an interval on the real line, then the probability of an event is the area under the curve of the weighting function.

narrowly defined concept that is largely limited to discrete events, e.g., flipping a coin. While we can assign weights to coin-toss events to deal with those biased coins, the extension to continuous events becomes problematic. By thinking of probability as a measure, we can generalize the notion to apply to intervals, areas, volumes, and so on.

Second, viewing probability as a measure forces us to disentangle an **event** from **measures**. An event is a subset in the sample space. It has nothing to do with the measure (e.g., a ruler) you use to measure the event. The measure, on the other hand, specifies the weighting function you apply to measure the event when computing the probability. For example, let $\Omega = [-1, 1]$ be an interval, and let $E = [a, b]$ be an event. We can define two weighting functions $f(x)$ and $g(x)$. Correspondingly, we will have two different probability measures $\mathbb{F}$ and $\mathbb{G}$ such that

$$\mathbb{F}([a, b]) = \int_E d\mathbb{F} = \int_a^b f(x)\,dx,$$

$$\mathbb{G}([a, b]) = \int_E d\mathbb{G} = \int_a^b g(x)\,dx. \tag{2.20}$$

To make sense of these notations, consider only $\mathbb{P}[[a, b]]$ and not $\mathbb{F}([a, b])$ and $\mathbb{G}([a, b])$. As you can see, the event for both measures is $E = [a, b]$ but the measures are different. Therefore, the values of the probability are different.

Example 2.35. (Two probability laws are different if their weighting functions are different.) Consider two different weighting functions for throwing a die. The first one assigns probability as the following:

$$\mathbb{P}[\{1\}] = \frac{1}{12}, \ \mathbb{P}[\{2\}] = \frac{2}{12}, \ \mathbb{P}[\{3\}] = \frac{3}{12},$$

$$\mathbb{P}[\{4\}] = \frac{4}{12}, \ \mathbb{P}[\{5\}] = \frac{1}{12}, \ \mathbb{P}[\{6\}] = \frac{1}{12},$$

whereas the second function assigns the probability like this:

$$\mathbb{P}[\{1\}] = \frac{2}{12}, \ \mathbb{P}[\{2\}] = \frac{2}{12}, \ \mathbb{P}[\{3\}] = \frac{2}{12},$$

$$\mathbb{P}[\{4\}] = \frac{2}{12}, \ \mathbb{P}[\{5\}] = \frac{2}{12}, \ \mathbb{P}[\{6\}] = \frac{2}{12}.$$

Let an event $E = \{1, 2\}$. Let $\mathbb{F}$ be the measure using the first set of probabilities, and let $\mathbb{G}$ be the measure of the second set of probabilities. Then,

$$\mathbb{F}(E) = \mathbb{F}(\{1,2\}) = \frac{1}{12} + \frac{2}{12} = \frac{3}{12},$$
$$\mathbb{G}(E) = \mathbb{G}(\{1,2\}) = \frac{2}{12} + \frac{2}{12} = \frac{4}{12}.$$

Therefore, although the events are the same, the two different measures will give us two different probability values.

Remark. The notation $\int_E d\mathbb{F}$ in Equation (2.20) is known as the **Lebesgue integral**. You should be aware of this notation, but the theory of Lebesgue measure is beyond the scope of this book.

2.2.4 Measure zero sets

Understanding the measure perspective on probability allows us to understand another important concept of probability, namely **measure zero sets**. To introduce this concept, we pose the question: What is the probability of obtaining a single point, say $\{0.5\}$, when the sample space is $\Omega = [0, 1]$?

The answer to this question is rooted in the **compatibility** between the measure and the sample space. In other words, the measure has to be meaningful for the events in the sample space. Using $\Omega = [0, 1]$, since Ω is an interval, an appropriate measure would be the length of this interval. You may add different weighting functions to define your measure, but ultimately, the measure must be an integral. If you use a "counter" as a measure, then the counter and the interval are not compatible because you cannot count on the real line.

Now, suppose that we define a measure for $\Omega = [0, 1]$ using a weighting function $f(x)$. This measure is determined by an integration. Then, for $E = \{0.5\}$, the measure is

$$\mathbb{P}[E] = \mathbb{P}[\{0.5\}] = \int_{0.5}^{0.5} f(x)\, dx = 0.$$

In fact, for any weighting function the integral will be zero because the length of the set E is zero.[1] An event that gives us zero probability is known as an **event with measure 0**. **Figure 2.20** shows an example.

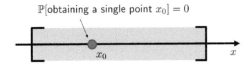

$\mathbb{P}[\text{obtaining a single point } x_0] = 0$

x_0 x

Figure 2.20: The probability of obtaining a single point in a continuous interval is zero.

---

[1] We assume that f is continuous throughout $[0, 1]$. If f is discontinuous at $x = 0.5$, some additional considerations will apply.

What are measure zero sets?

- A set E (non-empty) is called a measure zero set when $\mathbb{P}[E] = 0$.
- For example, $\{0\}$ is a measure zero set when we use a continuous measure $\mathbb{F}$.
- But $\{0\}$ can have a positive measure when we use a discrete measure $\mathbb{G}$.

Example 2.36(a). Consider a fair die with $\Omega = \{1,2,3,4,5,6\}$. Then the set $\{1\}$ has a probability of $\frac{1}{6}$. The sample space does not have a measure zero event because the measure we use is a counter.

Example 2.36(b). Consider an interval with $\Omega = [1,6]$. Then the set $\{1\}$ has measure 0 because it is an isolated point with respect to the sample space.

Example 2.36(c). For any intervals, $\mathbb{P}[[a,b]] = \mathbb{P}[(a,b)]$ because the two end points have measure zero: $\mathbb{P}[\{a\}] = \mathbb{P}[\{b\}] = 0$.

Formal definitions of measure zero sets

The following discussion of the formal definitions of measure zero sets is optional for the first reading of this book.

We can formally define measure zero sets as follows:

Definition 2.19. *Let Ω be the sample space. A set $A \in \Omega$ is said to have **measure zero** if for any given $\epsilon > 0$,*

- *There exists a countable number of subsets A_n such that $A \subseteq \cup_{n=1}^{\infty} A_n$, and*
- $\sum_{n=1}^{\infty} \mathbb{P}[A_n] < \epsilon$.

You may need to read this definition carefully. Suppose we have an event A. We construct a set of neighbors $A_1, \ldots, A_\infty$ such that A is included in the union $\cup_{n=1}^{\infty} A_n$. If the sum of the all $\mathbb{P}[A_n]$ is still less than ϵ, then the set A will have a measure zero.

To understand the difference between a measure for a continuous set and a countable set, consider **Figure 2.21**. On the left side of **Figure 2.21** we show an interval Ω in which there is an isolated point x_0. The measure for this Ω is the length of the interval (relative to whatever weighting function you use). We define a small neighborhood $A_0 = (x_0 - \frac{\epsilon}{2}, x_0 + \frac{\epsilon}{2})$ surrounding x_0. The length of this interval is not more than ϵ. We then shrink ϵ. However, regardless of how small ϵ is, since x_0 is an isolated point, it is always included in the neighborhood. Therefore, the definition is satisfied, and so $\{x_0\}$ has measure zero.

Example 2.37. Let $\Omega = [0,1]$. The set $\{0.5\} \subset \Omega$ has measure zero, i.e., $\mathbb{P}[\{0.5\}] = 0$. To see this, we draw a small interval around 0.5, say $[0.5 - \epsilon/3, 0.5 + \epsilon/3]$. Inside this interval, there is really nothing to measure besides the point 0.5. Thus we have found an interval such that it contains 0.5, and the probability is $\mathbb{P}[[0.5 - \epsilon/3, 0.5 + \epsilon/3]] = 2\epsilon/3 < \epsilon$. Therefore, by definition, the set $\{0.5\}$ has measure 0.

The situation is very different for the right-hand side of **Figure 2.21**. Here, the measure is not the length but a counter. So if we create a neighborhood surrounding the isolated point x_0, we can always make a count. As a result, if you shrink ϵ to become a very small number (in this case less than $\frac{1}{4}$), then $\mathbb{P}[\{x_0\}] < \epsilon$ will no longer be true. Therefore, the set $\{x_0\}$ has a non-zero measure when we use the counter as the measure.

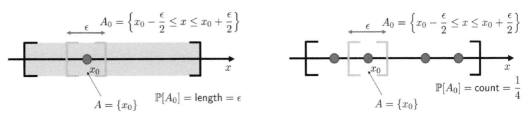

Figure 2.21: [Left] For a continuous sample space, a single point event $\{x_0\}$ can always be surrounded by a neighborhood A_0 whose size $\mathbb{P}[A_0] < \epsilon$. [Right] If you change the sample space to discrete elements, then a single point event $\{x_0\}$ can still be surrounded by a neighborhood A_0. However, the size $\mathbb{P}[A_0] = 1/4$ is a fixed number and will not work for *any* ϵ.

When we make probabilistic claims without considering the measure zero sets, we say that an event happens **almost surely**.

Definition 2.20. *An event $A \in \mathbb{R}$ is said to hold* **almost surely (a.s.)** *if*

$$\mathbb{P}[A] = 1 \tag{2.21}$$

except for all measure zero sets in $\mathbb{R}$.

Therefore, if a set A contains measure zero subsets, we can simply ignore them because they do not affect the probability of events. In this book, we will omit "a.s." if the context is clear.

Example 2.38(a). Let $\Omega = [0,1]$. Then $\mathbb{P}[(0,1)] = 1$ almost surely because the points 0 and 1 have measure zero in Ω.

Example 2.38(b). Let $\Omega = \{x \mid x^2 \leq 1\}$ and let $A = \{x \mid x^2 < 1\}$. Then $\mathbb{P}[A] = 1$ almost surely because the circumference has measure zero in Ω.

Practice Exercise 2.12. Let $\Omega = \{f : \mathbb{R} \to [-1,1] \mid f(t) = \cos(\omega_0 t + \theta)\}$, where ω_0 is a fixed constant and θ is random. Construct a measure zero event and an almost sure event.

Solution. Let
$$E = \{f : \mathbb{R} \to [-1, 1] \mid f(t) = \cos(\omega_0 t + k\pi/2)\}$$
for any integer k. That is, E contains all the functions with a phase of $\pi/2$, $2\pi/2$, $3\pi/2$, etc. Then E will have measure zero because it is a countable set of isolated functions. The event E^c will have probability $\mathbb{P}[E^c] = 1$ almost surely because E has measure zero.

This is the end of the discussion. Please join us again.

2.2.5 Summary of the probability space

After the preceding long journey through theory, let us summarize.

First, it is extremely important to understand our slogan: **probability is a measure of the size of a set**. This slogan is precise, but it needs clarification. When we say probability is a **measure**, we are thinking of it as being the probability law $\mathbb{P}$. Of course, in practice, we always think of probability as the **number** returned by the measure. However, the difference is not crucial. Also, "size" not only means the number of elements in the set, but it also means the relative weight of the set in the sample space. For example, if we use a weight function to weigh the set elements, then size would refer to the overall weight of the set.

When we put all these pieces together, we can understand why a probability space must consist of the three components

$$(\Omega, \mathcal{F}, \mathbb{P}), \tag{2.22}$$

where Ω is the sample space that defines all possible outcomes, $\mathcal{F}$ is the event space generated from Ω, and $\mathbb{P}$ is the probability law that maps an event to a number in $[0, 1]$. Can we drop one or more of the three components? We cannot! If we do not specify the sample space Ω, then there is no way to define the events. If we do not have a complete event space $\mathcal{F}$, then some events will become undefined, and further, if the probability law is applied only to outcomes, we will not be able to define the probability for events. Finally, if we do not specify the probability law, then we do not have a way to assign probabilities.

2.3 Axioms of Probability

We now turn to a deeper examination of the properties. Our motivation is simple. While the definition of probability law has achieved its goal of assigning a probability to an event, there must be restrictions on how the assignment can be made. For example, if we set $\mathbb{P}[\{H\}] = 1/3$, then $\mathbb{P}[\{T\}]$ must be $2/3$; otherwise, the sum of having a head and a tail will be greater than 1. The necessary restrictions on assigning a probability to an event are collectively known as the **axioms of probability**.

Definition 2.21. *A* **probability law** *is a function* $\mathbb{P}: \mathcal{F} \to [0,1]$ *that maps an event A to a real number in* $[0,1]$. *The function must satisfy the* **axioms of probability***:*

   I. **Non-negativity***:* $\mathbb{P}[A] \geq 0$, *for any* $A \subseteq \Omega$.

   II. **Normalization***:* $\mathbb{P}[\Omega] = 1$.

   III. **Additivity***: For any disjoint sets* $\{A_1, A_2, \ldots\}$, *it must be true that*

$$\mathbb{P}\left[\bigcup_{i=1}^{\infty} A_i\right] = \sum_{i=1}^{\infty} \mathbb{P}[A_i]. \tag{2.23}$$

An axiom is a proposition that serves as a premise or starting point in a logical system. Axioms are not definitions, nor are they theorems. They are believed to be true or true within a certain context. In our case, the axioms are true within the context of Bayesian probability. The Kolmogorov probability relies on another set of axioms. We will not dive into the details of these historical issues; in this book, we will confine our discussion to the three axioms given above.

2.3.1 Why these three probability axioms?

Why do we need three axioms? Why not just two axioms? Why these three particular axioms? The reasons are summarized in the box below.

Why these three axioms?

- Axiom I (Non-negativity) ensures that probability is never negative.
- Axiom II (Normalization) ensures that probability is never greater than 1.
- Axiom III (Additivity) allows us to add probabilities when two events do not overlap.

Axiom I is called the **non-negativity** axiom. It ensures that a probability value cannot be negative. Non-negativity is a must for probability. It is meaningless to say that the probability of getting an event is a negative number.

Axiom II is called the **normalization** axiom. It ensures that the probability of observing all possible outcomes is 1. This gives the upper limit of the probability. The upper limit does not have to be 1. It could be 10 or 100. As long as we are consistent about this upper limit, we are good. However, for historical reasons and convenience, we choose 1 to be the upper limit.

Axiom III is called the **additivity** axiom and is the most critical one among the three. The additivity axiom defines how set operations can be translated into probability operations. In a nutshell, it says that if we have a set of disjoint events, the probabilities can be added. From the measure perspective, Axiom III makes sense because if $\mathbb{P}$ measures the size of an event, then two disjoint events should have their probabilities added. If two disjoint events do not allow their probabilities to be added, then there is no way to measure a combined event. Similarly, if the probabilities can somehow be added even for overlapping events, there will be inconsistencies because there is no systematic way to handle the overlapping regions.

The **countable additivity** stated in Axiom III can be applied to both a finite number or an infinite number of sets. The finite case states that for any two disjoint sets A and B, we have

$$\mathbb{P}[A \cup B] = \mathbb{P}[A] + \mathbb{P}[B]. \tag{2.24}$$

In other words, if A and B are disjoint, then the probability of observing either A or B is the sum of the two individual probabilities. **Figure 2.22** illustrates this idea.

Example 2.39. Let's see why Axiom III is critical. Consider throwing a fair die with $\Omega = \{1, 2, 3, 4, 5, 6\}$. The probability of getting $\{4, 6\}$ is

$$\mathbb{P}[\{4, 6\}] = \mathbb{P}[\{4\} \cup \{6\}] = \mathbb{P}[\{4\}] + \mathbb{P}[\{6\}] = \frac{1}{6} + \frac{1}{6} = \frac{2}{6}.$$

In this equation, the second equality holds because the events $\{4\}$ and $\{6\}$ are disjoint. If we do not have Axiom III, then we cannot **add** probabilities.

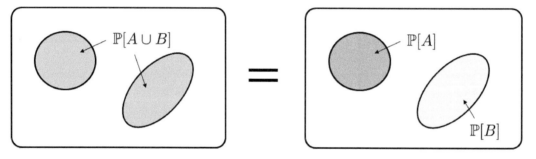

Figure 2.22: Axiom III says $\mathbb{P}[A \cup B] = \mathbb{P}[A] + \mathbb{P}[B]$ if $A \cap B = \emptyset$.

2.3.2 Axioms through the lens of measure

Axioms are "rules" we must abide by when we construct a measure. Therefore, any valid measure must be compatible with the axioms, regardless of whether we have a weighting function or not. In the following two examples, we will see how the weighting functions are used in the axioms.

Example 2.40. Consider a sample space with $\Omega = \{\clubsuit, \heartsuit, \maltese\}$. The probability for each outcome is

$$\mathbb{P}[\{\clubsuit\}] = \frac{2}{6}, \quad \mathbb{P}[\{\heartsuit\}] = \frac{1}{6}, \quad \mathbb{P}[\{\maltese\}] = \frac{3}{6}.$$

Suppose we construct two disjoint events $E_1 = \{\clubsuit, \heartsuit\}$ and $E_2 = \{\maltese\}$. Then Axiom

---

III says

$$\mathbb{P}[E_1 \cup E_2] = \mathbb{P}[E_1] + \mathbb{P}[E_2] = \left(\frac{2}{6} + \frac{1}{6}\right) + \frac{3}{6} = 1.$$

Note that in this calculation, the measure $\mathbb{P}$ is still a measure $\mathbb{P}$. If we endow it with a nonuniform weight function, then $\mathbb{P}$ applies the corresponding weights to the corresponding outcomes. This process is compatible with the axioms. See **Figure 2.23** for a pictorial illustration.

Example 2.41. Suppose the sample space is an interval $\Omega = [0,1]$. The two events are $E_1 = [a,b]$ and $E_2 = [c,d]$. Assume that the measure $\mathbb{P}$ uses a weighting function $f(x)$. Then, by Axiom III, we know that

$$\begin{aligned}
\mathbb{P}[E_1 \cup E_2] &= \mathbb{P}[E_1] + \mathbb{P}[E_2] \\
&= \mathbb{P}[[a,b]] + \mathbb{P}[[c,d]] && \text{(by Axiom 3)} \\
&= \int_a^b f(x)\,dx + \int_c^d f(x)\,dx, && \text{(apply the measure).}
\end{aligned}$$

As you can see, there is no conflict between the axioms and the measure. **Figure 2.24** illustrates this example.

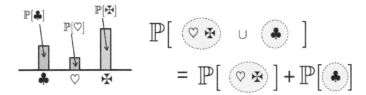

Figure 2.23: Applying weighting functions to the measures: Suppose we have three elements in the set. To compute the probability $\mathbb{P}[\{\heartsuit, \maltese\} \cup \{\clubsuit\}]$, we can write it as the sum of $\mathbb{P}[\{\heartsuit, \maltese\}]$ and $\mathbb{P}[\{\clubsuit\}]$.

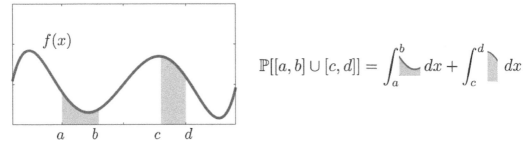

Figure 2.24: The axioms are compatible with the measure, even if we use a weighting function.

2.3.3 Corollaries derived from the axioms

The union of A and B is equivalent to the logical operator "OR". Once the logical operation "OR" is defined, all other logical operations can be defined. See the following examples.

CHAPTER 2. PROBABILITY

> **Corollary 2.1.** *Let $A \in \mathcal{F}$ be an event. Then,*
>
> *(a)* $\mathbb{P}[A^c] = 1 - \mathbb{P}[A]$.
>
> *(b)* $\mathbb{P}[A] \leq 1$.
>
> *(c)* $\mathbb{P}[\emptyset] = 0$.

Proof. (a) Since $\Omega = A \cup A^c$, by finite additivity we have $\mathbb{P}[\Omega] = \mathbb{P}[A \cup A^c] = \mathbb{P}[A] + \mathbb{P}[A^c]$. By the normalization axiom, we have $\mathbb{P}[\Omega] = 1$. Therefore, $\mathbb{P}[A^c] = 1 - \mathbb{P}[A]$.

(b) We prove by contradiction. Assume $\mathbb{P}[A] > 1$. Consider the complement A^c where $A \cup A^c = \Omega$. Since $\mathbb{P}[A^c] = 1 - \mathbb{P}[A]$, we must have $\mathbb{P}[A^c] < 0$ because by hypothesis $\mathbb{P}[A] > 1$. But $\mathbb{P}[A^c] < 0$ violates the non-negativity axiom. So we must have $\mathbb{P}[A] \leq 1$.

(c) Since $\Omega = \Omega \cup \emptyset$, by the first corollary we have $\mathbb{P}[\emptyset] = 1 - \mathbb{P}[\Omega] = 0$.
□

> **Corollary 2.2 (Unions of Two Non-Disjoint Sets).** *For any A and B in $\mathcal{F}$,*
> $$\mathbb{P}[A \cup B] = \mathbb{P}[A] + \mathbb{P}[B] - \mathbb{P}[A \cap B]. \tag{2.25}$$

This statement is different from Axiom III because A and B are not necessarily disjoint.

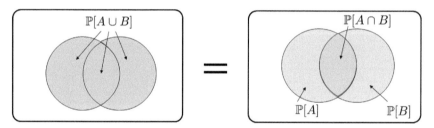

Figure 2.25: For any A and B, $\mathbb{P}[A \cup B] = \mathbb{P}[A] + \mathbb{P}[B] - \mathbb{P}[A \cap B]$.

Proof. First, observe that $A \cup B$ can be partitioned into three disjoint subsets as $A \cup B = (A \backslash B) \cup (A \cap B) \cup (B \backslash A)$. Since $A \backslash B = A \cap B^c$ and $B \backslash A = B \cap A^c$, by finite additivity we have that

$$\mathbb{P}[A \cup B] = \mathbb{P}[A \backslash B] + \mathbb{P}[A \cap B] + \mathbb{P}[B \backslash A] = \mathbb{P}[A \cap B^c] + \mathbb{P}[A \cap B] + \mathbb{P}[B \cap A^c]$$
$$\stackrel{(a)}{=} \mathbb{P}[A \cap B^c] + \mathbb{P}[A \cap B] + \mathbb{P}[B \cap A^c] + \mathbb{P}[A \cap B] - \mathbb{P}[A \cap B]$$
$$\stackrel{(b)}{=} \mathbb{P}[A \cap (B^c \cup B)] + \mathbb{P}[(A^c \cup A) \cap B] - \mathbb{P}[A \cap B]$$
$$= \mathbb{P}[A \cap \Omega] + \mathbb{P}[\Omega \cap B] - \mathbb{P}[A \cap B] = \mathbb{P}[A] + \mathbb{P}[B] - \mathbb{P}[A \cap B],$$

where in (a) we added and subtracted a term $\mathbb{P}[A \cap B]$, and in (b) we used finite additivity so that $\mathbb{P}[A \cap B^c] + \mathbb{P}[A \cap B] = \mathbb{P}[(A \cap B^c) \cup (A \cap B)] = \mathbb{P}[A \cap (B^c \cup B)]$.
□

Example 2.42. The corollary is easy to understand if we consider the following example. Let $\Omega = \{1, 2, 3, 4, 5, 6\}$ be the sample space of a fair die. Let $A = \{1, 2, 3\}$ and $B = \{3, 4, 5\}$. Then

$$\mathbb{P}[A \cup B] = \mathbb{P}[\{1, 2, 3, 4, 5\}] = \frac{5}{6}.$$

We can also use the corollary to obtain the same result:

$$\begin{aligned} \mathbb{P}[A \cup B] &= \mathbb{P}[A] + \mathbb{P}[B] - \mathbb{P}[A \cap B] \\ &= \mathbb{P}[\{1, 2, 3\}] + \mathbb{P}[\{3, 4, 5\}] - \mathbb{P}[\{3\}] \\ &= \frac{3}{6} + \frac{3}{6} - \frac{1}{6} = \frac{5}{6}. \end{aligned}$$

Corollary 2.3 (Inequalities). *Let A and B be two events in $\mathcal{F}$. Then,*

(a) $\mathbb{P}[A \cup B] \leq \mathbb{P}[A] + \mathbb{P}[B]$. (Union Bound)

(b) If $A \subseteq B$, then $\mathbb{P}[A] \leq \mathbb{P}[B]$.

Proof. (a) Since $\mathbb{P}[A \cup B] = \mathbb{P}[A] + \mathbb{P}[B] - \mathbb{P}[A \cap B]$ and by non-negativity axiom $\mathbb{P}[A \cap B] \geq 0$, we must have $\mathbb{P}[A \cup B] \leq \mathbb{P}[A] + \mathbb{P}[B]$. (b) If $A \subseteq B$, then there exists a set $B \backslash A$ such that $B = A \cup (B \backslash A)$. Therefore, by finite additivity we have $\mathbb{P}[B] = \mathbb{P}[A] + \mathbb{P}[B \backslash A] \geq \mathbb{P}[A]$. Since $\mathbb{P}[B \backslash A] \geq 0$, it follows that $\mathbb{P}[A] + \mathbb{P}[B \backslash A] \geq \mathbb{P}[A]$. Thus we have $\mathbb{P}[B] \geq \mathbb{P}[A]$. $\square$

Union bound is a frequently used tool for analyzing probabilities when the intersection $A \cap B$ is difficult to evaluate. Part (b) is useful when considering two events of different "sizes." For example, in the bus-waiting example, if we let $A = \{t \leq 5\}$, and $B = \{t \leq 10\}$, then $\mathbb{P}[A] \leq \mathbb{P}[B]$ because we have to wait for the first 5 minutes to go into the remaining 5 minutes.

Practice Exercise 2.13. Let the events A and B have $\mathbb{P}[A] = x$, $\mathbb{P}[B] = y$ and $\mathbb{P}[A \cup B] = z$. Find the following probabilities: $\mathbb{P}[A \cap B]$, $\mathbb{P}[A^c \cup B^c]$, and $\mathbb{P}[A \cap B^c]$.

Solution.

(a) Note that $z = \mathbb{P}[A \cup B] = \mathbb{P}[A] + \mathbb{P}[B] - \mathbb{P}[A \cap B]$. Thus, $\mathbb{P}[A \cap B] = x + y - z$.

(b) We can take the complement to obtain the result:

$$\mathbb{P}[A^c \cup B^c] = 1 - \mathbb{P}[(A^c \cup B^c)^c] = 1 - \mathbb{P}[A \cap B] = 1 - x - y + z.$$

(c) $\mathbb{P}[A \cap B^c] = \mathbb{P}[A] - \mathbb{P}[A \cap B] = x - (x + y - z) = z - y$.

Practice Exercise 2.14. Consider a sample space

$$\Omega = \{f : \mathbb{R} \to \mathbb{R} \mid f(x) = ax, \text{for all } a \in \mathbb{R}, x \in \mathbb{R}\}.$$

There are two events: $A = \{f \mid f(x) = ax,\ a \geq 0\}$, and $B = \{f \mid f(x) = ax,\ a \leq 0\}$. So, basically, A is the set of all straight lines with positive slope, and B is the set of straight lines with negative slope. Show that the union bound is tight.

Solution. First of all, we note that

$$\mathbb{P}[A \cup B] = \mathbb{P}[A] + \mathbb{P}[B] - \mathbb{P}[A \cap B].$$

The intersection is

$$\mathbb{P}[A \cap B] = \mathbb{P}[\{f \mid f(x) = 0\}].$$

Since this is a point set in the real line, it has measure zero. Thus, $\mathbb{P}[A \cap B] = 0$ and hence $\mathbb{P}[A \cup B] = \mathbb{P}[A] + \mathbb{P}[B]$. So the union bound is tight.

Closing remark. The development of today's probability theory is generally credited to Andrey Kolmogorov's 1933 book *Foundations of the Theory of Probability*. We close this section by citing one of the tables of the book. The table summarizes the correspondence between set theory and random events.

Theory of sets	Random events
A and B are disjoint, i.e., $A \cap B = \emptyset$	Events A and B are incompatible
$A_1 \cap A_2 \cdots \cap A_N = \emptyset$	Events $A_1, \ldots, A_N$ are incompatible
$A_1 \cap A_2 \cdots \cap A_N = X$	Event X is defined as the simultaneous occurrence of events $A_1, \ldots, A_N$
$A_1 \cup A_2 \cdots \cup A_N = X$	Event X is defined as the occurrence of at least one of the events $A_1, \ldots, A_N$
A^c	The opposite event A^c consisting of the non-occurrence of event A
$A = \emptyset$	Event A is impossible
$A = \Omega$	Event A must occur
$A_1, \ldots, A_N$ form a partition of Ω	The experiment consists of determining which of the events $A_1, \ldots, A_N$ occurs
$B \subset A$	From the occurrence of event B follows the inevitable occurrence of A

Table 2.2: Kolmogorov's summary of set theory results and random events.

2.4 Conditional Probability

In many practical data science problems, we are interested in the relationship between two or more events. For example, an event A may cause B to happen, and B may cause C to happen. A legitimate question in probability is then: If A has happened, what is the probability that B also happens? Of course, if A and B are correlated events, then knowing one event can tell us something about the other event. If the two events have no relationship, knowing one event will not tell us anything about the other.

In this section, we study the concept of **conditional probability**. There are three sub-topics in this section. We summarize the key points below.

The three main messages of this section are:

- Section 2.4.1: **Conditional probability**. Conditional probability of A given B is $\mathbb{P}[A|B] = \frac{\mathbb{P}[A \cap B]}{\mathbb{P}[B]}$.

- Section 2.4.2: **Independence**. Two events are **independent** if the occurrence of one does not influence the occurrence of the other: $\mathbb{P}[A|B] = \mathbb{P}[A]$.

- Section 2.4.3: **Bayes' theorem and the law of total probability**. Bayes' theorem allows us to switch the order of the conditioning: $\mathbb{P}[A|B]$ vs. $\mathbb{P}[B|A]$, whereas the law of total probability allows us to decompose an event into smaller events.

2.4.1 Definition of conditional probability

We start by defining **conditional probability**.

Definition 2.22. *Consider two events A and B. Assume $\mathbb{P}[B] \neq 0$. The* **conditional probability** *of A given B is*

$$\mathbb{P}[A \mid B] \stackrel{\text{def}}{=} \frac{\mathbb{P}[A \cap B]}{\mathbb{P}[B]}. \tag{2.26}$$

According to this definition, the conditional probability of A given B is the ratio of $\mathbb{P}[A \cap B]$ to $\mathbb{P}[B]$. It is the probability that A happens when we know that B has already happened. Since B has already happened, the event that A has also happened is represented by $A \cap B$. However, since we are only interested in the relative probability of A with respect to B, we need to normalize using B. This can be seen by comparing $\mathbb{P}[A \mid B]$ and $\mathbb{P}[A \cap B]$:

$$\mathbb{P}[A \mid B] = \frac{\mathbb{P}[A \cap B]}{\mathbb{P}[B]} \quad \text{and} \quad \mathbb{P}[A \cap B] = \frac{\mathbb{P}[A \cap B]}{\mathbb{P}[\Omega]}. \tag{2.27}$$

The difference is illustrated in **Figure 2.26**: The intersection $\mathbb{P}[A \cap B]$ calculates the overlapping area of the two events. We make no assumptions about the cause-effect relationship.

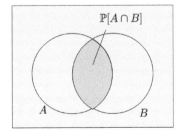
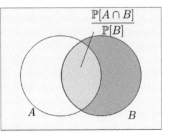

Figure 2.26: Illustration of conditional probability and its comparison with $\mathbb{P}[A \cap B]$.

What justifies this ratio? Suppose that B has already happened. Then, anything outside B will immediately become irrelevant as far as the relationship between A and B is concerned. So when we ask: "What is the probability that A happens given that B has happened?", we are effectively asking for the probability that $A \cap B$ happens under the condition that B has happened. Note that we need to consider $A \cap B$ because we know that B has already happened. If we take A only, then there exists a region $A \backslash B$ which does not contain anything about B. However, since we know that B has happened, $A \backslash B$ is impossible. In other words, among the elements of A, only those that appear in $A \cap B$ are meaningful.

Example 2.43. Let

$$A = \{\text{Purdue gets Big Ten championship}\},$$
$$B = \{\text{Purdue wins 15 games consecutively}\}.$$

In this example,

$$\mathbb{P}[A] = \text{Prob. that Purdue gets the championship,}$$
$$\mathbb{P}[B] = \text{Prob. that Purdue wins 15 games consecutively,}$$
$$\mathbb{P}[A \cap B] = \text{Prob. that Purdue gets the championship and wins 15 games,}$$
$$\mathbb{P}[A \,|\, B] = \text{Prob. that Purdue gets the championship given that}$$
$$\text{Purdue won 15 games.}$$

If Purdue has won 15 games consecutively, then it is unlikely that Purdue will get the championship because the sample space of all possible competition results is large. However, if we have already won 15 games consecutively, then the denominator of the probability becomes much smaller. In this case, the conditional probability is high.

Example 2.44. Consider throwing a die. Let

$$A = \{\text{getting a 3}\} \quad \text{and} \quad B = \{\text{getting an odd number}\}.$$

Find $\mathbb{P}[A \,|\, B]$ and $\mathbb{P}[B \,|\, A]$.

Solution. The following probabilities are easy to calculate:

$$\mathbb{P}[A] = \mathbb{P}[\{3\}] = \frac{1}{6}, \quad \text{and} \quad \mathbb{P}[B] = \mathbb{P}[\{1,3,5\}] = \frac{3}{6}.$$

Also, the intersection is

$$\mathbb{P}[A \cap B] = \mathbb{P}[\{3\}] = \frac{1}{6}.$$

Given these values, the conditional probability of A given B can be calculated as

$$\mathbb{P}[A \,|\, B] = \frac{\mathbb{P}[A \cap B]}{\mathbb{P}[B]} = \frac{\frac{1}{6}}{\frac{3}{6}} = \frac{1}{3}.$$

In other words, if we know that we have an odd number, then the probability of obtaining a 3 has to be computed over $\{1, 3, 5\}$, which give us a probability $\frac{1}{3}$. If we do not know that we have an odd number, then the probability of obtaining a 3 has to be computed from the sample space $\{1, 2, 3, 4, 5, 6\}$, which will give us $\frac{1}{6}$.

The other conditional probability is

$$\mathbb{P}[B \mid A] = \frac{\mathbb{P}[A \cap B]}{\mathbb{P}[A]} = 1.$$

Therefore, if we know that we have rolled a 3, then the probability for this number being an odd number is 1.

Example 2.45. Consider the situation shown in **Figure 2.27**. There are 12 points with equal probabilities of happening. Find the probabilities $\mathbb{P}[A|B]$ and $\mathbb{P}[B|A]$.

Solution. In this example, we can first calculate the individual probabilities:

$$\mathbb{P}[A] = \frac{5}{12}, \quad \text{and} \quad \mathbb{P}[B] = \frac{6}{12}, \quad \text{and} \quad \mathbb{P}[A \cap B] = \frac{2}{12}.$$

Then the conditional probabilities are

$$\mathbb{P}[A|B] = \frac{\mathbb{P}[A \cap B]}{\mathbb{P}[B]} = \frac{\frac{2}{12}}{\frac{6}{12}} = \frac{1}{3},$$

$$\mathbb{P}[B|A] = \frac{\mathbb{P}[A \cap B]}{\mathbb{P}[A]} = \frac{\frac{2}{12}}{\frac{5}{12}} = \frac{2}{5}.$$

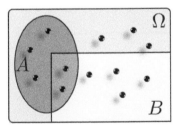 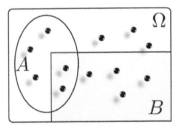 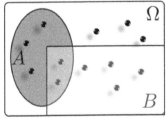

Figure 2.27: Visualization of Example 2.45: [Left] All the sets. [Middle] $P(A|B)$ is the ratio between dots inside the light yellow region over those in yellow, which is $\frac{2}{6}$. [Right] $\mathbb{P}[A|B]$ is the ratio between dots inside the light pink region over those in pink, which is $\frac{2}{5}$.

Example 2.46. Consider a tetrahedral (4-sided) die. Let X be the first roll and Y be the second roll. Let B be the event that $\min(X, Y) = 2$ and M be the event that $\max(X, Y) = 3$. Find $\mathbb{P}[M|B]$.

Solution. As shown in **Figure 2.28**, the event B is highlighted in green. (Why?) Similarly, the event M is highlighted in blue. (Again, why?) Therefore, the probability is

$$\mathbb{P}[M|B] = \frac{\mathbb{P}[M \cap B]}{\mathbb{P}[B]} = \frac{\frac{2}{16}}{\frac{5}{16}} = \frac{2}{5}.$$

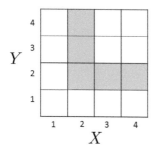 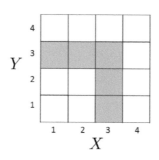 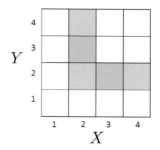

Figure 2.28: Visualization of Example 2.46. [Left] Event B. [Middle] Event M. [Right] $\mathbb{P}(M|B)$ is the ratio of the number of blue squares inside the green region to the total number of green squares, which is $\frac{2}{5}$.

Remark. Notice that if $\mathbb{P}[B] \leq \mathbb{P}[\Omega]$, then $\mathbb{P}[A \,|\, B]$ is always larger than or equal to $\mathbb{P}[A \cap B]$, i.e.,

$$\mathbb{P}[A|B] \geq \mathbb{P}[A \cap B].$$

Conditional probabilities are legitimate probabilities

Conditional probabilities are legitimate probabilities. That is, given B, the probability $\mathbb{P}[A|B]$ satisfies Axioms I, II, III.

Theorem 2.6. *Let $\mathbb{P}[B] > 0$. The conditional probability $\mathbb{P}[A \,|\, B]$ satisfies Axioms I, II, and III.*

Proof. Let's check the axioms:

- Axiom I: We want to show

$$\mathbb{P}[A \,|\, B] = \frac{\mathbb{P}[A \cap B]}{\mathbb{P}[B]} \geq 0.$$

Since $\mathbb{P}[B] > 0$ and Axiom I requires $\mathbb{P}[A \cap B] \geq 0$, we therefore have $\mathbb{P}[A \,|\, B] \geq 0$.

- Axiom II:

$$\mathbb{P}[\Omega \,|\, B] = \frac{\mathbb{P}[\Omega \cap B]}{\mathbb{P}[B]}$$

$$= \frac{\mathbb{P}[B]}{\mathbb{P}[B]} = 1.$$

- Axiom III: Consider two disjoint sets A and C. Then,

$$\mathbb{P}[A \cup C \,|\, B] = \frac{\mathbb{P}[(A \cup C) \cap B]}{\mathbb{P}[B]}$$

$$= \frac{\mathbb{P}[(A \cap B) \cup (C \cap B)]}{\mathbb{P}[B]}$$

$$\stackrel{(a)}{=} \frac{\mathbb{P}[A \cap B]}{\mathbb{P}[B]} + \frac{\mathbb{P}[C \cap B]}{\mathbb{P}[B]}$$

$$= \mathbb{P}[A|B] + \mathbb{P}[C|B],$$

where (a) holds because if A and C are disjoint then $(A \cap B) \cap (C \cap B) = \emptyset$.

□

To summarize this subsection, we highlight the essence of conditional probability.

What are conditional probabilities?

- Conditional probability of A given B is the ratio $\frac{\mathbb{P}[A \cap B]}{\mathbb{P}[B]}$.
- It is again a **measure**. It measures the relative size of A **inside** B.
- Because it is a measure, it must satisfy the three axioms.

2.4.2 Independence

Conditional probability deals with situations where two events A and B are related. What if the two events are unrelated? In probability, we have a technical term for this situation: statistical **independence**.

Definition 2.23. *Two events A and B are statistically* **independent** *if*

$$\mathbb{P}[A \cap B] = \mathbb{P}[A]\mathbb{P}[B]. \tag{2.28}$$

Why define independence in this way? Recall that $\mathbb{P}[A \,|\, B] = \frac{\mathbb{P}[A \cap B]}{\mathbb{P}[B]}$. If A and B are independent, then $\mathbb{P}[A \cap B] = \mathbb{P}[A]\,\mathbb{P}[B]$ and so

$$\mathbb{P}[A \,|\, B] = \frac{\mathbb{P}[A \cap B]}{\mathbb{P}[B]} = \frac{\mathbb{P}[A]\,\mathbb{P}[B]}{\mathbb{P}[B]} = \mathbb{P}[A]. \tag{2.29}$$

This suggests an interpretation of independence: If the occurrence of B provides no additional information about the occurrence of A, then A and B are independent.

Therefore, we can define independence via conditional probability:

Definition 2.24. *Let A and B be two events such that $\mathbb{P}[A] > 0$ and $\mathbb{P}[B] > 0$. Then*

A and B are **independent** if

$$\mathbb{P}[A \mid B] = \mathbb{P}[A] \quad or \quad \mathbb{P}[B \mid A] = \mathbb{P}[B]. \tag{2.30}$$

The two statements are equivalent as long as $\mathbb{P}[A] > 0$ and $\mathbb{P}[B] > 0$. This is because $\mathbb{P}[A|B] = \mathbb{P}[A \cap B]/\mathbb{P}[B]$. If $\mathbb{P}[A|B] = \mathbb{P}[A]$ then $\mathbb{P}[A \cap B] = \mathbb{P}[A]\mathbb{P}[B]$, which implies that $\mathbb{P}[B|A] = \mathbb{P}[A \cap B]/\mathbb{P}[A] = \mathbb{P}[B]$.

A pictorial illustration of independence is given in **Figure 2.29**. The key message is that if two events A and B are independent, then $\mathbb{P}[A|B] = \mathbb{P}[A]$. The conditional probability $\mathbb{P}[A|B]$ is the ratio of $\mathbb{P}[A \cap B]$ over $\mathbb{P}[B]$, which is the intersection over B (the blue set). The probability $\mathbb{P}[A]$ is the yellow set over the sample space Ω.

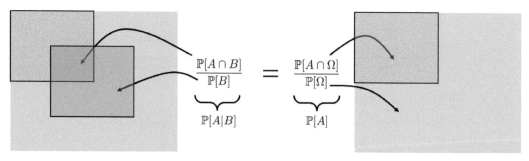

Figure 2.29: Independence means that the conditional probability $\mathbb{P}[A|B]$ is the same as $\mathbb{P}[A]$. This implies that the ratio of $\mathbb{P}[A \cap B]$ over $\mathbb{P}[B]$, and the ratio of $\mathbb{P}[A \cap \Omega]$ over $\mathbb{P}[\Omega]$ are the same.

Disjoint versus independent

$$\text{Disjoint} \not\Leftrightarrow \text{Independent}. \tag{2.31}$$

The statement says that disjoint and independent are two completely different concepts.

If A and B are disjoint, then $A \cap B = \emptyset$. This only implies that $\mathbb{P}[A \cap B] = 0$. However, it says nothing about whether $\mathbb{P}[A \cap B]$ can be factorized into $\mathbb{P}[A]\mathbb{P}[B]$. If A and B are independent, then we have $\mathbb{P}[A \cap B] = \mathbb{P}[A]\mathbb{P}[B]$. But this does not imply that $\mathbb{P}[A \cap B] = 0$. The only condition under which Disjoint $\Leftrightarrow$ Independence is when $\mathbb{P}[A] = 0$ or $\mathbb{P}[B] = 0$. **Figure 2.30** depicts the situation. When two sets are independent, the conditional probability (which is a ratio) remains unchanged compared to unconditioned probability. When two sets are disjoint, they simply do not overlap.

Practice Exercise 2.15. Throw a die twice. Are A and B independent, where

$$A = \{\text{1st die is 3}\} \quad \text{and} \quad B = \{\text{2nd die is 4}\}.$$

Solution. We can show that

$$\mathbb{P}[A \cap B] = \mathbb{P}[(3,4)] = \tfrac{1}{36}, \quad \mathbb{P}[A] = \tfrac{1}{6}, \quad \text{and} \quad \mathbb{P}[B] = \tfrac{1}{6}.$$

So $\mathbb{P}[A \cap B] = \mathbb{P}[A]\mathbb{P}[B]$. Thus, A and B are independent.

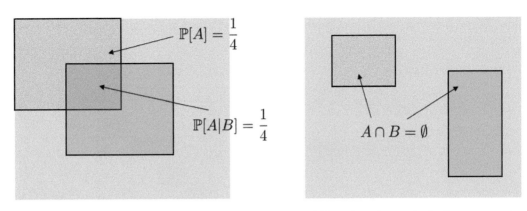

Figure 2.30: Independent means that the conditional probability, which is a ratio, is the same as the unconditioned probability. Disjoint means that the two sets do not overlap.

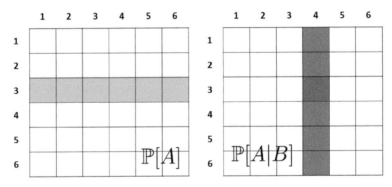

Figure 2.31: The two events A and B are independent because $\mathbb{P}[A] = \frac{1}{6}$ and $\mathbb{P}[A|B] = \frac{1}{6}$.

A pictorial illustration of this example is shown in **Figure 2.31**. The two events are independent because A is one row in the 2D space, which yields a probability of $\frac{1}{6}$. The conditional probability $\mathbb{P}[A|B]$ is the coordinate $(3, 4)$ over the event B, which is a column. It happens that $\mathbb{P}[A|B] = \frac{1}{6}$. Thus, the two events are independent.

Practice Exercise 2.16. Throw a die twice. Are A and B independent?

$$A = \{\text{1st die is 3}\} \quad \text{and} \quad B = \{\text{sum is 7}\}.$$

Solution. Note that

$$\mathbb{P}[A \cap B] = \mathbb{P}[(3, 4)] = \tfrac{1}{36}, \qquad \mathbb{P}[A] = \tfrac{1}{6},$$
$$\mathbb{P}[B] = \mathbb{P}[(1, 6), (2, 5), (3, 4), (4, 3), (5, 2), (6, 1)] = \tfrac{1}{6}.$$

So $\mathbb{P}[A \cap B] = \mathbb{P}[A]\,\mathbb{P}[B]$. Thus, A and B are independent.

A pictorial illustration of this example is shown in **Figure 2.32**. Notice that whether the two events intersect is not how we determine independence (that only determines disjoint or not). The key is whether the conditional probability (which is the ratio) remains unchanged compared to the unconditioned probability.

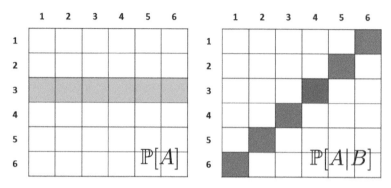

Figure 2.32: The two events A and B are independent because $\mathbb{P}[A] = \frac{1}{6}$ and $\mathbb{P}[A \cap B] = \frac{1}{6}$.

If we let $B = \{\text{sum is 8}\}$, then the situation is different. The intersection $A \cap B$ has a probability $\frac{1}{5}$ relative to B, and therefore $\mathbb{P}[A|B] = \frac{1}{5}$. Hence, the two events A and B are dependent. If you like a more intuitive argument, you can imagine that B has happened, i.e., the sum is 8. Then the probability for the first die to be 1 is 0 because there is no way to construct 8 when the first die is 1. As a result, we have eliminated one choice for the first die, leaving only five options. Therefore, since B has influenced the probability of A, they are dependent.

Practice Exercise 2.17. Throw a die twice. Let

$$A = \{\text{max is 2}\} \quad \text{and} \quad B = \{\text{min is 2}\}.$$

Are A and B independent?

Solution. Let us first list out A and B:

$$A = \{(1,2), (2,1), (2,2)\},$$
$$B = \{(2,2), (2,3), (2,4), (2,5), (2,6), (3,2), (4,2), (5,2), (6,2)\}.$$

Therefore, the probabilities are

$$\mathbb{P}[A] = \frac{3}{36}, \quad \mathbb{P}[B] = \frac{9}{36}, \quad \text{and} \quad \mathbb{P}[A \cap B] = \mathbb{P}[(2,2)] = \frac{1}{36}.$$

Clearly, $\mathbb{P}[A \cap B] \neq \mathbb{P}[A]\mathbb{P}[B]$ and so A and B are dependent.

What is independence?

- Two events are independent when the **ratio** $\mathbb{P}[A \cap B]/\mathbb{P}[B]$ **remains unchanged** compared to $\mathbb{P}[A]$.
- Independence $\neq$ disjoint.

2.4.3 Bayes' theorem and the law of total probability

Theorem 2.7 (Bayes' theorem). *For any two events A and B such that $\mathbb{P}[A] > 0$ and $\mathbb{P}[B] > 0$,*

$$\mathbb{P}[A \mid B] = \frac{\mathbb{P}[B \mid A]\,\mathbb{P}[A]}{\mathbb{P}[B]}.$$

Proof. By the definition of conditional probabilities, we have

$$\mathbb{P}[A \mid B] = \frac{\mathbb{P}[A \cap B]}{\mathbb{P}[B]} \quad \text{and} \quad \mathbb{P}[B \mid A] = \frac{\mathbb{P}[B \cap A]}{\mathbb{P}[A]}.$$

Rearranging the terms yields

$$\mathbb{P}[A \mid B]\mathbb{P}[B] = \mathbb{P}[B \mid A]\mathbb{P}[A],$$

which gives the desired result by dividing both sides by $\mathbb{P}[B]$. $\square$

Bayes' theorem provides two views of the intersection $\mathbb{P}[A \cap B]$ using two different conditional probabilities. We call $\mathbb{P}[B \mid A]$ the **conditional probability** and $\mathbb{P}[A \mid B]$ the **posterior probability**. The order of A and B is arbitrary. We can also call $\mathbb{P}[A \mid B]$ the conditional probability and $\mathbb{P}[B \mid A]$ the posterior probability. The context of the problem will make this clear.

Bayes' theorem provides a way to switch $\mathbb{P}[A|B]$ and $\mathbb{P}[B|A]$. The next theorem helps us decompose an event into smaller events.

Theorem 2.8 (Law of Total Probability). *Let $\{A_1, \ldots, A_n\}$ be a partition of Ω, i.e., $A_1, \ldots, A_n$ are disjoint and $\Omega = A_1 \cup \cdots \cup A_n$. Then, for any $B \subseteq \Omega$,*

$$\mathbb{P}[B] = \sum_{i=1}^{n} \mathbb{P}[B \mid A_i]\,\mathbb{P}[A_i]. \tag{2.32}$$

Proof. We start from the right-hand side.

$$\sum_{i=1}^{n} \mathbb{P}[B \mid A_i]\,\mathbb{P}[A_i] \overset{(a)}{=} \sum_{i=1}^{n} \mathbb{P}[B \cap A_i] \overset{(b)}{=} \mathbb{P}\left[\bigcup_{i=1}^{n}(B \cap A_i)\right]$$
$$\overset{(c)}{=} \mathbb{P}\left[B \cap \left(\bigcup_{i=1}^{n} A_i\right)\right] \overset{(d)}{=} \mathbb{P}[B \cap \Omega] = \mathbb{P}[B],$$

where (a) follows from the definition of conditional probability, (b) is due to Axiom III, (c) holds because of the distributive property of sets, and (d) results from the partition property of $\{A_1, A_2, \ldots, A_n\}$. $\square$

Interpretation. The law of total probability can be understood as follows. If the sample space Ω consists of disjoint subsets $A_1, \ldots, A_n$, we can compute the probability $\mathbb{P}[B]$ by summing over its portion $\mathbb{P}[B \cap A_1], \ldots, \mathbb{P}[B \cap A_n]$. However, each intersection can be written as

$$\mathbb{P}[B \cap A_i] = \mathbb{P}[B \mid A_i]\mathbb{P}[A_i]. \tag{2.33}$$

In other words, we write $\mathbb{P}[B \cap A_i]$ as the **conditional probability** $\mathbb{P}[B \mid A_i]$ times the **prior probability** $\mathbb{P}[A_i]$. When we sum all these intersections, we obtain the overall probability. See **Figure 2.33** for a graphical portrayal.

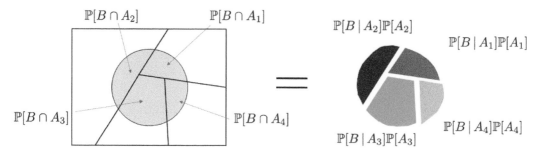

Figure 2.33: The law of total probability decomposes the probability $\mathbb{P}[B]$ into multiple conditional probabilities $\mathbb{P}[B \mid A_i]$. The probability of obtaining each $\mathbb{P}[B \mid A_i]$ is $\mathbb{P}[A_i]$.

Corollary 2.4. *Let $\{A_1, A_2, \ldots, A_n\}$ be a partition of Ω, i.e., $A_1, \ldots, A_n$ are disjoint and $\Omega = A_1 \cup A_2 \cup \cdots \cup A_n$. Then, for any $B \subseteq \Omega$,*

$$\mathbb{P}[A_j \mid B] = \frac{\mathbb{P}[B \mid A_j]\,\mathbb{P}[A_j]}{\sum_{i=1}^{n} \mathbb{P}[B \mid A_i]\,\mathbb{P}[A_i]}. \tag{2.34}$$

Proof. The result follows directly from Bayes' theorem:

$$\mathbb{P}[A_j \mid B] = \frac{\mathbb{P}[B \mid A_j]\,\mathbb{P}[A_j]}{\mathbb{P}[B]} = \frac{\mathbb{P}[B \mid A_j]\,\mathbb{P}[A_j]}{\sum_{i=1}^{n} \mathbb{P}[B \mid A_i]\,\mathbb{P}[A_i]}.$$

$\square$

Example 2.47. Suppose there are three types of players in a tennis tournament: A, B, and C. Fifty percent of the contestants in the tournament are A players, 25% are B players, and 25% are C players. Your chance of beating the contestants depends on the class of the player, as follows:

$$0.3 \text{ against an } A \text{ player}$$
$$0.4 \text{ against a } B \text{ player}$$
$$0.5 \text{ against a } C \text{ player}$$

If you play a match in this tournament, what is the probability of your winning the match? Supposing that you have won a match, what is the probability that you played against an A player?

Solution. We first list all the known probabilities. We know from the percentage of players that

$$\mathbb{P}[A] = 0.5, \quad \mathbb{P}[B] = 0.25, \quad \mathbb{P}[C] = 0.25.$$

Now, let W be the event that you win the match. Then the conditional probabilities are defined as follows:

$$\mathbb{P}[W|A] = 0.3, \quad \mathbb{P}[W|B] = 0.4, \quad \mathbb{P}[W|C] = 0.5.$$

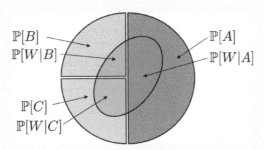

Therefore, by the law of total probability, we can show that the probability of winning the match is

$$\begin{aligned}
\mathbb{P}[W] &= \mathbb{P}[W \mid A]\,\mathbb{P}[A] + \mathbb{P}[W \mid B]\,\mathbb{P}[B] + \mathbb{P}[W \mid C]\,\mathbb{P}[C] \\
&= (0.3)(0.5) + (0.4)(0.25) + (0.5)(0.25) = 0.375.
\end{aligned}$$

Given that you have won the match, the probability of A given W is

$$\mathbb{P}[A|W] = \frac{\mathbb{P}[W|A]\mathbb{P}[A]}{\mathbb{P}[W]} = \frac{(0.3)(0.5)}{0.375} = 0.4.$$

Example 2.48. Consider the communication channel shown below. The probability of sending a 1 is p and the probability of sending a 0 is $1-p$. Given that 1 is sent, the probability of receiving 1 is $1-\eta$. Given that 0 is sent, the probability of receiving 0 is $1-\varepsilon$. Find the probability that a 1 has been correctly received.

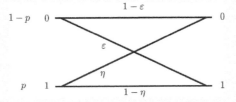

Solution. Define the events

$$S_0 = \text{``0 is sent''}, \quad \text{and} \quad R_0 = \text{``0 is received''}.$$
$$S_1 = \text{``1 is sent''}, \quad \text{and} \quad R_1 = \text{``1 is received''}.$$

Then, the probability that 1 is received is $\mathbb{P}[R_1]$. However, $\mathbb{P}[R_1] \neq 1 - \eta$ because $1 - \eta$

is the conditional probability that 1 is received given that 1 is sent. It is possible that we receive 1 as a result of an error when 0 is sent. Therefore, we need to consider the probability that both S_0 and S_1 occur. Using the law of total probability we have

$$\mathbb{P}[R_1] = \mathbb{P}[R_1 \mid S_1] \, \mathbb{P}[S_1] + \mathbb{P}[R_1 \mid S_0] \, \mathbb{P}[S_0]$$
$$= (1 - \eta)p + \varepsilon(1 - p).$$

Now, suppose that we have received 1. What is the probability that 1 was originally sent? This is asking for the posterior probability $\mathbb{P}[S_1 \mid R_1]$, which can be found using Bayes' theorem

$$\mathbb{P}[S_1 \mid R_1] = \frac{\mathbb{P}[R_1 \mid S_1] \, \mathbb{P}[S_1]}{\mathbb{P}[R_1]} = \frac{(1 - \eta)p}{(1 - \eta)p + \varepsilon(1 - p)}.$$

When do we need to use Bayes' theorem and the law of total probability?

- Bayes' theorem **switches** the role of the conditioning, from $\mathbb{P}[A|B]$ to $\mathbb{P}[B|A]$. Example:

$$\mathbb{P}[\text{win the game} \mid \text{play with A}] \quad \text{and} \quad \mathbb{P}[\text{play with A} \mid \text{win the game}].$$

- The law of total probability **decomposes** an event into smaller events. Example:

$$\mathbb{P}[\text{win}] = \mathbb{P}[\text{win} \mid A]\mathbb{P}[A] + \mathbb{P}[\text{win} \mid B]\mathbb{P}[B].$$

2.4.4 The Three Prisoners problem

Now that you are familiar with the concepts of conditional probabilities, we would like to challenge you with the following problem, known as the **Three Prisoners problem**. If you understand how this problem can be resolved, you have mastered conditional probability.

Once upon a time, there were three prisoners A, B, and C. One day, the king decided to pardon two of them and sentence the last one, as in this figure:

$A \qquad B \qquad C$

Figure 2.34: The Three Prisoners problem: The king says that he will pardon two prisoners and sentence one.

One of the prisoners, prisoner A, heard the news and wanted to ask a friendly guard about his situation. The guard was honest. He was allowed to tell prisoner A that prisoner B would be pardoned or that prisoner C would be pardoned, but he could not tell A whether he would be pardoned. Prisoner A thought about the problem, and he began to hesitate to ask the guard. Based on his present state of knowledge, his probability of being pardoned is $\frac{2}{3}$. However, if he asks the guard, this probability will be reduced to $\frac{1}{2}$ because the guard would tell him that one of the two other prisoners would be pardoned, and would tell him which one it would be. Prisoner A reasons that his chance of being pardoned would then drop because there are now only two prisoners left who may be pardoned, as illustrated in **Figure 2.35**:

Figure 2.35: The Three Prisoners problem: If you do not ask the guard, your chance of being released is 2/3. If you ask the guard, the guard will tell you which one of the other prisoners will be released. Your chance of being released apparently drops to 1/2.

Should prisoner A ask the guard? What has gone wrong with his reasoning? This problem is tricky in the sense that the verbal argument of prisoner A seems flawless. If he asked the guard, indeed, the game would be reduced to two people. However, this does not seem correct, because regardless of what the guard says, the probability for A to be pardoned should remain unchanged. Let's see how we can solve this puzzle.

Let X_A, X_B, X_C be the events of sentencing prisoners A, B, C, respectively. Let G_B be the event that the guard says that the prisoner B is released. Without doing anything, we know that

$$\mathbb{P}[X_A] = \frac{1}{3}, \qquad \mathbb{P}[X_B] = \frac{1}{3}, \qquad \mathbb{P}[X_C] = \frac{1}{3}.$$

Conditioned on these events, we can compute the following conditional probabilities that the guard says B is pardoned:

$$\mathbb{P}[G_B \mid X_A] = \frac{1}{2}, \qquad \mathbb{P}[G_B \mid X_B] = 0, \qquad \mathbb{P}[G_B \mid X_C] = 1.$$

Why are these conditional probabilities? $\mathbb{P}[G_B \mid X_B] = 0$ quite straightforward. If the king decides to sentence B, the guard has no way of saying that B will be pardoned. Therefore, $\mathbb{P}[G_B \mid X_B]$ must be zero. $\mathbb{P}[G_B \mid X_C] = 1$ is also not difficult. If the king decides to sentence C, then the guard has no way to tell you that B will be pardoned because the guard cannot say anything about prisoner A. Finally, $\mathbb{P}[G_B \mid X_A] = \frac{1}{2}$ can be understood as follows: If the king decides to sentence A, the guard can either tell you B or C. In other words, the guard flips a coin.

With these conditional probabilities ready, we can determine the probability. This is the conditional probability $\mathbb{P}[X_A \mid G_B]$. That is, supposing that the guard says B is pardoned, what is the probability that A will be sentenced? This is the actual scenario that A is facing. Solving for this conditional probability is not difficult. By Bayes' theorem we know that

$$\mathbb{P}[X_A \mid G_B] = \frac{\mathbb{P}[G_B \mid X_A]\mathbb{P}[X_A]}{\mathbb{P}[G_B]},$$

and $\mathbb{P}[G_B] = \mathbb{P}[G_B|X_A]\mathbb{P}[X_A] + \mathbb{P}[G_B|X_B]\mathbb{P}[X_B] + \mathbb{P}[G_B|X_C]\mathbb{P}[X_C]$ according to the law of total probability. Substituting the numbers into these equations, we have that

$$\mathbb{P}[G_B] = \mathbb{P}[G_B|X_A]\mathbb{P}[X_A] + \mathbb{P}[G_B|X_B]\mathbb{P}[X_B] + \mathbb{P}[G_B|X_C]\mathbb{P}[X_C]$$
$$= \frac{1}{2} \times \frac{1}{3} + 0 \times \frac{1}{3} + 1 \times \frac{1}{3} = \frac{1}{2},$$
$$\mathbb{P}[X_A \mid G_B] = \frac{\mathbb{P}[G_B \mid X_A]\mathbb{P}[X_A]}{\mathbb{P}[G_B]} = \frac{\frac{1}{2} \times \frac{1}{3}}{\frac{1}{2}} = \frac{1}{3}.$$

Therefore, given that the guard says B is pardoned, the probability that A will be sentenced remains $\frac{1}{3}$. In fact, what you can show in this example is that $\mathbb{P}[X_A \mid G_B] = \frac{1}{3} = \mathbb{P}[X_A]$. Therefore, the presence or absence of the guard does not alter the probability. This is because what the guard says is independent of whether the prisoners will be pardoned. The lesson we learn from this problem is not to rely on verbal arguments. We need to write down the conditional probabilities and spell out the steps.

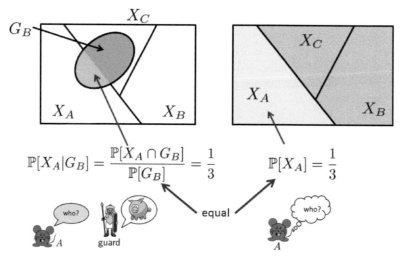

Figure 2.36: The Three Prisoners problem is resolved by noting that $\mathbb{P}[X_A|G_B] = \mathbb{P}[X_A]$. Therefore, the events X_A and G_B are independent.

How to resolve the Three Prisoners problem?

- The key is that G_A, G_B, G_C do not form a **partition**. See **Figure 2.36**.
- $G_B \neq X_B$. When G_B happens, the remaining set is not $X_A \cup X_C$.
- The ratio $\mathbb{P}[X_A \cap G_B]/\mathbb{P}[G_B]$ equals $\mathbb{P}[X_A]$. This is **independence**.

2.5 Summary

By now, we hope that you have become familiar with our slogan **probability is a measure of the size of a set**. Let us summarize:

- **Probability** = a probability law $\mathbb{P}$. You can also view it as the **value** returned by $\mathbb{P}$.

- **Measure** = a ruler, a scale, a stopwatch, or another measuring device. It is a tool that tells you how large or small a set is. The measure has to be compatible with the set. If a set is finite, then the measure can be a counter. If a set is a continuous interval, then the measure can be the length of the interval.

- **Size** = the relative weight of the set for the sample space. Measuring the size is done by using a weighting function. Think of a fair coin versus a biased coin. The former has a uniform weight, whereas the latter has a nonuniform weight.

- **Set** = an event. An event is a subset in the sample space. A probability law $\mathbb{P}$ always maps a **set** to a number. This is different from a typical function that maps a number to another number.

If you understand what this slogan means, you will understand why probability can be applied to discrete events, continuous events, events in n-D spaces, etc. You will also understand the notion of **measure zero** and the notion of **almost sure**. These concepts lie at the foundation of modern data science, in particular, theoretical machine learning.

The second half of this chapter discusses the concept of **conditional probability**. Conditional probability is a metaconcept that can be applied to any measure you use. The motivation of conditional probability is to restrict the probability to a subevent happening in the sample space. If B has happened, the probability for A to *also* happen is $\mathbb{P}[A \cap B]/\mathbb{P}[B]$. If two events are not influencing each other, then we say that A and B are independent. According to Bayes' theorem, we can also switch the order of A given B and B given A, according to Bayes' theorem. Finally, the law of total probability gives us a way to decompose events into subevents.

We end this chapter by mentioning a few terms related to conditional probabilities that will become useful later. Let us use the tennis tournament as an example:

- $\mathbb{P}[W \mid A]$ = **conditional probability** = Given that you played with player A, what is the probability that you will win?

- $\mathbb{P}[A]$ = **prior probability** = Without even entering the game, what is the chance that you will face player A?

- $\mathbb{P}[A \mid W]$ = **posterior probability** = After you have won the game, what is the probability that you have actually played with A?

In many practical engineering problems, the question of interest is often the last one. That is, supposing that you have observed something, what is the most likely cause of that event? For example, supposing we have observed this particular dataset, what is the best Gaussian model that would fit the dataset? Questions like these require some analysis of conditional probability, prior probability, and posterior probability.

2.6   References

Introduction to Probability

2-1 Dimitri P. Bertsekas and John N. Tsitsiklis, *Introduction to Probability*, Athena Scientific, 2nd Edition, 2008. Chapter 1.

2-2 Mark D. Ward and Ellen Gundlach, *Introduction to Probability*, W.H. Freeman and Company, 2016. Chapter 1 – Chapter 6.

2-3 Roy D. Yates and David J. Goodman, *Probability and Stochastic Processes*, 3rd Edition, Wiley 2013, Chapter 1.

2-4 John A. Gubner, *Probability and Random Processes for Electrical and Computer Engineers*, Cambridge University Press, 2006. Chapter 2.

2-5 Sheldon Ross, *A First Course in Probability*, Prentice Hall, 8th Edition, 2010. Chapter 2 and Chapter 3.

2-6 Ani Adhikari and Jim Pitman, *Probability for Data Science*, http://prob140.org/textbook/content/README.html. Chapters 1 and 2.

2-7 Alberto Leon-Garcia, *Probability, Statistics, and Random Processes for Electrical Engineering*, Prentice Hall, 3rd Edition, 2008. Chapter 2.1 – 2.7.

2-8 Athanasios Papoulis and S. Unnikrishna Pillai, *Probability, Random Variables and Stochastic Processes*, McGraw-Hill, 4th Edition, 2001. Chapter 2.

2-9 Henry Stark and John Woods, *Probability and Random Processes With Applications to Signal Processing*, Prentice Hall, 3rd Edition, 2001. Chapter 1.

Measure-Theoretic Probability

2-10 Alberto Leon-Garcia, *Probability, Statistics, and Random Processes for Electrical Engineering*, Prentice Hall, 3rd Edition, 2008. Chapter 2.8 and 2.9.

2-11 Henry Stark and John Woods, *Probability and Random Processes With Applications to Signal Processing*, Prentice Hall, 3rd Edition, 2001. Appendix D.

2-12 William Feller, *An Introduction to Probability Theory and Its Applications*, Wiley and Sons, 3rd Edition, 1950.

2-13 Andrey Kolmogorov, *Foundations of the Theory of Probability*, 2nd English Edition, Dover 2018. (Translated from Russian to English. Originally published in 1950 by Chelsea Publishing Company New York.)

2-14 Patrick Billingsley, *Probability and Measure*, Wiley, 3rd Edition, 1995.

Real Analysis

2-15 Tom M. Apostol, *Mathematical Analysis*, Pearson, 1974.

2-16 Walter Rudin, *Principles of Mathematical Analysis*, McGraw Hill, 1976.

2.7 Problems

Exercise 1.
A space S and three of its subsets are given by $S = \{1, 3, 5, 7, 9, 11\}$, $A = \{1, 3, 5\}$, $B = \{7, 9, 11\}$, and $C = \{1, 3, 9, 11\}$. Find $A \cap B \cap C$, $A^c \cap B$, $A \backslash C$, and $(A \backslash B) \cup B$.

Exercise 2.
Let $A = (-\infty, r]$ and $B = (-\infty, s]$ where $r \leq s$. Find an expression for $C = (r, s]$ in terms of A and B. Show that $B = A \cup C$, and $A \cap C = \emptyset$.

Exercise 3. (VIDEO SOLUTION)
Simplify the following sets.

 (a) $[1, 4] \cap ([0, 2] \cup [3, 5])$

 (b) $([0, 1] \cup [2, 3])^c$

 (c) $\bigcap_{i=1}^{\infty}(-1/n, +1/n)$

 (d) $\bigcup_{i=1}^{\infty}[5, 8 - (2n)^{-1}]$

Exercise 4.
We will sometimes deal with the relationship between two sets. We say that A implies B when A is a subset of B (why?). Show the following results.

 (a) Show that if A implies B, and B implies C, then A implies C.

 (b) Show that if A implies B, then B^c implies A^c.

Exercise 5.
Show that if $A \cup B = A$ and $A \cap B = A$, then $A = B$.

Exercise 6.
A space S is defined as $S = \{1, 3, 5, 7, 9, 22\}$, and three subsets as $A = \{1, 3, 5\}$, $B = \{7, 9, 11\}$, $C = \{1, 3, 9, 11\}$. Assume that each element has probability $1/6$. Find the following probabilities:

 (a) $\mathbb{P}[A]$
 (b) $\mathbb{P}[B]$
 (c) $\mathbb{P}[C]$
 (d) $\mathbb{P}[A \cup B]$
 (e) $\mathbb{P}[A \cup C]$
 (f) $\mathbb{P}[(A \backslash C) \cup B]$

Exercise 7. (VIDEO SOLUTION)
A collection of 26 letters, a-z, is mixed in a jar. Two letters are drawn at random, one after the other. What is the probability of drawing a vowel (a,e,i,o,u) and a consonant in either order? What is the sample space?

Exercise 8.
Consider an experiment consisting of rolling a die twice. The outcome of this experiment is an ordered pair whose first element is the first value rolled and whose second element is the second value rolled.

(a) Find the sample space.

(b) Find the set A representing the event that the value on the first roll is greater than or equal to the value on the second roll.

(c) Find the set B corresponding to the event that the first roll is a six.

(d) Let C correspond to the event that the first valued rolled and the second value rolled differ by two. Find $A \cap C$.

Note that A, B, and C should be subsets of the sample space specified in Part (a).

Exercise 9.
A pair of dice are rolled.

(a) Find the sample space Ω

(b) Find the probabilities of the events: (i) the sum is even, (ii) the first roll is equal to the second, (iii) the first roll is larger than the second.

Exercise 10.
Let A, B and C be events in an event space. Find expressions for the following:

(a) Exactly one of the three events occurs.

(b) Exactly two of the events occurs.

(c) Two or more of the events occur.

(d) None of the events occur.

Exercise 11.
A system is composed of five components, each of which is either working or failed. Consider an experiment that consists of observing the status of each component, and let the outcomes of the experiment be given by all vectors $(x_1, x_2, x_3, x_4, x_5)$, where x_i is 1 if component i is working and 0 if component i is not working.

(a) How many outcomes are in the sample space of this experiment?

(b) Suppose that the system will work if components 1 and 2 are both working, or if components 3 and 4 are both working, or if components 1, 3, and 5 are all working. Let W be the event that the system will work. Specify all of the outcomes in W.

(c) Let A be the event that components 4 and 5 have both failed. How many outcomes are in the event A?

(d) Write out all outcomes in the event $A \cap W$.

Exercise 12. (VIDEO SOLUTION)
A number x is selected at random in the interval $[-1, 2]$. Let the events $A = \{x \mid x < 0\}$, $B = \{x \mid |x - 0.5| < 0.5\}$, $C = \{x \mid x > 0.75\}$. Find (a) $\mathbb{P}[A \mid B]$, (b) $\mathbb{P}[B \mid C]$, (c) $\mathbb{P}[A \mid C^c]$, (d) $\mathbb{P}[B \mid C^c]$.

Exercise 13. (VIDEO SOLUTION)
Let the events A and B have $\mathbb{P}[A] = x$, $\mathbb{P}[B] = y$ and $\mathbb{P}[A \cup B] = z$. Find the following probabilities: (a) $\mathbb{P}[A \cap B]$, (b) $\mathbb{P}[A^c \cap B^c]$, (c) $\mathbb{P}[A^c \cup B^c]$, (d) $\mathbb{P}[A \cap B^c]$, (e) $\mathbb{P}[A^c \cup B]$.

Exercise 14.

(a) By using the fact that $\mathbb{P}[A \cup B] \leq \mathbb{P}[A] + \mathbb{P}[B]$, show that $\mathbb{P}[A \cup B \cup C] \leq \mathbb{P}[A] + \mathbb{P}[B] + \mathbb{P}[C]$.

(b) By using the fact that $\mathbb{P}\left[\bigcup_{k=1}^{n} A_k\right] \leq \sum_{k=1}^{n} \mathbb{P}[A_k]$, show that

$$\mathbb{P}\left[\bigcap_{k=1}^{n} A_k\right] \geq 1 - \sum_{k=1}^{n} \mathbb{P}[A_k^c].$$

Exercise 15.
Use the distributive property of set operations to prove the following generalized distributive law:

$$A \cup \left(\bigcap_{i=1}^{n} B_i\right) = \bigcap_{i=1}^{n} (A \cup B_i).$$

Hint: Use mathematical induction. That is, show that the above is true for $n = 2$ and that it is also true for $n = k + 1$ when it is true for $n = k$.

Exercise 16.
The following result is known as the Bonferroni's Inequality.

(a) Prove that for any two events A and B, we have

$$\mathbb{P}(A \cap B) \geq \mathbb{P}(A) + \mathbb{P}(B) - 1.$$

(b) Generalize the above to the case of n events $A_1, A_2, \ldots, A_n$, by showing that

$$\mathbb{P}(A_1 \cap A_2 \cap \cdots \cap A_n) \geq \mathbb{P}(A_1) + \mathbb{P}(A_2) + \cdots + \mathbb{P}(A_n) - (n-1).$$

Hint: You may use the generalized Union Bound $\mathbb{P}(\bigcup_{i=1}^{n} A_i) \leq \sum_{i=1}^{n} \mathbb{P}(A_i)$.

Exercise 17. (VIDEO SOLUTION)
Let A, B, C be events with probabilities $\mathbb{P}[A] = 0.5$, $\mathbb{P}[B] = 0.2$, $\mathbb{P}[C] = 0.4$. Find

(a) $\mathbb{P}[A \cup B]$ if A and B are independent.

(b) $\mathbb{P}[A \cup B]$ if A and B are disjoint.

(c) $\mathbb{P}[A \cup B \cup C]$ if A, B and C are independent.

(d) $\mathbb{P}[A \cup B \cup C]$ if A, B and C are pairwise disjoint; can this happen?

Exercise 18. (VIDEO SOLUTION)
A block of information is transmitted repeated over a noisy channel until an error-free block is received. Let $M \geq 1$ be the number of blocks required for a transmission. Define the following sets.

(i) $A = \{M \text{ is even}\}$

(ii) $B = \{M \text{ is a multiple of 3}\}$

(iii) $C = \{M \text{ is less than or equal to 6}\}$

Assume that the probability of requiring one additional block is half of the probability without the additional block. That is:

$$\mathbb{P}[M = k] = \left(\frac{1}{2}\right)^k, \qquad k = 1, 2, \ldots.$$

Determine the following probabilities.

(a) $\mathbb{P}[A]$, $\mathbb{P}[B]$, $\mathbb{P}[C]$, $\mathbb{P}[C^c]$

(b) $\mathbb{P}[A \cap B]$, $\mathbb{P}[A \backslash B]$, $\mathbb{P}[A \cap B \cap C]$

(c) $\mathbb{P}[A \,|\, B]$, $\mathbb{P}[B \,|\, A]$

(d) $\mathbb{P}[A \,|\, B \cap C]$, $\mathbb{P}[A \cap B \,|\, C]$

Exercise 19. (VIDEO SOLUTION)
A binary communication system transmits a signal X that is either a $+2$-voltage signal or a -2-voltage signal. A malicious channel reduces the magnitude of the received signal by the number of heads it counts in two tosses of a coin. Let Y be the resulting signal. Possible values of Y are listed below.

	2 Heads	1 Head	No Head
$X = -2$	$Y = 0$	$Y = -1$	$Y = -2$
$X = +2$	$Y = 0$	$Y = +1$	$Y = +2$

Assume that the probability of having $X = +2$ and $X = -2$ is equal.

(a) Find the sample space of Y, and hence the probability of each value of Y.

(b) What are the probabilities $\mathbb{P}[X = +2 \,|\, Y = 1]$ and $\mathbb{P}[Y = 1 \,|\, X = -2]$?

Exercise 20. (VIDEO SOLUTION)
A block of 100 bits is transmitted over a binary communication channel with a probability of bit error $p = 10^{-2}$.

(a) If the block has 1 or fewer errors, then the receiver accepts the block. Find the probability that the block is accepted.

(b) If the block has more than 1 error, then the block is retransmitted. What is the probability that 4 blocks are transmitted?

Exercise 21. (VIDEO SOLUTION)
A machine makes errors in a certain operation with probability p. There are two types of errors. The fraction of errors that are type A is α and the fraction that are type B is $1 - \alpha$.

(a) What is the probability of k errors in n operations?

(b) What is the probability of k_1 type A errors in n operations?

(c) What is the probability of k_2 type B errors in n operations?

(d) What is the joint probability of k_1 type A errors and k_2 type B errors in n operations? Hint: There are $\binom{n}{k_1}\binom{n-k_1}{k_2}$ possibilities of having k_1 type A errors and k_2 type B errors in n operations. (Why?)

Exercise 22. (VIDEO SOLUTION)
A computer manufacturer uses chips from three sources. Chips from sources A, B and C are defective with probabilities 0.005, 0.001 and 0.01, respectively. The proportions of chips from A, B and C are 0.5, 0.1 and 0.4 respectively. If a randomly selected chip is found to be defective, find

(a) the probability that the chips are from A.

(b) the probability that the chips are from B.

(c) the probability that the chips are from C.

Exercise 23. (VIDEO SOLUTION)
In a lot of 100 items, 50 items are defective. Suppose that m items are selected for testing. We say that the manufacturing process is malfunctioning if the probability that one or more items are tested to be defective. Call this failure probability p. What should be the minimum m such that $p \geq 0.99$?

Exercise 24. (VIDEO SOLUTION)
One of two coins is selected at random and tossed three times. The first coin comes up heads with probability $p_1 = 1/3$ and the second coin with probability $p_2 = 2/3$.

(a) What is the probability that the number of heads is $k = 3$?

(b) Repeat (a) for $k = 0, 1, 2$.

(c) Find the probability that coin 1 was tossed given that k heads were observed, for $k = 0, 1, 2, 3$.

(d) In part (c), which coin is more probably when 2 heads have been observed?

Exercise 25. (VIDEO SOLUTION)
Consider the following communication channel. A source transmits a string of binary symbols through a noisy communication channel. Each symbol is 0 or 1 with probability p and $1 - p$, respectively, and is received incorrectly with probability ε_0 and ε_1. Errors in different symbols transmissions are independent.

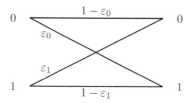

Denote S as the source and R as the receiver.

(a) What is the probability that a symbol is correctly received? Hint: Find

$$\mathbb{P}[R = 1 \cap S = 1] \quad \text{and} \quad \mathbb{P}[R = 0 \cap S = 0].$$

(b) Find the probability of receiving 1011 conditioned on that 1011 was sent, i.e.,

$$\mathbb{P}[R = 1011 \,|\, S = 1011].$$

(c) To improve reliability, each symbol is transmitted three times, and the received string is decoded by the majority rule. In other words, a 0 (or 1) is transmitted as 000 (or 111, respectively), and it is decoded at the receiver as a 0 (or 1) if and only if the received three-symbol string contains at least two 0s (or 1s, respectively). What is the probability that the symbol is correctly decoded, given that we send a 0?

(d) Suppose that the scheme of part (c) is used. What is the probability that a 0 was sent if the string 101 was received?

(e) Suppose the scheme of part (c) is used and given that a 0 was sent. For what value of ε_0 is there an improvement in the probability of correct decoding? Assume that $\varepsilon_0 \neq 0$.

Chapter 3

Discrete Random Variables

When working on a data analysis problem, one of the biggest challenges is the disparity between the theoretical tools we learn in school and the *actual data* our boss hands to us. By actual data, we mean a collection of numbers, perhaps organized or perhaps not. When we are given the dataset, the first thing we do would certainly not be to define the Borel σ-field and then define the measure. Instead, we would normally compute the mean, the standard deviation, and perhaps some scores about the skewness.

The situation is best explained by the landscape shown in **Figure 3.1**. On the one hand, we have well-defined probability tools, but on the other hand, we have a set of practical "battle skills" for processing data. Often we view them as two separate entities. As long as we can pull the statistics from the dataset, why bother about the theory? Alternatively, we have a set of theories, but we will never verify them using the actual datasets. How can we bridge the two? What are the missing steps in the probability theory we have learned so far? The goal of this chapter (and the next) is to fill this gap.

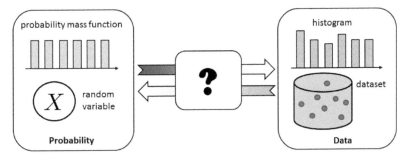

Figure 3.1: The landscape of probability and data. Often we view probability and data analysis as two different entities. However, probability and data analysis are inseparable. The goal of this chapter is to link the two.

Three concepts to bridge the gap between theory and practice

The starting point of our discussion is a probability space $(\Omega, \mathcal{F}, \mathbb{P})$. It is an abstract concept, but we hope we have convinced you in Chapter 2 of its significance. However, the probability space is certainly not "user friendly" because no one would write a Python program to implement those theories. How do we make the abstract probability space more convenient so that we can model practical scenarios?

The first step is to recognize that the sample space and the event space are all based on *statements*, for example, "getting a head when flipping a coin" or "winning the game." These statements are not numbers, but we (engineers) love numbers. Therefore, we should ask a very basic question: How do we convert a statement to a number? The answer is the concept of **random variables**.

Key Concept 1: What are random variables?

　　Random variables are mappings from outcomes to numbers.

Now, suppose that we have constructed a random variable that translates statements to numbers. The next task is to endow the random variable with probabilities. More precisely, we need to assign probabilities to the random variable so that we can perform computations. This is done using the concept called **probability mass function** (PMF).

Key Concept 2: What are probability mass functions (PMFs)?

　　Probability mass functions are the ideal histograms of random variables.

The best way to think about a PMF is a histogram, something we are familiar with. A histogram has two axes: The x-axis denotes the set of **states** and the y-axis denotes the **probability**. For each of the states that the random variable possesses, the histogram tells us the probability of getting a particular state. The PMF is the *ideal* histogram of a random variable. It provides a complete characterization of the random variable. If you have a random variable, you must specify its PMF. Vice versa, if you tell us the PMF, you have specified a random variable.

We ask the third question about pulling information from the probability mass function, such as the mean and standard deviation. How do we obtain these numbers from the PMF? We are also interested in operations on the mean and standard deviations. For example, if a professor offers ten bonus points to the entire class, how will it affect the mean and standard deviation? If a store provides 20% off on all its products, what will happen to its mean retail price and standard deviation? However, the biggest question is perhaps the difference between the mean we obtain from a PMF and the mean we obtain from a histogram. Understanding this difference will immediately help us build a bridge from theory to practice.

Key Concept 3: What is expectation?

　　Expectation = Mean = Average computed from a PMF.

Organization of this chapter

The plan for this chapter is as follows. We will start with the basic concepts of random variables in Section 3.1. We will formally define the random variables and discuss their relationship with the abstract probability space. Once this linkage is built, we can put the abstract probability space aside and focus on the random variables. In Section 3.2 we will define the probability mass function (PMF) of a random variable, which tells us the probability of obtaining a state of the random variable. PMF is closely related to the histogram of a dataset. We will explain the connection. In Section 3.3 we take a small detour to consider the cumulative distribution functions (CDF). Then, we discuss the mean and standard deviation in Section 3.4. Section 3.5 details a few commonly used random variables, including Bernoulli, binomial, geometric, and Poisson variables.

3.1 Random Variables

3.1.1 A motivating example

Consider an experiment with 4 outcomes $\Omega = \{\clubsuit, \diamondsuit, \heartsuit, \spadesuit\}$. We want to construct the probability space $(\Omega, \mathcal{F}, \mathbb{P})$. The sample space Ω is already defined. The event space $\mathcal{F}$ is the set of all possible subsets in Ω, which, in our case, is a set of 2^4 subsets. For the probability law $\mathbb{P}$, let us assume that the probability of obtaining each outcome is

$$\mathbb{P}[\{\clubsuit\}] = \frac{1}{6}, \quad \mathbb{P}[\{\diamondsuit\}] = \frac{2}{6}, \quad \mathbb{P}[\{\heartsuit\}] = \frac{2}{6}, \quad \mathbb{P}[\{\spadesuit\}] = \frac{1}{6}.$$

Therefore, we have constructed a probability space $(\Omega, \mathcal{F}, \mathbb{P})$ where everything is perfectly defined. So, in principle, they can live together happily forever.

A lazy data scientist comes, and there is a (small) problem. The data scientist does not want to write the symbols $\clubsuit, \diamondsuit, \heartsuit, \spadesuit$. There is nothing wrong with his motivation because all of us want efficiency. How can we help him? Well, the easiest solution is to *encode* each symbol with a number, for example, $\clubsuit \leftarrow 1$, $\diamondsuit \leftarrow 2$, $\heartsuit \leftarrow 3$, $\spadesuit \leftarrow 4$, where the arrow means that we assign a number to the symbol. But we can express this more formally by defining a function $X : \Omega \to \mathbb{R}$ with

$$X(\clubsuit) = 1, \quad X(\diamondsuit) = 2, \quad X(\heartsuit) = 3, \quad X(\spadesuit) = 4.$$

There is nothing new here: we have merely converted the symbols to numbers, with the help of a function X. However, with X defined, the probabilities can be written as

$$\mathbb{P}[X = 1] = \frac{1}{6}, \quad \mathbb{P}[X = 2] = \frac{2}{6}, \quad \mathbb{P}[X = 3] = \frac{2}{6}, \quad \mathbb{P}[X = 4] = \frac{1}{6}.$$

This is much more convenient, and so the data scientist is happy.

3.1.2 Definition of a random variable

The story above is exactly the motivation for random variables. Let us define a random variable formally.

> **Definition 3.1.** A **random variable** X *is a function* $X : \Omega \to \mathbb{R}$ *that maps an outcome* $\xi \in \Omega$ *to a number* $X(\xi)$ *on the real line.*

This definition may be puzzling at first glance. Why should we overcomplicate things by defining a *function* and calling it a *variable*?

If you recall the story above, we can map the notations of the story to the notations of the definition as follows.

Symbol	Meaning
Ω	sample space = the set containing ♣, ◇, ♡, ♠
ξ	an element in the sample space, which is one of ♣, ◇, ♡, ♠
X	a function that maps ♣ to the number 1, ◇ to the number 2, etc
$X(\xi)$	a number on the real line, e.g., $X(♣) = 1$

This explains our informal definition of random variables:

> **Key Concept 1: What are random variables?**
>
> Random variables are mappings from outcomes to numbers.

The random variable X is a *function*. The input to the function is an outcome of the sample space, whereas the output is a number on the real line. This type of function is somewhat different from an ordinary function that often translates a number to another number. Nevertheless, X is a function.

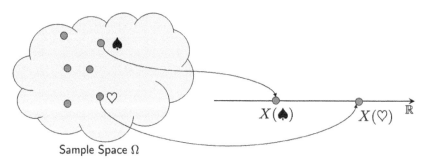

Sample Space Ω

Figure 3.2: A random variable is a mapping from the outcomes in the sample space to numbers on the real line. We can think of a random variable X as a translator that translates a statement to a number.

Why do we call this function X a *variable*? X **is a variable because** X **has multiple states**. As we illustrate in **Figure 3.2**, the mapping X translates every outcome ξ to a number. There are multiple numbers, which are the states of X. Each state has a certain probability for X to land on. Because X is not deterministic, we call it a *random* variable.

> **Example 3.1.** Suppose we flip a fair coin so that $\Omega = \{\text{head}, \text{tail}\}$. We can define the random variable $X : \Omega \to \mathbb{R}$ as
>
> $$X(\text{head}) = 1, \quad \text{and} \quad X(\text{tail}) = 0.$$

Therefore, when we write $\mathbb{P}[X=1]$ we actually mean $\mathbb{P}[\{\text{head}\}]$. Is there any difference between $\mathbb{P}[\{\text{Head}\}]$ and $\mathbb{P}[X=1]$? No, because they are describing two identical events. Note that the assignment of the value is totally up to you. You can say "head" is equal to the value 102. This is allowed and legitimate, but it isn't very convenient.

Example 3.2. Flip a coin 2 times. The sample space Ω is

$$\Omega = \{(\text{head},\text{head}), (\text{head},\text{tail}), (\text{tail},\text{head}), (\text{tail},\text{tail})\}.$$

Suppose that X is a random variable that maps an outcome to a number representing the sum of "head," i.e.,
$$X(\cdot) = \text{number of heads}.$$

Then, for the 4 ξ's in the sample space there are only 3 distinct numbers. More precisely, if we let $\xi_1 = (\text{head},\text{head})$, $\xi_2 = (\text{head},\text{tail})$, $\xi_3 = (\text{tail},\text{head})$, $\xi_4 = (\text{tail},\text{tail})$, then, we have

$$X(\xi_1) = 2, \;\; X(\xi_2) = 1, \;\; X(\xi_3) = 1, \;\; X(\xi_4) = 0.$$

A pictorial illustration of this random variable is shown in **Figure 3.3**. This example shows that the mapping defined by the random variable is not necessarily a one-to-one mapping because multiple outcomes can be mapped to the same number.

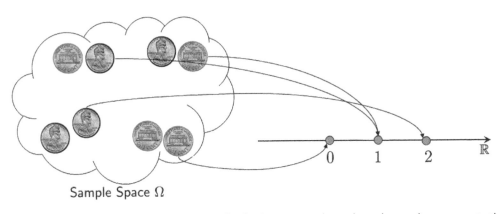

Figure 3.3: A random variable that maps a pair of coins to a number, where the number represents the number of heads.

3.1.3 Probability measure on random variables

By now, we hope that you understand Key Concept 1: **A random variable is a mapping from a statement to a number.** However, we are now facing another difficulty. We knew how to measure the size of an event using the probability law $\mathbb{P}$ because $\mathbb{P}(\cdot)$ takes an event $E \in \mathcal{F}$ and sends it to a number between $[0,1]$. After the translation X, we cannot send the output $X(\xi)$ to $\mathbb{P}(\cdot)$ because $\mathbb{P}(\cdot)$ "eats" a set $E \in \mathcal{F}$ and not a number $X(\xi) \in \mathbb{R}$. Therefore, when we write $\mathbb{P}[X=1]$, how do we measure the size of the event $X=1$?

This question appears difficult but is actually quite easy to answer. Since the probability law $\mathbb{P}(\cdot)$ is always applied to an **event**, we need to define an event for the random variable X. If we write the sets clearly, we note that "$X = a$" is equivalent to the set

$$E = \left\{ \xi \in \Omega \, \middle| \, X(\xi) = a \right\}.$$

This is the set that contains all possible ξ's such that $X(\xi) = a$. Therefore, when we say "find the probability of $X = a$," we are effectively asking the size of the set $E = \{ \xi \in \Omega \mid X(\xi) = a \}$.

How then do we measure the size of E? Since E is a subset in the sample space, E is measurable by $\mathbb{P}$. All we need to do is to determine what E is for a given a. This, in turn, requires us to find the **pre-image** $X^{-1}(a)$, which is defined as

$$X^{-1}(a) \stackrel{\text{def}}{=} \left\{ \xi \in \Omega \, \middle| \, X(\xi) = a \right\}.$$

Wait a minute, is this set just equal to E? Yes, the event E we are seeking is exactly the pre-image $X^{-1}(a)$. As such, the probability measure of E is

$$\mathbb{P}[X = a] = \mathbb{P}[X^{-1}(a)].$$

Figure 3.4 illustrates a situation where two outcomes ξ_1 and ξ_2 are mapped to the same value a on the real line. The corresponding event is the set $X^{-1}(a) = \{\xi_1, \xi_2\}$.

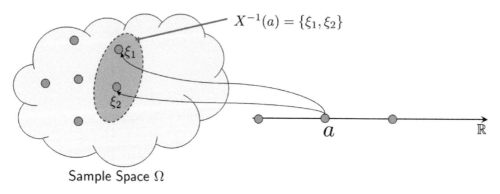

Figure 3.4: When computing the probability of $\mathbb{P}[\{\xi \in \Omega \mid X(\xi) = a\}]$, we effectively take the inverse mapping $X^{-1}(a)$ and compute the probability of the event $\mathbb{P}[\{\xi \in X^{-1}(a)\}] = \mathbb{P}[\{\xi_1, \xi_2\}]$.

Example 3.3. Suppose we throw a die. The sample space is

$$\Omega = \{1, 2, 3, 4, 5, 6\}.$$

There is a natural mapping X that maps $X(1) = 1$, $X(2) = 2$ and so on. Thus,

$$\mathbb{P}[X \leq 3] \overset{(a)}{=} \mathbb{P}[X = 1] + \mathbb{P}[X = 2] + \mathbb{P}[X = 3]$$
$$\overset{(b)}{=} \mathbb{P}[X^{-1}(1)] + \mathbb{P}[X^{-1}(2)] + \mathbb{P}[X^{-1}(3)]$$
$$\overset{(c)}{=} \mathbb{P}[\{1\}] + \mathbb{P}[\{2\}] + \mathbb{P}[\{3\}] = \frac{3}{6}.$$

In this derivation, step (a) is based on Axiom III, where the three events are disjoint. Step (b) is the pre-image due to the random variable X. Step (c) is the list of actual events in the event space. Note that there is no hand-waving argument in this derivation. Every step is justified by the concepts and theorems we have learned so far.

Example 3.4. Throw a die twice. The sample space is then

$$\Omega = \{(1,1), (1,2), \ldots, (6,6)\}.$$

These elements can be translated to 36 outcomes:

$$\xi_1 = (1,1), \xi_2 = (1,2), \ldots, \xi_{36} = (6,6).$$

Let

$$X = \text{sum of two numbers}.$$

Then, if we want to find the probability of getting $X = 7$, we can trace back and ask: Among the 36 outcomes, which of those ξ_i's will give us $X(\xi) = 7$? Or, what is the set $X^{-1}(7)$? To this end, we can write

$$\mathbb{P}[X = 7] = \mathbb{P}[\{(1,6), (2,5), (3,4), (4,3), (5,2), (6,1)\}]$$
$$= \mathbb{P}[(1,6)] + \mathbb{P}[(2,5)] + \mathbb{P}[(3,4)]$$
$$+ \mathbb{P}[(4,3)] + \mathbb{P}[(5,2)] + \mathbb{P}[(6,1)]$$
$$= \frac{1}{36} + \frac{1}{36} + \frac{1}{36} + \frac{1}{36} + \frac{1}{36} + \frac{1}{36} = \frac{1}{6}.$$

Again, in this example, you can see that all the steps are fully justified by the concepts we have learned so far.

Closing remark. In practice, when the problem is clearly defined, we can skip the inverse mapping $X^{-1}(a)$. However, this does not mean that the probability triplet $(\Omega, \mathcal{F}, \mathbb{P})$ is gone; it is still present. The triplet is now just the background of the problem.

The set of all possible values returned by X is denoted as $X(\Omega)$. Since X is not necessarily a bijection, the size of $X(\Omega)$ is not necessarily the same as the size of Ω. The elements in $X(\Omega)$ are often denoted as a or x. We call a or x one of the **states** of X. Be careful not to confuse x and X. The variable X is the random variable; it is a function. The variable x is a state assigned by X. A random variable X has multiple states. When we write $\mathbb{P}[X = x]$, we describe the probability of a random variable X taking a particular state x. It is exactly the same as $\mathbb{P}[\{\xi \in \Omega \mid X(\xi) = x\}]$.

3.2 Probability Mass Function

Random variables are mappings that translate events to numbers. After the translation, we have a set of numbers denoting the **states** of the random variables. Each state has a different probability of occurring. The probabilities are summarized by a function known as the probability mass function (PMF).

3.2.1 Definition of probability mass function

Definition 3.2. *The* **probability mass function (PMF)** *of a random variable X is a function which specifies the probability of obtaining a number $X(\xi) = x$. We denote a PMF as*

$$p_X(x) = \mathbb{P}[X = x]. \tag{3.1}$$

The set of all possible states of X is denoted as $X(\Omega)$.

Do not get confused by the sample space Ω and the set of states $X(\Omega)$. The sample space Ω contains all the possible outcomes of the experiments, whereas $X(\Omega)$ is the translation by the mapping X. The event $X = a$ is the set $X^{-1}(a) \subseteq \Omega$. Therefore, when we say $\mathbb{P}[X = x]$ we really mean $\mathbb{P}[X^{-1}(x)]$.

The probability mass function is a histogram summarizing the probability of each of the states X takes. Since it is a histogram, a PMF can be easily drawn as a bar chart.

Example 3.5. Flip a coin twice. The sample space is $\Omega = \{$HH, HT, TH, TT$\}$. We can assign a random variable $X =$ number of heads. Therefore,

$$X(\text{“HH”}) = 2, X(\text{“TH”}) = 1, X(\text{“HT”}) = 1, X(\text{“TT”}) = 0.$$

So the random variable X takes three states: 0, 1, 2. The PMF is therefore

$$p_X(0) = \mathbb{P}[X = 0] = \mathbb{P}[\{\text{“TT”}\}] = \frac{1}{4},$$

$$p_X(1) = \mathbb{P}[X = 1] = \mathbb{P}[\{\text{“TH”}, \text{“HT”}\}] = \frac{1}{2},$$

$$p_X(2) = \mathbb{P}[X = 2] = \mathbb{P}[\{\text{“HH”}\}] = \frac{1}{4}.$$

3.2.2 PMF and probability measure

In Chapter 2, we learned that probability is a measure of the size of a set. We introduced a **weighting function** that weights each of the elements in the set. The PMF is the weighing function for discrete random variables. Two random variables are different when their PMFs are different because they are constructing two different measures.

To illustrate the idea, suppose there are two dice. They each have probability masses as follows.

$$\mathbb{P}[\{1\}] = \frac{1}{12}, \ \mathbb{P}[\{2\}] = \frac{2}{12}, \ \mathbb{P}[\{3\}] = \frac{3}{12}, \ \mathbb{P}[\{4\}] = \frac{4}{12}, \ \mathbb{P}[\{5\}] = \frac{1}{12}, \ \mathbb{P}[\{6\}] = \frac{1}{12},$$

$$\mathbb{P}[\{1\}] = \frac{2}{12}, \ \mathbb{P}[\{2\}] = \frac{2}{12}, \ \mathbb{P}[\{3\}] = \frac{2}{12}, \ \mathbb{P}[\{4\}] = \frac{2}{12}, \ \mathbb{P}[\{5\}] = \frac{2}{12}, \ \mathbb{P}[\{6\}] = \frac{2}{12},$$

Let us define two random variables, X and Y, for the two dice. Then, the PMFs p_X and p_Y can be defined as

$$p_X(1) = \frac{1}{12}, \ p_X(2) = \frac{2}{12}, \ p_X(3) = \frac{3}{12}, \ p_X(4) = \frac{4}{12}, \ p_X(5) = \frac{1}{12}, \ p_X(6) = \frac{1}{12},$$

$$p_Y(1) = \frac{2}{12}, \ p_Y(2) = \frac{2}{12}, \ p_Y(3) = \frac{2}{12}, \ p_Y(4) = \frac{2}{12}, \ p_Y(5) = \frac{2}{12}, \ p_Y(6) = \frac{2}{12}.$$

These two probability mass functions correspond to two different probability measures, let's say $\mathbb{F}$ and $\mathbb{G}$. Define the event $E = \{\text{between 2 and 3}\}$. Then, $\mathbb{F}(E)$ and $\mathbb{G}(E)$ will lead to two different results:

$$\mathbb{F}(E) = \mathbb{P}[2 \leq X \leq 3] = p_X(2) + p_X(3) = \frac{1}{12} + \frac{2}{12} = \frac{3}{12},$$

$$\mathbb{G}(E) = \mathbb{P}[2 \leq Y \leq 3] = p_Y(2) + p_Y(3) = \frac{2}{12} + \frac{2}{12} = \frac{4}{12}.$$

Note that even though for some particular events two final results could be the same (e.g., $2 \leq X \leq 4$ and $2 \leq Y \leq 4$), the underlying measures are completely different.

Figure 3.5 shows another example of two different measures $\mathbb{F}$ and $\mathbb{G}$ on the same sample space $\Omega = \{\clubsuit, \diamondsuit, \heartsuit, \spadesuit\}$. Since the PMFs of the two measures are different, even when given the same event E, the resulting probabilities will be different.

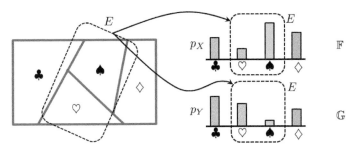

Figure 3.5: If we want to measure the size of a set E, using two different PMFs is equivalent to using two different measures. Therefore, the probabilities will be different.

Does $p_X = p_Y$ imply $X = Y$? If two random variables X and Y have the same PMF, does it mean that the random variables are the same? The answer is no. Consider a random variable with a symmetric PMF, e.g.,

$$p_X(-1) = \frac{1}{4}, \quad p_X(0) = \frac{1}{2}, \quad p_X(1) = \frac{1}{4}. \tag{3.2}$$

Suppose $Y = -X$. Then, $p_Y(-1) = \frac{1}{4}$, $p_Y(0) = \frac{1}{2}$, and $p_Y(1) = \frac{1}{4}$, which is the same as p_X. However, X and Y are two different random variables. If the sample space is $\{\clubsuit, \diamondsuit, \heartsuit\}$, we can define the mappings $X(\cdot)$ and $Y(\cdot)$ as

$$X(\clubsuit) = -1, \quad X(\diamondsuit) = 0, \quad X(\heartsuit) = +1,$$

$$Y(\clubsuit) = +1, \quad Y(\diamondsuit) = 0, \quad Y(\heartsuit) = -1.$$

Therefore, when we say $p_X(-1) = \frac{1}{4}$, the underlying event is ♣. But when we say $p_Y(-1) = \frac{1}{4}$, the underlying event is ♡. The two random variables are different, although their PMFs have exactly the same shape.

3.2.3 Normalization property

Here we must mention one important property of a probability mass function. This property is known as the **normalization property**, which is a useful tool for a sanity check.

Theorem 3.1. *A PMF should satisfy the condition that*

$$\sum_{x \in X(\Omega)} p_X(x) = 1. \tag{3.3}$$

Proof. The proof follows directly from Axiom II, which states that $\mathbb{P}[\Omega] = 1$. Since x covers all numerical values X can take, and since each x is distinct, by Axiom III we have

$$\sum_{x \in X(\Omega)} \mathbb{P}[X = x] = \sum_{x \in X(\Omega)} \mathbb{P}[\{\xi \in \Omega \,|\, X(\xi) = x\}]$$

$$= \mathbb{P}\left[\bigcup_{\xi \in \Omega} \{\xi \in \Omega \,|\, X(\xi) = x\}\right] = \mathbb{P}[\Omega] = 1.$$

□

Practice Exercise 3.1. Let $p_X(k) = c\left(\frac{1}{2}\right)^k$, where $k = 1, 2, \ldots$. Find c.

Solution. Since $\sum_{k \in X(\Omega)} p_X(k) = 1$, we must have

$$\sum_{k=1}^{\infty} \left(\frac{1}{2}\right)^k = 1.$$

Evaluating the geometric series on the right-hand side, we can show that

$$\sum_{k=1}^{\infty} c\left(\frac{1}{2}\right)^k = \frac{c}{2} \sum_{k=0}^{\infty} \left(\frac{1}{2}\right)^k$$

$$= \frac{c}{2} \cdot \frac{1}{1 - \frac{1}{2}}$$

$$= c \implies c = 1.$$

Practice Exercise 3.2. Let $p_X(k) = c \cdot \sin\left(\frac{\pi}{2}k\right)$, where $k = 1, 2, \ldots$. Find c.

Solution. The reader may might be tempted to sum $p_X(k)$ over all the possible k's:

$$\sum_{k=1}^{\infty} \sin\left(\frac{\pi}{2}k\right) = 1 + 0 - 1 + 0 + \cdots \overset{?}{=} 0.$$

However, a more careful inspection reveals that $p_X(k)$ is actually negative when $k = 3, 7, 11, \ldots$. This cannot happen because a probability mass function must be non-negative. Therefore, the problem is not defined, and so there is no solution.

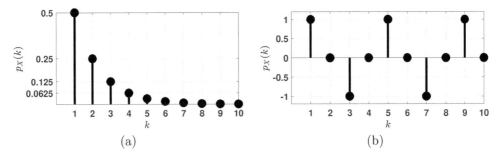

(a)   (b)

Figure 3.6: (a) The PMF of $p_X(k) = c\left(\frac{1}{2}\right)^k$, for $k = 1, 2, \ldots$. (b) The PMF of $p_X(k) = \sin\left(\frac{\pi}{2}k\right)$, where $k = 1, 2, \ldots$. Note that this is not a valid PMF because probability cannot have negative values.

3.2.4   PMF versus histogram

PMFs are closely related to histograms. A histogram is a plot that shows the frequency of a state. As we see in **Figure 3.6**, the x-axis is a collection of states, whereas the y-axis is the frequency. So a PMF is indeed a histogram.

Viewing a PMF as a histogram can help us understand a random variable. For better or worse, treating a random variable as a histogram could help you differentiate a random variable from a variable. An ordinary variable only has one state, but a random variable has multiple states. At any particular instance, we do not know which state will show up before our observation. However, we do know the probability. For example, in the coin-flip example, while we do not know whether we will get "HH," we know that the chance of getting "HH" is $1/4$. Of course, having a probability of $1/4$ does not mean that we will get "HH" once every four trials. It only means that if we run an infinite number of experiments, then $1/4$ of the experiments will give us "HH."

The linkage between PMF and histogram can be quite practical. For example, while we do not know the true underlying distribution of the 26 letters of the English alphabet, we can collect a large number of words and plot the histogram. The example below illustrates how we can empirically define a random variable from the data.

Example. There are 26 English letters, but the frequencies of the letters in writing are different. If we define a random variable X as a letter we randomly draw from an English text, we can think of X as an object with 26 different states. The mapping associated with the random variable is straightforward: $X(\text{"a"}) = 1$, $X(\text{"b"}) = 2$, etc. The probability of landing on a particular state approximately follows a histogram shown in **Figure 3.7**. The histogram provides meaningful values of the probabilities, e.g., $p_X(1) = 0.0847$, $p_X(2) = 0.0149$, etc. The true probability of the states may not be exactly these values. However, when we have enough samples, we generally expect the histogram to approach the theoretical PMF. The MATLAB and Python codes used to generate this histogram are shown below.

```
% MATLAB code to generate the histogram
load('ch3_data_English');
bar(f/100,'FaceColor',[0.9,0.6,0.0]);
```

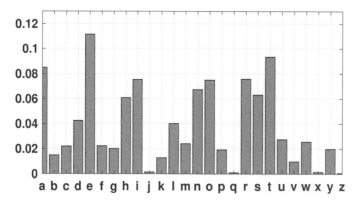

Figure 3.7: The frequency of the 26 English letters. Data source: Wikipedia.

```
xticklabels({'a','b','c','d','e','f','g','h','i','j','k','l',...
    'm','n','o','p','q','r','s','t','u','v','w','x','y','z'});
xticks(1:26);
yticks(0:0.02:0.2);
axis([1 26 0 0.13]);
```

```
# Python code generate the histogram
import numpy as np
import matplotlib.pyplot as plt
f = np.loadtxt('./ch3_data_english.txt')
n = np.arange(26)
plt.bar(n, f/100)
ntag = ['a','b','c','d','e','f','g','h','i','j','k','l','m',...
    'n','o','p','q','r','s','t','u','v','w','x','y','z']
plt.xticks(n, ntag)
```

PMF = ideal histograms

If a random variable is more or less a histogram, why is the PMF such an important concept? The answer to this question has two parts. The first part is that the histogram generated from a dataset is always an **empirical** histogram, so-called because the dataset comes from observation or experience rather than theory. Thus the histograms may vary slightly every time we collect a dataset.

As we increase the number of data points in a dataset, the histogram will eventually converge to an **ideal** histogram, or a **distribution**. For example, counting the number of heads in 100 coin flips will fluctuate more in percentage terms than counting the heads in 10 million coin flips. The latter will almost certainly have a histogram that is closer to a 50–50 distribution. Therefore, the "histogram" generated by a random variable can be considered the ultimate histogram or the limiting histogram of the experiment.

To help you visualize the difference between a PMF and a histogram, we show in **Figure 3.8** an experiment in which a die is thrown N times. Assuming that the die is fair, the PMF is simply $p_X(k) = 1/6$ for $k = 1, \ldots, 6$, which is a uniform distribution across the 6 states. Now, we can throw the die many times. As N increases, we observe that the

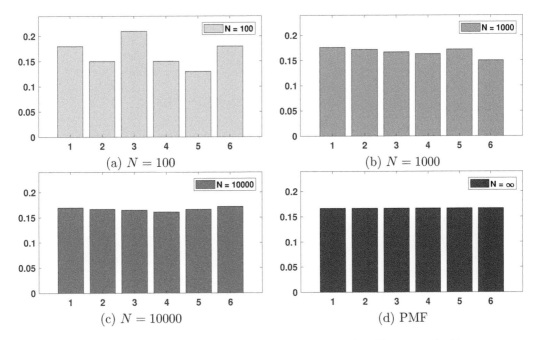

Figure 3.8: Histogram and PMF, when throwing a fair die N times. As N increases, the histograms are becoming more similar to the PMF.

histogram becomes more like the PMF. You can imagine that when N goes to infinity, the histogram will eventually become the PMF. Therefore, when given a dataset, one way to think of it is to treat the data as random realizations drawn from a certain PMF. The more data points you have, the closer the histogram will become to the PMF.

The MATLAB and Python codes used to generate **Figure 3.8** are shown below. The two commands we use here are `randi` (in MATLAB), which generates random integer numbers, and `hist`, which computes the heights and bin centers of a histogram. In Python, the corresponding commands are `np.random.randint` and `plt.hist`. Note that because of the different indexing schemes in MATLAB and Python, we offset the maximum index in `np.random.randint` to 7 instead of 6. Also, we shift the x-axes so that the bars are centered at the integers.

```
% MATLAB code to generate the histogram
x = [1 2 3 4 5 6];
q = randi(6,100,1);
figure;
[num,val] = hist(q,x-0.5);
bar(num/100,'FaceColor',[0.8, 0.8,0.8]);
axis([0 7 0 0.24]);
```

```
# Python code generate the histogram
import numpy as np
import matplotlib.pyplot as plt
q = np.random.randint(7,size=100)
plt.hist(q+0.5,bins=6)
```

This **generative** perspective is illustrated in **Figure 3.9**. We assume that the underlying latent random variable has some PMF that can be described by a few parameters, e.g., the mean and variance. Given the data points, if we can infer these parameters, we might retrieve the entire PMF (up to the uncertainty level intrinsic to the dataset). We refer to this inverse process as statistical inference.

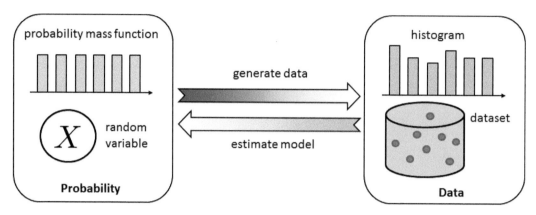

Figure 3.9: When analyzing a dataset, one can treat the data points are samples drawn according to a latent random variable with certain a PMF. The dataset we observe is often finite, and so the histogram we obtain is empirical. A major task in data analysis is statistical inference, which tries to retrieve the model information from the available measurements.

Returning to the question of why we need to understand the PMFs, the second part of the answer is the difference between **synthesis** and **analysis**. In synthesis, we start with a known random variable and generate samples according to the PMF underlying the random variable. For example, on a computer, we often start with a Gaussian random variable and generate random numbers according to the histogram specified by the Gaussian random variable. Synthesis is useful because we can predict what will happen. We can, for example, create millions of training samples to train a deep neural network. We can also evaluate algorithms used to estimate statistical quantities such as mean, variance, moments, etc., because the synthesis approach provides us with ground truth. In supervised learning scenarios, synthesis is vital to ensuring sufficient training data.

The other direction of synthesis is analysis. The goal is to start with a dataset and deduce the statistical properties of the dataset. For example, suppose we want to know whether the underlying model is indeed a Gaussian model. If we know that it is a Gaussian (or if we choose to use a Gaussian), we want to know the parameters that define this Gaussian. The analysis direction addresses this model selection and parameter estimation problem. Moving forward, once we know the model and the parameters, we can make a prediction or do recovery, both of which are ubiquitous in machine learning.

We summarize our discussions below, which is Key Concept 2 of this chapter.

Key Concept 2: What are probability mass functions (PMFs)?

PMFs are the ideal histograms of random variables.

3.2.5 Estimating histograms from real data

> The following discussions about histogram estimation can be skipped if it is your first time reading the book.

If you have a dataset, how would you plot the histogram? Certainly, if you have access to MATLAB or Python, you can call standard functions such as `hist` (in MATLAB) or `np.histogram` (in Python). However, when plotting a histogram, you need to specify the number of bins (or equivalently the width of bins). If you use larger bins, then you will have fewer bins with many elements in each bin. Conversely, if the bin width is too small, you may not have enough samples to fill the histogram. **Figure 3.10** illustrates two histograms in which the bins are respectively too large and too small.

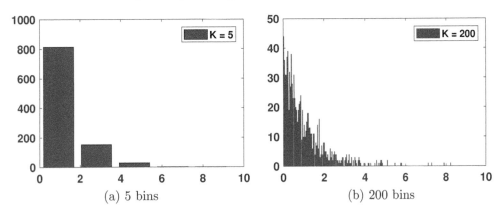

(a) 5 bins   (b) 200 bins

Figure 3.10: The width of the histogram has substantial influence on the information that can be extracted from the histogram.

The MATLAB and Python codes used to generate **Figure 3.10** are shown below. Note that here we are using an exponential random variable (to be discussed in Chapter 4). In MATLAB, calling an exponential random variable is done using `exprnd`, whereas in Python the command is `np.random.exponential`. For this experiment, we can specify the number of bins k, which can be set to $k = 200$ or $k = 5$. To suppress the Python output of the array, we can add a semicolon `;`. A final note is that `lambda` is a reserved variable in Python. Use something else.

```
% MATLAB code used to generate the plots
lambda = 1;
k       = 1000;
X       = exprnd(1/lambda,[k,1]);
[num,val] = hist(X,200);
bar(val,num,'FaceColor',[1, 0.5,0.5]);
```

```
# Python code used to generate the plots
import numpy as np
import matplotlib.pyplot as plt
lambd = 1
```

```
k       = 1000
X       = np.random.exponential(1/lambd, size=k)
plt.hist(X,bins=200);
```

In statistics, there are various rules to determine the bin width of a histogram. We mention a few of them here. Let K be the number of bins and N the number of samples.

- Square-root: $K = \sqrt{N}$
- Sturges' formula: $K = \log_2 N + 1$.
- Rice Rule: $K = 2\sqrt[3]{N}$
- Scott's normal reference rule: $K = \frac{\max X - \min X}{h}$, where $h = \frac{3.5\sqrt{\mathrm{Var}[X]}}{\sqrt[3]{N}}$ is the bin width.

For the example data shown in **Figure 3.10**, the histograms obtained using the above rules are given in **Figure 3.11**. As you can see, different rules have different suggested bin widths. Some are more conservative, e.g., using fewer bins, whereas some are less conservative. In any case, the suggested bin widths do seem to provide better histograms than the original ones in **Figure 3.10**. However, no bin width is the best for all purposes.

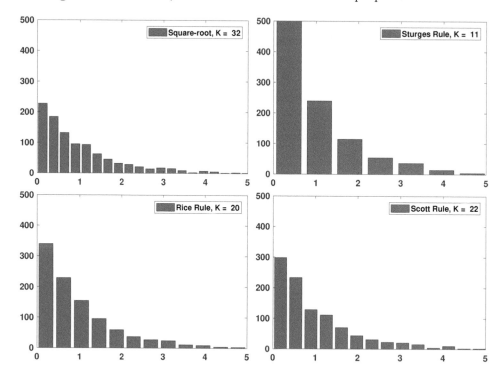

Figure 3.11: Histograms of a dataset using different bin width rules.

Beyond these predefined rules, there are also algorithmic tools to determine the bin width. One such tool is known as **cross-validation**. Cross-validation means defining some kind of **cross-validation score** that measures the statistical risk associated with the histogram. A histogram having a lower score has a lower risk, and thus it is a better histogram.

Note that the word "better" is relative to the optimality criteria associated with the cross-validation score. If you do not agree with our cross-validation score, our optimal bin width is not necessarily the one you want. In this case, you need to specify your optimality criteria.

Theoretically, deriving a meaningful cross-validation score is beyond the scope of this book. However, it is still possible to understand the principle. Let h be the bin width of the histogram, K the number of bins, and N the number of samples. Given a dataset, we follow this procedure:

- Step 1: Choose a bin width h.

- Step 2: Construct a histogram from the data, using the bin width h. The histogram will have the empirical PMF values $\widehat{p}_1, \widehat{p}_2, \ldots, \widehat{p}_K$, which are the heights of the histograms normalized so that the sum is 1.

- Step 3: Compute the cross-validation score (see Wasserman, *All of Statistics*, Section 20.2):

$$J(h) = \frac{2}{(N-1)h} - \frac{N+1}{(N-1)h} \left(\widehat{p}_1^2 + \widehat{p}_2^2 + \cdots + \widehat{p}_K^2 \right) \qquad (3.4)$$

- Repeat Steps 1, 2, 3, until we find an h that minimizes $J(h)$.

Note that when we use a different h, the PMF values $\widehat{p}_1, \widehat{p}_2, \ldots, \widehat{p}_K$ will change, and the number of bins K will also change. Therefore, when changing h, we are changing not only the terms in $J(h)$ that explicitly contain h but also terms that are implicitly influenced.

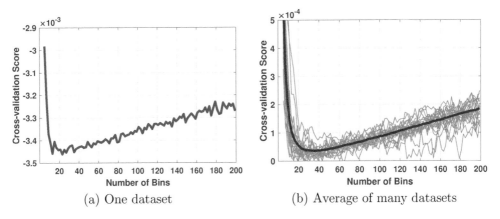

(a) One dataset (b) Average of many datasets

Figure 3.12: Cross-validation score for the histogram. (a) The score of one particular dataset. (b) The scores for many different datasets generated by the same model.

For the dataset we showed in **Figure 3.10**, the cross-validation score $J(h)$ is shown in **Figure 3.12**. We can see that although the curve is noisy, there is indeed a reasonably clear minimum happening around $20 \leq K \leq 30$, which is consistent with some of the rules.

The MATLAB and Python codes we used to generate **Figure 3.12** are shown below. The key step is to implement Equation (3.4) inside a for-loop, where the loop goes through the range of bins we are interested in. To obtain the PMF values $\widehat{p}_1, \ldots, \widehat{p}_K$, we call `hist` in MATLAB and `np.histogram` in Python. The bin width `h` is the number of samples `n` divided by the number of bins `m`.

```
% MATLAB code to perform the cross validation
lambda = 1;
n = 1000;
X = exprnd(1/lambda,[n,1]);
m = 6:200;
J = zeros(1,195);
for i=1:195
    [num,binc] = hist(X,m(i));
    h = n/m(i);
    J(i) = 2/((n-1)*h)-((n+1)/((n-1)*h))*sum( (num/n).^2 );
end
plot(m,J,'LineWidth',4,'Color',[0.9,0.2,0.0]);
```

```
# Python code to perform the cross validation
import numpy as np
import matplotlib.pyplot as plt
lambd = 1
n      = 1000
X      = np.random.exponential(1/lambd, size=n)
m      = np.arange(5,200)
J      = np.zeros((195))
for i in range(0,195):
  hist,bins = np.histogram(X,bins=m[i])
  h = n/m[i]
  J[i] = 2/((n-1)*h)-((n+1)/((n-1)*h))*np.sum((hist/n)**2)
plt.plot(m,J);
```

In **Figure 3.12**(b), we show another set of curves from the same experiment. The difference here is that we assume access to the true generative model so that we can generate the many datasets of the same distribution. In this experiment we generated $T = 1000$ datasets. We compute the cross-validation score $J(h)$ for each of the datasets, yielding T score functions $J^{(1)}(h), \ldots, J^{(T)}(h)$. We subtract the minimum because different realizations have different offsets. Then we compute the average:

$$\overline{J}(h) = \frac{1}{T} \sum_{t=1}^{T} \left\{ J^{(t)}(h) - \min_{h} \left\{ J^{(t)}(h) \right\} \right\}. \tag{3.5}$$

This gives us a smooth red curve as shown in **Figure 3.12**(b). The minimum appears to be at $N = 25$. This is the optimal N, concerning the cross-validation score, on the average of all datasets.

All rules, including cross-validation, are based on optimizing for a certain objective. Your objective could be different from our objective, and so our optimum is not necessarily your optimum. Therefore, cross-validation may not be the best. It depends on your problem.

End of the discussion.

3.3 Cumulative Distribution Functions (Discrete)

While the probability mass function (PMF) provides a complete characterization of a discrete random variable, the PMFs themselves are technically not "functions" because the impulses in the histogram are essentially delta functions. More formally, a PMF $p_X(k)$ should actually be written as

$$p_X(x) = \sum_{k \in X(\Omega)} \underbrace{p_X(k)}_{\text{PMF values}} \cdot \underbrace{\delta(x-k)}_{\text{delta function}}.$$

This is a train of delta functions, where the height is specified by the probability mass $p_X(k)$. For example, a random variable with PMF values

$$p_X(0) = \frac{1}{4}, \; p_X(1) = \frac{1}{2}, \; p_X(2) = \frac{1}{4}$$

will be expressed as

$$p_X(x) = \frac{1}{4}\delta(x) + \frac{1}{2}\delta(x-1) + \frac{1}{4}\delta(x-2).$$

Since delta functions need to be integrated to generate values, the typical things we want to do, e.g., integration and differentiation, are not as straightforward in the sense of Riemann-Stieltjes.

The way to handle the unfriendliness of the delta functions is to consider mild modifications of the PMF. This notation of "cumulative" distribution functions will allow us to resolve the delta function problems. We will defer the technical details to the next chapter. For the time being, we will briefly introduce the idea to prepare you for the technical discussion later.

3.3.1 Definition of the cumulative distribution function

Definition 3.3. *Let X be a discrete random variable with $\Omega = \{x_1, x_2, \ldots\}$. The* **cumulative distribution function** *(CDF) of X is*

$$F_X(x_k) \stackrel{\text{def}}{=} \mathbb{P}[X \le x_k] = \sum_{\ell=1}^{k} p_X(x_\ell). \tag{3.6}$$

If $\Omega = \{\ldots, -1, 0, 1, 2, \ldots\}$, then the CDF of X is

$$F_X(k) \stackrel{\text{def}}{=} \mathbb{P}[X \le k] = \sum_{\ell=-\infty}^{k} p_X(\ell). \tag{3.7}$$

A CDF is essentially the cumulative sum of a PMF from $-\infty$ to x, where the variable x' in the sum is a dummy variable.

Example 3.6. Consider a random variable X with PMF $p_X(0) = \frac{1}{4}$, $p_X(1) = \frac{1}{2}$ and $p_X(4) = \frac{1}{4}$. The CDF of X can be computed as

$$F_X(0) = \mathbb{P}[X \le 0] = p_X(0) = \frac{1}{4},$$

$$F_X(1) = \mathbb{P}[X \le 1] = p_X(0) + p_X(1) = \frac{3}{4},$$

$$F_X(4) = \mathbb{P}[X \le 4] = p_X(0) + p_X(1) + p_X(4) = 1.$$

As shown in **Figure 3.13**, the CDF of a discrete random variable is a staircase function.

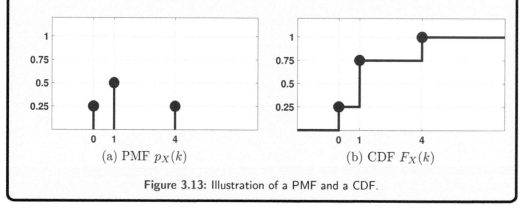

(a) PMF $p_X(k)$ (b) CDF $F_X(k)$

Figure 3.13: Illustration of a PMF and a CDF.

The MATLAB code and the Python code used to generate **Figure 3.13** are shown below. The CDF is computed using the command cumsum in MATLAB and np.cumsum in Python.

```
% MATLAB code to generate a PMF and a CDF
p = [0.25 0.5 0.25];
x = [0 1 4];
F = cumsum(p);

figure(1);
stem(x,p,'.','LineWidth',4,'MarkerSize',50);
figure(2);
stairs([-4 x 10],[0 F 1],'.-','LineWidth',4,'MarkerSize',50);
```

```
% Python code to generate a PMF and a CDF
import numpy as np
import matplotlib.pyplot as plt
p = np.array([0.25, 0.5, 0.25])
x = np.array([0, 1, 4])
F = np.cumsum(p)

plt.stem(x,p,use_line_collection=True); plt.show()
plt.step(x,F); plt.show()
```

Why is CDF a better-defined function than PMF? There are technical reasons associated with whether a function is integrable. Without going into the details of these discussions, a short answer is that delta functions are defined through integrations; they are not functions. A delta function is defined as a function such that $\delta(x) = 0$ everywhere except at $x = 0$, and $\int_\Omega \delta(x)\, dx = 1$. On the other hand, a staircase function is always well-defined. The discontinuous points of a staircase can be well defined if we specify the gap between two consecutive steps. For example, in **Figure 3.13**, as soon as we specify the gap 1/4, 1/2, and 1/4, the staircase function is completely defined.

Example. Figure 3.14 shows the empirical histogram of the English letters and the corresponding empirical CDF. We want to differentiate PMF versus histogram and CDF versus empirical CDF. The empirical CDF is the CDF computed from a finite dataset.

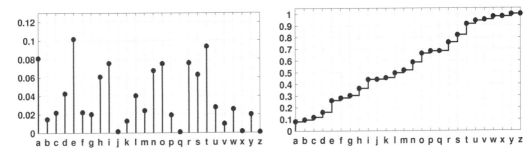

Figure 3.14: PMF and a CDF of the frequency of English letters.

3.3.2 Properties of the CDF

We observe from the example in Figure 3.13 that a CDF has several properties. First, being a staircase function, the CDF is non-decreasing. It can stay constant for a while, but it never drops. Second, the minimum value of a CDF is 0, whereas the maximum value is 1. It is 0 for any value that is smaller than the first state; it is 1 for any value that is larger than the last state. Third, the gap at each jump is exactly the probability mass at that state. Let us summarize these observations in the following theorem.

Theorem 3.2. *If X is a discrete random variable, then the CDF of X has the following properties:*

(i) *The CDF is a sequence of* **increasing** *unit steps.*

(ii) *The* **maximum** *of the CDF is when $x = \infty$: $F_X(+\infty) = 1$.*

(iii) *The* **minimum** *of the CDF is when $x = -\infty$: $F_X(-\infty) = 0$.*

(iv) *The unit steps have* **jumps** *at positions where $p_X(x) > 0$.*

Proof. Statement (i) can be seen from the summation

$$F_X(x) = \sum_{x' \leq x} p_X(x').$$

Since the probability mass function is non-negative, the value of F_X is larger when the value of the argument is larger. That is, $x \leq y$ implies $F_X(x) \leq F_X(y)$. The second statement (ii) is true because the summation includes all possible states. So we have

$$F_X(+\infty) = \sum_{x'=-\infty}^{\infty} p_X(x') = 1.$$

Similarly, for the third statement (iii),

$$F_X(-\infty) = \sum_{x' \leq -\infty} p_X(x').$$

The summation is taken over an empty set, and so $F_X(-\infty) = 0$. Statement (iv) is true because the cumulative sum changes only when there is a non-zero mass in the PMF. □

As we can see in the proof, the basic argument of the CDF is the cumulative sum of the PMF. By definition, a cumulative sum always adds mass. This is why the CDF is always increasing, has 0 at $-\infty$, and has 1 at $+\infty$. This last statement deserves more attention. It implies that the unit step always has a **solid dot on the left**-hand side and an **empty dot on the right**-hand side, because when the CDF jumps, the final value is specified by the "$\leq$" sign in Equation (3.6). The technical term for this property is **right continuous**.

3.3.3 Converting between PMF and CDF

> **Theorem 3.3.** *If X is a discrete random variable, then the PMF of X can be obtained from the CDF by*
>
> $$p_X(x_k) = F_X(x_k) - F_X(x_{k-1}), \qquad (3.8)$$
>
> *where we assumed that X has a countable set of states $\{x_1, x_2, \ldots\}$. If the sample space of the random variable X contains integers from $-\infty$ to $+\infty$, then the PMF can be defined as*
>
> $$p_X(k) = F_X(k) - F_X(k-1). \qquad (3.9)$$

> **Example 3.7.** Continuing with the example in **Figure 3.13**, if we are given the CDF
>
> $$F_X(0) = \frac{1}{4}, \qquad F_X(1) = \frac{3}{4}, \qquad F_X(4) = 1,$$
>
> how do we find the PMF? We know that the PMF will have non-negative values only at $x = 0, 1, 4$. For each of these x, we can show that
>
> $$p_X(0) = F_X(0) - F_X(-\infty) = \frac{1}{4} - 0 = \frac{1}{4},$$
> $$p_X(1) = F_X(1) - F_X(0) = \frac{3}{4} - \frac{1}{4} = \frac{1}{2},$$
> $$p_X(4) = F_X(4) - F_X(1) = 1 - \frac{3}{4} = \frac{1}{4}.$$

3.4 Expectation

When analyzing data, it is often useful to extract certain key parameters such as the mean and the standard deviation. The mean and the standard deviation can be seen from the lens of random variables. In this section, we will formalize the idea using **expectation**.

3.4.1 Definition of expectation

Definition 3.4. *The* **expectation** *of a random variable X is*

$$\mathbb{E}[X] = \sum_{x \in X(\Omega)} x\, p_X(x). \tag{3.10}$$

Expectation is the mean of the random variable X. Intuitively, we can think of $p_X(x)$ as the percentage of times that the random variable X attains the value x. When this percentage is multiplied by x, we obtain the contribution of each x. Summing over all possible values of x then yields the mean. To see this more clearly, we can write the definition as

$$\mathbb{E}[X] = \underbrace{\sum_{x \in X(\Omega)}}_{\text{sum over all states}} \underbrace{x}_{\text{a state } X \text{ takes}} \underbrace{p_X(x)}_{\text{the percentage}} .$$

Figure 3.15 illustrates a PMF that contains five states $x_1, \ldots, x_5$. Corresponding to each state are $p_X(x_1), \ldots, p_X(x_5)$. For this PMF to make sense, we must assume that $p_X(x_1) + \cdots + p_X(x_5) = 1$. To simplify notation, let us define $p_i \stackrel{\text{def}}{=} p_X(x_i)$. Then the expectation of X is just the sum of the products: value (x_i) times height (p_i). This gives $\mathbb{E}[X] = \sum_{i=1}^{5} x_i p_X(x_i)$.

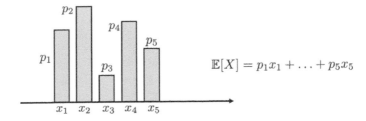

Figure 3.15: The expectation of a random variable is the sum of $x_i p_i$.

We emphasize that the definition of the expectation is exactly the same as the usual way we calculate the average of a dataset. When we calculate the average of a dataset $\mathcal{D} = \{x^{(1)}, x^{(2)}, \ldots, x^{(N)}\}$, we sum up these N samples and divide by the number of samples. This is what we called the empirical average or the sample average:

$$\text{average} = \frac{1}{N} \sum_{n=1}^{N} x^{(n)}. \tag{3.11}$$

Of course, in a typical dataset, these N samples often take distinct values. But suppose that among these N samples there are only K different values. For example, if we throw a die a million times, every sample we record will be one of the six numbers. This situation is illustrated in **Figure 3.16**, where we put the samples into the correct bin storing these values. In this case, to calculate the average we are effectively doing a binning:

$$\text{average} = \frac{1}{N} \sum_{k=1}^{K} \text{value } x_k \ \times \ \text{number of samples with value } x_k. \tag{3.12}$$

Equation (3.12) is *exactly* the same as Equation (3.11), as long as the samples can be grouped into K different values. With a little calculation, we can rewrite Equation (3.12) as

$$\text{average} = \underbrace{\sum_{k=1}^{K}}_{\text{sum of all states}} \ \underbrace{\text{value } x_k}_{\text{a state } X \text{ takes}} \ \times \ \underbrace{\frac{\text{number of samples with value } x_k}{N}}_{\text{the percentage}},$$

which is the same as the definition of expectation.

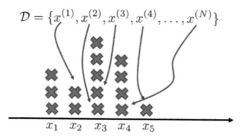

$$\mathcal{D} = \{x^{(1)}, x^{(2)}, x^{(3)}, x^{(4)}, \ldots, x^{(N)}\}$$

$$x_1 \quad x_2 \quad x_3 \quad x_4 \quad x_5$$

Figure 3.16: If we have a dataset $\mathcal{D}$ containing N samples, and if there are only K distinct values, we can effectively put these N samples into K bins. Thus, the "average" (which is the sum divided by the number N) is exactly the same as our definition of expectation.

The difference between $\mathbb{E}[X]$ and the average is that $\mathbb{E}[X]$ is computed from the *ideal* histogram, whereas average is computed from the *empirical* histogram. When the number of samples N approaches infinity, we expect the average to approximate $\mathbb{E}[X]$. However, when N is small, the empirical average will have random fluctuations around $\mathbb{E}[X]$. Every time we experiment, the empirical average may be slightly different. Therefore, we can regard $\mathbb{E}[X]$ as the *true average* of a certain random variable, and the empirical average as a *finite-sample average* based on the particular experiment we are working with. This summarizes Key Concept 3 of this chapter.

Key Concept 3: What is expectation?

Expectation = Mean = Average computed from a PMF.

If we are given a dataset on a computer, computing the mean can be done by calling the command `mean` in MATLAB and `np.mean` in Python. The example below shows the case of finding the mean of 10000 uniformly distributed random numbers.

```
% MATLAB code to compute the mean of a dataset
X  = rand(10000,1);
mX = mean(X);
```

```
# Python code to compute the mean of a dataset
import numpy as np
X  = np.random.rand(10000)
mX = np.mean(X)
```

Example 3.8. Let X be a random variable with PMF $p_X(0) = 1/4$, $p_X(1) = 1/2$ and $p_X(2) = 1/4$. We can show that the expectation is

$$\mathbb{E}[X] = (0)\underbrace{\left(\frac{1}{4}\right)}_{p_X(0)} + (1)\underbrace{\left(\frac{1}{2}\right)}_{p_X(1)} + (2)\underbrace{\left(\frac{1}{4}\right)}_{p_X(2)} = 1.$$

On MATLAB and Python, if we know the PMF then computing the expectation is straight-forward. Here is the code to compute the above example.

```
% MATLAB code to compute the expectation
p = [0.25 0.5 0.25];
x = [0 1 2];
EX = sum(p.*x);
```

```
# Python code to compute the expectation
import numpy as np
p = np.array([0.25, 0.5, 0.25])
x = np.array([0, 1, 2])
EX = np.sum(p*x)
```

Example 3.9. Flip an unfair coin, where the probability of getting a head is $\frac{3}{4}$. Let X be a random variable such that $X = 1$ means getting a head. Then we can show that $p_X(1) = \frac{3}{4}$ and $p_X(0) = \frac{1}{4}$. The expectation of X is therefore

$$\mathbb{E}[X] = (1)p_X(1) + (0)p_X(0) = (1)\left(\frac{3}{4}\right) + (0)\left(\frac{1}{4}\right) = \frac{3}{4}.$$

Center of mass. How would you interpret the result of this example? Does it mean that, on average, we will get 3/4 heads (but there is not anything called 3/4 heads!). Recall the definition of a random variable: it is a translator that translates a descriptive state to a number on the real line. Thus the expectation, which is an operation defined on the real line, can only tell us what is happening on the real line, not in the original sample

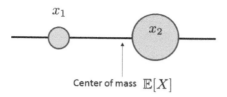

Center of mass $\mathbb{E}[X]$

Figure 3.17: Center of mass. If a state x_2 is more influential than another state x_1, the center of mass $\mathbb{E}[X]$ will lean towards x_2.

space. On the real line, the expectation can be regarded as the **center of mass**, which is the point where the "forces" between the two states are "balanced". In **Figure 3.17** we depict a random variable with two states x_1 and x_2. The state x_1 has less influence (because $p_X(x_1)$ is smaller) than x_2. Therefore the center of mass is shifted towards x_2. This result shows us that the value $\mathbb{E}[X]$ is not necessarily in the sample space. $\mathbb{E}[X]$ is a deterministic number with nothing to do with the sample space.

Example 3.10. Let X be a random variable with PMF $p_X(k) = \frac{1}{2^k}$, for $k = 1, 2, 3, \ldots$. The expectation is

$$\mathbb{E}[X] = \sum_{k=1}^{\infty} k p_X(k) = \sum_{k=1}^{\infty} k \cdot \frac{1}{2^k}$$

$$= \frac{1}{2} \sum_{k=1}^{\infty} k \cdot \frac{1}{2^{k-1}} = \frac{1}{2} \cdot \frac{1}{(1 - \frac{1}{2})^2} = 2.$$

On MATLAB and Python, if you want to verify this answer you can use the following code. Here, we approximate the infinite sum by a finite sum of $k = 1, \ldots, 100$.

```
% MATLAB code to compute the expectation
k = 1:100;
p = 0.5.^k;
EX = sum(p.*k);
```

```
# Python code to compute the expectation
import numpy as np
k = np.arange(100)
p = np.power(0.5,k)
EX = np.sum(p*k)
```

Example 3.11. Roll a die twice. Let X be the first roll and Y be the second roll. Let $Z = \max(X, Y)$. To compute the expectation $\mathbb{E}[Z]$, we first construct the sample space. Since there are two rolls, we can construct a table listing all possible pairs of outcomes. This will give us $\{(1, 1), (1, 2), \ldots, (6, 6)\}$. Now, we calculate Z, which is the max of the two rolls. So if we have $(1, 3)$, then the max will be 3, whereas if we have $(5, 2)$, then the max will be 5. We can complete a table as shown below.

	1	2	3	4	5	6
1	1	2	3	4	5	6
2	2	2	3	4	5	6
3	3	3	3	4	5	6
4	4	4	4	4	5	6
5	5	5	5	5	5	6
6	6	6	6	6	6	6

This table tell us that Z has 6 states. The PMF of Z can be determined by counting the number of times a state shows up in the table. Thus, we can show that

$$p_Z(1) = \frac{1}{36}, \ p_Z(2) = \frac{3}{36}, \ p_Z(3) = \frac{5}{36},$$
$$p_Z(4) = \frac{7}{36}, \ p_Z(5) = \frac{9}{36}, \ p_Z(6) = \frac{11}{36}.$$

The expectation of Z is therefore

$$\mathbb{E}[Z] = (1)\left(\frac{1}{36}\right) + (2)\left(\frac{3}{36}\right) + (3)\left(\frac{5}{36}\right)$$
$$+ (4)\left(\frac{7}{36}\right) + (5)\left(\frac{9}{36}\right) + (6)\left(\frac{11}{36}\right)$$
$$= \frac{161}{36}.$$

Example 3.12. Consider a game in which we flip a coin 3 times. The reward of the game is

- $1 if there are 2 heads
- $8 if there are 3 heads
- $0 if there are 0 or 1 head

There is a cost associated with the game. To enter the game, the player has to pay $1.50. We want to compute the net gain, on average.

To answer this question, we first note that the sample space contains 8 elements: HHH, HHT, HTH, THH, THT, TTH, HTT, TTT. Let X be the number of heads. Then the PMF of X is

$$p_X(0) = \frac{1}{8}, \ \ p_X(1) = \frac{3}{8}, \ \ p_X(2) = \frac{3}{8}, \ \ p_X(3) = \frac{1}{8}.$$

We then let Y be the reward. The PMF of Y can be found by "adding" the probabilities of X. This yields

$$p_Y(0) = p_X(0) + p_X(1) = \frac{4}{8}, \ \ p_Y(1) = p_X(2) = \frac{3}{8}, \ \ p_Y(8) = p_X(3) = \frac{1}{8}.$$

The expectation of Y is

$$\mathbb{E}[X] = (0)\left(\frac{4}{8}\right) + (1)\left(\frac{3}{8}\right) + (8)\left(\frac{1}{8}\right) = \frac{11}{8}.$$

Since the cost of the game is $\frac{12}{8}$, the net gain (on average) is $-\frac{1}{8}$.

3.4.2 Existence of expectation

Does every PMF have an expectation? No, because we can construct a PMF such that the expectation is undefined.

Example 3.13. Consider a random variable X with the following PMF:

$$p_X(k) = \frac{6}{\pi^2 k^2}, \qquad k = 1, 2, \ldots.$$

Using a result from algebra, one can show that $\sum_{k=1}^{\infty} \frac{1}{k^2} = \frac{\pi^2}{6}$. Therefore, $p_X(k)$ is a legitimate PMF because $\sum_{k=1}^{\infty} p_X(k) = 1$. However, the expectation diverges, because

$$\mathbb{E}[X] = \sum_{k=1}^{\infty} k p_X(k)$$

$$= \frac{6}{\pi^2} \sum_{k=1}^{\infty} \frac{1}{k} \to \infty,$$

where the limit is due to the harmonic series[a]: $1 + \frac{1}{2} + \frac{1}{3} + \cdots = \infty$.

---

[a] https://en.wikipedia.org/wiki/Harmonic_series_(mathematics)

A PMF has an expectation when it is **absolutely summable**.

Definition 3.5. *A discrete random variable X is **absolutely summable** if*

$$\mathbb{E}[|X|] \stackrel{\text{def}}{=} \sum_{x \in X(\Omega)} |x|\, p_X(x) < \infty. \tag{3.13}$$

This definition tells us that not all random variables have a finite expectation. This is a very important mathematical result, but its practical implication is arguably limited. Most of the random variables we use in practice are absolutely summable. Also, note that the property of absolute summability applies to discrete random variables. For continuous random variables, we have a parallel concept called **absolute integrability**, which will be discussed in the next chapter.

3.4.3 Properties of expectation

The expectation of a random variable has several useful properties. We list them below. Note that these properties apply to both discrete and continuous random variables.

Theorem 3.4. *The expectation of a random variable X has the following properties:*

(i) **Function.** *For any function g,*

$$\mathbb{E}[g(X)] = \sum_{x \in X(\Omega)} g(x)\, p_X(x).$$

(ii) **Linearity.** *For any function g and h,*

$$\mathbb{E}[g(X) + h(X)] = \mathbb{E}[g(X)] + \mathbb{E}[h(X)].$$

(iii) **Scale.** *For any constant c,*

$$\mathbb{E}[cX] = c\mathbb{E}[X].$$

(iv) **DC Shift.** *For any constant c,*

$$\mathbb{E}[X + c] = \mathbb{E}[X] + c.$$

Proof of (i): A pictorial proof of (i) is shown in **Figure 3.18**. The key idea is a change of variable.

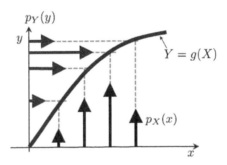

Figure 3.18: By letting $g(X) = Y$, the PMFs are not changed. What changes are the states.

When we have a function $Y = g(X)$, the PMF of Y will have impulses moved from x (the horizontal axis) to $g(x)$ (the vertical axis). The PMF values (i.e., the probabilities or the height of the stems), however, are not changed. If the mapping $g(X)$ is many-to-one, multiple PMF values will add to the same position. Therefore, when we compute $\mathbb{E}[g(X)]$, we compute the expectation along the vertical axis.

Practice Exercise 3.3. Prove statement (iii): For any constant c, $\mathbb{E}[cX] = c\mathbb{E}[X]$.

Solution. Recall the definition of expectation:

$$\mathbb{E}[cX] = \sum_{x \in X(\Omega)} (cx) p_X(x) = c \underbrace{\sum_{x \in X(\Omega)} x p_X(x)}_{=\mathbb{E}[X]} = c\mathbb{E}[X].$$

Statement (iii) is illustrated in **Figure 3.19**. Here, we assume that the original PMF has 3 states $X = 0, 1, 2$. We multiply X by a constant $c = 3$. This changes X to $cX = 0, 3, 6$. However, since the probabilities are not changed, the height of the PMF values remains. Therefore, when computing the expectation, we just multiply $\mathbb{E}[X]$ by c to get $c\mathbb{E}[X]$.

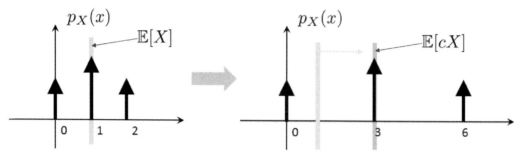

Figure 3.19: Pictorial representation of $\mathbb{E}[cX] = c\mathbb{E}[X]$. When we multiply X by c, we fix the probabilities but make the spacing between states wider/narrower.

Practice Exercise 3.4. Prove statement (ii): For any function g and h, $\mathbb{E}[g(X) + h(X)] = \mathbb{E}[g(X)] + \mathbb{E}[h(X)]$.

Solution. Recall the definition of expectation:

$$\mathbb{E}[g(X) + h(X)] = \sum_{x \in X(\Omega)} [g(x) + h(x)]p_X(x)$$

$$= \underbrace{\sum_{x \in X(\Omega)} g(x)p_X(x)}_{=\mathbb{E}[g(X)]} + \underbrace{\sum_{x \in X(\Omega)} h(x)p_X(x)}_{=\mathbb{E}[h(X)]}$$

$$= \mathbb{E}[g(X)] + \mathbb{E}[h(X)].$$

Practice Exercise 3.5. Prove statement (iv): For any constant c, $\mathbb{E}[X + c] = \mathbb{E}[X] + c$.

Solution. Recall the definition of expectation:

$$\mathbb{E}[X + c] = \sum_{x \in X(\Omega)} (x + c)p_X(x)$$

$$= \underbrace{\sum_{x \in X(\Omega)} x p_X(x)}_{=\mathbb{E}[X]} + c \cdot \underbrace{\sum_{x \in X(\Omega)} p_X(x)}_{=1}$$

$$= \mathbb{E}[X] + c.$$

This result is illustrated in **Figure 3.20**. As we add a constant to the random variable, its PMF values remain the same but their positions are shifted. Therefore, when computing the mean, the mean will be shifted accordingly.

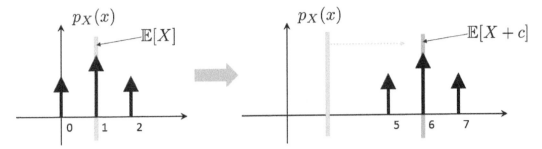

Figure 3.20: Pictorial representation of $\mathbb{E}[X+c] = \mathbb{E}[X]+c$. When we add c to X, we fix the probabilities and shift the entire PMF to the left or to the right.

Example 3.14. Let X be a random variable with four equally probable states $0, 1, 2, 3$. We want to compute the expectation $\mathbb{E}[\cos(\pi X/2)]$. To do so, we note that

$$\mathbb{E}[\cos(\pi X/2)] = \sum_{x \in X(\Omega)} \cos\left(\frac{\pi X}{2}\right) p_X(x)$$

$$= (\cos 0)\left(\frac{1}{4}\right) + (\cos\frac{\pi}{2})\left(\frac{1}{4}\right) + (\cos\frac{2\pi}{2})\left(\frac{1}{4}\right) + (\cos\frac{3\pi}{2})\left(\frac{1}{4}\right)$$

$$= \frac{1 + 0 + (-1) + 0}{4} = 0.$$

Example 3.15. Let X be a random variable with $\mathbb{E}[X] = 1$ and $\mathbb{E}[X^2] = 3$. We want to find the expectation $\mathbb{E}[(aX + b)^2]$. To do so, we realize that

$$\mathbb{E}[(aX + b)^2] \overset{(a)}{=} \mathbb{E}[a^2X^2 + 2abX + b^2] \overset{(b)}{=} a^2\mathbb{E}[X^2] + 2ab\mathbb{E}[X] + b^2 = 3a^2 + 2ab + b^2,$$

where (a) is due to expansion of the square, and (b) holds in two steps. The first step is to apply statement (ii) for individual functions of expectations, and the second step is to apply statement (iii) for scalar multiple of the expectations.

3.4.4 Moments and variance

Based on the concept of expectation, we can define a **moment**:

Definition 3.6. *The kth* **moment** *of a random variable* X *is*

$$\mathbb{E}[X^k] = \sum_x x^k p_X(x). \tag{3.14}$$

Essentially, the kth moment is the expectation applied to X^k. The definition follows from statement (i) of the expectation's properties. Using this definition, we note that $\mathbb{E}[X]$ is the first moment and $\mathbb{E}[X^2]$ is the second moment. Higher-order moments can be defined, but in practice they are less commonly used.

Example 3.16. Flip a coin 3 times. Let X be the number of heads. Then

$$p_X(0) = \frac{1}{8}, \ p_X(1) = \frac{3}{8}, \ p_X(2) = \frac{3}{8}, \ p_X(3) = \frac{1}{8}.$$

The second moment $\mathbb{E}[X^2]$ is

$$\mathbb{E}[X^2] = (0)^2 \left(\frac{1}{8}\right) + (1)^2 \left(\frac{3}{8}\right) + (2)^2 \left(\frac{3}{8}\right) + (4)^2 \left(\frac{1}{8}\right) = 3.$$

Example 3.17. Consider a random variable X with PMF

$$p_X(k) = \frac{1}{2^k}, \qquad k = 1, 2, \ldots.$$

The second moment $\mathbb{E}[X^2]$ is

$$\mathbb{E}[X^2] = \sum_{k=1}^{\infty} k^2 \left(\frac{1}{2}\right)^k = \frac{1}{2^2} \sum_{k=1}^{\infty} k(k-1+1) \left(\frac{1}{2}\right)^{k-2}$$

$$= \frac{1}{2^2} \sum_{k=1}^{\infty} k(k-1) \left(\frac{1}{2}\right)^{k-2} + \frac{1}{2^2} \sum_{k=1}^{\infty} k \left(\frac{1}{2}\right)^{k-2}$$

$$= \frac{1}{2^2} \left(\frac{2}{(1-\frac{1}{2})^3}\right) + \frac{1}{2} \left(\frac{1}{(1-\frac{1}{2})^2}\right) = 6.$$

Using the second moment, we can define the **variance** of a random variable.

Definition 3.7. *The* **variance** *of a random variable X is*

$$\mathrm{Var}[X] = \mathbb{E}[(X - \mu)^2], \qquad (3.15)$$

where $\mu = \mathbb{E}[X]$ is the expectation of X.

We denote σ^2 by $\mathrm{Var}[X]$. The square root of the variance, σ, is called the standard deviation of X. Like the expectation $\mathbb{E}[X]$, the variance $\mathrm{Var}[X]$ is computed using the ideal histogram PMF. It is the limiting object of the usual standard deviation we calculate from a dataset.

On a computer, computing the variance of a dataset is done by calling built-in commands such as `var` in MATLAB and `np.var` in Python. The standard deviation is computed using `std` and `np.std`, respectively.

```
% MATLAB code to compute the variance
X = rand(10000,1);
vX = var(X);
sX = std(X);
```

```
% Python code to compute the variance
import numpy as np
```

```
X = np.random.rand(10000)
vX = np.var(X)
sX = np.std(X)
```

What does the variance mean? It is a measure of the *deviation* of the random variable X relative to its mean. This deviation is quantified by the squared difference $(X - \mu)^2$. The expectation operator takes the average of the deviation, giving us a deterministic number $\mathbb{E}[(X - \mu)^2]$.

Theorem 3.5. *The variance of a random variable X has the following properties:*

(i) **Moment.**

$$\text{Var}[X] = \mathbb{E}[X^2] - \mathbb{E}[X]^2.$$

(ii) **Scale.** *For any constant c,*

$$\text{Var}[cX] = c^2 \text{Var}[X].$$

(iii) **DC Shift.** *For any constant c,*

$$\text{Var}[X + c] = \text{Var}[X].$$

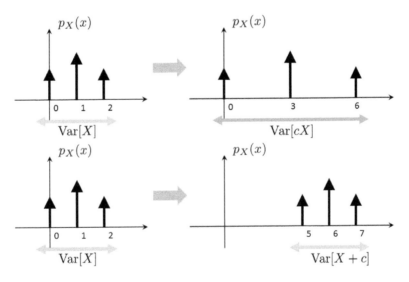

Figure 3.21: Pictorial representations of $\text{Var}[cX] = c^2 \text{Var}[X]$ and $\text{Var}[X + c] = \text{Var}[X]$.

Practice Exercise 3.6. Prove Theorem 3.5 above.

Solution. For statement (i), we show that

$$\text{Var}[X] = \mathbb{E}[(X - \mu)^2] = \mathbb{E}[X^2 - 2X\mu + \mu^2] = \mathbb{E}[X^2] - \mu^2.$$

Statement (ii) holds because $\mathbb{E}[cX] = c\mu$ and

$$\text{Var}[cX] = \mathbb{E}[(cX - \mathbb{E}[cX])^2]$$
$$= \mathbb{E}[(cX - c\mu)^2] = c^2\mathbb{E}[(X - \mu)^2] = c^2\text{Var}[X].$$

Statement (iii) holds because

$$\text{Var}[X + c] = \mathbb{E}[((X + c) - \mathbb{E}[X + c])^2] = \mathbb{E}[(X - \mathbb{E}[X])^2] = \text{Var}[X].$$

The properties above are useful in various ways. The first statement provides a link connecting variance and the second moment. Statement (ii) implies that when X is scaled by c, the variance should be scaled by c^2 because of the square in the second moment. Statement (iii) says that when X is shifted by a scalar c, the variance is unchanged. This is true because no matter how we shift the mean, the fluctuation of the random variable remains the same.

Practice Exercise 3.7. Flip a coin with probability p to get a head. Let X be a random variable denoting the outcome. The PMF of X is

$$p_X(0) = 1 - p, \qquad p_X(1) = p.$$

Find $\mathbb{E}[X]$, $\mathbb{E}[X^2]$ and $\text{Var}[X]$.

Solution. The expectation of X is

$$\mathbb{E}[X] = (0)p_X(0) + (1)p_X(1) = (0)(1 - p) + (1)(p) = p.$$

The second moment is

$$\mathbb{E}[X^2] = (0)^2 p_X(0) + (1)^2 p_X(1) = p.$$

The variance is

$$\text{Var}[X] = \mathbb{E}[X^2] - \mathbb{E}[X]^2 = p - p^2 = p(1 - p).$$

3.5 Common Discrete Random Variables

In the previous sections, we have conveyed three key concepts: one about the random variable, one about the PMF, and one about the mean. The next step is to introduce a few commonly used discrete random variables so that you have something concrete in your "toolbox." As we have mentioned before, these predefined random variables should be studied from a **synthesis** perspective (sometimes called **generative**). The plan for this section is to introduce several models, derive their theoretical properties, and discuss examples.

Note that some extra effort will be required to understand the *origins* of the random variables. The origins of random variables are usually overlooked, but they are more important than the equations. For example, we will shortly discuss the Poisson random variable

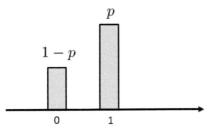

Figure 3.22: A Bernoulli random variable has two states with probability p and $1 - p$.

and its PMF $p_X(k) = \frac{\lambda^k e^{-\lambda}}{k!}$. Why is the Poisson random variable defined in this way? If you know how the Poisson PMF was originally derived, you will understand the assumptions made during the derivation. Consequently, you will know why Poisson is a good model for internet traffic, recommendation scores, and image sensors for computer vision applications. You will also know under what situation the Poisson model will fail. Understanding the *physics* behind the probability models is the focus of this section.

3.5.1 Bernoulli random variable

We start discussing the simplest random variable, namely the **Bernoulli random variable**. A Bernoulli random variable is a *coin-flip* random variable. The random variable has two states: either 1 or 0. The probability of getting 1 is p, and the probability of getting 0 is $1 - p$. See **Figure 3.22** for an illustration. Bernoulli random variables are useful for all kinds of binary state events: coin flip (H or T), binary bit (1 or 0), true or false, yes or no, present or absent, Democrat or Republican, etc.

To make these notions more precise, we define a Bernoulli random variable as follows.

Definition 3.8. *Let X be a* **Bernoulli random variable**. *Then, the PMF of X is*

$$p_X(0) = 1 - p, \qquad p_X(1) = p,$$

where $0 < p < 1$ is called the Bernoulli parameter. We write

$$X \sim \text{Bernoulli}(p)$$

to say that X is drawn from a Bernoulli distribution with a parameter p.

In this definition, the parameter p controls the probability of obtaining 1. In a coin-flip event, p is usually $\frac{1}{2}$, meaning that the coin is fair. However, for biased coins p is not necessarily $\frac{1}{2}$. For other situations such as binary bits (0 or 1), the probability of obtaining 1 could be very different from the probability of obtaining 0.

In MATLAB and Python, generating Bernoulli random variables can be done by calling the binomial random number generator `np.random.binomial` (Python) and `binornd` (MATLAB). When the parameter `n` is equal to 1, the binomial random variable is equivalent to a Bernoulli random variable. The MATLAB and Python codes to synthesize a Bernoulli random variable are shown below.

```
% MATLAB code to generate 1000 Bernoulli random variables
p = 0.5;
n = 1;
X = binornd(n,p,[1000,1]);
[num, ~] = hist(X, 10);
bar(linspace(0,1,10), num,'FaceColor',[0.4, 0.4, 0.8]);
```

```
# Python code to generate 1000 Bernoulli random variables
import numpy as np
import matplotlib.pyplot as plt
p = 0.5
n = 1
X = np.random.binomial(n,p,size=1000)
plt.hist(X,bins='auto')
```

An alternative method in Python is to call `stats.bernoulli.rvs` to generate random Bernoulli numbers.

```
# Python code to call scipy.stats library
import numpy as np
import matplotlib.pyplot as plt
import scipy.stats as stats
p = 0.5
X = stats.bernoulli.rvs(p,size=1000)
plt.hist(X,bins='auto');
```

Properties of Bernoulli random variables

Let us now derive a few key statistical properties of a Bernoulli random variable.

Theorem 3.6. *If $X \sim \text{Bernoulli}(p)$, then*

$$\mathbb{E}[X] = p, \qquad \mathbb{E}[X^2] = p, \qquad \text{Var}[X] = p(1-p).$$

Proof. The expectation can be computed as

$$\mathbb{E}[X] = (1)p_X(1) + (0)p_X(0) = (1)(p) + (0)(1-p) = p.$$

The second moment is

$$\mathbb{E}[X^2] = (1^2)(p) + (0^2)(1-p) = p.$$

Therefore, the variance is

$$\text{Var}[X] = \mathbb{E}[X^2] - \mu^2 = p - p^2 = p(1-p).$$

□

A useful property of the Python code is that we can construct an object **rv**. Then we can call **rv**'s attributes to determine its mean, variance, etc.

```
# Python code to generate a Bernoulli rv object
import numpy as np
import matplotlib.pyplot as plt
import scipy.stats as stats
p = 0.5
rv = stats.bernoulli(p)
mean, var = rv.stats(moments='mv')
print(mean, var)
```

In both MATLAB and Python, we can plot the PMF of a Bernoulli random variable, such as the one shown in **Figure 3.23**. To do this in MATLAB, we call the function `binopdf`, with the evaluation points specified by x.

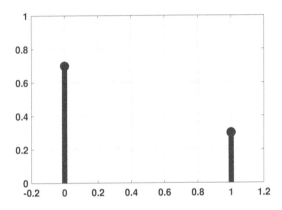

Figure 3.23: An example of a theoretical PMF (not the empirical histogram) plotted by MATLAB.

```
% MATLAB code to plot the PMF of a Bernoulli
p = 0.3;
x = [0,1];
f = binopdf(x,1,p);
stem(x, f, 'bo', 'LineWidth', 8);
```

In Python, we construct a random variable rv. With rv, we can call its PMF rv.pmf:

```
# Python code to plot the PMF of a Bernoulli
import numpy as np
import matplotlib.pyplot as plt
import scipy.stats as stats
p = 0.3
rv = stats.bernoulli(p)
x = np.linspace(0, 1, 2)
f = rv.pmf(x)
plt.plot(x, f, 'bo', ms=10);
plt.vlines(x, 0, f, colors='b', lw=5, alpha=0.5);
```

139

When will a Bernoulli random variable have the maximum variance?

Let us take a look at the variance of the Bernoulli random variable. For any given p, the variance is $p(1-p)$. This is a quadratic equation. If we let $V(p) = p(1-p)$, we can show that the maximum is attained at $p = 1/2$. To see this, take the derivative of $V(p)$ with respect to p. This will give us $\frac{d}{dp}V(p) = 1 - 2p$. Equating to zero yields $1 - 2p = 0$, so $p = 1/2$. We know that $p = 1/2$ is a maximum and not a minimum point because the second order derivative $V''(p) = -2$, which is negative. Therefore $V(p)$ is maximized at $p = 1/2$. Now, since $0 \le p \le 1$, we also know that $V(0) = 0$ and $V(1) = 0$. Therefore, the variance is minimized at $p = 0$ and $p = 1$. **Figure 3.24** shows a graph of the variance.

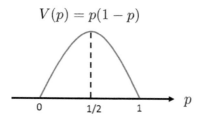

$$V(p) = p(1-p)$$

Figure 3.24: The variance of a Bernoulli reaches maximum at $p = 1/2$.

Does this result make sense? Why is the variance maximized at $p = 1/2$? If we think about this problem more carefully, we realize that a Bernoulli random variable represents a coin-flip experiment. If the coin is biased such that it always gives heads, on the one hand, it is certainly a bad coin. However, on the other hand, the variance is zero because there is nothing to vary; you will certainly get heads. The same situation happens if the coin is biased towards tails. However, if the coin is fair, i.e., $p = 1/2$, then the variance is large because we only have a 50% chance of getting a head or a tail whenever we flip a coin. Nothing is certain in this case. Therefore, the maximum variance happening at $p = 1/2$ matches our intuition.

Rademacher random variable

A slight variation of the Bernoulli random variable is the **Rademacher random variable**, which has two states: $+1$ and -1. The probability getting $+1$ and -1 is $1/2$. Therefore, the PMF of a Rademacher random variable is

$$p_X(-1) = \frac{1}{2}, \quad \text{and} \quad p_X(+1) = \frac{1}{2}.$$

Practice Exercise 3.8. Show that if X is a Rademacher random variable then $(X + 1)/2 \sim \text{Bernoulli}(1/2)$. Also show the converse: If $Y \sim \text{Bernoulli}(1/2)$ then $2Y - 1$ is a Rademacher random variable.

Solution. Since X can either be $+1$ or -1, we show that if $X = +1$ then $(X+1)/2 = 1$ and if $X = -1$ then $(X + 1)/2 = 0$. The probabilities of getting $+1$ and -1 are equal. Thus, the probabilities of getting $(X + 1)/2 = 1$ and 0 are also equal. So the resulting random variable is Bernoulli$(1/2)$. The other direction can be proved similarly.

Bernoulli in social networks: the Erdős-Rényi graph

The study of networks is a big branch of modern data science. It includes social networks, computer networks, traffic networks, etc. The history of network science is very long, but one of the most basic models of a network is the Erdős-Rényi graph, named after Paul Erdős and Alfréd Rényi. The underlying probabilistic model of the Erdős-Rényi graph is the Bernoulli random variable.

To see how a graph can be constructed from a Bernoulli random variable, we first introduce the concept of a **graph**. A graph contains two elements: nodes and edges. For node i and node j, we denote the edge connecting i and j as A_{ij}. Therefore, if we have N nodes, then we can construct a matrix A of size $N \times N$. We call this matrix the **adjacency matrix**. For example, the adjacency matrix

$$A = \begin{bmatrix} 0 & 1 & 1 & 0 \\ 1 & 0 & 0 & 0 \\ 1 & 0 & 0 & 1 \\ 0 & 0 & 1 & 0 \end{bmatrix}$$

will have edges for node pairs $(1, 2)$, $(1, 3)$, and $(3, 4)$. Note that in this example we assume that the adjacency matrix is symmetric, meaning that the graph is undirected. The "1" in the adjacency matrix indicates there is an edge, and "0" indicates there is no edge. So A represents a binary graph.

The Erdős-Rényi graph model says that the probability of getting an edge is an **independent** Bernoulli random variable. That is

$$A_{ij} \sim \text{Bernoulli}(p),$$

for $i < j$. If we model the graph in this way, then the parameter p will control the density of the graph. High values of p mean that there is a higher chance for an edge to be present.

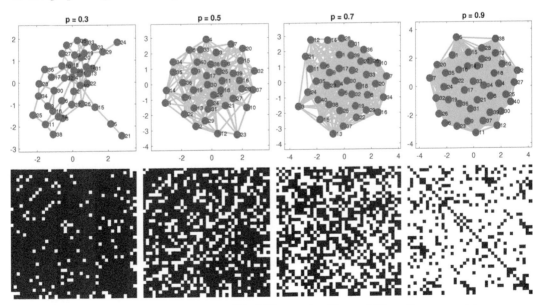

Figure 3.25: The Erdős-Rényi graph. [Top] The graphs. [Bottom] The adjacency matrices.

To illustrate the idea of an Erdős-Rényi graph, we show in **Figure 3.25** a graph of 40 nodes. The edges are randomly selected by flipping a Bernoulli random variable with parameter $p = 0.3, 0.5, 0.7, 0.9$. As we can see in the figure, a small value of p gives a graph with very sparse connectivity, whereas a large value of p gives a very densely connected graph. The bottom row of **Figure 3.25** shows the corresponding adjacency matrices. Here, a white pixel denotes "1" in the matrix and a black pixel denotes "0" in the matrix.

While Erdős-Rényi graphs are elementary, their variations can be realistic models of social networks. The **stochastic block model** is one such model. In a stochastic block model, nodes form small communities within a large network. For example, there are many majors in a university. Students within the same major tend to have more interactions than with students of another major. The stochastic block model achieves this goal by partitioning the nodes into communities. Within each community, the nodes can have a high degree of connectivity. Across different communities, the connectivity will be much lower. **Figure 3.26** illustrates a network and the corresponding adjacency matrix. In this example, the network has three communities.

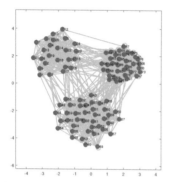 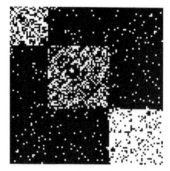

Figure 3.26: A stochastic block model containing three communities. [Left] The graph. [Right] The adjacency matrix.

In network analysis, one of the biggest problems is determining the community structure and recovering the underlying probabilities. The former task is about grouping the nodes into blocks. This is a nontrivial problem because in practice the nodes are never arranged nicely, as shown in **Figure 3.26**. For example, why should Alice be node 1 and Bob be node 2? Since we never know the correct ordering of the nodes, partitioning the nodes into blocks requires various estimation techniques such as clustering or iterative estimation. Recovering the underlying probability is also not easy. Given an adjacency matrix, why can we assume that the underlying network is a stochastic block model? Even if the model is correct, there will be imperfect grouping in the previous step. As such, estimating the underlying probability in the presence of these uncertainties would pose additional challenges.

Today, network analysis remains one of the hottest areas in data science. Its importance derives from its broad scope and impact. It can be used to analyze social networks, opinion polls, marketing, or even genome analysis. Nevertheless, the starting point of these advanced subjects is the Bernoulli random variable, the random variable of a coin flip!

3.5.2 Binomial random variable

Suppose we flip the coin n times count the number of heads. Since each coin flip is a random variable (Bernoulli), the sum is also a random variable. It turns out that this new random variable is the **binomial random variable**.

Definition 3.9. *Let X be a **binomial random variable**. Then, the PMF of X is*

$$p_X(k) = \binom{n}{k} p^k (1-p)^{n-k}, \qquad k = 0, 1, \ldots, n,$$

where $0 < p < 1$ is the binomial parameter, and n is the total number of states. We write

$$X \sim \text{Binomial}(n, p)$$

to say that X is drawn from a binomial distribution with a parameter p of size n.

To understand the meaning of a binomial random variable, consider a simple experiment consisting of flipping a coin three times. We know that all possible cases are HHH, HHT, HTH, THH, TTH, THT, HTT and TTT. Now, suppose we define $X =$ number of heads. We want to write down the probability mass function. Effectively, we ask: What is the probability of getting 0 head, one head, two heads, and three heads? We can, of course, count and get the answer right away for a fair coin. However, suppose the coin is unfair, i.e., the probability of getting a head is p whereas that of a tail is $1 - p$. The probability of getting each of the 8 cases is shown in **Figure 3.27** below.

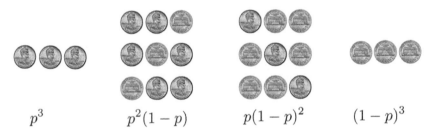

$$p^3 \qquad\qquad p^2(1-p) \qquad\qquad p(1-p)^2 \qquad\qquad (1-p)^3$$

Figure 3.27: The probability of getting k heads out of $n = 3$ coins.

Here are the detailed calculations. Let us start with $X = 3$.

$$\begin{aligned}
p_X(3) &= \mathbb{P}[\{\text{HHH}\}] \\
&= \mathbb{P}[\{\text{H}\} \cap \{\text{H}\} \cap \{\text{H}\}] \\
&\overset{(a)}{=} \mathbb{P}[\{\text{H}\}]\mathbb{P}[\{\text{H}\}]\mathbb{P}[\{\text{H}\}] \\
&\overset{(b)}{=} p^3,
\end{aligned}$$

where (a) holds because the three events are independent. (Recall that if A and B are independent then $\mathbb{P}[A \cap B] = \mathbb{P}[A]\mathbb{P}[B]$.) (b) holds because each $\mathbb{P}[\{\text{H}\}] = p$ by definition. With exactly the same argument, we can show that $p_X(0) = \mathbb{P}[\{\text{TTT}\}] = (1-p)^3$.

Now, let us look at $p_X(2)$, i.e., 2 heads. This probability can be calculated as follows:

$$p_X(2) = \mathbb{P}[\{HHT\} \cup \{HTH\} \cup \{THH\}]$$
$$\stackrel{(c)}{=} \mathbb{P}[\{HHT\}] + \mathbb{P}[\{HTH\}] + \mathbb{P}[\{THH\}]$$
$$\stackrel{(d)}{=} p^2(1-p) + p^2(1-p) + p^2(1-p) = 3p^2(1-p),$$

where (c) holds because the three events HHT, HTH and THH are disjoint in the sample space. Note that we are not using the independence argument in (c) but the disjoint argument. We should not confuse the two. The step in (d) uses independence, because each coin flip is independent.

The above calculation shows an interesting phenomenon: Although the three events HHT, HTH, and THH are different (in fact, disjoint), the number of heads in all the cases is the same. This happens because when counting the number of heads, the *ordering* of the heads and tails does not matter. So the same problem can be formulated as finding the number of combinations of { 2 heads and 1 tail }, which in our case is $\binom{3}{2} = 3$.

To complete the story, let us also try $p_X(1)$. This probability is

$$p_X(1) = \mathbb{P}[\{TTH\} \cup \{HTT\} \cup \{THT\}] = 3p(1-p)^2.$$

Again, we see that the combination $\binom{3}{1} = 3$ appears in front of the $p(1-p)^2$.

In general, the way to interpret the binomial random variable is to decouple the probabilities p, $(1-p)$, and the number of combinations $\binom{n}{k}$:

$$p_X(k) = \underbrace{\binom{n}{k}}_{\text{number of combinations}} \underbrace{p^k}_{\text{prob getting } k \text{ H's}} \underbrace{(1-p)^{n-k}}_{\text{prob getting } n-k \text{ T's}}.$$

The running index k should go with $0, 1, \ldots, n$. It starts with 0 because there could be zero heads in the sample space. Furthermore, we note that in this definition, two parameters are driving a binomial random variable: the number of Bernoulli trials n and the underlying probability for each coin flip p. As such, the notation for a binomial random variable is Binomial(n, p), with two arguments.

The histogram of a binomial random variable is shown in **Figure 3.28**(a). Here, we consider the example where $n = 10$ and $p = 0.5$. To generate the histogram, we use 5000 samples. In MATLAB and Python, generating binomial random variables as in **Figure 3.28**(a) can be done by calling `binornd` and `np.random.binomial`.

```
% MATLAB code to generate 5000 Binomial random variables
p = 0.5;
n = 10;
X = binornd(n,p,[5000,1]);
[num, ~] = hist(X, 10);
bar( num,'FaceColor',[0.4, 0.4, 0.8]);
```

```
# Python code to generate 5000 Binomial random variables
import numpy as np
import matplotlib.pyplot as plt
```

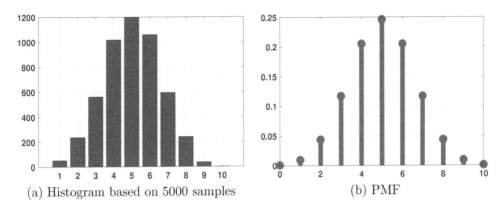

(a) Histogram based on 5000 samples   (b) PMF

Figure 3.28: An example of a binomial distribution with $n = 10$, $p = 0.5$.

```
p = 0.5
n = 10
X = np.random.binomial(n,p,size=5000)
plt.hist(X,bins='auto');
```

Generating the ideal PMF of a binomial random variable as shown in **Figure 3.28**(b) can be done by calling `binopdf` in MATLAB. In Python, we can define a random variable rv through `stats.binom`, and call the PMF using `rv.pmf`.

```
% MATLAB code to generate a binomial PMF
p = 0.5;
n = 10;
x = 0:10;
f = binopdf(x,n,p);
stem(x, f, 'o', 'LineWidth', 8, 'Color', [0.8, 0.4, 0.4]);
```

```
# Python code to generate a binomial PMF
import numpy as np
import matplotlib.pyplot as plt
import scipy.stats as stats
p = 0.5
n = 10
rv = stats.binom(n,p)
x  = np.arange(11)
f  = rv.pmf(x)
plt.plot(x, f, 'bo', ms=10);
plt.vlines(x, 0, f, colors='b', lw=5, alpha=0.5);
```

The shape of the binomial PMF is shown in **Figure 3.29**. In this set of figures, we vary one of the two parameters n and p while keeping the other fixed. In **Figure 3.29**(a), we fix $n = 60$ and plot three sets of $p = 0.1, 0.5, 0.9$. For small p the PMF is skewed towards the left, and for large p the PMF is skewed toward the right. **Figure 3.29**(b) shows the PMF for a fixed $p = 0.5$. As we increase n, the centroid of the PMF moves towards the right. Thus we should expect the mean of a binomial random variable to increase with p. Another interesting observation is that as n increases, the shape of the PMF approaches the Gaussian function (the bell-shaped curve). We will explain the reason for this when we discuss the Central Limit Theorem.

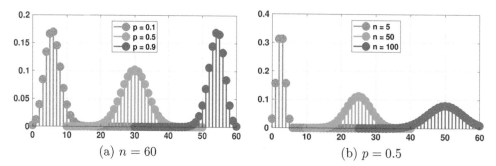

(a) $n = 60$ (b) $p = 0.5$

Figure 3.29: PMFs of a binomial random variable $X \sim \text{Binomial}(n, p)$. (a) We assume that $n = 60$. By varying the probability p, we see that the PMF shifts from the left to the right, and the shape changes. (b) We assume that $p = 0.5$. By varying the number of trials, the PMF shifts and the shape becomes more "bell-shaped."

The expectation, second moment, and variance of a binomial random variable are summarized in Theorem 3.7.

Theorem 3.7. *If* $X \sim \text{Binomial}(n, p)$, *then*

$$\mathbb{E}[X] = np,$$
$$\mathbb{E}[X^2] = np(np + (1 - p)),$$
$$\text{Var}[X] = np(1 - p).$$

We will prove that $\mathbb{E}[X] = np$ using the first principle. For $\mathbb{E}[X^2]$ and $\text{Var}[X]$, we will skip the proofs here and will introduce a "shortcut" later.

Proof. Let us start with the definition.

$$\mathbb{E}[X] = \sum_{k=0}^{n} k \cdot \binom{n}{k} p^k (1 - p)^{n-k}$$

$$= \sum_{k=0}^{n} k \cdot \frac{n!}{k!(n-k)!} p^k (1 - p)^{n-k}$$

$$= \underbrace{0 \cdot \frac{n!}{0!(n-0)!} p^0 (1 - p)^{n-0}}_{0} + \sum_{k=1}^{n} k \cdot \frac{n!}{k!(n-k)!} p^k (1 - p)^{n-k}$$

$$= \sum_{k=1}^{n} \frac{n!}{(k-1)!(n-k)!} p^k (1 - p)^{n-k}.$$

Note that we have shifted the index from $k = 0$ to $k = 1$. Now let us apply a trick:

$$\mathbb{E}[X] = \sum_{k=1}^{n} \frac{n!}{(k-1)!(n-k)!} p^k (1-p)^{n-k}$$

$$= \sum_{k=1}^{n} \frac{n!}{(k-1)!(n-k-1+1)!} p^k (1-p)^{n-k}.$$

Using this trick, we can show that

$$\sum_{k=1}^{n} \frac{n!}{(k-1)!(n-k-1+1)!} p^k (1-p)^{n-k}$$

$$= \sum_{k=1}^{n} \frac{n!}{(k-1)!((n-1)-(k-1))!} p^k (1-p)^{n-k}$$

$$= \sum_{k=1}^{n} \frac{n(n-1)!}{(k-1)!((n-1)-(k-1))!} p^k (1-p)^{n-k}$$

$$= np \sum_{k=1}^{n} \frac{(n-1)!}{(k-1)!((n-1)-(k-1))!} p^{k-1} (1-p)^{n-k}$$

With a simple substitution of $\ell = k - 1$, the above equation can be rewritten as

$$\mathbb{E}[X] = np \cdot \sum_{\ell=0}^{n-1} \frac{(n-1)!}{\ell!((n-1)-\ell)!} p^\ell (1-p)^{n-1-\ell}$$

$$= np \cdot \underbrace{\sum_{\ell=0}^{n-1} \binom{n-1}{k} p^\ell (1-p)^{n-1-\ell}}_{\text{summing PMF of Binomial}(n-1,p)} = np.$$

$\square$

In MATLAB, the mean and variance of a binomial random variable can be found by calling the command binostat(n,p) (MATLAB).

In Python, the command is rv = stats.binom(n,p) followed by calling rv.stats.

```
% MATLAB code to compute the mean and var of a binomial rv
p = 0.5;
n = 10;
[M,V] = binostat(n, p)
```

```
# Python code to compute the mean and var of a binomial rv
import scipy.stats as stats
p = 0.5
n = 10
rv = stats.binom(n,p)
M, V = rv.stats(moments='mv')
print(M, V)
```

An alternative view of the binomial random variable. As we discussed, the origin of a binomial random variable is the sum of a sequence of Bernoulli random variables. Because of this intrinsic definition, we can derive some useful results by exploiting this fact. To do so, let us define $I_1, \ldots, I_n$ as a sequence of Bernoulli random variables with $I_j \sim \text{Bernoulli}(p)$ for all $i = 1, \ldots, n$. Then the resulting variable

$$X = I_1 + I_2 + \cdots + I_n$$

is a binomial random variable of size n and parameter p. Using this definition, we can compute the expectation as follows:

$$
\begin{aligned}
\mathbb{E}[X] &= \mathbb{E}[I_1 + I_2 + \cdots + I_n] \\
&\overset{(a)}{=} \mathbb{E}[I_1] + \mathbb{E}[I_2] + \cdots + \mathbb{E}[I_n] \\
&= p + p + \cdots + p \\
&= np.
\end{aligned}
$$

In this derivation, the step (a) depends on a useful fact about expectation (which we have not yet proved): For any two random variables X and Y, it holds that $\mathbb{E}[X+Y] = \mathbb{E}[X] + E[Y]$. Therefore, we can show that the expectation of X is np. This line of argument not only simplifies the proof but also provides a good intuition of the expectation. If each coin flip has an expectation of $\mathbb{E}[I_i] = p$, then the expectation of the sum should be simply n times of p, given np.

How about the variance? Again, we are going to use a very useful fact about variance: If two random variables X and Y are independent, then $\text{Var}[X + Y] = \text{Var}[X] + \text{Var}[Y]$. With this result, we can show that

$$
\begin{aligned}
\text{Var}[X] &= \text{Var}[I_1 + \cdots + I_n] \\
&= \text{Var}[I_1] + \cdots + \text{Var}[I_n] \\
&= p(1 - p) + \cdots + p(1 - p) \\
&= np(1 - p).
\end{aligned}
$$

Finally, using the fact that $\text{Var}[X] = \mathbb{E}[X^2] - \mu^2$, we can show that

$$
\begin{aligned}
\mathbb{E}[X^2] &= \text{Var}[X] + \mu^2 \\
&= np(1 - p) + (np)^2.
\end{aligned}
$$

Practice Exercise 3.9. Show that the binomial PMF sums to 1.

Solution. We use the binomial theorem to prove this result:

$$\sum_{k=0}^{n} p_X(k) = \sum_{k=0}^{n} \binom{n}{k} p^k (1 - p)^{n-k} = (p + (1 - p))^n = 1.$$

The CDF of the binomial random variable is not very informative. It is basically the cumulative sum of the PMF:

$$F_X(k) = \sum_{\ell=0}^{k} \binom{n}{\ell} p^\ell (1 - p)^{n-\ell}.$$

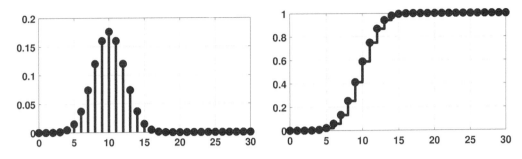

Figure 3.30: PMF and CDF of a binomial random variable $X \sim \text{Binomial}(n, p)$.

The shapes of the PMF and the CDF is shown in **Figure 3.30**.

In MATLAB, plotting the CDF of a binomial can be done by calling the function binocdf. You may also call f = binopdf(x,n,p), and define F = cumsum(f) as the cumulative sum of the PMF. In Python, the corresponding command is rv = stats.binom(n,p) followed by rv.cdf.

```
% MATLAB code to compute the mean and var of a binomial rv
x = 0:10;
p = 0.5;
n = 10;
F = binocdf(x,n,p);
figure; stairs(x,F,'.-','LineWidth',4,'MarkerSize',30);
```

```
# Python code to compute the mean and var of a binomial rv
import numpy as np
import matplotlib.pyplot as plt
import scipy.stats as stats
p = 0.5
n = 10
rv = stats.binom(n,p)
x   = np.arange(11)
F   = rv.cdf(x)
plt.plot(x, F, 'bo', ms=10);
plt.vlines(x, 0, F, colors='b', lw=5, alpha=0.5);
```

3.5.3 Geometric random variable

In some applications, we are interested in trying a binary experiment until we succeed. For example, we may want to keep calling someone until the person picks up the call. In this case, the random variable can be defined as the outcome of many failures followed by a final success. This is called the **geometric random variable**.

Definition 3.10. *Let X be a **geometric random variable**. Then, the PMF of X is*

$$p_X(k) = (1 - p)^{k-1} p, \qquad k = 1, 2, \dots,$$

> *where $0 < p < 1$ is the geometric parameter. We write*
>
> $$X \sim \text{Geometric}(p)$$
>
> *to say that X is drawn from a geometric distribution with a parameter p.*

A geometric random variable is easy to understand. We define it as Bernoulli trials with $k - 1$ consecutive failures followed by one success. This can be seen from the definition:

$$p_X(k) = \underbrace{(1-p)^{k-1}}_{k-1 \text{ failures}} \underbrace{p}_{\text{final success}}.$$

Note that in geometric random variables, there is no $\binom{n}{k}$ because we must have $k - 1$ consecutive failures before one success. There is no alternative combination of the sequence.

The histogram and PMF of a geometric random variable are illustrated in **Figure 3.31**. Here, we assume that $p = 0.5$.

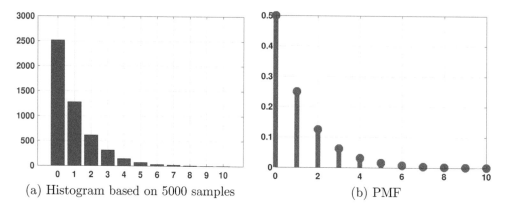

(a) Histogram based on 5000 samples   (b) PMF

Figure 3.31: An example of a geometric distribution with $p = 0.5$.

In MATLAB, generating geometric random variables can be done by calling the commands geornd. In Python, it is np.random.geometric.

```
% MATLAB code to generate 1000 geometric random variables
p = 0.5;
X = geornd(p,[5000,1]);
[num, ~] = hist(X, 0:10);
bar(0:10, num, 'FaceColor',[0.4, 0.4, 0.8]);
```

```
# Python code to generate 1000 geometric random variables
import numpy as np
import matplotlib.pyplot as plt
p = 0.5
X = np.random.geometric(p,size=1000)
plt.hist(X,bins='auto');
```

To generate the PMF plots, in MATLAB we call geopdf and in Python we call rv = stats.geom followed by rv.pmf.

```
% MATLAB code to generate geometric PMF
p = 0.5; x = 0:10;
f = geopdf(x,p);
stem(x, f, 'o', 'LineWidth', 8, 'Color', [0.8, 0.4, 0.4]);
```

```
# Python code to generate 1000 geometric random variables
import numpy as np
import matplotlib.pyplot as plt
import scipy.stats as stats
x  = np.arange(1,11)
rv = stats.geom(p)
f  = rv.pmf(x)
plt.plot(x, f, 'bo', ms=8, label='geom pmf')
plt.vlines(x, 0, f, colors='b', lw=5, alpha=0.5)
```

Practice Exercise 3.10. Show that the geometric PMF sums to one.

Solution. We can apply infinite series to show the result:

$$\sum_{k=1}^{\infty} p_X(k) = \sum_{k=1}^{\infty} (1-p)^{k-1} p$$

$$= p \cdot \sum_{k=1}^{\infty} (1-p)^{k-1}, \qquad \ell = k - 1$$

$$= p \cdot \sum_{\ell=0}^{\infty} (1-p)^{\ell}$$

$$= p \cdot \frac{1}{1-(1-p)} = 1.$$

It is interesting to compare the shape of the PMFs for various values of p. In **Figure 3.32** we show the PMFs. We vary the parameter $p = 0.25, 0.5, 0.9$. For small p, the PMF starts with a low value and decays at a slow speed. The opposite happens for a large p, where the PMF starts with a high value and decays rapidly.

Furthermore, we can derive the following properties of the geometric random variable.

Theorem 3.8. If $X \sim \text{Geometric}(p)$, then

$$\mathbb{E}[X] = \frac{1}{p}, \qquad \mathbb{E}[X^2] = \frac{2}{p^2} - \frac{1}{p}, \tag{3.16}$$

$$\text{Var}[X] = \frac{1-p}{p^2}.$$

Proof. We will prove that the mean is $1/p$ and leave the second moment and variance as

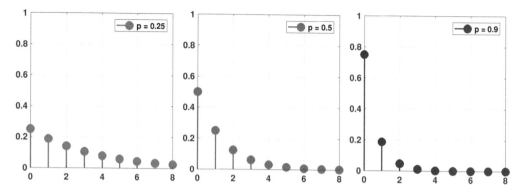

Figure 3.32: PMFs of a geometric random variable $X \sim$ Geometric(p).

an exercise.

$$\mathbb{E}[X] = \sum_{k=1}^{\infty} kp(1-p)^{k-1} = p \left(\sum_{k=1}^{\infty} k(1-p)^{k-1} \right) \overset{(a)}{=} p \left(\frac{1}{(1-(1-p))^2} \right) = \frac{1}{p},$$

where (a) follows from the infinite series identity in Chapter 1.

$\square$

3.5.4 Poisson random variable

In many physical systems, the arrivals of events are typically modeled as a Poisson random variable, e.g., photon arrivals, electron emissions, and telephone call arrivals. In social networks, the number of conversations per user can also be modeled as a Poisson. In e-commerce, the number of transactions per paying user is again modeled using a Poisson.

Definition 3.11. *Let X be a* **Poisson random variable.** *Then, the PMF of X is*

$$p_X(k) = \frac{\lambda^k}{k!} e^{-\lambda}, \qquad k = 0, 1, 2, \dots,$$

where $\lambda > 0$ is the Poisson rate. We write

$$X \sim \text{Poisson}(\lambda)$$

to say that X is drawn from a Poisson distribution with a parameter λ.

In this definition, the parameter λ determines the **rate** of the arrival. The histogram and PMF of a Poisson random variable are illustrated in **Figure 3.33**. Here, we assume that $\lambda = 1$.

The MATLAB code and Python code used to generate the histogram are shown below.

```
% MATLAB code to generate 5000 Poisson numbers
lambda = 1;
X = poissrnd(lambda,[5000,1]);
```

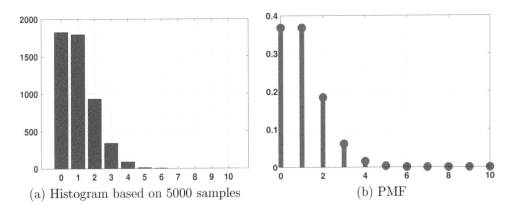

(a) Histogram based on 5000 samples   (b) PMF

Figure 3.33: An example of a Poisson distribution with $\lambda = 1$.

```
[num, ~] = hist(X, 0:10);
bar(0:10, num, 'FaceColor',[0.4, 0.4, 0.8]);
```

```
# Python code to generate 5000 Poisson random variables
import numpy as np
import matplotlib.pyplot as plt
lambd = 1
X = np.random.poisson(lambd,size=5000)
plt.hist(X,bins='auto');
```

For the PMF, in MATLAB we can call `poisspdf`, and in Python we can call `rv.pmf` with `rv = stats.poisson`.

```
% MATLAB code to plot the Poisson PMF
lambda = 1;
x = 0:10;
f = poisspdf(x,lambda);
stem(x, f, 'o', 'LineWidth', 8, 'Color', [0.8, 0.4, 0.4]);
```

```
# Python code to plot the Poisson PMF
import numpy as np
import matplotlib.pyplot as plt
import scipy.stats as stats
x = np.arange(0,11)
rv = stats.poisson(lambd)
f = rv.pmf(x)
plt.plot(x, f, 'bo', ms=8, label='geom pmf')
plt.vlines(x, 0, f, colors='b', lw=5, alpha=0.5)
```

The shape of the Poisson PMF changes with λ. As illustrated in **Figure 3.34**, $p_X(k)$ is more concentrated at lower values for smaller λ and becomes spread out for larger λ. Thus, we should expect that the mean and variance of a Poisson random variable will change together as a function of λ. In the same figure, we show the CDF of a Poisson random variable. The CDF of a Poisson is

$$F_X(k) = \mathbb{P}[X \le k] = \sum_{\ell=0}^{k} \frac{\lambda^\ell}{\ell!} e^{-\lambda}. \tag{3.17}$$

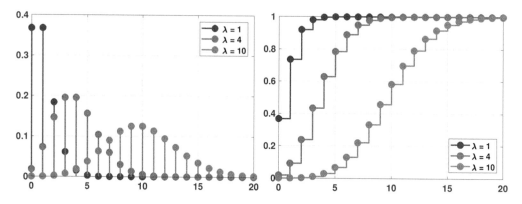

Figure 3.34: A Poisson random variable using different λ's. [Left] Probability mass function $p_X(k)$. [Right] Cumulative distribution function $F_X(k)$.

Example 3.18. Let X be a Poisson random variable with parameter λ. Find $\mathbb{P}[X > 4]$ and $\mathbb{P}[X \le 5]$.

Solution.

$$\mathbb{P}[X > 4] = 1 - \mathbb{P}[X \le 4] = 1 - \sum_{k=0}^{4} \frac{\lambda^k}{k!} e^{-\lambda},$$

$$\mathbb{P}[X \le 5] = \sum_{k=0}^{5} \frac{\lambda^k}{k!} e^{-\lambda}.$$

Practice Exercise 3.11. Show that the Poisson PMF sums to 1.

Solution. We use the exponential series to prove this result:

$$\sum_{k=0}^{\infty} p_X(k) = \sum_{k=0}^{\infty} \frac{\lambda^k}{k!} e^{-\lambda} = e^{-\lambda} \cdot \underbrace{\sum_{k=0}^{\infty} \frac{\lambda^k}{k!}}_{=e^\lambda} = 1.$$

Poisson random variables in practice

(1) Computational photography. In computational photography, the Poisson random variable is one of the most widely used models for photon arrivals. The reason pertains to the origin of the Poisson random variable, which we will discuss shortly. When photons are emitted from the source, they travel through the medium as a sequence of independent events. During the integration period of the camera, the photons are accumulated to generate a voltage that is then translated to digital bits.

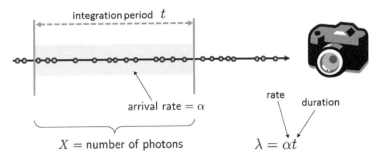

Figure 3.35: The Poisson random variable can be used to model photon arrivals.

If we assume that the photon arrival rate is α (photons per second), and suppose that the total amount of integration time is t, then the average number of photons that the sensor can see is αt. Let X be the number of photons seen during the integration time. Then if we follow the Poisson model, we can write down the PMF of X:

$$\mathbb{P}[X = k] = \frac{(\alpha t)^k}{k!} e^{-\alpha t}.$$

Therefore, if a pixel is bright, meaning that α is large, then X will have a higher likelihood of landing on a large number.

(2) Traffic model. The Poisson random variable can be used in many other problems. For example, we can use it to model the number of passengers on a bus or the number of spam phone calls. The required modification to **Figure 3.35** is almost trivial: merely replace the photons with your favorite cartoons, e.g., a person or a phone, as shown in **Figure 3.36**. In the United States, shared-ride services such as Uber and Lyft need to model the vacant cars and the passengers. As long as they have an arrival rate and certain degrees of independence between events, the Poisson random variable will be a good model.

As you can see from these examples, the Poisson random variable has broad applicability. Before we continue our discussion of its applications, let us introduce a few concepts related to the Poisson random variable.

Properties of a Poisson random variable

We now derive the mean and variance of a Poisson random variable.

Theorem 3.9. *If* $X \sim \text{Poisson}(\lambda)$, *then*

$$\mathbb{E}[X] = \lambda, \qquad \mathbb{E}[X^2] = \lambda + \lambda^2, \tag{3.18}$$
$$\text{Var}[X] = \lambda.$$

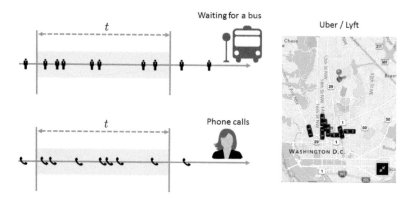

Figure 3.36: The Poisson random variable can be used to model passenger arrivals and the number of phone calls, and can be used by Uber or Lyft to provide shared rides.

Proof. Let us first prove the mean. It can be shown that

$$\mathbb{E}[X] = \sum_{k=0}^{\infty} k \cdot \frac{\lambda^k}{k!} e^{-\lambda} = \sum_{k=1}^{\infty} \frac{\lambda^k}{(k-1)!} e^{-\lambda}$$

$$= \lambda e^{-\lambda} \sum_{k=1}^{\infty} \frac{\lambda^{k-1}}{(k-1)!} = \lambda e^{-\lambda} \sum_{\ell=0}^{\infty} \frac{\lambda^\ell}{\ell!} = \lambda e^{-\lambda} e^{\lambda} = \lambda.$$

The second moment can be computed as

$$\mathbb{E}[X^2] = \sum_{k=0}^{\infty} k^2 \cdot \frac{\lambda^k}{k!} e^{-\lambda}$$

$$= \sum_{k=0}^{\infty} k \cdot \frac{\lambda^k}{(k-1)!} e^{-\lambda}$$

$$= \sum_{k=0}^{\infty} (k-1+1) \cdot \frac{\lambda^k}{(k-1)!} e^{-\lambda}$$

$$= \sum_{k=1}^{\infty} (k-1) \cdot \frac{\lambda^k}{(k-1)!} e^{-\lambda} + \sum_{k=1}^{\infty} \frac{\lambda^k}{(k-1)!} e^{-\lambda}$$

$$= \lambda^2 \cdot \underbrace{\sum_{k=2}^{\infty} \frac{\lambda^{k-2} e^{-\lambda}}{(k-2)!}}_{=1} + \lambda \cdot \underbrace{\sum_{k=1}^{\infty} \frac{\lambda^{k-1} e^{-\lambda}}{(k-1)!}}_{=1}.$$

The variance can be computed using $\mathrm{Var}[X] = \mathbb{E}[X^2] - \mu^2$.

$\square$

To compute the mean and variance of a Poisson random variable, we can call `poisstat` in MATLAB and `rv.stats(moments='mv')` in Python.

```
% MATLAB code to compute Poisson statistics
lambda = 1;
[M,V] = poisstat(lambda);
```

```
# Python code to compute Poisson statistics
import scipy.stats as stats
lambd = 1
rv = stats.poisson(lambd)
M, V = rv.stats(moments='mv')
```

The Poisson random variable is special in the sense that the mean and the variance are equal. That is, if the mean arrival number is higher, the variance is also higher. This is very different from some other random variables, e.g., the normal random variable where the mean and variance are independent. For certain engineering applications such as photography, this plays an important role in defining the signal-to-noise ratio. We will come back to this point later.

Origin of the Poisson random variable

We now address one of the most important questions about the Poisson random variable: Where does it come from? Answering this question is useful because the derivation process will reveal the underlying assumptions that lead to the Poisson PMF. When you change the problem setting, you will know when the Poisson PMF will hold and when the Poisson PMF will fail.

Our approach to addressing this problem is to consider the photon arrival process. (As we have shown, there is conceptually no difference if you replace the photons with pedestrians, passengers, or phone calls.) Our derivation follows the argument of J. Goodman, *Statistical Optics*, Section 3.7.2.

To begin with, we consider a photon arrival process. The total number of photons observed over an integration time t is defined as $X(t)$. Because $X(t)$ is a Poisson random variable, its arguments must be integers. The probability of observing $X(t) = k$ is therefore $\mathbb{P}[X(t) = k]$. **Figure 3.37** illustrates the notations and concepts.

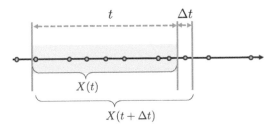

Figure 3.37: Notations for deriving the Poisson PMF.

We propose three hypotheses with the photon arrival process:

- For sufficiently small Δt, the probability of a small impulse occurring in the time interval $[t, t + \Delta t]$ is equal to the product of Δt and the rate λ, i.e.,

$$\mathbb{P}[X(t + \Delta t) - X(t) = 1] = \lambda \Delta t.$$

This is a linearity assumption, which typically holds for a short duration of time.

- For sufficiently small Δt, the probability that more than one impulse falls in Δt is negligible. Thus, we have that $\mathbb{P}[X(t + \Delta t) - X(t) = 0] = 1 - \lambda\Delta t$.

- The number of impulses in non-overlapping time intervals is independent.

The significance of these three hypotheses is that if the underlying photon arrival process violates any of these assumptions, then the Poisson PMF will not hold. One example is the presence of scattering effects, where a photon has a certain probability of going off due to the scattering medium and a certain probability of coming back. In this case, the events will no longer be independent.

Assuming that these hypotheses hold, then at time $t + \Delta t$, the probability of observing $X(t + \Delta t) = k$ can be computed as

$$
\begin{aligned}
&\mathbb{P}[X(t + \Delta t) = k] \\
&= \mathbb{P}[X(t) = k] \cdot \underbrace{(1 - \lambda\Delta t)}_{=\mathbb{P}[X(t+\Delta t)-X(t)=0]} + \mathbb{P}[X(t) = k - 1] \cdot \underbrace{(\lambda\Delta t)}_{=\mathbb{P}[X(t+\Delta t)-X(t)=1]} \\
&= \mathbb{P}[X(t) = k] - \mathbb{P}[X(t) = k]\lambda\Delta t + \mathbb{P}[X(t) = k - 1]\lambda\Delta t.
\end{aligned}
$$

By rearranging the terms we show that

$$
\frac{\mathbb{P}[X(t + \Delta t) = k] - \mathbb{P}[X(t) = k]}{\Delta t} = \lambda\left(\mathbb{P}[X(t) = k - 1] - \mathbb{P}[X(t) = k]\right).
$$

Setting the limit of $\Delta t \to 0$, we arrive at an ordinary differential equation

$$
\frac{d}{dt}\mathbb{P}[X(t) = k] = \lambda\left(\mathbb{P}[X(t) = k - 1] - \mathbb{P}[X(t) = k]\right). \tag{3.19}
$$

We claim that the Poisson PMF, i.e.,

$$
\mathbb{P}[X(t) = k] = \frac{(\lambda t)^k}{k!}e^{-\lambda t},
$$

would solve this differential equation. To see this, we substitute the PMF into the equation. The left-hand side gives us

$$
\begin{aligned}
\frac{d}{dt}\mathbb{P}[X(t) = k] &= \frac{d}{dt}\left(\frac{(\lambda t)^k}{k!}e^{-\lambda t}\right) \\
&= \lambda k\frac{(\lambda t)^{k-1}}{k!}e^{-\lambda t} + (-\lambda)\frac{(\lambda t)^k}{k!}e^{-\lambda t} \\
&= \lambda\frac{(\lambda t)^{k-1}}{(k-1)!}e^{-\lambda t} - \lambda\frac{(\lambda t)^k}{k!}e^{-\lambda t} \\
&= \lambda\left(\mathbb{P}[X(t) = k - 1] - \mathbb{P}[X(t) = k]\right),
\end{aligned}
$$

which is the right-hand side of the equation. To retrieve the basic form of Poisson, we can just set $t = 1$ in the PMF so that

$$
\mathbb{P}[X(1) = k] = \frac{\lambda^k}{k!}e^{-\lambda}.
$$

> **The origin of Poisson random variables**
> - We assume independent arrivals.
> - Probability of seeing one event is linear with the arrival rate.
> - Time interval is short enough so that you see either one event or no event.
> - Poisson is derived by solving a differential equation based on these assumptions.
> - Poisson becomes invalid when these assumptions are violated, e.g., in the case of scattering of photons due to turbid medium.

There is an alternative approach to deriving the Poisson PMF. The idea is to drive the parameter n in the binomial random variable to infinity while pushing p to zero. In this limit, the binomial PMF will converge to the Poisson PMF. We will discuss this shortly. However, we recommend the physics approach we have just described because it has a rich meaning and allows us to validate our assumptions.

Poisson approximation to binomial

We present one additional result about the Poisson random variable. The result shows that Poisson can be regarded as a limiting distribution of a binomial random variable.

> **Theorem 3.10. (Poisson approximation to binomial).** *For small p and large n,*
>
> $$\binom{n}{k} p^k (1-p)^{n-k} \approx \frac{\lambda^k}{k!} e^{-\lambda},$$
>
> *where $\lambda \stackrel{\text{def}}{=} np$.*

Before we prove the result, let us see how close the approximation can be. In **Figure 3.38**, we show a binomial distribution and a Poisson approximation. The closeness of the approximation can easily be seen.

In MATLAB, the code to approximate a binomial distribution with a Poisson formula is shown below. Here, we draw 10,000 random binomial numbers and plot their histogram. On top of the plot, we use `poisspdf` to compute the Poisson PMF. This gives us **Figure 3.38**. A similar set of commands can be called in Python.

```
% MATLAB code to approximate binomial using Poisson
n = 1000; p = 0.05;
X = binornd(n,p,[10000,1]);
t = 0:100;
[num,val] = hist(X,t);
lambda = n*p;
f_pois = poisspdf(t,lambda);
bar(num/10000,'FaceColor',[0.9 0.9 0],'BarWidth',1); hold on;
plot(f_pois, 'LineWidth', 4);
```

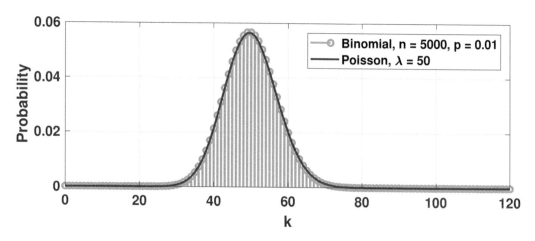

Figure 3.38: Poisson approximation of binomial distribution.

```
# Python code to approximate binomial using Poisson
import numpy as np
import matplotlib.pyplot as plt
import scipy.stats as stats
n = 1000; p = 0.05
rv1 = stats.binom(n,p)
X   = rv1.rvs(size=10000)
plt.figure(1); plt.hist(X,bins=np.arange(0,100));
rv2 = stats.poisson(n*p)
f   = rv2.pmf(bin)
plt.figure(2); plt.plot(f);
```

Proof. Let $\lambda = np$. Then,

$$\binom{n}{k} p^k (1-p)^{n-k} = \frac{n!}{k!(n-k)!} \left(\frac{\lambda}{n}\right)^k \left(1 - \frac{\lambda}{n}\right)^{n-k}$$

$$= \frac{\lambda^k}{k!} \frac{n(n-1)\cdots(n-k+1)}{n \cdot n \cdots n} \left(1 - \frac{\lambda}{n}\right)^{n-k}$$

$$= \frac{\lambda^k}{k!} \underbrace{(1)\left(1 - \frac{1}{n}\right)\cdots\left(1 - \frac{k-1}{n}\right)}_{\to 1 \text{ as } n \to \infty} \underbrace{\left(1 - \frac{\lambda}{n}\right)^{-k}}_{\to 1 \text{ as } n \to \infty} \left(1 - \frac{\lambda}{n}\right)^n$$

$$= \frac{\lambda^k}{k!} \left(1 - \frac{\lambda}{n}\right)^n.$$

We claim that $\left(1 - \frac{\lambda}{n}\right)^n \to e^{-\lambda}$. This can be proved by noting that

$$\log(1+x) \approx x, \qquad x \ll 1.$$

It then follows that $\log\left(1 - \frac{\lambda}{n}\right) \approx -\frac{\lambda}{n}$. Hence, $\left(1 - \frac{\lambda}{n}\right)^n \approx e^{-\lambda}$

$\square$

Example 3.19. Consider an optical communication system. The bit arrival rate is 10^9 bits/sec, and the probability of having one error bit is 10^{-9}. Suppose we want to find the probability of having five error bits in one second.

Let X be the number of error bits. In one second there are 10^9 bits. Since we do not know the location of these 5 bits, we have to enumerate all possibilities. This leads to a binomial distribution. Using the binomial distribution, we know that the probability of having k error bits is

$$\mathbb{P}[X = k] = \binom{n}{k} p^k (1-p)^{n-k}$$
$$= \binom{10^9}{k} (10^{-9})^k (1 - 10^{-9})^{10^9 - k}.$$

This quantity is difficult to calculate in floating-point arithmetic.

Using the Poisson to binomial approximation, we can see that the probability can be approximated by

$$\mathbb{P}[X = k] \approx \frac{\lambda^k}{k!} e^{-\lambda},$$

where $\lambda = np = 10^9 (10^{-9}) = 1$. Setting $k = 5$ yields $\mathbb{P}[X = 5] \approx 0.003$.

Photon arrival statistics

Poisson random variables are useful in computer vision, but you may skip this discussion if it is your first reading of the book.

The strong connection between Poisson statistics and physics makes the Poisson random variable a very good fit for many physical experiments. Here we demonstrate an application in modeling photon shot noise.

An image sensor is a photon sensitive device which is used to detect incoming photons. In the simplest setting, we can model a pixel in the object plane as $X_{m,n}$, for some 2D coordinate $[m, n] \in \mathbb{R}^2$. Written as an array, an $M \times N$ image in the object plane can be visualized as

$$\boldsymbol{X} = \text{object} = \begin{bmatrix} X_{1,1} & X_{1,2} & \cdots & X_{1,N} \\ \vdots & \vdots & \ddots & \vdots \\ X_{M,1} & X_{M,2} & \cdots & X_{M,N} \end{bmatrix}.$$

Without loss of generality, we assume that $X_{m,n}$ is normalized so that $0 \le X_{m,n} \le 1$ for every coordinate $[m, n]$. To model the brightness, we multiply $X_{m,n}$ by a scalar $\alpha > 0$. If a pixel $\alpha X_{m,n}$ has a large value, then it is a bright pixel; conversely, if $\alpha X_{m,n}$ has a small value, then it is a dark pixel. At a particular pixel location $[m, n] \in \mathbb{R}^2$, the observed pixel value $Y_{m,n}$ is a random variable following the Poisson statistics. This situation is illustrated in **Figure 3.39**, where we see that an object-plane pixel will generate an observed pixel through the Poisson PMF.[1]

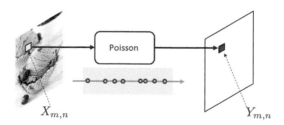

Figure 3.39: The image formation process is governed by the Poisson random variable. Given a pixel in the object plane $X_{m,n}$, the observed pixel $Y_{m,n}$ is a Poisson random variable with mean $\alpha X_{m,n}$. Therefore, a brighter pixel will have a higher Poisson mean, whereas a darker pixel will have a lower Poisson mean.

Written as an array, the image is

$$
\begin{aligned}
\boldsymbol{Y} &= \text{observed image} \\
&= \text{Poisson}\Big\{ \alpha \boldsymbol{X} \Big\} \\
&= \begin{bmatrix}
\text{Poisson}\{\alpha X_{1,1}\} & \text{Poisson}\{\alpha X_{1,2}\} & \cdots & \text{Poisson}\{\alpha X_{1,N}\} \\
\text{Poisson}\{\alpha X_{2,1}\} & \text{Poisson}\{\alpha X_{2,2}\} & \cdots & \text{Poisson}\{\alpha X_{2,N}\} \\
\vdots & \vdots & \ddots & \vdots \\
\text{Poisson}\{\alpha X_{M,1}\} & \text{Poisson}\{\alpha X_{M,2}\} & \cdots & \text{Poisson}\{\alpha X_{M,N}\}
\end{bmatrix}.
\end{aligned}
$$

Here, by Poisson$\{\alpha X_{m,n}\}$ we mean that $Y_{m,n}$ is a random integer with probability mass

$$
\mathbb{P}[Y_{m,n} = k] = \frac{[\alpha X_{m,n}]^k}{k!} e^{-\alpha X_{m,n}}.
$$

Note that this model implies that the images seen by our cameras are more or less an array of Poisson random variables. (We say "more or less" because of other sources of uncertainties such as read noise, dark current, etc.) Because the observed pixels $Y_{m,n}$ are random variables, they fluctuate about the mean values, and hence they are noisy. We refer to this type of random fluctuation as the **shot noise**. The impact of the shot noise can be seen in **Figure 3.40**. Here, we vary the sensor gain level α. We see that for small α the image is dark and has much random fluctuation. As α increases, the image becomes brighter and the fluctuation becomes smaller.

In MATLAB, simulating the Poisson photon arrival process for an image requires the image-processing toolbox. The command to read an image is `imread`. Depending on the data type, the input array could be unit8 integers. To convert them to floating-point numbers between 0 and 1, we use the command `im2double`. Drawing Poisson measurements from the clean image is done using `poissrnd`. Finally, we can use `imshow` to display the image.

---

[1]The color of an image is often handled by a **color filter array**, which can be thought of as a wavelength selector that allows a specific wavelength to pass through.

$\alpha = 10$ $\alpha = 100$ $\alpha = 1000$

Figure 3.40: Illustration of the Poisson random variable in photographing images. Here, α denotes the gain level of the sensor: Larger α means that there are more photons coming to the sensor.

```
% MATLAB code to simulate a photon arrival process
x0 = im2double(imread('cameraman.tif'));
X  = poissrnd(10*x0);
figure(1); imshow(x0, []);
figure(2); imshow(X, []);
```

Similar commands can be found in Python with the help of the `cv2` library. When reading an image, we call `cv2.imread`. The option 0 is used to read a gray-scale image; otherwise, we will have a 3-channel color image. The division `/255` ensures that the input array ranges between 0 to 1. Generating the Poisson random numbers can be done using `np.random.poisson`, or by calling the statistics library with `stats.poisson.rvs(10*x0)`. To display the images, we call `plt.imshow`, with the color map option set to `cmap = 'gray'`.

```
# Python code code to simulate a photon arrival process
import numpy as np
import matplotlib.pyplot as plt
import cv2
x0 = cv2.imread('./cameraman.tif', 0)/255
plt.figure(1); plt.imshow(x0,cmap='gray');
X  = np.random.poisson(10*x0)
plt.figure(2); plt.imshow(X, cmap='gray');
```

Why study Poisson? What is shot noise?

- The Poisson random variable is used to model photon arrivals.
- Shot noise is the random fluctuation of the photon counts at the pixels. Shot noise is present even if you have an ideal sensor.

Signal-to-noise ratio of Poisson

Now let us answer a question we asked before. A Poisson random variable has a variance equal to the mean. Thus, if the scene is brighter, the variance will be larger. How come our simulation in **Figure 3.40** shows that the fluctuation becomes smaller as the scene becomes brighter?

The answer to this question lies in the **signal-to-noise ratio** (SNR) of the Poisson random variable. The SNR of an image defines its quality. The higher the SNR, the better the image. The mathematical definition of SNR is the ratio between the signal power and the noise power. In our case, the SNR is

$$\text{SNR} = \frac{\text{signal power}}{\text{noise power}}$$

$$\overset{\text{def}}{=} \frac{\mathbb{E}[Y]}{\sqrt{\text{Var}[Y]}}$$

$$\overset{(a)}{=} \frac{\lambda}{\sqrt{\lambda}} = \sqrt{\lambda},$$

where $Y = Y_{m,n}$ is one of the observed pixels and $\lambda = \alpha X_{m,n}$ is the the corresponding object pixel. In this equation, the step (a) uses the properties of the Poisson random variable Y where $\mathbb{E}[Y] = \text{Var}[Y] = \lambda$. The result $\text{SNR} = \sqrt{\lambda}$ is very informative. It says that if the underlying mean photon flux (which is λ) increases, the SNR increases at a rate of $\sqrt{\lambda}$. So, yes, the variance becomes larger when the scene is brighter. However, the gain in signal $\mathbb{E}[Y]$ overrides the gain in noise $\sqrt{\text{Var}[Y]}$. As a result, the big fluctuation in bright images is compensated by the strong signal. Thus, to minimize the shot noise one has to use a longer exposure to increase the mean photon flux. When the scene is dark and the aperture is small, shot noise is unavoidable.

Poisson modeling is useful for describing the problem. However, the actual engineering question is that, given a noise observation $Y_{m,n}$, how would you reconstruct the clean image $X_{m,n}$? This is a very difficult **inverse problem**. The typical strategy is to exploit the spatial correlations between nearby pixels, e.g., usually smooth except along some sharp edges. Other information about the image, e.g., the likelihood of obtaining texture patterns, can also be leveraged. Modern image-processing methods are rich, ranging from classical filtering techniques to deep neural networks. Static images are easier to recover because we can often leverage multiple measurements of the same scene to boost the SNR. Dynamic scenes are substantially harder when we need to track the motion of any underlying objects. There are also newer image sensors with better photon sensitivity. The problem of imaging in the dark is an important research topic in **computational imaging**. New solutions are developed at the intersection of optics, signal processing, and machine learning.

The end of our discussions on photon statistics.

3.6 Summary

A **random variable** is so called because it can take more than one state. The probability mass function specifies the probability for it to land on a particular state. Therefore, whenever you think of a random variable you should immediately think of its PMF (or histogram if you prefer). The PMF is a unique characterization of a random variable. Two random variables with the same PMF are effectively the same random variables. (They are not identical because there could be measure-zero sets where the two differ.) Once you have the PMF, you can derive the CDF, expectation, moments, variance, and so on.

When your boss hands a dataset to you, which random variable (which model) should you use? This is a very practical and deep question. We highlight three steps for you to consider:

- (i) **Model selection**: Which random variable is the best fit for our problem? Sometimes we know by physics that, for example, photon arrivals or internet traffic follow a Poisson random variable. However, not all datasets can be easily described by simple models. The models we have learned in this chapter are called the **parametric** models because they are characterized by one or two parameters. Some datasets require nonparametric models, e.g., natural images, because they are just too complex. Some data scientists refer to deep neural networks as parametric models because the network weights are essentially the parameters. Some do not because when the number of parameters is on the order of millions, sometimes even more than the number of training samples, it seems more reasonable to call these models nonparametric. However, putting this debate aside, shortlisting a few candidate models based on prior knowledge is essential. Even if you use deep neural networks, selecting between convolutional structures versus long short-term memory models is still a legitimate task that requires an understanding of **your** problem.

- (ii) **Parameter estimation**: Suppose that you now have a candidate model; the next task is to estimate the model parameter using the available training data. For example, for Poisson we need to determine λ, and for binomial we need to determine (n, p). The estimation problem is an inverse problem. Often we need to use the PMF to construct certain optimization problems. By solving the optimization problem we will find the best parameter (for that particular candidate model). Modern machine learning is doing significantly better now than in the old days because optimization methods have advanced greatly.

- (iii) **Validation**. When each candidate model has been optimized to best fit the data, we still need to select the best model. This is done by running various testings. For example, we can construct a validation set and check which model gives us the best performance (such as classification rate or regression error). However, a model with the best validation score is not necessarily the best model. Your goal should be to seek a **good** model and not the **best** model because determining the best requires access to the testing data, which we do not have. Everything being equal, the common wisdom is to go with a simpler model because it is generally less susceptible to overfitting.

3.7 References

Probability textbooks

3-1 Dimitri P. Bertsekas and John N. Tsitsiklis, *Introduction to Probability*, Athena Scientific, 2nd Edition, 2008. Chapter 2.

3-2 Alberto Leon-Garcia, *Probability, Statistics, and Random Processes for Electrical Engineering*, Prentice Hall, 3rd Edition, 2008. Chapter 3.

3-3 Athanasios Papoulis and S. Unnikrishna Pillai, *Probability, Random Variables and Stochastic Processes*, McGraw-Hill, 4th Edition, 2001. Chapters 3 and 4.

3-4 John A. Gubner, *Probability and Random Processes for Electrical and Computer Engineers*, Cambridge University Press, 2006. Chapters 2 and3.

3-5 Sheldon Ross, *A First Course in Probability*, Prentice Hall, 8th Edition, 2010. Chapter 4.

3-6 Henry Stark and John Woods, *Probability and Random Processes With Applications to Signal Processing*, Prentice Hall, 3rd Edition, 2001. Chapters 2 and 4.

Advanced probability textbooks

3-7 William Feller, *An Introduction to Probability Theory and Its Applications*, Wiley and Sons, 3rd Edition, 1950.

3-8 Andrey Kolmogorov, *Foundations of the Theory of Probability*, 2nd English Edition, Dover 2018. (Translated from Russian to English. Originally published in 1950 by Chelsea Publishing Company New York.)

Cross-validation

3-9 Larry Wasserman, *All of Statistics*, Springer 2004. Chapter 20.

3-10 Mats Rudemo, "Empirical Choice of Histograms and Kernel Density Estimators," *Scandinavian Journal of Statistics*, Vol. 9, No. 2 (1982), pp. 65-78.

3-11 David W. Scott, *Multivariate Density Estimation: Theory, Practice, and Visualization*, Wiley, 1992.

Poisson statistics

3-12 Joseph Goodman, *Statistical Optics*, Wiley, 2015. Chapter 3.

3-13 Henry Stark and John Woods, *Probability and Random Processes With Applications to Signal Processing*, Prentice Hall, 3rd edition, 2001. Section 1.10.

3.8 Problems

Exercise 1. (VIDEO SOLUTION)
Consider an information source that produces numbers k in the set $S_X = \{1, 2, 3, 4\}$. Find and plot the PMF in the following cases:

(a) $p_k = p_1/k$, for $k = 1, 2, 3, 4$. Hint: Find p_1.

(b) $p_{k+1} = p_k/2$ for $k = 1, 2, 3$.

(c) $p_{k+1} = p_k/2^k$ for $k = 1, 2, 3$.

(d) Can the random variables in parts (a)-(c) be extended to take on values in the set $\{1, 2, \ldots\}$? Why or why not? Hint: You may use the fact that the series $1 + \frac{1}{2} + \frac{1}{3} + \cdots$ diverges.

Exercise 2. (VIDEO SOLUTION)
Two dice are tossed. Let X be the absolute difference in the number of dots facing up.

(a) Find and plot the PMF of X.

(b) Find the probability that $X \leq 2$.

(c) Find $\mathbb{E}[X]$ and $\mathrm{Var}[X]$.

Exercise 3. (VIDEO SOLUTION)
Let X be a random variable with PMF $p_k = c/2^k$ for $k = 1, 2, \ldots$.

(a) Determine the value of c.

(b) Find $\mathbb{P}(X > 4)$ and $\mathbb{P}(6 \leq X \leq 8)$.

(c) Find $\mathbb{E}[X]$ and $\mathrm{Var}[X]$.

Exercise 4.
Let X be a random variable with PMF $p_k = c/2^k$ for $k = -1, 0, 1, 2, 3, 4, 5$.

(a) Determine the value of c.

(b) Find $\mathbb{P}(1 \leq X < 3)$ and $\mathbb{P}(1 < X \leq 5)$.

(c) Find $\mathbb{P}[X^3 < 5]$.

(d) Find the PMF and the CDF of X.

Exercise 5. (VIDEO SOLUTION)
A modem transmits a $+2$ voltage signal into a channel. The channel adds to this signal a noise term that is drawn from the set $\{0, -1, -2, -3\}$ with respective probabilities $\{4/10, 3/10, 2/10, 1/10\}$.

(a) Find the PMF of the output Y of the channel.

(b) What is the probability that the channel's output is equal to the input of the channel?

(c) What is the probability that the channel's output is positive?

(d) Find the expected value and variance of Y.

Exercise 6.
On a given day, your golf score takes values from numbers 1 through 10, with equal probability of getting each one. Assume that you play golf for three days, and assume that your three performances are independent. Let X_1, X_2, and X_3 be the scores that you get, and let X be the minimum of these three numbers.

(a) Show that for any discrete random variable X, $p_X(k) = \mathbb{P}(X > k - 1) - \mathbb{P}(X > k)$.

(b) What is the probability $\mathbb{P}(X_1 > k)$ for $k = 1, \ldots, 10$?

(c) Use (a), determine the PMF $p_X(k)$, for $k = 1, \ldots, 10$.

(d) What is the average score improvement if you play just for one day compared with playing for three days and taking the minimum?

Exercise 7. (VIDEO SOLUTION)
Let
$$g(X) = \begin{cases} 1, & \text{if } X > 10 \\ 0, & \text{otherwise.} \end{cases} \quad \text{and} \quad h(X) = \begin{cases} X - 10, & \text{if } X - 10 > 0 \\ 0, & \text{otherwise.} \end{cases}$$

(a) Find $\mathbb{E}[g(X)]$ for X as in Problem 1(a) with $S_X = \{1, \ldots, 15\}$.

(b) Find $\mathbb{E}[h(X)]$ for X as in Problem 1(b) with $S_X = \{1, \ldots, 15\}$.

Exercise 8. (VIDEO SOLUTION)
A voltage X is uniformly distributed in the set $\{-3, \ldots, 3, 4\}$.

(a) Find the mean and variance of X.

(b) Find the mean and variance of $Y = -2X^2 + 3$.

(c) Find the mean and variance of $W = \cos(\pi X/8)$.

(d) Find the mean and variance of $Z = \cos^2(\pi X/8)$.

Exercise 9. (VIDEO SOLUTION)

(a) If X is Poisson(λ), compute $\mathbb{E}[1/(X+1)]$.

(b) If X is Bernoulli(p) and Y is Bernoulli(q), compute $\mathbb{E}[(X + Y)^3]$ if X and Y are independent.

(c) Let X be a random variable with mean μ and variance σ^2. Let $\Delta(\theta) = \mathbb{E}[(X - \theta)^2]$. Find θ that minimizes the error $\Delta(\theta)$.

(d) Suppose that $X_1, \ldots, X_n$ are independent uniform random variables in $\{0, 1, \ldots, 100\}$. Evaluate $\mathbb{P}[\min(X_1, \ldots, X_n) > \ell]$ for any $\ell \in \{0, 1, \ldots, 100\}$.

Exercise 10. (VIDEO SOLUTION)

(a) Consider the binomial probability mass function $p_X(k) = \binom{n}{k} p^k (1 - p)^{n-k}$. Show that the mean is $\mathbb{E}[X] = np$.

(b) Consider the geometric probability mass function $p_X(k) = p(1 - p)^k$ for $k = 0, 1, \ldots$. Show that the mean is $\mathbb{E}[X] = (1 - p)/p$.

(c) Consider the Poisson probability mass function $p_X(k) = \frac{\lambda^k}{k!} e^{-\lambda}$. Show that the variance is $\text{Var}[X] = \lambda$.

(d) Consider the uniform probability mass function $p_X(k) = \frac{1}{L}$ for $k = 1, \ldots, L$. Show that the variance is $\text{Var}[X] = \frac{L^2 - 1}{12}$. Hint: $1 + 2 + \cdots + n = \frac{n(n+1)}{2}$ and $1^2 + 2^2 + \cdots + n^2 = \frac{n^3}{3} + \frac{n^2}{2} + \frac{n}{6}$.

Exercise 11. (VIDEO SOLUTION)
An audio player uses a low-quality hard drive. The probability that the hard drive fails after being used for one month is $1/12$. If it fails, the manufacturer offers a free-of-charge repair for the customer. For the cost of each repair, however, the manufacturer has to pay \$20. The initial cost of building the player is \$50, and the manufacturer offers a 1-year warranty. Within one year, the customer can ask for a free repair up to 12 times.

(a) Let X be the number of months when the player fails. What is the PMF of X? Hint: $\mathbb{P}[X = 1]$ may not be very high because if the hard drive fails it will be fixed by the manufacturer. Once fixed, the drive can fail again in the remaining months. So saying $X = 1$ is equivalent to saying that there is only one failure in the entire 12-month period.

(b) What is the average cost per player?

Exercise 12. (VIDEO SOLUTION)
A binary communication channel has a probability of bit error of $p = 10^{-6}$. Suppose that transmission occurs in blocks of 10,000 bits. Let N be the number of errors introduced by the channel in a transmission block.

(a) What is the PMF of N?

(b) Find $\mathbb{P}[N = 0]$ and $\mathbb{P}[N \leq 3]$.

(c) For what value of p will the probability of 1 or more errors in a block be 99%?

Hint: Use the Poisson approximation to binomial random variables.

Exercise 13. (VIDEO SOLUTION)
The number of orders waiting to be processed is given by a Poisson random variable with parameter $\alpha = \lambda/n\mu$, where λ is the average number of orders that arrive in a day, μ is the number of orders that an employee can process per day, and n is the number of employees. Let $\lambda = 5$ and $\mu = 1$. Find the number of employees required so the probability that more than four orders are waiting is less than 10%.

Hint: You need to use trial and error for a few n's.

Exercise 14.
Let X be the number of photons counted by a receiver in an optical communication system. It is known that X is a Poisson random variable with a rate λ_1 when a signal is present and a Poisson random variable with the rate $\lambda_0 < \lambda_1$ when a signal is absent. The probability that the signal is present is p. Suppose that we observe $X = k$ photons. We want to determine a threshold T such that if $k \geq T$ we claim that the signal is present, and if $k < T$ we claim that the signal is absent. What is the value of T?

Chapter 4

Continuous Random Variables

If you are coming to this chapter from Chapter 3, we invite you to take a 30-second pause and switch your mind from discrete events to continuous events. Everything is continuous now. The sample space is continuous, the event space is continuous, and the probability measure is continuous. Continuous random variables are similar in many ways to discrete random variables. They are characterized by the probability density functions (the continuous version of the probability mass functions); they have cumulative distribution functions; they have means, moments, and variances. The most significant difference is perhaps the use of integration instead of summation, but this change is conceptually straightforward, aside from the difficulties associated with integrating functions. So why do we need a separate chapter for continuous random variables? There are several reasons.

- First, how would you define the probability of a continuous event? Note that we cannot count because a continuous event is uncountable. There is also nothing called the probability mass because there are infinitely many masses. To define the probability of continuous events, we need to go back to our "slogan": **probability is a measure of the size of a set**. Because probability is a measure, we can speak meaningfully about the probability of continuous events so long as we have a well-defined measure for them. Defining such a measure requires some effort. We will develop the intuitions and the formal definitions in Section 4.1. In Section 4.2, we will discuss the expectation and variance of continuous random variables.

- The second challenge is the **unification** between continuous and discrete random variables. Since the two types of random variables ultimately measure the size of a set, it is natural to ask whether we can unify them. Our approach to unifying them is based on the cumulative distribution functions (CDFs), which are well-defined functions for discrete and continuous random variables. Based on the CDF and the fundamental theorem of calculus, we can show that the probability density functions and probability mass functions can be derived from the derivative of the CDFs. These will be discussed in Section 4.3, and in Section 4.4 we will discuss some additional results about the mode and median.

- The third challenge is to understand several widely used continuous random variables. We will discuss the uniform random variable and the exponential random variable in Section 4.5. Section 4.6 deals with the important topic of the **Gaussian random variable**. Where does a Gaussian random variable come from? Why does it have a bell

171

shape? Why are Gaussian random variables so popular in data science? What are the useful properties of Gaussian random variables? What are the relationships between a Gaussian random variable and other random variables? These important questions will be answered in Section 4.6.

- The final challenge is the **transformation** of random variables. Imagine that you have a random variable X and a function g. What will the probability mass/density function of $g(X)$ be? Addressing this problem is essential because almost all practical engineering problems involve the transformation of random variables. For example, suppose we have voltage measurements and we would like to compute the power. This requires taking the square of the voltage. We will discuss the transformation in Section 4.7, and we will also discuss an essential application in generating random numbers in Section 4.8.

4.1 Probability Density Function

4.1.1 Some intuitions about probability density functions

Let's begin by outlining some intuitive reasoning, which is needed to define the probability of continuous events properly. These intuitions are based on the fact that probability is a **measure**. In the following discussion you will see a sequence of logical arguments for constructing such a measure for continuous events. Some arguments are discussed in Chapter 2, but now we place them in the context of continuous random variables.

Suppose we are given an event A that is a subset in the sample space Ω, as illustrated in **Figure 4.1**. In order to calculate the probability of A, the measure perspective suggests that we consider the relative size of the set

$$\mathbb{P}[\{x \in A\}] = \frac{\text{``size'' of } A}{\text{``size'' of } \Omega}.$$

The right-hand side of this equation captures everything about the probability: It is a measure of the size of a set. It is relative to the sample space. It is a number between 0 and 1. It can be applied to discrete sets, and it can be applied to continuous sets.

How do we measure the "size" of a continuous set? One possible way is by means of integrating the length, area, or volume covered by the set. Consider an example: Suppose that the sample space is the interval $\Omega = [0,5]$ and the event is $A = [2,3]$. To measure the "size" of A, we can integrate A to determine the length. That is,

$$\mathbb{P}[\{x \in [2,3]\}] = \frac{\text{``size'' of } A}{\text{``size'' of } \Omega} = \frac{\int_A dx}{\int_\Omega dx} = \frac{\int_2^3 dx}{\int_0^5 dx} = \frac{1}{5}.$$

Therefore, we have translated the "size" of a set to an integration. However, this definition is a very special case because when we calculate the "size" of a set, we treat all the elements in the set with equal importance. This is a strong assumption that will be relaxed later. But

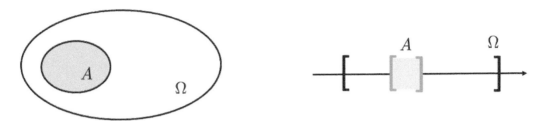

Figure 4.1: [Left] An event A in the sample space Ω. The probability that A happens can be calculated as the "size" of A relative to the "size" of Ω. [Right] A specific example on the real line. Note that the same definition of probability applies: The probability is the size of the interval A relative to that of the sample space Ω.

if you agree with this line of reasoning, we can rewrite the probability as

$$\mathbb{P}[\{x \in A\}] = \frac{\int_A dx}{\int_\Omega dx} = \frac{\int_A dx}{|\Omega|}$$

$$= \int_A \underbrace{\frac{1}{|\Omega|}}_{\text{equally important over } \Omega} dx.$$

This equation says that under our assumption (that all elements are equiprobable), the probability of A is calculated as the integration of A using an integrand $1/|\Omega|$ (note that $1/|\Omega|$ is a constant with respect to x). If we evaluate the probability of another event B, all we need to do is to replace A with B and compute $\int_B \frac{1}{|\Omega|} dx$.

What happens if we want to relax the "equiprobable" assumption? Perhaps we can adopt something similar to the probability mass function (PMF). Recall that a PMF p_X evaluated at a point x is the probability that the state x happens, i.e., $p_X(x) = \mathbb{P}[X = x]$. So, $p_X(x)$ is the relative frequency of x. Following the same line of thinking, we can define a function f_X such that $f_X(x)$ tells us something related to the "relative frequency". To this end, we can treat f_X as a continuous histogram with infinitesimal bin width as shown in **Figure 4.2**. Using this f_X, we can replace the constant function $1/|\Omega|$ with the new function $f_X(x)$. This will give us

$$\mathbb{P}[\{x \in A\}] = \int_A \underbrace{f_X(x)}_{\text{replace } 1/|\Omega|} dx. \tag{4.1}$$

If we compare it with a PMF, we note that when X is discrete,

$$\mathbb{P}[\{x \in A\}] = \sum_{x \in A} p_X(x).$$

Hence, f_X can be considered a continuous version of p_X, although we do not recommend this way of thinking for the following reason: $p_X(x)$ is a legitimate probability, but $f_X(x)$ is not a probability. Rather, f_X is the **probability per unit length**, meaning that we need to integrate f_X (times dx) in order to generate a probability value. If we only look at f_X at a point x, then this point is a measure-zero set because the length of this set is zero.

Equation (4.1) should be familiar to you from Chapter 2. The function $f_X(x)$ is precisely the weighting function we described in that chapter.

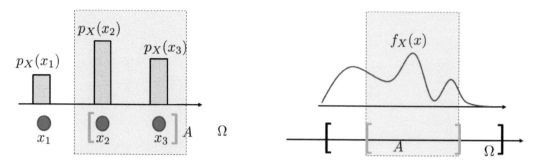

Figure 4.2: [Left] A probability mass function (PMF) tells us the relative frequency of a state when computing the probability. In this example, the "size" of A is $p_X(x_2) + p_X(x_3)$. [Right] A probability density function (PDF) is the infinitesimal version of the PMF. Thus, the "size" of A is the integration over the PDF.

What is a PDF?

- A PDF is the continuous version of a PMF.
- We integrate a PDF to compute the probability.
- We integrate instead of sum because continuous events are not countable.

To summarize, we have learned that when measuring the size of a continuous event, the discrete technique (counting the number of elements) does not work. Generalizing to continuous space requires us to integrate the event. However, since different elements in an event have different relative emphases, we use the probability density function $f_X(x)$ to tell us the relative frequency for a state x to happen. This PDF serves the role of the PMF.

4.1.2 More in-depth discussion about PDFs

A continuous random variable X is defined by its probability density function f_X. This function has to satisfy several criteria, summarized as follows.

Definition 4.1. *A probability density function f_X of a random variable X is a mapping $f_X : \Omega \to \mathbb{R}$, with the properties*

- **Non-negativity:** $f_X(x) \geq 0$ *for all $x \in \Omega$*
- **Unity:** $\int_\Omega f_X(x)\, dx = 1$
- **Measure of a set:** $\mathbb{P}[\{x \in A\}] = \int_A f_X(x)\, dx$

If all elements of the sample space are equiprobable, then the PDF is $f(x) = 1/|\Omega|$. You can easily check that it satisfies all three criteria.

Let us take a closer look at the three criteria:

- Non-negativity: The non-negativity criterion $f_X(x) \geq 0$ is reminiscent of Probability Axiom I. It says that no matter what x we are looking at, the probability density function f_X evaluated at x should never give a negative value. Axiom I ensures that we will not get a negative probability.

- Unity: The unity criterion $\int_\Omega f(x)\,dx = 1$ is reminiscent of Probability Axiom II, which says that measuring over the entire sample space will give 1.

- Measure of a set: The third criterion gives us a way to measure the size of an event A. It says that since each $x \in \Omega$ has a different emphasis when calculating the size of A, we need to scale the elements properly. This scaling is done by the PDF $f_X(x)$, which can be regarded as a histogram with a continuous x-axis. The third criterion is a consequence of Probability Axiom III, because if there are two events A and B that are disjoint, then $\mathbb{P}[\{x \in A\} \cup \{x \in B\}] = \int_A f_X(x)\,dx + \int_B f_X(x)\,dx$ because $f_X(x) \geq 0$ for all x.

If the random variable X takes real numbers in 1D, then a more "user-friendly" definition of the PDF can be given.

Definition 4.2. *Let X be a continuous random variable. The **probability density function (PDF)** of X is a function $f_X : \Omega \to \mathbb{R}$ that, when integrated over an interval $[a, b]$, yields the probability of obtaining $a \leq X \leq b$:*

$$\mathbb{P}[a \leq X \leq b] = \int_a^b f_X(x)\,dx. \tag{4.2}$$

This definition is just a rewriting of the previous definition by explicitly writing out the definition of A as an interval $[a, b]$. Here are a few examples.

Example 4.1. Let $f_X(x) = 3x^2$ with $\Omega = [0, 1]$. Let $A = [0, 0.5]$. Then the probability $\mathbb{P}[\{X \in A\}]$ is

$$\mathbb{P}[0 \leq X \leq 0.5] = \int_0^{0.5} 3x^2\,dx = \frac{1}{8}.$$

Example 4.2. Let $f_X(x) = 1/|\Omega|$ with $\Omega = [0, 5]$. Let $A = [3, 5]$. Then the probability $\mathbb{P}[\{X \in A\}]$ is

$$\mathbb{P}[3 \leq X \leq 5] = \int_3^5 \frac{1}{|\Omega|}\,dx = \int_3^5 \frac{1}{5}\,dx = \frac{2}{5}.$$

Example 4.3. Let $f_X(x) = 2x$ with $\Omega = [0, 1]$. Let $A = \{0.5\}$. Then the probability $\mathbb{P}[\{X \in A\}]$ is

$$\mathbb{P}[X = 0.5] = \mathbb{P}[0.5 \leq X \leq 0.5] = \int_{0.5}^{0.5} 2x\,dx = 0.$$

This example shows that evaluating the probability at an isolated point for a continuous random variable will yield 0.

Practice Exercise 4.1. Let X be the phase angle of a voltage signal. Without any prior knowledge about X we may assume that X has an equal probability of any value between 0 to 2π. Find the PDF of X and compute $\mathbb{P}[0 \leq X \leq \pi/2]$.

Solution. Since X has an equal probability for any value between 0 to 2π, the PDF of X is

$$f_X(x) = \frac{1}{2\pi}, \qquad \text{for } 0 \leq x \leq 2\pi.$$

Therefore, the probability $\mathbb{P}[0 \leq X \leq \pi/2]$ can be computed as

$$\mathbb{P}\left[0 \leq X \leq \frac{\pi}{2}\right] = \int_0^{\pi/2} \frac{1}{2\pi}\, dx = \frac{1}{4}.$$

Looking at Equation (4.2), you may wonder: If the PDF f_X is analogous to PMF p_X, why didn't we require $0 \leq f_X(x) \leq 1$ instead of requiring only $f_X(x) \geq 0$? This is an excellent question, and it points exactly to the difference between a PMF and a PDF. Notice that f_X is a mapping from the sample space Ω to the real line $\mathbb{R}$. It does not map Ω to $[0, 1]$. On the other hand, since $p_X(x)$ is the actual probability, it maps Ω to $[0, 1]$. Thus, $f_X(x)$ can take very large values but will not explode, because we have the unity constraint $\int_\Omega f_X(x)\, dx = 1$. Even if $f_X(x)$ takes a large value, it will be compensated by the small dx. If you recall, there is nothing like dx in the definition of a PMF. Whenever there is a probability mass, we need to sum or, putting it another way, the dx in the discrete case is always 1. Therefore, while the probability mass PMF must not exceed 1, a probability density PDF can exceed 1.

If $f_X(x) \geq 1$, then what is the meaning of $f_X(x)$? Isn't it representing the probability of having an element $X = x$? If it were a discrete random variable, then yes; $p_X(x)$ is the probability of having $X = x$ (so the probability mass cannot go beyond 1). However, for a continuous random variable, $f_X(x)$ is *not* the probability of having $X = x$. The probability of having $X = x$ (i.e., exactly at x) is 0 because an isolated point has zero measure in the continuous space. Thus, even though $f_X(x)$ takes a value larger than 1, the probability of X being x is zero.

At this point you can see why we call PDF a *density*, or density function, because each value $f_X(x)$ is the probability *per unit length*. If we want to calculate the probability of $x \leq X \leq x + \delta$, for example, then according to our definition, we have

$$\mathbb{P}[x \leq X \leq x + \delta] = \int_x^{x+\delta} f_X(x)\, dx \approx f_X(x) \cdot \delta.$$

Therefore, the probability of $\mathbb{P}[x \leq X \leq x + \delta]$ can be regarded as the "per unit length" density $f_X(x)$ multiplied with the "length" δ. As $\delta \to 0$, we can see that $\mathbb{P}[X = x] = 0$. See **Figure 4.3** for an illustration.

Why are PDFs called a density function?

- Because $f_X(x)$ is the probability **per unit length**.
- You need to integrate $f_X(x)$ to obtain a probability.

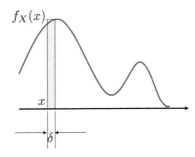

Figure 4.3: The probability $\mathbb{P}[x \leq X \leq x + \delta]$ can be approximated by the density $f_X(x)$ multiplied by the length δ.

Example 4.4. Consider a random variable X with PDF $f_X(x) = \frac{1}{2\sqrt{x}}$ for any $0 < x \leq 1$, and is 0 otherwise. We can show that $f_X(x) \to \infty$ as $x \to 0$. However, $f_X(x)$ remains a valid PDF because

$$\int_{-\infty}^{\infty} f_X(x)\, dx = \int_0^1 \frac{1}{2\sqrt{x}}\, dx = \sqrt{x}\, \Big|_0^1 = 1.$$

Remark. Since isolated points have zero measure in the continuous space, the probability of an open interval (a, b) is the same as the probability of a closed interval:

$$\mathbb{P}[[a, b]] = \mathbb{P}[(a, b)] = \mathbb{P}[(a, b]] = \mathbb{P}[[a, b)].$$

The exception is that when the PDF of $f_X(x)$ has a delta function at a or b. In this case, the probability measure at a or b will be non-zero. We will discuss this when we talk about the CDFs.

Practice Exercise 4.2. Let $f_X(x) = c(1 - x^2)$ for $-1 \leq x \leq 1$, and 0 otherwise. Find the constant c.

Solution. Since $\int_\Omega f_X(x)\, dx = 1$, it follows that

$$\int_\Omega f_X(x)\, dx = \int_{-1}^1 c(1 - x^2)\, dx = \frac{4c}{3} \Rightarrow c = 3/4.$$

Practice Exercise 4.3. Let $f_X(x) = x^2$ for $|x| \leq a$, and 0 otherwise. Find a.

Solution. Note that

$$\int_\Omega f_X(x)\, dx = \int_{-a}^a x^2\, dx = \frac{x^3}{3} \Big|_{-a}^a = \frac{2a^3}{3}.$$

Setting $\frac{2a^3}{3} = 1$ yields $a = \sqrt[3]{\frac{3}{2}}$.

4.1.3   Connecting with the PMF

The probability density function is more general than the probability mass function. To see this, consider a discrete random variable X with a PMF $p_X(x)$. Because p_X is defined on a countable set Ω, we can write it as a train of **delta functions** and define a corresponding PDF:

$$f_X(x) = \sum_{x_k \in \Omega} p_X(x_k)\, \delta(x - x_k).$$

Example 4.5. If X is a Bernoulli random variable with PMF $p_X(1) = p$ and $p_X(0) = 1 - p$, then the corresponding PDF can be written as

$$f_X(x) = p\, \delta(x - 1) + (1 - p)\, \delta(x - 0).$$

Example 4.6. If X is a binomial random variable with PMF $p_X(k) = \binom{n}{k} p^k (1-p)^{n-k}$, then the corresponding PDF can be written as

$$f_X(x) = \sum_{k=0}^{n} p_X(k)\, \delta(x - k)$$

$$= \sum_{k=0}^{n} \binom{n}{k} p^k (1 - p)^{n-k}\, \delta(x - k).$$

Strictly speaking, delta functions are not really functions. They are defined through integrations. They satisfy the properties that $\delta(x - x_k) = \infty$ if $x = x_k$, $\delta(x - x_k) = 0$ if $x \neq x_k$, and

$$\int_{x_k - \epsilon}^{x_k + \epsilon} \delta(x - x_k)\, dx = 1,$$

for any $\epsilon > 0$. Suppose we ignore the fact that delta functions are not functions and merely treat them as ordinary functions with some interesting properties. In this case, we can imagine that for every probability mass $p_X(x_k)$, there exists an interval $[a, b]$ such that there is one and only one state x_k that lies in $[a, b]$, as shown in **Figure 4.4**.

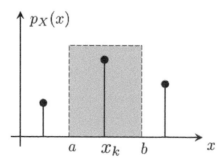

Figure 4.4: We can view a PMF as a train of impulses. When computing the probability $X = x_k$, we integrate the PMF over the interval $[a, b]$.

If we want to calculate the probability of obtaining $X = x_k$, we can show that

$$\mathbb{P}[X = x_k] \overset{(a)}{=} \mathbb{P}[a \leq X \leq b]$$

$$= \int_a^b f_X(x)\, dx$$

$$\overset{(b)}{=} \int_a^b p_X(x_k)\, \delta(x - x_k)\, dx$$

$$\overset{(c)}{=} p_X(x_k) \underbrace{\int_a^b \delta(x - x_k)\, dx}_{=1} = p_X(x_k).$$

Here, step (a) holds because within $[a, b]$, there is no other event besides $X = x_k$. Step (b) is just the definition of our $f_X(x)$ (inside the interval $[a, b]$). Step (c) shows that the delta function integrates to 1, thus leaving the probability mass $p_X(x_k)$ as the final result. Let us look at an example and then comment on this intuition.

Example 4.7. Let X be a discrete random variable with PMF

$$p_X(k) = \frac{1}{2^k}, \qquad k = 1, 2, \ldots$$

The continuous representation of the PMF can be written as

$$f_X(x) = \sum_{k=1}^{\infty} p_X(k)\, \delta(x - k) = \sum_{k=1}^{\infty} \left(\frac{1}{2^k} \right) \delta(x - k).$$

Suppose we want to compute the probability $\mathbb{P}[1 \leq X \leq 2]$. This can be computed as

$$\mathbb{P}[1 \leq X \leq 2] = \int_1^2 f_X(x)\, dx = \int_1^2 \sum_{k=1}^{\infty} \left(\frac{1}{2^k} \right) \delta(x - k)\, dx$$

$$= \int_1^2 \left\{ \frac{1}{2}\delta(x - 1) + \frac{1}{4}\delta(x - 2) + \cdots \right\} dx$$

$$= \frac{1}{2} \underbrace{\int_1^2 \delta(x - 1)\, dx}_{=1} + \frac{1}{4} \underbrace{\int_1^2 \delta(x - 2)\, dx}_{=1}$$

$$+ \frac{1}{8} \underbrace{\int_1^2 \delta(x - 3)\, dx}_{=0} + \underbrace{\cdots}_{=0}$$

$$= \frac{1}{2} + \frac{1}{4} = \frac{3}{4}.$$

However, if we want to compute the probability $\mathbb{P}[1 < X \leq 2]$, then the integration

---

limit will not include the number 1 and so the delta function will remain 0. Thus,

$$\mathbb{P}[1 < X \le 2] = \int_{1+}^{2} f_X(x)\, dx$$

$$= \frac{1}{2} \underbrace{\int_{1+}^{2} \delta(x-1)\, dx}_{=0} + \frac{1}{4} \underbrace{\int_{1+}^{2} \delta(x-2)\, dx}_{=1} = \frac{1}{4}.$$

Closing remark. To summarize, we see that a PMF can be "regarded" as a PDF. We are careful to put a quotation around "regarded" because PMF and PDF are defined for different events. A PMF uses a discrete measure (i.e., a counter) for countable events, whereas a PDF uses a continuous measure (i.e., integration) for continuous events. The way we link the two is by using the delta functions. Using the delta functions is valid, but the argument we provide here is intuitive rather than rigorous. It is not rigorous because the integration we use is still the Riemann-Stieltjes integration, which does not handle delta functions. Therefore, while you can treat a discrete PDF as a train of delta functions, it is important to remember the limitations of the integrations we use.

4.2 Expectation, Moment, and Variance

4.2.1 Definition and properties

As with discrete random variables, we can define **expectation** for continuous random variables. The definition is analogous: Just replace the summation with integration.

Definition 4.3. *The* **expectation** *of a continuous random variable X is*

$$\mathbb{E}[X] = \int_{\Omega} x\, f_X(x)\, dx. \tag{4.3}$$

Example 4.8. (Uniform random variable) Let X be a continuous random variable with PDF $f_X(x) = \frac{1}{b-a}$ for $a \le x \le b$, and 0 otherwise. The expectation is

$$\mathbb{E}[X] = \int_{\Omega} x f_X(x)\, dx = \int_{a}^{b} x \cdot \frac{1}{b-a}\, dx = \frac{1}{b-a} \underbrace{\int_{a}^{b} x\, dx}_{= \frac{x^2}{2}\big|_a^b}$$

$$= \frac{1}{b-a} \cdot \frac{b^2 - a^2}{2} = \frac{a+b}{2}.$$

Example 4.9. (**Exponential random variable**) Let X be a continuous random variable with PDF $f_X(x) = \lambda e^{-\lambda x}$, for $x \geq 0$. The expectation is

$$\mathbb{E}[X] = \int_0^\infty x\, \lambda e^{-\lambda x}\, dx$$

$$= -\int_0^\infty x\, de^{-\lambda x}$$

$$= \underbrace{-xe^{-\lambda x}\Big|_0^\infty}_{=0} + \int_0^\infty e^{-\lambda x}\, dx$$

$$= -\frac{1}{\lambda}\underbrace{e^{-\lambda x}\Big|_0^\infty}_{=-1} = \frac{1}{\lambda},$$

where the colored step is due to integration by parts.

If a function g is applied to the random variable X, the expectation can be found using the following theorem.

Theorem 4.1. *Let $g : \Omega \to \mathbb{R}$ be a function and X be a continuous random variable. Then*

$$\mathbb{E}[g(X)] = \int_\Omega g(x)\, f_X(x)\, dx. \tag{4.4}$$

Example 4.10. (**Uniform random variable**) Let X be a continuous random variable with $f_X(x) = \frac{1}{b-a}$ for $a \leq x \leq b$, and 0 otherwise. If $g(\cdot) = (\cdot)^2$, then

$$\mathbb{E}[g(X)] = \mathbb{E}[X^2] = \int_\Omega x^2 f_X(x)\, dx$$

$$= \frac{1}{b-a} \cdot \underbrace{\int_a^b x^2\, dx}_{=\frac{b^3-a^3}{3}} = \frac{a^2 + ab + b^2}{3}.$$

Practice Exercise 4.4. Let Θ be a continuous random variable with PDF $f_\Theta(\theta) = \frac{1}{2\pi}$ for $0 \leq \theta \leq 2\pi$ and is 0 otherwise. Let $Y = \cos(\omega t + \Theta)$. Find $\mathbb{E}[Y]$.

Solution. Referring to Equation (4.4), the function g is

$$g(\theta) = \cos(\omega t + \theta).$$

Therefore, the expectation $\mathbb{E}[Y]$ is

$$\mathbb{E}[Y] = \int_0^{2\pi} \cos(\omega t + \theta) \, f_\Theta(\theta) \, d\theta$$

$$= \frac{1}{2\pi} \int_0^{2\pi} \cos(\omega t + \theta) \, d\theta = 0,$$

where the last equality holds because the integral of a sinusoid over one period is 0.

Practice Exercise 4.5. Let $A \subseteq \Omega$. Let $\mathbb{I}_A(X)$ be an indicator function such that

$$\mathbb{I}_A(X) = \begin{cases} 1, & \text{if } X \in A, \\ 0, & \text{if } X \notin A. \end{cases}$$

Find $\mathbb{E}[\mathbb{I}_A(X)]$.

Solution. The expectation is

$$\mathbb{E}[\mathbb{I}_A(X)] = \int_\Omega \mathbb{I}_A(x) f_X(x) \, dx$$

$$= \int_{x \in A} f_X(x) \, dx$$

$$= \mathbb{P}[X \in A].$$

So the probability of $\{X \in A\}$ can be equivalently represented in terms of expectation.

Practice Exercise 4.6. Is it true that $\mathbb{E}[1/X] = 1/\mathbb{E}[X]$?

Solution. No. This is because

$$\mathbb{E}\left[\frac{1}{X}\right] = \int_\Omega \frac{1}{x} f_X(x) \, dx$$

$$\neq \frac{1}{\int_\Omega x f_X(x) \, dx}$$

$$= \frac{1}{\mathbb{E}[X]}.$$

All the properties of expectation we learned in the discrete case can be translated to the continuous case. Specifically, we have that

- $\mathbb{E}[aX] = a\mathbb{E}[X]$: A scalar multiple of a random variable will scale the expectation.
- $\mathbb{E}[X+a] = \mathbb{E}[X]+a$: Constant addition of a random variable will offset the expectation.
- $\mathbb{E}[aX + b] = a\mathbb{E}[X] + b$: Affine transformation of a random variable will translate to the expectation.

Practice Exercise 4.7. Prove the above three statements.

Solution. The third statement is just the sum of the first two statements, so we just need to show the first two:

$$\mathbb{E}[aX] = \int_\Omega axf_X(x)\,dx = a\int_\Omega xf_X(x)\,dx = a\mathbb{E}[X],$$

$$\mathbb{E}[X+a] = \int_\Omega (x+a)f_X(x)\,dx = \int_\Omega xf_X(x)\,dx + a = \mathbb{E}[X]+a.$$

4.2.2 Existence of expectation

As we discussed in the discrete case, not all random variables have an expectation.

Definition 4.4. *A random variable X has an expectation if it is* **absolutely integrable,** *i.e.,*

$$\mathbb{E}[|X|] = \int_\Omega |x|f_X(x)\,dx < \infty. \tag{4.5}$$

Being absolutely integrable implies that the expectation is that $\mathbb{E}[|X|]$ is the upper bound of $\mathbb{E}[X]$.

Theorem 4.2. *For any random variable X,*

$$|\mathbb{E}[X]| \le \mathbb{E}[|X|]. \tag{4.6}$$

Proof. Note that $f_X(x) \ge 0$. Therefore,

$$-|x|\,f_X(x) \le x\,f_X(x) \le |x|, f_X(x), \qquad \forall x.$$

Thus, integrating all three terms yields

$$-\int_\Omega |x|f_X(x)\,dx \le \int_\Omega x\,f_X(x)\,dx \le \int_\Omega |x|f_X(x)\,dx,$$

which is equivalent to $-\mathbb{E}[|X|] \le \mathbb{E}[X] \le \mathbb{E}[|X|]$.

$\square$

Example 4.11. Here is a random variable whose expectation is undefined. Let X be a random variable with PDF

$$f_X(x) = \frac{1}{\pi(1+x^2)}, \qquad x \in \mathbb{R}.$$

This random variable is called the **Cauchy random variable.** We can show that

$$\mathbb{E}[X] = \int_{-\infty}^{\infty} x \cdot \frac{1}{\pi(1+x^2)}\,dx = \frac{1}{\pi}\int_0^\infty \frac{x}{(1+x^2)}\,dx + \frac{1}{\pi}\int_{-\infty}^0 \frac{x}{(1+x^2)}\,dx.$$

The first integral gives

$$\int_0^\infty \frac{x}{(1+x^2)}\,dx = \frac{1}{2}\log(1+x^2)\Big|_0^\infty = \infty,$$

and the second integral gives $-\infty$. Since neither integral is finite, the expectation is undefined. We can also check the absolutely integrability criterion:

$$\mathbb{E}[|X|] = \int_{-\infty}^\infty |x| \cdot \frac{1}{\pi(1+x^2)}\,dx$$

$$\overset{(a)}{=} 2\int_0^\infty \frac{x}{\pi(1+x^2)}\,dx \geq 2\int_1^\infty \frac{x}{\pi(1+x^2)}\,dx$$

$$\overset{(b)}{\geq} 2\int_1^\infty \frac{x}{\pi(x^2+x^2)}\,dx = \frac{1}{\pi}\log(x)\Big|_1^\infty = \infty,$$

where in (a) we use the fact that the function being integrated is even, and in (b) we lower-bound $\frac{1}{1+x^2} \geq \frac{1}{x^2+x^2}$ if $x > 1$.

4.2.3 Moment and variance

The moment and variance of a continuous random variable can be defined analogously to the moment and variance of a discrete random variable, replacing the summations with integrations.

Definition 4.5. *The **kth moment** of a continuous random variable X is*

$$\mathbb{E}[X^k] = \int_\Omega x^k f_X(x)\,dx. \tag{4.7}$$

Definition 4.6. *The **variance** of a continuous random variable X is*

$$\mathrm{Var}[X] = \mathbb{E}[(X-\mu)^2] = \int_\Omega (x-\mu)^2 f_X(x)\,dx, \tag{4.8}$$

where $\mu \overset{\text{def}}{=} \mathbb{E}[X]$.

It is not difficult to show that the variance can also be expressed as

$$\mathrm{Var}[X] = \mathbb{E}[X^2] - \mu^2,$$

because

$$\begin{aligned}
\mathrm{Var}[X] &= \mathbb{E}[(X-\mu)^2] \\
&= \mathbb{E}[X^2] - 2\mathbb{E}[X]\mu + \mu^2 \\
&= \mathbb{E}[X^2] - \mu^2.
\end{aligned}$$

Practice Exercise 4.8. (Uniform random variable) Let X be a continuous random variable with PDF $f_X(x) = \frac{1}{b-a}$ for $a \le x \le b$, and 0 otherwise. Find $\text{Var}[X]$.

Solution. We have shown that $\mathbb{E}[X] = \frac{a+b}{2}$ and $\mathbb{E}[X^2] = \frac{a^2+ab+b^2}{3}$. Therefore, the variance is

$$\text{Var}[X] = \mathbb{E}[X^2] - \mathbb{E}[X]^2$$
$$= \frac{a^2 + ab + b^2}{3} - \left(\frac{a+b}{2}\right)^2$$
$$= \frac{(b-a)^2}{12}.$$

Practice Exercise 4.9. (Exponential random variable) Let X be a continuous random variable with PDF $f_X(x) = \lambda e^{-\lambda x}$ for $x \ge 0$, and 0 otherwise. Find $\text{Var}[X]$.

Solution. We have shown that $\mathbb{E}[X] = \frac{1}{\lambda}$. The second moment is

$$\mathbb{E}[X^2] = \int_0^\infty x^2 \, \lambda e^{-\lambda x} \, dx$$
$$= \left[-x^2 e^{-\lambda x}\right]_0^\infty + \int_0^\infty 2x e^{-\lambda x} \, dx$$
$$= \frac{2}{\lambda} \int_0^\infty x\lambda e^{-\lambda x} \, dx$$
$$= \frac{2}{\lambda} \cdot \frac{1}{\lambda} = \frac{2}{\lambda^2}.$$

Therefore,

$$\text{Var}[X] = \mathbb{E}[X^2] - \mathbb{E}[X]^2$$
$$= \frac{2}{\lambda^2} - \frac{1}{\lambda^2} = \frac{1}{\lambda^2}.$$

4.3 Cumulative Distribution Function

When we discussed discrete random variables, we introduced the concept of cumulative distribution functions (CDFs). One of the motivations was that if we view a PMF as a train of delta functions, they are technically not well-defined functions. However, it turns out that the CDF is always a well-defined function. In this section, we will complete the story by first discussing the CDF for continuous random variables. Then, we will come back and show you how the CDF can be derived for discrete random variables.

4.3.1 CDF for continuous random variables

Definition 4.7. *Let X be a continuous random variable with a sample space $\Omega = \mathbb{R}$. The* **cumulative distribution function (CDF)** *of X is*

$$F_X(x) \stackrel{\text{def}}{=} \mathbb{P}[X \le x] = \int_{-\infty}^{x} f_X(x')\,dx'. \tag{4.9}$$

The interpretation of the CDF can be seen from **Figure 4.5**. Given a PDF f_X, the CDF F_X evaluated at x is the integration of f_X from $-\infty$ up to a point x. The integration of f_X from $-\infty$ to x is nothing but the area under the curve of f_X. Since f_X is non-negative, the larger value x we use to evaluate in $F_X(x)$, the more area under the curve we are looking at. In the extreme when $x = -\infty$, we can see that $F_X(-\infty) = 0$, and when $x = +\infty$ we have that $F_X(+\infty) = \int_{-\infty}^{\infty} f_X(x)\,dx = 1$.

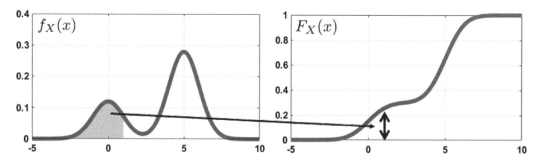

Figure 4.5: A CDF is the integral of the PDF. Thus, the height of a stem in the CDF corresponds to the area under the curve of the PDF.

Practice Exercise 4.10. (Uniform random variable) Let X be a continuous random variable with PDF $f_X(x) = \frac{1}{b-a}$ for $a \le x \le b$, and is 0 otherwise. Find the CDF of X.

Solution. The CDF of X is given by

$$F_X(x) = \begin{cases} 0, & x \le a, \\ \int_{-\infty}^{x} f_X(x')\,dx' = \int_{a}^{x} \frac{1}{b-a}\,dx' = \frac{x-a}{b-a}, & a < x \le b, \\ 1, & x > b. \end{cases}$$

As you can see from this practice exercise, we explicitly break the CDF into three segments. The first segment gives $F_X(x) = 0$ because for any $x \le a$, there is nothing to integrate, since $f_X(x) = 0$ for any $x \le a$. Similarly, for the last segment, $F_X(x) = 1$ for all $x > b$ because once x goes beyond b, the integration will cover all the non-zeros of f_X. **Figure 4.6** illustrates the PDF and CDF for this example.

In MATLAB, we can generate the PDF and CDF using the commands `pdf` and `cdf` respectively. For the particular example shown in **Figure 4.6**, the following code can be used. A similar set of commands can be implemented in Python.

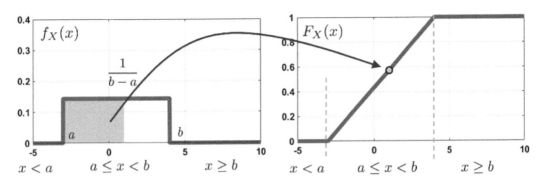

Figure 4.6: Example: $f_X(x) = 1/(b-a)$ for $a \leq x \leq b$. The CDF has three segments.

```matlab
% MATLAB code to generate the PDF and CDF
unif = makedist('Uniform','lower',-3,'upper',4);
x   = linspace(-5, 10, 1500)';
f   = pdf(unif, x);
F   = cdf(unif, x);
figure(1); plot(x, f, 'LineWidth', 6);
figure(2); plot(x, F, 'LineWidth', 6);
```

```python
# Python code to generate the PDF and CDF
import numpy as np
import matplotlib.pyplot as plt
import scipy.stats as stats
x = np.linspace(-5,10,1500)
f = stats.uniform.pdf(x,-3,4)
F = stats.uniform.cdf(x,-3,4)
plt.plot(x,f); plt.show()
plt.plot(x,F); plt.show()
```

Practice Exercise 4.11. (Exponential random variable) Let X be a continuous random variable with PDF $f_X(x) = \lambda e^{-\lambda x}$ for $x \geq 0$, and 0 otherwise. Find the CDF of X.

Solution. Clearly, for $x < 0$, we have $F_X(x) = 0$. For $x \geq 0$, we can show that

$$F_X(x) = \int_0^x f_X(x')\, dx' = \int_0^x \lambda e^{-\lambda x'}\, dx' = 1 - e^{-\lambda x}.$$

Therefore, the complete CDF is (see **Figure 4.7** for illustration):

$$F_X(x) = \begin{cases} 0, & x < 0, \\ 1 - e^{-\lambda x}, & x \geq 0. \end{cases}$$

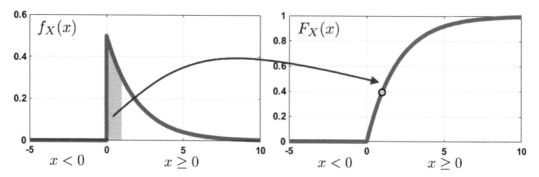

Figure 4.7: Example: $f_X(x) = \lambda e^{-\lambda x}$ for $x \geq 0$. The CDF has two segments.

The MATLAB code and Python code to generate this figure are shown below.

```
% MATLAB code to generate the PDF and CDF
pd = makedist('exp',2);
x  = linspace(-5, 10, 1500)';
f  = pdf(pd, x);
F  = cdf(pd, x);
figure(1); plot(x, f, 'LineWidth', 6);
figure(2); plot(x, F, 'LineWidth', 6);
```

```
# Python code to generate the PDF and CDF
import numpy as np
import matplotlib.pyplot as plt
import scipy.stats as stats
x = np.linspace(-5,10,1500)
f = stats.expon.pdf(x,2)
F = stats.expon.cdf(x,2)
plt.plot(x,f); plt.show()
plt.plot(x,F); plt.show()
```

4.3.2 Properties of CDF

Let us now describe the properties of a CDF. If we compare these with those for the discrete cases, we see that the continuous cases simply replace the summations by integrations. Therefore, we should expect to inherit most of the properties from the discrete cases.

> **Proposition 4.1.** Let X be a random variable (either continuous or discrete), then the CDF of X has the following properties:
>
> (i) The CDF is **nondecreasing**.
>
> (ii) The **maximum** of the CDF is when $x = \infty$: $F_X(+\infty) = 1$.
>
> (iii) The **minimum** of the CDF is when $x = -\infty$: $F_X(-\infty) = 0$.

Proof. For (i), we notice that $F_X(x) = \int_{-\infty}^{x} f_X(x') \, dx'$. Therefore, if $s \leq t$ then

$$F_X(s) = \int_{-\infty}^{s} f_X(x') \, dx' \leq \int_{-\infty}^{t} f_X(x') \, dx' = F_X(t).$$

Thus it shows that F_X is nondecreasing. (It does not need to be increasing because a CDF can have a steady state.) For (ii) and (iii), we can show that

$$F_X(+\infty) = \int_{-\infty}^{+\infty} f_X(x') \, dx' = 1, \quad \text{and} \quad F_X(-\infty) = \int_{-\infty}^{-\infty} f_X(x') \, dx' = 0. \qquad \square$$

Example 4.12. We can show that the CDF we derived for the uniform random variable satisfies these three properties. To see this, we note that

$$F_X(x) = \frac{x - a}{b - a}, \quad a \leq x \leq b.$$

The derivative of this function $F_X'(x) = \frac{1}{b-a} > 0$ for $a \leq x \leq b$. Also, note that $F_X(x) = 0$ for $x < a$ and $x > b$, so F_X is nondecreasing. The other two properties follow because if $x = b$, then $F_X(b) = 1$, and if $x = a$ then $F_X(a) = 0$. Together with the nondecreasing property, we show (ii) and (iii).

Proposition 4.2. *Let X be a continuous random variable. If the CDF F_X is continuous at any $a \leq x \leq b$, then*

$$\mathbb{P}[a \leq X \leq b] = F_X(b) - F_X(a). \tag{4.10}$$

Proof. The proof follows from the definition of the CDF, which states that

$$F_X(b) - F_X(a) = \int_{-\infty}^{b} f_X(x') \, dx' - \int_{-\infty}^{a} f_X(x') \, dx'$$

$$= \int_{a}^{b} f_X(x') \, dx' = \mathbb{P}[a \leq X \leq b]. \qquad \square$$

This result provides a very handy tool for calculating the probability of an event $a \leq X \leq b$ using the CDF. It says that $\mathbb{P}[a \leq X \leq b]$ is the difference between $F_X(b)$ and $F_X(a)$. So, if we are given F_X, calculating the probability of $a \leq X \leq b$ just involves evaluating the CDF at a and b. The result also shows that for a continuous random variable X, $\mathbb{P}[X = x_0] = F_X(x_0) - F_X(x_0) = 0$. This is consistent with our arguments from the measure's point of view.

Example 4.13. (Exponential random variable) We showed that the exponential random variable X with a PDF $f_X(x) = \lambda e^{-\lambda x}$ for $x \geq 0$ (and $f_X(x) = 0$ for $x < 0$) has a CDF given by $F_X(x) = 1 - e^{-\lambda x}$ for $x \geq 0$. Suppose we want to calculate the probability $\mathbb{P}[1 \leq X \leq 3]$. Then the PDF approach gives us

$$\mathbb{P}[1 \leq X \leq 3] = \int_1^3 f_X(x)\, dx = \int_1^3 \lambda e^{-\lambda x}\, dx = -e^{-\lambda x}\Big|_1^3 = e^{-3\lambda} - e^{-\lambda}.$$

If we take the CDF approach, we can show that

$$\mathbb{P}[1 \leq X \leq 3] = F_X(3) - F_X(1)$$
$$= (1 - e^{-\lambda}) - (1 - e^{-3\lambda}) = e^{-3\lambda} - e^{-\lambda},$$

which yields the same as the PDF approach.

Example 4.14. Let X be a random variable with PDF $f_X(x) = 2x$ for $0 \leq x \leq 1$, and is 0 otherwise. We can show that the CDF is

$$F_X(x) = \int_0^x f_X(t)\, dt = \int_0^x 2t\ dt = t^2\Big|_0^x = x^2, \qquad 0 \leq x \leq 1.$$

Therefore, to compute the probability $\mathbb{P}[1/3 \leq X \leq 1/2]$, we have

$$\mathbb{P}\left[\frac{1}{3} \leq X \leq \frac{1}{2}\right] = F_X\left(\frac{1}{2}\right) - F_X\left(\frac{1}{3}\right) = \left(\frac{1}{2}\right)^2 - \left(\frac{1}{3}\right)^2 = \frac{5}{36}.$$

$\square$

A CDF can be used for both continuous and discrete random variables. However, before we can do that, we need a tool to handle the discontinuities. The following definition is a summary of the three types of continuity.

Definition 4.8. *A function $F_X(x)$ is said to be*

- **Left-continuous** *at $x = b$ if $F_X(b) = F_X(b^-) \overset{\text{def}}{=} \lim_{h \to 0} F_X(b - h)$;*

- **Right-continuous** *at $x = b$ if $F_X(b) = F_X(b^+) \overset{\text{def}}{=} \lim_{h \to 0} F_X(b + h)$;*

- **Continuous** *at $x = b$ if it is both right-continuous and left-continuous at $x = b$. In this case, we have*

$$\lim_{h \to 0} F_X(b - h) = \lim_{h \to 0} F_X(b + h) = F(b).$$

In this definition, the step size $h > 0$ is shrinking to zero. The point $b - h$ stays at the left of b, and $b + h$ stays at the right of b. Thus, if we set the limit $h \to 0$, $b - h$ will approach a point b^- whereas $b + h$ will approach a point b^+. If it happens that $F_X(b^-) = F_X(b)$ then we say that F_X is left-continuous at b. If $F_X(b^+) = F_X(b)$ then we say that F_X is right-continuous at b. These are summarized in **Figure 4.8**.

Whenever F_X has a discontinuous point, it can be left-continuous, right-continuous, or neither. ("Neither" happens if $F_X(b)$ take a value other than $F_X(b^+)$ or $F_X(b^-)$. You can

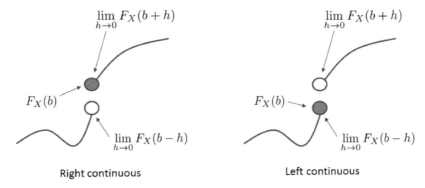

$$\lim_{h\to 0} F_X(b+h) \qquad\qquad \lim_{h\to 0} F_X(b+h)$$

$$F_X(b) \qquad\qquad F_X(b)$$

$$\lim_{h\to 0} F_X(b-h) \qquad\qquad \lim_{h\to 0} F_X(b-h)$$

Right continuous $\qquad\qquad$ Left continuous

Figure 4.8: The definition of left- and right-continuous at a point b.

always create a nasty function that satisfies this condition.) For continuous functions, it is necessary that $F_X(b^-) = F_X(b^+)$. If this happens, there is no gap between the two points.

Theorem 4.3. *For any random variable X (discrete or continuous), $F_X(x)$ is always* **right-continuous.** *That is,*

$$F_X(b) = F_X(b^+) \overset{\text{def}}{=} \lim_{h\to 0} F_X(b+h) \qquad (4.11)$$

Right-continuous means that if $F_X(x)$ is piecewise, it must have a **solid left end and an empty right end.** Figure 4.9 shows an example of a valid CDF and an invalid CDF.

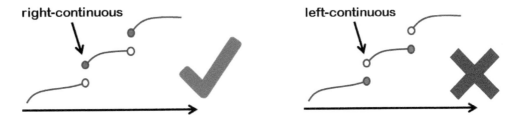

right-continuous $\qquad\qquad$ **left-continuous**

Figure 4.9: A CDF must be right-continuous.

The reason why F_X is always right-continuous is that the inequality $X \le x$ has a closed right-hand limit. Imagine the following situation: A discrete random variable X has four states: $1, 2, 3, 4$. Then,

$$\lim_{h\to 0} F_X(3+h) = \lim_{h\to 0} \sum_{k=1}^{\text{"}3+h\text{"}} p_X(k) = p_X(1) + p_X(2) + p_X(3) = F_X(3).$$

Similarly, if you have a continuous random variable X with a PDF f_X, then

$$\lim_{h\to 0} F_X(b+h) = \lim_{h\to 0} \int_{-\infty}^{b+h} f_X(t)\, dt = \int_{-\infty}^{b} f_X(t)\, dt = F_X(b).$$

In other words, the "≤" ensures that the rightmost state is included. If we defined CDF using <, we would have gotten left-hand continuous, but this would be inconvenient because the < requires us to deal with limits whenever we evaluate $X < x$.

Theorem 4.4. *For any random variable X (discrete or continuous), $\mathbb{P}[X = b]$ is*

$$\mathbb{P}[X = b] = \begin{cases} F_X(b) - F_X(b^-), & \text{if } F_X \text{ is discontinuous at } x = b \\ 0, & \text{otherwise.} \end{cases} \tag{4.12}$$

This proposition states that when $F_X(x)$ is discontinuous at $x = b$, then $\mathbb{P}[X = b]$ is the difference between $F_X(b)$ and the limit from the left. In other words, the height of the gap determines the probability at the discontinuity. If $F_X(x)$ is continuous at $x = b$, then $F_X(b) = \lim_{h \to 0} F_X(b - h)$ and so $\mathbb{P}[X = b] = 0$.

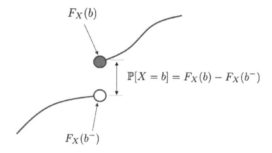

Figure 4.10: Illustration of Equation (4.12). Since the CDF is discontinuous at a point $x = b$, the gap $F_X(b) - F_X(b^-)$ will define the probability $\mathbb{P}[X = b]$.

Example 4.15. Consider a random variable X with a PDF

$$f_X(x) = \begin{cases} x, & 0 \le x \le 1, \\ \frac{1}{2}, & x = 3, \\ 0, & \text{otherwise.} \end{cases}$$

The CDF $F_X(x)$ will consist of a few segments. The first segment is $0 \le x < 1$. We can show that

$$F_X(x) = \int_0^x f_X(t)\, dt = \int_0^x t\ dt = \frac{t^2}{2}\bigg|_0^x = \frac{x^2}{2}, \quad 0 \le x < 1.$$

The second segment is when $1 \le x < 3$. Since there is no new f_X to integrate, the CDF stays at $F_X(x) = F_X(1) = \frac{1}{2}$ for $1 \le x < 3$. The third segment is $x > 3$. Because this range has covered the entire sample space, we have $F_X(x) = 1$ for $x > 3$. How about $x = 3$? We can show that

$$F_X(3) = F_X(3^+) = 1.$$

Therefore, to summarize, the CDF is

$$F_X(x) = \begin{cases} 0, & x < 0, \\ \frac{x^2}{2}, & 0 \le x < 1, \\ \frac{1}{2}, & 1 \le x < 3, \\ 1, & x \ge 3. \end{cases}$$

A graphical illustration is shown in **Figure 4.11**.

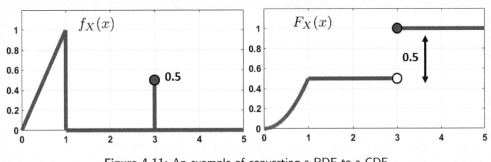

Figure 4.11: An example of converting a PDF to a CDF.

4.3.3 Retrieving PDF from CDF

Thus far, we have only seen how to obtain $F_X(x)$ from $f_X(x)$. In order to go in the reverse direction, we recall the fundamental theorem of calculus. This states that if a function f is continuous, then

$$f(x) = \frac{d}{dx} \int_a^x f(t)\, dt$$

for some constant a. Using this result for CDF and PDF, we have the following:

Theorem 4.5. *The **probability density function** (PDF) is the derivative of the cumulative distribution function (CDF):*

$$f_X(x) = \frac{dF_X(x)}{dx} = \frac{d}{dx} \int_{-\infty}^x f_X(x')\, dx', \tag{4.13}$$

provided F_X is differentiable at x. If F_X is not differentiable at $x = x_0$, then,

$$f_X(x_0) = \mathbb{P}[X = x_0]\delta(x - x_0).$$

Example 4.16. Consider a CDF

$$F_X(x) = \begin{cases} 0, & x < 0, \\ 1 - \frac{1}{4}e^{-2x}, & x \ge 0. \end{cases}$$

We want to find the PDF $f_X(x)$. To do so, we first show that $F_X(0) = \frac{3}{4}$. This corresponds to a discontinuity at $x = 0$, as shown in **Figure 4.12**.

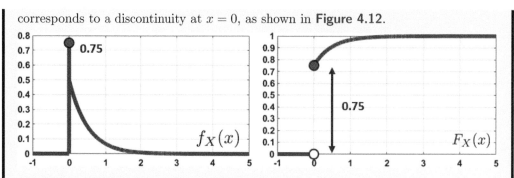

Figure 4.12: An example of converting a PDF to a CDF.

Because of the discontinuity, we need to consider three cases:

$$f_X(x) = \begin{cases} \frac{dF_X(x)}{dx}, & x < 0, \\ \mathbb{P}[X = 0]\,\delta(x - 0), & x = 0, \\ \frac{dF_X(x)}{dx}, & x > 0. \end{cases}$$

When $x < 0$, $F_X(x) = 0$, so $\frac{dF_X(x)}{dx} = 0$.

When $x > 0$, $F_X(x) = 1 - \frac{1}{4}e^{-2x}$, so

$$\frac{dF_X(x)}{dx} = \frac{1}{2}e^{-2x}.$$

When $x = 0$, the probability $\mathbb{P}[X = 0]$ is determined by the gap between the solid dot and the empty dot. This yields

$$\mathbb{P}[X = 0] = F_X(0) - \lim_{h \to 0} F_X(0 - h)$$
$$= \frac{3}{4} - 0 = \frac{3}{4}.$$

Therefore, the overall PDF is

$$f_X(x) = \begin{cases} 0, & x < 0, \\ \frac{3}{4}\delta(x - 0), & x = 0, \\ \frac{1}{2}e^{-2x}, & x > 0. \end{cases}$$

Figure 4.12 illustrates this example.

4.3.4 CDF: Unifying discrete and continuous random variables

The CDF is always a well-defined function. It is integrable everywhere. If the underlying random variable is continuous, the CDF is also continuous. If the underlying random variable is discrete, the CDF is a staircase function. We have seen enough CDFs for continuous random variables. Let us (re)visit a few discrete random variables.

Example 4.17. (Geometric random variable) Consider a geometric random variable with PMF $p_X(k) = (1-p)^{k-1}p$, for $k = 1, 2, \ldots$.

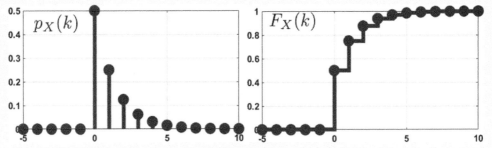

Figure 4.13: PMF and CDF of a geometric random variable.

We can show that the CDF is

$$F_X(k) = \sum_{\ell=1}^{k} p_X(\ell)$$

$$= \sum_{\ell=1}^{k} (1-p)^{\ell-1}p$$

$$= p \cdot \frac{1 - (1-p)^k}{1 - (1-p)}$$

$$= 1 - (1-p)^k.$$

For a sanity check, we can try to retrieve the PMF from the CDF:

$$p_X(k) = F_X(k) - F_X(k-1)$$
$$= (1 - (1-p)^k) - (1 - (1-p)^{k-1})$$
$$= (1-p)^{k-1}p.$$

A graphical portrayal of this example is shown in **Figure 4.13**.

If we treat the PMFs as delta functions in the above example, then the continuous definition also applies. Since the CDF is a piecewise constant function, the derivative is exactly a delta function. For some problems, it is easier to start with CDF and then compute the PMF or PDF. Here is an example.

Example 4.18. Let X_1, X_2 and X_3 be three independent discrete random variables with sample space $\Omega = \{1, 2, \ldots, 10\}$. Define $X = \max\{X_1, X_2, X_3\}$. We want to find the PMF of X. To tackle this problem, we first observe that the PMF for X_1 is $p_{X_1}(k) = \frac{1}{10}$. Thus, the CDF of X_1 is

$$F_{X_1}(k) = \sum_{\ell=1}^{k} p_{X_1}(\ell) = \frac{k}{10}.$$

Then, we can show that the CDF of X is

$$F_X(k) = \mathbb{P}[X \le k] = \mathbb{P}[\max\{X_1, X_2, X_3\} \le k]$$

$$\stackrel{(a)}{=} \mathbb{P}[X_1 \le k \cap X_2 \le k \cap X_3 \le k]$$

$$\stackrel{(b)}{=} \mathbb{P}[X_1 \le k]\mathbb{P}[X_2 \le k]\mathbb{P}[X_3 \le k]$$

$$= \left(\frac{k}{10}\right)^3,$$

where in (a) we use the fact that $\max\{X_1, X_2, X_3\} \le k$ if and only if all three elements are less than k, and in (b) we use independence. Consequently, the PMF of X is

$$p_X(k) = F_X(k) - F_X(k-1) = \left(\frac{k}{10}\right)^3 - \left(\frac{k-1}{10}\right)^3.$$

What is a CDF?

- CDF is $F_X(x) = \mathbb{P}[X \le x]$. It is the cumulative sum of the PMF/PDF.

- CDF is either a staircase function, a smooth function, or a hybrid. Unlike a PDF, which is not defined for discrete random variables, the CDF is always well defined.

- CDF $\xrightarrow{\frac{d}{dx}}$ PDF.

- CDF $\xleftarrow{\int}$ PDF.

- Gap of jump in CDF = height of delta in PDF.

4.4 Median, Mode, and Mean

There are three statistical quantities that we are frequently interested in: mean, mode, and median. We all know how to compute these from a dataset. For example, to compute the median of a dataset, we sort the data and pick the number that sits in the 50th percentile. However, the median computed in this way is the **empirical median**, i.e., it is a value computed from a particular dataset. If the data is generated from a random variable (with a given PDF), how do we compute the mean, median, and mode?

4.4.1 Median

Imagine you have a sequence of numbers as shown below.

n	1	2	3	4	5	6	7	8	9	$\cdots$	100
x_n	1.5	2.5	3.1	1.1	-0.4	-4.1	0.5	2.2	-3.4	$\cdots$	-1.4

How do we compute the median? We first sort the sequence (either in ascending order or descending order), and then pick the middle one. On computer, we permute the samples

$$\{x_{1'}, x_{2'}, \ldots, x_{N'}\} = \text{sort}\{x_1, x_2, \ldots, x_N\},$$

such that $x_{1'} < x_{2'} < \ldots < x_{N'}$ is ordered. The median is the one positioned at the middle. There are, of course, built-in commands such as median in MATLAB and np.median in Python to perform the median operation.

Now, how do we compute the median if we are given a random variable X with a PDF $f_X(x)$? The answer is by integrating the PDF.

Definition 4.9. *Let X be a continuous random variable with PDF f_X. The* **median** *of X is a point $c \in \mathbb{R}$ such that*

$$\int_{-\infty}^{c} f_X(x)\, dx = \int_{c}^{\infty} f_X(x)\, dx. \tag{4.14}$$

Why is the median defined in this way? This is because $\int_{-\infty}^{c} f_X(x)\, dx$ is the area under the curve on the left of c, and $\int_{c}^{\infty} f_X(x)\, dx$ is the area under the curve on the right of c. The area under the curve tells us the percentage of numbers that are less than the cutoff. Therefore, if the left area equals the right area, then c must be the median.

How to find the median from the PDF

- Find a point c that separates the PDF into two equal areas

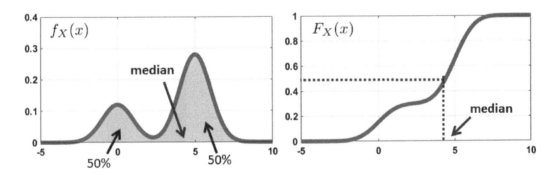

Figure 4.14: [Left] The median is computed as the point such that the two areas under the curve are equal. [Right] The median is computed as the point such that F_X hits 0.5.

The median can also be evaluated from the CDF as follows.

Theorem 4.6. *The* **median** *of a random variable X is the point c such that*

$$F_X(c) = \frac{1}{2}. \tag{4.15}$$

Proof. Since $F_X(x) = \int_{-\infty}^{x} f_X(x')\, dx'$, we have

$$F_X(c) = \int_{-\infty}^{c} f_X(x)\, dx = \int_{c}^{\infty} f_X(x)\, dx = 1 - F_X(c).$$

Rearranging the terms shows that $F_X(c) = \frac{1}{2}$. □

197

CHAPTER 4. CONTINUOUS RANDOM VARIABLES

How to find median from CDF

- Find a point c such that $F_X(c) = 0.5$.

Example 4.19. (**Uniform random variable**) Let X be a continuous random variable with PDF $f_X(x) = \frac{1}{b-a}$ for $a \leq x \leq b$, and is 0 otherwise. We know that the CDF of X is $F_X(x) = \frac{x-a}{b-a}$ for $a \leq x \leq b$. Therefore, the median of X is the number $c \in \mathbb{R}$ such that $F_X(c) = \frac{1}{2}$. Substituting into the CDF yields $\frac{c-a}{b-a} = \frac{1}{2}$, which gives $c = \frac{a+b}{2}$.

Example 4.20. (**Exponential random variable**) Let X be a continuous random variable with PDF $f_X(x) = \lambda e^{-\lambda x}$ for $x \geq 0$. We know that the CDF of X is $F_X(x) = 1 - e^{-\lambda x}$ for $x \geq 0$. The median of X is the point c such that $F_X(c) = \frac{1}{2}$. This gives $1 - e^{-\lambda c} = \frac{1}{2}$, which is $c = \frac{\log 2}{\lambda}$.

4.4.2 Mode

The mode is the peak of the PDF. We can see this from the definition below.

Definition 4.10. *Let X be a continuous random variable. The mode is the point c such that $f_X(x)$ attains the maximum:*

$$c = \underset{x \in \Omega}{argmax} \ f_X(x) = \underset{x \in \Omega}{argmax} \ \frac{d}{dx}F_X(x). \tag{4.16}$$

The second equality holds because $f_X(x) = F_X'(x) = \frac{d}{dx}\int_{-\infty}^{x} f_X(t) \, dt$. A pictorial illustration of mode is given in **Figure 4.15**. Note that the mode of a random variable is not unique, e.g., a mixture of two identical Gaussians with different means has two modes.

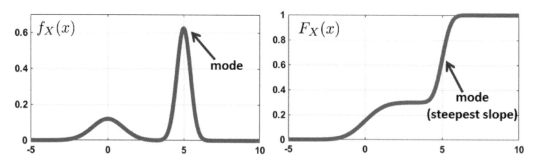

Figure 4.15: [Left] The mode appears at the peak of the PDF. [Right] The mode appears at the steepest slope of the CDF.

How to find mode from PDF

- Find a point c such that $f_X(c)$ is maximized.

How to find mode from CDF

- Continuous: Find a point c such that $F_X(c)$ has the steepest slope.
- Discrete: Find a point c such that $F_X(c)$ has the biggest gap in a jump.

Example 4.21. Let X be a continuous random variable with PDF $f_X(x) = 6x(1-x)$ for $0 \le x \le 1$. The mode of X happens at $\operatorname*{argmax}_{x} f_X(x)$. To find this maximum, we take the derivative of f_X. This gives

$$0 = \frac{d}{dx} f_X(x) = \frac{d}{dx} 6x(1-x) = 6(1-2x).$$

Setting this equal to zero yields $x = \frac{1}{2}$.

To ensure that this point is a maximum, we take the second-order derivative:

$$\frac{d^2}{dx^2} f_X(x) = \frac{d}{dx} 6(1-2x) = -12 < 0.$$

Therefore, we conclude that $x = \frac{1}{2}$ is a maximum point. Hence, the mode of X is $x = \frac{1}{2}$.

4.4.3 Mean

We have defined the mean as the expectation of X. Here, we show how to compute the expectation from the CDF. To simplify the demonstration, let us first assume that $X > 0$.

Lemma 4.1. Let $X > 0$. Then $\mathbb{E}[X]$ can be computed from F_X as

$$\mathbb{E}[X] = \int_0^\infty (1 - F_X(t)) \, dt. \tag{4.17}$$

Proof. The trick is to change the integration order:

$$
\int_0^\infty (1 - F_X(t)) \, dt = \int_0^\infty [1 - \mathbb{P}[X \le t]] \, dt = \int_0^\infty \mathbb{P}[X > t] \, dt
$$
$$
= \int_0^\infty \int_t^\infty f_X(x) \, dx \, dt \overset{(a)}{=} \int_0^\infty \int_0^x f_X(x) \, dt \, dx
$$
$$
= \int_0^\infty \int_0^x dt \, f_X(x) \, dx = \int_0^\infty x f_X(x) \, dx = \mathbb{E}[X].
$$

Here, step (a) is due to the change of integration order. See **Figure 4.16** for an illustration. $\square$

We draw a picture to illustrate the above lemma. As shown in **Figure 4.17**, the mean of a positive random variable $X > 0$ is equivalent to the area above the CDF.

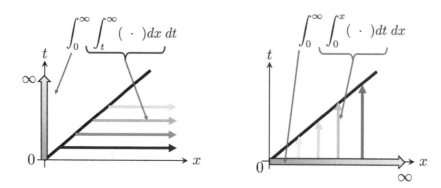

Figure 4.16: The double integration can be evaluated by x then t, or t then x.

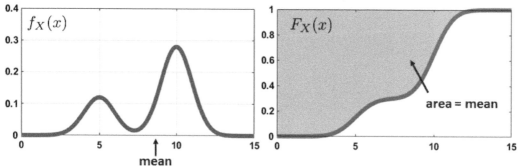

Figure 4.17: The mean of a **positive** random variable $X > 0$ can be calculated by integrating the CDF's complement.

Lemma 4.2. *Let $X < 0$. Then $\mathbb{E}[X]$ can be computed from F_X as*

$$\mathbb{E}[X] = \int_{-\infty}^{0} F_X(t) \, dt. \tag{4.18}$$

Proof. The idea here is also to change the integration order.

$$\int_{-\infty}^{0} F_X(t) \, dt = \int_{-\infty}^{0} \mathbb{P}[X \le t] \, dt = \int_{-\infty}^{0} \int_{-\infty}^{t} f_X(x) \, dx \, dt$$

$$= \int_{-\infty}^{0} \int_{x}^{0} f_X(x) \, dt \, dx = \int_{-\infty}^{0} x f_X(x) \, dx = \mathbb{E}[X].$$

$\square$

Theorem 4.7. *The mean of a random variable X can be computed from the CDF as*

$$\mathbb{E}[X] = \int_{0}^{\infty} (1 - F_X(t)) \, dt - \int_{-\infty}^{0} F_X(t) \, dt. \tag{4.19}$$

Proof. For any random variable X, we can partition $X = X^+ - X^-$ where X^+ and X^- are the positive and negative parts, respectively. Then, the above two lemmas will give us

$$\mathbb{E}[X] = \mathbb{E}[X^+ - X^-] = \mathbb{E}[X^+] - \mathbb{E}[X^-]$$

$$= \int_0^\infty (1 - F_X(t)) \ dt - \int_{-\infty}^0 F_X(t) \ dt.$$

$\square$

As illustrated in **Figure 4.18**, this equation is equivalent to computing the areas above and below the CDF and taking the difference.

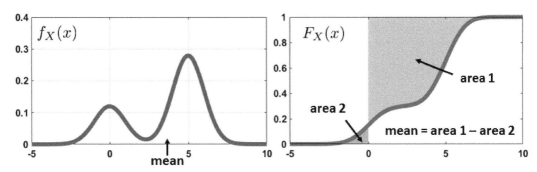

Figure 4.18: The mean of a random variable X can be calculated by computing the area in the CDF.

How to find the mean from the CDF

- A formula is given by Equation (4.20):

$$\mathbb{E}[X] = \int_0^\infty (1 - F_X(t)) \ dt - \int_{-\infty}^0 F_X(t) \ dt. \qquad (4.20)$$

- This result is not commonly used, but the proof technique of switching the integration order is important.

4.5 Uniform and Exponential Random Variables

There are many useful continuous random variables. In this section, we discuss two of them: uniform random variables and exponential random variables. In the next section, we will discuss the Gaussian random variables. Similarly to the way we discussed discrete random variables, we take a generative / synthesis perspective when studying continuous random variables. We assume we have access to the PDF of the random variables so we can derive the theoretical mean and variance. The opposite direction, namely inferring the underlying model parameters from a dataset, will be discussed later.

4.5.1   Uniform random variables

Definition 4.11. *Let X be a continuous* **uniform random variable.** *The PDF of X is*

$$f_X(x) = \begin{cases} \frac{1}{b-a}, & a \leq x \leq b, \\ 0, & \text{otherwise,} \end{cases} \qquad (4.21)$$

where $[a,b]$ is the interval on which X is defined. We write

$$X \sim \text{Uniform}(a,b)$$

to mean that X is drawn from a uniform distribution on an interval $[a,b]$.

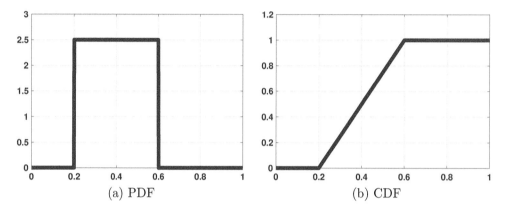

(a) PDF	(b) CDF

Figure 4.19: The PDF and CDF of $X \sim \text{Uniform}(0.2, 0.6)$.

The shape of the PDF of a uniform random variable is shown in **Figure 4.19**. In this figure, we assume that the random variables $X \sim \text{Uniform}(0.2, 0.6)$ are taken from the sample space $\Omega = [0, 1]$. Note that the height of the uniform distribution is greater than 1, since

$$f_X(x) = \begin{cases} \frac{1}{0.6-0.2} = 2.5, & 0.2 \leq x \leq 0.6, \\ 0, & \text{otherwise.} \end{cases}$$

There is nothing wrong with this PDF, because $f_X(x)$ is the probability *per unit length*. If we integrate $f_X(x)$ over any sub-interval between 0.2 and 0.6, we can show that the probability is between 0 and 1.

The CDF of a uniform random variable can be determined by integrating $f_X(x)$:

$$\begin{aligned} F_X(x) &= \int_{-\infty}^{x} f_X(t) \, dt \\ &= \int_{a}^{x} \frac{1}{b-a} \, dt \\ &= \frac{x-a}{b-a}, \qquad a \leq x \leq b. \end{aligned}$$

Therefore, the complete CDF is

$$F_X(x) = \begin{cases} 0, & x < a, \\ \frac{x-a}{b-a}, & a \leq x \leq b, \\ 1, & x > b. \end{cases}$$

The corresponding CDF for the PDF we showed in **Figure 4.19**(a) is shown in **Figure 4.19**(b). It can be seen that although the height of the PDF exceeds 1, the CDF grows linearly and saturates at 1.

Remark. The uniform distribution can also be defined for discrete random variables. In this case, the probability mass function is given by

$$p_X(k) = \frac{1}{b-a+1}, \quad k = a, a+1, \ldots, b.$$

The presence of "1" in the denominator of the PMF is because k runs from a to b, including the two endpoints.

In MATLAB and Python, generating uniform random numbers can be done by calling commands `unifrnd` (MATLAB), and `stats.uniform.rvs` (Python). For discrete uniform random variables, in MATLAB the command is `unidrnd`, and in Python the command is `stats.randint`.

```
% MATLAB code to generate 1000 uniform random numbers
a = 0; b = 1;
X = unifrnd(a,b,[1000,1]);
hist(X);
```

```
# Python code to generate 1000 uniform random numbers
import scipy.stats as stats
a = 0; b = 1;
X = stats.uniform.rvs(a,b,size=1000)
plt.hist(X);
```

To compute the empirical average and variance of the random numbers in MATLAB we can call the command `mean` and `var`. The corresponding command in Python is `np.mean` and `np.var`. We can also compute the median and mode, as shown below.

```
% MATLAB code to compute empirical mean, var, median, mode
X = unifrnd(a,b,[1000,1]);
M = mean(X);
V = var(X);
Med = median(X);
Mod = mode(X);
```

```
# Python code to compute empirical mean, var, median, mode
X = stats.uniform.rvs(a,b,size=1000)
M = np.mean(X)
V = np.var(X)
```

```
Med = np.median(X)
Mod = stats.mode(X)
```

The mean and variance of a uniform random variable are given by the theorem below.

Theorem 4.8. *If* $X \sim \text{Uniform}(a, b)$, *then*

$$\mathbb{E}[X] = \frac{a + b}{2} \quad and \quad \text{Var}[X] = \frac{(b - a)^2}{12}. \tag{4.22}$$

Proof. We have derived these results before. Here is a recap for completeness:

$$\mathbb{E}[X] = \int_{-\infty}^{\infty} x f_X(x)\, dx = \int_a^b \frac{x}{b - a}\, dx = \frac{a + b}{2},$$

$$\mathbb{E}[X^2] = \int_{-\infty}^{\infty} x^2 f_X(x)\, dx = \int_a^b \frac{x^2}{b - a}\, dx = \frac{a^2 + ab + b^2}{3},$$

$$\text{Var}[X] = \mathbb{E}[X^2] - \mathbb{E}[X]^2 = \frac{(b - a)^2}{12}.$$

□

The result should be intuitive because it says that the mean is the midpoint of the PDF.

When will we encounter a uniform random variable? Uniform random variables are one of the most elementary continuous random variables. Given a uniform random variable, we can construct any random variable by using an appropriate transformation. We will discuss this technique as part of our discussion about generating random numbers.

In MATLAB, computing the mean and variance of a uniform random variable can be done using the command `unifstat`. The Python coommand is `stats.uniform.stats`.

```
% MATLAB code to compute mean and variance
a = 0; b = 1;
[M,V] = unifstat(a,b)
```

```
# Python code to compute mean and variance
import scipy.stats as stats
a = 0; b = 1;
M, V = stats.uniform.stats(a,b,moments='mv')
```

To evaluate the probability $\mathbb{P}[\ell \leq X \leq u]$ for a uniform random variable, we can call `unifcdf` in MATLAB and

```
% MATLAB code to compute the probability P(0.2 < X < 0.3)
a = 0; b = 1;
F = unifcdf(0.3,a,b) - unifcdf(0.2,a,b)
```

```
# Python code to compute the probability P(0.2 < X < 0.3)
a = 0; b = 1;
F = stats.uniform.cdf(0.3,a,b)-stats.uniform.cdf(0.2,a,b)
```

An alternative is to define an object rv = stats.uniform, and call the CDF attribute:

```
# Python code to compute the probability P(0.2 < X < 0.3)
a = 0; b = 1;
rv = stats.uniform(a,b)
F = rv.cdf(0.3)-rv.cdf(0.2)
```

4.5.2 Exponential random variables

Definition 4.12. *Let X be an **exponential random variable**. The PDF of X is*

$$f_X(x) = \begin{cases} \lambda e^{-\lambda x}, & x \geq 0, \\ 0, & otherwise, \end{cases} \tag{4.23}$$

where $\lambda > 0$ is a parameter. We write

$$X \sim \text{Exponential}(\lambda)$$

to mean that X is drawn from an exponential distribution of parameter λ.

In this definition, the parameter λ of the exponential random variable determines the rate of decay. A large λ implies a faster decay. The PDF of an exponential random variable is illustrated in **Figure 4.20**. We show two values of λ. Note that the initial value $f_X(0)$ is

$$f_X(0) = \lambda e^{-\lambda 0} = \lambda.$$

Therefore, as long as $\lambda > 1$, $f_X(0)$ will exceed 1.

The CDF of an exponential random variable can be determined by

$$F_X(x) = \int_{-\infty}^{x} f_X(t) \, dt$$

$$= \int_{0}^{x} \lambda e^{-\lambda t} \, dt = 1 - e^{-\lambda x}, \qquad x \geq 0.$$

Therefore, if we consider the entire real line, the CDF is

$$F_X(x) = \begin{cases} 0, & x < 0, \\ 1 - e^{-\lambda x}, & x \geq 0. \end{cases}$$

The corresponding CDFs for the PDFs shown in **Figure 4.20**(a) are shown in **Figure 4.20**(b). For larger λ, the PDF $f_X(x)$ decays faster but the CDF $F_X(x)$ increases faster.

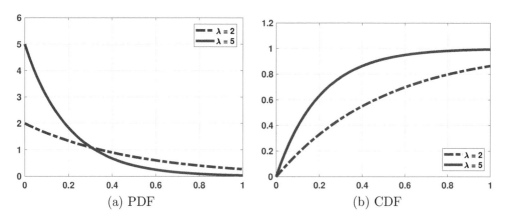

(a) PDF (b) CDF

Figure 4.20: (a) The PDF and (c) the CDF of $X \sim$ Exponential(λ).

In MATLAB, the code used to generate **Figure 4.20**(a) is shown below. There are multiple ways of doing this. An alternative way is to call `exppdf`, which will return the same result. In Python, the corresponding command is `stats.expon.pdf`. Note that in Python the parameter λ is specified in `scale` option.

```
% MATLAB code to plot the exponential PDF
lambda1 = 1/2;   lambda2 = 1/5;
x = linspace(0,1,1000);
f1 = pdf('exp',x, lambda1);
f2 = pdf('exp',x, lambda2);
plot(x, f1, 'LineWidth', 4, 'Color', [0 0.2 0.8]); hold on;
plot(x, f2, 'LineWidth', 4, 'Color', [0.8 0.2 0]);
```

```
# Python code to plot the exponential PDF
lambd1 = 1/2
lambd2 = 1/5
x = np.linspace(0,1,1000)
f1 = stats.expon.pdf(x,scale=lambd1)
f2 = stats.expon.pdf(x,scale=lambd2)
plt.plot(x, f1)
plt.plot(x, f2)
```

To plot the CDF, we replace `pdf` by `cdf`. Similarly, in Python we replace `expon.pdf` by `expon.cdf`.

```
% MATLAB code to plot the exponential CDF
F = cdf('exp',x, lambda1);
plot(x, F, 'LineWidth', 4, 'Color', [0 0.2 0.8]);
```

```
# Python code to plot the exponential CDF
F = stats.expon.cdf(x,scale=lambd1)
plt.plot(x, F)
```

Theorem 4.9. *If $X \sim$ Exponential(λ), then*

$$\mathbb{E}[X] = \frac{1}{\lambda} \quad and \quad \text{Var}[X] = \frac{1}{\lambda^2}. \tag{4.24}$$

Proof. We have discussed this proof before. Here is a recap for completeness:

$$\mathbb{E}[X] = \int_{-\infty}^{\infty} x f_X(x) \, dx = \int_{0}^{\infty} \lambda x e^{-\lambda x} \, dx$$

$$= -\int_{0}^{\infty} x \, de^{-\lambda x}$$

$$= -x e^{-\lambda x} \Big|_{0}^{\infty} + \int_{0}^{\infty} e^{-\lambda x} \, dx = \frac{1}{\lambda},$$

$$\mathbb{E}[X^2] = \int_{-\infty}^{\infty} x^2 f_X(x) \, dx = \int_{0}^{\infty} \lambda x^2 e^{-\lambda x} \, dx$$

$$= -\int_{0}^{\infty} x^2 \, de^{-\lambda x}$$

$$= -x^2 e^{-\lambda x} \Big|_{0}^{\infty} + \int_{0}^{\infty} 2x e^{-\lambda x} \, dx$$

$$= 0 + \frac{2}{\lambda} \mathbb{E}[X] = \frac{2}{\lambda^2}.$$

Thus, $\text{Var}[X] = \mathbb{E}[X^2] - \mathbb{E}[X]^2 = \frac{1}{\lambda^2}$.

$\square$

Computing the mean and variance of an exponential random variable in MATLAB and Python follows the similar procedures that we described above.

4.5.3 Origin of exponential random variables

Exponential random variables are closely related to Poisson random variables. Recall that the definition of a Poisson random variable is a random variable that describes the number of events that happen in a certain period, e.g., photon arrivals, number of pedestrians, phone calls, etc. We summarize the origin of an exponential random variable as follows.

What is the origin of exponential random variables?

- An exponential random variable is the **interarrival time** between two consecutive Poisson events.

- That is, an exponential random variable is how much time it takes to go from N Poisson counts to $N + 1$ Poisson counts.

An example will clarify this concept. Imagine that you are waiting for a bus, as illustrated in **Figure 4.21**. Passengers arrive at the bus stop with an arrival rate λ per unit time. Thus, for some time t, the average number of people that arrive is λt. Let N be a random variable denoting the number of people. We assume that N is Poisson with a parameter λt. That is, for any duration t, the probability of observing n people follows the PMF

$$\mathbb{P}[N = n] = \frac{(\lambda t)^n}{n!} e^{-\lambda t}.$$

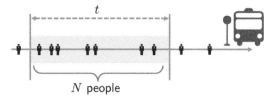

Figure 4.21: For any fixed period of time t, the number of people N is modeled as a Poisson random variable with a parameter λt.

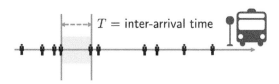

Figure 4.22: The interarrival time T between two consecutive Poisson events is an exponential random variable.

Let T be the interarrival time between two people, by which we mean the time between two consecutive arrivals, as shown in **Figure 4.22**. Note that T is a random variable because T depends on N, which is itself a random variable. To find the PDF of T, we first find the CDF of T. We note that

$$\mathbb{P}[T > t] \stackrel{(a)}{=} \mathbb{P}[\text{interarrival time } > t]$$
$$\stackrel{(b)}{=} \mathbb{P}[\text{no arrival in } t] \stackrel{(c)}{=} \mathbb{P}[N = 0] = \frac{(\lambda t)^0}{0!} e^{-\lambda t} = e^{-\lambda t}.$$

In this set of arguments, (a) holds because T is the interarrival time, and (b) holds because interarrival time is between two consecutive arrivals. If the interarrival time is larger than t, there is no arrival during the period. Equality (c) holds because N is the number of passengers.

Since $\mathbb{P}[T > t] = 1 - F_T(t)$, where $F_T(t)$ is the CDF of T, we can show that

$$F_T(t) = 1 - e^{-\lambda t},$$
$$f_T(t) = \frac{d}{dt} F_T(t) = \lambda e^{-\lambda t}.$$

Therefore, the interarrival time T follows an exponential distribution.

Since exponential random variables are tightly connected to Poisson random variables, we should expect them to be useful for modeling temporal events. We discuss two examples.

4.5.4 Applications of exponential random variables

Example 4.22. (**Photon arrivals**) Single-photon image sensors are designed to operate in the photon-limited regime. The number-one goal of using these sensors is to count the number of arriving photons precisely. However, for some applications not all single-photon image sensors are used to count photons. Some are used to measure the time between two photon arrivals, such as time-of-flight systems. In this case, we are interested in measuring the time it takes for a pulse to bounce back to the sensor. The more time it takes for a pulse to come back, the greater the distance between the object and the sensor. Other applications utilize the time information. For example, high-dynamic-range imaging can be achieved by recording the time between two photon arrivals because brighter regions have a higher Poisson rate λ and darker regions have a lower λ.

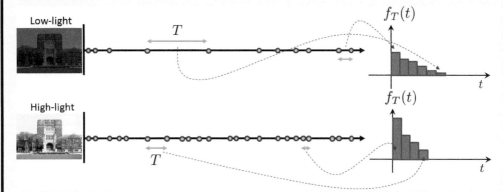

The figure above illustrates an example of high-dynamic-range imaging. When the scene is bright, the large λ will generate more photons. Therefore, the interarrival time between the consecutive photons will be relatively short. If we plot the histogram of the interarrival time, we observe that most of the interarrival time will be concentrated at small values. Dark regions behave in the opposite manner. The interarrival time will typically be much longer. In addition, because there is more variation in the photon arrival times, the histogram will look shorter and wider. Nevertheless, both cases are modeled by the exponential random variable.

Example 4.23. (**Energy-efficient escalator**) Many airports today have installed variable-speed escalators. These escalators change their speeds according to the traffic. If there are no passengers for more than a certain period (say, 60 seconds), the escalator will switch from the full-speed mode to the low-speed mode. For moderately busy escalators, the variable-speed configuration can save energy. The interesting data-science problem is to determine, given a traffic pattern, e.g., the one shown in **Figure 4.23**, whether we can predict the amount of energy savings?

We will not dive into the details of this problem, but we can briefly discuss the principle. Consider a fixed arrival rate λ (say, the average from 07:00 to 08:00). The interarrival time, according to our discussion above, follows an exponential distribution.

So we know that

$$f_T(t) = \lambda e^{-\lambda t}.$$

Suppose that the escalator switches to low-speed mode when the interarrival time exceeds τ. Then we can define a new variable Y to denote the amount of time that the escalator will operate in the low-speed mode. This new variable is

$$Y = \begin{cases} T - \tau, & T > \tau, \\ 0, & T \leq \tau. \end{cases}$$

In other words, if the interarrival time T is more than τ, then the amount of time saved Y takes the value $T - \tau$, but if the interarrival time is less than τ, then there is no saving.

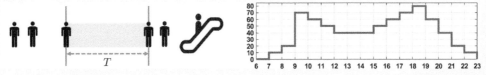

Figure 4.23: The variable-speed escalator problem. [Left] We model the passengers as independent Poisson arrivals. Thus, the interarrival time is exponential. [Right] A hypothetical passenger arrival rate (number of people per minute), from 06:00 to 23:00.

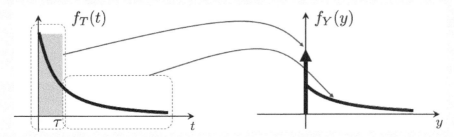

Figure 4.24: The escalator problem requires modeling the cutoff threshold τ such that if $T > \tau$, the savings are $Y = T - \tau$. If $T < \tau$, then $Y = 0$. The left-hand side of the figure shows how the PDF of Y is constructed.

The PDF of Y can be computed according to **Figure 4.24**. There are two parts to the calculation. When $Y = 0$, there is a probability mass such that

$$f_Y(0) = \mathbb{P}[Y = 0] = \int_0^\tau f_T(t)\, dt = \int_0^\tau \lambda e^{-\lambda t}\, dt = 1 - e^{-\lambda \tau}.$$

For other values of y, we can show that

$$f_Y(y) = f_T(y + \tau) = \lambda e^{-\lambda(y+\tau)}.$$

Therefore, to summarize, we can show that the PDF of Y is

$$f_Y(y) = \begin{cases} (1 - e^{-\lambda \tau})\delta(y), & y = 0, \\ \lambda e^{-\lambda(y+\tau)}, & y > 0. \end{cases}$$

Consequently, we can compute $\mathbb{E}[Y]$ and $\text{Var}[Y]$ and analyze how these values change for λ (which itself changes with the time of day). Furthermore, we can analyze the amount of savings in terms of dollars. We leave these problems as an exercise.

Closing remark. The photon arrival problem and the escalator problem are two of many examples we can find in which exponential random variables are useful for modeling a problem. We did not go into the details of the problems because each of them requires some additional modeling to address the real practical problem. We encourage you to explore these problems further. Our message is simple: Many problems can be modeled by exponential random variables, most of which are associated with time.

4.6 Gaussian Random Variables

We now discuss *the* most important continuous random variable — the **Gaussian random variable** (also known as the **normal random variable**). We call it the most important random variable because it is widely used in almost all scientific disciplines. Many of us have used Gaussian random variables before, and perhaps its bell shape is the first lesson we learn in statistics. However, there are many mysteries about Gaussian random variables which you may have missed, such as: Where does the Gaussian random variable come from? Why does it take a bell shape? What are the properties of a Gaussian random variable? The objective of this section is to explain everything you need to know about a Gaussian random variable.

4.6.1 Definition of a Gaussian random variable

> **Definition 4.13.** *A* **Gaussian random variable** *is a random variable X such that its PDF is*
> $$f_X(x) = \frac{1}{\sqrt{2\pi\sigma^2}} \exp\left\{-\frac{(x-\mu)^2}{2\sigma^2}\right\}, \tag{4.25}$$
> *where (μ, σ^2) are parameters of the distribution. We write*
> $$X \sim Gaussian(\mu, \sigma^2) \qquad or \qquad X \sim \mathcal{N}(\mu, \sigma^2)$$
> *to say that X is drawn from a Gaussian distribution of parameter (μ, σ^2).*

Gaussian random variables have two parameters (μ, σ^2). It is noteworthy that the mean is μ and the variance is σ^2 — these two parameters are exactly the first moment and the second central moment of the random variable. Most other random variables do not have this property.

Note that a Gaussian random variable is positive from $-\infty$ to ∞. Thus, $f_X(x)$ has a non-zero value for any x, even though the value may be extremely small. A Gaussian random variable is also symmetric about μ. If $\mu = 0$, then $f_X(x)$ is an even function.

The shape of the Gaussian is illustrated in **Figure 4.25**. When we fix the variance and change the mean, the PDF of the Gaussian moves left or right depending on the sign of the mean. When we fix the mean and change the variance, the PDF of the Gaussian changes its width. Since any PDF should integrate to unity, a wider Gaussian means that the PDF is shorter. Note also that if σ is very small, it is possible that $f_X(x) > 1$ although the integration over Ω will still be 1.

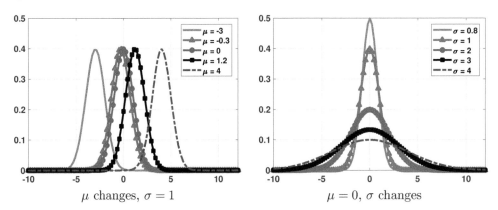

$$\mu \text{ changes, } \sigma = 1 \qquad \mu = 0, \sigma \text{ changes}$$

Figure 4.25: A Gaussian random variable with different μ and σ.

On a computer, plotting the Gaussian PDF can be done by calling the function pdf('norm',x) in MATLAB, and stats.norm.pdf in Python.

```
% MATLAB to generate a Gaussian PDF
x     = linspace(-10,10,1000);
mu    = 0; sigma = 1;
f     = pdf('norm',x,mu,sigma);
plot(x, f);
```

```
# Python to generate a Gaussian PDF
import numpy as np
import matplotlib.pyplot as plt
import scipy.stats as stats
x  = np.linspace(-10,10,1000)
mu = 0; sigma = 1;
f  = stats.norm.pdf(x,mu,sigma)
plt.plot(x,f)
```

Our next result concerns the mean and variance of a Gaussian random variable. You may wonder why we need this theorem when we already know that μ is the mean and σ^2 is the variance. The answer is that we have not proven these two facts.

Theorem 4.10. *If $X \sim Gaussian(\mu, \sigma^2)$, then*

$$\mathbb{E}[X] = \mu, \quad and \quad \text{Var}[X] = \sigma^2. \tag{4.26}$$

Proof. The expectation can be derived via substitution:

$$\mathbb{E}[X] = \frac{1}{\sqrt{2\pi\sigma^2}} \int_{-\infty}^{\infty} x e^{-\frac{(x-\mu)^2}{2\sigma^2}} \, dx$$

$$\overset{(a)}{=} \frac{1}{\sqrt{2\pi\sigma^2}} \int_{-\infty}^{\infty} (y+\mu) e^{-\frac{y^2}{2\sigma^2}} \, dy$$

$$= \frac{1}{\sqrt{2\pi\sigma^2}} \int_{-\infty}^{\infty} y e^{-\frac{y^2}{2\sigma^2}} \, dy + \frac{1}{\sqrt{2\pi\sigma^2}} \int_{-\infty}^{\infty} \mu e^{-\frac{y^2}{2\sigma^2}} \, dy$$

$$\overset{(b)}{=} 0 + \mu \left(\frac{1}{\sqrt{2\pi\sigma^2}} \int_{-\infty}^{\infty} e^{-\frac{y^2}{2\sigma^2}} \, dy \right)$$

$$\overset{(c)}{=} \mu,$$

where in (a) we substitute $y = x - \mu$, in (b) we use the fact that the first integrand is odd so that the integration is 0, and in (c) we observe that integration over the entire sample space of the PDF yields 1.

The variance is also derived by substitution.

$$\text{Var}[X] = \frac{1}{\sqrt{2\pi\sigma^2}} \int_{-\infty}^{\infty} (x-\mu)^2 e^{-\frac{(x-\mu)^2}{2\sigma^2}} \, dx$$

$$\overset{(a)}{=} \frac{\sigma^2}{\sqrt{2\pi}} \int_{-\infty}^{\infty} y^2 e^{-\frac{y^2}{2}} \, dy$$

$$= \frac{\sigma^2}{\sqrt{2\pi}} \left(-y e^{-\frac{y^2}{2}} \Big|_{-\infty}^{\infty} \right) + \frac{\sigma^2}{\sqrt{2\pi}} \int_{-\infty}^{\infty} e^{-\frac{y^2}{2}} \, dy$$

$$= 0 + \sigma^2 \left(\frac{1}{\sqrt{2\pi}} \int_{-\infty}^{\infty} e^{-\frac{y^2}{2}} \, dy \right)$$

$$= \sigma^2,$$

where in (a) we substitute $y = (x-\mu)/\sigma$.

4.6.2 Standard Gaussian

We need to evaluate the probability $\mathbb{P}[a \leq X \leq b]$ of a Gaussian random variable X in many practical situations. This involves the integration of the Gaussian PDF, i.e., determining the CDF. Unfortunately, there is no closed-form expression of $\mathbb{P}[a \leq X \leq b]$ in terms of (μ, σ^2). This leads to what we call the standard Gaussian.

> **Definition 4.14.** *The* **standard Gaussian** *(or standard normal) random variable X has a PDF*
> $$f_X(x) = \frac{1}{\sqrt{2\pi}} e^{-\frac{x^2}{2}}. \tag{4.27}$$
> *That is, $X \sim \mathcal{N}(0,1)$ is a Gaussian with $\mu = 0$ and $\sigma^2 = 1$.*

The CDF of the standard Gaussian can be determined by integrating the PDF. We have a special notation for this CDF. **Figure 4.26** illustrates the idea.

Definition 4.15. *The* **CDF** *of the standard Gaussian is defined as the* $\Phi(\cdot)$ *function*

$$\Phi(x) \stackrel{\text{def}}{=} F_X(x) = \frac{1}{\sqrt{2\pi}} \int_{-\infty}^{x} e^{-\frac{t^2}{2}} \, dt. \tag{4.28}$$

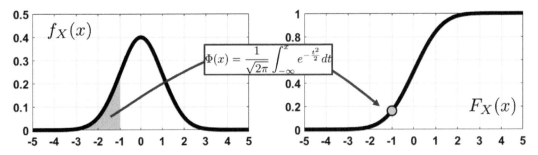

Figure 4.26: Definition of the CDF of the standard Gaussian $\Phi(x)$.

```
% MATLAB code to generate standard Gaussian PDF and CDF
x = linspace(-5,5,1000);
f = normpdf(x,0,1);
F = normcdf(x,0,1);
figure; plot(x, f);
figure; plot(x, F);
```

```
# Python code to generate standard Gaussian PDF and CDF
import numpy as np
import matplotlib.pyplot as plt
import scipy.stats as stats
x = np.linspace(-10,10,1000)
f = stats.norm.pdf(x)
F = stats.norm.cdf(x)
plt.plot(x,f); plt.show()
plt.plot(x,F); plt.show()
```

The standard Gaussian's CDF is related to a so-called **error function** defined as

$$\text{erf}(x) = \frac{2}{\sqrt{\pi}} \int_{0}^{x} e^{-t^2} \, dt. \tag{4.29}$$

It is easy to link $\Phi(x)$ with $\text{erf}(x)$:

$$\Phi(x) = \frac{1}{2}\left[1 + \text{erf}\left(\frac{x}{\sqrt{2}}\right)\right], \quad \text{and} \quad \text{erf}(x) = 2\Phi(x\sqrt{2}) - 1.$$

With the standard Gaussian CDF, we can define the CDF of an arbitrary Gaussian.

Theorem 4.11 (CDF of an arbitrary Gaussian). *Let $X \sim \mathcal{N}(\mu, \sigma^2)$. Then*

$$F_X(x) = \Phi\left(\frac{x - \mu}{\sigma}\right). \tag{4.30}$$

Proof. We start by expressing $F_X(x)$:

$$F_X(x) = \mathbb{P}[X \le x]$$

$$= \int_{-\infty}^{x} \frac{1}{\sqrt{2\pi\sigma^2}} e^{-\frac{(t-\mu)^2}{2\sigma^2}} \, dt.$$

Substituting $y = \frac{t-\mu}{\sigma}$, and using the definition of standard Gaussian, we have

$$\int_{-\infty}^{x} \frac{1}{\sqrt{2\pi\sigma^2}} e^{-\frac{(t-\mu)^2}{2\sigma^2}} \, dt = \int_{-\infty}^{\frac{x-\mu}{\sigma}} \frac{1}{\sqrt{2\pi}} e^{-\frac{y^2}{2}} \, dy$$

$$= \Phi\left(\frac{x-\mu}{\sigma}\right). \qquad \square$$

If you would like to verify this on a computer, you can try the following code.

```
% MATLAB code to verify standardized Gaussian
x = linspace(-5,5,1000);
mu = 3; sigma = 2;
f1 = normpdf((x-mu)/sigma,0,1); % standardized
f2 = normpdf(x, mu, sigma);     % raw
```

```
# Python code to verify standardized Gaussian
import numpy as np
import matplotlib.pyplot as plt
import scipy.stats as stats
x = np.linspace(-5,5,1000)
mu = 3; sigma = 2;
f1 = stats.norm.pdf((x-mu)/sigma,0,1) # standardized
f2 = stats.norm.cdf(x,mu,sigma)       # raw
```

An immediate consequence of this result is that

$$\mathbb{P}[a < X \le b] = \Phi\left(\frac{b - \mu}{\sigma}\right) - \Phi\left(\frac{a - \mu}{\sigma}\right). \tag{4.31}$$

To see this, note that

$$\mathbb{P}[a < X \le b] = \mathbb{P}[X \le b] - \mathbb{P}[X \le a]$$

$$= \Phi\left(\frac{b - \mu}{\sigma}\right) - \Phi\left(\frac{a - \mu}{\sigma}\right).$$

The inequality signs of the two end points are not important. That is, the statement also holds for $\mathbb{P}[a \le X \le b]$ or $\mathbb{P}[a < X < b]$, because X is a continuous random variable at every x. Thus, $\mathbb{P}[X = a] = \mathbb{P}[X = b] = 0$ for any a and b. Besides this, Φ has several properties of interest. See if you can prove these:

Corollary 4.1. *Let* $X \sim \mathcal{N}(\mu, \sigma^2)$. *Then the following results hold:*

- $\Phi(y) = 1 - \Phi(-y)$.
- $\mathbb{P}[X \geq b] = 1 - \Phi\left(\frac{b-\mu}{\sigma}\right)$.
- $\mathbb{P}[|X| \geq b] = 1 - \Phi\left(\frac{b-\mu}{\sigma}\right) + \Phi\left(\frac{-b-\mu}{\sigma}\right)$.

4.6.3 Skewness and kurtosis

In modern data analysis we are sometimes interested in high-order moments. Here we consider two useful quantities: **skewness** and **kurtosis**.

Definition 4.16. *For a random variable* X *with PDF* $f_X(x)$, *define the following* **central moments** *as*

$$mean = \mathbb{E}[X] \overset{\text{def}}{=} \mu,$$

$$variance = \mathbb{E}\left[(X-\mu)^2\right] \overset{\text{def}}{=} \sigma^2,$$

$$skewness = \mathbb{E}\left[\left(\frac{X-\mu}{\sigma}\right)^3\right] \overset{\text{def}}{=} \gamma,$$

$$kurtosis = \mathbb{E}\left[\left(\frac{X-\mu}{\sigma}\right)^4\right] \overset{\text{def}}{=} \kappa, \qquad excess\ kurtosis \overset{\text{def}}{=} \kappa - 3.$$

As you can see from the definitions above, skewness is the third central moment, whereas kurtosis is the fourth central moment. Both skewness and kurtosis can be regarded as "deviations" from a standard Gaussian —not in terms of mean and variance but in terms of shape.

Skewness measures the **asymmetry** of the distribution. **Figure 4.27** shows three different distributions: one with left skewness, one with right skewness, and one symmetric. The skewness of a curve is

- Skewed towards left: positive
- Skewed towards right: negative
- Symmetric: zero

What is skewness?

- $\mathbb{E}\left[\left(\frac{X-\mu}{\sigma}\right)^3\right]$.
- Measures the **asymmetry** of the distribution.
- Gaussian has skewness 0.

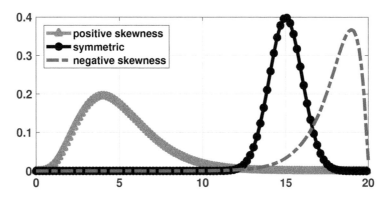

Figure 4.27: Skewness of a distribution measures the asymmetry of the distribution. In this example the skewnesses are: orange = 0.8943, black = 0, blue = -1.414.

Kurtosis measures how **heavy-tailed** the distribution is. There are two forms of kurtosis: one is the standard kurtosis, which is the fourth central moment, and the other is the **excess** kurtosis, which is $\kappa_{\text{excess}} = \kappa - 3$. The constant 3 comes from the kurtosis of a standard Gaussian. Excess kurtosis is more widely used in data analysis. The interpretation of kurtosis is the comparison to a Gaussian. If the kurtosis is positive, the distribution has a tail that decays faster than a Gaussian. If the kurtosis is negative, the distribution has a tail that decays more slowly than a Gaussian. **Figure 4.28** illustrates the (excess) kurtosis of three different distributions.

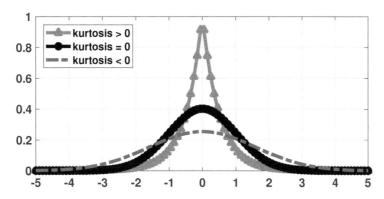

Figure 4.28: Kurtosis of a distribution measures how heavy-tailed the distribution is. In this example, the (excess) kurtoses are: orange = 2.8567, black = 0, blue = −0.1242.

What is kurtosis?

- $\kappa = \mathbb{E}\left[\left(\frac{X-\mu}{\sigma}\right)^4\right]$.

- Measures how **heavy-tailed** the distribution is. Gaussian has kurtosis 3.

- Some statisticians prefer **excess kurtosis** $\kappa - 3$, so that Gaussian has excess kurtosis 0.

Random variable	Mean μ	Variance σ^2	Skewness γ	Excess kurtosis $\kappa - 3$
Bernoulli	p	$p(1-p)$	$\frac{1-2p}{\sqrt{p(1-p)}}$	$\frac{1}{1-p}+\frac{1}{p}-6$
Binomial	np	$np(1-p)$	$\frac{1-2p}{\sqrt{np(1-p)}}$	$\frac{6p^2-6p+1}{np(1-p)}$
Geometric	$\frac{1}{p}$	$\frac{1-p}{p^2}$	$\frac{2-p}{\sqrt{1-p}}$	$\frac{p^2-6p+6}{1-p}$
Poisson	λ	λ	$\frac{1}{\sqrt{\lambda}}$	$\frac{1}{\lambda}$
Uniform	$\frac{a+b}{2}$	$\frac{(b-a)^2}{12}$	0	$-\frac{6}{5}$
Exponential	$\frac{1}{\lambda}$	$\frac{1}{\lambda^2}$	2	6
Gaussian	μ	σ^2	0	0

Table 4.1: The first few moments of commonly used random variables.

On a computer, computing the **empirical** skewness and kurtosis is done by built-in commands. Their implementations are based on the finite-sample calculations

$$\gamma \approx \frac{1}{N}\sum_{n=1}^{N}\left(\frac{X_n-\mu}{\sigma}\right)^3,$$

$$\kappa \approx \frac{1}{N}\sum_{n=1}^{N}\left(\frac{X_n-\mu}{\sigma}\right)^4.$$

The MATLAB and Python built-in commands are shown below, using a gamma distribution as an example.

```
% MATLAB code to compute skewness and kurtosis
X = random('gamma',3,5,[10000,1]);
s = skewness(X);
k = kurtosis(X);
```

```
# Python code to compute skewness and kurtosis
import scipy.stats as stats
X = stats.gamma.rvs(3,5,size=10000)
s = stats.skew(X)
k = stats.kurtosis(X)
```

Example 4.24. To further illustrate the behavior of skewness and kurtosis, we consider an example using the gamma random variable X. The PDF of X is given by the equation

$$f_X(x) = \frac{1}{\Gamma(k)\theta^k}x^{k-1}e^{-\frac{x}{\theta}}, \tag{4.32}$$

where $\Gamma(\cdot)$ is known as the gamma function. If k is an integer, the gamma function is just the factorial: $\Gamma(k) = (k-1)!$. A gamma random variable is parametrized by two parameters (k, θ). As k increases or decreases, the shape of the PDF will change. For example, when $k = 1$, the distribution is simplified to an exponential distribution.

Without going through the (tedious) integration, we can show that the skewness and the (excess) kurtosis of $\text{Gamma}(k, \theta)$ are

$$\text{skewness} = \frac{2}{\sqrt{k}},$$

$$(\text{excess}) \ \text{kurtosis} = \frac{6}{k}.$$

As we can see from these results, the skewness and kurtosis diminish as k grows. This can be confirmed from the PDF of $\text{Gamma}(k, \theta)$ as shown in **Figure 4.29**.

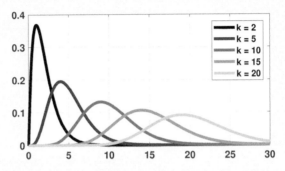

Figure 4.29: The PDF of a gamma distribution $\text{Gamma}(k, \theta)$, where $\theta = 1$. The skewness and the kurtosis are decaying to zero.

Example 4.25. Let us look at a real example. On April 15, 1912, RMS *Titanic* sank after hitting an iceberg. The disaster killed 1502 out of 2224 passengers and crew. A hundred years later, we want to analyze the data. At https://www.kaggle.com/c/titanic/ there is a dataset collecting the identities, age, gender, etc., of the passengers. We partition the dataset into two: one for those who died and the other one for those who survived. We plot the histograms of the ages of the two groups and compute several statistics of the dataset. **Figure 4.30** shows the two datasets.

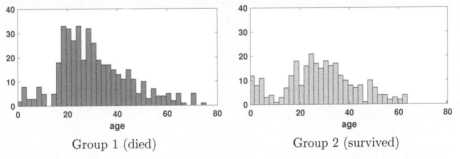

Group 1 (died)   Group 2 (survived)

Figure 4.30: The Titanic dataset https://www.kaggle.com/c/titanic/.

Statistics	Group 1 (Died)	Group 2 (Survived)
Mean	30.6262	28.3437
Standard Deviation	14.1721	14.9510
Skewness	0.5835	0.1795
Excess Kurtosis	0.2652	−0.0772

Note that the two groups of people have very similar means and standard deviations. In other words, if we only compare the mean and standard deviation, it is nearly impossible to differentiate the two groups. However, the skewness and kurtosis provide more information related to the shape of the histograms. For example, Group 1 has more positive skewness, whereas Group 2 is almost symmetrical. One interpretation is that more young people offered lifeboats to children and older people. The kurtosis of Group 1 is slightly positive, whereas that of Group 2 is slightly negative. Therefore, high-order moments can sometimes be useful for data analysis.

4.6.4   Origin of Gaussian random variables

The Gaussian random variable has a long history. Here, we provide one perspective on why Gaussian random variables are so useful. We give some intuitive arguments but leave the formal mathematical treatment for later when we introduce the Central Limit Theorem.

Let's begin with a numerical experiment. Consider throwing a fair die. We know that this will give us a (discrete) uniform random variable X. If we repeat the experiment many times we can plot the histogram, and it will return us a plot of 6 impulses with equal height, as shown in **Figure 4.31**(a).

Now, suppose we throw two dice. Call them X_1 and X_2, and let $Z = X_1 + X_2$, i.e., the sum of two dice. We want to find the distribution of Z. To do so, we first list out all the possible outcomes in the sample space; this gives us $\{(1,1), (1,2), \ldots, (6,6)\}$. We then sum the numbers, which gives us a list of states of Z: $\{2, 3, 4, \ldots, 12\}$. The probability of getting these states is shown in **Figure 4.31**(b), which has a triangular shape. The triangular shape makes sense because to get the state "2", we must have the pair $(1,1)$, which is quite unlikely. However, if we want to get the state 7, it would be much easier to get a pair, e.g., $(6,1), (5,2), (4,3), (3,4), (2,5), (1,6)$ would all do the job.

Now, what will happen if we throw 5 dice and consider $Z = X_1 + X_2 + \cdots + X_5$? It turns out that the distribution will continue to evolve and give something like **Figure 4.31**(c). This is starting to approximate a bell shape. Finally, if we throw 100 dice and consider $Z = X_1 + X_2 + \cdots + X_{100}$, the distribution will look like **Figure 4.31**(d). The shape is becoming a Gaussian! This numerical example demonstrates a fascinating phenomenon: As we sum more random variables, the distribution of the sum will converge to a Gaussian.

If you are curious about how we plot the above figures, the following MATLAB and Python code can be useful.

```
% MATLAB code to show the histogram of Z = X1+X2+X3
N  = 10000;
X1 = randi(6,1,N);
X2 = randi(6,1,N);
X3 = randi(6,1,N);
Z  = X1 + X2 + X3;
histogram(Z, 2.5:18.5);
```

```
# Python code to show the histogram of Z = X1+X2+X3
import numpy as np
import matplotlib.pyplot as plt
N = 10000
X1 = np.random.randint(1,6,size=N)
X2 = np.random.randint(1,6,size=N)
X3 = np.random.randint(1,6,size=N)
Z  = X1 + X2 + X3
plt.hist(Z,bins=np.arange(2.5,18.5))
```

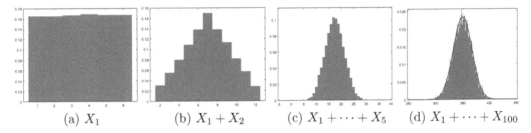

(a) X_1 (b) $X_1 + X_2$ (c) $X_1 + \cdots + X_5$ (d) $X_1 + \cdots + X_{100}$

Figure 4.31: When adding uniform random variables, the overall distribution approaches a Gaussian as the number of summed variables increase.

Can we provide a more formal description of this? Yes, but we need some new mathematical tools that we have not yet developed. So, for the time being, we will outline the flow of the arguments and leave the technical details to a later chapter. Suppose we have two independent random variables with identical distributions, e.g., X_1 and X_2, where both are uniform. This gives us PDFs $f_{X_1}(x)$ and $f_{X_2}(x)$ that are two identical rectangular functions. By what operation can we combine these two rectangular functions and create a triangle function? The key lies in the concept of **convolution**. If you convolve two rectangle functions, you will get a triangle function. Here we define the convolution of f_X as

$$(f_X * f_X)(x) = \int_{-\infty}^{\infty} f_X(\tau) f_X(x - \tau)\, d\tau.$$

In fact, for any pair of random variables X_1 and X_2 (not necessarily uniform random variables), the sum $Z = X_1 + X_2$ will have a PDF given by the convolution of the two PDFs. We have not yet proven this, but if you trust what we are saying, we can effectively generalize this argument to many random variables. If we have N random variables, then the sum $Z = X_1 + X_2 + \cdots + X_N$ will have a PDF that is the result of N convolutions of all the individual PDFs.

What is the PDF of $X + Y$?

- Summing $X + Y$ is equivalent to convolving the PDFs $f_X * f_Y$.
- If you sum many random variables, you convolve all their PDFs.

How do we analyze these convolutions? We need a second set of tools related to Fourier transforms. The Fourier transform of a PDF is known as the *characteristic function*, which we will discuss later, but the name is not important now. What matters is the important property of the Fourier transform, that a convolution in the original space is multiplication in the Fourier space. That is,

$$\mathcal{F}\{(f_X * f_X * \cdots * f_X)\} = \mathcal{F}\{f_X\} \cdot \mathcal{F}\{f_X\} \cdots \mathcal{F}\{f_X\}.$$

Multiplication in the Fourier space is much easier to analyze. In particular, for independent and identically distributed random variables, the multiplication will easily translate to addition in the exponent. Then, by truncating the exponent to the second order, we can show that the limiting object in the Fourier space is approaching a Gaussian. Finally, since the inverse Fourier transform of a Gaussian remains a Gaussian, we have shown that the infinite convolution will give us a Gaussian.

Here is some numerical evidence for what we have just described. Recall that the Fourier transform of a rectangle function is the sinc function. Therefore, if we have an infinite convolution of rectangular functions, equivalently, we have an infinite product of sinc functions in the Fourier space. Multiplying sinc functions is reasonably easy. See **Figure 4.32** for the first three sincs. It is evident that with just three sinc functions, the shape closely approximates a Gaussian.

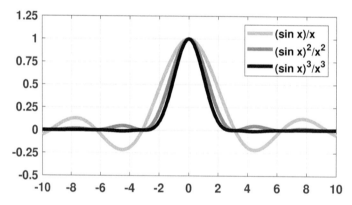

Figure 4.32: Convolving the PDF of a uniform distribution is equivalent to multiplying their Fourier transforms in the Fourier space. As the number of convolutions grows, the product is gradually becoming Gaussian.

How about distributions that are not rectangular? We invite you to numerically visualize the effect when you convolve the function many times. You will see that as the number of convolutions grows, the resulting function will become more and more like a Gaussian. Regardless of what the input random variables are, as long as you add them, the sum will have a distribution that looks like a Gaussian:

$$X_1 + X_2 + \cdots + X_N \rightsquigarrow \text{Gaussian}.$$

We use the notation $\rightsquigarrow$ to emphasize that the convergence is not the usual form of convergence. We will make this precise later.

The implication of this line of discussion is important. Regardless of the underlying true physical process, if we are only interested in the sum (or average), the distribution will be more or less Gaussian. In most engineering problems, we are looking at the sum or average. For example, when generating an image using an image sensor, the sensor will add a certain amount of read noise. Read noise is caused by the random fluctuation of the electrons in the transistors due to thermal distortions. For high-photon-flux situations, we are typically interested in the average read noise rather than the electron-level read noise. Thus Gaussian random variables become a reasonable model for that. In other applications, such as imaging through a turbulent medium, the random phase distortions (which alter the phase of the wavefront) can also be modeled as a Gaussian random variable. Here is the summary of the origin of a Gaussian random variable:

What is the origin of Gaussian?

- When we **sum** many independent random variables, the resulting random variable is a Gaussian.

- This is known as the **Central Limit Theorem**. The theorem applies to *any* random variable.

- Summing random variables is equivalent to **convolving** the PDFs. Convolving PDFs infinitely many times yields the bell shape.

4.7 Functions of Random Variables

One common question we encounter in practice is the transformation of random variables. The question can be summarized as follows: Given a random variable X with PDF $f_X(x)$ and CDF $F_X(x)$, and supposing that $Y = g(X)$ for some function g, what are $f_Y(y)$ and $F_Y(y)$? This is a prevalent question. For example, we measure the voltage V, and we want to analyze the power $P = V^2/R$. This involves taking the square of a random variable. Another example: We know the distribution of the phase Θ, but we want to analyze the signal $\cos(\omega t + \Theta)$. This involves a cosine transformation. How do we convert one variable to another? Answering this question is the goal of this section.

4.7.1 General principle

We will first outline the general principle for tackling this type of problem. In the following subsection, we will give a few concrete examples.

Suppose we are given a random variable X with PDF $f_X(x)$ and CDF $F_X(x)$. Let $Y = g(X)$ for some known and fixed function g. For simplicity, we assume that g is monotonically increasing. In this case, the CDF of Y can be determined as follows.

$$F_Y(y) \stackrel{(a)}{=} \mathbb{P}[Y \le y] \stackrel{(b)}{=} \mathbb{P}[g(X) \le y]$$
$$\stackrel{(c)}{=} \mathbb{P}[X \le g^{-1}(y)]$$
$$\stackrel{(d)}{=} F_X(g^{-1}(y)).$$

This sequence of steps is not difficult to understand. Step (a) is the definition of CDF. Step (b) substitutes $g(X)$ for Y. Step (c) uses the fact that since g is invertible, we can apply the inverse of g to both sides of $g(X) \leq y$ to yield $X \leq g^{-1}(y)$. Step (d) is the definition of the CDF, but this time applied to $\mathbb{P}[X \leq \clubsuit] = F_X(\clubsuit)$, for some $\clubsuit$.

It will be useful to visualize the situation in **Figure 4.33**. Here, we consider a uniformly distributed X so that the CDF $F_X(x)$ is a straight line. According to F_X, any samples drawn according to F_X are equally likely, as illustrated by the yellow dots on the x-axis. As we transform the X's through $Y = g(X)$, we increase/decrease the spacing between two samples. Therefore, some samples become more concentrated while some become less concentrated. The distribution of these transformed samples (the yellow dots on the y-axis) forms a new CDF $F_Y(y)$. The result $F_Y(y) = F_X(g^{-1}(y))$ holds when we look at Y. The samples are traveling with g^{-1} in order to go back to F_X. Therefore, we need g^{-1} in the formula.

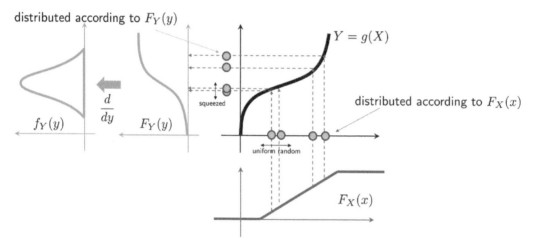

Figure 4.33: When transforming a random variable X to $Y = g(X)$, the distributions are defined according to the spacing between samples. In this figure, a uniformly distributed X will become squeezed by some parts of g and widened in other parts of g.

Why should we use the CDF and not the PDF in **Figure 4.33**? The advantage of the CDF is that it is an increasing function. Therefore, no matter what the function g is, the input and the output functions will still be increasing. If we use the PDF, then the non-monotonic behavior of the PDF will interact with another nonlinear function g. It becomes much harder to decouple the two.

We can carry out the integrations to determine $F_X(g^{-1}(y))$. It can be shown that

$$F_X(g^{-1}(y)) = \int_{-\infty}^{g^{-1}(y)} f_X(x')\, dx', \tag{4.33}$$

and hence, by the fundamental theorem of calculus, we have

$$f_Y(y) = \frac{d}{dy}F_Y(y) = \frac{d}{dy}F_X(g^{-1}(y)) = \frac{d}{dy}\int_{-\infty}^{g^{-1}(y)} f_X(x')\, dx'$$

$$= \left(\frac{d\, g^{-1}(y)}{dy}\right) \cdot f_X(g^{-1}(y)), \tag{4.34}$$

where the last step is due to the chain rule. Based on this line of reasoning we can summarize a "recipe" for this problem.

How to find the PDF of $Y = g(X)$
- Step 1: Find the CDF $F_Y(y)$, which is $F_Y(y) = F_X(g^{-1}(y))$.
- Step 2: Find the PDF $f_Y(y)$, which is $f_Y(y) = \left(\frac{d\,g^{-1}(y)}{dy}\right) \cdot f_X(g^{-1}(y))$.

This recipe works when g is a one-to-one mapping. If g is not one-to-one, e.g., $g(x) = x^2$ implies $g^{-1}(y) = \pm\sqrt{y}$, then we will have some issues with the above two steps. When this happens, then instead of writing $X \leq g^{-1}(y)$ we need to determine the set $\{x \mid g(x) \leq y\}$.

4.7.2 Examples

Example 4.26. (Linear transform) Let X be a random variable with PDF $f_X(x)$ and CDF $F_X(x)$. Let $Y = 2X + 3$. Find $f_Y(y)$ and $F_Y(y)$. Express the answers in terms of $f_X(x)$ and $F_X(x)$.

Solution. We first note that

$$
\begin{aligned}
F_Y(y) &= \mathbb{P}[Y \leq y] \\
&= \mathbb{P}[2X + 3 \leq y] \\
&= \mathbb{P}\left[X \leq \frac{y-3}{2}\right] = F_X\left(\frac{y-3}{2}\right).
\end{aligned}
$$

Therefore, the PDF is

$$
\begin{aligned}
f_Y(y) &= \frac{d}{dy}F_Y(y) \\
&= \frac{d}{dy}F_X\left(\frac{y-3}{2}\right) \\
&= F_X'\left(\frac{y-3}{2}\right)\frac{d}{dy}\left(\frac{y-3}{2}\right) = \frac{1}{2}f_X\left(\frac{y-3}{2}\right).
\end{aligned}
$$

Follow-Up. (Linear transformation of a Gaussian random variable). Suppose X is a Gaussian random variable with zero mean and unit variance, and let $Y = aX + b$. Then the CDF and PDF of Y are respectively

$$
F_Y(y) = F_X\left(\frac{y-b}{a}\right) = \Phi\left(\frac{y-b}{a}\right),
$$

$$
f_Y(y) = \frac{1}{a}f_X\left(\frac{y-b}{a}\right) = \frac{1}{\sqrt{2\pi}a}e^{-\frac{(y-b)^2}{2a^2}}.
$$

Follow-Up. (Linear transformation of an exponential random variable). Suppose X is an exponential random variable with parameter λ, and let $Y = aX + b$. Then the CDF and

PDF of Y are respectively

$$F_Y(y) = F_X\left(\frac{y-b}{a}\right)$$

$$= 1 - e^{-\frac{\lambda}{a}(y-b)}, \qquad y \geq b,$$

$$f_Y(y) = \frac{1}{a} f_X\left(\frac{y-b}{a}\right)$$

$$= \frac{\lambda}{a} e^{-\frac{\lambda}{a}(y-b)}, \qquad y \geq b.$$

Example 4.27. Let X be a random variable with PDF $f_X(x)$ and CDF $F_X(x)$. Supposing that $Y = X^2$, find $f_Y(y)$ and $F_Y(y)$. Express the answers in terms of $f_X(x)$ and $F_X(x)$.

Solution. We note that

$$F_Y(y) = \mathbb{P}[Y \leq y] = \mathbb{P}[X^2 \leq y] = \mathbb{P}[-\sqrt{y} \leq X \leq \sqrt{y}]$$
$$= F_X(\sqrt{y}) - F_X(-\sqrt{y}).$$

Therefore, the PDF is

$$f_Y(y) = \frac{d}{dy} F_Y(y)$$

$$= \frac{d}{dy}\left(F_X(\sqrt{y}) - F_X(-\sqrt{y})\right)$$

$$= F_X'(\sqrt{y})\frac{d}{dy}\sqrt{y} - F_X'(-\sqrt{y})\frac{d}{dy}(-\sqrt{y})$$

$$= \frac{1}{2\sqrt{y}}\left(f_X(\sqrt{y}) + f_X(-\sqrt{y})\right).$$

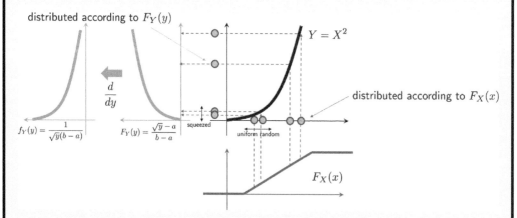

Figure 4.34: When transforming a random variable X to $Y = X^2$, the CDF becomes $F_Y(y) = \frac{\sqrt{y}-a}{b-a}$ and the PDF becomes $f_Y(y) = \frac{1}{\sqrt{y}(b-a)}$.

Follow Up. (Square of a uniform random variable) Suppose X is a uniform random variable in $[a, b]$ (assume $a > 0$), and let $Y = X^2$. Then the CDF and PDF of Y are respectively

$$F_Y(y) = \frac{\sqrt{y} - a}{b - a}, \qquad a^2 \le y \le b^2,$$

$$f_Y(y) = \frac{1}{\sqrt{y}(b - a)}, \qquad a^2 \le y \le b^2.$$

Example 4.28. Let $X \sim \text{Uniform}(0, 2\pi)$. Suppose $Y = \cos X$. Find $f_Y(y)$ and $F_Y(y)$.

Solution. First, we need to find the CDF of X. This can be done by noting that

$$F_X(x) = \int_{-\infty}^{x} f_X(x') \, dx' = \int_0^x \frac{1}{2\pi} \, dx' = \frac{x}{2\pi}.$$

Thus, the CDF of Y is

$$
\begin{aligned}
F_Y(y) &= \mathbb{P}[Y \le y] = \mathbb{P}[\cos X \le y] \\
&= \mathbb{P}[\cos^{-1} y \le X \le 2\pi - \cos^{-1} y] \\
&= F_X(2\pi - \cos^{-1} y) - F_X(\cos^{-1} y) \\
&= 1 - \frac{\cos^{-1} y}{\pi}.
\end{aligned}
$$

The PDF of Y is

$$
\begin{aligned}
f_Y(y) &= \frac{d}{dy} F_Y(y) = \frac{d}{dy}\left(1 - \frac{\cos^{-1} y}{\pi}\right) \\
&= \frac{1}{\pi\sqrt{1 - y^2}},
\end{aligned}
$$

where we used the fact that $\frac{d}{dy}\cos^{-1} y = \frac{-1}{\sqrt{1-y^2}}$.

Example 4.29. Let X be a random variable with PDF

$$f_X(x) = ae^x e^{-ae^x}.$$

Let $Y = e^X$, and find $f_Y(y)$.

Solution. We first note that

$$
\begin{aligned}
F_Y(y) &= \mathbb{P}[Y \le y] = \mathbb{P}[e^X \le y] \\
&= \mathbb{P}[X \le \log y] = \int_{-\infty}^{\log y} ae^x e^{-ae^x} \, dx.
\end{aligned}
$$

To find the PDF, we recall the fundamental theorem of calculus. This gives us

$$f_Y(y) = \frac{d}{dy} \int_{-\infty}^{\log y} ae^x e^{-ae^x} \, dx$$

$$= \left(\frac{d}{dy} \log y \right) \left(\frac{d}{d \log y} \int_{-\infty}^{\log y} ae^x e^{-ae^x} \, dx \right)$$

$$= \frac{1}{y} ae^{\log y} e^{-ae^{\log y}} = ae^{-ay}.$$

Closing remark. The transformation of random variables is a fundamental technique in data science. The approach we have presented is the most rudimentary yet the most intuitive. The key is to visualize the transformation and how the random samples are allocated after the transformation. Note that the density of the random samples is related to the slope of the CDF. Therefore, if the transformation maps many samples to similar values, the slope of the CDF will be steep. Once you understand this picture, the transformation will be a lot easier to understand.

Is it possible to replace the paper-and-pencil derivation of a transformation with a computer? If the objective is to transform random realizations, then the answer is yes because your goal is to transform numbers to numbers, which can be done on a computer. For example, transforming a sample x_1 to $\sqrt{x_1}$ is straightforward on a computer. However, if the objective is to derive the theoretical expression of the PDF, then the answer is no. Why might we want to derive the theoretical PDF? We might want to analyze the mean, variance, or other statistical properties. We may also want to reverse-engineer and determine a transformation that can yield a specific PDF. This would require a paper-and-pencil derivation. In what follows, we will discuss a handy application of the transformations.

What are the rules of thumb for transformation of random variables?

- Always find the CDF $F_Y(y) = \mathbb{P}[g(X) \le y]$. Ask yourself: What are the values of X such that $g(X) \le y$? Think of the cosine example.

- Sometimes you do not need to solve for $F_Y(y)$ explicitly. The fundamental theorem of calculus can help you find $f_Y(y)$.

- Draw pictures. Ask yourself whether you need to squeeze or stretch the samples.

4.8 Generating Random Numbers

Most scientific computing software nowadays has built-in random number generators. For common types of random variables, e.g., Gaussian or exponential, these random number generators can easily generate numbers according to the chosen distribution. However, if we are given an arbitrary PDF (or PMF) that is not among the list of predefined distributions, how can we generate random numbers according to the PDF or PMF we want?

4.8.1 General principle

Generating random numbers according to the desired distribution can be formulated as an inverse problem. Suppose that we can generate uniformly random numbers according to Uniform(0,1). This is a fragile assumption, and this process can be done on almost all computers today. Let us call this random variable U and its realization u. Suppose that we also have a desired distribution $f_X(x)$ (and its CDF $F_X(x)$). We can put the two random variables U and X on the two axes of **Figure 4.35**, yielding an input-output relationship. The inverse problem is: By using what transformation g, such that $X = g(U)$, can we make sure that X is distributed according to $f_X(x)$ (or $F_X(x)$)?

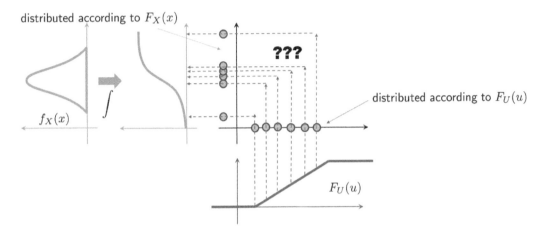

Figure 4.35: Generating random numbers according to a known CDF. The idea is to first generate a uniform(0,1) random variable, then do an inverse mapping F_X^{-1}.

Theorem 4.12. *The transformation g that can turn a uniform random variable into a random variable following a distribution $F_X(x)$ is given by*

$$g(u) = F_X^{-1}(u). \tag{4.35}$$

That is, if $g = F_X^{-1}$, then $g(U)$ will be distributed according to f_X (or F_X).

Proof. First, we know that if $U \sim \text{Uniform}(0, 1)$, then $f_U(u) = 1$ for $0 \le u \le 1$, so

$$F_U(u) = \int_{-\infty}^{u} f_U(u) \, du = u,$$

for $0 \le u \le 1$. Let $g = F_X^{-1}$ and define $Y = g(U)$. Then the CDF of Y is

$$
\begin{aligned}
F_Y(y) = \mathbb{P}[Y \le y] &= \mathbb{P}[g(U) \le y] \\
&= \mathbb{P}[F_X^{-1}(U) \le y] \\
&= \mathbb{P}[U \le F_X(y)] = F_X(y).
\end{aligned}
$$

Therefore, we have shown that the CDF of Y is the CDF of X. $\qquad\square$

The theorem above states that if we want a distribution F_X, then the transformation should be $g = F_X^{-1}$. This suggests a two-step process for generating random numbers.

How do we generate random numbers from an arbitrary distribution F_X?

- Step 1: Generate a random number $U \sim \text{Uniform}(0,1)$.
- Step 2: Let

$$Y = F_X^{-1}(U). \tag{4.36}$$

Then the distribution of Y is F_X.

4.8.2 Examples

Example 4.30. How can we generate Gaussian random numbers with mean μ and variance σ^2 from uniform random numbers?

First, we generate $U \sim \text{Uniform}(0,1)$. The CDF of the ideal distribution is

$$F_X(x) = \Phi\left(\frac{x - \mu}{\sigma}\right).$$

Therefore, the transformation g is

$$g(U) = F_X^{-1}(U) = \sigma\Phi^{-1}(U) + \mu.$$

In **Figure 4.36**, we plot the CDF of F_X and the transformation g.

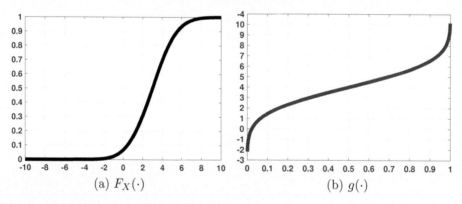

(a) $F_X(\cdot)$ (b) $g(\cdot)$

Figure 4.36: To generate random numbers according to Gaussian$(0,1)$, we plot its CDF in (a) and the transformation g in (b).

To visualize the random variables before and after the transformation, we plot the histograms in **Figure 4.37**.

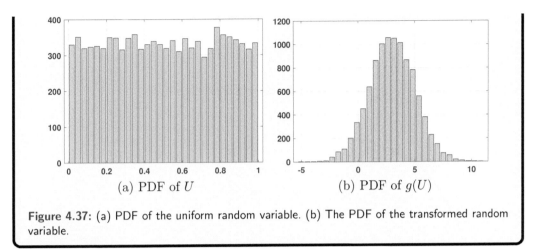

(a) PDF of U (b) PDF of $g(U)$

Figure 4.37: (a) PDF of the uniform random variable. (b) The PDF of the transformed random variable.

The MATLAB and Python codes used to generate the histograms above are shown below.

```
% MATLAB code to generate Gaussian from uniform
mu    = 3;
sigma = 2;
U     = rand(10000,1);
gU    = sigma*icdf('norm',U,0,1)+mu;
figure; hist(U);
figure; hist(gU);
```

```
# Python code to generate Gaussian from uniform
import numpy as np
import matplotlib.pyplot as plt
import scipy.stats as stats

mu = 3
sigma = 2
U  = stats.uniform.rvs(0,1,size=10000)
gU = sigma*stats.norm.ppf(U)+mu
plt.hist(U); plt.show()
plt.hist(gU); plt.show()
```

Example 4.31. How can we generate exponential random numbers with parameter λ from uniform random numbers?

First, we generate $U \sim \text{Uniform}(0, 1)$. The CDF of the ideal distribution is

$$F_X(x) = 1 - e^{-\lambda x}.$$

Therefore, the transformation g is

$$g(U) = F_X^{-1}(U) = -\frac{1}{\lambda}\log(1-U).$$

The CDF of the exponential random variable and the transformation g are shown in **Figure 4.38**.

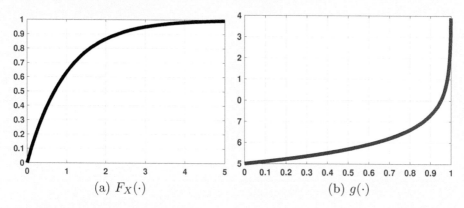

(a) $F_X(\cdot)$ (b) $g(\cdot)$

Figure 4.38: To generate random numbers according to Exponential(1), we plot its CDF in (a) and the transformation g in (b).

The PDF of the uniform random variable U and the PDF of the transformed variable $g(U)$ are shown in **Figure 4.39**.

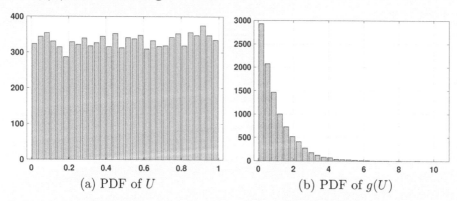

(a) PDF of U (b) PDF of $g(U)$

Figure 4.39: (a) PDF of the uniform random variable. (b) The PDF of the transformed random variable.

The MATLAB and Python codes for this transformation are shown below.

```
% MATLAB code to generate exponential random variables
lambda = 1;
U       = rand(10000,1);
gU      = -(1/lambda)*log(1-U);
```

```
# Python code to generate exponential random variables
import numpy as np
```

```
import scipy.stats as stats

lambd = 1;
U     = stats.uniform.rvs(0,1,size=10000)
gU    = -(1/lambd)*np.log(1-U)
```

Example 4.32. How can we generate the 4 integers $1, 2, 3, 4$, according to the histogram $[0.1\ 0.5\ 0.3\ 0.1]$, from uniform random numbers?

First, we generate $U \sim \text{Uniform}(0, 1)$. The CDF of the ideal distribution is

$$F_X(x) = \begin{cases} 0.1, & x = 1, \\ 0.1 + 0.5 = 0.6, & x = 2, \\ 0.1 + 0.5 + 0.3 = 0.9, & x = 3, \\ 0.1 + 0.5 + 0.3 + 0.1 = 1.0, & x = 4. \end{cases}$$

This CDF is not invertible. However, we can still define the "inverse" mapping as

$$g(U) = F_X^{-1}(U)$$

$$= \begin{cases} 1, & 0.0 \le U \le 0.1, \\ 2, & 0.1 < U \le 0.6, \\ 3, & 0.6 < U \le 0.9, \\ 4, & 0.9 < U \le 1.0. \end{cases}$$

For example, if $0.1 < U \le 0.6$, then on the black curve shown in **Figure 4.40**(a), we are looking at the second vertical line from the left. This will go to "2" on the x-axis. Therefore, the inversely mapped value is 2 for $0.1 < U \le 0.6$.

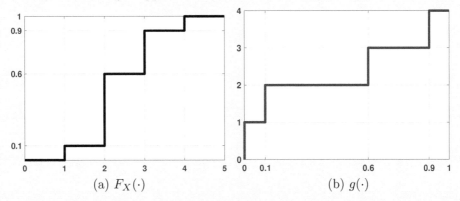

(a) $F_X(\cdot)$ (b) $g(\cdot)$

Figure 4.40: To generate random numbers according to a predefined histogram, we first define the CDF in (a) and the corresponding transformation in (b).

The PDFs of the transformed variables, before and after, are shown in **Figure 4.41**.

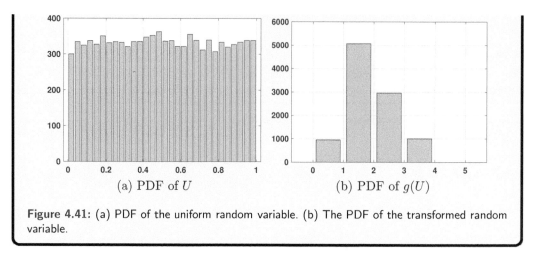

(a) PDF of U (b) PDF of $g(U)$

Figure 4.41: (a) PDF of the uniform random variable. (b) The PDF of the transformed random variable.

In MATLAB, the above PDFs can be plotted using the commands below. In Python, we need to use the logical comparison `np.logical_and` to identify the indices. An alternative is to use `gU[((U<=0.5)*(U>=0.0)).astype(np.bool)]=1`.

```
% MATLAB code to generate the desired random variables
U  = rand(10000,1);
gU = zeros(10000,1);
gU((U>=0)   & (U<=0.1)) = 1;
gU((U>0.1) & (U<=0.6)) = 2;
gU((U>0.6) & (U<=0.9)) = 3;
gU((U>0.9) & (U<=1))   = 4;
```

```
# Python code to generate the desired random variables
import numpy as np
import scipy.stats as stats

U  = stats.uniform.rvs(0,1,size=10000)
gU = np.zeros(10000)
gU[np.logical_and(U >= 0.0, U <= 0.1)] = 1
gU[np.logical_and(U > 0.1, U <= 0.6)]  = 2
gU[np.logical_and(U > 0.6, U <= 0.9)]  = 3
gU[np.logical_and(U > 0.9, U <= 1)]    = 4
```

4.9 Summary

Let us summarize this chapter by revisiting the four bullet points from the beginning of the chapter.

- **Definition of a continuous random variable.** Continuous random variables are *measured* by lengths, areas, and volumes, which are all defined by integrations. This makes them different from discrete random variables, which are measured by counts (and summations). Because of the different measures being used to define random variables, we consequently have different ways of defining expectation, variance, moments, etc., all in terms of integrations.

- **Unification of discrete and continuous random variables.** The unification is done by the CDF. The CDF of a discrete random variable can be written as a train of step functions. After taking the derivative, we will obtain the PDF, which is a train of impulses.

- **Origin of Gaussian random variables.** The origin of the Gaussian random variable lies in the fact that many observable events in engineering are sums of independent events. The summation of independent random variables is equivalent to taking convolutions of the PDFs. At the limit, they will converge to a bell-shaped function, which is the Gaussian. Gaussians are everywhere because we observe sums more often than we observe individual states.

- **Transformation of random variables.** Transformation of random variables is done in the CDF space. The transformation can be used to generate random numbers according to a predefined distribution. Specifically, if we want to generate random numbers according to F_X, then the transformation is $g = F_X^{-1}$.

4.10 References

PDF, CDF, expectation

4-1 Dimitri P. Bertsekas and John N. Tsitsiklis, *Introduction to Probability*, Athena Scientific, 2nd Edition, 2008. Chapter 3.1, 3.2.

4-2 Alberto Leon-Garcia, *Probability, Statistics, and Random Processes for Electrical Engineering*, Prentice Hall, 3rd Edition, 2008. Chapter 4.1 - 4.3.

4-3 Athanasios Papoulis and S. Unnikrishna Pillai, *Probability, Random Variables and Stochastic Processes*, McGraw-Hill, 4th Edition, 2001. Chapter 4.

4-4 John A. Gubner, *Probability and Random Processes for Electrical and Computer Engineers*, Cambridge University Press, 2006. Chapter 4.1, 4.2, 5.1, 5.3, 5.5.

4-5 Sheldon Ross, *A First Course in Probability*, Prentice Hall, 8th Edition, 2010. Chapter 4.10, 5.1, 5.2, 5.3.

4-6 Henry Stark and John Woods, *Probability and Random Processes With Applications to Signal Processing*, Prentice Hall, 3rd edition, 2001. Chapter 2.4, 2.5, 4.1, 4.4.

Gaussian random variables

4-7 Dimitri P. Bertsekas and John N. Tsitsiklis, *Introduction to Probability*, Athena Scientific, 2nd Edition, 2008. Chapter 3.3.

4-8 Alberto Leon-Garcia, *Probability, Statistics, and Random Processes for Electrical Engineering*, Prentice Hall, 3rd Edition, 2008. Chapter 4.4.

4-9 Sheldon Ross, *A First Course in Probability*, Prentice Hall, 8th Edition, 2010. Chapter 5.4.

4-10 Mark D. Ward and Ellen Gundlach, *Introduction to Probability*, W.H. Freeman and Company, 2016. Chapter 35.

Transformation of random variables

4-11 Dimitri P. Bertsekas and John N. Tsitsiklis, *Introduction to Probability*, Athena Scientific, 2nd Edition, 2008. Chapter 4.1.

4-12 Alberto Leon-Garcia, *Probability, Statistics, and Random Processes for Electrical Engineering*, Prentice Hall, 3rd Edition, 2008. Chapter 4.5.

4-13 Athanasios Papoulis and S. Unnikrishna Pillai, *Probability, Random Variables and Stochastic Processes*, McGraw-Hill, 4th Edition, 2001. Chapter 5.

4-14 John A. Gubner, *Probability and Random Processes for Electrical and Computer Engineers*, Cambridge University Press, 2006. Chapter 5.4.

4-15 Sheldon Ross, *A First Course in Probability*, Prentice Hall, 8th Edition, 2010. Chapter 5.7.

4-16 Henry Stark and John Woods, *Probability and Random Processes With Applications to Signal Processing*, Prentice Hall, 3rd edition, 2001. Chapter 3.1, 3.2.

Advanced probability textbooks

4-17 William Feller, *An Introduction to Probability Theory and Its Applications*, Wiley and Sons, 3rd Edition, 1950.

4-18 Andrey Kolmogorov, *Foundations of the Theory of Probability*, 2nd English Edition, Dover 2018. (Translated from Russian to English. Originally published in 1950 by Chelsea Publishing Company New York.)

4.11   Problems

Exercise 1. (VIDEO SOLUTION)
Let X be a Gaussian random variable with $\mu = 5$ and $\sigma^2 = 16$.

(a) Find $\mathbb{P}[X > 4]$ and $\mathbb{P}[2 \le X \le 7]$.

(b) If $\mathbb{P}[X < a] = 0.8869$, find a.

(c) If $\mathbb{P}[X > b] = 0.1131$, find b.

(d) If $\mathbb{P}[13 < X \le c] = 0.0011$, find c.

Exercise 2. (VIDEO SOLUTION)
Compute $\mathbb{E}[Y]$ and $\mathbb{E}[Y^2]$ for the following random variables:

(a) $Y = A\cos(\omega t + \theta)$, where $A \sim \mathcal{N}(\mu, \sigma^2)$.

(b) $Y = a\cos(\omega t + \Theta)$, where $\Theta \sim \text{Uniform}(0, 2\pi)$.

(c) $Y = a\cos(\omega T + \theta)$, where $T \sim \text{Uniform}\left(-\frac{\pi}{\omega}, \frac{\pi}{\omega}\right)$.

Exercise 3. (VIDEO SOLUTION)
Consider a CDF

$$F_X(x) = \begin{cases} 0, & \text{if } x < -1, \\ 0.5, & \text{if } -1 \le x < 0, \\ (1+x)/2, & \text{if } 0 \le x < 1, \\ 1, & \text{otherwise.} \end{cases}$$

(a) Find $\mathbb{P}[X < -1]$, $\mathbb{P}[-0.5 < X < 0.5]$ and $\mathbb{P}[X > 0.5]$.

(b) Find $f_X(x)$.

Exercise 4. (VIDEO SOLUTION)
A random variable X has CDF:

$$F_X(x) = \begin{cases} 0, & \text{if } x < 0, \\ 1 - \frac{1}{4}e^{-2x}, & \text{if } x \ge 0. \end{cases}$$

(a) Find $\mathbb{P}[X \le 2]$, $\mathbb{P}[X = 0]$, $\mathbb{P}[X < 0]$, $\mathbb{P}[2 < X < 6]$ and $\mathbb{P}[X > 10]$.

(b) Find $f_X(x)$.

Exercise 5. (VIDEO SOLUTION)
A random variable X has PDF

$$f_X(x) = \begin{cases} cx(1-x^2), & 0 \le x \le 1, \\ 0, & \text{otherwise.} \end{cases}$$

Find c, $F_X(x)$, and $\mathbb{E}[X]$.

Exercise 6. (VIDEO SOLUTION)
A continuous random variable X has a cumulative distribution

$$F_X(x) = \begin{cases} 0, & x < 0, \\ 0.5 + c\sin^2(\pi x/2), & 0 \le x \le 1, \\ 1, & x > 1. \end{cases}$$

(a) What values can c assume?

(b) Find $f_X(x)$.

Exercise 7. (VIDEO SOLUTION)
A continuous random variable X is uniformly distributed in $[-2, 2]$.

(a) Let $Y = \sin(\pi X/8)$. Find $f_Y(y)$.

(b) Let $Z = -2X^2 + 3$. Find $f_Z(z)$.

Hint: Compute $F_Y(y)$ from $F_X(x)$, and use $\frac{d}{dy}\sin^{-1} y = \frac{1}{\sqrt{1-y^2}}$.

Exercise 8.
Let $Y = e^X$.

(a) Find the CDF and PDF of Y in terms of the CDF and PDF of X.

(b) Find the PDF of Y when X is a Gaussian random variable. In this case, Y is said to be a lognormal random variable.

Exercise 9.
The random variable X has the PDF

$$f_X(x) = \begin{cases} \frac{1}{2\sqrt{x}}, & 0 \le x \le 1, \\ 0, & \text{otherwise.} \end{cases}$$

Let Y be a new random variable

$$Y = \begin{cases} 0, & X < 0, \\ \sqrt{X}, & 0 \le X \le 1, \\ 1, & X > 1. \end{cases}$$

Find $F_Y(y)$ and $f_Y(y)$, for $-\infty < y < \infty$.

Exercise 10.
A random variable X has the PDF

$$f_X(x) = \begin{cases} 2xe^{-x^2}, & x \geq 0, \\ 0, & x < 0. \end{cases}$$

Let

$$Y = g(X) = \begin{cases} 1 - e^{-X^2}, & X \geq 0, \\ 0, & X < 0. \end{cases}$$

Find the PDF of Y.

Exercise 11.
A random variable X has the PDF

$$f_X(x) = \frac{1}{2}e^{-|x|}, \qquad -\infty < x < \infty.$$

Let $Y = g(X) = e^{-X}$. Find the PDF of Y.

Exercise 12.
A random variable X has the PDF

$$f_X(x) = \frac{1}{\sqrt{2\pi\sigma^2}}e^{-\frac{x^2}{2\sigma^2}}, \qquad -\infty < x < \infty.$$

Find the PDF of Y where

$$Y = g(X) = \begin{cases} X, & |X| > K, \\ -X, & |X| < K. \end{cases}$$

Exercise 13.
A random variable X has the PDF

$$f_X(x) = \frac{1}{x^2\sqrt{2\pi}}e^{-\frac{x^2}{2}}, \qquad -\infty < x < \infty.$$

Let $Y = g(X) = \frac{1}{X}$. Find the PDF of Y.

Exercise 14.
A random variable X has the CDF

$$F_X(x) = \begin{cases} 0, & x < 0, \\ x^\alpha, & 0 \leq x \leq 1, \\ 1, & x > 1, \end{cases}$$

with $\alpha > 0$. Find the CDF of Y if

$$Y = g(X) = -\log X.$$

Exercise 15.

Energy efficiency is an important aspect of designing electrical systems. In some modern buildings (e.g., airports), traditional escalators are being replaced by a new type of "smart" escalator which can automatically switch between a normal operating mode and a standby mode depending on the flow of pedestrians.

(a) The arrival of pedestrians can be modeled as a Poisson random variable. Let N be the number of arrivals, and let λ be the arrival rate (people per minute). For a period of t minutes, show that the probability that there are n arrivals is

$$\mathbb{P}(N = n) = \frac{(\lambda t)^n}{n!} e^{-\lambda t}.$$

(b) Let T be a random variable denoting the interarrival time (i.e., the time between two consecutive arrivals). Show that

$$\mathbb{P}(T > t) = e^{-\lambda t}.$$

Also, determine $F_T(t)$ and $f_T(t)$. Sketch $f_T(t)$.

(Hint: Note that $\mathbb{P}(T > t) = \mathbb{P}(\text{no arrival in } t \text{ minutes})$.)

(c) Suppose that the escalator will go into standby mode if there are no pedestrians for $t_0 = 30$ seconds. Let Y be a random variable denoting the amount of time that the escalator is in standby mode. That is, let

$$Y = \begin{cases} 0, & \text{if } T \le t_0, \\ T - t_0, & \text{if } T > t_0. \end{cases}$$

Find $\mathbb{E}[Y]$.

Chapter 5

Joint Distributions

When you go to a concert hall, sometimes you may want to see a solo violin concert, but other times you may want to see a symphony. Symphonies are appealing because many instruments are playing together. Random variables are similar. While single random variables are useful for modeling simple events, we use multiple random variables to describe complex events. The multiple random variables can be either independent or correlated. When many random variables are present in the problem, we enter the subject of **joint distribution**.

What are joint distributions?

In the simplest sense, joint distributions are extensions of the PDFs and PMFs we studied in the previous chapters. We summarize them as follows.

> Joint distributions are **high-dimensional** PDFs (or PMFs or CDFs).

What do we mean by a high-dimensional PDF? We know that a single random variable is characterized by a 1-dimensional PDF $f_X(x)$. If we have a pair of random variables, then we use a 2-dimensional function $f_{X,Y}(x,y)$, and if we have a triplet of random variables, we use a 3-dimensional function $f_{X,Y,Z}(x,y,z)$. In general, the dimensionality of the PDF grows as the number of variables:

$$\underbrace{f_X(x)}_{\text{one variable}} \implies \underbrace{f_{X_1,X_2}(x_1,x_2)}_{\text{two variables}} \implies \cdots \implies \underbrace{f_{X_1,\ldots,X_N}(x_1,\ldots,x_N)}_{N \text{ variables}}.$$

For busy engineers like us, $f_{X_1,\ldots,X_N}(x_1,\ldots,x_N)$ is not a friendly notation. A more concise way to write $f_{X_1,\ldots,X_N}(x_1,\ldots,x_N)$ is to define a *vector* of random variables $\boldsymbol{X} = [X_1, X_2, \ldots, X_N]^T$ with a vector of states $\boldsymbol{x} = [x_1, x_2, \ldots, x_N]^T$, and to define the PDF as

$$f_{\boldsymbol{X}}(\boldsymbol{x}) = f_{X_1,\ldots,X_N}(x_1,\ldots,x_N).$$

Under what circumstance will we encounter creatures like $f_{\boldsymbol{X}}(\boldsymbol{x})$? Believe it or not, these high-dimensional PDFs are *everywhere*. In 2010, computer-vision scientists created the ImageNet dataset, containing 14 million images with ground-truth class labels. This enormous dataset has enabled a great blossoming of machine learning over the past several

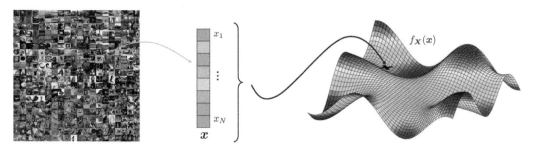

Figure 5.1: Joint distributions are ubiquitous in modern data analysis. For example, an image from a dataset can be represented by a high-dimensional vector $\boldsymbol{x}$. Each vector has a certain probability of being present. This probability is described by the high-dimensional joint PDF $f_{\boldsymbol{X}}(\boldsymbol{x})$. The goal of this chapter is to understand the properties of this $f_{\boldsymbol{X}}$.

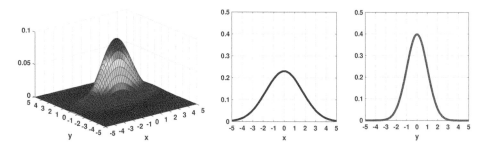

Figure 5.2: A 2-dimensional PDF $f_{X,Y}(x,y)$ of a pair of random variables (X,Y) and their respective 1D PDFs $f_X(x)$ and $f_Y(y)$.

decades, in which many advances in deep learning have been made. Fundamentally, the ImageNet dataset provides a large collection of *samples* drawn from a latent distribution that is high-dimensional. Each sample in the ImageNet dataset is a $224 \times 224 \times 3$ image (the three numbers stand for the image's height, width, and color). If we convert this image into a vector, then the sample will have a dimension of $224 \times 224 \times 3 = 150{,}528$. In other words, the sample is a vector $\boldsymbol{x} \in \mathbb{R}^{150528 \times 1}$. The probability of obtaining a particular sample $\boldsymbol{x}$ is determined by probability density function $f_{\boldsymbol{X}}(\boldsymbol{x})$. For example, it is more likely to get an image containing trees than one containing a Ferrari. The manifold generated by $f_{\boldsymbol{X}}(\boldsymbol{x})$ can be extremely complex, as illustrated in **Figure 5.1**.

The story of ImageNet is just one of the many instances for which we use a joint distribution $f_{\boldsymbol{X}}(\boldsymbol{x})$. Joint distributions are ubiquitous. If you do data science, you *must* understand joint distributions. However, extending a 1-dimensional function $f_X(x)$ to a 2-dimensional function $f_{X,Y}(x,y)$ and then to a N-dimensional function $f_{\boldsymbol{X}}(\boldsymbol{x})$ is not trivial. The goal of this chapter is to guide you through these important steps.

Plan of Part 1 of this chapter: Two variables

This chapter is broadly divided into two halves. In the first half, we will look at **a pair of random variables**.

- **Definition of** $f_{X,Y}(x,y)$**.** The first thing we need to learn is the definition of a joint distribution with two variables. Since we have two variables, the **joint probability density function** (or probability mass function) is a 2-dimensional function. A point on this 2D function is the probability density evaluated by a pair of variables $X = x$ and $Y = y$, as illustrated in **Figure 5.2**. However, how do we formally define this 2D function? How is it related to the probability measure? Is there a way we can retrieve $f_X(x)$ and $f_Y(y)$ from $f_{X,Y}(x, y)$, as illustrated on the right-hand sides of **Figure 5.2**? These questions will be answered in Section 5.1.

- **Joint expectation** $\mathbb{E}[XY]$. When we have a pair of random variables, how should we define the expectation? In Section 5.2, we will show that the most natural way to define the joint expectation is in terms of $\mathbb{E}[XY]$, i.e., the expectation of the product. There is a surprising and beautiful connection between this "expectation of the product" and the cosine angle between two vectors, thereby showing that $\mathbb{E}[XY]$ is the **correlation** between X and Y.

- The reason for studying a pair of random variables is to spell out the cause-effect relationship between the variables. This cannot be done without conditional distributions; this will be explained in Section 5.3. Conditional distributions provide an extremely important computational tool for decoupling complex events into simpler events. Such decomposition allows us to solve difficult joint expectation problems via simple **conditional expectations**; this subject will be covered in Section 5.4.

- If you recall our discussions about the origin of a Gaussian random variable, we claimed that the PDF of $X + Y$ is the **convolution** between f_X and f_Y. Why is this so? We will answer this question in terms of joint distributions in Section 5.5.

Plan of Part 2 of this chapter: N variables

The second half of the chapter focuses on the general case of N random variables. This requires the definitions of a random vector $\boldsymbol{X} = [X_1, \dots, X_N]^T$, a joint distribution $f_{\boldsymbol{X}}(\boldsymbol{x})$, and the corresponding expectations $\mathbb{E}[\boldsymbol{X}]$. To make our discussions concrete, we will focus on the case of **high-dimensional Gaussian** random variables and discuss the following topics.

- **Covariance matrices/correlation matrices.** If a pair of random variables can define the correlation through the expectation of the product $\mathbb{E}[X_1 X_2]$, then for a vector of random variables we can consider a matrix of correlations in the form

$$
\boldsymbol{R} = \begin{bmatrix}
\mathbb{E}[X_1 X_1] & \mathbb{E}[X_1 X_2] & \cdots & \mathbb{E}[X_1 X_N] \\
\mathbb{E}[X_2 X_1] & \mathbb{E}[X_2 X_2] & \cdots & \mathbb{E}[X_2 X_N] \\
\vdots & \vdots & \ddots & \vdots \\
\mathbb{E}[X_N X_1] & \mathbb{E}[X_N X_2] & \cdots & \mathbb{E}[X_N X_N]
\end{bmatrix}.
$$

What are the properties of the matrix? How does it affect the shape of the high-dimensional Gaussian? If we have a dataset of vectors, how do we estimate this matrix from the data? We will answer these questions in Section 5.6 and Section 5.7.

- **Principal-component analysis.** Given the covariance matrix, we can perform some very useful data analyses, such as the principal-component analysis in Section 5.8. The question we will ask is: Among the many components, which one is the principal component? If we can find the principal component(s), we can effectively perform dimensionality reduction by projecting a high-dimensional vector into low-dimensional representations. We will introduce an application for face detection.

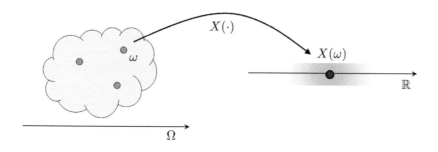

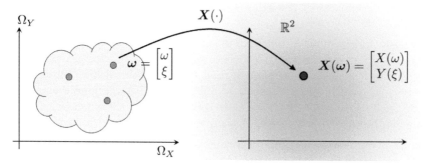

Figure 5.3: When there is a pair of random variables, we can regard the sample space as a set of coordinates. The random variables are 2D mappings from a coordinate ω in $\Omega_X \times \Omega_Y$ to another coordinate $X(\omega)$ in $\mathbb{R}^2$.

5.1 Joint PMF and Joint PDF

Probability is a measure of the size of a set. This principle applies to discrete random variables, continuous random variables, single random variables, and multiple random variables. In situations with a pair of random variables, the measure should be applied to the coordinate (X, Y) represented by the random variables X and Y. Consequently, when measuring the probability, we either count these coordinates or integrate the area covered by these coordinates. In this section, we formalize this notion of measuring 2D events.

5.1.1 Probability measure in 2D

Consider two random variables X and Y. Let the sample space of X and Y be Ω_X and Ω_Y, respectively. Define the **Cartesian product** of Ω_X and Ω_Y as $\Omega_X \times \Omega_Y = \{(x, y) \mid x \in \Omega_X \text{ and } y \in \Omega_Y\}$. That is, $\Omega_X \times \Omega_Y$ contains all possible pairs (X, Y).

Example 5.1. If $\Omega_X = \{1, 2\}$ and $\Omega_Y = \{4, 5\}$, then $\Omega_X \times \Omega_Y = \{(1, 4), (1, 5), (2, 4), (2, 5)\}$.

> **Example 5.2.** If $\Omega_X = [3,4]$ and $\Omega_Y = [1,2]$, then $\Omega_X \times \Omega_Y =$ a rectangle with two diagonal vertices as $(3,1)$ and $(4,2)$.

Random variables are mappings from the sample space to the real line. If $\omega \in \Omega_X$ is mapped to $X(\omega) \in \mathbb{R}$, and $\xi \in \Omega_Y$ is mapped to $Y(\xi) \in \mathbb{R}$, then a coordinate $\omega = (\omega, \xi)$ in the sample space $\Omega_X \times \Omega_Y$ should be mapped to a coordinate $(X(\omega), Y(\xi))$ in the 2D plane.

$$\boldsymbol{\omega} \overset{\text{def}}{=} \begin{bmatrix} \omega \\ \xi \end{bmatrix} \longmapsto \begin{bmatrix} X(\omega) \\ Y(\xi) \end{bmatrix} \overset{\text{def}}{=} \boldsymbol{X}(\boldsymbol{\omega}).$$

We denote such a vector-to-vector mapping as $\boldsymbol{X}(\cdot) : \Omega_X \times \Omega_Y \to \mathbb{R} \times \mathbb{R}$, as illustrated in **Figure 5.3**.

Therefore, if we have an event $\mathcal{A} \in \mathbb{R}^2$, the probability that $\mathcal{A}$ happens is

$$\mathbb{P}[\mathcal{A}] = \mathbb{P}[\{\boldsymbol{\omega} \mid \boldsymbol{X}(\boldsymbol{\omega}) \in \mathcal{A}\}]$$

$$= \mathbb{P}\left[\left\{ \begin{bmatrix} \omega \\ \xi \end{bmatrix} \;\middle|\; \begin{bmatrix} X(\omega) \\ Y(\xi) \end{bmatrix} \in \mathcal{A} \right\}\right]$$

$$= \mathbb{P}\left[\left\{ \begin{bmatrix} \omega \\ \xi \end{bmatrix} \in \boldsymbol{X}^{-1}(\mathcal{A}) \right\}\right]$$

$$= \mathbb{P}[\boldsymbol{\omega} \in \boldsymbol{X}^{-1}(\mathcal{A})].$$

In other words, we take the coordinate $\boldsymbol{X}(\boldsymbol{\omega})$ and find its inverse image $\boldsymbol{X}^{-1}(\mathcal{A})$. The size of this inverse image $\boldsymbol{X}^{-1}(\mathcal{A})$ in the sample space $\Omega_X \times \Omega_Y$ is then the probability. We summarize this general principle as follows.

> **How to measure probability in 2D**
>
> For a pair of random variables $\boldsymbol{X} = (X, Y)$, the probability of an event $\mathcal{A}$ is measured in the product space $\Omega_X \times \Omega_Y$ with the size
>
> $$\mathbb{P}[\{\boldsymbol{\omega} \mid \boldsymbol{X}^{-1}(\mathcal{A})\}].$$

This definition is quite abstract. To make it more concrete, we will look at discrete and continuous random variables.

5.1.2 Discrete random variables

Suppose that the random variables X and Y are discrete. Let $\mathcal{A} = \{X(\omega) = x, \ Y(\xi) = y\}$ be a discrete event. Then the above definition tells us that the probability of $\mathcal{A}$ is

$$\mathbb{P}[\mathcal{A}] = \mathbb{P}\left[(\omega, \xi) \;\middle|\; X(\omega) = x, \text{ and } Y(\xi) = y\right] = \underbrace{\mathbb{P}[X = x \text{ and } Y = y]}_{\overset{\text{def}}{=} p_{X,Y}(x,y)}.$$

We define this probability as the **joint probability mass function** (joint PMF) $p_{X,Y}(x,y)$.

Definition 5.1. *Let X and Y be two discrete random variables. The* **joint PMF** *of X and Y is defined as*

$$p_{X,Y}(x,y) = \mathbb{P}[X = x \text{ and } Y = y] = \mathbb{P}\left[(\omega, \xi) \,\middle|\, X(\omega) = x, \text{ and } Y(\xi) = y\right]. \quad (5.1)$$

We sometimes write the joint PMF as $p_{X,Y}(x,y) = \mathbb{P}[X = x, \, Y = y]$.

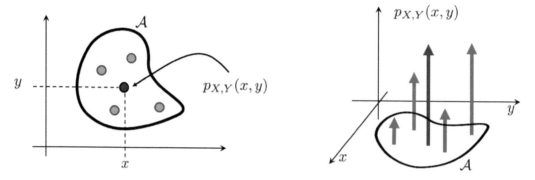

Figure 5.4: A joint PMF for a pair of discrete random variables consists of an array of impulses. To measure the size of the event $\mathcal{A}$, we sum all the impulses inside $\mathcal{A}$.

Figure 5.4 shows a graphical portrayal of the joint PMF. In a nutshell, $p_{X,Y}(x,y)$ can be considered as a 2D extension of a single variable PMF. The probabilities are still represented by the impulses, but the domain of these impulses is now a 2D plane. If we have an event $\mathcal{A}$, then the size of the event is

$$\mathbb{P}[\mathcal{A}] = \sum_{(x,y)\in\mathcal{A}} p_{X,Y}(x,y).$$

Example 5.3. Let X be a coin flip, Y be a die. The sample space of X is $\{0,1\}$, whereas the sample space of Y is $\{1,2,3,4,5,6\}$. The joint PMF, according to our definition, is the probability $\mathbb{P}[X = x \text{ and } Y = y]$, where x takes a binary state and Y takes one of the 6 states. The following table summarizes all the 12 states of the joint distribution.

	\multicolumn{6}{c}{Y}
	1	2	3	4	5	6
$X = 0$	$\frac{1}{12}$	$\frac{1}{12}$	$\frac{1}{12}$	$\frac{1}{12}$	$\frac{1}{12}$	$\frac{1}{12}$
$X = 1$	$\frac{1}{12}$	$\frac{1}{12}$	$\frac{1}{12}$	$\frac{1}{12}$	$\frac{1}{12}$	$\frac{1}{12}$

In this table, since there are 12 coordinates, and each coordinate has an equal chance of appearing, the probability for each coordinate becomes $1/12$. Therefore, the joint PMF of X and Y is

$$p_{X,Y}(x,y) = \frac{1}{12}, \quad x = 0,1, \quad y = 1,2,3,4,5,6.$$

In this example, we observe that if X and Y are not interacting with each other (formally, **independent**), the joint PMF is the product of the two individual probabilities.

Example 5.4. In the previous example, if we define $\mathcal{A} = \{X+Y=3\}$, the probability $\mathbb{P}[\mathcal{A}]$ is

$$\mathbb{P}[\mathcal{A}] = \sum_{(x,y)\in\mathcal{A}} p_{X,Y}(x,y) = p_{X,Y}(0,3) + p_{X,Y}(1,2)$$
$$= \frac{2}{12}.$$

If $\mathcal{B} = \{\min(X,Y) = 1\}$, the probability $\mathbb{P}[\mathcal{B}]$ is

$$\mathbb{P}[\mathcal{B}] = \sum_{(x,y)\in\mathcal{B}} p_{X,Y}(x,y)$$
$$= p_{X,Y}(1,1) + p_{X,Y}(1,2) + p_{X,Y}(1,3)$$
$$+ p_{X,Y}(1,4) + p_{X,Y}(1,5) + p_{X,Y}(1,6)$$
$$= \frac{6}{12}.$$

5.1.3 Continuous random variables

The continuous version of the joint PMF is called the **joint probability density function (joint PDF)**, denoted by $f_{X,Y}(x,y)$. A joint PDF is analogous to a joint PMF. For example, integrating it will give us the probability.

Definition 5.2. *Let X and Y be two continuous random variables. The **joint PDF** of X and Y is a function $f_{X,Y}(x,y)$ that can be integrated to yield a probability*

$$\mathbb{P}[\mathcal{A}] = \int_{\mathcal{A}} f_{X,Y}(x,y)\, dx\, dy, \tag{5.2}$$

for any event $\mathcal{A} \subseteq \Omega_X \times \Omega_Y$.

Pictorially, we can view $f_{X,Y}$ as a 2D function where the height at a coordinate (x,y) is $f_{X,Y}(x,y)$, as can be seen from **Figure 5.5**. To compute the probability that $(X,Y) \in \mathcal{A}$, we integrate the function $f_{X,Y}$ with respect to the area covered by the set $\mathcal{A}$. For example, if the set $\mathcal{A}$ is a rectangular box $\mathcal{A} = [a,b] \times [c,d]$, then the integration becomes

$$\mathbb{P}[\mathcal{A}] = \mathbb{P}[a \le X \le b, \ c \le Y \le d]$$
$$= \int_c^d \int_a^b f_{X,Y}(x,y)\, dx\, dy.$$

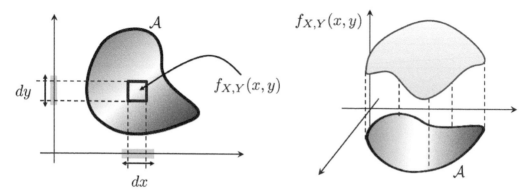

Figure 5.5: A joint PDF for a pair of continuous random variables is a surface in the 2D plane. To measure the size of the event $\mathcal{A}$, we integrate $f_{X,Y}(x,y)$ inside $\mathcal{A}$.

Example 5.5. Consider a uniform joint PDF $f_{X,Y}(x,y)$ defined on $[0,2]^2$ with $f_{X,Y}(x,y) = \frac{1}{4}$. Let $\mathcal{A} = [a,b] \times [c,d]$. Find $\mathbb{P}[\mathcal{A}]$.

Solution.

$$\mathbb{P}[\mathcal{A}] = \mathbb{P}[a \le X \le b, \ c \le X \le d]$$
$$= \int_c^d \int_a^b f_{X,Y}(x,y) \, dx \, dy = \int_c^d \int_a^b \frac{1}{4} \, dx \, dy = \frac{(d-c)(b-a)}{4}.$$

Practice Exercise 5.1. In the previous example, let $\mathcal{B} = \{X + Y \le 2\}$. Find $\mathbb{P}[\mathcal{B}]$.

Solution.

$$\mathbb{P}[\mathcal{B}] = \int_{\mathcal{B}} f_{X,Y}(x,y) \, dx \, dy$$
$$= \int_0^2 \int_0^{2-y} f_{X,Y}(x,y) \, dx \, dy$$
$$= \int_0^2 \int_0^{2-y} \frac{1}{4} \, dx \, dy$$
$$= \int_0^2 \frac{2-y}{4} \, dy = \frac{1}{2}.$$

Here, the limits of the integration can be determined from **Figure 5.6**. The inner integration (with respect to x) should start from 0 and end at $2 - y$, which is the line defining the set $x + y \le 2$. Since the inner integration is performed for every y, we need to enumerate all the possible y's to complete the outer integration. This leads to the outer limit from 0 to 2.

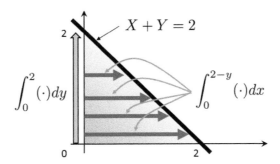

Figure 5.6: To calculate $\mathbb{P}[X + Y \leq 2]$, we perform a 2D integration over a triangle.

5.1.4 Normalization

The normalization property of a two-dimensional PMF and PDF is the property that, when we enumerate all outcomes of the sample space, we obtain 1.

Theorem 5.1. *Let* $\Omega = \Omega_X \times \Omega_Y$. *All joint PMFs and joint PDFs satisfy*

$$\sum_{(x,y)\in\Omega} p_{X,Y}(x,y) = 1 \quad or \quad \int_\Omega f_{X,Y}(x,y)\, dx\, dy = 1. \tag{5.3}$$

Example 5.6. Consider a joint uniform PDF defined in the shaded area $[0,3] \times [0,3]$ with PDF defined below. Find the constant c.

$$f_{X,Y}(x,y) = \begin{cases} c & \text{if } (x,y) \in [0,3] \times [0,3], \\ 0 & \text{otherwise.} \end{cases}$$

Solution. To find the constant c, we note that

$$1 = \int_0^3 \int_0^3 f_{X,Y}(x,y)\, dx\, dy$$

$$= \int_0^3 \int_0^3 c\, dx\, dy = 9c.$$

Equating the two sides gives us $c = \frac{1}{9}$.

Practice Exercise 5.2. Consider a joint PDF

$$f_{X,Y}(x,y) = \begin{cases} ce^{-x}e^{-y} & 0 \leq y \leq x < \infty, \\ 0 & \text{otherwise.} \end{cases}$$

Find the constant c. Tip: Consider the area of integration as shown in **Figure 5.7**.

Solution. There are two ways to take the integration shown in **Figure 5.7**. We choose the inner integration w.r.t. y first.

$$\int_{\Omega} f_{X,Y}(x,y) \, dx \, dy = \int_{0}^{\infty} \int_{0}^{x} ce^{-x} e^{-y} \, dy \, dx$$

$$= \int_{0}^{\infty} ce^{-x}(1 - e^{-x})$$

$$= \frac{c}{2}.$$

Therefore, $c = 2$.

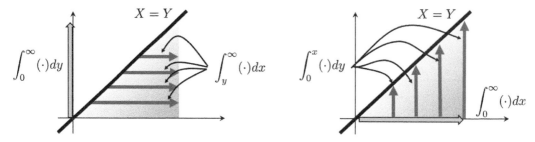

Figure 5.7: To integrate the probability $\mathbb{P}[0 \leq Y \leq X]$, we perform a 2D integration over a triangle. The two subfigures show the two ways of integrating the triangle. [Left] $\int \, dx$ first, and then $\int \, dy$. [Right] $\int \, dy$ first, and then $\int \, dx$.

5.1.5   Marginal PMF and marginal PDF

If we only sum / integrate for one random variable, we obtain the PMF / PDF of the other random variable. The resulting PMF / PDF is called the marginal PMF / PDF.

Definition 5.3. *The **marginal PMF** is defined as*

$$p_X(x) = \sum_{y \in \Omega_Y} p_{X,Y}(x,y) \quad and \quad p_Y(y) = \sum_{x \in \Omega_X} p_{X,Y}(x,y), \tag{5.4}$$

*and the **marginal PDF** is defined as*

$$f_X(x) = \int_{\Omega_Y} f_{X,Y}(x,y) \, dy \quad and \quad f_Y(y) = \int_{\Omega_X} f_{X,Y}(x,y) \, dx. \tag{5.5}$$

Since $f_{X,Y}(x,y)$ is a two-dimensional function, when integrating over y from $-\infty$ to ∞, we project $f_{X,Y}(x,y)$ onto the x-axis. Therefore, the resulting function depends on x only.

Example 5.7. Consider the joint PDF $f_{X,Y}(x,y) = \frac{1}{4}$ shown below. Find the marginal PDFs.

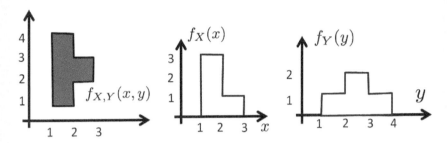

Solution. If we integrate over x and y, we have

$$f_X(x) = \begin{cases} 3, & \text{if } 1 < x \le 2, \\ 1, & \text{if } 2 < x \le 3, \\ 0, & \text{otherwise.} \end{cases} \quad \text{and} \quad f_Y(y) = \begin{cases} 1, & \text{if } 1 < x \le 2, \\ 2, & \text{if } 2 < x \le 3, \\ 1, & \text{if } 3 < x \le 4, \\ 0, & \text{otherwise.} \end{cases}$$

So the marginal PDFs are the projection of the joint PDFs onto the x- and y-axes.

Practice Exercise 5.3. A joint Gaussian random variable (X, Y) has a joint PDF given by

$$f_{X,Y}(x,y) = \frac{1}{2\pi\sigma^2} \exp\left\{ -\frac{((x-\mu_X)^2 + (y-\mu_Y)^2)}{2\sigma^2} \right\}.$$

Find the marginal PDFs $f_X(x)$ and $f_Y(y)$.

Solution.

$$f_X(x) = \int_{-\infty}^{\infty} f_{X,Y}(x,y)\, dy = \int_{-\infty}^{\infty} \frac{1}{2\pi\sigma^2} \exp\left\{ -\frac{((x-\mu_X)^2 + (y-\mu_Y)^2)}{2\sigma^2} \right\} dy$$

$$= \frac{1}{\sqrt{2\pi\sigma^2}} \exp\left\{ -\frac{(x-\mu_X)^2}{2\sigma^2} \right\} \cdot \int_{-\infty}^{\infty} \frac{1}{\sqrt{2\pi\sigma^2}} \exp\left\{ -\frac{(y-\mu_Y)^2}{2\sigma^2} \right\} dy.$$

Recognizing that the last integral is equal to unity because it integrates a Gaussian PDF over the real line, it follows that

$$f_X(x) = \frac{1}{\sqrt{2\pi\sigma^2}} \exp\left\{ -\frac{(x-\mu_X)^2}{2\sigma^2} \right\}.$$

Similarly, we have

$$f_Y(y) = \frac{1}{\sqrt{2\pi\sigma^2}} \exp\left\{ -\frac{(y-\mu_Y)^2}{2\sigma^2} \right\}.$$

5.1.6 Independent random variables

Two random variables are said to be independent if and only if the joint PMF or PDF can be factorized as a product of the marginal PMF / PDFs.

> **Definition 5.4.** *Random variables X and Y are* **independent** *if and only if*
>
> $$p_{X,Y}(x,y) = p_X(x)\, p_Y(y), \quad or \quad f_{X,Y}(x,y) = f_X(x)\, f_Y(y).$$

This definition is consistent with the definition of independence of two events. Recall that two events A and B are independent if and only if $\mathbb{P}[A \cap B] = \mathbb{P}[A]\mathbb{P}[B]$. Letting $A = \{X = x\}$ and $B = \{Y = y\}$, we see that if A and B are independent then $\mathbb{P}[X = x \cap Y = y]$ is the product $\mathbb{P}[X = x]\mathbb{P}[Y = y]$. This is precisely the relationship $p_{X,Y}(x,y) = p_X(x)\, p_Y(y)$.

Example 5.8. Consider two random variables with a joint PDF given by

$$f_{X,Y}(x,y) = \frac{1}{2\pi\sigma^2} \exp\left\{ -\frac{(x - \mu_X)^2 + (y - \mu_Y)^2}{2\sigma^2} \right\}.$$

Are X and Y independent?

Solution. We know that

$$f_{X,Y}(x,y) = \underbrace{\frac{1}{\sqrt{2\pi}\sigma} \exp\left\{ -\frac{(x - \mu_X)^2}{2\sigma^2} \right\}}_{f_X(x)} \times \underbrace{\frac{1}{\sqrt{2\pi}\sigma} \exp\left\{ -\frac{(y - \mu_Y)^2}{2\sigma^2} \right\}}_{f_Y(y)}.$$

Therefore, the random variables X and Y are independent.

Practice Exercise 5.4. Let X be a coin and Y be a die. Then the joint PMF is given by the table below.

	Y					
	1	2	3	4	5	6
$X = 0$	$\frac{1}{12}$	$\frac{1}{12}$	$\frac{1}{12}$	$\frac{1}{12}$	$\frac{1}{12}$	$\frac{1}{12}$
$X = 1$	$\frac{1}{12}$	$\frac{1}{12}$	$\frac{1}{12}$	$\frac{1}{12}$	$\frac{1}{12}$	$\frac{1}{12}$

Are X and Y independent?

Solution. For any x and y, we have that

$$p_{X,Y}(x,y) = \frac{1}{12} = \underbrace{\frac{1}{2}}_{p_X(x)} \times \underbrace{\frac{1}{6}}_{p_Y(y)}.$$

Therefore, the random variables X and Y are independent.

Example 5.9. Consider two random variables X and Y with a joint PDF given by[a]

$$f_{X,Y}(x,y) \propto \exp\left\{-(x-y)^2\right\} = \exp\left\{-x^2 + 2xy - y^2\right\}$$
$$= \underbrace{\exp\left\{-x^2\right\}}_{f_X(x)} \underbrace{\exp\left\{2xy\right\}}_{\text{extra term}} \underbrace{\exp\left\{-y^2\right\}}_{f_Y(y)}.$$

This PDF cannot be factorized into a product of two marginal PDFs. Therefore, the random variables are dependent.

___
[a]We use the notation "$\propto$" to denote "proportional to". It implies that the normalization constant is omitted.

We can extrapolate the definition of independence to multiple random variables. If there are many random variables $X_1, X_2, \ldots, X_N$, they will have a joint PDF

$$f_{X_1,\ldots,X_N}(x_1,\ldots,x_N).$$

If these random variables $X_1, X_2, \ldots, X_N$ are independent, then the joint PDF can be factorized as

$$f_{X_1,\ldots,X_N}(x_1,\ldots,x_N) = f_{X_1}(x_1) \cdot f_{X_2}(x_2) \cdots f_{X_N}(x_N)$$
$$= \prod_{n=1}^{N} f_{X_n}(x_n).$$

This gives us the definition of independence for N random variables.

Definition 5.5. *A sequence of random variables* $X_1, \ldots, X_N$ *is* **independent** *if and only if their joint PDF (or joint PMF) can be factorized.*

$$f_{X_1,\ldots,X_N}(x_1,\ldots,x_N) = \prod_{n=1}^{N} f_{X_n}(x_n). \tag{5.6}$$

Example 5.10. Throw a die 4 times. Let X_1, X_2, X_3 and X_4 be the outcomes. Then, since these four throws are independent, the probability mass function of any quadrable (x_1, x_2, x_3, x_4) is

$$p_{X_1,X_2,X_3,X_4}(x_1,x_2,x_3,x_4) = p_{X_1}(x_1)\, p_{X_2}(x_2)\, p_{X_3}(x_3)\, p_{X_4}(x_4).$$

For example, the probability of getting $(1, 5, 2, 6)$ is

$$p_{X_1,X_2,X_3,X_4}(1,5,2,6) = p_{X_1}(1)\, p_{X_2}(5)\, p_{X_3}(2)\, p_{X_4}(6) = \left(\frac{1}{6}\right)^4.$$

The example above demonstrates an interesting phenomenon. If the N random variables are independent, and if they all have the same distribution, then the joint PDF/PMF is just one of the individual PDFs taken to the power N. Random variables satisfying this property are known as **independent and identically distributed** random variables.

Definition 5.6 (Independent and Identically Distributed (i.i.d.)). *A collection of random variables $X_1, \ldots, X_N$ is called independent and identically distributed (i.i.d.) if*

- *All $X_1, \ldots, X_N$ are independent; and*
- *All $X_1, \ldots, X_N$ have the same distribution, i.e., $f_{X_1}(x) = \cdots = f_{X_N}(x)$.*

If $X_1, \ldots, X_N$ are i.i.d., we have that

$$f_{X_1,\ldots,X_N}(x_1, \ldots, x_1) = \prod_{n=1}^{N} f_{X_1}(x_n),$$

where the particular choice of X_1 is unimportant because $f_{X_1}(x) = \cdots = f_{X_N}(x)$.

Why is i.i.d. so important?

- If a set of random variables are i.i.d., then the joint PDF can be written as a product of PDFs.
- Integrating a joint PDF is difficult. Integrating a product of PDFs is much easier.

Example 5.11. Let $X_1, X_2, \ldots, X_N$ be a sequence of i.i.d. Gaussian random variables where each X_i has a PDF

$$f_{X_i}(x) = \frac{1}{\sqrt{2\pi}} \exp\left\{-\frac{x^2}{2}\right\}.$$

The joint PDF of $X_1, X_2, \ldots, X_N$ is

$$f_{X_1,\ldots,X_N}(x_1, \ldots, x_N) = \prod_{i=1}^{N} \left\{ \frac{1}{\sqrt{2\pi}} \exp\left\{-\frac{x_i^2}{2}\right\} \right\}$$

$$= \left(\frac{1}{\sqrt{2\pi}}\right)^N \exp\left\{-\sum_{i=1}^{N} \frac{x_i^2}{2}\right\},$$

which is a function depending not on the individual values of $x_1, x_2, \ldots, x_N$ but on the sum $\sum_{i=1}^{N} x_i^2$. So we have "compressed" an N-dimensional function into a 1D function.

Example 5.12. Let θ be a deterministic number that was sent through a noisy channel. We model the noise as an additive Gaussian random variable with mean 0 and variance σ^2. Supposing we have observed measurements $X_i = \theta + W_i$, for $i = 1, \ldots, N$, where $W_i \sim \text{Gaussian}(0, \sigma^2)$, then the PDF of each X_i is

$$f_{X_i}(x) = \frac{1}{\sqrt{2\pi\sigma^2}} \exp\left\{-\frac{(x-\theta)^2}{2\sigma^2}\right\}.$$

Thus the joint PDF of $(X_1, X_2, \ldots, X_N)$ is

$$f_{X_1,\ldots,X_N}(x_1,\ldots,x_N) = \prod_{i=1}^{N}\left\{\frac{1}{\sqrt{2\pi\sigma^2}}\exp\left\{-\frac{(x_i-\theta)^2}{2\sigma^2}\right\}\right\}$$

$$= \left(\frac{1}{\sqrt{2\pi\sigma^2}}\right)^N \exp\left\{-\sum_{i=1}^{N}\frac{(x_i-\theta)^2}{2\sigma^2}\right\}.$$

Essentially, this joint PDF tells us the probability density of seeing sample data $x_1,\ldots,x_N$.

5.1.7 Joint CDF

We now introduce the cumulative distribution function (CDF) for multiple variables.

Definition 5.7. *Let X and Y be two random variables. The **joint CDF** of X and Y is the function $F_{X,Y}(x,y)$ such that*

$$F_{X,Y}(x,y) = \mathbb{P}[X \le x \cap Y \le y]. \tag{5.7}$$

This definition can be more explicitly written as follows.

Definition 5.8. *If X and Y are discrete, then*

$$F_{X,Y}(x,y) = \sum_{y'\le y}\sum_{x'\le x} p_{X,Y}(x',y'). \tag{5.8}$$

If X and Y are continuous, then

$$F_{X,Y}(x,y) = \int_{-\infty}^{y}\int_{-\infty}^{x} f_{X,Y}(x',y')\, dx'\, dy'. \tag{5.9}$$

If the two random variables are **independent**, then we have

$$F_{X,Y}(x,y) = \int_{-\infty}^{x} f_X(x')\, dx' \int_{-\infty}^{y} f_Y(y')\, dy' = F_X(x)F_Y(y).$$

Example 5.13. Let X and Y be two independent uniform random variables Uniform$(0,1)$. Find the joint CDF.

Solution.

$$F_{X,Y}(x,y) = \int_0^x f_X(x')\, dx' \int_0^y f_Y(y')\, dy' = \int_0^x 1\, dx' \int_0^y 1\, dy' = xy.$$

Practice Exercise 5.5. Let X and Y be two independent uniform random variables Gaussian(μ, σ^2). Find the joint CDF.

Solution. Let $\Phi(\cdot)$ be the CDF of the standard Gaussian.

$$F_{X,Y}(x, y) = F_X(x) F_Y(y)$$

$$= \int_{-\infty}^{x} f_X(x') \, dx' \int_{-\infty}^{y} f_Y(y') \, dy' = \Phi\left(\frac{x - \mu}{\sigma}\right) \Phi\left(\frac{y - \mu}{\sigma}\right).$$

Here are a few properties of the CDF:

$$F_{X,Y}(x, -\infty) = \int_{-\infty}^{-\infty} \int_{-\infty}^{x} f_{X,Y}(x', y') \, dx' \, dy' = \int_{-\infty}^{x} 0 \, dx' = 0,$$

$$F_{X,Y}(-\infty, y) = \int_{-\infty}^{y} \int_{-\infty}^{-\infty} f_{X,Y}(x', y') \, dx' \, dy' = \int_{-\infty}^{y} 0 \, dy' = 0,$$

$$F_{X,Y}(-\infty, -\infty) = \int_{-\infty}^{-\infty} \int_{-\infty}^{-\infty} f_{X,Y}(x', y') \, dx' \, dy' = 0,$$

$$F_{X,Y}(\infty, \infty) = \int_{-\infty}^{\infty} \int_{-\infty}^{\infty} f_{X,Y}(x', y') \, dx' \, dy' = 1.$$

In addition, we can obtain the marginal CDF as follows.

Proposition 5.1. *Let X and Y be two random variables. The **marginal CDF** is*

$$F_X(x) = F_{X,Y}(x, \infty), \tag{5.10}$$
$$F_Y(y) = F_{X,Y}(\infty, y). \tag{5.11}$$

Proof. We prove only the first case. The second case is similar.

$$F_{X,Y}(x, \infty) = \int_{-\infty}^{x} \int_{-\infty}^{\infty} f_{X,Y}(x', y') \, dy' \, dx' = \int_{-\infty}^{y} f_X(x') \, dx' = F_X(x). \qquad \square$$

By the fundamental theorem of calculus, we can derive the PDF from the CDF.

Definition 5.9. *Let $F_{X,Y}(x, y)$ be the joint CDF of X and Y. Then, the joint PDF is*

$$f_{X,Y}(x, y) = \frac{\partial^2}{\partial y \, \partial x} F_{X,Y}(x, y). \tag{5.12}$$

The order of the partial derivatives can be switched, yielding a symmetric result:

$$f_{X,Y}(x, y) = \frac{\partial^2}{\partial x \, \partial y} F_{X,Y}(x, y).$$

Example 5.14. Let X and Y be two uniform random variables with joint CDF $F_{X,Y}(x,y) = xy$ for $0 \leq x \leq 1$ and $0 \leq y \leq 1$. Find the joint PDF.

Solution.

$$f_{X,Y}(x,y) = \frac{\partial^2}{\partial x \partial y} F_{X,Y}(x,y) = \frac{\partial^2}{\partial x \partial y} xy = 1,$$

which is consistent with the definition of a joint uniform random variable.

Practice Exercise 5.6. Let X and Y be two exponential random variables with joint CDF

$$F_{X,Y}(x,y) = (1 - e^{-\lambda x})(1 - e^{-\lambda y}), \qquad x \geq 0,\ y \geq 0.$$

Find the joint PDF.

Solution.

$$f_{X,Y}(x,y) = \frac{\partial^2}{\partial x \partial y} F_{X,Y}(x,y) = \frac{\partial^2}{\partial x \partial y}(1 - e^{-\lambda x})(1 - e^{-\lambda y})$$

$$= \frac{\partial}{\partial x}\left((1 - e^{-\lambda x})(\lambda e^{-\lambda y})\right) = \lambda e^{-\lambda x} \lambda e^{-\lambda y}.$$

which is consistent with the definition of a joint exponential random variable.

5.2 Joint Expectation

5.2.1 Definition and interpretation

When we have a single random variable, the expectation is defined as

$$\mathbb{E}[X] = \int_\Omega x f_X(x)\, dx.$$

For a pair of random variables, what would be a good way of defining the expectation? Certainly, we cannot just replace $f_X(x)$ by $f_{X,Y}(x,y)$ because the integration has to become a double integration. However, if it is a double integration, where should we put the variable y? It turns out that a useful way of defining the expectation for X and Y is as follows.

Definition 5.10. *Let X and Y be two random variables. The **joint expectation** is*

$$\mathbb{E}[XY] = \sum_{y \in \Omega_Y} \sum_{x \in \Omega_X} xy \cdot p_{X,Y}(x,y) \tag{5.13}$$

if X and Y are discrete, or

$$\mathbb{E}[XY] = \int_{y \in \Omega_Y} \int_{x \in \Omega_X} xy \cdot f_{X,Y}(x,y)\, dx\, dy \qquad (5.14)$$

if X and Y are continuous. Joint expectation is also called **correlation**.

The double summation and integration on the right-hand side of the equation is nothing but the state times the probability. Here, the state is the product xy, and the probability is the joint PMF $p_{X,Y}(x,y)$ (or PDF). Therefore, as long as you agree that joint expectation should be defined as $\mathbb{E}[XY]$, the double summation and the double integration make sense.

The biggest mystery here is $\mathbb{E}[XY]$. You may wonder why the joint expectation should be defined as the expectation of the *product* $\mathbb{E}[XY]$. Why not the sum $\mathbb{E}[X + Y]$, or the difference $\mathbb{E}[X - Y]$, or the quotient $\mathbb{E}[X/Y]$? Why are we so deeply interested in X times Y? These are excellent questions. That the joint expectation is defined as the product has to do with the correlation between two random variables. We will take a small detour into linear algebra.

Let us consider two discrete random variables X and Y, both with N states. So X will take the states $\{x_1, x_2, \ldots, x_N\}$ and Y will take the states $\{y_1, y_2, \ldots, y_N\}$. Let's define them as two vectors: $\boldsymbol{x} \overset{\text{def}}{=} [x_1, \ldots, x_N]^T$ and $\boldsymbol{y} \overset{\text{def}}{=} [y_1, \ldots, y_N]^T$. Since X and Y are random variables, they have a joint PMF $p_{X,Y}(x,y)$. The array of the PMF values can be written as a matrix:

$$\text{PMF as a matrix} = \boldsymbol{P} \overset{\text{def}}{=} \begin{bmatrix} p_{X,Y}(x_1,y_1) & p_{X,Y}(x_1,y_2) & \cdots & p_{X,Y}(x_1,y_N) \\ p_{X,Y}(x_2,y_1) & p_{X,Y}(x_2,y_2) & \cdots & p_{X,Y}(x_2,y_N) \\ \vdots & \vdots & \ddots & \vdots \\ p_{X,Y}(x_N,y_1) & p_{X,Y}(x_N,y_2) & \cdots & p_{X,Y}(x_N,y_N) \end{bmatrix}.$$

Let's try to write the joint expectation in terms of matrices and vectors. The definition of a joint expectation tells us that

$$\mathbb{E}[XY] = \sum_{i=1}^{N} \sum_{j=1}^{N} x_i y_j \cdot p_{X,Y}(x_i, y_j),$$

which can be written as

$$\mathbb{E}[XY] = \underbrace{\begin{bmatrix} x_1 & \cdots & x_N \end{bmatrix}}_{\boldsymbol{x}^T} \underbrace{\begin{bmatrix} p_{X,Y}(x_1,y_1) & \cdots & p_{X,Y}(x_1,y_N) \\ \vdots & \ddots & \vdots \\ p_{X,Y}(x_N,y_1) & \cdots & p_{X,Y}(x_N,y_N) \end{bmatrix}}_{\boldsymbol{P}} \underbrace{\begin{bmatrix} y_1 \\ \vdots \\ y_N \end{bmatrix}}_{\boldsymbol{y}} = \boldsymbol{x}^T \boldsymbol{P} \boldsymbol{y}.$$

This is a *weighted* inner product between $\boldsymbol{x}$ and $\boldsymbol{y}$ using the weight matrix $\boldsymbol{P}$.

Why correlation is defined as $\mathbb{E}[XY]$

- $\mathbb{E}[XY]$ is a weighted inner product between the states:

$$\mathbb{E}[XY] = \boldsymbol{x}^T \boldsymbol{P} \boldsymbol{y}.$$

- x and y are the states of the random variables X and Y.
- The inner product measures the similarity between two vectors.

Example 5.15. Let X be a discrete random variable with N states, where each state has an equal probability. Thus, $p_X(x) = 1/N$ for all x. Let $Y = X$ be another variable. Then the joint PMF of (X, Y) is

$$p_{X,Y}(x, y) = \begin{cases} \frac{1}{N}, & x = y, \\ 0, & x \neq y. \end{cases}$$

It follows that the joint expectation is

$$\mathbb{E}[XY] = \sum_{i=1}^{N} \sum_{j=1}^{N} x_i y_j \cdot p_{X,Y}(x_i, y_j) = \frac{1}{N} \sum_{i=1}^{N} x_i y_i.$$

Equivalently, we can obtain the result via the inner product by defining

$$\boldsymbol{P} = \begin{bmatrix} \frac{1}{N} & 0 & \cdots & 0 \\ 0 & \frac{1}{N} & \cdots & 0 \\ \vdots & \vdots & \ddots & \vdots \\ 0 & \cdots & \cdots & \frac{1}{N} \end{bmatrix} = \frac{1}{N} \boldsymbol{I}.$$

In this case, the weighted inner product is

$$\boldsymbol{x}^T \boldsymbol{P} \boldsymbol{y} = \frac{\boldsymbol{x}^T \boldsymbol{y}}{N} = \frac{1}{N} \sum_{i=1}^{N} x_i y_i = \mathbb{E}[XY].$$

How do we understand the inner product? Ignoring the matrix $\boldsymbol{P}$ for a moment, we recall an elementary result in linear algebra.

Definition 5.11. Let $\boldsymbol{x} \in \mathbb{R}^N$ and $\boldsymbol{y} \in \mathbb{R}^N$ be two vectors. Define the **cosine angle** $\cos \theta$ as

$$\cos \theta = \frac{\boldsymbol{x}^T \boldsymbol{y}}{\|\boldsymbol{x}\| \|\boldsymbol{y}\|}, \tag{5.15}$$

where $\|\boldsymbol{x}\| = \sqrt{\sum_{i=1}^{N} x_i^2}$ is the **norm** of the vector $\boldsymbol{x}$, and $\|\boldsymbol{y}\| = \sqrt{\sum_{i=1}^{N} y_i^2}$ is the norm of the vector $\boldsymbol{y}$.

This definition can be understood as the geometry between two vectors, as illustrated in **Figure 5.8**. If the two vectors $\boldsymbol{x}$ and $\boldsymbol{y}$ are parallel so that $\boldsymbol{x} = \alpha \boldsymbol{y}$ for some α, then the angle $\theta = 0$. If $\boldsymbol{x}$ and $\boldsymbol{y}$ are orthogonal so that $\boldsymbol{x}^T \boldsymbol{y} = 0$, then $\theta = \pi/2$. Therefore, the inner product $\boldsymbol{x}^T \boldsymbol{y}$ tells us the degree of correlation between the vectors $\boldsymbol{x}$ and $\boldsymbol{y}$.

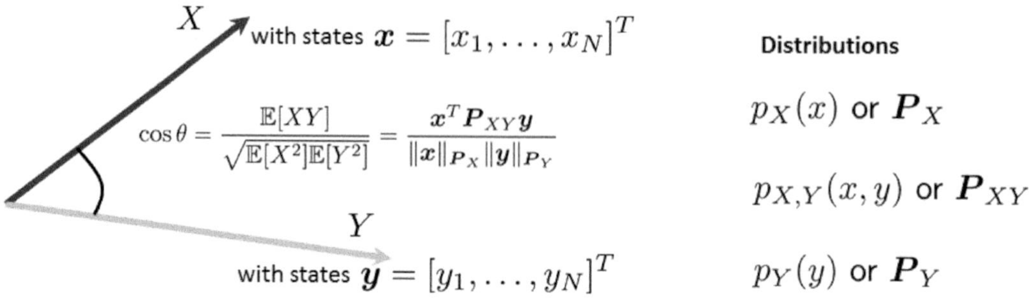

X with states $\boldsymbol{x} = [x_1, \ldots, x_N]^T$

Distributions

$$\cos\theta = \frac{\mathbb{E}[XY]}{\sqrt{\mathbb{E}[X^2]\mathbb{E}[Y^2]}} = \frac{\boldsymbol{x}^T \boldsymbol{P}_{XY}\boldsymbol{y}}{\|\boldsymbol{x}\|_{\boldsymbol{P}_X}\|\boldsymbol{y}\|_{\boldsymbol{P}_Y}}$$

$p_X(x)$ or $\boldsymbol{P}_X$

Y

with states $\boldsymbol{y} = [y_1, \ldots, y_N]^T$

$p_{X,Y}(x, y)$ or $\boldsymbol{P}_{XY}$

$p_Y(y)$ or $\boldsymbol{P}_Y$

Figure 5.8: The geometry of joint expectation. $\mathbb{E}[XY]$ gives us the cosine angle between the two random variables. This, in turn, tells us the correlation between the two random variables.

Now let's come back to our discussion about the joint expectation. The cosine angle definition tells us that if $\mathbb{E}[XY] = \boldsymbol{x}^T \boldsymbol{P}\boldsymbol{y}$, the following form would make sense:

$$\cos\theta = \frac{\boldsymbol{x}^T \boldsymbol{P}\boldsymbol{y}}{\|\boldsymbol{x}\|\|\boldsymbol{y}\|} = \frac{\mathbb{E}[XY]}{\|\boldsymbol{x}\|\|\boldsymbol{y}\|}.$$

That is, as long as we can find out the norms $\|\boldsymbol{x}\|$ and $\|\boldsymbol{y}\|$, we will be able to interpret $\mathbb{E}[XY]$ from the cosine angle perspective. But what would be a reasonable definition of $\|\boldsymbol{x}\|$ and $\|\boldsymbol{y}\|$? We define the norm by first considering the variance of the random variable X and Y:

$$\mathbb{E}[X^2] = \sum_{i=1}^{N} x_i x_i \cdot p_X(x_i)$$

$$= \underbrace{\begin{bmatrix} x_1 & \cdots & x_N \end{bmatrix}}_{\boldsymbol{x}^T} \underbrace{\begin{bmatrix} p_X(x_1) & \cdots & 0 \\ \vdots & \ddots & \vdots \\ 0 & \cdots & p_X(x_N) \end{bmatrix}}_{\boldsymbol{P}_X} \underbrace{\begin{bmatrix} x_1 \\ \vdots \\ x_N \end{bmatrix}}_{\boldsymbol{x}}$$

$$= \boldsymbol{x}^T \boldsymbol{P}_X \boldsymbol{x} = \|\boldsymbol{x}\|_{\boldsymbol{P}_X}^2,$$

where $\boldsymbol{P}_X$ is the diagonal matrix storing the probability masses of the random variable X. It is not difficult to show that $\boldsymbol{P}_X = \mathrm{diag}(\boldsymbol{P}\mathbf{1})$ by following the definition of the marginal distributions (which are the column and row sums of the joint PMF). Similarly we can define

$$\mathbb{E}[Y^2] = \sum_{j=1}^{N} y_j y_j \cdot p_Y(y_j)$$

$$= \underbrace{\begin{bmatrix} y_1 & \cdots & y_N \end{bmatrix}}_{\boldsymbol{y}^T} \underbrace{\begin{bmatrix} p_Y(y_1) & \cdots & 0 \\ \vdots & \ddots & \vdots \\ 0 & \cdots & p_Y(y_N) \end{bmatrix}}_{\boldsymbol{P}_Y} \underbrace{\begin{bmatrix} y_1 \\ \vdots \\ y_N \end{bmatrix}}_{\boldsymbol{y}}$$

$$= \boldsymbol{y}^T \boldsymbol{P}_Y \boldsymbol{y} = \|\boldsymbol{y}\|_{\boldsymbol{P}_Y}^2.$$

Therefore, one way to define the cosine angle is to start with

$$\cos\theta = \frac{\boldsymbol{x}^T \boldsymbol{P}_{XY} \boldsymbol{y}}{\|\boldsymbol{x}\|_{\boldsymbol{P}_X} \|\boldsymbol{y}\|_{\boldsymbol{P}_Y}},$$

where $\boldsymbol{P}_{XY} = \boldsymbol{P}$, $\|\boldsymbol{x}\|_{\boldsymbol{P}_X} = \sqrt{\boldsymbol{x}^T \boldsymbol{P}_X \boldsymbol{x}}$ and $\|\boldsymbol{y}\|_{\boldsymbol{P}_Y} = \sqrt{\boldsymbol{y}^T \boldsymbol{P}_Y \boldsymbol{y}}$. But writing it in terms of the expectation, we observe that this cosine angle is exactly

$$\cos\theta = \frac{\boldsymbol{x}^T \boldsymbol{P}_{XY} \boldsymbol{y}}{\|\boldsymbol{x}\|_{\boldsymbol{P}_X} \|\boldsymbol{y}\|_{\boldsymbol{P}_Y}}$$
$$= \frac{\mathbb{E}[XY]}{\sqrt{\mathbb{E}[X^2]}\sqrt{\mathbb{E}[Y^2]}}.$$

Therefore, $\mathbb{E}[XY]$ defines the cosine angle between the two random variables, which, in turn, defines the correlation between the two. A large $|\mathbb{E}[XY]|$ means that X and Y are highly correlated, and a small $|\mathbb{E}[XY]|$ means that X and Y are not very correlated. If $\mathbb{E}[XY] = 0$, then the two random variables are uncorrelated. Therefore, $\mathbb{E}[XY]$ tells us how the two random variables are related to each other.

To further convince you that $\frac{\mathbb{E}[XY]}{\sqrt{\mathbb{E}[X^2]}\sqrt{\mathbb{E}[Y^2]}}$ can be interpreted as a cosine angle, we show that

$$-1 \leq \frac{\mathbb{E}[XY]}{\sqrt{\mathbb{E}[X^2]}\sqrt{\mathbb{E}[Y^2]}} \leq 1,$$

because if this ratio can go beyond $+1$ and -1, it makes no sense to call it a cosine angle. The argument follows from a very well-known inequality in probability, called the Cauchy-Schwarz inequality (for expectation), which states that $-1 \leq \frac{\mathbb{E}[XY]}{\sqrt{\mathbb{E}[X^2]}\sqrt{\mathbb{E}[Y^2]}} \leq 1$:

Theorem 5.2 (Cauchy-Schwarz inequality). *For any random variables X and Y,*

$$(\mathbb{E}[XY])^2 \leq \mathbb{E}[X^2]\mathbb{E}[Y^2]. \tag{5.16}$$

The following proof can be skipped if you are reading the book the first time.

Proof. Let $t \in \mathbb{R}$ be a constant. Consider

$$\mathbb{E}[(X + tY)^2] = \mathbb{E}[X^2 + 2tXY + t^2 Y^2].$$

Since $\mathbb{E}[(X + tY)^2] \geq 0$ for any t, it follows that

$$\mathbb{E}[X^2 + 2tXY + t^2 Y^2] \geq 0.$$

Expanding the left-hand side yields

$$t^2 \mathbb{E}[Y^2] + 2t\mathbb{E}[XY] + \mathbb{E}[X^2] \geq 0.$$

This is a quadratic equation in t, and we know that for any quadratic equation $at^2+bt+c \geq 0$ we must have $b^2 - 4ac \leq 0$. Therefore, in our case, we have that

$$(2\mathbb{E}[XY])^2 - 4\mathbb{E}[Y^2]\mathbb{E}[X^2] \leq 0,$$

which means $(\mathbb{E}[XY])^2 \leq \mathbb{E}[X^2]\mathbb{E}[Y^2]$. The equality holds when $\mathbb{E}[(X + tY)^2] = 0$. In this case, $X = -tY$ for some t, i.e., the random variable X is a scaled version of Y so that the vector formed by the states of X is parallel to that of Y. □

End of the proof.

5.2.2 Covariance and correlation coefficient

In many practical problems, we prefer to work with central moments, i.e., $\mathbb{E}[(X - \mu_X)^2]$ instead of $\mathbb{E}[X^2]$. This essentially means that we subtract the mean from the random variable. If we adopt such a centralized random variable, we can define the **covariance** as follows.

Definition 5.12. *Let X and Y be two random variables. Then the* **covariance** *of X and Y is*
$$\text{Cov}(X,Y) = \mathbb{E}[(X - \mu_X)(Y - \mu_Y)], \tag{5.17}$$
where $\mu_X = \mathbb{E}[X]$ and $\mu_Y = \mathbb{E}[Y]$.

It is easy to show that if $X = Y$, then the covariance simplifies to the variance:

$$\text{Cov}(X,X) = \mathbb{E}[(X - \mu_X)(X - \mu_X)] = \text{Var}[X].$$

Thus, covariance is a generalization of variance. The former can handle a pair of variables, whereas the latter is only for a single variable. We can also demonstrate the following result.

Theorem 5.3. *Let X and Y be two random variables. Then*
$$\text{Cov}(X,Y) = \mathbb{E}[XY] - \mathbb{E}[X]\mathbb{E}[Y]. \tag{5.18}$$

Proof. Just apply the definition of covariance:
$$\text{Cov}(X,Y) = \mathbb{E}[(X - \mu_X)(Y - \mu_Y)]$$
$$= \mathbb{E}[XY - X\mu_Y - Y\mu_X + \mu_X\mu_Y] = \mathbb{E}[XY] - \mu_X\mu_Y. \quad □$$

The next theorem concerns the sum of two random variables.

Theorem 5.4. *For any X and Y,*

a. $\mathbb{E}[X + Y] = \mathbb{E}[X] + \mathbb{E}[Y]$.

b. $\text{Var}[X + Y] = \text{Var}[X] + 2\text{Cov}(X,Y) + \text{Var}[Y]$.

Proof. Recall the definition of joint expectation:

$$\mathbb{E}[X+Y] = \sum_y \sum_x (x+y)p_{X,Y}(x,y)$$

$$= \sum_y \sum_x x p_{X,Y}(x,y) + \sum_y \sum_x y p_{X,Y}(x,y)$$

$$= \sum_x x \left(\sum_y p_{X,Y}(x,y) \right) + \sum_y y \left(\sum_x p_{X,Y}(x,y) \right)$$

$$= \sum_x x p_X(x) + \sum_y y p_Y(y)$$

$$= \mathbb{E}[X] + \mathbb{E}[Y].$$

Similarly,

$$\mathrm{Var}[X+Y] = \mathbb{E}[(X+Y)^2] - \mathbb{E}[X+Y]^2$$

$$= \mathbb{E}[(X+Y)^2] - (\mu_X + \mu_Y)^2$$

$$= \mathbb{E}[X^2 + 2XY + Y^2] - (\mu_X^2 + 2\mu_X\mu_Y + \mu_Y^2)$$

$$= \mathbb{E}[X^2] - \mu_X^2 + \mathbb{E}[Y^2] - \mu_Y^2 + 2(\mathbb{E}[XY] - \mu_X\mu_Y)$$

$$= \mathrm{Var}[X] + 2\mathrm{Cov}(X,Y) + \mathrm{Var}[Y].$$

$\square$

With covariance defined, we can now define the **correlation coefficient** ρ, which is the cosine angle of the centralized variables. That is,

$$\rho = \cos\theta$$

$$= \frac{\mathbb{E}[(X-\mu_X)(Y-\mu_Y)]}{\sqrt{\mathbb{E}[(X-\mu_X)^2]\mathbb{E}[(Y-\mu_Y)^2]}}.$$

Recognizing that the denominator of this expression is just the variance of X and Y, we define the correlation coefficient as follows.

Definition 5.13. *Let X and Y be two random variables. The **correlation coefficient** is*

$$\rho = \frac{\mathrm{Cov}(X,Y)}{\sqrt{\mathrm{Var}[X]\mathrm{Var}[Y]}}. \qquad (5.19)$$

Since $-1 \le \cos\theta \le 1$, ρ is also between -1 and 1. The difference between ρ and $\mathbb{E}[XY]$ is that ρ is *normalized* with respect to the variance of X and Y, whereas $\mathbb{E}[XY]$ is not normalized. The correlation coefficient has the following properties:

- ρ is always between -1 and 1, i.e., $-1 \le \rho \le 1$. This is due to the cosine angle definition.
- When $X = Y$ (fully correlated), $\rho = +1$.
- When $X = -Y$ (negatively correlated), $\rho = -1$.
- When X and Y are uncorrelated, $\rho = 0$.

5.2.3 Independence and correlation

If two random variables X and Y are independent, the joint expectation can be written as a product of two individual expectations.

> **Theorem 5.5.** *If X and Y are independent, then*
>
> $$\mathbb{E}[XY] = \mathbb{E}[X]\mathbb{E}[Y].\tag{5.20}$$

Proof. We only prove the discrete case because the continuous can be proved similarly. If X and Y are independent, we have $p_{X,Y}(x,y) = p_X(x)\, p_Y(y)$. Therefore,

$$\mathbb{E}[XY] = \sum_y \sum_x xy p_{X,Y}(x,y) = \sum_y \sum_x xy p_X(x) p_Y(y)$$

$$= \left(\sum_x x p_X(x)\right)\left(\sum_y y p_Y(y)\right) = \mathbb{E}[X]\mathbb{E}[Y].$$

$\square$

In general, for any two independent random variables and two functions f and g,

$$\mathbb{E}[f(X)g(Y)] = \mathbb{E}[f(X)]\mathbb{E}[g(Y)].$$

The following theorem illustrates a few important relationships between independence and correlation.

> **Theorem 5.6.** *Consider the following two statements:*
>
> *a. X and Y are independent;*
>
> *b. $\text{Cov}(X,Y) = 0$.*
>
> *Statement (a) implies statement (b), but (b) does not imply (a). Thus, independence is a stronger condition than correlation.*

Proof. We first prove that (a) implies (b). If X and Y are independent, then $\mathbb{E}[XY] = \mathbb{E}[X]\mathbb{E}[Y]$. In this case,

$$\text{Cov}(X,Y) = \mathbb{E}[XY] - \mathbb{E}[X]\mathbb{E}[Y] = \mathbb{E}[X]\mathbb{E}[Y] - \mathbb{E}[X]\mathbb{E}[Y] = 0.$$

To prove that (b) does not imply (a), we show a counterexample. Consider a discrete random variable Z with PMF

$$p_Z(z) = \begin{bmatrix} \frac{1}{4} & \frac{1}{4} & \frac{1}{4} & \frac{1}{4} \end{bmatrix}.$$

Let X and Y be

$$X = \cos\frac{\pi}{2}Z \quad \text{and} \quad Y = \sin\frac{\pi}{2}Z.$$

Then we can show that $\mathbb{E}[X] = 0$ and $\mathbb{E}[Y] = 0$. The covariance is

$$
\begin{aligned}
\operatorname{Cov}(X, Y) &= \mathbb{E}[(X - 0)(Y - 0)] \\
&= \mathbb{E}\left[\cos\frac{\pi}{2}Z \sin\frac{\pi}{2}Z\right] \\
&= \mathbb{E}\left[\frac{1}{2}\sin\pi Z\right] \\
&= \frac{1}{2}\left[(\sin\pi 0)\frac{1}{4} + (\sin\pi 1)\frac{1}{4} + (\sin\pi 2)\frac{1}{4} + (\sin\pi 3)\frac{1}{4}\right] = 0.
\end{aligned}
$$

The next step is to show that X and Y are dependent. To this end, we only need to show that $p_{X,Y}(x, y) \neq p_X(x)p_Y(y)$. The joint PMF $p_{X,Y}(x, y)$ can be found by noting that

$$
\begin{aligned}
Z = 0 &\Rightarrow X = 1,\ Y = 0, \\
Z = 1 &\Rightarrow X = 0,\ Y = 1, \\
Z = 2 &\Rightarrow X = -1,\ Y = 0, \\
Z = 3 &\Rightarrow X = 0,\ Y = -1.
\end{aligned}
$$

Thus, the PMF is

$$
p_{X,Y}(x, y) = \begin{bmatrix} 0 & \frac{1}{4} & 0 \\ \frac{1}{4} & 0 & \frac{1}{4} \\ 0 & \frac{1}{4} & 0 \end{bmatrix}.
$$

The marginal PMFs are

$$
p_X(x) = \begin{bmatrix} \frac{1}{4} & \frac{1}{2} & \frac{1}{4} \end{bmatrix}, \quad p_Y(y) = \begin{bmatrix} \frac{1}{4} & \frac{1}{2} & \frac{1}{4} \end{bmatrix}.
$$

The product $p_X(x)\, p_Y(y)$ is

$$
p_X(x)p_Y(y) = \begin{bmatrix} \frac{1}{16} & \frac{1}{8} & \frac{1}{16} \\ \frac{1}{8} & \frac{1}{4} & \frac{1}{8} \\ \frac{1}{16} & \frac{1}{8} & \frac{1}{16} \end{bmatrix}.
$$

Therefore, $p_{X,Y}(x, y) \neq p_X(x)p_Y(y)$, although $\mathbb{E}[XY] = \mathbb{E}[X]\mathbb{E}[Y]$.

□

What is the relationship between independent and uncorrelated?

- Independent $\Rightarrow$ uncorrelated.

- Independent $\nLeftarrow$ uncorrelated.

5.2.4 Computing correlation from data

We close this section by discussing a very practical problem: Given a dataset containing two columns of data points, how do we determine whether the two columns are correlated?

Recall that the correlation coefficient is defined as

$$
\rho = \frac{\mathbb{E}[XY] - \mu_X\mu_Y}{\sigma_X\sigma_Y}.
$$

If we have a dataset containing $(x_n, y_i)_{n=1}^N$, then the correlation coefficient can be approximated by

$$\widehat{\rho} = \frac{\frac{1}{N}\sum_{n=1}^N x_n y_n - \overline{x}\,\overline{y}}{\sqrt{\frac{1}{N}\sum_{n=1}^N (x_n - \overline{x})^2}\sqrt{\frac{1}{N}\sum_{n=1}^N (y_n - \overline{y})^2}},$$

where $\overline{x} = \frac{1}{N}\sum_{n=1}^N x_n$ and $\overline{y} = \frac{1}{N}\sum_{n=1}^N y_n$ are the means. This equation should not be a surprise because essentially all terms are the empirical estimates. Thus, $\widehat{\rho}$ is the empirical correlation coefficient determined from the dataset. As $N \to \infty$, we expect $\widehat{\rho} \to \rho$.

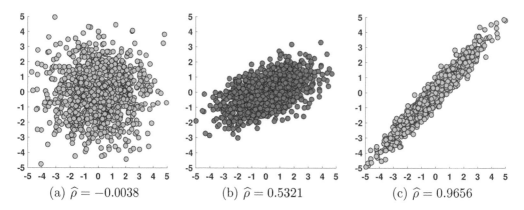

(a) $\widehat{\rho} = -0.0038$ (b) $\widehat{\rho} = 0.5321$ (c) $\widehat{\rho} = 0.9656$

Figure 5.9: Visualization of correlated variables. Each of these figures represent a scattered plot of a dataset containing $(x_n, y_n)_{n=1}^N$. (a) is uncorrelated. (b) is somewhat correlated. (c) is strongly correlated.

Figure 5.9 shows three example datasets. We plot the (x_n, y_n) pairs as coordinates in the 2D plane. The first dataset contains samples that are almost uncorrelated. We can see that x_n does not tell us anything about y_n. The second dataset is moderately correlated. The third dataset is highly correlated: If we know x_n, we are almost certain to know the corresponding y_n, with a small number of perturbations.

On a computer, computing the correlation coefficient can be done using built-in commands such as `corrcoef` in MATLAB and `stats.pearsonr` in Python. The codes to generate the results in **Figure 5.9**(b) are shown below.

```
% MATLAB code to compute the correlation coefficient
x = mvnrnd([0,0],[3 1; 1 1],1000);
figure(1); scatter(x(:,1),x(:,2));
rho = corrcoef(x)
```

```
# Python code to compute the correlation coefficient
import numpy as np
import scipy.stats as stats
import matplotlib.pyplot as plt
x = stats.multivariate_normal.rvs([0,0], [[3,1],[1,1]], 10000)
plt.figure(); plt.scatter(x[:,0],x[:,1])
rho,_ = stats.pearsonr(x[:,0],x[:,1])
print(rho)
```

5.3 Conditional PMF and PDF

Whenever we have a pair of random variables X and Y that are correlated, we can define their conditional distributions, which quantify the probability of $X = x$ given $Y = y$. In this section, we discuss the concepts of conditional PMF and PDF.

5.3.1 Conditional PMF

We start by defining the conditional PMF for a pair of discrete random variables.

> **Definition 5.14.** *Let X and Y be two discrete random variables. The* **conditional PMF** *of X given Y is*
>
> $$p_{X|Y}(x|y) = \frac{p_{X,Y}(x,y)}{p_Y(y)}. \tag{5.21}$$

The simplest way to understand this is to view $p_{X|Y}(x|y)$ as $\mathbb{P}[X = x \,|\, Y = y]$. That is, given that $Y = y$, what is the probability for $X = x$? To see why this perspective makes sense, let us recall the definition of a conditional probability:

$$
\begin{aligned}
p_{X|Y}(x|y) &= \frac{p_{X,Y}(x,y)}{p_Y(y)} \\
&= \frac{\mathbb{P}[X = x \cap Y = y]}{\mathbb{P}[Y = y]} = \mathbb{P}[X = x \,|\, Y = y].
\end{aligned}
$$

As we can see, the last two equalities are essentially the definitions of conditional probability and the joint PMF.

How should we understand the notation $p_{X|Y}(x|y)$? Is it a one-variable function in x or a two-variable function in (x, y)? What does $p_{X|Y}(x|y)$ tell us? To answer these questions, let us first try to understand the randomness exhibited in a conditional PMF. In $p_{X|Y}(x|y)$, the random variable Y is *fixed* to a specific value $Y = y$. Therefore there is nothing random about Y. All the possibilities of Y have already been taken care of by the denominator $p_Y(y)$. Only the variable x in $p_{X|Y}(x|y)$ has randomness. What do we mean by "fixed at a value $Y = y$"? Consider the following example.

> **Example 5.16.** Suppose there are two coins. Let
>
> $$X = \text{the sum of the values of two coins},$$
> $$Y = \text{the value of the first coin}.$$
>
> Clearly, X has 3 states: 0, 1, 2, and Y has two states: either 0 or 1. When we say $p_{X|Y}(x|1)$, we refer to the probability mass function of X when fixing $Y = 1$. If we do not impose this condition, the probability mass of X is simple:
>
> $$p_X(x) = \left[\frac{1}{4}, \frac{1}{2}, \frac{1}{4}\right].$$

However, if we include the conditioning, then

$$p_{X|Y}(x|1) = \frac{p_{X,Y}(x,1)}{p_Y(1)}$$

$$= \frac{[0, \frac{2}{4}, \frac{1}{4}]}{\frac{1}{6}} = \left[0, \frac{2}{3}, \frac{1}{3}\right].$$

To put this in plain words, when $Y = 1$, there is no way for X to take the state 0. The chance for X to take the state 1 is 2/3 because either $(0,1)$ or $(1,0)$ can give $X = 1$. The chance for X to take the state 2 is 1/3 because it has to be $(1,1)$ in order to give $X = 2$. Therefore, when we say "conditioned on $Y = 1$", we mean that we limit our observations to cases where $Y = 1$. Since Y is already fixed at $Y = 1$, there is nothing random about Y. The only variable is X. This example is illustrated in **Figure 5.10**.

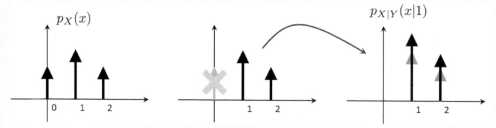

Figure 5.10: Suppose X is the sum of two coins with PMF $0.25, 0.5, 0.25$. Let Y be the first coin. When X is unconditioned, the PMF is just $[0.25, 0.5, 0.25]$. When X is conditioned on $Y = 1$, then "$X = 0$" cannot happen. Therefore, the resulting PMF $p_{X|Y}(x|1)$ only has two states. After normalization we obtain the conditional PMF $[0, 0.66, 0.33]$.

Since Y is already fixed at a particular value $Y = y$, $p_{X|Y}(x|y)$ is a probability mass function of x (we want to emphasize again that it is x and not y). So $p_{X|Y}(x|y)$ is a one-variable function in x. It is not the same as the usual PMF $p_X(x)$. $p_{X|Y}(x|y)$ is conditioned on $Y = y$. For example, $p_{X|Y}(x|1)$ is the PMF of X restricted to the condition that $Y = 1$. In fact, it follows that

$$\sum_{x \in \Omega_X} p_{X|Y}(x|y) = \sum_{x \in \Omega_X} \frac{p_{X,Y}(x,y)}{p_Y(y)}$$

$$= \frac{\sum_{x \in \Omega_X} p_{X,Y}(x,y)}{p_Y(y)} = \frac{p_Y(y)}{p_Y(y)} = 1,$$

but this tells us that $p_{X|Y}(x|y)$ is a legitimate probability mass of X. If we sum over the y's instead, then we will hit a bump:

$$\sum_{y \in \Omega_Y} p_{X|Y}(x|y) = \sum_{y \in \Omega_Y} \frac{p_{X,Y}(x,y)}{p_Y(y)} \neq 1.$$

Therefore, while $p_{X|Y}(x|y)$ is a legitimate probability mass function of X, it is not a probability mass function of Y.

Example 5.17. Consider a joint PMF given in the following table. Find the conditional PMF $p_{X|Y}(x|1)$ and the marginal PMF $p_X(x)$.

	Y= 1	2	3	4
X = 1	$\frac{1}{20}$	$\frac{1}{20}$	$\frac{1}{20}$	$\frac{0}{20}$
2	$\frac{1}{20}$	$\frac{2}{20}$	$\frac{3}{20}$	$\frac{1}{20}$
3	$\frac{1}{20}$	$\frac{2}{20}$	$\frac{3}{20}$	$\frac{1}{20}$
4	$\frac{0}{20}$	$\frac{1}{20}$	$\frac{1}{20}$	$\frac{1}{20}$

Solution. To find the marginal PMF, we sum over all the y's for every x:

$$x = 1: \quad p_X(1) = \sum_{y=1}^{4} p_{X,Y}(1, y) = \frac{1}{20} + \frac{1}{20} + \frac{1}{20} + \frac{0}{20} = \frac{3}{20},$$

$$x = 2: \quad p_X(2) = \sum_{y=1}^{4} p_{X,Y}(2, y) = \frac{1}{20} + \frac{2}{20} + \frac{3}{20} + \frac{1}{20} = \frac{7}{20},$$

$$x = 3: \quad p_X(3) = \sum_{y=1}^{4} p_{X,Y}(3, y) = \frac{1}{20} + \frac{2}{20} + \frac{3}{20} + \frac{1}{20} = \frac{7}{20},$$

$$x = 4: \quad p_X(4) = \sum_{y=1}^{4} p_{X,Y}(4, y) = \frac{0}{20} + \frac{1}{20} + \frac{1}{20} + \frac{1}{20} = \frac{3}{20}.$$

Hence, the marginal PMF is

$$p_X(x) = \begin{bmatrix} \frac{3}{20} & \frac{7}{20} & \frac{7}{20} & \frac{3}{20} \end{bmatrix}.$$

The conditional PMF $p_{X|Y}(x|1)$ is

$$p_{X|Y}(x|1) = \frac{p_{X,Y}(x, 1)}{p_Y(1)} = \frac{\begin{bmatrix} \frac{1}{20} & \frac{1}{20} & \frac{1}{20} & \frac{0}{20} \end{bmatrix}}{\frac{3}{20}} = \begin{bmatrix} \frac{1}{3} & \frac{1}{3} & \frac{1}{3} & 0 \end{bmatrix}.$$

Practice Exercise 5.7. Consider two random variables X and Y defined as follows.

$$Y = \begin{cases} 10^2, & \text{with prob } 5/6, \\ 10^4, & \text{with prob } 1/6. \end{cases} \qquad X = \begin{cases} 10^{-4}Y, & \text{with prob } 1/2, \\ 10^{-3}Y, & \text{with prob } 1/3, \\ 10^{-2}Y, & \text{with prob } 1/6. \end{cases}$$

Find $p_{X|Y}(x|y)$, $p_X(x)$ and $p_{X,Y}(x, y)$.

Solution. Since Y takes two different states, we can enumerate $Y = 10^2$ and $Y = 10^4$.

This gives us

$$
p_{X|Y}(x|10^2) = \begin{cases} 1/2, & \text{if } x = 0.01, \\ 1/3, & \text{if } x = 0.1, \\ 1/6, & \text{if } x = 1. \end{cases}
$$

$$
p_{X|Y}(x|10^4) = \begin{cases} 1/2, & \text{if } x = 1, \\ 1/3, & \text{if } x = 10, \\ 1/6, & \text{if } x = 100. \end{cases}
$$

The joint PMF $p_{X,Y}(x,y)$ is

$$
p_{X,Y}(x,10^2) = p_{X|Y}(x|10^2)p_Y(10^2) = \begin{cases} \left(\frac{1}{2}\right)\left(\frac{5}{6}\right), & x = 0.01, \\ \left(\frac{1}{3}\right)\left(\frac{5}{6}\right), & x = 0.1, \\ \left(\frac{1}{6}\right)\left(\frac{5}{6}\right), & x = 1. \end{cases}
$$

$$
p_{X,Y}(x,10^4) = p_{X|Y}(x|10^4)p_Y(10^4) = \begin{cases} \left(\frac{1}{2}\right)\left(\frac{1}{6}\right), & x = 1, \\ \left(\frac{1}{3}\right)\left(\frac{1}{6}\right), & x = 10, \\ \left(\frac{1}{6}\right)\left(\frac{1}{6}\right), & x = 100. \end{cases}
$$

Therefore, the joint PMF is given by the following table.

10^4	0	0	$\frac{1}{12}$	$\frac{1}{18}$	$\frac{1}{36}$
10^2	$\frac{5}{12}$	$\frac{5}{18}$	$\frac{5}{36}$	0	0
	0.01	0.1	1	10	100

The marginal PMF $p_X(x)$ is thus

$$
p_X(x) = \sum_y p_{X,Y}(x,y)
$$

$$
= \begin{bmatrix} \frac{5}{12} & \frac{5}{18} & \frac{2}{9} & \frac{1}{18} & \frac{1}{36} \end{bmatrix}.
$$

In the previous two examples, what is the probability $\mathbb{P}[X \in A \,|\, Y = y]$ or the probability $\mathbb{P}[X \in A]$ for some events A? The answers are giving by the following theorem.

Theorem 5.7. *Let X and Y be two discrete random variables. Let A be an event.*

$$
\mathbb{P}[X \in A \,|\, Y = y] = \sum_{x \in A} p_{X|Y}(x|y)
$$

and

$$
\mathbb{P}[X \in A] = \sum_{x \in A} \sum_{y \in \Omega_Y} p_{X|Y}(x|y)p_Y(y) = \sum_{y \in \Omega_Y} \mathbb{P}[X \in A \,|\, Y = y]p_Y(y).
$$

Proof. The first statement is based on the fact that if A contains a finite number of elements, then $\mathbb{P}[X \in A]$ is equivalent to the sum $\sum_{x \in A} \mathbb{P}[X = x]$. Thus,

$$\mathbb{P}[X \in A \mid Y = y] = \frac{\mathbb{P}[X \in A \cap Y = y]}{\mathbb{P}[Y = y]}$$
$$= \frac{\sum_{x \in A} \mathbb{P}[X = x \cap Y = y]}{\mathbb{P}[Y = y]}$$
$$= \sum_{x \in A} p_{X|Y}(x|y).$$

The second statement holds because the inner summation $\sum_{y \in \Omega_Y} p_{X|Y}(x|y) p_Y(y)$ is just the marginal PMF $p_X(x)$. Thus the outer summation yields the probability. □

Example 5.18. Let us follow up on Example 5.17. What is the probability that $\mathbb{P}[X > 2|Y = 1]$? What is the probability that $\mathbb{P}[X > 2]$?

Solution. Since the problem asks about the conditional probability, we know that it can be computed by using the conditional PMF. This gives us

$$\mathbb{P}[X > 2|Y = 1] = \sum_{x>2} p_{X|Y}(x|1)$$
$$= \underbrace{p_{X|Y}(1|1)} + \underbrace{p_{X|Y}(2|1)} + \underbrace{p_{X|Y}(3|1)}_{\frac{1}{3}} + \underbrace{p_{X|Y}(4|1)}_{0} = \frac{1}{3}.$$

The other probability is

$$\mathbb{P}[X > 2] = \sum_{x>2} p_X(x) = \underbrace{p_X(1)} + \underbrace{p_X(2)} + \underbrace{p_X(3)}_{\frac{8}{20}} + \underbrace{p_X(4)}_{\frac{3}{20}} = \frac{11}{20}.$$

What is the rule of thumb for conditional distribution?
- The PMF/PDF should *match* with the probability you are finding.
- If you want to find the conditional probability $\mathbb{P}[X \in A|Y = y]$, use the conditional PMF $p_{X|Y}(x|y)$.
- If you want to find the probability $\mathbb{P}[X \in A]$, use the marginal PMF $p_X(x)$.

Finally, we define the conditional CDF for discrete random variables.

Definition 5.15. *Let X and Y be discrete random variables. Then the* **conditional CDF** *of X given $Y = y$ is*

$$F_{X|Y}(x|y) = \mathbb{P}[X \le x \mid Y = y] = \sum_{x' \le x} p_{X|Y}(x'|y). \tag{5.22}$$

5.3.2 Conditional PDF

We now discuss the conditioning of a continuous random variable.

Definition 5.16. *Let X and Y be two continuous random variables. The **conditional PDF** of X given Y is*

$$f_{X|Y}(x|y) = \frac{f_{X,Y}(x,y)}{f_Y(y)}. \qquad (5.23)$$

Example 5.19. Let X and Y be two continuous random variables with a joint PDF

$$f_{X,Y}(x,y) = \begin{cases} 2e^{-x}e^{-y}, & 0 \le y \le x < \infty, \\ 0, & \text{otherwise.} \end{cases}$$

Find the conditional PDFs $f_{X|Y}(x|y)$ and $f_{Y|X}(y|x)$.

Solution. We first find the marginal PDFs.

$$f_X(x) = \int_{-\infty}^{\infty} f_{X,Y}(x,y)\,dy = \int_0^x 2e^{-x}e^{-y}\,dy = 2e^{-x}(1 - e^{-x}),$$

$$f_Y(y) = \int_{-\infty}^{\infty} f_{X,Y}(x,y)\,dx = \int_y^{\infty} 2e^{-x}e^{-y}\,dx = 2e^{-2y}.$$

Thus, the conditional PDFs are

$$f_{X|Y}(x|y) = \frac{f_{X,Y}(x,y)}{f_Y(y)}$$
$$= \frac{2e^{-x}e^{-y}}{2e^{-2y}} = e^{-(x+y)}, \quad x \ge y,$$

$$f_{Y|X}(y|x) = \frac{f_{X,Y}(x,y)}{f_X(x)}$$
$$= \frac{2e^{-x}e^{-y}}{2e^{-x}(1 - e^{-x})} = \frac{e^{-y}}{1 - e^{-x}}, \quad 0 \le y < x.$$

Where does the conditional PDF come from? We cannot duplicate the argument we used for the discrete case because the denominator of a conditional PMF becomes $\mathbb{P}[Y = y] = 0$ when Y is continuous. To answer this question, we first define the conditional CDF for continuous random variables.

Definition 5.17. *Let X and Y be continuous random variables. Then the **conditional CDF** of X given $Y = y$ is*

$$F_{X|Y}(x|y) = \frac{\int_{-\infty}^x f_{X,Y}(x',y)\,dx'}{f_Y(y)}. \qquad (5.24)$$

Why should the conditional CDF of continuous random variable be defined in this way? One way to interpret $F_{X|Y}(x|y)$ is as the limiting perspective. We can define the **conditional CDF** as

$$F_{X|Y}(x|y) = \lim_{h \to 0} \mathbb{P}(X \leq x \,|\, y \leq Y \leq y + h)$$

$$= \lim_{h \to 0} \frac{\mathbb{P}(X \leq x \cap y \leq Y \leq y + h)}{\mathbb{P}[y \leq Y \leq y + h]}.$$

With some calculations, we have that

$$\lim_{h \to 0} \frac{\mathbb{P}(X \leq x \cap y \leq Y \leq y + h)}{\mathbb{P}[y \leq Y \leq y + h]} = \lim_{h \to 0} \frac{\int_{-\infty}^{x} \int_{y}^{y+h} f_{X,Y}(x', y') \, dy' \, dx'}{\int_{y}^{y+h} f_Y(y') \, dy'}$$

$$= \lim_{h \to 0} \frac{\int_{-\infty}^{x} f_{X,Y}(x', y') \, dx' \cdot h}{f_Y(y) \cdot h}$$

$$= \frac{\int_{-\infty}^{x} f_{X,Y}(x', y') \, dx'}{f_Y(y)}.$$

The key here is that the small step size h in the numerator and the denominator will cancel each other out. Now, given the conditional CDF, we can verify the definition of the conditional PDF. It holds that

$$f_{X|Y}(x|y) = \frac{d}{dx} F_{X|Y}(x|y)$$

$$= \frac{d}{dx} \left\{ \frac{\int_{-\infty}^{x} f_{X,Y}(x', y) \, dx'}{f_Y(y)} \right\} \overset{(a)}{=} \frac{f_{X,Y}(x, y)}{f_Y(y)},$$

where (a) follows from the fundamental theorem of calculus.

Just like the conditional PMF, we can calculate the probabilities using the conditional PDFs. In particular, if we evaluate the probability where $X \in A$ given that Y takes a particular value $Y = y$, then we can integrate the conditional PDF $f_{X|Y}(x|y)$, with respect to x.

Theorem 5.8. *Let X and Y be continuous random variables, and let A be an event.*

(i) $\mathbb{P}[X \in A \,|\, Y = y] = \int_A f_{X|Y}(x|y) \, dx,$

(ii) $\mathbb{P}[X \in A] = \int_{\Omega_Y} \mathbb{P}[X \in A \,|\, Y = y] f_Y(y) \, dy.$

Example 5.20. Let X be a random bit such that

$$X = \begin{cases} +1, & \text{with prob } 1/2, \\ -1, & \text{with prob } 1/2. \end{cases}$$

Suppose that X is transmitted over a noisy channel so that the observed signal is

$$Y = X + N,$$

where $N \sim \text{Gaussian}(0, 1)$ is the noise, which is independent of the signal X. Find the probabilities $\mathbb{P}[X = +1 \,|\, Y > 0]$ and $\mathbb{P}[X = -1 \,|\, Y > 0]$.

Solution. First, we know that

$$f_{Y|X}(y|+1) = \frac{1}{\sqrt{2\pi}} e^{-\frac{(y-1)^2}{2}} \qquad \text{and} \qquad f_{Y|X}(y|-1) = \frac{1}{\sqrt{2\pi}} e^{-\frac{(y+1)^2}{2}}.$$

Therefore, integrating y from 0 to ∞ gives us

$$\mathbb{P}[Y > 0 \,|\, X = +1] = \int_0^\infty \frac{1}{\sqrt{2\pi}} e^{-\frac{(y-1)^2}{2}} \, dy$$

$$= 1 - \int_{-\infty}^0 \frac{1}{\sqrt{2\pi}} e^{-\frac{(y-1)^2}{2}} \, dy$$

$$= 1 - \Phi\left(\frac{0-1}{1}\right) = 1 - \Phi(-1).$$

Similarly, we have $\mathbb{P}[Y > 0 \,|\, X = -1] = 1 - \Phi(+1)$. The probability we want to find is $\mathbb{P}[X = +1 \,|\, Y > 0]$, which can be determined using Bayes' theorem.

$$\mathbb{P}[X = +1 \,|\, Y > 0] = \frac{\mathbb{P}[Y > 0 \,|\, X = +1]\mathbb{P}[X = +1]}{\mathbb{P}[Y > 0]}.$$

The denominator can be found by using the law of total probability:

$$\mathbb{P}[Y > 0] = \mathbb{P}[Y > 0 \,|\, X = +1]\mathbb{P}[X = +1]$$

$$+ \mathbb{P}[Y > 0 \,|\, X = -1]\mathbb{P}[X = -1]$$

$$= 1 - \frac{1}{2}\left(\Phi(+1) + \Phi(-1)\right)$$

$$= \frac{1}{2},$$

since $\Phi(+1) + \Phi(-1) = \Phi(+1) + 1 - \Phi(+1) = 1$. Therefore,

$$\mathbb{P}[X = +1 \,|\, Y > 0] = 1 - \Phi(-1)$$

$$= 0.8413.$$

The implication is that if $Y > 0$, the probability $\mathbb{P}[X = +1 \,|\, Y > 0] = 0.8413$. The complement of this result gives $\mathbb{P}[X = -1 \,|\, Y > 0] = 1 - 0.8413 = 0.1587$.

Practice Exercise 5.8. Find $\mathbb{P}[Y > y]$, where

$$X \sim \text{Uniform}[1, 2], \quad Y \,|\, X \sim \text{Exponential}(x).$$

Solution. The tricky part of this problem is the tendency to confuse the two variables X and Y. Once you understand their roles the problem becomes easy. First notice that $Y \,|\, X \sim \text{Exponential}(x)$ is a conditional distribution. It says that given $X = x$, the probability distribution of Y is exponential, with the parameter x. Thus, we have that

$$f_{Y|X}(y|x) = xe^{-xy}.$$

Why? Recall that if $Y \sim \text{Exponential}(\lambda)$ then $f_Y(y) = \lambda e^{-\lambda y}$. Now if we replace λ with x, we have xe^{-xy}. So the role of x in this conditional density function is as a parameter.

Given this property, we can compute the conditional probability:

$$\mathbb{P}[Y > y \,|\, X = x] = \int_y^\infty f_{Y|X}(y'|x)\,dy'$$

$$= \int_y^\infty xe^{-xy'}\,dy' = \left[-e^{-xy'}\right]_{y'=y}^\infty = e^{-xy}.$$

Finally, we can compute the marginal probability:

$$\mathbb{P}[Y > y] = \int_{\Omega_X} \mathbb{P}[Y > 0 | X = x']f_X(x')\,dx'$$

$$= \int_0^1 e^{-x'y}\,dx' = \left[\frac{1}{y}e^{-x'y}\right]_{x'=0}^{x'=1} = \frac{1}{y}\left(1 - e^{-y}\right).$$

We can double-check this result by noting that the problem asks about the probability $\mathbb{P}[Y > y]$. Thus, the answer must be a function of y but not of x.

5.4 Conditional Expectation

5.4.1 Definition

When dealing with two dependent random variables, at times we would like to determine the expectation of a random variable when the second random variable takes a particular state. The **conditional expectation** is a formal way of doing so.

Definition 5.18. *The* **conditional expectation** *of X given $Y = y$ is*

$$\mathbb{E}[X \,|\, Y = y] = \sum_x x p_{X|Y}(x|y) \tag{5.25}$$

for discrete random variables, and

$$\mathbb{E}[X \,|\, Y = y] = \int_{-\infty}^\infty x f_{X|Y}(x|y)\,dx \tag{5.26}$$

for continuous random variables.

There are two points to note here. First, the expectation of $\mathbb{E}[X \mid Y = y]$ is taken with respect to $f_{X|Y}(x|y)$. We assume that the random variable Y is already fixed at the state $Y = y$. Thus, the only source of randomness is X. Secondly, since the expectation $\mathbb{E}[X \mid Y = y]$ has eliminated the randomness of X, the resulting function is in y.

What is conditional expectation?

- $\mathbb{E}[X|Y = y]$ is the expectation using $f_{X|Y}(x|y)$.
- The integration is taken w.r.t. x, because $Y = y$ is given and fixed.

5.4.2 The law of total expectation

Theorem 5.9. *The law of total expectation states that*

$$\mathbb{E}[X] = \sum_y \mathbb{E}[X|Y = y]p_Y(y), \quad or \quad \mathbb{E}[X] = \int_{-\infty}^{\infty} \mathbb{E}[X|Y = y]f_Y(y) \, dy. \qquad (5.27)$$

Proof. We will prove the discrete case only, as the continuous case can be proved by replacing summation with integration.

$$\mathbb{E}[X] = \sum_x x p_X(x) = \sum_x x \left(\sum_y p_{X,Y}(x,y) \right)$$

$$= \sum_x \sum_y x p_{X|Y}(x|y) p_Y(y)$$

$$= \sum_y \left(\sum_x x p_{X|Y}(x|y) \right) p_Y(y) = \sum_y \mathbb{E}[X|Y = y]p_Y(y).$$

$\square$

Figure 5.11 illustrates the idea behind the proof. Essentially, we *decompose* the expectation $\mathbb{E}[X]$ into "subexpectations" $\mathbb{E}[X|Y = y]$. The probability of each subexpectation is $p_Y(y)$. By summing the subexpectation multiplied by $p_Y(y)$, we obtain the overall expectation.

What is the law of total expectation?

- The law of total expectation is a *decomposition* rule.
- It decomposes $\mathbb{E}[X]$ into smaller/easier conditional expectations.

This law can also be written in a more compact form.

Corollary 5.1. *Let X and Y be two random variables. Then*

$$\mathbb{E}[X] = \mathbb{E}_Y \left[\mathbb{E}_{X|Y}[X|Y] \right]. \qquad (5.28)$$

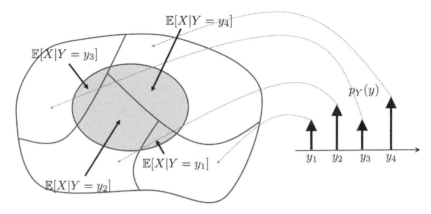

Figure 5.11: The expectation $\mathbb{E}[X]$ can be decomposed into a set of subexpectations. This gives us $\mathbb{E}[X] = \sum_y \mathbb{E}[X|Y = y]p_Y(y)$.

Proof. The previous theorem states that $\mathbb{E}[X] = \sum_y \mathbb{E}[X|Y = y]p_Y(y)$. If we treat $\mathbb{E}[X|Y = y]$ as a function of y, for instance $h(y)$, then

$$\mathbb{E}[X] = \sum_y \mathbb{E}[X|Y = y]p_Y(y) = \sum_y h(y)p_Y(y) = \mathbb{E}[h(Y)] = \mathbb{E}\left[\mathbb{E}[X|Y]\right]. \qquad \square$$

Example 5.21. Suppose there are two classes of cars. Let X be the speed of a car and C be the class. When $C = 1$, we know that $X \sim \text{Gaussian}(\mu_1, \sigma_1)$. We know that $\mathbb{P}[C = 1] = p$. When $C = 2$, $X \sim \text{Gaussian}(\mu_2, \sigma_2)$. Also, $\mathbb{P}[C = 2] = 1 - p$. If you see a car on the freeway, what is its average speed?

Solution. The problem has given us everything we need. In particular, we know that the conditional PDFs are:

$$f_{X|C}(x\,|\,1) = \frac{1}{\sqrt{2\pi\sigma_1^2}}\exp\left\{-\frac{(x-\mu_1)^2}{2\sigma_1^2}\right\},$$

$$f_{X|C}(x\,|\,2) = \frac{1}{\sqrt{2\pi\sigma_2^2}}\exp\left\{-\frac{(x-\mu_2)^2}{2\sigma_2^2}\right\}.$$

Therefore, conditioned on C, we have two expectations:

$$\mathbb{E}[X\,|\,C = 1] = \int_{-\infty}^{\infty} x\,f_{X|C}(x\,|\,1)\,dx = \mu_1,$$

$$\mathbb{E}[X\,|\,C = 2] = \int_{-\infty}^{\infty} x\,f_{X|C}(x\,|\,2)\,dx = \mu_2.$$

The overall expectation $\mathbb{E}[X]$ is

$$\mathbb{E}[X] = \mathbb{E}[X\,|\,C = 1]\mathbb{P}[C = 1] + \mathbb{E}[X\,|\,C = 2]\mathbb{P}[C = 2]$$
$$= p\mu_1 + (1-p)\mu_2.$$

Practice Exercise 5.9. Consider a joint PMF given by the following table. Find $\mathbb{E}[X|Y = 10^2]$ and $\mathbb{E}[X|Y = 10^4]$.

Y	10^4	0	0	$\frac{1}{12}$	$\frac{1}{18}$	$\frac{1}{36}$
	10^2	$\frac{5}{12}$	$\frac{5}{18}$	$\frac{5}{36}$	0	0
		0.01	0.1	1	10	100
				X		

Solution. To find the conditional expectation, we first need to know the conditional PMF.

$$p_{X|Y}(x|10^2) = \begin{bmatrix} \frac{1}{2} & \frac{1}{3} & \frac{1}{6} & 0 & 0 \end{bmatrix},$$
$$p_{X|Y}(x|10^4) = \begin{bmatrix} 0 & 0 & \frac{1}{2} & \frac{1}{3} & \frac{1}{6} \end{bmatrix}.$$

Therefore, the conditional expectations are

$$\mathbb{E}[X \,|\, Y = 10^2] = (10^{-2})\left(\frac{1}{2}\right) + (10^{-1})\left(\frac{1}{3}\right) + (1)\left(\frac{1}{6}\right)$$
$$= \frac{123}{600},$$
$$\mathbb{E}[X \,|\, Y = 10^4] = (1)\left(\frac{1}{2}\right) + (10)\left(\frac{1}{3}\right) + (100)\left(\frac{1}{6}\right)$$
$$= \frac{123}{6}.$$

From the conditional expectations we can also find $\mathbb{E}[X]$:

$$\mathbb{E}[X] = \mathbb{E}[X \,|\, Y = 10^2]p_Y(10^2)$$
$$+ \mathbb{E}[X \,|\, Y = 10^4]p_Y(10^4)$$
$$= \left(\frac{123}{600}\right)\left(\frac{5}{6}\right) + \left(\frac{123}{6}\right)\left(\frac{1}{6}\right)$$
$$= 3.5875.$$

Example 5.22. Consider two random variables X and Y. The random variable X is Gaussian-distributed with $X \sim \text{Gaussian}(\mu, \sigma^2)$. The random variable Y has a conditional distribution $Y|X \sim \text{Gaussian}(X, X^2)$. Find $\mathbb{E}[Y]$.

Solution. The notation $Y|X \sim \text{Gaussian}(X, X^2)$ means that given the variable X, the other variable Y has a conditional distribution $\text{Gaussian}(X, X^2)$. That is, the variable Y is a Gaussian with mean X and variance X^2. How can the mean be a random variable X and the variance be another random variable X^2? Because X is the conditional variable. $Y|X$ means that you have already chosen one state of X. Given that particular state, the distribution of Y follows $f_{Y|X}$. Therefore, for this problem, we know the PDFs:

$$f_X(x) = \frac{1}{\sqrt{2\pi\sigma^2}} \exp\left\{ -\frac{(x-\mu)^2}{2\sigma^2} \right\},$$

$$f_{Y|X}(y|x) = \frac{1}{\sqrt{2\pi x^2}} \exp\left\{ -\frac{(y-x)^2}{2x^2} \right\}.$$

The conditional expectation of Y given X is

$$\mathbb{E}[Y|X=x] = \int_{-\infty}^{\infty} y \frac{1}{\sqrt{2\pi x^2}} \exp\left\{ -\frac{(y-x)^2}{2x^2} \right\} dy$$

$$= \mathbb{E}[\text{Gaussian}(x, x^2)] = x.$$

The last equality holds because we are computing the expectation of a Gaussian random variable with mean x. Finally, applying the law of total expectation, we can show that

$$\mathbb{E}[Y] = \int_{-\infty}^{\infty} \mathbb{E}[Y|X=x] f_X(x)\, dx$$

$$= \int_{-\infty}^{\infty} x \frac{1}{\sqrt{2\pi\sigma^2}} \exp\left\{ -\frac{(x-\mu)^2}{2\sigma^2} \right\} dx$$

$$= \mathbb{E}[\text{Gaussian}(\mu, \sigma^2)] = \mu,$$

where the last equality is based on the fact that it is the mean of a Gaussian.

Practice Exercise 5.10. Find $\mathbb{E}[\sin(X+Y)]$, if $X \sim \text{Gaussian}(0,1)$, and $Y\,|\,X \sim$ Uniform$[x-\pi, x+\pi]$.

Solution. We know that the conditional density is

$$f_{Y|X}(y|x) = \frac{1}{2\pi}, \qquad x-\pi \le y \le x+\pi.$$

Therefore, we can compute the probability

$$\mathbb{E}[\sin(X+Y)|X=x] = \int_{x-\pi}^{x+\pi} \sin(x+y) f_{Y|X}(y|x)\, dy$$

$$= \frac{1}{2\pi} \underbrace{\int_{x-\pi}^{x+\pi} \sin(x+y)\, dy}_{=0} = 0.$$

Hence, the overall expectation is

$$\mathbb{E}[\sin(X+Y)] = \int_0^1 \underbrace{\mathbb{E}[\sin(X+Y)|X=x]}_{=0} \frac{1}{\sqrt{2\pi}} e^{-\frac{x^2}{2}}\, dx = 0.$$

5.5 Sum of Two Random Variables

One typical problem we encounter in engineering is to determine the PDF of the sum of two random variables X and Y, i.e., $X + Y$. Such a problem arises naturally when we want to evaluate the average of many random variables, e.g., the sample mean of a collection of data points. This section will discuss a general principle for determining the PDF of a sum of two random variables.

5.5.1 Intuition through convolution

First, consider two random variables, X and Y, both discrete uniform random variables in the range of $0, 1, 2, 3$. That is, $p_X(x) = p_Y(y) = [1/4, 1/4, 1/4, 1/4]$. Since this is such a simple problem we can enumerate all the possible cases of the sum $Z = X + Y$. The resulting probabilities are shown in the following table.

$Z = X + Y$	Cases, written in terms of (X, Y)	Probability
0	(0,0)	1/16
1	(0,1), (1,0)	2/16
2	(1,1), (2,0), (0,2)	3/16
3	(3,0), (2,1), (1,2), (0,3)	4/16
4	(3,1), (2,2), (1,3)	3/16
5	(3,2), (2,3)	2/16
6	(3,3)	1/16

Clearly, the PMF of Z is not $f_Z(z) = f_X(x) + f_Y(y)$. (Caution! Do not write this.) The PMF of Z looks like a triangle distribution. How can we get to this triangle distribution from two uniform distributions? The key is the idea of convolution. Let us start with the PMF of X, which is $p_X(x)$. Let us also flip $p_Y(y)$ over the y-axis. As we shift the flipped p_Y, we multiply and add the PMF values as shown in **Figure 5.12**. This gives us

$$
\begin{aligned}
p_Z(0) &= \mathbb{P}[X + Y = 0] \\
&= \mathbb{P}[(X, Y) = (0, 0)] \\
&= p_X(0) p_Y(0) \\
&= \frac{1}{16}.
\end{aligned}
$$

Now, if we shift towards the right by 1, we have

$$
\begin{aligned}
p_Z(1) &= \mathbb{P}[X + Y = 1] \\
&= \mathbb{P}[(X, Y) = (0, 1) \cup (0, 1)] \\
&= p_X(0) p_Y(1) + p_X(1) p_Y(0) = \frac{2}{16}.
\end{aligned}
$$

By continuing our argument, you can see that we will obtain the same PMF as the one shown in the table.

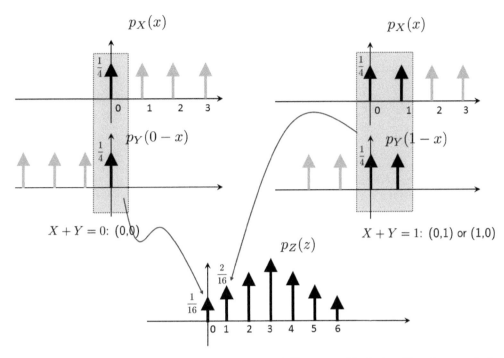

Figure 5.12: When summing two random variables X and Y, we are effectively taking the convolutions of the two respective PMF / PDFs.

5.5.2 Main result

We can show that for any arbitrary random variable X and Y, the sum $Z = X + Y$ has a distribution that is the convolution of two individual PDFs.

Theorem 5.10. *Let X and Y be two independent random variables with PDFs $f_X(x)$ and $f_Y(y)$ respectively. Let $Z = X + Y$. The PDF of Z is given by*

$$f_Z(z) = (f_X * f_Y)(z) = \int_{-\infty}^{\infty} f_X(z - y) f_Y(y)\, dy, \qquad (5.29)$$

where "$*$" denotes the convolution.

Proof. We begin by analyzing the CDF of Z. The CDF of Z is

$$F_Z(z) = \mathbb{P}[Z \le z] = \mathbb{P}[X + Y \le z].$$

We now draw a picture to illustrate the line under which we want to integrate. As shown in **Figure 5.13**, the equation $X + Y \le z$ defines a straight line in the xy plane. You can think of it as $Y \le -X + z$, so that the slope is -1 and the y-intercept is z.

Now, shall we take the upper half of the triangle or the lower half? Since the equation is $Y \le -X + z$, a value of Y has to be less than that of the line. Another easy way to check is to assume $z > 0$ so that we have a positive y-intercept. Then we check where the origin

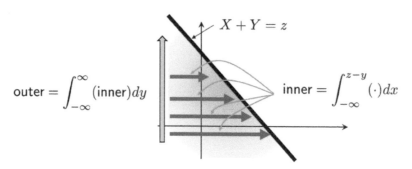

Figure 5.13: The shaded region highlights the set $X + Y \leq Z$. To integrate the PDF over this region, we first take the inner integration over dx and then take the outer integration over dy.

$(0,0)$ belongs. In this case, if $z > 0$, the origin $(0,0)$ will satisfy the equation $Y \leq -X + z$, and so it must be included. Thus, we conclude that the area is below the line.

Once we have determined the area to be integrated, we can write down the integration:

$$\mathbb{P}[X + Y \leq z] = \int_{-\infty}^{\infty} \int_{-\infty}^{z-y} f_{X,Y}(x,y) \, dx \, dy$$

$$= \int_{-\infty}^{\infty} \int_{-\infty}^{z-y} f_X(x) f_Y(y) \, dx \, dy, \quad \text{(independence)}$$

where the integration limits are just a rewrite of $X + Y \leq z$ (in this case since we are integrating x first we have $X \leq -Y + z$). Then, by the fundamental theorem of calculus, we can show that

$$f_Z(z) = \frac{d}{dz} F_Z(z) = \frac{d}{dz} \int_{-\infty}^{\infty} \int_{-\infty}^{z-y} f_X(x) f_Y(y) \, dx \, dy$$

$$= \int_{-\infty}^{\infty} \left(\frac{d}{dz} \int_{-\infty}^{z-y} f_X(x) f_Y(y) \, dx \right) dy$$

$$= \int_{-\infty}^{\infty} f_X(z-y) f_Y(y) \, dy = (f_X * f_Y)(z),$$

where "$*$" denotes the convolution.

How is convolution related to random variables?

- If you sum X and Y, the resulting PDF is the convolution of f_X and f_Y.
- E.g., convolving two uniform random variables gives you a triangle PDF.

5.5.3 Sum of common distributions

Theorem 5.11 (Sum of two Poissons). *Let $X_1 \sim Poisson(\lambda_1)$ and $X_2 \sim Poisson(\lambda_2)$. Then*

$$X_1 + X_2 \sim Poisson(\lambda_1 + \lambda_2). \tag{5.30}$$

Proof. Let us apply the convolution principle.

$$
\begin{aligned}
p_Y(k) &= \mathbb{P}[X_1 + X_2 = k] \\
&= \mathbb{P}[X_1 = \ell \cap X_2 = k - \ell] \\
&= \sum_{\ell=0}^{k} \frac{\lambda_1^\ell e^{-\lambda_1}}{\ell!} \cdot \frac{\lambda_2^{k-\ell} e^{-\lambda_2}}{(k-\ell)!} \\
&= e^{-(\lambda_1+\lambda_2)} \sum_{\ell=0}^{k} \frac{\lambda_1^\ell}{\ell!} \cdot \frac{\lambda_2^{k-\ell}}{(k-\ell)!} \\
&= e^{-(\lambda_1+\lambda_2)} \cdot \frac{1}{k!} \underbrace{\sum_{\ell=0}^{k} \frac{k!}{\ell!(k-\ell)!} \lambda_1^\ell \lambda_2^{k-\ell}}_{=\sum_{\ell=0}^{k} \binom{k}{\ell} \lambda_1^\ell \lambda_2^{k-\ell}} \\
&= \frac{(\lambda_1+\lambda_2)^k}{k!} e^{-(\lambda_1+\lambda_2)},
\end{aligned}
$$

where the last step is based on the binomial identity $\sum_{\ell=0}^{k} \binom{k}{\ell} a^\ell b^{k-\ell} = (a+b)^k$.

$\square$

> **Theorem 5.12 (Sum of two Gaussians).** Let X_1 and X_2 be two Gaussian random variables such that
>
> $$X_1 \sim Gaussian(\mu_1, \sigma_1^2) \quad and \quad X_2 \sim Gaussian(\mu_2, \sigma_2^2).$$
>
> Then
>
> $$X_1 + X_2 \sim Gaussian(\mu_1 + \mu_2, \sigma_1^2 + \sigma_2^2). \tag{5.31}$$

Proof. Let us apply the convolution principle by defining $Z = X_1 + X_2$. Then,

$$
\begin{aligned}
f_Z(z) &= \int_{-\infty}^{\infty} f_{X_1}(t) f_{X_2}(z - t)\, dt \\
&= \int_{-\infty}^{\infty} \frac{1}{\sqrt{2\pi\sigma^2}} \exp\left\{ -\frac{(t-\mu_1)^2}{2\sigma^2} \right\} \cdot \frac{1}{\sqrt{2\pi\sigma^2}} \exp\left\{ -\frac{(z-t-\mu_2)^2}{2\sigma^2} \right\} dt \\
&= \frac{1}{\sqrt{2\pi\sigma^2}} \int_{-\infty}^{\infty} \frac{1}{\sqrt{2\pi\sigma^2}} \exp\left\{ -\frac{(t-\mu_1)^2 + (z-t-\mu_2)^2}{2\sigma^2} \right\} dt.
\end{aligned}
$$

We now complete the square:

$$
\begin{aligned}
(t-\mu_1)^2 + (z-t-\mu_2)^2 &= [t^2 - 2\mu_1 t + \mu_1^2] + [t^2 + 2t(\mu_2 - z) + (\mu_2 - z)^2] \\
&= 2t^2 - 2t(\mu_1 - \mu_2 + z) + \mu_1^2 + (\mu_2 - z)^2 \\
&= 2\left[t^2 - 2t \cdot \frac{\mu_1 - \mu_2 + z}{2} \right] + \mu_1^2 + (\mu_2 - z)^2 \\
&= 2\left[t - \frac{\mu_1 - \mu_2 + z}{2} \right]^2 - 2\left[\frac{\mu_1 - \mu_2 + z}{2} \right]^2 + \mu_1^2 + (\mu_2 - z)^2.
\end{aligned}
$$

The last term can be simplified to

$$-2\left[\frac{\mu_1 - \mu_2 + z}{2}\right]^2 + \mu_1^2 + (\mu_2 - z)^2$$

$$= -\frac{\mu_1^2 - 2\mu_1(\mu_2 - z) + (\mu_2 - z)^2}{2} + \mu_1^2 + (\mu_2 - z)^2$$

$$= \frac{\mu_1^2 + 2\mu_1(\mu_2 - z) + (\mu_2 - z)^2}{2} = \frac{(\mu_1 + \mu_2 - z)^2}{2}.$$

Substituting these into the integral, we can show that

$$f_Z(z) = \frac{1}{\sqrt{2\pi\sigma^2}} \int_{-\infty}^{\infty} \frac{1}{\sqrt{2\pi\sigma^2}} \exp\left\{-\frac{2\left[t - \frac{\mu_1 - \mu_2 + z}{2}\right]^2 + \frac{(\mu_1 + \mu_2 - z)^2}{2}}{2\sigma^2}\right\} dt$$

$$= \frac{1}{\sqrt{2\pi\sigma^2}} \exp\left\{-\frac{(\mu_1 + \mu_2 - z)^2}{2(2\sigma^2)}\right\} \underbrace{\int_{-\infty}^{\infty} \frac{1}{\sqrt{2\pi\sigma^2}} \exp\left\{-\frac{\left[t - \frac{\mu_1 - \mu_2 + z}{2}\right]^2}{\sigma^2}\right\} dt}_{=\frac{1}{\sqrt{2}}}$$

$$= \frac{1}{\sqrt{2\pi(2\sigma^2)}} \exp\left\{-\frac{(\mu_1 + \mu_2 - z)^2}{2(2\sigma^2)}\right\}.$$

Therefore, we have shown that the resulting distribution is a Gaussian with mean $\mu_1 + \mu_2$ and variance $2\sigma^2$. $\qquad\square$

Practice Exercise 5.11. Let X and Y be independent, and let

$$f_X(x) = \begin{cases} xe^{-x}, & x \geq 0, \\ 0, & x < 0, \end{cases} \quad \text{and} \quad f_Y(y) = \begin{cases} ye^{-y}, & y \geq 0, \\ 0, & y < 0. \end{cases}$$

Find the PDF of $Z = X + Y$.

Solution. Using the results derived above, we see that

$$f_Z(z) = \int_{-\infty}^{\infty} f_X(z - y) f_Y(y) \, dy$$

$$= \int_{-\infty}^{z} f_X(z - y) f_Y(y) \, dy,$$

where the upper limit z came from the fact that $x \geq 0$. Therefore, since $Z = X + Y$, we must have $Z - Y = X \geq 0$ and so $Z \geq Y$. This is portrayed graphically in **Figure 5.14**. Substituting the PDFs into the integration yields

$$f_Z(z) = \int_{0}^{z} (z - y)e^{-(z-y)} ye^{-y} \, dy = \frac{z^3}{6} e^{-z}, \quad z \geq 0.$$

For $z < 0$, $f_Z(z) = 0$.

The functions of two random variables are not limited to summation. The following example illustrates the case of the product of two random variables.

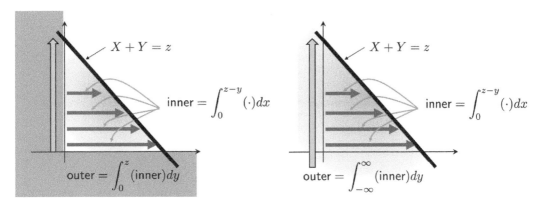

Figure 5.14: [Left] The outer integral goes from 0 to z because the triangle stops at $y = z$. [Right] If the triangle is unbounded, then the integral goes from $-\infty$ to ∞.

Example 5.23. Let X and Y be two independent random variables such that

$$f_X(x) = \begin{cases} 2x, & \text{if } 0 \leq x \leq 1, \\ 0, & \text{otherwise,} \end{cases} \quad \text{and} \quad f_Y(y) = \begin{cases} 1, & \text{if } 0 \leq y \leq 1, \\ 0, & \text{otherwise.} \end{cases}$$

Let $Z = XY$. Find $f_Z(z)$.

Solution. The CDF of Z can be evaluated as

$$F_Z(z) = \mathbb{P}[Z \leq z] = \mathbb{P}[XY \leq z] = \int_{-\infty}^{\infty} \int_{-\infty}^{\frac{z}{y}} f_X(x) f_Y(y) \, dx \, dy.$$

Taking the derivative yields

$$f_Z(z) = \frac{d}{dz} F_Z(z) = \frac{d}{dz} \int_{-\infty}^{\infty} \int_{-\infty}^{\frac{z}{y}} f_X(x) f_Y(y) \, dx \, dy$$

$$\overset{(a)}{=} \int_{-\infty}^{\infty} \frac{1}{y} f_X\left(\frac{z}{y}\right) f_Y(y) \, dy,$$

where (a) holds by the fundamental theorem of calculus. The upper and lower limit of this integration can be determined by noting that

$$0 \leq \frac{z}{y} = x \leq 1,$$

which implies that $z \leq y$. Since $y \leq 1$, we have that $z \leq y \leq 1$. Therefore, the PDF is

$$f_Z(z) = \int_z^1 \frac{1}{y} f_X\left(\frac{z}{y}\right) f_Y(y) \, dy$$

$$= \int_z^1 \frac{2z}{y^2} \, dy = 2(1 - z), \quad z \geq 0.$$

For $z < 0$, $f_Z(z) = 0$.

Closing remark. For some random variables, summing two i.i.d. copies remain the same random variable (but with different parameters). For other random variables, summing two i.i.d. copies gives a different random variable. **Table 5.1** summarizes some of the most commonly used random variable pairs.

X_1	X_2	Sum $X_1 + X_2$
Bernoulli(p)	Bernoulli(p)	Binomial$(2, p)$
Binomial(n, p)	Binomial(m, p)	Binomial$(m + n, p)$
Poisson(λ_1)	Poisson(λ_2)	Poisson$(\lambda_1 + \lambda_2)$
Exponential(λ)	Exponential(λ)	Erlang$(2, \lambda)$
Gaussian(μ_1, σ_1^2)	Gaussian(μ_2, σ_2^2)	Gaussian$(\mu_1 + \mu_2, \sigma_1^2 + \sigma_2^2)$

Table 5.1: Common distributions of the sum of two random variables.

5.6 Random Vectors and Covariance Matrices

We now enter the second part of this chapter. In the first part, we were mainly interested in a pair of random variables. In the second part, however, we will study vectors of N random variables. To understand a vector of random variables, we will not drill down to the integrations of the PDFs (which you would certainly not enjoy). Instead, we will blend linear algebra tools and probabilistic tools to learn a few practical data analysis techniques.

5.6.1 PDF of random vectors

Joint distributions can be generalized to more than two random variables. The most convenient way is to consider a vector of random variables and their corresponding states.

$$\boldsymbol{X} = \begin{bmatrix} X_1 \\ X_2 \\ \vdots \\ X_N \end{bmatrix} \quad \text{and} \quad \boldsymbol{x} = \begin{bmatrix} x_1 \\ x_2 \\ \vdots \\ x_N \end{bmatrix}.$$

Our notation here is unconventional since bold upper case letters usually represent matrices. Here, $\boldsymbol{X}$ denotes a vector, specifically a random vector. Its state is a vector $\boldsymbol{x}$. In this chapter, we will use the following notational convention: $\boldsymbol{X}$ and $\boldsymbol{Y}$ represent random vectors while $\boldsymbol{A}$ represents a matrix.

One way to think about $\boldsymbol{X}$ is to imagine that if you put your hand into the sample space, you will pick up a vector $\boldsymbol{x}$. This random realization $\boldsymbol{x}$ has N entries, and so you need to specify the probability of getting all these entries *simultaneously*. Accordingly, we should expect that $\boldsymbol{X}$ is characterized by an N-dimensional PDF

$$f_{\boldsymbol{X}}(\boldsymbol{x}) = f_{X_1, X_2, \ldots, X_N}(x_1, x_2, \ldots, x_N).$$

Essentially, this PDF tells us the probability density for random variable $X_1 = x_1$, random variable $X_2 = x_2$, etc. It is a coordinate-wise description. For example, if $\boldsymbol{X}$ contains three elements such that $\boldsymbol{X} = [X_1, X_2, X_3]^T$, and if the state we are looking at is $\boldsymbol{x} = [3, 1, 7]^T$, then $f_{\boldsymbol{X}}(\boldsymbol{x})$ is the probability density such that this 3D coordinate (X_1, X_2, X_3) takes the value $[3, 1, 7]^T$.

To compute the probability, we can integrate $f_{\boldsymbol{X}}(\boldsymbol{x})$ with respect to $\boldsymbol{x}$. Let $\mathcal{A}$ be the event. Then

$$\mathbb{P}[\boldsymbol{X} \in \mathcal{A}] = \int_{\mathcal{A}} f_{\boldsymbol{X}}(\boldsymbol{x}) \, d\boldsymbol{x}$$
$$= \int \cdots \int_{\mathcal{A}} f_{X_1,\ldots,X_N}(x_1,\ldots,x_N) \, dx_1 \ldots dx_N.$$

If the random coordinates $X_1, \ldots, X_N$ are **independent**, the PDF can be written as a product of N individual PDFs:

$$f_{X_1,\ldots,X_N}(x_1,\ldots,x_N) = f_{X_1}(x_1)f_{X_2}(x_2)\cdots f_{X_N}(x_N), \text{ and so}$$
$$\mathbb{P}[\boldsymbol{X} \in \mathcal{A}] = \int \cdots \int_{\mathcal{A}} f_{X_1}(x_1)f_{X_2}(x_2)\cdots f_{X_N}(x_N) \, dx_1 \cdots dx_N.$$

However, this does not necessarily simplify the calculation unless $\mathcal{A}$ is separable, e.g., $\mathcal{A} = [a_1, b_1] \times [a_2, b_2] \times \cdots \times [a_N, b_N]$. In this case the integration becomes

$$\mathbb{P}[\boldsymbol{X} \in \mathcal{A}] = \prod_{i=1}^{N}\left[\int_{a_i}^{b_i} f_{X_i}(x_i) \, dx_i\right],$$

which is obviously manageable.

Example 5.24. Let $\boldsymbol{X} = [X_1,\ldots,X_N]^T$ be a vector of zero-mean unit variance Gaussian random vectors. Let $\mathcal{A} = [-1, 2]^N$. Then

$$\mathbb{P}[\boldsymbol{X} \in \mathcal{A}] = \int_{\mathcal{A}} f_{\boldsymbol{X}}(\boldsymbol{x})d\boldsymbol{x}$$
$$= \int \cdots \int_{\mathcal{A}} f_{X_1,\cdots,X_N}(x_1,\ldots,x_N) \, dx_1 \cdots dx_N$$
$$= \left[\int_{-1}^{2} f_{X_1}(x_1) \, dx_1\right]^N = [\Phi(2) - \Phi(-1)]^N,$$

where $\Phi(\cdot)$ is the standard Gaussian CDF.

As you can see from the definition of a vector random variable, computing the probability typically involves integrating a high-dimensional function, which is tedious. However, the good news is that in practice we seldom need to perform such calculations. Often we are more interested in the mean and the covariance of the random vectors because they usually carry geometric meanings. The next subsection explores this topic.

5.6.2   Expectation of random vectors

Let $\boldsymbol{X} = [X_1, \dots, X_N]^T$ be a random vector. We define the **expectation of a random vector** as follows.

Definition 5.19. *Let* $\boldsymbol{X} = [X_1, \dots, X_N]^T$ *be a random vector. The expectation is*

$$\boldsymbol{\mu} \overset{\text{def}}{=} \mathbb{E}[\boldsymbol{X}] = \begin{bmatrix} \mathbb{E}[X_1] \\ \mathbb{E}[X_2] \\ \vdots \\ \mathbb{E}[X_N] \end{bmatrix}. \tag{5.32}$$

The resulting vector is called the **mean vector**. Since the mean vector is a vector of individual elements, we need to compute the marginal PDFs before computing the expectations:

$$\mathbb{E}[\boldsymbol{X}] = \begin{bmatrix} \mathbb{E}[X_1] \\ \vdots \\ \mathbb{E}[X_N] \end{bmatrix} = \begin{bmatrix} \int_\Omega x_1 f_{X_1}(x_1)\, dx_1 \\ \vdots \\ \int_\Omega x_N f_{X_N}(x_N)\, dx_N \end{bmatrix},$$

where the marginal PDF is determined by

$$f_{X_n}(x_n) = \int_\Omega f_{\boldsymbol{X}_{\backslash n}}(\boldsymbol{x}_{\backslash n}) d\boldsymbol{x}_{\backslash n}.$$

In the equation above, $\boldsymbol{x}_{\backslash n} = [x_1, \dots, x_{n-1}, x_{n+1}, \dots, x_N]^T$ contains all the elements without x_n. For example, if the PDF is $f_{X_1, X_2, X_3}(x_1, x_2, x_3)$, then

$$\mathbb{E}[X_1] = \int x_1 \underbrace{\int f_{X_1, X_2, X_3}(x_1, x_2, x_3)\, dx_2\, dx_3}_{f_{X_1}(x_1)}\, dx_1.$$

Again, this will become tedious when there are many variables.

While the definition of the expectation may be challenging to understand, some problems using it are straightforward. We will first demonstrate the case of independent Poisson random variables, and then we will discuss joint Gaussians.

Example 5.25. Let $\boldsymbol{X} = [X_1, \dots, X_N]^T$ be a random vector such that X_n are independent Poissons with $X_n \sim \text{Poisson}(\lambda_n)$. Then

$$\mathbb{E}[\boldsymbol{X}] = \begin{bmatrix} \mathbb{E}[X_1] \\ \vdots \\ \mathbb{E}[X_N] \end{bmatrix} = \begin{bmatrix} \sum_{k=0}^\infty k \cdot \frac{\lambda_1^k e^{-\lambda_1}}{k!} \\ \vdots \\ \sum_{k=0}^\infty k \cdot \frac{\lambda_N^k e^{-\lambda_N}}{k!} \end{bmatrix} = \begin{bmatrix} \lambda_1 \\ \vdots \\ \lambda_N \end{bmatrix}.$$

On computers, computing the mean vector can be done using built-in commands such as `mean` in MATLAB and `np.mean` in Python. However, caution is needed when performing the calculation. In MATLAB, `mean` computes along first dimension (rows index). Thus, if we have an $N \times 2$ array, applying `mean` will give us a 1×2 vector. To obtain the column mean vector of size $N \times 1$, we need to specify the direction as `mean(X,2)`. Similarly, in Python, when calling `np.mean`, we need to specify the axis.

```
% MATLAB code to compute a mean vector
X    = randn(100,2);
mX   = mean(X,2);
```

```
# Python code to compute a mean vector
import numpy as np
import scipy.stats as stats
X = stats.multivariate_normal.rvs([0,0],[[1,0],[0,1]],100)
mX = np.mean(X,axis=1)
```

5.6.3 Covariance matrix

Definition 5.20. *The **covariance matrix** of a random vector* $\boldsymbol{X} = [X_1, \ldots, X_N]^T$ *is*

$$
\boldsymbol{\Sigma} \stackrel{\text{def}}{=} \mathrm{Cov}(\boldsymbol{X}) = \begin{bmatrix} \mathrm{Var}[X_1] & \mathrm{Cov}(X_1, X_2) & \cdots & \mathrm{Cov}(X_1, X_N) \\ \mathrm{Cov}[X_2, X_1] & \mathrm{Var}[X_2] & \cdots & \mathrm{Cov}(X_2, X_N) \\ \vdots & \vdots & \ddots & \vdots \\ \mathrm{Cov}(X_N, X_1) & \mathrm{Cov}(X_N, X_2) & \cdots & \mathrm{Var}[X_N] \end{bmatrix}. \tag{5.33}
$$

A more compact way of writing the covariance matrix is

$$
\boldsymbol{\Sigma} = \mathrm{Cov}(\boldsymbol{X}) = \mathbb{E}[(\boldsymbol{X} - \boldsymbol{\mu})(\boldsymbol{X} - \boldsymbol{\mu})^T],
$$

where $\boldsymbol{\mu} = \mathbb{E}[\boldsymbol{X}]$ is the mean vector. The notation $\boldsymbol{ab}^T$ means the **outer product**, defined as

$$
\boldsymbol{ab}^T = \begin{bmatrix} a_1 \\ \vdots \\ a_N \end{bmatrix} \begin{bmatrix} b_1 & \cdots & b_N \end{bmatrix} = \begin{bmatrix} a_1 b_1 & a_1 b_2 & \cdots & a_1 b_N \\ \vdots & \vdots & \ddots & \vdots \\ a_N b_1 & a_N b_2 & \cdots & a_N b_N \end{bmatrix}.
$$

It is easy to show that $\mathrm{Cov}(\boldsymbol{X}) = \mathrm{Cov}(\boldsymbol{X})^T$, i.e., they are symmetric.

Theorem 5.13. *If the coordinates* $X_1, \ldots, X_N$ *are independent, then the covariance matrix* $\mathrm{Cov}(\boldsymbol{X}) = \boldsymbol{\Sigma}$ *is a diagonal matrix:*

$$
\boldsymbol{\Sigma} = \mathrm{Cov}(\boldsymbol{X}) = \begin{bmatrix} \mathrm{Var}[X_1] & 0 & \cdots & 0 \\ 0 & \mathrm{Var}[X_2] & \cdots & 0 \\ \vdots & \vdots & \ddots & \vdots \\ 0 & 0 & \cdots & \mathrm{Var}[X_N] \end{bmatrix}.
$$

Proof. If all X_i's are independent, then $\mathrm{Cov}(X_i, X_j) = 0$ for all $i \neq j$. Substituting this into the definition of the covariance matrix, we obtain the result.

$\square$

If we ignore the mean vector $\boldsymbol{\mu}$, we obtain the **autocorrelation matrix $\boldsymbol{R}$**.

Definition 5.21. *Let $\boldsymbol{X} = [X_1, \ldots, X_N]^T$ be a random vector. The autocorrelation matrix is*

$$\boldsymbol{R} = \mathbb{E}[\boldsymbol{X}\boldsymbol{X}^T] = \begin{bmatrix} \mathbb{E}[X_1 X_1] & \mathbb{E}[X_1 X_2] & \cdots & \mathbb{E}[X_1 X_N] \\ \mathbb{E}[X_2 X_1] & \mathbb{E}[X_2 X_2] & \cdots & \mathbb{E}[X_2 X_N] \\ \vdots & \vdots & \ddots & \vdots \\ \mathbb{E}[X_N X_1] & \mathbb{E}[X_N X_2] & \cdots & \mathbb{E}[X_N X_N] \end{bmatrix}. \tag{5.34}$$

We state without proof that

$$\boldsymbol{\Sigma} = \boldsymbol{R} - \boldsymbol{\mu}\boldsymbol{\mu}^T,$$

which corresponds to the single-variable case where $\sigma^2 = \mathbb{E}[X^2] - \mu^2$.

On computers, computing the covariance matrix is done using built-in commands `cov` in MATLAB and `np.cov` in Python. Like the mean vectors, when computing the covariance, we need to specify the direction. For example, for an $N \times 2$ data matrix $\boldsymbol{X}$, the covariance needs to be a 2×2 matrix. If we compute the covariance along the wrong direction, we will obtain an $N \times N$ matrix, which is incorrect.

```
% MATLAB code to compute covariance matrix
X    = randn(100,2);
covX = cov(X);
```

```
# Python code to compute covariance matrix
import numpy as np
import scipy.stats as stats
X = stats.multivariate_normal.rvs([0,0],[[1,0],[0,1]],100)
covX = np.cov(X,rowvar=False)
print(covX)
```

5.6.4 Multidimensional Gaussian

With the above tools in hand, we can now define a high-dimensional Gaussian. The PDF of a high-dimensional Gaussian is defined as follows.

Definition 5.22. *A d-dimensional* **joint Gaussian** *has the PDF*

$$f_{\boldsymbol{X}}(\boldsymbol{x}) = \frac{1}{\sqrt{(2\pi)^d |\boldsymbol{\Sigma}|}} \exp\left\{ -\frac{1}{2}(\boldsymbol{x} - \boldsymbol{\mu})^T \boldsymbol{\Sigma}^{-1}(\boldsymbol{x} - \boldsymbol{\mu}) \right\}, \tag{5.35}$$

where d denotes the dimensionality of the vector $\boldsymbol{x}$.

The mean vector and the covariance matrix of a joint Gaussian is readily available from the definition.

$$\mathbb{E}[\boldsymbol{X}] = \boldsymbol{\mu} \qquad \text{and} \qquad \text{Cov}(\boldsymbol{X}) = \boldsymbol{\Sigma}.$$

It is easy to show that if $\boldsymbol{X}$ is a scalar X, then $d = 1$, $\boldsymbol{\mu} = \mu$, and $\boldsymbol{\Sigma} = \sigma^2$. Substituting these into the above definition returns us the familiar 1D Gaussian.

The d-dimensional Gaussian is a generalization of the 1D Gaussian(s). Suppose that X_i and X_j are **independent** for all $i \neq j$. Then $\mathbb{E}[X_i X_j] = \mathbb{E}[X_i]\mathbb{E}[X_j]$ and hence $\text{Cov}(X_i, X_j) = 0$. Consequently, the covariance matrix $\boldsymbol{\Sigma}$ is a diagonal matrix:

$$\boldsymbol{\Sigma} = \begin{bmatrix} \sigma_1^2 & \cdots & 0 \\ \vdots & \ddots & \vdots \\ 0 & \cdots & \sigma_d^2 \end{bmatrix},$$

where $\sigma_i^2 = \text{Var}[X_i]$. When this occurs, the exponential term in the Gaussian PDF is

$$(\boldsymbol{x} - \boldsymbol{\mu})^T \boldsymbol{\Sigma}^{-1}(\boldsymbol{x} - \boldsymbol{\mu}) = \begin{bmatrix} x_1 - \mu_1 \\ \vdots \\ x_d - \mu_d \end{bmatrix}^T \begin{bmatrix} \sigma_1^2 & \cdots & 0 \\ \vdots & \ddots & \vdots \\ 0 & \cdots & \sigma_d^2 \end{bmatrix}^{-1} \begin{bmatrix} x_1 - \mu_1 \\ \vdots \\ x_d - \mu_d \end{bmatrix} = \sum_{i=1}^{d} \frac{(x_i - \mu_i)^2}{\sigma_i^2}.$$

Moreover, the determinant $|\boldsymbol{\Sigma}|$ is

$$|\boldsymbol{\Sigma}| = \left| \begin{bmatrix} \sigma_1^2 & \cdots & 0 \\ \vdots & \ddots & \vdots \\ 0 & \cdots & \sigma_d^2 \end{bmatrix} \right| = \prod_{i=1}^{d} \sigma_i^2.$$

Substituting these results into the joint Gaussian PDF, we obtain

$$f_{\boldsymbol{X}}(\boldsymbol{x}) = \prod_{i=1}^{n} \frac{1}{\sqrt{(2\pi)\sigma_i^2}} \exp\left\{ -\frac{(x - \mu_i)^2}{2\sigma_i^2} \right\},$$

which is a product of individual Gaussians.

The Gaussian has different offsets and orientations for different choices of $\boldsymbol{\mu}$ and $\boldsymbol{\Sigma}$. **Figure 5.15** shows a few examples. Note that for $\boldsymbol{\Sigma}$ to be valid $\boldsymbol{\Sigma}$ has to be "symmetric positive semi-definite", the meaning of which will be explained shortly.

Generating random numbers from a multidimensional Gaussian can be done by calling built-in commands. In MATLAB, we use mvnrnd. In Python, we have a similar command.

```
% MATLAB code to generate random numbers from multivariate Gaussian
mu    = [0 0];
Sigma = [.25 .3; .3 1];
X     = mvnrnd(mu,Sigma,100);
```

```
# Python code to generate random numbers from multivariate Gaussian
import numpy as np
import scipy.stats as stats
X = stats.multivariate_normal.rvs([0,0],[[0.25,0.3],[0.3,1.0]],100)
```

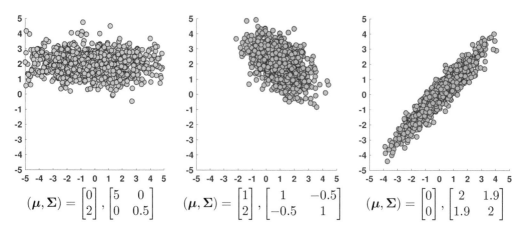

Figure 5.15: Visualization of 2D Gaussians with different means and covariances.

To display the data points and overlay with the contour, we can use MATLAB commands such as `contour`. The resulting plot looks like the one shown in **Figure 5.16**. In Python the corresponding command is `plt.contour`. To set up the plotting environment we use the commands `np.meshgrid`. The grid points are used to evaluate the PDF values, thus giving us the contour.

```matlab
% MATLAB code: Overlay random numbers with the Gaussian contour.
X   = mvnrnd([0 0],[.25 .3; .3 1],1000);
x1 = -2.5:.01:2.5;
x2 = -3.5:.01:3.5;
[X1,X2] = meshgrid(x1,x2);
F = mvnpdf([X1(:) X2(:)],[0 0],[.25 .3; .3 1]);
F = reshape(F,length(x2),length(x1));
figure(1);
scatter(x(:,1),x(:,2),'rx', 'LineWidth', 1.5); hold on;
contour(x1,x2,F,[.001 .01 .05:.1:.95 .99 .999], 'LineWidth', 2);
```

```python
# Python code: Overlay random numbers with the Gaussian contour.
import numpy as np
import scipy.stats as stats
import matplotlib.pyplot as plt
X = stats.multivariate_normal.rvs([0,0],[[0.25,0.3],[0.3,1.0]],1000)
x1 = np.arange(-2.5, 2.5, 0.01)
x2 = np.arange(-3.5, 3.5, 0.01)
X1, X2 = np.meshgrid(x1,x2)
Xpos = np.empty(X1.shape + (2,))
Xpos[:,:,0] = X1
Xpos[:,:,1] = X2
F = stats.multivariate_normal.pdf(Xpos,[0,0],[[0.25,0.3],[0.3,1.0]])
plt.scatter(X[:,0],X[:,1])
plt.contour(x1,x2,F)
```

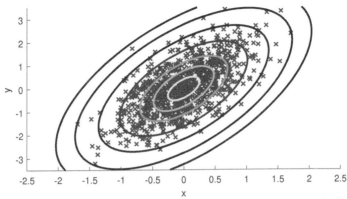

Figure 5.16: 1000 random numbers drawn from a 2D Gaussian, overlaid with the contour plot.

5.7 Transformation of Multidimensional Gaussians

As we have seen in **Figure 5.15**, the shape and orientation of a multidimensional Gaussian are determined by the mean vector $\boldsymbol{\mu}$ and the covariance matrix $\boldsymbol{\Sigma}$. This means that if we can somehow transform the mean vector and the covariance matrix, we will get another Gaussian. A few practical questions are:

- How do we shift and rotate a Gaussian random variable?
- If we have an arbitrary Gaussian, how do we go back to zero-mean unit-variance Gaussian?
- How do we generate random vectors according to a predefined Gaussian?

These questions come up frequently in data analysis. Answering the first two questions will help us transform Gaussians back and forth, while answering the last question will help us with generating random samples.

5.7.1 Linear transformation of mean and covariance

Suppose we have an arbitrary (not necessarily a Gaussian) random vector $\boldsymbol{X} = [X_1, \ldots, X_N]^T$ with mean $\boldsymbol{\mu}_X$ and covariance $\boldsymbol{\Sigma}_X$. Entries of $\boldsymbol{X}$ are not necessarily independent. Let $\boldsymbol{A} \in \mathbb{R}^{N \times N}$ be a transformation, and let $\boldsymbol{Y} = \boldsymbol{AX}$. That is,

$$
\boldsymbol{Y} =
\begin{bmatrix} Y_1 \\ Y_2 \\ \vdots \\ Y_N \end{bmatrix}
=
\begin{bmatrix}
a_{11} & a_{12} & \cdots & a_{1N} \\
a_{21} & a_{22} & \cdots & a_{2N} \\
\vdots & \vdots & \ddots & \vdots \\
a_{N1} & a_{N2} & \cdots & a_{NN}
\end{bmatrix}
\begin{bmatrix} X_1 \\ X_2 \\ \vdots \\ X_N \end{bmatrix}
= \boldsymbol{AX}.
$$

Then we can show the following result.

Theorem 5.14. *The mean vector and covariance matrix of* $\boldsymbol{Y} = \boldsymbol{AX}$ *are*

$$\boldsymbol{\mu}_Y = \boldsymbol{A\mu}_X, \qquad \boldsymbol{\Sigma}_Y = \boldsymbol{A\Sigma}_X \boldsymbol{A}^T. \tag{5.36}$$

Proof. We first show the mean. Consider the nth element of $\boldsymbol{Y}$:

$$\mathbb{E}[Y_n] = \mathbb{E}\left[\sum_{k=1}^N a_{nk} X_k\right] = \sum_{k=1}^N a_{nk} \mathbb{E}[X_k].$$

Therefore,

$$\boldsymbol{\mu}_Y = \begin{bmatrix} \mathbb{E}[Y_1] \\ \mathbb{E}[Y_2] \\ \vdots \\ \mathbb{E}[Y_N] \end{bmatrix} = \begin{bmatrix} \sum_{k=1}^N a_{1k}\mathbb{E}[X_k] \\ \sum_{k=1}^N a_{2k}\mathbb{E}[X_k] \\ \vdots \\ \sum_{k=1}^N a_{Nk}\mathbb{E}[X_k] \end{bmatrix}$$

$$= \begin{bmatrix} a_{11} & a_{12} & \cdots & a_{1N} \\ a_{21} & a_{22} & \cdots & a_{2N} \\ \vdots & \vdots & \ddots & \vdots \\ a_{N1} & a_{N2} & \cdots & a_{NN} \end{bmatrix} \begin{bmatrix} \mathbb{E}[X_1] \\ \mathbb{E}[X_2] \\ \vdots \\ \mathbb{E}[X_N] \end{bmatrix} = \boldsymbol{A\mu}_X.$$

The covariance matrix follows from the fact that

$$\begin{aligned} \boldsymbol{\Sigma}_Y &= \mathbb{E}[(\boldsymbol{Y} - \boldsymbol{\mu}_Y)(\boldsymbol{Y} - \boldsymbol{\mu}_Y)^T] \\ &= \mathbb{E}[(\boldsymbol{AX} - \boldsymbol{A\mu}_X)(\boldsymbol{AX} - \boldsymbol{A\mu}_X)^T] \\ &= \mathbb{E}[\boldsymbol{A}(\boldsymbol{X} - \boldsymbol{\mu}_X)(\boldsymbol{X} - \boldsymbol{\mu}_X)^T \boldsymbol{A}^T] \\ &= \boldsymbol{A}\mathbb{E}[(\boldsymbol{X} - \boldsymbol{\mu}_X)(\boldsymbol{X} - \boldsymbol{\mu}_X)^T]\boldsymbol{A}^T \\ &= \boldsymbol{A\Sigma}_X \boldsymbol{A}^T. \end{aligned}$$

$\square$

What if we shift the random vector by defining $\boldsymbol{Y} = \boldsymbol{X} + \boldsymbol{b}$? We state the following result without proof (try proving it as an exercise).

Theorem 5.15. *The mean vector and covariance matrix of* $\boldsymbol{Y} = \boldsymbol{X} + \boldsymbol{b}$ *are*

$$\boldsymbol{\mu}_Y = \boldsymbol{\mu}_X + \boldsymbol{b}, \qquad \boldsymbol{\Sigma}_Y = \boldsymbol{\Sigma}_X. \tag{5.37}$$

For a Gaussian random vector, the linear transformations either shifts the Gaussian or rotates the Gaussian, as shown in **Figure 5.17**:

- If we add $\boldsymbol{b}$ to $\boldsymbol{X}$, the resulting operation is a translation.
- If we multiply $\boldsymbol{A}$ by $\boldsymbol{X}$, then the resulting operation is a rotation and scaling.

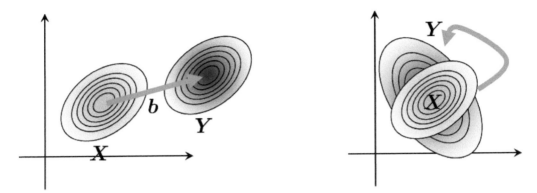

Figure 5.17: Transforming a Gaussian. [Left] Translation by a vector b. [Right] Rotation and scaling by a matrix X.

How to rotate, scale, and translate a Gaussian random variable
- We rotate and scale a Gaussian by $Y = AX$.
- We translate a Gaussian by $Y = X + b$.

5.7.2 Eigenvalues and eigenvectors

As our next step, we need to understand **eigendecomposition**. You can easily find relevant background in any undergraduate linear algebra textbook. Here we provide a summary for completeness.

When applying a matrix A to a vector x, a typical engineering question is: what x would be invariant to A? Or in other words, for what x can we make sure that $Ax = \lambda x$, for some scalar λ? If we can find such a vector x, we say that x is the **eigenvector** of A. Eigenvectors are useful for seeking principal components of datasets or finding efficient signal representations. They are defined as follows:

Definition 5.23. *Given a square matrix $A \in \mathbb{R}^{N \times N}$, the vector $u \in \mathbb{R}^N$ (with $u \neq 0$) is called the **eigenvector** of A if*

$$Au = \lambda u, \qquad (5.38)$$

*for some $\lambda \in \mathbb{R}$. The scalar λ is called the **eigenvalue** associated with u.*

An $N \times N$ matrix has N eigenvectors and N eigenvalues. Therefore, the above equation can be generalized to

$$Au_i = \lambda_i u_i,$$

for $i = 1, \dots, N$, or more compactly as $AU = \Lambda U$. The eigenvalues $\lambda_1, \dots, \lambda_N$ are not necessarily distinct. There are matrices with identical eigenvalues, the identity matrix being a trivial example. On the other hand, not all square matrices have eigenvectors. For example, the matrix $\begin{bmatrix} 0 & 1 \\ 0 & 0 \end{bmatrix}$ does not have an eigenvalue. Matrices that have eigenvalues must be **diagonalizable**.

There are a number of equivalent conditions for λ to be an eigenvalue:

- There exists $\boldsymbol{u} \neq 0$ such that $\boldsymbol{A}\boldsymbol{u} = \lambda\boldsymbol{u}$;
- There exists $\boldsymbol{u} \neq 0$ such that $(\boldsymbol{A} - \lambda\boldsymbol{I})\boldsymbol{u} = \boldsymbol{0}$;
- $(\boldsymbol{A} - \lambda\boldsymbol{I})$ is not invertible;
- $\det(\boldsymbol{A} - \lambda\boldsymbol{I}) = 0$.

We are mostly interested in symmetric matrices. If $\boldsymbol{A}$ is symmetric, then all the eigenvalues are real, and the following result holds.

Theorem 5.16. *If $\boldsymbol{A}$ is symmetric, all the eigenvalues are real, and there exists $\boldsymbol{U}$ such that $\boldsymbol{U}^T\boldsymbol{U} = \boldsymbol{I}$ and $\boldsymbol{A} = \boldsymbol{U}\boldsymbol{\Lambda}\boldsymbol{U}^T$. Then*

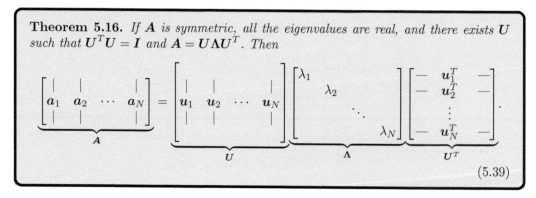

$$(5.39)$$

We call such a decomposition the **eigendecomposition**. In MATLAB, we can compute the eigenvalues of a matrix by using the `eig` command. In Python, the corresponding command is `np.linalg.eig`. Note that in our demonstration below we symmetrize the matrix. This step is needed, for otherwise the eigenvalues will contain complex numbers.

```
% MATLAB Code to perform eigendecomposition
A = randn(100,100);
A = (A + A')/2;        % symmetrize because A is not symmetric
[U,S] = eig(A);        % eigendecomposition
s = diag(S);           % extract eigenvalue
```

```
# Python Code to perform eigendecomposition
import numpy as np
A = np.random.randn(100,100)
A = (A + np.transpose(A))/2
S, U = np.linalg.eig(A)
s = np.diag(S)
```

The condition that $\boldsymbol{U}^T\boldsymbol{U} = \boldsymbol{I}$ is the result of an **orthonormal** matrix. Equivalently, $\boldsymbol{u}_i^T\boldsymbol{u}_j = 1$ if $i = j$ and $\boldsymbol{u}_i^T\boldsymbol{u}_j = 0$ if $i \neq j$. Since $\{\boldsymbol{u}_i\}_{i=1}^N$ is orthonormal, it can serve as a basis of any vector in $\mathbb{R}^n$:

$$\boldsymbol{x} = \sum_{j=1}^N \alpha_j \boldsymbol{u}_j,$$

where $\alpha_j = \boldsymbol{u}_j^T\boldsymbol{x}$ is called the **basis coefficient**. Basis vectors are useful in that they can provide alternative **representations** of a vector.

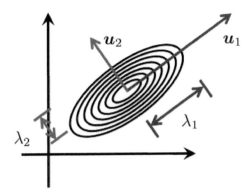

Figure 5.18: The center and the radius of the ellipse is determined by μ and Σ.

The geometry of the joint Gaussian is determined by its eigenvalues and eigenvectors. Consider the eigendecomposition of Σ:

$$\Sigma = U \Lambda U^T$$

$$= \begin{bmatrix} | & | & & | \\ u_1 & u_2 & \cdots & u_d \\ | & | & & | \end{bmatrix} \begin{bmatrix} \lambda_1 & 0 & \cdots & 0 \\ 0 & \lambda_2 & \cdots & 0 \\ \vdots & \vdots & \ddots & \vdots \\ 0 & \cdots & \cdots & \lambda_d \end{bmatrix} \begin{bmatrix} - & u_1^T & - \\ - & u_2^T & - \\ & \vdots & \\ - & u_d^T & - \end{bmatrix},$$

for some unitary matrix U and diagonal matrix Λ. The columns of U are called the eigenvectors, and the entries of Λ are called the eigenvalues. Since Σ is symmetric, all λ_i's are real. In addition, since Σ is positive semi-definite, all λ_i's are non-negative. Accordingly, the volume defined by the multidimensional Gaussian is always a convex object, e.g., an ellipse in 2D or an ellipsoid in 3D.

The orientation of the axes is defined by the column vectors u_i. In the case of $d = 2$, the major axis is defined by u_1 and the minor axis is defined by u_2. The corresponding radii of each axis are specified by the eigenvalues λ_1 and λ_2. **Figure 5.18** provides an illustration.

5.7.3 Covariance matrices are always positive semi-definite

> The following subsection about positive semi-definite matrices can be skipped if it is your first time reading the book.

Now that we understand eigendecomposition, what can we do with it? Here is one practical problem. Given a matrix Σ, how do you know that it is a valid covariance matrix? For example, if we give you a singular matrix, then Σ^{-1} may not exist. Checking the validity of Σ requires the concept of **positive semi-definite**.

Given a square matrix $A \in \mathbb{R}^{N \times N}$, it is important to check the positive semi-definiteness of A. There are two practical scenarios where we need positive semi-definiteness. (1) If we are estimating the covariance matrix Σ from a dataset, we need to ensure that $\Sigma = \mathbb{E}[(X - \mu)(X - \mu)^T]$ is positive semi-definite because all covariance matrices are positive semi-definite. Otherwise, the matrix we estimate is not a legitimate covariance matrix. (2) If we solve an optimization problem involving a function $f(x) = x^T A x$, then having A being positive semi-definite, we can guarantee that the problem is convex. Convex problems ensure that a local minimum is also global, and convex problems can be solved efficiently using known algorithms.

> **Definition 5.24 (Positive Semi-Definite).** *A matrix $A \in \mathbb{R}^{N \times N}$ is positive semi-definite if*
>
> $$x^T A x \geq 0 \tag{5.40}$$
>
> *for any $x \in \mathbb{R}^N$. A is **positive definite** if $x^T A x > 0$ for any $x \in \mathbb{R}^N$.*

Using eigendecomposition, it is not difficult to show that positive semi-definiteness is equivalent to having non-negative eigenvalues.

> **Theorem 5.17.** *A matrix $A \in \mathbb{R}^{N \times N}$ is **positive semi-definite** if and only if*
>
> $$\lambda_i(A) \geq 0 \tag{5.41}$$
>
> *for all $i = 1, \ldots, N$, where $\lambda_i(A)$ denotes the ith eigenvalue of A.*

Proof. By the definitions of eigenvalue and eigenvector, we have that

$$A u_i = \lambda_i u_i,$$

where λ_i is the eigenvalue and u_i is the corresponding eigenvector. If A is positive semi-definite, then $u_i^T A u_i \geq 0$ since u_i is a particular vector in $\mathbb{R}^n$. So we have

$$0 \leq u_i^T A u_i = \lambda \|u_i\|^2,$$

and hence $\lambda_i \geq 0$. Conversely, if $\lambda_i \geq 0$ for all i, then since $A = \sum_{i=1}^{N} \lambda_i u_i u_i^T$ we can conclude that

$$x^T A x = x^T \left(\sum_{i=1}^{N} \lambda_i u_i u_i^T \right) x = \sum_{i=1}^{N} \lambda_i (u_i^T x)^2 \geq 0.$$

$\square$

The following corollary shows that if $A \in \mathbb{R}^{n \times n}$ is positive definite, it must be invertible. Being invertible also means that the columns of A are linearly independent.

> **Corollary 5.2.** *If a matrix $A \in \mathbb{R}^{N \times N}$ is **positive definite** (but not semi-definite), then A must be invertible, i.e., there exists $A^{-1} \in \mathbb{R}^{N \times N}$ such that*
>
> $$A^{-1} A = A A^{-1} = I. \tag{5.42}$$

The next theorem tells us that the covariance matrix is always positive semi-definite.

> **Theorem 5.18.** *The covariance matrix* $\mathrm{Cov}(\boldsymbol{X}) = \boldsymbol{\Sigma}$ *is* **symmetric positive semi-definite**, *i.e.,*
> $$\boldsymbol{\Sigma}^T = \boldsymbol{\Sigma}, \quad \text{and} \quad \boldsymbol{v}^T \boldsymbol{\Sigma} \boldsymbol{v} \geq 0, \quad \forall \boldsymbol{v} \in \mathbb{R}^d.$$

Proof. Symmetry follows immediately from the definition, because $\mathrm{Cov}(X_i, X_j) = \mathrm{Cov}(X_j, X_i)$. The positive semi-definiteness comes from the fact that

$$
\begin{aligned}
\boldsymbol{v}^T \boldsymbol{\Sigma} \boldsymbol{v} &= \boldsymbol{v}^T \mathbb{E}[(\boldsymbol{X} - \boldsymbol{\mu})(\boldsymbol{X} - \boldsymbol{\mu})^T] \boldsymbol{v} \\
&= \mathbb{E}[\boldsymbol{v}^T (\boldsymbol{X} - \boldsymbol{\mu})(\boldsymbol{X} - \boldsymbol{\mu})^T \boldsymbol{v}] \\
&= \mathbb{E}[\boldsymbol{b}^T \boldsymbol{b}] = \mathbb{E}[\|\boldsymbol{b}\|^2] \geq 0,
\end{aligned}
$$

where $\boldsymbol{b} = (\boldsymbol{X} - \boldsymbol{\mu})^T \boldsymbol{v}$. $\qquad\square$

> End of the discussion.

5.7.4 Gaussian whitening

Besides checking positive semi-definiteness, another typical problem we encounter is how to generate random samples according to some Gaussian distributions.

From Gaussian$(\boldsymbol{0}, \boldsymbol{I})$ to Gaussian$(\boldsymbol{\mu}, \boldsymbol{\Sigma})$. If we are given zero-mean unit-variance Gaussian $\boldsymbol{X} \sim \mathrm{Gaussian}(\boldsymbol{0}, \boldsymbol{I})$, how do we generate $\boldsymbol{Y} \sim \mathrm{Gaussian}(\boldsymbol{\mu}, \boldsymbol{\Sigma})$ from $\boldsymbol{X}$?

The idea is to define a transformation

$$\boldsymbol{Y} = \boldsymbol{\Sigma}^{\frac{1}{2}} \boldsymbol{X} + \boldsymbol{\mu},$$

where $\boldsymbol{\Sigma}^{\frac{1}{2}} = \boldsymbol{U} \boldsymbol{\Lambda}^{\frac{1}{2}} \boldsymbol{U}^T$. Then the mean of $\boldsymbol{Y}$ is

$$
\begin{aligned}
\mathbb{E}[\boldsymbol{Y}] &= \mathbb{E}[\boldsymbol{\Sigma}^{\frac{1}{2}} \boldsymbol{X} + \boldsymbol{\mu}] \\
&= \boldsymbol{\Sigma}^{\frac{1}{2}} \mathbb{E}[\boldsymbol{X}] + \boldsymbol{\mu} = \boldsymbol{\Sigma}^{\frac{1}{2}} \boldsymbol{0} + \boldsymbol{\mu} = \boldsymbol{\mu},
\end{aligned}
$$

and the covariance matrix is

$$
\begin{aligned}
\mathbb{E}[(\boldsymbol{Y} - \boldsymbol{\mu})(\boldsymbol{Y} - \boldsymbol{\mu})^T] &= \mathbb{E}[(\boldsymbol{\Sigma}^{\frac{1}{2}} \boldsymbol{X} + \boldsymbol{\mu} - \boldsymbol{\mu})(\boldsymbol{\Sigma}^{\frac{1}{2}} \boldsymbol{X} + \boldsymbol{\mu} - \boldsymbol{\mu})^T] \\
&= \mathbb{E}[(\boldsymbol{\Sigma}^{\frac{1}{2}} \boldsymbol{X})(\boldsymbol{\Sigma}^{\frac{1}{2}} \boldsymbol{X})^T] = \boldsymbol{\Sigma}^{\frac{1}{2}} \mathbb{E}[\boldsymbol{X} \boldsymbol{X}^T] \boldsymbol{\Sigma}^{\frac{1}{2}} \\
&= \boldsymbol{\Sigma}^{\frac{1}{2}} \boldsymbol{I} \boldsymbol{\Sigma}^{\frac{1}{2}} = \boldsymbol{\Sigma}.
\end{aligned}
$$

> **Theorem 5.19.** *Let $\boldsymbol{X}$ be $\boldsymbol{X} \sim \mathrm{Gaussian}(\boldsymbol{0}, \boldsymbol{I})$. Consider a mean vector $\boldsymbol{\mu}$ and a covariance matrix $\boldsymbol{\Sigma}$ with eigendecomposition $\boldsymbol{\Sigma} = \boldsymbol{U} \boldsymbol{\Lambda} \boldsymbol{U}^T$. If*
> $$\boldsymbol{Y} = \boldsymbol{\Sigma}^{\frac{1}{2}} \boldsymbol{X} + \boldsymbol{\mu}, \tag{5.43}$$
> *where $\boldsymbol{\Sigma}^{\frac{1}{2}} = \boldsymbol{U} \boldsymbol{\Lambda}^{\frac{1}{2}} \boldsymbol{U}^T$, then $\boldsymbol{Y} \sim \mathrm{Gaussian}(\boldsymbol{\mu}, \boldsymbol{\Sigma})$.*

CHAPTER 5. JOINT DISTRIBUTIONS

Therefore, the two steps for doing this Gaussian whitening are:

- Step 1: Generate samples $\{x_1, \ldots, x_N\}$ that are distributed according to Gaussian$(0, I)$.
- Step 2: Define y_n where

$$y_n = \Sigma^{\frac{1}{2}} x_n + \mu.$$

These two steps are portrayed in **Figure 5.19**.

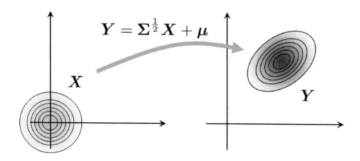

Figure 5.19: Generating an arbitrary Gaussian from Gaussian$(0, I)$.

Example 5.26. Consider a set of $N = 1000$ i.i.d. Gaussian$(0, I)$ data points as shown in **Figure 5.20**, for example,

$$x_1 = \begin{bmatrix} 0.5377 \\ 1.8399 \end{bmatrix}, \qquad x_2 = \begin{bmatrix} -2.2588 \\ 0.8622 \end{bmatrix}, \qquad \ldots, \qquad x_{1000} = \begin{bmatrix} 0.3188 \\ -1.3077 \end{bmatrix}.$$

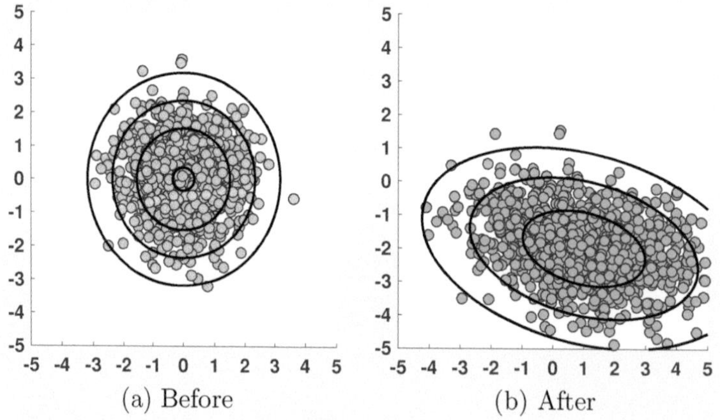

(a) Before

(b) After

Figure 5.20: Generating arbitrary Gaussian random variables from Gaussian$(0, I)$.

Transform these data points so that the new distribution is a Gaussian with

$$\mu = \begin{bmatrix} 1 \\ -2 \end{bmatrix} \quad \text{and} \quad \Sigma = \begin{bmatrix} 3 & -0.5 \\ -0.5 & 1 \end{bmatrix}.$$

Solution. To perform the transformation, we first perform eigendecomposition of $\Sigma = U\Lambda U^T$. Then $\Sigma^{\frac{1}{2}} = U\Lambda^{\frac{1}{2}}U^T$. For our problem, we compute

$$\Sigma^{\frac{1}{2}} = \begin{bmatrix} 1.722 & -0.1848 \\ -0.1848 & 0.9828 \end{bmatrix}.$$

Multiplying this matrix to yield $y_n = \Sigma^{\frac{1}{2}}x_n + \mu$, we obtain

$$y_1 = \begin{bmatrix} 1.5870 \\ -0.2971 \end{bmatrix}, \quad y_2 = \begin{bmatrix} -3.0495 \\ -0.7351 \end{bmatrix}, \quad \dots, \quad y_{1000} = \begin{bmatrix} 1.7907 \\ -3.3441 \end{bmatrix}.$$

In MATLAB, the above whitening procedure can be realized using the following commands.

```
% MATLAB code to perform the whitening
x     = mvnrnd([0,0],[1 0; 0 1],1000);
Sigma = [3 -0.5; -0.5 1];
mu    = [1; -2];
y     = Sigma^(0.5)*x' + mu;
```

The Python implementation is similar, although one needs to be careful with the more complicated syntax. For example, `Sigma^(0.5)` in MATLAB does the eigen-based matrix power automatically, whereas in Python we need to call a specific built-in command `fractional_matrix_power`. In MATLAB, broadcasting a vector to a matrix can be recognized. In Python, we need to call `repmat` explicitly to control the shape of the mean vectors.

```
# Python code to perform the whitening
import numpy as np
import scipy.stats as stats
from scipy.linalg import fractional_matrix_power

x      = np.random.multivariate_normal([0,0],[[1,0],[0,1]],1000)
mu     = np.array([1,-2])
Sigma  = np.array([[3, -0.5],[-0.5, 1]])
Sigma2 = fractional_matrix_power(Sigma,0.5)
y      = np.dot(Sigma2, x.T) + np.matlib.repmat(mu,1000,1).T
```

From Gaussian(μ, Σ) to Gaussian$(0, I)$. The reverse direction can be done as follows. Supposing that we have $Y \sim$ Gaussian(μ, Σ), we define

$$X = \Sigma^{-\frac{1}{2}}(Y - \mu). \tag{5.44}$$

Then

$$\mathbb{E}[X] = \mathbb{E}[\Sigma^{-\frac{1}{2}}(Y - \mu)]$$
$$= \Sigma^{-\frac{1}{2}}(\mathbb{E}[Y] - \mu) = 0.$$

CHAPTER 5. JOINT DISTRIBUTIONS

The covariance is

$$
\begin{aligned}
\mathrm{Cov}(\boldsymbol{X}) &= \mathbb{E}[(\boldsymbol{X}-\boldsymbol{\mu}_X)(\boldsymbol{X}-\boldsymbol{\mu}_X)^T] \\
&= \mathbb{E}[\boldsymbol{X}\boldsymbol{X}^T] \\
&= \mathbb{E}\left[\boldsymbol{\Sigma}^{-\frac{1}{2}}(\boldsymbol{Y}-\boldsymbol{\mu})(\boldsymbol{Y}-\boldsymbol{\mu})^T\boldsymbol{\Sigma}^{-\frac{T}{2}}\right] \\
&= \boldsymbol{\Sigma}^{-\frac{1}{2}}\mathbb{E}\left[(\boldsymbol{Y}-\boldsymbol{\mu})(\boldsymbol{Y}-\boldsymbol{\mu})^T\right]\boldsymbol{\Sigma}^{-\frac{T}{2}} \\
&= \boldsymbol{\Sigma}^{-\frac{1}{2}}\boldsymbol{\Sigma}\boldsymbol{\Sigma}^{-\frac{1}{2}} = \boldsymbol{I}.
\end{aligned}
$$

The following theorem summarizes this result.

Theorem 5.20. *Let* $\boldsymbol{Y}$ *be a Gaussian* $\boldsymbol{Y} \sim Gaussian(\boldsymbol{\mu},\boldsymbol{\Sigma})$*. If*

$$\boldsymbol{X} = \boldsymbol{\Sigma}^{-\frac{1}{2}}(\boldsymbol{Y}-\boldsymbol{\mu}), \tag{5.45}$$

then $\boldsymbol{X} \sim Gaussian(\boldsymbol{0},\boldsymbol{I})$*.*

Thus the two steps of doing this reversed Gaussian whitening are:

- Step 1: Assuming that $\boldsymbol{y}_1,\ldots,\boldsymbol{y}_N$ are distributed as Gaussian$(\boldsymbol{\mu},\boldsymbol{\Sigma})$, estimate $\boldsymbol{\mu}$ and $\boldsymbol{\Sigma}$.
- Step 2: Define $\boldsymbol{x}_n$ where

$$\boldsymbol{x}_n = \boldsymbol{\Sigma}^{\frac{1}{2}}(\boldsymbol{y}_n-\boldsymbol{\mu}). \tag{5.46}$$

These two steps are shown pictorially in **Figure 5.21**.

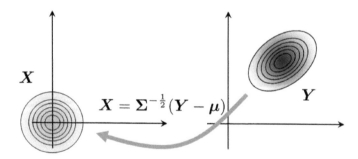

Figure 5.21: Converting an arbitrary Gaussian back to Gaussian$(\boldsymbol{0},\boldsymbol{I})$.

In practice, if we are given $\{\boldsymbol{y}_n\}_{n=1}^N$, we need to estimate $\boldsymbol{\mu}$ and $\boldsymbol{\Sigma}$. The estimations are quite straightforward.

$$\widehat{\boldsymbol{\mu}} = \frac{1}{N}\sum_{n=1}^N \boldsymbol{y}_n,$$

$$\widehat{\boldsymbol{\Sigma}} = \frac{1}{N}\sum_{n=1}^N (\boldsymbol{y}_n-\widehat{\boldsymbol{\mu}})(\boldsymbol{y}_n-\widehat{\boldsymbol{\mu}})^T.$$

On computers, these can be obtained using the command **mean** and cov. Once we have calculated $\widehat{\boldsymbol{\mu}}$ and $\widehat{\boldsymbol{\Sigma}}$, we can define $\boldsymbol{x}_n$ as

$$\boldsymbol{x}_n = \widehat{\boldsymbol{\Sigma}}^{-\frac{1}{2}}\left(\boldsymbol{y}_n - \widehat{\boldsymbol{\mu}}\right).$$

On computers, the codes for the whitening procedure that uses the estimated mean and covariance are shown below.

```
% MATLAB code to perform whitening
y     = mvnrnd([1; -2],[3 -0.5; -0.5 1],100);
mY    = mean(y);
covY = cov(y);
x     = covY^(-0.5)*(y-mY)';
```

```
# Python code to perform whitening
import numpy as np
import scipy.stats as stats
from scipy.linalg import fractional_matrix_power
y   = np.random.multivariate_normal([1,-2],[[3,-0.5],[-0.5,1]],100)
mY = np.mean(y,axis=0)
covY  = np.cov(y,rowvar=False)
covY2 = fractional_matrix_power(covY,-0.5)
x     = np.dot(covY2, (y-np.matlib.repmat(mY,100,1)).T)
```

5.8 Principal-Component Analysis

We have studied the covariance matrix $\boldsymbol{\Sigma}$ in some depth. It has many other uses besides transforming Gaussian random variables, and in this section we present one of them, called the **principal-component analysis** (PCA). PCA is a widely used tool for **dimension reduction**. Instead of using N features to describe a data point, PCA allows us to use the leading p principal components to describe the same data point. In many problems in machine learning, this makes the learning task easier and the inference task more efficient.

5.8.1 The main idea: Eigendecomposition

PCA can be summarized in one sentence:

> The key idea of PCA is the eigendecomposition of the covariance matrix $\boldsymbol{\Sigma}$.

This is a condensed summary of PCA: It is just the eigendecomposition of the covariance. However, before we discuss the computational procedure, we will explain why we would want to perform the eigendecomposition of the covariance matrix.

Consider a set of data points $\{x^{(1)}, \ldots, x^{(N)}\}$, where each $x^{(n)} \in \mathbb{R}^d$ is a d-dimensional vector. The dimension d is often high. For example, if we have an image of size $1024 \times 1024 \times 3$, then $d = 3{,}145{,}728$ — not a huge number, but enough to make you feel dizzy. The goal of PCA is to find a **low-dimensional representation** in $\mathbb{R}^p$ where $p \ll d$. If we can find this low-dimensional representation, we can represent the d-dimensional input using only p coefficients. Since $p \ll d$, we can "compress" the data by using a compact representation. In modern data science, such a dimension reduction scheme is useful for handling large-scale datasets.

Mathematically, we define a set of **basis vector** $v_1, \ldots, v_p$, where each $v_i \in \mathbb{R}^d$. Our goal is to approximate an input data point $x^{(n)} \in \mathbb{R}^d$ by these basis vectors:

$$x^{(n)} \approx \sum_{i=1}^{p} \alpha_i v_i,$$

where $\{\alpha_i\}_{i=1}^{p}$ are called the **representation coefficients**. The representation described by this equation is a **linear** representation. Linear representation is extremely common in practice. For example, a data point $x^{(n)} = [7, 1, 4]^T$ can be represented as

$$\underbrace{\begin{bmatrix} 7 \\ 1 \\ 4 \end{bmatrix}}_{x^{(n)}} = \underbrace{3}_{\alpha_1} \underbrace{\begin{bmatrix} 1 \\ -1 \\ 0 \end{bmatrix}}_{v_1} + \underbrace{4}_{\alpha_2} \underbrace{\begin{bmatrix} 1 \\ 1 \\ 1 \end{bmatrix}}_{v_2}.$$

Therefore, the 3-dimensional input $x^{(n)}$ can now be represented by two coefficients $\alpha_1 = 3$ and $\alpha_2 = 4$. This is called **dimensionality reduction**.

Pictorially, if we have already determined the basis vectors, we can compute the coefficients for every data point in the dataset. However, not all basis vectors are good. As illustrated in **Figure 5.22**, an elongated dataset will be of the greatest benefit if the basis vectors are oriented according to the data geometry. If we can find such basis vectors, then the data points will have a large coefficient and a small coefficient, corresponding to the major and the minor axes. Dimensionality reduction can thus be achieved by, for example, only keeping the larger coefficients.

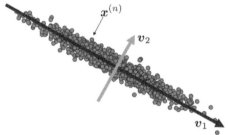

Figure 5.22: PCA aims at finding a low-dimensional representation of a high-dimensional dataset. In this figure, the 2D data points can be well represented by the 1D space spanned by v_1.

The challenge here is that, given the dataset $\{x^{(1)}, \ldots, x^{(N)}\}$, we need to determine both the basis vectors $\{v_i\}_{i=1}^{p}$ and the coefficients $\{\alpha_i\}_{i=1}^{p}$. Fortunately, this can be formulated as an eigendecomposition problem.

To see how this problem can be thus formulated, we consider the simplest case as illustrated in **Figure 5.22**, where we want to find *the* leading principal component. That is, we find $(\alpha, \boldsymbol{v})$ such that $\boldsymbol{x} \approx \alpha \boldsymbol{v}$. This amounts to solving the optimization problem

$$(\widehat{\boldsymbol{v}}, \widehat{\alpha}) = \underset{\|\boldsymbol{v}\|_2 = 1, \alpha}{\operatorname{argmin}} \left\| \begin{bmatrix} | \\ \boldsymbol{x} \\ | \end{bmatrix} - \alpha \begin{bmatrix} | \\ \boldsymbol{v} \\ | \end{bmatrix} \right\|^2.$$

The notation "argmin" means the argument that minimizes the function. The equation says that we find the $(\alpha, \boldsymbol{v})$ that minimizes the distance between $\boldsymbol{x}$ and $\alpha \boldsymbol{v}$. The constraint $\|\boldsymbol{v}\|_2 = 1$ limits the search to within a unit circle; otherwise our solution will not be unique.

Solving the optimization problem is not difficult. If we take the derivative w.r.t. α and set it to zero, we have that

$$2\boldsymbol{v}^T(\boldsymbol{x} - \alpha\boldsymbol{v}) = 0 \qquad \Rightarrow \qquad \alpha = \boldsymbol{v}^T\boldsymbol{x}.$$

Substituting $\alpha = \boldsymbol{x}^T\boldsymbol{v}$ into the objective function again, we show that

$$\underset{\|\boldsymbol{v}\|_2=1}{\operatorname{argmin}} \ \|\boldsymbol{x} - \alpha\boldsymbol{v}\|^2 = \underset{\|\boldsymbol{v}\|_2=1}{\operatorname{argmin}} \ \left\{ \boldsymbol{x}^T\boldsymbol{x} - 2\alpha\boldsymbol{x}^T\boldsymbol{v} + \alpha^2\cancel{\boldsymbol{v}^T\boldsymbol{v}} \right\}, \qquad \|\boldsymbol{v}\|_2 = 1$$

$$= \underset{\|\boldsymbol{v}\|_2=1}{\operatorname{argmin}} \ \left\{ -2\alpha\boldsymbol{x}^T\boldsymbol{v} + \alpha^2 \right\}, \qquad \text{drop } \boldsymbol{x}^T\boldsymbol{x}$$

$$= \underset{\|\boldsymbol{v}\|_2=1}{\operatorname{argmin}} \ \left\{ -2(\boldsymbol{x}^T\boldsymbol{v})\boldsymbol{x}^T\boldsymbol{v} + (\boldsymbol{x}^T\boldsymbol{v})^2 \right\}, \qquad \text{substitute } \alpha = \boldsymbol{x}^T\boldsymbol{v}$$

$$= \underset{\|\boldsymbol{v}\|_2=1}{\operatorname{argmax}} \ \left\{ \boldsymbol{v}^T\boldsymbol{x}\boldsymbol{x}^T\boldsymbol{v} \right\}, \qquad \text{change min to max.}$$

Let us pause for a second. We have shown that if we have *one* data point $\boldsymbol{x}$, the leading principal component $\boldsymbol{v}$ can be determined by maximizing $\boldsymbol{v}^T\boldsymbol{x}\boldsymbol{x}^T\boldsymbol{v}$. What have we gained? We have transformed the original optimization, which contains two variables $(\boldsymbol{v}, \alpha)$, to a new optimization that contains one variable $\boldsymbol{v}$. Thus if we know how to solve the one-variable problem we are done.

However, there is one more issue we need to address before we discuss how to solve for the problem. The issue is that the formulation is about *one data sample*, not the entire dataset. To include all the samples, we need to assume that $\boldsymbol{x}$ is a realization of a random vector $\boldsymbol{X}$. Then the above optimization can be formulated in the expectation sense as

$$\underset{\|\boldsymbol{v}\|_2=1}{\operatorname{argmin}} \ \mathbb{E}\|\boldsymbol{X} - \alpha\boldsymbol{v}\|^2 = \underset{\|\boldsymbol{v}\|_2=1}{\operatorname{argmax}} \ \boldsymbol{v}^T\mathbb{E}\left\{ \boldsymbol{X}\boldsymbol{X}^T \right\}\boldsymbol{v}$$

$$= \underset{\|\boldsymbol{v}\|_2=1}{\operatorname{argmax}} \ \boldsymbol{v}^T\boldsymbol{\Sigma}\boldsymbol{v},$$

where $\boldsymbol{\Sigma} \overset{\text{def}}{=} \mathbb{E}[\boldsymbol{X}^T\boldsymbol{X}]$.[1] Therefore, if we can maximize $\boldsymbol{v}^T\boldsymbol{\Sigma}\boldsymbol{v}$ we will be able to determine the principal component.

Now comes the main result. The following theorem shows that the maximization is equivalent to eigendecomposition. The proof requires Lagrange multipliers, which are beyond the scope of this book.

---

[1] Here we assume that $\boldsymbol{X}$ is zero-mean, i.e., $\mathbb{E}[\boldsymbol{X}] = 0$. If it is not, then we can subtract the mean by considering $\underset{\|\boldsymbol{v}\|_2=1}{\operatorname{argmax}} \ \boldsymbol{v}^T\mathbb{E}\left\{ (\boldsymbol{X} - \boldsymbol{\mu})(\boldsymbol{X} - \boldsymbol{\mu})^T \right\}\boldsymbol{v}$.

Theorem 5.21. *Let* $\mathbf{\Sigma}$ *be a* $d \times d$ *matrix with eigendecomposition* $\mathbf{\Sigma} = \mathbf{U}\mathbf{S}\mathbf{U}^T$. *Then the optimization*

$$\widehat{\mathbf{v}} = \underset{\|\mathbf{v}\|_2=1}{\text{argmax}} \ \mathbf{v}^T \mathbf{\Sigma} \mathbf{v} \tag{5.47}$$

has a solution $\widehat{\mathbf{v}} = \mathbf{u}_1$, *i.e., the first column of the eigenvector matrix* $\mathbf{U}$.

The following proof requires an understanding of Lagrange multipliers and constrained optimizations. It is not essential for understanding this chapter.

We want to prove that the solution to the problem

$$\widehat{\mathbf{v}} = \underset{\|\mathbf{v}\|_2=1}{\text{argmax}} \ \mathbf{v}^T \mathbf{\Sigma} \mathbf{v}$$

is the eigenvector of the matrix $\mathbf{\Sigma}$. To show that, we first write down the Lagrangian:

$$L(\mathbf{v}, \lambda) = \mathbf{v}^T \mathbf{\Sigma} \mathbf{v} - \lambda(\|\mathbf{v}\|^2 - 1)$$

Taking the derivative w.r.t. $\mathbf{v}$ and setting to zero yields

$$\nabla_{\mathbf{v}} L(\mathbf{v}, \lambda) = 2\mathbf{\Sigma}\mathbf{v} - 2\lambda\mathbf{v} = \mathbf{0}.$$

This is equivalent to $\mathbf{\Sigma}\mathbf{v} = \lambda\mathbf{v}$. So if $\mathbf{\Sigma} = \mathbf{U}\mathbf{S}\mathbf{U}^T$, then by letting $\mathbf{v} = \mathbf{u}_i$ and $\lambda = s_i$ we can satisfy the condition since $\mathbf{\Sigma}\mathbf{u}_i = \mathbf{U}\mathbf{S}\mathbf{U}^T\mathbf{u}_i = \mathbf{U}\mathbf{S}\mathbf{e}_i = s_i\mathbf{u}_i$.

End of the proof.

This theorem can be extended to the second (and other) principal components of the covariance matrix. In fact, given the covariance matrix $\mathbf{\Sigma}$ we can follow the procedure outlined in **Figure 5.23** to determine the principal components. The eigendecomposition of a $d \times d$ matrix $\mathbf{\Sigma}$ will give us a $d \times d$ eigenvector matrix $\mathbf{U}$ and an eigenvalue matrix $\mathbf{S}$. To keep the p leading eigenvectors, we truncate the $\mathbf{U}$ matrix to only use the first p eigenvectors. Here, we assume that the eigenvectors are ordered according to the magnitude of the eigenvalues, from large to small.

In practice, if we are given a dataset $\{\mathbf{x}^{(1)}, \dots, \mathbf{x}^{(N)}\}$, we can first estimate the covariance matrix $\mathbf{\Sigma}$ by

$$\widehat{\mathbf{\Sigma}} = \frac{1}{N} \sum_{n=1}^{N} (\mathbf{x}^{(n)} - \widehat{\boldsymbol{\mu}})(\mathbf{x}^{(n)} - \widehat{\boldsymbol{\mu}})^T,$$

where $\widehat{\boldsymbol{\mu}} = \frac{1}{N} \sum_{n=1}^{N} \mathbf{x}^{(n)}$ is the mean vector. Afterwards, we can compute the eigendecomposition of $\widehat{\mathbf{\Sigma}}$ by

$$[\mathbf{U}, \mathbf{S}] = \text{eig}(\widehat{\mathbf{\Sigma}}).$$

On a computer, the principal components are obtained through eigendecomposition. A MATLAB example and a Python example are shown below. We explicitly show the two principal components in this example. The magnitudes of these two vectors are determined by the eigenvalues `diag(s)`.

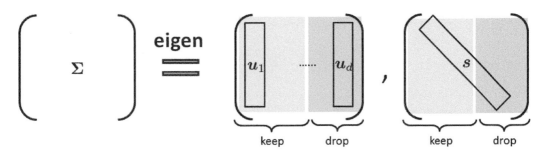

keep   drop   keep   drop

Figure 5.23: The principal components are the eigenvectors of the covariance matrix. In this figure Σ denotes the covariance matrix, $u_1, \ldots, u_p$ denote the p leading eigenvectors, and s denotes the diagonal of the eigenvalue matrix.

```matlab
% MATLAB code to perform the principal-component analysis
x = mvnrnd([0,0],[2 -1.9; -1.9 2],1000);
covX = cov(x);
[U,S] = eig(covX);
u(:,1) % Principle components
u(:,2) % Principle components
```

```python
# Python code to perform the principal-component analysis
import numpy as np
x  = np.random.multivariate_normal([1,-2],[[3,-0.5],[-0.5,1]],1000)
covX = np.cov(x,rowvar=False)
S, U = np.linalg.eig(covX)
print(U)
```

Example 5.27. Suppose we have a dataset containing $N = 1000$ samples, drawn from an unknown distribution. The first few samples are

$$x_1 = \begin{bmatrix} 0.5254 \\ -0.6930 \end{bmatrix}, \quad x_2 = \begin{bmatrix} -0.4040 \\ 0.3724 \end{bmatrix}, \quad \ldots, \quad x_{1000} = \begin{bmatrix} 1.4165 \\ -1.5463 \end{bmatrix}.$$

We can compute the mean and covariance using MATLAB commands **mean** and **cov**. This will return us

$$\widehat{\mu} = \begin{bmatrix} 0.0561 \\ -0.0303 \end{bmatrix} \quad \text{and} \quad \widehat{\Sigma} = \begin{bmatrix} 2.0460 & -1.9394 \\ -1.9394 & 2.0426 \end{bmatrix}.$$

Applying eigendecomposition on $\widehat{\Sigma}$, we show that

$$[U, S] = \text{eig}(\widehat{\Sigma}),$$

$$\implies U = \begin{bmatrix} -0.7068 & -0.7074 \\ -0.7074 & 0.7068 \end{bmatrix} \quad \text{and} \quad S = \begin{bmatrix} 0.1049 & 0 \\ 0 & 3.9837 \end{bmatrix}.$$

Therefore, we have obtained two principal components

$$u_1 = \begin{bmatrix} -0.7068 \\ -0.7074 \end{bmatrix} \quad \text{and} \quad u_2 = \begin{bmatrix} -0.7074 \\ 0.7068 \end{bmatrix}.$$

As seen in the figure below, these two principal components make sense. The vector u_1 is the orange line and is the minor axis. The vector u_2 is the blue line and is the major axis. Again, the ordering of the vectors is determined by the eigenvalues. Since u_2 has a larger eigenvalue ($=3.9837$), it is the leading principal component.

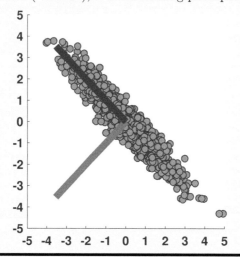

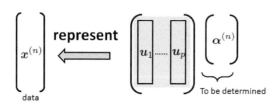

Figure 5.24: To determine the representation coefficients, we solve an inverse problem by finding the vector α in the equation $x^{(n)} = U_p \alpha^{(n)}$.

Why do we call our method principal component *analysis*? The analysis part comes from the fact that we can compress a data vector $x^{(n)}$ from a high dimension d to a low dimension p. Defining $U_p = [u_1, \ldots, u_p]$, a matrix containing the p leading eigenvectors of the matrix U, we solve the inverse problem:

$$x^{(n)} = U_p \alpha^{(n)},$$

where the goal is to determine the coefficient vector $\alpha^{(n)} \in \mathbb{R}^p$. Since U_p is an orthonormal matrix (i.e., $U_p^T U_p = I$), it follows that

$$U_p^T x^{(n)} = \underbrace{U_p^T U_p}_{=I} \alpha^{(n)},$$

as illustrated in **Figure 5.24**. Hence,

$$\boldsymbol{\alpha}^{(n)} = \boldsymbol{U}_p^T \boldsymbol{x}^{(n)}.$$

This equation is a **projection** operation that projects a data point $\boldsymbol{x}^{(n)}$ onto the space spanned by the p leading principal components. Repeating the procedure for all the data points $\boldsymbol{x}^{(1)}, \ldots, \boldsymbol{x}^{(N)}$ in the dataset, we have compressed the dataset.

Example 5.28. Using the example above, we can show that

$$\boldsymbol{\alpha}^{(1)} = \boldsymbol{U}^T \boldsymbol{x}^{(1)} = \begin{bmatrix} 0.1189 \\ -0.8615 \end{bmatrix}, \quad \boldsymbol{\alpha}^{(2)} = \begin{bmatrix} 0.0221 \\ 0.5491 \end{bmatrix}, \quad \ldots, \quad \boldsymbol{\alpha}^{(1000)} = \begin{bmatrix} 0.0927 \\ -2.0950 \end{bmatrix}.$$

The principal-component analysis says that since the leading components represent the data, we only need to keep the blue-colored values because they are the coefficients associated with the leading principal component.

5.8.2 The eigenface problem

As a concrete example of PCA, we consider a computer vision problem called the **eigenface** problem. In 2001, researchers at Yale University published the Yale Database, and a few years later they extended it to a larger one (`http://vision.ucsd.edu/~leekc/ExtYaleDatabase/ExtYaleB.html`). The dataset, now known as the Yale Face Dataset, contains 16,128 images of 28 human subjects under nine poses and 64 illumination conditions. The sizes of the images are $d = 168 \times 192 = 32,256$ pixels. Treating these $N = 16,128$ images as vectors in $\mathbb{R}^{32,256 \times 1}$, we have 16,128 of these vectors. Let us call them $\{\boldsymbol{x}^{(1)}, \ldots, \boldsymbol{x}^{(N)}\}$.

Following the procedure we described above, we estimate the covariance matrix by computing

$$\widehat{\boldsymbol{\Sigma}} = \mathbb{E}[(\boldsymbol{X} - \widehat{\boldsymbol{\mu}})(\boldsymbol{X} - \widehat{\boldsymbol{\mu}})^T] \approx \frac{1}{N} \sum_{n=1}^{N} (\boldsymbol{x}^{(n)} - \widehat{\boldsymbol{\mu}})(\boldsymbol{x}^{(n)} - \widehat{\boldsymbol{\mu}})^T, \tag{5.48}$$

where $\widehat{\boldsymbol{\mu}} = \mathbb{E}[\boldsymbol{X}] \approx \frac{1}{N} \sum_{n=1}^{N} \boldsymbol{x}^{(n)}$ is the mean vector. Note that the size of $\widehat{\boldsymbol{\mu}}$ is $32,256 \times 1$ and the size of $\widehat{\boldsymbol{\Sigma}}$ is $32,256 \times 32,256$.

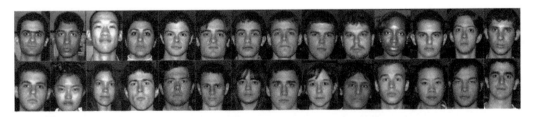

Figure 5.25: The extended Yale Face Database B.

Once we obtain an estimate of the covariance matrix, we can perform an eigendecomposition to get

$$[\boldsymbol{U}, \boldsymbol{S}] = \text{eig}(\widehat{\boldsymbol{\Sigma}}).$$

The columns of $\boldsymbol{U}$, i.e., $\{\boldsymbol{u}_i\}_{i=1}^{d}$, are the eigenvectors of $\widehat{\boldsymbol{\Sigma}}$. These eigenvectors are the **basis** of a testing face image.

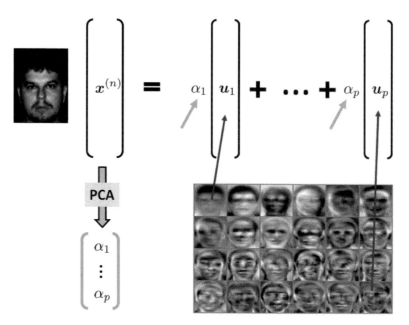

Figure 5.26: Given a face image, the learned basis vectors (from the eigendecomposition of the covariance matrix) can be used to compress the image x into a feature vector α where the dimension of α is significantly lower than that of x.

With the basis vectors $u_1, \ldots, u_p$ we can project every image in the dataset using a low-dimensional representation. Specifically, for an image x we compute the coefficients

$$\alpha_i = u_i^T x, \qquad i = 1, \ldots, p$$

or more compactly $\alpha = U^T x$. Note that the dimension of x is $d \times 1$ (which in our case is $d = 32{,}526$), and the dimensions of α can be as few as $p = 100$. Therefore, we are using a 100-dimensional vector to represent a 32,526-dimensional data. This is a huge dimensionality reduction.

The process repeats for all the samples $x^{(1)}, \ldots, x^{(N)}$. This gives us a collection of representation coefficients $\alpha^{(1)}, \ldots, \alpha^{(N)}$, where each $\alpha^{(n)}$ is 100-dimensional (see **Figure 5.26**). Notice that the basis vectors u_i appear more or less "face images," but they are the features of the faces. PCA says that a real face can be written as a linear combination of these basis vectors.

How to solve the eigenface problem

- Compute the covariance matrix of all the images.
- Apply eigendecomposition to the covariance matrix.
- Project onto the basis vectors and find the coefficients.
- The coefficients are the low-dimensional representation of the images.
- We use the coefficients to perform downstream tasks, such as classification.

5.8.3   What cannot be analyzed by PCA?

PCA is a dimension reduction tool. It compresses a raw data vector $x \in \mathbb{R}^d$ into a smaller feature vector $\alpha \in \mathbb{R}^p$. The advantage is that the downstream learning problems are much easier because $p \ll d$. For example, classification using α is more efficient than classification using x since there is very little information loss from x to α.

There are three limitations of PCA:

- **PCS fails when the raw data are not orthogonal.** The basis vectors u_i returned by PCA are **orthogonal**, meaning that $u_i^T u_j = 0$ as long as $i \neq j$. As a result, if the data intrinsically have this orthogonality property, then PCA will work very well. However, if the data live in a space such as a donut shape as illustrated in **Figure 5.27**, then PCA will fail. Here, by failure, we mean that p is not much smaller than d. To handle datasets behaving like **Figure 5.27** we need advanced tools. One of these is the kernel-PCA. The idea is to apply a nonlinear transformation to the data before you run PCA.

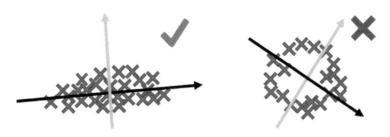

Figure 5.27: [Left] PCA works when the data has redundant dimensions or is living on orthogonal spaces. [Right] PCA fails when the data does not have easily decomposable spaces.

- **Basis vectors returned by PCA are not interpretable.** A temptation with PCA is to think that the basis vectors u_i offer meaningful information because they are the "principal components". However, since PCA is the eigendecomposition of the covariance matrix, which is purely a mathematical operation, there is no guarantee that the basis vectors contain any semantic meaning. If we look at the basis vectors shown in **Figure 5.26**, there is almost no information one can draw. Therefore, in the data-science literature alternative methods such as non-negative matrix factorization and the more recent deep neural network embedding are more attractive because the feature vectors sometimes (not always) have meanings.

- **PCA does not return you the most influential "component".** Imagine that you are analyzing medical data for research on a disease, in which each data vector $x^{(n)}$ contains height, weight, BMI, blood pressure, etc. When you run PCA on the dataset, you will obtain some "principal components". However, these principal components will likely have everything, e.g., the height entry of the principal component will have some values, the weight will have some values, etc. If you have found a principal component, it does not mean that you have identified the leading risk factor of the disease. If you want to identify the leading risk factor of the disease, e.g., whether the height or weight is more important, you need to resort to advanced tools such as variable selection or the LASSO type of regression analysis (see Chapter 7).

Closing remark. PCAs are powerful computational tools based on the simplest concept of covariance matrices because, as our derivation showed, covariance matrices encode the "variation" of the data. Therefore, by finding a vector that aligns with the maximum variation of the data, we can find the principal component.

5.9 Summary

As you were reading this chapter, you may have felt that the first and second parts discuss distinctly different subjects, and in fact many books treat them as separate topics. We take a different approach. We think that they are essentially the same thing if you understand the following chain of distributions:

$$\underbrace{f_X(x)}_{\text{one variable}} \implies \underbrace{f_{X_1, X_2}(x_1, x_2)}_{\text{two variables}} \implies \cdots \implies \underbrace{f_{X_1, \ldots, X_N}(x_1, \ldots, x_N)}_{N \text{ variables}}.$$

The first part exclusively deals with two variables. The generalization from two variables to N variables is straightforward for PDFs and CDFs:

- PDF: $f_{X_1, X_2}(x_1, x_2) \implies f_{X_1, \ldots, X_N}(x_1, \ldots, x_N)$.
- CDF: $F_{X_1, X_2}(x_1, x_2) \implies F_{X_1, \ldots, X_N}(x_1, \ldots, x_N)$.

The joint expectation can also be generalized from two variables to N variables:

$$\begin{bmatrix} \mathrm{Var}[X_1^2] & \mathrm{Cov}(X_1, X_2) \\ \mathrm{Cov}(X_2, X_1) & \mathrm{Var}[X_2^2] \end{bmatrix} \implies \begin{bmatrix} \mathrm{Var}[X_1^2] & \cdots & \mathrm{Cov}(X_1, X_N) \\ \vdots & \ddots & \vdots \\ \mathrm{Cov}(X_N, X_1) & \cdots & \mathrm{Var}[X_N^2] \end{bmatrix}.$$

Conditional PDFs and conditional expectations are powerful tools for *decomposing* complex events into simpler events. Specifically, the law of total expectation,

$$\mathbb{E}[X] = \int \mathbb{E}[X|Y = y] f_Y(y) \, dy = \mathbb{E}_Y[\mathbb{E}_{X|Y}[X|Y]],$$

is instrumental for evaluating variables defined through conditional relationships. The idea is also extendable to more random variables, such as

$$\mathbb{E}[X_1] = \int \int \mathbb{E}[X_1|X_2 = x_2, X_3 = x_3] f_{X_2, X_3}(x_2, x_3) \, dx_2 \, dx_3,$$

where $\mathbb{E}[X_1|X_2 = x_2, X_3 = x_3]$ can be evaluated through

$$\mathbb{E}[X_1|X_2 = x_2, X_3 = x_3] = \int x_1 f_{X_1|X_2, X_3}(x_1 \mid x_2, x_3) \, dx_1.$$

This type of chain relationship can generalize to other high-order cases.

It is important to remember that for any high-dimensional random variables, the characterization is always made by the PDF $f_{\boldsymbol{X}}(\boldsymbol{x})$ (or the CDF). We did not go into the details of analyzing $f_{\boldsymbol{X}}(\boldsymbol{x})$ but have only discussed the mean vector $\mathbb{E}[\boldsymbol{X}] = \boldsymbol{\mu}$ and the covariance matrix $\text{Cov}(\boldsymbol{X}) = \boldsymbol{\Sigma}$. We have been focusing exclusively on the high-dimensional Gaussian random variables

$$f_{\boldsymbol{X}}(\boldsymbol{x}) = \frac{1}{\sqrt{(2\pi)^d |\boldsymbol{\Sigma}|}} \exp\left\{ -\frac{1}{2}(\boldsymbol{x} - \boldsymbol{\mu})^T \boldsymbol{\Sigma}(\boldsymbol{x} - \boldsymbol{\mu}) \right\},$$

because they are ubiquitous in data science today. We discussed the linear transformations from a zero-mean unit-variance Gaussian to another Gaussian, and vice versa.

5.10 References

Joint Distributions and Correlation

5-1 Dimitri P. Bertsekas and John N. Tsitsiklis, *Introduction to Probability*, Athena Scientific, 2nd Edition, 2008. Chapters 2.5, 3.4, 4.2.

5-2 Alberto Leon-Garcia, *Probability, Statistics, and Random Processes for Electrical Engineering*, Prentice Hall, 3rd Edition, 2008. Chapters 5.1 – 5.6.

5-3 Athanasios Papoulis and S. Unnikrishna Pillai, *Probability, Random Variables and Stochastic Processes*, McGraw-Hill, 4th Edition, 2001. Chapters 6.1 – 6.4.

5-4 John A. Gubner, *Probability and Random Processes for Electrical and Computer Engineers*, Cambridge University Press, 2006. Chapters 7.1 – 7.2.

5-5 Sheldon Ross, *A First Course in Probability*, Prentice Hall, 8th Edition, 2010. Chapters 6.1 – 6.3.

5-6 Henry Stark and John Woods, *Probability and Random Processes With Applications to Signal Processing*, Prentice Hall, 3rd Edition, 2001. Chapter 2.6.

Conditional Distributions and Expectations

5-7 Dimitri P. Bertsekas and John N. Tsitsiklis, *Introduction to Probability*, Athena Scientific, 2nd Edition, 2008. Chapters 2.6, 3.5, 3.6, 4.3.

5-8 Alberto Leon-Garcia, *Probability, Statistics, and Random Processes for Electrical Engineering*, Prentice Hall, 3rd Edition, 2008. Chapter 5.7.

5-9 Athanasios Papoulis and S. Unnikrishna Pillai, *Probability, Random Variables and Stochastic Processes*, McGraw-Hill, 4th Edition, 2001. Chapters 6.6 – 6.7.

5-10 John A. Gubner, *Probability and Random Processes for Electrical and Computer Engineers*, Cambridge University Press, 2006. Chapters 7.3 – 7.5.

5-11 Sheldon Ross, *A First Course in Probability*, Prentice Hall, 8th Edition, 2010. Chapters 7.5 – 7.6.

5-12 Henry Stark and John Woods, *Probability and Random Processes With Applications to Signal Processing*, Prentice Hall, 3rd Edition, 2001. Chapter 4.2.

Sum of Random Variables

5-13 Dimitri P. Bertsekas and John N. Tsitsiklis, *Introduction to Probability*, Athena Scientific, 2nd Edition, 2008. Chapter 4.5.

5-14 Alberto Leon-Garcia, *Probability, Statistics, and Random Processes for Electrical Engineering*, Prentice Hall, 3rd Edition, 2008. Chapter 7.1.

5-15 Henry Stark and John Woods, *Probability and Random Processes With Applications to Signal Processing*, Prentice Hall, 3rd Edition, 2001. Chapters 3.3 and 3.4.

Vector Random Variables

5-16 Alberto Leon-Garcia, *Probability, Statistics, and Random Processes for Electrical Engineering*, Prentice Hall, 3rd Edition, 2008. Chapters 6.1 – 6.6.

5-17 John A. Gubner, *Probability and Random Processes for Electrical and Computer Engineers*, Cambridge University Press, 2006. Chapters 8.1 – 8.3, 9.

5-18 Henry Stark and John Woods, *Probability and Random Processes With Applications to Signal Processing*, Prentice Hall, 3rd Edition, 2001. Chapters 5.1 – 5.6.

Principal-Component Analysis

PCA is often taught in machine learning courses. For first-time readers, we suggest reviewing the linear algebraic tools in Moon and Stirling. Then, the tutorial by Shlens and the chapter in Bishop would be sufficient to cover most of the materials. More advanced topics, such as kernel PCA, can be found in the following references.

5-19 Todd K. Moon and Wynn C. Stirling, *Mathematical Methods and Algorithms for Signal Processing*, Prentice-Hall, 2000. Chapter 7.

5-20 Christopher Bishop, *Pattern Recognition and Machine Leanring*, Springer, 2006. Chapter 12.

5-21 Jonathon Shlens (2014) "A Tutorial on Principal Component Analysis", `https://arxiv.org/pdf/1404.1100.pdf`

5-22 Paul Honeine (2014), "An eigenanalysis of data centering in machine learning", `https://arxiv.org/pdf/1407.2904.pdf`

5-23 Quan Wang (2012), "Kernel Principal Component Analysis and its Applications", `https://arxiv.org/abs/1207.3538`

5-24 Schölkopf et al. (2005), "Kernel Principal Component Analysis", `https://link.springer.com/chapter/10.1007/BFb0020217`

5.11 Problems

Exercise 1. (VIDEO SOLUTION)
Alex and Bob each flips a fair coin twice. Use "1" to denote heads and "0" to denote tails. Let X be the maximum of the two numbers Alex gets, and let Y be the minimum of the two numbers Bob gets.

(a) Find and sketch the joint PMF $p_{X,Y}(x, y)$.

(b) Find the marginal PMF $p_X(x)$ and $p_Y(y)$.

(c) Find the conditional PMF $P_{X|Y}(x \mid y)$. Does $P_{X|Y}(x \mid y) = P_X(x)$? Why or why not?

Exercise 2.
Two fair dice are rolled. Find the joint PMF of X and Y when

(a) X is the larger value rolled, and Y is the sum of the two values.

(b) X is the smaller, and Y is the larger value rolled.

Exercise 3.
The amplitudes of two signals X and Y have joint PDF

$$f_{XY}(x, y) = e^{-x/2} y e^{-y^2}$$

for $x > 0, y > 0$.

(a) Find the joint CDF.

(b) Find $\mathbb{P}(X^{1/2} > Y)$.

(c) Find the marginal PDFs.

Exercise 4. (VIDEO SOLUTION)
Find the marginal CDFs $F_X(x)$ and $F_Y(y)$ and determine whether or not X and Y are independent, if

$$F_{XY}(x, y) = \begin{cases} x - 1 - \dfrac{e^{-y} - e^{-xy}}{y}, & \text{if } 1 \le x \le 2, y \ge 0 \\ 1 - \dfrac{e^{-y} - e^{-2y}}{y}, & \text{if } x > 2, y \ge 0, \\ 0, & \text{otherwise.} \end{cases}$$

Exercise 5. (VIDEO SOLUTION)

(a) Find the marginal PDF $f_X(x)$ if

$$f_{XY}(x, y) = \frac{\exp\{-|y - x| - x^2/2\}}{2\sqrt{2\pi}}.$$

315

(b) Find the marginal PDF $f_Y(y)$ if

$$f_{XY}(x,y) = \frac{4e^{-(x-y)^2/2}}{y^2\sqrt{2\pi}}.$$

Exercise 6. (VIDEO SOLUTION)
Let X, Y be two random variables with joint CDF

$$F_{X,Y}(x,y) = \frac{y + e^{-x(y+1)}}{y+1}.$$

Show that

$$\frac{\partial^2}{\partial x \partial y}F_{X,Y}(x,y) = \frac{\partial^2}{\partial y \partial x}F_{X,Y}(x,y).$$

What is the implication of this result?

Exercise 7. (VIDEO SOLUTION)
Let X and Y be two random variables with joint PDF

$$f_{X,Y}(x,y) = \frac{1}{2\pi}e^{-\frac{1}{2}(x^2+y^2)}.$$

(a) Find the PDF of $Z = \max(X, Y)$.

(b) Find the PDF of $Z = \min(X, Y)$.

You may leave your answers in terms of the $\Phi(\cdot)$ function.

Exercise 8.
The random vector (X, Y) has a joint PDF

$$f_{XY}(x,y) = 2e^{-x}e^{-2y}$$

for $x > 0$, $y > 0$. Find the probability of the following events:

(a) $\{X + Y \le 8\}$.

(b) $\{X - Y \le 10\}$.

(c) $\{X^2 < Y\}$.

Exercise 9.
Let X and Y be zero-mean, unit-variance independent Gaussian random variables. Find the value of r for which the probability that (X, Y) falls inside a circle of radius r is $1/2$.

Exercise 10.
The input X to a communication channel is $+1$ or -1 with probabilities p and $1 - p$, respectively. The received signal Y is the sum of X and noise N, which has a Gaussian distribution with zero mean and variance $\sigma^2 = 0.25$.

(a) Find the joint probability $\mathbb{P}(X = j, \, Y \leq y)$.

(b) Find the marginal PMF of X and the marginal PDF of Y.

(c) Suppose we are given that $Y > 0$. Which is more likely, $X = 1$ or $X = -1$?

Exercise 11. (VIDEO SOLUTION)
Let

$$f_{X,Y}(x,y) = \begin{cases} ce^{-x}e^{-y}, & \text{if } 0 \leq y \leq x < \infty, \\ 0, & \text{otherwise.} \end{cases}$$

(a) Find c.

(b) Find $f_X(x)$ and $f_Y(y)$.

(c) Find $\mathbb{E}[X]$ and $\mathbb{E}[Y]$, $\text{Var}[X]$ and $\text{Var}[Y]$.

(d) Find $\mathbb{E}[XY]$, $\text{Cov}(X, Y)$ and ρ.

Exercise 12. (VIDEO SOLUTION)
In class, we have used the Cauchy-Schwarz inequality to show that $-1 \leq \rho \leq 1$. This exercise asks you to prove the Cauchy-Schwarz inequality:

$$(\mathbb{E}[XY])^2 \leq \mathbb{E}[X^2]\mathbb{E}[Y^2].$$

Hint: Consider the expectation $\mathbb{E}[(tX + Y)^2]$. Note that this is a quadratic equation in t and $\mathbb{E}[(tX + Y)^2] \geq 0$ for all t. Consider the discriminant of this quadratic equation.

Exercise 13. (VIDEO SOLUTION)
Let $\Theta \sim \text{Uniform}[0, 2\pi]$.

(a) If $X = \cos \Theta$, $Y = \sin \Theta$. Are X and Y uncorrelated?

(b) If $X = \cos(\Theta/4)$, $Y = \sin(\Theta/4)$. Are X and Y uncorrelated?

Exercise 14. (VIDEO SOLUTION)
Let X and Y have a joint PDF

$$f_{X,Y}(x,y) = c(x + y),$$

for $0 \leq x \leq 1$ and $0 \leq y \leq 1$.

(a) Find c, $f_X(x)$, $f_Y(y)$, and $\mathbb{E}[Y]$.

(b) Find $f_{Y|X}(y|x)$.

(c) Find $\mathbb{P}[Y > X \,|\, X > 1/2]$.

(d) Find $\mathbb{E}[Y|X = x]$.

(e) Find $\mathbb{E}[\mathbb{E}[Y|X]]$, and compare with the $\mathbb{E}[Y]$ computed in (a).

Exercise 15. (VIDEO SOLUTION)
Use the law of total expectation to compute the following:

1. $\mathbb{E}[\sin(X+Y)]$, where $X \sim \mathcal{N}(0,1)$, and $Y \,|\, X \sim \text{Uniform}[x - \pi, x + \pi]$

2. $\mathbb{P}[Y < y]$, where $X \sim \text{Uniform}[0,1]$, and $Y \,|\, X \sim \text{Exponential}(x)$

3. $\mathbb{E}[Xe^Y]$, where $X \sim \text{Uniform}[-1,1]$, and $Y \,|\, X \sim \mathcal{N}(0, x^2)$

Exercise 16.
Let $Y = X + N$, where X is the input, N is the noise, and Y is the output of a system. Assume that X and N are independent random variables. It is given that $\mathbb{E}[X] = 0$, $\text{Var}[X] = \sigma_X^2$, $\mathbb{E}[N] = 0$, and $\text{Var}[N] = \sigma_N^2$.

(a) Find the correlation coefficient ρ between the input X and the output Y.

(b) Suppose we estimate the input X by a linear function $g(Y) = aY$. Find the value of a that minimizes the mean squared error $\mathbb{E}[(X - aY)^2]$.

(c) Express the resulting mean squared error in terms of $\eta = \sigma_X^2 / \sigma_N^2$.

Exercise 17. (VIDEO SOLUTION)
Two independent random variables X and Y have PDFs

$$f_X(x) = \begin{cases} e^{-x}, & x \geq 0, \\ 0, & x < 0, \end{cases} \qquad f_Y(y) = \begin{cases} 0, & y > 0, \\ e^y, & y \leq 0. \end{cases}$$

Find the PDF of $Z = X - Y$.

Exercise 18.
Let X and Y be two independent random variables with densities

$$f_X(x) = \begin{cases} xe^{-x}, & x \geq 0, \\ 0, & x < 0, \end{cases} \quad \text{and} \quad f_Y(y) = \begin{cases} ye^{-y}, & y \geq 0, \\ 0, & y < 0. \end{cases}$$

Find the PDF of $Z = X + Y$.

Exercise 19.
The random variables X and Y have the joint PDF

$$f_{XY}(x,y) = e^{-(x+y)}$$

for $0 < y < x < 1$. Find the PDF of $Z = X + Y$.

Exercise 20.
The joint density function of X and Y is given by

$$f_{XY}(x,y) = e^{-(x+y)}$$

for $x > 0, y > 0$. Find the PDF of the random variable $Z = X/Y$.

Chapter 6

Sample Statistics

When we think about probability, the first thing that likely comes to mind is flipping a coin, throwing a die, or playing a card game. These are excellent examples of the subject. However, they seldom fit in the context of modern data science, which is concerned with drawing conclusions from data. In our opinion, **the power of probability is its ability to summarize microstates using macro descriptions**. This statement will take us some effort to elaborate. We study probability because we want to analyze the uncertainties. However, when we have many data points, analyzing the uncertainties of each data point (the microstates) is computationally very difficult. Probability is useful here because it allows us to bypass the microstates and summarize the macro behavior. Instead of reporting the states of each individual, we report their sample average. Instead of offering the worst-case guarantee, we offer a probabilistic guarantee. You ask: so what? If we can offer you a performance guarantee at 99.99% confidence but one-tenth of the cost of a 100% performance guarantee, would you consider our offer? The goal of this chapter is to outline the concepts of these probabilistic arguments.

The significance of sample average

Imagine that you have a box containing many tiny magnets. (You can also think of a dataset containing two classes of labels.) In condensed matter physics, these are known as the **spin glasses**. The orientations of the magnets depend on the magnetic field. Under an extreme condition where the magnetic field is strong, all magnets will point in the same direction. When the magnetic field is not as strong, some will align with the field but some will not, as we show in **Figure 6.1**.

If we try to study every single magnet in this box, the correlation of the magnets will force us to consider a joint distribution, since if one magnet points to the right it is likely that another magnet will also point to the right. The simultaneous description of all magnets is modeled through a joint probability distribution

$$f_{X_1, X_2, \ldots, X_N}(x_1, x_2, \ldots, x_N).$$

Like any joint PDF, this PDF tells us the probability density that the magnets will take a collection of states simultaneously. If N is large (say, on the order of millions), this joint distribution will be very complicated.

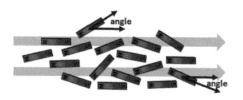

Experiment 1			Experiment M	
ID	angle		ID	angle
X_1	10.6°		X_1	21.3°
X_2	7.5°	...	X_2	17.1°
$\vdots$	$\vdots$		$\vdots$	$\vdots$
X_{10000}	23.5°		X_{10000}	3.8°
average	$\overline{X}_N$		average	$\overline{X}_N$

Figure 6.1: Imagine that we have a box of magnets and we want to measure their orientation angles. The data points have individual randomness and correlations. Studying each one individually could be computationally infeasible, as we need to estimate the joint PDF $f_{X_1,\ldots,X_N}(x_1,\ldots,x_N)$ across all the data points. Probability offers a tool to summarize these individual states using a macro description. For example, we can analyze the sample average $\overline{X}_N$ of the data points and derive conclusions from the PDF of $\overline{X}_N$, i.e., $f_{\overline{X}_N}(x)$. The objective of this chapter is to present a few probabilistic tools to analyze macro descriptions, such as the sample average.

Since the joint PDF is very difficult to obtain computationally, physicists proposed to study the sample statistics. Instead of looking at the individual states, they look at the **sample average** of the states. If we define $X_1,\ldots,X_N$ as the states of the magnets, then the sample average is

$$\overline{X}_N = \frac{1}{N}\sum_{n=1}^{N} X_n.$$

Since each magnet is random, the sample average is also random, and therefore it is granted a PDF:

$$f_{\overline{X}_N}(x).$$

Thus, $\overline{X}_N$ has a PDF, a mean, a variance, and so on.

We call $\overline{X}_N$ a sample statistic. It is called a **statistic** because it is a summary of the microstates, and a **sample** statistic because the statistic is based on random samples, not on the underlying theoretical distributions. We are interested in knowing the behavior of $\overline{X}_N$ because it is the summary of the observations. If we know the PDF of $\overline{X}_N$, we will know the mean, the variance, and the value of $\overline{X}_N$ when the magnetic field increases or decreases.

Why study the sample average $\overline{X}_N$?

- Analyzing individual variables is not feasible because the joint PDF can be extremely high-dimensional.
- Sample average is a macro description of the data.
- If you know the behavior of the sample average, you know most of the data.

Probabilistic guarantee versus worst-case guarantee

Besides the sample average, we are also interested in the difference between a probabilistic guarantee and a deterministic guarantee.

Consider the **birthday paradox** (see Chapter 1 for details). Suppose there are 50 students in a room. What is the probability that at least two students have the same birthday? A naive thought would suggest that we need 366 students to guarantee a pair of the same birthday because there are 365 days. So, with only 50 students, it would seem unlikely to have a pair with the same birthday. However, it turns out that with just 50 students, the probability of having at least one pair with the same birthday is more than 97%. **Figure 6.2** below shows a calculation by a computer, where we plot the estimated probability as a function of the number of students. What is more surprising is that with as few as 23 students, the probability is greater than 50%. There is no need for there to be 365 students in order to offer a guarantee.

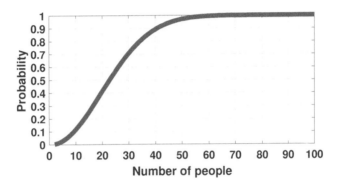

Figure 6.2: The birthday paradox asks the question of how many people we need to ask in order to have at least two of them having the same birthday. While we tend to think that the answer is 366 (because there are 365 days), the actual probability, as we have calculated (see Chapter 1), is more than 97%, even if we have only asked 50 people. The curve above shows the probability of having at least one pair of people having the same birthday as a function of the number of people. The plot highlights the gap between the **worst-case** performance and an **average-case** performance.

Why does this happen? Certainly, we can trace back to the formulae in Chapter 1 and argue through the lens of combinations and permutations. However, the more important message is about the difference between the **worst-case guarantee** and the **average-case guarantee**.

Worst case versus average case

- Worst-case guarantee: You need to ensure that the worst one is protected. This requires an exhaustive search until hitting 100%. It is a deterministic guarantee.

- Average-case guarantee: You guarantee that with a high probability (e.g., 99.99%), the undesirable event does not happen. This is a probabilistic guarantee.

Is there a difference between 99.99% and 100%? If the probability is 99.99%, there is one failure every 10,000 trials on average. You are unlikely to fail, but it is still possible. A 100% guarantee says that no matter how many trials you make you will not fail. The 99.99% guarantee is much weaker (yes, much weaker, not just a little bit weaker) than the deterministic guarantee. However, in practice, people might be willing to pay for the risk in exchange for efficiency. This is the principle behind insurance. Automobile manufacturing also uses this principle — your chance of purchasing a defective car is non-zero, but if the manufacturer can sell enough cars to compensate for the maintenance cost of fixing your car, they might be willing to offer a limited warranty in exchange for a lower selling price.

How do we analyze the probabilistic guarantee, e.g., for the sample average? Remember that the sample average $\overline{X}_N$ is a random variable. Since it is a random variable, it has a mean, variance, and PDF.[1] To measure the probabilistic guarantee, we consider the event

$$\mathcal{B} \stackrel{\text{def}}{=} \{|\overline{X}_N - \mu| \geq \epsilon\},$$

where $\mu = \mathbb{E}[\overline{X}_N]$ is the true population mean, and $\epsilon > 0$ is a constant. This probability is illustrated in **Figure 6.3**, assuming that $\overline{X}_N$ has the PDF of a Gaussian. The probability of $\mathcal{B}$ is the two tails under the PDF. Therefore, $\mathcal{B}$ is a **bad** event because in principle $\overline{X}_N$ should be close to μ. The probability $\mathbb{P}[\mathcal{B}]$ measures situations where $\overline{X}_N$ stays very far from μ. If we can show that $\mathbb{P}[\mathcal{B}]$ is small (e.g., $< 0.01\%$), then we can say that we have obtained a probabilistic guarantee at 99.99%.

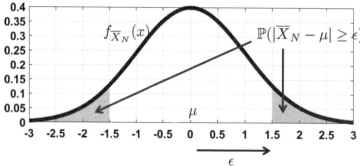

Figure 6.3: The probabilistic guarantee of a sample average $\overline{X}_N$ is established by computing the probability of the tails. In this example, we assume that $f_{\overline{X}_N}(x)$ take a Gaussian shape, and we define $\epsilon = 1$. Anything belonging to $|\overline{X}_N - \mu| \geq \epsilon$ is called a **undesired** event $\mathcal{B}$. If the probability of a undesired event is small, we say that we can offer a probabilistic guarantee.

The moment we compute $\mathbb{P}[|\overline{X}_N - \mu| \geq \epsilon]$, we enter the race of probabilistic guarantee (e.g., 99.99%). Why? If the probability $\mathbb{P}[|\overline{X}_N - \mu| \geq \epsilon]$ is less than 0.01%, it still does not exclude the possibility that something bad will happen once every 10,000 trials on average. The chance is low, but it is still possible. We will learn some mathematical tools for analyzing this type of probabilistic guarantee.

Plan for this chapter

With these two main themes in mind, we now discuss the organization of this chapter. There are four sections: two for mathematical tools and two for main results.

- **Moment-generating functions**: We have seen in Chapter 5 that the PDF of a sum of two random variables $X + Y$ is the **convolution** of the two PDFs $f_X * f_Y$. Convolutions are non-trivial, especially when we have more random variables to sum. The moment-generating functions provide a convenient way of summing N random variables. They are the transform domain techniques (e.g., Fourier transforms). Since convolutions in

---

[1] Not all random variables have mean and variance, e.g., a Cauchy random variable, but most of them do.

time are multiplications in frequency, the moment-generating functions allow us to multiply PDFs in the transformed space. In this way, we can sum as many random variables as we want. We will discuss this idea in Section 6.1.

> **Key Concept 1: Why study moment-generating functions?**
>
> Moment-generating functions help us determine the PDF of $X_1 + X_2 + \cdots + X_N$.

- **Probability inequalities**: When analyzing sample statistics such as $\overline{X}_N$, evaluating the exact probability could be difficult because it requires integrating the PDFs. However, if our ultimate goal is to estimate the probability, deriving an upper bound might be sufficient to achieve the goal. The probability inequalities are designed for this purpose. In Section 6.2, we discuss several of the most basic probability inequalities. We will use some of them to prove the law of large numbers.

> **Key Concept 2: How can probability inequalities be useful?**
>
> Probability inequalities help us upper-bound the bad event $\mathbb{P}[|\overline{X}_N - \mu| \geq \epsilon]$.

- **Law of large numbers**: This is the first main result of the chapter. The law of large numbers says that the sample average $\overline{X}_N$ converges to the population mean μ when the number of samples grows to infinity. The law of large numbers comes in two versions: the **weak** law of large numbers and the **strong** law of large numbers. The difference is the type of convergence they guarantee. The weak law is based on **convergence in probability**, whereas the strong law is based on **almost sure convergence**. We will discuss these types of convergence in Section 6.3.

> **Key Concept 3: What is the law of large numbers?**
>
> There is a weak law and a strong law of large numbers. The weak law of large numbers says that $\overline{X}_N$ converges to the true mean μ, as N grows:
>
> $$\lim_{N \to \infty} \mathbb{P}[|\overline{X}_N - \mu| > \epsilon] = 0.$$

- **Central Limit Theorem**: The Central Limit Theorem says that the probability of $\overline{X}_N$ can be approximated by the probability of a Gaussian. You can also think of this as saying that the CDF of $\overline{X}_N$ is converging to a distribution that can be well approximated by a bell-shaped Gaussian. If we have many random variables and their sum is becoming a Gaussian, we can ignore the individual PDFs and focus on the Gaussian. Thus it explains why Gaussian is so popular. We will discuss this theorem in detail in Section 6.4.

> **Key Concept 4: What is the Central Limit Theorem?**
>
> The CDF of $\overline{X}_N$ can be approximated by the CDF of a Gaussian, as N grows.

6.1 Moment-Generating and Characteristic Functions

Consider two independent random variables X and Y with PDFs $f_X(x)$ and $f_Y(y)$, respectively. Let $Z = X + Y$ be the sum of the two random variables. We know from Chapter 5 that the PDF of Z, f_Z, is the convolution of f_X and f_Y. However, we think you will agree that convolutions are not easy to compute. Especially when the sum involves more random variables, computing the convolution would be tedious. So how should we proceed in this case? One approach is to use some kind of "frequency domain" method that transforms the PDFs to another domain and then perform multiplication instead of the convolution to make the calculations easy or at least easier. The moment-generating functions and the characteristic functions are designed for this purpose.

6.1.1 Moment-generating function

> **Definition 6.1.** *For any random variable X, the* **moment-generating function** *(MGF)* $M_X(s)$ *is*
> $$M_X(s) = \mathbb{E}\left[e^{sX}\right]. \tag{6.1}$$

The definition says that the moment-generating function (MGF) is the expectation of the random variable taken to the power e^{sX} for some s. Effectively, it is the expectation of a **function** of random variables. The meaning of the expectation can be seen by writing out the definition. For the discrete case, the MGF is

$$M_X(s) = \sum_{x \in \Omega} e^{sx} p_X(x), \tag{6.2}$$

whereas in the continuous case, the MGF is

$$M_X(s) = \int_{-\infty}^{\infty} e^{sx} f_X(x)\, dx. \tag{6.3}$$

The continuous case should remind us of the definition of a Laplace transform. For any function $f(t)$, the Laplace transform is

$$\mathcal{L}[f](s) = \int_0^{\infty} f(t)e^{-st}\, dt.$$

From this perspective, we can interpret the MGF as the **Laplace transform** of the PDF. The argument s of the output can be regarded as the coordinate in the Laplace space. If $s = -j\omega$, then $M_X(j\omega)$ becomes the Fourier transform of the PDF.

> **Example 6.1.** Consider a random variable X with three states $0, 1, 2$ and with probability masses $\frac{2}{6}, \frac{3}{6}, \frac{1}{6}$ respectively. Find the MGF.

Solution. The moment-generating function is

$$M_X(s) = \mathbb{E}[e^{sX}] = e^{s0} \cdot \frac{2}{6} + e^{s1} \cdot \frac{3}{6} + e^{s2} \cdot \frac{1}{6}$$

$$= \frac{1}{3} + \frac{e^s}{2} + \frac{e^{2s}}{6}.$$

Practice Exercise 6.1. Find the MGF for a Poisson random variable.

Solution. The MGF of Poisson random variable can be found as

$$M_X(s) = \mathbb{E}[e^{sX}] = \sum_{x=0}^{\infty} e^{sx} \frac{\lambda^x e^{-\lambda}}{x!} = \sum_{x=0}^{\infty} \frac{(\lambda e^s)^x}{x!} e^{-\lambda} = e^{\lambda e^s} e^{-\lambda}.$$

Practice Exercise 6.2. Find the MGF for an exponential random variable.

Solution. The MGF of an exponential random variable can be found as

$$M_X(s) = \mathbb{E}[e^{sX}] = \int_0^{\infty} e^{sx} \lambda e^{-\lambda x} \, dx = \int_0^{\infty} \lambda e^{(s-\lambda)x} \, dx = \frac{\lambda}{\lambda - s}, \qquad \text{if } \lambda > s.$$

Why are moment-generating functions so called? The following theorem reveals the reason.

Theorem 6.1. *The MGF has the properties that*

- $M_X(0) = 1$,
- $\frac{d}{ds} M_X(s)|_{s=0} = \mathbb{E}[X]$, $\frac{d^2}{ds^2} M_X(s)|_{s=0} = \mathbb{E}[X^2]$,
- $\frac{d^k}{ds^k} M_X(s)|_{s=0} = \mathbb{E}[X^k]$, *for any positive integer k.*

Proof. The first property can be proved by noting that

$$M_X(0) = \mathbb{E}[e^{0X}] = \mathbb{E}[1] = 1.$$

The third property holds because

$$\frac{d^k}{ds^k} M_X(s) = \int_{-\infty}^{\infty} \frac{d^k}{ds^k} e^{sx} f_X(x) \, dx = \int_{-\infty}^{\infty} x^k e^{sx} f_X(x) \, dx.$$

Setting $s = 0$ yields

$$\frac{d^k}{ds^k} M_X(s)|_{s=0} = \int_{-\infty}^{\infty} x^k f_X(x) \, dx = \mathbb{E}[X^k].$$

The second property is a special case of the third property.

$\square$

CHAPTER 6. SAMPLE STATISTICS

The theorem tells us that if we take the derivative of the MGF and set $s = 0$, we will obtain the moment. The order of the moment depends on the order of the derivative. As a result, the MGF can "generate moments" by taking derivatives. This happens because of the exponential function e^{sx}. Since $\frac{d}{ds}e^{sx} = xe^{sx}$, the variable x appears whenever we take the derivative.

Practice Exercise 6.3. Let X be a Bernoulli random variable with parameter p. Find the first two moments using MGF.

Solution. The MGF of a Bernoulli random variable is

$$
\begin{aligned}
M_X(s) = \mathbb{E}[e^{sX}] \\
= e^{s0}p_X(0) + e^{s1}p_X(1) \\
= (1)(1-p) + (e^s)(p) \\
= 1 - p + pe^s.
\end{aligned}
$$

The first and the second moment, using the derivative approach, are

$$
\mathbb{E}[X] = \frac{d}{ds}M_X(s)\Big|_{s=0} = \frac{d}{ds}\left(1 - p + pe^s\right)\Big|_{s=0} = pe^s\Big|_{s=0} = p,
$$

$$
\mathbb{E}[X^2] = \frac{d^2}{ds^2}M_X(s)\Big|_{s=0} = \frac{d^2}{ds^2}\left(1 - p + pe^s\right)\Big|_{s=0} = pe^s\Big|_{s=0} = p.
$$

To facilitate our discussions of MGF, we summarize a few MGFs in the table below.

Distribution	PMF / PDF	$\mathbb{E}[X]$	$\text{Var}[X]$	$M_X(s)$
Bernoulli	$p_X(1) = p$ and $p_X(0) = 1 - p$	p	$p(1-p)$	$1 - p + pe^s$
Binomial	$p_X(k) = \binom{n}{k}p^k(1-p)^{n-k}$	np	$np(1-p)$	$(1 - p + pe^s)^n$
Geometric	$p_X(k) = p(1-p)^{k-1}$	$\frac{1}{p}$	$\frac{1-p}{p^2}$	$\frac{pe^s}{1 - (1-p)e^s}$
Poisson	$p_X(k) = \frac{\lambda^k e^{-\lambda}}{k!}$	λ	λ	$e^{\lambda(e^s - 1)}$
Gaussian	$f_X(x) = \frac{1}{\sqrt{2\pi\sigma^2}}\exp\left\{-\frac{(x-\mu)^2}{2\sigma^2}\right\}$	μ	σ^2	$\exp\left\{\mu s + \frac{\sigma^2 s^2}{2}\right\}$
Exponential	$f_X(x) = \lambda\exp\{-\lambda x\}$	$\frac{1}{\lambda}$	$\frac{1}{\lambda^2}$	$\frac{\lambda}{\lambda - s}$
Uniform	$f_X(x) = \frac{1}{b-a}$	$\frac{a+b}{2}$	$\frac{(b-a)^2}{12}$	$\frac{e^{sb} - e^{sa}}{s(b-a)}$

Table 6.1: Moment-generating functions of common random variables.

6.1.2 Sum of independent variables via MGF

MGFs are most useful when analyzing the PDF of a sum of two random variables. The following theorem highlights the result.

> **Theorem 6.2.** *Let X and Y be independent random variables. Let $Z = X + Y$. Then*
>
> $$M_Z(s) = M_X(s)M_Y(s). \tag{6.4}$$

Proof. By the definition of MGF, we have that

$$M_Z(s) = \mathbb{E}\left[e^{s(X+Y)}\right] \overset{(a)}{=} \mathbb{E}\left[e^{sX}\right] \mathbb{E}\left[e^{sY}\right] = M_X(s)M_Y(s),$$

where (a) is valid because X and Y are independent.

□

> **Corollary 6.1.** *Consider independent random variables $X_1, \ldots, X_N$. Let $Z = \sum_{n=1}^{N} X_n$ be the sum of random variables. Then the MGF of Z is*
>
> $$M_Z(s) = \prod_{n=1}^{N} M_{X_n}(s). \tag{6.5}$$
>
> *If these random variables are further assumed to be identically distributed, the MGF is*
>
> $$M_Z(s) = \left(M_{X_1}(s)\right)^N. \tag{6.6}$$

Proof. This follows immediately from the previous theorem:

$$M_Z(s) = \mathbb{E}[e^{s(X_1+\cdots+X_N)}] = \mathbb{E}[e^{sX_1}]\mathbb{E}[e^{sX_2}]\cdots\mathbb{E}[e^{sX_N}] = \prod_{n=1}^{N} M_{X_n}(s).$$

If the random variables $X_1, \ldots, X_N$ are i.i.d., then the product simplifies to

$$\prod_{n=1}^{N} M_{X_n}(s) = \prod_{n=1}^{N} M_{X_1}(s) = \left(M_{X_1}(s)\right)^N.$$

□

> **Theorem 6.3 (Sum of Bernoulli = binomial).** *Let $X_1, \ldots, X_N$ be a sequence of i.i.d. Bernoulli random variables with parameter p. Let $Z = X_1 + \cdots + X_N$ be the sum. Then Z is a binomial random variable with parameters (N, p).*

Proof. Let us consider a sequence of i.i.d. Bernoulli random variables $X_n \sim \text{Bernoulli}(p)$ for $n = 1, \ldots, N$. Let $Z = X_1 + \cdots + X_N$. The moment-generating function of Z is

$$M_Z(s) = \mathbb{E}[e^{s(X_1+\cdots+X_N)}] = \prod_{n=1}^{N} \mathbb{E}[e^{sX_n}]$$

$$= \prod_{n=1}^{N} \left(pe^{s1} + (1-p)e^{s0}\right) = \left(pe^s + (1-p)\right)^N.$$

Now, let us check the moment-generating function of a binomial random variable: If $Z \sim$ Binomial(N, p), then

$$M_Z(s) = \mathbb{E}[e^{sZ}] = \sum_{n=0}^{N} e^{sk} \binom{N}{k} p^k (1-p)^{N-k}$$

$$= \sum_{n=0}^{N} \binom{N}{k} (pe^s)^k (1-p)^{N-k} = (pe^s + (1-p))^N,$$

where the last equality holds because $\sum_{n=0}^{N} \binom{N}{k} a^k b^{N-k} = (a+b)^N$. Therefore, the two moment-generating functions are identical. □

Theorem 6.4 (Sum of binomial = binomial). *Let X_1, ..., X_N be a sequence of i.i.d. binomial random variables with parameters (n, p). Let $Z = X_1 + \cdots + X_N$ be the sum. Then Z is a binomial random variable with parameters (Nn, p).*

Proof. The MGF of a binomial random variable is

$$M_{X_i}(s) = (pe^s + (1-p))^n.$$

If we have N of these random variables, then $Z = X_1 + \cdots + X_N$ will have the MGF

$$M_Z(s) = \prod_{i=1}^{N} M_{X_i}(s) = (pe^s + (1-p))^{Nn}.$$

Note that this is just the MGF of another binomial random variable with parameter (Nn, p). □

Theorem 6.5 (Sum of Poisson = Poisson). *Let X_1, ..., X_N be a sequence of i.i.d. Poisson random variables with parameter λ. Let $Z = X_1 + \cdots + X_N$ be the sum. Then Z is a Poisson random variable with parameters $N\lambda$.*

Proof. The MGF of a Poisson random variable is

$$M_X(s) = \mathbb{E}[e^{sX}] = \sum_{k=0}^{\infty} e^{sk} \frac{\lambda^k}{k!} e^{-\lambda}$$

$$= e^{-\lambda} \sum_{k=0}^{\infty} \frac{(\lambda e^s)^k}{k!}$$

$$= e^{-\lambda} e^{\lambda e^s} = e^{\lambda(e^s - 1)}.$$

Assume that we have a sum of N i.i.d. Poisson random variables. Then, by the main theorem, we have that

$$M_Z(s) = [M_X(s)]^N = e^{N\lambda(e^s - 1)}.$$

Therefore, the resulting random variable Z is a Poisson with parameter $N\lambda$. □

Theorem 6.6 (Sum of Gaussian = Gaussian). *Let X_1, ..., X_N be a sequence of independent Gaussian random variables with parameters (μ_1, σ_1^2), ..., (μ_N, σ_N^2). Let $Z = X_1 + \cdots + X_N$ be the sum. Then Z is a Gaussian random variable:*

$$Z = Gaussian\left(\sum_{n=1}^{N} \mu_n, \sum_{n=1}^{N} \sigma_n^2 \right). \tag{6.7}$$

Proof. We skip the proof of the MGF of a Gaussian. It can be shown that

$$M_X(s) = \exp\left\{ \mu s + \frac{\sigma^2 s^2}{2} \right\}.$$

When we have a sequence of Gaussian random variables, then

$$\begin{aligned} M_Z(s) &= \mathbb{E}[e^{s(X_1 + \cdots + X_N)}] \\ &= M_{X_1}(s) \cdots M_{X_N}(s) \\ &= \left(\exp\left\{ \mu_1 s + \frac{\sigma_1^2 s^2}{2} \right\} \right) \cdots \left(\exp\left\{ \mu_N s + \frac{\sigma_N^2 s^2}{2} \right\} \right) \\ &= \exp\left\{ \left(\sum_{n=1}^{N} \mu_n \right) s + \left(\sum_{n=1}^{N} \sigma_n^2 \right) \frac{s^2}{2} \right\}. \end{aligned}$$

Therefore, the resulting random variable Z is also a Gaussian. The mean and variance of Z are $\sum_{n=1}^{N} \mu_n$ and $\sum_{n=1}^{N} \sigma_n^2$, respectively. $\qquad \square$

6.1.3   Characteristic functions

Moment-generating functions are the Laplace transforms of the PDFs. However, since the Laplace transform is defined on the entire right half-plane, not all PDFs can be transformed. One way to mitigate this problem is to restrict s to the imaginary axis, $s = j\omega$. This will give us the **characteristic function**.

Definition 6.2 (Usual definition). *The* **characteristic function** *of a random variable X is*

$$\Phi_X(j\omega) = \mathbb{E}[e^{j\omega X}]. \tag{6.8}$$

However, we note that since ω can take any value in $(-\infty, \infty)$, it does not matter if we consider $\mathbb{E}[e^{-j\omega X}]$ or $\mathbb{E}[e^{j\omega X}]$. This leads to the following equivalent definition of the characteristic function:

Definition 6.3 (Alternative definition (for this book)). *The* **characteristic function** *of a random variable X is*

$$\Phi_X(j\omega) = \mathbb{E}[e^{-j\omega X}]. \tag{6.9}$$

If we follow this definition, we see that the characteristic function can be written as

$$\Phi_X(j\omega) = \mathbb{E}[e^{-j\omega X}] = \int_{-\infty}^{\infty} e^{-j\omega x} f_X(x) \, dx. \tag{6.10}$$

This is exactly the **Fourier transform** of the PDF. The reason for introducing this alternative characteristic function is that $\mathbb{E}[e^{-j\omega X}]$ is the Fourier transform of $f_X(x)$ but $\mathbb{E}[e^{j\omega X}]$ is the inverse Fourier transform of $f_X(x)$. The former is more convenient (in terms of notation) for students who have taken a course in signals and systems. However, we should stress that the usual way of defining the characteristic function is $\mathbb{E}[e^{j\omega X}]$.

A list of common Fourier transforms is shown in the table below. Additional identities can be found in standard signals and systems textbooks.

Fourier Transforms $f(t) \longleftrightarrow F(\omega)$

1.	$e^{-at}u(t) \longleftrightarrow \frac{1}{a+j\omega}, \ a>0$	10.	$\text{sinc}^2(\frac{Wt}{2}) \longleftrightarrow \frac{2\pi}{W}\Delta(\frac{\omega}{2W})$
2.	$e^{at}u(-t) \longleftrightarrow \frac{1}{a-j\omega}, \ a>0$	11.	$e^{-at}\sin(\omega_0 t)u(t) \longleftrightarrow \frac{\omega_0}{(a+j\omega)^2+\omega_0^2}$
3.	$e^{-a|t|} \longleftrightarrow \frac{2a}{a^2+\omega^2}, \ a>0$	12.	$e^{-at}\cos(\omega_0 t)u(t) \longleftrightarrow \frac{a+j\omega}{(a+j\omega)^2+\omega_0^2}$
4.	$\frac{a^2}{a^2+t^2} \longleftrightarrow \pi a e^{-a|\omega|}, \ a>0$	13.	$e^{-\frac{t^2}{2\sigma^2}} \longleftrightarrow \sqrt{2\pi}\sigma e^{-\frac{\sigma^2\omega^2}{2}}$
5.	$te^{-at}u(t) \longleftrightarrow \frac{1}{(a+j\omega)^2}, \ a>0$	14.	$\delta(t) \longleftrightarrow 1$
6.	$t^n e^{-at}u(t) \longleftrightarrow \frac{n!}{(a+j\omega)^{n+1}}, \ a>0$	15.	$1 \longleftrightarrow 2\pi\delta(\omega)$
7.	$\text{rect}(\frac{t}{\tau}) \longleftrightarrow \tau\,\text{sinc}(\frac{\omega\tau}{2})$	16.	$\delta(t-t_0) \longleftrightarrow e^{-j\omega t_0}$
8.	$\text{sinc}(Wt) \longleftrightarrow \frac{\pi}{W}\text{rect}(\frac{w}{2W})$	17.	$e^{j\omega_0 t} \longleftrightarrow 2\pi\delta(\omega-\omega_0)$
9.	$\Delta(\frac{t}{\tau}) \longleftrightarrow \frac{\tau}{2}\text{sinc}^2(\frac{\omega\tau}{4})$	18.	$f(t)e^{j\omega_0 t} \longleftrightarrow F(\omega-\omega_0)$

$$\text{sinc}(t) = \frac{\sin(t)}{t} \qquad \text{rect}(t) = \begin{cases} 1, & -0.5 \le t \le 0.5, \\ 0, & \text{otherwise.} \end{cases} \qquad \Delta(t) = \begin{cases} 1-2|t|, & -0.5 \le t \le 0.5, \\ 0, & \text{otherwise.} \end{cases}$$

Table 6.2: Fourier transform pairs of commonly used functions.

Example 6.2. Let X be a random variable with PDF $f_X(x) = \lambda e^{-\lambda x}$ for $x \ge 0$. Find the characteristic function.

Solution. The Fourier transform pair is

$$\lambda e^{-\lambda x} \longrightarrow \lambda \cdot \mathcal{F}\left\{e^{-\lambda x}\right\} = \lambda \cdot \frac{1}{\lambda + j\omega}.$$

Therefore, the characteristic function is $\Phi_X(j\omega) = \frac{\lambda}{\lambda+j\omega}$.

Example 6.3. Let X and Y be independent, and let

$$f_X(x) = \begin{cases} \lambda e^{-\lambda x}, & x \geq 0, \\ 0, & x < 0, \end{cases} \qquad f_Y(y) = \begin{cases} \lambda e^{-\lambda y}, & y \geq 0, \\ 0, & y < 0. \end{cases}$$

Find the PDF of $Z = X + Y$.

Solution. The characteristic function of X and Y can be found from the Fourier table:

$$\Phi_X(j\omega) = \frac{\lambda}{\lambda + j\omega} \qquad \text{and} \qquad \Phi_Y(j\omega) = \frac{\lambda}{\lambda + j\omega}.$$

Therefore, the characteristic function of Z is

$$\Phi_Z(j\omega) = \Phi_X(j\omega)\Phi_Y(j\omega) = \frac{\lambda^2}{(\lambda + j\omega)^2}.$$

By inverse Fourier transform, we have that

$$f_Z(z) = \mathcal{F}^{-1}\left\{\frac{\lambda^2}{(\lambda + j\omega)^2}\right\} = \lambda^2 z e^{-\lambda z}, \quad z \geq 0.$$

Why $\Phi_X(j\omega)$ but not $M_X(s)$? As we said, the function is not always defined. Recall that the expectation $\mathbb{E}[X]$ exists only when $f_X(x)$ is absolutely integrable, or $\mathbb{E}[|X|] < \infty$. For a characteristic function, the expectation is valid because $\mathbb{E}[|e^{j\omega X}|] = \mathbb{E}[1] = 1$. However, for a function, $\mathbb{E}[|e^{sX}|]$ could be unbounded. To see a counterexample, we consider the Cauchy distribution.

Theorem 6.7. *Consider the Cauchy distribution with PDF*

$$f_X(x) = \frac{1}{\pi(x^2 + 1)}. \tag{6.11}$$

The MGF of X is undefined but the characteristic function is well defined.

Proof. The MGF is

$$M_X(s) = \int_{-\infty}^{\infty} e^{sx} \frac{1}{\pi(x^2+1)} \, dx \geq \int_1^{\infty} e^{sx} \frac{1}{\pi(x^2+1)} \, dx$$

$$\geq \int_1^{\infty} \frac{(sx)^3}{6\pi(x^2+1)} \, dx, \quad \text{because} \quad e^{sx} \geq \frac{(sx)^3}{6}$$

$$\geq \int_1^{\infty} \frac{(sx)^3}{6\pi(2x^2)} \, dx = \frac{s^3}{12\pi} \int_1^{\infty} x \, dx = \infty.$$

Therefore, the MGF is undefined. On the other hand, by the Fourier table we know that

$$\Phi_X(j\omega) = \mathcal{F}\left\{\frac{1}{\pi(x^2+1)}\right\} = e^{-|\omega|}.$$

$\square$

Example 6.4. Let $X_0, X_1, \ldots$ be a sequence of independent random variables with PDF

$$f_{X_k}(x) = \frac{a_k}{\pi(a_k^2 + x^2)}, \quad a_k = \frac{1}{2^{k+1}} \quad \text{for } k = 0, 1, \ldots.$$

Find the PDF of Y, where $Y = \sum_{k=0}^{\infty} X_k$.

Solution. From the Fourier transform table, we know that

$$\frac{a_k}{\pi(a_k^2 + x^2)} = \frac{1}{a_k \pi} \cdot \frac{a_k^2}{(a_k^2 + x^2)} \xleftrightarrow{\mathcal{F}} \frac{1}{a_k \pi} \cdot \pi a_k e^{-a_k|\omega|} = e^{-a_k|\omega|}.$$

The characteristic function of Y is

$$\Phi_Y(j\omega) = \prod_{k=0}^{\infty} \Phi_{X_k}(j\omega) = \exp\left\{-|\omega| \sum_{k=0}^{\infty} a_k\right\}.$$

Since $\sum_{k=0}^{\infty} a_k = \sum_{k=0}^{\infty} \frac{1}{2^{k+1}} = \frac{1}{2} + \frac{1}{4} + \cdots = 1$, the characteristic function becomes $\Phi_Y(j\omega) = e^{-|\omega|}$. The inverse Fourier transform gives us

$$e^{-|\omega|} = \frac{1}{\pi} \cdot \pi e^{-|\omega|} \xleftrightarrow{\mathcal{F}} \frac{1}{\pi} \cdot \frac{1}{1+x^2}.$$

Therefore the PDF of Y is

$$f_Y(y) = \frac{1}{\pi(1+y^2)}.$$

Example 6.5. Two random variables X and Y have the PDFs

$$f_X(x) = \begin{cases} e^{-x}, & x \geq 0, \\ 0, & x < 0, \end{cases} \quad \text{and} \quad f_Y(y) = \begin{cases} e^{-y}, & y \geq 0, \\ 0, & y < 0. \end{cases}$$

Find the PDF of $Z = \max(X,Y) - \min(X,Y)$.

Solution. We first show that

$$Z = \max(X,Y) - \min(X,Y) = |X - Y|.$$

Suppose $X > Y$, then $\max(X,Y) = X$ and $\min(X,Y) = Y$. So $Z = X - Y$. If $X < Y$, then $\max(X,Y) = Y$ and $\min(X,Y) = X$. So $Z = Y - X$. Combining the two cases gives us $Z = |X - Y|$. Now, consider the Fourier transform of the PDFs:

$$e^{-x} \xleftrightarrow{\mathcal{F}} \frac{1}{1+j\omega}.$$

Let $U = X - Y$, and let $Z = |U|$. The characteristic function is

$$\Phi_U(j\omega) = \mathbb{E}[e^{-j\omega(X-Y)}] = \mathbb{E}[e^{-j\omega X}]\mathbb{E}[e^{j\omega Y}]$$

$$= \frac{1}{1+j\omega} \cdot \frac{1}{1-j\omega} = \frac{1}{1+\omega^2} \xleftrightarrow{\mathcal{F}} f_U(u) = \frac{1}{2}e^{-|u|}.$$

With the PDF of U, we can find the CDF of Z:

$$F_Z(z) = \mathbb{P}[Z \leq z] = \mathbb{P}[|U| \leq z]$$

$$= \int_{-z}^{z} f_U(u)\, du$$

$$= \int_{-z}^{z} \frac{1}{2}e^{-|u|}\, du$$

$$= 2\int_{0}^{z} \frac{1}{2}e^{-u}\, du = 1 - e^{-z}.$$

Hence, the PDF is

$$f_Z(z) = \frac{d}{dz}F_Z(z) = e^{-z}.$$

Closing remark. Moment-generating functions and characteristic functions are useful mathematical tools. In this section, we have confined our discussion to using them to compute the sum of two random variables. Later sections and chapters will explain further uses for these functions. For example, we use the MGFs when proving Chernoff's bound and proving the Central Limit Theorem.

6.2 Probability Inequalities

Moment-generating functions and characteristic functions are powerful tools for handling the sum of random variables. We now introduce another set of tools, known as the **probability inequalities,** that allow us to do approximations. We will highlight a few basic probability inequalities in this section.

6.2.1 Union bound

The first inequality is the union bound we had introduced when we discussed the axioms of probabilities. The union bound states the following:

Theorem 6.8 (Union Bound). *Let $A_1, \ldots, A_N$ be a collection of sets. Then*

$$\mathbb{P}\left[\bigcup_{n=1}^{N} A_n\right] \leq \sum_{n=1}^{N} \mathbb{P}[A_n]. \tag{6.12}$$

Proof. We can prove this by induction. First, if $N = 2$,

$$\mathbb{P}[A_1 \cup A_2] = \mathbb{P}[A_1] + \mathbb{P}[A_2] - \mathbb{P}[A_1 \cap A_2] \le \mathbb{P}[A_1] + \mathbb{P}[A_2],$$

because $\mathbb{P}[A_1 \cap A_2]$ is a probability and so it must be non-negative. Thus we have proved the base case. Assume that the statement is true for $N = K$. We need to prove that the statement is also true for $N = K + 1$. To this end, we note that

$$\mathbb{P}\left[\bigcup_{n=1}^{K+1} A_n\right] = \mathbb{P}\left[\left(\bigcup_{n=1}^{K} A_n\right) \cup A_{K+1}\right]$$

$$= \mathbb{P}\left[\bigcup_{n=1}^{K} A_n\right] + \mathbb{P}[A_{K+1}] - \mathbb{P}\left[\left(\bigcup_{n=1}^{K} A_n\right) \cap A_{K+1}\right]$$

$$\le \mathbb{P}\left[\bigcup_{n=1}^{K} A_n\right] + \mathbb{P}[A_{K+1}].$$

Then, according to our hypothesis for $N = K$, it follows that

$$\mathbb{P}\left[\bigcup_{n=1}^{K} A_n\right] \le \sum_{n=1}^{K} \mathbb{P}[A_n].$$

Putting these together,

$$\mathbb{P}\left[\bigcup_{n=1}^{K+1} A_n\right] \le \sum_{n=1}^{K} \mathbb{P}[A_n] + \mathbb{P}[A_{K+1}] = \sum_{n=1}^{K+1} \mathbb{P}[A_n].$$

Therefore, by the principle of induction, we have proved the statement.

$\square$

Remark. The tightness of the union bound depends on the amount of **overlapping** between the events $A_1, \ldots, A_n$, as illustrated in **Figure 6.4**. If the events are disjoint, the union bound is tight. If the events are overlapping significantly, the union is loose. The idea of the union bound is the principle of divide and conquer. We decompose the system into smaller events for a system of n variables and use the union bound to upper-limit the overall probability. If the probability of each event is small, the union bound tells us that the overall probability of the system will also be small.

 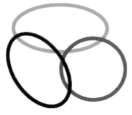

Figure 6.4: Conditions under which the union bound is loose or tight. [Left] The union bound is loose when the sets are overlapping. [Right] The union bound is tight when the sets are (nearly) disjoint.

Example 6.6. Let $X_1, \ldots, X_N$ be a sequence of i.i.d. random variables with CDF $F_{X_n}(x)$ and let $Z = \min(X_1, \ldots, X_N)$. Find an upper bound on the CDF of Z.

Solution. Note that $Z = \min(X_1, \ldots, X_N) \leq z$ is equivalent to at least one of the X_n's being less than z. Thus, we have that

$$Z = \min(X_1, \ldots, X_N) \leq z \iff X_1 \leq z \cup \cdots \cup X_N \leq z.$$

Substituting this result into the CDF,

$$\begin{aligned}
F_Z(z) &= \mathbb{P}[Z \leq z] \\
&= \mathbb{P}[\min(X_1, \ldots, X_N) \leq z] \\
&= \mathbb{P}[X_1 \leq z \cup \cdots \cup X_N \leq z] \\
&\leq \mathbb{P}[X_1 \leq z] + \cdots + \mathbb{P}[X_N \leq z] \\
&= N \cdot F_X(z).
\end{aligned}$$

6.2.2 The Cauchy-Schwarz inequality

The second inequality we study here is the **Cauchy-Schwarz inequality**, which we previously mentioned in Chapter 5. We review it for the sake of completeness.

Theorem 6.9 (Cauchy-Schwarz inequality). *Let X and Y be two random variables. Then*

$$\mathbb{E}[XY]^2 \leq \mathbb{E}[X^2]\mathbb{E}[Y^2]. \tag{6.13}$$

Proof. Let $f(s) = \mathbb{E}[(sX + Y)^2]$ for any real s. Then

$$\begin{aligned}
f(s) &= \mathbb{E}[(sX + Y)^2] \\
&= \mathbb{E}[s^2 X^2 + 2sXY + Y^2] \\
&= \mathbb{E}[X^2]s^2 + 2\mathbb{E}[XY]s + \mathbb{E}[Y^2].
\end{aligned}$$

This is a quadratic equation, and $f(s) \geq 0$ for all s because $\mathbb{E}[(sX + Y)^2] \geq 0$.

Recall that for a quadratic equation $\phi(x) = ax^2 + bx + c$, if the function $\phi(x) \geq 0$ then $b^2 - 4ac \leq 0$. Substituting this result into our problem, we show that

$$(2\mathbb{E}[XY])^2 - 4\mathbb{E}[X^2]\mathbb{E}[Y^2] \leq 0.$$

This implies that

$$\mathbb{E}[XY]^2 \leq \mathbb{E}[X^2]\mathbb{E}[Y^2],$$

which completes the proof. $\square$

Remark. As shown in Chapter 5, the Cauchy-Schwarz inequality is useful in analyzing $\mathbb{E}[XY]$. For example, we can use the Cauchy-Schwarz inequality to prove that the correlation coefficient ρ is bounded between -1 and 1.

6.2.3 Jensen's inequality

Our next inequality is **Jensen's inequality**. To motivate the inequality, we recall that

$$\text{Var}[X] = \mathbb{E}[X^2] - \mathbb{E}[X]^2.$$

Since $\text{Var}[X] \geq 0$ for any X, it follows that

$$\underbrace{\mathbb{E}[X^2]}_{=\mathbb{E}[g(X)]} \quad \geq \quad \underbrace{\mathbb{E}[X]^2}_{=g(\mathbb{E}[X])}. \tag{6.14}$$

Jensen's inequality is a generalization of the above result by recognizing that the inequality does not only hold for the function $g(X) = X^2$ but also for any **convex** function g. The theorem is stated as follows:

Theorem 6.10 (Jensen's inequality). *Let X be a random variable, and let $g : \mathbb{R} \to \mathbb{R}$ be a **convex** function. Then*

$$\mathbb{E}[g(X)] \geq g(\mathbb{E}[X]). \tag{6.15}$$

If the function g is **concave**, then the inequality sign is flipped: $\mathbb{E}[g(X)] \leq g(\mathbb{E}[X])$. The way to remember this result is to remember that $\mathbb{E}[X^2] - \mathbb{E}[X]^2 = \text{Var}[X] \geq 0$.

Now, what is a convex function? Informally, a function g is **convex** if, when we pick any two points on the function and connect them with a straight line, the line will be above the function for that segment. This definition is illustrated in **Figure 6.5**. Consider an interval $[x, y]$, and the line segment connecting $g(x)$ and $g(y)$. If the function $g(\cdot)$ is convex, then the entire line segment should be above the curve.

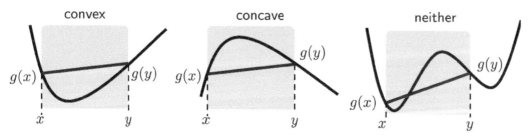

Figure 6.5: Illustration of a convex function, a concave function, and a function that is neither convex nor concave.

The definition of a convex function essentially follows the above picture:

Definition 6.4. *A function g is **convex** if*

$$g(\lambda x + (1 - \lambda)y) \leq \lambda g(x) + (1 - \lambda)g(y), \tag{6.16}$$

for any $0 \leq \lambda \leq 1$.

Here λ represents a "sweeping" constant that goes from 0 to 1. When $\lambda = 1$ then $\lambda x + (1 - \lambda)y$ simplifies to x, and when $\lambda = 0$ then $\lambda x + (1 - \lambda)y$ simplifies to y.

The definition is easy to understand. The left-hand side $g(\lambda x + (1-\lambda)y)$ is the function evaluated at any points in the interval $[x, y]$. The right-hand side is the red straight line we plotted in **Figure 6.5**. It connects the two points $g(x)$ and $g(y)$. Convexity means that the red line is entirely above the curve.

For twice-differentiable 1D functions, convexity can be described by the curvature of the function. A function is convex if

$$g''(x) \geq 0. \tag{6.17}$$

This is self-explanatory because if the curvature is non-negative for all x, then the slope of g has to keep increasing.

Example 6.7. The following functions are convex or concave:

- $g(x) = \log x$ is concave, because $g'(x) = \frac{1}{x}$ and $g''(x) = -\frac{1}{x^2} \leq 0$ for all x.
- $g(x) = x^2$ is convex, because $g'(x) = 2x$ and $g''(x) = 2$ is positive.
- $g(x) = e^{-x}$ is convex, because $g'(x) = -e^{-x}$ and $g''(x) = e^{-x} \geq 0$.

Why is Jensen inequality valid for a convex function? Consider the illustration in **Figure 6.6**. Suppose we have a random variable X taking some PDF $f_X(x)$. There is a convex function $g(\cdot)$ that maps the random variable X to $g(X)$. Since $g(\cdot)$ is convex, a PDF like the one we see in **Figure 6.6** will become skewed. (You can map the left tail to the new left tail, the peak to the new peak, and the right tail to the new right tail.) As you can see from the figure, the new random variable $g(X)$ has a mean $\mathbb{E}[g(X)]$ that is greater than the mapped old mean $g(\mathbb{E}[X])$. Jensen's inequality captures this phenomenon by stating that $\mathbb{E}[g(X)] \geq g(\mathbb{E}[X])$ for any convex function $g(\cdot)$.

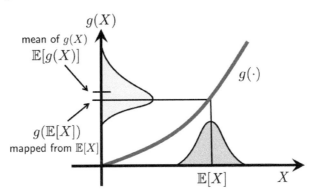

Figure 6.6: Jensen's inequality states that if there is a convex function $g(\cdot)$ that maps a random variable X to a new random variable $g(X)$, the new mean $\mathbb{E}[g(X)]$ will be greater than the mapped old mean $g(\mathbb{E}[X])$.

Proving Jensen's inequality is straightforward for a two-state discrete random variable. Define a random variable X with states x and y. The probabilities for these two states are $\mathbb{P}[X = x] = \lambda$ and $\mathbb{P}[X = y] = 1 - \lambda$. Then

$$\mathbb{E}[X] = \sum_{x' \in \{x,y\}} x' p_X(x') = \lambda x + (1 - \lambda)y.$$

Now, let $g(\cdot)$ be a convex function. We know from the expectation that

$$\mathbb{E}[g(X)] = \sum_{x' \in \{x,y\}} g(x')p_X(x') = g(x)\lambda + (1-\lambda)g(y).$$

By convexity of the function $g(\cdot)$, it follows that

$$\underbrace{g(\lambda x + (1-\lambda)y)}_{=g(\mathbb{E}[X])} \leq \underbrace{\lambda f(x) + (1-\lambda)g(y)}_{=\mathbb{E}[g(X)]},$$

where in the underbrace we substitute the definitions using the expectation. Therefore, for any two-state discrete random variables, the proof of Jensen's inequality follows directly from the convexity. If the discrete random variable takes more than two states, we can prove the theorem by induction. For continuous random variables, we can prove the theorem using the following approach.

> You may skip the proof of Jensen's inequality if this is your first time reading the book.

Here we present an alternative proof of Jensen's inequality that does not require proof by induction. The idea is to recognize that if the function g is convex we can find a tangent line $L(X) = aX + b$ at the point $\mathbb{E}[X]$ that is uniformly lower than $g(X)$, i.e., $g(X) \geq L(X)$ for all X. Then we can prove the result with a simple geometric argument. **Figure 6.7** illustrates this idea.

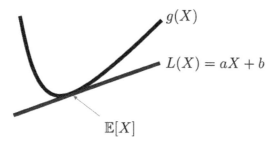

Figure 6.7: Geometric illustration of the proof of Jensen's inequality. Suppose $g(\cdot)$ is a convex function. For any point X on $g(\cdot)$, we can find a tangent line $L(X) = aX + b$. Since the black curve is always above the tangent, it follows that $\mathbb{E}[g(X)] \geq \mathbb{E}[L(X)]$ for any X. Also, note that at a particular point $\mathbb{E}[X]$, the black curve and the red line touch, and so we have $L(\mathbb{E}[X]) = g(\mathbb{E}[X])$.

Proof of Jensen's inequality. Consider $L(X)$ as defined above. Since g is convex, $g(X) \geq L(X)$ for all X. Therefore,

$$\begin{aligned}
\mathbb{E}[g(X)] &\geq \mathbb{E}[L(X)] \\
&= \mathbb{E}[aX + b] \\
&= a\mathbb{E}[X] + b \\
&= L(\mathbb{E}[X]) = g(\mathbb{E}[X]),
\end{aligned}$$

where the last equality holds because L is a tangent line to g where they meet at $\mathbb{E}[X]$. $\square$

What are (a, b) in the proof? By Taylor expansion,

$$g(X) \approx g(\mathbb{E}[X]) + g'(\mathbb{E}[X])(X - \mathbb{E}[X])$$
$$\stackrel{\text{def}}{=} L(X).$$

Therefore, if we want to be precise, then $a = g'(\mathbb{E}[X])$ and $b = g(\mathbb{E}[X]) - g'(\mathbb{E}[X])\mathbb{E}[X]$.

The end of the proof.

Example 6.8. By Jensen's inequality, we have that

(a) $\mathbb{E}[X^2] \geq \mathbb{E}[X]^2$, because $g(x) = x^2$ is convex.

(b) $\mathbb{E}\left[\frac{1}{X}\right] \geq \frac{1}{\mathbb{E}[X]}$, because $g(x) = \frac{1}{x}$ is convex.

(c) $\mathbb{E}[\log X] \leq \log \mathbb{E}[X]$, because $g(x) = \log x$ is concave.

6.2.4 Markov's inequality

Our next inequality, **Markov's inequality**, is an elementary inequality that links probability and expectation.

Theorem 6.11 (Markov's inequality). *Let $X \geq 0$ be a non-negative random variable. Then, for any $\varepsilon > 0$, we have*

$$\mathbb{P}[X \geq \varepsilon] \leq \frac{\mathbb{E}[X]}{\varepsilon}. \tag{6.18}$$

Markov's inequality concerns the **tail** of the random variable. As illustrated in **Figure 6.8**, $\mathbb{P}[X \geq \varepsilon]$ measures the probability that the random variable takes a value greater than ε. Markov's inequality asserts that this probability $\mathbb{P}[X \geq \varepsilon]$ is upper-bounded by the ratio $\mathbb{E}[X]/\varepsilon$. This result is useful because it relates the probability and the expectation. In many problems the probability $\mathbb{P}[X \geq \varepsilon]$ could be difficult to evaluate if the PDF is complicated. The expectation, on the other hand, is usually easier to evaluate.

Proof. Consider $\varepsilon\mathbb{P}[X \geq \varepsilon]$. It follows that

$$\varepsilon\mathbb{P}[X \geq \varepsilon] = \int_\varepsilon^\infty \varepsilon\, f_X(x)\, dx \leq \int_\varepsilon^\infty x f_X(x)\, dx,$$

where the inequality is valid because for any $x \geq \varepsilon$ the integrand (which is non-negative) will always increase (or at least not decrease). It then follows that

$$\int_\varepsilon^\infty x f_X(x)\, dx \leq \int_0^\infty x f_X(x)\, dx = \mathbb{E}[X]. \qquad \square$$

A pictorial interpretation of Markov's inequality is shown in **Figure 6.9**. For $X > 0$, it is not difficult to show that $\mathbb{E}[X] = \int_0^\infty 1 - F_X(x)\, dx$. Then, in the CDF plot, we see that $\varepsilon \cdot \mathbb{P}[X \geq \varepsilon]$ is a rectangle covering the top left corner. This area is clearly smaller than the area covered by the function $1 - F_X(x)$.

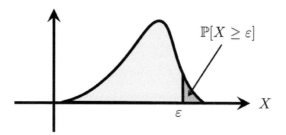

Figure 6.8: Markov's inequality provides an upper bound to the tail of a random variable. The inequality states that the probability $\mathbb{P}[X \geq \varepsilon]$ is upper bounded by the ratio $\mathbb{E}[X]/\varepsilon$.

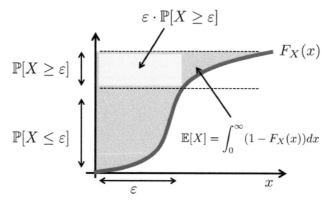

Figure 6.9: The proof of Markov's inequality follows from the fact that $\varepsilon \cdot \mathbb{P}[X \geq \varepsilon]$ occupies the top left corner marked by the yellow rectangle. The expectation is the area above the CDF so that $\mathbb{E}[X] = \int_0^\infty 1 - F_X(x)\, dx$. Since the yellow rectangle is smaller than the orange shaded area, it follows that $\varepsilon \cdot \mathbb{P}[X \geq \varepsilon] \leq \mathbb{E}[X]$, which is Markov's inequality.

Practice Exercise 6.4. Prove that if $X > 0$, then $\mathbb{E}[X] = \int_0^\infty 1 - F_X(x)\, dx$.

Solution. We start from the right-hand side:

$$\int_0^\infty 1 - F_X(x)\, dx = \int_0^\infty 1 - \mathbb{P}[X \leq x]\, dx$$

$$= \int_0^\infty \mathbb{P}[X \geq x]\, dx$$

$$= \int_0^\infty \int_x^\infty f_X(t)\, dt\, dx$$

$$= \int_0^\infty \int_0^t f_X(t)\, dx\, dt$$

$$= \int_0^\infty t f_X(t)\, dt = \mathbb{E}[X].$$

The change in the integration order is illustrated below.

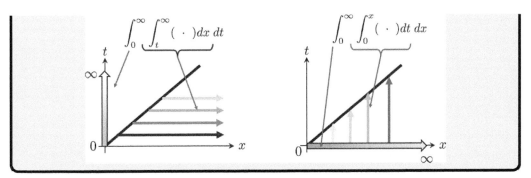

How tight is Markov's inequality? It is possible to create a random variable such that the equality is met (see Exercise 6.14). However, in general, the estimate provided by the upper bound is not tight. Here is an example.

Practice Exercise 6.5. Let $X \sim \text{Uniform}(0, 4)$. Verify Markov's inequality for $\mathbb{P}[X \geq 2]$, $\mathbb{P}[X \geq 3]$ and $\mathbb{P}[X \geq 4]$.

Solution. First, we observe that $\mathbb{E}[X] = 2$. Then

$$\mathbb{P}[X \geq 2] = 0.5, \qquad \frac{\mathbb{E}[X]}{2} = 1,$$

$$\mathbb{P}[X \geq 3] = 0.25, \qquad \frac{\mathbb{E}[X]}{3} = 0.67,$$

$$\mathbb{P}[X \geq 4] = 0, \qquad \frac{\mathbb{E}[X]}{4} = 0.5.$$

Therefore, although the upper bounds are all valid, they are very loose.

If Markov's inequality is not tight, why is it useful? It turns out that while Markov's inequality is not tight, its variations can be powerful. We will come back to this point when we discuss Chernoff's bound.

6.2.5 Chebyshev's inequality

The next inequality is a simple extension of Markov's inequality. The result is known as Chebyshev's inequality.

Theorem 6.12 (Chebyshev's inequality). *Let X be a random variable with mean μ. Then for any $\varepsilon > 0$ we have*

$$\mathbb{P}[|X - \mu| \geq \varepsilon] \leq \frac{\text{Var}[X]}{\varepsilon^2}. \tag{6.19}$$

The tail measured by Chebyshev's inequality is illustrated in **Figure 6.10**. Since the event $|X - \mu| \geq \varepsilon$ involves an absolute value, the probability measures the two-sided tail. Chebyshev's inequality states that this tail probability is upper-bounded by $\text{Var}[X]/\varepsilon^2$.

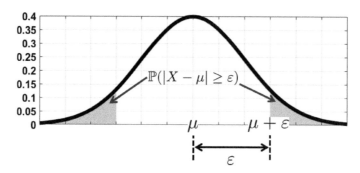

Figure 6.10: Chebyshev's inequality states that the two-sided tail probability $\mathbb{P}[|X - \mu| \geq \varepsilon]$ is upper-bounded by $\mathrm{Var}[X]/\varepsilon^2$

Proof. We apply Markov's inequality to show that

$$\mathbb{P}[|X - \mu| \geq \varepsilon] = \mathbb{P}[(X - \mu)^2 \geq \varepsilon^2]$$
$$\leq \frac{\mathbb{E}[(X - \mu)^2]}{\varepsilon^2} = \frac{\mathrm{Var}[X]}{\varepsilon^2}.$$

$\square$

An alternative form of Chebyshev's inequality is obtained by letting $\varepsilon = k\sigma$. In this case, we have

$$\mathbb{P}[|X - \mu| \geq k\sigma] \leq \frac{\sigma^2}{k^2\sigma^2} = \frac{1}{k^2}.$$

Therefore, if a random variable is k times the standard deviation away from the mean, then the probability bound drops to $1/k^2$.

Practice Exercise 6.6. Let $X \sim \mathrm{Uniform}(0, 2\sqrt{2})$. Find the bound of Chebyshev's inequality for the probability $\mathbb{P}[|X - \mu| \geq 1]$.

Solution. Note that $\mathbb{E}[X] = 2$ and $\sigma^2 = (2\sqrt{2})^2/12 = 2/3$. Therefore, we have

$$\mathbb{P}[|X - \mu| \geq 1] \leq \frac{\sigma^2}{\varepsilon^2} = \frac{2}{3},$$

which is a valid upper bound, but not very useful.

Practice Exercise 6.7. Let $X \sim \mathrm{Exponential}(1)$. Find the bound of Chebyshev's inequality for the probability $\mathbb{P}[X \geq \varepsilon]$.

Solution. Note that $\mathbb{E}[X] = 1$ and $\sigma^2 = 1$. Thus we have

$$\mathbb{P}[X \geq \varepsilon] = \mathbb{P}[X - \mu \geq \varepsilon - \mu] \leq \mathbb{P}[|X - \mu| \geq \varepsilon - \mu]$$
$$\leq \frac{\sigma^2}{(\varepsilon - \mu)^2} = \frac{1}{(\varepsilon - 1)^2}.$$

We can compare this with the exact probability, which is

$$\mathbb{P}[X \geq \varepsilon] = 1 - F_X(\varepsilon) = e^{-\varepsilon}.$$

Again, the estimate given by Chebyshev's inequality is acceptable but too conservative.

Corollary 6.2. *Let $X_1, \ldots, X_N$ be i.i.d. random variables with mean $\mathbb{E}[X_n] = \mu$ and variance $\mathrm{Var}[X_n] = \sigma^2$. Let $\overline{X}_N = \frac{1}{N} \sum_{n=1}^{N} X_n$ be the sample mean. Then*

$$\mathbb{P}\left[\left| \overline{X}_N - \mu \right| > \epsilon \right] \leq \frac{\sigma^2}{N\epsilon^2}. \qquad (6.20)$$

Proof. We can first show that $\mathbb{E}[\overline{X}_N] = \mu$ and $\mathrm{Var}[\overline{X}_N]$ satisfies

$$\mathrm{Var}[\overline{X}_N] = \frac{1}{N^2} \sum_{n=1}^{N} \mathrm{Var}[X_n] = \frac{\sigma^2}{N}.$$

Then by Chebyshev's inequality,

$$\mathbb{P}\left[\left| \overline{X}_N - \mu \right| > \epsilon \right] \leq \frac{\mathrm{Var}[\overline{X}_N]}{\epsilon^2} = \frac{\sigma^2}{N\epsilon^2}.$$

$\square$

The consequence of this corollary is that the upper bound $\sigma^2 N / \epsilon^2$ will converge to zero as $N \to \infty$. Therefore, the probability of getting the event $\{ |\overline{X}_N - \mu| > \epsilon \}$ is vanishing. It means that the sample average $\overline{X}_N$ is converging to the true population mean μ, in the sense that the probability of failing is shrinking.

6.2.6 Chernoff's bound

We now introduce a powerful inequality or a set of general procedures that gives us some highly useful inequalities. The idea is named for Herman Chernoff, although it was actually due to his colleague Herman Rubin.

Theorem 6.13 (Chernoff's bound). *Let X be a random variable. Then, for any $\varepsilon \geq 0$, we have that*

$$\mathbb{P}[X \geq \varepsilon] \leq e^{-\varphi(\varepsilon)}, \qquad (6.21)$$

where[a]

$$\varphi(\varepsilon) = \max_{s>0} \left\{ s\varepsilon - \log M_X(s) \right\}, \qquad (6.22)$$

and $M_X(s)$ is the moment-generating function.

---
[a]$\varphi(\varepsilon)$ is called the Fenchel-Legendre dual function of $\log M_X$. See references [6-14].

Proof. There are two tricks in the proof of Chernoff's bound. The first trick is a nonlinear transformation. Since e^{sx} is an increasing function for any $s > 0$ and x, we have that

$$\mathbb{P}[X \geq \varepsilon] = \mathbb{P}[e^{sX} \geq e^{s\varepsilon}]$$
$$\overset{(a)}{\leq} \frac{\mathbb{E}[e^{sX}]}{e^{s\varepsilon}}$$
$$\overset{(b)}{=} e^{-s\varepsilon} M_X(s)$$
$$= e^{-s\varepsilon + \log M_X(s)},$$

where the inequality (a) is due to Markov's inequality. Step (b) just uses the definition of MGF that $\mathbb{E}[e^{sX}] = M_X(s)$.

Now for the second trick. Note that the above result holds for all s. That means it must also hold for the s that minimizes $e^{-s\varepsilon + \log M_X(s)}$. This implies that

$$\mathbb{P}[X \geq \varepsilon] \leq \min_{s>0} \left\{ e^{-s\varepsilon + \log M_X(s)} \right\}.$$

Again, since e^x is increasing, the minimizer of the above probability is also the maximizer of this function:

$$\varphi(\varepsilon) = \max_{s>0} \left\{ s\varepsilon - \log M_X(s) \right\}.$$

Thus, we conclude that $\mathbb{P}[X \geq \varepsilon] \leq e^{-\varphi(\varepsilon)}$.

$\square$

6.2.7 Comparing Chernoff and Chebyshev

Let's consider an example of how Chernoff's bound can be useful.

Suppose that we have a random variable $X \sim \text{Gaussian}(0, \sigma^2/N)$. The number N can be regarded as the number of samples. For example, if $Y_1, \ldots, Y_N$ are N Gaussian random variables with mean 0 and variance σ^2, then the average $X = \frac{1}{N} \sum_{n=1}^{N} Y_n$ will have mean 0 and variance σ^2/N. Therefore, as N grows, the variance of X will become smaller and smaller.

First, since the random variable is Gaussian, we can show the following:

> **Lemma 6.1.** *Let $X \sim \text{Gaussian}(0, \frac{\sigma^2}{N})$ be a Gaussian random variable. Then, for any $\varepsilon > 0$,*
>
> $$\mathbb{P}[X \geq \varepsilon] = 1 - \Phi\left(\frac{\sqrt{N}\varepsilon}{\sigma}\right), \tag{6.23}$$
>
> *where Φ is the standard Gaussian's CDF.*

Note that this is the **exact** result: If you tell me ε, N, and σ, then the probability $\mathbb{P}[X \geq \varepsilon]$ is exactly the one shown on the right-hand side. No approximation, no randomness.

Proof. Since X is Gaussian, the probability is

$$\mathbb{P}[X \geq \varepsilon] = \int_\varepsilon^\infty \frac{1}{\sqrt{2\pi(\sigma^2/N)}} \exp\left\{-\frac{x^2}{2(\sigma^2/N)}\right\} dx$$

$$= 1 - \int_{-\infty}^\varepsilon \frac{1}{\sqrt{2\pi(\sigma^2/N)}} \exp\left\{-\frac{x^2}{2(\sigma^2/N)}\right\} dx$$

$$= 1 - \int_{-\infty}^{\frac{\varepsilon}{\sqrt{\sigma^2/N}}} \frac{1}{\sqrt{2\pi}} \exp\left\{-\frac{x^2}{2}\right\} dx$$

$$= 1 - \Phi\left(\frac{\varepsilon}{\sqrt{\sigma^2/N}}\right) = 1 - \Phi\left(\frac{\sqrt{N}\varepsilon}{\sigma}\right).$$

$\square$

Let us compute the bound given by Chebyshev's inequality.

Lemma 6.2. *Let $X \sim Gaussian(0, \frac{\sigma^2}{N})$ be a Gaussian random variable. Then, for any $\varepsilon > 0$, Chebyshev's inequality implies that*

$$\mathbb{P}[X \geq \varepsilon] \leq \frac{\sigma^2}{N\varepsilon^2}. \tag{6.24}$$

Proof. We apply Chebyshev's inequality by assuming that $\mu = 0$:

$$\mathbb{P}[X \geq \varepsilon] = \mathbb{P}[X - \mu \geq \varepsilon - \mu] \leq \mathbb{P}[|X - \mu| \geq \varepsilon - \mu]$$

$$\leq \frac{\mathbb{E}[(X - \mu)^2]}{(\varepsilon - \mu)^2} = \frac{\sigma^2}{N\varepsilon^2}.$$

$\square$

We now compute Chernoff's bound.

Theorem 6.14. *Let $X \sim Gaussian(0, \frac{\sigma^2}{N})$ be a Gaussian random variable. Then, for any $\varepsilon > 0$, Chernoff's bound implies that*

$$\mathbb{P}[X \geq \varepsilon] \leq \exp\left\{-\frac{\varepsilon^2 N}{2\sigma^2}\right\}. \tag{6.25}$$

Proof. The MGF of a zero-mean Gaussian random variable with variance σ^2/N is $M_X(s) = \exp\left\{\frac{\sigma^2 s^2}{2N}\right\}$. Therefore, the function φ can be written as

$$\varphi(\varepsilon) = \max_{s>0}\left\{s\varepsilon - \log M_X(s)\right\}$$

$$= \max_{s>0}\left\{s\varepsilon - \frac{\sigma^2 s^2}{2N}\right\}.$$

To maximize the function we take the derivative and set it to zero. This yields

$$\frac{d}{ds}\left\{s\varepsilon - \frac{\sigma^2 s^2}{2N}\right\} = 0 \quad \Rightarrow \quad s^* = \frac{N\varepsilon}{\sigma^2}.$$

Note that this s^* is a maximizer because $s\varepsilon - \frac{\sigma^2 s^2}{2N}$ is a concave function.

Substituting s^* into $\varphi(\varepsilon)$,

$$\varphi(\varepsilon) = \max_{s>0} \left\{ \frac{s\varepsilon - \sigma^2 s^2}{2N} \right\}$$

$$= s^*\varepsilon - \frac{\sigma^2 (s^*)^2}{2N} = \left(\frac{N\varepsilon}{\sigma^2} \right)\varepsilon - \frac{\sigma^2}{2N}\left(\frac{N\varepsilon}{\sigma^2} \right)^2 = \frac{\varepsilon^2 N}{2\sigma^2},$$

and hence

$$\mathbb{P}[X \geq \varepsilon] \leq e^{-\varphi(\varepsilon)} = \exp\left\{ -\frac{\varepsilon^2 N}{2\sigma^2} \right\}.$$

□

Figure 6.11 shows the comparison between the exact probability, the bound provided by Chebyshev's inequality, and Chernoff's bound:

- **Exact:** $\mathbb{P}[X \geq \varepsilon] = 1 - \Phi\left(\frac{\sqrt{N}\varepsilon}{\sigma} \right)$.

- **Chebyshev:** $\mathbb{P}[X \geq \varepsilon] \leq \frac{\sigma^2}{N\varepsilon^2}$,

- **Chernoff:** $\mathbb{P}[X \geq \varepsilon] \leq \exp\left\{ -\frac{\varepsilon^2 N}{2\sigma^2} \right\}$.

In this numerical experiment, we set $\varepsilon = 0.1$, and $\sigma = 1$. We vary the number N. As we can see from the figure, the bound provided by Chebyshev is valid but very loose. It does not even capture the tail as N grows. On the other hand, Chernoff's bound is reasonably tight. However, one should note that the tightness of Chernoff is only valid for **large** N. When N is small, it is possible to construct random variables such that Chebyshev is tighter.

The MATLAB code used to generate this plot is illustrated below.

```
% MATLAB code to compare the probability bounds
epsilon = 0.1;
sigma   = 1;
N       = logspace(1,3.9,50);
p_exact = 1-normcdf(sqrt(N)*epsilon/sigma);
p_cheby = sigma^2./(epsilon^2*N);
p_chern = exp(-epsilon^2*N/(2*sigma^2));

loglog(N, p_exact, '-o', 'Color', [1 0.5 0], 'LineWidth', 2); hold on;
loglog(N, p_cheby, '-', 'Color', [0.2 0.7 0.1], 'LineWidth', 2);
loglog(N, p_chern, '-', 'Color', [0.2 0.0 0.8], 'LineWidth', 2);
```

What could go wrong if we insist on using Chebyshev's inequality? Consider the following example.

Example 6.9. Let $X \sim \text{Gaussian}(0, \sigma^2/N)$. Suppose that we want the probability to be no greater than a confidence level of α:

$$\mathbb{P}[X \geq \varepsilon] \leq \alpha.$$

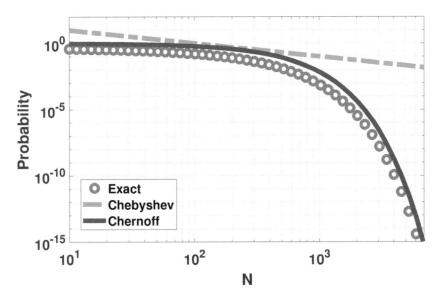

Figure 6.11: Comparison between Chernoff's bound and Chebyshev's bound. The random variable we use is $X \sim \text{Gaussian}(0, \sigma^2/N)$. As N grows, we show the probability bounds predicted by the two methods.

Let $\alpha = 0.05$, $\varepsilon = 0.1$, and $\sigma = 1$. Find the N using (i) Chebyshev's inequality and (ii) Chernoff's inequality.

Solution: (i) Chebyshev's inequality implies that

$$\mathbb{P}[X \geq \varepsilon] \leq \frac{\sigma^2}{N\varepsilon^2} \leq \alpha,$$

which means that

$$N \geq \frac{\sigma^2}{\alpha\varepsilon^2}.$$

If we plug in $\alpha = 0.05$, $\varepsilon = 0.1$, and $\sigma = 1$, then $N \geq 2000$.

(ii) For Chernoff's inequality, it holds that

$$\mathbb{P}[X \geq \varepsilon] \leq \exp\left\{-\frac{\varepsilon^2 N}{2\sigma^2}\right\} \leq \alpha,$$

which means that

$$N \geq -\frac{2\sigma^2}{\varepsilon^2}\log\alpha$$

Plugging in $\alpha = 0.05$, $\varepsilon = 0.1$, and $\sigma = 1$, we have that $N \geq 600$. This is more than 3 times smaller than the one predicted by Chebyshev's inequality. Which one is correct? Both are correct but Chebyshev's inequality is overly conservative. If $N \geq 600$ can make $\mathbb{P}[X \geq \varepsilon] \leq \alpha$, then certainly $N \geq 2000$ will work too. However, $N \geq 2000$ is too loose.

6.2.8 Hoeffding's inequality

Chernoff's bound can be used to derive many powerful inequalities. Here we present an inequality for bounded random variables. This result is known as Hoeffding's inequality.

> **Theorem 6.15 (Hoeffding's inequality).** *Let $X_1, \ldots, X_N$ be i.i.d. random variables with $0 \leq X_n \leq 1$, and $\mathbb{E}[X_n] = \mu$. Then*
>
> $$\mathbb{P}\left[\left|\overline{X}_N - \mu\right| > \epsilon\right] \leq 2e^{-2\epsilon^2 N}, \tag{6.26}$$
>
> *where $\overline{X}_N = \frac{1}{N}\sum_{n=1}^{N} X_n$.*

> You may skip the proof of Hoeffding's inequality if this is your first time reading the book.

Proof. (Hoeffding's inequality) First, we show that

$$\mathbb{P}\left[\overline{X}_N - \mu > \epsilon\right] = \mathbb{P}\left[\frac{1}{N}\sum_{n=1}^{N} X_n - \mu > \epsilon\right] = \mathbb{P}\left[\sum_{n=1}^{N}(X_n - \mu) > N\epsilon\right]$$

$$= \mathbb{P}\left[e^{s\sum_{n=1}^{N}(X_n - \mu)} \geq e^{s\epsilon N}\right]$$

$$\leq \frac{\mathbb{E}[e^{s\sum_{n=1}^{N}(X_n - \mu)}]}{e^{s\epsilon N}} = \left(\frac{\mathbb{E}[e^{s(X_n - \mu)}]}{e^{s\epsilon}}\right)^N.$$

Let $Z_n = X_n - \mu$. Then $-\mu \leq Z_n \leq 1 - \mu$. At this point we use Hoeffding Lemma (see below) that $\mathbb{E}[e^{sZ_n}] \leq e^{\frac{s^2}{8}}$ because $b - a = (1 - \mu) - (-\mu) = 1$. Thus,

$$\mathbb{P}\left[\overline{X}_N - \mu > \epsilon\right] \leq \left(\frac{\mathbb{E}[e^{sZ_n}]}{e^{s\epsilon}}\right)^N \leq \left(\frac{e^{\frac{s^2}{8}}}{e^{s\epsilon}}\right)^N = e^{\frac{s^2 N}{8} - s\epsilon N}, \qquad \forall s.$$

This result holds for all s, and thus it holds for the s that minimizes the right-hand side. This implies that

$$\mathbb{P}\left[\overline{X}_N - \mu > \epsilon\right] \leq \min_s \left\{\exp\left\{\frac{s^2 N}{8} - s\epsilon N\right\}\right\}.$$

Minimizing the exponent gives $\frac{d}{ds}\left\{\frac{s^2 N}{8} - s\epsilon N\right\} = \frac{sN}{4} - \epsilon N = 0$. Thus we have $s = 4\epsilon$. Hence,

$$\mathbb{P}\left[\overline{X}_N - \mu > \epsilon\right] \leq \exp\left\{\frac{(4\epsilon)^2 N}{8} - (4\epsilon)\epsilon N\right\} = e^{-2\epsilon^2 N}.$$

By symmetry, $\mathbb{P}\left[\overline{X}_N - \mu < -\epsilon\right] \leq e^{-2\epsilon^2 N}$. Then by union bound we show that

$$\mathbb{P}\left[\left|\overline{X}_N - \mu\right| > \epsilon\right] = \mathbb{P}\left[\overline{X}_N - \mu > \epsilon\right] + \mathbb{P}\left[\overline{X}_N - \mu < -\epsilon\right]$$

$$\leq e^{-2\epsilon^2 N} + e^{-2\epsilon^2 N}$$

$$= 2e^{-2\epsilon^2 N}. \qquad \square$$

Lemma 6.3 (**Hoeffding's lemma**). *Let* $a \leq X \leq b$ *be a random variable with* $\mathbb{E}[X] = 0$. *Then*

$$M_X(s) \stackrel{\text{def}}{=} \mathbb{E}\left[e^{sX}\right] \leq \exp\left\{\frac{s^2(b-a)^2}{8}\right\}. \tag{6.27}$$

Proof. Since $a \leq X \leq b$, we can write X as a linear combination of a and b:

$$X = \lambda b + (1 - \lambda)a,$$

where $\lambda = \frac{X-a}{b-a}$. Since $\exp(\cdot)$ is a convex function, it follows that $e^{\lambda b + (1-\lambda)a} \leq \lambda e^b + (1-\lambda)e^a$. (Recall that h is convex if $h(\lambda x + (1 - \lambda)y) \leq \lambda h(x) + (1 - \lambda)h(y)$.) Therefore, we have

$$e^{sX} \leq \lambda e^{sb} + (1 - \lambda)e^{sa}$$
$$= \frac{X - a}{b - a}e^{sb} + \frac{b - X}{b - a}e^{sa}.$$

Taking expectations on both sides of the equation,

$$\mathbb{E}[e^{sX}] \leq \frac{-a}{b - a}e^{sb} + \frac{b}{b - a}e^{sa},$$

because $\mathbb{E}[X] = 0$. Now, if we let $\theta = -\frac{a}{b-a}$, then

$$\frac{-a}{b - a}e^{sb} + \frac{b}{b - a}e^{sa} = \theta e^{sb} + (1 - \theta)e^{sa}$$

$$= e^{sa}\left(1 - \theta + \theta e^{s(b-a)}\right) = \left(1 - \theta + \theta e^{s(b-a)}\right)e^{-s\theta(b-a)}$$

$$= (1 - \theta + \theta e^u)\, e^{-\theta u} = e^{-\theta u + \log(1 - \theta + \theta e^u)},$$

where we let $u = s(b - a)$. This can be simplified as $\mathbb{E}[e^{sX}] \leq \mathbb{E}[e^{\phi(u)}]$ by defining

$$\phi(u) = -\theta u + \log(1 - \theta + \theta e^u).$$

The final step is to approximate $\phi(u)$. To this end, we use Taylor approximation:

$$\phi(u) = \phi(0) + u\phi'(0) + \frac{u^2}{2}\phi''(\xi),$$

for some $\xi \in [a, b]$. Since $\phi(0) = 0$, $\phi'(0) = 0$, and $\phi''(u) \leq \frac{1}{4}$ for all u, it follows that

$$\phi(u) = \frac{u^2}{2}\phi''(\xi) \leq \frac{u^2}{8} = \frac{s^2(b-a)^2}{8}. \qquad \square$$

End of the proof.

349

What is so special about the Hoeffding's inequality?

- Since Hoeffding's inequality is derived from Chernoff's bound, it inherits the tightness. Hoeffding's inequality is much stronger than Chebyshev's inequality in bounding the tail distributions.

- Hoeffding's inequality is one of the few inequalities that do not require $\mathbb{E}[X]$ and $\mathrm{Var}[X]$ on the right-hand side.

- A downside of the inequality is that boundedness is not always easy to satisfy. For example, if X_n is a Gaussian random variable, Hoeffding does not apply. There are more advanced inequalities for situations like these.

Interpreting Hoeffding's inequality. One way to interpret Hoeffding's inequality is to write the equation as

$$\mathbb{P}\big[\,|\overline{X}_N - \mu| > \epsilon\big] \leq \underbrace{2e^{-2\epsilon^2 N}}_{\delta},$$

which is equivalent to

$$\mathbb{P}\big[\,|\overline{X}_N - \mu| \leq \epsilon\big] \geq 1 - \delta.$$

This means that with a probability at least $1 - \delta$, we have

$$\overline{X}_N - \epsilon \leq \mu \leq \overline{X}_N + \epsilon.$$

If we let $\delta = 2e^{-2\epsilon^2 N}$, this becomes

$$\overline{X}_N - \sqrt{\frac{1}{2N}\log\frac{2}{\delta}} \leq \mu \leq \overline{X}_N + \sqrt{\frac{1}{2N}\log\frac{2}{\delta}}. \tag{6.28}$$

This inequality is a **confidence interval** (see Chapter 9). It says that with probability at least $1 - \delta$, the interval $[\overline{X}_N - \epsilon,\ \overline{X}_N + \epsilon]$ includes the true population mean μ.

There are two questions one can ask about the confidence interval:

- Given N and δ, what is the confidence interval? Equation (6.28) tells us that if we know N, to achieve a probability of at least $1 - \delta$ the confidence interval will follow Equation (6.28). For example, if $N = 10{,}000$ and $\delta = 0.01$, $\sqrt{\frac{1}{2N}\log\frac{2}{\delta}} = 0.016$. Therefore, with a probability at least 99%, the true population mean μ will be included in the interval

$$\overline{X}_N - 0.16 \leq \mu \leq \overline{X}_N + 0.16.$$

- If we want to achieve a certain confidence interval, what is the N we need? If we are given ϵ and δ, the N we need is

$$\delta \leq 2e^{-2\epsilon^2 N} \quad \Rightarrow \quad N \geq \frac{\log\frac{2}{\delta}}{2\epsilon^2}.$$

For example, if $\delta = 0.01$ and $\epsilon = 0.01$, the N we need is $N \geq 26{,}500$.

When is Hoeffding's inequality used? Hoeffding's inequality is fundamental in modern machine learning theory. In this field, one often wants to quantify how well a learning algorithm performs with respect to the complexity of the model and the number of training samples. For example, if we choose a complex model, we should expect to use more training samples or overfit otherwise. Hoeffding's inequality provides an asymptotic description of the training error, testing error, and the number of training samples. The inequality is often used to compare the theoretical performance limit of one model versus another model. Therefore, although we do not need to use Hoeffding's inequality in this book, we hope you appreciate its tightness.

Closing Remark. We close this section by providing the historic context of Chernoff's inequality. Herman Chernoff, the discoverer of Chernoff's inequality, wrote the following many years after the publication of the original paper in 1952.

"In working on an artificial example, I discovered that I was using the Central Limit Theorem for large deviations where it did not apply. This led me to derive the asymptotic upper and lower bounds that were needed for the tail probabilities. [Herman] Rubin claimed he could get these bounds with much less work, and I challenged him. He produced a rather simple argument, using Markov's inequality, for the upper bound. Since that seemed to be a minor lemma in the ensuing paper I published (Chernoff, 1952), I neglected to give him credit. I now consider it a serious error in judgment, especially because his result is stronger for the upper bound than the asymptotic result I had derived." — Herman Chernoff, "A career in statistics," in Lin et al., *Past, Present, and Future of Statistical Science* (2014), p. 35.

6.3 Law of Large Numbers

In this section, we present our first main result: the law of large numbers. We will discuss two versions of the law: the weak law and the strong law. We will also introduce two forms of convergence: convergence in probability and almost sure convergence.

6.3.1 Sample average

The law of large numbers is a probabilistic statement about the **sample average**. Suppose that we have a collection of i.i.d. random variables $X_1, \ldots, X_N$. The sample average of these N random variables is defined as follows:

Definition 6.5. *The **sample average** of a sequence of random variables $X_1, \ldots, X_N$ is*

$$\overline{X}_N = \frac{1}{N} \sum_{n=1}^{N} X_n. \tag{6.29}$$

If the random variables $X_1, \ldots, X_N$ are i.i.d. so that they have the same **population mean** $\mathbb{E}[X_n] = \mu$ (for $n = 1, \ldots, N$), then by the linearity of the expectation,

$$\mathbb{E}\left[\overline{X}_N\right] = \frac{1}{N} \sum_{n=1}^{N} \mathbb{E}[X_n] = \mu.$$

Therefore, the mean of $\overline{X}_N$ is the population mean μ.

The sample average, $\overline{X}_N$, plays an important role in statistics. For example, by surveying 10,000 Americans, we can find a sample average of their ages. Since we never have access to the true population mean, the sample average is an estimate, and since $\overline{X}_N$ is only an estimate, we need to ask how good the estimate is.

One reason we ask this question is that $\overline{X}_N$ is a finite-sample "approximation" of μ. More importantly, the root of the problem is that $\overline{X}_N$ itself is a random variable because $X_1, \ldots, X_N$ are all random variables. Since $\overline{X}_N$ is a random variable, there is a PDF of $\overline{X}_N$; there is a CDF of $\overline{X}_N$; there is $\mathbb{E}[\overline{X}_N]$; and there is $\mathrm{Var}[\overline{X}_N]$. Since $\overline{X}_N$ is a random variable, it has uncertainty. To say that we are confident about $\overline{X}_N$, we need to ensure that the uncertainty is within some tolerable range.

How do we control the uncertainty? We can compute the variance. If $X_1, \ldots, X_N$ are i.i.d. random variables with the same variance $\mathrm{Var}[X_n] = \sigma^2$ (for $n = 1, \ldots, N$), then

$$\mathrm{Var}\left[\overline{X}_N\right] = \frac{1}{N^2} \sum_{n=1}^{N} \mathrm{Var}[X_n] = \frac{1}{N^2} \sum_{n=1}^{N} \sigma^2 = \frac{\sigma^2}{N}.$$

Therefore, the variance will shrink to 0 as N grows. In other words, the more samples we use to construct the sample average, the less deviation the random variable $\overline{X}_N$ will have.

Visualizing the sample average

To help you visualize the randomness of $\overline{X}_N$, we consider an experiment of drawing N Bernoulli random variables $X_1, \ldots, X_N$ with parameter $p = 1/2$. Since X_n is Bernoulli, it follows that

$$\mathbb{E}[X_n] = p \qquad \text{and} \qquad \mathrm{Var}[X_n] = p(1 - p).$$

We construct a sample average $\overline{X}_N = \frac{1}{N} \sum_{n=1}^{N} X_n$. Since X_n is a Bernoulli random variable, we know everything about $\overline{X}_N$. First, $\overline{X}_N$ is a binomial random variable, since $\overline{X}_N$ is the sum of Bernoulli random variables. Second, the mean and variance of $\overline{X}_N$ are respectively

$$\mu_{\overline{X}_N} \stackrel{\text{def}}{=} \mathbb{E}[\overline{X}_N] = \frac{1}{N} \sum_{n=1}^{N} \mathbb{E}[X_n] = p,$$

$$\sigma_{\overline{X}_N}^2 \stackrel{\text{def}}{=} \mathrm{Var}[\overline{X}_N] = \frac{1}{N^2} \sum_{n=1}^{N} \mathrm{Var}[X_n] = \frac{p(1 - p)}{N}.$$

In **Figure 6.12**, we plot the random variables $\overline{X}_N$ (the black crosses) for every N. You can see that at each N, e.g., $N = 100$, there are many possible observations for $\overline{X}_N$ because $\overline{X}_N$ itself is a random variable. As N increases, we see that the deviation of the random variables becomes smaller. In the same plot, we show the bounds $\mu \pm 3\sigma_{\overline{X}_N}$, which are three standard deviations from the mean. We can see clearly that the bounds provide a very good envelope covering the random variables. As N goes to infinity, we can see that the standard deviation goes to zero, and so $\overline{X}_N$ approaches the true mean.

For your reference, the MATLAB code and the Python code we used to generate the plot are shown below.

```
% MATLAB code to illustrate the weak law of large numbers
Nset = round(logspace(2,5,100));
```

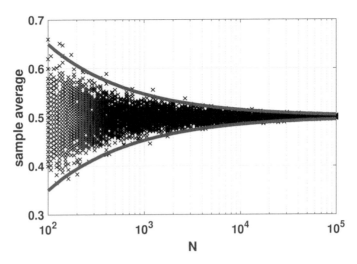

Figure 6.12: The weak law of large numbers. In this plot, we assume that $X_1, \ldots, X_N$ are i.i.d. Bernoulli random variables with a parameter p. The black crosses in the plot are the sample averages $\overline{X}_N = \frac{1}{N}\sum_{n=1}^{N} X_n$. The red curves are the ideal bounds $\mu_{\overline{X}_N} \pm 3\sigma_{\overline{X}_N}$, where $\mu_{\overline{X}_N} = p$ and $\sigma_{\overline{X}_N} = \sqrt{p(1-p)/N}$. As N grows, we observe that the variance shrinks to zero. Therefore, the sample average is converging to the true population mean.

```
for i=1:length(Nset)
    N = Nset(i);
    p = 0.5;
    x(:,i) = binornd(N, p, 1000,1)/N;
end
y = x(1:10:end,:)';
semilogx(Nset, y, 'kx'); hold on;
semilogx(Nset, p+3*sqrt(p*(1-p)./Nset), 'r', 'LineWidth', 4);
semilogx(Nset, p-3*sqrt(p*(1-p)./Nset), 'r', 'LineWidth', 4);
```

```
# Python code to illustrate the weak law of large numbers
import numpy as np
import matplotlib.pyplot as plt
import scipy.stats as stats
import numpy.matlib
p = 0.5
Nset = np.round(np.logspace(2,5,100)).astype(int)
x = np.zeros((1000,Nset.size))
for i in range(Nset.size):
  N = Nset[i]
  x[:,i] = stats.binom.rvs(N, p, size=1000)/N
Nset_grid = np.matlib.repmat(Nset, 1000, 1)

plt.semilogx(Nset_grid, x,'ko');
plt.semilogx(Nset, p + 3*np.sqrt((p*(1-p))/Nset), 'r', linewidth=6)
plt.semilogx(Nset, p - 3*np.sqrt((p*(1-p))/Nset), 'r', linewidth=6)
```

Note the outliers for each N in **Figure 6.12**. For example, at $N = 10^2$ we see a point located near 0.7 on the y-axis. This point is outside three standard deviations. Is it normal? Yes. Being outside three standard deviations only says that the probability of having this outlier is **small**. It does not say that the outlier is **impossible**. Having a small probability does not exclude the possibility. By contrast, if you say that something will surely not happen you mean that there is not even a small probability. The former is a weaker statement than the latter. Therefore, even though we establish a three standard deviation envelope, there are points falling outside the envelope. As N grows, the chance of having a bad outlier becomes smaller. Therefore, the greater the N, the smaller the chance we will get an outlier.

If the random variables X_n are i.i.d., the above phenomenon is universal. Below is an example of the Poisson case.

Practice Exercise 6.8. Let $X_n \sim \text{Poisson}(\lambda)$. Define the sample average as $\overline{X}_N = \frac{1}{N} \sum_{n=1}^{N} X_n$. Find the mean and variance of $\overline{X}_N$.

Solution. Since X_n is Poisson, we know that $\mathbb{E}[X_n] = \lambda$ and $\text{Var}[X_n] = \lambda$. So

$$\mathbb{E}[\overline{X}_N] = \frac{1}{N} \sum_{n=1}^{N} \mathbb{E}[X_n] = \frac{1}{N} \sum_{n=1}^{N} \lambda = \lambda,$$

$$\text{Var}[\overline{X}_N] = \frac{1}{N^2} \sum_{n=1}^{N} \text{Var}[X_n] = \frac{1}{N^2} \sum_{n=1}^{N} \lambda = \frac{\lambda}{N}.$$

Therefore, as $N \to \infty$, the variance $\text{Var}[\overline{X}_N] \to 0$.

6.3.2 Weak law of large numbers (WLLN)

The analysis of **Figure 6.12** shows us something important, namely that the convergence in a probabilistic way is different from that in a deterministic way. We now describe one fundamental result related to probabilistic convergence, known as the weak law of large numbers.

Theorem 6.16 (Weak law of large numbers). *Let $X_1, \ldots, X_N$ be a set of i.i.d. random variables with mean μ and variance σ^2. Assume $\mathbb{E}[X^2] < \infty$. Let $\overline{X}_N = \frac{1}{N} \sum_{n=1}^{N} X_n$. Then for any $\varepsilon > 0$,*

$$\lim_{N \to \infty} \mathbb{P}\left[|\overline{X}_N - \mu| > \varepsilon \right] = 0. \tag{6.30}$$

Proof. By Chebyshev's inequality,

$$\mathbb{P}\left[|\overline{X}_N - \mu| > \varepsilon \right] \leq \frac{\text{Var}[\overline{X}_N]}{\varepsilon^2} = \frac{\text{Var}[X_n]}{N\varepsilon^2}.$$

Therefore, setting $N \to \infty$ we have

$$\lim_{N \to \infty} \mathbb{P}\left[|\overline{X}_N - \mu| > \varepsilon \right] = \lim_{N \to \infty} \frac{\text{Var}[X_n]}{N\varepsilon^2} = 0.$$

$\square$

Example 6.10. Consider a set of i.i.d. random variables $X_1, \ldots, X_N$ where

$$X_n \sim \text{Gaussian}(\mu, \sigma^2).$$

Verify that the sample average $\overline{X}_N = \frac{1}{N} \sum_{n=1}^{N} X_n$ follows the weak law of large numbers.

Solution: Since X_n is a Gaussian, the sample average $\overline{X}_N$ is also a Gaussian:

$$\overline{X}_N \sim \text{Gaussian}\left(\mu, \frac{\sigma^2}{N}\right).$$

Consider the probability $\mathbb{P}\left[|\overline{X}_N - \mu| > \varepsilon\right]$ for each N:

$$
\begin{aligned}
\delta_N &\overset{\text{def}}{=} \mathbb{P}\left[|\overline{X}_N - \mu| > \varepsilon\right] \\
&= \mathbb{P}\left[\overline{X}_N - \mu > \varepsilon\right] + \mathbb{P}\left[\overline{X}_N - \mu < -\varepsilon\right] \\
&= 1 - \Phi\left(\frac{\varepsilon\sqrt{N}}{\sigma}\right) + \Phi\left(-\frac{\varepsilon\sqrt{N}}{\sigma}\right) \\
&= 2\Phi\left(-\frac{\varepsilon\sqrt{N}}{\sigma}\right).
\end{aligned}
$$

If we set $\sigma = 1$ and $\varepsilon = 0.1$, then

$$\delta_1 = 2\Phi\left(-\frac{0.1 \cdot 1}{1}\right) = 0.9203, \qquad \delta_5 = 2\Phi\left(-\frac{0.1 \cdot \sqrt{5}}{1}\right) = 0.8231,$$

$$\delta_{10} = 2\Phi\left(-\frac{0.1 \cdot \sqrt{10}}{1}\right) = 0.7518, \qquad \delta_{100} = 2\Phi\left(-\frac{0.1 \cdot \sqrt{100}}{1}\right) = 0.3173,$$

$$\delta_{1000} = 2\Phi\left(-\frac{0.1 \cdot \sqrt{1000}}{1}\right) = 0.0016.$$

As you can see, the sequence $\delta_1, \delta_2, \ldots, \delta_N, \ldots$ rapidly converges to 0 as N grows. In fact, since $\Phi(z)$ is a increasing function for $z < 0$ with $\Phi(-\infty) = 0$, it follows that

$$\lim_{N \to \infty} \mathbb{P}\left[|\overline{X}_N - \mu| > \varepsilon\right] = \lim_{N \to \infty} 2\Phi\left(-\frac{\varepsilon\sqrt{N}}{\sigma}\right) = 0.$$

The weak law of large numbers is portrayed graphically in **Figure 6.13**. In this figure we draw several PDFs of the sample average $\overline{X}_N$. The shapes of the PDFs are getting narrower as the variance of the random variable shrinks. Since the PDFs become narrower, the probability $\mathbb{P}[|\overline{X}_N - \mu| > \varepsilon]$ becomes more unlikely. At the limit when $N \to \infty$, the probability vanishes. The weak law of large numbers asserts that this happens for any set of i.i.d. random variables. It says that the sequence of probability values $\delta_N \overset{\text{def}}{=} \mathbb{P}[|\overline{X}_N - \mu| > \varepsilon]$

will converge to zero.

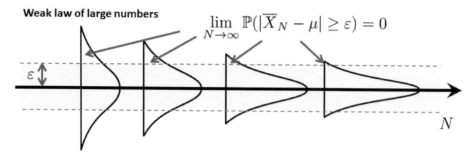

Figure 6.13: The weak law of large numbers states that as N increases, the variance of the sample average $\overline{X}_N$ shrinks. As a result, the probability $\mathbb{P}[|\overline{X}_N - \mu| > \varepsilon]$ decreases and eventually vanishes. Note that the convergence here is that of the sequence of probabilities $\mathbb{P}[|\overline{X}_N - \mu| > \varepsilon]$, which is just a sequence of numbers.

What is the weak law of large numbers?

Let $\overline{X}_N$ be the sample average of i.i.d. random variables $X_1, \ldots, X_N$.

$$\lim_{N \to \infty} \mathbb{P}\left[|\overline{X}_N - \mu| > \varepsilon\right] = 0. \tag{6.31}$$

- For details, see Theorem 6.16.
- The WLLN concerns the sequence of probability **values** $\delta_N = \mathbb{P}[|\overline{X}_N - \mu| > \varepsilon]$.
- The probabilities converge to zero as N grows.
- It is weak because having a small probability does not exclude the possibility of happening.

6.3.3 Convergence in probability

The example above tells us that in order to show convergence, we need to first compute the probability δ_n of each event and then take the limit of the sequence, e.g., the one shown in the table below:

δ_1	δ_5	δ_{10}	δ_{100}	δ_{1000}	δ_{10000}
0.9203	0.8231	0.7518	0.3173	0.0016	1.5240×10^{-23}

Therefore, the convergence is the convergence of the **probability**. Since $\{\delta_1, \delta_2, \ldots\}$ is a sequence of real numbers (between 0 and 1), any convergence results for real numbers apply here.

Note that the convergence controls only the probabilities. Probability means chance. Therefore, having the limit converging to zero only means that the chance of happening is becoming smaller and smaller. However, at any N, there is still a chance that some bad event can happen.

What do we mean by a bad event? Assume that X_n are fair coins. The sample average $\overline{X}_N = (1/N)\sum_{n=1}^{N} X_n$ is more or less equal to $1/2$ as N grows. However, even if N is a large number, say $N = 1000$, we are still not certain that the sample average is **exactly** $1/2$. It is possible, though very unlikely, that we obtain 1000 heads or 1000 tails (so that the sample average is "1" or "0"). The bottom line is: Having a probability converging to zero only means that for any tolerance level we can always find an N large enough so that the probability is smaller than that tolerance.

The type of convergence described by the weak law of large numbers is known as the **convergence in probability**.

Definition 6.6. *A sequence of random variables $A_1, \ldots, A_N$* **converges in probability** *to a deterministic number α if for every $\varepsilon > 0$,*

$$\lim_{N\to\infty} \mathbb{P}\left[|A_N - \alpha| > \varepsilon\right] = 0. \tag{6.32}$$

We write $A_N \xrightarrow{p} \alpha$ to denote convergence in probability.

The following two examples illustrate how to prove convergence in probability.

Example 6.11. Let $X_1, \ldots, X_N$ be i.i.d. random variables with $X_n \sim \text{Uniform}(0,1)$. Define $A_N = \min(X_1, \ldots, X_N)$. Show that A_N converges in probability to zero.

Solution. (Without determining the PDF of A_N, we notice that as N increases, the value of A_N will likely decrease. Therefore, we should expect A_N to converge to zero.) Pick an $\varepsilon > 0$. It follows that

$$\begin{aligned}
\mathbb{P}[|A_N - 0| \geq \varepsilon] &= \mathbb{P}[\min(X_1, \ldots, X_N) \geq \varepsilon], \qquad \text{because } X_n \geq 0 \\
&= \mathbb{P}[X_1 \geq \varepsilon \text{ and } \cdots \text{ and } X_N \geq \varepsilon] \\
&= \mathbb{P}(X_1 \geq \varepsilon) \cdots \mathbb{P}(X_N \geq \varepsilon) = (1-\varepsilon)^N.
\end{aligned}$$

Setting the limit of $N \to \infty$, we conclude that

$$\lim_{N\to\infty} \mathbb{P}[|A_N - 0| \geq \varepsilon] = \lim_{N\to\infty} (1-\varepsilon)^N = 0.$$

Therefore, A_N converges to zero in probability.

Practice Exercise 6.9. Let $X \sim \text{Exponential}(1)$. By evaluating the CDF, we know that $\mathbb{P}[X \geq x] = e^{-x}$. Let $A_N = X/N$. Prove that A_N converges to zero in probability.

Solution. For any $\varepsilon > 0$,

$$\begin{aligned}
\mathbb{P}[|A_N - 0| \geq \varepsilon] &= \mathbb{P}[A_N \geq \varepsilon] \\
&= \mathbb{P}[X \geq N\varepsilon] \\
&= e^{-N\varepsilon}.
\end{aligned}$$

Putting $N \to \infty$ on both sides of the equation gives us

$$\lim_{N \to \infty} \mathbb{P}[|A_N - 0| \geq \varepsilon] = \lim_{N \to \infty} e^{-N\varepsilon} = 0.$$

Thus, A_N converges to zero in probability.

Example 6.12. Construct an example such that A_N converges in probability to something, but $\mathbb{E}[A_N]$ does not converge to the same thing.

Solution. Consider a sequence of random variables A_N such that

$$\mathbb{P}[A_N = \alpha] = \begin{cases} 1 - \frac{1}{N}, & \alpha = 0, \\ \frac{1}{N}, & \alpha = N^2, \\ 0, & \text{otherwise.} \end{cases}$$

The PDF of the random variable A_N is shown in **Figure 6.14**.

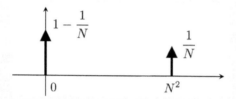

Figure 6.14: Probability density function of the random variable A_N.

We first show that A_N converges in probability to zero. Let $\varepsilon > 0$ be a fixed constant. Since $\varepsilon > 0$,

$$\mathbb{P}[A_N \geq \varepsilon] = \frac{1}{N}$$

for any $N > \sqrt{\varepsilon}$. Therefore, we have that

$$\lim_{N \to \infty} \mathbb{P}[|A_N - 0| \geq \varepsilon] = \lim_{N \to \infty} \mathbb{P}[A_N \geq \varepsilon]$$

$$= \lim_{N \to \infty} \frac{1}{N} = 0.$$

Hence, A_N converges to 0 in probability.

However, $\mathbb{E}[A_N]$ does not converge to zero, because

$$\mathbb{E}[A_N] = 0 \cdot \left(1 - \frac{1}{N}\right) + N^2 \cdot \frac{1}{N}$$

$$= N.$$

So $\mathbb{E}[A_N]$ goes to infinity as N grows.

6.3.4 Can we prove WLLN using Chernoff's bound?

The following discussion of using Chernoff's bound to prove WLLN can be skipped if this is your first time reading the book.

In proving WLLN we use Chebyshev's inequality. Can we use Chernoff's inequality (or Hoeffding's) to prove the result? Yes, we can use them. However, notice that the task here is to prove convergence, not to find the *best* convergence. Finding the best convergence means finding the fastest decay rate of the probability sequence. Chernoff's bound (and Hoeffding's inequality) offers a better decay rate. However, Chernoff's bound needs to be customized for individual random variables. For example, Chernoff's bound for Gaussian is different from Chernoff's bound for exponential. This result makes Chebyshev the most convenient bound because it only requires the variance to be bounded.

What if we insist on using Chernoff's bound in proving the WLLN? We can do that for specific random variables. Let's consider two examples. The first example is the Gaussian random variable where $X_n \sim \mathcal{N}(0, \sigma^2)$. We know that $\overline{X}_N \sim \mathcal{N}(0, \sigma^2/N)$. Chernoff's bound shows that

$$\mathbb{P}\left[|\overline{X}_N - \mu| > \varepsilon\right] \leq 2 \exp\left\{-\frac{\varepsilon^2 N}{2\sigma^2}\right\},$$

Taking the limit on both sides, we have

$$\lim_{N \to \infty} \mathbb{P}\left[|\overline{X}_N - \mu| > \varepsilon\right] = \lim_{N \to \infty} 2 \exp\left\{-\frac{\varepsilon^2 N}{2\sigma^2}\right\} = 0.$$

Note that the rate of convergence here is exponential. The rate of convergence offered by Chebyshev is only linear. Of course, you may argue that since X_n is Gaussian we have closed-form expressions about the probability, so we do not need Chernoff's bound. This is a legitimate point, and so here is an example where we do not have a closed-form expression for the probability.

Consider a sequence of arbitrary i.i.d. random variables $X_1, \ldots, X_N$ with $0 \leq X_n \leq 1$. Then Hoeffding's inequality tells us that

$$\mathbb{P}\left[|\overline{X}_N - \mu| > \varepsilon\right] \leq 2 \exp\left\{-2\varepsilon^2 N\right\}.$$

Taking the limit on both sides, we have

$$\lim_{N \to \infty} \mathbb{P}\left[|\overline{X}_N - \mu| > \varepsilon\right] = \lim_{N \to \infty} 2 \exp\left\{-2\varepsilon^2 N\right\} = 0.$$

Again, we obtain a WLLN result, this time for i.i.d. random variables $X_1, \ldots, X_N$ with $0 \leq X_n \leq 1$.

As you can see from these two examples, WLLN can be proved in multiple ways depending on how general the random variables need to be.

End of the discussions.

6.3.5   Does the weak law of large numbers always hold?

> The following discussion of the failure of the weak law of large numbers can be skipped if this is your first time reading the book.

The weak law of large numbers does not always hold. Recall that when we prove the weak law of large numbers using Chebyshev's inequality, we implicitly require that the variance $\mathrm{Var}[\overline{X}_N]$ is finite. (Look at the condition that $\mathbb{E}[X^2] < \infty$.) Thus for distributions whose variance is unbounded, Chebyshev's inequality does not hold. One example is the Cauchy distribution. The PDF of a Cauchy distribution is

$$f_X(x) = \frac{\gamma}{\pi(\gamma^2 + x^2)},$$

where γ is a parameter. Letting $\gamma = 1$,

$$\mathbb{E}[X^2] = \int_{-\infty}^{\infty} \frac{x^2}{\pi(1+x^2)}\, dx = \frac{1}{\pi}\int_{-\infty}^{\infty} 1 - \frac{1}{1+x^2}\, dx$$

$$= \frac{1}{\pi}\int_{-\infty}^{\infty} dx - \frac{1}{\pi}\int_{-\infty}^{\infty}\frac{1}{1+x^2}\, dx = \frac{1}{\pi}\Big[x - \tan^{-1}(x)\Big]\Big|_{x=-\infty}^{\infty} = \infty.$$

Since the second moment is unbounded, the variance of X will also be unbounded.

A perceptive reader may observe that even if $\mathbb{E}[X^2]$ is unbounded, it does not mean that the tail probability is unbounded. This is correct. However, for Cauchy distributions, we can show that the sample average $\overline{X}_N$ does not converge to the mean when $N \to \infty$ (and so the WLLN fails). To see this, we note that

$$\frac{1}{\pi(1+x^2)} \leftrightarrow e^{-|\omega|}.$$

So for the sample average $\overline{X}_N = \frac{1}{N}\sum_{n=1}^{N} X_n$, the characteristic function is

$$\mathbb{E}[e^{-j\omega\overline{X}_N}] = \mathbb{E}[e^{-\frac{j\omega}{N}\sum_{n=1}^{N} X_n}] = \prod_{n=1}^{N} \mathbb{E}[e^{-\frac{j\omega}{N}X_n}] = \left[e^{-\frac{|\omega|}{N}}\right]^N = e^{-|\omega|},$$

which remains a Cauchy distribution with $\gamma = 1$. Therefore, we have that

$$\mathbb{P}[|\overline{X}_N| \leq \varepsilon] = \int_{-\infty}^{\varepsilon} \frac{1}{\pi(1+x^2)}\, dx$$

$$= \int_{-\infty}^{0} \frac{1}{\pi(1+x^2)}\, dx + \int_{0}^{\varepsilon} \frac{1}{\pi(1+x^2)}\, dx = \frac{1}{2} + \frac{1}{\pi}\tan^{-1}(\varepsilon).$$

Thus no matter how many samples we have, $\mathbb{P}[|\overline{X}_N| \leq \varepsilon]$ will never converge to 1 (so $\mathbb{P}[|\overline{X}_N| > \varepsilon]$ will never converge to 0). Therefore, WLLN does not hold.

> End of the discussion.

6.3.6 Strong law of large numbers

Since there is a "weak" law of large numbers, you will not be surprised to learn that there is a strong law of large numbers. The strong law is *more restrictive* than the weak law. Any sequence satisfying the strong law will satisfy the weak law, but not vice versa. Since the strong law is "stronger", the proof is more involved.

Theorem 6.17 (Strong law of large numbers). *Let* $X_1, \ldots, X_N$ *be a sequence of i.i.d. random variables with common mean* μ *and variance* σ^2. *Assume* $\mathbb{E}[X^4] < \infty$. *Let* $\overline{X}_N = \frac{1}{N} \sum_{n=1}^{N} X_n$ *be the sample average. Then*

$$\mathbb{P}\left[\lim_{N \to \infty} \overline{X}_N = \mu \right] = 1. \tag{6.33}$$

The strong law flips the order of limit and probability. As you can see, the difference between the strong law and the weak law is the order of the limit and the probability. In the weak law, the limit is **outside** the probability, whereas, in the strong law, the limit is **inside** the probability. This switch in order makes the interpretation of the result fundamentally different. In the final analysis, the weak law concerns the limit of a sequence of probabilities (which are just real numbers between 0 and 1). However, the strong law concerns the limit of a sequence of random variables. The strong law answers the question, what is the **limiting object** of the sample average as N grows?

The strong law concerns the limiting object, not a sequence of numbers. What is the "limiting object"? If we denote $\overline{X}_N$ as the sample average using N samples, then we know that $\overline{X}_1$ is a random variable, $\overline{X}_2$ is a random variable, and all $\overline{X}_n$'s are random variables. So we have a sequence of random variables. As N goes to infinity, we can ask about the limiting object $\lim_{N \to \infty} \overline{X}_N$. However, even without any deep analysis, you should be able to see that $\lim_{N \to \infty} \overline{X}_N$ is another random variable. The strong law says that this limiting object will "successfully" become a deterministic number μ, after a finite number of "failures".

The strong law asserts that there are a finite number of failures. Let us explain "success" and "failure". $\overline{X}_N$ is a random variable, so it fluctuates. However, as N goes to infinity, the strong law says that the number of times where $\overline{X}_N \neq \mu$ will be zero. That is, there is a finite number of times where $\overline{X}_N \neq \mu$ (i.e., fail), and afterward, you will be **perfectly** fine (i.e., success). Yes, perfectly fine means 100%. The weak law only guarantees 99.99%.

A good example for differentiating the weak law and the strong law is an electronic dictionary that improves itself every time you use it. The weak law says that if you use the dictionary for a long period, the probability of making an error will become small. You will still get an error once in a while, but the probability is very small. This is a 99.99% guarantee, and it is the weak law. The strong law says that the number of failures is finite. After you have gone through this finite number of failures, you will be completely free of error. This is a 100% guarantee by the strong law. When will you hit this magical number? The strong law does not say when; it only asserts the existence of this number. However, this existence is already good enough in many ways. It gives a certificate of assurance, whereas the weak law still has uncertainty.

Strong law $\neq$ deterministic. If the strong law offers a 100% guarantee, does it mean that it is a deterministic guarantee? No, the strong law is still a probabilistic statement because we are still using $\mathbb{P}[\cdot]$ to measure an event. The event can include measure-zero subsets, and the measure-zero subsets can be huge. For example, the set of rational numbers on the real line is a measure-zero set when measuring the probability using an integration. The strong law does not handle those measure-zero subsets.

6.3.7 Almost sure convergence

> The discussion below can be skipped if this is your first time reading the book.

The type of convergence used by the strong law of large numbers is the **almost sure convergence**. It is defined formally as follows.

> **Definition 6.7.** *A sequence of random variables $A_1, \ldots, A_N$* **converges almost surely** *to α if*
>
> $$\mathbb{P}\left[\lim_{N \to \infty} A_N = \alpha\right] = 1. \tag{6.34}$$
>
> *We write $A_N \overset{a.s.}{\to} \alpha$ to denote almost sure convergence.*

To prove almost sure convergence, one needs to show that the sequence A_N will demonstrate $A_N \neq \alpha$ for a finite number of times. Afterward, A_N needs to demonstrate $A_N = \alpha$.

> **Example 6.13.**[a] Construct a sequence of events that converges almost surely.
>
> **Solution.** Let $X_1, \ldots, X_N$ be i.i.d. random variables such that $X_n \sim \text{Uniform}(0, 1)$. Define $A_N = \min(X_1, \ldots, X_N)$. Since A_N is nonincreasing and is bounded below by zero, it must have a limit. Let us call this limit
>
> $$A \overset{\text{def}}{=} \lim_{N \to \infty} A_N.$$
>
> Then we can show that
>
> $$\begin{aligned}
\mathbb{P}[A \geq \epsilon] &= \mathbb{P}[\min(X_1, X_2, \ldots) \geq \epsilon] \\
&\overset{(a)}{\leq} \mathbb{P}[\min(X_1, X_2, \ldots, X_N) \geq \epsilon] \\
&\overset{(b)}{=} \mathbb{P}[X_1 \geq \epsilon \text{ and } X_2 \geq \epsilon \text{ and } \cdots \text{ and } X_N \geq \epsilon] \\
&= (1 - \epsilon)^N,
\end{aligned}$$
>
> where (a) holds because there are more elements in $(X_1, X_2, \ldots)$ than in $(X_1, X_2, \ldots, X_N)$. Therefore, the minimum value of the former is less than the minimum value of the latter. (b) holds because if $\min(X_1, X_2, \ldots, X_N) \geq \epsilon$, then $X_n \geq \epsilon$ for all n.

Since $\mathbb{P}[A \geq \epsilon] \leq (1 - \epsilon)^N$ for any N, the statement still holds as $N \to \infty$. Thus,

$$\mathbb{P}[A \geq \epsilon] \leq \lim_{N \to \infty} (1 - \epsilon)^N = 0.$$

This shows $\mathbb{P}[A \geq \epsilon] = 0$ for any positive ϵ. So $\mathbb{P}[A > 0] = 0$, and hence $\mathbb{P}[A = 0] = 1$. Since A is the limit of A_N, we conclude that

$$\mathbb{P}\left[\lim_{N \to \infty} A_N = 0\right] = \mathbb{P}[A = 0] = 1.$$

So A_N converges to 0 almost surely.

---

[a]This example is modified from Bertsekas and Tsitsiklis, *Introduction to Probability*, Chapter 5.5.

Example 6.14.[a] Construct an example where a sequence of events converges in probability but does not converge almost surely.

Solution. Consider a discrete time arrival process. The set of times is partitioned into consecutive intervals of the form

$$I_1 = \{2, 3\},$$
$$I_2 = \{4, 5, 6, 7\},$$
$$I_3 = \{8, 9, 10, \ldots, 15\},$$
$$\vdots$$
$$I_k = \{2^k, 2^k + 1, \ldots, 2^{k+1} - 1\}.$$

Therefore, the length of each interval is $|I_1| = 2$, $|I_2| = 4$, ..., $|I_k| = 2^k$.

During each interval, there is exactly one arrival. Define Y_n as a binary random variable such that for every $n \in I_k$,

$$Y_n = \begin{cases} 1, & \text{with probability } \frac{1}{|I_k|}, \\ 0, & \text{with probability } 1 - \frac{1}{|I_k|}. \end{cases}$$

For example, if $n \in \{2, 3\}$, then $\mathbb{P}[Y_n = 1] = \frac{1}{2}$. If $n \in \{4, 5, 6, 7\}$, then $\mathbb{P}[Y_n = 1] = \frac{1}{4}$. In general, we have that

$$\lim_{n \to \infty} \mathbb{P}[Y_n = 1] = \lim_{n \to \infty} \frac{1}{|I_k|} = \lim_{n \to \infty} \frac{1}{2^k} = 0,$$

and hence

$$\lim_{n \to \infty} \mathbb{P}[Y_n = 0] = \lim_{n \to \infty} 1 - \frac{1}{2^k} = 1.$$

Therefore, Y_n converges to 0 in probability.

However, when we carry out the experiment, there is exactly one arrival per interval according to the problem conditions. Since we have an infinite number of intervals $I_1, I_2, \ldots$, we will have an infinite number of arrivals in total. As a result, $Y_n = 1$ for infinitely many times. We do not know which Y_n will equal 1 and which Y_n will equal to 0. However, we know that there are infinitely many Y_n that are equal to 1. Therefore, in the sequence $Y_1, Y_2, \ldots, Y_n, \ldots$, we must have that the tail of the sequence is 1. (If Y_n stops being 1 after some n, then we will not have an infinite number of arrivals in total.)

Since $Y_n = 1$ when n is large enough, it follows that

$$\mathbb{P}\left[\lim_{n \to \infty} Y_n = 1\right] = 1.$$

Equivalently, we can say that the sequence Y_n will never take the value 0 when n is large enough. Thus,

$$\mathbb{P}\left[\lim_{n \to \infty} Y_n = 0\right] = 0.$$

Therefore, Y_n does not converge to 0 almost surely.

------

[a] This example is modified from Bertsekas and Tsitsiklis, *Introduction to Probability*, Chapter 5.5.

End of the discussions.

6.3.8   Proof of the strong law of large numbers

The strong law of large numbers can be proved in several ways. We present a proof based on Bertsekas and Tsitsiklis, *Introduction to Probability*, Problems 5.16 and 5.17, which require a finite fourth moment $\mathbb{E}[X_n^4] < \infty$. An alternative proof that requires only $\mathbb{E}[X_n] < \infty$ is from Billingsley, *Probability and Measure*, Theorem 22.1.

The proof of the strong law of large numbers is beyond the scope of this book. This section is optional.

Lemma 6.4. *Consider non-negative random variables $X_1, \ldots, X_N$. Assume that*

$$\mathbb{E}\left[\sum_{n=1}^{\infty} X_n\right] < \infty. \tag{6.35}$$

Then $X_n \overset{a.s.}{\to} 0$.

Proof. Let $S = \sum_{n=1}^{N} X_n$. Note that S is a random variable, and our assumption is that $\mathbb{E}[S] < \infty$. Thus, we argue that $S < \infty$ with probability 1. If not, then S will have a positive probability of being ∞. But if this happens, we will have $\mathbb{E}[S] = \infty$ because (by the law of total expectation):

$$\mathbb{E}[S] = \underbrace{\mathbb{E}[S \mid S = \text{infinite}]}_{=\infty} \mathbb{P}[S = \text{infinite}] + \mathbb{E}[S \mid S = \text{finite}]\mathbb{P}[S = \text{finite}].$$

Now, since S is finite, the sequence $\{X_1, \ldots, X_N, \ldots\}$ must converge to zero. Otherwise, if X_n is converging to some constants $c > 0$, then summing the tail of the sequence (which contains infinitely many terms) gives infinity:

$$S = \underbrace{X_1 + \cdots + X_N}_{=\text{finite}} + \underbrace{X_N + \cdots +}_{=\text{infinite}}.$$

Since the probability of S being finite is 1, it follows that $\{X_1, \ldots, X_N\}$ is converging to zero with probability 1.

$\square$

Theorem 6.18 (Strong law of large numbers). *Let $X_1, \ldots, X_N$ be a sequence of i.i.d. random variables with common mean μ and variance σ^2. Assume $\mathbb{E}[X_n^4] < \infty$. Let $\overline{X}_N = \frac{1}{N} \sum_{n=1}^{N} X_n$ be the sample average. Then*

$$\mathbb{P}\left[\lim_{N \to \infty} \overline{X}_N = \mu \right] = 1. \tag{6.36}$$

Proof. We first prove the case where $\mathbb{E}[X_n] = 0$. To establish that $\overline{X}_N \to 0$ with probability 1, we use the lemma to show that

$$\mathbb{E}\left[\sum_{N=1}^{\infty} |\overline{X}_N| \right] < \infty.$$

But to show $\mathbb{E}[\sum_{N=1}^{\infty} |\overline{X}_N|] < \infty$, we note that $|x| \leq 1 + x^4$. Therefore, $\mathbb{E}[\sum_{N=1}^{\infty} |\overline{X}_N|] \leq 1 + \mathbb{E}[\sum_{N=1}^{\infty} \overline{X}_N^4]$, and hence we just need to show that

$$\mathbb{E}\left[\sum_{N=1}^{\infty} \overline{X}_N^4 \right] < \infty.$$

Let us expand the term $\mathbb{E}[\overline{X}_N^4]$ as follows:

$$\mathbb{E}[\overline{X}_N^4] = \frac{1}{N^4} \sum_{n_1=1}^{N} \sum_{n_2=1}^{N} \sum_{n_3=1}^{N} \sum_{n_4=1}^{N} \mathbb{E}[X_{n_1} X_{n_2} X_{n_3} X_{n_4}].$$

There are five possibilities for $\mathbb{E}[X_{n_1} X_{n_2} X_{n_3} X_{n_4}]$:

- All indices are different. Then

$$\mathbb{E}[X_{n_1} X_{n_2} X_{n_3} X_{n_4}] = \mathbb{E}[X_{n_1}]\mathbb{E}[X_{n_2}]\mathbb{E}[X_{n_3}]\mathbb{E}[X_{n_4}] = 0 \cdot 0 \cdot 0 \cdot 0 = 0.$$

- One index is different from other three indices. For example, if n_1 is different from n_2, n_3, n_4, then

$$\mathbb{E}[X_{n_1} X_{n_2} X_{n_3} X_{n_4}] = \mathbb{E}[X_{n_1}]\mathbb{E}[X_{n_2} X_{n_3} X_{n_4}] = 0 \cdot \mathbb{E}[X_{n_2} X_{n_3} X_{n_4}] = 0.$$

- Two indices are identical. For example, if $n_1 = n_3$, and $n_2 = n_4$, then

$$\mathbb{E}[X_{n_1} X_{n_2} X_{n_3} X_{n_4}] = \mathbb{E}[X_{n_1} X_{n_3}]\mathbb{E}[X_{n_2} X_{n_4}] = \mathbb{E}[X_{n_1}^2 X_{n_2}^2].$$

There are altogether $3N(N-1)$ of these cases: $N(N-1)$ comes from choosing N followed by choosing $N-1$, and 3 accounts for $n_1 = n_2 \neq n_3 = n_4$, $n_1 = n_3 \neq n_2 = n_4$, and $n_1 = n_4 \neq n_2 = n_3$.

- Two indices are identical, and two indices are different. For example, if $n_1 = n_3$ but n_2 and n_4 are different. Then

$$\mathbb{E}[X_{n_1} X_{n_2} X_{n_3} X_{n_4}] = \mathbb{E}[X_{n_1} X_{n_3}]\mathbb{E}[X_{n_2}]\mathbb{E}[X_{n_4}]$$
$$= \mathbb{E}[X_{n_1}^2] \cdot 0 \cdot 0 = 0.$$

- All indices are identical. If $n_1 = n_2 = n_3 = n_4$, then

$$\mathbb{E}[X_{n_1} X_{n_2} X_{n_3} X_{n_4}] = \mathbb{E}[X_{n_1}^4].$$

There are altogether N cases of this.

Therefore, it follows that

$$\mathbb{E}[\overline{X}_N^4] = \frac{N\mathbb{E}[X_1^4] + 3N(N-1)\mathbb{E}[X_1^2 X_2^2]}{N^4}.$$

Since $xy \le (x^2 + y^2)/2$, it follows that

$$\mathbb{E}[X_1^2 X_2^2] \le \mathbb{E}[(X_1^2)^2 + (X_2^2)^2]/2$$
$$= \mathbb{E}[X_1^4 + X_2^4]/2$$
$$= \mathbb{E}[X_1^4].$$

Substituting into the previous result,

$$\mathbb{E}[\overline{X}_N^4] \le \frac{N\mathbb{E}[X_1^4] + 3N(N-1)\mathbb{E}[X_1^4]}{N^4}$$
$$\le \frac{3N^2}{N^4}\mathbb{E}[X_1^4]$$
$$= \frac{3}{N^2}\mathbb{E}[X_1^4].$$

Now, let us complete the proof.

$$\mathbb{E}\left[\sum_{N=1}^{\infty} \overline{X}_N^4\right] \le \mathbb{E}\left[\sum_{N=1}^{\infty} \frac{3}{N^2}\mathbb{E}[X_1^4]\right] < \infty,$$

because $\sum_{N=1}^{\infty}(1/N^2)$ is the Bassel problem with a solution that $\sum_{N=1}^{\infty}(1/N^2) = \pi^2/6$. Consequently, we have shown that $\mathbb{E}\left[\sum_{N=1}^{\infty} \overline{X}_N^4\right] < \infty$, which implies $\mathbb{E}\left[\sum_{N=1}^{\infty} |\overline{X}_N|\right] < \infty$. Then, by the lemma, we have $\overline{X}_N$ converging to 0 with probability 1, which proves the result.

If $\mathbb{E}[X_n] = \mu$, then just replace X_n with $Y_n = X_n - \mu$ in the above arguments. Then we can show that $\overline{Y}_N$ converges to 0 with probability 1, which is equivalent to $\overline{X}_N$ converging to μ with probability 1.

> End of the proof of strong law of large numbers.

6.4 Central Limit Theorem

The law of large numbers tells us the **mean** of the sample average $\overline{X}_N = (1/N) \sum_{n=1}^{N} X_n$. However, if you recall our experiment of throwing N dice and inspecting the PDF of the sum of the numbers, you may remember that the convolution of an infinite number of uniform distributions gives us a Gaussian distribution. For example, we show a sequence of experiments in **Figure 6.15**. In each experiment, we throw N dice and count the sum. Therefore, if each face of the die is denoted as X_n, then the sum is $X_1 + \cdots + X_N$. We plot the PDF of the sum. As you can see in the figure, $X_1 + \cdots + X_N$ converges to a Gaussian. This phenomenon is explained by the **Central Limit Theorem (CLT)**.

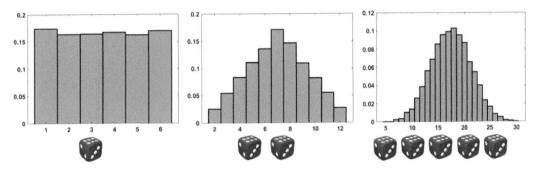

Figure 6.15: Pictorial illustration of the Central Limit Theorem. Suppose we throw a die and record the face. [Left] If we only have one die, then the distribution of the face is uniform. [Middle] If we throw two dice, the distribution is the convolution of two uniform distributions. This will give us a triangle distribution. [Right] If we throw five dice, the distribution is becoming similar to a Gaussian. The Central Limit Theorem says that as N goes to infinity, the distribution of the sum will converge to a Gaussian.

What does the Central Limit Theorem say? Let $\overline{X}_N$ be the sample average, and let $Z_N = \sqrt{N} \left(\frac{\overline{X}_N - \mu}{\sigma} \right)$ be the normalized variable. The Central Limit Theorem is as follows:

Central Limit Theorem:

The CDF of Z_N is converging pointwise to the CDF of Gaussian(0,1).

Note that we are very careful here. We are not saying that the PDF of Z_N is converging to the PDF of a Gaussian, nor are we saying that the random variable Z_N is converging to a Gaussian random variable. We are only saying that the **values** of the CDF are converging pointwise. The difference is subtle but important.

To understand the difficulty and the core ideas, we first present the concept of convergence in distribution.

CHAPTER 6. SAMPLE STATISTICS

6.4.1 Convergence in distribution

Definition 6.8. *Let $Z_1, \ldots, Z_N$ be random variables with CDFs $F_{Z_1}, \ldots, F_{Z_N}$ respectively. We say that a sequence of $Z_1, \ldots, Z_N$ **converges in distribution** to a random variable Z with CDF F_Z if*

$$\lim_{N \to \infty} F_{Z_N}(z) = F_Z(z), \qquad (6.37)$$

for every continuous point z of F_Z. We write $Z_N \overset{d}{\to} Z$ to denote convergence in distribution.

This definition involves many concepts, which we will discuss one by one. However, the definition can be summarized in a nutshell as follows.

Convergence in distribution = values of the CDF converge.

Example 1. (Bernoulli) Consider flipping a fair coin N times. Denote each coin flip as a Bernoulli random variable $X_n \sim \text{Bernoulli}(p)$, where $n = 1, 2, \ldots, N$. Define Z_N as the sum of N Bernoulli random variables, so that

$$Z_N = \sum_{n=1}^{N} X_n.$$

We know that the resulting random variable Z_N is a binomial random variable with mean Np and variance $Np(1-p)$. Let us plot the PDF $f_{Z_N}(z)$ as shown in **Figure 6.16**.

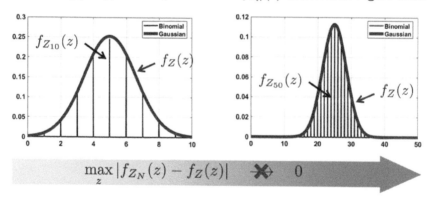

Figure 6.16: Convergence in distribution. The convergence in distribution concerns the convergence of the values of the CDF (not the PDF). In this figure, we let $Z_N = X_1 + \cdots + X_N$, where X_N is a Bernoulli random variable with parameter p. Since a sum of Bernoulli random variables is a binomial, Z_N is a binomial random variable with parameters (N, p). We plot the PDF of Z_N, which is a train of delta functions, and compare it with the Gaussian PDF. Observe that the error, $\max_z |f_{Z_N}(z) - f_Z(z)|$, does *not* converge to 0. The PDF of Z_N is a binomial. A binomial is always a binomial. It will not turn into a Gaussian.

The first thing we notice in the figure is that as N increases, the PDF of the binomial has an envelope that is "very Gaussian". So one temptation is to say that the random

368

variable Z_N is converging to another random variable Z. In addition, we would think that the PDFs converge in the sense that for *all* z,

$$f_{Z_N}(z) = \binom{N}{z}p^z(1-p)^{N-z} \longrightarrow f_Z(z) = \frac{1}{\sqrt{2\pi\sigma^2}}\exp\left\{-\frac{(z-\mu)^2}{2\sigma^2}\right\},$$

where $\mu = Np$ and $\sigma^2 = Np(1-p)$.

Unfortunately this argument does not work, because $f_Z(z)$ is continuous but $f_{Z_N}(z)$ is discrete. The sample space of Z_N and the sample space of Z are completely different. In fact, if we write f_{Z_N} as an impulse train, we observe that

$$f_{Z_N}(z) = \sum_{i=0}^{N}\binom{N}{i}p^i(1-p)^{N-i}\delta(z-i).$$

Clearly, no matter how big the N is, the difference $|f_{Z_N}(z) - f_Z(z)|$ will never go to zero for non-integer values of z. Mathematically, we can show that

$$\max_z |f_{Z_N}(z) - f_Z(z)| \not\longrightarrow 0,$$

as $N \to \infty$. Z_N is a binomial random variable regardless of N. It will not become a Gaussian.

If $f_{Z_N}(z)$ is not converging to a Gaussian PDF, how do we explain the convergence? The answer is to look at the CDF. For discrete PDFs such as a binomial random variable, the CDF is a staircase function. What we can show is that

$$F_{Z_N}(z) = \sum_{i=0}^{z}\binom{N}{i}p^i(1-p)^{N-i} \longrightarrow F_Z(z) = \int_{-\infty}^{z}\frac{1}{\sqrt{2\pi\sigma^2}}\exp\left\{-\frac{(t-\mu)^2}{2\sigma^2}\right\}\,dt.$$

The difference between the PDF convergence and the CDF convergence is that the PDF does not allow a meaningful "distance" between a discrete function and continuous function. For CDF, the distance is well defined by taking the difference between the staircase function and the continuous function. For example, we can compute

$$|F_{Z_N}(z) - F_Z(z)|, \qquad \text{for all continuous points } z \text{ of } F_Z,$$

and show that

$$\max_z |F_{Z_N}(z) - F_Z(z)| \longrightarrow 0.$$

We need to pay attention to the set of z's. We do not evaluate all z's but only the z's that are continuous points of F_Z. If F_Z is Gaussian, this does not matter because all z's are continuous. However, for CDFs containing discontinuous points, our definition of convergence in distribution will ignore these discontinuous points because they have a measure zero.

Example 2. (Poisson) Consider $X_n \sim \text{Poisson}(\lambda)$, and consider $X_1, \ldots, X_N$. Define $Z_N = \sum_{n=1}^{N} X_n$. It follows that $\mathbb{E}[Z_N] = \sum_{n=1}^{N}\mathbb{E}[X_n] = N\lambda$ and $\text{Var}[Z_N] = \sum_{n=1}^{N}\text{Var}[X_n] = N\lambda$. Moreover, we know that the sum of Poissons remains a Poisson. Therefore, the PDF of Z_N is

$$f_{Z_N}(z) = \sum_{k=0}^{\infty}\frac{(N\lambda)^k}{k!}e^{-N\lambda}\delta(z-k) \qquad \text{and} \qquad f_Z(z) = \frac{1}{\sqrt{2\pi\sigma^2}}\exp\left\{-\frac{(z-\mu)^2}{2\sigma^2}\right\},$$

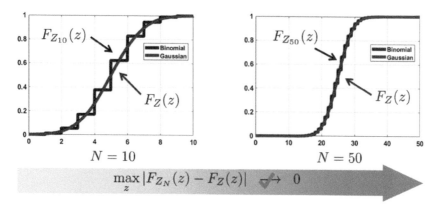

Figure 6.17: Convergence in distribution. This is the same as **Figure 6.16**, but this time we plot the CDF of Z_N. The CDF is a staircase function. We compare it with the Gaussian CDF. Observe that the error, $\max_z |F_{Z_N}(z) - F_Z(z)|$, converges to zero as N grows. Convergence in distribution says that the sequence of CDFs $F_{Z_N}(z)$ will converge to the limiting CDF $F_Z(z)$, at all continuous points of $F_Z(z)$.

where $\mu = N\lambda$ and $\sigma^2 = N\lambda$. Again, f_{Z_N} does not converge to f_Z. However, if we compare the CDF, we can see from **Figure 6.18** that the CDF of the Poisson is becoming better approximated by the Gaussian.

Interpreting "convergence in distribution". After seeing two examples, you should now have some idea of what "convergence in distribution" means. This concept applies to the CDFs. When we write

$$\lim_{N\to\infty} F_{Z_N}(z) = F_Z(z), \tag{6.38}$$

we mean that $F_{Z_N}(z)$ is converging to the value $F_Z(z)$, and this relationship holds for all the continuous z's of F_Z. It does not say that the random variable Z_N is becoming another random variable Z.

$$Z_N \xrightarrow{d} Z \text{ is equivalent to } \lim_{N\to\infty} F_{Z_N}(z) = F_Z(z).$$

Example 3. (Exponential) So far, we have studied the sum of discrete random variables. Now, let's take a look at continuous random variables. Consider $X_n \sim \text{Exponential}(\lambda)$, and let $X_1, \ldots, X_N$ be i.i.d. copies. Define $Z_N = \sum_{n=1}^N X_n$. Then $\mathbb{E}[Z_N] = \sum_{n=1}^N \mathbb{E}[X_n] = N/\lambda$ and $\text{Var}[Z_N] = \frac{N}{\lambda^2}$. How about the PDF of Z_N? Using the characteristic functions, we know that

$$f_{X_n}(x) = \lambda e^{-\lambda x} \xleftrightarrow{\mathcal{F}} \Phi_{X_n}(j\omega) = \frac{\lambda}{\lambda + j\omega}.$$

Therefore, the product is

$$\Phi_{Z_N}(j\omega) = \prod_{n=1}^N \Phi_{X_n}(j\omega) = \frac{\lambda^N}{(\lambda + j\omega)^N} = \frac{\lambda^N}{(\lambda + j\omega)^N} \times \frac{(N-1)!}{(N-1)!}$$

$$= \frac{\lambda^N}{(N-1)!} \cdot \frac{(N-1)!}{(\lambda + j\omega)^N} \xleftrightarrow{\mathcal{F}} \frac{\lambda^N}{(N-1)!} z^{N-1} e^{-\lambda z} = f_{Z_N}(z).$$

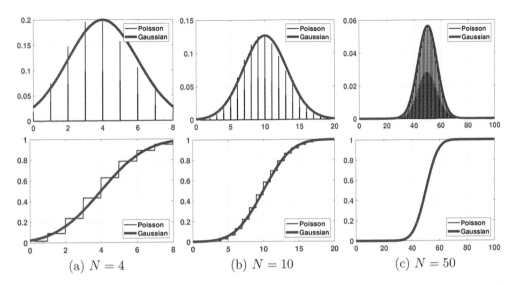

Figure 6.18: Convergence in distribution for a sum of Poisson random variables. Here we assume that $X_1, \ldots, X_N$ are i.i.d. Poisson with a parameter λ. We let $Z_N = \sum_{n=1}^{N} X_n$ be the sum, and compute the corresponding PDF (top row) and CDFs (bottom row). Just as with the binomial example, the PDFs of the Poisson do not converge but the CDFs of the Poisson converge to the CDF of a Gaussian.

This resulting PDF $f_{Z_N}(z) = \frac{\lambda^N}{(N-1)!} z^{N-1} e^{-\lambda z}$ is known as the **Erlang distribution**. The CDF of the Erlang distribution is

$$F_{Z_N}(z) = \int_{-\infty}^{z} f_{Z_N}(t) \, dt$$

$$= \int_{0}^{z} \frac{\lambda^N}{(N-1)!} t^{N-1} e^{-\lambda t} \, dt$$

$$= \text{Gamma function}(z, N),$$

where the last integral is known as the incomplete gamma function, evaluated at z.

Given all these, we can now compare the PDF and the CDF of Z_N versus Z. **Figure 6.19** shows the PDFs and the CDFs of Z_N for various N values. In this experiment we set $\lambda = 1$. As we can see from the experiment, the Erlang distribution's PDF and CDF converge to a Gaussian. In fact, for continuous random variables such as exponential random variables, we indeed have the random variable Z_N converging to the random variable Z. This is quite different from discrete random variables, where Z_N does not converge to Z but only F_{Z_N} converges to F_Z.

Is $\xrightarrow{d}$ stronger than $\xrightarrow{p}$? Convergence in distribution is actually weaker than convergence in probability. Consider a continuous random variable X with a symmetric PDF $f_X(x)$ such that $f_X(x) = f_X(-x)$. It holds that the PDF of $-X$ has the same PDF. If we define the sequence $Z_N = X$ if N is odd and $Z_N = -X$ if N is even, and let $Z = X$, then $F_{Z_N}(z) = F_Z(z)$ for every z because the PDF of X and $-X$ are identical. Therefore, $Z_N \xrightarrow{d} Z$. However, $Z_N \xcancel{\xrightarrow{p}} Z$ because Z_N oscillates between the random variables X and $-X$. These two random variables are different (although they have the same CDF) because $\mathbb{P}[X = -X] = \mathbb{P}[\{\omega : X(\omega) = -X(\omega)\}] = \mathbb{P}[\{\omega : X(\omega) = 0\}] = 0$.

371

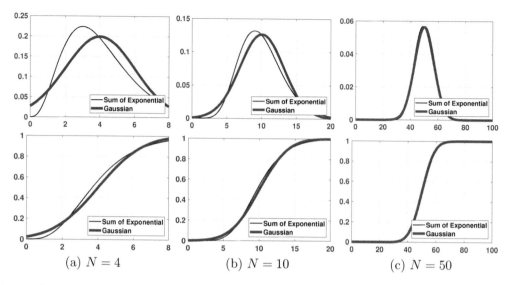

(a) $N = 4$ (b) $N = 10$ (c) $N = 50$

Figure 6.19: Convergence in distribution for a sum of exponential random variables. Here we assume that $X_1, \ldots, X_N$ are i.i.d. exponentials with a parameter λ. We define $Z_N = \sum_{n=1}^{N} X_n$ be the sum. It is known that the sum of exponentials is an Erlang. We compute the corresponding PDF (top row) and CDFs (bottom row). Unlike the previous two examples, in this example we see that both PDFs and CDFs of the Erlang distribution are converging to a Gaussian.

6.4.2 Central Limit Theorem

Theorem 6.19 (Central Limit Theorem). *Let $X_1, \ldots, X_N$ be i.i.d. random variables of mean $\mathbb{E}[X_n] = \mu$ and variance $\mathrm{Var}[X_n] = \sigma^2$. Also, assume that $\mathbb{E}[|X_n^3|] < \infty$. Let $\overline{X}_N = (1/N) \sum_{n=1}^{N} X_n$ be the sample average, and let $Z_N = \sqrt{N} \left(\frac{\overline{X}_N - \mu}{\sigma} \right)$. Then*

$$\lim_{N \to \infty} F_{\overline{Z}_N}(z) = F_Z(z), \tag{6.39}$$

where $Z = Gaussian(0, 1)$.

In plain words, the Central Limit Theorem says that the sample average (which is a random variable) has a CDF converging to the CDF of a Gaussian. Therefore, if we want to evaluate probabilities associated with the sample average, we can approximate the probability by the probability of a Gaussian.

As we discussed above, the Central Limit Theorem does not mean that the random variable Z_N is converging to a Gaussian random variable, nor does it mean that the PDF of Z_N is converging to the PDF of a Gaussian. It only means that the CDF of Z_N is converging to the CDF of a Gaussian. Many people think that the Central Limit Theorem means "sample average converges to Gaussian". This is incorrect for the above reasons. However, it is not completely wrong. For continuous random variables where both PDF and CDF are continuous, we will not run into situations where the PDF is a train of delta functions. In this case, convergence in CDF can be translated to convergence in PDF.

The power of the Central Limit Theorem is that the result holds for **any** distribution of $X_1, \ldots, X_N$. That is, regardless of the distribution of $X_1, \ldots, X_N$, the CDF of $\overline{X}_N$ is approaching a Gaussian.

Summary of the Central Limit Theorem

- $X_1, \ldots, X_N$ are i.i.d. random variables, with mean μ and variance σ^2. They are not necessarily Gaussians.

- Define the sample average as $\overline{X}_N = (1/N) \sum_{n=1}^{N} X_n$, and let $Z_N = \sqrt{N} \left(\frac{\overline{X} - \mu}{\sigma} \right)$.

- The Central Limit Theorem says $Z_N \xrightarrow{d}$ Gaussian$(0, 1)$. Equivalently, the theorem says that $N\overline{X}_N \xrightarrow{d}$ Gaussian(μ, σ^2).

- So if we want to evaluate the probability of $\overline{X}_N \in \mathcal{A}$ for some set $\mathcal{A}$, we can approximate the probability by evaluating the Gaussian:

$$\mathbb{P}[\overline{X}_N \in \mathcal{A}] \approx \int_{\mathcal{A}} \frac{1}{\sqrt{2\pi(\sigma^2/N)}} \exp \left\{ -\frac{(y - \mu)^2}{2(\sigma^2/N)} \right\} \, dy.$$

- CLT does **not** say that the PDF of $\overline{X}_N$ is becoming a Gaussian PDF.

- CLT only says that the CDF of $\overline{X}_N$ is becoming a Gaussian CDF.

If the set $\mathcal{A}$ is an interval, we can use the standard Gaussian CDF to compute the probability.

Corollary 6.3. *Let $X_1, \ldots, X_N$ be i.i.d. random variables with mean μ and variance σ^2. Define the sample average as $\overline{X}_N = (1/N) \sum_{n=1}^{N} X_n$. Then*

$$\mathbb{P}[a \leq \overline{X}_N \leq b] \approx \Phi \left(\sqrt{N} \frac{b - \mu}{\sigma} \right) - \Phi \left(\sqrt{N} \frac{a - \mu}{\sigma} \right), \tag{6.40}$$

where $\Phi(z) = \int_{-\infty}^{z} \frac{1}{\sqrt{2\pi}} e^{-\frac{x^2}{2}} \, dx$ is the CDF of the standard Gaussian.

Proof. By the Central Limit Theorem, we know that $\overline{X}_N \xrightarrow{d}$ Gaussian$(\mu, \frac{\sigma^2}{N})$. Therefore,

$$\mathbb{P}[a \leq \overline{X}_N \leq b] \approx \int_a^b \frac{1}{\sqrt{2\pi(\sigma^2/N)}} \exp \left\{ -\frac{(y - \mu)^2}{2(\sigma^2/N)} \right\} \, dy$$

$$= \int_{\sqrt{N}\frac{a-\mu}{\sigma}}^{\sqrt{N}\frac{b-\mu}{\sigma}} \frac{1}{\sqrt{2\pi}} e^{-\frac{y^2}{2}} \, dy = \Phi \left(\sqrt{N} \frac{b - \mu}{\sigma} \right) - \Phi \left(\sqrt{N} \frac{a - \mu}{\sigma} \right).$$

$\square$

A graphical illustration of the CLT is shown in **Figure 6.20**, where we use a binomial random variable (which is the sum of i.i.d. Bernoulli) as an example. The CLT does not say that the binomial random variable is becoming a Gaussian. It only says that the probability covered by the binomial can be approximated by the Gaussian.

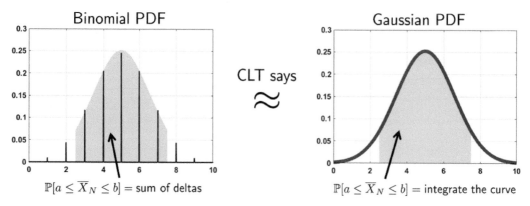

$\mathbb{P}[a \leq \overline{X}_N \leq b] = $ sum of deltas $\qquad \mathbb{P}[a \leq \overline{X}_N \leq b] = $ integrate the curve

Figure 6.20: The Central Limit Theorem says that if we want to evaluate the probability $\mathbb{P}[a \leq \overline{X}_N \leq b]$, where $\overline{X}_N = (1/N)\sum_{n=1}^{N} X_n$ is the sample average of i.i.d. random variables $X_1, \ldots, X_N$, we can approximate the probability by integrating the Gaussian PDF.

The following proof of the Central Limit Theorem can be skipped if this is your first time reading the book.

Proof of the Central Limit Theorem. We now give a "proof" of the Central Limit Theorem. Technically speaking, this proof does not prove the convergence of the CDF as the theorem claims; it only proves that the moment-generating function converges. The actual proof of the CDF convergence is based on the Berry-Esseen Theorem, which is beyond the scope of this book. However, what we prove below is still useful because it gives us some intuition about why Gaussian is the limiting random variable we should consider in the first place.

Let $Z_N = \sqrt{N}\left(\frac{\overline{X}_N - \mu}{\sigma}\right)$. It follows that $\mathbb{E}[Z_N] = 0$ and $\text{Var}[Z_N] = 1$. Therefore, if we can show that Z_N is converging to a standard Gaussian random variable $Z \sim \text{Gaussian}(0,1)$, then by the linear transformation property of Gaussian, $Y = \frac{\sigma}{\sqrt{N}}Z + \mu$ will be Gaussian$(\mu, \sigma^2/N)$.

Our proof is based on analyzing the moment-generating function of Z_N. In particular,

$$M_{Z_N}(s) \stackrel{\text{def}}{=} \mathbb{E}[e^{sZ_N}] = \mathbb{E}\left[e^{s\sqrt{N}\left(\frac{\overline{X}_N - \mu}{\sigma}\right)}\right] = \prod_{n=1}^{N} \mathbb{E}\left[e^{\frac{s}{\sigma\sqrt{N}}(X_n - \mu)}\right].$$

Expanding the exponential term using the Taylor expansion (Chapter 1.2),

$$\prod_{n=1}^{N} \mathbb{E}\left[e^{\frac{s}{\sigma\sqrt{N}}(X_n - \mu)}\right]$$

$$= \prod_{n=1}^{N} \mathbb{E}\left[1 + \frac{s}{\sigma\sqrt{N}}(X_n - \mu) + \frac{s^2}{2\sigma^2 N}(X_n - \mu)^2 + \mathcal{O}\left(\frac{(X_n - \mu)^3}{\sigma^3 N\sqrt{N}}\right)\right]$$

$$= \prod_{n=1}^{N} \left[1 + \frac{s}{\sigma\sqrt{N}}\mathbb{E}[X_n - \mu] + \frac{s^2}{2\sigma^2 N}\mathbb{E}\left[(X_n - \mu)^2\right]\right] = \left(1 + \frac{s^2}{2N}\right)^N.$$

It remains to show that $\left(1 + \frac{s^2}{2N}\right)^N \to e^{s^2/2}$. If we can show that, we have shown that the MGF of Z_N is also the MGF of Gaussian$(0,1)$. To this end, we consider $\log(1+x)$. By the Taylor approximation, we have that

$$\log(1+x) \approx \log(1) + \left(\frac{d}{dx}\log x\big|_{x=1}\right)x + \left(\frac{d^2}{dx^2}\log x\big|_{x=1}\right)\frac{x^2}{2} + \mathcal{O}(x^3).$$

Therefore, we have $\log\left(1 + \frac{s^2}{2N}\right) \approx \frac{s^2}{2N} - \frac{s^4}{4N^2}$. As $N \to \infty$, the limit becomes

$$\lim_{N\to\infty} N\log\left(1 + \frac{s^2}{2N}\right) \approx \frac{s^2}{2} - \lim_{N\to\infty}\frac{s^4}{4N} = \frac{s^2}{2},$$

and so taking the exponential on both sides yields $\lim_{N\to\infty}\left(1+\frac{s^2}{2N}\right)^N = e^{\frac{s^2}{2}}$. Therefore, we conclude that $\lim_{N\to\infty} M_{Z_N}(s) = e^{\frac{s^2}{2}}$, and so Z_N is converging to a Gaussian.

$\square$

Limitation of our proof. The limitation of our proof lies in the issue of whether the integration and the limit are interchangeable:

$$\lim_{N\to\infty} M_{Z_N}(s) = \lim_{N\to\infty}\left\{\int f_{Z_N}(z)e^{sz}\,dz\right\}$$
$$\stackrel{?}{=} \int\left(\lim_{N\to\infty} f_{Z_N}(z)\right)e^{sz}\,dz.$$

If they were, then proving $\lim_{N\to\infty} M_{Z_N}(s) = M_Z(s)$ is sufficient to claim $f_{Z_N}(z) \to f_Z(z)$. However, we know that the latter is not true in general. For example, if $f_{Z_N}(z)$ is a train of delta functions, then the limit and the integration are not interchangeable.

Berry-Esseen Theorem. The formal way of proving the Central Limit Theorem is to prove the Berry-Esseen Theorem. The theorem states that

$$\sup_{z\in\mathbb{R}}\left|F_{Z_N}(z) - F_Z(z)\right| \le C\frac{\beta}{\sigma^3\sqrt{N}},$$

where β and C are universal constants. Here, you can more or less treat the supremum operator as the maximum. The left-hand side represents the **worst-case** error of the CDF F_{Z_N} compared to the limiting CDF F_Z. The right-hand side involves several constants C, β, and σ, but they are fixed.

As N goes to infinity, the right-hand side will converge to zero. Therefore, if we can prove this result, then we have proved the actual Central Limit Theorem. In addition, we have found the rate of convergence since the right-hand side tells us that the error drops at the rate of $1/\sqrt{N}$, which is not particularly fast but is sufficient for our purpose. Unfortunately, proving the Berry-Esseen theorem is not easy. One of the difficulties, for example, is that one needs to deal with the infinite convolutions in the time domain or the frequency domain.

Interpreting our proof. If our proof is not completely valid, why do we mention it? For one thing, it provides us with some useful intuition. For most of the (well-behaving) random variables whose moments are finite, the exponential term in the moment-generating function can be truncated to the second-order polynomial. Since a second-order polynomial is a Gaussian, it naturally concludes that as long as we can perform such truncation the truncated random variable will be Gaussian.

To convince you that the Gaussian MGF is the second-order approximation to other MGFs, we use Bernoulli as an example. Let $X_1, \ldots, X_N$ be i.i.d. Bernoulli with a parameter p. Then the moment-generating function of $\overline{X}_N = (1/N) \sum_{n=1}^{N} X_n$ would be:

$$M_{\overline{X}_N}(s) = \mathbb{E}[e^{s\overline{X}}] = \mathbb{E}[e^{s\frac{1}{N}\sum_{n=1}^{N} X_n}] = \prod_{n=1}^{N} \mathbb{E}[e^{\frac{s}{N} X_n}]$$

$$= (1 - p + pe^{\frac{s}{N}})^N \approx \left(1 - p + p\left(1 + \frac{s}{N} + \frac{s^2}{2N^2}\right)\right)^N$$

$$= \left(1 + \frac{sp}{N} + \frac{s^2 p}{2N^2}\right)^N.$$

Using the logarithmic approximation, it follows that

$$\log M_{\overline{X}_N}(s) = N \log \left(1 + \frac{sp}{N} + \frac{s^2 p}{2N^2}\right)$$

$$\approx N \left(\frac{sp}{N} + \frac{s^2 p}{2N^2}\right) - \frac{N}{2} \left(\frac{sp}{N} + \frac{s^2 p}{2N^2}\right)^2$$

$$\approx sp + \frac{s^2 p(1 - p)}{2N} \stackrel{\text{def}}{=} \log M_Y(s).$$

Taking the exponential on both sides, we have that

$$M_Y(s) = \exp\left\{sp + \frac{s^2 p(1 - p)}{2N}\right\},$$

which is the MGF of a Gaussian random variable $Y \sim \text{Gaussian}\left(p, \frac{p(1-p)}{N}\right)$.

Figure 6.21 shows several MGFs. In each of the subfigures we plot the exact MGF $M_{\overline{X}_N}(s) = (1-p+pe^{\frac{s}{N}})^N$ as a function of s. (The parameter p in this example is $p = 0.5$.) We vary the number N, and we inspect how the shape of $M_{\overline{X}_N}(s)$ changes. On top of the exact MGFs, we plot the Gaussian approximations $M_Y(s) = \exp\left\{sp + \frac{s^2 p(1-p)}{2N}\right\}$. According to our calculation, this Gaussian approximation is the second-order approximation to the exact MGF. The figures show the effect of the second-order approximation. For example, in (a) when $N = 2$ the Gaussian is a quadratic approximation of the exact MGF. For (b) and (c), as N increases, the approximation improves.

The reason why the second-order approximation works for Gaussian is that when N increases, the higher order moments of $\overline{X}_N$ vanish and only the leading first two moments survive. The MGFs are becoming flat because $M_Y(s) = \exp\left\{sp + \frac{s^2 p(1-p)}{2N}\right\}$ converges to $\exp\{sp\}$ when $N \to \infty$. Taking the inverse Laplace transform, $M_Y(s) = \exp\{sp\}$ corresponds to a delta function. This makes sense because as N grows, the variance of the $\overline{X}$ shrinks.

> End of the discussion.

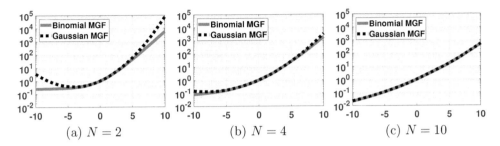

(a) $N = 2$ (b) $N = 4$ (c) $N = 10$

Figure 6.21: Explanation of the Central Limit Theorem using the function. In this set of plots, we show the MGF of the random variable $\overline{X}_N = (1/N)\sum_{n=1}^{N} X_n$, where $X_1, \ldots, X_N$ are i.i.d. Bernoulli random variables. The exact MGF of $\overline{X}_N$ is the binomial, whereas the approximated MGF is the Gaussian. We observe that as N increases, the Gaussian approximation to the exact MGF improves.

6.4.3 Examples

Example 6.15. Prove the equivalence of a few statements.

- $\sqrt{N}\left(\frac{\overline{X}_N - \mu}{\sigma}\right) \overset{d}{\to} \text{Gaussian}(0, 1)$

- $\sqrt{N}(\overline{X}_N - \mu) \overset{d}{\to} \text{Gaussian}(0, \sigma^2)$

- $\sqrt{N}\overline{X}_N \overset{d}{\to} \text{Gaussian}(\mu, \sigma^2)$

Solution. The proof is based on the linear transformation property of Gaussian random variables. For example, if the first statement is true, then the second statement is also true because

$$\lim_{N \to \infty} F_{\sqrt{N}(\overline{X}_N - \mu)}(z) = \lim_{N \to \infty} \mathbb{P}[\sqrt{N}(\overline{X}_N - \mu) \le z] = \lim_{N \to \infty} \mathbb{P}\left[\sqrt{N}\left(\frac{\overline{X}_N - \mu}{\sigma}\right) \le \frac{z}{\sigma}\right]$$

$$= \int_{-\infty}^{z/\sigma} \frac{1}{\sqrt{2\pi}} e^{-\frac{t^2}{2}} \, dt = \int_{-\infty}^{z} \frac{1}{\sqrt{2\pi\sigma^2}} e^{-\frac{t^2}{2\sigma^2}} \, dt.$$

The other results can be proved similarly.

Example 6.16. Suppose $X_n \sim \text{Poisson}(10)$ for $n = 1, \ldots, N$, and let $\overline{X}_N$ be the sample average. Use the Central Limit Theorem to approximate $\mathbb{P}[9 \le \overline{X}_N \le 11]$ for $N = 20$.

Solution. We first show that

$$\mathbb{E}[\overline{X}_N] = \mathbb{E}\left[\frac{1}{N}\sum_{n=1}^{N} X_n\right] = \frac{1}{N}\sum_{n=1}^{N} \mathbb{E}[X_n] = 10,$$

$$\text{Var}[\overline{X}_N] = \frac{1}{N^2}\sum_{n=1}^{N} \text{Var}[X_n] = \frac{1}{N}\text{Var}[X_n] = \frac{10}{20} = \frac{1}{2}.$$

Therefore, the Central Limit Theorem implies that $\overline{X}_N \xrightarrow{d}$ Gaussian $\left(10, \frac{1}{2}\right)$. The probability is

$$\mathbb{P}[9 \leq \overline{X}_N \leq 11] \approx \Phi\left(\frac{11 - 10}{\sqrt{1/2}}\right) - \Phi\left(\frac{9 - 10}{\sqrt{1/2}}\right)$$

$$= \Phi\left(\frac{1}{\sqrt{0.5}}\right) - \Phi\left(-\frac{1}{\sqrt{0.5}}\right) = 0.9214 - 0.0786 = 0.8427.$$

We can also do an exact calculation to verify our approximation. Let $S_N = \sum_{n=1}^{N} X_n$ so that $\overline{X}_N = \frac{S_N}{N}$. Since a sum of Poisson remains a Poisson, it follows that

$$S_N \sim \text{Poisson}(10N) = \text{Poisson}(200).$$

Consequently,

$$\mathbb{P}[9 \leq \overline{X}_N \leq 11] = \mathbb{P}[180 \leq S_N \leq 220]$$

$$= \sum_{\ell=0}^{220} \frac{200^{\ell} e^{-200}}{\ell!} - \sum_{\ell=0}^{180} \frac{200^{\ell} e^{-200}}{\ell!} = 0.9247 - 0.0822 = 0.8425.$$

Note that this is an exact calculation subject to numerical errors when evaluating the finite sums.

Example 6.17. Suppose you have collected $N = 100$ data points from an unknown distribution. The only thing you know is that the true population mean is $\mu = 500$ and the standard deviation is $\sigma = 80$. (Note that this distribution is not necessarily a Gaussian.)

(a) Find the probability that the sample mean will be inside the interval $(490, 510)$.

(b) Find an interval such that 95% of the sample average is covered.

Solution. To solve (a), we note that $\overline{X}_N \xrightarrow{d}$ Gaussian $\left(500, \left(\frac{80}{\sqrt{100}}\right)^2\right)$. Therefore,

$$\mathbb{P}[490 \leq \overline{X}_N \leq 510] = \Phi\left(\frac{510 - 500}{\frac{80}{\sqrt{100}}}\right) - \Phi\left(\frac{490 - 500}{\frac{80}{\sqrt{100}}}\right)$$

$$= \Phi(1.25) - \Phi(-1.25) = 0.7888.$$

To solve (b), we know that $\Phi(x) = 0.025$ implies that $x = -1.96$, and $\Phi(x) = 0.975$ implies that $x = +1.96$. So

$$\frac{y - 500}{\frac{80}{\sqrt{100}}} = \pm 1.96 \quad \Rightarrow \quad y = 484.32 \quad \text{or} \quad y = 515.68.$$

Therefore, $\mathbb{P}[484.32 \leq \overline{X}_N \leq 515.68] = 0.95$.

6.4.4 Limitation of the Central Limit Theorem

If we recall the statement of the Central Limit Theorem (Berry-Esseen), we observe that the theorem states only that

$$\lim_{N\to\infty} \mathbb{P}\left[\sqrt{N}\left(\frac{\overline{X}_N - \mu}{\sigma}\right) \le \varepsilon\right] = \lim_{N\to\infty} F_{Z_N}(\varepsilon) = F_Z(\varepsilon) = \Phi(\varepsilon).$$

Rearranging the terms,

$$\lim_{N\to\infty} \mathbb{P}\left[\overline{X}_N \le \mu + \frac{\sigma\varepsilon}{\sqrt{N}}\right] = \Phi(\varepsilon).$$

This implies that the approximation is good only when the deviation ε is *small*.

Let us consider an example to illustrate this idea. Consider a set of i.i.d. exponential random variables $X_1,\ldots,X_N$, where $X_n \sim \text{Exponential}(\lambda)$. Let $S_N = X_1 + \cdots + X_N$ be the sum, and let $\overline{X} = S_N/N$ be the sample average. Then, according to Chapter 6.4.1, S_N is an Erlang distribution $S_N \sim \text{Erlang}(N, \lambda)$ with a PDF

$$f_{S_N}(x) = \frac{\lambda^N}{(N-1)!} x^{N-1} e^{-\lambda x}.$$

Practice Exercise 6.10. Let $S_N \sim \text{Erlang}(N, \lambda)$ with a PDF $f_{S_N}(x)$. Show that if $Y_N = aS_N + b$ for any constants a and b, then

$$f_{Y_N}(y) = \frac{1}{a} f_{S_N}\left(\frac{y-b}{a}\right).$$

Solution: This is a simple transformation of random variables:

$$F_{Y_N}(y) = \mathbb{P}[Y \le y] = \mathbb{P}[aS_N + b \le y] = \mathbb{P}\left[S_N \le \frac{y-b}{a}\right] = \int_{-\infty}^{\frac{y-b}{a}} f_{S_N}(x)\,dx.$$

Hence, using the fundamental theorem of calculus,

$$f_{Y_N}(y) = \frac{d}{dy} \int_{-\infty}^{\frac{y-b}{a}} f_{S_N}(x)\,dx = \frac{1}{a} f_{S_N}\left(\frac{y-b}{a}\right).$$

We are interested in knowing the statistics of $\overline{X}_N$ and comparing it with a Gaussian. To this end, we construct a normalized variable

$$Z_N = \frac{\overline{X}_N - \mu}{\sigma/\sqrt{N}},$$

where $\mu = \mathbb{E}[X_n] = \frac{1}{\lambda}$ and $\sigma^2 = \text{Var}[X_n] = \frac{1}{\lambda^2}$. Then

$$Z_N = \frac{S_N/N - \mu}{\sigma/\sqrt{N}} = \frac{S_N - N\mu}{\sigma\sqrt{N}} = \frac{\lambda}{\sqrt{N}} S_N - \sqrt{N}$$

Using the result of the practice exercise, by mapping $a = \frac{\lambda}{\sqrt{N}}$ and $b = -\sqrt{N}$, it follows that

$$f_{Z_N}(z) = \frac{\sqrt{N}}{\lambda} f_{S_N}\left(\frac{z + \sqrt{N}}{\frac{\lambda}{\sqrt{N}}}\right).$$

Now we compare Z_N with the standard Gaussian $Z \sim \text{Gaussian}(0,1)$. According to the Central Limit Theorem, the standard Gaussian is a good approximation to the normalized sample average Z_N. To compare the two results, we conduct a numerical experiment. We let $\lambda = 1$ and we vary N. We plot the PDF $f_{Z_N}(z)$ as a function of z, for different N's, in **Figure 6.22**. In addition, we plot the PDF $f_Z(z)$, which is the standard Gaussian.

The plot in **Figure 6.22** shows that while the Central Limit Theorem provides a good approximation, the approximation is only good for values that are close to the mean. For the **tails**, the Gaussian approximation is not as good.

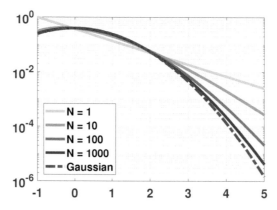

Figure 6.22: CLT fails at the tails. We note that $X_1, \ldots, X_N$ are i.i.d. exponential with a parameter $\lambda = 1$. We plot the PDFs of the normalized sample average $Z_N = \frac{\bar{X}_N - \mu}{\sigma/\sqrt{N}}$ by varying N. We plot the PDF of the standard Gaussian $Z \sim \text{Gaussian}(0,1)$ on the same grid. Note that the Gaussian approximation is good for values that are close to the mean. For the tails, the Gaussian approximation is not very accurate.

The limitation of the Central Limit Theorem is attributable to the fact that Gaussian is a second-order approximation. If a random variable has a very large third moment, the second-order approximation may not be sufficient. In this case, we need a much larger N to drive the third moment to a small value and make the Gaussian approximation valid.

When will the Central Limit Theorem fail?

- The Central Limit Theorem fails when N is small.
- The Central Limit Theorem fails if the third moment is large. As an extreme case, a Cauchy random variable does not have a finite third moment. The Central Limit Theorem is not valid for this case.
- The Central Limit Theorem can only approximate the probability for input values near the mean. It does not approximate the tails, for which we need to use Chernoff's bound.

6.5 Summary

Why do we need to study the sample average? Because it is the summary of the dataset. In machine learning, one of the most frequently asked questions is about the number of training samples required to train a model. The answer can be found by analyzing the average number of successes and failures as the number of training samples grows. For example, if we define f as the classifier that takes a data point $\boldsymbol{x}_n$ and predicts a label $f(\boldsymbol{x}_n)$, we hope that it will match with the true label y_n. If we define an error

$$
E_n = \begin{cases} 1, & f(\boldsymbol{x}_n) = y_n \quad \text{correct classification,} \\ 0, & f(\boldsymbol{x}_n) \neq y_n \quad \text{incorrect classification,} \end{cases}
$$

then E_n is a Bernoulli random variable, and the total loss $\mathcal{E} = \frac{1}{N} \sum_{n=1}^{N} E_n$ will be the training loss. But what is $\frac{1}{N} \sum_{n=1}^{N} E_n$? It is exactly the sample average of E_n. Therefore, by analyzing the sample average $\mathcal{E}$ we will learn something about the generalization capability of our model.

How should we study the sample average? By understanding the law of large numbers and the Central Limit Theorem, as we have seen in this chapter.

- Law of large numbers: $\overline{X}$ converges to the true mean μ as N grows.
- Central Limit Theorem: The CDF of $\overline{X}$ can be approximated by the CDF of a Gaussian, as N grows.

Performance guarantee? The other topic we discussed in this chapter is the concept of convergence type. There are essentially four types of convergence, ranked in the order of restrictions.

- **Deterministic convergence**: A sequence of deterministic numbers converges to another deterministic number. For example, the sequence $1, \frac{1}{2}, \frac{1}{3}, \frac{1}{4}, \ldots$ converges to 0 deterministically. There is nothing random about it.
- **Almost sure convergence**: Randomness exists, and there is a probabilistic convergence. Almost sure convergence means that there is zero probability of failure after a finite number of failures.
- **Convergence in probability**: The sequence of probability values converges, i.e., the chance of failure is going to zero. However, you can still fail even if your N is large.
- **Convergence in distribution**: The probability values can be approximated by the CDF of a Gaussian.

6.6 References

Moment-Generating and Characteristic Functions

6-1 Dimitri P. Bertsekas and John N. Tsitsiklis, *Introduction to Probability*, Athena Scientific, 2nd Edition, 2008. Chapter 4.4.

6-2 Alberto Leon-Garcia, *Probability, Statistics, and Random Processes for Electrical Engineering*, Prentice Hall, 3rd Edition, 2008. Chapters 4.5 and 4.7.

6-3 Athanasios Papoulis and S. Unnikrishna Pillai, *Probability, Random Variables and Stochastic Processes*, McGraw-Hill, 4th Edition, 2001. Chapters 5.5 and 7.2.

6-4 Henry Stark and John Woods, *Probability and Random Processes With Applications to Signal Processing*, Prentice Hall, 3rd Edition, 2001. Chapters 4.5 and 4.7.

6-5 Sheldon Ross, *A First Course in Probability*, Prentice Hall, 8th Edition, 2010. Chapter 7.7.

6-6 John A. Gubner, *Probability and Random Processes for Electrical and Computer Engineers*, Cambridge University Press, 2006. Chapter 4.3.

Basic probability inequality

6-7 Dimitri P. Bertsekas and John N. Tsitsiklis, *Introduction to Probability*, Athena Scientific, 2nd Edition, 2008. Chapter 5.1.

6-8 Alberto Leon-Garcia, *Probability, Statistics, and Random Processes for Electrical Engineering*, Prentice Hall, 3rd Edition, 2008. Chapters 6 and 8.

6-9 Athanasios Papoulis and S. Unnikrishna Pillai, *Probability, Random Variables and Stochastic Processes*, McGraw-Hill, 4th Edition, 2001. Chapter 7.4.

6-10 Sheldon Ross, *A First Course in Probability*, Prentice Hall, 8th Edition, 2010. Chapter 8.2.

6-11 Larry Wasserman, *All of Statistics*, Springer 2003. Chapter 4.

Concentration inequalities

6-12 Larry Wasserman, *All of Statistics*, Springer 2003. Chapter 4.

6-13 Martin Wainwright, *High-Dimensional Statistics*, Cambridge University Press, 2019. Chapter 2.1.

6-14 Stephane Boucheron, Gabor Lugosi and Pascal Massart, *Concentration Inequalities*, Oxford University Press, 2013. Chapters 2.1 and 2.2.

Law of large numbers

6-15 Dimitri P. Bertsekas and John N. Tsitsiklis, *Introduction to Probability*, Athena Scientific, 2nd Edition, 2008. Chapters 5.2, 5.3, 5.5.

6-16 Alberto Leon-Garcia, *Probability, Statistics, and Random Processes for Electrical Engineering*, Prentice Hall, 3rd Edition, 2008. Chapters 7.1, 7.2, 7.4

6-17 Athanasios Papoulis and S. Unnikrishna Pillai, *Probability, Random Variables and Stochastic Processes*, McGraw-Hill, 4th Edition, 2001. Chapter 7.4.

6-18 Sheldon Ross, *A First Course in Probability*, Prentice Hall, 8th Edition, 2010. Chapter 8.2, 8.4.

6-19 John A. Gubner, *Probability and Random Processes for Electrical and Computer Engineers*, Cambridge University Press, 2006. Chapters 3.3, 14.1, 14.3.

6-20 Larry Wasserman, *All of Statistics*, Springer 2003. Chapter 5.1 - 5.3.

6-21 Patrick Billingsley, *Probability and Measure*, Wiley 1995. Section 22.

Central Limit Theorem

6-22 Dimitri P. Bertsekas and John N. Tsitsiklis, *Introduction to Probability*, Athena Scientific, 2nd Edition, 2008. Chapter 5.4.

6-23 Alberto Leon-Garcia, *Probability, Statistics, and Random Processes for Electrical Engineering*, Prentice Hall, 3rd Edition, 2008. Chapter 7.3.

6-24 Athanasios Papoulis and S. Unnikrishna Pillai, *Probability, Random Variables and Stochastic Processes*, McGraw-Hill, 4th Edition, 2001. Chapter 7.4.

6-25 Sheldon Ross, *A First Course in Probability*, Prentice Hall, 8th Edition, 2010. Chapter 8.3.

6-26 John A. Gubner, *Probability and Random Processes for Electrical and Computer Engineers*, Cambridge University Press, 2006. Chapters 5.6, 14.2.

6-27 Larry Wasserman, *All of Statistics*, Springer 2003. Chapter 5.4.

6-28 Patrick Billingsley, *Probability and Measure*, Wiley 1995. Section 27.

6.7   Problems

Exercise 1. (VIDEO SOLUTION)
Let X, Y, Z be three independent random variables:

$$X \sim \text{Bernoulli}(p), \qquad Y \sim \text{Exponential}(\alpha), \qquad Z \sim \text{Poisson}(\lambda)$$

Find the function for the following random variables.

(a) $U = Y + Z$

(b) $U = 2Z + 3$

(c) $U = XY$

(d) $U = 2XY + (1 - X)Z$

Exercise 2. (VIDEO SOLUTION)
Two random variables X and Y have the joint PMF

$$\mathbb{P}(X = n, Y = m) = \frac{\lambda_1^{n+m} \lambda_2^m}{(n+m)!m!} e^{-(\lambda_1 + \lambda_2)}, \qquad m = 0, 1, 2, \ldots, \ n \geq -m.$$

Let $Z = X + Y$. Find the function $M_Z(s)$ and the PMF of Z.

Exercise 3. (VIDEO SOLUTION)
Let $X_0, X_1, \ldots$ be a sequence of independent random variables with PDF

$$f_{X_k}(x) = \frac{a_k}{\pi(a_k^2 + x^2)}, \qquad a_k = \frac{1}{2^{k+1}},$$

for $k = 0, 1, \ldots$. Find the PDF of Y, where

$$Y = \sum_{k=0}^{\infty} X_k.$$

Hint: You may find the characteristic function useful.

Exercise 4.
The random variables X and Y are independent and have PDFs

$$f_X(x) = \begin{cases} e^{-x}, & x \geq 0, \\ 0, & x < 0, \end{cases} \qquad \text{and} \qquad f_Y(y) = \begin{cases} 0, & y > 0, \\ e^y, & y \leq 0. \end{cases}$$

Find the PDF of $Z = X + Y$. (Hint: Use the characteristic function and the moment-generating function.)

Exercise 5.
A discrete random variable X has a PMF

$$p_X(k) = \frac{1}{2^k}, \qquad k = 1, 2, \ldots.$$

Find the characteristic function $\Phi_X(j\omega)$.

Exercise 6.
Let $T_1, T_2, \ldots$ be i.i.d. random variables with PDF

$$f_{T_k}(t) = \begin{cases} \lambda e^{-\lambda t}, & t \geq 0, \\ 0, & t < 0, \end{cases}$$

for $k = 1, 2, 3, \ldots$. Let $S_n = \sum_{k=1}^{n} T_k$. Find the PDF of S_n.

Exercise 7. (VIDEO SOLUTION)
In this exercise we will prove a variant of Chebyshev when the variance σ^2 is unknown but X is bounded between $a \leq X \leq b$.

(a) Let $\gamma \in \mathbb{R}$. Find a γ that minimizes $\mathbb{E}[(X-\gamma)^2]$. Hence, show that $\mathbb{E}[(X-\gamma)^2] \geq \mathrm{Var}[X]$ for any γ.

(b) Let $\gamma = (a+b)/2$. Show that

$$\mathbb{E}[(X-\gamma)^2] = \mathbb{E}[(X-a)(X-b)] + \frac{(b-a)^2}{4}.$$

(c) From (a) and (b), show that $\mathrm{Var}[X] \leq \frac{(b-a)^2}{4}$.

(d) Show that for any $\varepsilon > 0$,

$$\mathbb{P}[|X - \mu| > \varepsilon] \leq \frac{(b-a)^2}{4\varepsilon^2}.$$

Exercise 8.
The random variables X and Y are independent with PDFs

$$f_X(x) = \frac{1}{\pi(1+x^2)} \quad \text{and} \quad f_Y(y) = \frac{1}{\pi(1+y^2)},$$

respectively. Find the PDF of $Z = X - Y$. (Hint: Use the characteristic function.)

Exercise 9.
A random variable X has the characteristic function

$$\Phi_X(j\omega) = e^{-j\omega/(1-j\omega)}.$$

Find the mean and variance of X.

Exercise 10.
Show that for any random variables X and Y,

$$\mathbb{P}[|X - Y| > \epsilon] \leq \frac{1}{\epsilon^2}\mathbb{E}[(X - Y)^2].$$

Exercise 11.
Let X be an exponential random variable with a parameter λ. Let $\mu = \mathbb{E}[X]$ and $\sigma^2 = \mathrm{Var}[X]$. Compute $\mathbb{P}[|X - \mu| \geq k\sigma]$ for any $k > 1$. Compare this to the bound obtained by Chebyshev's inequality.

Exercise 12.
Let $X_1, \ldots, X_N$ be i.i.d. Bernoulli with a parameter p. Let $\alpha > 0$ and define

$$\epsilon = \sqrt{\frac{1}{2N}\log\left(\frac{2}{\alpha}\right)}.$$

Let $\overline{X}_N = \frac{1}{N}\sum_{n=1}^{N} X_n$. Define an interval

$$\mathcal{I} = \left[\overline{X}_N - \epsilon, \ \overline{X}_N + \epsilon\right].$$

Use Hoeffding's inequality to show that

$$\mathbb{P}[\mathcal{I} \text{ contains } p] \geq 1 - \alpha.$$

Exercise 13.
Let $Z \sim \mathrm{Gaussian}(0, 1)$. Prove that for any $\epsilon > 0$,

$$\mathbb{P}[|Z| > \epsilon] \leq \sqrt{\frac{2}{\pi}}\frac{e^{-\frac{\epsilon^2}{2}}}{\epsilon}.$$

Hint: Note that $\epsilon\mathbb{P}[|Z| > \epsilon] = 2\epsilon\mathbb{P}[Z > \epsilon]$, and then follow the procedure we used to prove Markov's inequality.

Exercise 14.
(a) Give a non-negative random variable $X \geq 0$ such that Markov's inequality is met with equality. Hint: Consider a discrete random variable.

(b) Give a random variable X such that Chebyshev's inequality is met with equality.

Exercise 15.
Consider a random variable X such that

$$\mathbb{E}[e^{sX}] \leq e^{\frac{s^2\sigma^2}{2}}.$$

(a) Show that for any t,

$$\mathbb{P}[X \geq t] \leq \exp\left\{-\frac{t^2}{2\sigma^2}\right\}.$$

Hint: Use Chernoff's bound.

(b) Show that

$$\mathbb{E}[X^2] \leq 4\sigma^2.$$

Hint: First prove that $\mathbb{E}[X^2] = \int_0^\infty \mathbb{P}[X^2 \geq t]\, dt$. Then use part (a) above.

Exercise 16.
Let $X_1, \ldots, X_N$ be i.i.d. uniform random variables distributed over $[0, 1]$. Suppose $Y_1, \ldots, Y_N$ are defined as follows.

(a) $Y_n = X_n/n$

(b) $Y_n = (X_n)^n$

(c) $Y_n = \max(X_1, \ldots, X_n)$

(d) $Y_n = \min(X_1, \ldots, X_n)$

For (a), (b), (c), and (d), show that Y_n converges in probability to some limit. Identify the limit in each case.

Exercise 17.
Let $\lambda_n = \frac{1}{n}$ for $n = 1, 2, \ldots$. Let $X_n \sim \text{Poisson}(\lambda_n)$. Show that X_n converges in probability to 0.

Exercise 18.
Let $Y_1, Y_2, \ldots$ be a sequence of random variables such that

$$Y_n = \begin{cases} 0, & \text{with probability } 1 - \frac{1}{n}, \\ 2^n, & \text{with probability } \frac{1}{n}. \end{cases}$$

Does Y_n converge in probability to 0?

Exercise 19. (VIDEO SOLUTION)
A Laplace random variable has a PDF

$$f_X(x) = \frac{\lambda}{2} e^{-\lambda|x|}, \quad \lambda > 0,$$

and the variance is $\text{Var}[X] = \frac{2}{\lambda^2}$. Let $X_1, \ldots, X_{500}$ be a sequence of i.i.d. Laplace random variables. Let

$$M_{500} = \frac{X_1 + \cdots + X_{500}}{500}.$$

(a) Find $\mathbb{E}[X]$. Express your answer in terms of λ.

(b) Let $\lambda = 10$. Using Chebyshev's inequality, find a lower bound of

$$\mathbb{P}[-0.1 \le M_{500} \le 0.1].$$

(c) Let $\lambda = 10$. Using the Central Limit Theorem, find the probability

$$\mathbb{P}\left[-0.1 \le M_{500} \le 0.1\right].$$

You may leave your answer in terms of the $\Phi(\cdot)$ function.

Exercise 20. (VIDEO SOLUTION)
Let $X_1, \ldots, X_N$ be a sequence of i.i.d. random variables such that $X_n = \pm 1$ with equal probability. Let

$$\overline{X}_N = \frac{1}{\sqrt{N}} \sum_{n=1}^{N} X_n.$$

Prove the Central Limit Theorem for this particular sequence of random variables by showing that

(a) $\mathbb{E}[\overline{X}_N] = 0$, $\text{Var}[\overline{X}_N] = 1$.

(b) The moment-generating function of $\overline{X}_N$ is $M_{\overline{X}_N}(s) \to e^{\frac{s^2}{2}}$ as $N \to \infty$.

Exercise 21. (VIDEO SOLUTION)
Let $X_1, \ldots, X_N$ be a sequence of i.i.d. random variables with mean and variance

$$\mathbb{E}[X_n] = \mu \quad \text{and} \quad \text{Var}[X_n] = \sigma^2, \quad n = 1, \ldots, N.$$

The distribution of X_n is, unknown. Let

$$M_N = \frac{1}{N} \sum_{n=1}^{N} X_n.$$

Use the Central Limit Theorem to estimate the probability $\mathbb{P}[M_N > 2\mu]$.

Chapter 7

Regression

Starting with this chapter, we will discuss several combat skills — techniques that we use to do the actual data analysis. The theme of this topic is **learning** and **inference**, which are both at the core of modern data science. The word "learning" can be broadly interpreted as seeking the best model to explain the data, and the word "inference" refers to prediction and recovery. Here, prediction means that we use the observed data to forecast or generalize to unseen situations, whereas recovery means that we try to restore the missing data in our current observations. In this chapter we will learn **regression**, one of the most widely used learning and inference techniques.

Regression is a process for finding the relationship between the inputs and the outputs. In a regression problem, we consider a set of **input data** $\{x_1, \ldots, x_N\}$ and a set of **output data** $\{y_1, \ldots, y_N\}$. We call the set of these input-output pairs $\mathcal{D} \stackrel{\text{def}}{=} \{(x_1, y_1), \ldots, (x_N, y_N)\}$ the **training data**. The true relationship between an x_n and a y_n is unknown. We do not know, you do not know, only God knows. We denote this unknown relationship as a mapping $f(\cdot)$ that takes x_n and maps it to y_n,

$$y_n = f(x_n),$$

as illustrated in **Figure 7.1**.

Figure 7.1: A regression problem is about finding the best approximation to the input-output relationship of the data.

Since we do not know $f(\cdot)$, finding it from a set of finite number of data points $\mathcal{D} = \{(x_1, y_1), \ldots, (x_N, y_N)\}$ is infeasible — there are infinitely many ways we can make $y_n = f(x_n)$ for every $n = 1, \ldots, N$. The idea of regression is to add a **structure** to the problem. Instead of looking for $f(\cdot)$, we find a proxy $g_{\boldsymbol{\theta}}(\cdot)$. This proxy $g_{\boldsymbol{\theta}}(\cdot)$ takes a certain **parametric** form. For example, we can postulate that (x_n, y_n) has a linear relationship, and so

$$g_{\boldsymbol{\theta}}(x_n) = \underbrace{\theta_1}_{\text{parameter}} x_n + \underbrace{\theta_0}_{\text{parameter}}, \qquad n = 1, \ldots, N.$$

This equation is a straight line with a slope θ_1 and a y-intercept θ_0. We call $\boldsymbol{\theta} = [\theta_1, \theta_0]$ the **parameter** of the model $f(\cdot)$. To emphasize that the function we are using here is **parameterized** by $\boldsymbol{\theta}$, we denote the function by $g_{\boldsymbol{\theta}}(\cdot)$.

Of course, any model we choose is our *guess*. It will never be the true model. There is always a difference between what our model tells us and what we have observed. We denote this "difference" or "error" by e_n and define it as:

$$e_n = y_n - g_{\boldsymbol{\theta}}(x_n), \quad n = 1, \ldots, N.$$

The purpose of regression is to find the best $\boldsymbol{\theta}$ such that the error is minimized. For example, consider a minimization of the sum-square error:

$$\widehat{\boldsymbol{\theta}} = \underset{\boldsymbol{\theta} \in \mathbb{R}^d}{\operatorname{argmin}} \ \underbrace{\sum_{n=1}^{N} (y_n - g_{\boldsymbol{\theta}}(x_n))^2}_{\text{training loss } \mathcal{E}_{\text{train}}(\boldsymbol{\theta})}.$$

The sum of the squared error is just one of the many possible ways we can define the **training loss** $\mathcal{E}_{\text{train}}(\boldsymbol{\theta})$. We will discuss different ways to define the training loss in this chapter, but the point should be evident. For a given dataset $\mathcal{D} = \{(x_1, y_1), \ldots, (x_N, y_N)\}$, regression tries to find a function $g_{\boldsymbol{\theta}}(\cdot)$ such that the training loss is minimized. The optimization variable is the parameter $\boldsymbol{\theta}$. If the function $g_{\boldsymbol{\theta}}(\cdot)$ is a linear function in $\boldsymbol{\theta}$, we call the regression a **linear regression**.

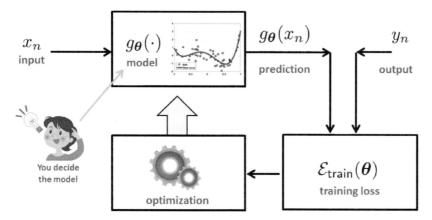

Figure 7.2: A regression problem involves several steps: picking a model $g_{\boldsymbol{\theta}}$, defining the training loss $\mathcal{E}_{\text{train}}(\boldsymbol{\theta})$, and solving the optimization to update $\boldsymbol{\theta}$.

A summary of the regression process is shown in **Figure 7.2**. Given the training data $\mathcal{D} = \{(x_1, y_1), \ldots, (x_N, y_N)\}$, the user picks a model $g_{\boldsymbol{\theta}}(\cdot)$ to make a prediction. We compare the predicted value $g_{\boldsymbol{\theta}}(x_n)$ with the observed value y_n, and compute the training loss $\mathcal{E}_{\text{train}}(\boldsymbol{\theta})$. The training loss $\mathcal{E}_{\text{train}}(\boldsymbol{\theta})$ is a function of the model parameter $\boldsymbol{\theta}$. Different model parameters $\boldsymbol{\theta}$ give different training loss. We solve an optimization problem to find the best model parameter. In practice, we often iterate the process for a few times until the training loss is settled down.

> **What is regression?**
>
> Given the data points $(x_1, y_1), \ldots, (x_N, y_N)$, regression is the process of finding the parameter $\boldsymbol{\theta}$ of a function $g_{\boldsymbol{\theta}}(\cdot)$ such that the **training loss** is minimized:
>
> $$\hat{\boldsymbol{\theta}} = \underset{\boldsymbol{\theta} \in \mathbb{R}^d}{\text{argmin}} \underbrace{\sum_{n=1}^{N} \mathcal{L}\left(y_n, \, g_{\boldsymbol{\theta}}(x_n)\right)}_{\text{training loss } \mathcal{E}_{\text{train}}(\boldsymbol{\theta})}, \qquad (7.1)$$
>
> where $\mathcal{L}(\cdot, \cdot)$ is the loss between a pair of true observation y_n and the prediction $g_{\boldsymbol{\theta}}(x_n)$. One common choice of $\mathcal{L}(\cdot, \cdot)$ is $\mathcal{L}(g_{\boldsymbol{\theta}}(x_n), y_n) = (g_{\boldsymbol{\theta}}(x_n) - y_n)^2$.

Example 1. Fitting the data

Suppose we have a set of data points $(x_1, y_1), (x_2, y_2), \ldots, (x_N, y_N)$, where x_n's are the inputs and y_n's are the outputs. These pairs of data points can be plotted in a scatter plot, as shown in **Figure 7.3**. We want to find the curve that best fits the data.

To solve this problem, we first need to choose a model, for example

$$g_{\boldsymbol{\theta}}(x_n) = \theta_0 + \theta_1 x_n + \theta_2 x_n^2 + \theta_3 x_n^3 + \theta_4 x_n^4.$$

We call the coefficients $\boldsymbol{\theta} = [\theta_0, \theta_1, \theta_2, \theta_3, \theta_4]$ the **regression coefficients**. They can be found by solving the optimization problem

$$\underset{\theta_0, \theta_1, \theta_2, \theta_3, \theta_4}{\text{minimize}} \sum_{n=1}^{N} \left(y_n - (\theta_0 + \theta_1 x_n + \theta_2 x_n^2 + \theta_3 x_n^3 + \theta_4 x_n^4) \right)^2.$$

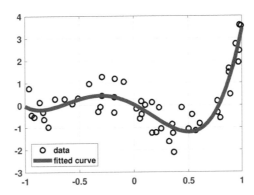

Figure 7.3: Regression can be used to fit the dataset using curves. In this example, we use a fourth-th order polynomial $g_{\boldsymbol{\theta}}(x) = \sum_{p=0}^{4} \theta_p x_n^p$ to fit a 50-point dataset.

This optimization asks for the best $\boldsymbol{\theta} = [\theta_0, \ldots, \theta_4]^T$ such that the training loss is minimized. Solving the minimization problem would require some effort, but if we imagine that we have solved it we can find the best curve, which is $g_{\boldsymbol{\theta}}(x) = \sum_{p=0}^{4} \theta_p x_n^p$ with the optimal $\boldsymbol{\theta}$ plugged in. The red curve in **Figure 7.3** shows an example in which we have used a fourth-order polynomial to fit a dataset comprising 50 data points. We will learn how to solve the problem in this chapter.

Example 2. Predicting the stock market

Imagine that you have bought some shares in the stock market. You have looked at the past data, and you want to predict the price of the shares over the next few days. How would you do it besides just eyeballing the data?

First, you would plot the data points on a graph. Mathematically, we can denote these data points as $\{x_1, x_2, \ldots, x_N\}$, where the indices $n = 1, 2, \ldots, N$ can be treated as time stamps. We assume a simple model to describe the relationship between the x_n's, say

$$x_n \approx a x_{n-1} + b x_{n-2},$$

for some parameters $\theta = (a, b)$.[1] This model assumes that the current value x_n can be approximated by a linear combination of two previous values x_{n-1} and x_{n-2}. Therefore, if we have x_1 and x_2 we should be able to predict x_3, and if we have x_2 and x_3 we should be able to predict x_4, etc. The magic of this prediction comes from the parameters a and b. If we know a and b, the prediction can be done by simply plugging in the numbers.

The regression problem here is to estimate the parameters a and b from the data. Since we are given a set of training data $\{x_1, x_2, \ldots, x_N\}$, we can check whether our predicted value $\widehat{x}_3$ is close to the true x_3, and whether our predicted value $\widehat{x}_4$ is close to the true x_4, etc. This leads to the optimization

$$(\widehat{a}, \widehat{b}) = \underset{a,b}{\operatorname{argmin}} \sum_{n=1}^{N} \left(x_n - \underbrace{(a x_{n-1} + b x_{n-2})}_{=\text{prediction}} \right)^2,$$

where we use initial conditions that $x_0 = x_{-1} = 0$. The optimization problem requires us to minimize the disparity between x_n and the predicted value $a x_{n-1} + b x_{n-2}$, for all n. By finding the (a, b) that minimizes this objective function, we will accomplish our goal of estimating the best (a, b).

Figure 7.4 shows an example of predicting a random process using the above model. If the parameters a and b are properly determined, we will obtain a reasonably well-fitted curve to the data. A simple extrapolation to the future timestamp would suffice for the forecast task.

Plan for this chapter

What are the key ingredients of regression?

- **Learning**: Formulate the regression problem as an optimization problem, and solve it by finding the best parameters.

- **Inference**: Use the estimated parameters and models to predict the unseen data points.

Regression is too broad a topic to be covered adequately in a single chapter. Accordingly, we will present a few principles and a few practical algorithmic techniques that are broadly applicable to many (definitely not all) regression tasks. These include the following.

---

[1] Caution: If you lose money in the stock market by following this naive model, please do not cry. This model is greatly oversimplified and probably wrong.

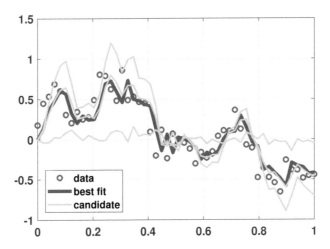

Figure 7.4: An autoregression model aims at learning the model parameters based on the previous samples. This example illustrates fitting the data using the model $x_n = ax_{n-1}+bx_{n-2}$, for $n = 1, \ldots, N$.

- The **principle of regression** (Section 7.1). We explain the formulation of a regression problem via optimization. There are a few steps involved in developing this concept. First, we will exclusively focus on **linear models** because these models are easier to analyze than nonlinear models but are still rich enough for many practical problems. We will discuss how to solve the linear regression problem and some applications of the solutions. We then address the issue of outliers using a concept called the **robust linear regression**.

- **Overfitting** (Section 7.2). The biggest practical challenge of regression is **overfitting**. Overfitting occurs when a model fits too closely to the training samples so that it fails to **generalize**. We will delve deeply into the roots of overfitting and show that overfitting depends on three factors: the number of training samples N, the model complexity d, and the magnitude of noise σ^2.

- **Bias-variance trade-off** (Section 7.3). We will present one of the most fundamental results in learning theory, known as the **bias-variance** trade-off. It applies to *all* regression problems, not just to linear models. Understanding this trade-off will help you understand the fundamental limits of your problem so that you know what to expect from the model.

- **Regularization** (Section 7.4). In this section we discuss a technique for combatting overfitting known as **regularization**. Regularization is carried out by adding an extra term to the regression objective function. By solving the modified optimization, the regression solution is improved in two ways: (i) regularization makes the regression solution less sensitive to noise perturbations, and (ii) it alleviates the fitting difficulty when we have only a few training samples. We will discuss two regularization strategies: the **ridge regression** and the **LASSO regression**.

Much of this chapter deals with optimization. If this is your first time reading this book, we encourage you to have a reference book on linear algebra at hand.

7.1 Principles of Regression

We start by recalling our discussion in the introduction. The purpose of regression can be summarized in a simple statement:

> Given the data points $(x_1, y_1), \ldots, (x_N, y_N)$, find the parameter $\boldsymbol{\theta}$ of a function $g_{\boldsymbol{\theta}}(\cdot)$ such that the training loss is minimized:
>
> $$\widehat{\boldsymbol{\theta}} = \underset{\boldsymbol{\theta} \in \mathbb{R}^d}{\operatorname{argmin}} \; \underbrace{\sum_{n=1}^{N} \mathcal{L}\left(y_n, \; g_{\boldsymbol{\theta}}(x_n)\right)}_{\text{training loss } \mathcal{E}_{\text{train}}(\boldsymbol{\theta})}, \qquad (7.2)$$
>
> where $\mathcal{L}(\cdot, \cdot)$ is the loss between a pair of true observation y_n and the prediction $g_{\boldsymbol{\theta}}(x_n)$.

When the context makes it clear, we will drop the subscript $\boldsymbol{\theta}$ in $g_{\boldsymbol{\theta}}(\cdot)$ with the understanding that the function $g(\cdot)$ is parameterized by $\boldsymbol{\theta}$.

As you can see, regression finds a function $g(\cdot)$ that *best approximates* the input-output relationship between x_n and y_n. There are two choices we need to make when formulating a regression problem:

- **Function $g(\cdot)$**: What is the *family* of functions we want to use? This could be a line, a polynomial, or a set of basis functions. If it is a polynomial, what is its order? We need to make all these decisions before running the regression. A poor choice of function family can lead to a poor regression result.

- **Loss "$\mathcal{L}(\cdot, \cdot)$"**: How do we measure the closeness between y_n and $g(x_n)$? Are we measuring in terms of the squared error $(y_n - g(x_n))^2$, or the absolute difference $|y_n - g(x_n)|$, or something else? Again, a poor choice of distance function can create a false sense of closeness because you might be optimizing for a wrong objective.

Before we delve into the details, we need to discuss briefly the connection between regression and probability. A regression problem can be solved without knowing probability, so why is regression discussed in a book on probability?

This question is related to how much we know about the statistical model and what kind of optimality we are seeking. A full answer requires some understanding of maximum likelihood estimation and maximum a posteriori estimation, which will be explained in Chapter 8. As a quick preview of our results, we summarize the key ideas below:

> **How is regression related to probability?**
>
> - If you know the statistical relationship between x_n and y_n, then we can construct a regression problem that maximizes the **likelihood** of the underlying distribution. Such regression solution is optimal with respect to the likelihood.
>
> - We can construct a regression problem that can minimize the expectation of the

squared error. This regression solution is **mean-squared optimal.**

- If you are a Bayesian and you know the prior distribution of x_n, then we can construct a regression problem that maximizes the posterior distribution. The solution to this regression problem is **Bayesian optimal.**

- If you know nothing about the statistics of x_n and y_n, you can still run the regression and get something, and this "something" can be very useful. However, you cannot claim statistical optimality of this "something".

See Chapter 8 for additional discussion.

It is important to understand that a regression problem is at the intersection of **optimization** and **statistics**. The need for optimization is clear because we need to minimize the error. The statistical need is to generalize to unknown data. If there is no statistical relationship between x_n and y_n (for all n), whatever model we obtain from the regression will only work for the N training samples. The model will not generalize because knowing x_n will not help us know y_n. In other words, if there is no statistical relationship between x_n and y_n, you can fit perfectly to the training data but you will fail miserably to fit the testing data.

7.1.1 Intuition: How to fit a straight line?

In this subsection we want to give you the basic idea of how regression is formulated. To keep things simple, we will discuss how to fit data using a straight line.

Consider a collection of data points $\mathcal{D} = \{(x_1, y_1), \ldots, (x_N, y_N)\}$, where x_n's are the inputs and y_n's are the observations, for example, in the table below.

n	x_n	y_n
1	0.6700	3.0237
2	0.3474	2.3937
3	0.6695	3.5548
$\vdots$	$\vdots$	$\vdots$
$N-1$	0.2953	2.6396
N	0.6804	3.2536

Let us consider the linear regression problem. The goal of linear regression is to find the **straight line** that best fits the datasets. All straight lines on a 2D graph are plots of the equation

$$g(x) = ax + b,$$

where a is the **slope** of the line and b is the y-**intercept** of the line. We denote this line by $g(\cdot)$. Note that this function g is characterized by two parameters (a, b) because once (a, b) are known the line is determined. If we change (a, b), the line will change as well. Therefore, by finding the *best* line we are essentially searching for the best (a, b) such that the training error is minimized.

The pictorial meaning of linear regression can easily be seen in **Figure 7.5**, which shows $N = 50$ data points according to some latent distributions. Given these 50 data points, we construct several possible *candidates* for the regression model. These candidates are characterized by the parameters (a, b). For example, the parameters $(a, b) = (1, 2)$ and $(a, b) = (-2, 3)$ represent two different straight lines in the candidate pool. The goal of the regression is to find the best line from these candidates. Note that since we limit ourselves to straight lines, the candidate set will not include polynomials or trigonometric functions. These functions are outside the family we are considering.

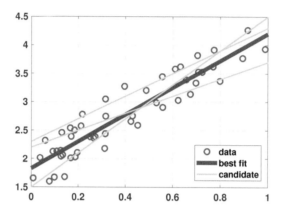

Figure 7.5: The objective of least squares fitting (or linear regression) is to find a line that best fits the dataset.

Given these candidate functions, we need to measure the the training loss. This can be defined in multiple ways, such as

- **Sum-squared loss** $\mathcal{E}_{\text{train}}(\boldsymbol{\theta}) = \sum_{n=1}^{N}(y_n - g(x_n))^2$.

- **Sum-absolute loss** $\mathcal{E}_{\text{train}}(\boldsymbol{\theta}) = \sum_{n=1}^{N}|y_n - g(x_n)|$.

- **Cross-entropy loss** $\mathcal{E}_{\text{train}}(\boldsymbol{\theta}) = -\sum_{n=1}^{N}(y_n \log g(x_n) + (1 - y_n) \log(1 - g(x_n)))$.

- **Perceptual loss** $\mathcal{E}_{\text{train}}(\boldsymbol{\theta}) = \sum_{n=1}^{N} \max(-y_n g(x_n), 0)$, when y_n and $g(x_n)$ are binary taking values ± 1. This is a reasonable training error because if y_n matches with $g(x_n)$, then $y_n g(x_n) = 1$ and so $\max(-y_n g(x_n), 0) = 0$. But if y_n does not match with $g(x_n)$, then $y_n g(x_n) = -1$ and hence $\max(-y_n g(x_n), 0) = 1$. Thus, the loss captures the sum of all the mismatched pairs.

Choosing the loss function is problem-specific. It is also where probability enters the picture because, without any knowledge about the distributions of x_n and y_n, there is no way to choose the best training loss. You can still pick one, as we will do, but it will not be granted any probabilistic guarantees.

Among these possible choices of the training error, we are going to focus on the sum-squared loss because it is **convex** and **differentiable**. This makes the computation easy, since we can run any textbook optimization algorithm. The regression problem under the sum-squared loss is:

$$\left(\widehat{a}, \widehat{b}\right) = \underset{(a, b)}{\operatorname{argmin}} \ \sum_{n=1}^{N}\left(y_n - \underbrace{(ax_n + b)}_{=g(x_n)}\right)^2. \tag{7.3}$$

In this equation, the symbol "argmin" means "argument minimize", which returns the argument that minimizes the cost function on the right. The interpretation of the equation is that we seek the (a, b) that minimize the sum $\sum_{n=1}^{N}(y_n - (ax_n + b))^2$. Since we are minimizing the squared error, this linear regression problem is also known as the **least squares fitting** problem. The idea is summarized in the following box.

What is linear least squares fitting?

- Find a line $g(x) = ax + b$ that best fits the training data $\{(x_n, y_n)\}_{n=1}^{N}$.
- The optimality criterion is to minimize the squared error

$$\mathcal{E}_{\text{train}}(\boldsymbol{\theta}) = \sum_{n=1}^{N}\left(y_n - g(x_n)\right)^2, \tag{7.4}$$

  where $\boldsymbol{\theta} = (a, b)$ is the model parameter.

- There exist other optimality criteria. Squared error is convex and differentiable.

7.1.2 Solving the linear regression problem

Let's consider how to solve the linear regression problem given by Equation (7.3). The problem is the following:

$$\left(\widehat{a}, \widehat{b}\right) = \underset{(a,b)}{\operatorname{argmin}}\ \mathcal{E}_{\text{train}}(a, b). \tag{7.5}$$

As with any two-dimensional optimization problem, the optimal point $(\widehat{a}, \widehat{b})$ should have a zero gradient, meaning that

$$\frac{\partial}{\partial a}\mathcal{E}_{\text{train}}(a, b) = 0 \quad \text{and} \quad \frac{\partial}{\partial b}\mathcal{E}_{\text{train}}(a, b) = 0.$$

This should be familiar to you, even if you have only learned basic calculus. This pair of equations says that, at a minimum point, the directional slopes should be zero no matter which direction you are looking at.

The derivative with respect to a is

$$\frac{\partial}{\partial a}\mathcal{E}_{\text{train}}(a, b)$$

$$= \frac{\partial}{\partial a}\left\{\sum_{n=1}^{N}\left(y_n - (ax_n + b)\right)^2\right\}$$

$$= \frac{\partial}{\partial a}\left\{\left(y_1 - (ax_1 + b)\right)^2 + \left(y_2 - (ax_2 + b)\right)^2 + \cdots + \left(y_N - (ax_N + b)\right)^2\right\}$$

$$= 2\left(y_1 - (ax_1 + b)\right)(-x_1) + \cdots + 2\left(y_N - (ax_N + b)\right)(-x_N)$$

$$= 2\left(-\sum_{n=1}^{N}x_n y_n + a\sum_{n=1}^{N}x_n^2 + b\sum_{n=1}^{N}x_n\right).$$

Similarly, the derivative with respect to b is

$$\frac{\partial}{\partial b}\mathcal{E}_{\text{train}}(a,b) = \frac{\partial}{\partial b}\left\{\sum_{n=1}^{N}\left(y_n - (ax_n + b)\right)^2\right\}$$

$$= 2\left(y_1 - (ax_1 + b)\right)(-1) + \cdots + 2\left(y_N - (ax_N + b)\right)(-1)$$

$$= 2\left(-\sum_{n=1}^{N}y_n + a\sum_{n=1}^{N}x_n + b\sum_{n=1}^{N}1\right).$$

Setting these two equations to zero, we have that

$$2\left(-\sum_{n=1}^{N}y_n x_n + a\sum_{n=1}^{N}x_n^2 + b\sum_{n=1}^{N}x_n\right) = 0,$$

$$2\left(-\sum_{n=1}^{N}y_n + a\sum_{n=1}^{N}x_n + b\sum_{n=1}^{N}1\right) = 0.$$

Rearranging the terms, the pair can be equivalently written as

$$\begin{bmatrix} \sum_{n=1}^{N}x_n^2 & \sum_{n=1}^{N}x_n \\ \sum_{n=1}^{N}x_n & N \end{bmatrix}\begin{bmatrix} a \\ b \end{bmatrix} = \begin{bmatrix} \sum_{n=1}^{N}x_n y_n \\ \sum_{n=1}^{N}y_n \end{bmatrix}.$$

Therefore, if we can solve this system of linear equations, we will have the linear regression solution.

Remark. It is easy to see that the solution achieves the minimum instead of the maximum, since the second-order derivatives are positive:

$$\frac{\partial^2}{\partial a^2}\mathcal{E}_{\text{train}}(a,b) = \sum_{n=1}^{N}x_n^2 \geq 0 \qquad \text{and} \qquad \frac{\partial^2}{\partial b^2}\mathcal{E}_{\text{train}}(a,b) = \sum_{n=1}^{N}1 > 0.$$

The following theorem summarizes this intermediate result.

Theorem 7.1. *The solution of the problem Equation (7.5)*

$$\left(\widehat{a}, \widehat{b}\right) = \underset{(a,b)}{argmin}\ \sum_{n=1}^{N}\left(y_n - (ax_n + b)\right)^2$$

satisfies the equation

$$\begin{bmatrix} \sum_{n=1}^{N}x_n^2 & \sum_{n=1}^{N}x_n \\ \sum_{n=1}^{N}x_n & N \end{bmatrix}\begin{bmatrix} \widehat{a} \\ \widehat{b} \end{bmatrix} = \begin{bmatrix} \sum_{n=1}^{N}x_n y_n \\ \sum_{n=1}^{N}y_n \end{bmatrix}. \tag{7.6}$$

Matrix-vector form of linear regression

The regression can be written as

$$
\underbrace{\begin{bmatrix} y_1 \\ \vdots \\ y_N \end{bmatrix}}_{y} = \underbrace{\begin{bmatrix} x_1 & 1 \\ \vdots & \vdots \\ x_N & 1 \end{bmatrix}}_{X} \underbrace{\begin{bmatrix} a \\ b \end{bmatrix}}_{\theta} + \underbrace{\begin{bmatrix} e_1 \\ \vdots \\ e_N \end{bmatrix}}_{e}.
$$

With X, y, θ and e, we can write the linear regression problem compactly as

$$
y = X\theta + e.
$$

Therefore, the training loss $\mathcal{E}_{\text{train}}(\theta)$ can be defined as

$$
\mathcal{E}_{\text{train}}(\theta) = \|y - X\theta\|^2
$$

$$
= \left\| \begin{bmatrix} y_1 \\ \vdots \\ y_N \end{bmatrix} - \begin{bmatrix} x_1 & 1 \\ \vdots & \vdots \\ x_N & 1 \end{bmatrix} \begin{bmatrix} a \\ b \end{bmatrix} \right\|^2 = \sum_{n=1}^{N} \left(y_n - (ax_n + b) \right)^2.
$$

Now, taking the gradient with respect to θ yields[2]

$$
\nabla_\theta \mathcal{E}_{\text{train}}(\theta) = \nabla_\theta \left\{ \|y - X\theta\|^2 \right\}
$$

$$
= -2X^T(y - X\theta).
$$

Equating this to zero, we obtain

$$
X^T(y - X\theta) = 0 \qquad \Longleftrightarrow \qquad X^T X \theta = X^T y. \tag{7.7}
$$

Equation (7.7) is called the **normal equation**.

The normal equation is a convenient way of constructing the system of linear equations. Using the 2-by-2 system shown in Equation (7.6) as an example, we note that

$$
X^T X = \begin{bmatrix} x_1 & \cdots & x_N \\ 1 & \cdots & 1 \end{bmatrix} \begin{bmatrix} x_1 & 1 \\ \vdots & \vdots \\ x_N & 1 \end{bmatrix} = \begin{bmatrix} \sum_{n=1}^{N} x_n^2 & \sum_{n=1}^{N} x_n \\ \sum_{n=1}^{N} x_n & N \end{bmatrix},
$$

$$
X^T y = \begin{bmatrix} x_1 & \cdots & x_N \\ 1 & \cdots & 1 \end{bmatrix} \begin{bmatrix} y_1 \\ \vdots \\ y_N \end{bmatrix} = \begin{bmatrix} \sum_{n=1}^{N} x_n y_n \\ \sum_{n=1}^{N} y_n \end{bmatrix}.
$$

Therefore, as long as you can construct the X matrix, forming the 2-by-2 system in Equation (7.6) is straightforward: start with $y = X\theta$ and then multiply the matrix transpose X^T to both sides. The resulting system is what you need. There is nothing to memorize.

---

[2]This is a basic vector calculus result. For details, you may consult standard texts such as the University of Waterloo's matrix cookbook. https://www.math.uwaterloo.ca/~hwolkowi/matrixcookbook.pdf

Running linear regression on a computer

On a computer, solving the linear regression for a line is straightforward. Let us look at the MATLAB code first.

```
% MATLAB code to fit data points using a straight line
N = 50;
x = rand(N,1)*1;
a = 2.5;                        % true parameter
b = 1.3;                        % true parameter
y = a*x + b + 0.2*rand(size(x)); % Synthesize training data

X    = [x(:) ones(N,1)];        % construct the X matrix
theta = X\y(:);                 % solve y = X theta

t    = linspace(0, 1, 200);     % interpolate and plot
yhat = theta(1)*t + theta(2);
plot(x,y,'o','LineWidth',2); hold on;
plot(t,yhat,'r','LineWidth',4);
```

In this piece of MATLAB code, we need to define the data matrix $\boldsymbol{X}$. Here, x(:) is the column vector that stores all the values $(x_1, \ldots, x_N)$. The all-one vector ones(N,1) is the second column in our $\boldsymbol{X}$ matrix. The command X\y(:) is equivalent to solving the normal equation

$$\boldsymbol{X}^T \boldsymbol{X} \boldsymbol{\theta} = \boldsymbol{X}^T \boldsymbol{y}.$$

The last few lines are used to plot the predicted curve. Note that theta(1) and theta(2) are the entries of the solution $\boldsymbol{\theta}$. The result of this program is exactly the plot shown in **Figure 7.5** above.

In Python, the program is quite similar. The command we use to solve the inversion is np.linalg.lstsq.

```
# Python code to fit data points using a straight line
import numpy as np
import matplotlib.pyplot as plt

N = 50
x = np.random.rand(N)
a = 2.5                         # true parameter
b = 1.3                         # true parameter
y = a*x + b + 0.2*np.random.randn(N)   # Synthesize training data

X = np.column_stack((x, np.ones(N)))   # construct the X matrix
theta = np.linalg.lstsq(X, y, rcond=None)[0] # solve y = X theta

t = np.linspace(0,1,200)               # interpolate and plot
yhat = theta[0]*t + theta[1]
plt.plot(x,y,'o')
plt.plot(t,yhat,'r',linewidth=4)
```

7.1.3 Extension: Beyond a straight line

Regression is a powerful technique. Although we have discussed its usefulness for fitting straight lines, the same concept can fit other curves.

To generalize the regression formulation, we consider a d-dimensional regression coefficient vector $\boldsymbol{\theta} = [\theta_0, \ldots, \theta_{d-1}]^T \in \mathbb{R}^d$ and a general linear model

$$g_{\boldsymbol{\theta}}(x_n) = \sum_{p=0}^{d-1} \theta_p \phi_p(x_n).$$

Here, the mappings $\{\phi_p(\cdot)\}_{p=0}^{d-1}$ can be considered as a nonlinear transformation that takes the input x_n and maps it to another value. For example, $\phi_p(\cdot) = (\cdot)^p$ will map an input x to a pth power x^p.

We can now write the system of linear equations as

$$\underbrace{\begin{bmatrix} y_1 \\ y_2 \\ \vdots \\ y_N \end{bmatrix}}_{\boldsymbol{y}} = \underbrace{\begin{bmatrix} \phi_0(x_1) & \phi_1(x_1) & \cdots & \phi_{d-1}(x_1) \\ \phi_0(x_2) & \phi_1(x_2) & \cdots & \phi_{d-1}(x_2) \\ \vdots & & \cdots & \vdots \\ \phi_0(x_N) & \phi_1(x_N) & \cdots & \phi_{d-1}(x_N) \end{bmatrix}}_{\boldsymbol{X}} \underbrace{\begin{bmatrix} \theta_0 \\ \theta_1 \\ \vdots \\ \theta_{d-1} \end{bmatrix}}_{\boldsymbol{\theta}} + \underbrace{\begin{bmatrix} e_1 \\ e_2 \\ \vdots \\ e_N \end{bmatrix}}_{\boldsymbol{e}}. \tag{7.8}$$

Let us look at some examples.

Example 7.1. (Quadratic fitting) Consider the linear regression problem using a **quadratic** equation:

$$y_n = a x_n^2 + b x_n + c, \qquad n = 1, \ldots, N.$$

Express this equation in matrix-vector form.

Solution. The matrix-vector expression is

$$\begin{bmatrix} y_1 \\ y_2 \\ \vdots \\ y_N \end{bmatrix} = \begin{bmatrix} x_1^2 & x_1 & 1 \\ x_2^2 & x_2 & 1 \\ \vdots & \vdots & \vdots \\ x_N^2 & x_N & 1 \end{bmatrix} \begin{bmatrix} a \\ b \\ c \end{bmatrix} + \begin{bmatrix} e_1 \\ e_2 \\ \vdots \\ e_N \end{bmatrix}.$$

This is again in the form of $\boldsymbol{y} = \boldsymbol{X}\boldsymbol{\theta} + \boldsymbol{e}$.

The MATLAB and Python programs for Example 7.1 are shown below. A numerical example is illustrated in **Figure 7.6**.

```
% MATLAB code to fit data using a quadratic equation
N = 50;
x = rand(N,1)*1;
a = -2.5;
b = 1.3;
c = 1.2;
```

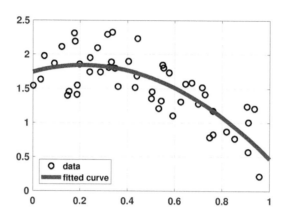

Figure 7.6: Example: Our goal is to fit the dataset of 50 data points shown above. The model we use is $g_\theta(x_n) = ax_n^2 + bx_n + c$, for $n = 1, \ldots, N$.

```
y = a*x.^2 + b*x + c + 1*rand(size(x));

N    = length(x);
X    = [ones(N,1) x(:) x(:).^2];
beta = X\y(:);
t    = linspace(0, 1, 200);
yhat = theta(3)*t.^2 + theta(2)*t + theta(1);
plot(x,y,   'o','LineWidth',2); hold on;
plot(t,yhat,'r','LineWidth',6);
```

```
# Python code to fit data using a quadratic equation
import numpy as np
import matplotlib.pyplot as plt

N = 50
x = np.random.rand(N)
a = -2.5
b = 1.3
c = 1.2
y = a*x**2 + b*x + c + 0.2*np.random.randn(N)

X = np.column_stack((np.ones(N), x, x**2))
theta = np.linalg.lstsq(X, y, rcond=None)[0]
t = np.linspace(0,1,200)
yhat = theta[0] + theta[1]*t + theta[2]*t**2
plt.plot(x,y,'o')
plt.plot(t,yhat,'r',linewidth=4)
```

The generalization to polynomials of arbitrary order is to replace the model with

$$g_\theta(x_n) = \sum_{p=0}^{d-1} \theta_p x^p,$$

where $p = 0, 1, \ldots, d-1$ represent the orders of the polynomials and $\theta_0, \ldots, \theta_{d-1}$ are the **regression coefficients**. In this case, the matrix system is

$$
\begin{bmatrix} y_1 \\ y_2 \\ \vdots \\ y_N \end{bmatrix} = \begin{bmatrix} 1 & x_1 & \cdots & x_1^{d-1} \\ 1 & x_2 & \cdots & x_2^{d-1} \\ \vdots & \cdots & \vdots & \vdots \\ 1 & x_N & \cdots & x_N^{d-1} \end{bmatrix} \begin{bmatrix} \theta_0 \\ \theta_1 \\ \vdots \\ \theta_{d-1} \end{bmatrix} + \begin{bmatrix} e_1 \\ e_2 \\ \vdots \\ e_N \end{bmatrix},
$$

which again is in the form of $\boldsymbol{y} = \boldsymbol{X}\boldsymbol{\theta} + \boldsymbol{e}$.

Example 7.2. (Legendre polynomial fitting) Let $\{L_p(\cdot)\}_{p=0}^{d-1}$ be a set of Legendre polynomials (see discussions below), and consider the linear regression problem using

$$
y_n = \sum_{p=0}^{d-1} \theta_p L_p(x), \qquad n = 1, \ldots, N.
$$

Express this equation in matrix-vector form.

Solution. The matrix-vector expression is

$$
\begin{bmatrix} y_1 \\ y_2 \\ \vdots \\ y_N \end{bmatrix} = \begin{bmatrix} L_0(x_1) & L_1(x_1) & \cdots & L_{d-1}(x_1) \\ L_0(x_2) & L_1(x_2) & \cdots & L_{d-1}(x_2) \\ \vdots & \cdots & \vdots & \vdots \\ L_0(x_N) & L_1(x_N) & \cdots & L_{d-1}(x_N) \end{bmatrix} \begin{bmatrix} \theta_0 \\ \theta_1 \\ \vdots \\ \theta_{d-1} \end{bmatrix} + \begin{bmatrix} e_1 \\ e_2 \\ \vdots \\ e_N \end{bmatrix}.
$$

Legendre polynomials are **orthogonal** polynomials. In conventional polynomials, the functions $\{x, x^2, x^3, \ldots, x^p\}$ are not orthogonal. As we increase p, the set of functions $\{x, x^2, x^3, \ldots, x^p\}$ will have redundancy, which will eventually result in the matrix $\boldsymbol{X}$ being noninvertible.

The pth-order Legendre polynomial is denoted by $L_p(x)$. Using the Legendre polynomials as the building block of the regression problem, the model is expressed as

$$
g_{\boldsymbol{\theta}}(x) \overset{\text{def}}{=} \sum_{p=0}^{d-1} \theta_p L_p(x)
$$

$$
= \theta_0 L_0(x) + \theta_1 \underbrace{L_1(x)}_{=x} + \theta_2 \underbrace{L_2(x)}_{=\frac{1}{2}(3x^2-1)} + \cdots + \theta_{d-1} L_{d-1}(x),
$$

where $L_0(\cdot)$, $L_1(\cdot)$ and $L_2(\cdot)$ are the Legendre polynomials of order 0, 1 and 2, respectively. As an example, the first few leading Legendre polynomials are

$$
L_0(x) = 1,
$$
$$
L_1(x) = x,
$$
$$
L_2(x) = \frac{1}{2}(3x^2 - 1),
$$
$$
L_3(x) = \frac{1}{2}(5x^3 - 3x).
$$

The order of the Legendre polynomials is always the same as that of the ordinary polynomials. The shapes of these polynomials are shown in **Figure 7.7**(a).

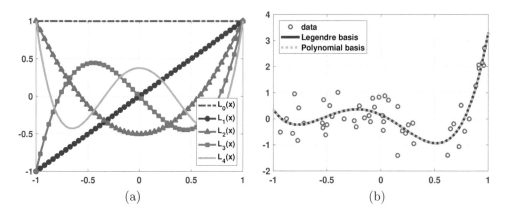

Figure 7.7: (a) The first 5 leading Legendre polynomials plotted in the range of $-1 \leq x \leq 1$. (b) Fitting the data using an ordinary polynomial and a Legendre polynomial.

Figure 7.7(b) demonstrates a fitting problem using the Legendre polynomials. You can see that the fitting is just as good as that of the ordinary polynomials (which should be the case). However, if we compare the coefficients, we observe that the magnitude of the Legendre coefficients is smaller (see **Table 7.1**). In general, as the order of polynomials increases and the noise grows, the ordinary polynomials will become increasingly difficult to fit the data.

	θ_4	θ_3	θ_2	θ_1	θ_0
Ordinary polynomials	5.3061	3.3519	−3.6285	−1.8729	0.1540
Legendre polynomials	1.2128	1.3408	0.6131	0.1382	0.0057

Table 7.1: The regression coefficients of an ordinary polynomial and a Legendre polynomial. Note that while both polynomials can fit the data, the Legendre polynomial coefficients have smaller magnitudes.

Calling Legendre polynomials for regression is not difficult in MATLAB and Python. Specifically, one can call `legendreP` in MATLAB and `scipy.special.eval_legendre` in Python.

```
% MATLAB code to fit data using Legendre polynomials
N = 50;
x = 1*(rand(N,1)*2-1);
a = [-0.001 0.01 +0.55 1.5 1.2];
y = a(1)*legendreP(0,x) + a(2)*legendreP(1,x) + ...
    + a(3)*legendreP(2,x) + a(4)*legendreP(3,x) + ...
    + a(5)*legendreP(4,x) + 0.5*randn(N,1);

X = [legendreP(0,x(:)) legendreP(1,x(:)) ...
     legendreP(2,x(:)) legendreP(3,x(:)) ...
```

```
        legendreP(4,x(:))];
beta = X\y(:);

t     = linspace(-1, 1, 200);
yhat = beta(1)*legendreP(0,t) + beta(2)*legendreP(1,t) + ...
       + beta(3)*legendreP(2,t) + beta(4)*legendreP(3,t) + ...
       + beta(5)*legendreP(4,t);
plot(x,y,'ko','LineWidth',2,'MarkerSize',10); hold on;
plot(t,yhat,'LineWidth',6,'Color',[0.9 0 0]);
```

```
import numpy as np
import matplotlib.pyplot as plt
from scipy.special import eval_legendre

N = 50
x = np.linspace(-1,1,N)
a = np.array([-0.001, 0.01, 0.55, 1.5, 1.2])
y = a[0]*eval_legendre(0,x) + a[1]*eval_legendre(1,x) + \
    a[2]*eval_legendre(2,x) + a[3]*eval_legendre(3,x) + \
    a[4]*eval_legendre(4,x) + 0.2*np.random.randn(N)

X = np.column_stack((eval_legendre(0,x), eval_legendre(1,x), \
                     eval_legendre(2,x), eval_legendre(3,x), \
                     eval_legendre(4,x)))
theta = np.linalg.lstsq(X, y, rcond=None)[0]
t     = np.linspace(-1, 1, 50);
yhat  = theta[0]*eval_legendre(0,t) + theta[1]*eval_legendre(1,t) + \
        theta[2]*eval_legendre(2,t) + theta[3]*eval_legendre(3,t) + \
        theta[4]*eval_legendre(4,t)

plt.plot(x,y,'o',markersize=12)
plt.plot(t,yhat, linewidth=8)
plt.show()
```

The idea of fitting a set of data using the Legendre polynomials belongs to the larger family of **basis functions**. In general, we can use a set of basis functions to model the data:

$$g_\theta(x) \stackrel{\text{def}}{=} \sum_{p=0}^{d-1} \theta_p \phi_p(x),$$

where $\{\phi_p(x)\}_{p=0}^{d-1}$ are the basis functions and $\{\theta_p\}_{p=0}^{d-1}$ are the regression coefficients. The constant θ_0 is often called the **bias** of the regression.

Choice of the $\phi_p(x)$ can be extremely broad. One can choose the ordinary polynomials $\phi_p(x) = x^p$ or the Legendre polynomial $\phi_p(x) = L_p(x)$. Other choices are also available:

- Fourier basis: $\phi_p(x) = e^{j\omega_p x}$, where ω_p is the pth carrier frequency.

- Sinusoid basis: $\phi_p(x) = \sin(\omega_p x)$, which is same as the Fourier basis but taking the imaginary part.

- Gaussian basis: $\phi_p(x) = \frac{1}{\sqrt{2\pi\sigma_p^2}} \exp\left\{-\frac{(x-\mu_p)^2}{2\sigma_p^2}\right\}$, where (μ_p, σ_p) are the model parameters.

Evidently, by choosing different basis functions we have different ways to fit the data. There is no definitive answer as to which functions are better. Statistical techniques such as model selections are available, but experience will tell you to align with one and not the other. It is frequently more useful to have some domain knowledge rather than resorting to various computational techniques.

How to fit data using basis functions

- Construct this equation:

$$
\underbrace{\begin{bmatrix} y_1 \\ y_2 \\ \vdots \\ y_N \end{bmatrix}}_{y} = \underbrace{\begin{bmatrix} \phi_0(x_1) & \phi_1(x_1) & \cdots & \phi_{d-1}(x_1) \\ \phi_0(x_2) & \phi_1(x_2) & \cdots & \phi_{d-1}(x_2) \\ \vdots & & \cdots & \vdots \\ \phi_0(x_N) & \phi_1(x_N) & \cdots & \phi_{d-1}(x_N) \end{bmatrix}}_{X} \underbrace{\begin{bmatrix} \theta_0 \\ \theta_1 \\ \vdots \\ \theta_{d-1} \end{bmatrix}}_{\theta} + \underbrace{\begin{bmatrix} e_1 \\ e_2 \\ \vdots \\ e_N \end{bmatrix}}_{e}, \tag{7.9}
$$

- The functions $\phi_p(x)$ are the basis functions, e.g., $\phi_p(x) = x^p$ for ordinary polynomials.

- You can replace the polynomials with the Legendre polynomials.

- You can also replace the polynomials with other basis functions.

- Solve for θ by
$$
\widehat{\theta} = \underset{\theta}{\mathrm{argmin}} \; \|y - X\theta\|^2.
$$

Example 7.3. (**Autoregressive model**) Consider a two-tap autoregressive model:

$$
y_n = ay_{n-1} + by_{n-2}, \qquad n = 1, 2, \ldots, N
$$

where we assume $y_0 = y_{-1} = 0$. Express this equation in the matrix-vector form.

Solution. The matrix-vector form of the equation is

$$
\underbrace{\begin{bmatrix} y_1 \\ y_2 \\ \vdots \\ y_N \end{bmatrix}}_{=y} = \underbrace{\begin{bmatrix} y_0 & y_{-1} \\ y_1 & y_0 \\ \vdots & \vdots \\ y_{N-1} & y_{N-2} \end{bmatrix}}_{=X} \underbrace{\begin{bmatrix} a \\ b \end{bmatrix}}_{=\theta} + \begin{bmatrix} e_1 \\ e_2 \\ \vdots \\ e_N \end{bmatrix}.
$$

In general, we can append more previous samples to predict the future. The general expression is

$$y_n = \sum_{\ell=1}^{L} \theta_\ell \, y_{n-\ell}, \qquad n = 1, 2, \ldots, N,$$

where $\ell = 1, 2, \ldots, L$ denote the previous L samples of the data and $\{\theta_1, \ldots, \theta_L\}$ are the regression coefficients. If we do this we see that the matrix expression is

$$\underbrace{\begin{bmatrix} y_1 \\ y_2 \\ y_3 \\ y_4 \\ \vdots \\ y_N \end{bmatrix}}_{=y} = \underbrace{\begin{bmatrix} y_0 & y_{-1} & y_{-2} & \cdots & y_{1-L} \\ y_1 & y_0 & y_{-1} & \cdots & y_{2-L} \\ y_2 & y_1 & y_0 & \cdots & y_{3-L} \\ y_3 & y_2 & y_1 & \cdots & y_{4-L} \\ \vdots & \vdots & \vdots & \vdots & \vdots \\ y_{N-1} & y_{N-2} & y_{N-3} & \vdots & y_{N-L} \end{bmatrix}}_{=X} \underbrace{\begin{bmatrix} \theta_1 \\ \theta_2 \\ \vdots \\ \theta_L \end{bmatrix}}_{=\boldsymbol{\theta}} + \begin{bmatrix} e_1 \\ e_2 \\ e_3 \\ e_4 \\ \vdots \\ e_N \end{bmatrix}.$$

Observe the pattern associated with this matrix $\boldsymbol{X}$. Each column is a one-entry shifted version of the previous column. This matrix is called a **Toeplitz matrix**.

The MATLAB (and Python) code for calling and using the Toeplitz matrix is shown below.

```
% MATLAB code for auto-regressive model
N = 500;
y = cumsum(0.2*randn(N,1)) + 0.05*randn(N,1);   % generate data

L = 100;                                         % use previous 100 samples
c = [0; y(1:400-1)];
r = zeros(1,L);
X = toeplitz(c,r);                               % Toeplitz matrix
theta = X\y(1:400);                              % solve y = X theta
yhat = X*theta;                                  % prediction
plot(y(1:400),    'ko','LineWidth',2);hold on;
plot(yhat(1:400),'r','LineWidth',4);
```

```
# Python code for auto-regressive model
import numpy as np
import matplotlib.pyplot as plt
from scipy.linalg import toeplitz

N = 500
y = np.cumsum(0.2*np.random.randn(N)) + 0.05*np.random.randn(N)

L = 100
c = np.hstack((0, y[0:400-1]))
r = np.zeros(L)
X = toeplitz(c,r)
theta = np.linalg.lstsq(X, y[0:400], rcond=None)[0]
yhat  = np.dot(X, theta)
```

```
plt.plot(y[0:400], 'o')
plt.plot(yhat[0:400],linewidth=4)
```

The plots generated by the above programs are shown in **Figure 7.8**(a). Note that we are doing an **interpolation**, because we are predicting the values within the training dataset.

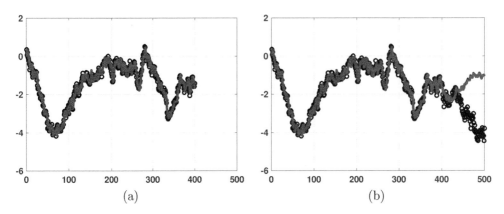

(a)   (b)

Figure 7.8: Autoregressive model on a simulated dataset, using $L = 100$ coefficients. (a) Training data. Note that the model trains very well on this dataset. (b) Testing data. When tested on future data, the autoregressive model can still predict for a few samples but loses track when the time elapsed grows.

We now consider **extrapolation**. Given the training data, we can find the regression coefficients by solving the above linear equation. This gives us $\boldsymbol{\theta}$. To predict the future samples we need to return to the equation

$$\widehat{y}_n = \sum_{\ell=1}^{L} \theta_\ell \underbrace{\widehat{y}_{n-\ell}}_{=\text{previous estimate}} , \qquad n = 1, 2, \ldots, N,$$

where $\widehat{y}_{n-\ell}$ are the previous estimates. For example, if we are given 100 days of stock prices, then predicting the 101st day's price should be based on the L days before the 101st. A simple for-loop suffices for such a calculation.

Figure 7.8(b) shows a numerical example of extrapolating data using the autoregressive model. In this experiment we use $N = 400$ samples to train an autoregressive model of order $L = 100$. We then predict the data for another 100 data points. As you can see from the figure, the first few samples still look reasonable. However, as time increases, the model starts to lose track of the real trend.

Is there any way we can improve the autoregressive model? A simple way is to increase the memory L so that we can use a long history to predict the future. This boils down to the long-term running average of the curve, which works well in many cases. However, if the testing data does not follow the same distribution as the training data (which is often the case in the real stock market because unexpected news can change the stock price), then even the long-term average will not be a good forecast. That is why data scientists on Wall Street make so much money: they have advanced mathematical tools for modeling the stock market. Nevertheless, we hope that the autoregressive model provides you with a new perspective for analyzing data.

The summary below highlights the main ideas of the autoregressive model.

What is the autoregressive model?

- It solves this problem

$$\underbrace{\begin{bmatrix} y_1 \\ y_2 \\ y_3 \\ \vdots \\ y_N \end{bmatrix}}_{=\boldsymbol{y}} = \underbrace{\begin{bmatrix} y_0 & y_{-1} & y_{-2} & \cdots & y_{1-L} \\ y_1 & y_0 & y_{-1} & \cdots & y_{2-L} \\ y_2 & y_1 & y_0 & \cdots & y_{3-L} \\ \vdots & \vdots & \vdots & \vdots & \vdots \\ y_{N-1} & y_{N-2} & y_{N-3} & \vdots & y_{N-L} \end{bmatrix}}_{=\boldsymbol{X}} \underbrace{\begin{bmatrix} \theta_1 \\ \theta_2 \\ \vdots \\ \theta_L \end{bmatrix}}_{=\boldsymbol{\theta}} + \underbrace{\begin{bmatrix} e_1 \\ e_2 \\ e_3 \\ \vdots \\ e_N \end{bmatrix}}_{=\boldsymbol{e}}. \tag{7.10}$$

- The number of taps in the past history would affect the memory and hence the long-term forecast.
- Solve for $\boldsymbol{\theta}$ by

$$\widehat{\boldsymbol{\theta}} = \underset{\boldsymbol{\theta} \in \mathbb{R}^d}{\operatorname{argmin}} \ \|\boldsymbol{y} - \boldsymbol{X}\boldsymbol{\theta}\|^2. \tag{7.11}$$

7.1.4 Overdetermined and underdetermined systems

The sub-section requires knowledge of some concepts in linear algebra that can be found in standard references.[a]

---

[a]Carl Meyer, *Matrix Analysis and Applied Linear Algebra*, SIAM, 2000.

Let us now consider the theoretical properties of the least squares linear regression problem, which is an optimization:

$$\widehat{\boldsymbol{\theta}} = \underset{\boldsymbol{\theta} \in \mathbb{R}^d}{\operatorname{argmin}} \|\boldsymbol{y} - \boldsymbol{X}\boldsymbol{\theta}\|^2. \tag{P1}$$

We observe that the objective value of this optimization problem can go to zero if and only if the minimizer $\widehat{\boldsymbol{\theta}}$ is the solution of the system of linear equations

$$\text{Find } \boldsymbol{\theta} \text{ such that } \boldsymbol{y} = \boldsymbol{X}\boldsymbol{\theta}. \tag{P2}$$

We emphasize that Problem (P1) and Problem (P2) are two different problems. Even if we cannot solve Problem (P2), Problem (P1) is still well defined, but the objective value will not go to zero. This subsection aims to draw the connection between the two problems and discuss the respective solutions. We will start with Problem (P2) by considering two shapes of the matrix $\boldsymbol{X}$.

Overdetermined system

Problem (P2) is called **overdetermined** if $\boldsymbol{X} \in \mathbb{R}^{N \times d}$ is tall and skinny, i.e., $N > d$. This happens when you have more rows than columns, or equivalently when you have more equations than unknowns. When $N > d$, Problem (P2) has a unique solution $\widehat{\boldsymbol{\theta}} = (\boldsymbol{X}^T \boldsymbol{X})^{-1} \boldsymbol{X}^T \boldsymbol{y}$ if and only if $X^T X$ is invertible, or equivalently if and only if the columns of X are linearly in-dependent. A technical description of this is that X has a **full rank**, denoted by rank$(X) = d$. When rank$(X) = d$, Problem (P1) has a unique global minimizer $\hat{\theta} = (X^T X)^{-1} X^T y$, which is the same as the unique solution of Problem (P2).

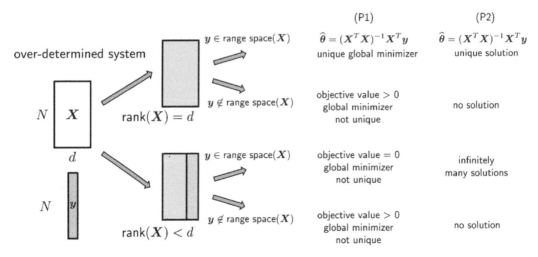

Figure 7.9: Hierarchy of the solutions of an overdetermined system. An overdetermined system uses a tall and skinny matrix X. The rank of a matrix X is defined as the largest number of independent columns we can find in X. If rank$(X) = d$, the matrix $X^T X$ is invertible, and Problem (P2) will have a unique solution. If rank$(X) < d$, then the solution depends on whether the particular observation y lives in the range space of X. If yes, Problem (P2) will have infinitely many solutions because there is a nontrivial null space. If no, Problem (P2) will have no solution because the system is incompatible.

If the columns of X are linearly dependent so that $X^T X$ is not invertible, we say that X is **rank-deficient** (denoted as rank$(X) < d$). In this case, Problem (P2) may not have a solution. We say that it *may* not have a solution because it is still *possible* to have a solution. It all depends on whether y can be written as a linear combination of the linearly independent columns of X.

If yes, we say that y lives in the **range space** of X. The range space of X is defined as the set of vectors $\{z \mid z = X\alpha, \text{ for some } \alpha\}$. If rank$(X) = d$, all y will live in the range space of X. But if rank$(X) < d$, only some of the y will live in the range space of X. When this happens, the matrix X must have a nontrivial **null space**. The null space of X is defined as the set of vectors $\{z \mid Xz = 0\}$. A nontrivial null space will give us infinitely many solutions to Problem (P2). This is because if α is the solution found in the range space so that $y = X\alpha$, then we can pick any z from the null space such that $Xz = 0$. This will lead to another solution $\alpha + z$ such that $X(\alpha + z) = X\alpha + 0 = y$. Since we have infinitely many choices of such z's, there will be infinitely many solutions to Problem (P2).

Although there are infinitely many solutions to Problem (P2), all of them are the global minimizers of Problem (P1). They can make the objective value equal to zero because the equality $y = X\theta$ holds. However, the solutions to Problem (P2) are not unique since the objective function is convex but not strictly convex.

If y does not live in the range space of X, we say that Problem (P2) is **incompatible**. If a system of linear equations is incompatible, there is no solution. However, even when this happens, we can still solve the optimization Problem (P1), but the objective value will not reach 0. The minimizer is a global minimizer because the objective function is convex, but the minimizer is not unique.

Underdetermined system

Problem (P2) is called **underdetermined** if X is fat and short, i.e., $N < d$. This happens when you have more columns than rows, or equivalently when you have more unknowns than equations. In this case, $X^T X$ is not invertible, and so we cannot use $\widehat{\theta} = (X^T X)^{-1} X^T y$ as the solution. However, if $\text{rank}(X) = N$, then *any* y will live in the range space of X. But because X is fat and short, there exists a nontrivial null space. Therefore, Problem (P2) will have *infinitely* many solutions, attributed to the vectors generated by the null space. For this set of infinitely many solutions, the corresponding Problem (P1) will have a global minimizer, and the objective value will be zero. However, the minimizer is not unique. This is the first case in **Figure 7.10**.

under-determined system

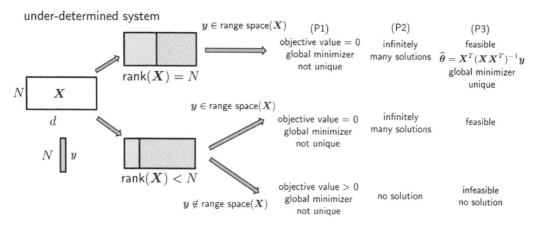

Figure 7.10: Hierarchy of the solutions of an underdetermined system. An underdetermined system uses a fat and short matrix X. The rank of a matrix X is defined as the largest number of independent columns we can find in X. If $\text{rank}(X) = N$, we will have infinitely many solutions. If $\text{rank}(X) < N$, then the solutions depends on whether the particular observation y lives in the range space of X. If yes, Problem (P2) will have infinitely many solutions because there is a nontrivial null space. If no, Problem (P2) will have no solution because the system is incompatible.

There are two other cases in **Figure 7.10**, which occur when $\text{rank}(X) < N$:

- (i) If y is in the range space of X, Problem (P2) will have infinitely many solutions. Since Problem (P2) remains feasible, the objective function of Problem (P1) will go to zero.

- (ii) If y is not in the range space of X, the system in Problem (P2) is incompatible and there will be no solution. The objective value of Problem (P1) will not go to zero.

If an underdetermined system has infinitely many solutions, we need to pick and choose. One of the possible approaches is to consider the optimization

$$\widehat{\theta} = \underset{\theta \in \mathbb{R}^d}{\text{argmin}} \ \|\theta\|^2 \ \text{ subject to } \ X\theta = y. \tag{P3}$$

This optimization is different from Problem (P1), which is an **unconstrained** optimization. Our goal is to minimize the deviation between $X\theta$ and y. Problem (P3) is **constrained**. Since

411

we assume that Problem (P2) has infinitely many solutions, the constraint set $y = X\theta$ is feasible. Among all the feasible choices, we pick the one that minimizes the squared norm. Therefore, the solution to Problem (P3) is called the **minimum-norm** least squares. Theorem 7.2 below summarizes the solution. If y does not live in the range space of X, then Problem (P2) does not have a solution. Therefore, the constraint in P3 is infeasible, and hence the optimization problem does not have a minimizer.

Theorem 7.2. *Consider the* **underdetermined** *linear regression problem where $N < d$:*

$$\widehat{\theta} = \underset{\theta \in \mathbb{R}^d}{\operatorname{argmin}} \ \|\theta\|^2 \ \text{subject to} \ y = X\theta,$$

where $X \in \mathbb{R}^{N \times d}$, $\theta \in \mathbb{R}^d$, and $y \in \mathbb{R}^N$. If rank$(X) = N$, then the linear regression problem will have a unique global minimum

$$\widehat{\theta} = X^T (XX^T)^{-1} y. \tag{7.12}$$

This solution is called the **minimum-norm** *least-squares solution.*

Proof. The proof of the theorem requires some knowledge of constrained optimization. Consider the Lagrangian of the problem:

$$\mathcal{L}(\theta, \lambda) = \|\theta\|^2 + \lambda^T (X\theta - y),$$

where λ is called the Lagrange multiplier. The solution of the constrained optimization is the stationary point of the Lagrangian. To find the stationary point, we take the derivatives with respect to θ and λ. This yields

$$\nabla_\theta \mathcal{L} = 2\theta + X^T \lambda = 0,$$
$$\nabla_\lambda \mathcal{L} = X\theta - y = 0.$$

The first equation gives us $\theta = -X^T \lambda / 2$. Substituting it into the second equation, and assuming that rank$(X) = N$ so that $X^T X$ is invertible, we have

$$X\left(-X^T \lambda / 2\right) - y = 0,$$

which implies that $\lambda = -2(XX^T)^{-1} y$. Therefore, $\theta = X^T (XX^T)^{-1} y$. $\qquad \square$

The end of this subsection. Please join us again.

7.1.5 Robust linear regression

This subsection is optional for a first reading of the book.

The linear regression we have discussed so far is based on an important criterion, namely the **squared error** criterion. We chose the squared error as the training loss because it is differentiable and convex. Differentiability allows us to take the derivative and locate the minimum point. Convexity allows us to claim a global minimizer (also unique if the objective function is strictly convex). However, such a nice criterion suffers from a serious drawback: the issue of **outliers**.

Consider **Figure 7.11**. In **Figure 7.11**(a), we show a regression problem for $N = 50$ data points. Our basis functions are the ordinary polynomials in the fourth order. Everything looks fine in the figure. We intervene in the data by randomly altering a few of them so that their values are off. There are only a handful of these outliers. We run the same regression analysis again, but we observe (see **Figure 7.11**(b)) that our fitted curve has been distorted quite significantly.

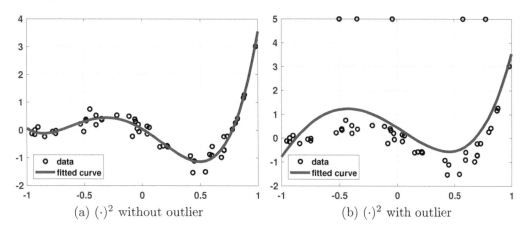

(a) $(\cdot)^2$ without outlier   (b) $(\cdot)^2$ with outlier

Figure 7.11: Linear regression using the squared error as the training loss suffers from outliers. (a) The regression performs well when there is no outlier. (b) By adding only a few outliers, the regression curve has already been distorted.

This occurs because of the squared error. By the definition of a squared error, our training loss is

$$\mathcal{E}_{\text{train}}(\boldsymbol{\theta}) = \sum_{n=1}^{N} \left(y_n - g_{\boldsymbol{\theta}}(x_n) \right)^2.$$

Without loss of generality, let us assume that one of these error terms is large because of an outlier. Then the training loss becomes

$$\mathcal{E}_{\text{train}}(\boldsymbol{\theta}) = \underbrace{\left(y_1 - g_{\boldsymbol{\theta}}(x_1) \right)^2}_{\text{small}} + \underbrace{\left(y_2 - g_{\boldsymbol{\theta}}(x_2) \right)^2}_{\text{small}} + \underbrace{\left(y_3 - g_{\boldsymbol{\theta}}(x_3) \right)^2}_{\text{large}} + \cdots + \underbrace{\left(y_N - g_{\boldsymbol{\theta}}(x_N) \right)^2}_{\text{small}}.$$

Here is the daunting fact: If one or a few of these individual error terms are large, the square operation will *amplify* them. As a result, the error you see is not just large but large^2. Moreover, since we put the squares to the small errors as well, we have small^2 instead of small. When you try to weigh the relative significance between the outliers and the normal data points, the outliers suddenly have a very large contribution to the error. Since the goal of linear regression is to minimize the *total* loss, the presence of the outliers will drive the optimization solution to compensate for the large error.

One possible solution is to replace the squared error by the **absolute error**, such that

$$\mathcal{E}_{\text{train}}(\boldsymbol{\theta}) = \sum_{n=1}^{N} \left| y_n - g_{\boldsymbol{\theta}}(x_n) \right|.$$

This is a simple modification, but it is very effective. The reason is that the absolute error keeps the small just as small, and keeps the large just as large. There is no amplification. Therefore, while the outliers still contribute to the overall loss, their contributions are less prominent. (If you have a lot of strong outliers, even the absolute error will fail. If this happens, you should go back to your data collection process and find out what has gone wrong.)

When we use the absolute error as the training loss, the resulting regression problem is the **least absolute deviation** regression (or simply the **robust regression**). The tricky thing about the least absolute deviation is that the training loss is not differentiable. In other words, we cannot take the derivative and find the optimal solution. The good news is that there exists an alternative approach for solving this problem: using **linear programming** (implemented via the **simplex method**).

Solving the robust regression problem

Let us focus on the linear model

$$g_{\boldsymbol{\theta}}(\boldsymbol{x}_n) = \boldsymbol{x}_n^T \boldsymbol{\theta},$$

where $\boldsymbol{x}_n = [\phi_0(x_n), \ldots, \phi_{d-1}(x_n)]^T \in \mathbb{R}^d$ is the nth input vector for some basis functions $\{\phi_p\}_{p=0}^{d-1}$, and $\boldsymbol{\theta} = [\theta_0, \ldots, \theta_{d-1}]^T \in \mathbb{R}^d$ is the parameter. Substituting this into the training loss, the optimization problem is

$$\underset{\boldsymbol{\theta} \in \mathbb{R}^d}{\text{minimize}} \sum_{n=1}^{N} \left| y_n - \boldsymbol{x}_n^T \boldsymbol{\theta} \right|.$$

Here is an important trick. The idea is to express the problem as an equivalent problem

$$\underset{\boldsymbol{\theta} \in \mathbb{R}^d, \boldsymbol{u} \in \mathbb{R}^N}{\text{minimize}} \sum_{n=1}^{N} u_n$$
$$\text{subject to } u_n = |y_n - \boldsymbol{x}_n^T \boldsymbol{\theta}|, \quad n = 1, \ldots, N.$$

There is a small but important difference between this problem and the previous one. In the first problem, there is only one optimization variable $\boldsymbol{\theta}$. In the new problem, we introduce an additional variable $\boldsymbol{u} = [u_1, \ldots, u_N]^T$ and add a constraint $u_n = |y_n - \boldsymbol{x}_n^T \boldsymbol{\theta}|$ for $n = 1, \ldots, N$. We introduce $\boldsymbol{u}$ so that we can have some additional degrees of freedom. At the optimal solution, u_n must equal to $|y_n - \boldsymbol{x}_n^T \boldsymbol{\theta}|$, and so the corresponding $\boldsymbol{\theta}$ is the solution of the original problem.

Now we note that $x = |a|$ is equivalent to $x \geq a$ and $x \geq -a$. Therefore, the constraint can be equivalently written as

$$\underset{\boldsymbol{\theta} \in \mathbb{R}^d, \boldsymbol{u} \in \mathbb{R}^N}{\text{minimize}} \sum_{n=1}^{N} u_n, \tag{7.13}$$
$$\text{subject to } u_n \geq -(y_n - \boldsymbol{x}_n^T \boldsymbol{\theta}), \quad n = 1, \ldots, N$$
$$u_n \geq (y_n - \boldsymbol{x}_n^T \boldsymbol{\theta}), \quad n = 1, \ldots, N.$$

In other words, we have rewritten the equality constraint as a pair of inequality constraints by removing the absolute signs.

The optimization in Equation (7.13) is in the form of a standard **linear programming** problem. A linear programming problem takes the form of

$$\underset{\boldsymbol{x} \in \mathbb{R}^k}{\text{minimize}} \quad \boldsymbol{c}^T \boldsymbol{x} \tag{7.14}$$

$$\text{subject to} \quad \boldsymbol{A}\boldsymbol{x} \leq \boldsymbol{b},$$

for some vectors $\boldsymbol{c} \in \mathbb{R}^k$, $\boldsymbol{b} \in \mathbb{R}^m$, and matrix $\boldsymbol{A} \in \mathbb{R}^{m \times k}$. Linear programming is a standard optimization problem that you can find in most optimization textbooks. On a computer, if we know $\boldsymbol{c}$, $\boldsymbol{b}$ and $\boldsymbol{A}$, solving the linear programming problem can be done using built-in commands. For MATLAB, the command is `linprog`. For Python, the command is `scipy.optimize.linprog`. We will discuss a concrete example shortly.

```
% MATLAB command for linear programming
x = linprog(c, A, b);
```

```
# Python command for linear programming
linprog(c, A, b, bounds=(None,None), method="revised simplex")
```

Given Equation (7.13), the question becomes how to convert it into the standard linear programming format. This requires two steps. The first step uses the **objective function**:

$$\sum_{n=1}^{N} u_n = \sum_{p=0}^{d-1} (0)(\theta_p) + \sum_{n=1}^{N} (1)(u_n)$$

$$= \underbrace{\begin{bmatrix} 0 & 0 & \cdots & 0 & 1 & 1 & \cdots & 1 \end{bmatrix}}_{= \boldsymbol{c}^T} \begin{bmatrix} \boldsymbol{\theta} \\ \boldsymbol{u} \end{bmatrix}.$$

Therefore, the vector $\boldsymbol{c}$ has d 0's followed by N 1's.

The second step concerns the **constraint**. It can be shown that $u_n \geq -(y_n - \boldsymbol{x}_n^T \boldsymbol{\theta})$ is equivalent to $\boldsymbol{x}_n^T \boldsymbol{\theta} - u_n \leq y_n$. Written in the matrix form, we have

$$\begin{bmatrix} \boldsymbol{x}_1^T & -1 & 0 & \cdots & 0 \\ \boldsymbol{x}_2^T & 0 & -1 & \cdots & 0 \\ \vdots & \vdots & \vdots & \cdots & \vdots \\ \boldsymbol{x}_N^T & 0 & 0 & \cdots & -1 \end{bmatrix} \begin{bmatrix} \boldsymbol{\theta} \\ u_1 \\ \vdots \\ u_N \end{bmatrix} \leq \begin{bmatrix} y_1 \\ y_2 \\ \vdots \\ y_N \end{bmatrix},$$

which is equivalent to

$$\begin{bmatrix} \boldsymbol{X} & -\boldsymbol{I} \end{bmatrix} \begin{bmatrix} \boldsymbol{\theta} \\ \boldsymbol{u} \end{bmatrix} \leq \boldsymbol{y}, \tag{7.15}$$

where $\boldsymbol{I} \in \mathbb{R}^{N \times N}$ is the identity matrix.

Similarly, the other constraint $u_n \geq (y_n - \boldsymbol{x}_n^T \boldsymbol{\theta})$ is equivalent to $-\boldsymbol{x}_n^T \boldsymbol{\theta} - u_n \leq -y_n$. Written in the matrix form, we have

$$\begin{bmatrix} -\boldsymbol{x}_1^T & -1 & 0 & \cdots & 0 \\ -\boldsymbol{x}_2^T & 0 & -1 & \cdots & 0 \\ \vdots & \vdots & \vdots & \cdots & \vdots \\ -\boldsymbol{x}_N^T & 0 & 0 & \cdots & -1 \end{bmatrix} \begin{bmatrix} \boldsymbol{\theta} \\ u_1 \\ \vdots \\ u_N \end{bmatrix} \leq \begin{bmatrix} -y_1 \\ -y_2 \\ \vdots \\ -y_N \end{bmatrix},$$

which is equivalent to

$$\begin{bmatrix} -\boldsymbol{X} & -I \end{bmatrix} \begin{bmatrix} \boldsymbol{\theta} \\ \boldsymbol{u} \end{bmatrix} \leq -\boldsymbol{y}$$

Putting everything together, we have finally arrived at the linear programming problem

$$\underset{\boldsymbol{\theta} \in \mathbb{R}^d, \boldsymbol{u} \in \mathbb{R}^N}{\text{minimize}} \quad \begin{bmatrix} \boldsymbol{0}_d & \boldsymbol{1}_N \end{bmatrix} \begin{bmatrix} \boldsymbol{\theta} \\ \boldsymbol{u} \end{bmatrix}$$

$$\text{subject to} \quad \begin{bmatrix} \boldsymbol{X} & -I \\ -\boldsymbol{X} & -I \end{bmatrix} \begin{bmatrix} \boldsymbol{\theta} \\ \boldsymbol{u} \end{bmatrix} \leq \begin{bmatrix} \boldsymbol{y} \\ -\boldsymbol{y} \end{bmatrix},$$

where $\boldsymbol{0}_d \in \mathbb{R}^d$ is an all-zero vector, and $\boldsymbol{1}_N \in \mathbb{R}^N$ is an all-one vector. It is this problem that solves the robust linear regression.

Let us look at how to implement linear programming to solve the robust regression optimization. As an example, we continue with the polynomial fitting problem in which there are outliers. We choose the ordinary polynomials as the basis functions. To construct the linear programming problem, we need to define the matrix $\boldsymbol{A}$ and the vectors $\boldsymbol{c}$ and $\boldsymbol{b}$ according to the linear programming form. This is done using the following MATLAB program.

```
% MATLAB code to demonstrate robust regression
N = 50;
x = linspace(-1,1,N)';
a = [-0.001 0.01 0.55 1.5 1.2];
y = a(1)*legendreP(0,x) + a(2)*legendreP(1,x) + ...
    a(3)*legendreP(2,x) + a(4)*legendreP(3,x) + ...
    a(5)*legendreP(4,x) + 0.2*randn(N,1);
idx = [10, 16, 23, 37, 45];
y(idx) = 5;

X   = [x(:).^0 x(:).^1 x(:).^2 x(:).^3 x(:).^4];
A   = [X -eye(N); -X -eye(N)];
b   = [y(:); -y(:)];
c   = [zeros(1,5) ones(1,N)]';
theta = linprog(c, A, b);

t    = linspace(-1,1,200)';
yhat = theta(1) + theta(2)*t(:) + ...
       theta(3)*t(:).^2 + theta(4)*t(:).^3 + ...
       theta(5)*t(:).^4;
plot(x,y,    'ko','LineWidth',2); hold on;
plot(t,yhat,'r','LineWidth',4);
```

In this set of commands, the basis vectors are defined as $\boldsymbol{x}_n^T = [\phi_4(x_n), \ldots, \phi_0(x_n)]^T$, for $n = 1, \ldots, N$. The matrix $\boldsymbol{I}$ is constructed by using the command eye(N), which constructs the identity matrix of size $N \times N$. The rest of the commands are self-explanatory. Note that the solution to the linear programming problem consists of both $\boldsymbol{\theta}$ and $\boldsymbol{u}$. To squeeze $\boldsymbol{\theta}$ we need to locate the first d entries. The remainder is $\boldsymbol{u}$.

Commands for Python are similar, although we need to call np.hstack and np.vstack to construct the matrices and vectors. The main routine is linprog in the scipy.optimize library. Note that for this particular example, the bounds are `bounds=(None,None)`, or otherwise Python will search in the positive quadrant.

```python
# Python code to demonstrate robust regression
import numpy as np
import matplotlib.pyplot as plt
from scipy.special import eval_legendre
from scipy.optimize import linprog

N = 50
x = np.linspace(-1,1,N)
a = np.array([-0.001, 0.01, 0.55, 1.5, 1.2])
y = a[0]*eval_legendre(0,x) + a[1]*eval_legendre(1,x) + \
    a[2]*eval_legendre(2,x) + a[3]*eval_legendre(3,x) + \
    a[4]*eval_legendre(4,x) + 0.2*np.random.randn(N)
idx = [10,16,23,37,45]
y[idx] = 5
X = np.column_stack((np.ones(N), x, x**2, x**3, x**4))
A = np.vstack((np.hstack((X, -np.eye(N))), np.hstack((-X, -np.eye(N)))))
b = np.hstack((y,-y))
c = np.hstack((np.zeros(5), np.ones(N)))
res = linprog(c, A, b, bounds=(None,None), method="revised simplex")
theta = res.x
t     = np.linspace(-1,1,200)
yhat = theta[0]*np.ones(200) + theta[1]*t + theta[2]*t**2 + \
       theta[3]*t**3 + theta[4]*t**4
plt.plot(x,y,'o',markersize=12)
plt.plot(t,yhat, linewidth=8)
plt.show()
```

The result of this experiment is shown in **Figure 7.12**. It is remarkable to see that the robust regression result is almost as good as the result would be without outliers.

If robust linear regression performs so well, why don't we use it all the time? Why is least squares regression still more popular? The answer has a lot to do with the computational complexity and the uniqueness of the solution. Linear programming requires an algorithm for a solution. While we have very fast linear programming solvers today, the computational cost of solving a linear program is still much higher than solving a least-squares problem (which is essentially a matrix inversion).

The other issue with robust linear regression is the uniqueness of the solution. Linear programming is known to have degenerate solutions when the constraint set (a high-dimensional polygon) touches the objective function (which is a line) at one of its edges. The least-squares fitting does not have this problem because the optimization surface is a parabola. Unless the matrix $X^T X$ is noninvertible, the solution is guaranteed to be the unique global minimum. Linear programming does not have this convenient property. We can have multiple solutions θ that give the same objective value. If you try to interpret your result by inspecting the magnitude of the θ's, the nonuniqueness of the solution would cause problems because your interpretation can be swiped immediately if the linear programming gives you a nonunique solution.

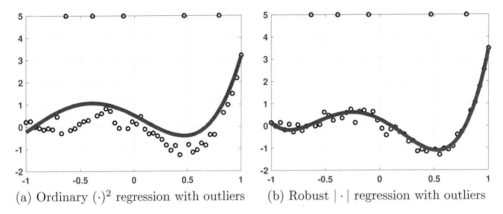

(a) Ordinary $(\cdot)^2$ regression with outliers   (b) Robust $|\cdot|$ regression with outliers

Figure 7.12: (a) Ordinary linear regression using $(\cdot)^2$ as the training loss. In the absence of any outlier, the regression performs well. (b) Robust linear regression using $|\cdot|$ as the training loss. Note that even in the presence of outliers, the robustness regression perform reasonably well.

> End of this subsection. Please join us again.

Closing remark. The principle of linear regression is primarily to set up a function to fit the data. This, in turn, is about finding a set of good basis functions and minimizing the appropriate training loss. Selecting the basis is usually done in several ways:

- The problem forces you to choose certain basis functions. For example, suppose you are working on a disease dataset. The variates are height, weight, and BMI. You do not have any choice here because your goal is to see which factor contributes the most to the cause of the disease.

- There are known basis functions that work. For example, suppose you are working on a speech dataset. Physics tells us that Fourier bases are excellent representations of these sinusoidal functions. So it would make more sense to use the Fourier basis than the polynomials.

- Sometimes the basis can be learned from the data. For example, you can run principal-component analysis (PCA) to extract the basis. Then you can run the linear regression to compute the coefficients. This is a data-driven approach and could apply to some problems.

7.2 Overfitting

The regression principle we have discussed in the previous section is a powerful technique for data analysis. However, there are many ways in which things can fall apart. We have seen the problem of outliers, where perturbations of one or a few data points would result in a big change in the regression result, and we discussed some techniques to overcome the outlier problem, e.g., using robust regression. In addition to outliers, there are other causes of the failure of the regression.

In this section, we examine the relationship between the number of training samples and the complexity of the model. For example, if we decide to use polynomials as the basis functions and we have only $N = 20$ data points, what should be the order of the polynomials? Shall we use the 5th-order polynomial, or shall we use the 20th-order? Our goal in this section is to acquire an understanding of the general problem known as **overfitting**. Then we will discuss methods for mitigating overfitting in Section 7.4.

7.2.1 Overview of overfitting

Imagine that we have a dataset containing $N = 20$ training samples. We know that the data are generated from a fourth-order polynomial with Legendre polynomials as the basis. On top of these samples, we also know that a small amount of noise corrupts each sample, for example, Gaussian noise of standard deviation $\sigma = 0.1$.

We have two options here for fitting the data:

- Option 1: $h(x) = \sum_{p=0}^{4} \theta_p L_p(x)$, which is a 4th-order polynomial.

- Option 2: $g(x) = \sum_{p=0}^{50} \theta_p L_p(x)$, which is a 50th-order polynomial.

Model 2 is more expressive because it has more degrees of freedom. Let us fit the data using these two models. **Figure 7.13** shows the results. However, what is going on with the 50th-order polynomial? It has gone completely wild. How can the regression ever choose such a terrible model?

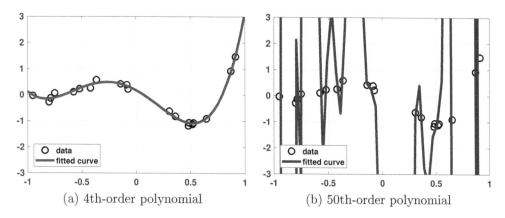

(a) 4th-order polynomial (b) 50th-order polynomial

Figure 7.13: Fitting data using a 4th-order polynomial and a 50th-order polynomial.

Here is an even bigger surprise: If we compute the training loss, we get

$$\mathcal{E}_{\text{train}}(h) = \frac{1}{N} \sum_{n=1}^{N} \left(y_n - h(x_n) \right)^2 = 0.0063,$$

$$\mathcal{E}_{\text{train}}(g) = \frac{1}{N} \sum_{n=1}^{N} \left(y_n - g(x_n) \right)^2 = 5.7811 \times 10^{-24}.$$

Thus, while Model 2 looks wild in the figure, it has a much lower training loss than Model 1. So according to the training loss, Model 2 fits better.

Any sensible person at this point will object, since Model 2 cannot possibly be better, for the following reason. It is not because it "looks bad", but because if you test the model with an unseen sample it is almost certain that the **testing error** will explode. For example, in **Figure 7.13**(a) if we look at $x = 0$, we would expect the predicted value to be close to $y = 0$. However, **Figure 7.13**(b) suggests that the predicted value is going to negative infinity. It would be hard to believe that the negative infinity is a better prediction than the other one. We refer to this general phenomenon of fitting very well to the training data but generalizing poorly to the testing data as **overfitting**.

> **What is overfitting?**
> Overfitting means that a model fits too closely to the training samples so that it fails to generalize.

Overfitting occurs as a consequence of an imbalance between the following three factors:

- **Number of training samples** N. If you have many training samples, you should learn very well, even if the model is complex. Conversely, if the model is complex but does not have enough training samples, you will overfit it. The most serious problem in regression is often insufficient training data.

- **Model order** d. This refers to the complexity of the model. For example, if your model uses a polynomial, d refers to the order of the polynomial. If your training set is too small, you need to use a less complex model. The general rule of thumb is: "less is more".

- **Noise variance** σ^2. This refers to the variance of the error e_n you add to the data. The model we assumed in the previous numerical experiment is that

$$y_n = g(x_n) + e_n, \qquad n = 1, \ldots, N.$$

where $e_n \sim \text{Gaussian}(0, \sigma^2)$. If σ increases, it is inevitable that the fitting will become more difficult. Hence it would require more training samples, and perhaps a less complex model would work better.

7.2.2 Analysis of the linear case

Let us spell out the details of these factors one by one. To make our discussion concrete, we will use linear regression as a case study. The general analysis will be presented in the next section.

Notations

- **Ground Truth Model.** To start with, we assume that we have a population set $\mathcal{D}$ containing infinitely many samples (x, y) drawn according to some latent distributions. The relationship between x and y is defined through an *unknown* target function

$$y = f(x) + e,$$

where $e \sim \text{Gaussian}(0, \sigma^2)$ is the noise. For our analysis, we assume that $f(\cdot)$ is linear, so that

$$f(\boldsymbol{x}) = \boldsymbol{x}^T \boldsymbol{\theta}^*,$$

where $\boldsymbol{\theta}^* \in \mathbb{R}^d$ is the ground truth model parameter. Notice that $f(\cdot)$ is deterministic, but e is random. Therefore, any randomness we see in y is due to e.

- **Training and Testing Set.** From $\mathcal{D}$, we construct two datasets: the training data set $\mathcal{D}_{\text{train}}$ that contains training samples $\{(\boldsymbol{x}_1, y_1), \ldots, (\boldsymbol{x}_N, y_N)\}$ and the testing dataset $\mathcal{D}_{\text{test}}$ that contains $\{(\boldsymbol{x}_1, y_1), \ldots, (\boldsymbol{x}_M, y_M)\}$. Both $\mathcal{D}_{\text{train}}$ and $\mathcal{D}_{\text{test}}$ are subsets of $\mathcal{D}$.

- **Predictive Model.** We consider a predictive model $g_{\boldsymbol{\theta}}(\cdot)$. For simplicity, we assume that $g_{\boldsymbol{\theta}}(\cdot)$ is also linear:

$$g_{\boldsymbol{\theta}}(\boldsymbol{x}) = \boldsymbol{x}^T \boldsymbol{\theta}.$$

Given the training dataset $\mathcal{D} = \{(\boldsymbol{x}_1, y_1), \ldots, (\boldsymbol{x}_N, y_N)\}$, we construct a linear regression problem:

$$\widehat{\boldsymbol{\theta}} = \underset{\boldsymbol{\theta} \in \mathbb{R}^d}{\text{argmin}} \ \|\boldsymbol{X}\boldsymbol{\theta} - \boldsymbol{y}\|^2.$$

Throughout our analysis, we assume that $N \geq d$ so that we have more training data than the number of unknowns. We further assume that $\boldsymbol{X}^T\boldsymbol{X}$ is invertible, and so there is a unique global minimizer

$$\widehat{\boldsymbol{\theta}} = (\boldsymbol{X}^T\boldsymbol{X})^{-1}\boldsymbol{X}^T\boldsymbol{y}.$$

- **Training Error.** Given the estimated model parameter $\widehat{\boldsymbol{\theta}}$, we define the **in-sample** prediction as

$$\widehat{\boldsymbol{y}}_{\text{train}} = \boldsymbol{X}_{\text{train}}\widehat{\boldsymbol{\theta}},$$

where $\boldsymbol{X}_{\text{train}} = \boldsymbol{X}$ is the training data matrix. The in-sample prediction is the predicted value using the trained model for the training data. The corresponding error with respect to the ground truth is called the **training error**:

$$\mathcal{E}_{\text{train}}(\widehat{\boldsymbol{\theta}}) = \mathbb{E}_e\left[\frac{1}{N}\|\widehat{\boldsymbol{y}}_{\text{train}} - \boldsymbol{y}\|^2\right],$$

where N is the number of training samples in the training dataset. Note that the expectation is taken with respect to the noise vector $\boldsymbol{e}$, which follows the distribution $\text{Gaussian}(0, \sigma^2\boldsymbol{I})$.

- **Testing Error.** During testing, we construct a testing matrix $\boldsymbol{X}_{\text{test}}$. This gives us the estimated values $\widehat{\boldsymbol{y}}_{\text{test}}$:

$$\widehat{\boldsymbol{y}}_{\text{test}} = \boldsymbol{X}_{\text{test}}\widehat{\boldsymbol{\theta}}.$$

The out-sample prediction is the predicted value using the trained model for the testing data. The corresponding error with respect to the ground truth is called the **testing error**:

$$\mathcal{E}_{\text{test}}(\widehat{\boldsymbol{\theta}}) = \mathbb{E}_e\left[\frac{1}{M}\|\widehat{\boldsymbol{y}}_{\text{test}} - \boldsymbol{y}\|^2\right],$$

where M is the number of testing samples in the testing dataset.

Analysis of the training error

We first analyze the training error, which we defined as

$$\mathcal{E}_{\text{train}} = \mathbb{E}_e \left[\frac{1}{N} \|\widehat{\boldsymbol{y}} - \boldsymbol{y}\|^2 \right] \overset{\text{def}}{=} \text{MSE}(\widehat{\boldsymbol{y}}, \boldsymbol{y}). \tag{7.16}$$

For this particular choice of the training error, we call it the mean squared error (MSE). It measures the difference between $\widehat{\boldsymbol{y}}$ and $\boldsymbol{y}$.

Theorem 7.3. *Let $\boldsymbol{\theta}^* \in \mathbb{R}^d$ be the ground truth linear model parameter, and $\boldsymbol{X} \in \mathbb{R}^{N \times d}$ be a matrix such that $N \geq d$ and $\boldsymbol{X}^T \boldsymbol{X}$ is invertible. Assume that the data follows the linear model $\boldsymbol{y} = \boldsymbol{X}\boldsymbol{\theta}^* + \boldsymbol{e}$ where $\boldsymbol{e} \sim \text{Gaussian}(0, \sigma^2 \boldsymbol{I})$. Consider the linear regression problem $\widehat{\boldsymbol{\theta}} = \underset{\boldsymbol{\theta} \in \mathbb{R}^d}{\text{argmin}} \ \|\boldsymbol{X}\boldsymbol{\theta} - \boldsymbol{y}\|^2$, and the predicted value $\widehat{\boldsymbol{y}} = \boldsymbol{X}\widehat{\boldsymbol{\theta}}$. The mean squared* **training error** *of this linear model is*

$$\mathcal{E}_{\text{train}} \overset{\text{def}}{=} \text{MSE}(\widehat{\boldsymbol{y}}, \boldsymbol{y}) = \mathbb{E}_e \left[\frac{1}{N} \|\widehat{\boldsymbol{y}} - \boldsymbol{y}\|^2 \right] = \sigma^2 \left(1 - \frac{d}{N} \right). \tag{7.17}$$

The proof below depends on some results from linear algebra that may be difficult for first-time readers. We recommend you read the proof later.

Proof. Recall that the least squares linear regression solution is $\widehat{\boldsymbol{\theta}} = (\boldsymbol{X}^T \boldsymbol{X})^{-1} \boldsymbol{X}^T \boldsymbol{y}$. Since $\boldsymbol{y} = \boldsymbol{X}\boldsymbol{\theta}^* + \boldsymbol{e}$, we can substitute this into the predicted value $\widehat{\boldsymbol{y}}$ to show that

$$\widehat{\boldsymbol{y}} = \boldsymbol{X}\widehat{\boldsymbol{\theta}} = \underbrace{\boldsymbol{X}(\boldsymbol{X}^T\boldsymbol{X})^{-1}\boldsymbol{X}^T}_{=\boldsymbol{H}}\boldsymbol{y} = \boldsymbol{X}(\boldsymbol{X}^T\boldsymbol{X})^{-1}\boldsymbol{X}^T(\boldsymbol{X}\boldsymbol{\theta}^* + \boldsymbol{e}) = \boldsymbol{X}\boldsymbol{\theta}^* + \boldsymbol{H}\boldsymbol{e}.$$

Therefore, substituting $\widehat{\boldsymbol{y}} = \boldsymbol{X}\boldsymbol{\theta}^* + \boldsymbol{H}\boldsymbol{e}$ into the MSE,

$$\text{MSE}(\widehat{\boldsymbol{y}}, \boldsymbol{y}) \overset{\text{def}}{=} \mathbb{E}_e \left[\frac{1}{N} \|\widehat{\boldsymbol{y}} - \boldsymbol{y}\|^2 \right] = \mathbb{E}_e \left[\frac{1}{N} \|\boldsymbol{X}\boldsymbol{\theta}^* + \boldsymbol{H}\boldsymbol{e} - \boldsymbol{X}\boldsymbol{\theta}^* - \boldsymbol{e}\|^2 \right]$$

$$= \mathbb{E}_e \left[\frac{1}{N} \|(\boldsymbol{H} - \boldsymbol{I})\boldsymbol{e}\|^2 \right].$$

At this point we need to use a tool from linear algebra. One useful identity[3] is that for any $\boldsymbol{v} \in \mathbb{R}^N$,

$$\|\boldsymbol{v}\|^2 = \text{Tr}(\boldsymbol{v}\boldsymbol{v}^T).$$

---

[3]The reason for this identity is that

$$\boldsymbol{v} = \sum_{n=1}^{N} v_n^2 = \text{Tr} \left\{ \begin{bmatrix} v_1^2 & v_1 v_2 & \cdots & v_1 v_N \\ v_2 v_1 & v_2^2 & \cdots & v_2 v_N \\ \vdots & \vdots & \ddots & \vdots \\ v_N v_1 & v_N v_2 & \cdots & v_N^2 \end{bmatrix} \right\} = \text{Tr}\left\{ \boldsymbol{v}\boldsymbol{v}^T \right\}.$$

Using this identity, we have that

$$\mathbb{E}_e\left[\frac{1}{N}\left\|(\boldsymbol{H}-\boldsymbol{I})\boldsymbol{e}\right\|^2\right] = \frac{1}{N}\mathbb{E}_e\left[\text{Tr}\left\{(\boldsymbol{H}-\boldsymbol{I})\boldsymbol{e}\boldsymbol{e}^T(\boldsymbol{H}-\boldsymbol{I})^T\right\}\right]$$

$$= \frac{1}{N}\text{Tr}\left\{(\boldsymbol{H}-\boldsymbol{I})\mathbb{E}_e\left[\boldsymbol{e}\boldsymbol{e}^T\right](\boldsymbol{H}-\boldsymbol{I})^T\right\}$$

$$= \frac{\sigma^2}{N}\text{Tr}\left\{(\boldsymbol{H}-\boldsymbol{I})(\boldsymbol{H}-\boldsymbol{I})^T\right\},$$

where we used the fact that $\mathbb{E}[\boldsymbol{e}\boldsymbol{e}^T] = \sigma^2\boldsymbol{I}$. The special structure of $\boldsymbol{H}$ tells us that $\boldsymbol{H}^T = \boldsymbol{H}$ and $\boldsymbol{H}^T\boldsymbol{H} = \boldsymbol{H}$. Thus, we have $(\boldsymbol{H}-\boldsymbol{I})^T(\boldsymbol{H}-\boldsymbol{I}) = \boldsymbol{I} - \boldsymbol{H}$. In addition, using the cyclic property of trace $\text{Tr}(\boldsymbol{AB}) = \text{Tr}(\boldsymbol{BA})$, we have that

$$\text{Tr}(\boldsymbol{H}) = \text{Tr}(\boldsymbol{X}(\boldsymbol{X}^T\boldsymbol{X})^{-1}\boldsymbol{X}^T)$$

$$= \text{Tr}((\boldsymbol{X}^T\boldsymbol{X})^{-1}\boldsymbol{X}^T\boldsymbol{X}) = \text{Tr}(\boldsymbol{I}) = d.$$

Consequently,

$$\frac{\sigma^2}{N}\text{Tr}\left\{(\boldsymbol{H}-\boldsymbol{I})(\boldsymbol{H}-\boldsymbol{I})^T\right\} = \frac{\sigma^2}{N}\text{Tr}\left\{\boldsymbol{I}-\boldsymbol{H}\right\}$$

$$= \sigma^2\left(1-\frac{d}{N}\right).$$

This completes the proof.

$\square$

The end of the proof. Please join us again.

Practice Exercise 1. In the theorem above, we proved the MSE of the **prediction** $\boldsymbol{y}$. In this example, we would like to prove the MSE for the **parameter**. Prove that

$$\text{MSE}(\widehat{\boldsymbol{\theta}},\boldsymbol{\theta}^*) \overset{\text{def}}{=} \mathbb{E}_e\left[\left\|\widehat{\boldsymbol{\theta}}-\boldsymbol{\theta}^*\right\|^2\right] = \sigma^2\text{Tr}\left\{(\boldsymbol{X}^T\boldsymbol{X})^{-1}\right\}.$$

Solution. Let us start with the definition:

$$\text{MSE}(\widehat{\boldsymbol{\theta}},\boldsymbol{\theta}^*) = \mathbb{E}_e\left[\left\|(\boldsymbol{X}^T\boldsymbol{X})^{-1}\boldsymbol{X}^T\boldsymbol{y}-\boldsymbol{\theta}^*\right\|^2\right]$$

$$= \mathbb{E}_e\left[\left\|(\boldsymbol{X}^T\boldsymbol{X})^{-1}\boldsymbol{X}^T(\boldsymbol{X}\boldsymbol{\theta}^*+e)-\boldsymbol{\theta}^*\right\|^2\right]$$

$$= \mathbb{E}_e\left[\left\|\boldsymbol{\theta}^*+(\boldsymbol{X}^T\boldsymbol{X})^{-1}\boldsymbol{X}^T e-\boldsymbol{\theta}^*\right\|^2\right] = \mathbb{E}_e\left[\left\|(\boldsymbol{X}^T\boldsymbol{X})^{-1}\boldsymbol{X}^T e\right\|^2\right].$$

Continuing the calculation,

$$\mathbb{E}_e\left[\left\|(\boldsymbol{X}^T\boldsymbol{X})^{-1}\boldsymbol{X}^T e\right\|^2\right] = \mathbb{E}_e\left[\text{Tr}\left\{(\boldsymbol{X}^T\boldsymbol{X})^{-1}\boldsymbol{X}^T e \ e^T\boldsymbol{X}(\boldsymbol{X}^T\boldsymbol{X})^{-1}\right\}\right]$$

$$= \text{Tr}\left\{(\boldsymbol{X}^T\boldsymbol{X})^{-1}\boldsymbol{X}^T\mathbb{E}_e\left[ee^T\right]\boldsymbol{X}(\boldsymbol{X}^T\boldsymbol{X})^{-1}\right\}$$

$$= \text{Tr}\left\{(\boldsymbol{X}^T\boldsymbol{X})^{-1}\boldsymbol{X}^T \cdot \sigma^2\boldsymbol{I} \cdot \boldsymbol{X}(\boldsymbol{X}^T\boldsymbol{X})^{-1}\right\}$$

$$= \sigma^2\text{Tr}\left\{(\boldsymbol{X}^T\boldsymbol{X})^{-1}\boldsymbol{X}^T \cdot \boldsymbol{X}(\boldsymbol{X}^T\boldsymbol{X})^{-1}\right\} = \sigma^2\text{Tr}\left\{(\boldsymbol{X}^T\boldsymbol{X})^{-1}\right\}.$$

Analysis of the testing error

Similarly to the training error, we can analyze the testing error. The testing error is defined as

$$\mathcal{E}_{\text{test}} = \text{MSE}(\widehat{\boldsymbol{y}}, \boldsymbol{y}') \overset{\text{def}}{=} \mathbb{E}_{e,e'}\left[\frac{1}{M}\|\widehat{\boldsymbol{y}} - \boldsymbol{y}'\|^2\right], \tag{7.18}$$

where $\widehat{\boldsymbol{y}} = [\widehat{y}_1, \ldots, \widehat{y}_M]^T$ is a vector of M predicted values and $\boldsymbol{y}' = [y_1', \ldots, y_M']^T$ is a vector of M true values in the testing data.[4]

We would like to derive something concrete. To make our analysis simple, we consider a special case in which the testing set contains $(x_1, y_1'), \ldots, (x_N, y_N')$. That is, the inputs $x_1, \ldots, x_N$ are identical for both training and testing (for example, suppose that you measure the temperature on two different days but at the same time stamps.) In this case, we have $M = N$, and we have $\boldsymbol{X}_{\text{test}} = \boldsymbol{X}_{\text{train}} = \boldsymbol{X}$. However, the noise added to the testing data is still different from the noise added to the training data.

With these simplifications, we can derive the testing error as follows.

Theorem 7.4. *Let $\boldsymbol{\theta}^* \in \mathbb{R}^d$ be the ground truth linear model parameter, and $\boldsymbol{X} \in \mathbb{R}^{N \times d}$ be a matrix such that $N \geq d$ and $\boldsymbol{X}^T\boldsymbol{X}$ is invertible. Assume that the training data follows the linear model $\boldsymbol{y} = \boldsymbol{X}\boldsymbol{\theta}^* + e$, where $e \sim \text{Gaussian}(0, \sigma^2\boldsymbol{I})$. Consider the linear regression problem $\widehat{\boldsymbol{\theta}} = (\boldsymbol{X}^T\boldsymbol{X})^{-1}\boldsymbol{X}^T\boldsymbol{y}$, and let $\widehat{\boldsymbol{y}} = \boldsymbol{X}\widehat{\boldsymbol{\theta}}$. Let $\boldsymbol{X}_{\text{test}} = \boldsymbol{X}$ be the testing input data matrix, and define $\boldsymbol{y}' = \boldsymbol{X}_{\text{test}}\boldsymbol{\theta}^* + e' \in \mathbb{R}^N$, with $e' \sim \text{Gaussian}(0, \sigma^2\boldsymbol{I})$, be the testing output. Then, the mean squared **testing error** of this linear model is*

$$\mathcal{E}_{\text{test}} \overset{\text{def}}{=} \text{MSE}(\widehat{\boldsymbol{y}}, \boldsymbol{y}') = \mathbb{E}_{e,e'}\left[\frac{1}{N}\|\widehat{\boldsymbol{y}} - \boldsymbol{y}'\|^2\right] = \sigma^2\left(1 + \frac{d}{N}\right). \tag{7.19}$$

In this definition, the expectation is taken with respect to a joint distribution of (e, e'). This is because, in testing, the trained model is based on $\boldsymbol{y}$ of which the randomness is e. However, the testing data is based on $\boldsymbol{y}'$, where the randomness comes from e'. We assume that e and e' are independent i.i.d. Gaussian vectors.

---

[4]In practice, the number of testing samples M can be much larger than the number of training samples N. This probably does not agree with your experience, in which the testing dataset is often much smaller than the training dataset. The reason for this paradox is that the practical testing data set is only a finite subset of all the possible testing samples available. So the "testing error" we compute in practice approximates the true testing error. If you want to compute the true testing error, you need a very large testing dataset.

As with the previous proof, we recommend you study this proof later.

Proof. The MSE can be derived from the definition:

$$
\mathrm{MSE}(\widehat{\boldsymbol{y}}, \boldsymbol{y}') = \mathbb{E}_{e,e'}\left[\frac{1}{N}\left\|\widehat{\boldsymbol{y}} - \boldsymbol{y}'\right\|^2\right]
$$

$$
= \frac{1}{N}\mathbb{E}_{e,e'}\left[\left\|\boldsymbol{X}\boldsymbol{\theta}^* + \boldsymbol{H}\boldsymbol{e} - \boldsymbol{X}\boldsymbol{\theta}^* - \boldsymbol{e}'\right\|^2\right]
$$

$$
= \frac{1}{N}\mathbb{E}_{e,e'}\left[\left\|\boldsymbol{H}\boldsymbol{e} - \boldsymbol{e}'\right\|^2\right].
$$

Since each noise term e_n and e'_n is an i.i.d. copy of the same Gaussian random variable, by using the fact that

$$
\mathrm{Tr}(\boldsymbol{H}) = \mathrm{Tr}(\boldsymbol{X}(\boldsymbol{X}^T\boldsymbol{X})^{-1}\boldsymbol{X}^T)
$$

$$
= \mathrm{Tr}((\boldsymbol{X}^T\boldsymbol{X})^{-1}\boldsymbol{X}^T\boldsymbol{X}) = \mathrm{Tr}(\boldsymbol{I}) = d,
$$

we have that

$$
\mathbb{E}_{e,e'}\left[\left\|\boldsymbol{H}\boldsymbol{e} - \boldsymbol{e}'\right\|^2\right] = \mathbb{E}_e\left[\left\|\boldsymbol{H}\boldsymbol{e}\right\|^2\right] - \underbrace{\mathbb{E}_{e,e'}\left[2\boldsymbol{e}^T\boldsymbol{H}^T\boldsymbol{e}'\right]}_{=0} + \mathbb{E}_{e'}\left[\left\|\boldsymbol{e}'\right\|^2\right]
$$

$$
= \mathbb{E}_e\left[\mathrm{Tr}\left\{\boldsymbol{H}\boldsymbol{e}\boldsymbol{e}^T\boldsymbol{H}^T\right\}\right] + \mathbb{E}_{e'}\left[\mathrm{Tr}\left\{\boldsymbol{e}'\boldsymbol{e}'^T\right\}\right]
$$

$$
= \mathrm{Tr}\left\{\boldsymbol{H}\mathbb{E}_e\left[\boldsymbol{e}\boldsymbol{e}^T\right]\boldsymbol{H}^T\right\} + \mathrm{Tr}\{\mathbb{E}_{e'}\left[\boldsymbol{e}'\boldsymbol{e}'^T\right]\}
$$

$$
= \mathrm{Tr}\left\{\boldsymbol{H}\cdot\sigma^2\boldsymbol{I}_{N\times N}\cdot\boldsymbol{H}^T\right\} + \mathrm{Tr}\left\{\sigma^2\boldsymbol{I}_{N\times N}\right\}
$$

$$
= \sigma^2\mathrm{Tr}\left\{\boldsymbol{H}\boldsymbol{H}^T\right\} + \mathrm{Tr}\left\{\sigma^2\boldsymbol{I}_{N\times N}\right\}
$$

$$
= \sigma^2\mathrm{Tr}(\boldsymbol{I}_{d\times d}) + \sigma^2\mathrm{Tr}\left\{\boldsymbol{I}_{N\times N}\right\} = \sigma^2(d+N).
$$

Combining all the terms,

$$
\mathrm{MSE}(\widehat{\boldsymbol{y}}, \boldsymbol{y}') = \mathbb{E}_{e,e'}\left[\frac{1}{N}\left\|\widehat{\boldsymbol{y}} - \boldsymbol{y}'\right\|^2\right] = \sigma^2\left(1 + \frac{d}{N}\right),
$$

which completes the proof.

□

The end of the proof.

7.2.3 Interpreting the linear analysis results

Let us summarize the two main theorems. They state that, for $N \geq d$,

$$
\mathcal{E}_{\mathrm{train}} \overset{\mathrm{def}}{=} \mathrm{MSE}(\widehat{\boldsymbol{y}}, \boldsymbol{y}) = \mathbb{E}_e\left[\frac{1}{N}\left\|\widehat{\boldsymbol{y}} - \boldsymbol{y}\right\|^2\right] = \sigma^2\left(1 - \frac{d}{N}\right), \tag{7.20}
$$

$$
\mathcal{E}_{\mathrm{test}} \overset{\mathrm{def}}{=} \mathrm{MSE}(\widehat{\boldsymbol{y}}, \boldsymbol{y}') = \mathbb{E}_{e,e'}\left[\frac{1}{N}\left\|\widehat{\boldsymbol{y}} - \boldsymbol{y}'\right\|^2\right] = \sigma^2\left(1 + \frac{d}{N}\right). \tag{7.21}
$$

This pair of equations tells us **everything** about the overfitting issue.

> **How do $\mathcal{E}_{\text{train}}$ and $\mathcal{E}_{\text{test}}$ change w.r.t. σ^2?**
> - $\mathcal{E}_{\text{train}} \uparrow$ as $\sigma^2 \uparrow$. Thus noisier data are harder to fit.
> - $\mathcal{E}_{\text{test}} \uparrow$ as $\sigma^2 \uparrow$. Thus a noiser model is more difficult to generalize.

The reasons for these results should be clear from the following equations:

$$\mathcal{E}_{\text{train}} = \sigma^2 \left(1 - \frac{d}{N} \right),$$

$$\mathcal{E}_{\text{test}} = \sigma^2 \left(1 + \frac{d}{N} \right).$$

As σ^2 increases, the training error $\mathcal{E}_{\text{train}}$ grows linearly w.r.t. σ^2. Since the training error measures how good your model is compared with the training data, a larger $\mathcal{E}_{\text{train}}$ means it is more difficult to fit. For the testing case, $\mathcal{E}_{\text{test}}$ also grows linearly w.r.t. σ^2. This implies that the model would be more difficult to generalize if the model were trained using noisier data.

> **How do $\mathcal{E}_{\text{train}}$ and $\mathcal{E}_{\text{test}}$ change w.r.t. N?**
> - $\mathcal{E}_{\text{train}} \uparrow$ as $N \uparrow$. Thus more training samples make fitting harder.
> - $\mathcal{E}_{\text{test}} \downarrow$ as $N \uparrow$. Thus more training samples improve generalization.

The reason for this should also be clear from the following equations:

$$\mathcal{E}_{\text{train}} = \sigma^2 \left(1 - \frac{d}{N} \right),$$

$$\mathcal{E}_{\text{test}} = \sigma^2 \left(1 + \frac{d}{N} \right).$$

As N increases, the model sees more training samples. The goal of the model is to minimize the error with all the training samples. Thus the more training samples we have, the harder it will be to make everyone happy, so the training error grows as N grows. For testing, if the model is trained with more samples it is more resilient to noise. Hence the generalization improves.

> **How do $\mathcal{E}_{\text{train}}$ and $\mathcal{E}_{\text{test}}$ change w.r.t. d?**
> - $\mathcal{E}_{\text{train}} \downarrow$ as $d \uparrow$. Thus a more complex model makes fitting easier.
> - $\mathcal{E}_{\text{test}} \uparrow$ as $d \uparrow$. Thus a more complex model makes generalization harder.

These results are perhaps less obvious than the others. The following equations tell us that

$$\mathcal{E}_{\text{train}} = \sigma^2 \left(1 - \frac{d}{N} \right),$$

$$\mathcal{E}_{\text{test}} = \sigma^2 \left(1 + \frac{d}{N} \right). \tag{7.22}$$

For this linear regression model to work, d has to be less than N; otherwise, the matrix inversion $(\boldsymbol{X}^T\boldsymbol{X})^{-1}$ is invalid. However, as d grows while N remains fixed, we ask the linear regression to fit a larger and larger model while not providing any additional training samples. Equation (7.22) says that $\mathcal{E}_{\text{train}}$ will drop as d increases but $\mathcal{E}_{\text{test}}$ will increase as d increases. Therefore, a larger model will not generalize as well if N is fixed.

If $d > N$, then the optimization

$$\widehat{\boldsymbol{\theta}} = \operatorname*{argmin}_{\boldsymbol{\theta}\in\mathbb{R}^d} \ \|\boldsymbol{X}\boldsymbol{\theta} - \boldsymbol{y}\|^2$$

will have many global minimizers (see **Figure 7.10**), implying that the training error can go to zero. Our analysis of $\mathcal{E}_{\text{train}}$ and $\mathcal{E}_{\text{test}}$ does not cover this case because our proofs require $(\boldsymbol{X}^T\boldsymbol{X})^{-1}$ to exist. However, we can still extrapolate what will happen. When the training error is zero, it only means that we fit perfectly into the training data. Since the testing error grows as d grows (though not in the particular form shown in Equation (7.22)), we should expect the testing error to become worse.

Learning curve

The results we derived above can be summarized in the **learning curve** shown in **Figure 7.14**. In this figure we consider a simple problem where

$$y_n = \theta_0 + \theta_1 x_n + e_n,$$

for $e_n \sim \text{Gaussian}(0,1)$. Therefore, according to our theoretical derivations, we have $\sigma = 1$ and $d = 2$. For every N, we compute the average training error $\mathcal{E}_{\text{train}}$ and the average testing error $\mathcal{E}_{\text{test}}$, and then mark them on the figure. These are our empirical training and testing errors. On the same figure, we calculate the theoretical training and testing error according to Equation (7.22).

The MATLAB and Python codes used to generate this learning curve are shown below.

```
Nset = round(logspace(1,3,20));
E_train = zeros(1,length(Nset));
E_test  = zeros(1,length(Nset));
a = [1.3, 2.5];
for j = 1:length(Nset)
    N = Nset(j);
    x = linspace(-1,1,N)';
    E_train_temp = zeros(1,1000);
    E_test_temp  = zeros(1,1000);
    X = [ones(N,1), x(:)];
    for i = 1:1000
        y  = a(1) + a(2)*x + randn(size(x));
        y1 = a(1) + a(2)*x + randn(size(x));
        theta = X\y(:);
        yhat = theta(1) + theta(2)*x;
        E_train_temp(i) = mean((yhat(:)-y(:)).^2);
        E_test_temp(i)  = mean((yhat(:)-y1(:)).^2);
    end
    E_train(j) = mean(E_train_temp);
```

```
      E_test(j)  = mean(E_test_temp);
end
semilogx(Nset, E_train, 'kx', 'LineWidth', 2, 'MarkerSize', 16); hold on;
semilogx(Nset, E_test, 'ro', 'LineWidth', 2, 'MarkerSize', 8);
semilogx(Nset, 1-2./Nset, 'k', 'LineWidth', 4);
semilogx(Nset, 1+2./Nset, 'r', 'LineWidth', 4);
```

```
import numpy as np
import matplotlib.pyplot as plt

Nset = np.logspace(1,3,20)
Nset = Nset.astype(int)
E_train = np.zeros(len(Nset))
E_test  = np.zeros(len(Nset))
for j in range(len(Nset)):
  N = Nset[j]
  x = np.linspace(-1,1,N)
  a = np.array([1, 2])
  E_train_tmp = np.zeros(1000)
  E_test_tmp  = np.zeros(1000)
  for i in range(1000):
    y              = a[0] + a[1]*x + np.random.randn(N)
    X              = np.column_stack((np.ones(N), x))
    theta          = np.linalg.lstsq(X, y, rcond=None)[0]
    yhat           = theta[0] + theta[1]*x
    E_train_tmp[i] = np.mean((yhat-y)**2)
    y1             = a[0] + a[1]*x + np.random.randn(N)
    E_test_tmp[i]  = np.mean((yhat-y1)**2)
  E_train[j] = np.mean(E_train_tmp)
  E_test[j]  = np.mean(E_test_tmp)
plt.semilogx(Nset, E_train, 'kx')
plt.semilogx(Nset, E_test, 'ro')
plt.semilogx(Nset, (1-2/Nset), linewidth=4, c='k')
plt.semilogx(Nset, (1+2/Nset), linewidth=4, c='r')
```

The training error curve and the testing error curve behave in opposite ways as N increases. The training error $\mathcal{E}_{\text{train}}$ increases as N increases, because when we have more training samples it becomes harder for the model to fit all the data. By contrast, the testing error $\mathcal{E}_{\text{test}}$ decreases as N increases, because when we have more training samples the model becomes more robust to noise and unseen data. Therefore, the testing error improves.

As N goes to infinity, both the training error and the testing error converge. This is due to the law of large numbers, which says that the empirical training and testing errors should converge to their respective expected values. If the training error and the testing error converge to the same value, the training can generalize to testing. If they do not converge to the same value, there is a mismatch between the training samples and the testing samples.

It is important to pay attention to the gap between the converged values. We often assume that the training samples and the testing samples are drawn from the same distribution, and therefore the training samples are good representatives of the testing samples.

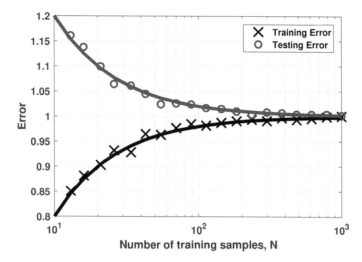

Figure 7.14: The learning curve is a pair of functions representing the training error and the testing error. As N increases we expect the training error to increase and the testing error to decrease. The two functions will converge to the same value as N goes to infinity. If they do not converge to the same value, there is an intrinsic mismatch between the training samples and the testing samples, e.g., the training samples are not representative enough for the dataset.

If the assumption is not true, there will be a gap between the converged training error and the testing error. Thus, what you claim in training cannot be transferred to the testing. Consequently, the learning curve provides you with a useful debugging tool to check how well your training compares with your testing.

Closing remark. In this section we have studied a very important concept in regression, overfitting. We emphasize that overfitting is not only caused by the complexity of the model but a combination of the three factors σ^2, N, and d. We close this section by summarizing the causes of overfitting:

What is the source of overfitting?

- Overfitting occurs because you have an imbalance between σ^2, N and d.
- Selecting the correct complexity for your model is the key to avoid overfitting.

7.3 Bias and Variance Trade-Off

Our linear analysis has provided you with a rough understanding of what we experience in overfitting. However, for general regression problems where the models are not necessarily linear, we need to go deeper. The goal of this section is to explain the trade-off between bias and variance. This analysis requires some patience as it involves many equations. We recommend skipping this section on a first reading and then returning to it later.

> If it is your first time reading it, we recommend you go through it slowly.

7.3.1 Decomposing the testing error

Notations

As we did at the beginning of Section 7.2, we consider a **ground truth model** that relates an input $\boldsymbol{x}$ and an output y:

$$y = f(\boldsymbol{x}) + e,$$

where $e \sim \text{Gaussian}(0, \sigma^2)$ is the noise. For example, if we use a linear model, then f could be $f(\boldsymbol{x}) = \boldsymbol{\theta}^T \boldsymbol{x}$, for some regression coefficients $\boldsymbol{\theta}$.

During **training**, we pick a prediction model $g_{\boldsymbol{\theta}}(\cdot)$ and try to predict the output when given a training sample $\boldsymbol{x}$:

$$\widehat{y} = g_{\boldsymbol{\theta}}(\boldsymbol{x}).$$

For example, we may choose $g_{\boldsymbol{\theta}}(\boldsymbol{x}) = \boldsymbol{\theta}^T \boldsymbol{x}$, which is also a linear model. We may also choose a linear model in another basis, e.g., $g_{\boldsymbol{\theta}}(\boldsymbol{x}) = \boldsymbol{\theta}^T \phi(\boldsymbol{x})$ for some transformations $\phi(\cdot)$. In any case, the goal of training is to minimize the training error:

$$\widehat{\boldsymbol{\theta}} = \underset{\boldsymbol{\theta}}{\arg\min} \ \frac{1}{N} \sum_{n=1}^{N} (g_{\boldsymbol{\theta}}(\boldsymbol{x}_n) - y_n)^2,$$

where the sum is taken over the training samples $\mathcal{D}_{\text{train}} = \{(\boldsymbol{x}_1, y_1), \ldots, (\boldsymbol{x}_N, y_N)\}$. Because the model parameter $\widehat{\boldsymbol{\theta}}$ is learned from the training dataset $\mathcal{D}_{\text{train}}$, the prediction model depends on $\mathcal{D}_{\text{train}}$. To emphasize this dependency, we write

$$g^{(\mathcal{D}_{\text{train}})} = \text{the model trained from } \left\{ (\boldsymbol{x}_1, y_1), \ldots, (\boldsymbol{x}_N, y_N) \right\}.$$

During **testing**, we consider a testing dataset $\mathcal{D}_{\text{test}} = \{(\boldsymbol{x}'_1, y'_1), \ldots, (\boldsymbol{x}'_M, y'_M)\}$. We put these testing samples into the trained model to predict an output:

$$\widehat{y}'_m = g^{(\mathcal{D}_{\text{train}})}(\boldsymbol{x}'_m), \qquad m = 1, \ldots, M. \qquad \text{(predicted value)}$$

Since the goal of regression is to make $g^{(\mathcal{D}_{\text{train}})}$ as close to f as possible, it is natural to expect $\widehat{y}'_m$ to be close to y'_m.

Testing error decomposition (noise-free)

So we can now compute the testing error — the error that we ultimately care about. In the noise-free condition, i.e., $e = 0$, the testing error is defined as

$$\mathcal{E}_{\text{test}}^{(\mathcal{D}_{\text{train}})} = \mathbb{E}_{\boldsymbol{x}'} \left[\left(g^{(\mathcal{D}_{\text{train}})}(\boldsymbol{x}') - f(\boldsymbol{x}') \right)^2 \right] \tag{7.23}$$

$$\approx \frac{1}{M} \sum_{m=1}^{M} \left(g^{(\mathcal{D}_{\text{train}})}(\boldsymbol{x}'_m) - f(\boldsymbol{x}'_m) \right)^2.$$

There are several components in this equation. First, $\boldsymbol{x}'$ is a testing sample drawn from a certain distribution. You can think of $\mathcal{D}_{\text{test}}$ as a finite subset drawn from this distribution.

Second, the error $\left(g^{(\mathcal{D}_{\text{train}})}(\boldsymbol{x}') - f(\boldsymbol{x}')\right)^2$ measures the deviation between our predicted value and the true value. Note that this error term is specific to one testing sample $\boldsymbol{x}'$. Therefore, we take expectation $\mathbb{E}_{\boldsymbol{x}'}$ to find the average of the error for the distribution of $\boldsymbol{x}'$.

The testing error $\mathcal{E}_{\text{test}}^{(\mathcal{D}_{\text{train}})}$ is a function that is dependent on the training set $\mathcal{D}_{\text{train}}$, because the model $g^{(\mathcal{D}_{\text{train}})}$ is trained from $\mathcal{D}_{\text{train}}$. Therefore, as we change the training set, we will have a different model g and hence a different testing error. To eliminate the randomness of the training set, we define the overall testing error as

$$\mathcal{E}_{\text{test}} = \mathbb{E}_{\mathcal{D}_{\text{train}}}\left[\mathcal{E}_{\text{test}}^{(\mathcal{D}_{\text{train}})}\right]$$

$$= \mathbb{E}_{\mathcal{D}_{\text{train}}}\left[\mathbb{E}_{\boldsymbol{x}'}\left[\left(g^{(\mathcal{D}_{\text{train}})}(\boldsymbol{x}') - f(\boldsymbol{x}')\right)^2\right]\right]. \tag{7.24}$$

Note that this definition of the testing error is consistent with the special case in Equation (7.18), in which the testing error involves a joint expectation over e and e'. The expectation over e accounts for the training samples, and the expectation over e' accounts for the testing samples.

Let us try to extract some meaning from the testing error. Our method will be to **decompose** the testing error into **bias** and **variance**.

Theorem 7.5. *Assume a noise-free condition. The testing error of a regression problem is given by*

$$\mathcal{E}_{test} = \mathbb{E}_{\boldsymbol{x}'}\Big[\underbrace{(\overline{g}(\boldsymbol{x}') - f(\boldsymbol{x}'))^2}_{=bias(\boldsymbol{x}')} + \underbrace{\mathbb{E}_{\mathcal{D}_{train}}[(g^{(\mathcal{D}_{train})}(\boldsymbol{x}') - \overline{g}(\boldsymbol{x}'))^2]}_{=var(\boldsymbol{x}')}\Big], \tag{7.25}$$

where $\overline{g}(\boldsymbol{x}') \overset{\text{def}}{=} \mathbb{E}_{\mathcal{D}_{train}}[g^{(\mathcal{D}_{train})}(\boldsymbol{x}')]$.

Proof. To simplify our notation, we will drop the subscript "train" in $\mathcal{D}_{\text{train}}$ when the context is clear. We have that

$$\mathcal{E}_{\text{test}} = \mathbb{E}_{\mathcal{D}}\left[\mathbb{E}_{\boldsymbol{x}'}\left[(g^{(\mathcal{D})}(\boldsymbol{x}') - f(\boldsymbol{x}'))^2\right]\right]$$

$$= \mathbb{E}_{\boldsymbol{x}'}\left[\mathbb{E}_{\mathcal{D}}\left[(g^{(\mathcal{D})}(\boldsymbol{x}') - f(\boldsymbol{x}'))^2\right]\right].$$

Continuing the calculation,

$$\mathcal{E}_{\text{test}} = \mathbb{E}_{\boldsymbol{x}'}\left[\mathbb{E}_{\mathcal{D}}\left[(g^{(\mathcal{D})}(\boldsymbol{x}') - \overline{g}(\boldsymbol{x}') + \overline{g}(\boldsymbol{x}') - f(\boldsymbol{x}'))^2\right]\right]$$

$$= \mathbb{E}_{\boldsymbol{x}'}\left[\mathbb{E}_{\mathcal{D}}\left[(g^{(\mathcal{D})}(\boldsymbol{x}') - \overline{g}(\boldsymbol{x}'))^2\right] + 2\mathbb{E}_{\mathcal{D}}\left[(g^{(\mathcal{D})}(\boldsymbol{x}') - \overline{g}(\boldsymbol{x}'))(\overline{g}(\boldsymbol{x}') - f(\boldsymbol{x}'))\right]\right.$$

$$\left. + \mathbb{E}_{\mathcal{D}}\left[(\overline{g}(\boldsymbol{x}') - f(\boldsymbol{x}'))^2\right]\right].$$

Since $\overline{g}(\boldsymbol{x}') \overset{\text{def}}{=} \mathbb{E}_{\mathcal{D}}[g^{(\mathcal{D})}(\boldsymbol{x}')]$, it follows that

$$2\mathbb{E}_{\mathcal{D}}\left[(g^{(\mathcal{D})}(\boldsymbol{x}') - \overline{g}(\boldsymbol{x}'))(\overline{g}(\boldsymbol{x}') - f(\boldsymbol{x}'))\right] = 0$$

because $\bar{g}(\boldsymbol{x}') - f(\boldsymbol{x}')$ is independent of $\mathcal{D}$, and

$$\mathbb{E}_{\mathcal{D}}\left[(\bar{g}(\boldsymbol{x}') - f(\boldsymbol{x}'))^2\right] = (\bar{g}(\boldsymbol{x}') - f(\boldsymbol{x}'))^2.$$

Therefore,

$$\mathcal{E}_{\text{test}} = \mathbb{E}_{\boldsymbol{x}'}\left[\mathbb{E}_{\mathcal{D}}\left[(g^{(\mathcal{D})}(\boldsymbol{x}') - \bar{g}(\boldsymbol{x}'))^2\right] + \left[(\bar{g}(\boldsymbol{x}') - f(\boldsymbol{x}'))^2\right]\right].$$

Thus, by defining two following terms we have proved the theorem.

$$\text{bias}(\boldsymbol{x}') \stackrel{\text{def}}{=} (\bar{g}(\boldsymbol{x}') - f(\boldsymbol{x}'))^2,$$
$$\text{var}(\boldsymbol{x}') \stackrel{\text{def}}{=} \mathbb{E}_{\mathcal{D}}[(g^{(\mathcal{D})}(\boldsymbol{x}') - \bar{g}(\boldsymbol{x}'))^2].$$

$\square$

Let's consider what this theorem implies. This result is a decomposition of the testing error into **bias** and **variance**. It is a universal result that applies to **all** regression models, not only linear cases. To summarize the meanings of bias and variance:

What are bias and variance?

- Bias = how far average predicted value is from the truth.
- Variance = how much fluctuation you have around the average.

Figure 7.15 gives a pictorial representation of bias and variance. In this figure, we construct four scenarios of bias and variance. Each cross represents the predictor $g^{(\mathcal{D}_{\text{train}})}$, with the true predictor f at the origin. **Figure 7.15**(a) shows the case with a low bias and a low variance. All these predictors $g^{(\mathcal{D}_{\text{train}})}$ are very close to the ground truth, and they have small fluctuations around their average. **Figure 7.15**(b) shows the case of a high bias and a low variance. It has a high bias because the entire group of $g^{(\mathcal{D}_{\text{train}})}$ is shifted to the corner. The bias, which is the distance from the truth to the average, is therefore large. The variance remains small because the fluctuation around the average is small. **Figure 7.15**(c) shows the case of a low bias but high variance. In this case, the fluctuation around the average is large. **Figure 7.15** shows the case of high bias and high variance. We want to avoid this case.

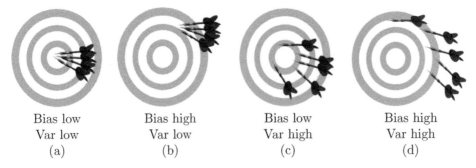

Bias low	Bias high	Bias low	Bias high
Var low	Var low	Var high	Var high
(a)	(b)	(c)	(d)

Figure 7.15: Imagine that you are throwing a dart with a target at the center. The four subfigures show the levels of bias and variance.

Testing error decomposition (noisy case)

Let us consider a situation when there is noise. In the presence of noise, the training and testing samples will follow the relationship

$$y = f(\boldsymbol{x}) + e,$$

where $e \sim \text{Gaussian}(0, \sigma^2)$. We assume that the noise is Gaussian to make the proof easier. We can consider other types of noise in theory, but the theoretical results will need to be modified.

In the presence of noise, the testing error is

$$\mathcal{E}_{\text{test}}(\boldsymbol{x}') \overset{\text{def}}{=} \mathbb{E}_{\mathcal{D}_{\text{train}},e} \left[\left(g^{(\mathcal{D}_{\text{train}})}(\boldsymbol{x}') - f(\boldsymbol{x}') + e \right)^2 \right]$$

$$= \mathbb{E}_{\mathcal{D}_{\text{train}},e} \left[\left(g^{(\mathcal{D}_{\text{train}})}(\boldsymbol{x}') - \overline{g}(\boldsymbol{x}') + \overline{g}(\boldsymbol{x}') - f(\boldsymbol{x}') + e \right)^2 \right],$$

where we take the joint expectation over the training dataset $\mathcal{D}_{\text{train}}$ and the error e. Continuing the calculation, and using the fact that $\mathcal{D}_{\text{train}}$ and e are independent (and $\mathbb{E}[e] = 0$), it follows that

$$\mathcal{E}_{\text{test}}(\boldsymbol{x}') = \mathbb{E}_{\mathcal{D}_{\text{train}},e} \left[\left(g^{(\mathcal{D}_{\text{train}})}(\boldsymbol{x}') - \overline{g}(\boldsymbol{x}') + \overline{g}(\boldsymbol{x}') - f(\boldsymbol{x}') + e \right)^2 \right]$$

$$= \mathbb{E}_{\mathcal{D}_{\text{train}},e} \left[\left(g^{(\mathcal{D})}(\boldsymbol{x}') - \overline{g}(\boldsymbol{x}') \right)^2 + \left(\overline{g}(\boldsymbol{x}') - f(\boldsymbol{x}') \right)^2 + e^2 \right]$$

$$= \underbrace{\mathbb{E}_{\mathcal{D}_{\text{train}}} \left[\left(g^{(\mathcal{D}_{\text{train}})}(\boldsymbol{x}') - \overline{g}(\boldsymbol{x}') \right)^2 \right]}_{=\text{var}(\boldsymbol{x}')} + \underbrace{\left(\overline{g}(\boldsymbol{x}') - f(\boldsymbol{x}') \right)^2}_{=\text{bias}(\boldsymbol{x}')} + \underbrace{\mathbb{E}_e \left[e^2 \right]}_{=\text{noise}}.$$

Taking the expectation of $\boldsymbol{x}'$ over the entire testing distribution gives us

$$\mathcal{E}_{\text{test}} = \mathbb{E}_{\boldsymbol{x}'} [\mathcal{E}_{\text{test}}(\boldsymbol{x}')] = \underbrace{\mathbb{E}_{\boldsymbol{x}'} [\text{var}(\boldsymbol{x}')]}_{\text{var}} + \underbrace{\mathbb{E}_{\boldsymbol{x}'} [\text{bias}(\boldsymbol{x}')]}_{\text{bias}} + \sigma^2.$$

The theorem below summarizes the results:

Theorem 7.6. *Assume a noisy condition where* $y = f(\boldsymbol{x}) + e$ *for some i.i.d. Gaussian noise* $e \sim \text{Gaussian}(0, \sigma^2)$. *The testing error of a regression problem is given by*

$$\mathcal{E}_{test} = \mathbb{E}_{\boldsymbol{x}'} \left[\underbrace{(\overline{g}(\boldsymbol{x}') - f(\boldsymbol{x}'))^2}_{=bias(\boldsymbol{x}')} \right] + \mathbb{E}_{\boldsymbol{x}'} \left[\underbrace{\mathbb{E}_{\mathcal{D}_{train}} [(g^{(\mathcal{D}_{train})}(\boldsymbol{x}') - \overline{g}(\boldsymbol{x}'))^2]}_{=var(\boldsymbol{x}')} \right] + \sigma^2, \quad (7.26)$$

where $\overline{g}(\boldsymbol{x}') \overset{\text{def}}{=} \mathbb{E}_{\mathcal{D}_{train}} [g^{(\mathcal{D}_{train})}(\boldsymbol{x}')]$.

7.3.2 Analysis of the bias

Let us examine the bias and variance in more detail. To discuss bias we must first understand the quantity

$$\overline{g}(\boldsymbol{x}') \overset{\text{def}}{=} \mathbb{E}_{\mathcal{D}_{\text{train}}} [g^{(\mathcal{D}_{\text{train}})}(\boldsymbol{x}')], \qquad (7.27)$$

which is known as the **average predictor**. The average predictor, as the equation suggests, is the expectation of the predictor $g^{(\mathcal{D}_{\text{train}})}$. Remember that $g^{(\mathcal{D}_{\text{train}})}$ is a predictor constructed from a specific training set $\mathcal{D}_{\text{train}}$. If tomorrow our training set $\mathcal{D}_{\text{train}}$ contains other data (that come from the same underlying distribution), $g^{(\mathcal{D}_{\text{train}})}$ will be different. The average predictor $\bar{g}$ is the average across these random fluctuations of the dataset $\mathcal{D}_{\text{train}}$. Here is an example:

Suppose we use a linear model with the ordinary polynomials as the bases. The data points are generated according to

$$y_n = \underbrace{\sum_{p=0}^{d-1} \theta_p x_n^p}_{\stackrel{\text{def}}{=} f(x_n) = \boldsymbol{\theta}^T \boldsymbol{x}_n} + e_n. \tag{7.28}$$

If we use a particular training set $\mathcal{D}_{\text{train}}$ and run the regression, we will be able to obtain one of the regression lines, as shown in **Figure 7.16**. Let us call this line $g^{(1)}$. We repeat the experiment by drawing another dataset, and call it $g^{(2)}$. We continue and eventually we will find a set of regression lines $g^{(1)}, g^{(2)}, \ldots, g^{(K)}$, where K denotes the number of training sets you are using to generate all the gray curves. The average predictor $\bar{g}$ is defined as

$$\bar{g}(\boldsymbol{x}') = \mathbb{E}_{\mathcal{D}_{\text{train}}}[g^{(\mathcal{D}_{\text{train}})}] \approx \frac{1}{K} \sum_{k=1}^{K} g^{(k)}(\boldsymbol{x}').$$

Thus if we take the average of all these gray curves we will obtain the average predictor, which is the red curve shown in **Figure 7.16**.

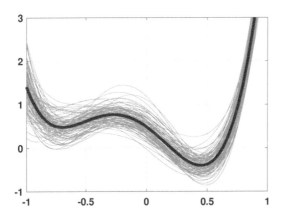

Figure 7.16: We run linear regression many times for different training datasets. Each one consists of different random realizations of noise. The gray curves are the regression lines returned by each of the training datasets. We then take the average of these gray curves to obtain the red curve, which is the average predictor.

If you are curious about how this plot was generated, the MATLAB and Python codes are given below.

```
% MATLAB code to visualize the average predictor
N = 20;
```

```
a = [5.7, 3.7, -3.6, -2.3, 0.05];
x = linspace(-1,1,N);
yhat = zeros(100,50);
for i=1:100
    X     = [x(:).^0, x(:).^1, x(:).^2, x(:).^3, x(:).^4];
    y     = X*a(:) + 0.5*randn(N,1);
    theta = X\y(:);
    t     = linspace(-1, 1, 50);
    yhat(i,:) = theta(1) + theta(2)*t(:)   + theta(3)*t(:).^2 ...
                         + theta(4)*t(:)^3 + theta(5)*t(:).^4;
end
figure;
plot(t, yhat, 'color', [0.6 0.6 0.6]); hold on;
plot(t, mean(yhat), 'LineWidth', 4, 'color', [0.8 0 0]);
axis([-1 1 -2 2]);
```

```
import numpy as np
import matplotlib.pyplot as plt
from scipy.special import eval_legendre
np.set_printoptions(precision=2, suppress=True)

N = 20
x = np.linspace(-1,1,N)
a = np.array([0.5, -2, -3, 4, 6])
yhat = np.zeros((50,100))
for i in range(100):
  y = a[0] + a[1]*x    + a[2]*x**2 + \
          a[3]*x**3 + a[4]*x**4 + 0.5*np.random.randn(N)
  X = np.column_stack((np.ones(N), x, x**2, x**3, x**4))

  theta = np.linalg.lstsq(X, y, rcond=None)[0]
  t = np.linspace(-1,1,50)
  Xhat = np.column_stack((np.ones(50), t, t**2, t**3, t**4))
  yhat[:,i] = np.dot(Xhat, theta)
  plt.plot(t, yhat[:,i], c='gray')
plt.plot(t, np.mean(yhat, axis=1), c='r', linewidth=4)
```

We now show an analytic calculation to verify **Figure 7.16**.

Example 7.4. Consider a linear model such that

$$y = x^T\theta + e. \tag{7.29}$$

What is the predictor $g^{(\mathcal{D}_{\text{train}})}(x')$? What is the average predictor $\bar{g}(x')$?

Solution. First, consider a training dataset $\mathcal{D}_{\text{train}} = \{(x_1,y_1),\ldots,(x_N,y_N)\}$. We assume that the x_n's are deterministic and fixed. Therefore, the source of randomness in the training set is caused by the noise $e \sim \text{Gaussian}(0,\sigma^2)$ and hence by the noisy

435

observation y.

The training set gives us the equation $\boldsymbol{y} = \boldsymbol{X}\boldsymbol{\theta} + \boldsymbol{e}$, where $\boldsymbol{X}$ is the matrix constructed from $\boldsymbol{x}_n$'s. The regression solution to this dataset is

$$\widehat{\boldsymbol{\theta}} = (\boldsymbol{X}^T\boldsymbol{X})^{-1}\boldsymbol{X}^T\boldsymbol{y},$$

which should actually be $\widehat{\boldsymbol{\theta}}^{(\mathcal{D}_{\text{train}})}$ because $\boldsymbol{y}$ is a dataset-dependent vector.

Consequently,

$$\begin{aligned}
g^{(\mathcal{D}_{\text{train}})}(\boldsymbol{x}') = \widehat{\boldsymbol{\theta}}^T\boldsymbol{x}' &= (\boldsymbol{x}')^T(\boldsymbol{X}^T\boldsymbol{X})^{-1}\boldsymbol{X}^T\boldsymbol{y} \\
&= (\boldsymbol{x}')^T(\boldsymbol{X}^T\boldsymbol{X})^{-1}\boldsymbol{X}^T(\boldsymbol{X}\boldsymbol{\theta} + \boldsymbol{e}) \\
&= (\boldsymbol{x}')^T\boldsymbol{\theta} + (\boldsymbol{x}')^T(\boldsymbol{X}^T\boldsymbol{X})^{-1}\boldsymbol{X}^T\boldsymbol{e}.
\end{aligned}$$

Since the randomness of $\mathcal{D}_{\text{train}}$ is caused by the noise, it follows that

$$\begin{aligned}
\overline{g}(\boldsymbol{x}') = \mathbb{E}_{\mathcal{D}_{\text{train}}}[g^{(\mathcal{D}_{\text{train}})}(\boldsymbol{x}')] &= \mathbb{E}_e[(\boldsymbol{x}')^T\boldsymbol{\theta} + (\boldsymbol{x}')^T(\boldsymbol{X}^T\boldsymbol{X})^{-1}\boldsymbol{X}^T\boldsymbol{e}] \\
&= (\boldsymbol{x}')^T\boldsymbol{\theta} + (\boldsymbol{x}')^T(\boldsymbol{X}^T\boldsymbol{X})^{-1}\boldsymbol{X}^T\mathbb{E}_e[\boldsymbol{e}] \\
&= (\boldsymbol{x}')^T\boldsymbol{\theta} + 0 = f(\boldsymbol{x}').
\end{aligned}$$

So the average predictor will return the ground truth. However, note that not all predictors will return the ground truth.

In the above example, we obtained an interesting result, namely that $\overline{g}(\boldsymbol{x}') = f(\boldsymbol{x}')$. That is, the average predictor equals the true predictor. However, in general, $\overline{g}(\boldsymbol{x}')$ does not necessarily equal $f(\boldsymbol{x}')$. If this occurs, we have a deviation $(\overline{g}(\boldsymbol{x}') - f(\boldsymbol{x}'))^2 > 0$. This deviation is called the **bias**. Bias is independent of the number of training samples because we have taken the **average** of the predictors. Therefore, bias is more of an intrinsic (or systematic) error due to the choice of the model.

What is bias?

- Bias is defined as $\text{bias} = \mathbb{E}_{\boldsymbol{x}'}[(\overline{g}(\boldsymbol{x}') - f(\boldsymbol{x}'))^2]$, where $\boldsymbol{x}'$ is a testing sample.
- It is the deviation from the average predictor to the true predictor.
- Bias is not necessarily a bad thing. A good predictor can have some bias as long as it helps to reduce the variance.

7.3.3 Variance

The other quantity in the game is the **variance**. Variance at a testing sample $\boldsymbol{x}'$ is defined as

$$\text{var}(\boldsymbol{x}') \overset{\text{def}}{=} \mathbb{E}_{\mathcal{D}_{\text{train}}}[(g^{(\mathcal{D}_{\text{train}})}(\boldsymbol{x}') - \overline{g}(\boldsymbol{x}'))^2]. \tag{7.30}$$

As the equation suggests, the variance measures the fluctuation between the predictor $g^{(\mathcal{D}_{\text{train}})}$ and the average predictor $\overline{g}$. **Figure 7.17** illustrates the polynomial-fitting problem we discussed above. In this figure we consider two levels of variance by varying the noise strength of e_n. The figure shows that as the observation becomes noisier, the predictor $g^{(\mathcal{D}_{\text{train}})}$ will have a larger fluctuation for the average predictor.

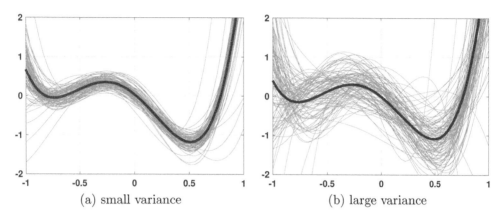

(a) small variance   (b) large variance

Figure 7.17: Variance measures the magnitude of fluctuation between the particular predictor $g^{(\mathcal{D}_{\text{train}})}$ and the average predictor $\overline{g}$.

Example 7.5. Continuing with Example 7.4, we ask: What is the variance?

Solution. We first determine the predictor and its average:

$$g^{(\mathcal{D}_{\text{train}})} = (\boldsymbol{X}^T\boldsymbol{X})^{-1}\boldsymbol{X}^T\boldsymbol{y} = \boldsymbol{\theta} + (\boldsymbol{X}^T\boldsymbol{X})^{-1}\boldsymbol{X}^T\boldsymbol{e}$$
$$\overline{g} = \mathbb{E}[g^{(\mathcal{D}_{\text{train}})}] = \mathbb{E}_e[\boldsymbol{\theta} + (\boldsymbol{X}^T\boldsymbol{X})^{-1}\boldsymbol{X}^T\boldsymbol{e}] = \boldsymbol{\theta},$$

so the prediction at a testing sample $\boldsymbol{x}'$ is

$$g^{(\mathcal{D}_{\text{train}})}(\boldsymbol{x}') = (\boldsymbol{x}')^T\boldsymbol{\theta} + (\boldsymbol{x}')^T(\boldsymbol{X}^T\boldsymbol{X})^{-1}\boldsymbol{X}^T\boldsymbol{e}$$
$$\overline{g}(\boldsymbol{x}') = (\boldsymbol{x}')^T\boldsymbol{\theta},$$

Consequently, the variance is

$$\mathbb{E}_{\mathcal{D}_{\text{train}}}\left[\left(g^{(\mathcal{D}_{\text{train}})}(\boldsymbol{x}') - \overline{g}(\boldsymbol{x}')\right)^2\right] = \mathbb{E}_e\left[\left((\boldsymbol{x}')^T\boldsymbol{\theta} + (\boldsymbol{x}')^T(\boldsymbol{X}^T\boldsymbol{X})^{-1}\boldsymbol{X}^T\boldsymbol{e} - (\boldsymbol{x}')^T\boldsymbol{\theta}\right)^2\right]$$

$$= \mathbb{E}_e\left[\left((\boldsymbol{x}')^T(\boldsymbol{X}^T\boldsymbol{X})^{-1}\boldsymbol{X}^T\boldsymbol{e}\right)^2\right].$$

Continuing the calculation,

$$\mathbb{E}_{\mathcal{D}_{\text{train}}}\left[\left(g^{(\mathcal{D}_{\text{train}})}(\boldsymbol{x}') - \overline{g}(\boldsymbol{x}')\right)^2\right] = (\boldsymbol{x}')^T(\boldsymbol{X}^T\boldsymbol{X})^{-1}\boldsymbol{X}^T\mathbb{E}_e[\boldsymbol{e}\boldsymbol{e}^T]\boldsymbol{X}(\boldsymbol{X}^T\boldsymbol{X})^{-1}\boldsymbol{x}'$$

$$= (\boldsymbol{x}')^T(\boldsymbol{X}^T\boldsymbol{X})^{-1}\boldsymbol{X}^T\sigma^2\boldsymbol{I}\boldsymbol{X}(\boldsymbol{X}^T\boldsymbol{X})^{-1}\boldsymbol{x}'$$

$$= \sigma^2(\boldsymbol{x}')^T(\boldsymbol{X}^T\boldsymbol{X})^{-1}\boldsymbol{x}'$$

$$= \sigma^2\text{Tr}\left\{(\boldsymbol{X}^T\boldsymbol{X})^{-1}(\boldsymbol{x}')(\boldsymbol{x}')^T\right\}.$$

What will happen if we use more samples so that N grows? As N grows, the matrix $\boldsymbol{X}$ will have more rows. Assuming that the magnitude of the entries remains unchanged, more rows in $\boldsymbol{X}$ will increase the magnitude of $\boldsymbol{X}^T\boldsymbol{X}$ because we are summing more terms. Consider a 2×2 ordinary polynomial system where

$$
\boldsymbol{X}^T\boldsymbol{X} = \begin{bmatrix} \sum_{n=1}^{N} x_n^2 & \sum_{n=1}^{N} x_n \\ \sum_{n=1}^{N} x_n & N \end{bmatrix}.
$$

As N grows, all the entries in the matrix grow. As a result, $(\boldsymbol{X}^T\boldsymbol{X})^{-1}$ will shrink in magnitude and thus drive the variance $\sigma^2 \mathrm{Tr}\left\{ (\boldsymbol{X}^T\boldsymbol{X})^{-1}(\boldsymbol{x}')(\boldsymbol{x}')^T \right\}$ to zero.

What is variance?

- Variance is the deviation between the predictor $g^{(\mathcal{D}_{\text{train}})}$ and its average $\overline{g}$.
- It can be reduced by using more training samples.

7.3.4 Bias and variance on the learning curve

The decomposition of the testing error into bias and variance is portrayed visually by the **learning curve** shown in **Figure 7.18**. This figure shows the testing error and the training error as functions of the number of training samples. As N increases, we observe that both testing and training errors converge to the same value. At any fixed N, the testing error is composed of bias and variance:

- The bias is the distance from the ground to the steady-state level. This value is fixed and is a constant w.r.t. N. In other words, regardless of how many training samples you have, the bias is always there. It is the best outcome you can achieve.

- The variance is the fluctuation from the steady-state level to the instantaneous state. It drops as N increases.

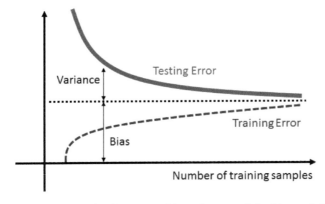

Figure 7.18: The learning curve can be decomposed into the sum of the bias and the variance. The bias is the testing error when $N = \infty$. For finite N, the difference between the testing error and the bias is the variance.

Figure 7.19 compares the learning curve of two models. The first case requires us to fit the data using a simple model (marked in purple). The training error and the testing error have small fluctuations around the steady-state because, for simple models, you need only a small number of samples to make the model happy. The second case requires us to fit the data using a complex model (marked in green). This set of curves has a much wider fluctuation because it is harder to train and harder to generalize. However, when we have enough training samples, the training error and the testing error will converge to a lower steady-state value. Therefore, you need to pay the price of using a complex model, but if you do, you will enjoy a lower testing error.

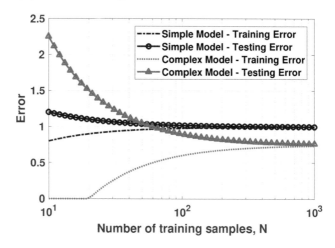

Figure 7.19: The generalization capability of a model is summarized by the training and testing errors of the model. If we use a simple model we will have an easier time with the training but the steady-state testing error will be high. In contrast, if we use a complex model we need to have a sufficient number of training samples to train the model well. However, when the complex model is well trained, the steady-state error will be lower.

The implication of all this is that you should choose the model by considering the number of data points. Never buy an expensive toy when you do not have the money! If you insist on using a complex model while you do not have enough training data, you will suffer from a poor testing error even if you feel good about it.

Closing remark. We close this section by revisiting the bias-variance trade-off:

$$\mathcal{E}_{\text{test}} = \mathbb{E}_{\boldsymbol{x}'}\left[\underbrace{(\overline{g}(\boldsymbol{x}') - f(\boldsymbol{x}'))^2}_{=\text{bias}(\boldsymbol{x}')}\right] + \mathbb{E}_{\boldsymbol{x}'}\left[\underbrace{\mathbb{E}_{\mathcal{D}_{\text{train}}}[(g^{(\mathcal{D}_{\text{train}})}(\boldsymbol{x}') - \overline{g}(\boldsymbol{x}'))^2]}_{=\text{var}(\boldsymbol{x}')}\right] + \sigma^2. \qquad (7.31)$$

The relationship among the three terms is summarized below:

What is the trade-off offered by the bias-variance analysis?

- Overfitting improves if $N \uparrow$: Variance drops as N grows. Bias is unchanged.
- Overfitting worsens if $\sigma^2 \uparrow$. If training noise grows, $g^{(\mathcal{D}_{\text{train}})}$ will have more fluctuations, so variance will grow.

- Overfitting worsens if the target function f is too complicated to be approximated by $\overline{g}$.

End of the section. Please join us again.

7.4 Regularization

Having discussed the source of the overfitting problem, we now discuss methods to allevi-ate overfitting. The method we focus on here is **regularization**. Regularization means that instead of seeking the model parameters by minimizing the training loss alone, we add a **penalty term** to force the parameters to "behave better". As a preview of the technique, we change the original training loss

$$\mathcal{E}_{\text{train}}(\boldsymbol{\theta}) = \underbrace{\sum_{n=1}^{N} \left(y_n - \sum_{p=0}^{d-1} \theta_p \phi_p(x_n) \right)^2}_{\text{data fidelity}}, \tag{7.32}$$

which consists of only the data fidelity term, to a modified training loss

$$\mathcal{E}_{\text{train}}(\boldsymbol{\theta}) = \underbrace{\sum_{n=1}^{N} \left(y_n - \sum_{p=0}^{d-1} \theta_p \phi_p(x_n) \right)^2}_{F(\boldsymbol{\theta}),\ \text{data fidelity}} + \underbrace{\lambda \cdot \sum_{p=0}^{d-1} \theta_p^2}_{\lambda \cdot R(\boldsymbol{\theta}),\ \text{regularization}}. \tag{7.33}$$

Putting this into the matrix form, we define the **data fidelity** term as

$$F(\boldsymbol{\theta}) = \|\boldsymbol{X}\boldsymbol{\theta} - \boldsymbol{y}\|^2. \tag{7.34}$$

The newly added term $R(\boldsymbol{\theta})$ is called the **regularization function** or the **penalty function**. It can take a variety of forms, e.g.,

- Ridge regression: $R(\boldsymbol{\theta}) = \sum_{p=0}^{d-1} \theta_p^2 = \|\boldsymbol{\theta}\|^2$.
- LASSO regression: $R(\boldsymbol{\theta}) = \sum_{p=0}^{d-1} |\theta_p| = \|\boldsymbol{\theta}\|_1$.

In this section we aim to understand the role of the regularization functions by studying these two examples of $R(\boldsymbol{\theta})$.

7.4.1 Ridge regularization

To explain the meaning of Equation (7.33) we write it in terms of matrices and vectors:

$$\underset{\boldsymbol{\theta} \in \mathbb{R}^d}{\text{minimize}} \quad \|\boldsymbol{X}\boldsymbol{\theta} - \boldsymbol{y}\|^2 + \lambda \|\boldsymbol{\theta}\|^2, \tag{7.35}$$

where λ is called the **regularization parameter**. It needs to be tuned by the user. We refer to Equation (7.35) as the **ridge regression**.[5]

---

[5] In signal processing and optimization, Equation (7.35) is called the Tikhonov regularization. We follow the statistics community in calling it the ridge regression.

How can the regularization function help to mitigate the overfitting problem? First let's find the solution to this problem.

Practice Exercise 1. Prove that the solution to Equation (7.35) is

$$\widehat{\boldsymbol{\theta}} = (\boldsymbol{X}^T\boldsymbol{X} + \lambda\boldsymbol{I})^{-1}\boldsymbol{X}^T\boldsymbol{y}. \qquad (7.36)$$

Solution. Take the derivative with respect to $\boldsymbol{\theta}$.[a] This yields

$$\nabla_{\boldsymbol{\theta}}\left\{\|\boldsymbol{X}\boldsymbol{\theta} - \boldsymbol{y}\|^2 + \lambda\|\boldsymbol{\theta}\|^2\right\} = 2\boldsymbol{X}^T(\boldsymbol{X}\boldsymbol{\theta} - \boldsymbol{y}) + 2\lambda\boldsymbol{\theta} = 0.$$

Rearranging the terms gives

$$(\boldsymbol{X}^T\boldsymbol{X} + \lambda\boldsymbol{I})\boldsymbol{\theta} = \boldsymbol{X}^T\boldsymbol{y}.$$

Taking the inverse of the matrix on both sides yields the solution.

---

[a]The solution here requires some basic matrix calculus. You may refer to the University of Waterloo's Matrix Cookbook https://www.math.uwaterloo.ca/~hwolkowi/matrixcookbook.pdf.

Let us compare the ridge regression solution with the vanilla regression solutions:

$$\widehat{\boldsymbol{\theta}}_{\text{vanilla}} = (\boldsymbol{X}^T\boldsymbol{X})^{-1}\boldsymbol{X}^T\boldsymbol{y},$$
$$\widehat{\boldsymbol{\theta}}_{\text{ridge}}(\lambda) = (\boldsymbol{X}^T\boldsymbol{X} + \lambda\boldsymbol{I})^{-1}\boldsymbol{X}^T\boldsymbol{y}.$$

Clearly, the only difference is the presence of the parameter λ:

- If $\lambda \to 0$, then $\widehat{\boldsymbol{\theta}}_{\text{ridge}}(0) = \widehat{\boldsymbol{\theta}}_{\text{vanilla}}$. This is because

$$\mathcal{E}_{\text{train}}(\boldsymbol{\theta}) = \|\boldsymbol{X}\boldsymbol{\theta} - \boldsymbol{y}\|^2 + \underbrace{\lambda\|\boldsymbol{\theta}\|^2}_{=0}.$$

  Hence, when $\lambda \to 0$, the regression problem goes back to the vanilla version, and so does the solution.

- $\lambda \to \infty$, then $\widehat{\boldsymbol{\theta}}_{\text{ridge}}(\infty) = 0$. This happens because

$$\mathcal{E}_{\text{train}}(\boldsymbol{\theta}) = \underbrace{\frac{1}{\lambda}\|\boldsymbol{X}\boldsymbol{\theta} - \boldsymbol{y}\|^2}_{=0} + \|\boldsymbol{\theta}\|^2.$$

  Since we are now minimizing $\|\boldsymbol{\theta}\|^2$, the solution will be $\boldsymbol{\theta} = 0$ because zero is the smallest value a squared function can achieve.

For any $0 < \lambda < \infty$, the net effect of $(\boldsymbol{X}^T\boldsymbol{X} + \lambda\boldsymbol{I})$ is the constant λ added to all the eigenvalues of $\boldsymbol{X}^T\boldsymbol{X}$. By taking the eigendecomposition of $\boldsymbol{X}^T\boldsymbol{X}$,

$$[\boldsymbol{U}, \boldsymbol{S}] = \texttt{eig}(\boldsymbol{X}^T\boldsymbol{X}),$$

we have that

$$\boldsymbol{X}^T\boldsymbol{X} + \lambda\boldsymbol{I} = \boldsymbol{U}\boldsymbol{S}\boldsymbol{U}^T + \lambda\boldsymbol{I}$$
$$= \boldsymbol{U}\boldsymbol{S}\boldsymbol{U}^T + \lambda\boldsymbol{U}\boldsymbol{U}^T = \boldsymbol{U}(\boldsymbol{S} + \lambda\boldsymbol{I})\boldsymbol{U}^T.$$

Therefore, if the eigenvalue matrix $\boldsymbol{S}$ has a zero eigenvalue it will be offset by λ:

$$\boldsymbol{S} = \begin{bmatrix} \clubsuit & & & \\ & \heartsuit & & \\ & & \spadesuit & \\ & & & 0 \end{bmatrix} \quad \longrightarrow \quad \boldsymbol{S} + \lambda\boldsymbol{I} = \begin{bmatrix} \clubsuit + \lambda & & & \\ & \heartsuit + \lambda & & \\ & & \spadesuit + \lambda & \\ & & & \lambda \end{bmatrix}$$

As a result, even if $\boldsymbol{X}^T\boldsymbol{X}$ is not invertible (or close to not invertible), the new matrix $\boldsymbol{X}^T\boldsymbol{X} + \lambda\boldsymbol{I}$ is guaranteed to be invertible.

Practice Exercise 2. You may be wondering what happens if $\boldsymbol{X}^T\boldsymbol{X}$ has a negative eigenvalue so that when we add a positive λ, the resulting matrix may have a zero eigenvalue. Prove that $\boldsymbol{X}^T\boldsymbol{X}$ will never have a negative eigenvalue, and $\boldsymbol{X}^T\boldsymbol{X} + \lambda\boldsymbol{I}$ always has positive eigenvalues.

Solution. Eigenvalues of a matrix $\boldsymbol{A}$ are nonnegative if and only if $\boldsymbol{v}^T\boldsymbol{A}\boldsymbol{v} \geq 0$ for any $\boldsymbol{v}$. Thus we need to check whether $\boldsymbol{v}^T\boldsymbol{X}^T\boldsymbol{X}\boldsymbol{v} \geq 0$ for all $\boldsymbol{v}$. However, this is easy:

$$\boldsymbol{v}^T\boldsymbol{X}^T\boldsymbol{X}\boldsymbol{v} = \|\boldsymbol{X}\boldsymbol{v}\|^2,$$

which must be nonnegative for any $\boldsymbol{v}$. Matrices satisfying this property are called **positive semidefinite**. Therefore, $\boldsymbol{X}^T\boldsymbol{X}$ is positive semidefinite.

Implementation

Solving the ridge regression is easy. First, we observe that the regularization function $R(\boldsymbol{\theta}) = \|\boldsymbol{\theta}\|^2$ is a quadratic function. Therefore, it can be combined with the data fidelity term as

$$\widehat{\boldsymbol{\theta}} = \underset{\boldsymbol{\theta} \in \mathbb{R}^d}{\text{argmin}} \ \|\boldsymbol{X}\boldsymbol{\theta} - \boldsymbol{y}\|^2 + \lambda\|\boldsymbol{\theta}\|^2$$

$$= \underset{\boldsymbol{\theta} \in \mathbb{R}^d}{\text{argmin}} \ \|\boldsymbol{X}\boldsymbol{\theta} - \boldsymbol{y}\|^2 + \|\sqrt{\lambda}\boldsymbol{I}\boldsymbol{\theta} - \boldsymbol{0}\|^2$$

$$= \underset{\boldsymbol{\theta} \in \mathbb{R}^d}{\text{argmin}} \ \left\| \begin{bmatrix} \boldsymbol{X} \\ \sqrt{\lambda}\boldsymbol{I} \end{bmatrix} \boldsymbol{\theta} - \begin{bmatrix} \boldsymbol{y} \\ \boldsymbol{0} \end{bmatrix} \right\|^2.$$

Therefore, all we need to do is to concatenate the matrix $\boldsymbol{X}$ with a $d \times d$ identity operator $\sqrt{\lambda}\boldsymbol{I}$, and concatenate $\boldsymbol{y}$ with a $d \times 1$ all-zero vector.

In MATLAB and Python, the implementation of the ridge regression is done by defining a new matrix A and a new vector b, as shown below:

```
% MATLAB command for ridge regression
A = [X; sqrt(lambda)*eye(d)];
b = [y(:); zeros(d,1)];
theta = A\b;
```

```
% MATLAB command for ridge regression
A = np.vstack((X, np.sqrt(lambd)*np.eye(d)))
b = np.hstack((y, np.zeros(d)))
theta = np.linalg.lstsq(A, b, rcond=None)[0]
```

Example 7.6. Consider a dataset of $N = 20$ data points. These data points are constructed from the model

$$y_n = 0.5 - 2x_n - 3x_n^2 + 4x_n^3 + 6x_N^4 + e_n, \qquad n = 1, \ldots, N,$$

where $e_n \sim \text{Gaussian}(0, 0.25^2)$ is the noise. Fit the data using

(a) Vanilla linear regression with a 4th-order polynomial.

(b) Vanilla linear regression with a 20th-order polynomial.

(c) Ridge regression with a 20th-order polynomial, by considering three choices of λ: $\lambda = 10^{-6}$, $\lambda = 10^{-3}$, and $\lambda = 10$.

Solution.

(a) We first fit the data using a 4th-order polynomial. This fitting is relatively straightforward. In the MATLAB / Python programs below, set $d = 4$ and $\lambda = 0$. The result is shown in **Figure 7.20**(a).

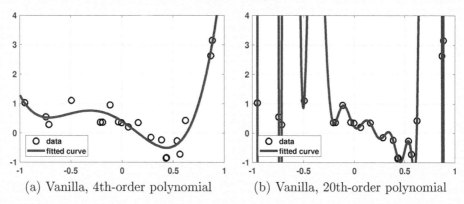

(a) Vanilla, 4th-order polynomial   (b) Vanilla, 20th-order polynomial

Figure 7.20: Overfitting occurs when the model is too complex for the number of training samples. When using a vanilla regression with a 20th-order polynomial, the curve overfits the data and causes a catastrophic fitting error.

(b) Suppose we use a 20th-order polynomial $g(x) = \sum_{p=0}^{20} \theta_p x^p$ to fit the data. We plot the result in **Figure 7.20**(b). Since the order of the polynomial is very high relative to the number of training samples, it comes as no surprise that the fitting is poor. This is overfitting, and we know the reason.

(c) Next, we consider a ridge regression using three choices of λ. The result is shown in **Figure 7.21**. If λ is too small, we observe that some overfitting still occurs. If λ is too large, then the curve underfits the data. For an appropriately chosen λ, it can be seen that the fitting is reasonably good.

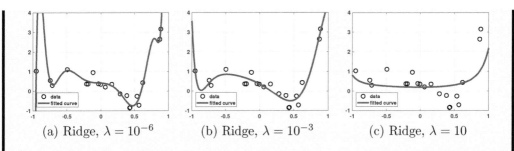

(a) Ridge, $\lambda = 10^{-6}$ (b) Ridge, $\lambda = 10^{-3}$ (c) Ridge, $\lambda = 10$

Figure 7.21: Ridge regression addresses the overfitting problem by adding a regularization term to the training loss. Depending on the strength of the parameter λ, the fitted curve can vary from overfitting to underfitting.

The MATLAB and Python codes used to generate the above plots are shown below.

```
% MATLAB code to demonstrate a ridge regression example
% Generate data
N = 20;
x = linspace(-1,1,N);
a = [0.5, -2, -3, 4, 6];
y = a(1)+a(2)*x(:).^2+a(3)*x(:).^2+a(4)*x(:).^3+a(5)*x(:).^4+0.25*randn(N,1);

% Ridge regression
lambda = 0.1;
d = 20;
X = zeros(N, d);
for p=0:d-1
    X(:,p+1) = x(:).^p;
end
A = [X; sqrt(lambda)*eye(d)];
b = [y(:); zeros(d,1)];
theta = A\b;

% Interpolate and display results
t    = linspace(-1, 1, 500);
Xhat = zeros(length(t), d);
for p=0:d-1
    Xhat(:,p+1) = t(:).^p;
end
yhat = Xhat*theta;
plot(x,y,   'ko','LineWidth',2, 'MarkerSize', 10); hold on;
plot(t,yhat,'LineWidth',4,'Color',[0.2 0.2 0.9]);
```

```
# Python code to demonstrate a ridge regression example
import numpy as np
import matplotlib.pyplot as plt
from scipy.special import eval_legendre
np.set_printoptions(precision=2, suppress=True)
```

```
N = 20
x = np.linspace(-1,1,N)
a = np.array([0.5, -2, -3, 4, 6])
y = a[0] + a[1]*x   + a[2]*x**2 + \
           a[3]*x**3 + a[4]*x**4 + 0.25*np.random.randn(N)
d = 20
X = np.zeros((N, d))
for p in range(d):
  X[:,p] = x**p

lambd = 0.1
A = np.vstack((X, np.sqrt(lambd)*np.eye(d)))
b = np.hstack((y, np.zeros(d)))
theta = np.linalg.lstsq(A, b, rcond=None)[0]

t    = np.linspace(-1, 1, 500)
Xhat = np.zeros((500,d))
for p in range(d):
  Xhat[:,p] = t**p
yhat = np.dot(Xhat, theta)

plt.plot(x,y,'o',markersize=12)
plt.plot(t,yhat, linewidth=4)
plt.show()
```

Why does ridge regression work?

- The penalty term $\|\boldsymbol{\theta}\|^2$ in

$$\widehat{\boldsymbol{\theta}}_{\text{ridge}} = \underset{\boldsymbol{\theta} \in \mathbb{R}^d}{\operatorname{argmin}} \ \|\boldsymbol{X}\boldsymbol{\theta} - \boldsymbol{y}\|^2 + \lambda\|\boldsymbol{\theta}\|^2$$

does not allow solutions with very $\|\boldsymbol{\theta}\|^2$.

- The penalty term adds a positive offset to the eigenvalues of $\boldsymbol{X}^T\boldsymbol{X}$.
- Since the denominator in $(\boldsymbol{X}^T\boldsymbol{X} + \lambda\boldsymbol{I})^{-1}\boldsymbol{X}^T\boldsymbol{y}$ becomes larger than that of $(\boldsymbol{X}^T\boldsymbol{X})^{-1}\boldsymbol{X}^T\boldsymbol{y}$, noise in $\boldsymbol{y}$ is less amplified.

Choosing the parameter

How should we choose the parameter λ? The honest answer is that there is no answer because the optimal λ can only be found if we have access to the **testing** samples. If we do, we can plot the MSE (the testing error) with respect to λ, as shown in **Figure 7.22**(a).

Of course in reality we do not have access to the testing data. However, we can reserve a small portion of the training samples and treat them as **validation samples**. Then we run the ridge regression for different choices of λ. The λ that minimizes the error on these validation samples is the one that you should deploy. If the training set is small, we can

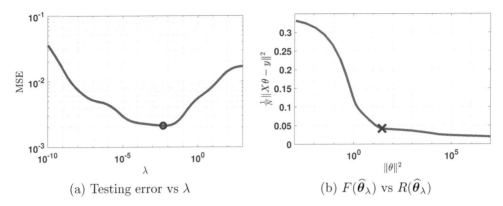

(a) Testing error vs λ (b) $F(\widehat{\boldsymbol{\theta}}_\lambda)$ vs $R(\widehat{\boldsymbol{\theta}}_\lambda)$

Figure 7.22: (a) Determining the optimal λ requires knowledge of the testing samples. In practice, we can replace the testing samples with the validation samples, which are subsets of the training data. Then by plotting the validation error as a function of λ we can determine the optimal λ. (b) The alternative is to plot $F(\widehat{\boldsymbol{\theta}}_\lambda)$ versus $R(\widehat{\boldsymbol{\theta}}_\lambda)$. The optimal λ can be found by locating the elbow point.

shuffle the validation samples randomly and compute the average. This scheme is known as **cross-validation**.

For some problems, there are "tactics" you may be able to employ for determining the optimal λ. The first approach is to ask yourself what would be the reasonable range of $\|\boldsymbol{\theta}\|^2$ or $\|\boldsymbol{X\theta} - \boldsymbol{y}\|^2$? Are you expecting them to be large or small? Approximately in what order of magnitude? If you have some clues about this, then you can plot the function $F(\widehat{\boldsymbol{\theta}}_\lambda) = \|\boldsymbol{X}\widehat{\boldsymbol{\theta}}_\lambda - \boldsymbol{y}\|^2$ as a function of $R(\widehat{\boldsymbol{\theta}}_\lambda) = \|\widehat{\boldsymbol{\theta}}_\lambda\|^2$, where $\widehat{\boldsymbol{\theta}}_\lambda$ is a shorthand notation for $\widehat{\boldsymbol{\theta}}_{\text{ridge}}(\lambda)$, which is the estimated parameter using a specific value of λ. **Figure 7.22**(b) shows an example of such a plot. As you can see, by varying λ we have different values of $F(\widehat{\boldsymbol{\theta}}_\lambda)$ and $R(\widehat{\boldsymbol{\theta}}_\lambda)$.

If you have some ideas about what $\|\boldsymbol{\theta}\|^2$ should be, say you want $\|\boldsymbol{\theta}\|^2 \leq \tau$, you can go to the $F(\widehat{\boldsymbol{\theta}}_\lambda)$ versus $R(\widehat{\boldsymbol{\theta}}_\lambda)$ curve and find a point such that $R(\widehat{\boldsymbol{\theta}}_\lambda) \leq \tau$. On the other hand, if you want $\|\boldsymbol{X\theta} - \boldsymbol{y}\|^2 \leq \epsilon$, you can also go to the $F(\widehat{\boldsymbol{\theta}}_\lambda)$ versus $R(\widehat{\boldsymbol{\theta}}_\lambda)$ curve and find a point such that $\|\boldsymbol{X\theta} - \boldsymbol{y}\|^2 \leq \epsilon$. In either case, you have the freedom to shift the difficulty of finding λ to that of finding τ or ϵ. Note that τ and ϵ have better physical interpretations. The quantity ϵ tells us the upper bound of the prediction error, and τ tells us the upper bound of the parameter magnitude. If you have been working on your dataset long enough, the historical data (and your experience) will help you determine these values.

Another feasible option suggested in the literature is finding the anchor point of the $F(\widehat{\boldsymbol{\theta}}_\lambda)$ and $R(\widehat{\boldsymbol{\theta}}_\lambda)$. The idea is that if the curve has a sharp elbow, the turning point would indicate a rapid increase/decrease in $F(\widehat{\boldsymbol{\theta}}_\lambda)$ (or $R(\widehat{\boldsymbol{\theta}}_\lambda)$).

How to determine λ

- Cross-validation: Reserve a few training samples as validation samples. Check the prediction error w.r.t. these validation samples. The λ that minimizes the validation error is the one you deploy.
- $\|\boldsymbol{\theta}\|^2 \leq \tau$: Plot the $F(\widehat{\boldsymbol{\theta}}_\lambda)$ and $R(\widehat{\boldsymbol{\theta}}_\lambda)$. Then go along the R-axis to find the

position where $R(\widehat{\boldsymbol{\theta}}_\lambda) \leq \tau$.

- $\|\boldsymbol{X}\boldsymbol{\theta} - \boldsymbol{y}\|^2 \leq \epsilon$: Plot the $F(\widehat{\boldsymbol{\theta}}_\lambda)$ and $R(\widehat{\boldsymbol{\theta}}_\lambda)$. Then go along the F-axis to find the position where $F(\widehat{\boldsymbol{\theta}}_\lambda) \leq \epsilon$.

- Find the elbow point of $F(\widehat{\boldsymbol{\theta}}_\lambda)$ and $R(\widehat{\boldsymbol{\theta}}_\lambda)$.

Bias and variance trade-off for ridge regression

We now discuss the **bias and variance trade-off** of the ridge regression.

Theorem 7.7. *Let* $\boldsymbol{y} = \boldsymbol{X}\boldsymbol{\theta} + \boldsymbol{e}$ *be the training data, where* $\boldsymbol{e}$ *is zero-mean and has a covariance* $\sigma^2 \boldsymbol{I}$. *Consider the ridge regression*

$$\widehat{\boldsymbol{\theta}}_\lambda = \underset{\boldsymbol{\theta} \in \mathbb{R}^d}{argmin} \ \|\boldsymbol{X}\boldsymbol{\theta} - \boldsymbol{y}\|^2 + \lambda\|\boldsymbol{\theta}\|^2. \tag{7.37}$$

Then the estimate has the properties that

$$\widehat{\boldsymbol{\theta}}_\lambda = (\boldsymbol{X}^T\boldsymbol{X} + \lambda\boldsymbol{I})^{-1}\boldsymbol{X}^T\boldsymbol{X}\boldsymbol{\theta} + (\boldsymbol{X}^T\boldsymbol{X} + \lambda\boldsymbol{I})^{-1}\boldsymbol{X}^T\boldsymbol{e},$$
$$\mathbb{E}[\widehat{\boldsymbol{\theta}}_\lambda] = (\boldsymbol{X}^T\boldsymbol{X} + \lambda\boldsymbol{I})^{-1}\boldsymbol{X}^T\boldsymbol{X}\boldsymbol{\theta} = \boldsymbol{W}_\lambda\boldsymbol{\theta},$$
$$\text{Cov}[\widehat{\boldsymbol{\theta}}_\lambda] = \sigma^2(\boldsymbol{X}^T\boldsymbol{X} + \lambda\boldsymbol{I})^{-1}\boldsymbol{X}^T\boldsymbol{X}(\boldsymbol{X}^T\boldsymbol{X} + \lambda\boldsymbol{I})^{-1},$$
$$MSE(\widehat{\boldsymbol{\theta}}_\lambda, \boldsymbol{\theta}) = \sigma^2 Tr\left\{\boldsymbol{W}_\lambda(\boldsymbol{X}^T\boldsymbol{X})^{-1}\boldsymbol{W}_\lambda^T\right\} + \boldsymbol{\theta}^T(\boldsymbol{W}_\lambda - \boldsymbol{I})^T(\boldsymbol{W}_\lambda - \boldsymbol{I})\boldsymbol{\theta},$$

where $\boldsymbol{W}_\lambda = (\boldsymbol{X}^T\boldsymbol{X} + \lambda\boldsymbol{I})^{-1}\boldsymbol{X}^T\boldsymbol{X}$.

Proof. The proof of this theorem involves some tedious matrix operations that will be omitted here. If you are interested in the proof you can consult van Wieringen's "Lecture notes on ridge regression", https://arxiv.org/pdf/1509.09169.pdf. □

The results of this theorem provide a way to assess the bias and variance. Specifically, from the MSE we know that

$$\text{MSE}(\widehat{\boldsymbol{\theta}}_\lambda, \boldsymbol{\theta}) = \mathbb{E}_e\left[\|\widehat{\boldsymbol{\theta}}_\lambda - \boldsymbol{\theta}\|^2\right]$$
$$= \|\mathbb{E}_e[\widehat{\boldsymbol{\theta}}_\lambda] - \boldsymbol{\theta}\|^2 + \text{Tr}\left\{\text{Cov}[\widehat{\boldsymbol{\theta}}_\lambda]\right\}$$
$$= \underbrace{\boldsymbol{\theta}^T(\boldsymbol{W}_\lambda - \boldsymbol{I})^T(\boldsymbol{W}_\lambda - \boldsymbol{I})\boldsymbol{\theta}}_{\text{bias}} + \underbrace{\sigma^2\text{Tr}\left\{\boldsymbol{W}_\lambda(\boldsymbol{X}^T\boldsymbol{X})^{-1}\boldsymbol{W}_\lambda^T\right\}}_{\text{variance}}.$$

The bias and variance are defined respectively as

$$\text{Bias}(\widehat{\boldsymbol{\theta}}_\lambda, \boldsymbol{\theta}) = \boldsymbol{\theta}^T(\boldsymbol{W}_\lambda - \boldsymbol{I})^T(\boldsymbol{W}_\lambda - \boldsymbol{I})\boldsymbol{\theta},$$
$$\text{Var}(\widehat{\boldsymbol{\theta}}_\lambda, \boldsymbol{\theta}) = \sigma^2\text{Tr}\left\{\boldsymbol{W}_\lambda(\boldsymbol{X}^T\boldsymbol{X})^{-1}\boldsymbol{W}_\lambda^T\right\}.$$

We can then plot the bias and variance as a function of λ. An example is shown in **Figure 7.23**.

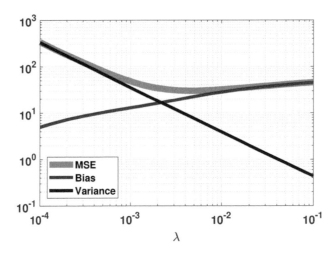

Figure 7.23: The bias and variance of the ridge regression behave in opposite ways as λ increases. The MSE is the sum of bias and variance.

The result in **Figure 7.23** can be summarized in three points:

- **Bias** $\uparrow$ as $\lambda \uparrow$. This is because a large λ pushes the solution towards $\boldsymbol{\theta} = 0$. Therefore, the bias with respect to the ground truth $\boldsymbol{\theta}$ will increase.

- **Variance** $\downarrow$ as $\lambda \uparrow$. Since variance is caused by noise, increasing λ forces the solution $\boldsymbol{\theta}$ to be small. Hence, it becomes less sensitive to noise.

- **MSE** reaches a minimum point somewhere in the middle. The MSE is the sum of bias and variance. Therefore, it drops to the minimum and then rises again as λ increases.

With appropriate choice of λ, we can show that the ridge regression can have a lower mean squared error than the vanilla regression. The following result is due to C. M. Theobald:[6]

Theorem 7.8. *For* $\lambda < 2\sigma^2 \|\boldsymbol{\theta}\|^{-2}$,

$$MSE\left(\widehat{\boldsymbol{\theta}}_{ridge}(\lambda), \boldsymbol{\theta}\right) < MSE\left(\widehat{\boldsymbol{\theta}}_{vanilla}, \boldsymbol{\theta}\right). \tag{7.38}$$

This theorem says that as long as λ is small enough, the ridge regression will have a lower MSE than the vanilla regression. Thus ridge regression is almost always helpful. Of course, the optimal λ is not provided by the theorem, which only tells us where to search for a good λ.

Why does ridge regression reduce the testing error?

- The regularization reduces the variance (see **Figure 7.23** when $\lambda > 0$)
- It pays the price of increasing the bias.

---

[6]Theobald, C. M. (1974). Generalizations of mean square error applied to ridge regression. *Journal of the Royal Statistical Society. Series B (Methodological)*, 36(1), 103-106.

- Usually, the drop in variance outweighs the increase in bias. So the overall MSE drops.

- Bias is not always a bad thing.

7.4.2 LASSO regularization

The ridge regression we discussed in the previous subsection is just one of the many possible ways of doing regularization. One alternative is to replace $\|\boldsymbol{\theta}\|^2$ by $\|\boldsymbol{\theta}\|_1$, where

$$\|\boldsymbol{\theta}\|_1 = \sum_{p=0}^{d-1} |\theta_p|. \tag{7.39}$$

This change from the sum-squares to sum-absolute-values has been main driving force in data science, machine learning, and signal processing for at least the past two decades. The optimization associated with $\|\boldsymbol{\theta}\|_1$ is

$$\underset{\boldsymbol{\theta}\in\mathbb{R}^d}{\text{minimize}} \quad \|\boldsymbol{X}\boldsymbol{\theta} - \boldsymbol{y}\|^2 + \lambda\|\boldsymbol{\theta}\|_1, \tag{7.40}$$

or

$$\mathcal{E}_{\text{train}}(\boldsymbol{\theta}) = \underbrace{\sum_{n=1}^{N}\left(y_n - \sum_{p=0}^{d-1}\theta_p\phi_p(x_n)\right)^2}_{F(\boldsymbol{\theta}),\ \text{data fidelity}} + \underbrace{\lambda\cdot\sum_{p=0}^{d-1}|\theta_p|}_{\lambda\cdot R(\boldsymbol{\theta}),\ \text{regularization}}. \tag{7.41}$$

Seeking a sparse solution

To understand the choice of $\|\cdot\|_1$, we need to introduce the concept of **sparsity**.

Definition 7.1. *A vector $\boldsymbol{\theta}$ is called* **sparse** *if it has only a few non-zero elements.*

As illustrated in **Figure 7.24**, a sparse $\boldsymbol{\theta}$ ensures that only a very few columns of the data matrix $\boldsymbol{X}$ are active. This is an attractive property because, in some of the regression problems, it is indeed possible to have just a few dominant factors. The LASSO regression says that if our problem possesses this sparse solution, then the $\|\cdot\|_1$ can help us find the sparse solution.

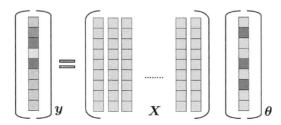

Figure 7.24: A vector $\boldsymbol{\theta}$ is sparse if it only contains a few non-zero elements. If $\boldsymbol{\theta}$ is sparse, then the observation $\boldsymbol{y}$ is determined by a few active components.

How can $\|\boldsymbol{\theta}\|_1$ promote sparsity? If we consider the sets

$$\Omega_1 = \{\boldsymbol{\theta} \mid \|\boldsymbol{\theta}\|_1 \leq \tau\} = \{(\theta_1, \theta_2) \mid |\theta_1| + |\theta_2| \leq \tau\},$$
$$\Omega_2 = \{\boldsymbol{\theta} \mid \|\boldsymbol{\theta}\|^2 \leq \tau\} = \{(\theta_1, \theta_2) \mid \theta_1^2 + \theta_2^2 \leq \tau\},$$

we note that Ω_1 has a diamond shape whereas Ω_2 has a circular shape. Since the data fidelity term $\|\boldsymbol{X}\boldsymbol{\theta} - \boldsymbol{y}\|^2$ is an ellipsoid, seeking the optimal value in the presence of the regularization term can be viewed as moving the ellipsoid until it touches the set defined by the regularization. As illustrated in **Figure 7.25**, since $\{\boldsymbol{\theta} \mid \|\boldsymbol{\theta}\|^2 \leq \tau\}$ is a circle, the solution will be somewhere in the middle. On the other hand, since $\{\boldsymbol{\theta} \mid \|\boldsymbol{\theta}\|_1 \leq \tau\}$ is a diamond, the solution will be one of the vertices. The difference between "somewhere in the middle" and "a vertex" is that the vertex is a sparse solution, since by the definition of a vertex one coordinate must be zero and the other coordinate must be non-zero. We can easily extrapolate this idea to the higher-dimensional spaces. In this case, we will see that the solution for the $\|\cdot\|_1$ problem has only a few non-zero entries.

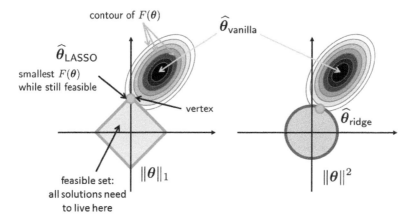

Figure 7.25: A vector $\boldsymbol{\theta}$ is sparse if it contains only a few non-zero elements. If $\boldsymbol{\theta}$ is sparse, then the observation $\boldsymbol{y}$ is determined by a few active components.

The optimization formulated in Equation (7.41) is known as the **least absolute shrinkage and selection operator** (LASSO). LASSO problems are difficult, but over the past two decades we have increased our understanding of the problem. The most significant breakthrough is that we now have algorithms to solve the LASSO problem efficiently. This is important because, unlike the ridge regression, where we have a (very simple) closed-form solution, the LASSO problem can only be solved using iterative algorithms.

What is so special about LASSO?

- LASSO regularization promotes a sparse solution.
- If the underlying model has a sparse solution, e.g., you choose a 50th-order polynomial, but the underlying model is a third-order polynomial, then there should only be three non-zero regression coefficients in your 50th-order polynomial. LASSO will help in this case.

- If the underlying model has a dense solution, then LASSO is of limited value. A ridge regression could be better.

- While $\|\boldsymbol{\theta}\|_1$ is not differentiable (at 0), there exist polynomial-time convex algorithms to solve the problem, e.g., interior-point methods.

Solving the LASSO problem

Today, there are many open-source packages to solve the LASSO problem. They are mostly developed in the **convex optimization** literature. One of the most user-friendly packages is the CVX package developed by S. Boyd and colleagues at Stanford University.[7] Once you have downloaded and installed the package, solving the optimization can be done literally by typing in the data fidelity term and the regularization term. An example is given below.

```
cvx_begin
    variable theta(d)
    minimize(sum_square(X*theta-y) + lambda*norm(theta,1))
cvx_end
```

As you can see, the program is extremely simple. You start by calling `cvx_begin` and end it with `cvx_end`. Inside the box we create a variable `beta(d)`, where d denotes the dimension of the vector `theta`. The main command is `minimize`. However, this line is almost self-explanatory. As long as you follow the syntax given by the user guidelines, you will be able to set it up properly.

In Python, we can call the `cvxpy` library.

```
import cvxpy as cvx
theta      = cvx.Variable(d)
objective = cvx.Minimize( cvx.sum_squares(X*theta-y) \
                        + lambd*cvx.norm1(theta) )
prob       = cvx.Problem(objective)
prob.solve()
```

To see a concrete example, we use the crime rate data obtained from `https://web.stanford.edu/~hastie/StatLearnSparsity/data.html`. A snapshot of the data is shown in the table below. In this dataset, the vector y is the crime rate, which is the last column of the table. The feature/basis vectors are `funding`, `hs`, `not-hs`, `college`.

city	crime rate	funding	hs	no-hs	college
1	478	40	74	11	31
2	494	32	72	11	43
3	643	57	71	18	16
4	341	31	71	11	25
⋮	⋮	⋮	⋮	⋮	⋮
50	940	66	67	26	18

---

[7]The MATLAB version is here: `http://cvxr.com/cvx/`. The Python version is here: `https://cvxopt.org/`. Follow the instructions to install the package.

We consider two optimizations:

$$\widehat{\boldsymbol{\theta}}_1(\lambda) = \underset{\boldsymbol{\theta}}{\operatorname{argmin}} \ \ \mathcal{E}_1(\boldsymbol{\theta}) \overset{\text{def}}{=} \|\boldsymbol{X}\boldsymbol{\theta} - \boldsymbol{y}\|^2 + \lambda\|\boldsymbol{\theta}\|_1,$$

$$\widehat{\boldsymbol{\theta}}_2(\lambda) = \underset{\boldsymbol{\theta}}{\operatorname{argmin}} \ \ \mathcal{E}_2(\boldsymbol{\theta}) \overset{\text{def}}{=} \|\boldsymbol{X}\boldsymbol{\theta} - \boldsymbol{y}\|^2 + \lambda\|\boldsymbol{\theta}\|^2.$$

As we have discussed, the first optimization uses the $\|\cdot\|_1$ regularized least squares, which is the LASSO problem. The second optimization is the standard $\|\cdot\|^2$ regularized least squares. Since both solutions depend on the parameter λ, we parameterize the solutions in terms of λ. Note that the optimal λ for $\widehat{\boldsymbol{\theta}}_1$ is not necessarily the optimal λ for $\widehat{\boldsymbol{\theta}}_2$.

One thing we would like to demonstrate in this example is visualizing the linear regression coefficients $\widehat{\boldsymbol{\theta}}_1(\lambda)$ and $\widehat{\boldsymbol{\theta}}_2(\lambda)$ as λ changes. To solve the optimization, we use CVX with the MATLAB and Python implementation is shown below.

```
data = load('./dataset/data_crime.txt');
y    = data(:,1);        % The observed crime rate
X    = data(:,3:end);    % Feature vectors
[N,d]= size(X);

lambdaset = logspace(-1,8,50);
theta_store   = zeros(d,50);
for i=1:length(lambdaset)
    lambda = lambdaset(i);
    cvx_begin
        variable theta(d)
        minimize( sum_square(X*theta-y) + lambda*norm(theta,1) )
%       minimize( sum_square(X*theta-y) + lambda*sum_square(theta) )
    cvx_end
    theta_store(:,i) = theta(:);
end

figure(1);
semilogx(lambdaset, theta_store, 'LineWidth', 4);
legend('funding','% high', '% no high', '% college', ...
       '% graduate', 'Location','NW');
xlabel('lambda');
ylabel('feature attribute');
```

```
import cvxpy as cvx
import numpy as np
import matplotlib.pyplot as plt

data = np.loadtxt("/content/data_crime.txt")
y = data[:,0]
X = data[:,2:7]
N,d = X.shape

lambd_set = np.logspace(-1,8,50)
```

```
theta_store = np.zeros((d,50))
for i in range(50):
  lambd = lambd_set[i]
  theta = cvx.Variable(d)
  objective   = cvx.Minimize( cvx.sum_squares(X*theta-y) \
                + lambd*cvx.norm1(theta) )
# objective   = cvx.Minimize( cvx.sum_squares(X*theta-y) \
                + lambd*cvx.sum_squares(theta) )
  prob        = cvx.Problem(objective)
  prob.solve()
  theta_store[:,i] = theta.value

for i in range(d):
  plt.semilogx(lambd_set, theta_store[i,:])
```

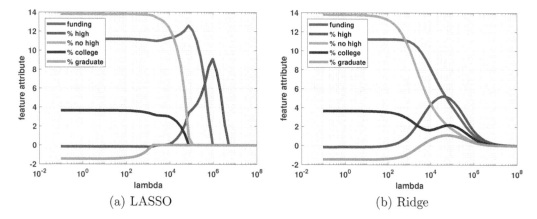

(a) LASSO   (b) Ridge

Figure 7.26: Ridge and LASSO regression on the crime-rate dataset. (a) The LASSO regression suggests that there are only a few active components as we change λ. (b) The ridge regression returns a set of dense solutions for all choices of λ.

Figure 7.26 shows some interesting differences between the two regression models.

- **Trajectory.** For the $\|\cdot\|^2$ estimate $\widehat{\boldsymbol{\theta}}_2(\lambda)$, the trajectory of the regression coefficients is smooth. This is attributable to the fact that the training loss $\mathcal{E}_2(\boldsymbol{\theta})$ is continuously differentiable in $\boldsymbol{\theta}$, and so the solution trajectory is smooth. By contrast, the $\|\cdot\|_1$ estimate $\widehat{\boldsymbol{\theta}}_1(\lambda)$ has a more disruptive trajectory.

- **Active members.** For the LASSO problem, $\widehat{\boldsymbol{\theta}}_1(\lambda)$ switches the active member as λ changes. For example, the feature `high-school` is the first one being activated when $\lambda \downarrow$. This implies that if we limit ourselves to only **one** feature, then `high-school` is the feature we should select. The ridge regression does not have this feature-selection property. How about when $\lambda = 10^6$? In this case, the LASSO has two active members: `funding` and `high-school`. This suggests that if there are two contributing factors, `funding` and `high-school` are the two. As $\lambda = 10^4$, we see that in LASSO, the green curve goes to zero but then the red curve rises. This means a correlation between high school and no high school, which should not be a surprise because they are complementary to each other.

- **Magnitude of solutions.** The magnitude of the solutions does not necessarily convey a clear conclusion because the feature vectors (e.g., high school) and the observable crime rate have different units.

- **Limiting solutions.** As $\lambda \to 0$, both $\widehat{\boldsymbol{\theta}}_1(\lambda)$ and $\widehat{\boldsymbol{\theta}}_2(\lambda)$ reach the same solution, because the training losses are identical when $\lambda = 0$.

LASSO for overfitting

Does LASSO help to mitigate the overfitting problem? Not always, but it often does. In **Figure 7.27** we consider fitting a dataset of $N = 20$ data points. The ground truth model we use is

$$y_n = L_0(x_n) + 0.5L_1(x_n) + 0.5L_2(x_n) + 1.5L_3(x_n) + L_4(x_n) + e_n,$$

where $e_n \sim \text{Gaussian}(0, \sigma^2)$ for $\sigma = 0.25$. When fitting the data, we purposely choose a 20th-order Legendre polynomial as the regression model. With only $N = 20$ data points, we can be almost certain that there is overfitting.

The MATLAB and Python codes for solving this LASSO problem are shown below.

```
% MATLAB code to demonstrate overfitting and LASSO
% Generate data
N = 20;
x = linspace(-1,1,N)';
a = [1, 0.5, 0.5, 1.5, 1];
y = a(1)*legendreP(0,x)+a(2)*legendreP(1,x)+a(3)*legendreP(2,x)+ ...
    a(4)*legendreP(3,x)+a(5)*legendreP(4,x)+0.25*randn(N,1);

% Solve LASSO using CVX
d = 20;
X = zeros(N, d);
for p=0:d-1
    X(:,p+1) = reshape(legendreP(p,x),N,1);
end
lambda = 2;
cvx_begin
    variable theta(d)
    minimize( sum_square( X*theta - y ) + lambda * norm(theta , 1) )
cvx_end

% Plot results
t    = linspace(-1, 1, 200);
Xhat = zeros(length(t), d);
for p=0:d-1
    Xhat(:,p+1) = reshape(legendreP(p,t),200,1);
end
yhat = Xhat*theta;
```

```
plot(x,y,    'ko','LineWidth',2, 'MarkerSize', 10); hold on;
plot(t,yhat,'LineWidth',6,'Color',[0.2 0.5 0.2]);
```

```
# Python code to demonstrate overfitting and LASSO
import cvxpy as cvx
import numpy as np
import matplotlib.pyplot as plt

# Setup the problem
N = 20
x = np.linspace(-1,1,N)
a = np.array([1, 0.5, 0.5, 1.5, 1])
y = a[0]*eval_legendre(0,x) + a[1]*eval_legendre(1,x) + \
    a[2]*eval_legendre(2,x) + a[3]*eval_legendre(3,x) + \
    a[4]*eval_legendre(4,x) + 0.25*np.random.randn(N)

# Solve LASSO using CVX
d = 20
lambd = 1
X = np.zeros((N, d))
for p in range(d):
  X[:,p] = eval_legendre(p,x)
theta       = cvx.Variable(d)
objective   = cvx.Minimize( cvx.sum_squares(X*theta-y) \
                             + lambd*cvx.norm1(theta) )
prob        = cvx.Problem(objective)
prob.solve()
thetahat = theta.value

# Plot the curves
t = np.linspace(-1, 1, 500)
Xhat = np.zeros((500,d))
for p in range(P):
  Xhat[:,p] = eval_legendre(p,t)
yhat = np.dot(Xhat, thetahat)
plt.plot(x, y, 'o')
plt.plot(t, yhat, linewidth=4)
```

Let us compare the various regression results. **Figure 7.27**(b) shows the vanilla regression, which as you can see fits the $N = 20$ data points very well. However, no one would believe that such a fitting curve can generalize to unseen data. **Figure 7.27**(c) shows the ridge regression result. When performing the analysis, we sweep a range of λ and pick the value $\lambda = 0.5$ so that the fitted curve is neither too "wild" nor too "flat". We can see that the fitting is improved. However, since the ridge regression only penalizes large-magnitude coefficients, the fitting is still not ideal. **Figure 7.27**(d) shows the LASSO regression result. Since the true model is a 4th-order polynomial and we use a 20th-order polynomial, the true solution is sparse. Therefore, LASSO is helpful, and hence we can pick a sparse solution.

The significance of LASSO is often not about the fitting of the data points but the

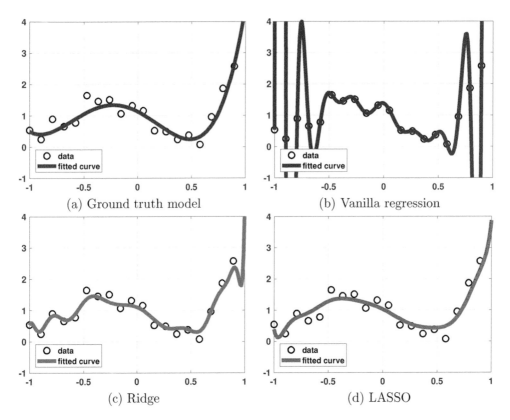

(a) Ground truth model   (b) Vanilla regression

(c) Ridge   (d) LASSO

Figure 7.27: We fit a dataset of $N = 20$ data points. (a) The ground truth model that generates the data. The model is a 4th-order ordinary polynomial. (b) Vanilla regression result, without any regularization. Note that there is severe overfitting because the model complexity is too high. (c) Ridge regression result, by setting $\lambda = 0.5$. (d) LASSO regression result, by setting $\lambda = 2$.

number of active coefficients. In **Figure 7.28** we show a comparison between the ground truth coefficients, the vanilla regression coefficients, the ridge regression coefficients, and the LASSO regression coefficients. It is evident that the LASSO solution contains a much smaller number of non-zeros compared to the ridge regression. Most of the high-order coefficients are zero. By contrast, the vanilla regression coefficients are wild. The ridge regression is better, but there are many non-zero high-order coefficients.

Closing remark. In this section, we discussed two regularization techniques: ridge regression and LASSO regression. Both techniques are about adding a penalty term to the training loss to constrain the regression coefficients. In the optimization literature, writings on ridge and LASSO regression are abundant, covering both algorithms and theoretical properties. An example of a theoretical question addressed in the literature is: Under what conditions is LASSO guaranteed to recover the correct support of the solution, i.e., locating the correct positions of the non-zeros? Problems like these are beyond the scope of this book.

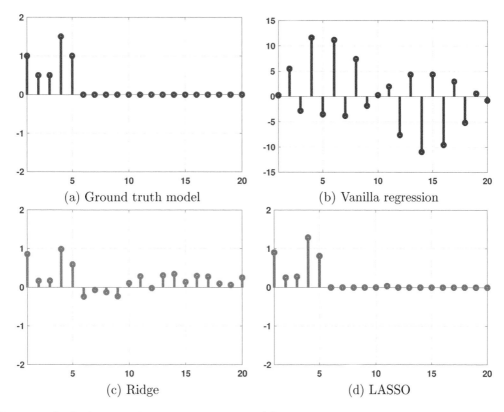

Figure 7.28: Coefficients of the regression models. (a) The ground truth model, which is a 4th-order polynomial. There are only 5 non-zero coefficients. (b) The vanilla regression coefficients. Note that the values are wild and large, although the curve fits the training data points very well. (c) The ridge regression coefficients. While the overall magnitudes are significantly improved from the vanilla, some high-order coefficients are still non-zero. (d) The LASSO regression coefficients. There are very few non-zeros, and the non-zeros match well with the ground truth.

7.5 Summary

Regression is one of the most widely used techniques in data science. The formulation of the regression problem is as simple as setting up a system of linear equations:

$$\underset{\boldsymbol{\theta}\in\mathbb{R}^d}{\text{minimize}} \quad \|\boldsymbol{X}\boldsymbol{\theta} - \boldsymbol{y}\|^2, \tag{7.42}$$

which has a closed-form solution. The biggest problems in practice are outliers, lack of training samples, and poor choice of the regression model.

- **Outliers:** We always recommend plotting the data whenever possible to check if there are obvious outliers. There are also statistical tests in which you can evaluate the validity of your samples. One simple way to debug outliers is to run the regression and check the prediction error against each training sample. If you have an outlier, and if your model is of reasonably low complexity, then a sample with an excessively large prediction error is an outlier. For example, if most of the training samples are within one standard deviation from your prediction but a few are substantially off, you will know which ones are the outliers. Robust linear regression is one technique for countering outliers, but an experienced data scientist can often reject outliers before running any regression algorithms. Domain knowledge is of great value for this purpose.

- **Lack of training samples**: As we have discussed in the overfitting section, it is extremely important to ensure that your model complexity is appropriate for the number of training samples. If the training set is small, do not use a complex model. Regularization techniques are valuable tools to mitigate overfitting. However, choosing a good regularization requires domain knowledge. For example, if you know that some features are not important, you need to scale them properly so as not to over-influence the regression solution.

- **Wrong model**: We have mentioned several times that regression can always return you a result because regression is an optimization problem. However, whether that result is meaningful depends on how meaningful your regression problem is. For example, if the noise is i.i.d. Gaussian, a data fidelity term with $\| \cdot \|^2$ would be a good choice; however, if the noise is i.i.d. Poisson, $\| \cdot \|^2$ would become a very bad model. We need a tighter connection with the statistics of the underlying data-generation model for problems like these. This is the subject of our next chapter, on parameter estimation.

7.6 References

Linear regression

Treatment of standard linear regression is abundant. In the context of machine learning and data science, the following references are useful.

7-1 Gareth James, Daniela Witten, Trevor Hastie, and Robert Tibshirani, *An Introduction to Statistical Learning with Applications in R*, Springer 2013, Chapter 3.

7-2 Stephen Boyd and Lieven Vandenberghe, *Convex Optimization*, Cambridge University Press, 2004. Chapter 6.

7-3 Trevor Hastie, Robert Tibshirani, and Jerome Friedman, *The Elements of Statistical Learning*, Springer, 2001. Chapter 3.

7-4 Christopher Bishop, *Pattern Recognition and Machine Learning*, Springer 2006. Chapter 3.1.

7-5 Yaser Abu-Mostafa, Malik Magdon-Ismail and Hsuan-Tien Lin, *Learning from Data*, AML Book, 2012. Chapter 3.2

Overfitting and Bias/Variance

The theory of overfitting and the trade-off between bias and variance can be found in multiple references. The following are basic treatments of the subject.

7-6 Yaser Abu-Mostafa, Malik Magdon-Ismail and Hsuan-Tien Lin, *Learning from Data*, AML Book, 2012. Chapter 4.

7-7 Christopher Bishop, *Pattern Recognition and Machine Learning*, Springer 2006. Chapter 3.2.

Ridge and LASSO regression

Ridge and LASSO regression are important tools in statistical learning today. The following two textbooks cover some of the perspectives of the statistical community and the signal processing community.

7-8 Trevor Hastie, Robert Tibshirani, and Martin Wainwright, *Statistical Learning with Sparsity: The LASSO and Generalizations*, CRC Press, 2015.

7-9 Michael Elad, *Sparse and Redundant Representations*, Springer, 2010. Chapters 1 and 3.

7.7 Problems

Exercise 1.

(a) Construct a dataset with $N = 20$ samples, following the model

$$y_n = \sum_{p=0}^{d-1} \theta_p L_p(x_n) + e_n, \tag{7.43}$$

where $\theta_0 = 1$, $\theta_1 = 0.5$, $\theta_2 = 0.5$, $\theta_3 = 1.5$, $\theta_4 = 1$, for $-1 < x < 1$. Here, $L_p(x)$ is the Legendre polynomial of the pth order. The $N = 20$ samples are random uniformly sampled from the interval $[-1, 1]$. The noise samples e_n are i.i.d. Gaussian with variance $\sigma^2 = 0.25^2$. Plot the dataset using the MATLAB or Python command scatter.

(b) Run the regression using the same model where $d = 5$, without any regularization. Plot the predicted curve and overlay with the training samples.

(c) Repeat (b) by running the regression with $d = 20$. Explain your observations.

(d) Increase the number of training samples N to $N = 50$, $N = 500$, and $N = 5000$, and repeat (c). Explain your observations.

(e) Construct a testing dataset with $M = 1000$ testing samples. For each of the regression models trained in (b)-(d), compute the testing error.

Exercise 2.
Consider a data generation model

$$x_n = \frac{1}{\sqrt{N}} \sum_{k=0}^{N-1} c_k e^{-j \frac{2\pi k n}{N}}, n = 0, \ldots, N - 1.$$

(a) Write the above equation in matrix-vector form

$$x = Wc.$$

What are the vectors c and x, and what is the matrix W?

(b) Show that W is orthogonal, i.e.,, $W^H W = I$, where W^H is the conjugate transpose of W.

(c) Using (b), derive the least squares regression solution if we want to estimate c from $x = Wc$.

Exercise 3.
Consider a simplified LASSO regression problem:

$$\widehat{\theta} = \underset{\theta \in \mathbb{R}^d}{\text{argmin}} \;\; \|y - \theta\|^2 + \lambda \|\theta\|_1. \tag{7.44}$$

Show that the solution is given by

$$\widehat{\theta} = \text{sign}(y) \cdot \max\left(|y| - \lambda, 0\right), \tag{7.45}$$

where $\cdot$ is the elementwise multiplication.

Exercise 4.
A one-dimensional signal is corrupted by blur and noise:

$$y_n = \sum_{\ell=0}^{L-1} h_\ell x_{n-\ell} + e_n.$$

(a) Formulate the least squares regression problem in matrix-vector form $y = Hx + e$. Find x, y and H.

(b) Consider a regularization function

$$R(x) = \sum_{n=2}^{N} (x_n - x_{n-1})^2.$$

Show that this regularization is equivalent to $R(x) = \|Dx\|^2$ for some D. Find D.

(c) Using the regularization in (b), derive the regularized least squares regression result:

$$\underset{x}{\text{minimize}} \;\; \|y - Hx\|^2 + \lambda \|Dx\|^2.$$

Exercise 5.
Let $\sigma(\cdot)$ be the sigmoid function

$$\sigma(a) = \frac{1}{1 + e^a}.$$

We want to use $\sigma(a)$ as a basis function.

(a) Show that the tanh function and the sigmoid function are related by

$$\tanh(a) = 2\sigma(2a) - 1.$$

(b) Show that a linear combination of sigmoid functions

$$y_n = \theta_0 + \sum_{p=1}^{d-1} \theta_p \sigma\left(\frac{x_n - \mu_j}{s}\right)$$

is equivalent to a linear combination of tanh functions

$$y_n = \alpha_0 + \sum_{p=1}^{d-1} \alpha_p \tanh\left(\frac{x_n - \mu_j}{2s}\right).$$

(c) Find the relationship between θ_p and α_p.

Exercise 6. (NHANES PART 1)(DATA DOWNLOAD)
The National Health and Nutrition Examination Survey (NHANES) is a program to assess the health and nutritional status of adults and children in the United States[8]. The complete survey result contains over 4,000 samples of health-related data of individuals who participated in the survey between 2011 and 2014. In the following exercises, we will focus on two categories of the data for each individual: height (in mm) and body mass index (BMI). The data is divided into two classes based on gender. Table 1 contains snippets of the data.

index	female bmi	female stature mm	index	male bmi	male stature mm
0	28.2	1563	0	30	1679
1	22.2	1716	1	25.6	1586
2	27.1	1484	2	24.2	1773
3	28.1	1651	3	27.4	1816

Table 7.2: Male and Female Data Snippets

Use `csv.reader` to read the training data files for the two data classes.

Important! Before proceeding to the problems,

- normalize the number in `male_stature_mm` and `female_stature_mm` by dividing them by 1000, and
- normalize that of `male_bmi` and `female_bmi` by dividing them by 10.

This will significantly reduce the numerical error.

Consider a linear model:

$$g_\theta = \theta^T x, \tag{7.46}$$

---

[8]https://www.cdc.gov/nchs/nhanes/index.htm

The regression problem we want to solve is

$$\widehat{\boldsymbol{\theta}} = \underset{\boldsymbol{\theta} \in \mathbb{R}^d}{\mathrm{argmin}} \ \sum_{n=1}^{N} (y_n - g_{\boldsymbol{\theta}}(\boldsymbol{x}_n))^2,$$

where $\mathcal{D} = \{(\boldsymbol{x}_n, y_n)\}_{n=1}^{N}$ is the training dataset. Putting the equation into the matrix form, we know that the optimization is equivalent to

$$\widehat{\boldsymbol{\theta}} = \underset{\boldsymbol{\theta} \in \mathbb{R}^d}{\mathrm{argmin}} \ \underbrace{\|\boldsymbol{y} - \boldsymbol{X}\boldsymbol{\theta}\|^2}_{\mathcal{E}_{\mathrm{train}}(\boldsymbol{\theta})}.$$

(a) Derive the solution $\widehat{\boldsymbol{\theta}}$. State the conditions under which the solution is the unique global minimum in terms of the rank of $\boldsymbol{X}$. Suggest two techniques that can be used when $\boldsymbol{X}^T\boldsymbol{X}$ is not invertible.

(b) For the NHANES dataset, assign $y_n = +1$ if the nth sample is a male and $y_n = -1$ if the nth sample is a female. Implement your answer in (a) with Python to solve the problem. Report your answer.

(c) Repeat (b), but this time use CVXPY. Report your answer, and compare with (b).

Exercise 7. (NHANES PART 2)(DATA DOWNLOAD)
We want to do a classification based on the linear model we found in the previous exercise. The classifier we will use is

$$\text{predicted label} = \mathrm{sign}(g_{\boldsymbol{\theta}}(\boldsymbol{x})), \tag{7.47}$$

where $\boldsymbol{x} \in \mathbb{R}^d$ is the a test sample. Here, we label $+1$ for male and -1 for female. Because the dataset we consider in this exercise has only two columns, the linear model is

$$g_{\boldsymbol{\theta}}(\boldsymbol{x}) = \theta_0 + \theta_1 x_1 + \theta_2 x_2,$$

where $\boldsymbol{x} = [1, x_1, x_2]^T$ is the input data and $\boldsymbol{\theta} = [\theta_0, \theta_1, \theta_2]^T$ is the parameter vector.

(a) First, we want to visualize the classifier.

  (i) Plot the training data points of the male and female classes. Mark the male class with blue circles and the female class with red dots.

  (ii) Plot the decision boundary $g_{\boldsymbol{\theta}}(\cdot)$ and overlay it with the data plotted in (a). Hint: $g_{\boldsymbol{\theta}}(\cdot)$ is a straight line in 2D. You can express x_2 in terms of x_1 and other parameters.

(b) (This problem requires knowledge of the content of Chapter 9). Report the classification accuracy. To do so, take testing data $\boldsymbol{x}$ and compute the prediction according to Equation (7.47).

  (i) What is the Type 1 error (False Alarm) of classifying males? That is, what is the percentage of testing samples that should be female but a male was predicted?

  (ii) What is the Type 2 error (Miss) of classifying males? That is, what is the percentage of testing samples that should be male but a female was predicted?

(iii) What is the precision and recall for this classifier? For the definitions of precision and recall, refer to Chapter 9.5.4.

Exercise 8. (NHANES PART 3)(DATA DOWNLOAD)
This exercise requires some background in optimization. Please refer to Reference [7.2, Chapter 9 and 10]. Consider the following three optimization problems:

$$\widehat{\boldsymbol{\theta}}_\lambda = \underset{\boldsymbol{\theta} \in \mathbb{R}^d}{\operatorname{argmin}} \ \|\boldsymbol{X}\boldsymbol{\theta} - \boldsymbol{y}\|_2^2 + \lambda\|\boldsymbol{\theta}\|_2^2, \tag{7.48}$$

$$\widehat{\boldsymbol{\theta}}_\alpha = \underset{\boldsymbol{\theta} \in \mathbb{R}^d}{\operatorname{argmin}} \ \|\boldsymbol{X}\boldsymbol{\theta} - \boldsymbol{y}\|_2^2 \ \text{subject to} \ \|\boldsymbol{\theta}\|_2^2 \le \alpha, \tag{7.49}$$

$$\widehat{\boldsymbol{\theta}}_\epsilon = \underset{\boldsymbol{\theta} \in \mathbb{R}^d}{\operatorname{argmin}} \ \|\boldsymbol{\theta}\|_2^2 \ \text{subject to} \ \|\boldsymbol{X}\boldsymbol{\theta} - \boldsymbol{y}\|_2^2 \le \epsilon. \tag{7.50}$$

(a) Set `lambd = np.arange(0.1,10,0.1)`. Plot

- $\|\boldsymbol{X}\widehat{\boldsymbol{\theta}}_\lambda - \boldsymbol{y}\|_2^2$ as a function of $\|\widehat{\boldsymbol{\theta}}_\lambda\|_2^2$.
- $\|\boldsymbol{X}\widehat{\boldsymbol{\theta}}_\lambda - \boldsymbol{y}\|_2^2$ as a function of λ.
- $\|\widehat{\boldsymbol{\theta}}_\lambda\|_2^2$ as a function of λ.

(b) (i) Write down the Lagrangian for each of the three problems. Note that the first problem does not have any Lagrange multiplier. For the second and third problems you may use the following notations:

- γ_α = the Lagrange multiplier of Equation (7.49), and
- γ_ϵ = the Lagrange multiplier of Equation (7.50).

(ii) State the first-order optimality conditions (the Karush-Kuhn-Tucker or KKT conditions) for each of the three problems. Express your answers in terms of $\boldsymbol{X}$, $\boldsymbol{\theta}$, $\boldsymbol{y}$, λ, α, ϵ, and the two Lagrange multipliers γ_α, γ_ϵ.

(iii) Fix $\lambda > 0$. We can solve Equation (7.48) to obtain $\widehat{\boldsymbol{\theta}}_\lambda$. Find α and the Lagrange multiplier γ_α in Equation (7.49) such that $\widehat{\boldsymbol{\theta}}_\lambda$ would satisfy the KKT conditions of Equation (7.49).

(iv) Fix $\lambda > 0$. We can solve Equation (7.48) to obtain $\widehat{\boldsymbol{\theta}}_\lambda$. Find ϵ and the Lagrange multiplier γ_ϵ in Equation (7.50) such that $\widehat{\boldsymbol{\theta}}_\lambda$ would satisfy the KKT conditions of Equation (7.50).

(v) Fix $\lambda > 0$. By using the α and γ_α you found in (iii), you can show that $\widehat{\boldsymbol{\theta}}_\lambda$ would satisfy the KKT conditions of Equation (7.49). Is it enough to claim that $\widehat{\boldsymbol{\theta}}_\lambda$ is the solution of Equation (7.49)? If yes, why? If no, what else do we need to show? Please elaborate through a proof, if needed.

Exercise 9.
Consider a training dataset $\mathcal{D}_{\text{train}} = \{(\boldsymbol{x}_1, y_1), \ldots, (\boldsymbol{x}_N, y_N)\}$ and a weight $\boldsymbol{w} = [w_1, \ldots, w_N]^T$. Find the regression solution to the following problem and discuss how you would choose the weight.

$$\widehat{\boldsymbol{\theta}} = \underset{\boldsymbol{\theta} \in \mathbb{R}^d}{\operatorname{argmin}} \ \sum_{n=1}^N w_n \left(y_n - \boldsymbol{x}_n^T \boldsymbol{\theta}\right)^2. \tag{7.51}$$

Exercise 10.

Consider a training dataset $\mathcal{D}_{\text{train}} = \{(\boldsymbol{x}_1, y_1), \ldots, (\boldsymbol{x}_N, y_N)\}$. Suppose that the input data $\boldsymbol{x}_n$ is corrupted by i.i.d. Gaussian noise $\boldsymbol{e}_n \sim \text{Gaussian}(0, \sigma^2 \boldsymbol{I}_d)$ so that the training set becomes $\mathcal{D}_{\text{train}} = \{(\boldsymbol{x}_1 + \boldsymbol{e}_1, y_1), \ldots, (\boldsymbol{x}_N + \boldsymbol{e}_N, y_N)\}$. Show that the (vanilla) least squares linear regression by taking the expectation over $\boldsymbol{e}_n$,

$$\widehat{\boldsymbol{\theta}} = \underset{\boldsymbol{\theta} \in \mathbb{R}^d}{\text{argmin}} \sum_{n=1}^{N} \mathbb{E}_{\boldsymbol{e}_n} \left[\left(y_n - (\boldsymbol{x}_n + \boldsymbol{e}_n)^T \boldsymbol{\theta} \right)^2 \right], \tag{7.52}$$

is equivalent to a ridge regression.

Chapter 8

Estimation

In this chapter, we discuss another set of important combat skills in data science, namely **estimation**. Estimation has a close relationship with regression. Regression primarily takes the optimization route, while estimation takes the probabilistic route. As we will see, at a certain point the two will merge. That is, under some specific statistical conditions, estimation processes will coincide with the regression.

Estimation is summarized pictorially in **Figure 8.1**. Imagine that we have some random samples $X_1, \ldots, X_N$. These samples are drawn from a distribution $f_X(x; \boldsymbol{\theta})$, where $\boldsymbol{\theta}$ is a parameter that characterizes the distribution. The parameter $\boldsymbol{\theta}$ is not known to us. The goal of estimation is to solve an inverse problem to recover the parameter based on the observations $X_1, \ldots, X_N$.

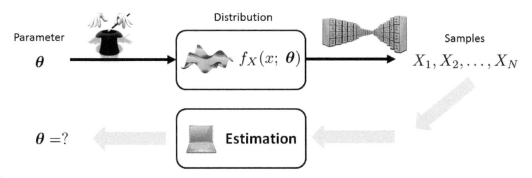

Figure 8.1: Estimation is an inverse problem of recovering the unknown parameters that were used by the distribution. In this figure, the PDF of X using a parameter $\boldsymbol{\theta}$ is denoted as $f_X(x; \boldsymbol{\theta})$. The forward data-generation process takes the parameter $\boldsymbol{\theta}$ and creates the random samples $X_1, \ldots, X_N$. Estimation takes these observed random samples and recovers the underlying model parameter $\boldsymbol{\theta}$.

> **What is estimation?**
>
> Estimation is an inverse problem with the goal of recovering the underlying parameter $\boldsymbol{\theta}$ of a distribution $f_X(x; \boldsymbol{\theta})$ based on the observed samples $X_1, \ldots, X_N$.

What are parameters?

Before we discuss the methods of estimation, let us clarify the meaning of the **parameter θ**. All probability density functions (PDFs) have parameters. For example, a Bernoulli random variable is characterized by a parameter p that defines the probability of getting a "head". A Gaussian random variable is characterized by two parameters: the mean μ and variance σ^2.

Example 8.1. (Parameter of a Bernoulli) If X_n is a Bernoulli random variable, then the PMF has a parameter θ:

$$p_{X_n}(x_n\,;\,\theta) = \theta^{x_n}(1-\theta)^{1-x_n}.$$

Remark. The PMF is expressed in this form because x_n is either 1 or 0:

$$p_{X_n}(x_n\,;\,\theta) = \begin{cases} \theta^1(1-\theta)^{1-1} = \theta, & \text{if} \quad x_n = 1, \\ \theta^0(1-\theta)^{1-0} = 1-\theta, & \text{if} \quad x_n = 0. \end{cases}$$

Example 8.2. (Parameter of a Gaussian) If X_n is a Gaussian random variable, the PDF is

$$f_{X_n}(x_n\,;\, \underbrace{\boldsymbol{\theta}}_{=(\mu,\sigma)}) = \frac{1}{\sqrt{2\pi\sigma^2}}\exp\left\{-\frac{(x_n-\mu)^2}{2\sigma^2}\right\},$$

where $\boldsymbol{\theta} = [\mu, \sigma]$ consists of both the mean and the variance. We can also designate the parameter θ to be the mean only. For example, if we know that $\sigma = 1$, then the PDF is

$$f_{X_n}(x_n\,;\, \underbrace{\theta}_{=\mu}) = \frac{1}{\sqrt{2\pi}}\exp\left\{-\frac{(x_n-\mu)^2}{2}\right\},$$

where θ is the mean.

Since all probability density functions have parameters, estimating them from the observed random variables is a well-defined inverse problem. Of course, there are better estimates and there are worse estimates. Let us look at the following example to develop our intuitions about estimation.

Figure 8.2 shows a dataset containing 1000 data points generated from a 2D Gaussian distribution with an unknown mean vector $\boldsymbol{\mu}$ and an unknown covariance matrix $\boldsymbol{\Sigma}$. We duplicate this dataset in the four subfigures. The estimation problem is to recover the unknown mean vector $\boldsymbol{\mu}$ and the covariance matrix $\boldsymbol{\Sigma}$. In the subfigures we propose four candidates, each with a different mean vector and a different covariance matrix. We draw the contour lines of the corresponding Gaussians. It can be seen that some Gaussians fit the data better than others. The goal of this chapter is to develop a systematic way of finding the best fit for the data.

Plan for this chapter

The discussions in this chapter concern the three elementary distributions:

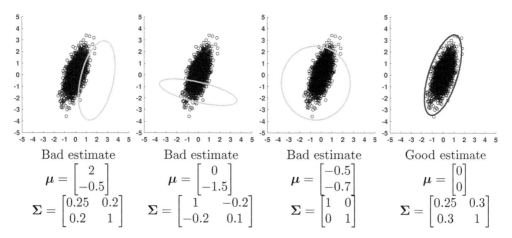

Figure 8.2: An estimation problem. Given a set of 1000 data points drawn from a Gaussian distribution with unknown mean $\boldsymbol{\mu}$ and covariance $\boldsymbol{\Sigma}$, we propose several candidate Gaussians and see which one would be the best fit to the data. Visually, we observe that the right-most Gaussian has the best fit. The goal of this chapter is to develop a systematic way of solving estimation problems of this type.

- Likelihood: $f_{\boldsymbol{X}|\boldsymbol{\Theta}}(\boldsymbol{x}|\boldsymbol{\theta})$, which is the conditional PDF of $\boldsymbol{X}$ given that the parameter is $\boldsymbol{\Theta}$.

- Prior: $f_{\boldsymbol{\Theta}}(\boldsymbol{\theta})$, which is the PDF of $\boldsymbol{\Theta}$.

- Posterior: $f_{\boldsymbol{\Theta}|\boldsymbol{X}}(\boldsymbol{\theta}|\boldsymbol{x})$, which is the conditional PDF of $\boldsymbol{\Theta}$ given the data $\boldsymbol{X}$.

Each of these density functions has its respective meaning, and consequently a set of different estimation techniques. In Section 8.1 we introduce the concept of **maximum-likelihood** (ML) estimation. As the name suggests, the estimate is constructed by maximizing the likelihood function. We will discuss a few examples of ML estimation and draw connections between ML estimation and regression. In Section 8.2 we will discuss several basic properties of an ML estimate. Specifically, we will introduce the ideas of unbiasedness, consistency, and the invariance principle.

The second topic discussed in this chapter is the **maximum-a-posteriori** (MAP) estimation, detailed in Section 8.3. In MAP, the parameter $\boldsymbol{\Theta}$ is a random variable. Since $\boldsymbol{\Theta}$ is a random variable, it has its own probability density function $f_{\boldsymbol{\Theta}}(\boldsymbol{\theta})$, which we call the **prior**. Given the likelihood and the prior, we can define the **posterior**. The MAP estimation finds the peak of the posterior distribution as a way to "explain" the data. Several important topics will be covered in Section 8.3. For example, we will discuss the choice of the prior via the concept of **conjugate prior**. We will also discuss how MAP is related to regularized regressions such as the ridge and LASSO regressions.

The third topic is the **minimum mean-square estimation** (MMSE), outlined in Section 8.4. The MMSE is a Bayesian approach. An important result that will be demonstrated is that the MMSE estimate is the conditional expectation of the posterior distribution. In other words, it is the mean of the posterior. An MMSE estimate has an important difference compared to a MAP estimate, namely that while an MMSE estimate is the mean of the posterior, a MAP estimate is the mode of the posterior. We discuss the formulation of the estimation problem and ways of solving the problem. We also discuss how the MMSE can be performed for multidimensional Gaussian distributions.

8.1 Maximum-Likelihood Estimation

Maximum-likelihood (ML) estimation, as the name suggests, is an estimation method that "maximizes" the "likelihood". Therefore, to understand the ML estimation, we first need to understand the meaning of likelihood, and why maximizing the likelihood would be useful.

8.1.1 Likelihood function

Consider a set of N data points $\mathcal{D} = \{x_1, x_2, \dots, x_N\}$. We want to describe these data points using a probability distribution. What would be the most general way of defining such a distribution?

Since we have N data points, and we do not know anything about them, the most general way to define a distribution is as a high-dimensional probability density function (PDF) $f_{\boldsymbol{X}}(\boldsymbol{x})$. This is a PDF of a random vector $\boldsymbol{X} = [X_1, \dots, X_N]^T$. A particular realization of this random vector is $\boldsymbol{x} = [x_1, \dots, x_N]^T$.

$f_{\boldsymbol{X}}(\boldsymbol{x})$ is the most general description for the N data points because $f_{\boldsymbol{X}}(\boldsymbol{x})$ is the **joint** PDF of all variables. It provides the complete statistical description of the vector $\boldsymbol{X}$. For example, we can compute the mean vector $\mathbb{E}[\boldsymbol{X}]$, the covariance matrix $\text{Cov}(\boldsymbol{X})$, the marginal distributions, the conditional distribution, the conditional expectations, etc. In short, if we know $f_{\boldsymbol{X}}(\boldsymbol{x})$, we know everything about $\boldsymbol{X}$.

The joint PDF $f_{\boldsymbol{X}}(\boldsymbol{x})$ is always **parameterized** by a certain parameter $\boldsymbol{\theta}$. For example, if we assume that $\boldsymbol{X}$ is drawn from a joint Gaussian distribution, then $f_{\boldsymbol{X}}(\boldsymbol{x})$ is parameterized by the mean vector $\boldsymbol{\mu}$ and the covariance matrix $\boldsymbol{\Sigma}$. So we say that the parameter $\boldsymbol{\theta}$ is $\boldsymbol{\theta} = (\boldsymbol{\mu}, \boldsymbol{\Sigma})$. To state the dependency on the parameter explicitly, we write

$$f_{\boldsymbol{X}}(\boldsymbol{x}; \boldsymbol{\theta}) = \text{PDF of the random vector } \boldsymbol{X} \text{ with a parameter } \boldsymbol{\theta}.$$

When you express the joint PDF as a function of $\boldsymbol{x}$ and $\boldsymbol{\theta}$, you have two variables to play with. The first variable is the **observation** $\boldsymbol{x}$, which is given by the measured data. We usually think about the probability density function $f_{\boldsymbol{X}}(\boldsymbol{x})$ in terms of $\boldsymbol{x}$, because the PDF is evaluated at $\boldsymbol{X} = \boldsymbol{x}$. In estimation, however, $\boldsymbol{x}$ is something that you cannot control. When your boss hands a dataset to you, $\boldsymbol{x}$ is already fixed. You can consider the probability of getting this particular $\boldsymbol{x}$, but you cannot change $\boldsymbol{x}$.

The second variable stated in $f_{\boldsymbol{X}}(\boldsymbol{x}; \boldsymbol{\theta})$ is the **parameter** $\boldsymbol{\theta}$. This parameter is what we want to find out, and it is the subject of interest in an estimation problem. Our goal is to find the optimal $\boldsymbol{\theta}$ that can offer the "best explanation" to data $\boldsymbol{x}$, in the sense that it can maximize $f_{\boldsymbol{X}}(\boldsymbol{x}; \boldsymbol{\theta})$.

The **likelihood function** is the PDF that shifts the emphasis to $\boldsymbol{\theta}$:

Definition 8.1. *Let $\boldsymbol{X} = [X_1, \dots, X_N]^T$ be a random vector drawn from a joint PDF $f_{\boldsymbol{X}}(\boldsymbol{x}; \boldsymbol{\theta})$, and let $\boldsymbol{x} = [x_1, \dots, x_N]^T$ be the realizations. The **likelihood function** is a function of the parameter $\boldsymbol{\theta}$ given the realizations $\boldsymbol{x}$:*

$$\mathcal{L}(\boldsymbol{\theta} \,|\, \boldsymbol{x}) \stackrel{\text{def}}{=} f_{\boldsymbol{X}}(\boldsymbol{x}; \boldsymbol{\theta}). \tag{8.1}$$

A word of caution: $\mathcal{L}(\boldsymbol{\theta} \,|\, \boldsymbol{x})$ is *not* a conditional PDF because $\boldsymbol{\theta}$ is not a random variable. The correct way to interpret $\mathcal{L}(\boldsymbol{\theta} \,|\, \boldsymbol{x})$ is to view it as a function of $\boldsymbol{\theta}$. This function changes its shape according the observed data $\boldsymbol{x}$. We will return to this point shortly.

Independent observations

While $f_{\boldsymbol{X}}(\boldsymbol{x})$ provides us with a complete picture of the $\boldsymbol{X}$, using $f_{\boldsymbol{X}}(\boldsymbol{x})$ is tedious. We need to describe how each X_n is generated and describe how X_n is related to X_m for all pairs of n and m. If the vector $\boldsymbol{X}$ contains N entries, then there are $N^2/2$ pairs of correlations we need to compute. When N is large, finding $f_{\boldsymbol{X}}(\boldsymbol{x})$ would be very difficult if not impossible.

In practice, $f_{\boldsymbol{X}}(\boldsymbol{x})$ may sometimes be overkill. For example, if we measure the inter-arrival time of a bus for several days, it is quite likely that the measurements will not be correlated. In this case, instead of using the full $f_{\boldsymbol{X}}(\boldsymbol{x})$, we can make assumptions about the data points. The assumption we will make is that all the data points are **independent** and that they are drawn from an **identical** distribution $f_X(x)$. The assumption that the data points are **independently and identically distributed** (i.i.d.) significantly simplifies the problem so that the joint PDF $f_{\boldsymbol{X}}$ can be written as a product of single PDFs f_{X_n}:

$$f_{\boldsymbol{X}}(\boldsymbol{x}) = f_{X_1,\ldots,X_N}(x_1,\ldots,x_N) = \prod_{n=1}^{N} f_{X_n}(x_n).$$

If you prefer a visualization, we can take a look at the covariance matrix, which goes from a full covariance matrix to a diagonal matrix and then to an identity matrix:

$$\begin{bmatrix} \mathrm{Var}[X_1] & \mathrm{Cov}(X_1,X_2) & \cdots & \mathrm{Cov}(X_1,X_N) \\ \mathrm{Cov}[X_2,X_1] & \mathrm{Var}[X_2] & \cdots & \mathrm{Cov}(X_2,X_N) \\ \vdots & \vdots & \ddots & \vdots \\ \mathrm{Cov}(X_N,X_1) & \mathrm{Cov}(X_N,X_2) & \cdots & \mathrm{Var}[X_N] \end{bmatrix} \underset{\text{independent}}{\Longrightarrow} \begin{bmatrix} \mathrm{Var}[X_1] & 0 & \cdots & 0 \\ 0 & \mathrm{Var}[X_2] & \cdots & 0 \\ \vdots & \vdots & \ddots & \vdots \\ 0 & 0 & \cdots & \mathrm{Var}[X_N] \end{bmatrix}$$

$$\underset{\text{identical}}{\Longrightarrow} \begin{bmatrix} \sigma^2 & 0 & \cdots & 0 \\ 0 & \sigma^2 & \cdots & 0 \\ \vdots & \vdots & \ddots & \vdots \\ 0 & 0 & \cdots & \sigma^2 \end{bmatrix}.$$

The assumption of i.i.d. is strong. Not all data can be modeled as i.i.d. (For example, photons passing through a scattering medium have correlated statistics.) However, if the i.i.d. assumption is valid, we can simplify the model significantly.

If the data points are i.i.d., then we can write the joint PDF as

$$f_{\boldsymbol{X}}(\boldsymbol{x};\,\boldsymbol{\theta}) = \prod_{n=1}^{N} f_{X_n}(x_n;\,\boldsymbol{\theta}).$$

This simplifies the likelihood function as a product of the individual PDFs.

Definition 8.2. *Given i.i.d. random variables $X_1,\ldots,X_N$ that all have the same PDF $f_{X_n}(x_n)$, the **likelihood function** is*

$$\mathcal{L}(\boldsymbol{\theta} \,|\, \boldsymbol{x}) \stackrel{\text{def}}{=} \prod_{n=1}^{N} f_{X_n}(x_n;\,\boldsymbol{\theta}). \tag{8.2}$$

In computation we often take the log of the likelihood function. We call the resulting function the **log-likelihood**.

Definition 8.3. *Given a set of i.i.d. random variables $X_1, \ldots, X_N$ with PDF $f_{X_n}(x;;\boldsymbol{\theta})$, the* **log-likelihood** *is defined as*

$$\log \mathcal{L}(\boldsymbol{\theta} \mid \boldsymbol{x}) = \log f_{\boldsymbol{X}}(\boldsymbol{x};\boldsymbol{\theta}) = \sum_{n=1}^{N} \log f_{X_n}(x_n;\boldsymbol{\theta}). \qquad (8.3)$$

Example 8.3. Find the log-likelihood of a sequence of i.i.d. Gaussian random variables $X_1, \ldots, X_N$ with mean μ and variance σ^2.

Solution. Since the random variables $X_1, \ldots, X_N$ are i.i.d. Gaussian, the PDF is

$$f_{\boldsymbol{X}}(\boldsymbol{x};\mu,\sigma^2) = \prod_{n=1}^{N} \left\{ \frac{1}{\sqrt{2\pi\sigma^2}} e^{-\frac{(x_n-\mu)^2}{2\sigma^2}} \right\}. \qquad (8.4)$$

Taking the log on both sides yields the log-likelihood function:

$$\log \mathcal{L}(\mu,\sigma^2 \mid \boldsymbol{x}) = \log f_{\boldsymbol{X}}(\boldsymbol{x};\mu,\sigma^2)$$

$$= \log \left\{ \prod_{n=1}^{N} \left\{ \frac{1}{\sqrt{2\pi\sigma^2}} e^{-\frac{(x_n-\mu)^2}{2\sigma^2}} \right\} \right\}$$

$$= \sum_{n=1}^{N} \log \left\{ \frac{1}{\sqrt{2\pi\sigma^2}} e^{-\frac{(x_n-\mu)^2}{2\sigma^2}} \right\}$$

$$= \sum_{n=1}^{N} \left\{ -\frac{1}{2}\log(2\pi\sigma^2) - \frac{(x_n-\mu)^2}{2\sigma^2} \right\}$$

$$= -\frac{N}{2}\log(2\pi\sigma^2) - \frac{1}{2\sigma^2}\sum_{n=1}^{N}(x_n-\mu)^2.$$

Practice Exercise 8.1. Find the log-likelihood of a sequence of i.i.d. Bernoulli random variables $X_1, \ldots, X_N$ with parameter θ.

Solution. If $X_1, \ldots, X_N$ are i.i.d. Bernoulli random variables, we have

$$f_{\boldsymbol{X}}(\boldsymbol{x};\theta) = \prod_{n=1}^{N} \left\{ \theta^{x_n}(1-\theta)^{1-x_n} \right\}.$$

Taking the log on both sides of the equation yields the log-likelihood function:

$$\log \mathcal{L}(\theta \mid \boldsymbol{x}) = \log \left\{ \prod_{n=1}^{N} \left\{ \theta^{x_n}(1-\theta)^{1-x_n} \right\} \right\}.$$

Hence,

$$
\log \mathcal{L}(\theta \mid \boldsymbol{x}) = \sum_{n=1}^{N} \log \left\{ \theta^{x_n} (1 - \theta)^{1-x_n} \right\}
$$

$$
= \sum_{n=1}^{N} x_n \log \theta + (1 - x_n) \log(1 - \theta)
$$

$$
= \left(\sum_{n=1}^{N} x_n \right) \cdot \log \theta + \left(N - \sum_{n=1}^{N} x_n \right) \cdot \log(1 - \theta).
$$

Visualizing the likelihood function

The likelihood function $\mathcal{L}(\boldsymbol{\theta} \mid \boldsymbol{x})$ is a function of $\boldsymbol{\theta}$, but its value also depends on the underlying measurements $\boldsymbol{x}$. It is extremely important to keep in mind the presence of both.

To help you visualize the effect of $\boldsymbol{\theta}$ and $\boldsymbol{x}$, we consider a set of i.i.d. Bernoulli random variables. As we have just shown in the practice exercise, the likelihood function of these i.i.d. random variables is

$$
\log \mathcal{L}(\theta \mid \boldsymbol{x}) = \underbrace{\left(\sum_{n=1}^{N} x_n \right)}_{S} \cdot \log \theta + \underbrace{\left(N - \sum_{n=1}^{N} x_n \right)}_{N-S} \cdot \log(1 - \theta), \tag{8.5}
$$

where we define $S = \sum_{n=1}^{N} x_n$ as the sum of the (binary) measurements.

To make the dependency on S and θ explicit, we write $\mathcal{L}(\theta \mid \boldsymbol{x})$ as

$$
\log \mathcal{L}(\theta \mid S) = S \log \theta + (N - S) \log(1 - \theta), \tag{8.6}
$$

which emphasizes the role of S in defining the log-likelihood function. We plot the surface of $L(\theta \mid S)$ as a function of S and θ, assuming that $N = 50$. As shown on the left-hand side of **Figure 8.3**, the surface $L(\theta|S)$ has a saddle shape. Along one direction the function goes up, whereas along another direction the function goes down. In the middle of **Figure 8.3**, we show a bird's-eye view of the surface, with the color-coding matched with the surface plot. As you can see, when plotted as a function of θ and $\boldsymbol{x}$ (in our case, we use a summary statistic $S = \sum_{n=1}^{N} x_n$), the two-dimensional plot tells us how the log-likelihood function changes when S changes. On the right-hand side of **Figure 8.3**, we show two particular cross sections of the two-dimensional plot. One cross section is taken from $S = 25$ and the other cross section is taken from $S = 12$. Since the total number of heads in this numerical experiment is assumed to be $N = 50$, the first cross section at $S = 25$ is obtained when half of the Bernoulli measurements are "1", whereas the second cross section at $S = 12$ is obtained when a quarter of the Bernoulli measurements are "1".

The cross sections tell us the log-likelihood function $\log \mathcal{L}(\theta|S)$ is a function defined specifically **for a given measurement** $\boldsymbol{x}$. As you can see from **Figure 8.3**, the log-likelihood function changes when S changes. Therefore, if our goal is to "find a θ that maximizes the log-likelihood function", then for a different $\boldsymbol{x}$ we will have a different answer. For example, according to **Figure 8.3**, the maximum for $\log \mathcal{L}(\theta|S = 25)$ occurs when $\theta \approx 0.5$, and the maximum for $\log \mathcal{L}(\theta|S = 12)$ occurs when $\theta \approx 0.24$. These are the **maximum-likelihood estimates** for the respective measurements.

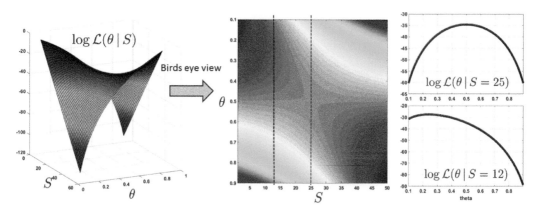

Figure 8.3: We plot the log-likelihood function as a function of $S = \sum_{n=1}^{N} x_n$ and θ. [Left] We show the surface plot of $\mathcal{L}(\theta|S) = S \log \theta + (N - S) \log(1 - \theta)$. Note that the surface has a saddle shape. [Middle] By taking a bird's-eye view of the surface plot, we obtain a 2-dimensional contour plot of the surface, where the color code matches the height of the log-likelihood function. [Right] We take two cross sections along $S = 25$ and $S = 12$. Observe how the shape changes.

We use the following MATLAB code to generate the surface plot:

```
% MATLAB code to generate the surface plot
N = 50;
S = 1:N;
theta = linspace(0.1,0.9,100);
[S_grid, theta_grid] = meshgrid(S, theta);
L = S_grid.*log(theta_grid) + (N-S_grid).*log(1-theta_grid);
s = surf(S,theta,L);
s.LineStyle   = '-';
colormap jet
view(65,15)
```

For the bird's-eye view plot, we replace `surf` with `imagesc(S,theta,L)`. For the cross section plots, we call the commands `plot(theta, L(:,12))` and `plot(theta, L(:,25))`.

8.1.2 Maximum-likelihood estimate

The likelihood is the PDF of $\boldsymbol{X}$ but viewed as a function of $\boldsymbol{\theta}$. The optimization problem of maximizing $\mathcal{L}(\boldsymbol{\theta} \,|\, \boldsymbol{x})$ is called the maximum-likelihood (ML) estimation:

> **Definition 8.4.** Let $\mathcal{L}(\boldsymbol{\theta})$ be the likelihood function of the parameter $\boldsymbol{\theta}$ given the measurements $\boldsymbol{x} = [x_1, \ldots, x_N]^T$. The **maximum-likelihood** estimate of the parameter $\boldsymbol{\theta}$ is a parameter that maximizes the likelihood:
>
> $$\widehat{\boldsymbol{\theta}}_{ML} \overset{\text{def}}{=} \underset{\boldsymbol{\theta}}{argmax} \ \mathcal{L}(\boldsymbol{\theta} \,|\, \boldsymbol{x}). \tag{8.7}$$

Example 8.4. Find the ML estimate for a set of i.i.d. Bernoulli random variables $\{X_1, \ldots, X_N\}$ with $X_n \sim \text{Bernoulli}(\theta)$ for $n = 1, \ldots, N$.

Solution. We know that the log-likelihood function of a set of i.i.d. Bernoulli random variables is given by

$$\log \mathcal{L}(\theta \,|\, \boldsymbol{x}) = \left(\sum_{n=1}^{N} x_n\right) \cdot \log \theta + \left(N - \sum_{n=1}^{N} x_n\right) \cdot \log(1 - \theta). \qquad (8.8)$$

Thus, to find the ML estimate, we need to solve the optimization problem

$$\widehat{\theta}_{\text{ML}} = \underset{\theta}{\operatorname{argmax}} \; \left\{ \left(\sum_{n=1}^{N} x_n\right) \cdot \log \theta + \left(N - \sum_{n=1}^{N} x_n\right) \cdot \log(1 - \theta) \right\}.$$

Taking the derivative with respect to θ and setting it to zero, we obtain

$$\frac{d}{d\theta} \left\{ \left(\sum_{n=1}^{N} x_n\right) \cdot \log \theta + \left(N - \sum_{n=1}^{N} x_n\right) \cdot \log(1 - \theta) \right\} = 0.$$

This gives us

$$\frac{\left(\sum_{n=1}^{N} x_n\right)}{\theta} - \frac{N - \sum_{n=1}^{N} x_n}{1 - \theta} = 0.$$

Rearranging the terms yields

$$\widehat{\theta}_{\text{ML}} = \frac{1}{N} \sum_{n=1}^{N} x_n.$$

Let's do a sanity check to see if this result makes sense. The solution to this problem says that $\widehat{\theta}_{\text{ML}}$ is the empirical average of the measurements. Assume that $N = 50$. Let us consider two particular scenarios as illustrated in **Figure 8.4**.

- **Scenario 1**: $\boldsymbol{x}$ is a vector of measurements such that $S \overset{\text{def}}{=} \sum_{n=1}^{N} x_n = 25$. Since $N = 50$, the formula tells us that $\widehat{\theta}_{\text{ML}} = \frac{25}{50} = 0.5$. This is the *best* guess based on the 50 measurements where 25 are heads. If you look at **Figure 8.3** and **Figure 8.4**, when $S = 25$, we are looking at a particular cross section in the 2D plot. The likelihood function we are inspecting is $\mathcal{L}(\theta|S = 25)$. For this likelihood function, the maximum occurs at $\theta = 0.5$.

- **Scenario 2**: $\boldsymbol{x}$ is a vector of measurements such that $S \overset{\text{def}}{=} \sum_{n=1}^{N} x_n = 12$. The formula tells us that $\widehat{\theta}_{\text{ML}} = \frac{12}{50} = 0.24$. This is again the *best* guess based on the 50 measurements where 12 are heads. Referring to **Figure 8.3** and **Figure 8.4**, we can see that the likelihood function corresponds to another cross section $\mathcal{L}(\theta|S = 12)$ where the maximum occurs at $\theta = 0.24$.

At this point, you may wonder why the shape of the likelihood function $\mathcal{L}(\theta \,|\, \boldsymbol{x})$ changes so radically as $\boldsymbol{x}$ changes? The answer can be found in **Figure 8.5**. Imagine that we have $N = 50$ measurements of which $S = 40$ give us heads. If these i.i.d. Bernoulli random

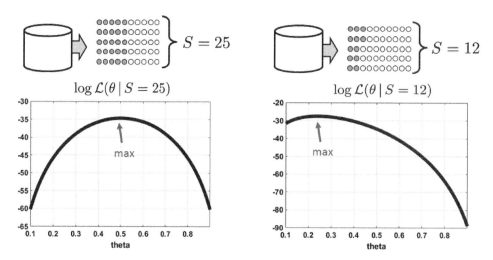

Figure 8.4: Illustration of how the maximum-likelihood estimate of a set of i.i.d. Bernoulli random variables is determined. The subfigures above show two particular scenarios at $S = 25$ and $S = 12$, assuming that $N = 50$. When $S = 25$, the likelihood function has a quadratic shape centered at $\theta = 0.5$. This point is also the peak of the likelihood function when $S = 25$. Therefore, the ML estimate is $\hat{\theta}_{\text{ML}} = 0.5$. The second case is when $S = 12$. The quadratic likelihood is shifted toward the left. The ML estimate is $\hat{\theta}_{\text{ML}} = 0.24$.

variables have a parameter $\theta = 0.5$, it is quite unlikely that we will get 40 out of 50 measurements to be heads. (If it were $\theta = 0.5$, we should get more or less 25 out of 50 heads.) When $S = 40$, and without any additional information about the experiment, the most logical guess is that the Bernoulli random variables have a parameter $\theta = 0.8$. Since the measurement S can be as extreme as 0 out of 50 or 50 out of 50, the likelihood function $\mathcal{L}(\theta \,|\, \boldsymbol{x})$ has to reflect these extreme cases. Therefore, as we change $\boldsymbol{x}$, we observe a big change in the shape of the likelihood function.

As you can see from **Figure 8.5**, $S = 40$ corresponds to the marked vertical cross section. As we determine the maximum-likelihood estimate, we search among all the possibilities, such as $\theta = 0.2$, $\theta = 0.5$, $\theta = 0.8$, etc. These possibilities correspond to the horizontal lines we drew in the figure. Among those horizontal lines, it is clear that the best estimate occurs when $\theta = 0.8$, which is also the ML estimate.

Visualizing ML estimation as N grows

Maximum-likelihood estimation can also be understood directly from the PDF instead of the likelihood function. To explain this perspective, let's do a quick exercise.

Practice Exercise 8.2. Suppose that X_n is a Gaussian random variable. Assume that $\sigma = 1$ is known but the mean θ is unknown. Find the ML estimate of the mean.

Solution. The ML estimate $\hat{\theta}_{\text{ML}}$ is

$$\hat{\theta}_{\text{ML}} = \underset{\theta}{\operatorname{argmax}} \ \log \mathcal{L}(\theta \,|\, \boldsymbol{x}).$$

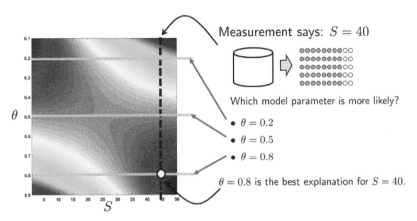

Figure 8.5: Suppose that we have a set of measurements such that $S = 40$. To determine the ML estimate, we look at the vertical cross section at $S = 40$. Among the different candidate parameters, e.g., $\theta = 0.2$, $\theta = 0.5$ and $\theta = 0.8$, we pick the one that has the maximum response to the likelihood function. For $S = 40$, it is more likely that the underlying parameter is $\theta = 0.8$ than $\theta = 0.2$ or $\theta = 0.5$.

With some calculation, we can show that

$$\widehat{\theta}_{\mathrm{ML}} = \underset{\theta}{\operatorname{argmax}} \ \log \left\{ \prod_{n=1}^{N} \frac{1}{\sqrt{2\pi}} \exp\left\{ -\frac{(x_n - \theta)^2}{2} \right\} \right\}$$

$$= \underset{\theta}{\operatorname{argmax}} \ -\frac{N}{2}\log(2\pi) - \frac{1}{2}\sum_{n=1}^{N}(x_n - \theta)^2.$$

Taking the derivative with respect to θ, we obtain

$$\frac{d}{d\theta}\left\{ -\frac{N}{2}\log(2\pi) - \frac{1}{2}\sum_{n=1}^{N}(x_n - \theta)^2 \right\} = 0.$$

This gives us $\sum_{n=1}^{N}(x_n - \theta) = 0$. Therefore, the ML estimate is

$$\widehat{\theta}_{\mathrm{ML}} = \frac{1}{N}\sum_{n=1}^{N} x_n.$$

Now we will draw the PDF and compare it with the measured data points. Our focus is to analyze how the ML estimate changes as N grows.

When $N = 1$. There is only one observation x_1. The best Gaussian that fits this sample must be the one that is centered at x_1. In fact, the optimization is[1]

$$\widehat{\theta}_{\mathrm{ML}} = \underset{\theta}{\operatorname{argmax}} \ \log \left\{ \frac{1}{\sqrt{2\pi\sigma^2}} \exp\left\{ -\frac{(x_1 - \theta)^2}{2\sigma^2} \right\} \right\} = \underset{\theta}{\operatorname{argmax}} \ -(x_1 - \theta)^2 = x_1.$$

---

[1]We skip the step of checking whether the stationary point is a maximum or a minimum, which can be done by evaluating the second-order derivative. In fact, since the function $-(x_1 - \theta)^2$ is concave in θ, a stationary point must be a maximum.

Therefore, the ML estimate is $\widehat{\theta}_{\mathrm{ML}} = x_1$. **Figure 8.6** illustrates this case. As we conduct the ML estimation, we imagine that there are a few candidate PDFs. The ML estimation says that among all these candidate PDFs we need to find one that can maximize the probability of obtaining the observation x_1. Since we only have one observation, we have no choice but to pick a Gaussian centered at x_1. Certainly the sample $X_1 = x_1$ could be bad, and we may find a wrong Gaussian. However, with only one sample there is no way for us to make better decisions.

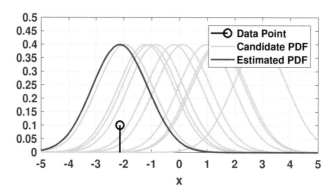

Figure 8.6: $N = 1$. Suppose that we are given one observed data point located around $x = -2.1$. To conduct the ML estimation we propose a few candidate PDFs, each being a Gaussian with unit variance but a different mean θ. The ML estimate is a parameter θ such that the corresponding PDF matches the best with the observed data. In this example the best match happens when the estimated Gaussian PDF is centered at x_1.

When $N = 2$. In this case we need to find a Gaussian that fits both x_1 and x_2. The probability of simultaneously observing x_1 and x_2 is determined by the joint distribution. By independence we then have

$$\widehat{\theta}_{\mathrm{ML}} = \underset{\theta}{\mathrm{argmax}} \ \log\left\{ \left(\frac{1}{\sqrt{2\pi\sigma^2}}\right)^2 \exp\left\{ -\frac{(x_1 - \theta)^2 + (x_2 - \theta)^2)}{2\sigma^2}\right\}\right\}$$

$$= \underset{\theta}{\mathrm{argmax}} \left\{ -\frac{(x_1 - \theta)^2 + (x_2 - \theta)^2}{2\sigma^2}\right\} = \frac{x_1 + x_2}{2},$$

where the last step is obtained by taking the derivative:

$$\frac{d}{d\theta}\left\{(x_1 - \theta)^2 + (x_2 - \theta)^2\right\} = 2(x_1 - \theta) + 2(x_2 - \theta).$$

Equating this with zero yields the solution $\theta = \frac{x_1 + x_2}{2}$. Therefore, the best Gaussian that fits the observations is Gaussian$(\frac{x_1 + x_2}{2}, \sigma^2)$.

Does this result make sense? When you have two data points x_1 and x_2, the ML estimation is trying to find a Gaussian that can best fit both of these two data points. Your best bet here is $\widehat{\theta}_{\mathrm{ML}} = (x_1 + x_2)/2$, because there are no other choices. If you choose $\widehat{\theta}_{\mathrm{ML}} = x_1$ or $\widehat{\theta}_{\mathrm{ML}} = x_2$, it cannot be a good estimate because you are not using both data points. As shown in **Figure 8.7**, for these two observed data points x_1 and x_2, the PDF marked in red (which is a Gaussian centered at $(x_1 + x_2)/2$) is indeed the best fit.

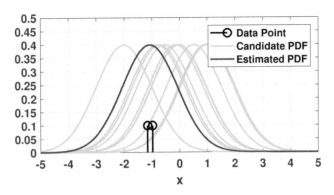

Figure 8.7: $N = 2$. Suppose that we are given two observed data points located around $x_1 = -0.98$ and $x_2 = -1.15$. To conduct the ML estimation we propose a few candidate PDFs, each being a Gaussian with unit variance but a different mean θ. The ML estimate is a parameter θ such that the corresponding PDF best matches the observed data. In this example the best match happens when the estimated Gaussian PDF is centered at $(x_1 + x_2)/2 \approx -1.07$.

When $N = 10$ and $N = 100$. We can continue the above calculation for $N = 10$ and $N = 100$. In this case the MLE is

$$\widehat{\theta}_{\mathrm{ML}} = \underset{\theta}{\operatorname{argmax}} \; \log \left\{ \left(\frac{1}{\sqrt{2\pi\sigma^2}} \right)^N \exp \left\{ -\frac{(x_1 - \theta)^2 + \cdots + (x_N - \theta)^2}{2\sigma^2} \right\} \right\}$$

$$= \underset{\theta}{\operatorname{argmax}} \; -\sum_{n=1}^{N} \frac{(x_n - \theta)^2}{2\sigma^2} = \frac{1}{N} \sum_{n=1}^{N} x_n.$$

where the optimization is solved by taking the derivative:

$$\frac{d}{d\theta} \sum_{n=1}^{N} (x_n - \theta)^2 = -2 \sum_{n=1}^{N} (x_n - \theta)$$

Equating this with zero yields the solution $\theta = \frac{1}{N} \sum_{n=1}^{N} x_n$.

The result suggests that for an arbitrary number of training samples the ML estimate is the sample average. These cases are illustrated in **Figure 8.8**. As you can see, the red curves (the estimated PDF) are always trying to fit as many data points as possible.

The above experiment tells us something about the ML estimation:

How does ML estimation work, intuitively?

- The likelihood function $\mathcal{L}(\theta|\boldsymbol{x})$ measures how "likely" it is that we will get $\boldsymbol{x}$ if the underlying parameter is θ.

- In the case of a Gaussian with an unknown mean, you move around the Gaussian until you find a good fit.

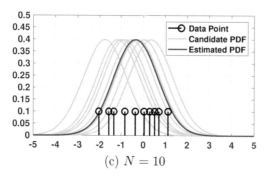
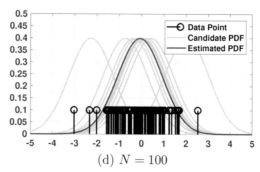

(c) $N = 10$ (d) $N = 100$

Figure 8.8: When $N = 10$ and $N = 100$, the ML estimation continues to evaluate the different candidate PDFs. For a given set of data points, the ML estimation picks the best PDF to fit the data points. In this Gaussian example it was shown that the optimal parameter is $\widehat{\theta}_{\mathsf{ML}} = (1/N) \sum_{n=1}^{N} x_n$, which is the sample average.

8.1.3   Application 1: Social network analysis

ML estimation has extremely broad applicability. In this subsection and the next we discuss two real examples. We start with an example in social network analysis.

In Chapter 3, when we discussed the Bernoulli random variables, we introduced the Erdős-Rényi graph — one of the simplest models for social networks. The Erdős-Rényi graph is a single-membership network that assumes that all users belong to the same cluster. Thus the connectivity between users is specified by a single parameter, which is also the probability of the Bernoulli random variable.

In our discussions in Chapter 3 we defined an adjacency matrix to represent a graph. The adjacency matrix is a binary matrix, with the (i, j)th entry indicating an edge connecting nodes i and j. Since the presence and absence of an edge is binary and random, we may model each element of the adjacency matrix as a Bernoulli random variable

$$X_{ij} \sim \text{Bernoulli}(p).$$

In other words, the edge X_{ij} linking user i and user j in the network is either $X_{ij} = 1$ with probability p, or $X_{ij} = 0$ with probability $1 - p$. In terms of notation, we define the matrix $\boldsymbol{X} \in \mathbb{R}^{N \times N}$ as the adjacency matrix, with the (i, j)th element being X_{ij}.

A few examples of a single-membership Erdős-Rényi graph are shown in **Figure 8.9**. As the figure shows, the network connectivity increases as the Bernoulli parameter p increases. This happens because p defines the "density" of the edges. If p is large, we have a greater chance of getting $X_{ij} = 1$, and so there is a higher probability that an edge is present between node i and node j. If p is small, the probability is lower.

Suppose that we are given *one* snapshot of the network, i.e., one realization $\boldsymbol{x} \in R^{N \times N}$ of the adjacency matrix $\boldsymbol{X} \in \mathbb{R}^{N \times N}$. The problem of recovering the latent parameter p can be formulated as an ML estimation.

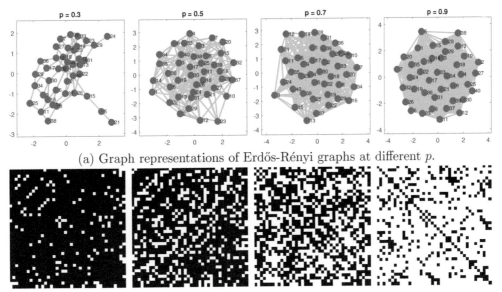

(a) Graph representations of Erdős-Rényi graphs at different p.

(b) Adjacent matrices of the corresponding graphs.

Figure 8.9: A single-membership Erdős-Rényi graph is a graph structure in which the edge between node i and node j is defined as a Bernoulli random variable with parameter p. As p increases, the graph has a higher probability of having more edges. The adjacent matrices shown in the bottom row are the mathematical representations of the graphs.

Example 8.5. Write down the log-likelihood function of the single-membership Erdős-Rényi graph ML estimation problem.

Solution. Based on the definition of the graph model, we know that

$$X_{ij} \sim \text{Bernoulli}(p).$$

Therefore, the probability mass function of X_{ij} is

$$\mathbb{P}[X_{ij} = 1] = p \quad \text{and} \quad \mathbb{P}[X_{ij} = 0] = 1 - p.$$

This can be compactly expressed as

$$f_{\mathbf{X}}(\mathbf{x}; p) = \prod_{i=1}^{N} \prod_{j=1}^{N} p^{x_{ij}} (1-p)^{1-x_{ij}}.$$

Hence, the log-likelihood is

$$\log \mathcal{L}(p \mid \mathbf{x}) = \sum_{i=1}^{N} \sum_{j=1}^{N} \left\{ x_{ij} \log p + (1 - x_{ij}) \log(1-p) \right\}.$$

Now that we have the log-likelihood function, we can proceed to estimate the parameter p. The solution to this is the ML estimate.

Practice Exercise 8.3. Solve the ML estimation problem:

$$\widehat{p}_{\mathrm{ML}} = \underset{p}{\operatorname{argmax}}\ \log \mathcal{L}(p \,|\, \boldsymbol{x}).$$

Solution. Using the log-likelihood we just derived, we have that

$$\widehat{p}_{\mathrm{ML}} = \sum_{i=1}^{N}\sum_{j=1}^{N} \left\{ x_{ij} \log p + (1 - x_{ij}) \log(1 - p) \right\}.$$

Taking the derivative and setting it to zero,

$$\frac{d}{dp} \log \mathcal{L}(p \,|\, \boldsymbol{x}) = \frac{d}{dp} \left\{ \sum_{i=1}^{N}\sum_{j=1}^{N} \left\{ x_{ij} \log p + (1 - x_{ij}) \log(1 - p) \right\} \right\}$$

$$= \sum_{i=1}^{N}\sum_{j=1}^{N} \left\{ \frac{x_{ij}}{p} - \frac{1 - x_{ij}}{1 - p} \right\} = 0.$$

Let $S = \sum_{i=1}^{N}\sum_{j=1}^{N} x_{ij}$. The equation above then becomes

$$\frac{S}{p} - \frac{N^2 - S}{1 - p} = 0.$$

Rearranging the terms yields $(1 - p)S = p(N^2 - S)$, which gives us

$$\widehat{p}_{\mathrm{ML}} = \frac{S}{N^2} = \frac{1}{N^2} \sum_{i=1}^{N}\sum_{j=1}^{N} x_{ij}. \tag{8.9}$$

On computers, visualizing the graphs and computing the ML estimates are reasonably straightforward. In MATLAB, you can call the command `graph` to build a graph from the adjacency matrix A. This will allow you to plot the graph. The computation, however, is done directly by the adjacency matrix. In the code below, you can see that we call `rand` to generate the Bernoulli random variables. The command `triu` extracts the upper triangular matrix from the matrix A. This ensures that we do not pick the diagonals. The symmetrization of A+A' ensures that the graph is indirectional, meaning that i to j is the same as j to i.

```
% MATLAB code to visualize a graph
n = 40;                # Number of nodes
p = 0.3                # probability
A = rand(n,n)<p;
A = triu(A,1);
A = A+A';              # Adj matrix
G = graph(A);          # Graph
plot(G);               # Drawing
p_ML = mean(A(:));     # ML estimate
```

In Python, the computation is done similarly with the help of the `networkx` library. The number of edges `m` is defined as $m = p\frac{n^2}{2}$. This is because for a graph with n nodes, there are at most $\frac{n^2}{2}$ unique pairs of indirected edges. Multiplying this number by the probability p will give us the number of edges m.

```
# Python code to visualize a graph
import networkx as nx
import numpy as np
n = 40                          # Number of nodes
p = 0.3                         # probability
m = np.round(((n ** 2)/2)*p)    # Number of edges
G = nx.gnm_random_graph(n,m)    # Graph
A = nx.adjacency_matrix(G)      # Adj matrix
nx.draw(G)                      # Drawing
p_ML = np.mean(A)               # ML estimate
```

As you can see in both the MATLAB and the Python code, the ML estimate $\widehat{p}_{\mathrm{ML}}$ is determined by taking the sample average. Thus the ML estimate, according to our calculation, is $\widehat{p}_{\mathrm{ML}} = \frac{1}{N^2} \sum_{i=1}^{N} \sum_{j=1}^{N} x_{ij}$.

8.1.4 Application 2: Reconstructing images

Being able to see in the dark is the holy grail of imaging. Many advanced sensing technologies have been developed over the past decade. In this example, we consider a single-photon image sensor. This is a counting device that counts the number of photons arriving at the sensor. Physicists have shown that a Poisson process can model the arrival of the photons. For simplicity we assume a homogeneous pattern of N pixels. The underlying intensity of the homogeneous pattern is a constant λ.

Suppose that we have a sensor with N pixels $X_1, \ldots, X_N$. According to the Poisson statistics, the probability of observing a pixel value is determined by the Poisson probability:

$$X_n \sim \mathrm{Poisson}(\lambda), \quad n = 1, \ldots, N,$$

or more explicitly,

$$\mathbb{P}[X_n = x_n] = \frac{\lambda^{x_n}}{x_n!} e^{-\lambda},$$

where x_n is the nth observed pixel value, and is an integer.

A single-photon image sensor is slightly more complicated in the sense that it does not report X_n but instead reports a truncated version of X_n. Depending on the number of incoming photons, the sensor reports

$$Y_n = \begin{cases} 1, & X_n \geq 1, \\ 0, & X_n = 0. \end{cases} \tag{8.10}$$

We call this type of sensors a **one-bit** single-photon image sensor (see **Figure 8.10**). Our question is: If we are given the measurements $X_1, \ldots, X_N$, can we estimate the underlying parameter λ?

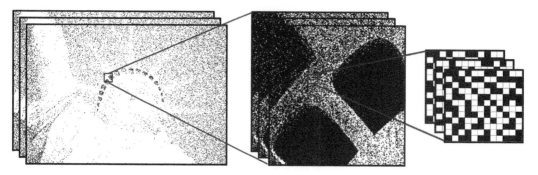

Figure 8.10: A one-bit single-photon image sensor captures an image with binary bits: It reports a "1" when the number of photons exceeds certain threshold, and "0" otherwise. The recovery problem here is to estimate the underlying image from the measurements.

Example 8.6. Derive the log-likelihood function of the estimation problem for the single-photon image sensors.

Solution. Since Y_n is a binary random variable, its probability is completely specified by the two states it takes:

$$\mathbb{P}[Y_n = 0] = \mathbb{P}[X_n = 0] = e^{-\lambda}$$
$$\mathbb{P}[Y_n = 1] = \mathbb{P}[X_n \neq 0] = 1 - e^{-\lambda}.$$

Thus, Y_n is a Bernoulli random variable with probability $1 - e^{-\lambda}$ of getting a value of 1, and probability $e^{-\lambda}$ of getting a value of 0. By defining y_n as a binary number taking values of either 0 or 1, it follows that the log-likelihood is

$$\log \mathcal{L}(\lambda \mid \boldsymbol{y}) = \log \left\{ \prod_{n=1}^{N} \left(1 - e^{-\lambda}\right)^{y_n} \left(e^{-\lambda}\right)^{1-y_n} \right\}$$
$$= \sum_{n=1}^{N} \left\{ y_n \log(1 - e^{-\lambda}) - \lambda(1 - y_n) \right\}.$$

Practice Exercise 8.4. Solve the ML estimation problem

$$\widehat{\lambda}_{\mathrm{ML}} = \operatorname*{argmax}_{\lambda} \ \log \mathcal{L}(\lambda \mid \boldsymbol{y}). \tag{8.11}$$

Solution. First, we define $S = \sum_{n=1}^{N} y_n$. This simplifies the log-likelihood function to

$$\log \mathcal{L}(\lambda \mid \boldsymbol{y}) = \sum_{n=1}^{N} \left\{ y_n \log(1 - e^{-\lambda}) - \lambda(1 - y_n) \right\}$$
$$= S \log(1 - e^{-\lambda}) - \lambda(N - S).$$

The ML estimation is

$$\widehat{\lambda}_{\mathrm{ML}} = \underset{\lambda}{\mathrm{argmax}} \ \ S\log(1 - e^{-\lambda}) - \lambda(N - S).$$

Taking the derivative w.r.t. λ yields

$$\frac{d}{d\lambda}\left\{S\log(1 - e^{-\lambda}) - \lambda(N - S)\right\} = \frac{S}{1 - e^{-\lambda}}e^{-\lambda} - (N - S).$$

Moving around the terms, it follows that

$$\frac{S}{1 - e^{-\lambda}}e^{-\lambda} - (N - S) = 0 \quad \Longrightarrow \quad \lambda = -\log\left(1 - \frac{S}{N}\right).$$

Therefore, the ML estimate is

$$\widehat{\lambda}_{\mathrm{ML}} = -\log\left(1 - \frac{1}{N}\sum_{n=1}^{N} y_n\right). \tag{8.12}$$

For real images, you can extrapolate the idea from y_n to $y_{i,j,t}$, which denotes the (i,j)th pixel located at time t. Defining $\boldsymbol{y}_t \in \mathbb{R}^{N \times N}$ as the tth frame of the observed data, we can use T frames to recover one image $\widehat{\boldsymbol{\lambda}}_{\mathrm{ML}} \in \mathbb{R}^{N \times N}$. It follows from the above derivation that the ML estimate is

$$\widehat{\boldsymbol{\lambda}}_{\mathrm{ML}} = -\log\left(1 - \frac{1}{T}\sum_{t=1}^{T} \boldsymbol{y}_t\right). \tag{8.13}$$

Figure 8.11 shows a pair of input-output images of a 256×256 image.

(a) Observed data (1-frame)   (b) ML estimate (using 100 frames)

Figure 8.11: ML estimation for a single-photon image sensor problem. The observed data consists of 100 frames of binary measurements $\boldsymbol{y}_1, \ldots, \boldsymbol{y}_T$, where $T = 100$. The ML estimate is constructed by $\boldsymbol{\lambda} = -\log(1 - \frac{1}{T}\sum_{t=1}^{T} \boldsymbol{y}_t)$.

On a computer the ML estimation can be done in a few lines of MATLAB code. The code in Python requires more work, as it needs to read images using the openCV library.

```matlab
% MATLAB code to recover an image from binary measurements
lambda = im2double(imread('cameraman.tif'));
T = 100;                                % 100 frames
x = poissrnd( repmat(lambda, [1,1,T]) );  % generate Poisson r.v.
y = (x>=1);                             % binary truncation
lambdahat = -log(1-mean(y,3));          % ML estimation
figure(1); imshow(x(:,:,1));
figure(2); imshow(lambdahat);
```

```python
# Python code to recover an image from binary measurements
import cv2
import numpy as np
import scipy.stats as stats
import matplotlib.pyplot as plt
lambd = cv2.imread('./cameraman.tif')                 # read image
lambd = cv2.cvtColor(lambd, cv2.COLOR_BGR2GRAY)/255   # gray scale
T = 100
lambdT = np.repeat(lambd[:, :, np.newaxis], T, axis=2)  # repeat image
x = stats.poisson.rvs(lambdT)                         # Poisson statistics
y = (x>=1).astype(float)                              # binary truncation
lambdhat = -np.log(1-np.mean(y,axis=2))               # ML estimation
plt.imshow(lambdhat,cmap='gray')
```

8.1.5 More examples of ML estimation

By now you should be familiar with the procedure for solving the ML estimation problem. We summarize the two steps as follows.

How to solve an ML estimation problem

- Write down the likelihood $\mathcal{L}(\boldsymbol{\theta} \,|\, \boldsymbol{x})$.

- Maximize the likelihood by solving $\widehat{\boldsymbol{\theta}}_{\mathrm{ML}} = \underset{\boldsymbol{\theta}}{\operatorname{argmax}}\ \log \mathcal{L}(\boldsymbol{\theta} \,|\, \boldsymbol{x})$.

Practice Exercise 8.5 (Gaussian). Suppose that we are given a set of i.i.d. Gaussian random variables $X_1, \ldots, X_N$, where both the mean μ and the variance σ^2 are unknown. Let $\boldsymbol{\theta} = [\mu, \sigma^2]^T$ be the parameter. Find the ML estimate of $\boldsymbol{\theta}$.

Solution. We first write down the likelihood. The likelihood of these i.i.d. Gaussian random variables is

$$\mathcal{L}(\boldsymbol{\theta}|\boldsymbol{x}) = \left(\frac{1}{\sqrt{2\pi\sigma^2}}\right)^N \exp\left\{-\frac{1}{2\sigma^2}\sum_{n=1}^{N}(x_n - \mu)^2\right\}.$$

To solve the ML estimation problem, we maximize the log-likelihood:

$$\widehat{\boldsymbol{\theta}}_{\mathrm{ML}} \stackrel{\text{def}}{=} \operatorname*{argmax}_{\boldsymbol{\theta}} \ \mathcal{L}(\boldsymbol{\theta} \,|\, \boldsymbol{x})$$

$$= \operatorname*{argmax}_{\mu,\sigma^2} \ \left\{ -\frac{N}{2}\log(2\pi\sigma^2) - \frac{1}{2\sigma^2}\sum_{n=1}^{N}(x_n-\mu)^2 \right\}.$$

Since we have two parameters, we need to take the derivatives for both.

$$\frac{d}{d\mu}\left\{ -\frac{N}{2}\log(2\pi\sigma^2) - \frac{1}{2\sigma^2}\sum_{n=1}^{N}(x_n-\mu)^2 \right\} = 0,$$

$$\frac{d}{d\sigma^2}\left\{ -\frac{N}{2}\log(2\pi\sigma^2) - \frac{1}{2\sigma^2}\sum_{n=1}^{N}(x_n-\mu)^2 \right\} = 0.$$

(Note that the derivative of the second equation is taken w.r.t. to σ^2 and not σ.) This pair of equations gives us

$$\frac{1}{\sigma^2}\sum_{n=1}^{N}(x_n-\mu) = 0, \text{ and } -\frac{N}{2}\cdot\frac{1}{2\pi\sigma^2}\cdot(2\pi) + \frac{1}{2\sigma^4}\sum_{n=1}^{N}(x_n-\mu)^2 = 0.$$

Rearranging the equations, we find that

$$\widehat{\mu}_{\mathrm{ML}} = \frac{1}{N}\sum_{n=1}^{N}x_n \quad \text{and} \quad \widehat{\sigma}^2_{\mathrm{ML}} = \frac{1}{N}\sum_{n=1}^{N}(x_n-\widehat{\mu}_{\mathrm{ML}})^2. \tag{8.14}$$

Practice Exercise 8.6. (Poisson) Given a set of i.i.d. Poisson random variables $X_1,\ldots,X_N$ with an unknown parameter λ, find the ML estimate of λ.

Solution. For a Poisson random variable, the likelihood function is

$$\mathcal{L}(\lambda \,|\, \boldsymbol{x}) = \prod_{n=1}^{N}\left\{ \frac{\lambda^{x_n}}{x_n!}e^{-\lambda} \right\}. \tag{8.15}$$

To solve the ML estimation problem, we note that

$$\widehat{\lambda}_{\mathrm{ML}} = \operatorname*{argmax}_{\lambda} \ \mathcal{L}(\lambda \,|\, \boldsymbol{x}) = \operatorname*{argmax}_{\lambda} \ \log\left\{ \prod_{n=1}^{N}\frac{\lambda^{x_n}}{x_n!}e^{-\lambda} \right\}$$

$$= \operatorname*{argmax}_{\lambda} \ \log\left\{ \frac{\lambda^{\sum_n x_n}}{\prod_n x_n!}e^{-N\lambda} \right\}.$$

Since $\prod_n x_n!$ is independent of λ, its presence or absence will not affect the optimization problem. Consequently we can drop the term. It follows that

$$\widehat{\lambda}_{\mathrm{ML}} = \underset{\lambda}{\mathrm{argmax}} \; \log\left\{\lambda^{\sum_n x_n} e^{-N\lambda}\right\}$$

$$= \underset{\lambda}{\mathrm{argmax}} \; \left(\sum_n x_n\right)\log\lambda - N\lambda.$$

Taking the derivative and setting it to zero yields

$$\frac{d}{d\lambda}\left\{\left(\sum_n x_n\right)\log\lambda - N\lambda\right\} = \frac{\sum_n x_n}{\lambda} - N = 0.$$

Rearranging the terms yields

$$\widehat{\lambda}_{\mathrm{ML}} = \frac{1}{N}\sum_{n=1}^{N} x_n. \tag{8.16}$$

The idea of ML estimation can also be extended to vector observations.

Example 8.7. (**High-dimensional Gaussian**) Suppose that we are given a set of i.i.d. d-dimensional Gaussian random vectors $\boldsymbol{X}_1,\ldots,\boldsymbol{X}_N$ such that

$$\boldsymbol{X}_n \sim \mathrm{Gaussian}(\boldsymbol{\mu},\boldsymbol{\Sigma}).$$

We assume that $\boldsymbol{\Sigma}$ is fixed and known, but $\boldsymbol{\mu}$ is unknown. Find the ML estimate of $\boldsymbol{\mu}$.
Solution. The likelihood function is

$$\mathcal{L}(\boldsymbol{\mu}\,|\,\{\boldsymbol{x}_n\}_{n=1}^N) = \prod_{n=1}^{N} f_{\boldsymbol{X}_n}(\boldsymbol{x}_n;\,\boldsymbol{\mu})$$

$$= \prod_{n=1}^{N}\left\{\frac{1}{\sqrt{(2\pi)^d|\boldsymbol{\Sigma}|}}\exp\left\{-\frac{1}{2}(\boldsymbol{x}_n-\boldsymbol{\mu})^T\boldsymbol{\Sigma}^{-1}(\boldsymbol{x}_n-\boldsymbol{\mu})\right\}\right\}$$

$$= \left(\frac{1}{\sqrt{(2\pi)^d|\boldsymbol{\Sigma}|}}\right)^N \exp\left\{-\frac{1}{2}\sum_{n=1}^{N}(\boldsymbol{x}_n-\boldsymbol{\mu})^T\boldsymbol{\Sigma}^{-1}(\boldsymbol{x}_n-\boldsymbol{\mu})\right\}.$$

Thus the log-likelihood function is

$$\log\mathcal{L}(\boldsymbol{\mu}\,|\,\{\boldsymbol{x}_n\}_{n=1}^N) = \frac{N}{2}\log|\boldsymbol{\Sigma}| + \frac{N}{2}\log(2\pi)^d + \sum_{n=1}^{N}\left\{\frac{1}{2}(\boldsymbol{x}_n-\boldsymbol{\mu})^T\boldsymbol{\Sigma}^{-1}(\boldsymbol{x}_n-\boldsymbol{\mu})\right\}.$$

The ML estimate is found by maximizing this log-likelihood function:

$$\widehat{\boldsymbol{\mu}}_{\mathrm{ML}} = \underset{\boldsymbol{\mu}}{\mathrm{argmax}} \; \log\mathcal{L}(\boldsymbol{\mu}\,|\,\{\boldsymbol{x}_n\}_{n=1}^N).$$

Taking the gradient of the function and setting it to zero, we have that

$$\frac{d}{d\boldsymbol{\mu}}\left\{\frac{N}{2}\log|\boldsymbol{\Sigma}| + \frac{N}{2}\log(2\pi)^d + \sum_{n=1}^{N}\left\{\frac{1}{2}(\boldsymbol{x}_n - \boldsymbol{\mu})^T\boldsymbol{\Sigma}^{-1}(\boldsymbol{x}_n - \boldsymbol{\mu})\right\}\right\} = 0.$$

The derivatives of the first two terms are zero because they do not depend on $\boldsymbol{\mu}$). Thus we have that:

$$\sum_{n=1}^{N}\left\{\boldsymbol{\Sigma}^{-1}(\boldsymbol{x}_n - \boldsymbol{\mu})\right\} = 0.$$

Rearranging the terms yields the ML estimate

$$\widehat{\boldsymbol{\mu}}_{\mathrm{ML}} = \frac{1}{N}\sum_{n=1}^{N}\boldsymbol{x}_n.$$

Example 8.8. (High-dimensional Gaussian) Assume the same problem setting as in Example 8.7, except that this time we assume that both the mean vector $\boldsymbol{\mu}$ and the covariance matrix $\boldsymbol{\Sigma}$ are unknown. Find the ML estimate for $\boldsymbol{\theta} = (\boldsymbol{\mu}, \boldsymbol{\Sigma})$.

Solution. The log-likelihood follows from Example 8.7:

$$\log \mathcal{L}(\boldsymbol{\mu} \mid \{\boldsymbol{x}_n\}_{n=1}^{N}) = \frac{N}{2}\log|\boldsymbol{\Sigma}| + \frac{N}{2}\log(2\pi)^d$$
$$+ \sum_{n=1}^{N}\left\{\frac{1}{2}(\boldsymbol{x}_n - \boldsymbol{\mu})^T\boldsymbol{\Sigma}^{-1}(\boldsymbol{x}_n - \boldsymbol{\mu})\right\}.$$

Finding the ML estimate requires taking the derivative with respect to both $\boldsymbol{\mu}$ and $\boldsymbol{\Sigma}$:

$$\frac{d}{d\boldsymbol{\mu}}\left\{\frac{N}{2}\log|\boldsymbol{\Sigma}| + \frac{N}{2}\log(2\pi)^d + \sum_{n=1}^{N}\left\{\frac{1}{2}(\boldsymbol{x}_n - \boldsymbol{\mu})^T\boldsymbol{\Sigma}^{-1}(\boldsymbol{x}_n - \boldsymbol{\mu})\right\}\right\} = 0,$$

$$\frac{d}{d\boldsymbol{\Sigma}}\left\{\frac{N}{2}\log|\boldsymbol{\Sigma}| + \frac{N}{2}\log(2\pi)^d + \sum_{n=1}^{N}\left\{\frac{1}{2}(\boldsymbol{x}_n - \boldsymbol{\mu})^T\boldsymbol{\Sigma}^{-1}(\boldsymbol{x}_n - \boldsymbol{\mu})\right\}\right\} = 0.$$

After some tedious algebraic steps (see Duda et al., *Pattern Classification*, Problem 3.14), we have that

$$\widehat{\boldsymbol{\mu}}_{\mathrm{ML}} = \frac{1}{N}\sum_{n=1}^{N}\boldsymbol{x}_n, \tag{8.17}$$

$$\widehat{\boldsymbol{\Sigma}}_{\mathrm{ML}} = \frac{1}{N}\sum_{n=1}^{N}(\boldsymbol{x}_n - \widehat{\boldsymbol{\mu}}_{\mathrm{ML}})(\boldsymbol{x}_n - \widehat{\boldsymbol{\mu}}_{\mathrm{ML}})^T. \tag{8.18}$$

8.1.6 Regression versus ML estimation

ML estimation is closely related to regression. To understand the connection, we consider a linear model that we studied in Chapter 7. This model describes the relationship between the inputs $x_1, \ldots, x_N$ and the observed outputs $y_1, \ldots, y_N$, via the equation

$$y_n = \sum_{p=0}^{d-1} \theta_p \phi_p(x_n) + e_n, \qquad n = 1, \ldots, N. \tag{8.19}$$

In this expression, $\phi_p(\cdot)$ is a transformation that extracts the "features" of the input vector x to produce a scalar. The coefficient θ_p defines the relative weight of the feature $\phi_p(x_n)$ in constructing the observed variable y_n. The error e_n defines the modeling error between the observation y_n and the prediction $\sum_{p=0}^{d-1} \theta_p \phi_p(x_n)$. We call this equation a linear model.

Expressed in matrix form, the linear model is

$$\underbrace{\begin{bmatrix} y_1 \\ y_2 \\ \vdots \\ y_N \end{bmatrix}}_{=y} = \underbrace{\begin{bmatrix} \phi_0(x_1) & \phi_1(x_1) & \cdots & \phi_{d-1}(x_1) \\ \phi_0(x_2) & \phi_1(x_2) & \cdots & \phi_{d-1}(x_2) \\ \vdots & & \cdots & \vdots \\ \phi_0(x_N) & \phi_1(x_N) & \cdots & \phi_{d-1}(x_N) \end{bmatrix}}_{=X} \underbrace{\begin{bmatrix} \theta_0 \\ \theta_1 \\ \vdots \\ \theta_{d-1} \end{bmatrix}}_{=\theta} + \underbrace{\begin{bmatrix} e_1 \\ e_2 \\ \vdots \\ e_N \end{bmatrix}}_{=e},$$

or more compactly as $y = X\theta + e$. Rearranging the terms, it is easy to show that

$$\sum_{n=1}^{N} e_n^2 = \sum_{n=1}^{N} \left(y_n - \sum_{p=0}^{d-1} \theta_p \phi_p(x_n) \right)^2$$

$$= \sum_{n=1}^{N} (y_n - [X\theta]_n)^2 = \|y - X\theta\|^2.$$

Now we make an *assumption*: that each noise e_n is an i.i.d. copy of a Gaussian random variable with zero mean and variance σ^2. In other words, the error vector e is distributed according to $e \sim \text{Gaussian}(0, \sigma^2 I)$. This assumption is not always true because there are many situations in which the error is not Gaussian. However, this assumption is necessary for us to make the connection between ML estimation and regression.

With this assumption, we ask, given the observations $y_1, \ldots, y_N$, what would be the ML estimate of the unknown parameter θ? We answer this question in two steps.

Example 8.9. Find the likelihood function of θ, given $y = [y_1, \ldots, y_N]^T$.

Solution. The PDF of y is given by a Gaussian:

$$f_Y(y; \theta) = \prod_{n=1}^{N} \left\{ \frac{1}{\sqrt{2\pi\sigma^2}} \exp\left\{ -\frac{(y_n - [X\theta]_n)^2}{2\sigma^2} \right\} \right\}$$

$$= \frac{1}{\sqrt{(2\pi\sigma^2)^N}} \exp\left\{ -\frac{1}{2\sigma^2} \sum_{n=1}^{N} (y_n - [X\theta]_n)^2 \right\}$$

$$= \frac{1}{\sqrt{(2\pi\sigma^2)^N}} \exp\left\{ -\frac{1}{2\sigma^2} \|y - X\theta\|^2 \right\}. \tag{8.20}$$

Therefore, the log-likelihood function is

$$
\log \mathcal{L}(\boldsymbol{\theta} \mid \boldsymbol{y}) = \log \left\{ \frac{1}{\sqrt{(2\pi\sigma^2)^N}} \exp\left\{ -\frac{1}{2\sigma^2} \|\boldsymbol{y} - \boldsymbol{X}\boldsymbol{\theta}\|^2 \right\} \right\}
$$
$$
= -\frac{N}{2} \log(2\pi\sigma^2) - \frac{1}{2\sigma^2} \|\boldsymbol{y} - \boldsymbol{X}\boldsymbol{\theta}\|^2.
$$

The next step is to solve the ML estimation by maximizing the log-likelihood.

Example 8.10. Solve the ML estimation problem stated in Example 8.9. Assume that $\boldsymbol{X}^T \boldsymbol{X}$ is invertible.

Solution.

$$
\widehat{\boldsymbol{\theta}}_{\mathrm{ML}} = \underset{\boldsymbol{\theta}}{\operatorname{argmax}} \ \log \mathcal{L}(\boldsymbol{\theta} \mid \boldsymbol{y})
$$
$$
= \underset{\boldsymbol{\theta}}{\operatorname{argmax}} \ \left\{ -\frac{N}{2} \log(2\pi\sigma^2) - \frac{1}{2\sigma^2} \|\boldsymbol{y} - \boldsymbol{X}\boldsymbol{\theta}\|^2 \right\}.
$$

Taking the derivative w.r.t. $\boldsymbol{\theta}$ yields

$$
\frac{d}{d\boldsymbol{\theta}} \left\{ -\frac{N}{2} \log(2\pi\sigma^2) - \frac{1}{2\sigma^2} \|\boldsymbol{y} - \boldsymbol{X}\boldsymbol{\theta}\|^2 \right\} = 0.
$$

Since $\frac{d}{d\boldsymbol{\theta}} \boldsymbol{\theta}^T \boldsymbol{A} \boldsymbol{\theta} = \boldsymbol{A} + \boldsymbol{A}^T$, it follows from the chain rule that

$$
\frac{d}{d\boldsymbol{\theta}} \left\{ -\frac{1}{2\sigma^2} \|\boldsymbol{y} - \boldsymbol{X}\boldsymbol{\theta}\|^2 \right\} = \frac{d}{d\boldsymbol{\theta}} \left\{ -\frac{1}{2\sigma^2} (\boldsymbol{y} - \boldsymbol{X}\boldsymbol{\theta})^T (\boldsymbol{y} - \boldsymbol{X}\boldsymbol{\theta}) \right\}
$$
$$
= \frac{1}{\sigma^2} \boldsymbol{X}^T (\boldsymbol{X}\boldsymbol{\theta} - \boldsymbol{y}).
$$

Substituting this result into the equation,

$$
\frac{1}{\sigma^2} \boldsymbol{X}^T (\boldsymbol{X}\boldsymbol{\theta} - \boldsymbol{y}) = 0.
$$

Rearranging terms we obtain $\boldsymbol{X}^T \boldsymbol{X} \boldsymbol{\theta} = \boldsymbol{X}^T \boldsymbol{y}$, of which the solution is

$$
\widehat{\boldsymbol{\theta}}_{\mathrm{ML}} = (\boldsymbol{X}^T \boldsymbol{X})^{-1} \boldsymbol{X}^T \boldsymbol{y}. \tag{8.21}
$$

Since the ML estimate in Equation (8.21) is the same as the regression solution (see Chapter 7), we conclude that the regression problem of a linear model is equivalent to solving an ML estimation problem.

The main difference between a linear regression problem and an ML estimation problem is the underlying statistical model, as illustrated in **Figure 8.12**. In linear regression, you do not care about the statistics of the noise term e_n. We choose $(\cdot)^2$ as the error because it is differentiable and convenient. In ML estimation, we choose $(\cdot)^2$ as the error because the noise is Gaussian. If the noise is not Gaussian, e.g., the noise follows a Laplace distribution, we need to choose $|\cdot|$ as the error. Therefore, you can always get a result by solving the linear regression. However, this result will only become meaningful if you provide additional

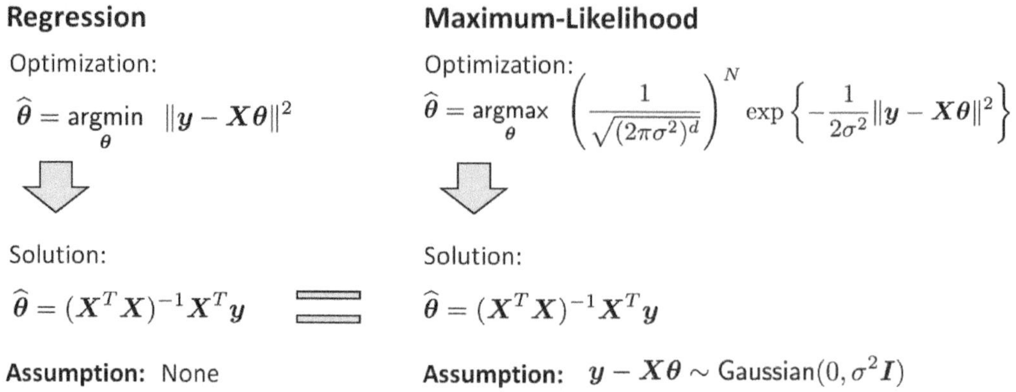

Regression

Optimization:

$$\widehat{\theta} = \underset{\theta}{\text{argmin}} \ \|y - X\theta\|^2$$

Solution:

$$\widehat{\theta} = (X^T X)^{-1} X^T y$$

Assumption: None

Maximum-Likelihood

Optimization:

$$\widehat{\theta} = \underset{\theta}{\text{argmax}} \ \left(\frac{1}{\sqrt{(2\pi\sigma^2)^d}}\right)^N \exp\left\{-\frac{1}{2\sigma^2}\|y - X\theta\|^2\right\}$$

Solution:

$$\widehat{\theta} = (X^T X)^{-1} X^T y$$

Assumption: $y - X\theta \sim \text{Gaussian}(0, \sigma^2 I)$

Figure 8.12: ML estimation is equivalent to a linear regression when the underlying statistical model for ML estimation is a Gaussian. Specifically, if the error term $e = y - X\theta$ is an independent Gaussian vector with zero mean and covariance matrix $\sigma^2 I$, then the resulting ML estimation is the same as linear regression. If the underlying statistical model is not Gaussian, then solving the regression is equivalent to applying a Gaussian ML estimation to a non-Gaussian problem. This will still give us a result, but that result will not maximize the likelihood, and thus it will not have any statistical guarantee.

information about the problem. For example, if you know that the noise is Gaussian, then the regression solution is also the ML solution. This is a statistical guarantee.

In practice, of course, we do not know whether the noise is Gaussian or not. At this point we have two courses of action: (i) Use your prior knowledge/domain expertise to determine whether a Gaussian assumption makes sense, or (ii) select an alternative model and see if the alternative model fits the data better. In practice, we should also question whether maximizing the likelihood is what we want. We may have some knowledge and therefore prefer the parameter θ, e.g., we want a sparse solution so that θ only contains a few non-zeros. In that case, maximizing the likelihood without any constraint may not be the solution we want.

ML estimation versus regression

- ML estimation requires a statistical assumption, whereas regression does not.
- Suppose that you use a linear model $y_n = \sum_{p=0}^{d-1} \theta_p \phi_p(x_n) + e_n$ where $e_n \sim$ Gaussian$(0, \sigma^2)$, for $n = 1, \ldots, N$.
- Then the likelihood function in the ML estimation is

$$\mathcal{L}(\theta \,|\, y) = \frac{1}{\sqrt{(2\pi\sigma^2)^N}} \exp\left\{-\frac{1}{2\sigma^2}\|y - X\theta\|^2\right\},$$

- The ML estimate $\widehat{\theta}_{\text{ML}}$ is $\widehat{\theta}_{\text{ML}} = (X^T X)^{-1} X^T y$, which is exactly the same as the regression solution. If the above statistical assumptions do not hold, then the regression solution will not maximize the likelihood.

8.2   Properties of ML Estimates

ML estimation is a very special type of estimation. Not all estimations are ML. If an estimate is ML, are there any theoretical properties we can analyze? For example, will ML estimates guarantee the recovery of the true parameter? If so, when will this happen? In this section we investigate these theoretical questions so that you will acquire a better understanding of the statistical nature of ML estimates.[2]

8.2.1   Estimators

We know that an ML estimate is defined as

$$\widehat{\theta}_{\mathrm{ML}}(\boldsymbol{x}) = \operatorname*{argmax}_{\theta}\ \mathcal{L}(\theta \,|\, \boldsymbol{x}). \tag{8.22}$$

We write $\widehat{\theta}_{\mathrm{ML}}(\boldsymbol{x})$ to emphasize that $\widehat{\theta}_{\mathrm{ML}}$ is a function of $\boldsymbol{x}$. The dependency of $\widehat{\theta}_{\mathrm{ML}}(\boldsymbol{x})$ on $\boldsymbol{x}$ should not be a surprise. For example, if the ML estimate is the sample average, we have that

$$\widehat{\theta}_{\mathrm{ML}}(x_1,\ldots,x_N) = \frac{1}{N}\sum_{n=1}^{N} x_n,$$

where $\boldsymbol{x} = [x_1,\ldots,x_N]^T$.

However, in this setting we should always remember that $x_1,\ldots,x_N$ are realizations of the i.i.d. random variables $X_1,\ldots,X_N$. Therefore, if we want to analzye the randomness of the variables, it is more reasonable to write $\widehat{\theta}_{\mathrm{ML}}$ as a random variable $\widehat{\Theta}_{\mathrm{ML}}$. For example, in the case of sample average, we have that

$$\widehat{\Theta}_{\mathrm{ML}}(X_1,\ldots,X_N) = \frac{1}{N}\sum_{n=1}^{N} X_n. \tag{8.23}$$

We call $\widehat{\Theta}_{\mathrm{ML}}$ the ML **estimator** of the true parameter θ.

Estimate versus estimator

- An **estimate** is a **number**, e.g., $\widehat{\theta}_{\mathrm{ML}} = \dfrac{1}{N}\sum_{n=1}^{N} x_n$. It is the random realization of a random variable.

- An **estimator** is a **random variable**, e.g., $\widehat{\Theta}_{\mathrm{ML}} = \dfrac{1}{N}\sum_{n=1}^{N} X_n$. It takes a set of random variables and generates another random variable.

---

[2]For notational simplicity, in this section we will focus on a scalar parameter θ instead of a vector parameter $\boldsymbol{\theta}$.

The ML estimators are one type of estimator, namely those that maximize the likelihood functions. If we do not want to maximize the likelihood we can still define an estimator. An estimator is any function that takes the data points $X_1, \ldots, X_N$ and maps them to a number (or a vector of numbers). That is, an estimator is

$$\widehat{\Theta}(X_1, \ldots, X_N).$$

We call $\widehat{\Theta}$ the **estimator** of the true parameter θ.

Example 8.11. Let $X_1, \ldots, X_N$ be Gaussian i.i.d. random variables with unknown mean θ and known variance σ^2. Construct two possible estimators.

Solution. We define two estimators:

$$\widehat{\Theta}_1(X_1, \ldots, X_N) = \frac{1}{N} \sum_{n=1}^{N} X_n,$$

$$\widehat{\Theta}_2(X_1, \ldots, X_N) = X_1,$$

In the first case, the estimator takes all the samples and constructs the sample average. The second estimator takes all the samples and returns on the first element. Both are legitimate estimators. However, $\widehat{\Theta}_1$ is the ML estimator, whereas $\widehat{\Theta}_2$ is not.

8.2.2 Unbiased estimators

While you can define estimators in any way you like, certain estimators are good and others are bad. By "good" we mean that the estimator can provide you with the information about the true parameter θ; otherwise, why would you even construct such an estimator? However, the difficulty here is that $\widehat{\Theta}$ is a **random variable** because it is constructed from $X_1, \ldots, X_N$. Therefore, we need to define different metrics to quantify the usefulness of the estimators.

Definition 8.5. *An estimator $\widehat{\Theta}$ is* **unbiased** *if*

$$\mathbb{E}[\widehat{\Theta}] = \theta. \tag{8.24}$$

Unbiasedness means that the **average** of the random variable $\widehat{\Theta}$ matches the true parameter θ. In other words, while we allow $\widehat{\Theta}$ to fluctuate, we expect the average to match the true θ. If this is not the case, using more measurements will not help us get closer to θ.

Example 8.12. Let $X_1, \ldots, X_N$ be i.i.d. Gaussian random variables with a unknown mean θ. It has been shown that the ML estimator is

$$\widehat{\Theta}_{\text{ML}} = \frac{1}{N} \sum_{n=1}^{N} X_n. \tag{8.25}$$

Is the ML estimator $\widehat{\Theta}_{\text{ML}}$ unbiased?

Solution: To check the unbiasedness, we look at the expectation:

$$\mathbb{E}[\widehat{\Theta}_{\mathrm{ML}}] = \frac{1}{N}\sum_{n=1}^{N}\mathbb{E}[X_n] = \frac{1}{N}\sum_{n=1}^{N}\theta = \theta.$$

Thus, $\widehat{\Theta}_{\mathrm{ML}} = \frac{1}{N}\sum_{n=1}^{N}X_n$ is an unbiased estimator of θ.

Example 8.13. Same as the example before, but this time we consider an estimator

$$\widehat{\Theta} = X_1 + X_2 + 5. \tag{8.26}$$

Is this estimator unbiased?

Solution: In this case,

$$\mathbb{E}[\widehat{\Theta}] = \mathbb{E}[X_1 + X_2 + 5] = \mathbb{E}[X_1] + \mathbb{E}[X_2] + 5 = 2\theta + 5 \neq \theta.$$

Therefore, the estimator is biased.

Example 8.14. Let $X_1, \ldots, X_N$ be i.i.d. Gaussian random variables with unknown mean μ and unknown variance σ^2. We have shown that the ML estimators are

$$\widehat{\mu}_{\mathrm{ML}} = \frac{1}{N}\sum_{n=1}^{N}X_n \quad \text{and} \quad \widehat{\sigma}_{\mathrm{ML}}^2 = \frac{1}{N}\sum_{n=1}^{N}(X_n - \widehat{\mu}_{\mathrm{ML}})^2.$$

It is easy to show that $\mathbb{E}[\widehat{\mu}_{\mathrm{ML}}] = \mu$. How about $\widehat{\sigma}_{\mathrm{ML}}^2$? Is it an unbiased estimator?

Solution: For simplicity we assume $\mu = 0$ so that $\mathbb{E}[X_n^2] = \mathbb{E}[(X_n - 0)^2] = \sigma^2$.
Note that

$$\mathbb{E}[\widehat{\sigma}_{\mathrm{ML}}^2] = \frac{1}{N}\sum_{n=1}^{N}\left\{\mathbb{E}[X_n^2] - 2\mathbb{E}[\widehat{\mu}_{\mathrm{ML}}X_n] + \mathbb{E}[\widehat{\mu}_{\mathrm{ML}}^2]\right\}$$

$$= \frac{1}{N}\sum_{n=1}^{N}\left\{\sigma^2 - 2\mathbb{E}\left[\frac{1}{N}\sum_{j=1}^{N}X_jX_n\right] + \mathbb{E}\left[\left(\frac{1}{N}\sum_{n=1}^{N}X_n\right)^2\right]\right\}.$$

By independence, we observe that $\mathbb{E}[X_jX_n] = \mathbb{E}[X_j]\mathbb{E}[X_n] = 0$, for any $j \neq n$. Therefore,

$$\mathbb{E}\left[\frac{1}{N}\sum_{j=1}^{N}X_jX_n\right] = \frac{1}{N}\mathbb{E}\left[X_1X_n + \cdots + X_NX_n\right]$$

$$= \frac{1}{N}(0 + \cdots + \sigma^2 + \cdots + 0) = \frac{\sigma^2}{N}.$$

Similarly, we have that

$$\mathbb{E}\left[\left(\frac{1}{N}\sum_{n=1}^{N}X_n\right)^2\right] = \frac{1}{N^2}\sum_{n=1}^{N}\left\{\mathbb{E}[X_n^2] + \sum_{j\neq n}\mathbb{E}[X_jX_n]\right\}$$

$$= \frac{1}{N^2}\sum_{n=1}^{N}\left\{\sigma^2 + 0\right\} = \frac{\sigma^2}{N}.$$

Combining everything, we arrive at the result:

$$\mathbb{E}[\widehat{\sigma}_{\text{ML}}^2] = \frac{1}{N}\sum_{n=1}^{N}\left\{\sigma^2 - 2\mathbb{E}\left[\frac{1}{N}\sum_{j=1}^{N}X_jX_n\right] + \mathbb{E}\left[\left(\frac{1}{N}\sum_{n=1}^{N}X_n\right)^2\right]\right\}$$

$$= \frac{1}{N}\sum_{n=1}^{N}\left\{\sigma^2 - \frac{2\sigma^2}{N} + \frac{\sigma^2}{N}\right\}$$

$$= \frac{N-1}{N}\sigma^2,$$

which is not equal to σ^2. Therefore, $\widehat{\sigma}_{\text{ML}}^2$ is a biased estimator of σ^2.

In the previous example, it is possible to construct an unbiased estimator for the variance. To do so, we can use

$$\widehat{\sigma}_{\text{unbias}}^2 = \frac{1}{N-1}\sum_{n=1}^{N}(X_n - \widehat{\mu}_{\text{ML}})^2, \tag{8.27}$$

so that $\mathbb{E}[\widehat{\sigma}_{\text{unbias}}^2] = \sigma^2$. However, note that $\widehat{\sigma}_{\text{unbias}}^2$ does not maximize the likelihood, so while you can get unbiasedness, you cannot maximize the likelihood. If you want to maximize the likelihood, you cannot get unbiasedness.

What is an unbiased estimator?

- An estimator $\widehat{\Theta}$ is unbiased if $\mathbb{E}[\widehat{\Theta}] = \theta$.

- Unbiased means that the statistical average of $\widehat{\Theta}$ is the true parameter θ.

- If $X_n \sim \text{Gaussian}(\theta, \sigma^2)$, then $\widehat{\Theta} = (1/N)\sum_{n=1}^{N}X_n$ is unbiased, but $\widehat{\Theta} = X_1$ is biased.

8.2.3 Consistent estimators

By definition, an estimator $\widehat{\Theta}(X_1, \ldots, X_N)$ is a function of N random variables $X_1, \ldots, X_N$. Therefore, $\widehat{\Theta}(X_1, \ldots, X_N)$ changes as N grows. In this subsection we analyze how $\widehat{\Theta}$ behaves when N changes. For notational simplicity we use the following notation:

$$\widehat{\Theta}_N = \widehat{\Theta}(X_1, \ldots, X_N). \tag{8.28}$$

Thus, as N increases, we use more random variables in defining $\widehat{\Theta}(X_1, \ldots, X_N)$.

Definition 8.6. *An estimator* $\widehat{\Theta}_N$ *is* **consistent** *if* $\widehat{\Theta}_N \xrightarrow{p} \theta$, *i.e.*,

$$\lim_{N\to\infty} \mathbb{P}\left[\left|\widehat{\Theta}_N - \theta\right| \geq \epsilon\right] = 0. \tag{8.29}$$

The definition here follows from our discussions of the law of large numbers in Chapter 6. The specific type of convergence is known as the **convergence in probability**. It says that as N grows, the estimator $\widehat{\Theta}$ will be close enough to θ so that the probability of getting a large deviation will diminish, as illustrated in **Figure 8.13**.

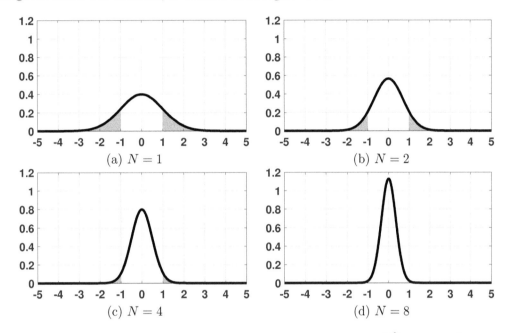

(a) $N = 1$

(b) $N = 2$

(c) $N = 4$

(d) $N = 8$

Figure 8.13: The four subfigures here illustrate the probability of error $\mathbb{P}\left[|\widehat{\Theta}_N - \theta| \geq \epsilon\right]$, which is represented by the areas shaded in blue. We assume that the estimator $\widehat{\Theta}_N$ is a Gaussian random variable following a distribution Gaussian$(0, \frac{\sigma^2}{N})$, where we set $\sigma = 1$. The threshold we use in this figure is $\epsilon = 1$. As N grows, we see that the probability of error diminishes. If the probability of error goes to zero, we say that the estimator is **consistent**.

The examples in **Figure 8.13** are typical situations for an estimator based on the sample average. For example, if we assume that $X_1, \ldots, X_N$ are i.i.d. Gaussian copies of Gaussian$(0, \sigma^2)$, then the estimator

$$\widehat{\Theta}(X_1, \ldots, X_N) = \frac{1}{N}\sum_{n=1}^{N} X_n$$

will follow a Gaussian distribution Gaussian$(0, \frac{\sigma^2}{N})$. (Please refer to Chapter 6 for the derivation.) Then, as N grows, the PDF of $\widehat{\Theta}_N$ becomes narrower and narrower. For a fixed ϵ, it follows that the probability of error will diminish to zero. In fact, we can prove that, for this example,

$$
\begin{aligned}
\mathbb{P}\left[\left|\widehat{\Theta}_N - \theta\right| \geq \epsilon\right] &= \mathbb{P}\left[\widehat{\Theta}_N - \theta \geq \epsilon\right] + \mathbb{P}\left[\widehat{\Theta}_N - \theta \leq -\epsilon\right] \\
&= \int_{\theta+\epsilon}^{\infty} \text{Gaussian}\left(z \mid \theta, \frac{\sigma^2}{N}\right) dz + \int_{-\infty}^{\theta-\epsilon} \text{Gaussian}\left(z \mid \theta, \frac{\sigma^2}{N}\right) dz \\
&= \int_{\theta+\epsilon}^{\infty} \frac{1}{\sqrt{2\pi\sigma^2/N}} e^{-\frac{(z-\theta)^2}{2\sigma^2/N}} dz + \int_{-\infty}^{\theta-\epsilon} \frac{1}{\sqrt{2\pi\sigma^2/N}} e^{-\frac{(z-\theta)^2}{2\sigma^2/N}} dz \\
&= \int_{\frac{\epsilon}{\sigma/\sqrt{N}}}^{\infty} \frac{1}{\sqrt{2\pi}} e^{-\frac{z^2}{2}} dz + \int_{-\infty}^{-\frac{\epsilon}{\sigma/\sqrt{N}}} \frac{1}{\sqrt{2\pi}} e^{-\frac{z^2}{2}} dz \\
&= 1 - \Phi\left(\frac{\epsilon}{\sigma/\sqrt{N}}\right) + \Phi\left(\frac{-\epsilon}{\sigma/\sqrt{N}}\right) \\
&= 2\Phi\left(\frac{-\epsilon}{\sigma/\sqrt{N}}\right).
\end{aligned}
$$

Therefore, as $N \to \infty$, it holds that $\frac{-\epsilon}{\sigma/\sqrt{N}} \to -\infty$. Hence,

$$
\lim_{N\to\infty} \mathbb{P}\left[\left|\widehat{\Theta}_N - \theta\right| \geq \epsilon\right] = \lim_{N\to\infty} 2\Phi\left(\frac{-\epsilon}{\sigma/\sqrt{N}}\right) = 0.
$$

This explains why in **Figure 8.13** the probability of error diminishes to zero as N grows. Therefore, we say that $\widehat{\Theta}_N$ is **consistent**.

In general, there are two ways to check whether an estimator is consistent:

- Prove **convergence in probability**. This is based on the definition of a consistent estimator. If we can prove that

$$
\lim_{N\to\infty} \mathbb{P}\left[|\widehat{\Theta}_N - \theta| \geq \epsilon\right] = 0, \tag{8.30}
$$

  then we say that the estimator is consistent.

- Prove **convergence in mean squared error**:

$$
\lim_{N\to\infty} \mathbb{E}[(\widehat{\Theta}_N - \theta)^2] = 0. \tag{8.31}
$$

To see why convergence in the mean squared error is sufficient to guarantee consistency, we recall Chebyshev's inequality in Chapter 6, which says that

$$
\mathbb{P}\left[|\widehat{\Theta}_N - \theta| \geq \epsilon\right] \leq \frac{\mathbb{E}[(\widehat{\Theta}_N - \theta)^2]}{\epsilon^2}.
$$

Thus, if $\lim_{N\to\infty} \mathbb{E}[(\widehat{\Theta}_N - \theta)^2] = 0$, convergence in probability will also hold. However, since mean square convergence is stronger than convergence in probability, being unable to show mean square convergence does not imply that an estimator is inconsistent.

Be careful not to confuse a consistent estimator and an unbiased estimator. The two are different concepts; one does not imply the other.

Consistent versus unbiased

- Consistent = If you have enough samples, then the estimator $\widehat{\Theta}$ will converge to the true parameter.

- Unbiasedness does not imply consistency. For example (Gaussian), if

$$\widehat{\Theta} = X_1,$$

then $\mathbb{E}[X_1] = \mu$. But $\mathbb{P}[|\widehat{\Theta} - \mu| > \epsilon]$ does not converge to 0 as N grows. So this estimator is inconsistent. (See Example 8.16 below.)

- Consistency does not imply unbiasedness. For example (Gaussian), if

$$\widehat{\Theta} = \frac{1}{N} \sum_{n=1}^{N} (X_n - \mu)^2$$

is a biased estimate for variance, but it is consistent. (See Example 8.17 below.)

Example 8.15. Let $X_1, \ldots, X_N$ be i.i.d. Gaussian random variables with an unknown mean μ and known variance σ^2. We know that the ML estimator for the mean is $\widehat{\mu}_{\text{ML}} = (1/N) \sum_{n=1}^{N} X_n$. Is $\widehat{\mu}_{\text{ML}}$ consistent?

Solution. We have shown that the ML estimator is

$$\widehat{\mu}_{\text{ML}} = \frac{1}{N} \sum_{n=1}^{N} X_n.$$

Since $\mathbb{E}[\widehat{\mu}_{\text{ML}}] = \mu$, and $\mathbb{E}[(\widehat{\mu}_{\text{ML}} - \mu)^2] = \text{Var}[\widehat{\mu}_{\text{ML}}] = \frac{\sigma^2}{N}$, it follows that

$$\mathbb{P}[|\widehat{\mu}_{\text{ML}} - \mu| \geq \epsilon] \leq \frac{\mathbb{E}[(\widehat{\mu}_{\text{ML}} - \mu)^2]}{\epsilon^2} = \frac{\sigma^2}{N\epsilon^2}.$$

Thus, when N goes to infinity, the probability converges to zero, and hence the estimator is consistent.

Example 8.16. Let $X_1, \ldots, X_N$ be i.i.d. Gaussian random variables with an unknown mean μ and known variance σ^2. Define an estimator $\widehat{\mu} = X_1$. Show that the estimator is unbiased but inconsistent.

Solution. We know that $\mathbb{E}[\widehat{\mu}] = \mathbb{E}[X_1] = \mu$. So $\widehat{\mu}$ is an unbiased estimator. However, we can show that

$$\mathbb{E}[(\widehat{\mu} - \mu)^2] = \mathbb{E}[(X_1 - \mu)^2] = \sigma^2.$$

Since this variance $\mathbb{E}[(\widehat{\mu} - \mu)^2]$ does not shrink as N increases, it follows that no matter how many samples we use we cannot make $\mathbb{E}[(\widehat{\mu} - \mu)^2]$ go to zero. To be more precise,

$$\mathbb{P}\left[|\widehat{\mu} - \mu| \geq \epsilon\right] = \mathbb{P}\left[|X_1 - \mu| \geq \epsilon\right]$$

$$= \mathbb{P}\left[X_1 \leq \mu - \epsilon\right] + \mathbb{P}\left[X_1 \geq \mu + \epsilon\right]$$

$$= \int_{-\infty}^{\mu-\epsilon} \frac{1}{\sqrt{2\pi\sigma^2}} e^{-\frac{(x-\mu)^2}{2\sigma^2}}\, dx + \int_{\mu+\epsilon}^{\infty} \frac{1}{\sqrt{2\pi\sigma^2}} e^{-\frac{(x-\mu)^2}{2\sigma^2}}\, dx$$

$$= 2\Phi\left(\frac{-\epsilon}{\sigma}\right),$$

which does not converge to zero as $N \to \infty$. So the estimator is inconsistent.

Example 8.17. Let $X_1, \ldots, X_N$ be i.i.d. Gaussian random variables with an unknown mean μ and an unknown variance σ^2. Is the ML estimate of the variance, i.e., $\widehat{\sigma}_{\text{ML}}^2$, consistent?

Solution. We know that the ML estimator for the mean is

$$\widehat{\mu}_{\text{ML}} = \frac{1}{N} \sum_{n=1}^{N} X_n,$$

and we have shown that it is an unbiased and consistent estimator of the mean. For the variance,

$$\widehat{\sigma}_{\text{ML}}^2 = \frac{1}{N} \sum_{n=1}^{N} (X_n - \widehat{\mu}_{\text{ML}})^2 = \frac{1}{N} \sum_{n=1}^{N} \left[X_n^2 - 2\widehat{\mu}_{\text{ML}} X_n + \widehat{\mu}_{\text{ML}}^2\right]$$

$$= \frac{1}{N} \sum_{n=1}^{N} X_n^2 - 2\widehat{\mu}_{\text{ML}} \cdot \frac{1}{N} \sum_{n=1}^{N} X_n + \widehat{\mu}_{\text{ML}}^2$$

$$= \frac{1}{N} \sum_{n=1}^{N} X_n^2 - \widehat{\mu}_{\text{ML}}^2.$$

Note that $\frac{1}{N} \sum_{n=1}^{N} X_n^2$ is the sample average of the second moment, and so by the weak law of large numbers it should converge in probability to $\mathbb{E}[X_n^2]$. Similarly, $\widehat{\mu}_{\text{ML}}$ will converge in probability to μ. Therefore, we have

$$\widehat{\sigma}_{\text{ML}}^2 = \frac{1}{N} \sum_{n=1}^{N} X_n^2 - \widehat{\mu}_{\text{ML}}^2 \xrightarrow{p} (\sigma^2 + \mu^2) - \mu^2 = \sigma^2.$$

Thus, we have shown that the ML estimator of the variance is biased but consistent.

> The following discussions about the consistency of ML estimators can be skipped.

As we have said, there are many estimators. Some estimators are consistent and some are not. The ML estimators are special. It turns out that under certain regularity conditions the ML estimators of i.i.d. observations are consistent.

Without proving this result formally, we highlight a few steps to illustrate the idea. Suppose that we have a set of i.i.d. data points $x_1, \ldots, x_N$ drawn from some distribution $f(x, | \theta_{\text{true}})$. To formulate the ML estimation, we consider the log-likelihood function (divided by N):

$$\frac{1}{N} \log \mathcal{L}(\theta \,|\, x) = \frac{1}{N} \sum_{n=1}^{N} \log f(x_n; \theta). \tag{8.32}$$

Here, the variable θ is unknown. We need to find it by maximizing the log-likelihood.

By the weak law of large numbers, we can show that the log-likelihood based on the N samples will converge in probability to

$$\underbrace{\frac{1}{N} \sum_{n=1}^{N} \log f(x_n; \theta)}_{g_N(\theta)} \xrightarrow{p} \mathbb{E}[\log f(x; \theta)]. \tag{8.33}$$

The expectation can be evaluated by integrating over the true distribution:

$$\mathbb{E}[\log f(x; \theta)] = \underbrace{\int \log f(x; \theta) \cdot f(x; \theta_{\text{true}}) dx}_{g(\theta)}.$$

where $f(x; \theta_{\text{true}})$ denotes the true distribution of the samples x_n's. From these two results we define two functions:

$$g_N(\theta) \overset{\text{def}}{=} \frac{1}{N} \sum_{n=1}^{N} \log f(x_n; \theta), \quad \text{and} \quad g(\theta) \overset{\text{def}}{=} \int \log f(x; \theta) \cdot f(x; \theta_{\text{true}}) dx,$$

and we know that $g_N(\theta) \xrightarrow{p} g(\theta)$.

We also know that $\widehat{\theta}_{\text{ML}}$ is the ML estimator, and so

$$\widehat{\theta}_{\text{ML}} = \underset{\theta}{\operatorname{argmax}} \; g_N(\theta).$$

Let θ^* be the maximizer of the limiting function, i.e.,

$$\theta^* = \underset{\theta}{\operatorname{argmax}} \; g(\theta).$$

Because $g_N(\theta) \xrightarrow{p} g(\theta)$, we can (loosely[3]) argue that $\widehat{\theta}_{\text{ML}} \xrightarrow{p} \theta^*$. If we can show that $\theta^* = \theta_{\text{true}}$, then we have shown that $\widehat{\theta}_{\text{ML}} \xrightarrow{p} \theta_{\text{true}}$, implying that $\widehat{\theta}_{\text{ML}}$ is consistent.

---

[3]To rigorously prove this statement we need some kind of regularity conditions on g_N and g. A more formal proof can be found in H. Vincent Poor, *An Introduction Signal Detection and Estimation*, Springer, 1998, Section IV.D.

To show that $\boldsymbol{\theta}^* = \boldsymbol{\theta}_{\text{true}}$, we note that

$$\frac{d}{d\boldsymbol{\theta}} \int \log f(\boldsymbol{x}; \boldsymbol{\theta}) \cdot f(\boldsymbol{x}; \boldsymbol{\theta}_{\text{true}}) \, d\boldsymbol{x} = \int \frac{d}{d\boldsymbol{\theta}} \log f(\boldsymbol{x}; \boldsymbol{\theta}) \cdot f(\boldsymbol{x}; \boldsymbol{\theta}_{\text{true}}) \, d\boldsymbol{x}$$

$$= \int \frac{f'(\boldsymbol{x}; \boldsymbol{\theta})}{f(\boldsymbol{x}; \boldsymbol{\theta})} \cdot f(\boldsymbol{x}; \boldsymbol{\theta}_{\text{true}}) \, d\boldsymbol{x}.$$

We ask whether this is equal to zero. Putting $\boldsymbol{\theta} = \boldsymbol{\theta}_{\text{true}}$, we have that

$$\int \frac{f'(\boldsymbol{x}; \boldsymbol{\theta}_{\text{true}})}{f(\boldsymbol{x}; \boldsymbol{\theta}_{\text{true}})} \cdot f(\boldsymbol{x}; \boldsymbol{\theta}_{\text{true}}) \, d\boldsymbol{x} = \int f'(\boldsymbol{x}; \boldsymbol{\theta}_{\text{true}}) \, d\boldsymbol{x}.$$

However, this integral can be simplified to

$$\int f'(\boldsymbol{x}; \boldsymbol{\theta}_{\text{true}}) \, d\boldsymbol{x} = \frac{d}{d\boldsymbol{\theta}} \underbrace{\int f(\boldsymbol{x}; \boldsymbol{\theta}) \, d\boldsymbol{x}}_{=1} \bigg|_{\boldsymbol{\theta}=\boldsymbol{\theta}_{\text{true}}} = 0.$$

Therefore, $\boldsymbol{\theta}_{\text{true}}$ is the maximizer for $g(\boldsymbol{\theta})$, and so $\boldsymbol{\theta}_{\text{true}} = \boldsymbol{\theta}^*$.

End of the discussion. Please join us again.

8.2.4 Invariance principle

Another useful property satisfied by the ML estimate is the **invariance principle**. The invariance principle says that a monotonic transformation of the true parameter is preserved for the ML estimates.

What is the invariance principle?

- There is a monotonic function h.
- There is an ML estimate $\widehat{\theta}_{\text{ML}}$ for θ.
- The monotonic function h maps the true parameter $\theta \longmapsto h(\theta)$.
- Then the same function will map the ML estimate $\widehat{\theta}_{\text{ML}} \longmapsto h(\widehat{\theta}_{\text{ML}})$.

The formal statement of the invariance principle is given by the theorem below.

Theorem 8.1. *If $\widehat{\theta}_{ML}$ is the ML estimate of θ, then for any one-to-one function h of θ, the ML estimate of $h(\theta)$ is $h(\widehat{\theta}_{ML})$.*

Proof. Define the likelihood function $\mathcal{L}(\theta)$ (we have dropped $\boldsymbol{x}$ to simplify the notation). Then, for any monotonic function h, we have that

$$\mathcal{L}(\theta) = \mathcal{L}(h^{-1}(h(\theta))).$$

Let $\widehat{\theta}_{\mathrm{ML}}$ be the ML estimate:

$$\widehat{\theta}_{\mathrm{ML}} = \operatorname*{argmax}_{\theta} \mathcal{L}(\theta) = \operatorname*{argmax}_{\theta} \mathcal{L}(h^{-1}(h(\theta))).$$

By the definition of ML, $\widehat{\theta}_{\mathrm{ML}}$ must maximize the likelihood. Therefore, $\mathcal{L}(h^{-1}(h(\theta)))$ is maximized when $h^{-1}(h(\theta)) = \widehat{\theta}_{\mathrm{ML}}$. This implies that $h(\theta) = h(\widehat{\theta}_{\mathrm{ML}})$ because h is monotonic. Since $h(\theta)$ is the parameter we try to estimate, the equality $h(\theta) = h(\widehat{\theta}_{\mathrm{ML}})$ implies that $h(\widehat{\theta}_{\mathrm{ML}})$ is the ML estimate of $h(\theta)$. $\qquad\square$

Example 8.18. Consider the single-photon image sensor example we discussed in Section 8.1. We consider a set of i.i.d. Bernoulli random variables with PMF

$$p_{X_n}(1) = 1 - e^{-\eta} \qquad \text{and} \qquad p_{X_n}(0) = e^{-\eta}. \tag{8.34}$$

Find the ML estimate through (a) direct calculation and (b) the invariance principle.

Solution. (a) Following the example in Equation (8.12), the ML estimate of η is

$$\widehat{\eta}_{\mathrm{ML}} = \operatorname*{argmax}_{\eta} \prod_{n=1}^{N} (1 - e^{-\eta})^{x_n} (e^{-\eta})^{1-x_n}$$

$$= -\log\left(1 - \frac{1}{N} \sum_{n=1}^{N} x_n\right).$$

(b) We can obtain the same result using the invariance principle. Since X_n is a binary random variable, we assume that it is a Bernoulli with parameter θ. Then the ML estimate of θ is

$$\widehat{\theta}_{\mathrm{ML}} = \operatorname*{argmax}_{\theta} \prod_{n=1}^{N} \theta^{x_n} (1 - \theta)^{1-x_n}$$

$$= \frac{1}{N} \sum_{n=1}^{N} x_n.$$

The relationship between θ and η is that $\theta = 1 - e^{-\eta}$, or $\eta = -\log(1 - \theta)$. So we let $h(\theta) = -\log(1 - \theta)$. The invariance principle says that the ML estimate of $h(\theta)$ is

$$\widehat{\eta}_{\mathrm{ML}} \overset{\text{def}}{=} \widehat{h(\theta)}_{\mathrm{ML}}$$

$$\overset{(i)}{=} h(\widehat{\theta}_{\mathrm{ML}})$$

$$= -\log\left(1 - \frac{1}{N} \sum_{n=1}^{N} x_n\right),$$

where (i) follows from the invariance principle.

The invariance principle can be very convenient, especially when the transformation h is complicated, so that a direct evaluation of the ML estimate is difficult.

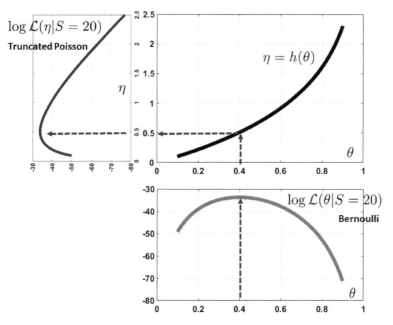

Figure 8.14: The invariance principle is a transformation of the ML estimate. In this example, we consider a Bernoulli log-likelihood function shown in the lowermost plot. For this log-likelihood, the ML estimate is $\widehat{\theta}_{\mathrm{ML}} = 0.4$. On the left-hand side we show another log-likelihood, derived for a truncated Poisson random variable. Note that the ML estimate is $\widehat{\eta}_{\mathrm{ML}} = 0.5108$. The invariance principle asserts that, instead of computing these ML estimates directly, we can first derive the relationship between η and θ for any θ. Since we know that $\theta = 1 - e^{-\eta}$, it follows that $\eta = -\log(1-\theta)$. We define this transformation as $\eta = h(\theta) = -\log(1-\theta)$. Then the ML estimate is $\widehat{\eta}_{\mathrm{ML}} = h(\widehat{\theta}_{\mathrm{ML}}) = h(0.4) = 0.5108$. The invariance principle saves us the trouble of computing the maximization of the more truncated Poisson likelihood.

The invariance principle is portrayed in **Figure 8.14**. We start with the Bernoulli log-likelihood

$$\log \mathcal{L}(\theta|S) = S \log \theta + (1 - S) \log(1 - \theta).$$

In this particular example we let $S = 20$, where S denotes the sum of the $N = 50$ Bernoulli random variables. The other log-likelihood is the truncated Poisson, which is given by

$$\log \mathcal{L}(\eta|S) = S \log(1 - e^{-\eta}) + (1 - S) \log(e^{-\eta}).$$

The transformation between the two is the function

$$\eta = h(\theta) = -\log(1 - \theta).$$

Putting everything into the figure, we see that the ML estimate ($\theta = 0.4$) is translated to $\eta = 0.5108$. The invariance principle asserts that this calculation can be done by $\widehat{\eta}_{\mathrm{ML}} = h(\widehat{\theta}_{\mathrm{ML}}) = h(0.4) = -0.5108$.

8.3 Maximum A Posteriori Estimation

In ML estimation, the parameter $\boldsymbol{\theta}$ is treated as a deterministic quantity. There are, however, many situations where we have some **prior knowledge** about $\boldsymbol{\theta}$. For example, we may not know exactly the speed of a car, but we may know that the speed is roughly 65 mph with a standard deviation of 5 mph. How do we incorporate such prior knowledge into the estimation problem?

In this section, we introduce the second estimation technique, known as the **maximum a posteriori** (MAP) estimation. MAP estimation links the likelihood and the prior. The key idea is to treat the parameter $\boldsymbol{\theta}$ as a random variable (vector) $\boldsymbol{\Theta}$ with a PDF $f_{\boldsymbol{\Theta}}(\boldsymbol{\theta})$.

8.3.1 The trio of likelihood, prior, and posterior

To understand how the MAP estimation works, it is important first to understand the role of the parameter $\boldsymbol{\theta}$, which changes from a deterministic quantity to a random quantity.

Recall the likelihood function we defined in the ML estimation; it is

$$\mathcal{L}(\boldsymbol{\theta} \,|\, \boldsymbol{x}) = f_{\boldsymbol{X}}(\boldsymbol{x}; \boldsymbol{\theta}),$$

if we assume that we have a set of i.i.d. observations $\boldsymbol{x} = [x_1, \ldots, x_N]^T$. By writing the PDF of $\boldsymbol{X}$ as $f_{\boldsymbol{X}}(\boldsymbol{x}; \boldsymbol{\theta})$, we emphasize that $\boldsymbol{\theta}$ is a deterministic but unknown parameter. There is nothing random about $\boldsymbol{\theta}$.

In MAP, we change the nature of $\boldsymbol{\theta}$ from deterministic to random. We replace $\boldsymbol{\theta}$ by $\boldsymbol{\Theta}$ and write

$$f_{\boldsymbol{X}}(\boldsymbol{x}; \boldsymbol{\theta}) \overset{\text{becomes}}{\Longrightarrow} f_{\boldsymbol{X}|\boldsymbol{\Theta}}(\boldsymbol{x}|\boldsymbol{\theta}). \tag{8.35}$$

The difference between the left-hand side and the right-hand side is subtle but important. On the left-hand side, $f_{\boldsymbol{X}}(\boldsymbol{x}; \boldsymbol{\theta})$ is the PDF of $\boldsymbol{X}$. This PDF is parameterized by $\boldsymbol{\theta}$. On the right-hand side, $f_{\boldsymbol{X}|\boldsymbol{\Theta}}(\boldsymbol{x}|\boldsymbol{\theta})$ is a **conditional** PDF of $\boldsymbol{X}$ given $\boldsymbol{\Theta}$. The values they provide are exactly the same. However, in $f_{\boldsymbol{X}|\boldsymbol{\Theta}}(\boldsymbol{x}|\boldsymbol{\theta})$, $\boldsymbol{\theta}$ is a realization of a random variable $\boldsymbol{\Theta}$.

Because $\boldsymbol{\Theta}$ is now a random variable (vector), we can define its PDF (yes, the PDF of $\boldsymbol{\Theta}$), and denote it by

$$f_{\boldsymbol{\Theta}}(\boldsymbol{\theta}), \tag{8.36}$$

which is called the **prior** distribution. The prior distribution of $\boldsymbol{\Theta}$ is unique in MAP estimation. There is nothing called a prior in ML estimation.

Multiplying $f_{\boldsymbol{X}|\boldsymbol{\Theta}}(\boldsymbol{x}|\boldsymbol{\theta})$ with the prior PDF $f_{\boldsymbol{\Theta}}(\boldsymbol{\theta})$, and using Bayes' Theorem, we obtain the **posterior** distribution:

$$f_{\boldsymbol{\Theta}|\boldsymbol{X}}(\boldsymbol{\theta}|\boldsymbol{x}) = \frac{f_{\boldsymbol{X}|\boldsymbol{\Theta}}(\boldsymbol{x}|\boldsymbol{\theta}) f_{\boldsymbol{\Theta}}(\boldsymbol{\theta})}{f_{\boldsymbol{X}}(\boldsymbol{x})}. \tag{8.37}$$

The posterior distribution is the PDF of $\boldsymbol{\Theta}$ given the measurements $\boldsymbol{X}$.

The likelihood, the prior, and the posterior can be confusing. Let us clarify their meanings.

- **Likelihood** $f_{X|\Theta}(x|\theta)$: This is the conditional probability density of X given the parameter Θ. Do not confuse the likelihood $f_{X|\Theta}(x|\theta)$ defined in the MAP context and the likelihood $f_X(x;|\theta)$ defined in the ML context. The former assumes that Θ is random whereas the latter assumes that θ is deterministic. They have the same values.

- **Prior** $f_\Theta(\theta)$: This is the prior distribution of Θ. It does not come from the data X but from our prior knowledge. For example, if we see a bike on the road, even before we take any measurement we will have a rough idea of its speed. This is the prior distribution.

- **Posterior** $f_{\Theta|X}(\theta|x)$: This is the posterior density of Θ given that we have observed X. Do not confuse $f_{\Theta|X}(\theta|x)$ and $\mathcal{L}(\theta\,|\,x)$. The posterior distribution $f_{\Theta|X}(\theta|x)$ is a PDF of Θ given $X = x$. The likelihood $\mathcal{L}(\theta\,|\,x)$ is not a PDF. If you integrate $f_{\Theta|X}(\theta|x)$ with respect to θ, you get 1, but if you integrate $\mathcal{L}(\theta\,|\,x)$ with respect to θ, you do not get 1.

What is the difference between ML and MAP?

Likelihood	ML	$f_X(x;\,\theta)$ The parameter θ is deterministic.
	MAP	$f_{X|\Theta}(x\,|\,\theta)$ The parameter Θ is random.
Prior	ML	There is no prior, because θ is deterministic.
	MAP	$f_\Theta(\theta)$ This is the PDF of Θ.
Optimization	ML	Find the peak of the likelihood $f_X(x;\,\theta)$.
	MAP	Find the peak of the posterior $f_{\Theta|X}(\theta\,|\,x)$.

Maximum a posteriori (MAP) estimation is a form of Bayesian estimation. Bayesian methods emphasize our prior knowledge or beliefs about the parameters. As we will see shortly, the prior has something valuable to offer, especially when we have very few data points.

8.3.2 Understanding the priors

Since the biggest difference between MAP and ML is the addition of the prior $f_\Theta(\theta)$, we need to take a closer look at what they mean. In **Figure 8.15** below, we show a set of six different priors. We ask two questions: (1) What do they mean? (2) Which one should we use?

What does the shape of a prior tell us?

It tells us **your** belief as to how the underlying parameter Θ should be distributed.

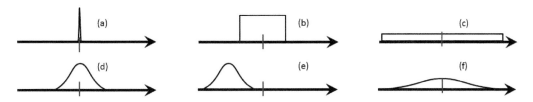

Figure 8.15: This figure illustrates six different examples of the prior distribution $f_\Theta(\boldsymbol{\theta})$, when the prior is a 1D parameter θ. The prior distribution $f_\Theta(\theta)$ is the PDF of Θ. (a) $f_\Theta(\theta) = \delta(\theta)$, which is a delta function. (b) $f_\Theta(\theta) = \frac{1}{b-a}$ for $a \le \theta \le b$. This is a uniform distribution. (c) This is also a uniform distribution, but the spread is very wide. (d) $f_\Theta(\theta) = \text{Gaussian}(0, \sigma^2)$, which is a zero-mean Gaussian. (e) The same Gaussian, but with a different mean. (f) A Gaussian with zero mean, but a large variance.

The meaning of this statement can be best understood from the examples shown in **Figure 8.15**:

- **Figure 8.15**(a). This is a delta prior $f_\Theta(\theta) = \delta(\theta)$ (or $f_\Theta(\theta) = \delta(\theta - \theta_0)$). If you use this prior, you are absolutely sure that the parameter Θ takes a specific value. There is no uncertainty about your belief. Since you are so confident about your prior knowledge, you will ignore the likelihood that is constructed from the data. No one will use a delta prior in practice.

- **Figure 8.15**(b). $f_\Theta(\theta) = \frac{1}{b-a}$ for $a \le \theta \le b$, and is zero otherwise. This is a bounded uniform prior. You do not have any preference for the parameter Θ, but you do know from your prior experience that $a \le \Theta \le b$.

- **Figure 8.15**(c). This prior is the same as (b) but is short and very wide. If you use this prior, it means that you know nothing about the parameter. So you give up the prior and let the likelihood dominate the MAP estimate.

- **Figure 8.15**(d). $f_\Theta(\theta) = \text{Gaussian}(0, \sigma^2)$. You use this prior when you know something about the parameter, e.g., that it is centered at certain location and you have some uncertainty.

- **Figure 8.15**(e). Same as (d), but the parameter is centered at some other location.

- **Figure 8.15**(f). Same as (d), but you have less confidence about the parameter.

As you can see from these examples, the shape of the prior tells us how **you** want Θ to be distributed. The choice you make will directly influence the MAP optimization, and hence the MAP estimate.

Since the prior is a subjective quantity in the MAP framework, you as the user have the freedom to choose whatever you like. For instance, if you have conducted a similar experiment before, you can use the results of the previous experiments as the current prior. Another strategy is to go with physics. For instance, we can argue that $\boldsymbol{\theta}$ should be sparse so that it contains as few non-zeros as possible. In this case, a sparsity-driven prior, such as $f_\Theta(\boldsymbol{\theta}) = \exp\{-\|\boldsymbol{\theta}\|_1\}$, could be a choice. The third strategy is to choose a prior that is computationally "friendlier", e.g., in quadratic form so that the MAP is differentiable. One such choice is the **conjugate prior**. We will discuss this later in Section 8.3.6.

> **Which prior should we choose?**
>
> - Based on **your** preference, e.g., you know from historical data that the parameter should behave in certain ways.
> - Based on physics, e.g., the parameter has a physical interpretation, so you need to abide by the physical laws.
> - Choose a prior that is computationally "friendlier". This is the topic of the **conjugate prior**, which is a prior that does not change the form of the posterior distribution. (We will discuss this later in Section 8.3.6.)

8.3.3 MAP formulation and solution

Our next task is to study how to formulate the MAP problem and how to solve it.

> **Definition 8.7.** *Let $X = [X_1, \ldots, X_N]^T$ be i.i.d. observations. Let Θ be a random parameter. The* **maximum-a-posteriori** *estimate of Θ is*
>
> $$\widehat{\theta}_{MAP} = \underset{\theta}{argmax}\ f_{\Theta|X}(\theta|x). \tag{8.38}$$

Philosophically speaking, ML and MAP have two different goals. ML considers a parametric model with a deterministic parameter. Its goal is to find the parameter that maximizes the likelihood for the data we have observed. MAP also considers a parametric model but the parameter Θ is random. Because Θ is random, we are finding one particular state θ of the parameter Θ that offers the best explanation **conditioned** on the data X we observe. In a sense, the two optimization problems are

$$\widehat{\theta}_{\text{ML}} = \underset{\theta}{\operatorname{argmax}}\ f_{X|\Theta}(x|\theta),$$

$$\widehat{\theta}_{\text{MAP}} = \underset{\theta}{\operatorname{argmax}}\ f_{\Theta|X}(\theta|x).$$

This pair of equations is interesting, as the pair tells us that the difference between the ML estimation and the MAP estimation is the flipped order of X and Θ.

There are two reasons we care about the posterior. First, in MAP the posterior allows us to incorporate the prior. ML does not allow a prior. A prior can be useful when the number of samples is small. Second, maximizing the posterior does have some physical interpretations. MAP asks for the probability of $\Theta = \theta$ *after* observing N training samples $X = x$. ML asks for the probability of observing $X = x$ *given* a parameter θ. Both are correct and legitimate criteria, but sometimes we might prefer one over the other.

To solve the MAP problem, we notice that

$$\widehat{\theta}_{\text{MAP}} = \underset{\theta}{\operatorname{argmax}}\ f_{\Theta|X}(\theta|x)$$

$$= \underset{\theta}{\operatorname{argmax}}\ \frac{f_{X|\Theta}(x|\theta)f_{\Theta}(\theta)}{f_X(x)}$$

$$= \underset{\theta}{\operatorname{argmax}}\ f_{X|\Theta}(x|\theta)f_{\Theta}(\theta), \qquad f_X(x) \text{ does not contain } \theta$$

$$= \underset{\theta}{\operatorname{argmax}}\ \log f_{X|\Theta}(x|\theta) + \log f_{\Theta}(\theta).$$

Therefore, what MAP adds is the prior $\log f_{\Theta}(\boldsymbol{\theta})$. If you use an uninformative prior, e.g., a prior with extremely wide support, then the MAP estimation will return more or less the same result as the ML estimation.

When does MAP = ML?

- The relation "=" does not make sense here, because $\boldsymbol{\theta}$ is random in MAP but deterministic in ML.
- Solution of MAP optimization = solution of ML optimization, when $f_{\Theta}(\boldsymbol{\theta})$ is uniform over the parameter space.
- In this case, $f_{\Theta}(\boldsymbol{\theta})$ = constant and so it can be dropped from the optimization.

Example 8.19. Let $X_1, \ldots, X_N$ be i.i.d. random variables with a PDF $f_{X_n|\Theta}(x_n|\theta)$ for all n, and Θ be a random parameter with PDF $f_{\Theta}(\theta)$:

$$f_{X_n|\Theta}(x_n|\theta) = \frac{1}{\sqrt{2\pi\sigma^2}} \exp\left\{-\frac{(x_n - \theta)^2}{2\sigma^2}\right\},$$

$$f_{\Theta}(\theta) = \frac{1}{\sqrt{2\pi\sigma_0^2}} \exp\left\{-\frac{(\theta - \mu_0)^2}{2\sigma_0^2}\right\}.$$

Find the MAP estimate.

Solution. The MAP estimate is

$$\widehat{\theta}_{\text{MAP}} = \underset{\theta}{\operatorname{argmax}} \left[\prod_{n=1}^{N} \frac{1}{\sqrt{2\pi\sigma^2}} \exp\left\{-\frac{(x_n - \theta)^2}{2\sigma^2}\right\}\right] \times \left[\frac{1}{\sqrt{2\pi\sigma_0^2}} \exp\left\{-\frac{(\theta - \mu_0)^2}{2\sigma_0^2}\right\}\right]$$

$$= \underset{\theta}{\operatorname{argmax}} \left(\frac{1}{\sqrt{2\pi\sigma^2}}\right)^N \times \frac{1}{\sqrt{2\pi\sigma_0^2}} \exp\left\{-\sum_{n=1}^{N} \frac{(x_n - \theta)^2}{2\sigma^2} - \frac{(\theta - \mu_0)^2}{2\sigma_0^2}\right\}.$$

Since the maximizer is not changed by any monotonic function, we apply logarithm to the above equations. This yields

$$\widehat{\theta}_{\text{MAP}} = \underset{\theta}{\operatorname{argmax}} \left\{-\frac{N}{2} \log\left(2\pi\sigma^2\right) - \frac{1}{2} \log(2\pi\sigma_0^2) \right.$$

$$\left. -\sum_{n=1}^{N} \frac{(x_n - \theta)^2}{2\sigma^2} - \frac{(\theta - \mu_0)^2}{2\sigma_0^2}\right\}.$$

Constants in the maximization do not matter. So by dropping the constant terms we obtain

$$\widehat{\theta}_{\text{MAP}} = \underset{\theta}{\operatorname{argmax}} \left\{-\sum_{n=1}^{N} \frac{(x_n - \theta)^2}{2\sigma^2} - \frac{(\theta - \mu_0)^2}{2\sigma_0^2}\right\}. \tag{8.39}$$

It now remains to solve the maximization. To this end we take the derivative w.r.t. θ

and show that

$$\frac{d}{d\theta}\left\{-\sum_{n=1}^{N}\frac{(x_n-\theta)^2}{2\sigma^2}-\frac{(\theta-\mu_0)^2}{2\sigma_0^2}\right\}=0.$$

This yields

$$\sum_{n=1}^{N}\frac{(x_n-\theta)}{\sigma^2}-\frac{\theta-\mu_0}{\sigma_0^2}=0.$$

Rearranging the terms gives us the final result:

$$\widehat{\theta}_{\text{MAP}}=\frac{\sigma_0^2\left(\frac{1}{N}\sum_{n=1}^{N}x_n\right)+\frac{\sigma^2}{N}\mu_0}{\sigma_0^2+\frac{\sigma^2}{N}}. \tag{8.40}$$

Practice Exercise 8.7. Prove that if $f_{\Theta}(\theta)=\delta(\theta-\theta_0)$, the MAP estimate is $\widehat{\theta}_{\text{MAP}}=\theta_0$.

Solution. If $f_{\Theta}(\theta)=\delta(\theta-\theta_0)$, then

$$\begin{aligned}\widehat{\theta}_{\text{MAP}}&=\underset{\theta}{\operatorname{argmax}}\ \log f_{\boldsymbol{X}|\Theta}(\boldsymbol{x}|\boldsymbol{\theta})+\log f_{\Theta}(\boldsymbol{\theta})\\&=\underset{\theta}{\operatorname{argmax}}\ \log f_{\boldsymbol{X}|\Theta}(\boldsymbol{x}|\boldsymbol{\theta})+\log\delta(\boldsymbol{\theta}-\boldsymbol{\theta}_0)\\&=\begin{cases}\underset{\theta}{\operatorname{argmax}}\ \log f_{\boldsymbol{X}|\Theta}(\boldsymbol{x}|\boldsymbol{\theta})-\infty, & \boldsymbol{\theta}\neq\boldsymbol{\theta}_0.\\\underset{\theta}{\operatorname{argmax}}\ \log f_{\boldsymbol{X}|\Theta}(\boldsymbol{x}|\boldsymbol{\theta})+0, & \boldsymbol{\theta}=\boldsymbol{\theta}_0.\end{cases}\end{aligned}$$

Thus, if $\widehat{\boldsymbol{\theta}}_{\text{MAP}}\neq\boldsymbol{\theta}_0$, the first case says that there is no solution, so we must go with the second case $\widehat{\boldsymbol{\theta}}_{\text{MAP}}=\boldsymbol{\theta}_0$. But if $\widehat{\boldsymbol{\theta}}_{\text{MAP}}=\boldsymbol{\theta}_0$, there is no optimization because we have already chosen $\widehat{\boldsymbol{\theta}}_{\text{MAP}}=\boldsymbol{\theta}_0$. This proves the result.

8.3.4 Analyzing the MAP solution

As we said earlier, MAP offers something that ML does not. To see this, we will use the result of the Gaussian random variables as an example and analyze the MAP solution as we change the parameters N and σ_0. Recall that if $X_1,\ldots,X_N$ are i.i.d. Gaussian random variables with unknown mean θ and known variance σ, the ML estimate is

$$\widehat{\theta}_{\text{ML}}=\frac{1}{N}\sum_{n=1}^{N}x_n.$$

Assuming that the parameter Θ is distributed according to a PDF Gaussian(μ_0, σ_0^2), we have shown in the previous subsection that

$$\widehat{\theta}_{\text{MAP}} = \frac{\sigma_0^2 \left(\frac{1}{N} \sum_{n=1}^{N} x_n \right) + \frac{\sigma^2}{N} \mu_0}{\sigma_0^2 + \frac{\sigma^2}{N}} = \frac{\sigma_0^2 \widehat{\theta}_{\text{ML}} + \frac{\sigma^2}{N} \mu_0}{\sigma_0^2 + \frac{\sigma^2}{N}}.$$

In what follows, we will take a look at the behavior of the MAP estimate $\widehat{\theta}_{\text{MAP}}$ as N and σ_0 change. The results of our discussion are summarized in **Figure 8.16**.

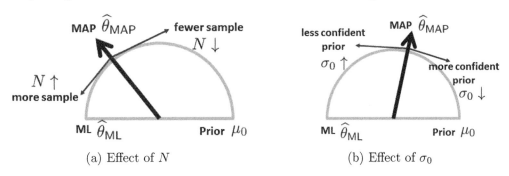

(a) Effect of N (b) Effect of σ_0

Figure 8.16: The MAP estimate $\widehat{\theta}_{\text{MAP}}$ swings between the ML estimate $\widehat{\theta}_{\text{ML}}$ and the prior μ_0. (a) When N increases, the likelihood is more reliable and so we lean towards the ML estimate. If N is small, we should trust the prior more than the ML estimate. (b) When σ_0 decreases, we become more confident about the prior and so we will use it. If σ_0 is large, we use more information from the ML estimate.

First, let's look at the effect of N.

How does N change $\widehat{\theta}_{\text{MAP}}$?

- As $N \rightarrow \infty$, the MAP estimate $\widehat{\theta}_{\text{MAP}} \rightarrow \widehat{\theta}_{\text{ML}}$: If we have enough samples, we trust the data.

- As $N \rightarrow 0$, the MAP estimate $\widehat{\theta}_{\text{MAP}} \rightarrow \theta_0$. If we do not have any samples, we trust the prior.

These two results can be demonstrated by taking the limits. As $N \rightarrow \infty$, the MAP estimate converges to

$$\lim_{N \to \infty} \widehat{\theta}_{\text{MAP}} = \lim_{N \to \infty} \frac{\sigma_0^2 \widehat{\theta}_{\text{ML}} + \frac{\sigma^2}{N} \mu_0}{\sigma_0^2 + \frac{\sigma^2}{N}} = \widehat{\theta}_{\text{ML}}. \tag{8.41}$$

This result is not surprising. When we have infinitely many samples, we will completely rely on the data and make our estimate. Thus, the MAP estimate is the same as the ML estimate.

When $N \rightarrow 0$, the MAP estimate converges to

$$\lim_{N \to 0} \widehat{\theta}_{\text{MAP}} = \lim_{N \to 0} \frac{\sigma_0^2 \widehat{\theta}_{\text{ML}} + \frac{\sigma^2}{N} \mu_0}{\sigma_0^2 + \frac{\sigma^2}{N}} = \mu_0. \tag{8.42}$$

This means that, when we do not have any samples, the MAP estimate $\widehat{\theta}_{\text{MAP}}$ will completely use the prior distribution, which has a mean μ_0.

The implication of this result is that MAP offers a natural swing between $\widehat{\theta}_{\mathrm{ML}}$ and $\widehat{\theta}_0$, controlled by N. Where does this N come from? If we recall the derivation of the result, we note that the N affects the likelihood term through the number of samples:

$$\widehat{\theta}_{\mathrm{MAP}} = \underset{\theta}{\mathrm{argmax}} \left\{ -\underbrace{\sum_{n=1}^{N} \frac{(x_n - \theta)^2}{2\sigma^2}}_{N \text{ terms here}} - \underbrace{\frac{(\theta - \mu_0)^2}{2\sigma_0^2}}_{1 \text{ term}} \right\}.$$

Thus, as N increases, the influence of the data term grows, and so the result will gradually shift towards $\widehat{\theta}_{\mathrm{ML}}$.

Figure 8.17 illustrates a numerical experiment in which we draw N random samples $x_1, \ldots, x_N$ according to a Gaussian distribution $\mathrm{Gaussian}(\theta, \sigma^2)$, with $\sigma = 1$. We assume that the prior distribution is $\mathrm{Gaussian}(\mu_0, \sigma_0^2)$, with $\mu_0 = 0$ and $\sigma_0 = 0.25$. The ML estimate of this problem is $\widehat{\theta}_{\mathrm{ML}} = \frac{1}{N} \sum_{n=1}^{N} x_n$, whereas the MAP estimate is given by Equation (8.40). The figure shows the resulting PDFs. A helpful analogy is that the prior and the likelihood are pulling a rope in two opposite directions. As N grows, the force of the likelihood increases and so the influence becomes stronger.

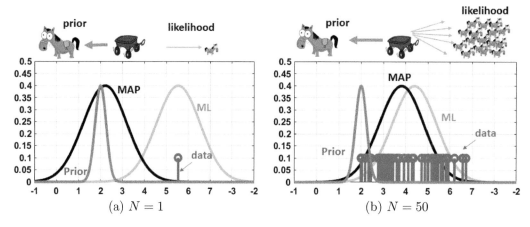

Figure 8.17: The subfigures show the prior distribution $f_\Theta(\theta)$ and the likelihood function $f_{X|\Theta}(x|\theta)$, given the observed data. (a) When $N = 1$, the estimated posterior distribution $f_{\Theta|X}(\theta|x)$ is pulled towards the prior. (b) When $N = 50$, the posterior is pulled towards the ML estimate. The analogy for the situation is that each data point is acting as a small force against the big force of the prior. As N grows, the small forces of the data points accumulate and eventually dominate.

We next look at the effect of σ_0.

How does σ_0 change $\widehat{\theta}_{\mathrm{MAP}}$?

- As $\sigma_0 \to \infty$, the MAP estimate $\widehat{\theta}_{\mathrm{MAP}} \to \widehat{\theta}_{\mathrm{ML}}$: If we have doubts about the prior, we trust the data.

- As $\sigma_0 \to 0$, the MAP estimate $\widehat{\theta}_{\mathrm{MAP}} \to \theta_0$. If we are absolutely sure about the prior, we ignore the data.

When $\sigma_0 \to \infty$, the limit of $\widehat{\theta}_{\text{MAP}}$ is

$$\lim_{\sigma_0 \to \infty} \widehat{\theta}_{\text{MAP}} = \lim_{\sigma_0 \to \infty} \frac{\sigma_0^2 \widehat{\theta}_{\text{ML}} + \frac{\sigma^2}{N} \mu_0}{\sigma_0^2 + \frac{\sigma^2}{N}} = \widehat{\theta}_{\text{ML}}. \tag{8.43}$$

The reason why this happens is that σ_0 is the uncertainty level of the prior. If σ_0 is high, we are not certain about the prior. In this case, MAP chooses to follow the ML estimate.

When $\sigma_0 \to 0$, the limit of $\widehat{\theta}_{\text{MAP}}$ is

$$\lim_{\sigma_0 \to 0} \widehat{\theta}_{\text{MAP}} = \lim_{\sigma_0 \to 0} \frac{\sigma_0^2 \widehat{\theta}_{\text{ML}} + \frac{\sigma^2}{N} \mu_0}{\sigma_0^2 + \frac{\sigma^2}{N}} = \mu_0. \tag{8.44}$$

Note that when $\sigma_0 \to 0$, we are essentially saying that we are absolutely sure about the prior. If we are so sure about the prior, there is no need to look at the data. In that case the MAP estimate is μ_0.

The way to understand the influence of σ_0 is to inspect the equation:

$$\widehat{\theta}_{\text{MAP}} = \operatorname*{argmax}_{\theta} \left\{ -\underbrace{\sum_{n=1}^{N} \frac{(x_n - \theta)^2}{2\sigma^2}}_{\text{fixed w.r.t. } \sigma_0} - \underbrace{\frac{(\theta - \mu_0)^2}{2\sigma_0^2}}_{\text{changes with } \sigma_0} \right\}.$$

Since σ_0 is purely a preference **you** decide, you can control how much trust to put onto the prior.

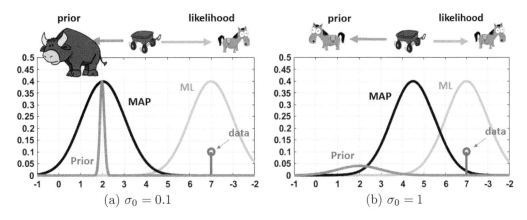

Figure 8.18: The subfigures show the prior distribution $f_\Theta(\theta)$ and the likelihood function $f_{X|\Theta}(x|\theta)$, given the observed data. (a) When $\sigma_0 = 0.1$, the estimated posterior distribution $f_{\Theta|X}(\theta|x)$ is pulled towards the prior. (b) When $\sigma_0 = 1$, the posterior is pulled towards the ML estimate. An analogy for the situation is that the strength of the prior depends on the magnitude of σ_0. If σ_0 is small the prior is strong, and so the influence is large. If σ_0 is large the prior is weak, and so the ML estimate will dominate.

Figure 8.18 illustrates a numerical experiment in which we compare $\sigma_0 = 0.1$ and $\sigma_0 = 1$. If σ_0 is small, the prior distribution $f_\Theta(\theta)$ becomes similar to a delta function. We can interpret it as a very confident prior, so confident that we wish to align with the prior. The situation can be imagined as a game of tug-of-war between a powerful bull and a horse, which the bull will naturally win. If σ_0 is large the prior distribution will become flat. It means that we are not very confident about the prior so that we will trust the data. In this case the MAP estimate will shift towards the ML estimate.

8.3.5 Analysis of the posterior distribution

When the likelihood is multiplied with the prior to form the posterior, what does the posterior distribution look like? To answer this question we continue our Gaussian example with a fixed variance σ and an unknown mean θ. The posterior distribution is proportional to

$$f_{\Theta|\boldsymbol{X}}(\theta|\boldsymbol{x}) = \frac{f_{\boldsymbol{X}|\Theta}(\boldsymbol{x}|\theta)f_{\Theta}(\theta)}{f_{\boldsymbol{X}}(\boldsymbol{x})} \propto f_{\boldsymbol{X}|\Theta}(\boldsymbol{x}|\theta)f_{\Theta}(\theta)$$

$$= \left[\prod_{n=1}^{N}\frac{1}{\sqrt{2\pi\sigma^2}}\exp\left\{-\frac{(x_n-\theta)^2}{2\sigma^2}\right\}\right]\cdot\left[\frac{1}{\sqrt{2\pi\sigma_0^2}}\exp\left\{-\frac{(\theta-\mu_0)^2}{2\sigma_0^2}\right\}\right]. \quad (8.45)$$

Performing the multiplication and completing the squares,

$$\sum_{n=1}^{N}\frac{(x_n-\theta)^2}{2\sigma^2}+\frac{(\theta-\mu_0)^2}{2\sigma_0^2}=\frac{(\theta-\widehat{\theta}_{\mathrm{MAP}})^2}{2\sigma_{\mathrm{MAP}}^2},$$

where

$$\widehat{\theta}_{\mathrm{MAP}}=\frac{\sigma_0^2\widehat{\theta}_{\mathrm{ML}}+\frac{\sigma^2}{N}\mu_0}{\sigma_0^2+\frac{\sigma^2}{N}}, \qquad \text{and} \qquad \frac{1}{\widehat{\sigma}_{\mathrm{MAP}}^2}=\frac{1}{\sigma_0^2}+\frac{N}{\sigma^2}. \quad (8.46)$$

In other words, the posterior distribution $f_{\Theta|\boldsymbol{X}}(\theta|\boldsymbol{x})$ is also a Gaussian with

$$f_{\Theta|\boldsymbol{X}}(\theta|\boldsymbol{x})=\mathrm{Gaussian}(\widehat{\theta}_{\mathrm{MAP}},\widehat{\sigma}_{\mathrm{MAP}}^2).$$

If $f_{\boldsymbol{X}|\Theta}(\boldsymbol{x}|\theta) = \mathbf{Gaussian}(\boldsymbol{x};\ \theta,\sigma)$, and $f_{\Theta}(\theta) = \mathbf{Gaussian}(\theta;\ \mu_0,\sigma_0^2)$, what is the posterior $f_{\Theta|\boldsymbol{X}}(\theta|\boldsymbol{x})$?

The posterior $f_{\Theta|\boldsymbol{X}}(\theta|\boldsymbol{x})$ is Gaussian$(\widehat{\theta}_{\mathrm{MAP}},\widehat{\sigma}_{\mathrm{MAP}}^2)$, where

$$\widehat{\theta}_{\mathrm{MAP}}=\frac{\sigma_0^2\widehat{\theta}_{\mathrm{ML}}+\frac{\sigma^2}{N}\mu_0}{\sigma_0^2+\frac{\sigma^2}{N}}, \qquad \text{and} \qquad \frac{1}{\widehat{\sigma}_{\mathrm{MAP}}^2}=\frac{1}{\sigma_0^2}+\frac{N}{\sigma^2}. \quad (8.47)$$

The posterior tells us how N and σ_0 will influence the MAP estimate. As N grows, the posterior mean and variance becomes

$$\lim_{N\to\infty}\widehat{\theta}_{\mathrm{MAP}}=\widehat{\theta}_{\mathrm{ML}}=\theta, \quad \text{and} \quad \lim_{N\to\infty}\widehat{\sigma}_{\mathrm{MAP}}=0.$$

As a result, the posterior distribution $f_{\Theta|\boldsymbol{X}}(\theta|\boldsymbol{x})$ will converge to a delta function centered at the ML estimate $\widehat{\theta}_{\mathrm{ML}}$. Therefore, as we try to solve the MAP problem by maximizing the posterior, the MAP estimate has to improve because $\widehat{\sigma}_{\mathrm{MAP}}\to 0$.

We can plot the posterior distribution Gaussian$(\widehat{\theta}_{\mathrm{MAP}},\widehat{\sigma}_{\mathrm{MAP}}^2)$ as a function of the number of samples N. **Figure 8.19** illustrates this example using the following configurations.

The likelihood is Gaussian with $\mu = 1$, $\sigma = 0.25$. The prior is Gaussian with $\mu_0 = 0$ and $\sigma = 0.25$. We construct the Gaussian according to Gaussian$(\widehat{\theta}_{\text{MAP}}, \widehat{\sigma}^2_{\text{MAP}})$ by varying N. The result shown in **Figure 8.19** confirms our prediction: As N grows, the posterior becomes more like a delta function whose mean is the true mean μ. The posterior estimator $\widehat{\theta}_{\text{MAP}}$, for each N, is the peak of the respective Gaussian.

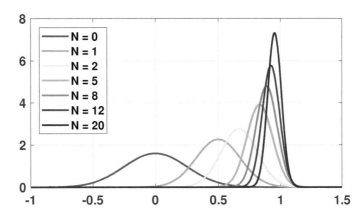

Figure 8.19: Posterior distribution $f_{\Theta|\boldsymbol{X}}(\theta|\boldsymbol{x}) = $ Gaussian$(\widehat{\theta}_{\text{MAP}}, \sigma^2_{\text{MAP}})$ as N grows. When N is small, the posterior distribution is dominated by the prior. As N increases, the posterior distribution changes its mean and its variance.

What is the pictorial interpretation of the MAP estimate?

- For every N, MAP has a posterior distribution $f_{\Theta|\boldsymbol{X}}(\theta|\boldsymbol{x})$.
- As N grows, $f_{\Theta|\boldsymbol{X}}(\theta|\boldsymbol{x})$ converges to a delta function centered at $\widehat{\boldsymbol{\theta}}_{\text{ML}}$.
- MAP tries to find the peak of $f_{\Theta|\boldsymbol{X}}(\theta|\boldsymbol{x})$. For large N, it returns $\widehat{\boldsymbol{\theta}}_{\text{ML}}$.

8.3.6 Conjugate prior

Choosing the prior is an important topic in a MAP estimation. We have elaborated two "engineering" solutions: Use your prior experience or follow the physics. In this subsection, we discuss the third option: to choose something computationally friendly. To explain what we mean by "computationally friendly", let us consider the following example, thanks to Avinash Kak.[4]

Consider a Bernoulli distribution with a PDF

$$f_{\boldsymbol{X}|\Theta}(\boldsymbol{x}|\theta) = \prod_{n=1}^{N} \theta^{x_n}(1-\theta)^{1-x_n}. \tag{8.48}$$

To compute the MAP estimate, we assume that we have a prior $f_{\Theta}(\theta)$. Therefore, the MAP

---

[4]Avinash Kak "ML, MAP, and Bayesian — The Holy Trinity of Parameter Estimation and Data Prediction", https://engineering.purdue.edu/kak/Tutorials/Trinity.pdf

estimate is given by

$$\widehat{\theta}_{\text{MAP}} = \underset{\theta}{\text{argmax}} \ f_{\boldsymbol{X}|\Theta}(\boldsymbol{x}|\theta) f_{\Theta}(\theta)$$

$$= \underset{\theta}{\text{argmax}} \ \left[\prod_{n=1}^{N} \theta^{x_n}(1-\theta)^{1-x_n} \right] \cdot f_{\Theta}(\theta)$$

$$= \underset{\theta}{\text{argmax}} \ \sum_{n=1}^{N} x_n \log \theta + (1-x_n) \log(1-\theta) + \log f_{\Theta}(\theta).$$

Let us consider three options for the prior. Which one would you use?

- **Candidate 1**: $f_{\Theta}(\theta) = \frac{1}{\sqrt{2\pi\sigma^2}} \exp\left\{ -\frac{(\theta-\mu)^2}{2\sigma^2} \right\}$, a Gaussian prior. If you choose this prior, the optimization problem will become

$$\widehat{\theta}_{\text{MAP}} = \underset{\theta}{\text{argmax}} \ \sum_{n=1}^{N} \left\{ x_n \log \theta + (1-x_n) \log(1-\theta) \right\} - \frac{(\theta-\mu)^2}{2\sigma^2}.$$

We can still take the derivative and set it to zero. This gives

$$\frac{\sum_{n=1}^{N} x_n}{\theta} - \frac{N - \sum_{n=1}^{N} x_n}{1-\theta} = \frac{\theta - \mu}{\sigma^2}.$$

Defining $S = \sum_{n=1}^{N} x_n$ and moving the terms around, we have

$$(1-\theta)\sigma^2 S - \theta\sigma^2(N-S) = \theta(1-\theta)(\theta-\mu).$$

This is a cubic polynomial problem that has a closed-form solution and is also solvable by a computer. But it's also tedious, at least to lazy engineers like ourselves.

- **Candidate 2**: $f_{\Theta}(\theta) = \frac{\lambda}{2} e^{-\lambda|\theta|}$, a Laplace prior. In this case, the optimization problem becomes

$$\widehat{\theta}_{\text{MAP}} = \underset{\theta}{\text{argmax}} \ \sum_{n=1}^{N} \left\{ x_n \log \theta + (1-x_n) \log(1-\theta) \right\} - \lambda|\theta|.$$

Welcome to convex optimization! There is no closed-form solution. If you want to solve this problem, you need to call a convex solver.

- **Candidate 3**: $f_{\Theta}(\theta) = \frac{1}{C} \theta^{\alpha-1}(1-\theta)^{\beta-1}$, a beta prior. This prior looks very complicated, but let's plug it into our optimization problem:

$$\widehat{\theta}_{\text{MAP}} = \underset{\theta}{\text{argmax}} \ \sum_{n=1}^{N} \left\{ x_n \log \theta \right.$$

$$\left. + (1-x_n) \log(1-\theta) \right\} + (\alpha-1) \log \theta + (\beta-1) \log(1-\theta)$$

$$= \underset{\theta}{\text{argmax}} \ (S+\alpha-1) \log \theta + (N-S+\beta-1) \log(1-\theta),$$

where $S = \sum_{n=1}^{N} x_n$. Taking the derivative and setting it to zero, we have

$$\frac{S + \alpha - 1}{\theta} = \frac{N - S + \beta - 1}{1 - \theta}.$$

Rearranging the terms we obtain the final estimate:

$$\widehat{\theta}_{\text{MAP}} = \frac{S + \alpha - 1}{N + \beta + \alpha - 2}. \tag{8.49}$$

There are a number of intuitions that we can draw from this beta prior, but most importantly, we have obtained a very simple solution. That is because the posterior distribution remains in the same form as the prior, after multiplying by the prior. Specifically, if we use the beta prior, the posterior distribution is

$$f_{\Theta|\boldsymbol{X}}(\theta|\boldsymbol{x}) \propto f_{\boldsymbol{X}|\Theta}(\boldsymbol{x}|\theta) f_{\Theta}(\theta)$$

$$= \left[\prod_{n=1}^{N} \theta^{x_n} (1 - \theta)^{1-x_n} \right] \cdot \frac{1}{C} \theta^{\alpha-1} (1 - \theta)^{\beta-1}$$

$$= \theta^{S+\alpha-1} (1 - \theta)^{N-S+\beta-1}.$$

This is still in the form of $\theta^{\star-1}(1 - \theta)^{\blacksquare-1}$, which is the same as the prior. When this happens, we call the prior a conjugate prior. In this example, the beta prior is a conjugate before the Bernoulli likelihood.

What is a conjugate prior?

- It is a prior such that when multiplied by the likelihood to form the posterior, the posterior $f_{\Theta|\boldsymbol{X}}(\theta|\boldsymbol{x})$ takes the same form as the prior $f_{\Theta}(\theta)$.

- Every likelihood has its conjugate prior.

- Conjugate priors are not necessarily good priors. They are just computationally friendly. Some of them have good physical interpretations.

We can make a few interpretations of the beta prior, in the context of Bernoulli likelihood. First, the beta distribution takes the form

$$f_{\Theta}(\theta) = \frac{1}{B(\alpha, \beta)} \theta^{\alpha-1} (1 - \theta)^{\beta-1}, \tag{8.50}$$

with $B(\alpha, \beta)$ is the beta function[5]. The shape of the beta distribution is shown in **Figure 8.20**. For different choices of α and β, the distribution has a peak located towards either side of the interval $[0, 1]$. For example, if α is large but β is small, the distribution $f_{\Theta}(\theta)$ leans towards 1 (the yellow curve).

As a user, you have the freedom to pick $f_{\Theta}(\theta)$. Even if you are restricted to the beta distribution, you still have plenty of degrees of freedom in choosing α and β so that your choice matches your belief. For example, if you know ahead of time that the Bernoulli experiment is biased towards 1 (e.g., the coin is more likely to come up heads), you can choose a large α and a small β. By contrast, if you believe that the coin is fair, you choose $\alpha = \beta$. The parameters α and β are known as the **hyperparameters** of the prior distribution. Hyperparameters are parameters for $f_{\Theta}(\theta)$.

---

[5]The beta function is defined as $B(\alpha, \beta) = \frac{\Gamma(\alpha)\Gamma(\beta)}{\Gamma(\alpha+\beta)}$, where Γ is the gamma function. For integer n, $\Gamma(n) = (n - 1)!$

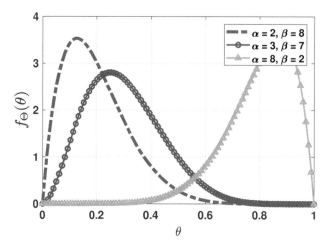

Figure 8.20: Beta distribution $f_\Theta(\theta)$ for various choices of α and β. When $(\alpha, \beta) = (2, 8)$, the beta distribution favors small θ. When $(\alpha, \beta) = (8, 2)$, the beta distribution favors large θ. By swinging between the (α, β) pairs, we obtain a prior that has a preference over θ.

Example 8.20. (Prior for Gaussian mean) Consider a Gaussian likelihood for a fixed variance σ^2 and unknown mean θ:

$$f_{\mathbf{X}|\Theta}(\mathbf{x}|\theta) = \left(\frac{1}{\sqrt{2\pi\sigma^2}}\right)^N \exp\left\{-\sum_{n=1}^{N}\frac{(x_n - \theta)^2}{2\sigma^2}\right\}.$$

Show that the conjugate prior is given by

$$f_\Theta(\theta) = \frac{1}{\sqrt{2\pi\sigma_0^2}}\exp\left\{-\frac{(\theta - \mu_0)^2}{2\sigma_0^2}\right\}. \tag{8.51}$$

Solution. We have shown this result previously. By some (tedious) completing squares, we show that

$$f_{\Theta|\mathbf{X}}(\theta|\mathbf{x}) = \frac{1}{\sqrt{2\pi\sigma_N^2}}\exp\left\{-\frac{(\theta - \mu_N)^2}{2\sigma_N^2}\right\},$$

where

$$\mu_N = \frac{\sigma^2}{N\sigma_0^2 + \sigma^2}\mu_0 + \frac{N\sigma_0^2}{N\sigma_0^2 + \sigma^2}\widehat{\theta}_{\mathrm{ML}},$$

$$\sigma_N^2 = \frac{\sigma^2\sigma_0^2}{\sigma^2 + N\sigma_0^2}.$$

Since $f_{\Theta|\mathbf{X}}(\theta|\mathbf{x})$ is in the same form as $f_\Theta(\theta)$, we know that $f_\Theta(\theta)$ is a conjugate prior.

Example 8.21. (Prior for Gaussian variance) Consider a Gaussian likelihood for a mean μ and unknown variance σ^2:

$$f_{\boldsymbol{X}|\sigma}(\boldsymbol{x}|\sigma) = \left(\frac{1}{\sqrt{2\pi\sigma^2}}\right)^N \exp\left\{-\sum_{n=1}^{N}\frac{(x_n-\mu)^2}{2\sigma^2}\right\}.$$

Find the conjugate prior.

Solution. We first define the precision $\theta = \frac{1}{\sigma^2}$. The likelihood is

$$f_{\boldsymbol{X}|\Theta}(\boldsymbol{x}|\theta) = \left(\frac{1}{\sqrt{2\pi\sigma^2}}\right)^N \exp\left\{-\sum_{n=1}^{N}\frac{(x_n-\mu)^2}{2\sigma^2}\right\}$$

$$= \frac{1}{(2\pi)^{N/2}} \theta^{N/2} \exp\left\{-\frac{\theta}{2}\sum_{n=1}^{N}(x_n-\mu)^2\right\}.$$

We propose to choose the prior $f_\Theta(\theta)$ as

$$f_\Theta(\theta) = \frac{1}{\Gamma(a)} b^a \theta^{a-1} \exp\left\{-b\theta\right\},$$

for some a and b. This $f_\Theta(\theta)$ is called the Gamma distribution $\text{Gamma}(\theta|a,b)$. We can show that $\mathbb{E}[\Theta] = \frac{a}{b}$ and $\text{Var}[\Theta] = \frac{a}{b^2}$. With some (tedious) completing squares, we show that the posterior is

$$f_{\Theta|\boldsymbol{X}}(\theta|\boldsymbol{x}) \propto \theta^{(a_0+N/2)-1} \exp\left\{-\left(b_0 + \frac{1}{2}\sum_{n=1}^{N}(x_n-\mu)^2\right)\theta\right\},$$

which is in the same form as the prior. So we know that our proposed $f_\Theta(\theta)$ is a conjugate prior.

The story of conjugate priors is endless because every likelihood has its conjugate prior. **Table 8.1** summarizes a few commonly used conjugate priors, their likelihoods, and their posteriors. The list can be expanded further to distributions with multiple parameters. For example, if a Gaussian has both unknown mean and variance, then there exists a conjugate prior consisting of a Gaussian multiplied by a Gamma. Conjugate priors also apply to multidimensional distributions. For example, the prior for the mean vector of a high-dimensional Gaussian is another high-dimensional Gaussian. The prior for the covariance matrix of a high-dimensional Gaussian is the Wishart prior. The prior for both the mean vector and the covariance matrix is the normal Wishart.

8.3.7 Linking MAP with regression

ML and regression represent the statistics and the optimization aspects of the same problem. With the parallel argument, MAP is linked to the **regularized** regression. The reason follows

Table of Conjugate Priors

Likelihood $f_{\boldsymbol{X}\mid\Theta}(\boldsymbol{x}\mid\theta)$	Conjugate Prior $f_\Theta(\theta)$	Posterior $f_{\Theta\mid\boldsymbol{X}}(\theta\mid\boldsymbol{x})$
Bernoulli(θ)	Beta(α,β)	Beta$(\alpha+S, \beta+N-S)$
Poisson(θ)	Gamma(α,β)	Gamma$\left(\alpha+S, \frac{\beta}{1+N}\right)$
Exponential(θ)	Gamma(α,β)	Gamma$\left(\alpha+N, \frac{\beta}{1+\beta S}\right)$
Gaussian(θ,σ^2)	Gaussian(μ_0,σ_0^2)	Gaussian$\left(\frac{\mu_0/\sigma_0^2+S/\sigma^2}{1/\sigma_0^2+N/\sigma^2}, \frac{1}{\frac{N}{\sigma^2}+\frac{1}{\sigma_0^2}}\right)$
Gaussian(μ,θ^2)	Inv. Gamma(α,β)	Gamma$\left(\alpha+\frac{N}{2}, \beta+\frac{1}{2}\sum_{n=1}^{N}(x_n-\mu)^2\right)$

Table 8.1: Commonly used conjugate priors. Here, $S = \sum_{n=1}^{N} x_n$ is the sum, and N is the number of observed samples.

immediately from the definition of MAP:

$$\widehat{\boldsymbol{\theta}}_{\mathrm{MAP}} = \operatorname*{argmax}_{\boldsymbol{\theta}} \ \underbrace{\log f_{\boldsymbol{X}\mid\Theta}(\boldsymbol{x}\mid\boldsymbol{\theta})}_{\text{data fidelity}} + \underbrace{\log f_\Theta(\boldsymbol{\theta})}_{\text{regularization}} .$$

To make this more explicit, we consider following linear regression problem:

$$\begin{bmatrix} y_1 \\ y_2 \\ \vdots \\ y_N \end{bmatrix} = \underbrace{\begin{bmatrix} \phi_0(x_1) & \phi_1(x_1) & \cdots & \phi_{d-1}(x_1) \\ \phi_0(x_2) & \phi_1(x_2) & \cdots & \phi_{d-1}(x_2) \\ \vdots & & \cdots & \vdots \\ \phi_0(x_N) & \phi_1(x_N) & \cdots & \phi_{d-1}(x_N) \end{bmatrix}}_{=\boldsymbol{X}} \underbrace{\begin{bmatrix} \theta_0 \\ \theta_1 \\ \vdots \\ \theta_{d-1} \end{bmatrix}}_{=\boldsymbol{\theta}} + \underbrace{\begin{bmatrix} e_1 \\ e_2 \\ \vdots \\ e_N \end{bmatrix}}_{=\boldsymbol{e}} .$$

If we assume that $\boldsymbol{e} \sim \text{Gaussian}(0, \sigma^2\boldsymbol{I})$, the likelihood is defined as

$$f_{\boldsymbol{Y}\mid\Theta}(\boldsymbol{y}\mid\boldsymbol{\theta}) = \frac{1}{\sqrt{(2\pi\sigma^2)^N}} \exp\left\{-\frac{1}{2\sigma^2}\|\boldsymbol{y}-\boldsymbol{X}\boldsymbol{\theta}\|^2\right\}. \tag{8.52}$$

In the ML setting, the ML estimate is the maximizer of the likelihood:

$$\widehat{\boldsymbol{\theta}}_{\mathrm{ML}} = \operatorname*{argmax}_{\boldsymbol{\theta}} \ \log f_{\boldsymbol{Y}\mid\Theta}(\boldsymbol{y}\mid\boldsymbol{\theta})$$

$$= \operatorname*{argmax}_{\boldsymbol{\theta}} \ -\frac{1}{2\sigma^2}\|\boldsymbol{y}-\boldsymbol{X}\boldsymbol{\theta}\|^2.$$

For MAP, we add a prior term so that the optimization becomes

$$\widehat{\boldsymbol{\theta}}_{\mathrm{MAP}} = \underset{\boldsymbol{\theta}}{\mathrm{argmax}} \quad \log f_{\boldsymbol{Y}|\boldsymbol{\Theta}}(\boldsymbol{y}|\boldsymbol{\theta}) + \log f_{\boldsymbol{\Theta}}(\boldsymbol{\theta})$$

$$= \underset{\boldsymbol{\theta}}{\mathrm{argmin}} \quad \frac{1}{2\sigma^2}\|\boldsymbol{y} - \boldsymbol{X}\boldsymbol{\theta}\|^2 - \log f_{\boldsymbol{\Theta}}(\boldsymbol{\theta}).$$

Therefore, the regularization of the regression is exactly $-\log f_{\boldsymbol{\Theta}}(\boldsymbol{\theta})$. We can perform reverse engineering to find out the corresponding prior for our favorite choices of the regularization.

Ridge regression. Suppose that

$$f_{\boldsymbol{\Theta}}(\boldsymbol{\theta}) = \exp\left\{-\frac{\|\boldsymbol{\theta}\|^2}{2\sigma_0^2}\right\}.$$

Taking the negative log on both sides yields

$$-\log f_{\boldsymbol{\Theta}}(\boldsymbol{\theta}) = \frac{\|\boldsymbol{\theta}\|^2}{2\sigma_0^2}.$$

Putting this into the MAP estimate,

$$\widehat{\boldsymbol{\theta}}_{\mathrm{MAP}} = \underset{\boldsymbol{\theta}}{\mathrm{argmin}} \quad \frac{1}{2\sigma^2}\|\boldsymbol{y} - \boldsymbol{X}\boldsymbol{\theta}\|^2 + \frac{1}{2\sigma_0^2}\|\boldsymbol{\theta}\|^2$$

$$= \underset{\boldsymbol{\theta}}{\mathrm{argmin}} \quad \|\boldsymbol{y} - \boldsymbol{X}\boldsymbol{\theta}\|^2 + \underbrace{\frac{\sigma^2}{\sigma_0^2}}_{=\lambda}\|\boldsymbol{\theta}\|^2,$$

where λ is the corresponding ridge regularization parameter. Therefore, the ridge regression is equivalent to a MAP estimation using a Gaussian prior.

How is MAP related to ridge regression?

- In MAP, define the prior as a Gaussian:

$$f_{\boldsymbol{\Theta}}(\boldsymbol{\theta}) = \exp\left\{-\frac{\|\boldsymbol{\theta}\|^2}{2\sigma_0^2}\right\}. \tag{8.53}$$

- The prior says that the solution $\boldsymbol{\theta}$ is naturally distributed according to a Gaussian with mean zero and variance σ_0^2.

LASSO regression. Suppose that

$$f_{\boldsymbol{\Theta}}(\boldsymbol{\theta}) = \exp\left\{-\frac{\|\boldsymbol{\theta}\|_1}{\alpha}\right\}.$$

Taking the negative log on both sides yields

$$-\log f_{\boldsymbol{\Theta}}(\boldsymbol{\theta}) = \frac{\|\boldsymbol{\theta}\|_1}{\alpha}.$$

Putting this into the MAP estimate we can show that

$$\widehat{\boldsymbol{\theta}}_{\text{MAP}} = \underset{\boldsymbol{\theta}}{\operatorname{argmin}} \quad \frac{1}{2\sigma^2} \|\boldsymbol{y} - \boldsymbol{X}\boldsymbol{\theta}\|^2 + \frac{1}{\alpha} \|\boldsymbol{\theta}\|_1$$

$$= \underset{\boldsymbol{\theta}}{\operatorname{argmin}} \quad \frac{1}{2} \|\boldsymbol{y} - \boldsymbol{X}\boldsymbol{\theta}\|^2 + \underbrace{\frac{\sigma^2}{\alpha}}_{=\lambda} \|\boldsymbol{\theta}\|_1.$$

To summarize:

How is MAP related to LASSO regression?

- LASSO is a MAP using the prior

$$f_{\boldsymbol{\Theta}}(\boldsymbol{\theta}) = \exp\left\{ -\frac{\|\boldsymbol{\theta}\|_1}{\alpha} \right\}. \tag{8.54}$$

At this point, you may be wondering what MAP buys us when regularized regression can already do the job. The answer is about the interpretation. While regularized regression can always return us a result, that is just a result. However, if you know that the parameter $\boldsymbol{\theta}$ is distributed according to some distributions $f_{\boldsymbol{\Theta}}(\boldsymbol{\theta})$, MAP offers a statistical perspective of the solution in the sense that it returns the peak of the posterior $f_{\boldsymbol{\Theta}|\boldsymbol{X}}(\boldsymbol{\theta}|\boldsymbol{x})$. For example, if we know that the data is generated from a linear model with Gaussian noise, and if we know that the true regression coefficients are drawn from a Gaussian, then the ridge regression is guaranteed to be optimal in the posterior sense. Similarly, if we know that there are outliers and have some ideas about the outlier statistics, perhaps the LASSO regression is a better choice.

It is also important to note the different optimalities offered by MAP versus ML versus regression. The optimality offered by regression is the training loss, which can always give us a result even if the underlying statistics do not match the optimization formulation, e.g., there are outliers, and you use unregularized least-squares minimization. You can get a result, but the outliers will heavily influence your solution. On the other hand, if you know the data statistics and choose to follow the ML, then the ML solution is optimal in the sense of optimizing the likelihood $f_{\boldsymbol{X}|\boldsymbol{\Theta}}(\boldsymbol{x}|\boldsymbol{\theta})$. If you further know the prior statistics, the MAP solution will be optimal, but this time it is optimal w.r.t. to the posterior $f_{\boldsymbol{\Theta}|\boldsymbol{X}}(\boldsymbol{\theta}|\boldsymbol{x})$. Since each of these is optimizing for a different goal, they are only good for their chosen objectives. For example, $\widehat{\boldsymbol{\theta}}_{\text{MAP}}$ can be a biased estimate if our goal is to maximize the likelihood. The $\widehat{\boldsymbol{\theta}}_{\text{ML}}$ is optimal for the likelihood but can be a bad choice for the posterior. Both $\widehat{\boldsymbol{\theta}}_{\text{MAP}}$ and $\widehat{\boldsymbol{\theta}}_{\text{ML}}$ can possibly achieve a reasonable mean-squared error, but their results may not make sense (e.g., if $\boldsymbol{\theta}$ is an image then $\widehat{\boldsymbol{\theta}}_{\text{MAP}}$ may over-smooth the image whereas $\widehat{\boldsymbol{\theta}}_{\text{ML}}$ amplifies noise). So it's incorrect to think that $\widehat{\boldsymbol{\theta}}_{\text{MAP}}$ is superior to $\widehat{\boldsymbol{\theta}}_{\text{ML}}$ because it is more general.

Here are some rules of thumb for MAP, ML, and regression:

When should I use regression, ML and MAP?

- **Regression:** If you are lazy and you know nothing about the statistics, do the regression with whatever regularization you prefer. It will give you a result. See if it makes sense with your data.

- **MAP**: If you know the statistics of the data, and if you have some preference for the prior distribution, go with MAP. It will offer you the optimal solution w.r.t. finding the peak of the posterior.

- **ML**: If you are interested in some simple-form solution, and you want those nice properties such as consistency and unbiasedness, then go with ML. It usually possesses the "friendly" properties so that you can derive the performance limit.

8.4 Minimum Mean-Square Estimation

First-time readers are often tempted to think that the maximum-likelihood estimation or the maximum a posteriori estimation are *the* best methods to estimate parameters. In some sense, this is true because both estimation procedures offer some form of optimal explanation for the observed variables. However, as we said above, being optimal with respect to the likelihood or the posterior only means optimal under the respective criteria. An ML estimate is not necessarily optimal for the posterior, whereas a MAP estimate is not necessarily optimal for the likelihood. Therefore, as we proceed to the third commonly used estimation strategy, we need to remind ourselves of the specific type of optimality we seek.

8.4.1 Positioning the minimum mean-square estimation

Mean-square error estimation, as it is termed, uses the mean-square error as the optimality criterion. The corresponding estimation process is known as the **minimum mean-square estimation (MMSE)**. MMSE is a **Bayesian** approach, meaning that it uses the prior $f_{\Theta}(\theta)$ as well as the likelihood $f_{X|\Theta}(x|\theta)$. As we will show shortly, the MMSE estimate of a set of i.i.d. observation $X = [X_1, \dots, X_N]^T$ is

$$\widehat{\theta}_{\text{MMSE}}(x) \stackrel{(a)}{=} \mathbb{E}_{\Theta|X}\left[\Theta | X = x\right] \qquad (a): \text{We will discuss this.}$$

$$= \int \theta \cdot f_{\Theta|X}(\theta|x)\, d\theta. \tag{8.55}$$

You may find this equation very surprising, because it says that the MMSE estimate is the **mean** of the posterior distribution $f_{\Theta|X}(\theta|x)$. Let's compare this result with the ML estimate and the MAP estimate:

$$\widehat{\theta}_{\text{ML}} = \text{peak of } f_{X|\Theta}(x \mid \theta),$$

$$\widehat{\theta}_{\text{MAP}} = \text{peak of } f_{\Theta X|}(\theta \mid x),$$

$$\widehat{\theta}_{\text{MMSE}} = \text{average of } f_{\Theta|X}(\theta \mid x).$$

Therefore, an MMSE estimate is not by any means universally superior or inferior to a MAP estimate or an ML estimate. It is just a different estimate with a different goal.

So how exactly are these estimates different? **Figure 8.21** illustrates a typical situation of asymmetric distribution. Here, we plot both the likelihood function $f_{X|\Theta}(x \mid \theta)$ and the posterior function $f_{\Theta X|}(\theta \mid x)$.

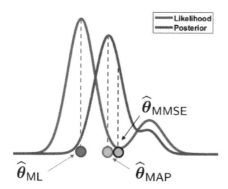

Figure 8.21: A typical example of an ML estimate, a MAP estimate and an MMSE estimate.

As shown in the figure, the ML estimate is the peak of the likelihood, whereas the MAP estimate is the peak of the posterior. The third estimate is the MMSE estimate, which is the average of the posterior distribution. It is easy to see that if the posterior distribution is symmetric and has a single peak, the peak is always the mean. Therefore, for single-peak symmetric distributions, MMSE and MAP estimates are identical.

What is so special about the MMSE estimate?

- MMSE is a Bayesian estimation, so it requires a prior.

- An MMSE estimate is the mean of the posterior distribution.

- MMSE estimate = MAP estimate if the posterior distribution is symmetric and has a single peak.

8.4.2 Mean squared error

The MMSE is based on minimizing the mean squared error (MSE). In this subsection we discuss the mean squared error in the Bayesian setting. In the deterministic setting, given an estimate $\widehat{\theta}$ and a ground truth θ, the MSE is defined as

$$\mathrm{MSE}(\underbrace{\theta}_{\text{ground truth}}, \underbrace{\widehat{\theta}}_{\text{estimate}}) = (\theta - \widehat{\theta})^2. \tag{8.56}$$

In any estimation problem, the estimate $\widehat{\theta}$ is always a function of the observed variables. Thus, we have

$$\widehat{\theta}(\boldsymbol{X}) = g(\boldsymbol{X}), \qquad \text{where} \qquad \boldsymbol{X} = [X_1, \dots, X_N]^T,$$

for some function $g(\cdot)$. Substituting this into the definition of MSE, and recognizing that $\boldsymbol{X}$ is drawn from a distribution $f_{\boldsymbol{X}}(\boldsymbol{x})$, we take the expectation to define the MSE as

$$\mathrm{MSE}(\theta, \widehat{\theta}) = (\theta - \widehat{\theta})^2$$

$$\Downarrow \text{replace } \widehat{\theta} \text{ by } g(\boldsymbol{X})$$

$$\mathrm{MSE}(\theta, \widehat{\theta}) = (\theta - g(\boldsymbol{X}))^2$$

$$\Downarrow \text{take expectation over } \boldsymbol{X}$$

$$\mathrm{MSE}(\theta, \widehat{\theta}) = \mathbb{E}_{\boldsymbol{X}} \left[(\theta - g(\boldsymbol{X}))^2 \right].$$

Thus we have arrived at the definition of MSE. We call this the **frequentist** version, because the parameter θ is deterministic.

Definition 8.8 (Mean squared error, frequentist). *The mean squared error of an estimate $g(X)$ w.r.t. the true parameter θ is*

$$MSE_{freq}(\theta, g(\cdot)) = \mathbb{E}_X \left[(\theta - g(X))^2 \right]. \tag{8.57}$$

If the parameter $\boldsymbol{\theta}$ is high-dimensional, so is the estimate $g(X)$, and the MSE is

$$MSE_{freq}(\boldsymbol{\theta}, \boldsymbol{g}(\cdot)) = \mathbb{E}_X \left[\| \boldsymbol{\theta} - \boldsymbol{g}(X) \|^2 \right]. \tag{8.58}$$

Note that in the above definition the MSE is measured between the true parameter θ and the estimator $g(\cdot)$. We use the function $g(\cdot)$ here because we have taken the expectation of all the possible inputs X. So we are not comparing θ with a value $g(X)$ but with the function $g(\cdot)$.

If we take a Bayesian approach such as the MAP, then θ itself is a random variable Θ, To compute the MSE, we then need to take the average across all the possible choices of ground truth Θ. This leads to

$$\text{MSE}(\theta, \widehat{\theta}) = \mathbb{E}_X \left[(\theta - g(X))^2 \right]$$

$$\Downarrow \text{ replace } \theta \text{ by } \Theta$$

$$\text{MSE}(\theta, \widehat{\theta}) = \mathbb{E}_X \left[(\Theta - g(X))^2 \right]$$

$$\Downarrow \text{ take expectation over } \Theta$$

$$\text{MSE}(\theta, \widehat{\theta}) = \mathbb{E}_{X, \Theta} \left[(\Theta - g(X))^2 \right].$$

Therefore, we have arrived at our definition of the MSE, in the Bayesian setting.

Definition 8.9 (Mean squared error, Bayesian). *The mean squared error of an estimate $g(X)$ w.r.t. the true parameter Θ is*

$$MSE_{Bayes}(\Theta, g(\cdot)) = \mathbb{E}_{\Theta, X} \left[(\Theta - g(X))^2 \right]. \tag{8.59}$$

If the parameter Θ is high-dimensional, so is the estimate $g(X)$, and the MSE is

$$MSE_{Bayes}(\boldsymbol{\Theta}, \boldsymbol{g}(\cdot)) = \mathbb{E}_{\boldsymbol{\Theta}, X} \left[\| \boldsymbol{\Theta} - \boldsymbol{g}(X) \|^2 \right]. \tag{8.60}$$

The difference between the Bayesian MSE and the frequentist MSE is the expectation over Θ, Practically speaking, the frequentist MSE is more of an evaluation metric than an objective function for solving an inverse problem. The reason is that in an inverse problem, we never have access to the true parameter θ. (If we knew θ, there would be no problem to solve.) Bayesian MSE is more meaningful. It says that we do not know the true parameter θ, but we know its statistics. We are trying to find the best $g(\cdot)$ that minimizes the error. Our solution will depend on the statistics of Θ but not on the unknown true parameter θ.

When we say *minimum* mean squared error estimation, we typically refer to the **Bayesian** MMSE. In this case, the problem we solve is

$$g(\cdot) = \underset{g(\cdot)}{\text{argmin}} \ \mathbb{E}_{\Theta, X} \left[(\Theta - g(X))^2 \right]. \tag{8.61}$$

As you can see from Definition 8.9, the goal of the Bayesian MMSE is to find a function $g : \mathbb{R}^N \to \mathbb{R}$ such that the joint expectation $\mathbb{E}_{\Theta,\boldsymbol{X}}\left[(\Theta - g(\boldsymbol{X}))^2\right]$ is minimized. In the case where $\boldsymbol{\Theta}$ is a vector, the problem becomes

$$\boldsymbol{g}(\cdot) = \underset{\boldsymbol{g}(\cdot)}{\operatorname{argmin}} \ \mathbb{E}_{\boldsymbol{\Theta},\boldsymbol{X}}\left[\|\boldsymbol{\Theta} - \boldsymbol{g}(\boldsymbol{X})\|^2\right], \tag{8.62}$$

where $\boldsymbol{g}(\cdot) : \mathbb{R}^{N \times d} \to \mathbb{R}^d$ if $\boldsymbol{\Theta}$ is a d-dimensional vector. The function $\boldsymbol{g}$ will take a sequence of N observed numbers and estimate the parameter $\boldsymbol{\Theta}$.

What is the Bayesian MMSE estimate?

The Bayesian MMSE estimate is obtained by minimizing the MSE:

$$g(\cdot) = \underset{g(\cdot)}{\operatorname{argmin}} \ \mathbb{E}_{\Theta,\boldsymbol{X}}\left[(\Theta - g(\boldsymbol{X}))^2\right]. \tag{8.63}$$

8.4.3 MMSE estimate = conditional expectation

Theorem 8.2. *The Bayesian MMSE estimate is*

$$\widehat{\theta}_{MMSE} = \underset{g(\cdot)}{\operatorname{argmin}} \ \mathbb{E}_{\Theta,\boldsymbol{X}}\left[(\Theta - g(\boldsymbol{X}))^2\right]$$
$$= \mathbb{E}_{\Theta|\boldsymbol{X}}[\Theta \mid \boldsymbol{X} = \boldsymbol{x}]. \tag{8.64}$$

Proof. First of all, we decompose the joint expectation:

$$\mathbb{E}_{\Theta,\boldsymbol{X}}\left[(\Theta - g(\boldsymbol{X}))^2\right] = \int \mathbb{E}_{\Theta|\boldsymbol{X}}\left[(\Theta - g(\boldsymbol{X}))^2 \mid \boldsymbol{X} = \boldsymbol{x}\right] f_{\boldsymbol{X}}(\boldsymbol{x}) \, d\boldsymbol{x}.$$

Since $f_{\boldsymbol{X}}(\boldsymbol{x}) \geq 0$ for all $\boldsymbol{x}$, and $\mathbb{E}_{\Theta|\boldsymbol{X}}\left[(\Theta - g(\boldsymbol{X}))^2 \mid \boldsymbol{X} = \boldsymbol{x}\right] \geq 0$ because it is a square, it follows that the integral is minimized when $\mathbb{E}_{\Theta|\boldsymbol{X}}\left[(\Theta - g(\boldsymbol{X}))^2 \mid \boldsymbol{X} = \boldsymbol{x}\right]$ is minimized.

The conditional expectation can be evaluated as

$$\mathbb{E}_{\Theta|\boldsymbol{X}}[(\Theta - g(\boldsymbol{X}))^2 \mid \boldsymbol{X} = \boldsymbol{x}]$$
$$= \mathbb{E}_{\Theta|\boldsymbol{X}}\left[\Theta^2 - 2\Theta g(\boldsymbol{X}) + g(\boldsymbol{X})^2 \mid \boldsymbol{X} = \boldsymbol{x}\right]$$
$$= \underbrace{\mathbb{E}_{\Theta|\boldsymbol{X}}\left[\Theta^2 \mid \boldsymbol{X} = \boldsymbol{x}\right]}_{\overset{\text{def}}{=}V(\boldsymbol{x})} - 2\underbrace{\mathbb{E}_{\Theta|\boldsymbol{X}}\left[\Theta \mid \boldsymbol{X} = \boldsymbol{x}\right]}_{\overset{\text{def}}{=}u(\boldsymbol{x})}g(\boldsymbol{x}) + g(\boldsymbol{x})^2$$
$$= V(\boldsymbol{x}) - 2u(\boldsymbol{x})g(\boldsymbol{x}) + g(\boldsymbol{x})^2 + u(\boldsymbol{x})^2 - u(\boldsymbol{x})^2$$
$$= V(\boldsymbol{x}) - u(\boldsymbol{x})^2 + (u(\boldsymbol{x}) - g(\boldsymbol{x}))^2$$
$$\geq V(\boldsymbol{x}) - u(\boldsymbol{x})^2, \qquad \forall g(\cdot),$$

where the last inequality holds because no matter what $g(\cdot)$ we choose, the square term $(u(\boldsymbol{x}) - g(\boldsymbol{x}))^2$ is non-negative. Therefore, $\mathbb{E}_{\Theta|\boldsymbol{X}}[(\Theta - g(\boldsymbol{X}))^2 \mid \boldsymbol{X} = \boldsymbol{x}]$ is lower-bounded by

$V(\boldsymbol{x}) - u(\boldsymbol{x})^2$, which is a bound that is independent of $g(\cdot)$. If we can find a $g(\cdot)$ such that this lower bound can be met, the corresponding $g(\cdot)$ is the minimizer.

To this end we only need to make $\mathbb{E}_{\Theta|\boldsymbol{X}}[(\Theta - g(\boldsymbol{X}))^2 \mid \boldsymbol{X} = \boldsymbol{x}]$ equal $V(\boldsymbol{x}) - u(\boldsymbol{x})^2$, but this is easy: the equality holds if and only if $(u(\boldsymbol{x}) - g(\boldsymbol{x}))^2 = 0$. In other words, if we choose $g(\cdot)$ such that $g(\boldsymbol{x}) = u(\boldsymbol{x})$, the corresponding $g(\cdot)$ is the minimizer. This $g(\cdot)$, by substituting the definition of $u(\boldsymbol{x})$, is

$$g(\boldsymbol{x}) = \mathbb{E}_{\Theta|\boldsymbol{X}}\left[\Theta \,\middle|\, \boldsymbol{X} = \boldsymbol{x}\right]. \tag{8.65}$$

This completes the proof.

□

What is the MMSE estimate?

The MMSE estimate is

$$\widehat{\theta}_{\text{MMSE}}(\boldsymbol{x}) = \mathbb{E}_{\Theta|\boldsymbol{X}}[\Theta \mid \boldsymbol{X} = \boldsymbol{x}]. \tag{8.66}$$

We emphasize that $\widehat{\theta}_{\text{MMSE}}(\boldsymbol{x})$ is a function of $\boldsymbol{x}$, because for a different set of observations $\boldsymbol{x}$ we will have a different estimated value. Since $\boldsymbol{x}$ is a random realization of the random vector $\boldsymbol{X}$, we can also define the MMSE **estimator** as

$$\widehat{\Theta}_{\text{MMSE}}(\boldsymbol{X}) = \mathbb{E}_{\Theta|\boldsymbol{X}}[\Theta \mid \boldsymbol{X}]. \tag{8.67}$$

In this notation, we emphasize that the estimator $\widehat{\Theta}_{\text{MMSE}}$ returns a random parameter. The input to the estimator is the random vector $\boldsymbol{X}$. Because we are not looking at a particular realization $\boldsymbol{X} = \boldsymbol{x}$ but the general $\boldsymbol{X}$, $\widehat{\Theta}_{\text{MMSE}}$ is a function of $\boldsymbol{X}$ and not $\boldsymbol{x}$.

Conditional expectation of what?

An MMSE estimator is the conditional expectation of Θ given $\boldsymbol{X} = \boldsymbol{x}$:

$$\mathbb{E}_{\Theta|\boldsymbol{X}}\left[\Theta \,\middle|\, \boldsymbol{X} = \boldsymbol{x}\right] = \int \theta \, f_{\Theta|\boldsymbol{X}}(\theta|\boldsymbol{x}) \, d\theta. \tag{8.68}$$

This is the expectation using the posterior distribution $f_{\Theta|\boldsymbol{X}}(\theta|\boldsymbol{x})$. It should be compared to the peak of the posterior, which returns us the MAP estimate. The posterior distribution is constructed through Bayes' theorem:

$$f_{\Theta|\boldsymbol{X}}(\theta|\boldsymbol{x}) = \frac{f_{\boldsymbol{X}|\Theta}(\boldsymbol{x}|\theta) f_{\Theta}(\theta)}{f_{\boldsymbol{X}}(\boldsymbol{x})}. \tag{8.69}$$

Therefore, to evaluate the expectation of the condition distribution, we need to include the normalization constant $f_{\boldsymbol{X}}(\boldsymbol{x})$, which was omitted in MAP.

> The discussion about the mean squared error and the vector estimates can be skipped if this is your first time reading the book.

What is the mean squared error when using the MMSE estimator?

- The mean squared error conditioned on the observation is

$$\mathrm{MSE}(\Theta, \widehat{\Theta}_{\mathrm{MMSE}}(\boldsymbol{X})) \overset{\text{def}}{=} \mathbb{E}_{\Theta|\boldsymbol{X}}[(\Theta - \widehat{\Theta}_{\mathrm{MMSE}}(\boldsymbol{X}))^2 \mid \boldsymbol{X}]$$
$$= \mathrm{Var}_{\Theta|\boldsymbol{X}}[\Theta|\boldsymbol{X}],$$

  which is the conditional variance.

- The overall mean squared error, unconditioned, is

$$\mathrm{MSE}(\Theta, \widehat{\Theta}_{\mathrm{MMSE}}(\cdot)) = \mathbb{E}_{\boldsymbol{X}}\left[\mathrm{Var}_{\Theta|\boldsymbol{X}}[\Theta|\boldsymbol{X}]\right]$$
$$= \mathrm{Var}_{\Theta}[\Theta].$$

Proof. Let us prove these two statements. The resulting MSE is obtained by substituting $\widehat{\Theta}_{\mathrm{MMSE}}(\boldsymbol{x}) = \mathbb{E}_{\Theta|\boldsymbol{X}}[\Theta \mid \boldsymbol{X}]$ into the $\mathrm{MSE}(\Theta, \widehat{\Theta}_{\mathrm{MMSE}}(\boldsymbol{X}))$. To this end, we have that

$$\mathbb{E}_{\Theta|\boldsymbol{X}}[(\Theta - \widehat{\Theta}_{\mathrm{MMSE}}(\boldsymbol{X}))^2 \mid \boldsymbol{X}] = V(\boldsymbol{X}) - u(\boldsymbol{X})^2$$
$$+ \underbrace{(u(\boldsymbol{X}) - \widehat{\Theta}_{\mathrm{MMSE}}(\boldsymbol{X}))^2}_{=0,\ \text{because}\ \widehat{\Theta}_{\mathrm{MMSE}}(\boldsymbol{X}) = \mathbb{E}_{\Theta|\boldsymbol{X}}[\Theta|\boldsymbol{X}] = u(\boldsymbol{X})}.$$

The variables V and u are defined as

$$V(\boldsymbol{X}) = \mathbb{E}_{\Theta|\boldsymbol{X}}[\Theta^2 \mid \boldsymbol{X}] = \text{2nd moment of } \Theta \text{ using } f_{\Theta|\boldsymbol{X}}(\theta|\boldsymbol{x}),$$
$$u(\boldsymbol{X}) = \mathbb{E}_{\Theta|\boldsymbol{X}}[\Theta \mid \boldsymbol{X}] = \text{1st moment of } \Theta \text{ using } f_{\Theta|\boldsymbol{X}}(\theta|\boldsymbol{x}).$$

Since $\mathrm{Var}[Z] = \mathbb{E}[Z^2] - \mathbb{E}[Z]^2$ for any random variable Z, it follows that

$$\mathbb{E}_{\Theta|\boldsymbol{X}}[(\Theta - \widehat{\Theta}_{\mathrm{MMSE}}(\boldsymbol{X}))^2 \mid \boldsymbol{X}] = V(\boldsymbol{X}) - u(\boldsymbol{X})^2$$
$$= \mathbb{E}_{\Theta|\boldsymbol{X}}[\Theta^2 \mid \boldsymbol{X}] - \left(\mathbb{E}_{\Theta|\boldsymbol{X}}[\Theta \mid \boldsymbol{X}]\right)^2$$
$$= \text{variance of } \Theta \text{ using } f_{\Theta|\boldsymbol{X}}(\theta|\boldsymbol{x})$$
$$\overset{\text{def}}{=} \mathrm{Var}_{\Theta|\boldsymbol{X}}[\Theta|\boldsymbol{X}].$$

Substituting this conditional variance into the MSE definition,

$$\mathrm{MSE}(\Theta, \widehat{\Theta}_{\mathrm{MMSE}}(\cdot)) = \int \mathbb{E}_{\Theta|\boldsymbol{X}}[(\Theta - \widehat{\Theta}_{\mathrm{MMSE}}(\boldsymbol{X}))^2 \mid \boldsymbol{X} = \boldsymbol{x}] f_{\boldsymbol{X}}(\boldsymbol{x}) \, d\boldsymbol{x}$$
$$= \int \mathrm{Var}_{\Theta|\boldsymbol{X}}[\Theta|\boldsymbol{X} = \boldsymbol{x}] f_{\boldsymbol{X}}(\boldsymbol{x}) \, d\boldsymbol{x}$$
$$= \mathrm{Var}_{\Theta}[\Theta].$$

$\square$

> **What happens if the parameter is a vector?**
> - The MMSE estimate is $\widehat{\boldsymbol{\theta}}_{\mathrm{MMSE}}(\boldsymbol{x}) = \mathbb{E}_{\boldsymbol{\Theta}|\boldsymbol{X}}[\boldsymbol{\Theta}|\boldsymbol{X} = \boldsymbol{x}]$.
> - The MSE is
>
> $$\mathrm{MSE}(\boldsymbol{\Theta}, \widehat{\boldsymbol{\Theta}}_{\mathrm{MMSE}}(\cdot)) = \mathrm{Tr}\left\{\mathbb{E}_{\boldsymbol{X}}\left\{\mathrm{Cov}(\boldsymbol{\Theta}|\boldsymbol{X})\right\}\right\}. \qquad (8.70)$$

Proof. The first statement, that the MMSE estimate is

$$\widehat{\boldsymbol{\theta}}_{\mathrm{MMSE}}(\boldsymbol{x}) = \mathbb{E}_{\boldsymbol{\Theta}|\boldsymbol{X}}[\boldsymbol{\Theta}|\boldsymbol{X} = \boldsymbol{x}],$$

is easy to understand since it just follows from the scalar case. The estimator is $\widehat{\boldsymbol{\Theta}}_{\mathrm{MMSE}}(\boldsymbol{X}) = \mathbb{E}_{\boldsymbol{\Theta}|\boldsymbol{X}}[\boldsymbol{\Theta}|\boldsymbol{X}]$. The corresponding MSE is

$$\mathrm{MSE}(\boldsymbol{\Theta}, \widehat{\boldsymbol{\Theta}}_{\mathrm{MMSE}}(\cdot)) = \mathbb{E}_{\boldsymbol{\Theta}, \boldsymbol{X}}[\|\boldsymbol{\Theta} - \widehat{\boldsymbol{\Theta}}_{\mathrm{MMSE}}(\boldsymbol{X})\|^2]$$
$$= \mathbb{E}_{\boldsymbol{X}}\left\{\mathbb{E}_{\boldsymbol{\Theta}|\boldsymbol{X}}[\|\boldsymbol{\Theta} - \widehat{\boldsymbol{\Theta}}_{\mathrm{MMSE}}(\boldsymbol{X})\|^2 \mid \boldsymbol{X}]\right\},$$

where we have used the law of total expectation to decompose the joint expectation. Using the matrix identity below, we have that

$$\mathbb{E}_{\boldsymbol{X}}\left\{\mathbb{E}_{\boldsymbol{\Theta}|\boldsymbol{X}}[\|\boldsymbol{\Theta} - \widehat{\boldsymbol{\Theta}}_{\mathrm{MMSE}}(\boldsymbol{X})\|^2 \mid \boldsymbol{X}]\right\}$$

$$= \mathbb{E}_{\boldsymbol{X}}\left\{\mathbb{E}_{\boldsymbol{\Theta}|\boldsymbol{X}}\left[\mathrm{Tr}\left\{(\boldsymbol{\Theta} - \widehat{\boldsymbol{\Theta}}_{\mathrm{MMSE}}(\boldsymbol{X}))(\boldsymbol{\Theta} - \widehat{\boldsymbol{\Theta}}_{\mathrm{MMSE}}(\boldsymbol{X}))^T\right\} \mid \boldsymbol{X}\right]\right\}$$

$$= \mathrm{Tr}\left\{\mathbb{E}_{\boldsymbol{X}}\left\{\mathbb{E}_{\boldsymbol{\Theta}|\boldsymbol{X}}\left[(\boldsymbol{\Theta} - \widehat{\boldsymbol{\Theta}}_{\mathrm{MMSE}}(\boldsymbol{X}))(\boldsymbol{\Theta} - \widehat{\boldsymbol{\Theta}}_{\mathrm{MMSE}}(\boldsymbol{X}))^T \mid \boldsymbol{X}\right]\right\}\right\}.$$

However, since the MMSE estimator is the condition expectation of the posterior, it follows that the inner expectation is the conditional covariance. Therefore, we arrive at the second statement:

$$\mathrm{MSE}(\boldsymbol{\Theta}, \widehat{\boldsymbol{\Theta}}_{\mathrm{MMSE}}(\cdot)) = \mathrm{Tr}\left\{\mathbb{E}_{\boldsymbol{X}}\left\{\mathbb{E}_{\boldsymbol{\Theta}|\boldsymbol{X}}\left[(\boldsymbol{\Theta} - \widehat{\boldsymbol{\Theta}}_{\mathrm{MMSE}}(\boldsymbol{X}))(\boldsymbol{\Theta} - \widehat{\boldsymbol{\Theta}}_{\mathrm{MMSE}}(\boldsymbol{X}))^T \mid \boldsymbol{X}\right]\right\}\right\}$$

$$= \mathrm{Tr}\left\{\mathbb{E}_{\boldsymbol{X}}\left\{\mathrm{Cov}(\boldsymbol{\Theta}|\boldsymbol{X})\right\}\right\}.$$

$\square$

To prove the two statements above, we need some tools from linear algebra. The two specific matrix identities are given by the following lemma:

> **Lemma 8.1.** *The following are matrix identities:*
>
> - *For any random vector $\boldsymbol{\Theta} \in \mathbb{R}^d$,*
>
> $$\|\boldsymbol{\Theta}\|^2 = Tr(\boldsymbol{\Theta}^T\boldsymbol{\Theta}) = Tr(\boldsymbol{\Theta}\boldsymbol{\Theta}^T).$$

- *For any random vector $\boldsymbol{\Theta} \in \mathbb{R}^d$,*

$$\mathbb{E}_{\boldsymbol{\Theta}}[Tr(\boldsymbol{\Theta}\boldsymbol{\Theta}^T)] = Tr(\mathbb{E}_{\boldsymbol{\Theta}}[\boldsymbol{\Theta}\boldsymbol{\Theta}^T]).$$

The proof of these two results is straightforward. The first is due to the cyclic property of the trace operator. The second statement is true because the trace is a linear operator that sums the diagonal of a matrix.

The end of the discussion. Please join us again.

Example 8.22. Let

$$f_{X|\Theta}(x|\theta) = \begin{cases} \theta e^{-\theta x}, & x \geq 0, \\ 0, & x < 0, \end{cases} \quad \text{and} \quad f_{\Theta}(\theta) = \begin{cases} \alpha e^{-\alpha\theta}, & \theta \geq 0, \\ 0, & \theta < 0. \end{cases}$$

Find the ML, MAP, and MMSE estimates for a single observation $X = x$.

Solution. We first find the posterior distribution:

$$\begin{aligned}
f_{\Theta|X}(\theta|x) &= \frac{f_{X|\Theta}(x|\theta)f_{\Theta}(\theta)}{f_X(x)} \\
&= \frac{\alpha\theta e^{-(\alpha+x)\theta}}{\int_0^\infty \alpha\theta e^{-(\alpha+x)\theta}\, d\theta} \\
&= \frac{\alpha\theta e^{-(\alpha+x)\theta}}{\frac{\alpha}{(\alpha+x)^2}} \\
&= (\alpha+x)^2 \theta e^{-(\alpha+x)\theta}.
\end{aligned}$$

The MMSE estimate is the conditional expectation of the posterior:

$$\begin{aligned}
\widehat{\theta}_{\text{MMSE}}(x) &= \mathbb{E}_{\Theta|X}[\Theta|X = x] \\
&= \int_0^\infty \theta f_{\Theta|X}(\theta|x)\, d\theta \\
&= \int_0^\infty \theta(\alpha+x)^2 \theta e^{-(\alpha+x)\theta}\, d\theta \\
&= (\alpha+x) \underbrace{\int_0^\infty \theta^2 \cdot (\alpha+x)e^{-(\alpha+x)\theta}\, d\theta}_{\text{2nd moment of exponential distribution}} \\
&= (\alpha+x) \cdot \frac{2}{(\alpha+x)^2} = \frac{2}{\alpha+x}.
\end{aligned}$$

The MAP estimate is the peak of the posterior:

$$\widehat{\theta}_{\text{MAP}}(x) = \underset{\theta}{\operatorname{argmax}} \quad \log f_{X|\Theta}(x|\theta) + \log f_{\Theta}(\theta)$$

$$= \underset{\theta}{\operatorname{argmax}} \quad -\theta x + \log \theta - \alpha\theta + \log \alpha.$$

Taking the derivative and setting it to zero yields $-x + \frac{1}{\theta} - \alpha = 0$. This implies that

$$\widehat{\theta}_{\text{MAP}}(x) = \frac{1}{\alpha + x}.$$

Finally, the ML estimate is

$$\widehat{\theta}_{\text{ML}}(x) = \underset{\theta}{\operatorname{argmax}} \quad \log f_{X|\Theta}(x|\theta) = \frac{1}{x}.$$

Practice Exercise 8.8. Following the previous example, derive the estimates for multiple observations $\boldsymbol{X} = \boldsymbol{x}$.

Solution. The posterior is

$$f_{\Theta|\boldsymbol{X}}(\theta|\boldsymbol{x}) = \frac{f_{\boldsymbol{X}|\Theta}(\boldsymbol{x}|\theta)f_{\Theta}(\theta)}{f_{\boldsymbol{X}}(\boldsymbol{x})}$$

$$= \frac{(\prod_{n=1}^{N} f_{X|\Theta}(x_n|\theta))f_{\Theta}(\theta)}{f_{\boldsymbol{X}}(\boldsymbol{x})}$$

$$= \frac{\alpha\theta e^{-(\alpha+\sum_{n=1}^{N} x_n)\theta}}{\int_{0}^{\infty} \alpha\theta e^{-(\alpha+\sum_{n=1}^{N} x_n)\theta} \, d\theta}$$

$$= \left(\alpha + \sum_{n=1}^{N} x_n\right)^2 \theta e^{-(\alpha+\sum_{n=1}^{N} x_n)\theta}.$$

Therefore, we are only replacing x by the sum $\sum_{n=1}^{N} x_n$ in the posterior. Hence, the estimates are:

$$\widehat{\theta}_{\text{MMSE}}(x) = \frac{2}{\alpha + \sum_{n=1}^{N} x_n},$$

$$\widehat{\theta}_{\text{MAP}}(x) = \frac{1}{\alpha + \sum_{n=1}^{N} x_n},$$

$$\widehat{\theta}_{\text{ML}}(x) = \frac{1}{\sum_{n=1}^{N} x_n}.$$

This example shows that as $N \to \infty$, the ML estimate $\widehat{\theta}_{\text{ML}}(x) \to 0$. The reason is that the likelihood is an exponential distribution. Therefore, the peak is always at 0. The posterior is an Erlang distribution, and therefore the peak is offset by α in the denominator. However, as $N \to \infty$ the posterior distribution is dominated by the likelihood, so the peak is shifted towards 0. Finally, since the Erlang distribution is asymmetric, the mean is different from the peak. Hence, the MMSE estimate is different from the MAP estimate.

8.4.4 MMSE estimator for multidimensional Gaussian

The multidimensional Gaussian has some very important uses in data science. Accordingly, we devote this subsection to the discussion of the MMSE estimate of a Gaussian. The main result is stated as follows.

What is the MMSE estimator for a multi-dimensional Gaussian?

Theorem 8.3. *Suppose* $\Theta \in \mathbb{R}^d$ *and* $X \in \mathbb{R}^N$ *are jointly Gaussian with a joint PDF*

$$\begin{bmatrix} \Theta \\ X \end{bmatrix} \sim Gaussian \left(\begin{bmatrix} \mu_\Theta \\ \mu_X \end{bmatrix}, \begin{bmatrix} \Sigma_{\Theta\Theta} & \Sigma_{\Theta X} \\ \Sigma_{X\Theta} & \Sigma_{XX} \end{bmatrix} \right).$$

The MMSE estimator is

$$\widehat{\Theta}_{MMSE}(X) = \mu_\Theta + \Sigma_{\Theta X} \Sigma_{XX}^{-1} (X - \mu_X). \tag{8.71}$$

The proof of this result is not difficult but it is tedious. The flow of the argument is:

- Step 1: Show that the posterior distribution $f_{\Theta|X}(\theta|x)$ is a Gaussian.
- Step 2: To do so we need to complete the squares for matrices.
- Step 3: Once we have the $f_{\Theta|X}(\theta|x)$, the posterior mean is the MMSE estimator.

The proof below can be skipped if this is your first time reading the book.

Proof. The posterior PDF is

$$f_{\Theta|X}(\theta|x) = \frac{f_{\Theta,X}(\theta,x)}{f_X(x)}$$

$$= \frac{\frac{1}{\sqrt{(2\pi)^{d+N}|\Sigma|}} \exp\left\{ -\frac{1}{2} \begin{bmatrix} \theta - \mu_\Theta \\ x - \mu_X \end{bmatrix}^T \begin{bmatrix} \Sigma_{\Theta\Theta} & \Sigma_{\Theta X} \\ \Sigma_{X\Theta} & \Sigma_{XX} \end{bmatrix}^{-1} \begin{bmatrix} \theta - \mu_\Theta \\ x - \mu_X \end{bmatrix} \right\}}{\frac{1}{\sqrt{(2\pi)^N |\Sigma_{XX}|}} \exp\left\{ -\frac{1}{2} \begin{bmatrix} x - \mu_X \end{bmatrix}^T \Sigma_{XX}^{-1} \begin{bmatrix} x - \mu_X \end{bmatrix} \right\}}.$$

Without loss of generality, we assume that $\mu_X = \mu_\Theta = 0$. Then the posterior becomes

$$f_{\Theta|X}(\theta|x) = \frac{1}{\sqrt{(2\pi)^d |\Sigma|/|\Sigma_{XX}|}}$$

$$\times \exp\underbrace{\left\{ -\frac{1}{2} \begin{bmatrix} \theta \\ x \end{bmatrix}^T \begin{bmatrix} \Sigma_{\Theta\Theta} & \Sigma_{\Theta X} \\ \Sigma_{X\Theta} & \Sigma_{XX} \end{bmatrix}^{-1} \begin{bmatrix} \theta \\ x \end{bmatrix} + \frac{1}{2} x^T \Sigma_{XX}^{-1} x \right\}}_{H(\theta,x)}.$$

The tedious task here is to simplify $H(\theta, x)$.

Regardless of what the 2-by-2 matrix inverse is, the matrix will take the form

$$\begin{bmatrix} \Sigma_{\Theta\Theta} & \Sigma_{\Theta X} \\ \Sigma_{X\Theta} & \Sigma_{XX} \end{bmatrix}^{-1} = \begin{bmatrix} A & B \\ C & D \end{bmatrix},$$

for some choices of matrices A, B, C and D. Therefore, the function $H(\boldsymbol{\theta}, \boldsymbol{x})$ can be written as

$$H(\boldsymbol{\theta}, \boldsymbol{x}) = -\frac{1}{2}\left\{\boldsymbol{\theta}^T A \boldsymbol{\theta} + \boldsymbol{\theta}^T B \boldsymbol{x} + \boldsymbol{x}^T C \boldsymbol{\theta} + \boldsymbol{x}^T D \boldsymbol{x} - \boldsymbol{x}^T \Sigma_{XX}^{-1} \boldsymbol{x}\right\}. \tag{8.72}$$

Our goal is to complete the square for $H(\boldsymbol{\theta}, \boldsymbol{x})$. To this end, we propose to write

$$H(\boldsymbol{\theta}, \boldsymbol{x}) = -\frac{1}{2}\left\{(\boldsymbol{\theta} - G\boldsymbol{x})^T A (\boldsymbol{\theta} - G\boldsymbol{x}) + Q(\boldsymbol{x})\right\}, \tag{8.73}$$

for some matrix G and function $Q(\cdot)$ of $\boldsymbol{x}$ only. If we compare Equation (8.72) and Equation (8.73), we observe that G must satisfy

$$G = -A^{-1} B.$$

Therefore, if we can determine A and B, we will know G. If we know G, we have completed the square for $H(\boldsymbol{\theta}, \boldsymbol{x})$. If we can complete the square for $H(\boldsymbol{\theta}, \boldsymbol{x})$, we can write

$$f_{\Theta|X}(\boldsymbol{\theta}|\boldsymbol{x}) = \underbrace{\frac{\exp\{-Q(\boldsymbol{x})/2\}}{\sqrt{(2\pi)^d |\Sigma|/|\Sigma_{XX}|}}}_{\text{constant in } \boldsymbol{\theta}} \times \underbrace{\exp\left\{-\frac{1}{2}(\boldsymbol{\theta} - G\boldsymbol{x})^T A(\boldsymbol{\theta} - G\boldsymbol{x})\right\}}_{\text{a Gaussian}}.$$

Hence, the MMSE estimate, which is the posterior mean $\mathbb{E}[\Theta|X = \boldsymbol{x}]$, is simply $G\boldsymbol{x}$:

$$\begin{aligned} \widehat{\boldsymbol{\theta}}_{\text{MMSE}}(\boldsymbol{x}) &= \mathbb{E}[\Theta|X = \boldsymbol{x}] \\ &= G\boldsymbol{x} \\ &= -A^{-1} B \boldsymbol{x}. \end{aligned}$$

So it remains to determine A and B by solving the tedious matrix inversion problem. The result is:[6]

$$\begin{aligned} A &= (\Sigma_{\Theta\Theta} - \Sigma_{\Theta X}\Sigma_{XX}^{-1}\Sigma_{X\Theta})^{-1}, \\ B &= -(\Sigma_{\Theta\Theta} - \Sigma_{\Theta X}\Sigma_{XX}^{-1}\Sigma_{X\Theta})^{-1}\Sigma_{\Theta X}\Sigma_{XX}^{-1}, \\ C &= (\Sigma_{XX} - \Sigma_{X\Theta}\Sigma_{\Theta\Theta}^{-1}\Sigma_{\Theta X})^{-1}\Sigma_{X\Theta}\Sigma_{\Theta\Theta}^{-1}, \\ D &= (\Sigma_{XX} - \Sigma_{X\Theta}\Sigma_{\Theta\Theta}^{-1}\Sigma_{\Theta X})^{-1}. \end{aligned}$$

Therefore, plugging everything into the equation,

$$\begin{aligned} \widehat{\boldsymbol{\theta}}_{\text{MMSE}}(\boldsymbol{x}) &= -A^{-1} B \boldsymbol{x} \\ &= \Sigma_{\Theta, X}\Sigma_{XX}^{-1}\boldsymbol{x}. \end{aligned}$$

For non-zero means, we can repeat the same arguments above and show that

$$\widehat{\boldsymbol{\theta}}_{\text{MMSE}}(\boldsymbol{x}) = \boldsymbol{\mu}_\Theta + \Sigma_{\Theta, X}\Sigma_{XX}^{-1}(\boldsymbol{x} - \boldsymbol{\mu}_X).$$

$\square$

---

[6]See Matrix Cookbook https://www.math.uwaterloo.ca/~hwolkowi/matrixcookbook.pdf Section 9.1.5 on the Schur complement.

End of the proof. Please join us again.

Practice Exercise 8.9. Suppose $\boldsymbol{\Theta} \in \mathbb{R}^d$ and $\boldsymbol{X} \in \mathbb{R}^N$ are jointly Gaussian with a joint PDF

$$\begin{bmatrix} \boldsymbol{\Theta} \\ \boldsymbol{X} \end{bmatrix} \sim \text{Gaussian} \left(\begin{bmatrix} \boldsymbol{\mu}_\Theta \\ \boldsymbol{\mu}_X \end{bmatrix}, \begin{bmatrix} \boldsymbol{\Sigma}_{\Theta\Theta} & \boldsymbol{\Sigma}_{\Theta X} \\ \boldsymbol{\Sigma}_{X\Theta} & \boldsymbol{\Sigma}_{XX} \end{bmatrix} \right).$$

We know that the MMSE estimator is

$$\widehat{\boldsymbol{\Theta}}_{\text{MMSE}}(\boldsymbol{X}) = \boldsymbol{\mu}_\Theta + \boldsymbol{\Sigma}_{\Theta X}\boldsymbol{\Sigma}_{XX}^{-1}(\boldsymbol{X} - \boldsymbol{\mu}_X). \tag{8.74}$$

Find the mean squared error when using the MMSE estimator.

Solution. Conditioned on $\boldsymbol{X} = \boldsymbol{x}$, according to Equation (8.70), the MMSE is

$$\text{MSE}(\boldsymbol{\Theta}, \widehat{\boldsymbol{\Theta}}(\boldsymbol{X})) = \text{Tr}\left\{\text{Cov}[\boldsymbol{\Theta}|\boldsymbol{X}]\right\}.$$

The conditional covariance $\text{Cov}[\boldsymbol{\Theta}|\boldsymbol{X}]$ is the covariance of the posterior distribution $f_{\boldsymbol{\Theta}|\boldsymbol{X}}(\boldsymbol{\theta}|\boldsymbol{x})$, which is

$$\begin{aligned} \text{Tr}\left\{\text{Cov}[\boldsymbol{\Theta}|\boldsymbol{X}]\right\} &= \text{Tr}\left\{\boldsymbol{A}\right\} \\ &= \text{Tr}\left\{(\boldsymbol{\Sigma}_{\Theta\Theta} - \boldsymbol{\Sigma}_{\Theta X}\boldsymbol{\Sigma}_{XX}^{-1}\boldsymbol{\Sigma}_{X\Theta})^{-1}\right\}. \end{aligned}$$

The overall mean squared error is

$$\begin{aligned} \text{MSE}\left(\boldsymbol{\Theta}, \widehat{\boldsymbol{\Theta}}(\cdot)\right) &= \mathbb{E}_{\boldsymbol{X}}\left[\text{MSE}(\boldsymbol{\Theta}, \widehat{\boldsymbol{\Theta}}(\boldsymbol{X}))\right] \\ &= \int \text{MSE}(\boldsymbol{\Theta}, \widehat{\boldsymbol{\Theta}}(\boldsymbol{x})) f_{\boldsymbol{X}}(\boldsymbol{x})\, d\boldsymbol{x} \\ &= \int \text{Tr}\left\{\text{Cov}[\boldsymbol{\Theta}|\boldsymbol{X}]\right\} f_{\boldsymbol{X}}(\boldsymbol{x})\, d\boldsymbol{x} \\ &= \int \text{Tr}\left\{(\boldsymbol{\Sigma}_{\Theta\Theta} - \boldsymbol{\Sigma}_{\Theta X}\boldsymbol{\Sigma}_{XX}^{-1}\boldsymbol{\Sigma}_{X\Theta})^{-1}\right\} f_{\boldsymbol{X}}(\boldsymbol{x})\, d\boldsymbol{x} \\ &= \text{Tr}\left\{(\boldsymbol{\Sigma}_{\Theta\Theta} - \boldsymbol{\Sigma}_{\Theta X}\boldsymbol{\Sigma}_{XX}^{-1}\boldsymbol{\Sigma}_{X\Theta})^{-1}\right\} \int f_{\boldsymbol{X}}(\boldsymbol{x})\, d\boldsymbol{x} \\ &= \text{Tr}\left\{(\boldsymbol{\Sigma}_{\Theta\Theta} - \boldsymbol{\Sigma}_{\Theta X}\boldsymbol{\Sigma}_{XX}^{-1}\boldsymbol{\Sigma}_{X\Theta})^{-1}\right\}. \end{aligned}$$

For multidimensional Gaussian, does MMSE = MAP?

The answer is *YES*.

Theorem 8.4. *Suppose $\boldsymbol{\Theta} \in \mathbb{R}^d$ and $\boldsymbol{X} \in \mathbb{R}^N$ are jointly Gaussian with a joint PDF*

$$\begin{bmatrix} \boldsymbol{\Theta} \\ \boldsymbol{X} \end{bmatrix} \sim \text{Gaussian} \left(\begin{bmatrix} \boldsymbol{\mu}_\Theta \\ \boldsymbol{\mu}_X \end{bmatrix}, \begin{bmatrix} \boldsymbol{\Sigma}_{\Theta\Theta} & \boldsymbol{\Sigma}_{\Theta X} \\ \boldsymbol{\Sigma}_{X\Theta} & \boldsymbol{\Sigma}_{XX} \end{bmatrix} \right).$$

The MAP estimate is

$$\widehat{\Theta}_{MAP}(\boldsymbol{X}) = \boldsymbol{\mu}_{\Theta} + \boldsymbol{\Sigma}_{\Theta X}\boldsymbol{\Sigma}_{XX}^{-1}(\boldsymbol{X} - \boldsymbol{\mu}_X). \tag{8.75}$$

Proof. The proof of this result is straightforward. If we return to the proof of the MMSE result, we note that

$$f_{\Theta|\boldsymbol{X}}(\boldsymbol{\theta}|\boldsymbol{x}) = \underbrace{\frac{\exp\{-Q(\boldsymbol{x})/2\}}{\sqrt{(2\pi)^d|\boldsymbol{\Sigma}|/|\boldsymbol{\Sigma}_{XX}|}}}_{\text{constant in } \boldsymbol{\theta}} \times \underbrace{\exp\left\{-\frac{1}{2}(\boldsymbol{\theta} - \boldsymbol{Gx})^T\boldsymbol{A}(\boldsymbol{\theta} - \boldsymbol{Gx})\right\}}_{\text{a Gaussian}}.$$

Therefore, the maximizer of this posterior distribution, which is the MAP estimate, is

$$\widehat{\boldsymbol{\theta}}_{\text{MAP}}(\boldsymbol{x}) = \underset{\boldsymbol{\theta}}{\operatorname{argmax}} \ f_{\Theta|\boldsymbol{X}}(\boldsymbol{\theta}|\boldsymbol{x})$$

$$= \underset{\boldsymbol{\theta}}{\operatorname{argmax}} \ -\frac{1}{2}(\boldsymbol{\theta} - \boldsymbol{Gx})^T\boldsymbol{A}(\boldsymbol{\theta} - \boldsymbol{Gx}).$$

Taking the derivative w.r.t. $\boldsymbol{\theta}$ and setting it zero, we have

$$\widehat{\boldsymbol{\theta}}_{\text{MAP}}(\boldsymbol{x}) = \boldsymbol{Gx} = \boldsymbol{\Sigma}_{\Theta,X}\boldsymbol{\Sigma}_{XX}^{-1}\boldsymbol{x}.$$

If the mean vectors are non-zero, we have $\widehat{\boldsymbol{\theta}}_{\text{MAP}}(\boldsymbol{x}) = \boldsymbol{\mu}_{\Theta} + \boldsymbol{\Sigma}_{\Theta X}\boldsymbol{\Sigma}_{XX}^{-1}(\boldsymbol{x} - \boldsymbol{\mu}_X)$.

$\square$

8.4.5 Linking MMSE and neural networks

The blossoming of deep neural networks since 2010 has created a substantial impact on modern data science. The basic idea of a neural network is to train a stack of matrices and nonlinear functions (known as the network weights and the neuron activation functions, respectively), among other innovative ideas, so that a certain training loss is minimized. Expressing this by equations, the goal of the learning is equivalent to solving the optimization problem

$$\widehat{g}(\cdot) = \underset{g(\cdot)}{\operatorname{argmin}} \ \mathbb{E}_{\boldsymbol{X},\Theta}\left[\|\Theta - g(\boldsymbol{X})\|^2\right], \tag{8.76}$$

where $\boldsymbol{X} \in \mathbb{R}^M$ is the input data and $\Theta \in \mathbb{R}^d$ is the ground truth prediction. We want to find $g(\cdot)$ such that the error is minimized.

The error we choose here is the ℓ_2-norm error $\|\cdot\|^2$. It is only one of many possible choices. You may recognize that this is **exactly** the same as the MMSE optimization. Therefore, the neural network we are finding here is the MMSE estimator. Since the MMSE estimator is the conditional expectation of the posterior distribution, the neural network approximates the mean of the posterior distribution.

Often the struggle we have with deep neural networks is whether we can find the optimal network parameters via optimization algorithms such as the stochastic gradient descent algorithms. However, if we think about this problem more deeply, the equivalence between the MMSE estimator and the posterior mean tells us that the hard part is related to the posterior distribution. In the high-dimensional landscape, it is close to impossible to determine the posterior and its mean. If we add to these difficulties and the nonconvexity of the function g, training a network is very challenging.

One misconception about neural networks is that if we can achieve a low training error, and if the model can also achieve a low testing error, then the network is good. This is a false sense of satisfaction. If a model can achieve very good training and testing errors, then the model is only good with respect to the error you choose. For example, if we choose the ℓ_2-norm error $\|\cdot\|^2$ and if our model achieves good training and testing errors (in terms of $\|\cdot\|^2$), we can conclude that the model does well with respect to $\|\cdot\|^2$. The more serious problem here, unfortunately, is that $\|\cdot\|^2$ is not necessarily a good metric of performance (for both training and testing) because training with $\|\cdot\|^2$ is equivalent to approximating the posterior mean. There is absolutely no reason to believe that in the high-dimensional landscape, the posterior mean is *the* optimal. If we choose the posterior **mode** or the posterior **median**, we will also obtain a result. Why are the modes and medians "worse" than the **mean**? In practice, it has been observed that training deep neural networks for image-processing tasks generally leads to over-smoothed images. This demonstrates how minimizing the mean squared error $\|\cdot\|^2$ can be a fundamental mismatch with the problem.

Is minimizing the MSE the best option?

- No. Minimizing the MSE is equivalent to finding the mean of the posterior. There is no reason why the mean is the "best".

- You can find the mode of the posterior, in which case you will get a MAP estimator.

- You can also find the median of the posterior, in which case you will get the minimum absolute error estimator.

- Ultimately, you need to define what is "good" and what is "bad".

- The same principle applies to deep neural networks. Especially in the regression setting, why is $\|\cdot\|^2$ a good evaluation metric for testing (not just training)?

8.5 Summary

In this chapter, we have discussed the basic principles of parameter estimation. The three building blocks are:

- **Likelihood** $f_{X|\Theta}(x|\theta)$: the PDF that we observe samples X conditioned on the unknown parameter Θ. In the frequentist world, Θ is a deterministic quantity. In the Bayesian world, Θ is random and so it has a PDF.

- **Prior** $f_\Theta(\theta)$: the PDF of Θ. The prior $f_\Theta(\theta)$ is used by all Bayesian computation.

- **Posterior** $f_{\Theta|X}(\theta|x)$: the PDF that the underlying parameter is $\Theta = \theta$ given that we have observed $X = x$.

The three building blocks give us several strategies to estimate the parameters:

- **Maximum likelihood (ML)** estimation: Maximize $f_{X|\Theta}(x|\theta)$.

- **Maximum a posteriori (MAP)** estimation: Maximize $f_{\Theta|X}(\theta|x)$.

- **Minimum mean-square estimation** (MMSE): Minimize the mean squared error, which is equivalent to finding the mean of $f_{\Theta|X}(\theta|x)$.

As discussed in this chapter, no single estimation strategy is universally "better" because one needs to specify the optimality criterion. If the goal is to minimize the mean squared error, then the MMSE estimator is the optimal strategy. If the goal is to maximize the likelihood without assuming any prior knowledge, the ML estimator would be the optimal strategy. It may appear that if we knew the ground truth parameter θ^* we could minimize the distance between the estimated parameter θ and the true value θ^*. If the parameter is a scalar, this will work. However, if the parameter is a vector, the noise of the distance becomes an issue. For example, if one cares about the mean absolute error (MAE), the optimal estimator would be the median of the posterior distribution instead of the mean of the posterior in the MMSE case. Therefore, it is the end user's responsibility to specify the optimality criterion.

Whenever we consider parameter estimation, we tend to think that it is about estimating the model parameters, such as the mean of a Gaussian PDF. While in many statistics problems this is indeed the case, parameter estimation can be much broader if we link it with regression. Specifically, a regularized linear regression problem can be formulated as a MAP estimation

$$\theta^* = \underset{\theta}{\operatorname{argmax}} \ \underbrace{\|X\theta - y\|^2}_{-\log f_{X|\Theta}(x|\theta)} + \ \underbrace{\lambda R(\theta)}_{-\log f_\Theta(\theta)} \ , \tag{8.77}$$

for some regularization $R(\theta)$, which is also the negative log of the prior. Expressed in this way, we recognize that the MAP estimation can be used to recover signals. For example, we can model X as a linear degradation process of certain imaging systems. Then solving the MAP estimation is equivalent to finding the best signal explaining the degraded observation using the posterior as the criterion. There is rich literature dealing with solving MAP estimation problems similar to these in subjects such as computational imaging, communication systems, remote sensing, radar engineering, and recommendation systems, to name a few.

8.6   References

Basic

8-1 Dimitri P. Bertsekas and John N. Tsitsiklis, *Introduction to Probability*, Athena Scientific, 2nd Edition, 2008. Chapter 8 and Chapter 9.

8-2 Alberto Leon-Garcia, *Probability, Statistics, and Random Processes for Electrical Engineering*, Prentice Hall, 3rd Edition, 2008. Chapter 6 and Chapter 8.

8-3 Athanasios Papoulis and S. Unnikrishna Pillai, *Probability, Random Variables and Stochastic Processes*, McGraw-Hill, 4th Edition, 2001. Chapter 8.

8-4 Henry Stark and John W. Woods, *Probability and Random Processes with Applications to Signal Processing*, Prentice Hall, 3rd Edition, 2002. Chapter 5.

8-5 Todd K. Moon and Wynn C. Stirling, *Mathematical Methods and Algorithms for Signal Processing*, Prentice-Hall, 2000. Chapter 12.

Theoretical analysis

8-6 H. Vincent Poor, *An Introduction Signal Detection and Estimation*, Springer, 1998.

8-7 Steven M. Kay, *Fundamentals of Statistical Signal Processing: Estimation Theory*, Prentice-Hall, 1993.

8-8 Bernard C. Levy, *Principles of Signal Detection and Parameter Estimation*, Springer, 2008.

8-9 Athanasios Papoulis and S. Unnikrishna Pillai, *Probability, Random Variables and Stochastic Processes*, McGraw-Hill, 2001. Chapter 8.

8-10 Larry Wasserman, *All of Statistics: A Concise Course in Statistical Inference*, Springer, 2010.

8-11 Erich L. Lehmann, *Elements of Large-Sample Theory*, Springer, 1999. Chapter 7.

8-12 George Casella and Roger L. Berger *Statistical Inference*, Duxbury, 2002. Chapter 7.

Machine-learning

8-13 Christopher Bishop, *Pattern Recognition and Machine Learning*, Springer, 2006. Chapter 2 and Chapter 3.

8-14 Richard O. Duda, Peter E. Hart and David G. Stork, *Pattern Classification*, Wiley 2001. Chapter 3.

8.7 Problems

Exercise 1.
Let $X_1, \ldots, X_N$ be a sequence of i.i.d. Bernoulli random variables with $\mathbb{P}[X_n = 1] = \theta$. Suppose that we have observed $x_1, \ldots, x_N$.

(a) Show that the PMF of X_n is $p_{X_n}(x_n \mid \theta) = \theta^{x_n}(1 - \theta)^{1-x_n}$. Find the joint PMF

$$p_{X_1, \ldots, X_N}(x_1, \ldots, x_N).$$

(b) Find the maximum likelihood estimate $\widehat{\theta}$, i.e.,

$$\widehat{\theta}_{\mathrm{ML}} = \underset{\theta}{\mathrm{argmax}} \ \log p_{X_1, \ldots, X_N}(x_1, \ldots, x_N).$$

Express your answer in terms of $x_1, \ldots, x_N$.

(c) Let $\theta = 1/2$. Use Chebyshev's inequality to find an upper bound for $\mathbb{P}[|\widehat{\Theta}_{\mathrm{ML}} - \theta| > 0.1]$.

Exercise 2.
Let $Y_n = \theta + W_n$ be the output of a noisy channel where the input is a scalar θ and $W_n \sim \mathcal{N}(0, 1)$ is an i.i.d. Gaussian noise. Suppose that we have observed $y_1, \ldots, y_N$.

(a) Express the PDF of Y_n in terms of θ and y_n. Find the joint PDF of $Y_1, \ldots, Y_N$.

(b) Find the maximum likelihood estimate $\widehat{\theta}_{\mathrm{ML}}$. Express your answer in terms of $y_1, \ldots, y_N$.

(c) Find $\mathbb{E}[\widehat{\Theta}_{\mathrm{ML}}]$.

Exercise 3.
Let $X_1, \ldots, X_N$ be a sequence of i.i.d. Gaussian random variables with unknown mean θ_1 and variance θ_2. Suppose that we have observations $x_1, \ldots, x_N$.

(a) Express the PDF of X_n in terms of x_n, θ_1 and θ_2. Find the joint PDF of $X_1, \ldots, X_N$.

(b) Find the maximum likelihood estimates of θ_1 and θ_2.

Exercise 4.
In this problem we study a single-photon image sensor. First, recall that photons arrive according to a Poisson distribution, i.e., the probability of observing k photons is

$$\mathbb{P}[Y = k] = \frac{\lambda^k e^{-\lambda}}{k!},$$

where λ is the (unknown) underlying photon arrival rate. When photons arrive at the single-photon detector, the detector generates a binary response "1" when one or more photons are detected, and "0" when no photon is detected.

(a) Let B be the random variable denoting the response of the single-photon detector. That is,

$$B = \begin{cases} 1, & Y \geq 1, \\ 0, & Y = 0. \end{cases}$$

Find the PMF of B.

(b) Suppose we have obtained T independent measurements with realizations $B_1 = b_1$, $B_2 = b_2, ..., B_T = b_T$. Show that the underlying photon arrival rate λ can be estimated by

$$\lambda = -\log\left(1 - \frac{\sum_{t=1}^{T} b_t}{T}\right).$$

(c) Get a random image from the internet and turn it into a grayscale array with values between 0 and 1. Write a MATLAB or Python program to synthetically generate a sequence of $T = 1000$ binary images. Then use the previous result to reconstruct the grayscale image.

Exercise 5.
Consider a deterministic vector $s \in \mathbb{R}^d$ and random vectors

$$f_{Y|\Theta}(y|\theta) = \text{Gaussian}(s\theta, \Sigma),$$
$$f_\Theta(\theta) = \text{Gaussian}(\mu, \sigma^2).$$

(a) Show that the posterior distribution is given by

$$f_{\Theta|Y}(\theta|y) = \text{Gaussian}(m, q^2), \tag{8.78}$$

where

$$d^2 = s^T \Sigma^{-1} s,$$
$$m = \left(d^2 + \frac{1}{\sigma^2}\right)^{-1}\left(s^T \Sigma^{-1} y + \frac{\mu}{\sigma^2}\right),$$
$$q^2 = \frac{1}{d^2 + \frac{1}{\sigma^2}}.$$

(b) Show that the MMSE estimate $\widehat{\theta}_{\text{MMSE}}(y)$ is given by

$$\widehat{\theta}_{\text{MMSE}}(y) = \frac{\sigma^2 s^T \Sigma^{-1} y + \mu}{\sigma^2 d^2 + 1}. \tag{8.79}$$

(c) Show that the MSE is given by

$$\text{MSE}(\Theta, \widehat{\Theta}_{\text{MMSE}}(Y)) = \frac{1}{d^2 + \frac{1}{\sigma^2}}. \tag{8.80}$$

What happens when $\sigma \to 0$?

(d) Give an interpretation of d^2. What happens when $d^2 \to 0$ and when $d^2 \to \infty$?

Exercise 6.
Prove the following identity:

$$
\begin{bmatrix} \Sigma_{\Theta\Theta} & \Sigma_{\Theta X} \\ \Sigma_{X\Theta} & \Sigma_{XX} \end{bmatrix}^{-1}
$$
$$
= \begin{bmatrix} (\Sigma_{\Theta\Theta} - \Sigma_{\Theta X}\Sigma_{XX}^{-1}\Sigma_{X\Theta})^{-1} & -(\Sigma_{\Theta\Theta} - \Sigma_{\Theta X}\Sigma_{XX}^{-1}\Sigma_{X\Theta})^{-1}\Sigma_{\Theta X}\Sigma_{XX}^{-1} \\ (\Sigma_{XX} - \Sigma_{X\Theta}\Sigma_{\Theta\Theta}^{-1}\Sigma_{\Theta X})^{-1}\Sigma_{X\Theta}\Sigma_{\Theta\Theta}^{-1} & (\Sigma_{XX} - \Sigma_{X\Theta}\Sigma_{\Theta\Theta}^{-1}\Sigma_{\Theta X})^{-1} \end{bmatrix}.
$$

Hint: You can perform reverse engineering by checking whether the product of the left-hand side and the right-hand side would give you the identity matrix.

Exercise 7.
Let X_1, X_2, X_3 and X_4 be four i.i.d. Poisson random variables with mean $\theta = 4$. Find the mean and variance of the following estimators $\widehat{\Theta}(\boldsymbol{X})$ for θ and determine whether they are biased or unbiased.

- $\widehat{\Theta}(\boldsymbol{X}) = (X_1 + X_2)/2$
- $\widehat{\Theta}(\boldsymbol{X}) = (X_3 + X_4)/2$
- $\widehat{\Theta}(\boldsymbol{X}) = (X_1 + 2X_2)/3$
- $\widehat{\Theta}(\boldsymbol{X}) = (X_1 + X_2 + X_3 + X_4)/4$

Exercise 8.
Let $X_1, \ldots, X_N$ be i.i.d. random variables with a uniform distribution of $[0, \theta]$. Consider the following estimator:

$$\widehat{\Theta}(\boldsymbol{X}) = \max(X_1, \ldots, X_N). \tag{8.81}$$

(a) Show that the PDF of $\widehat{\Theta}$ is $f_{\widehat{\Theta}}(z) = N[F_X(z)]^{N-1}f_X(z)$, where f_X and F_X are respectively the PDF and CDF of X_n.

(b) Show that $\widehat{\Theta}$ is a biased estimator.

(c) Is it a consistent estimator?

(d) Find a constant c so that $c\widehat{\Theta}$ is unbiased.

Exercise 9.
Let $X_1, \ldots, X_N$ be i.i.d. Gaussian random variables with unknown mean θ and known variance $\sigma = 1$.

(a) Show that the log-likelihood function is

$$\log \mathcal{L}(\theta \mid \boldsymbol{x}) = -\frac{N}{2}\log(2\pi) - \frac{1}{2}\sum_{n=1}^{N}(x_n - \theta)^2. \tag{8.82}$$

(b) Let $\overline{X^2} = \frac{1}{N}\sum_{n=1}^{N} x_n^2$ and $\overline{X} = \frac{1}{N}\sum_{n=1}^{N} x_n$. Show that $\overline{X^2} \geq (\overline{X})^2$.

(c) Use Python/MATLAB to plot the function $\log \mathcal{L}(\theta \,|\, \boldsymbol{x})$, when $\overline{X} = 1$, $\overline{X^2} = 2$, $N = 1000$.

Exercise 10.
Let $X_1, \ldots, X_N$ be i.i.d. uniform random variables over the interval $[0, \theta]$.
Let $T = \max(X_1, \ldots, X_N)$.

(a) Consider the estimator $h(\boldsymbol{X}) = \frac{1}{N} \sum_{n=1}^{N} X_n$. Is $h(\cdot)$ an unbiased estimator?

(b) Consider the estimator $g(\boldsymbol{X}) = \frac{2}{N} \sum_{n=1}^{N} X_n$. Is $g(\cdot)$ an unbiased estimator?

(c) Show that
$$\mathbb{E}[g(\boldsymbol{X})|T = t] = \left(\frac{N+1}{N}\right) t.$$

(d) Let $\widehat{g}(\boldsymbol{X}) = \mathbb{E}[g(\boldsymbol{X})|T] = \left(\frac{N+1}{N}\right) T$. Show that
$$\mathbb{E}[\widehat{g}(\boldsymbol{X})^2] = \left(\frac{(N+1)^2}{N(N+2)}\right) \theta^2.$$

(e) Show that
$$\mathbb{E}[(\widehat{g}(\boldsymbol{X}) - \theta)^2] = \left(\frac{1}{N(N+2)}\right) \theta^2.$$

Exercise 11.
The Kullback-Leibler divergence between two distributions $p_1(\boldsymbol{x})$ and $p_2(\boldsymbol{x})$ is defined as
$$\mathrm{KL}(p_1 \,\|\, p_2) = \int p_1(\boldsymbol{x}) \log \frac{p_1(\boldsymbol{x})}{p_2(\boldsymbol{x})} \, d\boldsymbol{x}. \tag{8.83}$$

Suppose we approximate p_1 using a distribution p_2. Let us choose $p_2 = \text{Gaussian}(\boldsymbol{\mu}, \boldsymbol{\Sigma})$. Show that $\boldsymbol{\mu}$ and $\boldsymbol{\Sigma}$, which minimize the KL divergence, are such that
$$\boldsymbol{\mu} = \mathbb{E}_{\boldsymbol{x} \sim p_1(\boldsymbol{x})}[\boldsymbol{x}] \qquad \text{and} \qquad \boldsymbol{\Sigma} = \mathbb{E}_{\boldsymbol{x} \sim p_1(\boldsymbol{x})}[(\boldsymbol{x} - \boldsymbol{\mu})(\boldsymbol{x} - \boldsymbol{\mu})^T].$$

Exercise 12.

(a) Recall that the trace operator is defined as $\mathrm{tr}[\boldsymbol{A}] = \sum_{i=1}^{d} [\boldsymbol{A}]_{i,i}$. Prove the matrix identity
$$\boldsymbol{x}^T \boldsymbol{A} \boldsymbol{x} = \mathrm{tr}[\boldsymbol{A}\boldsymbol{x}\boldsymbol{x}^T], \tag{8.84}$$
where $\boldsymbol{A} \in \mathbb{R}^{d \times d}$.

(b) Show that the likelihood function
$$p(\mathcal{D} \,|\, \boldsymbol{\Sigma}) = \prod_{n=1}^{N} \left\{ \frac{1}{(2\pi)^{d/2} |\boldsymbol{\Sigma}|^{1/2}} \exp\left\{ -\frac{1}{2}(\boldsymbol{x}_n - \boldsymbol{\mu})^T \boldsymbol{\Sigma}^{-1} (\boldsymbol{x}_n - \boldsymbol{\mu}) \right\} \right\} \tag{8.85}$$

can be written as
$$p(\mathcal{D}|\boldsymbol{\Sigma}) = \frac{1}{(2\pi)^{Nd/2}} |\boldsymbol{\Sigma}^{-1}|^{N/2} \exp\left\{ -\frac{1}{2} \mathrm{tr}\left[\boldsymbol{\Sigma}^{-1} \sum_{n=1}^{N} (\boldsymbol{x}_n - \boldsymbol{\mu})(\boldsymbol{x}_n - \boldsymbol{\mu})^T \right] \right\}. \tag{8.86}$$

(c) Let $\boldsymbol{A} = \boldsymbol{\Sigma}^{-1}\widehat{\boldsymbol{\Sigma}}_{\mathrm{ML}}$, and $\lambda_1, ..., \lambda_d$ be the eigenvalues of $\boldsymbol{A}$. Show that the result from part (b) leads to

$$p(\mathcal{D}|\boldsymbol{\Sigma}) = \frac{1}{(2\pi)^{Nd/2}|\widehat{\boldsymbol{\Sigma}}_{\mathrm{ML}}|^{N/2}} \left(\prod_{i=1}^{d}\lambda_i\right)^{N/2} \exp\left\{-\frac{N}{2}\sum_{i=1}^{d}\lambda_i\right\}. \tag{8.87}$$

Hint: For matrix $\boldsymbol{A}$ with eigenvalues $\lambda_1, ..., \lambda_d$, $\mathrm{tr}[\boldsymbol{A}] = \sum_{i=1}^{d}\lambda_i$.

(d) Find $\lambda_1, \ldots, \lambda_d$ such that Equation (8.87) is maximized.

(e) With the choice of λ_i given in (d), derive the ML estimate $\widehat{\boldsymbol{\Sigma}}_{\mathrm{ML}}$.

(f) What would be the alternative way of finding $\widehat{\boldsymbol{\Sigma}}_{\mathrm{ML}}$? You do not need to prove it. Just briefly describe the idea.

(g) $\widehat{\boldsymbol{\Sigma}}_{\mathrm{ML}}$ is a *biased* estimate of the covariance matrix because $\mathbb{E}[\widehat{\boldsymbol{\Sigma}}_{\mathrm{ML}}] \neq \boldsymbol{\Sigma}$. Can you suggest an unbiased estimate $\widehat{\boldsymbol{\Sigma}}_{\mathrm{unbias}}$ such that $\mathbb{E}[\widehat{\boldsymbol{\Sigma}}_{\mathrm{unbias}}] = \boldsymbol{\Sigma}$? You don't need to prove it. Just state the result.

Chapter 9

Confidence and Hypothesis

In Chapters 7 and 8 we learned about regression and estimation, which allow us to determine the underlying parameters of our statistical models. After obtaining the estimates, we would like to quantify the accuracy of the estimates and draw statistical conclusions. Additionally, we would like to understand the **confidence** of these estimates along with their **statistical significance**. This chapter presents a few principles that involve analyzing the confidence of the estimates and conducting hypothesis testing. There are two main questions that we will address:

- How good is our estimate? This is a fundamental question about the estimator $\widehat{\Theta}$, a random variable with a PDF, a mean, and a variance.[1] The estimator we construct today may be different from the estimator we construct tomorrow due to variations in the observed data. Therefore, the quality of the estimator depends on the randomness and the number of samples used to construct it. To measure the quality of the estimator we need to introduce an important concept known as the **confidence**.

- Is there statistical significance? Suppose that we ran a campaign and observed that there is a change in the statistics. On what basis do we claim that the change is statistically significant? How should the cutoff be determined? If we claim that a result is statistically significant but there is no significance in reality, how much error will we suffer? These questions are the subjects of **hypothesis testing**.

These two principal questions are critical for modern data science. If they are not properly answered, our statistical conclusions could potentially be flawed. A toy example:

Imagine that you are developing a COVID-19 vaccine. You tested the vaccine on three patients, and all of them show positive responses to the vaccine. You felt excited because your vaccine has a 100% success rate. You submit your vaccine application to FDA. Within 1 second your application is rejected. Why? The answer is obvious. You only have three testing samples. How reliable can these three samples be?

While you are laughing at this toy example, it raises deep statistical questions. First, why are three samples not enough? Well, it is because the **variance** of the estimator can potentially be huge. More samples are better because if the estimator is the sample average of the individual responses, the estimator will behave like a Gaussian according to the Central

---

[1]Not all random variables have a well-defined PDF, mean, and variance. E.g., a Cauchy variable does not have a mean.

Limit Theorem. The variance of this Gaussian will diminish as we have more samples. Therefore, if we want to control the variance of the estimator, we need more samples. Second, even if we have many samples, how confident is this estimator with respect to the *unknown* population parameter? Note that the population parameter is unknown, and so we cannot measure things such as the mean squared error. We need a tool to report confidence. Third, for simple estimators such as the sample average, we can approximate it by a **Gaussian**. However, if the estimator is more complicated, e.g., the sample median, how do we estimate the variance and the confidence? Fourth, suppose that we have expanded the vaccine test to, say, 951 patients, and we have obtained some statistics. To what extent can we declare that the vaccine is effective? We need a **decision rule** that turns the statistics into a binary decision. Finally, even if we declare that the vaccine is effective with a confidence of 95%, what about the remaining 5%? What if we want to push the confidence to 99%? What is the trade-off?

As you can see, these questions are the recurring themes of all data science problems. No matter if you are developing a medical diagnostic system, a computer vision algorithm, a speech recognition system, a recommendation system, a search engine, stock forecast, fraud detection, or robotics controls, you need to answer these questions. This chapter will introduce useful concepts related to data analysis in the form of **five basic principles**:

1. **Confidence interval** (Section 9.1). A confidence interval is a random interval that includes the true parameter. We will discuss how a confidence interval is constructed and the correct way to interpret the confidence interval.

2. **Bootstrapping** (Section 9.2). When constructing the confidence interval, we need the variance of the estimator. However, since we do not know the true distribution, we need an alternative way to estimate the variance. Bootstrapping is designed for this purpose.

3. **Hypothesis testing** (Section 9.3). Many statistical tasks require a binary decision at the end, e.g., there is a disease versus there is no disease. Hypothesis testing is a principle for making a systematic decision with statistical guarantees.

4. **Neyman-Pearson decision** (Section 9.4). The simple hypothesis testing procedure has many limitations that can only be resolved if we understand a more general framework. We will study such a framework, called the Neyman-Pearson decision rule.

5. **ROC and PR curves** (Section 9.5). No decision rule is perfect. There is always a trade-off between how much we can detect and how much we will miss. The receiver operating characteristic (ROC) curve and the precision-recall (PR) curve can give us more insight into this trade-off. We will establish the equivalence between the ROC and the PR curve and correct any misconceptions about them.

After reading this chapter, we hope that you will be able to apply these principles to your favorite data analysis problems correctly. With these principles, you can tell your customers or bosses the statistical significance of your conclusions. You will also be able to help your friends understand the many misconceptions that they may find on the internet.

9.1 Confidence Interval

The first topic we discuss in this chapter is the **confidence interval**. At a high level, the confidence interval tells us the quality of our estimator with respect to the number of samples. We begin this section by reviewing the randomness of an estimator. Then we develop the concept of the confidence interval. We discuss several methods for constructing and interpreting these confidence intervals.

9.1.1 The randomness of an estimator

Imagine that we have a dataset $\mathcal{X} = \{X_1, \ldots, X_N\}$, where we assume that X_n are i.i.d. copies drawn from a distribution $f_X(x; \theta)$. We want to construct an **estimator** $\widehat{\Theta}$ of θ from the dataset $\mathcal{X}$. For example, if f_X is a Gaussian distribution with an unknown mean θ, we would like to estimate θ using the sample average $\widehat{\Theta}$. In statistics, an estimator $\widehat{\Theta}$ is also known as a **statistic**, which is constructed from the samples. In this book we use the terms "estimator" and "statistic" interchangeably. Written as equations, an estimator is a function of the samples:

$$\underbrace{\widehat{\Theta}}_{\text{estimator}} = \underbrace{g(X_1, \ldots, X_N)}_{\text{function of } \mathcal{X}},$$

where g is a function that takes the samples $X_1, \ldots, X_N$ and returns a random variable $\widehat{\Theta}$. For example, the sample average

$$\widehat{\Theta} = \underbrace{\frac{1}{N} \sum_{n=1}^{N} X_n}_{g(X_1, \ldots, X_N)}$$

is an estimator because it is computed by summing the samples $X_1, \ldots, X_N$ and dividing it by N.

What is an estimator?

- An estimator $\widehat{\Theta}$ is a function of the samples $X_1, \ldots, X_N$:

$$\widehat{\Theta} = g(X_1, \ldots, X_N). \tag{9.1}$$

- $\widehat{\Theta}$ is a random variable. It has a PDF, CDF, mean, variance, etc.

By construction, $\widehat{\Theta}$ is a random variable because it is a function of the random samples. Therefore, $\widehat{\Theta}$ has its own PDF, CDF, mean, variance, etc. Since $\widehat{\Theta}$ is a random variable, we should report both the estimator's *value* and the estimator's *confidence* when reporting its performance. The confidence measures the quality of $\widehat{\Theta}$ when compared to the true parameter θ. It provides a measure of the reliability of the estimator $\widehat{\Theta}$. If $\widehat{\Theta}$ fluctuates a great deal we may not be confident of our estimates. Let's consider the following example.

Example 9.1. A class of 1000 students took a test. The distribution of the score is roughly a Gaussian with mean 50 and standard deviation 20. A teaching assistant was too lazy to calculate the true population mean. Instead, he sampled a subset of 5 scores listed as follows:

Student ID	1	2	3	4	5
Scores	11	97	1	78	82

He calculated the average, which is 53.8. This is a very good estimate of the class average (which is 50). What is wrong with his procedure?

Solution. He was just lucky. It quite possible that if he sampled another 5 scores, he would get something very different. For example, if he looks at the 11 to 15 student scores, he could get:

Student ID	11	12	13	14	15
Scores	44	29	19	27	15

In this case the average is 26.8.

Both 53.8 and 26.8 are legitimate estimates, but they are the random realizations of a random variable $\widehat{\Theta}$. This $\widehat{\Theta}$ has a PDF, CDF, mean, variance, etc. It may be misleading to simply report the estimated value from a particular instant, so the confidence of the estimator must be specified.

Distributions of $\widehat{\Theta}$. We next discuss the distribution of $\widehat{\Theta}$. **Figure 9.1** illustrates several key ideas. Suppose that the population distribution $f_X(x)$ is a mixture of two Gaussians. Let θ be the mean of this distribution (somewhere between the two peak locations). We sample $N = 50$ data points $X_1, \ldots, X_N$ from this distribution. However, the 50 data points we sample today could differ from the 50 data points we sample tomorrow. If we compute the sample average from each of these finite-sample distributions, we will obtain a set of sample averages $\widehat{\Theta}$. Notably, we have a *set* of $\widehat{\Theta}$ because today we have one $\widehat{\Theta}$ and tomorrow we have another $\widehat{\Theta}$. By plotting the histogram of the sample averages $\widehat{\Theta}$, we will have a distribution.

The histogram of $\widehat{\Theta}$ depends on several factors. According to Central Limit Theorem, the shape of $f_{\widehat{\Theta}}(\theta)$ is a Gaussian because $\widehat{\Theta}$ is the average of N i.i.d. random variables. If $\widehat{\Theta}$ is not the average of i.i.d. random variables, the shape is not necessarily a Gaussian. This results in additional complications, so we will discuss some tools for dealing with this problem. The spread of the sample distribution is mainly driven by the number of samples we have in each subdataset. As you can imagine, the more samples we have in a subdataset the more accurate the distribution. Thus you will have a more accurate sample average. The fluctuation of the sample average will also be smaller.

Before we continue, let's summarize the randomness of $\widehat{\Theta}$:

What is the randomness of $\widehat{\Theta}$?
- $\widehat{\Theta}$ is generated from a finite-sample dataset. Each time we draw a finite-sample dataset, we introduce randomness.

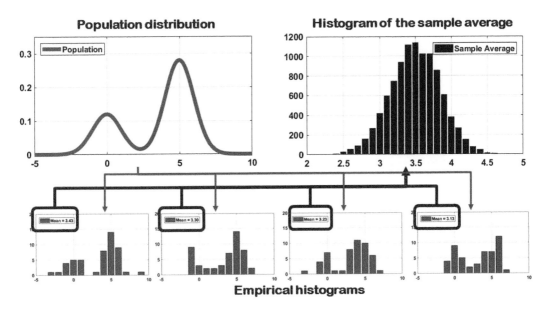

Figure 9.1: Pictorial illustration of the randomness of the estimator $\widehat{\Theta}$. Given a population, our datasets are usually a subset of the population. Computing the sample average from these finite-sample distributions introduces the randomness to $\widehat{\Theta}$. If we plot the histogram of the sample averages, we will obtain a distribution. The mean of this distribution is the population mean, but there is a nontrivial amount of fluctuation. The purpose of the concept of confidence interval is to quantify this fluctuation.

- If $\widehat{\Theta}$ is the sample average, the PDF is (roughly) a Gaussian. If $\widehat{\Theta}$ is not a sample average, the PDF is not necessarily a Gaussian.

- The spread of the fluctuation depends on the number of samples in each sub-dataset.

9.1.2 Understanding confidence intervals

The confidence interval is a probabilistic statement about $\widehat{\Theta}$. Instead of studying $\widehat{\Theta}$ as a *point*, we construct an *interval*

$$\mathcal{I} = \left[\widehat{\Theta} - \epsilon, \ \widehat{\Theta} + \epsilon\right], \tag{9.2}$$

for some ϵ to be determined. Note that this interval is a *random interval*: If we have a different realization of $\widehat{\Theta}$, we will have a different $\mathcal{I}$. We call $\mathcal{I}$ the **confidence interval** for the estimator $\widehat{\Theta}$.

Given this random interval, we ask: What is the probability that $\mathcal{I}$ includes θ? That means that we want to evaluate the probability

$$\mathbb{P}[\theta \in \mathcal{I}] = \mathbb{P}\left[\widehat{\Theta} - \epsilon \leq \theta \leq \widehat{\Theta} + \epsilon\right].$$

We emphasize that the randomness in this probability is caused by $\widehat{\Theta}$, not θ. This is because the interval $\mathcal{I}$ changes when we conduct a different experiment to obtain a different $\widehat{\Theta}$. The situation is similar to that illustrated on the left-hand side of **Figure 9.2**. The confidence interval $\mathcal{I}$ changes but the true parameter θ is fixed.

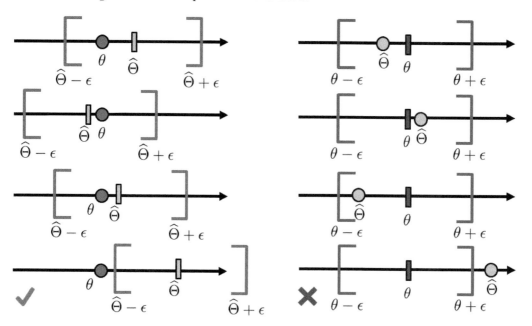

Figure 9.2: Confidence interval is the random interval $\mathcal{I} = [\widehat{\Theta} - \epsilon, \widehat{\Theta} + \epsilon]$, not the deterministic interval $[\theta - \epsilon, \theta + \epsilon]$. The random interval in the former case does not require any knowledge about the true parameter θ, whereas the latter requires θ. By claiming a 95% confidence interval, we say that there is 95% chance that the random interval will include the true parameter. So if you have 100 random realizations of the confidence intervals, then 95 on average will include the true parameter.

Confidence intervals can be confusing. Often the confusion arises because of the following identity:

$$\mathbb{P}\left[\widehat{\Theta} - \epsilon \leq \theta \leq \widehat{\Theta} + \epsilon\right] = \mathbb{P}\left[-\epsilon \leq \theta - \widehat{\Theta} \leq \epsilon\right]$$

$$= \mathbb{P}\left[-\epsilon - \theta \leq -\widehat{\Theta} \leq \epsilon - \theta\right]$$

$$= \mathbb{P}\left[\theta - \epsilon \leq \widehat{\Theta} \leq \theta + \epsilon\right]. \tag{9.3}$$

Although the values of the two probabilities are the same, the two events are interpreted differently. The right-hand side of **Figure 9.2** illustrates $\mathbb{P}[\theta - \epsilon \leq \widehat{\Theta} \leq \theta + \epsilon]$. The interval $[\theta - \epsilon, \theta + \epsilon]$ is fixed. What is the probability that the estimator $\widehat{\Theta}$ lies within this deterministic interval? To find this probability, we need to know the true parameter θ, which is not available. By contrast, the other probability $\mathbb{P}[\widehat{\Theta} - \epsilon \leq \theta \leq \widehat{\Theta} + \epsilon]$ does not require any knowledge about the true parameter θ. What is the probability that the true parameter is included inside the random interval? If the probability is high, we say that there is a good chance that our confidence interval will contain the true parameter. This is observed in the left-hand side of **Figure 9.2**.

In practice we often set $\mathbb{P}[\widehat{\Theta} - \epsilon \leq \theta \leq \widehat{\Theta} + \epsilon]$ to be greater than a certain confidence level, say 95%, and then we determine ϵ. Once we have determined ϵ, we can claim that with 95% probability the interval $[\widehat{\Theta} - \epsilon, \ \widehat{\Theta} + \epsilon]$ will include the unknown parameter θ. We do not need to know θ at any point in this process.

To make this more general, we define $1 - \alpha$ as the **confidence level** for some parameter α. For example, if we would like to have a 95% confidence level, we set $\alpha = 0.05$. Then the probability inequality

$$\mathbb{P}\left[\widehat{\Theta} - \epsilon \leq \theta \leq \widehat{\Theta} + \epsilon\right] \geq 1 - \alpha \tag{9.4}$$

tells us that there is at least a 95% chance that the random interval $\mathcal{I} = [\widehat{\Theta} - \epsilon, \ \widehat{\Theta} + \epsilon]$ will include the true parameter θ. In this case we say that $\mathcal{I}$ is a "**95% confidence interval**".

What is a 95% confidence interval?

- It is a random interval $[\widehat{\Theta} - \epsilon, \widehat{\Theta} + \epsilon]$ such that there is 95% probability for it to include the true parameter θ.
- It is not the deterministic interval $[\theta - \epsilon, \theta + \epsilon]$, because we never know θ.

Example 9.2. After analyzing the life expectancy of people in the United States, it was concluded that the 95% confidence interval is (77.8, 79.1) years old. Is the following claim valid?

About 95% of the people in the United States have a life expectancy between 77.8 years old and 79.1 years old.

Solution. No. The confidence interval tells us that with 95% probability the random interval (77.8, 79.1) will include the true average. We emphasize that (77.8, 79.1) is random because it is constructed from a small set of data points. If we survey another set of people we will have another interval.

Since we do not know the true average, we do not know the percentage of people whose life expectancy is between 77.8 years old and 79.1 years old. It could be that the true average is 80 years old, which is out of the range. It could also be that the true average is 77.9 years old, which is within the range, but only 10% of the population may have life expectancy in (77.8, 79.1).

Example 9.3. After studying the SAT scores of 1000 high school students, it was concluded that the 95% confidence interval is (1134, 1250) points. Is the following claim valid?

There is a 95% probability that the average SAT score in the population is in the range 1134 and 1250.

Solution. Yes, but it can be made clearer. The average SAT score in the population remains unknown. It is a constant and it is deterministic, so there is no probability associated with it. A better way to say this is: "There is 95% probability that the random interval 1134 and 1250 will include the average SAT score." We emphasize that the 95% probability is about the random interval, not the unknown parameter.

9.1.3 Constructing a confidence interval

Let's consider an example. Suppose that we have a set of i.i.d. observations $X_1, \ldots, X_N$ that are Gaussians with an unknown mean θ and a known variance σ^2. We consider the maximum-likelihood estimator, which is the sample average:

$$\widehat{\Theta} = \frac{1}{N} \sum_{n=1}^{N} X_n.$$

Our goal is to construct a confidence interval.

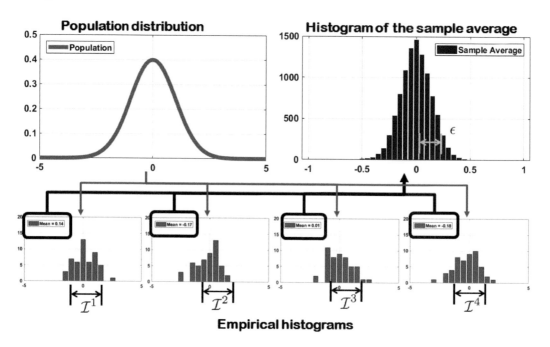

Figure 9.3: Conceptual illustration of how to construct a confidence interval. Starting with the population, we draw random subsets. Each random subset gives us an estimator, and correspondingly an interval.

Before we consider the equations, let's look at a graph illustrating what we want to achieve. **Figure 9.3** shows a population distribution, which is a Gaussian in this example. We draw N samples from the Gaussian to construct a random subset. Based on this random subset we construct the estimator $\widehat{\Theta}$. Since this estimator is based on the particular random subset we have, we can follow the same approach by drawing another random subset. To differentiate the estimators constructed by the different random subsets, let's call the estimators $\widehat{\Theta}^{(1)}$ and $\widehat{\Theta}^{(2)}$, respectively. For each estimator we construct an interval $[\widehat{\Theta} - \epsilon, \ \widehat{\Theta} + \epsilon]$ to obtain two different intervals:

$$\mathcal{I}^1 = [\widehat{\Theta}^{(1)} - \epsilon, \ \widehat{\Theta}^{(1)} + \epsilon] \qquad \text{and} \qquad \mathcal{I}^2 = [\widehat{\Theta}^{(2)} - \epsilon, \ \widehat{\Theta}^{(2)} + \epsilon].$$

If we can determine ϵ, we have found the confidence interval.

We can determine the confidence interval by observing the histogram of $\widehat{\Theta}$, which in our case is the histogram of the sample average, since the histogram of $\widehat{\Theta}$ is well-defined, especially if we are looking at the sample average. The histogram of the sample average is a Gaussian because the average of N i.i.d. Gaussian random variables is Gaussian. Therefore, the width of this Gaussian is determined by the answer to this question:

For what ϵ can we cover 95% of the histogram of $\widehat{\Theta}$?

To find the answer, we set up the following probability inequality:

$$\mathbb{P}\left[\frac{|\widehat{\Theta} - \mathbb{E}[\widehat{\Theta}]|}{\sqrt{\text{Var}[\widehat{\Theta}]}} \leq \epsilon\right] \geq 1 - \alpha.$$

This probability says that we want to find an ϵ such that the majority of $\widehat{\Theta}$ is living close to its mean. The level $1 - \alpha$ is our confidence level, which is typically 95%. Equivalently, we let $\alpha = 0.05$.

In the above equation, we can define the quotient as

$$\widehat{Z} \overset{\text{def}}{=} \frac{\widehat{\Theta} - \mathbb{E}[\widehat{\Theta}]}{\sqrt{\text{Var}[\widehat{\Theta}]}}.$$

We know that $\widehat{Z}$ is a zero-mean unit-variance Gaussian because it is the standardized variable. [Note: Not all normalized variables are Gaussian, but if $\widehat{\Theta}$ is a Gaussian the normalized variable will remain a Gaussian.] Thus, the probability inequality we are looking at is

$$\underbrace{\mathbb{P}\left[|\widehat{Z}| \leq \epsilon\right]}_{\text{two tails of a standard Gaussian}} \geq 1 - \alpha.$$

The PDF of $\widehat{Z}$ is shown in **Figure 9.4**. As you can see, to achieve 95% confidence we need to pick an appropriate ϵ such that the shaded area is less than 5%.

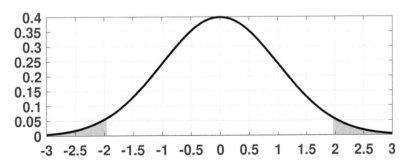

Figure 9.4: PDF of the random variable $\widehat{Z} = (\widehat{\Theta} - \mathbb{E}[\widehat{\Theta}])/\sqrt{\text{Var}[\widehat{\Theta}]}$. The shaded area denotes the $\alpha = 0.05$ confidence level.

Since $\mathbb{P}[\widehat{Z} \leq \epsilon]$ is the CDF of a Gaussian, it follows that

$$\mathbb{P}[|\widehat{Z}| \leq \epsilon] = \mathbb{P}[-\epsilon \leq \widehat{Z} \leq \epsilon]$$
$$= \mathbb{P}[\widehat{Z} \leq \epsilon] - \mathbb{P}[\widehat{Z} \leq -\epsilon]$$
$$= \Phi(\epsilon) - \Phi(-\epsilon).$$

Using the symmetry of the Gaussian, it follows that $\Phi(-\epsilon) = 1 - \Phi(\epsilon)$ and hence

$$\mathbb{P}[|\widehat{Z}| \leq \epsilon] = 2\Phi(\epsilon) - 1.$$

Equating this result with the probability inequality $\mathbb{P}[|\widehat{Z}| \leq \epsilon] \geq 1 - \alpha$, we have that

$$\epsilon \geq \Phi^{-1}\left(1 - \frac{\alpha}{2}\right).$$

The remainder of this problem is solvable on a computer. On MATLAB, we can call icdf to compute the inverse CDF of a standard Gaussian. On Python, the command is stats.norm.ppf. The commands are as shown below.

```
% MATLAB code to compute the width of the confidence interval
alpha = 0.05;
mu = 0; sigma = 1; % Standard Gaussian
epsilon = icdf('norm',1-alpha/2,mu,sigma)
```

```
# Python code to compute the width of the confidence interval
import scipy.stats as stats
alph = 0.05;
mu   = 0; sigma = 1; # Standard Gaussian
epsilon = stats.norm.ppf(1-alph/2, mu, sigma)
print(epsilon)
```

If everything is done properly, we see that for a 95% confidence level ($\alpha = 0.05$) the corresponding ϵ is $\epsilon = 1.96$.

After determining ϵ, it remains to determine $\mathbb{E}[\widehat{\Theta}]$ and $\text{Var}[\widehat{\Theta}]$ in order to complete the probability inequality. To this end, we note that

$$\mathbb{E}[\widehat{\Theta}] = \mathbb{E}\left[\frac{1}{N}\sum_{n=1}^{N}X_n\right] = \theta,$$

$$\text{Var}[\widehat{\Theta}] = \text{Var}\left[\frac{1}{N}\sum_{n=1}^{N}X_n\right] = \frac{\sigma^2}{N},$$

if we assume that the population distribution is Gaussian(θ, σ^2), where θ is unknown but σ is known. Substituting these into the probability inequality, we have that

$$\mathbb{P}\left[\frac{|\widehat{\Theta} - \mathbb{E}[\widehat{\Theta}]|}{\sqrt{\text{Var}[\widehat{\Theta}]}} \leq \epsilon\right] = \mathbb{P}\left[\widehat{\Theta} - \epsilon\frac{\sigma}{\sqrt{N}} \leq \theta \leq \widehat{\Theta} + \epsilon\frac{\sigma}{\sqrt{N}}\right]$$

$$= \mathbb{P}\left[\widehat{\Theta} - 1.96\frac{\sigma}{\sqrt{N}} \leq \theta \leq \widehat{\Theta} + 1.96\frac{\sigma}{\sqrt{N}}\right],$$

where we let $\epsilon = 1.96$ for a 95% confidence level. Therefore, the 95% confidence interval is

$$\left[\widehat{\Theta} - 1.96\frac{\sigma}{\sqrt{N}}, \quad \widehat{\Theta} + 1.96\frac{\sigma}{\sqrt{N}}\right]. \tag{9.5}$$

As you can see, we do not need to know the value of θ at any point of the derivation because the confidence interval in Equation (9.5) does not involve θ. This is an important difference with the other probability $\mathbb{P}[\theta - \epsilon \leq \widehat{\Theta} \leq \theta + \epsilon]$, which requires θ.

How to construct a confidence interval
- Compute the estimator $\widehat{\Theta}$.
- Determine the width of the confidence interval ϵ by inspecting the confidence level $1 - \alpha$. If $\widehat{\Theta}$ is Gaussian, then $\epsilon = \Phi^{-1}(1 - \frac{\alpha}{2})$.
- If $\widehat{\Theta}$ is not a Gaussian, replace the Gaussian CDF by the CDF of $\widehat{\Theta}$.
- The confidence interval is $[\widehat{\Theta} - \epsilon, \widehat{\Theta} + \epsilon]$.

9.1.4 Properties of the confidence interval

Some important properties of the confidence interval are listed below.

- **Probability of $\widehat{\Theta}$ is the same as probability of $\widehat{Z}$.** First, the two random variables $\widehat{\Theta}$ and $\widehat{Z}$ have a one-to-one correspondence. We proved the following in Chapter 6:

  If $\widehat{\Theta} \sim \text{Gaussian}(\theta, \frac{\sigma^2}{N})$, then

  $$\widehat{Z} \overset{\text{def}}{=} \frac{\widehat{\Theta} - \theta}{\sigma/\sqrt{N}} \sim \text{Gaussian}(0, 1). \qquad (9.6)$$

  For example, if $\widehat{\Theta} \sim \text{Gaussian}(\theta, \frac{\sigma^2}{N})$ with $N = 1$, $\theta = 1$ and $\sigma = 2$, then a 95% confidence level is

  $$0.95 \approx \mathbb{P}[-1.96 \leq \widehat{Z} \leq 1.96], \qquad (\widehat{Z} \text{ is within 1.96 std from } \widehat{Z}\text{'s mean})$$

  $$= \mathbb{P}[-1.96 \leq \frac{\widehat{\Theta} - \theta}{\sigma/\sqrt{N}} \leq 1.96]$$

  $$= \mathbb{P}\left[\theta - 1.96\frac{\sigma}{\sqrt{N}} \leq \widehat{\Theta} \leq \theta + 1.96\frac{\sigma}{\sqrt{N}}\right]$$

  $$= \mathbb{P}[-2.92 \leq \widehat{\Theta} \leq 4.92]. \qquad (\widehat{\Theta} \text{ is within 1.96 std from } \widehat{\Theta}\text{'s mean})$$

  Note that while the range for $\widehat{Z}$ is different from the range for $\widehat{\Theta}$, they both return the same probability. The only difference is that $\widehat{\Theta}$ is constructed before the normalization and $\widehat{Z}$ is constructed after the normalization.

- **Standard error.** In this estimation problem we know that $\widehat{\Theta}$ is the sample average. We assume that the mean θ is unknown but the variance $\text{Var}[\widehat{\Theta}]$ is known. The standard deviation of $\widehat{\Theta}$ is called the **standard error**:

  $$\text{se} = \sqrt{\text{Var}[\widehat{\Theta}]} = \frac{\sigma}{\sqrt{N}}. \qquad (9.7)$$

- **Critical value.** The value 1.96 in our example is often known as the **critical value**. It is defined as

  $$z_\alpha = \Phi^{-1}\left(1 - \frac{\alpha}{2}\right). \qquad (9.8)$$

The z_α value gives us a multiplier applied to the standard error that will result in a value within the confidence interval. This is because, by the definition of the confidence interval, the interval is

$$\left[\widehat{\Theta} - 1.96\frac{\sigma}{\sqrt{N}}, \quad \widehat{\Theta} + 1.96\frac{\sigma}{\sqrt{N}}\right] = \left[\widehat{\Theta} - z_\alpha\mathsf{se}, \quad \widehat{\Theta} + z_\alpha\mathsf{se}\right]$$

- **Margin of error.** The margin of error is defined as

$$\text{margin of error} = z_\alpha\frac{\sigma}{\sqrt{N}}. \tag{9.9}$$

The margin of error is also the width of the confidence interval. As the name implies, the margin of error tells us how much error the confidence interval includes when predicting the population parameter.

Practice Exercise 9.1. Suppose that the number of photos a Facebook user uploads per day is a random variable with $\sigma = 2$. In a set of 341 users, the sample average is 2.9. Find the 90% confidence interval of the population mean.

Solution. We set $\alpha = 0.1$. The z_α-value is

$$z_\alpha = \Phi^{-1}\left(1 - \frac{\alpha}{2}\right) = 1.6449.$$

The 90% confidence interval is then

$$\left[\widehat{\Theta} - 1.64\frac{2}{\sqrt{341}}, \quad \widehat{\Theta} + 1.64\frac{2}{\sqrt{341}}\right] = [2.72, 3.08].$$

Therefore, with 90% probability, the interval $[2.72, 3.08]$ includes the population mean.

Example 9.4. Professional cyber-athletes have a standard deviation of $\sigma = 73.4$ actions per minute. If we want to estimate the average actions per minute of the population, how many samples are needed to obtain a margin of error < 20 at 90% confidence?

Solution. With a 90% confidence level, the z_α-value is

$$z_\alpha = \Phi^{-1}\left(1 - \frac{\alpha}{2}\right) = \Phi^{-1}(0.95) = 1.645.$$

The margin of error is 20. So we have $z_\alpha\frac{\sigma}{\sqrt{N}} = 20$. Moving around the terms gives us

$$N \geq \left(z_\alpha\frac{\sigma}{20}\right)^2 = 36.45.$$

Therefore, we need at least $N = 37$ samples to ensure a margin of error of < 20 at a 90% confidence level.

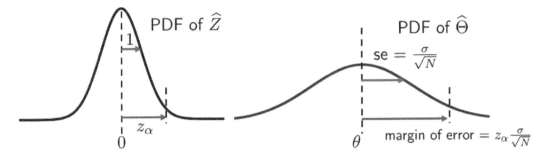

Figure 9.5: Relationships between the standard error se, the z_α value, and the margin of error. The confidence level α is the area under the curve for the tails of each PDF.

The concepts of standard error **se**, the z_α value, and the margin of error are summarized in **Figure 9.5**. The left-hand side is the PDF of $\widehat{Z}$. It is the normalized random variable, which is also the standard Gaussian. The right-hand side is the PDF of $\widehat{\Theta}$, the unnormalized random variable. The z_α value is located in the $\widehat{Z}$-space. It defines the range of $\widehat{Z}$ in the PDF within which we are confident about the true parameter. The corresponding value in the $\widehat{\Theta}$-space is the **margin of error**. This is found by multiplying z_α with the standard deviation of $\widehat{\Theta}$, known as the **standard error**. Correspondingly, in the $\widehat{Z}$-space the standard deviation is the unity.

Two further points about the confidence interval should be mentioned:

- **Number of Samples** N. The confidence interval is a function of N. As we increase the number of samples, the distribution of the estimator $\widehat{\Theta}$ becomes narrower. Specifically, if $\widehat{\Theta}$ follows a Gaussian distribution

$$\widehat{\Theta} \sim \text{Gaussian}\left(\theta, \ \frac{\sigma^2}{N}\right),$$

then $\widehat{\Theta} \xrightarrow{p} \theta$ as $N \to \infty$. **Figure 9.6** illustrates a few examples of $\widehat{\Theta}$ as N grows. In the limit when $N \to \infty$, we observe that the interval becomes

$$\left[\widehat{\Theta} - 1.96\frac{\sigma}{\sqrt{N}}, \quad \widehat{\Theta} + 1.96\frac{\sigma}{\sqrt{N}}\right] \longrightarrow \left[\widehat{\Theta}, \quad \widehat{\Theta}\right] = \widehat{\Theta}.$$

In this case, the statement $\theta \in \left[\widehat{\Theta} - 1.96\frac{\sigma}{\sqrt{N}}, \quad \widehat{\Theta} + 1.96\frac{\sigma}{\sqrt{N}}\right]$ becomes $\theta = \widehat{\Theta}$. That means the estimator $\widehat{\Theta}$ returns the correct true parameter θ. Of course, it is possible that $\mathbb{E}[\widehat{\Theta}] \neq \theta$, i.e., the estimator is biased. In that case, having more samples will approach another estimate that is not θ.

- **Distribution of** $\widehat{Z}$. When defining the confidence interval we constructed an intermediate variable

$$\widehat{Z} = \frac{\widehat{\Theta} - \theta}{\sigma/\sqrt{N}}.$$

Since X_n's are i.i.d. Gaussian, it follows that Z is also Gaussian. This gives us a way to calculate the probability using the standard Gaussian table. What happens when X_n's are *not* Gaussian? The good news is that even if X_n's are not Gaussian, for

555

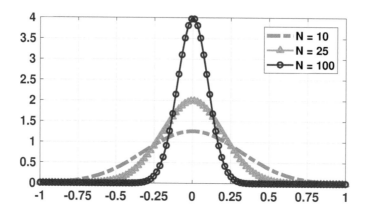

Figure 9.6: The PDF of $\widehat{\Theta}$ as the number of samples N grows. Here, we assume that X_n are i.i.d. Gaussian random variables with mean $\theta = 0$ and variance $\sigma^2 = 1$.

sufficiently large N, the random variable $\widehat{\Theta}$ is more or less Gaussian, because of the Central Limit Theorem. Therefore, even if X_n's are not Gaussian we can still use the Gaussian probability table to construct α and ϵ.

9.1.5 Student's t-distribution

In the discussions above, we estimate the population mean θ using the estimator $\widehat{\Theta}$. The assumption was that the variance σ^2 was known a priori and hence is fixed. In practice, however, there are many situations where σ^2 is not known. Thus we not only need to use the mean estimator $\widehat{\Theta}$ but also the variance estimator $\widehat{S}$, which can be defined as

$$\widehat{S}^2 \overset{\text{def}}{=} \frac{1}{N-1} \sum_{n=1}^{N} (X_n - \widehat{\Theta})^2,$$

where $\widehat{\Theta}$ is the estimator of the mean. What is the confidence interval for $\widehat{\Theta}$?

For a confidence interval to be valid, we expect it to take the form of

$$\mathcal{I} = \left[\widehat{\Theta} - z_\alpha \frac{\widehat{S}}{\sqrt{N}}, \ \ \widehat{\Theta} + z_\alpha \frac{\widehat{S}}{\sqrt{N}} \right],$$

which is essentially the confidence interval we have just derived but with σ replaced by $\widehat{S}$. However, there is a problem with this. When we derive the confidence interval assuming a known σ, the z_α value is determined by checking the standard Gaussian

$$\widehat{Z} = \frac{\widehat{\Theta} - \theta}{\sigma/\sqrt{N}},$$

which gives us $z_\alpha = \Phi^{-1}(1 - \alpha/2)$. The whole derivation is based on the fact that $\widehat{Z}$ is a standard Gaussian. Now that we have replaced σ by $\widehat{S}$, the new random variable

$$T \overset{\text{def}}{=} \frac{\widehat{\Theta} - \theta}{\widehat{S}/\sqrt{N}} \tag{9.10}$$

is *not* a standard Gaussian.

It turns out that the distribution of T is Student's t-**distribution** with $N-1$ degrees of freedom. The PDF of Student's t-distribution is given as follows.

Definition 9.1. *If X is a random variable following Student's t-**distribution** of ν degrees of freedom, then the PDF of X is*

$$f_X(x) = \frac{\Gamma\left(\frac{\nu+1}{2}\right)}{\sqrt{\nu\pi}\Gamma\left(\frac{\nu}{2}\right)}\left(1+\frac{x^2}{\nu}\right)^{-\frac{\nu+1}{2}}. \tag{9.11}$$

We may compare Student's t-distribution with the Gaussian distribution. **Figure 9.7** shows the standard Gaussian and several t distributions with $\nu = N-1$ degrees of freedom. Note that Student's t-distribution has a similar shape to the Gaussian but it has a heavier tail.

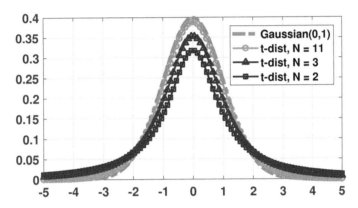

Figure 9.7: The PDF of Student's t-distribution with $\nu = N-1$ degrees of freedom.

Since $T = \frac{\widehat{\Theta}-\theta}{\widehat{S}/\sqrt{N}}$ is a t-random variable, to determine the z_α value we can follow the same procedure by considering the CDF of T. Let the CDF of the Student's t-distribution with ν degrees of freedom be

$$\Psi_\nu(z) = \text{CDF of } X \text{ at } z.$$

If we want $\mathbb{P}[|T| \leq z_\alpha] = 1 - \alpha$, it follows that

$$z_\alpha = \Psi_\nu^{-1}\left(1 - \frac{\alpha}{2}\right). \tag{9.12}$$

Therefore, the new confidence interval, assuming an unknown $\widehat{S}$, is

$$\mathcal{I} = \left[\widehat{\Theta} - z_\alpha\frac{\widehat{S}}{\sqrt{N}},\ \ \widehat{\Theta} + z_\alpha\frac{\widehat{S}}{\sqrt{N}}\right],$$

with z_α defined in Equation (9.12), using $\nu = N-1$.

Practice Exercise 9.2. A survey asked $N = 14$ people for their rating of a movie. Assume that the mean estimator is $\widehat{\Theta}$ and the variance estimator is $\widehat{S}$. Find the confidence interval.

Solution. If we use Student's t-distribution, it follows that

$$z_\alpha = \Psi_{13}^{-1}\left(1 - \frac{\alpha}{2}\right) = 2.16,$$

where the degrees of freedom are $\nu = 14 - 1 = 13$. Thus the confidence interval is

$$\mathcal{I} = \left[\widehat{\Theta} - 2.16\frac{\widehat{S}}{\sqrt{N}}, \quad \widehat{\Theta} + 2.16\frac{\widehat{S}}{\sqrt{N}}\right].$$

The MATLAB and Python codes to report the z_α value of a Student's t-distribution are shown below. They are both called through the inverse CDF function. In MATLAB it is `icdf`, and in Python it is `stats.t.ppf`.

```
% MATLAB code to compute the z_alpha value of t distribution
alpha = 0.05;
nu = 13;
z = icdf('norm',1-alpha/2,nu)
```

```
# Python code to compute the z_alpha value of t distribution
import scipy.stats as stats
alph = 0.05
nu   = 13
z = stats.t.ppf(1-alph/2, nu)
print(z)
```

Example 9.5. A class of 10 students took a midterm exam. Their scores are given in the following table.

Student	1	2	3	4	5	6	7	8	9	10
Score	72	69	75	58	67	70	60	71	59	65

Find the 95% confidence interval.

Solution. The mean and standard deviation of the datasets are respectively $\widehat{\Theta} = 66.6$ and $\widehat{S} = 5.61$. The critical z_α value is determined by Student's t-distribution:

$$z_\alpha = \Psi_9^{-1}\left(1 - \frac{\alpha}{2}\right) = 2.26.$$

The confidence interval is

$$\left[\widehat{\Theta} - z_\alpha \frac{\widehat{S}}{\sqrt{N}}, \quad \widehat{\Theta} + z_\alpha \frac{\widehat{S}}{\sqrt{N}}\right] = [62.59, 70.61].$$

Therefore, with 95% probability, the interval $[62.59, 70.61]$ will include the true population mean.

Remark 1. Make sure you understand the meaning of "population mean" in this example. Since we have ten students, isn't the population mean just the average of the ten scores? This is incorrect. In statistics, we assume that these ten students are the realizations of some underlying (unknown) random variable X with some PDF $f_X(x)$. The population mean θ is therefore the expectation $\mathbb{E}[X]$, where the expectation is taken w.r.t. f_X. The sample average $\widehat{\Theta}$, which is the average of the ten numbers, is an estimator of the population mean θ.

Remark 2. You may be wondering why we are using Student's t-distribution here when we do not even know the PDF of X. The answer is that it is an approximation. When X is Gaussian, the sample average $\widehat{\Theta}$ is a Student's t-distribution, assuming that the variance is approximated by the sample variance $\widehat{S}$. This result is attributed to the original paper of William Gosset, who developed Student's t-distribution.

The above example can be solved computationally. An implementation through Python is given below, and the MATLAB implementation is straightforward.

```
# Python code to generate a confidence interval
import numpy as np
import scipy.stats as stats
x = np.array([72, 69, 75, 58, 67, 70, 60, 71, 59, 65])
N         = x.size
Theta_hat = np.mean(x) # Sample mean
S_hat     = np.std(x)  # Sample standard deviation
nu        = x.size-1   # degrees of freedom
alpha     = 0.05       # confidence level
z    = stats.t.ppf(1-alph/2, nu)
CI_L = Theta_hat-z*S_hat/np.sqrt(N)
CI_U = Theta_hat+z*S_hat/np.sqrt(N)
print(CI_L, CI_U)
```

What is Student's t-distribution?
- It was developed by William Gosset in 1908. When he published the paper he used the pseudonym Student.
- We use Student's t-distribution to model the estimator $\widehat{\Theta}$'s PDF when the variance σ^2 is replaced by the sample variance $\widehat{S}^2$.
- Student's t-distribution has a heavier tail than a Gaussian.

9.1.6 Comparing Student's t-distribution and Gaussian

We now discuss an important theoretical result regarding the relationship between a Student's t-distribution and Gaussian distribution. The main result is that the standard Gaussian is a limiting distribution of the t distribution as the degrees of freedom $\nu \to \infty$.

> **Theorem 9.1.** *As $\nu \to \infty$, the Student's t-distribution approaches the standard Gaussian distribution:*
>
> $$\lim_{\nu \to \infty} \left\{ \frac{\Gamma\left(\frac{\nu+1}{2}\right)}{\sqrt{\nu\pi}\,\Gamma\left(\frac{\nu}{2}\right)} \left(1 + \frac{y^2}{\nu}\right)^{-\frac{\nu+1}{2}} \right\} = \frac{1}{\sqrt{2\pi}} e^{-\frac{t^2}{2}}. \qquad (9.13)$$

> The proof of the theorem requires Stirling's approximation, which is not essential for this book. Feel free to skip it if needed.

Proof. There are two results we need to use:

- Stirling's approximation:[2] $\Gamma(z) \approx \sqrt{\frac{2\pi}{z}} \left(\frac{z}{e}\right)^z$.

- Exponential approximation: $(1 + \frac{x}{k})^{-k} \to e^{-x}$, as $k \to \infty$.

We have that

$$\frac{\Gamma\left(\frac{\nu+1}{2}\right)}{\sqrt{\nu\pi}\,\Gamma\left(\frac{\nu}{2}\right)} \approx \frac{\sqrt{\frac{2\pi}{\frac{\nu+1}{2}}}\left(\frac{\nu+1}{2e}\right)^{\frac{\nu+1}{2}}}{\sqrt{\nu\pi}\sqrt{\frac{2\pi}{\frac{\nu}{2}}}\left(\frac{\nu}{2e}\right)^{\frac{\nu}{2}}}$$

$$= \frac{1}{\sqrt{\nu\pi}}\sqrt{\frac{\nu}{\nu+1}}\frac{1}{\sqrt{e}}\left(\frac{\nu+1}{\nu}\right)^{\frac{\nu}{2}}\frac{\sqrt{\nu+1}}{\sqrt{\nu}}$$

$$= \frac{1}{\sqrt{\nu\pi}}\frac{\sqrt{\nu}}{\sqrt{2e}}\left(\frac{\nu+1}{\nu}\right)^{\frac{\nu}{2}}$$

$$= \frac{1}{\sqrt{2\pi e}}\left(1 + \frac{1}{\nu}\right)^{\frac{\nu}{2}}.$$

Putting a limit of $\nu \to \infty$, we have that

$$\lim_{\nu \to \infty} \frac{1}{\sqrt{2\pi e}}\left(1 + \frac{1}{\nu}\right)^{\frac{\nu}{2}} = \frac{1}{\sqrt{2\pi e}}e^{\frac{1}{2}} = \frac{1}{\sqrt{2\pi}}.$$

The other limit follows from the fact that

$$\lim_{\nu \to \infty}\left(1 + \frac{t^2}{\nu}\right)^{-\frac{\nu+1}{2}} = e^{-\frac{t^2}{2}}.$$

Combining the two limits proves the theorem. $\qquad \square$

---

[2]K. G. Binmore, *Mathematical analysis: A straightforward approach.* Cambridge University Press, 1977. Section 17.7.2.

> End of the proof. Please join us again.

This theorem has several implications:

- When N is large, $S^2 \to \sigma^2$. The Gaussian approximation kicks in, and so Student's t-distribution is more or less the same as the Gaussian.

- Student's t-distribution is better for small N, usually $N \leq 30$. If $N \geq 30$, using the Gaussian approximation suffices.

- If X is Gaussian, Student's t-distribution is an excellent model. If X is not Gaussian, Student's t-distribution will have some issues unless N increases.

9.2 Bootstrapping

When estimating the confidence interval, we focus exclusively on the sample average $\widehat{\Theta} = (1/N) \sum_{n=1}^{N} X_n$. There are, however, many estimators that are not sample averages. For example, we might be interested in an estimator that estimates the sample median: $\widehat{\Theta} = \text{median}\{X_1, \ldots, X_N\}$. In such cases, the Gaussian-based analysis or the Student's t-based analysis we just derived would not work.

Stepping back a little further, it is important to understand the hierarchy of estimation. **Figure 9.8** illustrates a rough breakdown of the various techniques. On the left-hand side of the tree, we have three **point estimation** methods: MLE, MAP, and MMSE. They are so-called *point* estimation methods because they are reporting a point — a single value. This stands in contrast to the right-hand side of the tree, in which we report the **confidence interval**. Note that point estimates and confidence intervals do not conflict with each other. The point estimates are used for the actual engineering solution and the confidence intervals are used to report the confidence about the point estimates. Under the branch of confidence intervals we discussed sample average. However, if we want to study an estimator that is not the sample average, we need the technique known as the **bootstrapping** — a method for estimating the confidence interval. Notably, it does not give you a better point estimate.

As we have frequently emphasized, since $\widehat{\Theta}$ is a *random variable*, it has its own PDF, CDF, mean, variance, etc. The confidence interval introduced in the previous section provides one way to quantify the randomness of $\widehat{\Theta}$. Throughout the derivation of the confidence interval we need to estimate the variance $\text{Var}(\widehat{\Theta})$. For simple problems such as the sample average, analyzing $\text{Var}(\widehat{\Theta})$ is not difficult. However, if $\widehat{\Theta}$ is a more complicated statistic, e.g., the *median*, analyzing $\text{Var}(\widehat{\Theta})$ may not be as straightforward. **Bootstrapping** is a technique that is suitable for this purpose.

Why is it difficult to provide a confidence interval for estimators such as the median? A couple of difficulties arise:

- Many estimators do not have a simple expression for the variance. For simple estimators such as the sample average $\widehat{\Theta} = (1/N) \sum_{n=1}^{N} X_n$, the variance is σ^2/N. If the

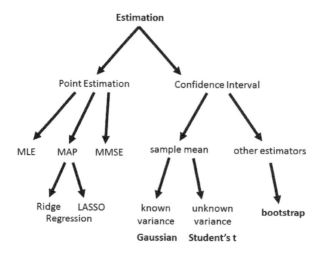

Figure 9.8: Hierarchy of estimation. Bootstrapping belongs to the category of confidence interval. It is used to report the confidence intervals for estimators that are not the sample averages.

estimator is the median $\widehat{\Theta} = \text{median}\{X_1, \ldots, X_N\}$, the variance of $\widehat{\Theta}$ will depend on the underlying distribution of the X_n's. If the estimator is something beyond the sample median, the variance of $\widehat{\Theta}$ can be even more complicated to determine. Therefore, techniques such as Central Limit Theorem do not apply here.

- We typically have only *one* set of data points. We cannot re-collect more i.i.d. samples to estimate the variance of the estimator. Therefore, our only option is to squeeze the information from the data we have been given.

When do we use bootstrapping?

- Bootstrapping is a technique to estimate the confidence interval.
- We use bootstrapping when the estimator does not have a simple expression for the variance.
- Bootstrapping allows us to estimate the variance without re-collecting more data.
- Bootstrapping does not improve your point estimates.

9.2.1 A brute force approach

Before we discuss the idea of bootstrapping, we need to elaborate on the difficulty of estimating the variance using repeated measurements. Suppose that we somehow have access to the population distribution. Let us denote the CDF of this population distribution by F_X, and the PDF by f_X. By having access to the population distribution we can synthetically generate as many samples X_n's as we want. This is certainly hypothetical, but let's assume that it is possible for now.

If we have full access to the population distribution, then we are able to draw K replicate datasets $\mathcal{X}^1, \ldots, \mathcal{X}^K$ from F_X:

$$\mathcal{X}^{(1)} = \{X_1^{(1)}, \ldots, X_N^{(1)}\} \sim F_X,$$
$$\mathcal{X}^{(2)} = \{X_1^{(2)}, \ldots, X_N^{(2)}\} \sim F_X, \qquad (9.14)$$
$$\vdots$$
$$\mathcal{X}^{(K)} = \{X_1^{(K)}, \ldots, X_N^{(K)}\} \sim F_X.$$

Each dataset $\mathcal{X}^{(K)}$ contains N data points, and by virtue of i.i.d. all the samples have the same underlying distribution F_X.

For each dataset we construct an estimator $\widehat{\Theta} = g(\cdot)$ for some function $g(\cdot)$. The estimator takes the data points of the dataset $\mathcal{X}$ and returns a value. Since we have K datasets, correspondingly we will have K estimators:

$$\widehat{\Theta}^{(1)} = g(\mathcal{X}^{(1)}) = g(X_1^{(1)}, \ldots, X_N^{(1)}),$$
$$\widehat{\Theta}^{(2)} = g(\mathcal{X}^{(2)}) = g(X_1^{(2)}, \ldots, X_N^{(2)}), \qquad (9.15)$$
$$\vdots$$
$$\widehat{\Theta}^{(K)} = g(\mathcal{X}^{(K)}) = g(X_1^{(K)}, \ldots, X_N^{(K)}).$$

Note that these estimators $g(\cdot)$ can be anything. It can be the sample average or it can be the sample median. There is no restriction.

Since we are interested in constructing the confidence interval for $\widehat{\Theta}$, we need to analyze the mean and variance of $\widehat{\Theta}$. The true mean and the estimated mean of $\widehat{\Theta}$ are

$$\mathbb{E}[\widehat{\Theta}] = \text{true mean of } \widehat{\Theta}, \qquad (9.16)$$
$$\mathbb{M}(\widehat{\Theta}) = \text{estimated mean based on } \widehat{\Theta}^{(1)}, \ldots, \widehat{\Theta}^{(K)}$$
$$\stackrel{\text{def}}{=} \frac{1}{K} \sum_{k=1}^{K} \widehat{\Theta}^{(k)} = \frac{1}{K} \sum_{k=1}^{K} g(\mathcal{X}^{(k)}), \qquad (9.17)$$

respectively. Similarly, the true variance and the estimated variance of $\widehat{\Theta}$ are

$$\text{Var}[\widehat{\Theta}] = \text{true variance of } \widehat{\Theta}, \qquad (9.18)$$
$$\mathbb{V}(\widehat{\Theta}) = \text{estimated variance based on } \widehat{\Theta}^{(1)}, \ldots, \widehat{\Theta}^{(K)}$$
$$\stackrel{\text{def}}{=} \frac{1}{K} \sum_{k=1}^{K} \left(\widehat{\Theta}^{(k)} - \mathbb{M}(\widehat{\Theta}) \right)^2$$
$$= \frac{1}{K} \sum_{k=1}^{K} \left(g(\mathcal{X}^{(k)}) - \mathbb{M}(\widehat{\Theta}) \right)^2. \qquad (9.19)$$

These two equations should be familiar: Since $\widehat{\Theta}$ is a random variable, and $\{\widehat{\Theta}^{(k)}\}$ are i.i.d. copies of $\widehat{\Theta}$, we can compute the average of $\widehat{\Theta}^{(1)}, \ldots, \widehat{\Theta}^{(K)}$ and the corresponding variance. As the number of repeated trials K approaches ∞, the estimated variance $\mathbb{V}(\widehat{\Theta})$ will converge to $\text{Var}(\widehat{\Theta})$ according to the law of large numbers.

We can summarize the procedure we have just outlined. To produce an estimate of the variance, we run the algorithm below.

Algorithm 1: Brute force method to generate an estimated variance

---

- Assume: We have access to F_X.
- Step 1: Generate datasets $\mathcal{X}^{(1)}, \ldots, \mathcal{X}^{(K)}$ from F_X.
- Step 2: Compute $\mathbb{M}(\widehat{\Theta})$ and $\mathbb{V}(\widehat{\Theta})$ based on the samples.
- Output: The estimated variance is $\mathbb{V}(\widehat{\Theta})$.

The problem, however, is that we only have *one* dataset $\mathcal{X}^{(1)}$. We do not have access to $\mathcal{X}^{(2)}, \ldots, \mathcal{X}^{(K)}$, and we do not have access to F_X. Therefore, we are not able to approximate the variance using the above brute force simulation. Bootstrapping is a computational technique to mimic the above simulation process by using the available data in $\mathcal{X}^{(1)}$.

9.2.2 Bootstrapping

The idea of bootstrapping is illustrated in **Figure 9.9**. Imagine that we have a population CDF F_X and PDF f_X. The dataset we have in hand, $\mathcal{X}$, is a collection of the random realizations of the random variable X. This dataset $\mathcal{X}$ contains N data points $\mathcal{X} = \{X_1, \ldots, X_N\}$.

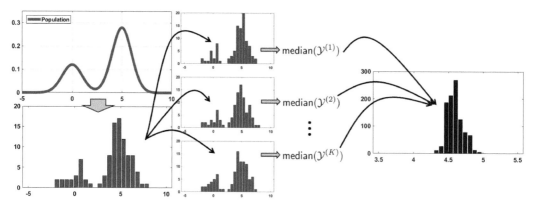

Figure 9.9: A conceptual illustration of bootstrapping. Given the observed dataset $\mathcal{X}$, we synthetically construct K bootstrapped datasets (colored in yellow) by sampling with replacement from $\mathcal{X}$. We then compute the estimators, e.g., computing the median, for every bootstrapped dataset. Finally, we construct the estimator's histogram (in blue) to compute the bootstrapped mean and variance.

In bootstrapping, we synthesize K bootstrapped datasets $\mathcal{Y}^{(1)}, \ldots, \mathcal{Y}^{(K)}$, where each bootstrapped dataset $\mathcal{Y}^{(k)}$ consists of N samples redrawn from $\mathcal{X}$. Essentially, we draw with replacement N samples from the observed dataset $\mathcal{X}$:

$$\mathcal{Y}^{(1)} = \{Y_1^{(1)}, \ldots, Y_N^{(1)}\} = N \text{ random samples from } \mathcal{X},$$

$$\vdots$$

$$\mathcal{Y}^{(K)} = \{Y_1^{(K)}, \ldots, Y_N^{(K)}\} = N \text{ random samples from } \mathcal{X}.$$

Afterward, we construct our estimator $\widehat{\Theta}$ according to our desired function $g(\cdot)$. For example, if $g(\cdot) =$ median, we have

$$\widehat{\Theta}_{\text{boot}}^{(1)} = g(\mathcal{Y}^{(1)}) = \text{median}(\mathcal{Y}^{(1)}),$$

$$\vdots$$

$$\widehat{\Theta}_{\text{boot}}^{(K)} = g(\mathcal{Y}^{(K)}) = \text{median}(\mathcal{Y}^{(K)}).$$

Then, we define the bootstrapped mean and the bootstrapped variance as

$$\mathbb{M}_{\text{boot}}(\widehat{\Theta}) = \frac{1}{K} \sum_{k=1}^{K} \widehat{\Theta}_{\text{boot}}^{(k)}, \tag{9.20}$$

$$\mathbb{V}_{\text{boot}}(\widehat{\Theta}) = \frac{1}{K} \sum_{k=1}^{K} \left(\widehat{\Theta}_{\text{boot}}^{(k)} - \mathbb{M}_{\text{boot}}(\widehat{\Theta}) \right)^2. \tag{9.21}$$

The procedure we have just outlined can be summarized as follows.

Algorithm 2: Bootstrapping to generate an estimated variance

- Assume: We do NOT have access to F_X, but we have one dataset $\mathcal{X}$.
- Step 1: Generate datasets $\mathcal{Y}^{(1)}, \ldots, \mathcal{Y}^{(K)}$ from $\mathcal{X}$, by sampling with replacement from $\mathcal{X}$.
- Step 2: Compute $\mathbb{M}_{\text{boot}}(\widehat{\Theta})$ and $\mathbb{V}_{\text{boot}}(\widehat{\Theta})$ based on the samples.
- Output: The bootstrapped variance is $\mathbb{V}_{\text{boot}}(\widehat{\Theta})$.

The only difference between this algorithm and the previous one is that we are not synthesizing data from the population but rather from the observed dataset $\mathcal{X}$.

What makes bootstrapping work? The basic principle of bootstrapping is based on three approximations:

$$\text{Var}_F(\widehat{\Theta}) \overset{(a)}{\approx} \mathbb{V}_{\text{full}}(\widehat{\Theta})$$

$$\overset{(b)}{\approx}$$

$$\text{Var}_{\widehat{F}}(\widehat{\Theta}) \overset{(c)}{\approx} \mathbb{V}_{\text{boot}}(\widehat{\Theta})$$

In this set of equations, the ultimate quantity we want to know is $\text{Var}_F(\widehat{\Theta})$, which is the variance of $\widehat{\Theta}$ under F. (By "under F" we mean that the variance was found by integrating with respect to the distribution F_X.) However, since we do not have access to F, we have to approximate $\text{Var}_F(\widehat{\Theta})$ by $\mathbb{V}_{\text{full}}(\widehat{\Theta})$. $\mathbb{V}_{\text{full}}(\widehat{\Theta})$ is the sample variance computed from the K hypothetical datasets $\mathcal{X}^{(1)}, \ldots, \mathcal{X}^{(K)}$. We call it "full" because we can generate as many hypothetical datasets as we want. It is marked as the approximation (a) above.

In the bootstrapping world, we approximate the underlying distribution F by some other distribution $\widehat{F}$. For example, if F is the CDF of a Gaussian distribution, we can choose $\widehat{F}$ to be the finite-sample staircase function approximating F. In our case, we use the observed dataset $\mathcal{X}$ to serve as a proxy $\widehat{F}$ to F. This is the second approximation, marked by (b). Normally, if you have a reasonably large $\mathcal{X}$, it is safe to assume that this finite-sample dataset $\mathcal{X}$ has a CDF $\widehat{F}$ that is close to the true CDF F.

The third approximation is to find a numerical estimate $\mathrm{Var}_{\widehat{F}}(\widehat{\Theta})$ via the simulation procedure we have just outlined. This is essentially the same line of argument for (a) but now applied to the bootstrapping world. We mark this approximation by (c). Its goal is to approximate $\mathrm{Var}_{\widehat{F}}(\widehat{\Theta})$ via $\mathbb{V}_{\mathrm{boot}}(\widehat{\Theta})$.

The three approximations have their respective influence on the accuracy of the bootstrapped variance:

How does bootstrapping work?

- It is based on three approximations:

- (a): A hypothetical approximation. The best we can do is that we have access to F. It is practically impossible to achieve, but it gives us intuition.

- (b): Approximate F by $\widehat{F}$, where $\widehat{F}$ is the empirical CDF of the observed data. This is usually the source of error. The approximation error reduces when you use more samples to approximate F.

- (c): Approximate the theoretical bootstrapped variance by a finite approximation. This approximation error is usually small because you can generate as many bootstrapped datasets as you want.

One "mysterious" property of bootstrapping is the sampling with replacement scheme used to synthesize the bootstrapped samples. The typical questions are:

- (1) **Why does sampling from the observed dataset $\mathcal{X}$ lead to meaningful bootstrapped datasets** $\mathcal{Y}^{(1)}, \ldots, \mathcal{Y}^{(K)}$? To answer this question we consider the following toy example. Suppose we have a dataset $\mathcal{X}$ containing $N = 20$ samples, as shown below.

  X = [0 0 0 0 0 0 1 1 1 1 2 2 2 2 2 2 2 2 2 2]

  This dataset is generated from a random variable X with a PDF $\widehat{f}$ having three states: 0 (30%), 1 (20%), 2 (50%). As we draw samples from $\mathcal{X}$, the percentage of the states will determine the likelihood of one state being drawn. For example, if we randomly pick a sample Y_n from $\mathcal{X}$, we have a 30% chance of having Y_n to be 0, 20% chance of having it to be 1, and 50% chance of having it to be 2. Therefore, the PDF of Y_n (the randomly drawn sample from $\mathcal{X}$) will be 0 (30%), 1 (20%), 2 (50%), the same as the original PDF. If you think about this problem more deeply, by "sampling with replacement" we essentially assign each X_n with an equal probability of $1/N$. If one of the states is more popular, the individual probabilities will add to form a higher probability mass.

- (2) **Why can't we do sampling without replacement, aka permutation?** We need to understand that sampling without replacement is the same as permuting the data in $\mathcal{X}$. By permuting the data in $\mathcal{X}$, the simple probability assignments such as $\mathbb{P}[X = 0] = \frac{6}{20}$, $\mathbb{P}[X = 1] = \frac{4}{20}$ and $\mathbb{P}[X = 2] = \frac{10}{20}$ will be destroyed. Moreover, permuting the data does not change the mean and variance of the data because we are only shuffling the order. As far as constructing the confidence interval is concerned, shuffling the order is not useful.

On computers it is easy to generate the bootstrapped dataset, along with their mean and variance. In MATLAB the key step is to call a `for` loop. Inside the `for` loop, we draw N random indices `randi` from 1 to N and pick the samples. The estimator `Thetahat` is then constructed by calling your target estimator function $g(\cdot)$. In this example the estimator is the median. After the `for` loop, we compute the mean and variance of $\widehat{\Theta}$. These are the bootstrapped mean and variance, respectively.

```
% MATLAB code to estimate a bootstrapped variance
X = [72, 69, 75, 58, 67, 70, 60, 71, 59, 65];
N = size(X,2);
K = 1000;
Thetahat = zeros(1,K);
for i=1:K                        % repeat K times
    idx = randi(N,[1, N]);       % sampling w/ replacement
    Y = X(idx);
    Thetahat(i) = median(Y);     % estimator
end
M = mean(Thetahat)               % bootstrapped mean
V = var(Thetahat)                % bootstrapped variance
```

The Python commands are similar. We call `np.random.randint` to generate random integers and we pick samples according to `Y = X[idx]`. After generating the bootstrapped dataset, we compute the bootstrap estimators `Thetahat`.

```
# Python code to estimate a bootstrapped variance
import numpy as np
X = np.array([72, 69, 75, 58, 67, 70, 60, 71, 59, 65])
N = X.size
K = 1000
Thetahat = np.zeros(K)
for i in range(K):
   idx = np.random.randint(N, size=N)
   Y = X[idx]
   Thetahat[i] = np.median(Y)
M = np.mean(Thetahat)
V = np.var(Thetahat)
```

After we have constructed the bootstrapped variance, we can define the bootstrapped standard error as

$$\widehat{se}_{\text{boot}} = \sqrt{\mathbb{V}_{\text{boot}}(\widehat{\Theta})}. \tag{9.22}$$

Accordingly we define the bootstrapped confidence interval as

$$\mathcal{I} = \left[\widehat{\Theta} - z_\alpha \widehat{se}_{\text{boot}}, \ \widehat{\Theta} + z_\alpha \widehat{se}_{\text{boot}}\right], \tag{9.23}$$

where z_α is the critical value of the Gaussian.

The validity of the confidence intervals constructed by bootstrapping is subject to the validity of z_α. If $\widehat{\Theta}$ is roughly a Gaussian, the bootstrapped confidence interval will be reasonably good. If $\widehat{\Theta}$ is not Gaussian, there are advanced methods to replace z_α with better estimates. This topic is beyond the scope of this book; we refer interested readers to Larry Wasserman, *All of Statistics*, Springer 2003, Chapter 8.

9.3 Hypothesis Testing

Imagine that you are a vaccine company developing COVID-19 vaccines. You gave the vaccine to 934 patients, and 928 patients have developed antigens. How confident can you be that your vaccine is effective? Questions like this are becoming more common nowadays in situations in which we need to make statistically informed choices between YES and NO. The subject of this section is **hypothesis testing** — a principled statistical procedure used to evaluate statements that should be accepted or rejected.

9.3.1 What is a hypothesis?

A hypothesis is a statement that requires testing by observation to determine whether it is true or false. A few examples:

- The coin is unbiased.
- Students entering the graduate program have GPA ≥ 3.
- More people like orange juice than lemonade.
- Algorithm A performs better than Algorithm B.

As you can see from these examples, a hypothesis is something we can test based on the data. Therefore, being "correct" or "wrong" depends on the statistics we have and the cutoff threshold. Accepting or rejecting a hypothesis does not mean that the statement is correct or wrong, since the truth is unknown. If we accept a hypothesis, we have made a *better* decision solely based on the statistical evidence. It is possible that tomorrow when you have collected more data we may reject a previously accepted hypothesis.

The procedure for testing whether a hypothesis should be accepted or rejected is known as **hypothesis testing**. In hypothesis testing, we often have two opposite hypotheses:

- H_0: Null hypothesis. It is the "status quo", or the current status.
- H_1: Alternative hypothesis. It is the alternative to the null hypothesis.

To better understand hypothesis testing, consider a courthouse. By default, any person being prosecuted is assumed to be innocent. The police need to show sufficient evidence in order to prove the person guilty. The null hypothesis is the *default* assumption. Hypothesis testing asks whether we have strong enough evidence to reject the null hypothesis. If our evidence is not strong enough, we must assume that the null hypothesis is possibly true.

> **Example 9.6.** Suggest a null hypothesis and an alternative hypothesis regarding whether a coin is unbiased.
>
> **Solution:** Let θ be the probability of getting a head.

- H_0: $\theta = 0.5$, and H_1: $\theta > 0.5$. This is a one-sided alternative.
- H_0: $\theta = 0.5$, and H_1: $\theta < 0.5$. This is another one-sided alternative.
- H_0: $\theta = 0.5$, and H_1: $\theta \neq 0.5$. This is a two-sided alternative.

Practice Exercise 9.3. Suggest a null and an alternative hypothesis regarding whether more than 62% of people in the United States use Microsoft Windows.

Solution: Let θ be the proportion of people using Microsoft Windows in United States.

- H_0: $\theta \geq 0.62$, and H_1: $\theta < 0.62$. This is a one-sided alternative.

Practice Exercise 9.4. Suggest a null and an alternative hypothesis regarding whether self-checkout at Walmart is faster than using a cashier.

Solution: Let θ be the proportion of people that check out faster with self-checkout..

- H_0: $\theta \geq 0.5$, and H_1: $\theta < 0.5$. This is a one-sided alternative.

9.3.2 Critical-value test

In hypothesis testing, there are two major approaches: the **critical-value test**, and the p-**value test**. The two tests are more or less equivalent. If you reject the null hypothesis using the critical-value test, you will reject the hypothesis using the p-value. In this subsection, we will discuss the critical-value test. Let us consider a toy problem:

Suppose that we have a 4-sided die and our goal is to test whether the die is unbiased. To do so, we define the null and the alternative hypotheses as

- H_0: $\theta = 0.25$, which is our default belief.
- H_1: $\theta > 0.25$, which is a one-sided alternative.

There is no particular reason for considering the one-sided alternative other than the fact that the calculation is slightly easier. You are welcome to consider the two-sided alternative.

We must obtain data prior to conducting any hypothesis testing. Let's assume that we have thrown the die $N = 1000$ times. We find that "3" appears 290 times (we could just as well have chosen 1, 2, or 4). We let $X_1, \ldots, X_{1000}$ be the $N = 1000$ binary random variables representing whether we have obtained a "3" or not. If the true probability is $\theta = 0.25$, then we will have $\mathbb{P}[X_n = 3] = \theta = 0.25$ and $\mathbb{P}[X_n \neq 3] = 1 - \theta = 0.75$. We know that we cannot access the true probability, so we can only construct an estimator of the probability:

$$\widehat{\Theta} = \frac{1}{N} \sum_{n=1}^{N} X_n.$$

In this experiment, we can show that $\widehat{\Theta} = 290/1000 = 0.29$.

To make our problem slightly easier, we *pretend* that we know the variance $\mathrm{Var}[X_n]$. In practice, we certainly do not know $\mathrm{Var}[X_n]$, and so we need to estimate the variance. If we knew the variance, it should be $\text{Var}[X_n] = \theta(1-\theta) = 0.25(1-0.25) = 0.1875$, because X_n is a Bernoulli random variable with a mean θ.

The question asked by hypothesis testing is: How far is "$\widehat{\Theta} = 0.29$" from "$\theta = 0.25$"? If the statistic generated by our data, $\widehat{\Theta} = 0.29$, is "far" from the hypothesized $\theta = 0.25$, then we need to reject H_0 because H_0 says that $\theta = 0.25$. However, if there is no strong evidence that $\theta > 0.25$, we will need to assume that H_0 may possibly be true. So the key question is what is meant by "far".

For many problems like this one, it is possible to analyze the PDF of $\widehat{\Theta}$. Since $\widehat{\Theta}$ is the sample average of a sequence of Bernoulli random variables, it follows that $\widehat{\Theta}$ is a binomial (with a scaling constant $1/N$). If N is large enough, e.g., $N \geq 30$, the Central Limit Theorem tells us that $\widehat{\Theta}$ is also very close to a Gaussian. Therefore, we can more or less claim that

$$\widehat{\Theta} \sim \text{Gaussian}\left(\theta, \frac{\sigma^2}{N}\right).$$

With a simple translation and scaling, we can normalize $\widehat{\Theta}$ to obtain $\widehat{Z}$:

$$\widehat{Z} = \frac{\widehat{\Theta} - \theta}{\sigma/\sqrt{N}} \sim \text{Gaussian}\,(0,1).$$

Figure 9.10 illustrates the range of values for this problem. There are two axes: the $\widehat{\Theta}$-axis (which is the estimator) and the $\widehat{Z}$-axis (which is the normalized variable). The values corresponding to each axis are shown in the figure. For example, $\widehat{\Theta} = 0.29$ is equivalent to $\widehat{Z} = 2.92$, and $\widehat{\Theta} = 0.25$ is equivalent to $\widehat{Z} = 0$, etc. Therefore, when we ask how far "$\widehat{\Theta} = 0.29$" is from "$\theta = 0.25$", we can map this question from the $\widehat{\Theta}$-axis to the $\widehat{Z}$-axis, and ask the relative position of $\widehat{Z}$ from the origin.

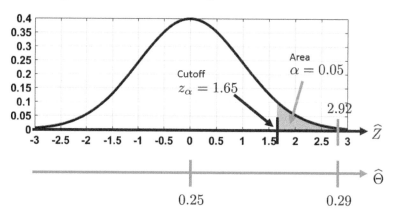

Figure 9.10: The mapping between $\widehat{\Theta}$ and $\widehat{Z}$. To decide whether we want to reject or keep H_0, the critical-value approach compares $\widehat{Z}$ relative to the critical value z_α.

On a computer, obtaining these values is quite straightforward. Using MATLAB, finding $\widehat{Z}$ can be done by calling the following commands. The Python code is analogous.

```
% MATLAB command to estimate the Z_hat value.
Theta_hat = 0.29;                    % Your estimate
```

```
theta     = 0.25;                       % Your hypothesis
sigma     = sqrt(theta*(1-theta));      % Known standard deviation
N         = 1000;                       % Number of samples
Z_hat     = (Theta_hat - theta)/(sigma/sqrt(N));
```

```
# Python command to estimate the Z_hat value
import numpy as np
Theta_hat = 0.29                    # Your estimate
theta     = 0.25                    # Your hypothesis
N         = 1000                    # Number of samples
sigma     = np.sqrt(theta*(1-theta)) # Known standard deviation
Z_hat = (Theta_hat - theta)/(sigma / np.sqrt(N))
print(Z_hat)
```

One essential element of hypothesis testing is the cutoff threshold, which is defined through the **critical level** α. It is the area under the curve of the PDF of $\widehat{Z}$. Typically, α is chosen to be a small value, such as $\alpha = 0.05$ (corresponding to a 5% margin). The corresponding cutoff is known as the **critical value**. It is defined as

$$z_\alpha = \text{cutoff location where area under the curve is } \alpha.$$

If $\widehat{Z}$ is Gaussian(0,1) and if we are looking at the right-hand tail, it follows that

$$z_\alpha = \Phi^{-1}\left(1 - \alpha\right). \tag{9.24}$$

In our example, we find that $z_{0.05} = 1.65$, which is marked in **Figure 9.10**.

On computers, determining the critical value z_α is straightforward. In MATLAB the command is `icdf`, and in Python the command is `stats.norm.ppf`.

```
% MATLAB code to compute the critical value
alpha = 0.05;
z_alpha = icdf('norm', 1-alpha, 0, 1);
```

```
# Python code to compute the critical value
import scipy.stats as stats
alpha = 0.05
z_alpha = stats.norm.ppf(1-alpha, 0, 1)
```

Do we have enough evidence to reject H_0 in this example? Of course! The estimated value $\widehat{\Theta} = 0.29$ is equivalent to $\widehat{Z} = 2.92$, which is much too far from the cutoff $z_\alpha = 1.65$. In other words, we conclude that at a 5% critical level we have strong evidence to believe that the die is biased. Therefore, we need to reject H_0.

This conclusion makes a lot of sense if you think about it carefully. The estimator $\widehat{\Theta} = 0.29$ is obtained from $N = 1000$ independent experiments. If we were only conducting $N = 20$ experiments, it might be consistent with the null hypothesis to have $\widehat{\Theta} = 0.29$. However, if we have $N = 1000$ experiments, having $\widehat{\Theta} = 0.29$ does not seem likely when there is no systematic bias. If there is no systematic bias, the estimator $\widehat{\Theta}$ should slightly jitter around $\widehat{\Theta} = 0.25$, but it is quite unlikely to vary wildly to $\widehat{\Theta} = 0.29$. Thus, based on the available statistics, we decide to reject the null hypothesis.

The decision based on comparing the critical value is known as the **critical-value test**. The idea (for testing a **right-hand** tail of a Gaussian random variable) is summarized in three steps:

How to conduct a critical-value test

- Set a critical value z_α. Compute $\widehat{Z} = (\widehat{\Theta} - \theta)/(\sigma/\sqrt{N})$.
- If $\widehat{Z} \geq z_\alpha$, then reject H_0.
- If $\widehat{Z} < z_\alpha$, then keep H_0.

If you are testing a **left-hand tail**, you can switch the order of the inequalities.

The critical-value test belongs to a larger family of testing procedures based on decision theory. To give you a preview of the general theory of hypothesis testing, we define a **decision rule**, a function that maps a realization of the estimator to a binary decision space. In our problem the estimator is $\widehat{Z}$ (or equivalently $\widehat{\Theta}$). We denote its realization by $\widehat{z}$. The binary decision space is $\{H_0, H_1\}$, corresponding to whether we want to claim H_0 or H_1. Claiming H_0 is equivalent to keeping H_0, and claiming H_1 is equivalent to rejecting H_0. For the critical-value test, the decision rule $\delta(\cdot) : \mathbb{R} \to \{0, 1\}$ is given by the equation (for testing a **right-hand** tail):

$$\delta(\widehat{z}) = \begin{cases} 1, & \text{if } \widehat{z} \geq z_\alpha, & \text{(claim } H_1), \\ 0, & \text{if } \widehat{z} < z_\alpha, & \text{(claim } H_0). \end{cases} \tag{9.25}$$

Example 9.7. It was found that only 35% of the children in a kindergarten eat broccoli. The teachers conducted a campaign to get more kids to eat broccoli, after which it was found that 390 kids out of 1009 kids reported that they had eaten broccoli. Has the campaign successfully increased the number of kids eating broccoli? Assume that the standard deviation is known.

Solution. We setup the null and the alternative hypothesis.

$$H_0: \quad \theta = 0.35, \qquad H_1: \quad \theta > 0.35.$$

We construct an estimator $\widehat{\Theta} = (1/N)\sum_{n=1}^{N} X_n$, where X_n is Bernoulli with probability θ. Based on θ, $\sigma^2 = \theta(1 - \theta) = 0.227$. (Again, in practice we do not know the true variance, but in this problem we pretend that we know it.)

By the Central Limit Theorem, $\widehat{\Theta}$ is roughly a Gaussian. We compute the test statistics $\widehat{\Theta} = \frac{390}{1009} = 0.387$. Standardization gives $\widehat{Z} = \frac{\widehat{\Theta} - \theta}{\sigma/\sqrt{N}} = 2.432$. At a 5% critical level, we have that $z_\alpha = 1.65$. So $\widehat{Z} = 2.432 > 1.65 = z_\alpha$, and hence we need to reject the null hypothesis. Even if we choose a 1% critical level so that $z_\alpha = 2.32$, our estimator $\widehat{Z} = 2.432 > 2.32 = z_\alpha$ will still reject the null hypothesis.

A graphical illustration of this problem is shown in **Figure 9.11**. It can be seen that $\widehat{\Theta} = 0.387$ is actually quite far away from the cutoff 1.65. Thus, we need to reject the null hypothesis.

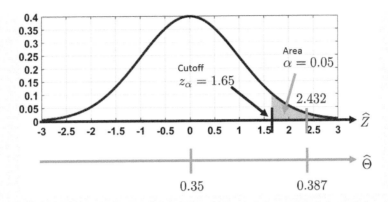

Figure 9.11: Example of a critical-value test. In this example, the test statistic $\widehat{\Theta} = 0.387$ is equivalent to $\widehat{Z} = 2.432$, which is significantly larger than the cutoff $z_\alpha = 1.65$. Therefore, we have strong evidence to reject the null hypothesis, because the probability of obtaining $\widehat{\Theta} = 0.387$ is very low if H_0 is true.

9.3.3 p-value test

An alternative to the critical-value test is the p-value test. Instead of looking at the cutoff value z_α, we inspect the probability of obtaining our observation if H_0 is true. To understand how the p-value test works, we consider another toy problem.

Suppose that we have two hypotheses about flipping a coin:

- H_0: $\theta = 0.9$, which is our default belief.
- H_1: $\theta < 0.9$, which is a one-sided alternative.

It was found that with $N = 150$ coin flips, the coin landed on heads 128 times. Thus the estimator is $\widehat{\Theta} = \frac{128}{150} = 0.853$. Then, by following our previous procedures, we have that

$$\widehat{Z} = \frac{\widehat{\Theta} - \theta}{\sigma/\sqrt{N}} = \frac{0.853 - 0.9}{\sqrt{\frac{0.9(1-0.9)}{150}}} = -1.92.$$

At this point we can follow the previous subsection by computing the critical value z_α and make the decision. However, let's take a different route. We want to know what is the **probability** under the curve if we integrate the PDF of $\widehat{Z}$ from $-\infty$ to -1.92. This is easy. Since $\widehat{Z}$ is Gaussian$(0, 1)$, it follows from the CDF of a Gaussian that

$$\underbrace{\mathbb{P}[\widehat{Z} \leq -1.92]}_{p\text{-value}} = 0.0274.$$

Referring to **Figure 9.12**, the value 0.0274 is the pink area under the curve, which is the PDF of $\widehat{Z}$. Since the area under the curve is less than the critical level α (say 5%), we reject the null hypothesis.

On computers, computing the p-value is done using the CDF commands.

```
% MATLAB code to compute the p-value
p = cdf('norm', -1.92, 0, 1);
```

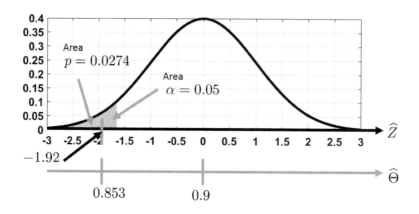

Figure 9.12: The p-value test asks us to look at the probability of $\widehat{Z} \leq \widehat{z}$. If this probability (the p-value) is less than the critical level α, we have significant evidence to reject the null hypothesis.

```
# Python code to compute the p-value
import scipy.stats as stats
p = stats.norm.cdf(-1.92,0,1)
```

In this example, the probability $\mathbb{P}[\widehat{Z} \leq -1.92]$ is known as the p-**value**. It is the probability of $\widehat{Z} \leq z$, under the distribution mandated by the null hypothesis, where z is the (normalized) estimated value based on data. Using our example, z is -1.92. By "distribution mandated by the null hypothesis" we mean that the PDF of $\widehat{Z}$ is the PDF that the null hypothesis wants. In the above example the PDF is Gaussian$(0, 1)$, corresponding to Gaussian$(\theta, \sigma/\sqrt{N})$ for $\widehat{\Theta}$.

More formally, the p-value for a left-hand tail test is defined as

$$p\text{-value}(\widehat{z}) = \mathbb{P}[\widehat{Z} \leq \widehat{z}],$$

where $\widehat{z}$ is the random realization of $\widehat{Z}$ estimated from the data. The **decision rule** based on the p-value is (for the **left-hand** tail):

$$\delta(\widehat{z}) = \begin{cases} 1, & \mathbb{P}[\widehat{Z} \leq \widehat{z}] < \alpha \quad (\text{claim } H_1), \\ 0, & \mathbb{P}[\widehat{Z} \leq \widehat{z}] \geq \alpha \quad (\text{claim } H_0). \end{cases} \tag{9.26}$$

If the alternative hypothesis is right-handed, then the probability becomes $\mathbb{P}[\widehat{Z} \geq \widehat{z}]$ instead.

Relationship between critical-value and p-value tests. There is a one-to-one correspondence between the p-value and the critical value. In the p-value test, if $\widehat{Z}$ is Gaussian, it follows that

$$p\text{-value} = \mathbb{P}[\widehat{Z} \leq \widehat{z}] = \Phi(\widehat{z}),$$

where Φ is CDF of the standard Gaussian. Taking the inverse, the corresponding $\widehat{z}$ is

$$\widehat{z} = \Phi^{-1}(p\text{-value}).$$

In practice, we do not need to take any inverse of the p-value to obtain $\widehat{z}$ because it is directly available from the data.

To test the p-value, we compare it with the critical level α by checking

$$p\text{-value} < \alpha.$$

Taking the inverse of both sides, it follows that the decision rule is equivalent to

$$\underbrace{\Phi^{-1}(p\text{-value})}_{\widehat{z}} < \underbrace{\Phi^{-1}(\alpha)}_{z_\alpha},$$

where the quantity on the right-hand side is the critical value z_α. Therefore, if the test statistic fails in the p-value test it will also fail in the critical-value test, and vice versa.

What is the difference between the critical-value test and p-value test?

- Critical-value test: Compare w.r.t. critical value, which is the cutoff on the Z-axis.
- p-value test: Compare w.r.t. α, which is the probability.
- Both will give you the same statistical conclusion. So it does not matter which one you use.

Example 9.8. We flip a coin for $N = 150$ times and find that 128 are heads. Consider two hypotheses

- H_0: $\theta = 0.9$, which is our default belief.
- H_1: $\theta \neq 0.9$, which is a two-sided alternative.

For a critical level of $\alpha = 0.05$, shall we keep or reject H_0?

Solution. We know that $\widehat{\Theta} = 128/150 = 0.853$. The normalized statistic is

$$\widehat{Z} = \frac{\widehat{\Theta} - \theta}{\sigma/\sqrt{N}} = \frac{0.853 - 0.9}{\sqrt{\frac{0.9(1-0.9)}{150}}} = -1.92.$$

To compute the p-value, we observe that the two-sided test means that we consider the two tails. Thus, we have

$$p\text{-value} = \mathbb{P}[|\widehat{Z}| > 1.92]$$
$$= 2 \times \mathbb{P}[\widehat{Z} > 1.92]$$
$$= 2 \times 0.0274 = 0.055.$$

For a critical level of $\alpha = 0.05$, the p-value is larger. This means that the probability of obtaining $|Z| > 1.92$ is not extreme enough. Therefore, we do not have sufficient evidence to reject the null hypothesis.

If we take the critical-value test, we will reach the same conclusion. The critical value for $\alpha = 0.05$ is determined by taking the inverse CDF at $1 - 0.025$, giving

$$z_\alpha = \Phi^{-1}\left(1 - \frac{\alpha}{2}\right) = 1.96.$$

Since $\widehat{Z} = 1.92$ has not passed this threshold, we conclude that there is not enough evidence to reject the null hypothesis.

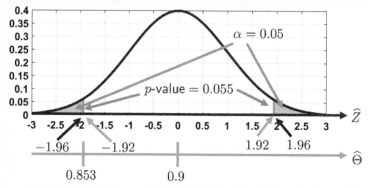

Figure 9.13: Example of a two-sided test using the p-value and the z_α-value.

9.3.4 Z-test and T-test

The critical-value test and the p-value tests are generic tools for hypothesis testing. In this subsection we introduce the Z-test and the T-test. It is important to understand that the Z-test and the T-test refer to the distributional assumptions we make about the variance. They define the **distribution** we use to conduct the test but not the *tools*. In fact, both the Z-test and the T-test can be implemented using the critical-value test or the p-value test. **Figure 9.14** illustrates the hierarchy of the tests.

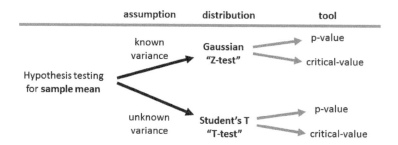

Figure 9.14: When conducting a hypothesis testing of the sample average, we may or may not know the variance. If we know the variance, we use the Gaussian distribution to conduct either a p-value test or a critical-value test. If we do not know the variance, we use Student's t-distribution.

The difference between the Gaussian distribution and the T distribution is mainly attributable to the knowledge about the population variance. If the variance is known, the distribution of the estimator (which in our case is the sample average) is Gaussian. If the variance is estimated from the sample, the distribution of the estimator will follow a Student's t-distribution.

To introduce the Z-test and the T-test we consider the following two examples. The first example is a Z-test.

Example 9.9 (Z-test). Suppose we have a Gaussian random variable with unknown mean θ and a known variance $\sigma = 11.6$. We draw $N = 25$ samples and construct an estimator $\widehat{\Theta} = 80.94$. We propose two hypotheses:

- H_0: $\theta = 85$, which is our default belief.
- H_1: $\theta < 85$, which is a one-sided alternative.

For a critical level of $\alpha = 0.05$, shall we keep or reject the null hypothesis?

Solution. The test statistic is

$$\widehat{Z} = \frac{\widehat{\Theta} - \theta}{\sigma/\sqrt{N}} = -1.75.$$

Since the individual samples are assumed to follow a Gaussian, the sample average $\widehat{\Theta}$ is also a Gaussian. Hence, $\widehat{Z}$ is distributed according to Gaussian$(0, 1)$.

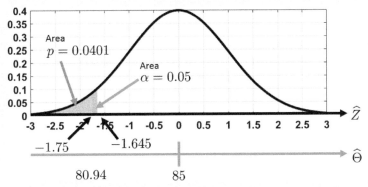

Figure 9.15: A one-sided Z-test using the p-value and the z_α-value.

For a critical level of 0.05, a one-sided critical value is

$$z_\alpha = \Phi^{-1}(1 - \alpha) = -1.645.$$

Since $\widehat{Z} = -1.75$, which is more extreme than the critical value, we conclude that we need to reject H_0.

If we use the p-value test, we have that the p-value is

$$\mathbb{P}[\widehat{Z} \leq -1.75] = \Phi(-1.75) = 0.0401.$$

Since the p-value is smaller than the critical level $\alpha = 0.05$, it implies that $\widehat{Z} = -1.75$ is more extreme. Hence, we reject H_0.

The following example is a T-test. In a T-test we do not know the population variance but only know the sample variance $\widehat{S}$. Thus the test statistic we use is a T random variable.

Example 9.10 (T-test). Suppose we have a Gaussian random variable with unknown mean θ and an unknown variance σ. We draw $N = 100$ samples and construct an estimator $\widehat{\Theta} = 130.1$, with a sample variance $\widehat{S} = 21.21$. We propose two hypotheses:

- H_0: $\theta = 120$, which is our default belief.
- H_1: $\theta \neq 120$, which is a two-sided alternative.

For a critical level of $\alpha = 0.05$, shall we keep or reject the null hypothesis?

Solution. The test statistic is

$$\widehat{T} = \frac{\widehat{\Theta} - \theta}{\widehat{S}/\sqrt{N}} = 4.762.$$

Note that while the sample average $\widehat{\Theta}$ is a Gaussian, the test statistic $\widehat{T}$ is distributed according to a T distribution with $N - 1$ degrees of freedom. For a critical level of 0.05, a two-sided critical value is

$$t_\alpha = \Psi_{99}^{-1}\left(1 - \frac{\alpha}{2}\right) = 1.984.$$

Since $\widehat{T} = 4.762$, which is more extreme than the critical value, we conclude that we need to reject H_0.

If we use the p-value test, we have that the p-value is

$$\mathbb{P}[|\widehat{T}| \geq 4.762] = 2 \times \mathbb{P}[\widehat{T} \geq 4.762]$$
$$= 3.28 \times 10^{-6}.$$

Since the p-value is (much) smaller than the critical level $\alpha = 0.05$, it implies that $|\widehat{T}| \geq 4.762$ is quite extreme. Hence, we reject H_0.

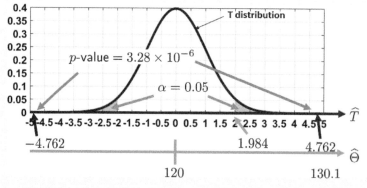

Figure 9.16: A two-sided T-test using the p-value and the z_α-value.

For this example, the MATLAB and Python commands to compute t_α and the p-value are

```
% MATLAB code to compute critical-value and p-value
t_alpha = icdf('t', 1-0.025, 99);
p = 1-cdf('t', 4.762, 99);
```

```
# Python code to compute critical value and p-value
import scipy.stats as stats
t_alpha = stats.t.ppf(1-0.025,99)
p = 1-stats.t.cdf(4.762,99)
```

What are the Z-test and the T-test?
- Both are hypothesis testings for the sample averages.
- Z-test: Assume known variance. Hence, use the Gaussian distribution.
- T-test: Assume unknown variance. Hence, use the Student's t-distribution.

Remark. We are exclusively analyzing the sample average in this section. There are other types of estimators we can analyze. For example, we can discuss the difference between the two means, the ratio of two random variables, etc. If you need tools for these more advanced problems, please refer to the reference section at the end of this chapter.

9.4 Neyman-Pearson Test

The hypothesis testing procedures we discussed in the previous section are elementary in the sense that we have not discussed much theory. This section aims to fill the gap so that you can understand hypothesis testing from a broader perspective. This generalization will also help to bridge statistics to other disciplines such as classification in machine learning and detection in signal processing. We call this theoretical analysis the **Neyman-Pearson framework**.

9.4.1 Null and alternative distributions

When we discussed hypothesis testing in the previous section, we focused exclusively on the null hypothesis H_0. Regardless of whether we are studying the Z-test or the T-test, using the critical value or the p-value, all the distributions are associated with the distribution under H_0.

What do we mean by "distribution under H_0"? Using $\widehat{\Theta}$ as an example, the PDF of $\widehat{\Theta}$ is assumed to be Gaussian$(\theta, \sigma^2/N)$. This Gaussian, centered at θ, is the distribution assumed under H_0. As we decide whether to keep or reject H_0, we look at the critical value and the p-value of the test statistic under Gaussian$(\theta, \sigma^2/N)$.

Importantly, the analysis of hypothesis testing is not just about H_0 — it is also about the alternative hypothesis H_1, which uses a different PDF. For example, H_1 could use Gaussian$(\theta', \sigma^2/N)$ for $\theta' > \theta$. Therefore, for the same testing statistic $\widehat{\Theta}$, we can check how close it is to H_1.

To capture both distributions, we define

$$f_0(y) = f_Y(y \mid H_0),$$
$$f_1(y) = f_Y(y \mid H_1).$$

The first PDF defines the distribution when the true model is H_0. The second PDF is the distribution when the true model is H_1.

Example 9.11. Consider an estimator $Y \sim$ Gaussian$(\theta, \sigma^2/N)$. Define two hypotheses $H_0 : \theta = 120$ and $H_1 : \theta > 120$. The two PDFs are then

$$f_0(y) = f_Y(y|H_0) = \text{Gaussian}(120, \sigma^2/N),$$
$$f_1(y) = f_Y(y|H_1) = \text{Gaussian}(\theta', \sigma^2/N), \quad \theta' > 120.$$

A graph of the two distributions is shown in **Figure 9.17**. In this figure we plot the PDF under the null hypothesis and the PDF under an alternative hypothesis. The decision is based on the null, where we marked the critical value.

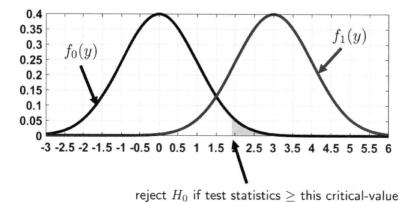

reject H_0 if test statistics $\geq$ this critical-value

Figure 9.17: The PDF of the estimator under hypotheses H_0 and H_1. The yellow region defines the rejection zone R_α. If the estimator has a realization $Y = y$ that falls into the rejection zone R_α, we need to reject H_0.

Students are frequently confused about the exact equation of the PDF under H_1. If the alternative hypothesis is defined as $\theta > 120$, shall we define the PDF as a Gaussian centered at 130 or 151.4? They are both valid alternative hypotheses. The answer is that we are going to express all equations based on θ'. For example, if we want to analyze the prediction error (this term will be explained later), the prediction error will be a function of θ'. If θ' is close to θ, we will expect a larger prediction error. However, if θ' is far away from θ, the prediction error may be small.

Whenever we discuss hypothesis testing, a decision rule is always implied. A decision rule is a mapping $\delta(\cdot)$ from sample space $\mathcal{Y}$ of the test statistic Y (or $\widehat{\Theta}$ if you prefer) to the binary space of $\{0, 1\}$:

$$\delta(y) = \begin{cases} 1, & \text{if } y \in R_\alpha, \quad (\text{we will reject } H_0), \\ 0, & \text{if } y \notin R_\alpha, \quad (\text{we will keep } H_0). \end{cases} \tag{9.27}$$

Here R_α is the **rejection zone**. For example, in a one-sided testing at a critical level α, the rejection zone is $R_\alpha = \{y \geq \Phi^{-1}(1 - \alpha)\}$. Therefore, as long as $y \geq \Phi^{-1}(1 - \alpha)$, we will reject the null hypothesis. Otherwise, we will keep the null hypothesis. A rejection zone can be one-sided, two-sided, or even more complicated.

Example 9.12. Consider $H_0 : \theta = 0.35$ and $H_1 : \theta > 0.35$. It was found that the sample average over 1009 samples is $\widehat{\Theta} = 0.387$, with $\sigma^2 = 0.227$. The normalized test statistic is $\widehat{Z} = \sqrt{N}(\widehat{\Theta} - \theta)/\sigma = 2.432$. At a 5% critical level, define the decision rule based on the critical-value approach.

Solution. If $\alpha = 0.05$, it follows that $z_\alpha = \Phi^{-1}(1 - 0.05) = 1.65$. Therefore, the decision rule is

$$\delta(\widehat{z}) = \begin{cases} 1, & \text{if } \widehat{z} \geq 1.65, \quad (\text{we will reject } H_0), \\ 0, & \text{if } \widehat{z} < 1.65, \quad (\text{we will keep } H_0), \end{cases}$$

where $\widehat{z}$ is the realization of $\widehat{Z}$. In this particular problem, we have $\widehat{z} = 2.432$. Thus, according to the decision rule, we need to reject H_0.

A decision rule is something *you* create. You do not need to follow the critical-value or the p-value procedure — you can create your own decision rule. For example, you can say "reject H_0 when $|y| > 0.000001$". There is nothing wrong with this decision rule except that you will almost always reject the null hypothesis (so it is a bad decision rule). See **Figure 9.18** for a graph of a similar example. If you follow the critical-value or the p-value procedures, it turns out that the resulting decision rule is equivalent to some form of *optimal* decision rule. This concept is the Neyman-Pearson framework, which we will explain shortly.

9.4.2 Type 1 and type 2 errors

Since hypothesis testing is about applying a decision rule to the test statistics, and since no decision rule is perfect, it is natural to ask about the error expected from a particular decision rule. In this subsection we define the decision error. However, the terminology varies from discipline to discipline. We will explain the decision error first through the statistics perspective and then through the signal processing perspective.

Two tables of the cases that can be generated by a binary decision-making process are shown in **Figure 9.19**. The columns of the tables are the true statements, i.e., whether the test statistic has a population distribution under H_0 or H_1. The rows of the tables are the statements predicted by the decision rule, i.e., whether we should declare the statistics are from H_0 or H_1. Each combination of the truth and prediction has a label:

- True positive: The truth is H_1, and you declare H_1.
- True negative: The truth is H_0, and you declare H_0.
- False positive: The truth is H_0, and you declare H_1.

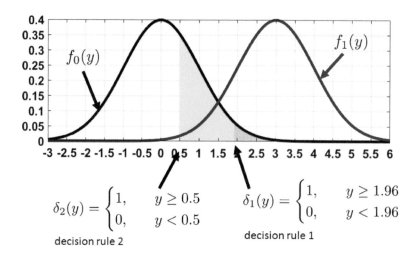

$$\delta_2(y) = \begin{cases} 1, & y \geq 0.5 \\ 0, & y < 0.5 \end{cases} \qquad \delta_1(y) = \begin{cases} 1, & y \geq 1.96 \\ 0, & y < 1.96 \end{cases}$$

decision rule 2   decision rule 1

Figure 9.18: Two possible decision rules $\delta_1(y)$ and $\delta_2(y)$. In this example, $\delta_1(y)$ is designed according to the critical-value approach at $\alpha = 0.025$, whereas $\delta_2(y)$ is arbitrarily designed. Both are valid decision rules, although δ_2 should not be used because it tends to reject the null hypothesis more often than desired.

- False negative: The truth is H_1, and you declare H_0.

Different communities have different ways of labeling these quantities. In the statistics community the false negative rate (i.e., the number of false negative cases divided by the total number of cases) is called the **type 2 error**, and the false positive rate is called the **type 1 error**. The true positive rate is called the **power** of the decision rule.

In the engineering community (e.g., radar engineering and signal processing) the objective is to detect whether a target (e.g., a missile or an enemy aircraft) is present. In this context, the false positive rate is known as the probability of **false alarm**, since personnel will be alerted when no target is present. The false negative rate is known as the probability of **miss** because you miss a target. If the truth is H_1 and the prediction is also H_1, we call this the probability of **detection**.

	Truth	
	H_0	H_1
Prediction H_0	True Negative	False Negative
H_1	False Positive	True Positive

	Truth	
	H_0	H_1
Prediction H_0		Type 2 Miss
H_1	Type 1 False Alarm	Power Detection

Figure 9.19: Terminologies used in labeling the prediction error. The terms "Type 1 error" and "Type 2 error" are commonly used by the statistics community, whereas the terms "false alarm", "miss" and "detection" are more often used in the engineering community.

The diagram in **Figure 9.20** will help to clarify these definitions. Given two hypotheses H_0 and H_1, there exists the corresponding distributions $f_0(y)$ and $f_1(y)$, which are the PDFs of the test statistics Y (or $\widehat{\Theta}$ if you prefer). Supposing that our decision rule is to declare H_1 when $Y \geq \eta$ for some η, for example, $\eta = 1.65$ for a 5% critical level, there are two areas under the curve that we need to consider.

- **Type 1 / False alarm.** The blue region under the curve represents the probability of declaring H_1 (i.e., we choose to reject the null) while the truth is actually H_0 (i.e., we should have not rejected the null). Mathematically, this probability is

$$p_F = \mathbb{P}[Y \geq \eta \mid H_0] = \int_{y \geq \eta} f_0(y)\, dy. \qquad (9.28)$$

- **Type 2 / Miss.** The pink region under the curve represents the probability of declaring H_0 (i.e., we choose to keep the null) while the truth is actually H_1 (i.e., we should have rejected the null). Mathematically, this probability is

$$p_M = \mathbb{P}[Y < \eta \mid H_1] = \int_{y < \eta} f_1(y)\, dy. \qquad (9.29)$$

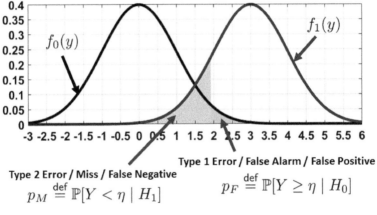

Figure 9.20: Definition of type 1 and type 2 errors.

The **power** of the decision rule is also known as the detection. It is defined as

$$p_D = \mathbb{P}[Y \geq \eta \mid H_1]. \qquad (9.30)$$

A plot illustrating the power of the decision rule is shown in **Figure 9.21**. Since p_D is the conditional probability of $Y \geq \eta$ given H_1, it is the complement of p_M, and so we have the identity

$$p_D = 1 - p_M.$$

Some communities refer to the above quantities in terms of the *counts* instead of the *probabilities*. The difference is that the probabilities are normalized to $[0, 1]$ whereas the counts are just the raw integers obtained from running an experiment. We prefer to use the probabilities because they are the *theoretical values*. If you tell us the distributions f_0 and f_1, we can report the probabilities. The counts, by contrast, are just another form of *sample statistics*. The number of counts today may be different from the number of counts tomorrow

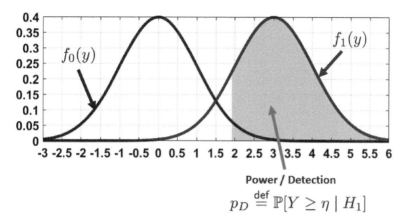

Power / Detection
$$p_D \overset{\text{def}}{=} \mathbb{P}[Y \geq \eta \mid H_1]$$

Figure 9.21: The power of the decision rule is the area under the curve of f_1, integrated for y inside the rejection zone.

because they are obtained from the experiments. The difference between probabilities and counts is analogous to the difference between PMFs and histograms.

Since the probability of errors changes as the decision rule changes, it is necessary to define p_F, p_D and p_M as functions of δ. In addition, hypothesis testing is not limited to one-sided tests. We can define the rejection zone as $R_\alpha = \{y \mid \text{reject } H_0 \text{ using a critical level } \alpha\}$. The probabilities p_F and p_M are defined as

$$p_F(\delta) = \int \delta(y) f_0(y) \, dy = \int_{y \in R_\alpha} f_0(y) \, dy, \tag{9.31}$$

$$p_M(\delta) = \int \delta(y) f_1(y) \, dy = \int_{y \notin R_\alpha} f_1(y) \, dy. \tag{9.32}$$

Using the property that $p_D = 1 - p_M$, we have that

$$p_D(\delta) = 1 - p_M(\delta) = \int_{y \in R_\alpha} f_1(y) \, dy. \tag{9.33}$$

Note that the rejection zone does not need to depend on α. You can arbitrarily define the rejection zone, and the probabilities p_F, p_M, and p_D can still be defined.

Example 9.13. Find $p_F(\delta_1)$ and $p_F(\delta_2)$ for the decision rule in **Figure 9.18**.

Solution. Since f_0 is a Gaussian with zero mean and unit variance, it follows that

$$p_F(\delta_1) = \int_{1.96}^{\infty} \frac{1}{\sqrt{2\pi}} e^{-\frac{y^2}{2}} \, dy = 1 - \Phi(1.92) = 0.025,$$

$$p_F(\delta_2) = \int_{0.5}^{\infty} \frac{1}{\sqrt{2\pi}} e^{-\frac{y^2}{2}} \, dy = 1 - \Phi(0.5) = 0.3085.$$

9.4.3 Neyman-Pearson decision

At this point you have probably observed something about the critical-value test and the p-value test. Among the four types of decision combinations, we are looking at the **false**

positive rate, or the probability of false alarm $p_F(\delta)$. The critical-value test requires us to find δ such that $p_F(\delta)$ is equal to α. That is, if you tell us the critical level α (e.g., $\alpha = 0.05$), we will find a decision rule (by telling you the cutoff) such that the false alarm rate is α. Consider an example:

Example 9.14. Let $\alpha = 0.05$. Assume that f_0 is a Gaussian with zero-mean and unit-variance. Let us do a one-sided test for $H_0 : \theta = 0$ versus $H_1 : \theta > 0$. Find δ such that $p_F(\delta) = \alpha$.

Solution. Let the decision rule δ be

$$\delta(y) = \begin{cases} 1, & y \geq \eta, \\ 0, & y < \eta. \end{cases}$$

Our goal is to find η. The probability of false alarm is

$$p_F(\delta) = \int_\eta^\infty \frac{1}{\sqrt{2\pi}} e^{-\frac{y^2}{2}} \, dy = 1 - \Phi(\eta).$$

Equating this to α, it follows that $1 - \Phi(\eta) = \alpha$ implies $\eta = \Phi^{-1}(1 - \alpha) = 1.65$. So the decision rule becomes

$$\delta(y) = \begin{cases} 1, & y \geq 1.65, \\ 0, & y < 1.65. \end{cases}$$

If you apply this decision rule, you are guaranteed that the false alarm rate is $\alpha = 0.05$.

But why should we aim for $p_F(\delta)$ *equal to* α? Isn't a lower false alarm rate better? Indeed, we would not mind having a lower false alarm, so we are happy to have any δ that satisfies $p_F(\delta) \leq \alpha$. However, changing the equality to an inequality means that we now have a set of δ instead of a unique δ. More important, we need to pay attention to the trade-off between $p_F(\delta)$ and $p_D(\delta)$. The smaller the $p_F(\delta)$ a decision rule δ provides, the smaller the $p_D(\delta)$ you can achieve. This is immediately apparent from **Figure 9.20** and **Figure 9.21**. (If you move the cutoff to the right, the gray area and the blue area will both shrink.) Therefore, the desired optimization should be formulated as: From all the decision rules δ that have a false alarm rate of no larger than α, we pick the one that maximizes the detection rate. The resulting decision rule is known as the **Neyman-Pearson decision rule**.

Definition 9.2. *The* **Neyman-Pearson decision rule** *is defined as the solution to the optimization*

$$\delta^* = \underset{\delta}{argmax} \; p_D(\delta),$$

$$subject \; to \; p_F(\delta) \leq \alpha. \qquad (9.34)$$

Figure 9.22 illustrates two decision rules $\delta^*(y)$ and $\delta(y)$. The first decision rule $\delta^*(y)$ is obtained according to the critical-value approach, with $\alpha = 0.025$. As we will prove shortly, this is also the optimal Neyman-Pearson decision rule for a one-sided hypothesis testing at $\alpha = 0.025$. The second decision rule $\delta(y)$ has a harsher cutoff, meaning that you need an extreme test statistic to reject the null hypothesis. Clearly, the p-value obtained by $\delta(y)$ is less than $\alpha = 0.025$. Thus, $\delta(y)$ is a valid decision rule according to the Neyman-Pearson formulation. However, $\delta(y)$ is not optimal because the detection rate is not maximized.

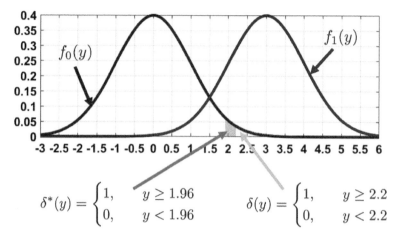

$$\delta^*(y) = \begin{cases} 1, & y \geq 1.96 \\ 0, & y < 1.96 \end{cases} \qquad \delta(y) = \begin{cases} 1, & y \geq 2.2 \\ 0, & y < 2.2 \end{cases}$$

Figure 9.22: Two decision rules $\delta(y)$ and $\delta^*(y)$. Assume that $\alpha = 0.025$. Then $\delta(y)$ is one of the many feasible choices in the Neyman-Pearson optimization, but $\delta^*(y)$ is the optimal solution.

Because of the complementary behavior of p_F and p_D, it follows that p_D is maximized when p_F hits the upper bound. If we want to maximize the detection rate we need to stretch the false alarm rate as much as possible. As a result, the Neyman-Pearson solution occurs when $p_F(\delta) = \alpha$, i.e., when the equality is met.

The Neyman-Pearson framework is a general framework for all distributions f_0 and f_1, as opposed to the critical-value and p-value examples, which are either Gaussian or Student's t-distribution. The solution to the Neyman-Pearson optimization is a decision rule known as the **likelihood ratio test**. The likelihood ratio is defined as follows.

Definition 9.3. *The* **likelihood ratio** *for two distributions $f_1(y)$ and $f_0(y)$ is*

$$L(y) = \frac{f_1(y)}{f_0(y)}. \tag{9.35}$$

It turns out that the solution to the Neyman-Pearson optimization takes the form of the likelihood ratio.

Theorem 9.2. *The solution to the* **Neyman-Pearson** *optimization is a decision rule that checks the likelihood ratio*

$$\delta^*(y) = \begin{cases} 1, & L(y) \geq \eta, \\ 0, & L(y) < \eta, \end{cases} \tag{9.36}$$

for some decision boundary η which is a function of the critical level α.

What is so special about Neyman-Pearson decision rule?

- It is the **optimal** decision. Its optimality is defined w.r.t. maximizing the detection rate while keeping a reasonable false alarm rate:

$$\delta^* = \underset{\delta}{\operatorname{argmax}} \ p_D(\delta),$$

$$\text{subject to } p_F(\delta) \leq \alpha.$$

- If your goal is to maximize the detection rate while maintaining the false alarm rate, you cannot do better than Neyman-Pearson.

- Its solution is the likelihood ratio test:

$$\delta^*(y) = \begin{cases} 1, & L(y) \geq \eta, \\ 0, & L(y) < \eta, \end{cases}$$

where $L(y) = f_1(y)/f_0(y)$ is the likelihood ratio.

- The critical-value test and the p-value test are special cases of the Neyman-Pearson test.

Deriving the solution to the Neyman-Pearson optimization can be skipped if this is your first time reading the book.

Proof. Given α, choose δ^* such that the false alarm rate is maximized: $p_F(\delta^*) = \alpha$. Then, by substituting the definition of δ^* into the false alarm rate,

$$\alpha = p_F(\delta^*) = \int_{-\infty}^{\infty} \delta^*(y) f_0(y) \, dy$$

$$= \int_{L(y) \geq \eta} 1 \cdot f_0(y) \, dy + \int_{L(y) < \eta} 0 \cdot f_0(y) \, dy. \tag{9.37}$$

Now, consider another decision rule δ that is not optimal but is feasible. That means that δ satisfies $p_F(\delta) \leq \alpha$. Therefore,

$$\alpha \geq p_F(\delta) = \int_{-\infty}^{\infty} \delta(y) f_0(y) \, dy$$

$$= \int_{L(y) \geq \eta} \delta(y) \cdot f_0(y) \, dy + \int_{L(y) < \eta} \delta(y) \cdot f_0(y) \, dy. \tag{9.38}$$

Our goal is to show that $p_D(\delta^*) \geq p_D(\delta)$, because by proving this result we can claim that δ^* maximizes the detection rate.

By combining Equation (9.37) and Equation (9.38), we have

$$0 \leq p_F(\delta^*) - p_F(\delta)$$

$$= \int_{L(x) \geq \eta} (1 - \delta(y)) f_0(y) \, dy - \int_{L(y) < \eta} \delta(y) f_0(y) \, dy. \tag{9.39}$$

Define $L(y) = \frac{f_1(y)}{f_0(y)}$. Then $L(y) \geq \eta$ if and only if $f_1(y) \geq \eta f_0(y)$. So,

$$
\begin{aligned}
p_D(\delta^*) - p_D(\delta) &= \int_{L(y) \geq \eta} (1 - \delta(y)) f_1(y)\, dy - \int_{L(y) < \eta} \delta(y) f_1(y)\, dy \\
&= \int_{L(y) \geq \eta} (1 - \delta(y)) \eta f_0(y)\, dy - \int_{L(y) < \eta} \delta(y) \eta f_0(y)\, dy \\
&= \eta \left[\int_{L(y) \geq \eta} (1 - \delta(y)) f_0(y)\, dy - \int_{L(y) < \eta} \delta(y) f_0(y)\, dy \right] \geq 0,
\end{aligned}
$$

where the last inequality holds because of Equation (9.39). Therefore, we conclude that δ^* maximizes p_D. $\qquad\square$

> **End of the proof. Please join us again.**

At this point, you may object that the likelihood ratio test (i.e., the Neyman-Pearson decision rule) is very different from the hypothesis testing examples we have seen in the previous chapter because now we need to handle the likelihood ratio $L(y)$. Rest assured that they are the same, as illustrated by the following example.

Example 9.15. Consider two hypotheses: $H_0 : Y \sim \text{Gaussian}(0, \sigma^2)$, and $H_1 : Y \sim \text{Gaussian}(\mu, \sigma^2)$, with $\mu > 0$. Construct the Neyman-Pearson decision rule (i.e., the likelihood ratio test).

Solution. Let us first define the likelihood functions. It is clear from the description that

$$
f_0(y) = \frac{1}{\sqrt{2\pi\sigma^2}} \exp\left\{-\frac{y^2}{2\sigma^2}\right\} \quad \text{and} \quad f_1(y) = \frac{1}{\sqrt{2\pi\sigma^2}} \exp\left\{-\frac{(y-\mu)^2}{2\sigma^2}\right\}.
$$

Therefore, the likelihood ratio is

$$
L(y) = \frac{f_1(y)}{f_0(y)} = \exp\left\{-\frac{1}{2\sigma^2}(\mu^2 - 2\mu y)\right\}.
$$

The likelihood ratio test states that the decision rule is

$$
\delta^*(y) = \begin{cases} 1, & L(y) \geq \eta, \\ 0, & L(y) < \eta. \end{cases}
$$

So it remains to simplify the condition $L(y) \gtrless \eta$. To this end, we observe that

$$
\begin{aligned}
L(y) \geq \eta \quad &\Longleftrightarrow \quad -\frac{1}{2\sigma^2}(\mu^2 - 2\mu y) \geq \log \eta \\
&\Longleftrightarrow \quad y \geq \underbrace{\frac{\mu}{2} - \frac{\sigma^2}{\mu} \log \eta}_{\overset{\text{def}}{=} \tau}.
\end{aligned}
$$

Therefore, instead of determining η, we just need to define τ because the decision rules based on η and τ are equivalent.

To determine τ, Neyman-Pearson states that $p_F(\delta) \leq \alpha$ (and at the optimal point the equality has to hold). Substituting this criterion into the decision rule,

$$\alpha = p_F(\delta) = \int_{L(y) \geq \eta} f_0(y) \, dy$$

$$= \int_{y \geq \tau} f_0(y) \, dy$$

$$= \int_{y \geq \tau} \frac{1}{\sqrt{2\pi\sigma^2}} e^{-\frac{y^2}{2\sigma^2}} \, dy$$

$$= 1 - \Phi\left(\frac{\tau}{\sigma}\right).$$

Taking the inverse of the CDF, we obtain τ:

$$\tau = \sigma \Phi^{-1}(1 - \alpha).$$

Putting everything together, the final decision rule is

$$\delta^*(y) = \begin{cases} 1, & y \geq \sigma\Phi^{-1}(1-\alpha), \\ 0, & y < \sigma\Phi^{-1}(1-\alpha). \end{cases}$$

So if $\alpha = 0.05$ we will reject H_0 when $y \geq 1.65\sigma$. We can also replace σ by $\sigma/\sqrt{N}$ if the estimator is constructed from multiple measurements.

The above example tells us that even though the likelihood ratio test may appear complicated at first glance, the decision is the same as the good old hypothesis testing rules we have derived. The flexibility we have gained with the likelihood ratio test is the variety of distributions we can handle. Instead of restricting ourselves to Gaussians or Student's t-distribution (which exclusively focuses on the sample averages), the likelihood ratio test allows us to consider any distributions. The exact decision rule could be less obvious, but the method is generalizable to a broad range of problems.

Practice Exercise 9.5. In a telephone system, the waiting time is defined as the inter-arrival time between two consecutive calls. However, it is known that sometimes the waiting time can be mistakenly recorded as the time between three consecutive calls (i.e., by skipping the second one). Since the interarrival time of an independent Poisson process is either an exponential random variable or an Erlang random variable, depending on how many occurrences we are counting, we define the hypotheses

$$f_0(y) = \begin{cases} e^{-y}, & y \geq 0, \\ 0, & y < 0, \end{cases} \quad \text{and} \quad f_1(y) = \begin{cases} ye^{-y}, & y \geq 0, \\ 0, & y < 0. \end{cases}$$

Suppose we are given one measurement $Y = y$. Find the Neyman-Pearson decision rule for $\alpha = 0.05$.

Solution. The likelihood ratio is

$$L(y) = \frac{f_1(y)}{f_0(y)} = \frac{ye^{-y}}{e^{-y}} = y, \qquad y \geq 0.$$

Substituting this into the decision rule, we have

$$\delta^*(y) = \begin{cases} 1, & L(y) \geq \eta \iff y \geq \eta, \\ 0, & L(y) < \eta \iff y < \eta. \end{cases}$$

It remains to determine η. Inspecting $p_F(\delta)$, we have that

$$\alpha = p_F(\delta^*) = \int_{L(y) \geq \eta} f_0(y)\, dy$$

$$= \int_{y \geq \eta} e^{-y}\, dy = e^{-\eta}.$$

Setting $e^{-\eta} = \alpha$, we have that $\alpha = -\log \alpha$. Hence, the decision rule is

$$\delta^*(y) = \begin{cases} 1, & L(y) \geq \eta \iff y \geq -\log \alpha, \\ 0, & L(y) < \eta \iff y < -\log \alpha. \end{cases}$$

For $\alpha = 0.05$, we reject the null hypothesis when $y \geq 2.9957$. **Figure 9.23** illustrates the hypothesis testing rule.

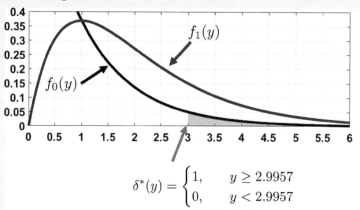

$$\delta^*(y) = \begin{cases} 1, & y \geq 2.9957 \\ 0, & y < 2.9957 \end{cases}$$

Figure 9.23: Neyman-Pearson decision rule at $\alpha = 0.05$.

Remark. This example is instructive in that we have only one measurement $Y = y$. If we have repeated measurements and take the average, then the Central Limit Theorem will kick in. In that case, we can resort to our favorite Gaussian distribution or Student's t-distribution instead of dealing with the exponential and the Erlang distributions. However, the example demonstrates the usefulness of Neyman-Pearson, especially when the distributions are complicated.

9.5 ROC and Precision-Recall Curve

Being a *binary* decision rule, the hypothesis testing procedure shares many similarities with a two-class classification algorithm.[3] Given a testing statistic or a testing sample, both the hypothesis testing and a classification algorithm will report YES or NO. Therefore, any performance evaluation metric developed for hypothesis testing is equally applicable to classification and vice versa.

The topic we study in this section is the **receiver operating characteristic** (ROC) curve and the **precision-recall** (PR) curve. The ROC curve and the PR curve are arguably *the* most popular metrics in modern machine learning, in particular for classification, detection, and segmentation tasks in computer vision. There are many unresolved questions about these two curves and there are many debates about how to use them. Our goal is not to add another voice to the debate; rather, we would like to fill in the gap between the hypothesis testing theory (particularly the Neyman-Pearson framework) and these two sets of curves. We will establish the equivalence between the two curves and leave the open-ended debates to you.

9.5.1 Receiver Operating Characteristic (ROC)

Our approach to understanding the ROC curve and the PR curve is based on the Neyman-Pearson framework. Under this framework, we know that the **optimal** decision rule w.r.t to the Neyman-Pearson criterion is the solution to the optimization

$$\delta^*(\alpha) = \underset{\delta}{\operatorname{argmax}} \ p_D(\delta)$$

$$\text{subject to} \quad p_F(\delta) \leq \alpha.$$

As a result of this optimization, the decision rule δ^* will achieve a certain false alarm rate $p_F(\delta^*)$ and detection rate $p_D(\delta^*)$. Clearly, the decision rule δ^* changes as we change the critical level α. Accordingly we write δ^* as $\delta^*(\alpha)$ to reflect this dependency.

What this observation implies is that as we sweep through the range of α's, we construct different decision rules, each one with a different p_F and p_D. If we denote the decision rules by $\delta_1, \delta_2, \ldots, \delta_M$, we have M pairs of false alarm rate p_F and detection rate p_D:

- Decision rule δ_1: False alarm rate $p_F(\delta_1)$ and detection rate $p_D(\delta_1)$.

- Decision rule δ_2: False alarm rate $p_F(\delta_2)$ and detection rate $p_D(\delta_2)$.

- $\quad \vdots$

- Decision rule δ_M: False alarm rate $p_F(\delta_M)$ and detection rate $p_D(\delta_M)$.

---

[3]In a classification algorithm, the goal is to look at the testing sample $\boldsymbol{y}$ and compute certain thresholding criteria. For example, a typical decision rule of a classification algorithm is $\delta(\boldsymbol{y}) = \begin{cases} 1, & \boldsymbol{w}^T \phi(\boldsymbol{y}) \geq \tau \\ 0, & \boldsymbol{w}^T \phi(\boldsymbol{y}) < \tau \end{cases}$. Here, you can think of the vector $\boldsymbol{w}$ as the regression coefficient, and $\phi(\cdot)$ is some kind of feature transform. The equation says that class 1 will be reported if the inner product is larger than a threshold τ, and class 0 will be reported otherwise. Therefore, a binary classification, when written in this form, is the same as a hypothesis testing procedure.

If we plot $p_D(\delta)$ on the y-axis as a function of $p_F(\delta)$ on the x-axis, we obtain a curve shown in **Figure 9.24** (see the example below for the problem setting). The black curve shown on the right is known as the **receiver operating characteristic** (ROC) curve.

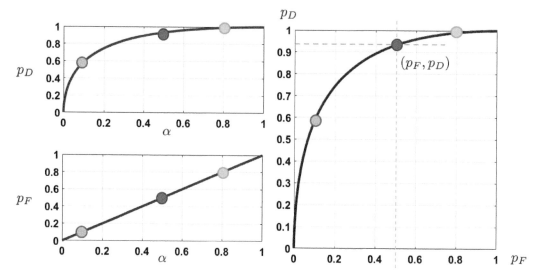

Figure 9.24: An example of an ROC curve, where we consider two hypotheses: $H_0 : Y \sim$ Gaussian$(0, 2)$, and $H_1 : Y \sim$ Gaussian$(3, 2)$. We construct the Neyman-Pearson decision rule for a range of critical levels α. For each α we compute the theoretical $p_F(\alpha)$ and $p_D(\alpha)$, shown on the left-hand side of the figure. The pair of (p_D, p_F) is then plotted as the right-hand side curve by sweeping the α's.

The setup of the figure follows the example below.

Example 9.16. We consider two hypotheses: $H_0 : Y \sim$ Gaussian$(0, 2)$, and $H_1 : Y \sim$ Gaussian$(3, 2)$. Derive the Neyman-Pearson decision rule and plot the ROC curve.

Solution. We construct a Neyman-Pearson decision rule:

$$\delta^*(y) = \begin{cases} 1, & y \geq \sigma\Phi^{-1}(1-\alpha), \\ 0, & y < \sigma\Phi^{-1}(1-\alpha). \end{cases}$$

where τ is a tunable threshold. For example, if $\alpha = 0.05$, then $\sigma\Phi^{-1}(1-0.05) = 3.2897$, and if $\alpha = 0.1$, then $\sigma\Phi^{-1}(1 - 0.1) = 2.5631$. Therefore, the false alarm rate and the detection rate are functions of the critical level α.

For this particular example, we have the false alarm rate and detection rate in closed form, as functions of α:

$$p_F(\alpha) = \int_{\sigma\Phi^{-1}(1-\alpha)}^{\infty} \frac{1}{\sqrt{2\pi\sigma^2}} e^{-\frac{y^2}{2\sigma^2}} \, dy$$

$$= 1 - \Phi\left(\frac{\sigma\Phi^{-1}(1-\alpha)}{\sigma}\right) = \alpha,$$

$$p_D(\alpha) = \int_{\sigma\Phi^{-1}(1-\alpha)}^{\infty} \frac{1}{\sqrt{2\pi\sigma^2}} e^{-\frac{(y-\mu)^2}{2\sigma^2}}\, dy$$

$$= 1 - \Phi\left(\Phi^{-1}(1-\alpha) - \frac{\mu}{\sigma}\right).$$

These give us the two curves on the left-hand side of **Figure 9.24**.

What is an ROC curve?
- It is a plot showing p_D on the y-axis and p_F on the x-axis.
- p_D = detection rate (also known as the power of the test).
- p_F = false alarm rate (also known as the type 1 error of the test).

The ROC curve tells us the behavior of the decision rule as we change the threshold α. A graphical illustration is shown in **Figure 9.25**. There are a few key observations we need to pay attention to:

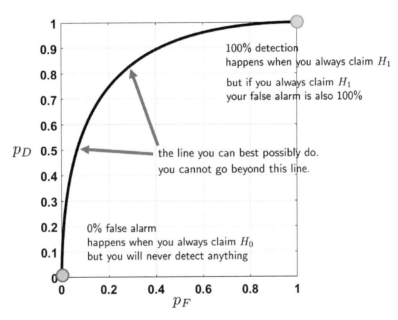

Figure 9.25: Interpreting the ROC curve.

- The ROC curve must go through $(0,0)$. This happens when you always keep the null hypothesis or always declare class 0, no matter what observations. If you always keep H_0, certainly you will not make any false positive (or false alarm), because you will never say H_0 is wrong. Therefore, the detection rate (or the power of the test) is also 0. This is a useless decision rule for both classification and hypothesis testing.

- The ROC curve must go through $(1,1)$. This happens when you always reject the null hypothesis, no matter what observations we have. If you always reject H_0, you will always say that "there is a target". As far as detection is concerned, you are perfect because you have not missed any targets. However, the false positive rate is also high because you will falsely declare a target when there is nothing. Therefore, this is also a useless decision rule.

- The ROC curve tells us the operating point of the decision rule as we change the threshold. A threshold is a universal concept for both hypothesis testing and classification. In hypothesis testing, we have the critical level α, say 0.05 or 0.1. In classification, we also have a threshold for judging whether a sample should be classified as class 1 or class 0. Often in classification, the intermediate estimates are probabilities or distances to decision boundaries. These real numbers need to be binarized to generate a binary decision. The ROC curve tells us that if you pick a threshold, your decision rule will have a certain p_F and p_D as predicted by the curve. If you want to tolerate a higher p_F, you can move along the curve to find your operating point.

- The ideal operating point on a ROC curve is when $p_F = 0$ and $p_D = 1$. However, this is a hypothetical situation that does not happen in any real decision rule.

9.5.2 Comparing ROC curves

Because of how the ROC curves are constructed, every binary decision rule has its own ROC curve. Typically, when one tries to compare classification algorithms, the **area under the curve** (**AUC**) occupied by the ROC curve is compared. A decision rule having a larger AUC is often a "better" decision rule.

To illustrate the idea of comparing estimators, we consider a trivial decision rule based on a blind guess.

Example 9.17. (A blind guess decision) Consider a decision rule that we reject H_0 with probability α and keep H_0 with probability $1 - \alpha$. We call this a blind guess, since the decision rule ignores observation y. Mathematically, this trivial decision rule is

$$\delta(y) = \begin{cases} 1, & \text{with probability } \alpha, \\ 0, & \text{with probability } 1 - \alpha. \end{cases}$$

Find p_F, p_D, and AUC.

Solution. For this decision rule we compute its false positive rate (or false alarm rate) and its true positive rate (or detection rate). However, since $\delta(y)$ is now random, we need to take the expectation over the two random states that $\delta(y)$ can take. This gives us

$$p_F(\alpha) = \mathbb{E}\left[\int \delta(y) f_0(y)\, dy\right]$$

$$= \int 1 \cdot f_0(y)\, dy \mathbb{P}[\delta(y) = 1] + \int 0 \cdot f_0(y)\, dy \mathbb{P}[\delta(y) = 0]$$

$$= \alpha \int f_0(y)\, dy = \alpha.$$

Similarly, the detection rate is

$$p_D(\alpha) = \mathbb{E}\left[\int \delta(y)f_1(y)\,dy\right] = \alpha\int f_1(y)\,dy = \alpha.$$

If we plot p_D as a function of p_F, we notice that the function is a straight line going from $(0,0)$ to $(1,1)$. This decision rule is useless. Comparing this with the Neyman-Pearson decision rule, it is clear that Neyman-Pearson has a larger AUC. The AUC for this trivial decision rule is the area of the triangle, which is 0.5.

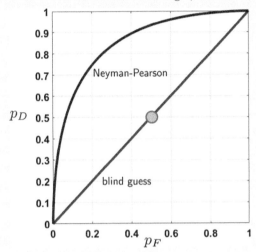

Figure 9.26: The ROC curve of the blind guess decision rule is a straight line. The AUC is 0.5.

If you set $\alpha = 0.5$, then the decision rule becomes

$$\delta(y) = \begin{cases} 1, & \text{with probability } \frac{1}{2}, \\ 0, & \text{with probability } \frac{1}{2}. \end{cases}$$

This is equivalent to flipping a fair coin with probability $1/2$ of declaring H_0 and $1/2$ declaring H_1. Its operating point is the yellow circle.

Computing the AUC can be done by calling special library functions. However, to spell out the details we demonstrate something more elementary. The program below is a piece of MATLAB code plotting two ROC curves corresponding to two different decision rules. The first decision rule is the trivial decision rule, where we have just shown that $p_F(\alpha) = p_D(\alpha) = \alpha$. The second decision rule is the Neyman-Pearson decision rule, for which we showed in **Figure 9.24** that $p_F(\alpha) = \alpha$ and $p_D(\alpha) = 1 - \Phi\left(\Phi^{-1}(1-\alpha) - \frac{\mu}{\sigma}\right)$. Using the MATLAB code below, we can plot the two ROC curves shown in **Figure 9.26**.

```
% MATLAB code to plot ROC curve
sigma = 2;  mu = 3;
alphaset = linspace(0,1,1000);
PF1 = zeros(1,1000); PD1 = zeros(1,1000);
PF2 = zeros(1,1000); PD2 = zeros(1,1000);
for i=1:1000
    alpha = alphaset(i);
```

```
   PF1(i) = alpha;
   PD1(i) = alpha;

   PF2(i) = alpha;
   PD2(i) = 1-normcdf(norminv(1-alpha)-mu/sigma);
end
figure;
plot(PF1, PD1,'LineWidth', 4, 'Color', [0.8, 0, 0]); hold on;
plot(PF2, PD2,'LineWidth', 4, 'Color', [0, 0, 0]); hold off;
```

To compute the AUC we perform a numerical integration:

$$\text{AUC} = \int p_D(\alpha) \cdot \mathrm{d}p_F(\alpha) \approx \sum_i p_D(\alpha_i) \cdot \Delta p_F(\alpha_i)$$
$$= \sum_i p_D(\alpha_i) \cdot \left[p_F(\alpha_i) - p_F(\alpha_{i-1}) \right],$$

where α_i is the ith critical level we use to plot the ROC curve. (We assume that the α's are sorted in ascending order.) In MATLAB, the commands are

```
auc1 = sum(PD1.*[0 diff(PF1)])
auc2 = sum(PD2.*[0 diff(PF2)])
```

The AUC of the two decision rules computed by MATLAB are 0.8561 and 0.5005, respectively. The small slack of 0.0005 is caused by the numerical approximation at the tail, which can be ignored as long as you are consistent for all the ROC curves.

The commands for Python are analogous to the commands for MATLAB.

```
# Python code to plot ROC curve
import numpy as np
import matplotlib.pyplot as plt
import scipy.stats as stats

sigma = 2; mu = 3;
alphaset = np.linspace(0,1,1000)
PF1 = np.zeros(1000); PD1 = np.zeros(1000)
PF2 = np.zeros(1000); PD2 = np.zeros(1000)
for i in range(1000):
  alpha = alphaset[i]
  PF1[i] = alpha
  PD1[i] = alpha
  PF2[i] = alpha
  PD2[i] = 1-stats.norm.cdf(stats.norm.ppf(1-alpha)-mu/sigma)
plt.plot(PF1,PD1)
plt.plot(PF2,PD2)
```

To compute the AUC, the Python code is (continuing from the previous code):

```
auc1 = np.sum(PD1 * np.append(0, np.diff(PF1)))
auc2 = np.sum(PD2 * np.append(0, np.diff(PF2)))
```

It is possible to get a decision rule that is worse than a blind guess. The following example illustrates a trivial setup.

Practice Exercise 9.6. (Flipped Neyman-Pearson). Consider two hypotheses

$$H_0 = \text{Gaussian}(0, \sigma^2),$$
$$H_1 = \text{Gaussian}(\mu, \sigma^2), \qquad \mu > 0.$$

Let α be the critical level. The Neyman-Pearson decision rule is

$$\delta^*(y) = \begin{cases} 1, & y \geq \sigma\Phi^{-1}(1-\alpha), \\ 0, & y < \sigma\Phi^{-1}(1-\alpha). \end{cases}$$

Now, consider a flipped Neyman-Pearson decision rule

$$\delta^+(y) = \begin{cases} 1, & y < \sigma\Phi^{-1}(1-\alpha), \\ 0, & y \geq \sigma\Phi^{-1}(1-\alpha). \end{cases}$$

Find p_F, p_D, and AUC for the new decision rule δ^+.

Solution. Since we flip the rejection zone, the probability of false alarm is

$$p_F(\alpha) = \int \delta^+(y) f_0(y) \, dy$$
$$= \int_{-\infty}^{\sigma\Phi^{-1}(1-\alpha)} \frac{1}{\sqrt{2\pi\sigma^2}} e^{-\frac{y^2}{2\sigma^2}} \, dy$$
$$= \Phi\left(\frac{\sigma\Phi^{-1}(1-\alpha)}{\sigma}\right)$$
$$= 1 - \alpha.$$

Similarly, the probability of detection is

$$p_D(\alpha) = \int \delta^+(y) f_1(y) \, dy$$
$$= \int_{-\infty}^{\sigma\Phi^{-1}(1-\alpha)} \frac{1}{\sqrt{2\pi\sigma^2}} e^{-\frac{(y-\mu)^2}{2\sigma^2}} \, dy$$
$$= \Phi\left(\frac{\sigma\Phi^{-1}(1-\alpha) - \mu}{\sigma}\right)$$
$$= \Phi\left(\Phi^{-1}(1-\alpha) - \frac{\mu}{\sigma}\right).$$

If you plot p_D as a function of p_F, you will obtain a curve shown in **Figure 9.27**. The AUC for this flipped decision rule is 0.1439, whereas that for Neyman-Pearson is 0.8561. The two numbers are complements of each other, meaning that their sum is unity.

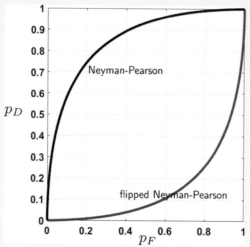

Figure 9.27: The ROC curve of a flipped Neyman-Pearson decision rule.

What if we arbitrarily construct a decision rule that is neither Neyman-Pearson nor the blind guess? The following example demonstrates one possible choice.

Practice Exercise 9.7. Consider two hypotheses

$$H_0 = \text{Gaussian}(0, \sigma^2),$$
$$H_1 = \text{Gaussian}(\mu, \sigma^2), \qquad \mu > 0.$$

Let α be the critical level. Consider the following decision rule:

$$\delta^{\clubsuit}(y) = \begin{cases} 1, & |y| \geq \sigma\Phi^{-1}(1-\alpha), \\ 0, & |y| < \sigma\Phi^{-1}(1-\alpha). \end{cases}$$

Find p_F, p_D, and AUC for the new decision rule $\delta^{\clubsuit}$.

Solution. The probability of false alarm is

$$p_F(\alpha) = \int \delta^{\clubsuit}(y) f_0(y) \, dy$$

$$= 1 - \int_{-\sigma\Phi^{-1}(1-\alpha)}^{\sigma\Phi^{-1}(1-\alpha)} \frac{1}{\sqrt{2\pi\sigma^2}} e^{-\frac{y^2}{2\sigma^2}} \, dy$$

$$= 1 - \Phi\left(\Phi^{-1}(1-\alpha)\right) + \Phi\left(-\Phi^{-1}(1-\alpha)\right)$$

$$= 2\alpha.$$

Similarly, the probability of detection is

$$p_D(\alpha) = \int \delta^{\clubsuit}(y) f_1(y) \, dy$$

$$= 1 - \int_{-\sigma\Phi^{-1}(1-\alpha)}^{\sigma\Phi^{-1}(1-\alpha)} \frac{1}{\sqrt{2\pi\sigma^2}} e^{-\frac{(y-\mu)^2}{2\sigma^2}} \, dy$$

$$= 1 - \Phi\left(\frac{\sigma\Phi^{-1}(1-\alpha) - \mu}{\sigma}\right) + \Phi\left(\frac{-\sigma\Phi^{-1}(1-\alpha) - \mu}{\sigma}\right)$$

$$= 1 - \Phi\left(\Phi^{-1}(1-\alpha) - \frac{\mu}{\sigma}\right) + \Phi\left(-\Phi^{-1}(1-\alpha) - \frac{\mu}{\sigma}\right).$$

If you plot p_D as a function of p_F, you will obtain a curve shown in **Figure 9.28**. The AUC for this proposed decision rule is 0.7534, whereas that of Neyman-Pearson is 0.8561. Therefore, the Neyman-Pearson decision rule is better.

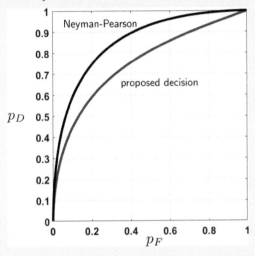

Figure 9.28: The ROC curve of a proposed decision rule.

The MATLAB code we used to generate **Figure 9.28** is shown below. Note that we need to separate the calculations of the two curves, because the proposed curve can only take $0 < \alpha < 0.5$. The Python code is implemented analogously.

```
% MATLAB code to generate the ROC curve.
sigma = 2;   mu = 3;
PF1 = zeros(1,1000); PD1 = zeros(1,1000);
PF2 = zeros(1,1000); PD2 = zeros(1,1000);
alphaset = linspace(0,0.5,1000);
for i=1:1000
    alpha = alphaset(i);
    PF1(i) = 2*alpha;
    PD1(i) = 1-(normcdf(norminv(1-alpha)-mu/sigma)-...
                normcdf(-norminv(1-alpha)-mu/sigma));
end
alphaset = linspace(0,1,1000);
```

```
for i=1:1000
    alpha = alphaset(i);
    PF2(i) = alpha;
    PD2(i) = 1-normcdf(norminv(1-alpha)-mu/sigma);
end
figure;
plot(PF1, PD1,'LineWidth', 4, 'Color', [0.8, 0, 0]); hold on;
plot(PF2, PD2,'LineWidth', 4, 'Color', [0, 0, 0]); hold off;
```

```python
import numpy as np
import matplotlib.pyplot as plt
import scipy.stats as stats

sigma = 2; mu = 3;
PF1 = np.zeros(1000); PD1 = np.zeros(1000)
PF2 = np.zeros(1000); PD2 = np.zeros(1000)

alphaset = np.linspace(0,0.5,1000)
for i in range(1000):
  alpha = alphaset[i]
  PF1[i] = 2*alpha
  PD1[i] = 1-(stats.norm.cdf(stats.norm.ppf(1-alpha)-mu/sigma) \
             -stats.norm.cdf(-stats.norm.ppf(1-alpha)-mu/sigma))

alphaset = np.linspace(0,1,1000)
for i in range(1000):
  alpha = alphaset[i]
  PF2[i] = alpha
  PD2[i] = 1-stats.norm.cdf(stats.norm.ppf(1-alpha)-mu/sigma)

plt.plot(PF1, PD1)
plt.plot(PF2, PD2)
```

9.5.3 The ROC curve in practice

If the Neyman-Pearson decision rule is the optimal rule, why don't we always use it? The problem is that in practice we may not have access to the distributions. For example, if we classify images, how do we know that the data follows a Gaussian distribution or a mixture of distributions? Consequently, the ROC curves we discussed in the subsections above are the *theoretical* ROC curves. In practice, we plot the *empirical* ROC curves.

Plotting an empirical ROC curve for a binary classification method (and hypothesis testing) is intuitive. The ingredients we need are a set of scores and a set of labels. The scores are the probability values determining the likelihood of a sample belonging to one class. Generally speaking, for empirical data this requires looking at the training data, building a model, and computing the likelihood. We will not go into the details of how a binary classifier is built. Instead, we assume that you have already built a binary classifier and have obtained the scores. Our goal is to show you how to plot the ROC curve.

The following MATLAB code uses a dataset `fisheriris`. The code builds a binary classifier and returns the scores.

```
% MATLAB code to train a classification algorithm.
% Do not worry if you cannot understand this code.
% It is not the focus on this book.
load fisheriris
pred = meas(51:end,1:2);
resp = (1:100)'>50;
mdl = fitglm(pred,resp,'Distribution','binomial','Link','logit');
scores = mdl.Fitted.Probability;
labels = [ones(1,50), zeros(1,50)];
save('ch9_ROC_example_data','scores','labels');
```

To give you an idea of how the scores of the classifier look, we plot the histogram of the scores in **Figure 9.29**. As you can see, there is no clear division between the two classes. No matter what threshold τ we use, some cases will be misclassified.

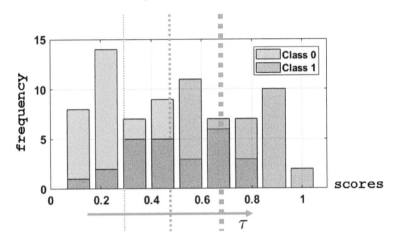

Figure 9.29: The distribution of probability scores obtained from a binary classifier for the dataset `fisheriris`. The green vertical lines represent the threshold for turning the scores into binary decisions. Any score greater than τ will be classified as Class 1, and any score that is less than τ will be classified as Class 0. These predicted labels would then be compared to the true labels to plot the ROC curve.

Recall that the ROC curve is a function of p_D versus p_F. Using terminology from statistics, p_D is the true positive rate and p_F is the false positive rate. By sweeping a range of decision thresholds (over the scores), we can compute the corresponding p_F's and p_D's. On a computer this can be done by setting up two columns of labels: the true label `labels` and the predicted labels `prediction`. For any threshold τ, we binarize the scores to turn them into a decision vector. Then we count the number of true positives, true negatives, false positives, and false negatives. The total of these numbers will give us p_F and p_D.

In MATLAB, the above description can be easily implemented by sweeping through the range of τ.

```
% MATLAB code to generate an empirical ROC curve
load ch9_ROC_example_data
```

```
tau = linspace(0,1,1000);
for i=1:1000
    idx    = (scores <= tau(i));
    predict = zeros(1,100);
    predict(idx)   = 1;
    true_positive  = 0; true_negative  = 0;
    false_positive = 0; false_negative = 0;
    for j=1:100
        if (predict(j)==1) && (labels(j)==1)
            true_positive = true_positive + 1;   end
        if (predict(j)==1) && (labels(j)==0)
            false_positive = false_positive + 1; end
        if (predict(j)==0) && (labels(j)==1)
            false_negative = false_negative + 1; end
        if (predict(j)==0) && (labels(j)==0)
            true_negative = true_negative + 1;   end
    end
    PF(i) = false_positive/50;
    PD(i) = true_positive/50;
end
plot(PF, PD, 'LineWidth', 4, 'Color', [0, 0, 0]);
```

The Python codes of this problem are similar. We give them here for completeness.

```
# Python code to generate an empirical ROC curve
import numpy as np
import matplotlib.pyplot as plt
import scipy.stats as stats
scores = np.loadtxt('ch9_ROC_example_data.txt')
labels = np.append(np.ones(50), np.zeros(50))
tau = np.linspace(0,1,1000)
PF = np.zeros(1000)
PD = np.zeros(1000)
for i in range(1000):
  idx = scores<= tau[i]
  predict = np.zeros(100)
  predict[idx] = 1
  true_positive  = 0;   true_negative  = 0
  false_positive = 0;   false_negative = 0
  for j in range(100):
    if (predict[j]==1) and (labels[j]==1): true_positive  += 1
    if (predict[j]==1) and (labels[j]==0): false_positive += 1
    if (predict[j]==0) and (labels[j]==1): false_negative += 1
    if (predict[j]==0) and (labels[j]==0): true_negative  += 1
  PF[i] = false_positive/50
  PD[i] = true_positive/50
plt.plot(PF, PD)
```

The empirical ROC curve for this problem is shown in **Figure 9.30**. Each point on the curve is a coordinate (p_F, p_D), evaluated at a particular threshold τ. Mathematically, the decision rule we used was

$$\delta(y) = \begin{cases} 1, & \texttt{score}(y) \geq \tau, \\ 0, & \texttt{score}(y) < \tau. \end{cases}$$

For every τ, we have a false alarm rate and a detection rate. Since this is an empirical dataset with only 100 samples, there are many occasions where p_F does not change but p_D increases, or p_D stays constant but p_F increases. For this particular example, we can compute the AUC, which is 0.7948.

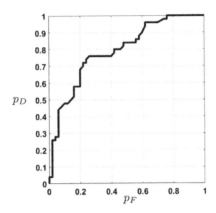

Figure 9.30: The empirical ROC curve for the dataset `fisheriris`, using a classifier based on the logistic regression.

Note that the empirical ROC is rough. It does not have the smooth **concave** shape of the theoretical ROC curve. One can prove that if the decision rule is Neyman-Pearson, i.e., if we conduct a likelihood ratio test, then the resulting ROC curve is concave. Otherwise, you can still obtain an empirical ROC curve for real datasets and classifiers. However, the shape is not necessarily concave.

9.5.4 The Precision-Recall (PR) curve

In modern data science, an alternative performance metric to the ROC curve is the **precision-recall (PR) curve**. The precision and recall are defined as follows.

> **Definition 9.4.** *Let TP = true positive, FP = false positive, FN = false negative. The* **precision** *is defined as*
>
> $$precision = \frac{TP}{TP + FP} = \frac{p_D}{p_D + p_F}, \tag{9.40}$$
>
> *and the* **recall** *is defined as*
>
> $$recall = \frac{TP}{TP + FN} = \frac{p_D}{p_D + p_M} = p_D. \tag{9.41}$$

In this definition, TP, FP, and FN are the *numbers* of samples that are classified as true positive, false positive, and false negative, respectively. However, both precision and recall are defined as ratios of numbers. The ratios can be equivalently defined through the *rates*. Using our terminology, this gives us the definitions in terms of p_D, p_F and p_M. Since $p_D = 1 - p_M$, it also holds that the recall is p_D.

Let us take a moment to consider the meanings of precision and recall. Precision is defined as

$$\text{precision} = \frac{\text{TP}}{\text{TP} + \text{FP}} = \frac{\# \text{ true positives}}{\text{total } \# \text{ positives you claim}}. \tag{9.42}$$

The numerator of the precision is the number of true positive samples and the denominator is the total number of positives that you claim. This includes the true positives and the false positives. Therefore, precision measures how *trustworthy* your claim is. There are two scenarios to consider:

- **High precision**: This means that among all the positives you claim, many of them are the true positives. Therefore, whatever you claim is trustworthy. One possibility for obtaining a high precision is that the critical level α of the Neyman-Pearson decision rule approaches 1. In other words, you are very accepting of the null hypotheses. Thus, whenever you reject, it will be a reliable reject.

- **Low precision**: This means that you are overclaiming the positives, and so there are many false positives. Thus, even though you claim many positives, not all are trustworthy. One reason why low precision occurs is that you are too eager to reject the null. Thus you tend to overkill the unnecessary cases.

A similar analysis can be applied to the recall. The recall is defined as

$$\text{recall} = \frac{\text{TP}}{\text{TP} + \text{FN}} = \frac{\# \text{ true positives}}{\text{total } \# \text{ positives in the distribution}}. \tag{9.43}$$

The difference between the recall and the precision is the denominator. For recall, the denominator is the total number of positives in the *distribution*. We are not interested in knowing what you have claimed but in knowing how many of them are there in the distribution. If you examine the definition using p_D, you can see that recall is the probability of detection — how successfully you can detect a target. A high recall and a low recall can occur in two situations:

- **High recall**: This means that you are very good at detecting the target or rejecting the null appropriately. A high recall can happen when the critical level α is low so that you never miss a target. However, if the critical level α is low, you will suffer from a low precision.

- **Low recall**: This means that you are too accepting of the null hypotheses, and so you never claim that there is a target. As a result the number of successful detections is low. However, having a low recall can buy you high precision because you do not reject the null unless it has extreme evidence (hence there is no false alarm.)

As you can see from the discussions above, the precision-recall has a trade-off, just as the ROC curve does. Since the PR curve and ROC curve are derived from p_F and p_D, there is a one-to-one correspondence. This can be proved by rearranging the terms in the previous theorem.

Theorem 9.3. *The* **false alarm rate** p_F *and the* **detection rate** p_D *can be expressed in terms of the precision and recall as*

$$p_F = \frac{\text{recall}(1 - \text{precision})}{\text{precision}}, \qquad (9.44)$$

$$p_D = \text{recall}.$$

This result implies that whenever we have an ROC curve we can convert it to a PR curve. Moreover, whenever we have a PR curve we can convert it to an ROC curve. Therefore, there is no additional information one can squeeze out by converting the curves. What we can claim, at most, is that the two curves offer different ways of interpreting the decision rule.

To illustrate the equivalence between an ROC curve and a PR curve, we plot two different decision rules in **Figure 9.31**. Any point on the ROC curve will have a corresponding point on the PR curve, and vice versa.

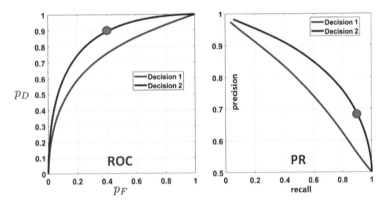

Figure 9.31: There is a one-to-one correspondence between the ROC curve and the PR curve.

The MATLAB and Python codes for generating the PR curve are straightforward. Assuming that we have run the code used to generate **Figure 9.28**, we plot the PR curve as follows (this will give us **Figure 9.31**).

```
% MATLAB code to generate a PR curve
precision1 = PD1./(PD1+PF1);
precision2 = PD2./(PD2+PF2);
recall1    = PD1;
recall2    = PD2;
plot(recall1, precision1, 'LineWidth', 4); hold on;
plot(recall2, precision2, 'LineWidth', 4); hold off;
```

Practice Exercise 9.8. Suppose that the decision rule is a blind guess:

$$\delta(y) = \begin{cases} 1, & \text{with probability } \alpha, \\ 0, & \text{with probability } 1 - \alpha, \end{cases}$$

Plot the ROC curve and the PR curve.

Solution: As we have shown earlier, $p_F(\alpha)$ and $p_D(\alpha)$ for this decision rule are $p_F(\alpha) = \alpha$ and $p_D(\alpha) = \alpha$. Therefore,

$$\text{precision} = \frac{p_D}{p_D + p_F} = \frac{\alpha}{\alpha + \alpha} = \frac{1}{2}, \quad \text{and} \quad \text{recall} = p_D = \alpha.$$

Thus the PR curve is a straight line with a level of 0.5.

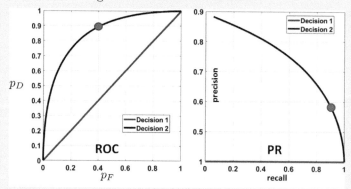

Figure 9.32: The PR curve of a blind-guess decision rule is a straight line.

Practice Exercise 9.9. Convert the ROC curve in **Figure 9.30** to a PR curve.

Solution: The conversion is done by first computing p_F and p_D. Defining the precision and recall in terms of p_F and p_D, we plot the PR curves below.

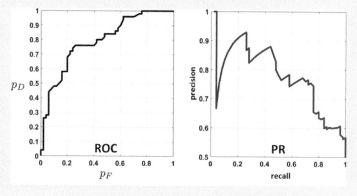

Figure 9.33: The PR curve of a real dataset.

As you can see from the figure, the PR curve behaves very differently from the ROC curve. It is sometimes argued that the two curves can be interpreted differently, even though they describe the same decision rule for the same dataset.

9.6 Summary

In this chapter, we have discussed five principles for quantifying the confidence of an estimator and making statistical decisions. To summarize the chapter, we clarify a few common misconceptions about these topics.

- **Confidence interval.** Students frequently become confused about the meaning of a confidence interval. It is not the interval that 95% of the samples will fall inside. It is also not the interval within which the estimator has a 95% chance to show up. A confidence interval is a **random interval** that has a 95% chance of including the population parameter. A better way to think about a confidence interval is to think of it as an alternative to a point estimate. A point estimate only gives a point, whereas a confidence interval extends the point to an interval. All the randomness of the point estimate is also there in the confidence interval. However, if the confidence interval is narrow, there is a good chance for the point estimate to be accurate.

- **Bootstrapping.** The most common misconception about bootstrapping is that it can create something from nothing. Another misconception is that bootstrapping can make your estimates better. Both beliefs are wrong. Bootstrapping is a technique for estimating the estimator's variance, and consequently it provides a confidence interval. Bootstrapping does not improve the point estimate, no matter how many bootstrapping samples you synthesize. Bootstrapping works because the sampling with the replacement step is equivalent to drawing samples from the empirical distribution. The whole process relies on the proximity between the empirical distribution and the true population. If you do not have enough samples and the empirical distribution does not approximate the population, bootstrapping will not work. Therefore, bootstrapping does not create something from nothing; it uses whatever you have and tells you how reliable the estimate is.

- **Hypothesis testing.** Students are often overwhelmed at first by the great number of tests one can use for hypothesis testing, e.g., p-value, critical value, Z-test, T-test, χ^2 test, F-test, etc. Our advice is to forget about them and remember that hypothesis testing is a court trial. Your job is to decide whether you have enough evidence to declare that the defendant is guilty. To reach a guilty verdict, you need to make sure that the test statistic is unlikely to happen. Therefore, the best practice is to draw the distributions of the test statistic and ask yourself how likely is it that the test statistic has such a value. When you draw the pictures of the distributions, you will know whether you should use a Gaussian Z, a Student's t, a χ^2, a F-statistic, etc. When you examine the likelihood of the test statistic, you will know whether you want to use the p-value or the critical value. If you follow this principle, you will never be confused by the oceans of tests you find in the textbooks.

- **Neyman-Pearson.** Beginners often find Neyman-Pearson abstract and do not understand why it is useful. In this chapter, however, we have explained why we need to understand Neyman-Pearson. It is a very general framework for many kinds of hypothesis testing problems. All it says is that if we want to maximize the detection rate while maintaining the false alarm rate, then the optimal testing procedure boils down to the critical-value test and the p-value test. This gives us a certificate that our usual hypothesis testing is optimal according to the Neyman-Pearson framework.

- **ROC and PR curves.** On the internet nowadays there is a huge quantity of articles, blogs, and tutorials about **how** to plot the ROC curve and the PR curve. Often these curves are explained through programming examples such as Python, R, or MATLAB. Our advice for studying the ROC curve and the PR curve is to go back to the Neyman-Pearson framework. These two curves do not come out of the blue. The ROC curve is the natural figure explaining the objective and the constraint in the Neyman-Pearson framework. By changing the coordinates, we obtain the PR curve. Therefore, the two curves are the same in terms of the amount of information, but they offer different interpretations.

9.7 References

Confidence Interval

9-1 Dimitri P. Bertsekas and John N. Tsitsiklis, *Introduction to Probability*, Athena Scientific, 2nd Edition, 2008. Chapter 9.1.

9-2 Michael J Evans and Jeffrey S. Rosenthal, *Probability and Statistics*, W. H. Freeman, 2nd Edition, 2009. Chapter 6.3.

9-3 Robert V. Hogg, Joseph W. McKean, and Allen T. Craig, *Introduction to Mathematical Statistics*, Pearson, 7th Edition, 2013. Chapter 4.2.

9-4 Larry Wasserman, *All of Statistics*, Springer 2003. Chapter 6.

9-5 Alberto Leon-Garcia, *Probability, Statistics, and Random Processes for Electrical Engineering*, Prentice Hall, 3rd Edition, 2008. Chapter 8.4.

Bootstrapping

9-6 Trevor Hastie, Robert Tibshirani, and Jerome Friedman, *Elements of Statistical Learning*, Springer, 2nd Edition. Chapter 8.2.

9-7 Larry Wasserman, *All of Statistics*, Springer 2003. Chapter 8.

9-8 Michael J Evans and Jeffrey S. Rosenthal, *Probability and Statistics*, W. H. Freeman, 2nd Edition, 2009. Chapter 6.4.

9-9 Robert V. Hogg, Joseph W. McKean, and Allen T. Craig, *Introduction to Mathematical Statistics*, Pearson, 7th Edition, 2013. Chapter 4.9.

Hypothesis Testing

9-10 Robert V. Hogg, Joseph W. McKean, and Allen T. Craig, *Introduction to Mathematical Statistics*, Pearson, 7th Edition, 2013. Chapter 4.5.

9-11 Athanasios Papoulis and S. Unnikrishna Pillai, *Probability, Random Variables and Stochastic Processes*, McGraw-Hill, 4th Edition, 2001. Chapter 8.

9-12 Alberto Leon-Garcia, *Probability, Statistics, and Random Processes for Electrical Engineering*, Prentice Hall, 3rd Edition, 2008. Chapter 8.5.

9-13 Dimitri P. Bertsekas and John N. Tsitsiklis, *Introduction to Probability*, Athena Scientific, 2nd Edition, 2008. Chapter 9.

9-14 Michael J Evans and Jeffrey S. Rosenthal, *Probability and Statistics*, W. H. Freeman, 2nd Edition, 2009. Chapter 6.3.

9-15 Larry Wasserman, *All of Statistics*, Springer 2003. Chapter 10.

9-16 Laura Simon, *Introduction to Mathematical Statistics*, Penn State University STAT 415 Textbook, Online materials. Accessed 12/2020. `https://online.stat.psu.edu/stat415/`

Neyman-Pearson and ROC curves

9-17 Robert V. Hogg, Joseph W. McKean, and Allen T. Craig, *Introduction to Mathematical Statistics*, Pearson, 7th Edition, 2013. Chapter 8.

9-18 H. Vincent Poor, *An Introduction Signal Detection and Estimation*, Springer, 1998.

9-19 Bernard C. Levy, *Principles of Signal Detection and Parameter Estimation*, Springer, 2008.

9-20 Steven M. Kay, *Fundamentals of Statistical Signal Processing: Estimation Theory*, Prentice-Hall, 1993.

9-21 Steven M. Kay, *Fundamentals of Statistical Signal Processing: Detection Theory*, Prentice-Hall, 1998.

9.8 Problems

Exercise 1.
Consider i.i.d. Gaussian random variables $X_1, \ldots, X_N$ with an unknown mean θ and a known variance $\sigma^2 = 1$. Suppose $N = 30$. Find the confidence level $1 - \alpha$ for the confidence intervals of the mean $\widehat{\Theta}$:

(a) $\mathcal{I} = [\widehat{\Theta} - \frac{2.14\sigma}{\sqrt{N}}, \widehat{\Theta} + \frac{2.14\sigma}{\sqrt{N}}]$

(b) $\mathcal{I} = [\widehat{\Theta} - \frac{1.85\sigma}{\sqrt{N}}, \widehat{\Theta} + \frac{1.85\sigma}{\sqrt{N}}]$

Exercise 2.

Suppose that we have conducted an experiment with $N = 100$ samples. A 95% confidence interval of the mean was $0.45 \leq \mu \leq 0.82$.

(a) Would a 99% confidence interval calculated from the sample data be wider or narrower?

(b) Is it correct to interpret the confidence interval as saying that there is a 95% chance that μ is between 0.49 and 0.82? You may answer yes, no, or partially correct. Explain.

(c) Is it correct to say that if we conduct the experiment 1000 times, there will be 950 confidence intervals that will contain μ? You may answer yes, no, or partially correct. Explain.

Exercise 3.

Suppose that we have conducted an experiment. We know that $\sigma = 25$. We obtained $N = 20$ samples and found that the sample mean is $\widehat{\Theta} = 1014$.

(a) Construct a 95% two-sided confidence interval of $\widehat{\Theta}$.

(b) Construct a 95% one-sided confidence interval (the lower tail) of $\widehat{\Theta}$.

Exercise 4.

Let $X_1, \ldots, X_N$ be i.i.d. Gaussian with $X_n \sim \text{Gaussian}(0, 1)$. Let $Y_n = e^{X_n}$, and suppose we have $N = 100$ samples. We want to compute a 95% confidence interval for skewness.

(a) Randomly subsample the dataset with $B = 30$ samples. Repeat the exercise 5 times. Plot the resulting histograms using MATLAB or Python.

(b) Repeat (a) for $M = 500$ times and compute the 95% bootstrapped confidence interval of the skewness.

(c) Try using a larger $B = 70$ and a smaller $B = 10$. Report the 95% bootstrapped confidence interval of the skewness.

Exercise 5.

Let $X_1, \ldots, X_N$ be i.i.d. uniform with $X_n \sim \text{Uniform}(0, \theta)$. Let $\widehat{\Theta} = \max\{X_1, \ldots, X_N\}$. Generate a dataset of $N = 50$ with $\theta = 1$.

(a) Find the distribution of the estimator $\widehat{\Theta}$.

(b) Show that $\mathbb{P}[\widehat{\Theta} = \theta] = 1 - (1 - (1/n))^N$. Thus, as $N \to \infty$, we have $\mathbb{P}[\widehat{\Theta} = \theta] = 0$.

(c) Use Python or MATLAB to generate the histogram of $\widehat{\Theta}$ from bootstrapping. How does the bootstrapped histogram look as N grows? Why?

Exercise 6.

Let X be a Gaussian random variable with unknown mean and unknown variance. It was found that with $N = 15$,

$$\sum_{n=1}^{N} X_n = 250, \qquad \sum_{n=1}^{N} X_n^2 = 10000.$$

Find a 95% confidence interval of the mean of X.

Exercise 7.
Let $\widehat{\Theta}$ be the sample mean of a dataset containing N samples. It is known that the samples are drawn from Gaussian$(\theta, 3^2)$. Find N such that

$$\mathbb{P}[\widehat{\Theta} - 1 \leq \theta \leq \widehat{\Theta} + 1] = 0.95.$$

Exercise 8.
Which of the following statements are valid hypothesis testing problems?

(a) H_0: $\mu = 25$ and H_1: $\mu \neq 25$.

(b) H_0: $\sigma > 10$ and H_1: $\sigma = 10$.

(c) H_0: $\overline{X} = 50$ and H_1: $\overline{X} \neq 50$.

(d) H_0: p-value $= 0.1$, H_1: p-value $= 0.5$.

Exercise 9.
It is claimed that the mean is $\theta = 12$ with a standard deviation 0.5. Consider H_0: $\theta = 12$ and H_1: $\theta < 12$. Ten samples are obtained, and it is found that $\widehat{\Theta} = 13.5$. With a 95% confidence level, should we accept or reject the null hypothesis?

Exercise 10.
Consider a hypothesis testing problem: H_0: $\theta = 175$ versus an alternative hypothesis H_1: $\theta > 175$. Assume $N = 10$ and $\sigma = 20$.

(a) Find the type 1 error if the critical region is $\widehat{\Theta} > 185$.

(b) Find the type 2 error if the true mean is 195.

Exercise 11.
Consider H_0: $\theta = 30000$ versus an alternative hypothesis H_1: $\theta > 30000$. Suppose $N = 16$, and let $\sigma = 1500$.

(a) If we want $\alpha = 0.01$, what is z_α?

(b) What is the type 2 error when $\theta = 31000$?

Exercise 12.
Let $W_n \sim$ Gaussian$(0, \sigma^2)$, and consider two hypotheses:

$$\begin{aligned}
H_0: & \quad X_n = \theta_0 + W_n, \quad n = 1, \ldots, N, \\
H_1: & \quad X_n = \theta_1 + W_n, \quad n = 1, \ldots, N.
\end{aligned}$$

Let $\overline{X} = (1/N) \sum_{n=1}^{N} X_n$.

(a) Show that the likelihood of observing $X_1, \ldots, X_N$ given H_0 is

$$f_{\boldsymbol{X}}(\boldsymbol{x}|H_0) = \frac{1}{(2\pi\sigma^2)^{N/2}} \exp\left\{ -\frac{1}{2\sigma^2} \sum_{n=1}^{N}(X_n - \theta_0)^2 \right\}.$$

(b) Find the likelihood $f_{\boldsymbol{X}}(\boldsymbol{x}|H_1)$ of observing $X_1, \ldots, X_N$ given H_1.

(c) The likelihood ratio test states that

$$\frac{f_{\boldsymbol{X}}(\boldsymbol{x}|H_1)}{f_{\boldsymbol{X}}(\boldsymbol{x}|H_0)} \underset{H_0}{\overset{H_1}{\gtrless}} \tau.$$

Show that the likelihood ratio test is given by

$$\overline{X} \underset{H_0}{\overset{H_1}{\gtrless}} \frac{\theta_0 + \theta_1}{2} + \frac{\sigma^2 \log \tau}{N(\theta_1 - \theta_0)}.$$

Chapter 10

Random Processes

In modern data science, many problems involve time. The stock market changes every minute; a speech signal changes every millisecond; a car changes its steering angle constantly; the examples are endless. A common theme among all these examples is randomness. We do not know whether a stock will go up or down tomorrow, although we may be able to make some predictions based on previous observations. We do not know the next word of a sentence, but we can guess based on the context. Random processes are tools that can be applied to these situations. We treat a random process as an infinitely long vector of random variables where the correlations between the individual variables define the statistical properties of the process. If we can determine these correlations, we will be able to summarize the past and predict the future.

The objective of this chapter is to introduce the basic concepts of **random processes**. Given the breadth of the subject, we can only cover the most elementary results, but they are sufficient for many engineering and data science problems. However, there are complex situations for which these elementary results will be insufficient. The references at the end of this chapter contain more in-depth discussions of random processes.

Plan of this chapter

We begin by outlining the definition of random processes and ways to characterize their randomness in Section 10.1. In Section 10.2 we discuss the mean function, the autocorrelation function, and the autocovariance function of a random process. In Section 10.3 we look at a special subclass of random processes known as the wide-sense stationary processes. Wide-sense stationary processes allow us to use tools in the Fourier domain to make statistical statements. Based on wide-sense stationary processes, we discuss power spectral density in Section 10.4. With this concept, we can ask what will happen to the random process when we pass it through a linear transformation. In Section 10.5 we discuss such interactions between the random process and a linear time-invariant system. Finally, we discuss a practical usage of random processes in the subject of optimal linear filters in Section 10.6.

10.1 Basic Concepts

10.1.1 Everything you need to know about a random process

Here is the single most important thing you need to remember about random processes:

> **What is a random process?**
> A random process is a **function** indexed by a **random key**.

That's it. Now you may be wondering what exactly a "function indexed by a **random key**" means. To help you see the picture, we consider two examples.

> **Example 10.1.** We consider a set of straight lines. We define two random variables a and b that are uniformly distributed in a certain range. We then define a function:
>
> $$f(t) = at + b, \qquad -2 \le t \le 2. \qquad (10.1)$$
>
> Clearly, $f(t)$ is a function of time t. But since a and b are random, $f(t)$ is also random. The randomness is caused by a and b. To emphasize this dependency, we write $f(t)$ as
>
> $$f(t, \xi) = a(\xi)t + b(\xi), \qquad -2 \le t \le 2,$$
>
> where $\xi \in \Omega$ denotes the random index of the constants (a, b) and Ω is the sample space of ξ. Therefore, by picking a different pair of constants $(a(\xi), b(\xi))$, we will have a different function $f(t, \xi)$, which in our case is a straight line of different slope and y-intercept.
>
>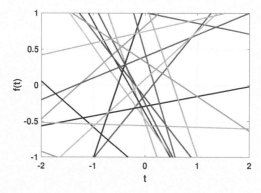
>
> Figure 10.1: The set of straight lines $f(x) = ax + b$ where $a, b \in \mathbb{R}$.
>
> As a special case of the example, suppose that the sample space contains only two pairs of constants: $(a, b) = (1.2, 0.6)$ and $(a, b) = (-0.75, 1.8)$. The probability of

getting either pair is $\frac{1}{2}$. Then the function $f(t, \xi)$ will take two forms:

$$f(t, \xi) = \begin{cases} 1.2t + 0.6, & \text{with probability } \frac{1}{2}, \\ -0.75t + 1.8, & \text{with probability } \frac{1}{2}. \end{cases}$$

Every time you pick a sample you pick one of the two functions, either $f(t, \xi_1)$ or $f(t, \xi_2)$. So we say that $f(t, \xi)$ is a random process because it is a function $f(t)$ indexed by a random key ξ.

Example 10.2. This example studies the function

$$f(t) = \cos(\omega_0 t + \Theta), \qquad -1 \leq t \leq 1,$$

where Θ is a random phase distributed uniformly over the range $[0, 2\pi]$. Depending on the randomness of Θ, the function $f(t)$ will take a different phase offset. To emphasize this dependency, we write

$$f(t, \xi) = \cos(\omega_0 t + \Theta(\xi)), \qquad -1 \leq t \leq 1. \tag{10.2}$$

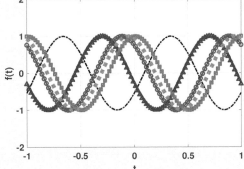

Figure 10.2: The set of phase-shifted cosines $f(t) = \cos(\omega_0 t + \theta)$ where $\theta \in [0, 2\pi]$.

Again, ξ denotes the index of the random variable Θ. Since Θ is drawn uniformly from the interval $[0, 2\pi]$, the following functions are two possible realizations:

$$f(t, \xi_1) = \cos\left(\omega_0 t + \frac{3\pi}{4}\right), \qquad -1 \leq t \leq 1,$$

$$f(t, \xi_2) = \cos\left(\omega_0 t - \frac{7\pi}{3}\right), \qquad -1 \leq t \leq 1.$$

Just as with the previous example, $f(t)$ is a function indexed by a random key ξ.

These two examples should give you a feeling for what to expect from a random process. A random process is quite similar to a random variable because they are both contained in a certain sample space. For (discrete) random variables, the sample space is a collection of outcomes $\{\xi_1, \xi_2, \ldots, \xi_N\}$. The random variable $X : \mathcal{F} \to \mathbb{R}$ is a mapping that maps ξ_n to $X(\xi_n)$, where $X(\xi_n)$ is a number. For random processes, the sample space is also

$\{\xi_1, \xi_2, \ldots, \xi_N\}$. However, the mapping X does not map ξ_n to a **number** $X(\xi_n)$ but to a **function** $X(t, \xi_n)$. A function has the time index t, which is absent in the number. Therefore, for the same ξ_n, $X(t_1, \xi_n)$ can take one value and $X(t_2, \xi_n)$ can take another value.

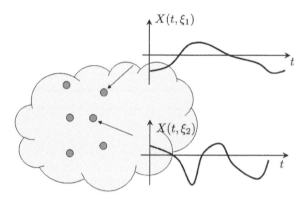

Figure 10.3: The sample space of a random process $X(t, \xi)$ contains many functions. Therefore, each random realization is a function.

Figure 10.3 shows the sample space of a random process. Each outcome in the sample space is a function. The probability of getting a function is specified by the probability mass or the probability density of the associated **random key** ξ. If you put your hand into the sample space, the sample you pick will be a function that will change with time and is indexed by the random key. From our discussions of joint random variables in Chapter 5, you can think of the function as a vector. When you pull a sample from the sample space, you pull the entire vector and not just an element.

10.1.2   Statistical and temporal perspectives

Since a random process is a function indexed by a random key, it is a two-dimensional object. It is a function both of time t and of the random key ξ. That's why we use the notation $X(t, \xi)$ to denote a random process. These two axes play different roles, as illustrated in **Figure 10.4**.

Temporal perspective: Let us fix the random key at $\xi = \xi_0$. This gives us a function $X(t, \xi_0)$. Since ξ is already fixed at ξ_0, we are looking at a particular realization drawn from the sample space. This realization is expressed as a function $X(t, \xi_0)$, which is just a deterministic function that evolves over time. There is no randomness associated with it. This is analogous to a random variable. While X itself is a random variable, by fixing the random key $\xi = \xi_0$, $X(\xi_0)$ is just a real number. For random processes, $X(t, \xi_0)$ now becomes a function.

Since $X(t, \xi_0)$ is a function that evolves over time, we view it along the **horizontal** axis. For example, we can study the sequence

$$X(t_1, \xi_0), X(t_2, \xi_0), \ldots, X(t_K, \xi_0),$$

where $t_1, \ldots, t_K$ are the time indices of the function. This sequence is deterministic and is just a sequence of numbers, although the numbers evolve as t changes.

Statistical perspective: The other perspective, which could be slightly more abstract, is the statistical perspective. Let us fix the time at $t = t_0$. The random key ξ can take any

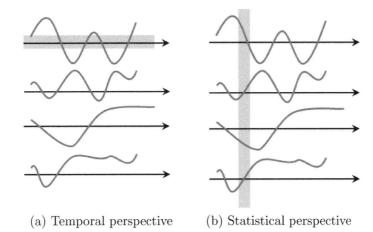

(a) Temporal perspective   (b) Statistical perspective

Figure 10.4: Temporal and statistical perspectives of a random process. For the temporal perspective (which we call the horizontal perspective), we fix the random key ξ and look at the function in **time**. For the statistical perspective (which we call the vertical perspective), we fix the time and look at the function at different **random keys**.

state defined in the sample space. So if the sample space contains $\{\xi_1, \ldots, \xi_N\}$, the sequence $\{X(t_0, \xi_1), \ldots, X(t_0, \xi_N)\}$ is a sequence of random variables, because the ξ's can go from one state to another state.

A good way to visualize the statistical perspective is the **vertical** perspective in which we write the sequence as a vertical column of random variables:

$$X(t_0, \xi_1)$$
$$X(t_0, \xi_2)$$
$$\vdots$$
$$X(t_0, \xi_N)$$

That is, if you fix the time at $t = t_0$, you are getting a sequence of random variables. The probability of getting a particular value $X(t_0)$ depends on which random state you land on.

Why do we bother to differentiate the temporal perspective and the statistical perspective? The reason is that the operations associated with the two are different, even if sometimes they give you the same result. For example, if we take the **temporal average** of the random process, we get a number:

$$\overline{X}(\xi) = \frac{1}{T} \int_0^T X(t, \xi)\, dt. \tag{10.3}$$

We call this the "temporal average" because we have integrated the function over time. The resulting value will not change with time. However, $\overline{X}(\xi)$ depends on the random key you provide. If you pick a different random realization, $\overline{X}(\xi)$ will take a different value. So the temporal average is a **random variable**.

On the other hand, if we take the statistical average of the random process, we get

$$\mathbb{E}[X(t)] = \int_\Omega X(t, \xi)\, p(\xi)\, d\xi, \tag{10.4}$$

617

where $p(\xi)$ is the PDF of the random key ξ. We call this the **statistical average** because we have taken the expectation over all possible random keys. The resulting object $\mathbb{E}[X(t)]$ is deterministic but a function of time.

No matter how you look at the temporal average or the statistical average, they are different with the following exception: that $\overline{X}(\xi) = \text{const}$ and $\mathbb{E}[X(t)] = \text{const}$, for example, $\overline{X}(\xi) = \mathbb{E}[X(t)] = 0$. This happens only for some special (and useful) random processes known as **ergodic** processes that allow us to approximate the statistical average using the temporal average, with some guarantees derived from the law of large numbers. We will return to this point later.

Example 10.3. Let $A \sim \text{Uniform}[0,1]$. Define

$$X(t,\xi) = A(\xi)\cos(2\pi t).$$

In this example, the magnitude $A(\xi)$ is a random variable depending on the random key ξ. For example if we draw ξ_1, perhaps we will get a value $A(\xi_1) = 0.5$. Then $X(t,\xi_1) = 0.5\cos(2\pi t)$. To take another example, if we draw ξ_2, we may get $A(\xi_2) = 1$. Then $X(t,\xi_2) = 1\cos(2\pi t)$. **Figure 10.5** shows a few random realizations of the cosines. We can look at $X(t,\xi)$ from the statistical and the temporal views.

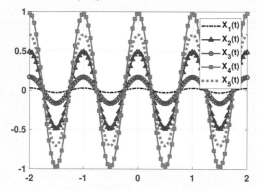

Figure 10.5: Five different realizations of the random process $X(t) = A\cos(2\pi t)$.

- **Statistical View**: Fix t (for example $t = 10$). In this case, we have

$$X(t,\xi) = A(\xi)\cos(2\pi(10))$$
$$= A(\xi)\cos(20\pi),$$

which is a random variable because $\cos(20\pi)$ is a constant. The randomness of X comes from the fact that $A(\xi) \sim \text{Uniform}[0,1]$.

- **Temporal View**: Fix ξ (for example $A(\xi) = 0.7$). In this case, we have

$$X(t,\xi) = 0.7\cos(2\pi t),$$

which is a deterministic function of t.

Example 10.4. Let A be a discrete random variable with a PMF

$$\mathbb{P}(A = +1) = \frac{1}{2} \quad \text{and} \quad \mathbb{P}(A = -1) = \frac{1}{2}.$$

We define the function $X[n, \xi] = A(\xi)(-1)^n$. In this example, A can only take two states. If $A = +1$, then $X[n, \xi] = (-1)^n$. If $A = -1$, then $X[n, \xi] = (-1)^{n+1}$.

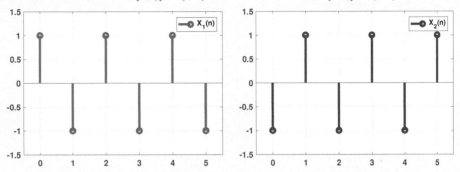

Figure 10.6: Realizations of the random process $X[n] = A(-1)^n$.

The graphical illustration of this example is shown in **Figure 10.6**. Again, we can look at $X[n, \xi]$ from two views.

- **Statistical View**: Fix n, say $n = 10$. Then,

$$X(\xi) = \begin{cases} (-1)^{10} = 1, & \text{with prob } 1/2, \\ (-1)^{11} = -1, & \text{with prob } 1/2, \end{cases}$$

  which is a Bernoulli random variable.

- **Temporal View**: Fix ξ. Then,

$$X[n] = \begin{cases} (-1)^n, & \text{if } A = +1, \\ (-1)^{n+1}, & \text{if } A = -1, \end{cases}$$

  which is a time series.

In this example, we see that the sample space of $X(n, \xi)$ consists of only two functions with probabilities

$$\mathbb{P}(X[n] = (-1)^n) = \frac{1}{2},$$

$$\mathbb{P}(X[n] = (-1)^{n+1}) = \frac{1}{2},$$

Therefore, if there is a sequence outside the sample space, e.g.,

$$\mathbb{P}\left(X[n] = \begin{bmatrix} 1 & 1 & 1 & -1 & 1 & -1 & \cdots \end{bmatrix}\right) = 0$$

then the probability of obtaining that sequence is 0.

What do we mean by statistical average and temporal average?

- Statistical average: Take the expectation of $X(t,\xi)$ over ξ. This is the vertical average.

- Temporal average: Take the expectation of $X(t,\xi)$ over t. This is the horizontal average.

- In general, statistical average $\neq$ temporal average.

10.2 Mean and Correlation Functions

Given a random variable, we often want to know the expectation and variance, and often we also want to know the expectation and variance for the random processes. Nevertheless, we need to consider the time axis. In this section, we discuss the **mean function** and the **autocorrelation function**.

10.2.1 Mean function

Definition 10.1. *The* **mean function** $\mu_X(t)$ *of a random process* $X(t)$ *is*

$$\mu_X(t) = \mathbb{E}\left[X(t)\right]. \tag{10.5}$$

Let's consider the "expectation" of $X(t)$. Recall that a random process is actually $X(t,\xi)$ where ξ is the random key. Therefore, the expectation is taken with respect to ξ, or to state it more explicitly,

$$\mu_X(t) = \mathbb{E}[X(t)] = \int_\Omega X(t,\xi) \, p(\xi) \, d\xi,$$

where $p(\xi)$ is the PDF of the random key. This is an abstract definition, but it is not difficult to understand if you follow the example below.

Example 10.5. Let $A \sim \text{Uniform}[0,1]$, and let $X(t) = A\cos(2\pi t)$. Find $\mu_X(t)$.

Solution. The solution to this problem is actually very simple:

$$\mu_X(t) = \mathbb{E}[X(t)] = \mathbb{E}[A\cos(2\pi t)]$$

$$= \cos(2\pi t)\mathbb{E}[A] = \frac{1}{2}\cos(2\pi t).$$

So the answer is $\mu_X(t) = \frac{1}{2}\cos(2\pi t)$.

We can link the equations to the definition more explicitly. To do so, we rewrite $X(t)$ as

$$X(t,\xi) = A(\xi)\cos(2\pi t).$$

Then we take the expectation over A:

$$\mu_X(t) = \int_\Omega X(t,a)\, p_A(a)\, da = \int_0^1 a\cos(2\pi t)\cdot 1\, da$$

$$= \cos(2\pi t)\left[\frac{a^2}{2}\right]_0^1 = \frac{1}{2}\cos(2\pi t).$$

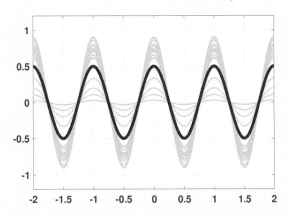

Figure 10.7: The mean function of $X(t) = A\cos(2\pi t)$.

An illustration is provided in **Figure 10.7**, in which we observe many random realizations of the random process $X(t,\xi)$. On top of these, we also see the mean function. The way to visualize the mean function is to use the **statistical perspective**. That is, fix a time t and look at all the possible values that the function can take. For example, if we fix $t = t_0$, then we will have a set of realizations of one random variable:

$$\left\{0.71\cos(2\pi t_0),\, 0.58\cos(2\pi t_0),\, \ldots,\, 0.93\cos(2\pi t_0)\right\} \rightarrow \text{take expectation}$$

Therefore, when we take the expectation, it is that of the underlying random variable. If we move to another timestamp $t = t_1$, we will have a different expectation because $\cos(2\pi t_0)$ now becomes $\cos(2\pi t_1)$.

The MATLAB/Python codes used to generate **Figure 10.7** are shown below. You can also replace the line `0.5*cos(2*pi*t)` by the mean function `mean(X)` (in MATLAB).

```
% MATLAB code for Example 10.5
x = zeros(1000,20);
t = linspace(-2,2,1000);
for i=1:20
    X(:,i) = rand(1)*cos(2*pi*t);
end
plot(t, X, 'LineWidth', 2, 'Color', [0.8 0.8 0.8]); hold on;
plot(t, 0.5*cos(2*pi*t), 'LineWidth', 4, 'Color', [0.6 0 0]);
```

```
# Python code for Example 10.5
x = np.zeros((1000,20))
```

```
t = np.linspace(-2,2,1000)
for i in range(20):
  x[:,i] = np.random.rand(1)*np.cos(2*np.pi*t)
plt.plot(t,x,color='gray')
plt.plot(t,0.5*np.cos(2*np.pi*t),color='red')
plt.show()
```

Example 10.6. Let $\Theta \sim \text{Uniform}[-\pi, \pi]$, and let $X(t) = \cos(\omega t + \Theta)$. Find $\mu_X(t)$.

Solution.

$$\mu_X(t) = \mathbb{E}\left[\cos(\omega t + \Theta)\right] = \int_{-\pi}^{\pi} \cos(\omega t + \theta) \cdot \frac{1}{2\pi} \, d\theta = 0.$$

Again, as in the previous example, we can try to map this simple calculation with the definition. Write $X(t)$ as

$$X(t, \xi) = \cos(\omega t + \Theta(\xi)).$$

Then the expectation is

$$\mu_X(t) = \int_{\Omega} \cos(\omega t + \theta) p_\Theta(\theta) \, d\theta$$

$$= \int_{-\pi}^{\pi} \cos(\omega t + \theta) \cdot \frac{1}{2\pi} \, d\theta = 0.$$

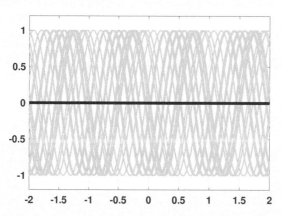

Figure 10.8: The mean function of $X(t) = \cos(\omega t + \Theta)$.

Figure 10.8 illustrates the random realizations for $X(t) = \cos(\omega t + \Theta)$ and the mean function. The zero mean should not be a surprise because if we take the **statistical average** (the vertical average) across all the possible values at any time instant, the positive and negative values of the realizations will make the mean zero.

We should emphasize that the statistical average is not the same as the temporal average, even if they give you the same value. Why do we say that? If we calculate the **temporal average** of the function $\cos(\omega t + \theta_0)$ for a specific value $\Theta = \theta_0$, then we have

$$\overline{X} = \frac{1}{T} \int_0^T \cos(\omega t + \theta_0)\, dt = 0,$$

assuming that T is a multiple of the cosine period. This implies that the temporal average is zero, which is the same as the statistical average. This gives us an example in which the statistical average and the temporal average have the same value, although we know they are two completely different things.

The MATLAB/Python codes used to generate **Figure 10.8** are shown below.

```
% MATLAB code for Example 10.6
x = zeros(1000,20);
t = linspace(-2,2,1000);
for i=1:20
X(:,i) = cos(2*pi*t+2*pi*rand(1));
end
plot(t, X, 'LineWidth', 2, 'Color', [0.8 0.8 0.8]); hold on;
plot(t, 0*cos(2*pi*t), 'LineWidth', 4, 'Color', [0.6 0 0]);
```

```
# Python code for Example 10.6
x = np.zeros((1000,20))
t = np.linspace(-2,2,1000)
for i in range(20):
  Theta = 2*np.pi*(np.random.rand(1))
  x[:,i] = np.cos(2*np.pi*t+Theta)
plt.plot(t,x,color='gray')
plt.plot(t,np.zeros((1000,1)),color='red')
plt.show()
```

Example 10.7. Let us consider a discrete-time random process. Let $X[n] = S^n$, where $S \sim$ Uniform$[0, 1]$. Find $\mu_X[n]$.

$$\mu_X[n] = \mathbb{E}[s^n] = \int_0^1 s^n\, ds = \frac{1}{n+1}.$$

In this example the randomness goes with the constant s. Thus, if we write $X[n]$ as

$$X[n, \xi] = [S(\xi)]^n,$$

the expectation is

$$\mathbb{E}[X[n]] = \int_\Omega s^n p_S(s)\, ds = \int_0^1 s^n \cdot 1\, ds = \frac{1}{n+1}.$$

The graphical illustration is provided in **Figure 10.9**.

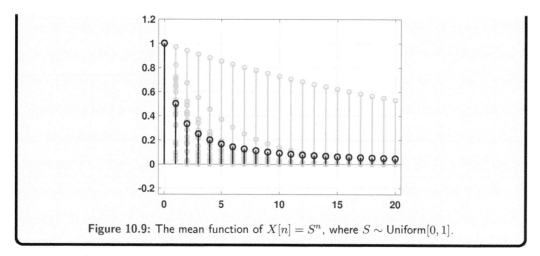

Figure 10.9: The mean function of $X[n] = S^n$, where $S \sim \text{Uniform}[0,1]$.

The MATLAB code used to generate **Figure 10.9** is shown below. We skip the Python implementation because it is straightforward.

```
% MATLAB code for Example 10.7
t = 0:20;
for i=1:20
    X(:,i) = rand(1).^t;
end
stem(t, X, 'LineWidth', 2, 'Color', [0.8 0.8 0.8]); hold on;
stem(t, 1./(t+1), 'LineWidth', 2, 'MarkerSize', 8);
```

10.2.2 Autocorrelation function

In random processes, the notions of "variance" and "covariance" are trickier than for random variables. Let us first define the concept of an **autocorrelation function**.

Definition 10.2. *The* **autocorrelation function** *of a random process* $X(t)$ *is*

$$R_X(t_1, t_2) = \mathbb{E}\left[X(t_1)X(t_2)\right]. \tag{10.6}$$

$R_X(t_1, t_2)$ is not difficult to calculate — just integrate $X(t_1)X(t_2)$ using the appropriate PDFs.

Example 10.8. Let $A \sim \text{Uniform}[0,1]$, $X(t) = A\cos(2\pi t)$. Find $R_X(t_1, t_2)$.

Solution.

$$R_X(t_1, t_2) = \mathbb{E}\left[A\cos(2\pi t_1)A\cos(2\pi t_2)\right]$$
$$= \mathbb{E}[A^2]\cos(2\pi t_1)\cos(2\pi t_2) = \frac{1}{3}\cos(2\pi t_1)\cos(2\pi t_2).$$

Example 10.9. Let $\Theta \sim$Uniform$[-\pi, \pi]$, $X(t) = \cos(\omega t + \Theta)$. Find $R_X(t_1, t_2)$.

Solution.

$$R_X(t_1, t_2) = \mathbb{E}\left[\cos(\omega t_1 + \Theta)\cos(\omega t_2 + \Theta)\right]$$

$$= \frac{1}{2\pi}\int_{-\pi}^{\pi}\cos(\omega t_1 + \theta)\cos(\omega t_2 + \theta)\,d\theta$$

$$\overset{(a)}{=} \frac{1}{2\pi}\int_{-\pi}^{\pi}\frac{1}{2}\left[\cos(\omega(t_1 + t_2) + 2\theta) + \cos(\omega(t_1 - t_2))\right]\,d\theta$$

$$= \frac{1}{2}\cos\left(\omega(t_1 - t_2)\right),$$

where in (a) we applied the trigonometric formula $\cos A \cos B = \frac{1}{2}[\cos(A+B)+\cos(A-B)]$.

As you can see, the calculations are not difficult. The tricky thing is the interpretation of $R_X(t_1, t_2)$.

How do we understand the meaning of $\mathbb{E}[X(t_1)X(t_2)]$?

$\mathbb{E}[X(t_1)X(t_2)]$ is analogous to the correlation $\mathbb{E}[XY]$ between X and Y.

The autocorrelation function $\mathbb{E}[X(t_1)X(t_2)]$ is analogous to the correlation $\mathbb{E}[XY]$ in relation to a pair of random variables. In our discussions of $\mathbb{E}[XY]$, we mentioned that $\mathbb{E}[XY]$ could be regarded as the inner product of two vectors, and so it is a measure of the closeness between X and Y. Now, if we substitute X and Y with $X(t_1)$ and $X(t_2)$ respectively, then we are effectively asking about the closeness between $X(t_1)$ and $X(t_2)$. So, in a nutshell, the autocorrelation function tells us the correlation between the function at two different time stamps.

What do we mean by the correlation between two timestamps? Remember that $X(t_1)$ and $X(t_2)$ are two random variables. Consider the following example.

Example 10.10. Let $X(t) = A\cos(2\pi t)$, where $A \sim$ Uniform$[0, 1]$. Find $\mathbb{E}[X(0)X(0.5)]$.

Solution. If $X(t) = A\cos(2\pi t)$, then

$$X(0) = A\cos(0) = A,$$
$$X(0.5) = A\cos(\pi) = -A.$$

When you have two random variables, you consider their correlations. Using this example, we have that

$$\mathbb{E}[X(0)X(0.5)] = -\mathbb{E}[A \cdot A] = -\mathbb{E}[A^2] = -\frac{1}{3}.$$

A picture will reveal what is happening. **Figure 10.10** presents the realizations of the random process $X(t) = A\cos(2\pi t)$. If we consider $X(0)$ and $X(0.5)$, each of them is a

625

random variable, and thus we can ask about their PDFs. It is obvious from the illustration that the random variable $X(0)$ has a PDF that is a uniform distribution from 0 to 1, whereas the random variable $X(0.5)$ has a PDF that is a uniform distribution from -1 to 0. Mathematically, the PDFs are

$$f_{X(0)}(x) = \begin{cases} 1, & 0 \le x \le 1, \\ 0, & \text{otherwise} \end{cases} \quad \text{and} \quad f_{X(0.5)}(x) = \begin{cases} 1, & -1 \le x \le 0, \\ 0, & \text{otherwise.} \end{cases}$$

Since $X(0)$ and $X(0.5)$ have their own PDFs, we can calculate their correlation. This will give us $\mathbb{E}[X(0)X(0.5)]$ which after some calculations is $\mathbb{E}[X(0)X(0.5)] = -\frac{1}{3}$.

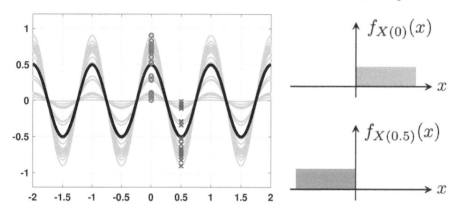

Figure 10.10: The autocorrelation between $X(0)$ and $X(0.5)$ should be regarded as the correlation between two random variables. Each random variable has its own PDF.

We can now consider the autocorrelation for any t_1 and t_2. When you are evaluating the autocorrelation function, you are not just evaluating at $t = 0$ and $t = 0.5$, you are also evaluating the correlation for all pairs of t_1 and t_2. Now you want to know what the correlation is between $t = 0$ and $t = 0.5$, $t = 2$ and $t = 3.1$, etc. Of course, there are infinitely many pairs of time instants. The point of the autocorrelation function is to tell you the correlation of **all** the pairs. In other words, if we tell you $R_X(t_1, t_2)$, you will be able to plug in a value of t_1 and a value of t_2 and tell us the correlation at (t_1, t_2). How is this possible? To find out, let's consider the following example.

Example 10.11. Let $A \sim \text{Uniform}[0, 1]$, $X(t) = A \cos(2\pi t)$. Find $R_X(0, 0.5)$, and draw $R_X(t_1, t_2)$.

Solution. From the previous example, we know that

$$R_X(t_1, t_2) = \frac{1}{3} \cos(2\pi t_1) \cos(2\pi t_2).$$

Therefore, $R_X(0, 0.5) = \frac{1}{3} \cos(2\pi 0) \cos(2\pi 0.5) = -\frac{1}{3}$, which is the same as if we had computed it from the first principle.

The autocorrelation function tells you how one point of a time series is correlated with another point of the time series. If $R_X(t_1, t_2)$ gives a high value, then it means the random variables at t_1 and t_2 have a strong correlation. To understand this, suppose we let $t_1 = 0$, and let us vary t_2. Then

$$R_X(0, t_2) = \frac{1}{3}\cos(2\pi 0)\cos(2\pi t_2)$$

$$= \frac{1}{3}\cos(2\pi t_2).$$

This is a periodic function that cycles through itself whenever t_2 is an integer. As we recall from **Figure 10.10**, if $t_2 = 0.5$, the random variable $X(t_2)$ will take only the negative values, but otherwise it is correlated with $X(0)$. On the other hand, if $t_2 = 0.25$, then **Figure 10.10** says that the random variable $X(t_2)$ is a constant 0, and so the correlation with $X(0)$ is zero.

Clearly, $R_X(t_1, t_2)$ is a 2-dimensional function of t_1 and t_2. You need to tell R_X which of the two time instants you want to compare, and then R_X will tell you the correlation. So no matter what happens, you must specify two time instants. Because $R_X(t_1, t_2)$ is a 2-dimensional function, we can visualize it by calculating all the possible values it takes. For example, if $R_X(t_1, t_2) = \frac{1}{3}\cos(2\pi t_1)\cos(2\pi t_2)$, we can plot R_X as a function of t_1 and t_2. **Figure 10.11** shows the plot.

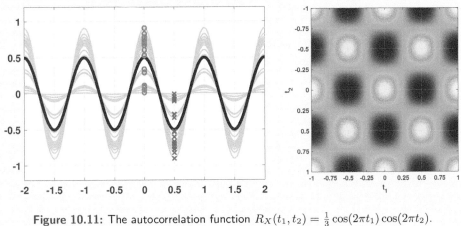

Figure 10.11: The autocorrelation function $R_X(t_1, t_2) = \frac{1}{3}\cos(2\pi t_1)\cos(2\pi t_2)$.

The MATLAB/Python code for **Figure 10.11** is shown below.

```
% MATLAB code for Example 10.11
t = linspace(-1,1,1000);
R = (1/3)*cos(2*pi*t(:)).*cos(2*pi*t);
imagesc(t,t,R);
```

```
# Python code for Example 10.11
import numpy as np
import matplotlib.pyplot as plt
t = np.linspace(-1,1,1000)
R = (1/3)*np.outer(np.cos(2*np.pi*t), np.cos(2*np.pi*t))
plt.imshow(R, extent=[-1, 1, -1, 1])
plt.show()
```

To understand the 2D function shown on the right hand side of **Figure 10.11**, we can take a closer look by drawing **Figure 10.12**. For any two time instants t_1 and t_2, we have two random variables $X(t_1)$ and $X(t_2)$. The joint expectation $\mathbb{E}[X(t_1)X(t_2)]$ will return us some value, and this is a point in the 2D plot $R_X(t_1, t_2)$. The value tells us the correlation between $X(t_1)$ and $X(t_2)$. In the example in which $t_1 = 0$ and $t_2 = 0.5$, the correlation is $-\frac{1}{3}$. Interestingly, if we pick another pair of time instants $t_1 = -0.5$ and $t_2 = 0$, the joint expectation is $\mathbb{E}[X(-0.5)X(0)] = -\frac{1}{3}$, which is the same value. However, this $-\frac{1}{3}$ is located at a different valley than $\mathbb{E}[X(0)X(0.5)]$ in the 2D plot.

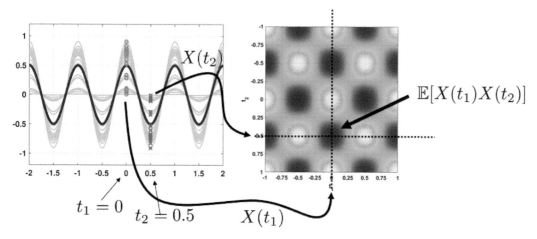

Figure 10.12: To understand the autocorrelation function, pick two time instants t_1 and t_2, and then evaluate the joint expectation $\mathbb{E}[X(t_1)X(t_2)]$.

The above example shows a periodic autocorrelation function. The fact that it is periodic is coincidental because the random process $X(t)$ is a periodic function. In general, an arbitrary random process can have an arbitrary autocorrelation function that is not periodic. There are, of course, various properties of the autocorrelation functions and special types of autocorrelation functions. We will study one of them, called the **wide-sense stationary processes**, later.

Example 10.12. Let $\Theta \sim \text{Uniform}[-\pi, \pi]$, $X(t) = \cos(\omega t + \Theta)$. Draw the autocorrelation function $R_X(t_1, t_2)$.

Solution. From the previous example we know that

$$R_X(t_1, t_2) = \frac{1}{2}\cos\left(\omega(t_1 - t_2)\right).$$

Figure 10.13 shows the realizations, and the mean and autocorrelation functions.

Note that the autocorrelation function has a structure: Every row is a shifted version of the previous row. We call this a **Toeplitz** structure. An autocorrelation with a Toeplitz structure is specified once we know any of the rows. A Toeplitz structure also implies that the autocorrelation function does not depend on the pair (t_1, t_2) but only on the difference $t_1 - t_2$. In other words, $R_X(0, 1)$ is the same as $R_X(11.6, 12.6)$, and so knowing $R_X(0, 1)$ is enough to know all $R_X(t_0, t_0 + t)$. Not all random processes have

---

a Toeplitz autocorrelation function. Random processes with a Toeplitz autocorrelation function are "nice" processes that we will study in detail later.

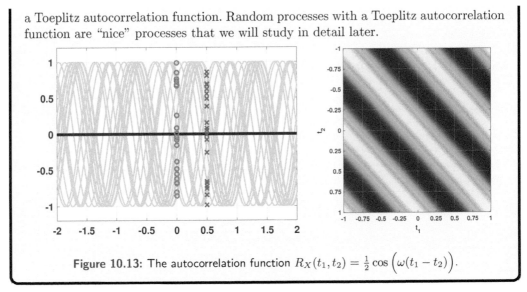

Figure 10.13: The autocorrelation function $R_X(t_1, t_2) = \frac{1}{2}\cos\left(\omega(t_1 - t_2)\right)$.

The MATLAB code used to generate **Figure 10.13** is shown below.

```
% MATLAB code for Example 10.12
t = linspace(-1,1,1000);
R = Toeplitz(0.5*cos(2*pi*t(:)));

imagesc(t,t,R);
grid on;
xticks(-1:0.25:1);
yticks(-1:0.25:1);
```

Practice Exercise 10.1. Let $\Theta \sim \text{Uniform}[0, 2\pi]$, $X(t) = \cos(\omega t + \Theta)$. Find the PDF of $X(0)$.

Solution. Let $Z = X(0) = \cos\Theta$. Then the CDF of Z is

$$
\begin{aligned}
F_Z(z) &= \mathbb{P}[Z \le z] \\
&= \mathbb{P}[\cos\Theta \le z] \\
&= \mathbb{P}[\cos^{-1} z \le \Theta \le 2\pi - \cos^{-1} z] \\
&= 1 - \frac{\cos^{-1} z}{\pi}.
\end{aligned}
$$

Then by the fundamental theorem of calculus,

$$
f_Z(z) = \frac{1}{\pi\sqrt{1 - z^2}}.
$$

A similar concept to the autocorrelation function is the autocovariance function. The idea is to remove the mean before computing the correlation. This is analogous to the covariance $\text{Cov}(X,Y) = \mathbb{E}[(X - \mu_X)(Y - \mu_Y)]$ as opposed to the correlation $\mathbb{E}[XY]$ in the random variable case.

Definition 10.3. *The* **autocovariance function** *of a random process $X(t)$ is*

$$C_X(t_1, t_2) = \mathbb{E}\left[(X(t_1) - \mu_X(t_1))(X(t_2) - \mu_X(t_2))\right]. \tag{10.7}$$

As one might expect, the autocovariance function is closely related to the autocorrelation function.

Theorem 10.1.
$$C_X(t_1, t_2) = R_X(t_1, t_2) - \mu_X(t_1)\mu_X(t_2). \tag{10.8}$$

Proof. Plugging in the definition, we have that

$$\begin{aligned}
C_X(t_1, t_2) &= \mathbb{E}\left[X(t_1)X(t_2) - X(t_1)\mu_X(t_2) - X(t_2)\mu_X(t_1) + \mu_X(t_1)\mu_X(t_2)\right] \\
&= R_X(t_1, t_2) - \mu_X(t_1)\mu_X(t_2) - \mu_X(t_1)\mu_X(t_2) + \mu_X(t_1)\mu_X(t_2) \\
&= R_X(t_1, t_2) - \mu_X(t_1)\mu_X(t_2). \qquad \square
\end{aligned}$$

Practice Exercise 10.2. If $X(t) = A\cos(2\pi t)$ for $A \sim \text{Uniform}[0, 1]$, find $C_X(t_1, t_2)$.

Solution.

$$\begin{aligned}
C_X(t_1, t_2) &= \frac{1}{3}\cos(2\pi t_1)\cos(2\pi t_2) - \frac{1}{2}\cos(2\pi t_1) \cdot \frac{1}{2}\cos(2\pi t_2) \\
&= \frac{1}{12}\cos(2\pi t_1)\cos(2\pi t_2).
\end{aligned}$$

Practice Exercise 10.3. Suppose $X(t) = \cos(\omega t + \Theta)$ for $\Theta \sim \text{Uniform}[-\pi, \pi]$. Find $C_X(t_1, t_2)$.

Solution.

$$\begin{aligned}
C_X(t_1, t_2) &= R_X(t_1, t_2) - \mu_X(t_1)\mu_X(t_2) \\
&= \frac{1}{2}\cos\left(\omega(t_1 - t_2)\right) - 0 \cdot 0 = \frac{1}{2}\cos\left(\omega(t_1 - t_2)\right).
\end{aligned}$$

In some problems we are interested in the correlation between two random processes $X(t)$ and $Y(t)$. This gives us the cross-correlation and the cross-covariance functions.

Definition 10.4. *The* **cross-correlation function** *of $X(t)$ and $Y(t)$ is*

$$R_{X,Y}(t_1, t_2) = \mathbb{E}\left[X(t_1)Y(t_2)\right]. \tag{10.9}$$

Definition 10.5. *The* **cross-covariance function** *of $X(t)$ and $Y(t)$ is*

$$C_{X,Y}(t_1, t_2) = \mathbb{E}\left[(X(t_1) - \mu_X(t_1))(Y(t_2) - \mu_Y(t_2))\right]. \qquad (10.10)$$

Remark. If $\mu_X(t_1) = \mu_Y(t_2) = 0$, then $C_{X,Y}(t_1, t_2) = R_{X,Y}(t_1, t_2) = \mathbb{E}[X(t_1)Y(t_2)]$.

10.2.3 Independent processes

How do we establish **independence** for two random processes? We know that for two random variables to be independent, the joint PDF can be written as a product of two PDFs:

$$f_{X,Y}(x, y) = f_X(x)f_Y(y). \qquad (10.11)$$

If we extrapolate this idea to random processes, a natural formulation would be

$$f_{X(t),Y(t)}(x, y) = f_{X(t)}(x)f_{Y(t)}(y). \qquad (10.12)$$

But this definition has a problem because $X(t)$ and $Y(t)$ are functions. It is not enough to just look at one time index, say $t = t_0$. The way to think about this situation is to consider a pair of random vectors $\boldsymbol{X}$ and $\boldsymbol{Y}$. When you say $\boldsymbol{X}$ and $\boldsymbol{Y}$ are independent, you require $f_{\boldsymbol{X},\boldsymbol{Y}}(\boldsymbol{x}, \boldsymbol{y}) = f_{\boldsymbol{X}}(\boldsymbol{x})f_{\boldsymbol{Y}}(\boldsymbol{y})$. The PDF $f_{\boldsymbol{X}}(\boldsymbol{x})$ itself is a joint distribution, i.e., $f_{\boldsymbol{X}}(\boldsymbol{x}) = f_{X_1,\dots,X_N}(x_1, \dots, x_N)$. Therefore, for random processes, we need something similar.

Definition 10.6. *Two random processes $X(t)$ and $Y(t)$ are* **independent** *if for any $t_1, \dots, t_N$,*

$$f_{X(t_1),\dots,X(t_N),Y(t_1),\dots,Y(t_N)}(x_1, \dots, x_N, y_1, \dots, y_N)$$
$$= f_{X(t_1),\dots,X(t_N)}(x_1, \dots, x_N) \times f_{Y(t_1),\dots,Y(t_N)}(y_1, \dots, y_N).$$

This definition is reminiscent of $f_{\boldsymbol{X},\boldsymbol{Y}}(\boldsymbol{x}, \boldsymbol{y}) = f_{\boldsymbol{X}}(\boldsymbol{x})f_{\boldsymbol{Y}}(\boldsymbol{y})$. The requirement here is that the factorization holds for **any** N, including very small N and very large N, because $X(t)$ and $Y(t)$ are infinitely long.

Independence means that the behavior of one process will not influence the behavior of the other process. We define **uncorrelated** as follows.

Definition 10.7. *Two random processes are $X(t)$ and $Y(t)$* **uncorrelated** *if*

$$\mathbb{E}\left[X(t_1)Y(t_2)\right] = \mathbb{E}\left[X(t_1)\right]\mathbb{E}\left[Y(t_2)\right], \qquad (10.13)$$

Independence implies uncorrelation, as we can see from the following. If $X(t)$ and $Y(t)$ are independent, it follows that

$$\mathbb{E}\left[X(t_1)Y(t_2)\right] = \int X(t_1, \xi)Y(t_2, \zeta)f_{X,Y}(\xi, \zeta)\, d\xi\, d\zeta$$

$$= \int X(t_1, \xi)Y(t_2, \zeta)f_X(\xi)f_Y(\zeta)\, d\xi\, d\zeta, \qquad \text{independence}$$

$$= \int X(t_1, \xi)f_X(\xi)\, d\xi \int Y(t_2, \zeta)f_Y(\zeta)\, d\zeta = \mathbb{E}[X(t_1)]\mathbb{E}[Y(t_2)].$$

If two random processes are uncorrelated, they are not necessarily independent.

Independent X and Y $\overset{\Rightarrow}{\nLeftarrow}$ uncorrelated X and Y

Example 10.13. Let $Y(t) = X(t) + N(t)$, where $X(t)$ and $N(t)$ are independent. Then

$$R_{X,Y}(t_1, t_2) = \mathbb{E}\left[X(t_1)Y(t_2)\right] = \mathbb{E}\left[X(t_1)\left(X(t_2) + N(t_2)\right)\right]$$
$$= R_X(t_1, t_2) + \mu_X(t_1)\mu_N(t_2).$$

10.3 Wide-Sense Stationary Processes

As we have seen in the previous sections, some random processes have a "nice" autocorrelation function, in the sense that the 2D function $R_X(t_1, t_2)$ has a Toeplitz structure. Random processes with this property are known as **wide-sense stationary** (WSS) processes. WSS processes belong to a very small subset in the entire universe of random processes, but they are practically the most useful ones. Before we discuss how to use them, we first present a formal definition of a WSS process.[1]

10.3.1 Definition of a WSS process

Definition 10.8. *A random process* $X(t)$ *is* **wide-sense stationary** *if:*

1. $\mu_X(t) = $ *constant, for all* t, *and*

2. $R_X(t_1, t_2) = R_X(t_1 - t_2)$ *for all* t_1, t_2.

There are two criteria that define a WSS process. The first criterion is that the mean is a constant. That is, the mean function does not change with time. The second criterion is that the autocorrelation function only depends on the difference $t_1 - t_2$ and not on the absolute starting point. For example, $R_X(0.1, 1.1)$ needs to be the same as $R_X(6.3, 7.3)$, because the intervals are both 1.

How can these two criteria be mapped to the Toeplitz structure we discussed in the previous examples? **Figure 10.14** shows the autocorrelation function $R_X(t_1, t_2)$, which is a 2D function. We take three cross sections corresponding to $t_2 = -0.13$, $t_2 = 0$ and $t_2 = 0.3$. As you can see from the figure, each $R_X(t_1, t_2)$ is a shifted version of another one. To obtain any value $R_X(t_1, t_2)$ on the function, there is no need to probe to the 2D map; you only need to probe to the red curve and locate the position marked as $t_1 - t_2$, and you will be able to obtain the value $R_X(t_1, t_2)$.

---

[1] Many textbooks introduce strictly stationary processes before discussing a wide-sense stationary process. We skip the former because, throughout our book, we only use WSS processes. Readers interested in strictly stationary processes can consult the references listed at the end of this chapter.

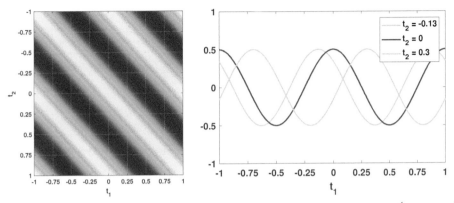

Figure 10.14: Cross sections of the autocorrelation function $R_X(t_1, t_2) = \frac{1}{2}\cos\left(\omega(t_1 - t_2)\right)$.

Not all random processes have a Toeplitz autocorrelation function. For example, the random process $X(t) = A\cos(2\pi t)$ is not a WSS process, because the autocorrelation function is

$$R_X(t_1, t_2) = \frac{1}{3}\cos(2\pi t_1)\cos(2\pi t_2),$$

which cannot be written as the difference $t_1 - t_2$.

Remark 1. WSS processes can also be defined using the autocovariance function instead of the autocorrelation function, because if a process is WSS, then the mean function is a constant. If the mean function is a constant, then $C_X(t_1, t_2) = R_X(t_1, t_2) - \mu^2$. So any geometric structure that R_X possesses will be translated to C_X, as the constant μ^2 will not influence the geometry. Therefore, it is equally valid to say that a WSS process has

$$C_X(t_1, t_2) = C_X(t_1 - t_2).$$

Remark 2. Because a WSS is completely characterized by the difference $t_1 - t_2$, there is no need to keep track of the absolute indices t_1 and t_2. We can rewrite the autocorrelation function as

$$R_X(\tau) = \mathbb{E}[X(t + \tau)X(t)]. \tag{10.14}$$

There is nothing new in this equation: It only says that instead of writing $R_X(t + \tau, t)$, we can write $R_X(\tau)$ because the time index t plays no role in terms of R_X. Thus from now on, for any WSS processes we will write the autocorrelation function as $R_X(\tau)$.

10.3.2 Properties of $R_X(\tau)$

When $X(t)$ is WSS, $R_X(\tau)$ has several important properties.

Corollary 10.1. $R_X(0) = $ *average power of $X(t)$.*

Proof. Since

$$R_X(0) = \mathbb{E}[X(t + 0)X(t)] = \mathbb{E}[X(t)^2],$$

and since $\mathbb{E}[X(t)^2]$ is the average power, $R_X(0)$ is the average power of $X(t)$. $\square$

CHAPTER 10. RANDOM PROCESSES

> **Corollary 10.2.** $R_X(\tau)$ *is symmetric. That is,* $R_X(\tau) = R_X(-\tau)$.

Proof. Note that $R_X(\tau) = \mathbb{E}[X(t+\tau)X(t)]$. By switching the order of multiplication in the expectation, we have

$$\mathbb{E}[X(t+\tau)X(t)] = \mathbb{E}[X(t)X(t+\tau)] = R_X(-\tau).$$

$\square$

> **Corollary 10.3.**
> $$\mathbb{P}(|X(t+\tau) - X(\tau)| > \epsilon) \le \frac{2(R_X(0) - R_X(\tau))}{\epsilon^2}.$$

This result says that if $R_X(\tau)$ is slowly decaying from $R_X(0)$, the probability of having a large deviation $|X(t+\tau) - X(\tau)|$ is small.

Proof.

$$\begin{aligned}
\mathbb{P}(|X(t+\tau) - X(\tau)| > \epsilon) &\le \mathbb{E}[(X(t+\tau) - X(\tau))^2]/\epsilon^2 \\
&= \left(\mathbb{E}[X(t+\tau)^2] - 2\mathbb{E}[X(t+\tau)X(t)] + \mathbb{E}[X(t)^2]\right)/\epsilon^2 \\
&= \left(2\mathbb{E}[X(t)^2] - 2\mathbb{E}[X(t+\tau)X(t)]\right)/\epsilon^2 \\
&= 2\left(R_X(0) - R_X(\tau)\right)/\epsilon^2.
\end{aligned}$$

$\square$

> **Corollary 10.4.** $|R_X(\tau)| \le R_X(0)$, *for all* τ.

Proof. By Cauchy's inequality $\mathbb{E}[XY]^2 \le \mathbb{E}[X^2]\mathbb{E}[Y^2]$, we can show that

$$\begin{aligned}
R_X(\tau)^2 &= \mathbb{E}[X(t)X(t+\tau)]^2 \\
&\le \mathbb{E}[X(t)^2]\mathbb{E}[X(t+\tau)^2] \\
&= \mathbb{E}[X(t)^2]^2 = R_X(0)^2.
\end{aligned}$$

$\square$

10.3.3 Physical interpretation of $R_X(\tau)$

How should we understand the autocorrelation function $R_X(\tau)$ for WSS processes? Certainly, by definition, $R_X(\tau) = \mathbb{E}[X(t+\tau)X(t)]$ means that we can analyze $R_X(\tau)$ from the statistical perspective. But in this section we want to take a slightly different approach by answering the question from a computational perspective.

Consider the following function:

$$\widehat{R}_X(\tau) \stackrel{\text{def}}{=} \frac{1}{2T} \int_{-T}^{T} X(t+\tau)X(t)\, dt. \tag{10.15}$$

634

This function is the **temporal average** of $X(t+\tau)X(t)$, as opposed to the statistical average. Why do we want to consider this temporal average? We first show the main result, that $\mathbb{E}[\widehat{R}_X(\tau)] = R_X(\tau)$.

Lemma 10.1. *Let $\widehat{R}_X(\tau) \stackrel{\text{def}}{=} \frac{1}{2T} \int_{-T}^{T} X(t+\tau)X(t)\, dt$. Then*

$$\mathbb{E}\left[\widehat{R}_X(\tau)\right] = R_X(\tau). \tag{10.16}$$

Proof.

$$\mathbb{E}\left[\widehat{R}_X(\tau)\right] = \frac{1}{2T} \int_{-T}^{T} \mathbb{E}\left[X(t+\tau)X(t)\right]\, dt$$

$$= \frac{1}{2T} \int_{-T}^{T} R_X(\tau)\, dt$$

$$= R_X(\tau)\frac{1}{2T} \int_{-T}^{T} dt = R_X(\tau).$$

$\square$

This lemma implies that if the signal $X(t)$ is long enough, we can approximate $R_X(\tau)$ by $\widehat{R}_X(\tau)$. The approximation is asymptotically consistent, in the sense that $\mathbb{E}[\widehat{R}_X(\tau)] = R_X(\tau)$. Now, the more interesting question is the interpretation of $\widehat{R}_X(\tau)$. What is it?

How should we understand $\widehat{R}_X(\tau)$?

$\widehat{R}_X(\tau)$ is the "unflipped convolution", or **correlation**, of $X(\tau)$ and $X(t+\tau)$.

Correlation is analogous to convolution. For **convolution**, the definition is

$$Y(\tau) = \int_{-T}^{T} X(\tau - t)X(t)\, dt, \tag{10.17}$$

whereas for **correlation**, the definition is

$$Y(\tau) = \int_{-T}^{T} X(\tau + t)X(t)\, dt. \tag{10.18}$$

Clearly, $\widehat{R}_X(\tau)$ is the latter. A graphical illustration of the difference between convolution and correlation is provided in **Figure 10.15**. The only difference between the two is that the correlation does not flip the function, whereas the convolution does flip the function.

The temporal correlation is easy to visualize. Starting with the function $X(t+\tau)$, if you make τ larger or smaller, then effectively you are shifting $X(t)$ left or right. The integration $\int_{-T}^{T} X(t+\tau)X(t)\, dt$ calculates the energy accumulated. If the integral is large, there is a strong correlation between $X(t)$ and $X(t+\tau)$. Otherwise the correlation is small. Here is an extreme example:

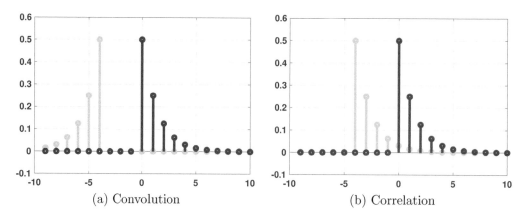

(a) Convolution   (b) Correlation

Figure 10.15: The difference between convolution and correlation. In convolution, the function $X(t)$ is flipped before we compute the result. For correlation, the function is not flipped.

Example 10.14. Consider a random process $X(t)$ such that for every t, $X(t)$ is an i.i.d. Gaussian random variable with zero mean and unit variance. Then

$$R_X(\tau) = \mathbb{E}[X(t+\tau)X(t)] = \begin{cases} \mathbb{E}[X^2(t)], & \tau = 0, \\ \mathbb{E}[X(t+\tau)]\mathbb{E}[X(t)], & \tau \neq 0. \end{cases}$$

Using the fact that $X(t)$ is i.i.d. Gaussian for all t, we can show that $\mathbb{E}[X^2(t)] = 1$ for any t, and $\mathbb{E}[X(t+\tau)]\mathbb{E}[X(t)] = 0$. Therefore, we have

$$R_X(\tau) = \begin{cases} 1, & \tau = 0, \\ 0. & \tau \neq 0. \end{cases}$$

The equation says that since the random process is i.i.d. Gaussian, shifting and integrating will give maximum correlation at the origin. As soon as the shift is not at the origin, the correlation is zero. This makes sense because the samples are just i.i.d. Gaussian. One pixel offset is enough to destroy any correlation.

Now let's calculate the temporal correlation. We know that

$$\widehat{R}_X(\tau) = \frac{1}{2T} \int_{-T}^{T} X(t+\tau)X(t)\, d\tau.$$

This equation says that we shift $X(t)$ to the left and right and then integrate. If τ is not zero, the product $X(t+\tau)X(t)$ will sometimes be positive and sometimes be negative. After integrating the entire period, we cancel out most of the terms. Let's plot the functions and see if all these steps make sense. In **Figure 10.16**(a), we show two random realizations of the random process $X(t)$. They are just i.i.d. Gaussian samples.

In **Figure 10.16**(b) we plot the temporal autocorrelation function $\widehat{R}_X(\tau)$. Since $\widehat{R}_X(\tau)$ itself is a random process, it has different realizations. We plot two random realizations, which are computed based on shifting and integrating $X(t)$. In the same plot, we also show the statistical expectation $R_X(\tau)$. As we can see from the plot, the temporal correlation and the statistical correlation match reasonably well except for the fluctuation in $\widehat{R}_X(\tau)$, which is expected because it is computed from a finite number of samples.

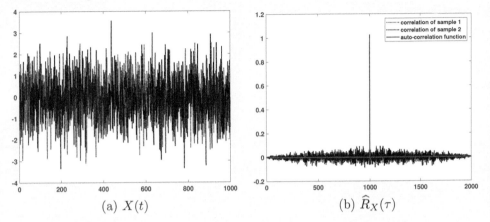

(a) $X(t)$ (b) $\widehat{R}_X(\tau)$

Figure 10.16: (a) A random process $X(t)$ with two different realizations. (b) As we calculate the temporal correlation of each of the two realizations, we obtain a noisy function that is nearly an impulse. If we take the average of many of these realizations, we obtain a pure delta function.

On a computer, the commands to do the autocorrelation function are xcorr in MATLAB and np.correlate in Python. Below are the codes used to generate **Figure 10.16**.

```
% MATLAB code to demonstrate autocorrelation
N      = 1000; % number of sample paths
T      = 1000; % number of time stamps
X      = 1*randn(N,T);
xc     = zeros(N,2*T-1);

for i=1:N
    xc(i,:) = xcorr(X(i,:))/T;
end
plot(xc(1,:),'b:', 'LineWidth', 2); hold on;
plot(xc(2,:),'k:', 'LineWidth', 2);
```

```
# Python code to demonstrate autocorrelation
N = 1000
T = 1000
X = np.random.randn(N,T)
xc= np.zeros((N,2*T-1))

for i in range(N):
  xc[i,:] = np.correlate(X[i,:],X[i,:],mode='full')/T
plt.plot(xc[0,:],'b:')
plt.plot(xc[1,:],'k:')
plt.show()
```

Under what conditions will $\widehat{R}_X(\tau) \to R_X(\tau)$ as $T \to \infty$? The answer to this question is provided by an important theorem called **Mean-Square Ergodic Theorem**, which can be thought of as the random process version of the weak law of large numbers. We leave the discussion of the mean ergodic theorem to the Appendix.

> **Everything you need to know about a WSS process**
> - The mean of a WSS process is a constant (does not need to be zero)
> - The correlation function only depends on the difference, so $R_X(t_1, t_2)$ is Toeplitz.
> - You can write $R_X(t_1, t_2)$ as $R_X(\tau)$, where $\tau = t_1 - t_2$.
> - $R_X(\tau)$ tells you how much correlation you have with someone located at a time instant τ from you.

10.4 Power Spectral Density

Beginning with this section we are going to focus on WSS processes. By WSS, we mean that the autocorrelation function $R_X(t_1, t_2)$ has a Toeplitz structure. Putting it in other words, we assume $R_X(t_1, t_2)$ can be simplified to $R_X(\tau)$, where $\tau = t_1 - t_2$. We call this property **time invariance**.

10.4.1 Basic concepts

Assuming that $R_X(\tau)$ is square integrable, i.e., $\int_{-\infty}^{\infty} R_X(\tau)^2 \, d\tau < \infty$, we can now define the Fourier transform of $R_X(\tau)$ which is called the **power spectral density**.

> **Theorem 10.2 (Einstein-Wiener-Khinchin Theorem).** *The power spectral density $S_X(\omega)$ of a WSS process is*
> $$S_X(\omega) = \int_{-\infty}^{\infty} R_X(\tau) \, e^{-j\omega\tau} \, d\tau$$
> $$= \mathcal{F}(R_X(\tau)),$$
> *assuming that $\int_{-\infty}^{\infty} R_X(\tau)^2 \, d\tau < \infty$ so that the Fourier transform of $R_X(\tau)$ exists.*

> **Practice Exercise 10.4.** Let $R_X(\tau) = e^{-2\alpha|\tau|}$. Find $S_X(\omega)$.
>
> **Solution.** Using the Fourier transform table,
> $$S_X(\omega) = \mathcal{F}\{R_X(\tau)\} = \frac{4\alpha}{4\alpha^2 + \omega^2}.$$
>
> **Figure 10.17** shows $R_X(\tau)$ and $S_X(\omega)$.

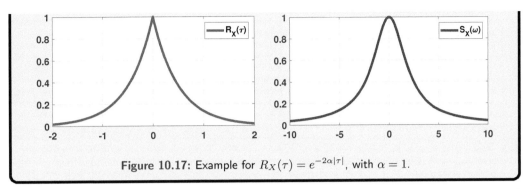

Figure 10.17: Example for $R_X(\tau) = e^{-2\alpha|\tau|}$, with $\alpha = 1$.

Why is Theorem 10.2 a **theorem** rather than a **definition**? This is because power spectral density has its definition. There is no way that you can get any "power" information merely by looking at the Fourier transform of $R_X(\tau)$. We will discuss the origin of the power spectral density later, but for now, we only need to know that $S_X(\omega)$ is the Fourier transform of $R_X(\tau)$.

Remark. The power spectral density is defined for WSS processes. If the process is not WSS, then R_X will be a 2D function instead of a 1D function of τ, so we cannot take the Fourier transform in τ. We will discuss this in detail shortly.

Practice Exercise 10.5. Let $X(t) = a\cos(\omega_0 t + \Theta)$, $\Theta \sim \text{Uniform}[0, 2\pi]$. Find $S_X(\omega)$.

Solution. We know that the autocorrelation function is

$$R_X(\tau) = \frac{a^2}{2}\cos(\omega_0\tau) = \frac{a^2}{2}\left(\frac{e^{j\omega_0\tau} + e^{-j\omega_0\tau}}{2}\right).$$

By taking the Fourier transform of both sides, we have

$$S_X(\omega) = \frac{a^2}{2}\left[\frac{2\pi\delta(\omega - \omega_0) + 2\pi\delta(\omega + \omega_0)}{2}\right]$$

$$= \frac{\pi a^2}{2}\left[\delta(\omega - \omega_0) + \delta(\omega + \omega_0)\right].$$

The result is shown in **Figure 10.18**.

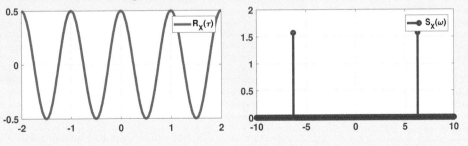

Figure 10.18: Example for $R_X(\tau) = \frac{a^2}{2}\cos(\omega_0\tau)$, with $a = 1$ and $\omega_0 = 2\pi$.

Practice Exercise 10.6. Let $S_X(\omega) = \frac{N_0}{2}\text{rect}(\frac{\omega}{2W})$. Find $R_X(\tau)$.

Solution. Since $S_X(\omega) = \mathcal{F}(R_X(\tau))$, the inverse holds:

$$R_X(\tau) = \frac{N_0}{2}\frac{W}{\pi}\text{sinc}(W\tau).$$

This example shows what we call the bandlimited **white noise**. The power spectral density $S_X(\omega)$ is uniform, meaning that it covers all frequencies (or wavelengths in optics). It is called "white noise" because white light is essentially a mixture of all wavelengths.

The bandwidth of the power spectral density W defines the zero crossings of $R_X(\tau)$. It is easy to show that when $W \to \infty$, $R_X(\tau)$ converges to a delta function. This happens when $X(t)$ is i.i.d. Gaussian. Therefore, the pure Gaussian noise random process is also known as the **white noise process**. Reshaping the i.i.d. Gaussian noise to an arbitrary power spectral density can be done by passing it through a linear filter, as we will explain later.

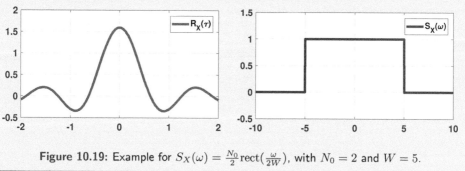

Figure 10.19: Example for $S_X(\omega) = \frac{N_0}{2}\text{rect}(\frac{\omega}{2W})$, with $N_0 = 2$ and $W = 5$.

Finding $S_X(\omega)$ from $R_X(\tau)$ is straightforward, at least in principle. The more interesting questions to ask are: (1) Why do we need to learn about power spectral density? (2) Why do we need WSS to define power spectral density?

How is power spectral density useful?

- Power spectral densities are useful when we pass a random process through some linear operations, e.g., convolution, running average, or running difference.

- Power spectral densities are the Fourier transforms of the autocorrelation functions. Fourier transforms are useful for speeding up computation and drawing random samples from a given power spectral density.

A random process itself is not interesting until we process it; there are many ways to do this. The most basic operation is to send the random process through a linear time-invariant system, e.g., a convolution. Convolution is equivalent to **filtering** the random process. For example, if the input process contains noise, we can design a linear time-invariant filter to denoise the random process. The power spectral density, which is the **Fourier transform** of the autocorrelation function, makes the filtering easier because everything can be done in the spectral (Fourier) domain. Moreover, we can analyze the performance and quantify the limit using standard results in Fourier analysis. For some specialized problems such as imaging through atmospheric turbulence, the distortions happen in the phase domain. This can be simulated by drawing samples from the power spectral density, e.g., the Kolmogorov spectrum or the von Kármán spectrum. Power spectral densities have many important engineering applications.

Why does the power spectral density require wide-sense stationarity?

- If a process is WSS, then R_X will have a Toeplitz structure.
- A Toeplitz matrix is important. If you do eigendecomposition to a Toeplitz matrix, the eigenvectors are the Fourier bases.
- So if R_X is Toeplitz, then you can diagonalize it using the Fourier transform.
- Therefore, the power spectral density can be defined.

Why does power spectral density require WSS? This has to do with the Toeplitz structure of the autocorrelation function. To make our discussion easier let us discretize the autocorrelation function $R_X(t_1, t_2)$ by considering $R_X[m, n]$. (You can do a mental calculation by converting t_1 to integer indices m, and t_2 to n. See any textbook on signals and systems if you need help. This is called the "discrete time signal".) Following the range of t_1 and t_2, $R_X[m, n]$ can be expressed as:

$$\boldsymbol{R} = \begin{bmatrix} R_X[0] & R_X[1] & \cdots & R_X[N-1] \\ R_X[1] & R_X[0] & \cdots & R_X[N-2] \\ \vdots & \vdots & \ddots & \vdots \\ R_X[N-1] & R_X[N-1] & \cdots & R_X[0] \end{bmatrix},$$

where we used the fact that $R_X[m, n] = R_X[m-n]$ for WSS processes and $R_X[k] = R_X[-k]$. We call the resulting matrix $\boldsymbol{R}$ the **autocorrelation matrix**, which is a discretized version of the autocorrelation function $R_X(t_1, t_2)$. Looking at $\boldsymbol{R}$, we again observe the Toeplitz structure. For example, **Figure 10.20** shows one Toeplitz structure and one non-Toeplitz structure.

Any Toeplitz matrix $\boldsymbol{R}$ can be diagonalized using the Fourier transforms. That is, we can write $\boldsymbol{R}$ as

$$\boldsymbol{R} = \boldsymbol{F}^H \boldsymbol{\Lambda} \boldsymbol{F},$$

where $\boldsymbol{F}$ is the (discrete) **Fourier transform matrix** and $\boldsymbol{\Lambda}$ is a diagonal matrix. This can be understood as the eigendecomposition of $\boldsymbol{R}$. The important point here is that only Toeplitz matrices can be eigendecomposed using the Fourier transforms; an arbitrary symmetric matrix cannot. **Figure 10.20** illustrates this point. If your matrix is Toeplitz, you can diagonalize it, and hence you can define the power spectral density, just as in the first example. If your matrix is not Toeplitz, then the power spectral density is undefined. To get the Toeplitz matrix, you must start with a WSS process.

Before moving on, we define **cross power spectral densities**, which will be useful in some applications.

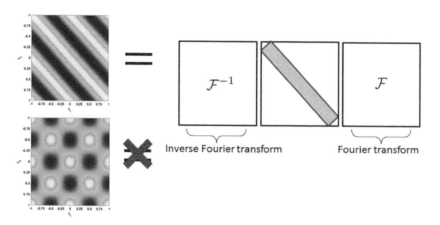

Figure 10.20: We show two autocorrelation functions $R_X[m, n]$ on the left-hand side. The first autocorrelation function comes from a WSS process that has a Toeplitz structure. The second autocorrelation function does not have Toeplitz structure. For the Toeplitz matrix, we can diagonalize it using the Fourier transform. The eigenvalues are the power spectral density.

Definition 10.9. *The* **cross power spectral density** *between two random processes $X(t)$ and $Y(t)$ is*

$$
\begin{aligned}
S_{X,Y}(\omega) = \mathcal{F}(R_{X,Y}(\tau)) & \quad where \quad R_{X,Y}(\tau) = \mathbb{E}[X(t+\tau)Y(t)], \\
S_{Y,X}(\omega) = \mathcal{F}(R_{Y,X}(\tau)) & \quad where \quad R_{Y,X}(\tau) = \mathbb{E}[Y(t+\tau)X(t)].
\end{aligned}
\tag{10.19}
$$

Remark. In general, $S_{X,Y}(\omega) \neq S_{Y,X}(\omega)$. Rather, since $R_{X,Y}(\tau) = R_{Y,X}(-\tau)$, we have $S_{X,Y}(\omega) = \overline{S_{Y,X}(\omega)}$.

10.4.2 Origin of the power spectral density

To understand the power spectral density, it is crucial to understand where it comes from and why it is the Fourier transform of the autocorrelation function.

We begin by assuming that $X(t)$ is a WSS random process with mean μ_X and autocorrelation $R_X(\tau)$. We now consider the notion of **power**. Consider a random process $X(t)$. The power within a period $[-T, T]$ is

$$
\widehat{P}_X = \frac{1}{2T} \int_{-T}^{T} |X(t)|^2 \, dt.
$$

$\widehat{P}_X$ defines the power because the integration alone is the energy, and the normalization by $1/2T$ gives us the power. However, there are two problems. First, since $X(t)$ is random, the power $\widehat{P}_X$ is also random. Is there a way we can eliminate the randomness? Second, T is a finite period of time. It does not capture the entire process, and so we do not know the power of the entire process.

A natural solution to these two problems is to consider

$$
P_X \stackrel{\text{def}}{=} \mathbb{E}\left[\lim_{T \to \infty} \frac{1}{2T} \int_{-T}^{T} |X(t)|^2 \, dt \right].
\tag{10.20}
$$

Here, we take the limit of T to infinity so that we can compute the power of the entire process. We also take the expectation to eliminate the randomness. Therefore, P_X can be regarded as the average power of the complete random process $X(t)$.

Next, we need one definition and one lemma. The definition defines $S_X(\omega)$, and the lemma will link $S_X(\omega)$ with the power P_X.

Definition 10.10. *The* **power spectral density** *(PSD) of a WSS process is defined as*

$$S_X(\omega) = \lim_{T \to \infty} \frac{\mathbb{E}\left[|\tilde{X}_T(\omega)|^2\right]}{2T}, \qquad (10.21)$$

where

$$\tilde{X}_T(\omega) = \int_{-T}^{T} X(t)e^{-j\omega t}\, dt \qquad (10.22)$$

is the Fourier transform of $X(t)$ limited to $[-T, T]$.

This definition is abstract, but in a nutshell, it simply considers everything in the Fourier domain. The ratio $|\tilde{X}_T(\omega)|^2/2T$ is the power, but in the frequency domain. The reason is that if $X(t)$ is Fourier transformable, then **Parseval's theorem** will hold. Parseval's theorem states that energy in the original space is conserved in the Fourier space. Since the ratio $|\tilde{X}_T(\omega)|^2/2T$ is the energy divided by time, it is the power. However, this is still not enough to help us understand power spectral density: We need a lemma.

Lemma 10.2. *Define*

$$P_X \stackrel{\text{def}}{=} \mathbb{E}\left[\lim_{T \to \infty} \frac{1}{2T} \int_{-T}^{T} |X(t)|^2\, dt\right].$$

Then

$$P_X = \frac{1}{2\pi} \int_{-\infty}^{\infty} S_X(\omega)\, d\omega. \qquad (10.23)$$

The lemma has to be read together with the previous definition. If we can prove the lemma, we know that by integrating $S_X(\omega)$ we will obtain the power. Therefore, $S_X(\omega)$ can be viewed as a **density function**, specifically the density function of the power. $S_X(\omega)$ is called the power **spectral** density because everything is defined in the Fourier domain. Putting this all together gives us "power spectral density".

Proof. First, we recall that P_X is the expectation of the average power of $X(t)$. Let

$$X_T(t) = \begin{cases} X(t) & -T \le t \le T, \\ 0 & \text{otherwise.} \end{cases}$$

It follows that integrating over $-\infty$ to ∞ is equivalent to

$$\int_{-\infty}^{\infty} |X_T(t)|^2\, dt = \int_{-T}^{T} |X(t)|^2\, dt.$$

By Parseval's theorem, energy is conserved in both the time and the frequency domain:

$$\int_{-\infty}^{\infty} |X_T(t)|^2 \, dt = \frac{1}{2\pi} \int_{-\infty}^{\infty} |\widetilde{X}_T(\omega)|^2 \, d\omega.$$

Therefore, P_X satisfies

$$P_X = \mathbb{E}\left[\lim_{T\to\infty} \frac{1}{2T} \int_{-T}^{T} |X(t)|^2 \, dt\right] = \mathbb{E}\left[\lim_{T\to\infty} \frac{1}{2\pi} \frac{1}{2T} \int_{-\infty}^{\infty} |\widetilde{X}_T(\omega)|^2 \, d\omega\right]$$

$$= \frac{1}{2\pi} \int_{-\infty}^{\infty} \underbrace{\lim_{T\to\infty} \frac{1}{2T} \mathbb{E}\left[|\widetilde{X}_T(\omega)|^2\right]}_{\stackrel{\text{def}}{=} S_X(\omega)} \, d\omega.$$

$\square$

The power spectral densities are functions whose integrations give us the power. If we want to determine the power of a random process, the **Einstein-Wiener-Khinchin theorem** (Theorem 10.2) says that $S_X(\omega)$ is just the Fourier transform of $R_X(\tau)$:

$$S_X(\omega) = \int_{-\infty}^{\infty} R_X(\tau) \, e^{-j\omega\tau} \, d\tau = \mathcal{F}(R_X(\tau)).$$

The proof of the Einstein-Wiener-Khinchin theorem is quite intricate, so we defer the proof to the Appendix. The significance of the theorem is that it turns an abstract quantity, the power spectral density, into a very easily computable quantity, namely the Fourier transform of the autocorrelation function. For now, we will happily use this theorem because it saves us a great deal of trouble when we want to determine the power spectral density from the first principles.

10.5 WSS Process through LTI Systems

Random processes have limited usefulness until we can apply operations to them. In this section we discuss how WSS processes respond to a **linear time-invariant** (LTI) system. This technique is most useful in signal processing, communication, speech analysis, and imaging. We will be brief here since you can find most of this information in any standard textbook on signals and systems.

10.5.1 Review of linear time-invariant systems

When we say a "system", we mean that there exists an **input-output** relationship as shown in **Figure 10.21**.

Linear time-invariant **(LTI)** systems are the simplest systems we use in engineering problems. An LTI system has two properties.

- **Linearity**. Linearity means that when two input random processes are **added and scaled**, the output random processes will also be added and scaled in exactly the same way. Mathematically, linearity says that if $X_1(t) \to Y_1(t)$ and $X_2(t) \to$

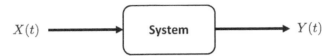

Figure 10.21: A system can be viewed as a black box that takes an input $X(t)$ and turns it into an output $Y(t)$.

$Y_2(t)$, then

$$aX_1(t) + bX_2(t) \rightarrow aY_1(t) + bY_2(t).$$

- **Time-invariant**: Time invariance means that if we **shift** the input random process by a certain time period, the output will be shifted in the same way. Mathematically, time invariance means that if $X(t) \rightarrow Y(t)$, then

$$X(t + \tau) \rightarrow Y(t + \tau).$$

If a system is linear time-invariant, the input-to-output relation is given by **convolution**:

The **convolution** between two functions $X(t)$ and $h(t)$ is defined as

$$Y(t) = h(t) * X(t) = \int_{-\infty}^{\infty} h(\tau)\, X(t - \tau)\, d\tau,$$

in which we call $h(t)$ the system response or **impulse response**.

The function $h(t)$ is called the impulse response because if $X(t) = \delta(t)$, then according to the convolution equation we have

$$Y(t) = \int_{-\infty}^{\infty} h(\tau)\, \delta(t - \tau)\, d\tau = h(t).$$

Therefore, if we send an impulse to the system, the output will be $h(t)$.

Convolution is commutative, meaning that $h(t) * X(t) = X(t) * h(t)$. Written as integrations, we have

$$\int_{-\infty}^{\infty} h(\tau)\, X(t - \tau)\, d\tau = \int_{-\infty}^{\infty} h(t - \tau)\, X(\tau)\, d\tau. \tag{10.24}$$

For LTI systems, $Y(t)$ can be determined through the Fourier transforms.

The **Fourier transform** of a (squared-integrable) function $X(t)$ is

$$X(\omega) = \mathcal{F}\{X(t)\} = \int_{-\infty}^{\infty} X(\tau)\, e^{-j\omega\tau}\, d\tau. \tag{10.25}$$

A basic property of convolution is that convolution in the **time domain** is equivalent to multiplication in the **Fourier domain**. Therefore

$$Y(\omega) = H(\omega)X(\omega), \tag{10.26}$$

where $H(\omega) = \mathcal{F}\{h(t)\}$ is the Fourier transform of $h(t)$, and $Y(\omega) = \mathcal{F}(Y(t))$ is the Fourier transform of $Y(t)$.

In the rest of this section we study the pair of input and output random processes that are defined as follows

- $X(t) =$ input. It is a WSS random process.
- $Y(t) =$ output. It is constructed by sending $X(t)$ through an LTI system with impulse response $h(t)$. Therefore, $Y(t) = h(t) * X(t)$.

10.5.2 Mean and autocorrelation through LTI Systems

Since $X(t)$ is WSS, the mean function of $X(t)$ stays constant, i.e., $\mu_X(t) = \mu_X$. The following theorem gives the mean function of the output.

Theorem 10.3. *If $X(t)$ passes through an LTI system to yield $Y(t)$, the mean function of $Y(t)$ is*

$$\mathbb{E}[Y(t)] = \mu_X \int_{-\infty}^{\infty} h(\tau)\, d\tau. \tag{10.27}$$

Proof. Suppose that $Y(t) = h(t) * X(t)$. Then,

$$\mu_Y(t) = \mathbb{E}[Y(t)] = \mathbb{E}\left[\int_{-\infty}^{\infty} h(\tau)X(t-\tau)\, d\tau\right]$$

$$= \int_{-\infty}^{\infty} h(\tau)\mathbb{E}[X(t-\tau)]\, d\tau$$

$$= \int_{-\infty}^{\infty} h(\tau)\mu_X\, d\tau = \mu_X \int_{-\infty}^{\infty} h(\tau)\, d\tau,$$

where the second to last equality is valid because $\mathbb{E}[X(t-\tau)] = \mu_X$. $\square$

The theorem suggests that if the input $X(t)$ has a constant mean, the output $Y(t)$ should also have a constant mean. This should not be a surprise because if the system is linear, a constant input will give a constant output.

Example 10.15. Consider a WSS random process $X(t)$ such that each sample is an i.i.d. Gaussian random variable with zero mean and unit variance. We send this process through an LTI system with impulse response $h(t)$, where

$$h(t) = \begin{cases} 10(1 - |t|), & -1 \le t \le 1, \\ 0, & \text{otherwise.} \end{cases}$$

The mean function of $X(t)$ is $\mu_X(t) = 0$, and that of $Y(t)$ is $\mu_Y(t) = 0$. **Figure 10.22** illustrates a numerical example, in which we see that the random processes $X(t)$ and $Y(t)$ have different shapes but the mean functions remain constant.

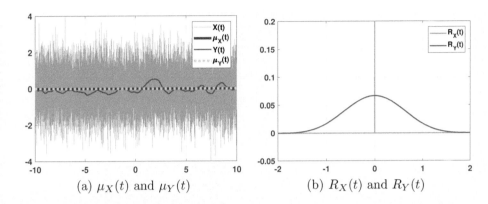

(a) $\mu_X(t)$ and $\mu_Y(t)$ (b) $R_X(t)$ and $R_Y(t)$

Figure 10.22: When sending a WSS random process through an LTI system, the mean and the autocorrelation functions are changed.

Next, we derive the autocorrelation function of a random process when sent through an LTI system.

Theorem 10.4. *If $X(t)$ passes through an LTI system to yield $Y(t)$, the* **autocorre-lation function** *of $Y(t)$ is*

$$R_Y(\tau) = \int_{-\infty}^{\infty} \int_{-\infty}^{\infty} h(s)h(r)R_X(\tau + s - r) \, ds \, dr. \tag{10.28}$$

Proof. We start with the definition of $Y(t)$:

$$R_Y(\tau) = \mathbb{E}[Y(t)Y(t+\tau)] = \mathbb{E}\left[\int_{-\infty}^{\infty} h(s)X(t-s) \, ds \int_{-\infty}^{\infty} h(r)X(t+\tau-r) \, dr\right]$$

$$\overset{(a)}{=} \int_{-\infty}^{\infty} \int_{-\infty}^{\infty} h(s)h(r)\mathbb{E}\left[X(t-s)X(t+\tau-r) \, ds \, dr\right]$$

$$= \int_{-\infty}^{\infty} \int_{-\infty}^{\infty} h(s)h(r)R_X(\tau+s-r) \, ds \, dr,$$

where in (a) we assume that integration and expectation are interchangeable.

□

A shorthand notation of the above formula is $R_Y(t) = [h \circledast (h * R_X)](t)$, where $*$ denotes the convolution and $\circledast$ denotes the correlation. **Figure 10.22**(b) shows the autocorrelation functions R_X and R_Y. In this example R_X is a delta function because for i.i.d. Gaussian noise the power spectral density is a constant. After convolving with the system response, the autocorrelation R_Y has a different shape.

10.5.3 Power spectral density through LTI systems

Denoting the Fourier transform of the impulse response by $H(\omega) = \mathcal{F}(h(t))$, we derive the power spectral density of the output.

Theorem 10.5. *If $X(t)$ passes through an LTI system to yield $Y(t)$, the* **power spectral density** *of $Y(t)$ is*

$$S_Y(\omega) = |H(\omega)|^2 S_X(\omega). \qquad (10.29)$$

Proof. By definition, the power spectral density $S_Y(\omega)$ is the Fourier transform of the autocorrelation function $R_Y(\omega)$. Therefore,

$$S_Y(\omega) = \int_{-\infty}^{\infty} R_Y(\tau)e^{-j\omega\tau}\, d\tau$$

$$= \int_{-\infty}^{\infty}\int_{-\infty}^{\infty}\int_{-\infty}^{\infty} h(s)h(r)R_X(\tau+s-r)\, ds\, dr e^{-j\omega\tau}\, d\tau.$$

Letting $u = \tau + s - r$, we have

$$S_Y(\omega) = \int_{-\infty}^{\infty}\int_{-\infty}^{\infty}\int_{-\infty}^{\infty} h(s)h(r)R_X(u)e^{-j\omega(u-s+r)}\, ds\, dr\, du$$

$$= \int_{-\infty}^{\infty} h(s)e^{j\omega s}\, ds \int_{-\infty}^{\infty} h(r)e^{-j\omega r}\, dr \int_{-\infty}^{\infty} R_X(u)e^{-j\omega u}\, du$$

$$= \overline{H(\omega)}H(\omega)S_X(\omega),$$

where $\overline{H(\omega)}$ is the complex conjugate of $H(\omega)$. $\qquad\square$

It is tempting to think that since $Y(t) = h(t) * X(t)$, the power spectral density should also be $S_Y(\omega) = H(\omega)X(\omega)$, but this is not true. The above result shows that we need an additional complex conjugate $\overline{H(\omega)}$ because $S_Y(\omega)$ is the **power**, which means the square of the signal. Note that R_X is "squared" because we have convolved it with itself, and R_Y is also squared. Therefore, to match R_X and R_Y, the impulse response h also needs to be squared in the Fourier domain.

Example 10.16. A WSS process $X(t)$ has a correlation function

$$R_X(\tau) = \text{sinc}(\pi\tau).$$

Suppose that $X(t)$ passes through an LTI system with input/output relationship

$$2\frac{d^2}{dt^2}Y(t) + 2\frac{d}{dt}Y(t) + 4Y(t) = 3\frac{d^2}{dt^2}X(t) - 3\frac{d}{dt}X(t) + 6X(t).$$

Find $R_Y(\tau)$.

Solution: The sinc function has a Fourier transform given by

$$\text{sinc}(Wt) \underset{\mathcal{F}}{\longleftrightarrow} \frac{\pi}{W}\text{rect}\left(\frac{\omega}{2W}\right).$$

Therefore, the autocorrelation function is

$$R_X(\tau) = \text{sinc}(\pi\tau) \underset{\mathcal{F}}{\longleftrightarrow} \frac{\pi}{\pi}\text{rect}\left(\frac{\omega}{2\pi}\right).$$

By taking the Fourier transform on both sides, we have

$$S_X(\omega) = \begin{cases} 1, & -\pi \leq \omega \leq \pi, \\ 0, & \text{elsewhere.} \end{cases}$$

The system response is found from the differential equation:

$$\begin{aligned} H(\omega) &= \frac{3(j\omega)^2 - 3(j\omega) + 6}{2(j\omega)^2 + 2(j\omega) + 4} \\ &= \frac{3\left[(2 - \omega^2) - j\omega\right]}{2\left[(2 - \omega^2) + j\omega\right]}. \end{aligned}$$

Taking the magnitude square yields

$$\begin{aligned} |H(\omega)|^2 &= \frac{3\left[(2 - \omega^2) - j\omega\right]}{2\left[(2 - \omega^2) + j\omega\right]} \frac{3\left[(2 - \omega^2) + j\omega\right]}{2\left[(2 - \omega^2) - j\omega\right]} \\ &= \frac{9}{4} \frac{(2 - \omega^2)^2 + \omega^2}{(2 - \omega^2)^2 + \omega^2} = \frac{9}{4}. \end{aligned}$$

Therefore, the output power spectral density is

$$S_Y(\omega) = |H(\omega)|^2 S_X(\omega) = \frac{9}{4} S_X(\omega).$$

Taking the inverse Fourier transform, we have

$$R_Y(\tau) = \frac{9}{4} \text{sinc}(\pi\tau).$$

Example 10.17. A random process $X(t)$ has zero mean and $R_X(t, s) = \min(t, s)$. Consider a new process $Y(t) = e^t X(e^{-2t})$.

1. Is $Y(t)$ WSS?

2. Suppose $Y(t)$ passes through a LTI system to yield an output $Z(t)$ according to

$$\frac{d}{dt} Z(t) + 2Z(t) = \frac{d}{dt} Y(t) + Y(t).$$

Find $R_Z(\tau)$.

Solution:

1. In order to verify whether $Y(t)$ is WSS, we need to check the mean function and the autocorrelation function. The mean function is

$$\mathbb{E}[Y(t)] = \mathbb{E}\left[e^t X(e^{-2t})\right] = e^t \mathbb{E}\left[X(e^{-2t})\right].$$

Since $X(t)$ has zero mean, $\mathbb{E}[X(t)] = 0$ for all t. This implies that if $u = e^{-2t}$, then $\mathbb{E}[X(u)] = 0$ because u is just another time instant. Thus $\mathbb{E}[X(e^{-2t})] = 0$, and hence $\mathbb{E}[Y(t)] = 0$.

The autocorrelation is

$$\mathbb{E}\left[Y(t+\tau)Y(t)\right] = \mathbb{E}\left[e^{t+\tau}X(e^{-2(t+\tau)})e^t X(e^{-2t})\right]$$
$$= e^{2t+\tau}\mathbb{E}\left[X(e^{-2(t+\tau)})X(e^{-2t})\right]$$
$$= e^{2t+\tau}R_X(e^{-2(t+\tau)}, e^{-2t}).$$

Substituting $R_X(t, s) = \min(t, s)$, we have that

$$e^{2t+\tau}R_X(e^{-2(t+\tau)}, e^{-2t}) = e^{2t+\tau}\min(e^{-2(t+\tau)}, e^{-2t})$$
$$= e^{2t+\tau}\begin{cases} e^{-2(t+\tau)}, & \tau \geq 0 \\ e^{-2t}, & \tau < 0 \end{cases}$$
$$= \begin{cases} e^{-\tau}, & \tau \geq 0 \\ e^{\tau}, & \tau < 0 \end{cases}$$
$$= e^{-|\tau|}.$$

So $R_Y(\tau) = e^{-|\tau|}$. Since $R_Y(\tau)$ is a function of τ, $Y(t)$ is WSS.

2. The system response is given by

$$H(\omega) = \frac{1+j\omega}{2+j\omega}.$$

The magnitude is therefore

$$|H(\omega)|^2 = \frac{1+\omega^2}{4+\omega^2}.$$

Hence, the output autocorrelation function is

$$R_Y(\tau) = e^{-|\tau|} \longleftrightarrow S_Y(\omega) = \frac{2}{1+\omega^2},$$

and

$$S_Z(\omega) = |H(\omega)|^2 S_Y(\omega)$$
$$= \frac{1+\omega^2}{4+\omega^2}\frac{2}{1+\omega^2} = \frac{2}{4+\omega^2}.$$

Therefore

$$R_Z(\tau) = \frac{1}{2}e^{-2|\tau|}.$$

10.5.4 Cross-correlation through LTI Systems

The above analyses are developed for the **autocorrelation** function. If we consider the cross-correlation between two random processes, say $X(t)$ and $Y(t)$, then the above results do not hold. In this section, we discuss the cross-correlation through LTI systems.

To begin with, we need to define WSS for a pair of random processes.

Definition 10.11. *Two random processes $X(t)$ and $Y(t)$ are **jointly WSS** if*

1. *$X(t)$ is WSS and $Y(t)$ is WSS, and*

2. *$R_{X,Y}(t_1, t_2) = \mathbb{E}[X(t_1)Y(t_2)]$ is a function of $t_1 - t_2$.*

If $X(t)$ and $Y(t)$ are jointly WSS, we write

$$R_{X,Y}(t_1, t_2) = R_{X,Y}(\tau) \stackrel{\text{def}}{=} \mathbb{E}[X(t+\tau)Y(\tau)].$$

The definition of "jointly WSS" is necessary here because $R_{X,Y}$ is defined by X and Y. Just knowing that $X(t)$ and $Y(t)$ are WSS does not allow one to say that $R_{X,Y}(t_1, t_2)$ can be written as the time difference.

If we flip the order of X and Y to consider $R_{Y,X}(\tau)$ and not $R_{X,Y}(\tau)$, then we need to flip the argument. The following lemma explains why.

Lemma 10.3. *For any random processes $X(t)$ and $Y(t)$, the **cross-correlation** $R_{X,Y}(\tau)$ is related to $R_{Y,X}(\tau)$ as*

$$R_{X,Y}(\tau) = R_{Y,X}(-\tau). \tag{10.30}$$

Proof. Recall the definition of $R_{Y,X}(-\tau) = \mathbb{E}[Y(t-\tau)X(t)]$. This can be simplified as follows:

$$\begin{aligned}
R_{Y,X}(-\tau) &= \mathbb{E}[Y(t-\tau)X(t)] \\
&= \mathbb{E}[X(t)Y(t-\tau)] \\
&= \mathbb{E}[X(t'+\tau)Y(t')] = R_{X,Y}(\tau),
\end{aligned}$$

where we substituted $t' = t - \tau$.

□

Example 10.18. Let $X(t)$ and $N(t)$ be two independent WSS random processes with expectations $\mathbb{E}[X(t)] = \mu_X$ and $\mathbb{E}[N(t)] = 0$, respectively. Let $Y(t) = X(t) + N(t)$. We want to show that $X(t)$ and $Y(t)$ are jointly WSS, and we want to find $R_{X,Y}(\tau)$.

Solution. Before we show the joint WSS property of $X(t)$ and $Y(t)$, we first show that $Y(t)$ is WSS:

$$\begin{aligned}
\mathbb{E}[Y(t)] &= \mathbb{E}[X(t) + N(t)] = \mu_X. \\
R_Y(t_1, t_2) &= \mathbb{E}[(X(t_1) + N(t_1))(X(t_2) + N(t_2))] \\
&= \mathbb{E}[(X(t_1)X(t_2)] + \mathbb{E}[(N(t_1)N(t_2)] \\
&= R_X(t_1 - t_2) + R_N(t_1 - t_2).
\end{aligned}$$

To show that $X(t)$ and $Y(t)$ are jointly WSS, we need to check the cross-correlation function:

$$
\begin{aligned}
R_{X,Y}(t_1, t_2) &= \mathbb{E}[X(t_1)Y(t_2)] \\
&= \mathbb{E}\left[X(t_1)(X(t_2) + N(t_2))\right] \\
&= \mathbb{E}\left[X(t_1)(X(t_2)\right] + \mathbb{E}\left[X(t_1)N(t_2)\right] \\
&= R_X(t_1, t_2) + \mathbb{E}[X(t_1)]\mathbb{E}[N(t_2)] \\
&= R_X(t_1, t_2).
\end{aligned}
$$

Since $R_{X,Y}(t_1, t_2)$ is a function of $t_1 - t_2$, and since $X(t)$ and $Y(t)$ are WSS, $X(t)$ and $Y(t)$ must be jointly WSS.

Finally, to find $R_{X,Y}(\tau)$, we substitute $\tau = t_1 - t_2$ and obtain $R_{X,Y}(\tau) = R_X(\tau)$.

Knowing the definition of jointly WSS, we consider the cross-correlation between $X(t)$ and $Y(t)$. Note that here we are asking about the cross-correlation between the input and the output of the same LTI system, as illustrated in **Figure 10.23**. The pair $X(t)$ and $Y(t) = h(t) * X(t)$ are special because $Y(t)$ is the convolved version of $X(t)$.

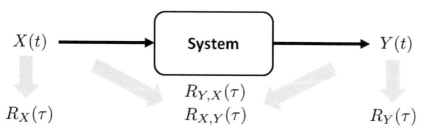

Figure 10.23: The source of the signals when defining $R_X(\tau)$, $R_{X,Y}(\tau)$, $R_{Y,X}(\tau)$ and $R_Y(\tau)$.

Theorem 10.6. *Let $X(t)$ and $Y(t)$ be jointly WSS processes, and let $Y(t) = h(t) * X(t)$. Then the* **cross-correlation** *$R_{Y,X}(\tau)$ is*

$$R_{Y,X}(\tau) = h(\tau) * R_X(\tau). \tag{10.31}$$

Proof. Recalling the definition of cross-correlation, we have

$$
\begin{aligned}
R_{Y,X}(\tau) &= \mathbb{E}[Y(t+\tau)X(t)] \\
&= \mathbb{E}\left[X(t)\int_{-\infty}^{\infty} X(t+\tau-r)h(r)\,dr\right] \\
&= \int_{-\infty}^{\infty} \mathbb{E}[X(t)X(t+\tau-r)]h(r)\,dr \\
&= \int_{-\infty}^{\infty} R_X(\tau-r)h(r)\,dr,
\end{aligned}
$$

which is the convolution $R_{Y,X}(\tau) = h(\tau) * R_X(\tau)$. $\qquad\square$

We next define the **cross power spectral density** of two jointly WSS processes as the Fourier transform of the cross-correlation function.

Definition 10.12. *The* **cross power spectral density** *of two jointly WSS processes* $X(t)$ *and* $Y(t)$ *is defined as*

$$S_{X,Y}(\omega) = \mathcal{F}[R_{X,Y}(\tau)],$$
$$S_{Y,X}(\omega) = \mathcal{F}[R_{Y,X}(\tau)].$$

The relationship between $S_{X,Y}$ and $S_{Y,X}$ can be seen from the following theorem.

Theorem 10.7. *For two jointly WSS random processes* $X(t)$ *and* $Y(t)$, *the cross power spectral density satisfies the property that*

$$S_{X,Y}(\omega) = \overline{S_{Y,X}(\omega)}, \qquad (10.32)$$

where $\overline{(\cdot)}$ *denotes the complex conjugate.*

Proof. Since $S_{X,Y}(\omega) = \mathcal{F}[R_{X,Y}(\tau)]$ by definition, it follows that

$$\mathcal{F}[R_{X,Y}(\tau)] = \int_{-\infty}^{\infty} R_{X,Y}(\tau)e^{-j\omega\tau}\,d\tau$$
$$= \int_{-\infty}^{\infty} R_{Y,X}(-\tau)e^{-j\omega\tau}\,d\tau$$
$$= \int_{-\infty}^{\infty} R_{X,Y}(\tau')e^{j\omega\tau'}\,d\tau',$$

which is exactly the conjugate $\overline{S_{Y,X}(\omega)}$. $\qquad\square$

When sending the random process through an LTI system, the cross-correlation power spectral density is given by the theorem below.

Theorem 10.8. *If* $X(t)$ *passes through an LTI system to yield* $Y(t)$, *then the* **cross power spectral density** *is*

$$S_{Y,X}(\omega) = H(\omega)S_X(\omega),$$
$$S_{X,Y}(\omega) = \overline{H(\omega)}S_X(\omega).$$

Proof. By taking the Fourier transform on $R_{Y,X}(\tau)$ we have that $S_{Y,X}(\omega) = H(\omega)S_X(\omega)$. Since $R_{X,Y}(\tau) = R_{Y,X}(-\tau)$, it holds that $S_{X,Y}(\omega) = \overline{H(\omega)}S_X(\omega)$. $\qquad\square$

Example 10.19. Let $X(t)$ be a WSS random process with

$$R_X(\tau) = e^{-\tau^2/2}, \quad H(\omega) = e^{-\omega^2/2}.$$

Find $S_{X,Y}(\omega)$, $R_{X,Y}(\tau)$, $S_Y(\omega)$ and $R_Y(\tau)$.

Solution. First, by the Fourier transform table we know that

$$S_X(\omega) = \sqrt{2\pi}e^{-\omega^2/2}.$$

Since $H(\omega) = e^{-\omega^2/2}$, we have

$$S_{X,Y}(\omega) = \overline{H(\omega)}S_X(\omega) = \sqrt{2\pi}e^{-\omega^2}.$$

The cross-correlation function is

$$R_{X,Y}(\omega) = \mathcal{F}^{-1}\left[\sqrt{2\pi}e^{-\omega^2}\right] = \frac{1}{\sqrt{2}}e^{-\frac{\tau^2}{4}}.$$

The power spectral density of $Y(t)$ is

$$S_Y(\omega) = |H(\omega)|^2 S_X(\omega) = \sqrt{2\pi}e^{-\frac{3\omega^2}{2}}.$$

Therefore, the autocorrelation function of $Y(t)$ is

$$R_Y(\tau) = \mathcal{F}^{-1}\left[\sqrt{2\pi}e^{-\frac{3\omega^2}{2}}\right] = \frac{1}{\sqrt{3}}e^{-\tau^2/6}.$$

10.6 Optimal Linear Filter

In the previous sections, we have built many tools to analyze random processes. Our next goal is to apply these techniques. To that end, we will discuss **optimal linear filter design**, which is a set of estimation techniques for predicting and recovering information from a time series.

10.6.1 Discrete-time random processes

We begin by introducing some notations. In the previous sections, we have been using **continuous-time** random processes to study statistics. In this section, we mainly focus on **discrete-time** random processes. The shift from continuous-time to discrete-time is straightforward as far as the theories are concerned — we switch the continuous-time index t to a discrete-time index n. However, shifting to discrete-time random processes can simplify many difficult problems because many discrete-time problems can be solved by matrices and vectors. This will make the computations and implementations much easier. To make this transition easier, we provide a few definitions and results without proof.

Notations for discrete-time random processes

- We denote the discrete-time indices by m and n, corresponding to the continuous-time indices t_1 and t_2, respectively.

- A discrete-time random process is denoted by $X[n]$.
- Its mean function and the autocorrelation function are

$$\mu_X[n] = \mathbb{E}[X[n]],$$
$$R_X[m,n] = \mathbb{E}[X[m]X[n]].$$

- We say that $X[n]$ is WSS if $\mu_X[n] = $ constant, and $R_X[m,n]$ is a function of $m - n$.
- If $X[n]$ is WSS, we write $R_X[m,n]$ as

$$R_X[m,n] = R_X[m-n] = R_X[k],$$

where $k = m - n$ is the interval.

- If $X[n]$ is WSS, we define the power spectral density as

$$S_X(e^{j\omega}) = \mathcal{F}\{R_X[k]\},$$

where $S_X(e^{j\omega})$ denotes the discrete-time Fourier transform.

When a random process $X[n]$ is sent through an LTI system with an impulse response $h[n]$, the output is

$$Y[n] = h[n] * X[n] = \sum_{k=-\infty}^{\infty} h[k]X[n-k]. \tag{10.33}$$

When a WSS process $X[n]$ passes through an LTI system $h[n]$ to yield an output $Y[n]$, the auto- and cross-correlation function and power spectral densities are

- $R_Y[k] = \mathbb{E}[Y[n+k]Y[n]]$, $S_Y(e^{j\omega}) = \mathcal{F}\{R_Y[k]\} = |H(e^{j\omega})|^2 S_X(e^{j\omega})$.
- $R_{XY}[k] = \mathbb{E}[X[n+k]Y[n]]$, $S_{XY}(e^{j\omega}) = \mathcal{F}\{R_{XY}[k]\} = \overline{H(e^{j\omega})}S_X(e^{j\omega})$.
- $R_{YX}[k] = \mathbb{E}[Y[n+k]X[n]]$, $S_{YX}(e^{j\omega}) = \mathcal{F}\{R_{YX}[k]\} = H(e^{j\omega})S_X(e^{j\omega})$.

10.6.2 Problem formulation

The problem we study here is known as the **optimal linear filter design**. Suppose that there is a WSS process $X[n]$ that we want to process. For example, if $X[n]$ is a corrupted version of some clean time-series, we may want to remove the noise by filtering (also known as averaging) $X[n]$. Conceptualizing the denoising process as a linear time-invariant system with an impulse response $h[n]$, our goal is to determine the optimal $h[n]$ such that the estimated time series $\widehat{Y}[n]$ is as close to the true time series $Y[n]$ as possible.

Referring to **Figure 10.24**, we refer to $X[n]$ as the **input function** and to $Y[n]$ as the **target function**. $X[n]$ and $Y[n]$ are related according to the equation

$$Y[n] = \underbrace{\sum_{k=0}^{K-1} h[k]X[n-k]}_{\widehat{Y}[n]} + E[n], \tag{10.34}$$

where $E[n]$ is a noise random process to model the error. The linear part of the equation is known as the **prediction** and is constructed by sending $X[n]$ through the system. For simplicity we assume that $X[n]$ is WSS. Thus, it follows that $Y[n]$ is also WSS. We may also assume that we can estimate $R_X[k]$, $R_{YX}[k]$, $R_{XY}[k]$ and $R_Y[k]$.

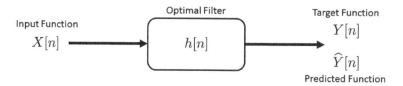

Figure 10.24: A schematic diagram illustrating the optimal linear filter problem: Given an input function $X[n]$, we want to design a filter $h[n]$ such that the prediction $\widehat{Y}[n]$ is close to the target function $Y[n]$.

Example 10.20. If we let $K = 3$, Equation (10.34) gives us

$$Y[n] = h[0]X[n] + h[1]X[n-1] + h[2]X[n-2] + E[n].$$

That is, the current sample $Y[n]$ is a linear combination of the previous samples $X[n]$, $X[n-1]$ and $X[n-2]$.

Given $X[n]$ and $Y[n]$, what would be the best guess of the impulse response $h[n]$ so that the prediction is as close to the true values as possible? From our discussions of linear regression, we know that this is equivalent to solving the optimization problem

$$\underset{\{h[k]\}_{k=0}^{K-1}}{\text{minimize}} \quad \left(Y[n] - \sum_{k=0}^{K-1} h[k]X[n-k]\right)^2. \tag{10.35}$$

The choice of the squared error is more or less arbitrary, depending on how we want to model $E[n]$. By using the square norm, we implicitly assume that the error is Gaussian. This may not be true, but it is commonly used because the squared norm is **differentiable**. We will follow this tradition.

The challenge associated with the minimization is that in most of the practical settings the random processes $X[n]$ and $Y[n]$ are changing rapidly because they are **random processes**. Therefore, even if we solve the optimization problem, the estimates $h[k]$ will be random variables since we are solving a random equation. To eliminate this randomness, we take the **expectation** over all the possible choices of $X[n]$ and $Y[n]$, yielding

$$\underset{\{h[k]\}_{k=0}^{K-1}}{\text{minimize}} \quad \left(Y[n] - \sum_{k=0}^{K-1} h[k]X[n-k]\right)^2,$$

$$\Downarrow$$

$$\underset{\{h[k]\}_{k=0}^{K-1}}{\text{minimize}} \ \mathbb{E}_{X,Y}\left[\left(Y[n] - \sum_{k=0}^{K-1} h[k]X[n-k]\right)^2\right].$$

The resulting impulse responses $h[k]$, derived by solving the above minimization, is known as the **optimal linear filter**. It is the best linear model for describing the input-output relationships between $X[n]$ and $Y[n]$.

What is the optimal linear filter?

The optimal linear filter is the solution to the optimization problem

$$\operatorname*{minimize}_{\{h[k]\}_{k=0}^{K-1}} \; \mathbb{E}_{X,Y}\left[\left(Y[n] - \sum_{k=0}^{K-1} h[k]X[n-k]\right)^2\right]. \qquad (10.36)$$

10.6.3 Yule-Walker equation

To solve the optimal linear filter problem, we first perform some (slightly tedious) algebra to obtain the following results:

Lemma 10.4. *Let $\widehat{Y}[n] = \sum_{k=0}^{K-1} h[k]X[n-k]$ be the prediction of $Y[n]$. The squared-norm error can be written as*

$$\mathbb{E}_{X,Y}\left[\left(Y[n] - \widehat{Y}[n]\right)^2\right]$$

$$= R_Y[0] - 2\sum_{k=0}^{K-1} h[k]R_{YX}[k] + \sum_{k=0}^{K-1}\sum_{j=0}^{K-1} h[k]h[j]R_X[j-k]. \qquad (10.37)$$

Thus we can express the error in terms of $R_{YX}[k]$, $R_X[k]$ and $R_Y[k]$.

Proof. We expand the error as follows:

$$\mathbb{E}_{X,Y}\left[\left(Y[n] - \widehat{Y}[n]\right)^2\right] = \mathbb{E}_Y\left[(Y[n])^2\right] - 2\mathbb{E}_{X,Y}\left[Y[n]\widehat{Y}[n]\right] + \mathbb{E}_X\left[(\widehat{Y}[n])^2\right].$$

The first term is the autocorrelation of $Y[n]$:

$$\mathbb{E}_Y\left[(Y[n])^2\right] = \mathbb{E}\left[Y[n+0]Y[n]\right] = R_Y[0]. \qquad (10.38)$$

The second term is

$$\mathbb{E}_{X,Y}\left[Y[n]\widehat{Y}[n]\right] = \mathbb{E}_{X,Y}\left[Y[n]\sum_{k=0}^{K-1} h[k]X[n-k]\right]$$

$$= \sum_{k=0}^{K-1} h[k]\mathbb{E}_{X,Y}\left[Y[n]X[n-k]\right]$$

$$= \sum_{k=0}^{K-1} h[k]R_{YX}[k]. \qquad (10.39)$$

The third term is

$$
\mathbb{E}_X\left[(\widehat{Y}[n])^2\right] = \mathbb{E}_X\left[\left(\sum_{k=0}^{K-1} h[k]X[n-k]\right)\left(\sum_{j=0}^{K-1} h[j]X[n-j]\right)\right]
$$

$$
= \mathbb{E}_X\left[\sum_{k=0}^{K-1}\sum_{j=0}^{K-1} h[k]h[j]X[n-k]X[n-j]\right]
$$

$$
= \sum_{k=0}^{K-1}\sum_{j=0}^{K-1} h[k]h[j]\mathbb{E}_X\left[X[n-k]X[n-j]\right]
$$

$$
= \sum_{k=0}^{K-1}\sum_{j=0}^{K-1} h[k]h[j]R_X[j-k]. \tag{10.40}
$$

This completes the proof.

$\square$

The significance of this theorem is that it allows us to write the error in terms of $R_{YX}[k]$, $R_X[k]$ and $R_Y[k]$. As we have mentioned, while we can solve the randomized optimization Equation (10.35), the resulting solution will be a random vector depending on the particular realizations $X[n]$ and $Y[n]$. Switching from Equation (10.35) to Equation (10.36) eliminates the randomness because we have taken the expectation. The resulting optimization according to the theorem is also convenient. Instead of seeking individual realizations, we only need to know the overall statistical description of the data through $R_{YX}[k]$, $R_X[k]$ and $R_Y[k]$. These can be estimated through modeling or pseudorandom signals.

The solution to the optimal linear filter problem is summarized by the **Yule-Walker equation**:

Theorem 10.9. *The solution $\{h[0],\ldots,h[K-1]\}$ to the optimal linear filter problem*

$$
\underset{\{h[k]\}_{k=0}^{K-1}}{\text{minimize}}\ \mathbb{E}_{X,Y}\left[\left(Y[n] - \sum_{k=0}^{K-1} h[k]X[n-k]\right)^2\right] \tag{10.41}
$$

is given by the following matrix equation:

$$
\begin{pmatrix} R_{YX}[0] \\ R_{YX}[1] \\ \vdots \\ R_{YX}[K-1] \end{pmatrix} = \begin{pmatrix} R_X[0] & R_X[1] & \cdots & R_X[K-1] \\ R_X[1] & R_X[0] & \cdots & \vdots \\ \vdots & \vdots & \ddots & \vdots \\ R_X[K-1] & R_X[k-2] & \cdots & R_X[0] \end{pmatrix} \begin{pmatrix} h[0] \\ h[1] \\ \vdots \\ h[K-1] \end{pmatrix}, \tag{10.42}
$$

which is known as the Yule-Walker equation.

Therefore, by solving the simple linear problem given by the Yule-Walker equation, we will find the optimal linear filter solution.

Proof. Since the error is a squared norm, the optimal solution is obtained by taking the derivative:

$$\frac{d}{dh[i]} \mathbb{E}_{X,Y}\left[\left(Y[n] - \widehat{Y}[n]\right)^2\right]$$

$$= \frac{d}{dh[i]} \left\{ R_Y[0] - 2\sum_{k=0}^{K-1} h[k]R_{YX}[k] + \sum_{k=0}^{K-1}\sum_{j=0}^{K-1} h[k]h[j]R_X[j-k] \right\}$$

$$= 0 - 2R_{YX}[i] + 2\sum_{k=0}^{K-1} h[k]R_X[i-k],$$

in which the derivative of the last term is computed by noting that

$$\frac{d}{dh[i]}\sum_{k=0}^{K-1}\sum_{j=0}^{K-1} h[k]h[j]R_X[j-k]$$

$$= \frac{d}{dh[i]}\sum_{j=0}^{K-1} h[j]^2 R_X[0] + \frac{d}{dh[i]}\sum_{k=0}^{K-1}\sum_{j\neq k} h[k]h[j]R_X[j-k]$$

$$= 2\sum_{k=0}^{K-1} h[k]R_X[i-k].$$

Equating the derivative to zero yields

$$R_{YX}[i] = \sum_{k=0}^{K-1} h[k]R_X[i-k], \qquad i = 0, \ldots, K-1,$$

and putting the above equations into the matrix-vector form we complete the proof.

□

The matrix in the Yule-Walker equation is a **Toeplitz** matrix, in which each row is a shifted version of the preceding row. This matrix structure is a consequence of a WSS process so that the autocorrelation function is determined by the time difference k and not by the starting and end times.

Remark. If we take the derivative of the loss w.r.t. $h[i]$, we have that

$$0 = \frac{d}{dh[i]} \mathbb{E}_{X,Y}\left[\left(Y[n] - \widehat{Y}[n]\right)^2\right] = -2\mathbb{E}\left[\left(Y[n] - \widehat{Y}[n]\right)X[n-i]\right].$$

This condition is known as the **orthogonality condition**, as it says that the error $Y[n] - \widehat{Y}[n]$ is orthogonal to the signal $X[n-i]$.

10.6.4 Linear prediction

We now demonstrate how to use the Yule-Walker equation in modeling an **autoregressive process**. The procedure in this simple example can be used in speech processing and time-series forecasting.

Suppose that we have a WSS random process $Y[n]$. We would like to predict the future samples by using the most recent K samples through an autoregressive model. Since the model is linear, we can write

$$\widehat{Y}[n] = \sum_{k=1}^{K} h[k]Y[n-k] + E[n]. \tag{10.43}$$

In this model, we say that the predicted value $\widehat{Y}[n]$ is a linear combination of the past K samples, albeit to approximation error $E[n]$.

The problem we need to solve is

$$\underset{h[k]}{\text{minimize}} \ \ \mathbb{E}\left[\left(Y[n] - \widehat{Y}[n]\right)^2\right].$$

Since $\widehat{Y}[n]$ is written in terms of the past samples of $Y[n]$ in this problem, in the Yule-Walker equation we can replace X with Y. Consequently, we can write the matrix equation from

$$\begin{pmatrix} R_{YX}[0] \\ R_{YX}[1] \\ \vdots \\ R_{YX}[K-1] \end{pmatrix} = \begin{pmatrix} R_X[0] & R_X[1] & \cdots & R_X[K-1] \\ R_X[1] & R_X[0] & \cdots & R_X[K-2] \\ \vdots & \vdots & \ddots & \vdots \\ R_X[K-1] & R_X[k-2] & \cdots & R_X[0] \end{pmatrix} \begin{pmatrix} h[0] \\ h[1] \\ \vdots \\ h[K-1] \end{pmatrix},$$

to

$$\underbrace{\begin{pmatrix} R_Y[1] \\ R_Y[2] \\ \vdots \\ R_Y[K] \end{pmatrix}}_{r} = \underbrace{\begin{pmatrix} R_Y[0] & R_Y[1] & \cdots & R_Y[K-1] \\ R_Y[1] & R_Y[0] & \cdots & R_Y[K-2] \\ \vdots & \vdots & \ddots & \vdots \\ R_Y[K-1] & R_Y[k-2] & \cdots & R_Y[0] \end{pmatrix}}_{R} \begin{pmatrix} h[0] \\ h[1] \\ \vdots \\ h[K-1] \end{pmatrix}. \tag{10.44}$$

On a computer, solving the Yule-Walker equation requires a few steps. First, we need to estimate the correlation

$$R_Y[k] = \mathbb{E}[Y[n+k]Y[n]] \approx \frac{1}{N}\sum_{n=1}^{N} Y[n+k]Y[n].$$

The averaging on the right-hand side is often done using xcorr in MATLAB or np.correlate in Python. A graphical illustration of the input and the autocorrelation function is shown in **Figure 10.25**.

After we have found $R_Y[n]$, we need to construct the Yule-Walker equation. For this linear prediction problem, the left-hand side of the Yule-Walker equation is the vector r, defined according to Equation (10.44). The Yule-Walker equation also requires the matrix R. This R can be constructed via the Toeplitz matrix as

$$R = \text{Toeplitz}\left\{R_Y[0], R_Y[1], \dots, R_Y[K-1]\right\}.$$

In MATLAB, we can call Toeplitz to construct the matrix. In Python, the command is lin.Toeplitz.

To solve the Yule-Walker equation, we need to invert the matrix R. There are built-in commands for such an operation. In MATLAB, the command is \ (the backslash), whereas in Python the command is np.linalg.lstsq.

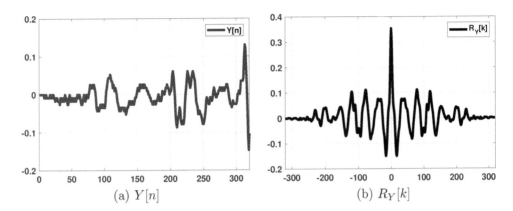

(a) $Y[n]$ (b) $R_Y[k]$

Figure 10.25: An example time-series and its autocorrelation function.

```
% MATLAB code to solve the Yule Walker Equation
y = load('data_ch10.txt');
K = 10;
N = 320;


y_corr = xcorr(y);
R      = Toeplitz(y_corr(N+[0:K-1]));
lhs    = y_corr(N+[1:K]);
h      = R\lhs;
```

```
# Python code to solve the Yule Walker Equation
y = np.loadtxt('./data_ch10.txt')
K = 10
N = 320


y_corr = np.correlate(y,y,mode='full')
R      = lin.Toeplitz(y_corr[N-1:N+K-1]) #call scipy.linalg
lhs    = y_corr[N:N+K]
h      = np.linalg.lstsq(R,lhs,rcond = None)[0]
```

Note that in both the MATLAB and Python codes the Toeplitz matrix R starts with the index N. This is because, as you can see from **Figure 10.25**, the origin of the autocorrelation function is the middle index of the computed autocorrelation function. For r, the starting index is $N + 1$ because the vector starts with $R_Y[1]$.

To predict the future samples, we recall the autoregressive model for this problem:

$$\widehat{Y}[n] = \sum_{k=0}^{K-1} h[k]Y[n-k].$$

Therefore, given $Y[n-1], Y[n-2], \ldots, Y[n-K]$, we can predict $\widehat{Y}[n]$. Then we insert this predicted $\widehat{Y}[n]$ into the sequence and increment the estimation problem to the next time index. By repeating the process, we will be able to predict the future samples of $Y[n]$.

Figure 10.26 illustrates the prediction results of the Yule-Walker equation. As you can see, the predictions are reasonably meaningful since the patterns follow the trend.

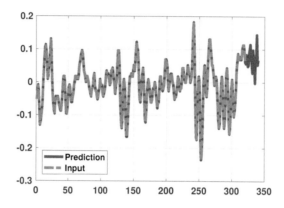

Figure 10.26: An example of the predictions made by the autoregressive model.

The MATLAB and Python codes are shown below.

```
% MATLAB code to predict the samples
z    = y(311:320);
yhat = zeros(340,1);
yhat(1:320) = y;

for t = 1:20
    predict     = z'*h;
    z           = [z(2:10); predict];
    yhat(320+t) = predict;
end

plot(yhat, 'r', 'LineWidth', 3); hold on;
plot(y,    'k', 'LineWidth', 4);
```

```
# Python code to predict the samples
z = y[310:320]
yhat = np.zeros((340,1))
yhat[0:320,0] = y

for t in range(20):
  predict = np.inner(np.reshape(z,(1,10)),h)
  z = np.concatenate((z[1:10], predict))
  yhat[320+t,0] = predict

plt.plot(yhat,'r')
plt.plot(y,'k')
plt.show()
```

10.6.5 Wiener filter

In the previous formulation, we notice that the impulse response has a **finite** length. There are, however, problems in which the impulse response is infinite. For example, a **recursive filter** $h[n]$ will be infinitely long. The extension from finite length to infinite length is straightforward. We can model the problem as

$$Y[n] = \sum_{k=-\infty}^{\infty} h[k]X[n-k] + E[n].$$

However, when $h[n]$ is infinitely long the Yule-Walker equation does not hold because the matrix $\mathbf{R}$ will be infinitely large. Nevertheless, the building block equation for Yule-Walker is still valid:

$$R_{YX}[i] = \sum_{k=-\infty}^{\infty} h[k]R_X[i-k]. \tag{10.45}$$

To maintain the spirit of the Yule-Walker equation while enabling computation, we recognize that the infinite sum on the right-hand side is, in fact, a **convolution**. Thus we can take the (discrete-time) Fourier transform of both sides to obtain

$$S_{YX}(e^{j\omega}) = H(e^{j\omega})S_X(e^{j\omega}). \tag{10.46}$$

Therefore, the corresponding optimal linear filter (in the Fourier domain) is

$$H(e^{j\omega}) = \frac{S_{YX}(e^{j\omega})}{S_X(e^{j\omega})}, \tag{10.47}$$

and

$$h[n] = \mathcal{F}^{-1}\left\{ \frac{S_{YX}(e^{-j\omega})}{S_X(e^{-j\omega})} \right\}.$$

The filter obtained in this way is known as the **Wiener filter**.

Example 10.21. (Denoising) Suppose $X[n] = Y[n] + W[n]$, where $W[n]$ is the noise term that is independent of $Y[n]$, as shown in **Figure 10.27**.

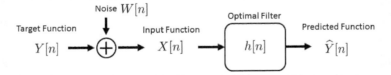

Figure 10.27: Design of a Wiener filter that takes an input function $X[n]$ and outputs an estimate $\widehat{Y}[n]$ that is close to the true function $Y[n]$.

Now, given the input function $X[n]$, can we construct the Wiener filter $h[n]$ such that the predicted function $\widehat{Y}[n]$ is as close to $Y[n]$ as possible? The Wiener filter for this problem is also the optimal denoising filter.

Solution. The following correlation functions can easily be seen:

$$
\begin{aligned}
R_X[k] &= \mathbb{E}[X[n+k]X[n]] \\
&= \mathbb{E}[(Y[n+k] + W[n+k])(Y[n] + W[n])] \\
&= \mathbb{E}[Y[n+k]Y[n]] + \mathbb{E}[Y[n+k]W[n]] \\
&\quad + \mathbb{E}[W[n+k]Y[n]] + \mathbb{E}[W[n+k]W[n]] \\
&= \mathbb{E}[Y[n+k]Y[n]] + 0 + 0 + \mathbb{E}[W[n+k]W[n]] \\
&= R_Y[k] + R_W[k].
\end{aligned}
$$

Similarly, we have

$$
\begin{aligned}
R_{YX}[k] &= \mathbb{E}[Y[n+k]X[n]] \\
&= \mathbb{E}[Y[n](Y[n+k] + W[n+k])] = R_Y[k].
\end{aligned}
$$

Consequently, the optimal linear filter is

$$
\begin{aligned}
H(e^{j\omega}) &= \frac{S_{YX}(e^{j\omega})}{S_X(e^{j\omega})} \\
&= \frac{\mathcal{F}\{R_{YX}[k]\}}{\mathcal{F}\{R_X[k]\}} \\
&= \frac{S_Y(e^{j\omega})}{S_Y(e^{j\omega}) + S_W(e^{j\omega})}.
\end{aligned}
$$

What is the Wiener filter for a denoising problem?

- Suppose the corrupted function $X[n]$ is related to the clean function $Y[n]$ through $X[n] = Y[n] + W[n]$, for some noise function $W[n]$.

- The Wiener filter is

$$
H(e^{j\omega}) = \frac{S_Y(e^{j\omega})}{S_Y(e^{j\omega}) + S_W(e^{j\omega})}. \tag{10.48}
$$

- To perform the filtering, the denoised function $\widehat{Y}[n]$ is

$$
\widehat{Y}[n] = \mathcal{F}^{-1}\left\{ H(e^{j\omega})X(e^{j\omega}) \right\}.
$$

Figure 10.28 shows an example of applying the Wiener filter to a noise removal problem. In this example we let $W[n]$ be an i.i.d. Gaussian process with standard deviation $\sigma = 0.05$ and mean $\mu = 0$. The noisy samples of random process $X[n]$ are defined as $X[n] = Y[n] + W[n]$, where $Y[n]$ is the clean function. As you can see from **Figure 10.28**(a), the Wiener filter is able to denoise the function reasonably well.

The optimal linear filter used for this denoising task is infinitely long. This can be seen in **Figure 10.28**(b), where the filter length is the same as the length of the observed time series $X[n]$. If $X[n]$ is longer, the filter $h[n]$ will also become longer. Therefore, finite-length approaches such as the Yule-Walker equation do not apply here.

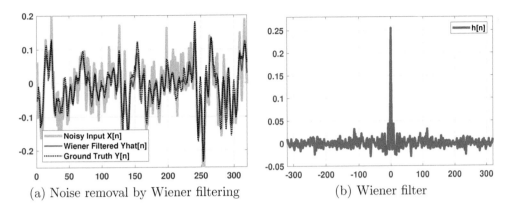

(a) Noise removal by Wiener filtering   (b) Wiener filter

Figure 10.28: (a) Applying a Wiener filter to denoise a function. (b) The Wiener filter used for the denoising task.

The MATLAB / Python codes used to generate **Figure 10.28**(a) are shown below. The main commands here are `scipy.fft` and `scipy.ifft`, which are available in the `scipy` library. The commands `Yhat = H.*fft(x, 639)` in MATLAB execute the Wiener filtering step. Here, we resample the function x to 639 samples so that it matches with the Wiener filter H. Similar commands in Python are `H * fft(x, 639)`.

```
% MATLAB code for Wiener filtering
w = 0.05*randn(320,1);
x = y + w;

Ry = xcorr(y);
Rw = xcorr(w);
Sy = fft(Ry);
Sw = fft(Rw);
H = Sy./(Sy + Sw);
Yhat = H.*fft(x, 639);
yhat = real(ifft(Yhat));

plot(x, 'LineWidth', 4, 'Color', [0.7, 0.7, 0.7]); hold on;
plot(yhat(1:320), 'r', 'LineWidth', 2);
plot(y, 'k:', 'LineWidth', 2);
```

```
# Python code for Wiener filtering
from scipy.fft import fft, ifft
w = 0.05*np.random.randn(320)
x = y + w

Ry = np.correlate(y,y,mode='full')
Rw = np.correlate(w,w,mode='full')
Sy = fft(Ry)
Sw = fft(Rw)
H  = Sy / (Sy+Sw)
Yhat = H * fft(x, 639)
```

```
yhat = np.real(ifft(Yhat))

plt.plot(x,color='gray')
plt.plot(yhat[0:320],'r')
plt.plot(y,'k:')
```

Example 10.22. (Deconvolution) Suppose that the corrupted function is generated according to a linear process given by

$$X[n] = \sum_{\ell=-\infty}^{\infty} g[\ell]Y[n-\ell] + W[n],$$

where $g[n]$ is the impulse response of some kind of degradation process and $W[n]$ is the Gaussian noise term, as shown in **Figure 10.29**. Find the optimal linear filter (i.e., the Wiener filter) to estimate $\widehat{Y}[n]$.

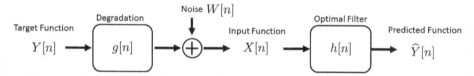

Figure 10.29: Design of a Wiener filter that takes an input function $X[n]$ and outputs an estimate $\widehat{Y}[n]$ that is close to the true function $Y[n]$.

Solution. To construct the Wiener filter, we first determine the cross-correlation function:

$$R_{YX}[k] = \mathbb{E}\left[Y[n+k]X[n]\right] = \mathbb{E}\left[Y[n+k]\sum_{\ell=-\infty}^{\infty} g[\ell]Y[n-\ell] + W[n]\right].$$

Using algebra, it follows that

$$\mathbb{E}\left[Y[n+k]\sum_{\ell=-\infty}^{\infty} g[\ell]Y[n-\ell] + W[n]\right]$$

$$= \sum_{\ell=-\infty}^{\infty} g[\ell]\mathbb{E}[Y[n+k]Y[n-\ell]] + \mathbb{E}[Y[n+k]W[n]]$$

$$= \sum_{\ell=-\infty}^{\infty} g[\ell]R_Y[k+\ell] + 0 = (g \circledast R_Y)[k],$$

which is the correlation between g and R_Y. Therefore, the cross power spectral density $S_{YX}(e^{j\omega})$ is

$$S_{YX}(e^{j\omega}) = \overline{G(e^{j\omega})}S_Y(e^{j\omega}).$$

666

The autocorrelation of this problem is

$$
\begin{aligned}
R_X[k] &= \mathbb{E}\left[X[n+k]X[n]\right] \\
&= \mathbb{E}\left[((g*Y)[n+k]+W[n+k])((g*Y)[n]+W[n])\right] \\
&= \mathbb{E}\left[(g*Y)[n+k](g*Y)[n]\right] + \mathbb{E}[W[n+k]W[n]] \\
&= (g \circledast (g*R_Y))[k] + R_W[k],
\end{aligned}
$$

where, according to the previous section, the first part is the correlation $\circledast$ followed by a convolution $*$. Therefore, the power spectral density of X is

$$
S_X(e^{j\omega}) = |G(e^{j\omega})|^2 S_Y(e^{j\omega}) + S_W(e^{j\omega}).
$$

Combining the results, the Wiener filter is

$$
H(e^{j\omega}) = \frac{S_{YX}(e^{j\omega})}{S_X(e^{j\omega})} = \frac{\overline{G(e^{j\omega})}S_Y(e^{j\omega})}{|G(e^{j\omega})|^2 S_Y(e^{j\omega}) + S_W(e^{j\omega})}.
$$

What is the Wiener filter for a deconvolution problem?

- Suppose that the corrupted function $X[n]$ is related to the clean function $Y[n]$ through $X[n] = (g*Y)[n] + W[n]$, for some degradation $g[n]$ and noise $W[n]$.

- The Wiener filter is

$$
H(e^{j\omega}) = \frac{\overline{G(e^{j\omega})}S_Y(e^{j\omega})}{|G(e^{j\omega})|^2 S_Y(e^{j\omega}) + S_W(e^{j\omega})}. \tag{10.49}
$$

- To perform the filtering, the estimated function $\widehat{Y}[n]$ is

$$
\widehat{Y}[n] = \mathcal{F}^{-1}\left\{H(e^{j\omega})X(e^{j\omega})\right\}.
$$

As an example of the deconvolution problem, we show a WSS function $Y[n]$ in **Figure 10.30**. This clean function $Y[n]$ is constructed by passing an i.i.d. noise process through an arbitrary LTI system so that the WSS property is guaranteed. Given this $Y[n]$, we construct a degradation process in which the impulse response is given by $g[n]$. In this example, we assume that $g[n]$ is a uniform function. We then add noise $W[n]$ to the time series to obtain the corrupted observation $X[n]$. The reconstruction by the Wiener filter is shown in **Figure 10.30**.

The MATLAB and Python codes used to generate **Figure 10.30** are shown below.

```
% MATLAB code to solve the Wiener deconvolution problem
load('ch10_wiener_deblur_data');
g = ones(32,1)/32;
w = 0.02*randn(320,1);
x = conv(y,g,'same') + w;

Ry = xcorr(y);
```

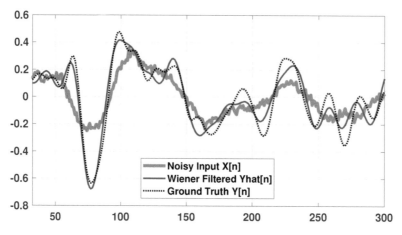

Figure 10.30: Reconstructing time series from degraded observations using a Wiener filter.

```
Rw = xcorr(w);
Sy = fft(Ry);
Sw = fft(Rw);
G  = fft(g,639);

H = (conj(G).*Sy)./(abs(G).^2.*Sy + Sw);
Yhat = H.*fft(x, 639);
yhat = real(ifft(Yhat));

figure;
plot(x, 'LineWidth', 4, 'Color', [0.5, 0.5, 0.5]); hold on;
plot(16:320+15, yhat(1:320), 'r', 'LineWidth', 2);
plot(1:320, y, 'k:', 'LineWidth', 2);
```

```python
# Python code to solve the Wiener deconvolution problem
y = np.loadtxt('./ch10_wiener_deblur_data.txt')
g = np.ones(64)/64
w = 0.02*np.random.randn(320)
x = np.convolve(y,g,mode='same') + w

Ry = np.correlate(y,y,mode='full')
Rw = np.correlate(w,w,mode='full')
Sy = fft(Ry)
Sw = fft(Rw)
G  = fft(g,639)
H = (np.conj(G)*Sy)/( np.power(np.abs(G),2)*Sy + Sw )

Yhat = H * fft(x, 639)
yhat = np.real(ifft(Yhat))

plt.plot(x,color='gray')
```

```
plt.plot(np.arange(32,320+32),yhat[0:320],'r')
plt.plot(y,'k:')
```

Caveat to Wiener filtering. In practice, the above Wiener filter needs to be modified because $S_Y(e^{j\omega})$ and $S_W(e^{j\omega})$ cannot be estimated from the data via the temporal correlation (as we did in the MATLAB/Python programs). The reason is that we never have access to $Y[n]$ and $W[n]$. In this case, one has to *guess* the power spectral densities $S_Y(e^{j\omega})$ and $S_W(e^{j\omega})$. The noise power $S_W(e^{j\omega})$ is usually not difficult to estimate. For example, in the program we showed above, the noise power spectral density is `Sw = 0.02^2*320` (MATLAB), which is the noise standard deviation times the number of samples.

The signal $S_Y(e^{j\omega})$ is often the hard part. In the absence of any knowledge about the ground truth's power spectral density, the Wiener filter does not work. However, for certain problems in which $S_Y(e^{j\omega})$ can be predetermined by prior knowledge, the Wiener filter is guaranteed to be optimal — optimal in the mean-squared-error sense over the entire time axis.

Wiener filter versus ridge regression. The Wiener filter equation can be interpreted as a ridge regression. Denoting the forward observation model by

$$x = Gy + w,$$

the corresponding ridge regression minimization is

$$\widehat{y} = \underset{y}{\operatorname{argmin}} \ \|x - Gy\|^2 + \lambda\|y\|^2$$
$$= (G^T G + \lambda I)^{-1} G^T x.$$

If G is a convolutional matrix, the above solution can be written in the Fourier domain (by using the Fourier transform as the eigenvectors):

$$\widehat{Y}(e^{j\omega}) = \underbrace{\left[\frac{\overline{G(e^{j\omega})}}{|G(e^{j\omega})|^2 + \lambda} \right]}_{H(e^{j\omega})} X(e^{j\omega}).$$

Comparing this "optimal linear filter" with the Wiener filter, we observe that the Wiener filter has slightly more generality:

$$\widehat{Y}(e^{j\omega}) = \left[\frac{\overline{G(e^{j\omega})}S_Y(e^{j\omega})}{|G(e^{j\omega})|^2 S_Y(e^{j\omega}) + S_W(e^{j\omega})} \right] X(e^{j\omega}).$$

Therefore, in the absence of $S_Y(e^{j\omega})$ and assuming that $S_W(e^{j\omega})$ is a constant (e.g., for Gaussian noise), the Wiener filter is exactly a ridge regression.

10.7 Summary

Random processes are very useful tools for analyzing random variables over time. In this chapter, we have introduced some of the most basic mechanisms:

- **Statistical versus temporal analysis**: The statistical analysis of a random process looks at the random process **vertically**. It treats $X(t)$ as a random variable and studies the randomness across different realizations. The temporal analysis is the **horizontal** perspective. It treats $X(t)$ as a function in time with a fixed random index. In general, statistical average $\neq$ temporal average.

- **Mean function** $\mu_X(t)$: The mean function is the expectation of the random process. At every time t, we take the expectation to obtain the expected value $\mathbb{E}[X(t)]$.

- **Autocorrelation function** $R_X(t_1, t_2)$. This is the joint expectation of the random process at two different time instants t_1 and t_2. The corresponding values $X(t_1)$ and $X(t_2)$ are two random variables, and so the joint expectation measures how correlated these two variables are.

- **Wide-sense stationary (WSS)**: This is a special class of random processes in which $\mu_X(t)$ is a constant and $R_X(t_1, t_2)$ is a function of $t_1 - t_2$. When this happens, the autocorrelation function (which is originally a 2D function) will have a Toeplitz structure. We write $R_X(t_1, t_2)$ as $R_X(\tau)$, where $\tau = t_1 - t_2$.

- **Power spectral density (PSD)**: This is the Fourier transform of the autocorrelation function $R_X(\tau)$, according to the Einstein-Wiener-Khinchin theorem. It is called the power spectral density because we can integrate it in the Fourier space to retrieve the power. This provides us with some convenient computational tools for analyzing data.

- Random process through a **linear time-invariant (LTI) system**: This tells us how a random process behaves after going through an LTI system. The analysis can be done at the realization level, where we look at each random process, or at the statistical level, where we look at the autocorrelation function and the PSD.

- **Optimal linear filter**: A set of techniques that can be used to retrieve signals by using the statistical information of the data and the system. We introduced two specific approaches: the Yule-Walker equation for a finite-length filter and the Wiener filter for an infinite-length filter. We demonstrated how these techniques could be applied to forecast a time series and recover a time series from corrupted measurements.

While we have covered some of the most basic ideas in random processes, there are also several topics we have not discussed. These include, but are not limited to: strictly stationary process, a more restrictive class of random process than WSS; Poisson process, a useful model for arrival analysis; Markov chain, a discrete-time random process where the current state only depends on the previous state. Readers interested in these materials should consult the references listed at the end of this chapter.

10.8 Appendix

The Einstein-Wiener-Khinchin theorem

The Einstein-Wiener-Khinchin theorem is a fundamental result. It states that for any wide-sense stationary process, the power spectral density $S_X(\omega)$ is the Fourier transform of the autocorrelation function.

Theorem 10.10 (The Einstein-Wiener-Khinchin theorem). *For a WSS random process $X(t)$,*

$$S_X(\omega) = \mathcal{F}\{R_X(\tau)\}, \tag{10.50}$$

whenever the Fourier transform of $R_X(\tau)$ exists.

Proof. First, let's recall the definition of $S_X(\omega)$:

$$S_X(\omega) \overset{\text{def}}{=} \lim_{T \to \infty} \frac{1}{2T} \mathbb{E}\left[|\widetilde{X}_T(\omega)|^2\right]. \tag{10.51}$$

By expanding the expectation, we have

$$\mathbb{E}[|\widetilde{X}_T(\omega)|^2] = \mathbb{E}\left[\left(\int_{-T}^{T} X(t)e^{-j\omega t}\,dt\right)\left(\int_{-T}^{T} X(\theta)e^{-j\omega\theta}\,d\theta\right)^*\right]$$

$$= \int_{-T}^{T}\int_{-T}^{T} \mathbb{E}\left[X(t)X(\theta)\right] e^{-j\omega(t-\theta)}\,dt\,d\theta = \int_{-T}^{T}\int_{-T}^{T} R_X(t-\theta)e^{-j\omega(t-\theta)}\,dt\,d\theta. \tag{10.52}$$

Our next step is to analyze $R_X(t-\theta)$. Define

$$Q_X(v) = \mathcal{F}\{R_X(\tau)\}. \tag{10.53}$$

Then, by inverse Fourier transform

$$R_X(\tau) = \frac{1}{2\pi}\int_{-\infty}^{\infty} Q_X(v)e^{jv\tau}\,dv,$$

and therefore

$$R_X(t-\theta) = \frac{1}{2\pi}\int_{-\infty}^{\infty} Q_X(v)e^{jv(t-\theta)}\,dv.$$

Substituting this into Equation (10.52) yields

$$\mathbb{E}[|\widetilde{X}_T(\omega)|^2] = \int_{-T}^{T}\int_{-T}^{T}\left(\frac{1}{2\pi}\int_{-\infty}^{\infty} Q_X(v)e^{jv(t-\theta)}\,dv\right)e^{-j\omega(t-\theta)}\,dt\,d\theta$$

$$= \frac{1}{2\pi}\int_{-\infty}^{\infty} Q_X(v)\left(\int_{-T}^{T} e^{jt(v-\omega)}\,dt\right)\left(\int_{-T}^{T} e^{j\theta(\omega-v)}\,d\theta\right)dv.$$

We now need to simplify the two inner integrals. Recall by Fourier pair that

$$\text{rect}\left(\frac{t}{T}\right) \quad \overset{\mathcal{F}}{\longleftrightarrow} \quad T\text{sinc}\left(\frac{\omega T}{2}\right).$$

This implies that

$$\int_{-T}^{T} e^{jt(v-\omega)}\, dt = \int_{-T}^{T} e^{-j(\omega-v)t}\, dt$$

$$= \int_{-\infty}^{\infty} \text{rect}(\frac{t}{2T})e^{-j(\omega-v)t}\, dt = 2T\, \text{sinc}((\omega-v)T) = 2T\, \frac{\sin((\omega-v)T)}{(\omega-v)T}.$$

Hence, we have

$$\mathbb{E}\left[|\tilde{X}_T(\omega)|^2\right] = \frac{1}{2\pi}\int_{-\infty}^{\infty} Q_X(v)\left(2T\,\frac{\sin((\omega-v)T)}{(\omega-v)T}\right)^2 dv. \tag{10.54}$$

and so

$$\frac{1}{2T}\mathbb{E}[|\tilde{X}_T(\omega)|^2] = \frac{2T}{2\pi}\int_{-\infty}^{\infty} Q_X(v)\left(\frac{\sin((\omega-v)T)}{(\omega-v)T}\right)^2 dv. \tag{10.55}$$

As $T \to \infty$ (see Lemma 10.5 below), we have

$$2T\left(\frac{\sin((\omega-v)T)}{(\omega-v)T}\right)^2 \quad \longrightarrow \quad 2\pi\delta(\omega-v).$$

Therefore,

$$\lim_{T\to\infty}\frac{1}{2T}\mathbb{E}\left[|\tilde{X}_T(\omega)|^2\right] = \frac{1}{2\pi}\int_{-\infty}^{\infty} Q_X(v)\left[\lim_{T\to\infty} 2T\left(\frac{\sin((\omega-v)T)}{(\omega-v)T}\right)^2\right] dv$$

$$= \int_{-\infty}^{\infty} Q_X(v)\delta(\omega-v)\, dv = Q_X(\omega).$$

Since $Q_X(\omega) = \mathcal{F}[R_X(\tau)]$, we conclude that

$$S_X(\omega) = \lim_{T\to\infty}\frac{1}{2T}\mathbb{E}[|\tilde{X}_T(\omega)|^2] = Q_X(\omega) = \mathcal{F}[R_X(\tau)].$$

Lemma 10.5.

$$\lim_{T\to\infty}\frac{1}{2\pi}\int_{-\infty}^{\infty} Q_X(v)2T\left(\frac{\sin((\omega-v)T)}{(\omega-v)T}\right)^2 dv = Q_X(\omega). \tag{10.56}$$

To prove this lemma, we first define $\delta_T(\omega) = 2T(\frac{\sin(\omega T)}{\omega T})^2$. It is sufficient to show that

$$\left|\lim_{T\to\infty}\frac{1}{2\pi}\int_{-\infty}^{\infty} Q_X(v)2T\left(\frac{\sin((\omega-v)T)}{(\omega-v)T}\right)^2 dv - Q_X(\omega)\right| \to 0 \quad \text{as} \quad T \to \infty. \tag{10.57}$$

We will proceed by demonstrating the following three facts about $\delta_T(\omega)$:

1.

$$\frac{1}{2\pi} \int_{-\infty}^{\infty} \delta_T(\omega)\, d\omega = 1$$

.

2. For any $\triangle > 0$,

$$\int_{\{\omega:|\omega|>\triangle\}} \delta_T(\omega)\, d\omega \to 0 \quad \text{as} \quad T \to \infty$$

3. For any $|\omega| \geq \triangle > 0$, we have $|\delta_T(\omega)| \leq \frac{2}{T\triangle^2}$

Proof of Fact 1.

$$\frac{1}{2\pi} \int_{-\infty}^{\infty} \delta_T(\omega)\, d\omega = \frac{1}{2\pi} \int_{-\infty}^{\infty} 2T \underbrace{\left(\frac{\sin(\omega T)}{\omega T}\right)^2}_{\text{sinc}^2(\omega T)}\, d\omega.$$

Note that

$$\Lambda\left(\frac{t}{4T}\right) \longleftrightarrow 2T\text{sinc}^2(\omega T).$$

Therefore,

$$\frac{1}{2\pi} \int_{-\infty}^{\infty} 2T\text{sinc}^2(\omega T)\, d\omega = \frac{1}{2\pi} \int_{-\infty}^{\infty} 2T\text{sinc}^2(\omega T)e^{j\omega 0}\, d\omega$$

$$= \Lambda\left(\frac{0}{4T}\right) = 1.$$

Proof of Fact 2. $\delta_T(\omega)$ is symmetric, so, it is sufficient to check only one side:

$$\int_{\triangle}^{\infty} \delta_T(\omega)\, d\omega = \int_{\triangle}^{\infty} 2T\left(\frac{\sin(\omega t)}{\omega T}\right)^2\, d\omega$$

$$= \frac{2T}{T^2} \int_{\triangle}^{\infty} \frac{\sin^2(\omega t)}{\omega^2}\, d\omega$$

$$\leq \frac{2}{T} \int_{\triangle}^{\infty} \frac{1}{\omega^2}\, d\omega \qquad |\sin(.)|^2 \leq 1$$

$$= \frac{2}{T}\left[-\frac{1}{\omega}\right]_{\triangle}^{\infty} = \frac{2}{T\triangle} \to 0 \quad \text{as} \quad T \to \infty.$$

Proof of Fact 3.

$$|\delta_T(\omega)| = 2T\left(\frac{\sin(\omega T)}{\omega T}\right)^2 \leq 2T\left(\frac{1}{(\omega T)^2}\right) = \frac{2}{\omega^2 T} \leq \frac{2}{T\triangle^2}.$$

Proof of Lemma. Consider $Q_X(\omega)$. By Property 1,

$$Q_X(\omega) = Q_X(\omega).\frac{1}{2\pi} \int_{-\infty}^{\infty} \delta_T(\omega - v)\, dv = \frac{1}{2\pi} \int_{-\infty}^{\infty} Q_X(\omega)\delta_T(\omega - v)\, dv.$$

Therefore,

$$\left| \frac{1}{2\pi} \int_{-\infty}^{\infty} Q_X(v)\delta_T(\omega - v)\, dv - Q_X(\omega) \right|$$

$$= \left| \frac{1}{2\pi} \int_{-\infty}^{\infty} Q_X(v)\delta_T(\omega - v)\, dv - \frac{1}{2\pi} \int_{-\infty}^{\infty} Q_X(\omega)\delta_T(\omega - v)\, dv \right|$$

$$= \frac{1}{2\pi} \left| \int_{-\infty}^{\infty} (Q_X(v) - Q_X(\omega))\, \delta_T(\omega - v)\, dv \right| \leq \frac{1}{2\pi} \int_{-\infty}^{\infty} |Q_X(v) - Q_X(\omega)|\delta_T(\omega - v)\, dv.$$

For any $\epsilon > 0$, let $\triangle$ be a constant such that

$$|\omega - v| < \triangle \quad \text{whenever} \quad |Q_X(v) - Q_X(\omega)| < \epsilon.$$

Then we can partition the above integral into

$$\frac{1}{2\pi} \int_{-\infty}^{\infty} |Q_X(\omega) - Q_X(v)|\delta_T(\omega - v)\, dv = \frac{1}{2\pi} \int_{\omega - \triangle}^{\omega + \triangle} |Q_X(\omega) - Q_X(v)|\delta_T(\omega - v)\, dv \quad (1)$$

$$+ \frac{1}{2\pi} \int_{\omega + \triangle}^{\infty} |Q_X(\omega) - Q_X(v)|\delta_T(\omega - v)\, dv \quad (2)$$

$$+ \frac{1}{2\pi} \int_{-\infty}^{\omega + \triangle} |Q_X(\omega) - Q_X(v)|\delta_T(\omega - v)\, dv. \quad (3)$$

Partition (1) above can be evaluated as follows:

$$\frac{1}{2\pi} \int_{\omega - \triangle}^{\omega + \triangle} |Q_X(\omega) - Q_X(v)|\delta_T(\omega - v)\, dv$$

$$\leq \frac{1}{2\pi} \int_{\omega - \triangle}^{\omega + \triangle} \epsilon\delta_T(\omega - v)\, dv$$

$$= \frac{\epsilon}{2\pi} \int_{\omega - \triangle}^{\omega + \triangle} \delta_T(\omega - v)\, dv$$

$$\leq \frac{\epsilon}{2\pi} \int_{-\infty}^{\infty} \delta_T(\omega - v)\, dv = \epsilon,$$

where the last inequality holds because $\delta_T(\omega - v) \geq 0$. Since ϵ can be arbitrarily small, the only possibility for

$$\frac{1}{2\pi} \int_{\omega - \triangle}^{\omega + \triangle} |Q_X(\omega) - Q_X(v)|\delta_T(\omega - v)\, dv$$

for all ϵ is that the integral is 0.

Partition (2) above can be evaluated as follows:

$$\frac{1}{2\pi} \int_{\omega + \triangle}^{\infty} |Q_X(\omega) - Q_X(v)|\delta_T(\omega - v)\, dv$$

$$\leq \frac{1}{2\pi} \int_{\omega + \triangle}^{\infty} (|Q_X(\omega)| + |Q_X(v)|)\, \delta_T(\omega - v)\, dv$$

$$= Q_X(\omega)\frac{1}{2\pi} \int_{\omega + \triangle}^{\infty} \delta_T(\omega - v)\, dv + \frac{1}{2\pi} \int_{\omega + \triangle}^{\infty} Q_X(v)\delta_T(\omega - v)\, dv.$$

By Property 2, $\frac{1}{2\pi}\int_{\omega+\triangle}^{\infty}\delta_T(\omega-v)\,dv \to 0$ as $T \to \infty$. By Property 3,

$$\frac{1}{2\pi}\int_{\omega+\triangle}^{\infty}Q_X(v)\delta_T(\omega-v)\,dv \le \frac{1}{2\pi}\frac{2}{T\triangle^2}\underbrace{\int_{\omega+\triangle}^{\infty}Q_X(v)\,dv}_{<\infty \text{ because } Q_X(v)=\mathcal{F}[R_X(\tau)]} \to 0.$$

Therefore, we conclude that

$$\frac{1}{2\pi}\int_{\omega+\triangle}^{\infty}Q_X(v)\delta_T(\omega-v)\,dv \to 0 \quad \text{as} \quad T \to \infty.$$

and hence (1), (2) and (3) all $\to 0$ as $T \to \infty$. So we have

$$\left|\lim_{T\to\infty}\frac{1}{2\pi}\int_{-\infty}^{\infty}Q_X(v)2T\left(\frac{\sin((\omega-v)T)}{(\omega-v)T}\right)^2 dv - Q_X(\omega)\right| \to 0 \quad \text{as} \quad T \to \infty,$$

which completes the proof.

10.8.1 The Mean-Square Ergodic Theorem

The mean-square ergodic theorem states that for any WSS random process, the **statistical average** is the same as the **temporal average**. This provides an important tool in practice because finding the statistical average is typically very difficult. With the mean ergodic theorem, one can easily estimate the statistical average using the temporal average.

> **Theorem 10.11 (Mean-Square Ergodic Theorem).** *Let $Y(t)$ be a WSS process, with mean $\mathbb{E}[Y(t)] = m$ and autocorrelation function $R_Y(\tau)$. Assume that the Fourier transform of $R_Y(\tau)$ exists. Define*
>
> $$M_T \overset{\text{def}}{=} \frac{1}{2T}\int_{-T}^{T}Y(t)\,dt. \tag{10.58}$$
>
> *Then $\mathbb{E}\left[\left|M_T - m\right|^2\right] \to 0$ as $T \to \infty$.*

Proof of Mean Ergodic Theorem. Let $X(t) = Y(t) - m$. It follows that

$$M_T - m = \frac{1}{2T}\int_{-T}^{T}Y(t)\,dt - m = \frac{1}{2T}\int_{-T}^{T}X(t)\,dt.$$

We define the finite-window approximation of $X(t)$:

$$X_T(t) = \begin{cases} X(t), & -T \le t \le T, \\ 0, & \text{elsewhere.} \end{cases}$$

Then the difference $M_T - m$ can be computed as

$$M_T - m = \frac{1}{2T}\int_{-T}^{T}X(t)\,dt = \frac{1}{2T}\int_{-\infty}^{\infty}X(t)e^{-j0t}\,dt = \frac{1}{2T}\widetilde{X}_T(\omega)\Big|_{\omega=0} = \frac{\widetilde{X}_T(0)}{2T}.$$

Taking the expectation of the squares yields

$$\mathbb{E}\left[|M_T - m|^2\right] = \frac{\mathbb{E}\left[|\widetilde{X}_T(0)|^2\right]}{4T^2}.$$

Recall from the Einstein-Wiener-Khinchin theorem,

$$\frac{1}{2T}\mathbb{E}\left[|\widetilde{X}_T(\omega)|^2\right] = \frac{1}{2\pi}\int_{-\infty}^{\infty} S_X(v)2T\left(\frac{\sin((\omega - v)T)}{(\omega - v)T}\right)^2 dv.$$

Putting the limit $T \to \infty$, if we have that

$$\lim_{T\to\infty}\frac{1}{2\pi}\int_{-\infty}^{\infty} S_X(v)2T\left(\frac{\sin((\omega - v)T)}{(\omega - v)T}\right)^2 dv = S_X(\omega),$$

then we will have

$$\frac{1}{2T}\mathbb{E}\left[|\widetilde{X}_T(\omega)|^2\right] \to S_X(\omega) \text{ and } \frac{1}{2T}\mathbb{E}\left[|\widetilde{X}_T(0)|^2\right] \to S_X(0).$$

Hence,

$$\lim_{T\to\infty}\mathbb{E}\left[|M_T - m|^2\right] = \lim_{T\to\infty}\frac{1}{2T}\mathbb{E}\left[|\widetilde{X}_T(0)|^2\right] = \lim_{T\to\infty}\frac{1}{2T}S_X(0) = 0.$$

This completes the proof.

10.9   References

Basic texts

The following textbooks are basic texts about random processes. They offer many complementary materials to our book. For example, we omitted the topics of straightly stationary processes and memoryless properties. We have also omitted a few classical examples, such as the random telegraph signal, the incremental independence of Poisson processes, and Markov chains. These materials can be found in the texts below.

10-1 John A. Gubner, *Probability and Random Processes for Electrical and Computer Engineers*, Cambridge University Press, Illustrated edition, 2006.

10-2 Alberto Leon-Garcia, *Probability, Statistics, and Random Processes For Electrical Engineering*, Pearson, 3rd Edition, 2007.

10-3 Athanasios Papoulis, S. Unnikrishna Pillai, *Probability, Random Variables and Stochastic Processes*, McGraw-Hill, 4th Edition, 2012.

10-4 Henry Stark and John Woods, *Probability and Random Processes With Applications to Signal Processing*, Prentice Hall, 3rd Edition, 2001.

10-5 Eugene Wong and Bruce Hajek, *Stochastic Processes in Engineering Systems*, Springer-Verlag, 1985.

10-6 Bruce Hajek, *Random Processes for Engineers*, Cambridge University Press, 2015.

10-7 Dimitri P. Bertsekas and John N. Tsitsiklis, *Introduction to Probability*, Athena Scientific, 2nd Edition, 2008.

10-8 Robert G. Gallager, *Stochastic Processes: Theory for Applications*, Cambridge University Press, 1st Edition, 2014.

Signal and systems / Fourier transforms

The following references are classic references on signal and systems.

10-9 Alan Oppenheim and Ronald Schafer, *Discrete-Time Signal Processing*, 2nd Edition, Prentice Hall 1999.

10-10 Alan Oppenheim and Alan Willsky, *Signals and Systems*, Pearson, 2nd Edition, 1996.

10-11 Martin Vetterli, Jelena Kovacevic, and Vivek K. Goyal, *Foundations of Signal Processing*, Cambridge University Press, 3rd Edition, 2014.

10-12 Todd K. Moon and Wynn C. Stirling, *Mathematical Methods and Algorithms for Signal Processing*, Prentice-Hall, 2000.

Engineering applications

10-13 John G. Proakis and Masoud Salehi, *Communication Systems Engineering*, Pearson, 2nd Edition, 2001.

10-14 Rodger E. Ziemer, William H. Tranter, *Principles of Communications*, Wiley, 7th Edition, 2014.

10-15 Joseph W. Goodman, *Statistical Optics*, Wiley, 2015.

10.10   Problems

Exercise 1. (VIDEO SOLUTION)
Consider the random process

$$X(t) = 2A\cos(t) + (B-1)\sin(t),$$

where A and B are two independent random variables with $\mathbb{E}[A] = \mathbb{E}[B] = 0$, and $\mathbb{E}[A^2] = \mathbb{E}[B^2] = 1$.

(a) Find $\mu_X(t)$.

(b) Find $R_X(t_1, t_2)$.

(c) Find $C_X(t_1, t_2)$.

Exercise 2. (VIDEO SOLUTION)
Let $X[n]$ be a discrete-time random process with mean function $m_X[n] = \mathbb{E}\{X[n]\}$ and correlation function $R_X[n, m] = \mathbb{E}\{X[n]X[m]\}$. Suppose that

$$Y[n] = \sum_{i=-\infty}^{\infty} h[n-i]X[i]. \tag{10.59}$$

(a) Find $\mu_Y[n]$.

(b) Find $R_{XY}[n, m]$.

Exercise 3. (VIDEO SOLUTION)
Let $Y(t) = X(t) - X(t-d)$.

(a) Find $R_{X,Y}(\tau)$ and $S_{X,Y}(\omega)$.

(b) Find $R_Y(\tau)$.

(c) Find $S_Y(\omega)$.

Exercise 4. (VIDEO SOLUTION)
Let $X(t)$ be a zero-mean WSS process with autocorrelation function $R_X(\tau)$. Let $Y(t) = X(t)\cos(\omega t + \Theta)$, where $\Theta \sim \text{uniform}(-\pi, \pi)$ and Θ is independent of the process $X(t)$.

(a) Find the autocorrelation function $R_Y(\tau)$.

(b) Find the cross-correlation function of $X(t)$ and $Y(t)$.

(c) Is $Y(t)$ WSS? Why or why not?

Exercise 5. (VIDEO SOLUTION)
A WSS process $X(t)$ with autocorrelation function

$$R_X(\tau) = 1/(1 + \tau^2)$$

is passed through an LTI system with impulse response

$$h(t) = 3\sin(\pi t)/(\pi t).$$

Let $Y(t)$ be the system output. Find $S_Y(\omega)$ and sketch $S_Y(\omega)$.

Exercise 6. (VIDEO SOLUTION)
A white noise $X(t)$ with power spectral density $S_X(\omega) = N_0/2$ is applied to a lowpass filter $h(t)$ with impulse response

$$h(t) = \frac{1}{RC}e^{-t/RC}, \qquad t > 0. \tag{10.60}$$

Find the followings.

(a) $S_{XY}(\omega)$.

(b) $R_{XY}(\tau)$.

(c) $S_Y(\omega)$.

(d) $R_Y(\tau)$.

Exercise 7. (VIDEO SOLUTION)
Consider a WSS process $X(t)$ with autocorrelation function

$$R_X(\tau) = \text{sinc}(\pi\tau).$$

The process is sent to an LTI system with input-output relationship

$$2\frac{d^2}{dt^2}Y(t) + 2\frac{d}{dt}Y(t) + 4Y(t) = 3\frac{d^2}{dt^2}X(t) - 3\frac{d}{dt}X(t) + 6X(t).$$

Find the autocorrelation function $R_Y(\tau)$.

Exercise 8. (VIDEO SOLUTION)
Given the functions $a(t)$, $b(t)$ and $c(t)$, let

$$g(t, 1) = a(t),$$
$$g(t, 2) = b(t),$$
$$g(t, 3) = c(t).$$

Let $X(t) = g(t, Z)$, where Z is a discrete random variable with PMF $\mathbb{P}[Z = 1] = p_1$, $\mathbb{P}[Z = 2] = p_2$ and $\mathbb{P}[Z = 3] = p_3$. Find, in terms of the p_1, p_2, p_3, $a(t)$, $b(t)$ and $c(t)$,

(a) $\mu_X(t)$.

(b) $R_X(t_1, t_2)$.

Exercise 9.
In the previous problem, let $a(t) = e^{-\lambda|t|}$, $b(t) = \sin(\pi t)$ and $c(t) = -1$.

(a) Choose p_1, p_2, p_3 so that $X(t)$ is WSS.

(b) Choose p_1, p_2, p_3 so that $X(t)$ is not WSS.

Exercise 10. (VIDEO SOLUTION)
Find the autocorrelation function $R_X(\tau)$ corresponding to each of the following power spectral densities:

(a) $\delta(\omega - \omega_0) + \delta(\omega + \omega_0)$.

(b) $e^{-\omega^2/2}$.

(c) $e^{-|\omega|}$.

Exercise 11. (VIDEO SOLUTION)
A WSS process $X(t)$ with autocorrelation function $R_X(\tau) = e^{-\tau^2/(2\sigma_T^2)}$ is passed through an LTI system with transfer function $H(\omega) = e^{-\omega^2/(2\sigma_H^2)}$. Denote the system output by $Y(t)$. Find the followings.

(a) $S_{XY}(\omega)$.

(b) $R_{XY}(\tau)$.

(c) $S_Y(\omega)$.

(d) $R_Y(\tau)$.

Exercise 12. (VIDEO SOLUTION)
A white noise $X(t)$ with power spectral density $S_X(\omega) = N_0/2$ is applied to a lowpass filter $h(t)$ with

$$H(\omega) = \begin{cases} 1 - \omega^2, & \text{if } |\omega| \leq \pi, \\ 0, & \text{otherwise.} \end{cases}$$

Find $\mathbb{E}[|Y(t)|^2]$, where $Y(t)$ is the output of the filter.

Exercise 13. (VIDEO SOLUTION)
Let $X(t)$ be a WSS process with correlation function

$$R_X(\tau) = \begin{cases} 1 - |\tau|, & \text{if } -1 \leq \tau \leq 1, \\ 0, & \text{otherwise.} \end{cases} \tag{10.61}$$

It is known that when $X(t)$ is input to a system with transfer function $H(\omega)$, the system output $Y(t)$ has a correlation function

$$R_Y(\tau) = \frac{\sin \pi \tau}{\pi \tau}. \tag{10.62}$$

Find the transfer function $H(\omega)$.

Exercise 14.

Consider the system

$$Y(t) = e^{-t} \int_{-\infty}^{t} e^{\tau} X(\tau) \, d\tau.$$

Assume that $X(t)$ is zero-mean white noise with power spectral density $S_X(\omega) = N_0/2$. Find the followings:

(a) $S_{XY}(\omega)$.

(b) $R_{XY}(\tau)$.

(c) $S_Y(\omega)$.

(d) $R_Y(\tau)$.

Chapter A

Appendix

Useful Identities

1. $\sum_{k=0}^{\infty} r^k = 1 + r + r^2 + \cdots = \frac{1}{1-r}$

2. $\sum_{k=1}^{n} k = 1 + 2 + 3 + \cdots + n = \frac{n(n+1)}{2}$

3. $e^x = \sum_{k=0}^{\infty} \frac{x^k}{k!} = 1 + \frac{x}{1!} + \frac{x^2}{2!} + \cdots$

4. $\sum_{k=1}^{\infty} k r^{k-1} = 1 + 2r + 3r^2 + \cdots = \frac{1}{(1-r)^2}$

5. $\sum_{k=1}^{n} k^2 = 1^2 + 2^2 + 3^3 + \cdots + n^2 = \frac{n^3}{3} + \frac{n^2}{2} + \frac{n}{6}$

6. $(a+b)^n = \sum_{k=0}^{n} \binom{n}{k} a^k b^{n-k}$

Common Distributions

Distribution	PMF / PDF	$\mathbb{E}[X]$	$\mathrm{Var}[X]$	$M_X(s)$
Bernoulli	$p_X(1) = p$ and $p_X(0) = 1 - p$	p	$p(1-p)$	$1 - p + pe^s$
Binomial	$p_X(k) = \binom{n}{k} p^k (1-p)^{n-k}$	np	$np(1-p)$	$(1 - p + pe^s)^n$
Geometric	$p_X(k) = p(1-p)^{k-1}$	$\frac{1}{p}$	$\frac{1-p}{p^2}$	$\frac{pe^s}{1 - (1-p)e^s}$
Poisson	$p_X(k) = \frac{\lambda^k e^{-\lambda}}{k!}$	λ	λ	$e^{\lambda(e^s - 1)}$
Gaussian	$f_X(x) = \frac{1}{\sqrt{2\pi\sigma^2}} \exp\left\{ -\frac{(x-\mu)^2}{2\sigma^2} \right\}$	μ	σ^2	$\exp\left\{ \mu s + \frac{\sigma^2 s^2}{2} \right\}$
Exponential	$f_X(x) = \lambda \exp\{-\lambda x\}$	$\frac{1}{\lambda}$	$\frac{1}{\lambda^2}$	$\frac{\lambda}{\lambda - s}$
Uniform	$f_X(x) = \frac{1}{b-a}$	$\frac{a+b}{2}$	$\frac{(b-a)^2}{12}$	$\frac{e^{sb} - e^{sa}}{s(b-a)}$

Sum of Two Random Variables

X_1	X_2	Sum $X_1 + X_2$
Bernoulli(p)	Bernoulli(p)	Binomial$(2, p)$
Binomial(n, p)	Binomial(m, p)	Binomial$(m + n, p)$
Poisson(λ_1)	Poisson(λ_2)	Poisson$(\lambda_1 + \lambda_2)$
Exponential(λ)	Exponential(λ)	Erlang$(2, \lambda)$
Gaussian(μ_1, σ_1^2)	Gaussian(μ_2, σ_2^2)	Gaussian$(\mu_1 + \mu_2,\ \sigma_1^2 + \sigma_2^2)$

Fourier Transform Table

$$F(\omega) = \int_{-\infty}^{\infty} f(t)\, e^{-j\omega t}\, dt.$$

	$f(t) \longleftrightarrow F(\omega)$		$f(t) \longleftrightarrow F(\omega)$
1.	$e^{-at}u(t) \longleftrightarrow \dfrac{1}{a + j\omega},\ a > 0$	10.	$\operatorname{sinc}^2\left(\dfrac{Wt}{2}\right) \longleftrightarrow \dfrac{2\pi}{W}\Delta\left(\dfrac{\omega}{2W}\right)$
2.	$e^{at}u(-t) \longleftrightarrow \dfrac{1}{a - j\omega},\ a > 0$	11.	$e^{-at}\sin(\omega_0 t)u(t) \longleftrightarrow \dfrac{\omega_0}{(a + j\omega)^2 + \omega_0^2},\ a > 0$
3.	$e^{-a|t|} \longleftrightarrow \dfrac{2a}{a^2 + \omega^2},\ a > 0$	12.	$e^{-at}\cos(\omega_0 t)u(t) \longleftrightarrow \dfrac{a + j\omega}{(a + j\omega)^2 + \omega_0^2},\ a > 0$
4.	$\dfrac{a^2}{a^2 + t^2} \longleftrightarrow \pi a e^{-a|\omega|},\ a > 0$	13.	$\exp\left\{-\dfrac{t^2}{2\sigma^2}\right\} \longleftrightarrow \sqrt{2\pi}\sigma \exp\left\{-\dfrac{\sigma^2 \omega^2}{2}\right\}$
5.	$te^{-at}u(t) \longleftrightarrow \dfrac{1}{(a + j\omega)^2},\ a > 0$	14.	$\delta(t) \longleftrightarrow 1$
6.	$t^n e^{-at}u(t) \longleftrightarrow \dfrac{n!}{(a + j\omega)^{n+1}},\ a > 0$	15.	$1 \longleftrightarrow 2\pi\delta(\omega)$
7.	$\operatorname{rect}\left(\dfrac{t}{\tau}\right) \longleftrightarrow \tau\operatorname{sinc}\left(\dfrac{\omega\tau}{2}\right)$	16.	$\delta(t - t_0) \longleftrightarrow e^{-jwt_0}$
8.	$\operatorname{sinc}(Wt) \longleftrightarrow \dfrac{\pi}{W}\operatorname{rect}\left(\dfrac{\omega}{2W}\right)$	17.	$e^{j\omega_0 t} \longleftrightarrow 2\pi\delta(\omega - \omega_0)$
9.	$\Delta\left(\dfrac{t}{\tau}\right) \longleftrightarrow \dfrac{\tau}{2}\operatorname{sinc}^2\left(\dfrac{\omega\tau}{4}\right)$	18.	$f(t)e^{j\omega_0 t} \longleftrightarrow F(\omega - \omega_0)$

Some definitions:

$$\operatorname{sinc}(t) = \frac{\sin(t)}{t}$$

$$\operatorname{rect}(t) = \begin{cases} 1, & -0.5 \leq t \leq 0.5, \\ 0, & \text{otherwise.} \end{cases}$$

$$\Delta(t) = \begin{cases} 1 - 2|t|, & -0.5 \leq t \leq 0.5, \\ 0, & \text{otherwise.} \end{cases}$$

Basic Trigonometric Identities

$$e^{j\theta} = \cos\theta + j\sin\theta$$

$$\sin 2\theta = 2\sin\theta\cos\theta$$

$$\cos 2\theta = 2\cos^2\theta - 1$$

$$\cos A \cos B = \frac{1}{2}(\cos(A+B) + \cos(A-B))$$

$$\sin A \sin B = -\frac{1}{2}(\cos(A+B) - \cos(A-B))$$

$$\sin A \cos B = \frac{1}{2}(\sin(A+B) + \sin(A-B))$$

$$\cos A \sin B = \frac{1}{2}(\sin(A+B) - \sin(A-B))$$

$$\cos(A+B) = \cos A \cos B - \sin A \sin B$$

$$\cos(A-B) = \cos A \cos B + \sin A \sin B$$

$$\sin(A+B) = \sin A \cos B + \cos A \sin B$$

$$\sin(A-B) = \sin A \cos B - \cos A \sin B$$

Index